ALMOST EVERYTHING THERE IS TO KNOW

BY HUNKIN

THE COMPLETE RUDIMENTS OF WISDOM
FROM THE OBSERVER COLOUR MAGAZINE

THE ANTIDOTE TO BORING REFERENCE BOOKS

PYRAMID BOOKS

First published in 1988 by Pyramid Books
An imprint of Octopus Publishing Group Ltd
Michelin House
81 Fulham Road
London SW3 6RB

This Anthology Copyright © Tim Hunkin
Based upon material variously © Tim Hunkin 1973–1987

ISBN: 1 871307 43 0

Printed in Austria

Introduction

The cartoons in this book were originally called *The Rudiments of Wisdom* and they appeared in *The Sunday Observer* colour supplement between 1973 and 1987. The very first ones were drawn for a Cambridge student newspaper called *Stop Press* in 1972.

The idea for the cartoon occurred to me after looking through the university library catalogue. Under words like 'odd', 'strange' and 'peculiar', there were a number of books such as *Strange But True* and *Oddities of Animal Life*. These books were full of obscure advice, odd facts and ridiculous information. At first, the cartoon was not meant to be taken at all seriously (the first one contained absurd advice on how to draw cows).

After leaving Cambridge, I took on a strange variety of commissions – firework displays, book illustrations and mechanical sculptures. One of these was building an exploding Christmas cake for an art gallery. A reporter from *The Observer* turned up at this event, looked at my portfolio and carried off the cartoons. The editor of the children's section of the magazine had been looking for a cartoon and took on *The Rudiments* for a trial period of six weeks. I stayed 14 years!

As I continued doing new subjects, the research became more and more enjoyable. I quickly began to mistrust books like Ripley's *Believe it or not*, with such dubious facts as 'the horse who was court marshalled' and 'the first man to wear trousers', and took to more reliable sources. Over the years the research became more difficult (as I ran out of simple subjects). I carried on for 14 years mainly because I was so addicted to the research (there aren't many jobs where you get paid to investigate anything you like).

I would like to thank the various editors of *The Young Observer* for putting up with me, correcting my odd spelling and keeping everything reasonably intelligible. I would also like to thank Tony Ellis for his comments – often justifiably caustic and occasionally enthusiastic and encouraging. I thank Nick Webb for originally encouraging me to get the book together and, finally, I thank Denise Brotherhood, Lowestoft Art College, Mike Ball, Adrian Mason and Sally Lloyd Jones who have all helped in getting it published.

Tim Hunkin

Tim Hunkin, June 1988.

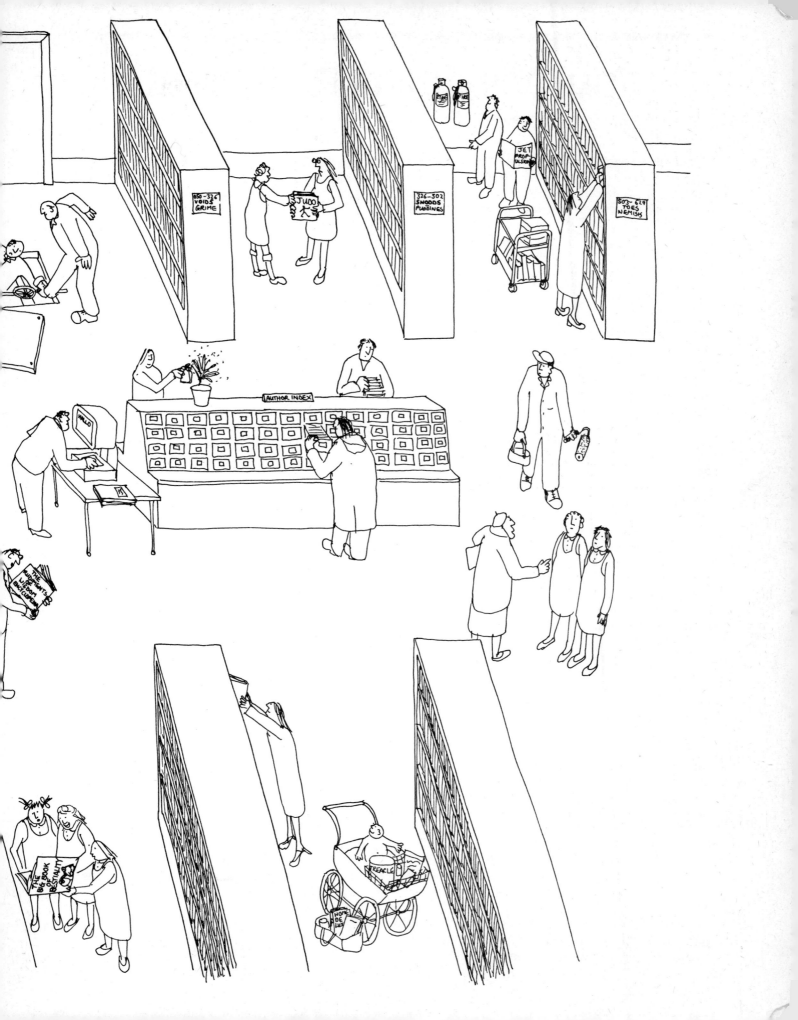

Sources of the Rudiments

Researching and discovering little-known facts, absurd advice and strange information needs patience and can be great fun. Here are some useful tips for anyone who fancies trying their hand at it.

Libraries
The range of books you find in public libraries is always patchy and one library is very different from another. They have a strong local flavour; Lowestoft, for instance, is good on fishing and shipping, while Holborn is good on business and economics. The sorts of books they hold also, to some extent, reflect the interests of the librarians and so are interestingly unpredictable (although you can be sure all have large sections on librarianship!).

The biggest public libraries in Britain are in provincial cities (Glasgow is the biggest); the public libraries in London are split into boroughs and are smaller.

Children's libraries are a surprisingly good source of detailed information about some subjects, particularly animals and common substances like rubber, tea, diamonds, etc.

Public libraries also keep a list of private college and company libraries in the area. These are often open to the public for reference and have comprehensive collections on their own specialities (college collections relate to their courses and company collections relate to their trade).

Copyright libraries, like the British Museum, where the public is not allowed direct access to the books and has to have them fetched by librarians, can be very slow and frustrating if you are not sure what you want.

Magazines
Recent scientific and technical magazines are particularly useful for up-to-date information. Books in these areas often need updating. Some general scientific magazines have an index which makes it possible to look up recent references to any subject.

I find the *New Scientist* the easiest scientific magazine to read. *The Times* index is useful for looking up the dates when things were in the news.

A vast number of specialist magazines are also published and large reference libraries subscribe to a surprising quantity (and keep the back numbers). They also keep lists of other libraries' subscriptions and can tell you where to go to find a particular magazine if they do not have it themselves.

Telephone
All government departments, most museums and most companies have press and public relations offices. They will send publicity material (occasionally informative), answer questions and provide current statistics. It is often more informative to ask to speak directly to an 'expert' than to public relations staff. It is important to get the name of the person you speak to – they sometimes don't phone back and need pestering.

Reference Books
I use a large number of reference books but most of them are rather unappetising. Encyclopedias are good sources – especially the earlier editions of the *Encyclopedia Britannica*. The articles are written by a large number of people and something of their personality remains. I never know what to expect from an article – some are ridiculously complicated, some are dreadfully boring and others are fascinating.

At the other end of the spectrum there are various books of 'extraordinary facts'. Although these are generally totally untrustworthy, there are a few notable exceptions, like *The Shell Book of Firsts* and the Guinness *Facts and Feats* series. Books from unlikely sources can be very good. For instance, I have a Marshall Cavendish part-work called *How it works* which is clear, comprehensive and up-to-date and better than anything else I've got on basic modern technology.

Remainder bookshops are also a good place to find useful books. The jumble of subject matter makes for interesting browsing and the ridiculously cheap prices reduce any inhibitions for trying unlikely subjects. Remainder bookshops exist because publishers now keep books in print for very short periods. As a result, there are many books which are no longer obtainable.

The most important thing to remember is – whenever you find a book that appeals to you, buy it immediately – next week it may be gone for good!

Tim Hunkin

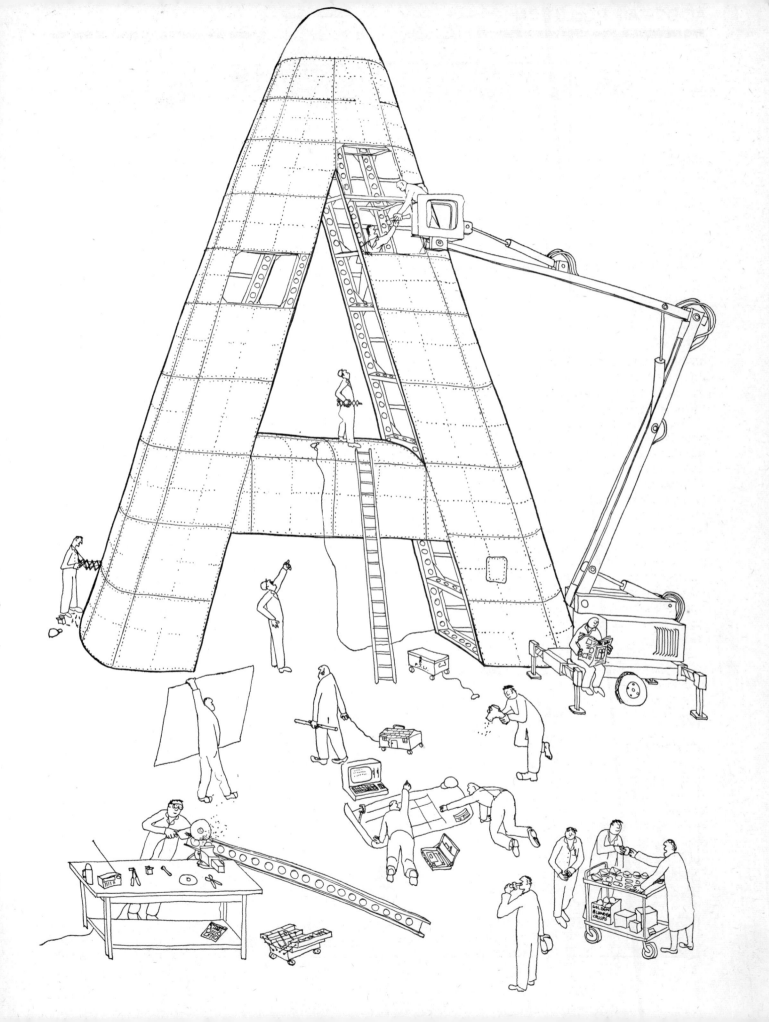

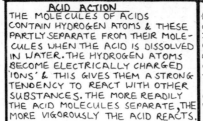

☆ ACIDS ☆
USEFUL ACTIVE CHEMICALS

ACID ACTION

THE MOLECULES OF ACIDS CONTAIN HYDROGEN ATOMS & THESE PARTLY SEPARATE FROM THEIR MOLECULES WHEN THE ACID IS DISSOLVED IN WATER. THE HYDROGEN ATOMS BECOME ELECTRICALLY CHARGED 'IONS' & THIS GIVES THEM A STRONG TENDENCY TO REACT WITH OTHER SUBSTANCES. THE MORE READILY THE ACID MOLECULES SEPARATE, THE MORE VIGOROUSLY THE ACID REACTS.

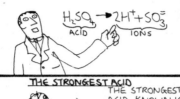

$$H_2SO_4 \rightarrow 2H^+ + SO_3^=$$
ACID — IONS

THE STRONGEST ACID

THE STRONGEST ACID KNOWN IS A SOLUTION OF ANTIMONY PENTA-FLUORIDE IN FLUOSULPHONIC ACID ($SbF_3 + FSO_3H$).

THE FIRST ACID

ALMOST THE ONLY ACID KNOWN TO THE ANCIENT CIVILISATIONS WAS VINEGAR. THIS WAS PRODUCED BY LEAVING WINE EXPOSED TO AIR TO CONTINUE FERMENTATION.

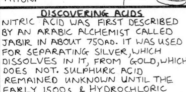

DISCOVERING ACIDS

NITRIC ACID WAS FIRST DESCRIBED BY AN ARABIC ALCHEMIST CALLED JABIR IN ABOUT 750AD. IT WAS USED FOR SEPARATING SILVER, WHICH DISSOLVES IN IT, FROM GOLD, WHICH DOES NOT. SULPHURIC ACID REMAINED UNKNOWN UNTIL THE EARLY 1500s & HYDROCHLORIC UNTIL THE 1600s.

IMPORTANT ACIDS

LIEBIG, A FAMOUS VICTORIAN CHEMIST, CLAIMED: 'WE MAY FAIRLY JUDGE THE COMMERCIAL PROSPERITY OF A COUNTRY FROM THE AMOUNT OF SULPHURIC ACID IT CONSUMES.' CERTAINLY THE INTRODUCTION OF THE LEAD CHAMBER PROCESS (c1836) FOR THE LARGE-SCALE MANUFACTURE OF THE ACID WAS THE BASIS OF THE VICTORIAN CHEMICAL INDUSTRY, BEING USED IN THE MAKING OF SODA, CHLORINE, HYDROCHLORIC & NITRIC ACIDS & MANY OTHER ESSENTIAL CHEMICALS.

POLLUTING ACIDS

ACID POLLUTION WAS CREATING PROBLEMS AS EARLY AS THE 1830s. THE LEBLANC PROCESS FOR MAKING SODA ($NaOH$) PRODUCED CLOUDS OF HYDROCHLORIC ACID GAS & THE MANUFACTURERS WERE FREQUENTLY SUED FOR DAMAGES. SOME TRIED TO ABATE THE NUISANCE BY BUILDING VERY HIGH CHIMNEYS, BUT A BETTER SOLUTION WAS DISCOVERED IN 1836. THE GAS WAS PASSED INTO TOWERS WHERE IT WAS ABSORBED BY DESCENDING STREAMS OF WATER. THIS LED TO THE ALKALI ACT OF 1863 WHICH REQUIRED AT LEAST 95% OF THE ACID TO BE ABSORBED.

HOW TO MAKE A PENCIL JUMP

LOOP ELASTIC BAND ROUND FOREFINGER & STRETCH WITH PENCIL HOLDING IT AS RIGHT. RELEASE THUMB & PENCIL WILL JUMP OUT.

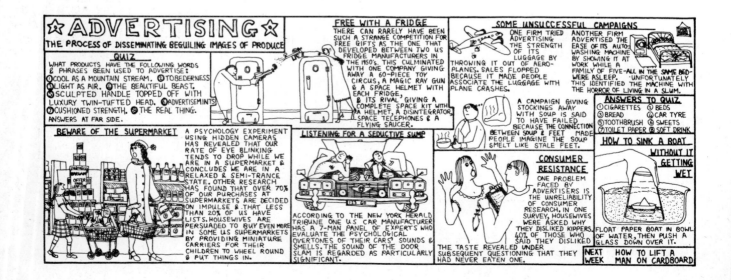

☆ ADVERTISING ☆
THE PROCESS OF DISSEMINATING BEGUILING IMAGES OF PRODUCE

QUIZ

WHAT PRODUCTS HAVE THE FOLLOWING WORDS & PHRASES BEEN USED TO ADVERTISE:
1. COOL AS A MOUNTAIN STREAM. 2. TOBEDERNESS 3. LIGHT AS AIR. 4. THE BEAUTIFUL BEAST. 5. SCULPTED HANDLE TOPPED OFF WITH LUXURY TWIN-TUFTED HEAD. 6. ADVERTISEMINTS 7. CUSHIONED STRENGTH. 8. THE REAL THING.
ANSWERS AT FAR SIDE.

FREE WITH A FRIDGE

THERE CAN RARELY HAVE BEEN SUCH A STRANGE COMPETITION FOR FREE GIFTS AS THE ONE THAT DEVELOPED BETWEEN TWO US FRIDGE MANUFACTURERS IN THE 1950's. THIS CULMINATED WITH ONE COMPANY GIVING AWAY A 60-PIECE TOY CIRCUS, A MAGIC RAY GUN & A SPACE HELMET WITH EACH FRIDGE, & ITS RIVAL GIVING A COMPLETE SPACE KIT WITH A HELMET, A DISINTEGRATOR, SPACE TELEPHONES & A FLYING SAUCER.

SOME UNSUCCESSFUL CAMPAIGNS

ONE FIRM TRIED ADVERTISING THE STRENGTH OF ITS LUGGAGE BY THROWING IT OUT OF AEROPLANES. SALES FLOPPED BECAUSE IT MADE PEOPLE ASSOCIATE THE LUGGAGE WITH PLANE CRASHES.

ANOTHER FIRM ADVERTISED THE EASE OF ITS AUTO-WASHING MACHINE BY SHOWING IT AT WORK WHILE A FAMILY OF FIVE-ALL IN THE SAME BED-WERE ASLEEP. UNFORTUNATELY THIS IDENTIFIED THE MACHINE WITH THE HORROR OF LIVING IN A SLUM.

A CAMPAIGN GIVING STOCKINGS AWAY WITH SOUP IS SAID TO HAVE FAILED BECAUSE THE CONNECTION BETWEEN SOUP & FEET MADE PEOPLE IMAGINE THE SOUP SMELT LIKE STALE FEET.

ANSWERS TO QUIZ
1. CIGARETTES 2. BEDS 3. BREAD 4. CAR TYRE 5. TOOTHBRUSH 6. SWEETS 7. TOILET PAPER 8. SOFT DRINK

BEWARE OF THE SUPERMARKET

A PSYCHOLOGY EXPERIMENT USING HIDDEN CAMERAS HAS REVEALED THAT OUR RATE OF EYE BLINKING TENDS TO DROP WHILE WE ARE IN A SUPERMARKET & CONCLUDES WE ARE IN A RELAXED & SEMI-TRANCE STATE. OTHER RESEARCH HAS FOUND THAT OVER 70% OF OUR PURCHASES AT SUPERMARKETS ARE DECIDED ON IMPULSE & THAT LESS THAN 20% OF US HAVE LISTS. HOUSEWIVES ARE PERSUADED TO BUY EVEN MORE IN SOME US SUPERMARKETS BY PROVIDING MINIATURE CARRIERS FOR THEIR CHILDREN TO WHEEL ROUND & PUT THINGS IN.

LISTENING FOR A SEDUCTIVE SLAM

ACCORDING TO THE NEW YORK HERALD TRIBUNE ONE US CAR MANUFACTURER HAS A 7-MAN PANEL OF EXPERTS WHO EVALUATE THE PSYCHOLOGICAL OVERTONES OF THEIR CARS' SOUNDS & SMELLS. THE SOUND OF THE DOOR SLAM IS REGARDED AS PARTICULARLY SIGNIFICANT.

CONSUMER RESISTANCE

ONE PROBLEM FACED BY ADVERTISERS IS THE UNRELIABILITY OF CONSUMER RESEARCH. IN ONE SURVEY, HOUSEWIVES WERE ASKED WHY THEY DISLIKED KIPPERS. 40% OF THOSE WHO SAID THEY DISLIKED THE TASTE REVEALED UNDER SUBSEQUENT QUESTIONING THAT THEY HAD NEVER EATEN ONE.

HOW TO SINK A ROAT WITHOUT IT GETTING WET

FLOAT PAPER BOAT IN BOWL OF WATER, THEN PUSH A GLASS DOWN OVER IT.

NEXT WEEK: HOW TO LIFT A MAN ON CARDBOARD

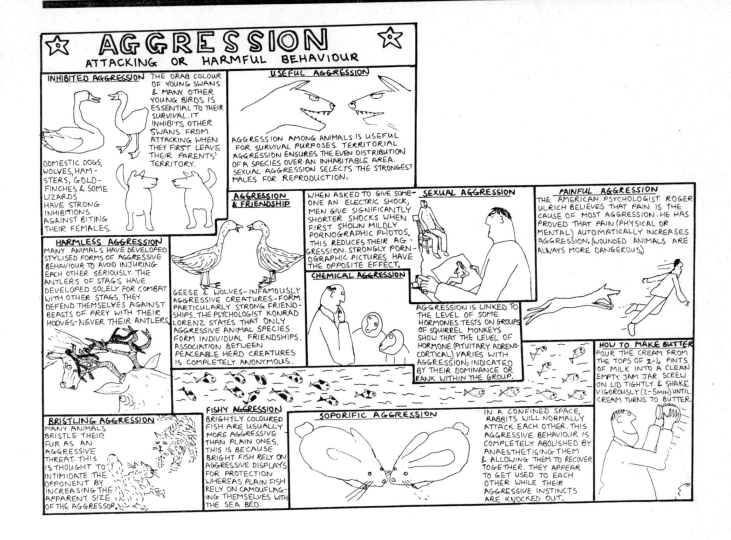

☆ AGGRESSION ☆
ATTACKING OR HARMFUL BEHAVIOUR

INHIBITED AGGRESSION

THE DRAB COLOUR OF YOUNG SWANS & MANY OTHER YOUNG BIRDS IS ESSENTIAL TO THEIR SURVIVAL. IT INHIBITS OTHER SWANS FROM ATTACKING WHEN THEY FIRST LEAVE THEIR PARENTS' TERRITORY.

DOMESTIC DOGS, WOLVES, HAMSTERS, GOLDFINCHES & SOME LIZARDS HAVE STRONG INHIBITIONS AGAINST BITING THEIR FEMALES.

USEFUL AGGRESSION

AGGRESSION AMONG ANIMALS IS USEFUL FOR SURVIVAL PURPOSES. TERRITORIAL AGGRESSION ENSURES THE EVEN DISTRIBUTION OF A SPECIES OVER AN INHABITABLE AREA. SEXUAL AGGRESSION SELECTS THE STRONGEST MALES FOR REPRODUCTION.

HARMLESS AGGRESSION

MANY ANIMALS HAVE DEVELOPED STYLISED FORMS OF AGGRESSIVE BEHAVIOUR TO AVOID INJURING EACH OTHER SERIOUSLY. THE ANTLERS OF STAGS HAVE DEVELOPED SOLELY FOR COMBAT WITH OTHER STAGS. THEY DEFEND THEMSELVES AGAINST BEASTS OF PREY WITH THEIR HOOVES- NEVER THEIR ANTLERS.

AGGRESSION & FRIENDSHIP

GEESE & WOLVES-INFAMOUSLY AGGRESSIVE CREATURES-FORM PARTICULARLY STRONG FRIENDSHIPS. THE PSYCHOLOGIST KONRAD LORENZ STATES THAT ONLY AGGRESSIVE ANIMAL SPECIES FORM INDIVIDUAL FRIENDSHIPS. ASSOCIATION BETWEEN PEACEABLE HERD CREATURES IS COMPLETELY ANONYMOUS.

WHEN ASKED TO GIVE SOMEONE AN ELECTRIC SHOCK, MEN GIVE SIGNIFICANTLY SHORTER SHOCKS WHEN FIRST SHOWN MILDLY PORNOGRAPHIC PHOTOS. THIS REDUCES THEIR AGGRESSION. STRONGLY PORNOGRAPHIC PICTURES HAVE THE OPPOSITE EFFECT.

CHEMICAL AGGRESSION

AGGRESSION IS LINKED TO THE LEVEL OF SOME HORMONES. TESTS ON GROUPS OF SQUIRREL MONKEYS SHOW THAT THE LEVEL OF HORMONE (PITUITARY ADRENO-CORTICAL) VARIES WITH AGGRESSION, INDICATED BY THEIR DOMINANCE OR RANK WITHIN THE GROUP.

SEXUAL AGGRESSION

PAINFUL AGGRESSION

THE AMERICAN PSYCHOLOGIST ROGER ULRICH BELIEVES THAT PAIN IS THE CAUSE OF MOST AGGRESSION. HE HAS PROVED THAT PAIN (PHYSICAL OR MENTAL) AUTOMATICALLY INCREASES AGGRESSION. (WOUNDED ANIMALS ARE ALWAYS MORE DANGEROUS)

HOW TO MAKE BUTTER

POUR THE CREAM FROM THE TOPS OF 2-4 PINTS OF MILK INTO A CLEAN EMPTY JAM JAR. SCREW ON LID TIGHTLY & SHAKE VIGOROUSLY (2-5min) UNTIL CREAM TURNS TO BUTTER.

BRISTLING AGGRESSION

MANY ANIMALS BRISTLE THEIR FUR AS AN AGGRESSIVE THREAT. THIS IS THOUGHT TO INTIMIDATE THE OPPONENT BY INCREASING THE APPARENT SIZE OF THE AGGRESSOR.

FISHY AGGRESSION

BRIGHTLY COLOURED FISH ARE USUALLY MORE AGGRESSIVE THAN PLAIN ONES. THIS IS BECAUSE BRIGHT FISH RELY ON AGGRESSIVE DISPLAYS FOR PROTECTION WHEREAS PLAIN FISH RELY ON CAMOUFLAGING THEMSELVES WITH THE SEA BED.

SOPORIFIC AGGRESSION

IN A CONFINED SPACE, RABBITS WILL NORMALLY ATTACK EACH OTHER. THIS AGGRESSIVE BEHAVIOUR IS COMPLETELY ABOLISHED BY ANAESTHETISING THEM & ALLOWING THEM TO RECOVER TOGETHER. THEY APPEAR TO GET USED TO EACH OTHER WHILE THEIR AGGRESSIVE INSTINCTS ARE KNOCKED OUT.

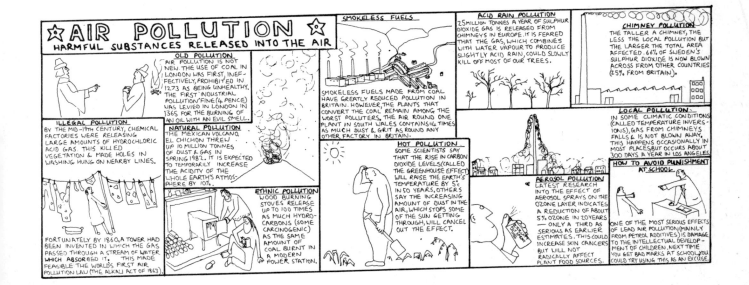

☆ AIR POLLUTION ☆
HARMFUL SUBSTANCES RELEASED INTO THE AIR

OLD POLLUTION

AIR POLLUTION IS NOT NEW. THE USE OF COAL IN LONDON WAS FIRST, INEFFECTIVELY, PROHIBITED IN 1273 AS BEING UNHEALTHY. THE FIRST INDUSTRIAL POLLUTION FINE (4 PENCE) WAS LEVIED IN LONDON IN 1365 FOR THE BURNING OF AN OIL WITH AN EVIL SMELL.

ILLEGAL POLLUTION

BY THE MID-19TH CENTURY, CHEMICAL FACTORIES WERE RELEASING LARGE AMOUNTS OF HYDROCHLORIC ACID GAS. THIS KILLED VEGETATION & MADE HOLES IN WASHING HUNG ON NEARBY LINES.

FORTUNATELY BY 1860, A TOWER HAD BEEN INVENTED IN WHICH THE GAS PASSED THROUGH A STREAM OF WATER WHICH ABSORBED IT. THIS MADE FEASIBLE THE WORLD'S FIRST AIR POLLUTION LAW (THE ALKALI ACT OF 1863).

NATURAL POLLUTION

THE MEXICAN VOLCANO, EL CHICHON THREW UP 10 MILLION TONNES OF DUST & GAS IN SPRING 1982. IT IS EXPECTED TO TEMPORARILY INCREASE THE ACIDITY OF THE WHOLE EARTH'S ATMOSPHERE BY 10%.

ETHNIC POLLUTION

WOOD BURNING STOVES RELEASE UP TO 100 TIMES AS MUCH HYDROCARBONS (SOME CARCINOGENIC) AS THE SAME AMOUNT OF COAL BURNT IN A MODERN POWER STATION.

SMOKELESS FUELS

SMOKELESS FUELS MADE FROM COAL HAVE GREATLY REDUCED POLLUTION IN BRITAIN. HOWEVER, THE PLANTS THAT CONVERT THE COAL REMAIN AMONG THE WORST POLLUTERS. THE AIR ROUND ONE PLANT IN SOUTH WALES CONTAINS 14 TIMES AS MUCH DUST & GRIT AS ROUND ANY OTHER FACTORY IN BRITAIN.

HOT POLLUTION

SOME SCIENTISTS SAY THAT THE RISE IN CARBON DIOXIDE LEVELS (CALLED THE GREENHOUSE EFFECT) WILL RAISE THE EARTH'S TEMPERATURE BY 5°C IN 50 YEARS. OTHERS SAY THE INCREASING AMOUNT OF DUST IN THE AIR, WHICH STOPS SOME OF THE SUN GETTING THROUGH, WILL CANCEL OUT THE EFFECT.

ACID RAIN POLLUTION

25 MILLION TONNES A YEAR OF SULPHUR DIOXIDE GAS IS RELEASED FROM CHIMNEYS IN EUROPE. IT IS FEARED THAT THE GAS, WHICH COMBINES WITH WATER VAPOUR TO PRODUCE SLIGHTLY ACID RAIN, COULD SLOWLY KILL OFF MOST OF OUR TREES.

AEROSOL POLLUTION

LATEST RESEARCH INTO THE EFFECT OF AEROSOL SPRAYS ON THE OZONE LAYER INDICATES A REDUCTION OF ABOUT 5% OZONE IN 20 YEARS — ONLY A THIRD AS SERIOUS AS EARLIER ESTIMATES. THIS COULD INCREASE SKIN CANCERS BUT WILL NOT RADICALLY AFFECT PLANT FOOD SOURCES.

CHIMNEY POLLUTION

THE TALLER A CHIMNEY, THE LESS THE LOCAL POLLUTION BUT THE LARGER THE TOTAL AREA AFFECTED. 66% OF SWEDEN'S SULPHUR DIOXIDE IS NOW BLOWN ACROSS FROM OTHER COUNTRIES (25% FROM BRITAIN).

LOCAL POLLUTION

IN SOME CLIMATIC CONDITIONS (CALLED TEMPERATURE INVERSIONS), GAS FROM CHIMNEYS FALLS & IS NOT BLOWN AWAY. THIS HAPPENS OCCASIONALLY IN MOST PLACES, BUT OCCURS ABOUT 300 DAYS A YEAR IN LOS ANGELES.

HOW TO AVOID PUNISHMENT AT SCHOOL

ONE OF THE MOST SERIOUS EFFECTS OF LEAD AIR POLLUTION (MAINLY FROM PETROL ADDITIVES) IS DAMAGE TO THE INTELLECTUAL DEVELOPMENT OF CHILDREN. NEXT TIME YOU GET BAD MARKS AT SCHOOL, YOU COULD TRY USING THIS AS AN EXCUSE.

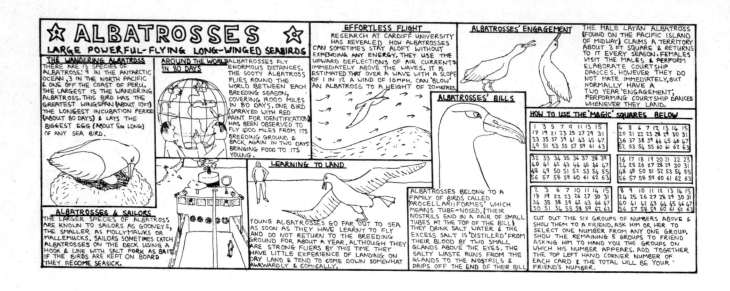

☆ ALBATROSSES ☆
LARGE POWERFUL-FLYING LONG-WINGED SEABIRDS

THE WANDERING ALBATROSS
THERE ARE 13 SPECIES OF ALBATROSS: 9 IN THE ANTARCTIC OCEAN, 3 IN THE NORTH PACIFIC & ONE OFF THE COAST OF PERU. THE LARGEST IS THE WANDERING ALBATROSS. THIS BIRD HAS THE GREATEST WINGSPAN (ABOUT 10FT) THE LONGEST INCUBATION PERIOD (ABOUT 80 DAYS) & LAYS THE BIGGEST EGG (ABOUT 5IN LONG) OF ANY SEA BIRD.

AROUND THE WORLD IN 80 DAYS
ALBATROSSES FLY ENORMOUS DISTANCES. THE SOOTY ALBATROSS FLIES ROUND THE WORLD BETWEEN EACH BREEDING SEASON, COVERING 19,000 MILES IN 80 DAYS. ONE BIRD (SPRAYED WITH RED PAINT FOR IDENTIFICATION) HAS BEEN OBSERVED TO FLY 1200 MILES FROM ITS BREEDING GROUND & BACK AGAIN IN TWO DAYS BRINGING FOOD TO ITS YOUNG.

ALBATROSSES & SAILORS
THE LARGER SPECIES OF ALBATROSS ARE KNOWN TO SAILORS AS GOONEYS, THE SMALLER AS MOLLYMAWKS OR MALLEMUCKS. SAILORS SOMETIMES CATCH ALBATROSSES ON THE DECK USING A HOOK & LINE WITH SALT PORK AS BAIT. IF THE BIRDS ARE KEPT ON BOARD THEY BECOME SEASICK.

EFFORTLESS FLIGHT
RESEARCH AT CARDIFF UNIVERSITY HAS REVEALED HOW ALBATROSSES CAN SOMETIMES STAY ALOFT WITHOUT EXPENDING ANY ENERGY. THEY USE THE UPWARD DEFLECTIONS OF AIR CURRENTS IMMEDIATELY ABOVE THE WAVES. IT IS ESTIMATED THAT OVER A WAVE WITH A SLOPE OF 1 IN 12 A WIND OF 16MPH, CAN 'BLOW' AN ALBATROSS TO A HEIGHT OF 20 METRES.

LEARNING TO LAND
YOUNG ALBATROSSES GO FAR OUT TO SEA AS SOON AS THEY HAVE LEARNT TO FLY AND DO NOT RETURN TO THE BREEDING GROUND FOR ABOUT A YEAR. ALTHOUGH THEY ARE STRONG FLIERS BY THIS TIME THEY HAVE LITTLE EXPERIENCE OF LANDING ON DRY LAND & TEND TO COME DOWN SOMEWHAT AWKWARDLY & COMICALLY.

ALBATROSSES' BILLS
ALBATROSSES BELONG TO A FAMILY OF BIRDS CALLED 'PROCELLARIIFORMES' WHICH MEANS TUBE-NOSED, (THEIR NOSTRILS END IN A PAIR OF SMALL TUBES AT THE TOP OF THE BILL) THEY DRINK SALT WATER & THE EXCESS SALT IS 'DISTILLED' FROM THEIR BLOOD BY TWO SMALL GLANDS ABOVE THE EYES. THE SALTY WASTE RUNS FROM THE GLANDS TO THE NOSTRILS & DRIPS OFF THE END OF THEIR BILL.

ALBATROSSES' ENGAGEMENT
THE MALE LAYAN ALBATROSS (FOUND ON THE PACIFIC ISLAND OF MIDWAY) CLAIMS A TERRITORY ABOUT 3 FT SQUARE & RETURNS TO IT EVERY SEASON. FEMALES VISIT THE MALES & PERFORM ELABORATE COURTSHIP DANCES. HOWEVER THEY DO NOT MATE IMMEDIATELY, BUT NORMALLY HAVE A TWO YEAR 'ENGAGEMENT', PERFORMING COURTSHIP DANCES WHENEVER THEY LAND.

HOW TO USE THE 'MAGIC' SQUARES BELOW

1	3	5	7	9	11	13	15
17	19	21	23	25	27	29	31
33	35	37	39	41	43	45	47
49	51	53	55	57	59	61	63

4	5	6	7	12	13	14	15
20	21	22	23	28	29	30	31
36	37	38	39	44	45	46	47
52	53	54	55	60	61	62	63

32	33	34	35	36	37	38	39
40	41	42	43	44	45	46	47
48	49	50	51	52	53	54	55
56	57	58	59	60	61	62	63

16	17	18	19	20	21	22	23
24	25	26	27	28	29	30	31
48	49	50	51	52	53	54	55
56	57	58	59	60	61	62	63

2	3	6	7	10	11	14	15
18	19	22	23	26	27	30	31
34	35	38	39	42	43	46	47
50	51	54	55	58	59	62	63

8	9	10	11	12	13	14	15
24	25	26	27	28	29	30	31
40	41	42	43	44	45	46	47
56	57	58	59	60	61	62	63

CUT OUT THE SIX GROUPS OF NUMBERS ABOVE & SHOW THEM TO A FRIEND. ASK HIM OR HER TO SELECT ONE NUMBER FROM ANY ONE GROUP. SHOW THE REMAINING 5 GROUPS TO FRIEND ASKING HIM TO HAND YOU THE GROUPS ON WHICH HIS NUMBER APPEARS. ADD TOGETHER THE TOP LEFT HAND CORNER NUMBER OF EACH CARD & THE TOTAL WILL BE YOUR FRIEND'S NUMBER.

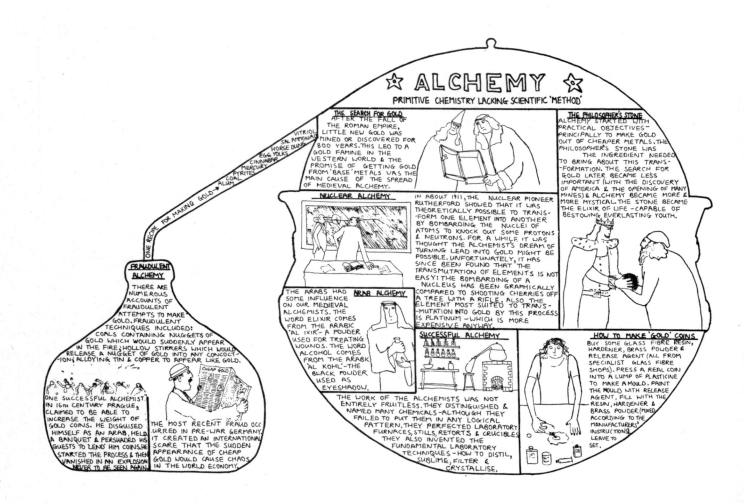

☆ ALCHEMY ☆
PRIMITIVE CHEMISTRY LACKING SCIENTIFIC 'METHOD'

THE SEARCH FOR GOLD
AFTER THE FALL OF THE ROMAN EMPIRE, LITTLE NEW GOLD WAS MINED OR DISCOVERED FOR 800 YEARS. THIS LED TO A GOLD FAMINE IN THE WESTERN WORLD & THE PROMISE OF GETTING GOLD FROM 'BASE' METALS WAS THE MAIN CAUSE OF THE SPREAD OF MEDIEVAL ALCHEMY.

THE PHILOSOPHER'S STONE
ALCHEMY STARTED WITH PRACTICAL OBJECTIVES— PRINCIPALLY TO MAKE GOLD OUT OF CHEAPER METALS. THE PHILOSOPHER'S STONE WAS THE INGREDIENT NEEDED TO BRING ABOUT THIS TRANS-FORMATION. THE SEARCH FOR GOLD LATER BECAME LESS IMPORTANT (WITH THE DISCOVERY OF AMERICA & THE OPENING OF MANY MINES) & ALCHEMY BECAME MORE & MORE MYSTICAL. THE STONE BECAME THE ELIXIR OF LIFE—CAPABLE OF BESTOWING EVERLASTING YOUTH.

NUCLEAR ALCHEMY
IN ABOUT 1911, THE NUCLEAR PIONEER RUTHERFORD SHOWED THAT IT WAS THEORETICALLY POSSIBLE TO TRANS-FORM ONE ELEMENT INTO ANOTHER BY BOMBARDING THE NUCLEI OF ATOMS TO KNOCK OUT SOME PROTONS & NEUTRONS. FOR A WHILE IT WAS THOUGHT THE ALCHEMIST'S DREAM OF TURNING LEAD INTO GOLD MIGHT BE POSSIBLE. UNFORTUNATELY, IT HAS SINCE BEEN FOUND THAT THE TRANSMUTATION OF ELEMENTS IS NOT EASY: THE BOMBARDING OF A NUCLEUS HAS BEEN GRAPHICALLY COMPARED TO SHOOTING CHERRIES OFF A TREE WITH A RIFLE. ALSO THE ELEMENT MOST SUITED TO TRANS-MUTATION INTO GOLD BY THIS PROCESS IS PLATINUM—WHICH IS MORE EXPENSIVE ANYWAY.

ARAB ALCHEMY
THE ARABS HAD SOME INFLUENCE ON OUR MEDIEVAL ALCHEMISTS. THE WORD ELIXIR COMES FROM THE ARABIC 'AL IXIR'- A POWDER USED FOR TREATING WOUNDS. THE WORD ALCOHOL COMES FROM THE ARABIC 'AL KOHL'-THE BLACK POWDER USED AS EYESHADOW.

SUCCESSFUL ALCHEMY
THE WORK OF THE ALCHEMISTS WAS NOT ENTIRELY FRUITLESS. THEY DISTINGUISHED & NAMED MANY CHEMICALS -ALTHOUGH THEY FAILED TO PUT THEM IN ANY LOGICAL PATTERN. THEY PERFECTED LABORATORY FURNACES, STILLS, RETORTS & CRUCIBLES. THEY ALSO INVENTED THE FUNDAMENTAL LABORATORY TECHNIQUES-HOW TO DISTIL, SUBLIME, FILTER & CRYSTALLISE.

HOW TO MAKE 'GOLD' COINS
BUY SOME GLASS FIBRE RESIN, HARDENER, BRASS POWDER & RELEASE AGENT (ALL FROM SPECIALIST GLASS FIBRE SHOPS). PRESS A REAL COIN INTO A LUMP OF PLASTICINE TO MAKE A MOULD. PAINT THE MOULD WITH RELEASE AGENT, FILL WITH THE RESIN, HARDENER & BRASS POWDER (MIXED ACCORDING TO THE MANUFACTURERS' INSTRUCTIONS) LEAVE TO SET.

ONE RECIPE FOR MAKING GOLD!
VITRIOL, SAL AMMONIAC, HORSE DUNG, EGG YOLKS, CINNABAR, MERCURY, PYRITES, COAL, ALUM

FRAUDULENT ALCHEMY
THERE ARE NUMEROUS ACCOUNTS OF FRAUDULENT ATTEMPTS TO MAKE GOLD. FRAUDULENT TECHNIQUES INCLUDED: COALS CONTAINING NUGGETS OF GOLD WHICH WOULD SUDDENLY APPEAR IN THE FIRE; HOLLOW STIRRERS WHICH WOULD RELEASE A NUGGET OF GOLD INTO ANY CONCOCT-ION; ALLOYING TIN & COPPER TO APPEAR LIKE GOLD.

ONE SUCCESSFUL ALCHEMIST IN 16TH CENTURY PRAGUE, CLAIMED TO BE ABLE TO INCREASE THE WEIGHT OF GOLD COINS. HE DISGUISED HIMSELF AS AN ARAB, HELD A BANQUET & PERSUADED HIS GUESTS TO LEND HIM COINS. HE STARTED THE PROCESS & THEN VANISHED IN AN EXPLOSION NEVER TO BE SEEN AGAIN.

THE MOST RECENT FRAUD OCCURRED IN PRE-WAR GERMANY. IT CREATED AN INTERNATIONAL SCARE THAT THE SUDDEN APPEARANCE OF CHEAP GOLD WOULD CAUSE CHAOS IN THE WORLD ECONOMY.

CHEAP GOLD

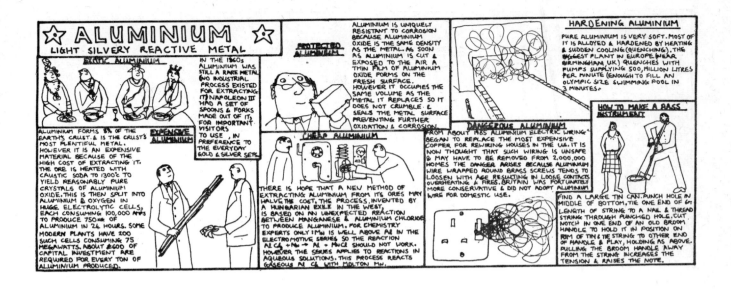

☆ ALUMINIUM ☆
LIGHT SILVERY REACTIVE METAL

EXOTIC ALUMINIUM

IN THE 1860s ALUMINIUM WAS STILL A RARE METAL (NO INDUSTRIAL PROCESS EXISTED FOR EXTRACTING IT) NAPOLEON III HAD A SET OF SPOONS & FORKS MADE OUT OF IT, FOR IMPORTANT VISITORS TO USE, IN PREFERENCE TO THE EVERYDAY GOLD & SILVER SETS.

EXPENSIVE ALUMINIUM

ALUMINIUM FORMS 8% OF THE EARTH'S CRUST & IS THE CRUST'S MOST PLENTIFUL METAL. HOWEVER IT IS AN EXPENSIVE MATERIAL BECAUSE OF THE HIGH COST OF EXTRACTING IT. THE ORE IS HEATED WITH CAUSTIC SODA TO 1300°C TO YIELD REASONABLY PURE CRYSTALS OF ALUMINIUM OXIDE. THIS IS THEN SPLIT INTO ALUMINIUM & OXYGEN IN HUGE ELECTROLYTIC CELLS, EACH CONSUMING 100,000 AMPS TO PRODUCE 750Kg OF ALUMINIUM IN 24 HOURS. SOME MODERN PLANTS HAVE 200 SUCH CELLS CONSUMING 75 MEGAWATTS. ABOUT £600 OF CAPITAL INVESTMENT ARE REQUIRED FOR EVERY TON OF ALUMINIUM PRODUCED.

PROTECTED ALUMINIUM

ALUMINIUM IS UNIQUELY RESISTANT TO CORROSION BECAUSE ALUMINIUM OXIDE IS THE SAME DENSITY AS THE METAL. AS SOON AS ALUMINIUM IS CUT & EXPOSED TO THE AIR A THIN FILM OF ALUMINIUM OXIDE FORMS ON THE FRESH SURFACE. HOWEVER IT OCCUPIES THE SAME VOLUME AS THE METAL IT REPLACES SO IT DOES NOT CRUMBLE & SEALS THE METAL SURFACE PREVENTING FURTHER OXIDATION & CORROSION.

CHEAP ALUMINIUM

THERE IS HOPE THAT A NEW METHOD OF EXTRACTING ALUMINIUM FROM ITS ORES MAY HALVE THE COST. THE PROCESS, INVENTED BY A HUNGARIAN EXILE IN THE WEST, IS BASED ON AN UNEXPECTED REACTION BETWEEN MANGANESE & ALUMINIUM CHLORIDE TO PRODUCE ALUMINIUM. FOR CHEMISTRY EXPERTS ONLY Mn IS WELL ABOVE Al IN THE ELECTROMOTIVE SERIES SO THE REACTION $AlCl_3 + Mn \rightarrow Al + MnCl_2$ SHOULD NOT WORK. HOWEVER THE SERIES APPLIES TO REACTIONS IN AQUEOUS SOLUTIONS. THIS PROCESS REACTS GASEOUS $AlCl_3$ WITH MOLTON Mn.

DANGEROUS ALUMINIUM

FROM ABOUT 1965 ALUMINIUM ELECTRIC WIRING BEGAN TO REPLACE THE MOST EXPENSIVE COPPER FOR REWIRING HOUSES IN THE U.S. IT IS NOW THOUGHT THAT SUCH WIRING IS UNSAFE & MAY HAVE TO BE REMOVED FROM 2,000,000 HOMES. THE DANGER ARISES BECAUSE ALUMINIUM WIRE WRAPPED ROUND BRASS SCREWS TENDS TO LOOSEN WITH AGE RESULTING IN LOOSE CONTACTS OVERHEATING & FIRES. BRITAIN WAS FORTUNATELY MORE CONSERVATIVE & DID NOT ADOPT ALUMINIUM WIRE FOR DOMESTIC USE.

HARDENING ALUMINIUM

PURE ALUMINIUM IS VERY SOFT. MOST OF IT IS ALLOYED & HARDENED BY HEATING & SUDDEN COOLING (QUENCHING). THE BIGGEST PLANT IN EUROPE (NEAR BIRMINGHAM, UK) QUENCHES WITH PUMPS SUPPLYING 500, MILLION LITRES PER MINUTE (ENOUGH TO FILL AN OLYMPIC SIZE SWIMMING POOL IN 3 MINUTES.

HOW TO MAKE A BASS INSTRUMENT

FIND A LARGE TIN CAN. PUNCH HOLE IN MIDDLE OF BOTTOM, TIE ONE END OF 6' LENGTH OF STRING TO A NAIL & THREAD STRING THROUGH PUNCHED HOLE. CUT NOTCH IN ONE END OF AN OLD BROOM HANDLE TO HOLD IT IN POSITION ON RIM OF TIN & THE STRING TO OTHER END OF HANDLE & PLAY, HOLDING AS ABOVE. PULLING THE BROOM HANDLE AWAY FROM THE STRING INCREASES THE TENSION & RAISES THE NOTE.

☆ AMERICAN WORDS ☆
UNITS OF THE AMERICAN LANGUAGE

YANKEE

YANKEE PROBABLY DERIVES FROM JAN KEES, A NAME ORIGINALLY USED TO MEAN 'A HOLLANDER' IN PARTS OF GERMANY. THE WORD CAME TO AMERICA FROM ENGLISH SAILORS WHO USED IT REFERRING TO DUTCH PIRATES. IT FIRST CAME INTO GENERAL USE IN THE COLONIES AS A DEROGATORY TERM MEANING 'A PERSON WHOSE COMMERCIAL ENTERPRISE OUTRUNS HIS MORAL SCRUPLES'. LATER THIS CAME TO BE REGARDED AS A COMPLIMENT.

BUM

IN AMERICA THE SOURCE OF THIS WORD IS THOUGHT TO BE 'BUMMELIN' (GERMAN FOR TO WASTE TIME) IT FIRST APPEARED AS BUMMER IN THE CIVIL WAR, USED TO DESCRIBE SOLDIERS WHO WENT FORAGING BY THEMSELVES. THE BRITISH USE OF THE WORD TO MEAN THE BACKSIDE WAS UNKNOWN IN AMERICA TILL VERY RECENTLY.

INVENTIONS

THE WORDS FOR MANY COMMON MATERIALS WERE COINED BY THEIR INVENTORS. THESE INCLUDE:

ASPIRIN

LINOLEUM

KEROSENE   CELLOPHANE   VASELINE

NYLON   ZIPPER

BULLDOZER

THE WORD BULLDOZER COMES FROM AMERICA. IT FIRST APPEARED IN 1871 USED IN A DESCRIPTION OF LOUISIANA VIGILANTES WHO SPECIALISED IN FLOGGING NEGROES SEEKING TO VOTE. ITS USE DESCRIBING AN EARTH PUSHING MACHINE IS CONSIDERABLY LATER.

LYNCH

LYNCH COMES FROM A VERY RESPECTABLE CAPTAIN W. LYNCH DURING THE AMERICAN REVOLUTION. HE SET UP A COURT IN VIRGINIA WITH OTHER IMPORTANT LOCAL CITIZENS BECAUSE THE WAR MADE IT IMPOSSIBLE TO SEND OFFENDERS TO THE PROPERLY CONSTITUTED COURTS IN WASHINGTON. HE NEVER INDULGED IN THE VIOLENCE OF LYNCHING, AS WE NOW USE THE WORD.

MORON

MORON WAS COINED BY AN AMERICAN DOCTOR IN 1910 TO DESIGNATE 'A FEEBLE MINDED INDIVIDUAL OF A MENTAL AGE BETWEEN 8 & 12 YEARS'. ITS USE SPREAD RAPIDLY TAKING ON A MUCH BROADER MEANING.

O.K.

O.K. PROBABLY STEMS FROM A VOGUE FOR ACRONYMS IN BOSTON NEWSPAPERS IN 1838 USED TO SIGNIFY 'ALL CORRECT'. HOWEVER ITS FAME DID NOT SPREAD TILL IT APPEARED IN THE POLITICAL CAMPAIGNS OF 1840, WHEN THE SUPPORTERS OF THE PRESIDENT, M.VAN BUREN, FOUNDED THE O.K. CLUB (ALSO STANDING FOR OLD KINDERHOOK THE VILLAGE WHERE HE WAS BORN.)

THE O.K. CLUB

HOW TO MAKE A POT PLANT WATERER

FIND A 6 in. STRIP OF ASBESTOS OR GLASS FIBRE FOR WICK. (A COTTON WICK WILL ALSO WORK BUT WILL ROT). TO INSERT WICK PLACE HAND OVER SOIL, INVERT POT & TAP TO RELEASE BALL OF SOIL FROM POT. SEPARATE HALF OF WICK INTO STRANDS & SPREAD OVER BOTTOM OF POT, PUSHING OTHER END THROUGH POT'S DRAINAGE HOLE. REPLACE SOIL & TAP POT TO ENSURE GOOD CONTACT BETWEEN WICK & SOIL. FINALLY PLACE POT IN TRAY OF WATER ON WOOD BLOCKS. THE PLANT WILL THEN WATER ITSELF FOR SEVERAL WEEKS.

FLOWER POT — SOIL — WICK — WOOD BLOCKS — WATER — TRAY

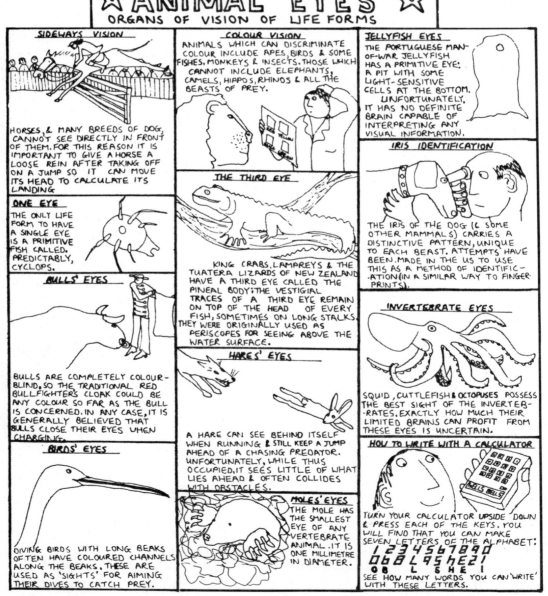

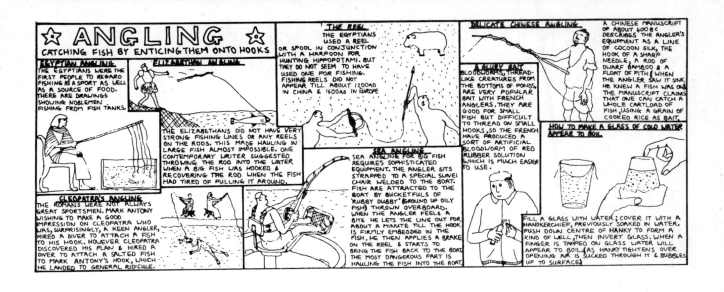

☆ ANGLING ☆
CATCHING FISH BY ENTICING THEM ONTO HOOKS

EGYPTIAN ANGLING
THE EGYPTIANS WERE THE FIRST PEOPLE TO REGARD FISHING AS A SPORT AS WELL AS A SOURCE OF FOOD. THERE ARE DRAWINGS SHOWING NOBLEMEN FISHING FROM FISH TANKS.

ELIZABETHAN ANGLING
THE ELIZABETHANS DID NOT HAVE VERY STRONG FISHING LINES OR ANY REELS ON THE RODS. THIS MADE HAULING IN LARGE FISH ALMOST IMPOSSIBLE. ONE CONTEMPORARY WRITER SUGGESTED THROWING THE ROD INTO THE WATER WHEN A BIG FISH WAS HOOKED & RECOVERING THE ROD WHEN THE FISH HAD TIRED OF PULLING IT AROUND.

CLEOPATRA'S ANGLING
THE ROMANS WERE NOT ALWAYS GREAT SPORTSMEN. MARK ANTONY WISHING TO MAKE A GOOD IMPRESSION ON CLEOPATRA WHO WAS, SURPRISINGLY, A KEEN ANGLER, HIRED A DIVER TO ATTACH A FISH TO HIS HOOK. HOWEVER CLEOPATRA DISCOVERED HIS PLAN & HIRED A DIVER TO ATTACH A SALTED FISH TO MARK ANTONY'S HOOK, WHICH HE LANDED TO GENERAL RIDICULE.

THE REEL
THE EGYPTIANS USED A REEL OR SPOOL IN CONJUNCTION WITH A HARPOON FOR HUNTING HIPPOPOTAMI. BUT THEY DO NOT SEEM TO HAVE USED ONE FOR FISHING. FISHING REELS DID NOT APPEAR TILL ABOUT 1200AD IN CHINA & 1600AD IN EUROPE

A GLUEY BAIT
BLOODWORMS, THREAD-LIKE CREATURES FROM THE BOTTOMS OF PONDS, ARE VERY POPULAR BAIT WITH FRENCH ANGLERS. THEY ARE GOOD FOR SMALL FISH BUT DIFFICULT TO THREAD ON SMALL HOOKS, SO THE FRENCH HAVE PRODUCED A SORT OF ARTIFICIAL BLOODWORM OF RED RUBBER SOLUTION WHICH IS MUCH EASIER TO USE.

SEA ANGLING
SEA ANGLING FOR BIG FISH REQUIRES SOPHISTICATED EQUIPMENT. THE ANGLER SITS STRAPPED TO A SPECIAL SWIVEL CHAIR WELDED TO THE BOAT. FISH ARE ATTRACTED TO THE BOAT BY BUCKETFULS OF 'RUBBY DUBBY' (GROUND UP OILY FISH) THROWN OVERBOARD. WHEN THE ANGLER FEELS A BITE HE LETS THE LINE OUT FOR ABOUT A MINUTE TILL THE HOOK IS FIRMLY EMBEDDED IN THE FISH, HE THEN APPLIES A BRAKE ON THE REEL & STARTS TO BRING THE FISH BACK TO THE BOAT. THE MOST DANGEROUS PART IS HAULING THE FISH INTO THE BOAT.

DELICATE CHINESE ANGLING
A CHINESE MANUSCRIPT OF ABOUT 400 BC DESCRIBES THE ANGLER'S EQUIPMENT AS A LINE OF COCOON SILK, THE HOOK OF A SHARP NEEDLE, A ROD OF DWARF BAMBOO & A FLOAT OF PITH (WHEN THE ANGLER SAW IT SINK HE KNEW A FISH WAS ON) THE MANUSCRIPT CLAIMS THAT ONE CAN CATCH A WHOLE CARTLOAD OF FISH USING A GRAIN OF COOKED RICE AS BAIT.

HOW TO MAKE A GLASS OF COLD WATER APPEAR TO BOIL
FILL A GLASS WITH WATER; COVER IT WITH A HANDKERCHIEF, PREVIOUSLY SOAKED IN WATER. PUSH DOWN CENTRE OF HANKY TO FORM A KIND OF WELL, THEN INVERT GLASS. WHEN A FINGER IS TAPPED ON GLASS WATER WILL APPEAR TO BOIL. (AS HANKY TIGHTENS OVER OPENING AIR IS SUCKED THROUGH IT & BUBBLES UP TO SURFACE.)

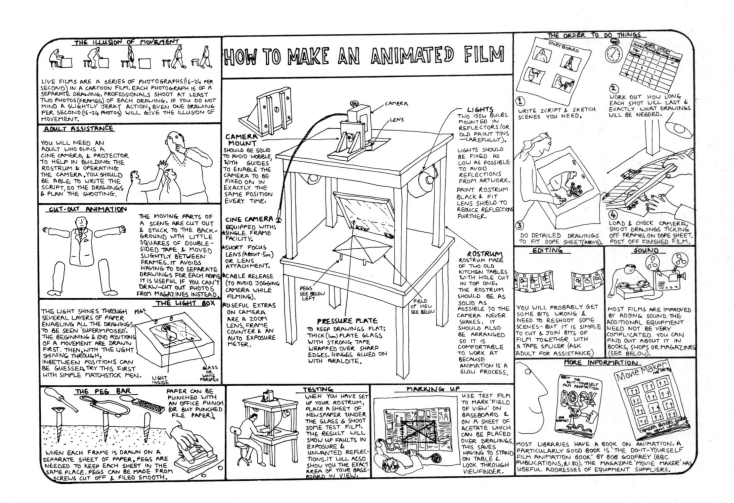

HOW TO MAKE AN ANIMATED FILM

THE ILLUSION OF MOVEMENT
LIVE FILMS ARE A SERIES OF PHOTOGRAPHS (16-24 PER SECOND) IN A CARTOON FILM. EACH PHOTOGRAPH IS OF A SEPARATE DRAWING. PROFESSIONALS SHOOT AT LEAST TWO PHOTOS (FRAMES) OF EACH DRAWING. IF YOU DO NOT MIND A SLIGHTLY JERKY ACTION, EVEN ONE DRAWING PER SECOND (16-24 PHOTOS) WILL GIVE THE ILLUSION OF MOVEMENT.

ADULT ASSISTANCE
YOU WILL NEED AN ADULT WHO OWNS A CINE CAMERA & PROJECTOR TO HELP IN BUILDING THE ROSTRUM & OPERATING THE CAMERA. YOU SHOULD BE ABLE TO WRITE THE SCRIPT, DO THE DRAWINGS & PLAN THE SHOOTING.

CUT-OUT ANIMATION
THE MOVING PARTS OF A SCENE ARE CUT OUT & STUCK TO THE BACKGROUND WITH LITTLE SQUARES OF DOUBLE-SIDED TAPE, & MOVED SLIGHTLY BETWEEN FRAMES. IT AVOIDS HAVING TO DO SEPARATE DRAWINGS FOR EACH FRAME. IT IS USEFUL IF YOU CAN'T DRAW — CUT OUT PHOTOS FROM MAGAZINES INSTEAD.

THE LIGHT BOX
THE LIGHT SHINES THROUGH SEVERAL LAYERS OF PAPER ENABLING ALL THE DRAWINGS TO BE SEEN 'SUPERIMPOSED'. THE BEGINNING & END POSITIONS OF A MOVEMENT ARE DRAWN FIRST. THEN, WITH THE LIGHT SHINING THROUGH, INBETWEEN POSITIONS CAN BE GUESSED. TRY THIS FIRST WITH SIMPLE MATCHSTICK MEN.

THE PEG BAR
PAPER CAN BE PUNCHED WITH AN OFFICE PUNCH (OR BUY PUNCHED FILE PAPER). WHEN EACH FRAME IS DRAWN ON A SEPARATE SHEET OF PAPER, PEGS ARE NEEDED TO KEEP EACH FRAME IN THE SAME PLACE. PEGS CAN BE MADE FROM SCREWS CUT OFF & FILED SMOOTH.

CAMERA MOUNT
SHOULD BE SOLID TO AVOID WOBBLE WITH GUIDES TO ENABLE THE CAMERA TO BE FIXED ON IN EXACTLY THE SAME POSITION EVERY TIME.

CINE CAMERA
EQUIPPED WITH:
• A SINGLE FRAME FACILITY.
• A SHORT FOCUS LENS (ABOUT 5m) OR LENS ATTACHMENT.
• A CABLE RELEASE (TO AVOID JOGGING CAMERA WHILE FILMING).
• USEFUL EXTRAS ON CAMERA ARE A ZOOM LENS, FRAME COUNTER & AN AUTO EXPOSURE METER.

PRESSURE PLATE
TO KEEP DRAWINGS FLAT: THICK (1cm) PLATE GLASS WITH STRONG TAPE WRAPPED OVER SHARP EDGES. HINGES GLUED ON WITH ARALDITE.

PEGS SEE BELOW LEFT

FIELD OF VIEW SEE BELOW

LIGHTS
TWO 150W BULBS MOUNTED IN REFLECTORS (OR OLD PAINT TINS — CAREFULLY). LIGHTS SHOULD BE FIXED AS LOW AS POSSIBLE TO AVOID REFLECTIONS FROM ARTWORK. PAINT ROSTRUM BLACK & FIT LENS SHIELD TO REDUCE REFLECTIONS FURTHER.

ROSTRUM
ROSTRUM MADE OF TWO OLD KITCHEN TABLES WITH HOLE CUT IN TOP ONE. THE ROSTRUM SHOULD BE AS SOLID AS POSSIBLE SO THE CAMERA NEVER SHAKES. IT SHOULD ALSO BE ARRANGED SO IT IS COMFORTABLE TO WORK AT BECAUSE ANIMATION IS A SLOW PROCESS.

THE ORDER TO DO THINGS

① WRITE SCRIPT & SKETCH SCENES YOU NEED.

② WORK OUT HOW LONG EACH SHOT WILL LAST & EXACTLY WHAT DRAWINGS WILL BE NEEDED.

③ DO DETAILED DRAWINGS TO FIT DOPE SHEET (ABOVE).

④ LOAD & CHECK CAMERA. SHOOT DRAWINGS, TICKING OFF FRAMES ON DOPE SHEET. POST OFF FINISHED FILM.

EDITING
YOU WILL PROBABLY GET SOME BITS WRONG & NEED TO RESHOOT SOME SCENES — BUT IT IS SIMPLE TO CUT & JOIN BITS OF FILM TOGETHER WITH A TAPE SPLICER (ASK ADULT FOR ASSISTANCE).

SOUND
MOST FILMS ARE IMPROVED BY ADDING SOUND. THE ADDITIONAL EQUIPMENT NEED NOT BE VERY COMPLICATED. YOU CAN FIND OUT ABOUT IT IN BOOKS, SHOPS OR MAGAZINES (SEE BELOW).

MORE INFORMATION
MOST LIBRARIES HAVE A BOOK ON ANIMATION. A PARTICULARLY GOOD BOOK IS 'THE DO-IT-YOURSELF FILM ANIMATION BOOK' BY BOB GODFREY (BBC PUBLICATIONS, £1.50). THE MAGAZINE 'MOVIE MAKER' HAS USEFUL ADDRESSES OF EQUIPMENT SUPPLIERS.

TESTING
WHEN YOU HAVE SET UP YOUR ROSTRUM, PLACE A SHEET OF NEWSPAPER UNDER THE GLASS & SHOOT SOME TEST FILM. THE RESULT WILL SHOW UP FAULTS IN EXPOSURE & UNWANTED REFLECTIONS. IT WILL ALSO SHOW YOU THE EXACT AREA OF YOUR BASEBOARD IN VIEW.

MARKING UP
USE TEST FILM TO MARK 'FIELD OF VIEW' ON BASEBOARD & ON A SHEET OF ACETATE WHICH CAN BE PLACED OVER DRAWINGS. THIS SAVES HAVING TO STAND ON TABLE & LOOK THROUGH VIEWFINDER.

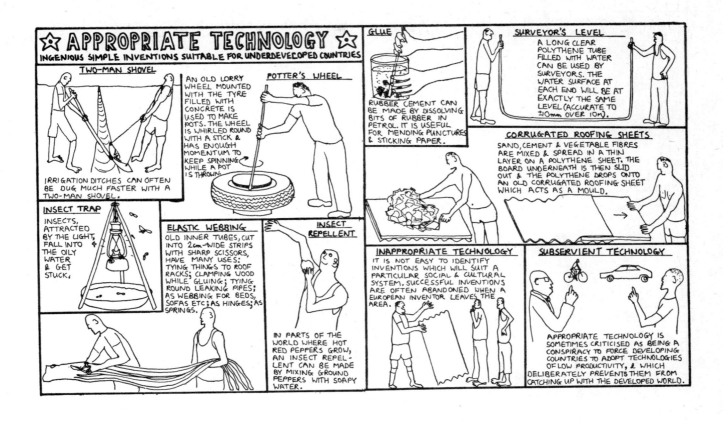

☆ APPROPRIATE TECHNOLOGY ☆

INGENIOUS SIMPLE INVENTIONS SUITABLE FOR UNDERDEVELOPED COUNTRIES

TWO-MAN SHOVEL

IRRIGATION DITCHES CAN OFTEN BE DUG MUCH FASTER WITH A TWO-MAN SHOVEL.

POTTER'S WHEEL

AN OLD LORRY WHEEL MOUNTED WITH THE TYRE FILLED WITH CONCRETE IS USED TO MAKE POTS. THE WHEEL IS WHIRLED ROUND WITH A STICK & HAS ENOUGH MOMENTUM TO KEEP SPINNING WHILE A POT IS THROWN.

INSECT TRAP

INSECTS, ATTRACTED BY THE LIGHT, FALL INTO THE OILY WATER & GET STUCK.

ELASTIC WEBBING

OLD INNER TUBES, CUT INTO 2cm-WIDE STRIPS WITH SHARP SCISSORS, HAVE MANY USES: TYING THINGS TO ROOF RACKS; CLAMPING WOOD WHILE GLUING; TYING ROUND LEAKING PIPES; AS WEBBING FOR BEDS, SOFAS ETC; AS HINGES; AS SPRINGS.

INSECT REPELLENT

IN PARTS OF THE WORLD WHERE HOT RED PEPPERS GROW, AN INSECT REPELLENT CAN BE MADE BY MIXING GROUND PEPPERS WITH SOAPY WATER.

GLUE

RUBBER CEMENT CAN BE MADE BY DISSOLVING BITS OF RUBBER IN PETROL. IT IS USEFUL FOR MENDING PUNCTURES & STICKING PAPER.

SURVEYOR'S LEVEL

A LONG CLEAR POLYTHENE TUBE FILLED WITH WATER CAN BE USED BY SURVEYORS. THE WATER SURFACE AT EACH END WILL BE AT EXACTLY THE SAME LEVEL (ACCURATE TO ±10mm OVER 10m).

CORRUGATED ROOFING SHEETS

SAND, CEMENT & VEGETABLE FIBRES ARE MIXED & SPREAD IN A THIN LAYER ON A POLYTHENE SHEET. THE BOARD UNDERNEATH IS THEN SLID OUT & THE POLYTHENE DROPS ONTO AN OLD CORRUGATED ROOFING SHEET WHICH ACTS AS A MOULD.

INAPPROPRIATE TECHNOLOGY

IT IS NOT EASY TO IDENTIFY INVENTIONS WHICH WILL SUIT A PARTICULAR SOCIAL & CULTURAL SYSTEM. SUCCESSFUL INVENTIONS ARE OFTEN ABANDONED WHEN A EUROPEAN INVENTOR LEAVES THE AREA.

SUBSERVIENT TECHNOLOGY

APPROPRIATE TECHNOLOGY IS SOMETIMES CRITICISED AS BEING A CONSPIRACY TO FORCE DEVELOPING COUNTRIES TO ADOPT TECHNOLOGIES OF LOW PRODUCTIVITY, & WHICH DELIBERATELY PREVENTS THEM FROM CATCHING UP WITH THE DEVELOPED WORLD.

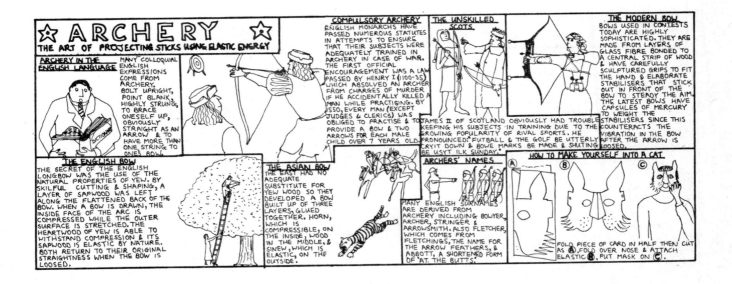

☆ ARCHERY ☆

THE ART OF PROJECTING STICKS USING ELASTIC ENERGY

ARCHERY IN THE ENGLISH LANGUAGE

MANY COLLOQUIAL ENGLISH EXPRESSIONS COME FROM ARCHERY. BOLT UPRIGHT, POINT BLANK, HIGHLY STRUNG, TO BRACE ONESELF UP, OBVIOUSLY STRAIGHT AS AN ARROW & TO HAVE MORE THAN ONE STRING TO ONE'S BOW.

THE ENGLISH BOW

THE SECRET OF THE ENGLISH LONGBOW WAS THE USE OF THE NATURAL PROPERTIES OF YEW. BY SKILFUL CUTTING & SHAPING, A LAYER OF SAPWOOD WAS LEFT ALONG THE FLATTENED BACK OF THE BOW. WHEN A BOW IS DRAWN, THE INSIDE FACE OF THE ARC IS COMPRESSED WHILE THE OUTER SURFACE IS STRETCHED. THE HEARTWOOD OF YEW IS ABLE TO WITHSTAND COMPRESSION & ITS SAPWOOD IS ELASTIC BY NATURE. BOTH RETURN TO THEIR ORIGINAL STRAIGHTNESS WHEN THE BOW IS LOOSED.

COMPULSORY ARCHERY

ENGLISH MONARCHS HAVE PASSED NUMEROUS STATUTES IN ATTEMPTS TO ENSURE THAT THEIR SUBJECTS WERE ADEQUATELY TRAINED IN ARCHERY IN CASE OF WAR. THE FIRST OFFICIAL ENCOURAGEMENT WAS A LAW PASSED BY HENRY I (1100-35) WHICH ABSOLVED AN ARCHER FROM CHARGES OF MURDER IF HE ACCIDENTALLY KILLED A MAN WHILE PRACTISING. BY 1550, EVERY MAN (EXCEPT JUDGES & CLERICS) WAS OBLIGED TO PRACTISE & TO PROVIDE A BOW & TWO ARROWS FOR EACH MALE CHILD OVER 7 YEARS OLD.

THE ASIAN BOW

THE EAST HAD NO ADEQUATE SUBSTITUTE FOR YEW WOOD SO THEY DEVELOPED A BOW BUILT UP OF THREE LAYERS, GLUED TOGETHER. HORN, WHICH IS COMPRESSIBLE, ON THE INSIDE, WOOD IN THE MIDDLE, & SINEW, WHICH IS ELASTIC, ON THE OUTSIDE.

THE UNSKILLED SCOTS

JAMES II OF SCOTLAND OBVIOUSLY HAD TROUBLE KEEPING HIS SUBJECTS IN TRAINING DUE TO THE GROWING POPULARITY OF RIVAL SPORTS. HE PRONOUNCED: "FUTBALL & THE GOLF BE UTTERLY CRYIT DOWN & BOWE MARKS BE MADE & SHUTING BE USYT ILK SUNDAY."

ARCHERS' NAMES

MANY ENGLISH SURNAMES ARE DERIVED FROM ARCHERY INCLUDING BOWYER, ARCHER, STRINGER & ARROWSMITH. ALSO FLETCHER WHICH COMES FROM FLETCHINGS, THE NAME FOR THE ARROW FEATHERS, & ABBOTT, A SHORTENED FORM OF 'AT. THE BUTTS'.

THE MODERN BOW

BOWS USED IN CONTESTS TODAY ARE HIGHLY SOPHISTICATED. THEY ARE MADE FROM LAYERS OF GLASS FIBRE BONDED TO A CENTRAL STRIP OF WOOD & HAVE CAREFULLY SCULPTURED GRIPS TO FIT THE HAND & ELABORATE STABILISERS THAT STICK OUT IN FRONT OF THE BOW TO STEADY THE AIM. THE LATEST BOWS HAVE CAPSULES OF MERCURY TO WEIGHT THE STABILISERS SINCE THIS COUNTERACTS THE VIBRATION IN THE BOW AFTER THE ARROW IS LOOSED.

HOW TO MAKE YOURSELF INTO A CAT

FOLD PIECE OF CARD IN HALF THEN CUT AS (A). FOLD OVER NOSE & ATTACH ELASTIC (B). PUT MASK ON (C).

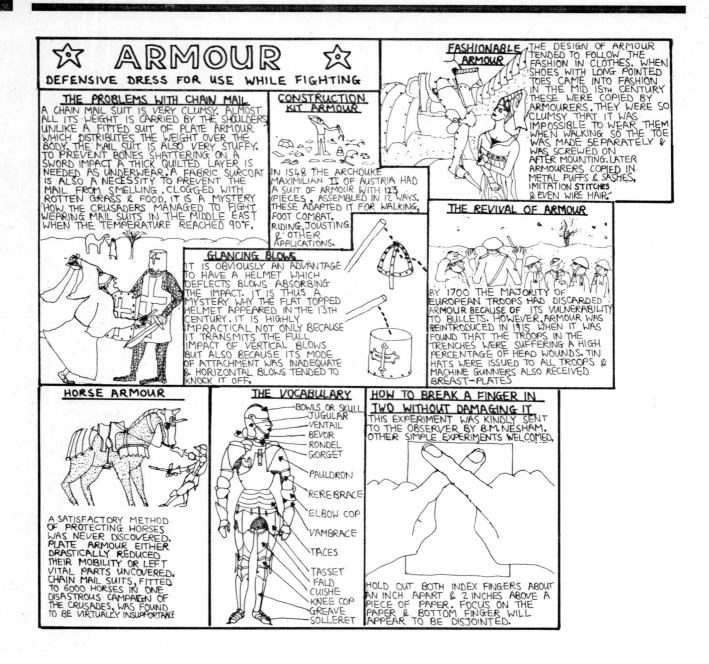

☆ ARMOUR ☆
DEFENSIVE DRESS FOR USE WHILE FIGHTING

THE PROBLEMS WITH CHAIN MAIL

A CHAIN MAIL SUIT IS VERY CLUMSY. ALMOST ALL ITS WEIGHT IS CARRIED BY THE SHOULDERS UNLIKE A FITTED SUIT OF PLATE ARMOUR WHICH DISTRIBUTES THE WEIGHT OVER THE BODY. THE MAIL SUIT IS ALSO VERY STUFFY. TO PREVENT BONES SHATTERING ON A SWORD IMPACT A THICK QUILTED LAYER IS NEEDED AS UNDERWEAR. A FABRIC SURCOAT IS ALSO A NECESSITY TO PREVENT THE MAIL FROM SMELLING, CLOGGED WITH ROTTEN GRASS & FOOD. IT IS A MYSTERY HOW THE CRUSADERS MANAGED TO FIGHT WEARING MAIL SUITS IN THE MIDDLE EAST WHEN THE TEMPERATURE REACHED 90°F.

CONSTRUCTION KIT ARMOUR

IN 1548 THE ARCHDUKE MAXIMILIAN II OF AUSTRIA HAD A SUIT OF ARMOUR WITH 123 PIECES, ASSEMBLED IN 12 WAYS. THESE ADAPTED IT FOR WALKING, FOOT COMBAT, RIDING, JOUSTING & OTHER APPLICATIONS.

GLANCING BLOWS

IT IS OBVIOUSLY AN ADVANTAGE TO HAVE A HELMET WHICH DEFLECTS BLOWS ABSORBING THE IMPACT. IT IS THUS A MYSTERY WHY THE FLAT TOPPED HELMET APPEARED IN THE 13TH CENTURY. IT IS HIGHLY IMPRACTICAL NOT ONLY BECAUSE IT TRANSMITS THE FULL IMPACT OF VERTICAL BLOWS BUT ALSO BECAUSE ITS MODE OF ATTACHMENT WAS INADEQUATE & HORIZONTAL BLOWS TENDED TO KNOCK IT OFF.

FASHIONABLE ARMOUR

THE DESIGN OF ARMOUR TENDED TO FOLLOW THE FASHION IN CLOTHES. WHEN SHOES WITH LONG POINTED TOES CAME INTO FASHION IN THE MID 15TH CENTURY THESE WERE COPIED BY ARMOURERS. THEY WERE SO CLUMSY THAT IT WAS IMPOSSIBLE TO WEAR THEM WHEN WALKING SO THE TOE WAS MADE SEPARATELY & WAS SCREWED ON AFTER MOUNTING. LATER ARMOURERS COPIED IN METAL PUFFS & SASHES, IMITATION STITCHES & EVEN WIRE HAIR.

THE REVIVAL OF ARMOUR

BY 1700 THE MAJORITY OF EUROPEAN TROOPS HAD DISCARDED ARMOUR BECAUSE OF ITS VULNERABILITY TO BULLETS. HOWEVER, ARMOUR WAS REINTRODUCED IN 1915 WHEN IT WAS FOUND THAT THE TROOPS IN THE TRENCHES WERE SUFFERING A HIGH PERCENTAGE OF HEAD WOUNDS. TIN HATS WERE ISSUED TO ALL TROOPS & MACHINE GUNNERS ALSO RECEIVED BREAST-PLATES.

HORSE ARMOUR

A SATISFACTORY METHOD OF PROTECTING HORSES WAS NEVER DISCOVERED. PLATE ARMOUR EITHER DRASTICALLY REDUCED THEIR MOBILITY OR LEFT VITAL PARTS UNCOVERED. CHAIN MAIL SUITS, FITTED TO 6000 HORSES IN ONE DISASTROUS CAMPAIGN OF THE CRUSADES, WAS FOUND TO BE VIRTUALLY INSUPPORTABLE.

THE VOCABULARY

- BOWLS OR SKULL
- JUGULAR
- VENTAIL
- BEVOR
- RONDEL
- GORGET
- PAULDRON
- REREBRACE
- ELBOW COP
- VAMBRACE
- TACES
- TASSET
- FALD
- CUISHE
- KNEE COP
- GREAVE
- SOLLERET

HOW TO BREAK A FINGER IN TWO WITHOUT DAMAGING IT

THIS EXPERIMENT WAS KINDLY SENT TO THE OBSERVER BY B.M. NESHAM. OTHER SIMPLE EXPERIMENTS WELCOMED.

HOLD OUT BOTH INDEX FINGERS ABOUT AN INCH APART & 2 INCHES ABOVE A PIECE OF PAPER. FOCUS ON THE PAPER & BOTTOM FINGER WILL APPEAR TO BE DISJOINTED.

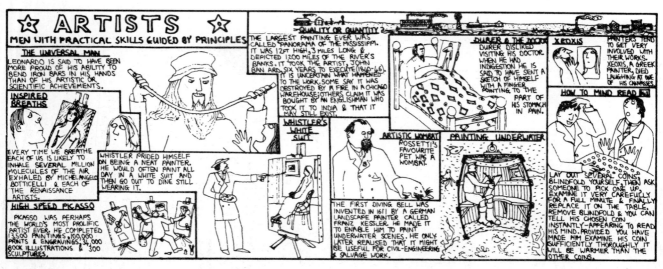

☆ ARTISTS ☆
MEN WITH PRACTICAL SKILLS GUIDED BY PRINCIPLES

THE UNIVERSAL MAN

LEONARDO IS SAID TO HAVE BEEN MORE PROUD OF HIS ABILITY TO BEND IRON BARS IN HIS HANDS THAN OF HIS ARTISTIC OR SCIENTIFIC ACHIEVEMENTS.

INSPIRED BREATHS

EVERY TIME WE BREATHE EACH OF US IS LIKELY TO INHALE SEVERAL MILLION MOLECULES OF THE AIR EXHALED BY MICHELANGELO, BOTTICELLI & EACH OF THE RENAISSANCE ARTISTS.

HIGH SPEED PICASSO

PICASSO WAS PERHAPS THE WORLD'S MOST PROLIFIC ARTIST EVER. HE COMPLETED 1,500 PAINTINGS, 100,000 PRINTS & ENGRAVINGS, 34,000 BOOK ILLUSTRATIONS & 300 SCULPTURES.

QUALITY OR QUANTITY?

THE LARGEST PAINTING EVER WAS CALLED 'PANORAMA OF THE MISSISSIPPI'. IT WAS 12FT HIGH, 3 MILES LONG & DEPICTED 1200 MILES OF THE RIVER'S BANKS. IT TOOK THE ARTIST, JOHN BANVARD, SIX YEARS TO EXECUTE (1840-46). IT IS UNCERTAIN WHAT HAPPENED TO THE WORK. SOME SAY IT WAS DESTROYED BY A FIRE IN A CHICAGO WAREHOUSE; OTHERS CLAIM IT WAS BOUGHT BY AN ENGLISHMAN WHO TOOK IT TO INDIA & THAT IT MAY STILL EXIST.

WHISTLER'S WHITE SUIT

WHISTLER PRIDED HIMSELF ON BEING A NEAT PAINTER. HE WOULD OFTEN PAINT ALL DAY IN A WHITE SUIT AND THEN GO OUT TO DINE STILL WEARING IT.

DÜRER & THE DOCTOR

DÜRER DISLIKED VISITING HIS DOCTOR. WHEN HE HAD INDIGESTION HE IS SAID TO HAVE SENT A SKETCH OF HIMSELF WITH A FINGER POINTING TO THE PART OF HIS STOMACH IN PAIN.

ARTISTIC WOMBAT

ROSSETTI'S FAVOURITE PET WAS A WOMBAT.

PAINTING UNDERWATER

THE FIRST DIVING BELL WAS INVENTED IN 1611 BY A GERMAN LANDSCAPE PAINTER CALLED FRANZ KESSLER. HE MADE IT TO ENABLE HIM TO PAINT UNDERWATER SCENES. HE ONLY LATER REALISED THAT IT MIGHT BE USEFUL FOR CIVIL-ENGINEERING & SALVAGE WORK.

ZEUXIS

PAINTERS TEND TO GET VERY INVOLVED WITH THEIR WORKS. ZEUXIS, A GREEK PAINTER, DIED LAUGHING AT ONE OF HIS CANVASES.

HOW TO MIND READ

LAY OUT SEVERAL COINS BLINDFOLD YOURSELF, THEN ASK SOMEONE TO PICK ONE UP. EXAMINE IT VERY CAREFULLY FOR A FULL MINUTE & FINALLY REPLACE IT ON THE TABLE. REMOVE BLINDFOLD & YOU CAN TELL HIS CHOSEN COIN INSTANTLY—APPEARING TO READ HIS MIND. PROVIDED YOU HAVE MADE HIM EXAMINE HIS COIN SUFFICIENTLY THOROUGHLY IT WILL BE WARMER THAN THE OTHER COINS.

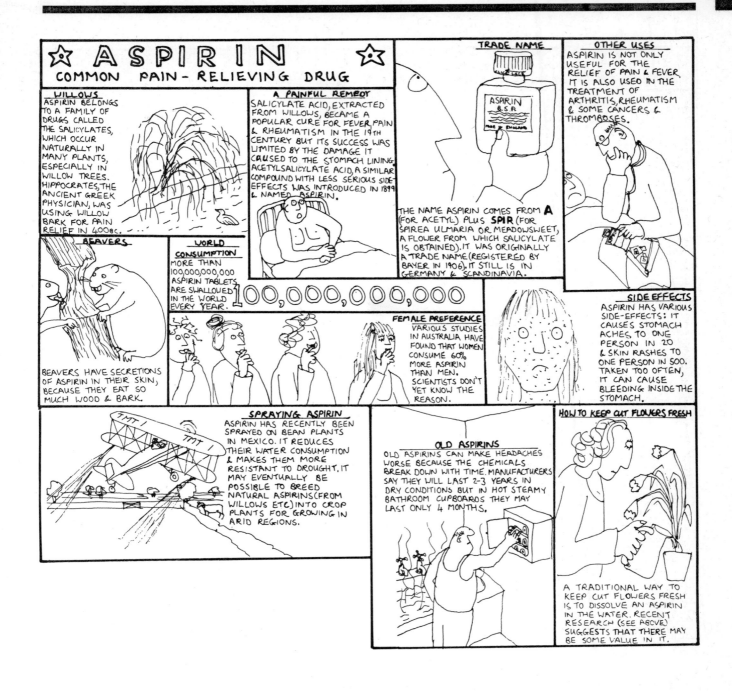

☆ ASPIRIN ☆
COMMON PAIN-RELIEVING DRUG

WILLOWS
ASPIRIN BELONGS TO A FAMILY OF DRUGS CALLED THE SALICYLATES, WHICH OCCUR NATURALLY IN MANY PLANTS, ESPECIALLY IN WILLOW TREES. HIPPOCRATES, THE ANCIENT GREEK PHYSICIAN, WAS USING WILLOW BARK FOR PAIN RELIEF IN 400BC.

A PAINFUL REMEDY
SALICYLATE ACID, EXTRACTED FROM WILLOWS, BECAME A POPULAR CURE FOR FEVER, PAIN & RHEUMATISM IN THE 19TH CENTURY BUT ITS SUCCESS WAS LIMITED BY THE DAMAGE IT CAUSED TO THE STOMACH LINING. ACETYLSALICYLATE ACID, A SIMILAR COMPOUND WITH LESS SERIOUS SIDE-EFFECTS WAS INTRODUCED IN 1899 & NAMED ASPIRIN.

TRADE NAME
THE NAME ASPIRIN COMES FROM **A** (FOR ACETYL) PLUS **SPIR** (FOR SPIREA ULMARIA OR MEADOWSWEET, A FLOWER FROM WHICH SALICYLATE IS OBTAINED). IT WAS ORIGINALLY A TRADE NAME (REGISTERED BY BAYER IN 1906). IT STILL IS IN GERMANY & SCANDINAVIA.

OTHER USES
ASPIRIN IS NOT ONLY USEFUL FOR THE RELIEF OF PAIN & FEVER, IT IS ALSO USED IN THE TREATMENT OF ARTHRITIS, RHEUMATISM & SOME CANCERS & THROMBOSES.

BEAVERS
BEAVERS HAVE SECRETIONS OF ASPIRIN IN THEIR SKIN, BECAUSE THEY EAT SO MUCH WOOD & BARK.

WORLD CONSUMPTION
MORE THAN 100,000,000,000 ASPIRIN TABLETS ARE SWALLOWED IN THE WORLD EVERY YEAR. 100,000,000,000,000

FEMALE PREFERENCE
VARIOUS STUDIES IN AUSTRALIA HAVE FOUND THAT WOMEN CONSUME 60% MORE ASPIRIN THAN MEN. SCIENTISTS DON'T YET KNOW THE REASON.

SIDE EFFECTS
ASPIRIN HAS VARIOUS SIDE-EFFECTS: IT CAUSES STOMACH ACHES TO ONE PERSON IN 20 & SKIN RASHES TO ONE PERSON IN 500. TAKEN TOO OFTEN, IT CAN CAUSE BLEEDING INSIDE THE STOMACH.

SPRAYING ASPIRIN
ASPIRIN HAS RECENTLY BEEN SPRAYED ON BEAN PLANTS IN MEXICO. IT REDUCES THEIR WATER CONSUMPTION & MAKES THEM MORE RESISTANT TO DROUGHT. IT MAY EVENTUALLY BE POSSIBLE TO BREED NATURAL ASPIRINS (FROM WILLOWS ETC) INTO CROP PLANTS FOR GROWING IN ARID REGIONS.

OLD ASPIRINS
OLD ASPIRINS CAN MAKE HEADACHES WORSE BECAUSE THE CHEMICALS BREAK DOWN WITH TIME. MANUFACTURERS SAY THEY WILL LAST 2-3 YEARS IN DRY CONDITIONS BUT IN HOT STEAMY BATHROOM CUPBOARDS THEY MAY LAST ONLY 4 MONTHS.

HOW TO KEEP CUT FLOWERS FRESH
A TRADITIONAL WAY TO KEEP CUT FLOWERS FRESH IS TO DISSOLVE AN ASPIRIN IN THE WATER. RECENT RESEARCH (SEE ABOVE) SUGGESTS THAT THERE MAY BE SOME VALUE IN IT.

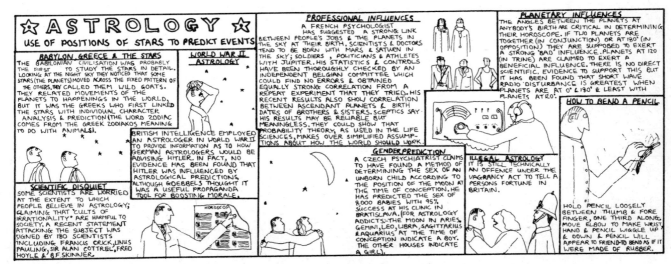

☆ ASTROLOGY ☆
USE OF POSITIONS OF STARS TO PREDICT EVENTS

BABYLON, GREECE & THE STARS
THE BABYLONIAN CIVILISATION WAS PROBABLY THE FIRST TO STUDY THE STARS IN DETAIL. LOOKING AT THE NIGHT SKY THEY NOTICED THAT SOME STARS (THE PLANETS) MOVED ACROSS THE FIXED PATTERN OF THE OTHERS. THEY CALLED THEM THE WILD GOATS. THEY RELATED MOVEMENTS OF THE PLANETS TO HAPPENINGS IN THE WORLD, BUT IT WAS THE GREEKS WHO FIRST LINKED THE STARS WITH INDIVIDUAL CHARACTER ANALYSIS & PREDICTION (THE WORD ZODIAC COMES FROM THE GREEK ZODIAKOS MEANING TO DO WITH ANIMALS).

WORLD WAR II ASTROLOGY
BRITISH INTELLIGENCE EMPLOYED AN ASTROLOGER IN WORLD WAR II TO PROVIDE INFORMATION AS TO HOW GERMAN ASTROLOGERS WOULD BE ADVISING HITLER. IN FACT, NO EVIDENCE HAS BEEN FOUND THAT HITLER WAS INFLUENCED BY ASTROLOGICAL PREDICTIONS, ALTHOUGH GOEBBELS THOUGHT IT WAS A USEFUL PROPAGANDA TOOL FOR BOOSTING MORALE.

SCIENTIFIC DISQUIET
SOME SCIENTISTS ARE WORRIED AT THE EXTENT TO WHICH PEOPLE BELIEVE IN ASTROLOGY; CLAIMING THAT 'CULTS OF IRRATIONALITY' ARE HARMFUL TO SOCIETY. A RECENT STATEMENT ATTACKING THE SUBJECT WAS SIGNED BY 180 SCIENTISTS INCLUDING FRANCIS CRICK, LINUS PAULING, SIR ALAN COTTREL, FRED HOYLE & B.F. SKINNER.

PROFESSIONAL INFLUENCES
A FRENCH PSYCHOLOGIST HAS SUGGESTED A STRONG LINK BETWEEN PEOPLE'S JOBS & THE PLANETS IN THE SKY AT THEIR BIRTH. SCIENTISTS & DOCTORS TEND TO BE BORN WITH MARS & SATURN IN THE SKY; SOLDIERS, POLITICIANS & ATHLETES WITH JUPITER. HIS STATISTICS & CONTROLS HAVE BEEN THOROUGHLY CHECKED BY AN INDEPENDENT BELGIAN COMMITTEE WHICH COULD FIND NO ERRORS & OBTAINED EQUALLY STRONG CORRELATION FROM A REPEAT EXPERIMENT THAT THEY TRIED. HIS RECENT RESULTS ALSO SHOW CORRELATION BETWEEN ASCENDANT PLANETS & BIRTH DATES OF BROTHERS & SISTERS. SCEPTICS SAY HIS RESULTS MAY BE RELIABLE BUT MEANINGLESS, THEY COULD SHOW THAT PROBABILITY THEORY, AS USED IN THE LIFE SCIENCES, MAKES OVER SIMPLIFIED ASSUMPTIONS ABOUT HOW THE WORLD SHOULD WORK.

GENDER PREDICTION
A CZECH PSYCHIATRIST CLAIMS TO HAVE FOUND A METHOD OF DETERMINING THE SEX OF AN UNBORN CHILD ACCORDING TO THE POSITION OF THE MOON AT THE TIME OF CONCEPTION. HE HAS PREDICTED THE SEX OF 8,000 BABIES WITH 95% SUCCESS AT HIS CLINIC IN BRATISLAVA. (FOR ASTROLOGY ADDICTS – THE MOON IN ARIES, GEMINI, LEO, LIBRA, SAGITTARIUS & AQUARIUS AT THE TIME OF CONCEPTION INDICATE A BOY. THE OTHER HOUSES INDICATE A GIRL).

PLANETARY INFLUENCES
THE ANGLES BETWEEN THE PLANETS AT ANYBODY'S BIRTH ARE CRITICAL IN DETERMINING THEIR HOROSCOPE. IF TWO PLANETS ARE TOGETHER (IN CONJUNCTION) OR AT 180° (IN OPPOSITION) THEY ARE SUPPOSED TO EXERT A STRONG 'BAD' INFLUENCE. PLANETS AT 120° (IN TRINE) ARE CLAIMED TO EXERT A BENEFICIAL INFLUENCE. THERE IS NO DIRECT SCIENTIFIC EVIDENCE TO SUPPORT THIS BUT IT HAS BEEN FOUND THAT SHORT WAVE RADIO DISTURBANCE IS GREATEST WHEN PLANETS ARE AT 0° & 180° & LEAST WITH PLANETS AT 120°.

ILLEGAL ASTROLOGY
IT IS STILL TECHNICALLY AN OFFENCE UNDER THE VAGRANCY ACT TO TELL A PERSON'S FORTUNE IN BRITAIN.

HOW TO BEND A PENCIL
HOLD PENCIL LOOSELY BETWEEN THUMB & FORE FINGER, ONE THIRD ALONG. MOVE ELBOW TO MAKE WRIST, HAND & PENCIL WIGGLE UP & DOWN & PENCIL WILL APPEAR TO FRIEND TO BEND AS IF IT WERE MADE OF RUBBER.

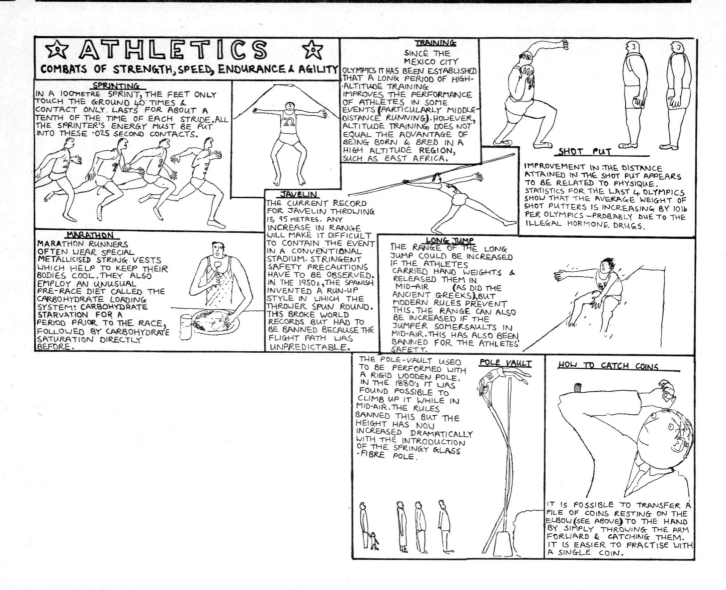

☆ ATHLETICS ☆
COMBATS OF STRENGTH, SPEED, ENDURANCE & AGILITY

SPRINTING
IN A 100METRE SPRINT, THE FEET ONLY TOUCH THE GROUND 40 TIMES & CONTACT ONLY. LASTS FOR ABOUT A TENTH OF THE TIME OF EACH STRIDE. ALL THE SPRINTER'S ENERGY MUST BE PUT INTO THESE .025 SECOND CONTACTS.

TRAINING
SINCE THE MEXICO CITY OLYMPICS IT HAS BEEN ESTABLISHED THAT A LONG PERIOD OF HIGH-ALTITUDE TRAINING IMPROVES THE PERFORMANCE OF ATHLETES IN SOME EVENTS (PARTICULARLY MIDDLE-DISTANCE RUNNING). HOWEVER, ALTITUDE TRAINING DOES NOT EQUAL THE ADVANTAGE OF BEING BORN & BRED IN A HIGH ALTITUDE REGION, SUCH AS EAST AFRICA.

SHOT PUT
IMPROVEMENT IN THE DISTANCE ATTAINED IN THE SHOT PUT APPEARS TO BE RELATED TO PHYSIQUE. STATISTICS FOR THE LAST 4 OLYMPICS SHOW THAT THE AVERAGE WEIGHT OF SHOT PUTTERS IS INCREASING BY 10lb PER OLYMPICS — PROBABLY DUE TO THE ILLEGAL HORMONE DRUGS.

MARATHON
MARATHON RUNNERS OFTEN WEAR SPECIAL METALLICISED STRING VESTS WHICH HELP TO KEEP THEIR BODIES COOL. THEY ALSO EMPLOY AN UNUSUAL PRE-RACE DIET CALLED THE CARBOHYDRATE LOADING SYSTEM: CARBOHYDRATE STARVATION FOR A PERIOD PRIOR TO THE RACE, FOLLOWED BY CARBOHYDRATE SATURATION DIRECTLY BEFORE.

JAVELIN
THE CURRENT RECORD FOR JAVELIN THROWING IS 95 METRES. ANY INCREASE IN RANGE WILL MAKE IT DIFFICULT TO CONTAIN THE EVENT IN A CONVENTIONAL STADIUM. STRINGENT SAFETY PRECAUTIONS HAVE TO BE OBSERVED. IN THE 1950s, THE SPANISH INVENTED A RUN-UP STYLE IN WHICH THE THROWER SPUN ROUND. THIS BROKE WORLD RECORDS BUT HAD TO BE BANNED BECAUSE THE FLIGHT PATH WAS UNPREDICTABLE.

LONG JUMP
THE RANGE OF THE LONG JUMP COULD BE INCREASED IF THE ATHLETES CARRIED HAND WEIGHTS & RELEASED THEM IN MID-AIR (AS DID THE ANCIENT GREEKS) BUT MODERN RULES PREVENT THIS. THE RANGE CAN ALSO BE INCREASED IF THE JUMPER SOMERSAULTS IN MID-AIR. THIS HAS ALSO BEEN BANNED FOR THE ATHLETES' SAFETY.

POLE VAULT
THE POLE-VAULT USED TO BE PERFORMED WITH A RIGID WOODEN POLE. IN THE 1880's IT WAS FOUND POSSIBLE TO CLIMB UP IT WHILE IN MID-AIR. THE RULES BANNED THIS BUT THE HEIGHT HAS NOW INCREASED DRAMATICALLY WITH THE INTRODUCTION OF THE SPRINGY GLASS-FIBRE POLE.

HOW TO CATCH COINS
IT IS POSSIBLE TO TRANSFER A PILE OF COINS RESTING ON THE ELBOW (SEE ABOVE) TO THE HAND BY SIMPLY THROWING THE ARM FORWARD & CATCHING THEM. IT IS EASIER TO PRACTISE WITH A SINGLE COIN.

☆ AUTOMOBILES ☆
VEHICLES DEPENDANT ON A VOLATILE SOURCE

THE FIRST PETROL SHORTAGE
EARLY MOTORISTS HAD GREAT DIFFICULTY IN OBTAINING THE PETROLEUM SPIRIT TO POWER THEIR VEHICLES. AT FIRST IT WAS SOLD ONLY BY PAINT-SHOPS & SUB POST-OFFICES IN 2 GALLON CANS. ROADSIDE PETROL PUMPS DID NOT APPEAR TILL THE 1920s. ATTEMPTS WERE MADE TO ENCOURAGE THE USE OF OTHER FUELS BY EXEMPTING THEM FROM TAX. BRITAIN TRIED BENZOLE (A GAS-WORKS BY-PRODUCT) & FRANCE TRIED ALCOHOL (MOSTLY FROM POTATOES), BUT NEITHER HAD MUCH SUCCESS.

REGISTRATION
REGISTRATION NUMBERS WERE FIRST INTRODUCED BY THE 1903 MOTORING ACT. THE MOTORING GENTRY OBJECTED STRONGLY TO BEING NUMBERED LIKE CONVICTS & LABELLED LIKE HACKNEY CARRIAGES; TO SOFTEN THIS BLOW TO THEIR PRIDE A CLAUSE WAS ADDED RAISING THE SPEED LIMIT FROM 12 TO 20 MPH.

MR. NIXON'S CAR
PROBABLY THE MOST EXPENSIVE CAR EVER MADE IS THE U.S. PRESIDENT'S BULLETPROOF LINCOLN CONTINENTAL. ITS MODIFICATIONS INCLUDED ONE INCH THICK GLASS & 2½ TONS OF ARMOUR PLATING & COST £208,000. EVEN IF ALL 4 TYRES ARE SHOT OUT IT CAN TRAVEL AT 50MPH ON INNER RUBBER EDGED STEEL DISCS.

FRIENDLY ADVICE
MAGISTRATES WERE AT FIRST HOSTILE TOWARDS MOTORISTS, ACCEPTING DUBIOUS EVIDENCE OF SPEEDING & IMPOSING THE MAXIMUM FINES. THE AA WAS FOUNDED IN 1906 SPECIFICALLY TO WARN MOTORISTS OF SPEED TRAPS. A LEGAL ACTION IN 1907 RULED OUT THIS INTERFERENCE WITH THE POLICE BUT THEY OVERCAME THIS BY WARNING DRIVERS: IF AN A.A. SCOUT FAILS TO SALUTE YOU, STOP & ASK THE REASON WHY.

MOTORING IN JAPAN
TOKYO HAS THE WORST TRAFFIC JAMS ANYWHERE IN THE WORLD. ONLY 9% OF THE CITY AREA IS ROADWAY (LONDON HAS 23% & WASHINGTON D.C. HAS 43%). IT ALSO HAS MORE FATAL ROAD ACCIDENTS, PER HEAD OF POPULATION, THAN ANY OTHER CAPITAL.

POLLUTION
JUST TWO GALLONS OF PETROL WOULD USE ALL THE AIR IN THE ABOVE ROOM WHILE COMBUSTING. THE EXHAUSTS OF U.S. CARS IN 1971 WERE ESTIMATED TO DISSEMINATE 60 MILLION TONS OF CARBON MONOXIDE, 12 MILLION TONS OF HYDROCARBONS, 6 MILLION TONS OF NITROUS OXIDE & 1 MILLION TONS EACH OF SULPHUR OXIDE & ASH. NO WONDER AMERICA IS WORRIED.

MOTORING IN RUSSIA
MOSCOW IS ONE OF THE LEAST CONGESTED CAPITALS WITH ONE CAR TO EVERY 29 INHABITANTS. RUSSIA MAKES THE WORLD'S HEAVIEST PRODUCTION CAR (THE ZIL 114, WEIGHING 3.12 TONS) & ALSO THE CAR WITH THE MOST COMPREHENSIVE STANDARD TOOL KIT (THE MOSKVICH). RUSSIA MUST ALSO HAVE THE CLEANEST CARS IN THE WORLD AS IT IS A CRIMINAL OFFENCE TO DRIVE A DIRTY CAR.

HOW TO EMPTY A BOWL OF WATER USING 4 MATCHES, 1 GLASS & HALF A CORK
ASK FATHER TO HELP YOU WITH THIS

STICK MATCHES INTO CORK & FLOAT CORK IN BOWL THEN LIGHT MATCHES & PUT GLASS OVER CORK. AS OXYGEN IN GLASS IS USED UP WATER WILL BE SUCKED IN.

NEXT WEEK HOW TO MAKE A HOLE THROUGH A HOLE IN A HOLE

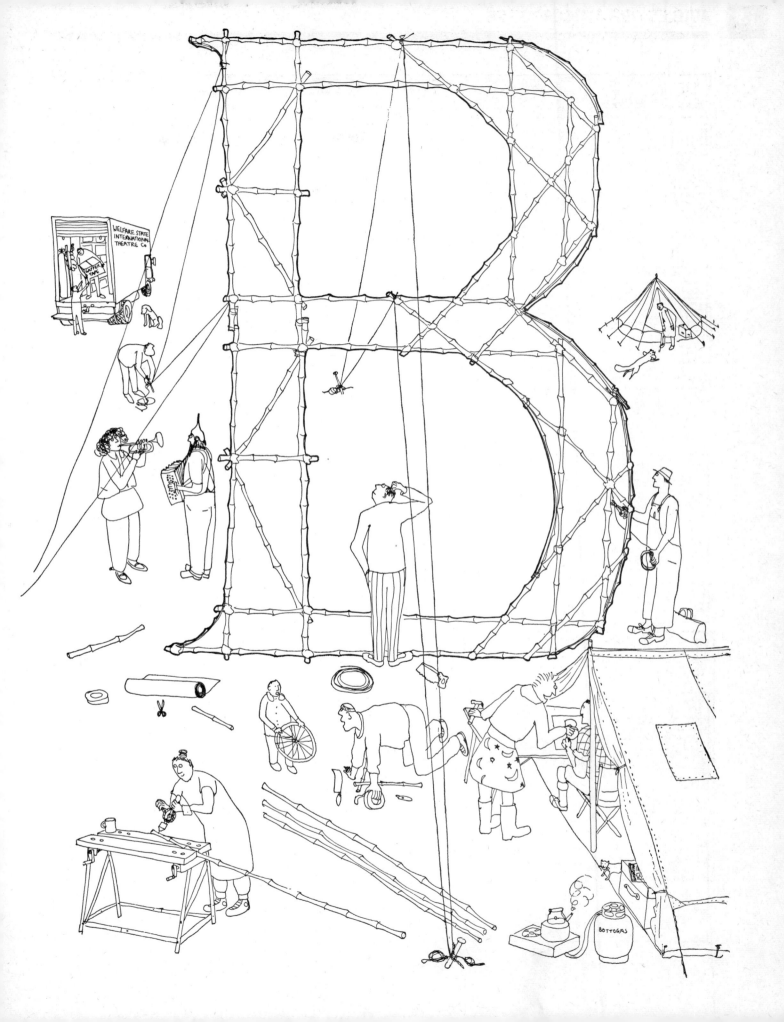

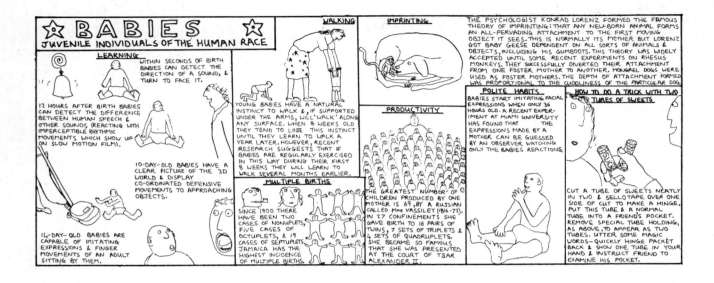

☆ BABIES ☆
JUVENILE INDIVIDUALS OF THE HUMAN RACE

LEARNING

WITHIN SECONDS OF BIRTH BABIES CAN DETECT THE DIRECTION OF A SOUND, & TURN TO FACE IT.

12 HOURS AFTER BIRTH BABIES CAN DETECT THE DIFFERENCE BETWEEN HUMAN SPEECH & OTHER SOUNDS (REACTING WITH IMPERCEPTIBLE RHYTHMIC MOVEMENTS WHICH SHOW UP ON SLOW MOTION FILM).

10-DAY-OLD BABIES HAVE A CLEAR PICTURE OF THE 3D WORLD & DISPLAY CO-ORDINATED DEFENSIVE MOVEMENTS TO APPROACHING OBJECTS.

14-DAY-OLD BABIES ARE CAPABLE OF IMITATING EXPRESSIONS & FINGER MOVEMENTS OF AN ADULT SITTING BY THEM.

WALKING

YOUNG BABIES HAVE A NATURAL INSTINCT TO WALK &, IF SUPPORTED UNDER THE ARMS, WILL 'WALK' ALONG ANY SURFACE. WHEN 8 WEEKS OLD THEY TEND TO LOSE THIS INSTINCT UNTIL THEY LEARN TO WALK A YEAR LATER. HOWEVER, RECENT RESEARCH SUGGESTS THAT IF BABIES ARE REGULARLY EXERCISED IN THIS WAY DURING THEIR FIRST 8 WEEKS THEY WILL LEARN TO WALK SEVERAL MONTHS EARLIER.

MULTIPLE BIRTHS

SINCE 1900 THERE HAVE BEEN TWO CASES OF NONUPLETS, FIVE CASES OF OCTUPLETS, & 19 CASES OF SEPTUPLETS. JAMAICA HAS THE HIGHEST INCIDENCE OF MULTIPLE BIRTHS.

IMPRINTING

THE GREATEST NUMBER OF CHILDREN PRODUCED BY ONE MOTHER IS 69 ,BY A RUSSIAN CALLED MME VASSILET (1816-72). IN 27 CONFINEMENTS SHE GAVE BIRTH TO 16 PAIRS OF TWINS, 7 SETS OF TRIPLETS & 4 SETS OF QUADRUPLETS. SHE BECAME SO FAMOUS THAT SHE WAS PRESENTED AT THE COURT OF TSAR ALEXANDER II.

PRODUCTIVITY

POLITE HABITS

BABIES START IMITATING FACIAL EXPRESSIONS WHEN ONLY 36 HOURS OLD. A RECENT EXPERIMENT AT MIAMI UNIVERSITY HAS FOUND THAT THE EXPRESSIONS MADE BY A MOTHER CAN BE GUESSED BY AN OBSERVER WATCHING ONLY THE BABIES REACTIONS.

THE PSYCHOLOGIST KONRAD LORENZ FORMED THE FAMOUS THEORY OF IMPRINTING: THAT ANY NEW-BORN ANIMAL FORMS AN ALL-PERVADING ATTACHMENT TO THE FIRST MOVING OBJECT IT SEES. THIS IS NORMALLY ITS MOTHER BUT LORENZ GOT BABY GEESE DEPENDENT ON ALL SORTS OF ANIMALS & OBJECTS, INCLUDING HIS GUMBOOTS. THIS THEORY WAS WIDELY ACCEPTED UNTIL SOME RECENT EXPERIMENTS ON RHESUS MONKEYS. THEY SUCCESSFULLY DIVERTED THEIR ATTACHMENT FROM ONE FOSTER MOTHER TO ANOTHER. MONGREL DOGS WERE USED AS FOSTER MOTHERS. THE DEPTH OF ATTACHMENT FORMED WAS PROPORTIONAL TO THE CUDDLINESS OF THE PARTICULAR DOG.

HOW TO DO A TRICK WITH TWO TUBES OF SWEETS

CUT A TUBE OF SWEETS NEATLY IN TWO & SELLOTAPE OVER ONE SIDE OF CUT TO MAKE A HINGE. PUT THIS TUBE & A NORMAL TUBE INTO A FRIEND'S POCKET. REMOVE SPECIAL TUBE HOLDING, AS ABOVE, TO APPEAR AS TWO TUBES. UTTER SOME MAGIC WORDS-QUICKLY HINGE PACKET BACK & SHOW ONE TUBE IN YOUR HAND & INSTRUCT FRIEND TO EXAMINE HIS POCKET.

☆ BABOONS ☆
LARGE MONKEYS OF VARIOUS SPECIES

HIGH LIFE

BABOONS ARE FOUND ONLY IN PARTS OF AFRICA & ARABIA AT HEIGHTS OF 3-4,000m. THEY LIVE IN TROOPS OF 200-300.

DIET

BABOONS ARE OMNIVOROUS, EATING FRUIT, GRAIN, ROOTS, BUDS, EGGS & MEAT. THEIR TEETH ARE NOT SO WELL ADAPTED FOR HUNTING AS THOSE OF THE CARNIVORES (DOGS, CATS etc). THEIR VICTIMS (EVEN SMALL DEER) ARE OFTEN EATEN ALIVE.

HAREMS

BABOON TROOPS ARE DIVIDED INTO STABLE HAREMS OF UP TO EIGHT FEMALES & THEIR CHILDREN. THE FEMALES ARE USUALLY INTER-RELATED & SELDOM LEAVE THE HAREM WHERE THEY WERE BORN. THE MALES COMPETE FOR EACH HAREM & OWNERSHIP CHANGES QUITE FREQUENTLY. THE MALE ATTEMPTS TO KEEP HOLD OF HIS HAREM BY GROOMING EACH OF THE FEMALES IN TURN (EVEN, BETWEEN BOUTS, WHEN FIGHTING OFF AN INTRUDING RIVAL). BUT THE FEMALES APPEAR TO PREFER GROOMING WITH EACH OTHER THAN WITH THE MALES.

LOYALTY

BABOONS ARE SURPRISINGLY LOYAL. RECENT RESEARCH HAS FOUND THAT IF TWO MALES & A FEMALE ARE INTRODUCED TO EACH OTHER SIMULTANEOUSLY, THE MALES WILL FIGHT FOR THE FEMALE. HOWEVER, IF ONE MALE IS INTRODUCED IS MIN BEFORE THE OTHER, THE SECOND MALE WILL NOT ATTEMPT TO INTERFERE WITH THE 'COUPLE'. THE FEMALE APPEARS NOT TO BE TEMPTED BY THE SECOND MALE, EVEN IF HE IS MUCH BIGGER & STRONGER THAN THE FIRST.

MANDRILLS

THE MANDRILL IS OFTEN SAID TO BE THE UGLIEST & MOST BRUTAL OF THE BABOONS. IT HAS A PURPLE NOSE WITH SWOLLEN BLUE CHEEKS & TECHNICOLOUR BUTTOCKS. IT DOES NOT OFTEN ATTACK MAN, BUT IS REGARDED AS A TYRANT OF THE FOREST, FEARING NOTHING (NOT EVEN THE SOUND OF GUNS).

☆ BACTERIA ☆
SIMPLE SELF-REPRODUCING BODIES

TOUGH BACTERIA

NEW BACTERIA, CAPABLE OF WITHSTANDING EXTRAORDINARY CONDITIONS, ARE CONTINUALLY BEING DISCOVERED. VARIETIES ARE NOW KNOWN WHICH CAN SURVIVE IN LIQUID HYDROGEN, IN SPACE (25 MILES FROM THE EARTH'S SURFACE), IN PRESSURES OF 6000 ATMOSPHERES, IN BOILING WATER & IN RADIATION OF 64 MILLION RONTGEN (A FATAL HUMAN DOSE IS 650R).

MICROBES ON JUPITER?

NASA RECENTLY ANNOUNCED THAT IT BELIEVES THERE MAY BE LIVING ORGANISMS ELSEWHERE IN THE SOLAR SYSTEM. THEY HAVE DISCOVERED A BACTERIUM THAT HAS NOT YET BEEN NAMED, BUT SURVIVES IN STRONG ALKALINE SOLUTIONS. SPECTOGRAPHIC STUDIES OF JUPITERS ATMOSPHERE INDICATE THE BACTERIUM MIGHT THRIVE ON THE PLANETS SURFACE.

EXOTOXINS

SOME BACTERIA MANUFACTURE & DEPOSIT POISONOUS CHEMICALS CALLED EXOTOXINS. AMONGST THESE ARE THE MOST TOXIC SUBSTANCES KNOWN. 10 MILLIGRAMS OF THE EXOTOXIN BOTULINUS (ABOUT 1/500 OF THE WEIGHT OF THIS PAGE) COULD THEORETICALLY DESTROY THE WORLDS ENTIRE HUMAN POPULATION.

LIFE WITHOUT BACTERIA

BACTERIA ARE RESPONSIBLE FOR FERMENTATION, CHEESE-MAKING & NUMEROUS CHEMICAL PROCESSES. EXPERIMENTS BREEDING ANIMALS IN STERILE ENVIRONMENTS HAVE FOUND THAT RABBIT & CHICKEN MEAT IS COMPLETELY TASTELESS IN THE ABSENCE OF BACTERIA. THEY ARE EVEN THOUGHT TO BE CLEANING UP THE ATMOSPHERE, CONVERTING CAR EXHAUST GASES BACK TO OXYGEN. H_2O & CO_2.

SOME EVIL USES FOR BACTERIA

IN ORDER TO ACT AS A POISON THE EXOTOXIN BOTULINUS HAS TO ENTER THE BLOODSTREAM. A FIENDISH GERMAN BACTERIOLOGIST MURDERED HIS WIFE BY PUTTING A TRACE OF TOXIN ON HER TOOTHPASTE & GIVING HER A NEW HARD-BRISTLE TOOTHBRUSH. THE POISON WAS IMPOSSIBLE TO TRACE AT THE AUTOPSY BUT HE WAS LATER CAUGHT HAVING MADE OTHER MISTAKES. ON A LARGER SCALE IT IS THOUGHT THAT ANY BREWERY COULD BE CONVERTED TO A TOXIN FACTORY IN A FEW WEEKS. FORTUNATELY THE DIFFICULTY OF INJECTING IT INTO AN ENEMY'S BLOOD RENDERS GERM WARFARE IMPRACTICAL.

AVOIDING THE COMMON COLD VIRUS

RECENT RESEARCH INTO THE VIRUSES RESPONSIBLE FOR THE COMMON COLD HAS REVEALED THAT THE FALLOUT FROM A SNEEZE RARELY CONTAINS AN ACTIVE VIRUS. HOWEVER 40% OF PEOPLE WITH COLDS HAVE ACTIVE VIRUSES ON THEIR HANDS, PICKED UP FROM THEIR EYES & NOSES. UNFORTUNATELY THE SIMPLE REMEDY OF REFUSING TO SHAKE HANDS WITH COLD RIDDEN PEOPLE IS INEFFECTIVE AS THE VIRUSES CAN STAY ALIVE FOR 3 HOURS IN EVERYTHING THEY TOUCH.

HOW TO MAKE A HOLE THROUGH A HOLE IN A HOLE

MOULD 2 HEMISPHERES OF CLAY OR PLASTICENE & GOUGE HOLES AS ABOVE. STICK HALVES TOGETHER & POINT A WILL BECOME A HOLE THROUGH A HOLE IN A HOLE.

☆ BADGERS ☆
PLANTIGRADE NOCTURNAL CARNIVORES

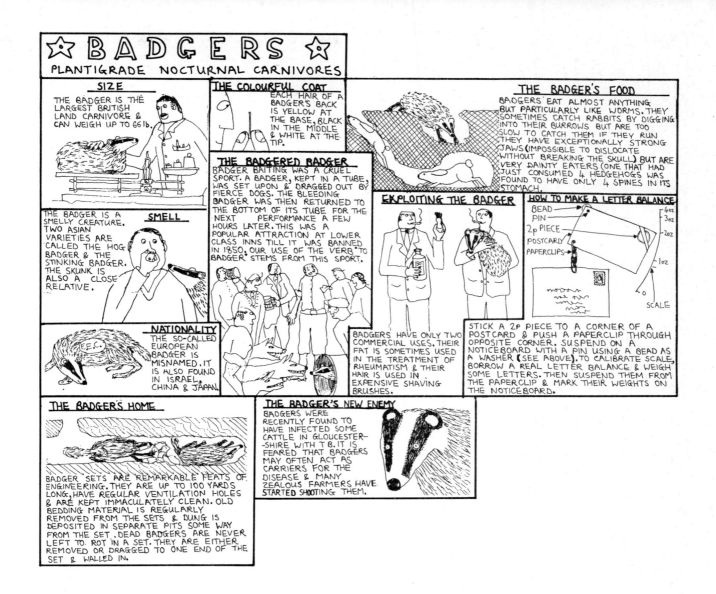

SIZE
THE BADGER IS THE LARGEST BRITISH LAND CARNIVORE & CAN WEIGH UP TO 66 lb.

THE COLOURFUL COAT
EACH HAIR OF A BADGER'S BACK IS YELLOW AT THE BASE, BLACK IN THE MIDDLE & WHITE AT THE TIP.

THE BADGERED BADGER
BADGER BAITING WAS A CRUEL SPORT. A BADGER, KEPT IN A TUBE, WAS SET UPON & DRAGGED OUT BY FIERCE DOGS. THE BLEEDING BADGER WAS THEN RETURNED TO THE BOTTOM OF ITS TUBE FOR THE NEXT PERFORMANCE A FEW HOURS LATER. THIS WAS A POPULAR ATTRACTION AT LOWER CLASS INNS TILL IT WAS BANNED IN 1850. OUR USE OF THE VERB 'TO BADGER' STEMS FROM THIS SPORT.

THE BADGER'S FOOD
BADGERS EAT ALMOST ANYTHING BUT PARTICULARLY LIKE WORMS. THEY SOMETIMES CATCH RABBITS BY DIGGING INTO THEIR BURROWS BUT ARE TOO SLOW TO CATCH THEM IF THEY RUN. THEY HAVE EXCEPTIONALLY STRONG JAWS (IMPOSSIBLE TO DISLOCATE WITHOUT BREAKING THE SKULL) BUT ARE VERY DAINTY EATERS (ONE THAT HAD JUST CONSUMED 4 HEDGEHOGS WAS FOUND TO HAVE ONLY 4 SPINES IN ITS STOMACH.

SMELL
THE BADGER IS A SMELLY CREATURE. TWO ASIAN VARIETIES ARE CALLED THE HOG BADGER & THE STINKING BADGER. THE SKUNK IS ALSO A CLOSE RELATIVE.

EXPLOITING THE BADGER
BADGERS HAVE ONLY TWO COMMERCIAL USES. THEIR FAT IS SOMETIMES USED IN THE TREATMENT OF RHEUMATISM & THEIR HAIR IS USED IN EXPENSIVE SHAVING BRUSHES.

HOW TO MAKE A LETTER BALANCE
BEAD
PIN
2p PIECE
POSTCARD
PAPERCLIPS

4oz
3oz
2oz
1oz
0
SCALE

STICK A 2p PIECE TO A CORNER OF A POSTCARD & PUSH A PAPERCLIP THROUGH OPPOSITE CORNER. SUSPEND ON A NOTICEBOARD WITH A PIN USING A BEAD AS A WASHER (SEE ABOVE). TO CALIBRATE SCALE, BORROW A REAL LETTER BALANCE & WEIGH SOME LETTERS. THEN SUSPEND THEM FROM THE PAPERCLIP & MARK THEIR WEIGHTS ON THE NOTICEBOARD.

NATIONALITY
THE SO-CALLED EUROPEAN BADGER IS MISNAMED. IT IS ALSO FOUND IN ISRAEL, CHINA & JAPAN.

THE BADGER'S HOME
BADGER SETS ARE REMARKABLE FEATS OF ENGINEERING. THEY ARE UP TO 100 YARDS LONG, HAVE REGULAR VENTILATION HOLES & ARE KEPT IMMACULATELY CLEAN. OLD BEDDING MATERIAL IS REGULARLY REMOVED FROM THE SETS & DUNG IS DEPOSITED IN SEPARATE PITS SOME WAY FROM THE SET. DEAD BADGERS ARE NEVER LEFT TO ROT IN A SET. THEY ARE EITHER REMOVED OR DRAGGED TO ONE END OF THE SET & WALLED IN.

THE BADGER'S NEW ENEMY
BADGERS WERE RECENTLY FOUND TO HAVE INFECTED SOME CATTLE IN GLOUCESTER-SHIRE WITH TB. IT IS FEARED THAT BADGERS MAY OFTEN ACT AS CARRIERS FOR THE DISEASE & MANY ZEALOUS FARMERS HAVE STARTED SHOOTING THEM.

☆ BALANCES ☆
DEVICES FOR MEASURING THE MASS OF OBJECTS

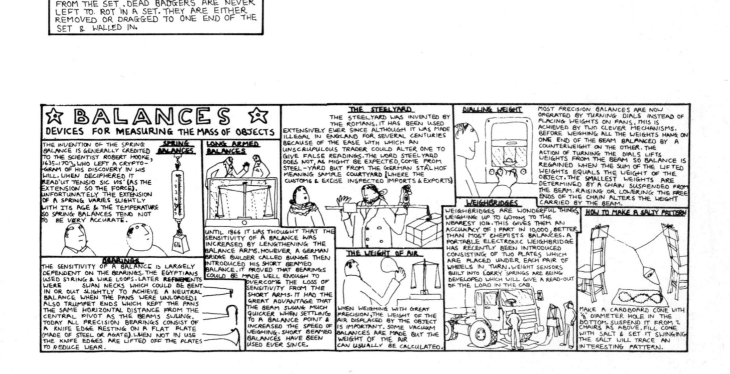

THE INVENTION OF THE SPRING BALANCE IS GENERALLY CREDITED TO THE SCIENTIST ROBERT HOOKE, 1635-1703, WHO LEFT A CRYPTO-GRAM OF HIS DISCOVERY IN HIS WILL. WHEN DECIPHERED IT READ 'UT TENSIO SIC VIS' (AS THE EXTENSION SO THE FORCE). UNFORTUNATELY THE EXTENSION OF A SPRING VARIES SLIGHTLY WITH ITS AGE & THE TEMPERATURE SO SPRING BALANCES TEND NOT TO BE VERY ACCURATE.

SPRING BALANCES
6 lb

BEARINGS
THE SENSITIVITY OF A BALANCE IS LARGELY DEPENDENT ON THE BEARINGS. THE EGYPTIANS USED STRING & WIRE LOOPS. LATER REFINEMENTS WERE SWAN NECKS WHICH COULD BE BENT IN OR OUT SLIGHTLY TO ACHIEVE A NEUTRAL BALANCE WHEN THE PANS WERE UNLOADED; ALSO TRUMPET ENDS WHICH KEPT THE PANS THE SAME HORIZONTAL DISTANCE FROM THE CENTRAL PIVOT AS THE BEAMS SWUNG. TODAY ALL PRECISION BEARINGS CONSIST OF A KNIFE EDGE RESTING ON A FLAT PLATE (MADE OF STEEL OR AGATE). WHEN NOT IN USE THE KNIFE EDGES ARE LIFTED OFF THE PLATES TO REDUCE WEAR.

LONG ARMED BALANCES
UNTIL 1866 IT WAS THOUGHT THAT THE SENSITIVITY OF A BALANCE WAS INCREASED BY LENGTHENING THE BALANCE ARMS. HOWEVER A GERMAN BRIDGE BUILDER CALLED BAULE THEN INTRODUCED HIS SHORT BEAMED BALANCE. IT PROVED THAT BEARINGS COULD BE MADE WELL ENOUGH TO OVERCOME THE LOSS OF SENSITIVITY FROM THE SHORT ARMS. IT HAD THE GREAT ADVANTAGE THAT THE BEAM SWUNG MUCH QUICKER WHEN SETTLING TO A BALANCE POINT & INCREASED THE SPEED OF WEIGHING. SHORT BEAMED BALANCES HAVE BEEN USED EVER SINCE.

THE STEELYARD
THE STEELYARD WAS INVENTED BY THE ROMANS. IT HAS BEEN USED EXTENSIVELY EVER SINCE ALTHOUGH IT WAS MADE ILLEGAL IN ENGLAND FOR SEVERAL CENTURIES BECAUSE OF THE EASE WITH WHICH AN UNSCRUPULOUS TRADER COULD ALTER ONE TO GIVE FALSE READINGS. THE WORD STEELYARD DOES NOT, AS MIGHT BE EXPECTED, COME FROM STEEL-YARD BUT FROM THE GERMAN STÅLHOF MEANING SAMPLE COURTYARD [WHERE THE CUSTOMS & EXCISE INSPECTED IMPORTS & EXPORTS]

THE WEIGHT OF AIR
WHEN WEIGHING WITH GREAT PRECISION, THE WEIGHT OF THE AIR DISPLACED BY THE OBJECT IS IMPORTANT. SOME VACUUM BALANCES ARE MADE BUT THE WEIGHT OF THE AIR CAN USUALLY BE CALCULATED.

DIALLING WEIGHT
MOST PRECISION BALANCES ARE NOW OPERATED BY TURNING DIALS INSTEAD OF PLACING WEIGHTS ON PANS. THIS IS ACHIEVED BY TWO CLEVER MECHANISMS. BEFORE WEIGHING ALL THE WEIGHTS HANG ON ONE END OF THE BEAM BALANCED BY A COUNTERWEIGHT ON THE OTHER. THE ACTION OF TURNING THE DIALS LIFTS WEIGHTS FROM THE BEAM SO BALANCE IS REGAINED WHEN THE SUM OF THE LIFTED WEIGHTS EQUALS THE WEIGHT OF THE OBJECT. THE SMALLEST WEIGHTS ARE DETERMINED BY A CHAIN SUSPENDED FROM THE BEAM. RAISING OR LOWERING THE FREE ENDS OF THE CHAIN ALTERS THE WEIGHT CARRIED BY THE BEAM.

WEIGHBRIDGES
WEIGHBRIDGES ARE WONDERFUL THINGS WEIGHING UP TO 40 TONS TO THE NEAREST 10 lb. THIS GIVES THEM AN ACCURACY OF 1 PART IN 10,000, BETTER THAN MOST CHEMISTS BALANCES. A PORTABLE ELECTRONIC WEIGHBRIDGE HAS RECENTLY BEEN INTRODUCED CONSISTING OF TWO PLATES WHICH ARE PLACED UNDER EACH PAIR OF WHEELS IN TURN. WEIGHT SENSORS BUILT INTO LORRY SPRINGS ARE BEING DEVELOPED WHICH WILL GIVE A READ-OUT OF THE LOAD IN THE CAB.

HOW TO MAKE A SALTY PATTERN
MAKE A CARDBOARD CONE WITH A ⅛" DIAMETER HOLE IN THE BOTTOM. SUSPEND IT FROM 2 CHAIRS AS ABOVE. FILL CONE WITH SALT & SET IT SWINGING. THE SALT WILL TRACE AN INTERESTING PATTERN.

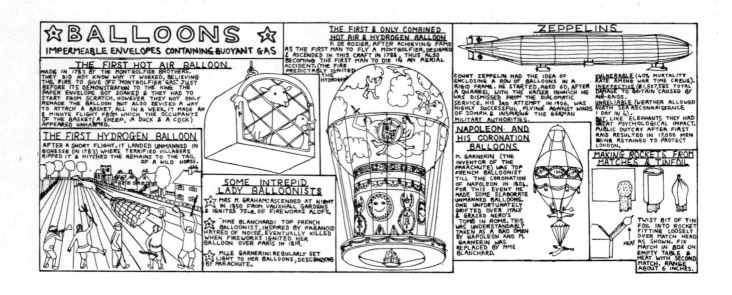

☆ BALLOONS ☆
IMPERMEABLE ENVELOPES CONTAINING BUOYANT GAS

THE FIRST HOT AIR BALLOON
MADE IN 1783 BY THE MONTGOLFIER BROTHERS. THEY DID NOT KNOW WHY IT WORKED, BELIEVING THE FIRE TO GIVE OFF 'MONTGOLFIER GAS'. JUST BEFORE ITS DEMONSTRATION TO THE KING THE PAPER ENVELOPE GOT SOAKED & THEY HAD TO START FROM SCRATCH. HOWEVER THEY NOT ONLY REMADE THE BALLOON BUT ALSO DEVISED A WAY TO ATTACH A BASKET, ALL IN A WEEK. IT MADE AN 8 MINUTE FLIGHT FROM WHICH THE OCCUPANTS OF THE BASKET (A SHEEP, A DUCK & A COCK) APPEARED UNHARMED.

THE FIRST HYDROGEN BALLOON
AFTER A SHORT FLIGHT, IT LANDED UNMANNED IN GONESSE (IN 1783) WHERE TERRIFIED VILLAGERS RIPPED IT & HITCHED THE REMAINS TO THE TAIL OF A WILD HORSE.

SOME INTREPID LADY BALLOONISTS
☆ MRS M. GRAHAM: ASCENDED AT NIGHT IN 1850 FROM VAUXHALL GARDENS & IGNITED 75LB. OF FIREWORKS ALOFT.

☆ MME BLANCHARD: TOP FRENCH BALLOONIST, INSPIRED BY PARANOID HATRED OF NOISE, EVENTUALLY KILLED WHEN FIREWORKS IGNITED HER BALLOON OVER PARIS IN 1819.

☆ MLLE GARNERIN: REGULARLY SET LIGHT TO HER BALLOONS, DESCENDING BY PARACHUTE.

THE FIRST & ONLY COMBINED HOT AIR & HYDROGEN BALLOON
P. DE ROZIER, AFTER ACHIEVING FAME AS THE FIRST MAN TO FLY, A MONTGOLFIER, DESIGNED & ASCENDED IN THIS CRAFT IN 1785, THUS ALSO BECOMING THE FIRST MAN TO DIE IN AN AERIAL ACCIDENT. (THE FIRE PREDICTABLY IGNITED THE HYDROGEN.)

NAPOLEON AND HIS CORONATION BALLOONS
M. GARNERIN (THE INVENTOR OF THE PARACHUTE) WAS TOP FRENCH BALLOONIST TILL THE CORONATION OF NAPOLEON IN 1804. FOR THIS EVENT HE MADE SOME ELABORATE UNMANNED BALLOONS. ONE UNFORTUNATELY DRIFTED OVER ITALY & GRAZED NERO'S TOMB IN ROME. THIS WAS UNDERSTANDABLY TAKEN AS A BAD OMEN BY NAPOLEON AND M. GARNERIN WAS REPLACED BY MME BLANCHARD.

ZEPPELINS
COUNT ZEPPELIN HAD THE IDEA OF ENCLOSING A ROW OF BALLOONS IN A RIGID FRAME. HE STARTED, AGED 60, AFTER A QUARREL WITH THE KAISER IN WHICH HE WAS DISMISSED FROM THE DIPLOMATIC SERVICE. HIS 3RD ATTEMPT, IN 1906, WAS HIGHLY SUCCESSFUL, FLYING AGAINST WINDS OF 20MPH & INSPIRING THE GERMAN MILITARY AUTHORITIES.

VULNERABLE (40% MORTALITY RATE AMONG WAR TIME CREWS). INEFFECTIVE (£1,527,585 TOTAL DAMAGE TO BRITAIN CAUSED BY AIR-RAIDS). UNRELIABLE (WEATHER ALLOWED NORTH SEA RECONNAISSANCE 1 DAY IN 4). BUT, LIKE ELEPHANTS THEY HAD GREAT PSYCHOLOGICAL IMPACT. PUBLIC OUTCRY AFTER FIRST RAID RESULTED IN 17,000 MEN BEING RETAINED TO PROTECT LONDON.

MAKING ROCKETS FROM MATCHES & TINFOIL
TWIST BIT OF TIN FOIL INTO ROCKET FITTING LOOSELY OVER MATCH HEAD AS SHOWN. FIX MATCH IN BOX ON EMPTY TABLE & HEAT WITH SECOND MATCH. RANGE ABOUT 6 INCHES.
HEAT

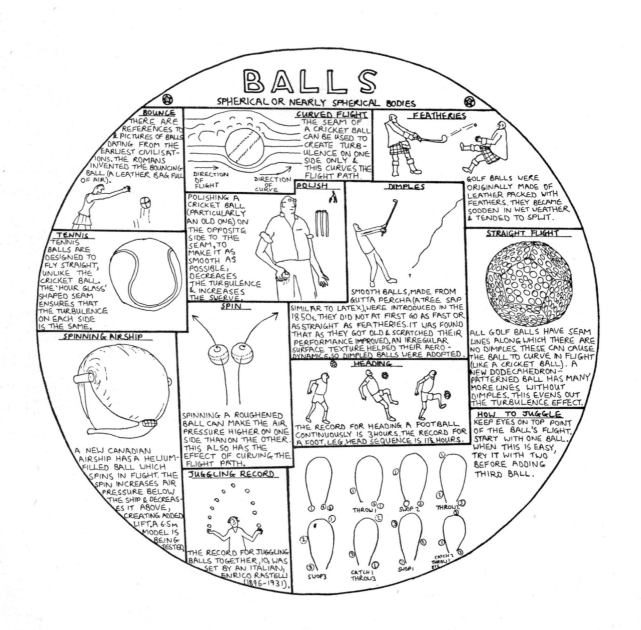

BALLS
SPHERICAL OR NEARLY SPHERICAL BODIES

BOUNCE
THERE ARE REFERENCES TO & PICTURES OF BALLS DATING FROM THE EARLIEST CIVILISATIONS. THE ROMANS INVENTED THE BOUNCING BALL (A LEATHER BAG FULL OF AIR).

TENNIS
TENNIS BALLS ARE DESIGNED TO FLY STRAIGHT, UNLIKE THE CRICKET BALL. THE 'HOUR GLASS' SHAPED SEAM ENSURES THAT THE TURBULENCE ON EACH SIDE IS THE SAME.

SPINNING AIRSHIP
A NEW CANADIAN AIRSHIP HAS A HELIUM-FILLED BALL WHICH SPINS IN FLIGHT. THE SPIN INCREASES AIR PRESSURE BELOW THE SHIP & DECREASES IT ABOVE, CREATING ADDED LIFT. A 6·5m MODEL IS BEING TESTED.

CURVED FLIGHT
THE SEAM OF A CRICKET BALL CAN BE USED TO CREATE TURBULENCE ON ONE SIDE ONLY & THIS CURVES THE FLIGHT PATH.

DIRECTION OF FLIGHT
DIRECTION OF CURVE

POLISH
POLISHING A CRICKET BALL (PARTICULARLY AN OLD ONE) ON THE OPPOSITE SIDE TO THE SEAM, TO MAKE IT AS SMOOTH AS POSSIBLE, DECREASES THE TURBULENCE & INCREASES THE SWERVE.

SPIN
SPINNING A ROUGHENED BALL CAN MAKE THE AIR PRESSURE HIGHER ON ONE SIDE THAN ON THE OTHER. THIS ALSO HAS THE EFFECT OF CURVING THE FLIGHT PATH.

JUGGLING RECORD
THE RECORD FOR JUGGLING BALLS TOGETHER, 10, WAS SET BY AN ITALIAN, ENRICO RASTELLI (1896-1931).

FEATHERIES
GOLF BALLS WERE ORIGINALLY MADE OF LEATHER PACKED WITH FEATHERS. THEY BECAME SODDEN IN WET WEATHER & TENDED TO SPLIT.

DIMPLES
SMOOTH BALLS, MADE FROM GUTTA PERCHA (A TREE SAP SIMILAR TO LATEX), WERE INTRODUCED IN THE 1850s. THEY DID NOT AT FIRST GO AS FAST OR AS STRAIGHT AS FEATHERIES. IT WAS FOUND THAT AS THEY GOT OLD & SCRATCHED THEIR PERFORMANCE IMPROVED, AN IRREGULAR SURFACE TEXTURE HELPED THEIR AERO-DYNAMICS, SO DIMPLED BALLS WERE ADOPTED.

HEADING
THE RECORD FOR HEADING A FOOTBALL CONTINUOUSLY IS 3 HOURS. THE RECORD FOR A FOOT, LEG, HEAD SEQUENCE IS 11½ HOURS.

STRAIGHT FLIGHT
ALL GOLF BALLS HAVE SEAM LINES ALONG WHICH THERE ARE NO DIMPLES. THESE CAN CAUSE THE BALL TO CURVE IN FLIGHT (LIKE A CRICKET BALL). A NEW DODECAHEDRON-PATTERNED BALL HAS MANY MORE LINES WITHOUT DIMPLES. THIS EVENS OUT THE TURBULENCE EFFECT.

HOW TO JUGGLE
KEEP EYES ON TOP POINT OF THE BALL'S FLIGHT. START WITH ONE BALL. WHEN THIS IS EASY, TRY IT WITH TWO BEFORE ADDING THIRD BALL.

THROW 1   SWOP 2   THROW 3
SWOP 3   CATCH 1 THROW 3   SWOP 1   CATCH 1 THROW 1 ETC

BAMBOO
GIANT GRASSES

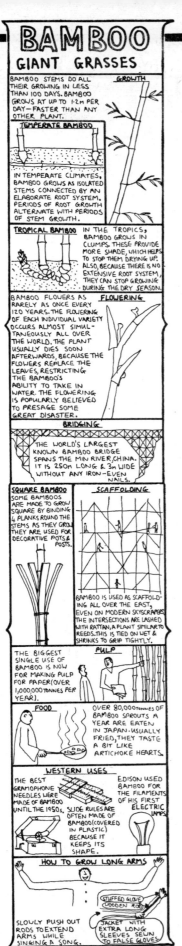

GROWTH
BAMBOO STEMS DO ALL THEIR GROWING IN LESS THAN 100 DAYS. BAMBOO GROWS AT UP TO 1·2m PER DAY — FASTER THAN ANY OTHER PLANT.

TEMPERATE BAMBOO
IN TEMPERATE CLIMATES, BAMBOO GROWS AS ISOLATED STEMS CONNECTED BY AN ELABORATE ROOT SYSTEM. PERIODS OF ROOT GROWTH ALTERNATE WITH PERIODS OF STEM GROWTH.

TROPICAL BAMBOO
IN THE TROPICS, BAMBOO GROWS IN CLUMPS. THESE PROVIDE MORE SHADE, WHICH HELPS TO STOP THEM DRYING UP. ALSO, BECAUSE THERE IS NO EXTENSIVE ROOT SYSTEM, THEY CAN STOP GROWING DURING THE DRY SEASON.

FLOWERING
BAMBOO FLOWERS AS RARELY AS ONCE EVERY 120 YEARS. THE FLOWERING OF EACH INDIVIDUAL VARIETY OCCURS ALMOST SIMULTANEOUSLY ALL OVER THE WORLD. THE PLANT USUALLY DIES SOON AFTERWARDS, BECAUSE THE FLOWERS REPLACE THE LEAVES, RESTRICTING THE BAMBOO'S ABILITY TO TAKE IN WATER. THE FLOWERING IS POPULARLY BELIEVED TO PRESAGE SOME GREAT DISASTER.

BRIDGING
THE WORLD'S LARGEST KNOWN BAMBOO BRIDGE SPANS THE MIN RIVER, CHINA. IT IS 250m LONG & 3m WIDE WITHOUT ANY IRON — EVEN NAILS.

SQUARE BAMBOO
SOME BAMBOOS ARE MADE TO GROW SQUARE BY BINDING 4 PLANKS ROUND THE STEMS AS THEY GROW. THEY ARE USED FOR DECORATIVE POTS & POSTS.

SCAFFOLDING
BAMBOO IS USED AS SCAFFOLDING ALL OVER THE EAST, EVEN ON MODERN SKYSCRAPERS. THE INTERSECTIONS ARE LASHED WITH RATTAN, A PLANT SIMILAR TO REEDS. THIS IS TIED ON WET & SHRINKS TO GRIP TIGHTLY.

PULP
THE BIGGEST SINGLE USE OF BAMBOO IS NOW FOR MAKING PULP FOR PAPER (OVER 1,000,000 TONNES PER YEAR).

FOOD
OVER 80,000 TONNES OF BAMBOO SPROUTS A YEAR ARE EATEN IN JAPAN. USUALLY FRIED, THEY TASTE A BIT LIKE ARTICHOKE HEARTS.

WESTERN USES
THE BEST GRAMOPHONE NEEDLES WERE MADE OF BAMBOO UNTIL THE 1950s. SLIDE RULES ARE OFTEN MADE OF BAMBOO (COVERED IN PLASTIC) BECAUSE IT KEEPS ITS SHAPE.

EDISON USED BAMBOO FOR THE FILAMENTS OF HIS FIRST ELECTRIC LAMPS.

HOW TO GROW LONG ARMS
SLOWLY PUSH OUT RODS TO EXTEND ARMS WHILE SINGING A SONG.

STUFFED GLOVE
WOODEN ROD
JACKET WITH EXTRA LONG SLEEVES SEWN TO FALSE GLOVES.

☆ BANKS ☆
INSTITUTIONS STORING & DEALING IN MONEY

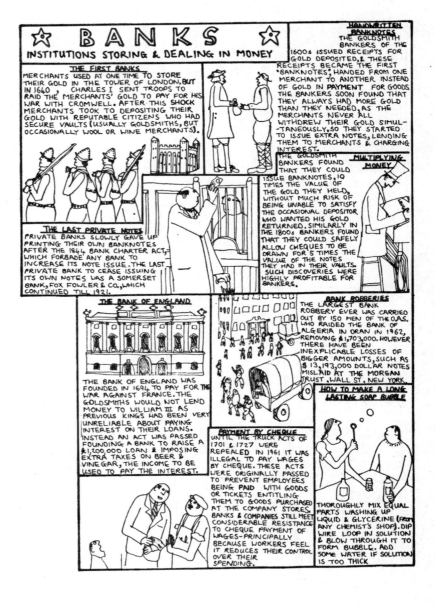

THE FIRST BANKS
MERCHANTS USED AT ONE TIME TO STORE THEIR GOLD IN THE TOWER OF LONDON, BUT IN 1640, CHARLES I SENT TROOPS TO RAID THE MERCHANTS' GOLD TO PAY FOR HIS WAR WITH CROMWELL. AFTER THIS SHOCK MERCHANTS TOOK TO DEPOSITING THEIR GOLD WITH REPUTABLE CITIZENS WHO HAD SECURE VAULTS (USUALLY GOLDSMITHS, BUT OCCASIONALLY WOOL OR WINE MERCHANTS).

THE LAST PRIVATE NOTES
PRIVATE BANKS SLOWLY GAVE UP PRINTING THEIR OWN BANKNOTES AFTER THE 1844 BANK CHARTER ACT, WHICH FORBADE ANY BANK TO INCREASE ITS NOTE ISSUE. THE LAST PRIVATE BANK TO CEASE ISSUING ITS OWN NOTES WAS A SOMERSET BANK, FOX FOWLER & CO., WHICH CONTINUED TILL 1921.

HANDWRITTEN BANKNOTES
THE GOLDSMITH BANKERS OF THE 1600s ISSUED RECEIPTS FOR GOLD DEPOSITED, & THESE RECEIPTS BECAME THE FIRST "BANKNOTES", HANDED FROM ONE MERCHANT TO ANOTHER INSTEAD OF GOLD IN PAYMENT FOR GOODS. THE BANKERS SOON FOUND THAT THEY ALWAYS HAD MORE GOLD THAN THEY NEEDED, AS THE MERCHANTS NEVER ALL WITHDREW THEIR GOLD SIMULTANEOUSLY, SO THEY STARTED TO ISSUE EXTRA NOTES, LENDING THEM TO MERCHANTS & CHARGING INTEREST.

MULTIPLYING MONEY
THE GOLDSMITH BANKERS FOUND THAT THEY COULD ISSUE BANKNOTES, 10 TIMES THE VALUE OF THE GOLD THEY HELD, WITHOUT MUCH RISK OF BEING UNABLE TO SATISFY THE OCCASIONAL DEPOSITOR WHO WANTED HIS GOLD RETURNED. SIMILARLY IN THE 1800s BANKERS FOUND THAT THEY COULD SAFELY ALLOW CHEQUES TO BE DRAWN FOR 5 TIMES THE VALUE OF THE NOTES THEY HAD IN THEIR VAULTS. SUCH DISCOVERIES WERE HIGHLY PROFITABLE FOR BANKERS.

THE BANK OF ENGLAND
THE BANK OF ENGLAND WAS FOUNDED IN 1694 TO PAY FOR THE WAR AGAINST FRANCE. THE GOLDSMITHS WOULD NOT LEND MONEY TO WILLIAM III AS PREVIOUS KINGS HAD BEEN VERY UNRELIABLE ABOUT PAYING INTEREST ON THEIR LOANS. INSTEAD AN ACT WAS PASSED FOUNDING A BANK TO RAISE A £1,200,000 LOAN & IMPOSING EXTRA TAXES ON BEER & VINEGAR, THE INCOME TO BE USED TO PAY THE INTEREST.

BANK ROBBERIES
THE LARGEST BANK ROBBERY EVER WAS CARRIED OUT BY 150 MEN OF THE O.A.S. WHO RAIDED THE BANK OF ALGERIA IN ORAN IN 1962, REMOVING £1,703,000. HOWEVER THERE HAVE BEEN INEXPLICABLE LOSSES OF BIGGER AMOUNTS, SUCH AS $13,193,000 DOLLAR NOTES MISLAID AT THE MORGAN TRUST, WALL ST. NEW YORK.

PAYMENT BY CHEQUE
UNTIL THE TRUCK ACTS OF 1701 & 1727 WERE REPEALED IN 1961 IT WAS ILLEGAL TO PAY WAGES BY CHEQUE. THESE ACTS WERE ORIGINALLY PASSED TO PREVENT EMPLOYEES BEING PAID WITH GOODS OR TICKETS ENTITLING THEM TO GOODS PURCHASED AT THE COMPANY STORES. BANKS & COMPANIES STILL MEET CONSIDERABLE RESISTANCE TO CHEQUE PAYMENT OF WAGES — PRINCIPALLY BECAUSE WORKERS FEEL IT REDUCES THEIR CONTROL OVER THEIR SPENDING.

HOW TO MAKE A LONG LASTING SOAP BUBBLE
THOROUGHLY MIX EQUAL PARTS WASHING UP LIQUID & GLYCERINE (FROM ANY CHEMIST'S SHOP). DIP WIRE LOOP IN SOLUTION & BLOW THROUGH IT TO FORM BUBBLE. ADD SOME WATER IF SOLUTION IS TOO THICK

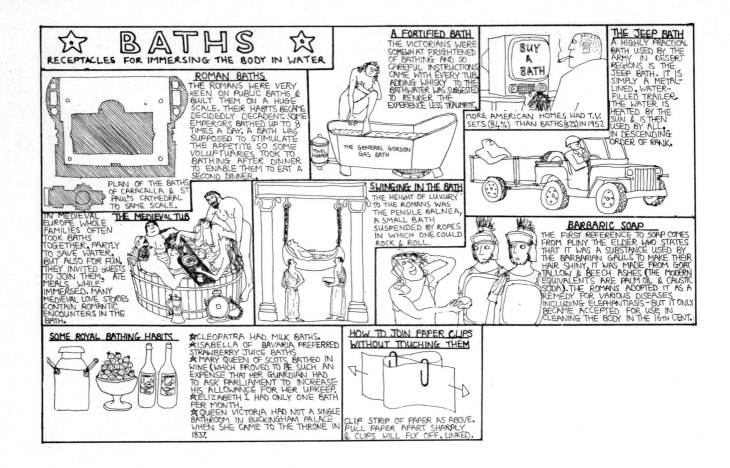

☆ BATHS ☆
RECEPTACLES FOR IMMERSING THE BODY IN WATER

ROMAN BATHS
THE ROMANS WERE VERY KEEN ON PUBLIC BATHS & BUILT THEM ON A HUGE SCALE. THEIR HABITS BECAME DECIDEDLY DECADENT. SOME EMPERORS BATHED UP TO 8 TIMES A DAY. A BATH WAS SUPPOSED TO STIMULATE THE APPETITE SO SOME VOLUPTUARIES TOOK TO BATHING AFTER DINNER TO ENABLE THEM TO EAT A SECOND DINNER.

PLAN OF THE BATHS OF CARACALLA & ST PAUL'S CATHEDRAL TO SAME SCALE.

THE MEDIEVAL TUB
IN MEDIEVAL EUROPE WHOLE FAMILIES OFTEN TOOK BATHS TOGETHER, PARTLY TO SAVE WATER, BUT ALSO FOR FUN. THEY INVITED GUESTS TO JOIN THEM, ATE MEALS WHILE IMMERSED. MANY MEDIEVAL LOVE STORIES CONTAIN ROMANTIC ENCOUNTERS IN THE BATH.

A FORTIFIED BATH
THE VICTORIANS WERE SOMEWHAT FRIGHTENED OF BATHING AND SO CAREFUL INSTRUCTIONS CAME WITH EVERY TUB. ADDING WHISKY TO THE BATHWATER WAS SUGGESTED TO RENDER THE EXPERIENCE LESS TRAUMATIC.

THE GENERAL GORDON GAS BATH

BUY A BATH

MORE AMERICAN HOMES HAD T.V. SETS (84%) THAN BATHS (82%) IN 1952

SWINGING IN THE BATH
THE HEIGHT OF LUXURY TO THE ROMANS WAS THE PENSILE BALNEA, A SMALL BATH SUSPENDED BY ROPES IN WHICH ONE COULD ROCK & ROLL.

THE JEEP BATH
A HIGHLY PRACTICAL BATH USED BY THE ARMY IN DESERT REGIONS IS THE JEEP BATH. IT IS SIMPLY A METAL-LINED, WATER-FILLED TRAILER. THE WATER IS HEATED BY THE SUN & IS THEN USED BY ALL, IN DESCENDING ORDER OF RANK.

BARBARIC SOAP
THE FIRST REFERENCE TO SOAP COMES FROM PLINY THE ELDER WHO STATES THAT IT WAS A SUBSTANCE USED BY THE BARBARIAN GAULS TO MAKE THEIR HAIR SHINY. IT WAS MADE FROM GOAT TALLOW & BEECH ASHES (THE MODERN EQUIVALENTS ARE PALM OIL & CAUSTIC SODA). THE ROMANS ADOPTED IT AS A REMEDY FOR VARIOUS DISEASES INCLUDING ELEPHANTIASIS – BUT IT ONLY BECAME ACCEPTED FOR USE IN CLEANING THE BODY IN THE 16th CENT.

SOME ROYAL BATHING HABITS
☆ CLEOPATRA HAD MILK BATHS.
☆ ISABELLA OF BAVARIA PREFERRED STRAWBERRY JUICE BATHS
☆ MARY QUEEN OF SCOTS BATHED IN WINE (WHICH PROVED TO BE SUCH AN EXPENSE THAT HER GUARDIAN HAD TO ASK PARLIAMENT TO INCREASE HIS ALLOWANCE FOR HER UPKEEP.
☆ ELIZABETH I HAD ONLY ONE BATH PER MONTH.
☆ QUEEN VICTORIA HAD NOT A SINGLE BATHROOM IN BUCKINGHAM PALACE WHEN SHE CAME TO THE THRONE IN 1837.

HOW TO JOIN PAPER CLIPS WITHOUT TOUCHING THEM
CLIP STRIP OF PAPER AS ABOVE. PULL PAPER APART SHARPLY & CLIPS WILL FLY OFF, LINKED.

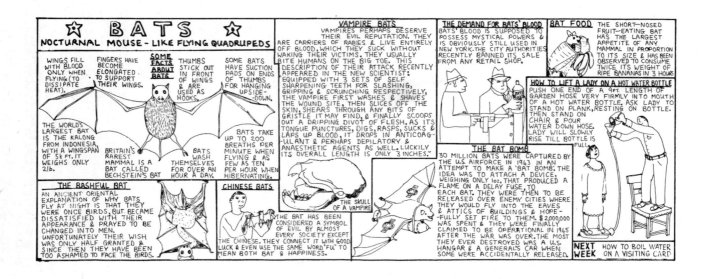

☆ BATS ☆
NOCTURNAL MOUSE-LIKE FLYING QUADRUPEDS

WINGS FILL WITH BLOOD ONLY WHEN FLYING (TO DISSIPATE HEAT).

FINGERS HAVE BECOME ELONGATED TO SUPPORT THEIR WINGS.

SOME FACTS ABOUT BATS

THUMBS STICK OUT IN FRONT OF WINGS & ARE USED AS HOOKS.

SOME BATS HAVE SUCTION PADS ON ENDS OF THUMBS FOR HANGING UPSIDE-DOWN.

THE WORLD'S LARGEST BAT IS THE KALONG FROM INDONESIA WITH A WINGSPAN OF 5½ FT. IT WEIGHS ONLY 2lb.

BRITAIN'S RAREST MAMMAL IS A BAT CALLED BECHSTEIN'S BAT

BATS WASH THEMSELVES FOR OVER AN HOUR A DAY.

BATS TAKE UP TO 200 BREATHS PER MINUTE WHEN FLYING & AS FEW AS TEN PER HOUR WHEN HIBERNATING.

THE BASHFUL BAT
AN ANCIENT ORIENTAL EXPLANATION OF WHY BATS FLY AT NIGHT IS THAT THEY WERE ONCE BIRDS, BUT BECAME DISSATISFIED WITH THEIR APPEARANCE & PRAYED TO BE CHANGED INTO MEN. UNFORTUNATELY THEIR WISH WAS ONLY HALF GRANTED & SINCE THEN THEY HAVE BEEN TOO ASHAMED TO FACE THE BIRDS.

CHINESE BATS
THE BAT HAS BEEN CONSIDERED A SYMBOL OF EVIL BY ALMOST EVERY SOCIETY EXCEPT THE CHINESE. THEY CONNECT IT WITH GOOD LUCK & EVEN USE THE SAME WORD "FU" TO MEAN BOTH BAT & HAPPINESS.

VAMPIRE BATS
VAMPIRES PERHAPS DESERVE THEIR EVIL REPUTATION. THEY ARE CARRIERS OF RABIES & LIVE ENTIRELY OFF BLOOD, WHICH THEY SUCK WITHOUT WAKING THEIR VICTIMS. THEY USUALLY BITE HUMANS ON THE BIG TOE. THIS DESCRIPTION OF THEIR ATTACK RECENTLY APPEARED IN THE NEW SCIENTIST: EQUIPPED WITH 3 SETS OF SELF SHARPENING TEETH FOR SLASHING, GRIPPING & SCRUNCHING RESPECTIVELY, THE VAMPIRE FIRST WASHES & SHAVES THE WOUND SITE, THEN SLICES OFF THE SKIN, SHEARS THROUGH ANY BITS OF GRISTLE IT MAY FIND, & FINALLY SCOOPS OUT A DRIPPING DIVOT OF FLESH. AS ITS TONGUE PUNCTURES, DIGS, RASPS, SUCKS & LAPS UP BLOOD, IT DROPS IN ANTICOAGULANT & PERHAPS DEPILATORY & ANAESTHETIC AGENTS AS WELL. LUCKILY ITS OVERALL LENGTH IS ONLY 3 INCHES."

THE SKULL OF A VAMPIRE

THE DEMAND FOR BATS' BLOOD
BATS' BLOOD IS SUPPOSED TO POSSESS MYSTICAL POWERS & IS OBVIOUSLY STILL USED IN NEW YORK. THE CITY AUTHORITIES RECENTLY BANNED ITS SALE FROM ANY RETAIL SHOP.

THE BAT BOMB
30 MILLION BATS WERE CAPTURED BY THE U.S. AIRFORCE IN 1943 IN AN ATTEMPT TO MAKE A 'BAT BOMB'. THE IDEA WAS TO ATTACH A DEVICE, WEIGHING ONLY 1oz, THAT PRODUCED A FLAME ON A DELAY FUSE, TO EACH BAT. THEY WERE THEN TO BE RELEASED OVER ENEMY CITIES WHERE THEY WOULD FLY INTO THE EAVES & ATTICS OF BUILDINGS & HOPE-FULLY SET FIRE TO THEM. $2,000,000 WAS SPENT & THEY WERE FINALLY CLAIMED TO BE OPERATIONAL IN 1945 AFTER THE WAR WAS OVER. THE MOST THEY EVER DESTROYED WAS A U.S. HANGAR & A GENERAL'S CAR WHEN SOME WERE ACCIDENTALLY RELEASED.

BAT FOOD
THE SHORT-NOSED FRUIT-EATING BAT HAS THE LARGEST APPETITE OF ANY MAMMAL IN PROPORTION TO ITS SIZE & HAS BEEN OBSERVED TO CONSUME TWICE ITS WEIGHT OF RIPE BANANAS IN 3 HOURS

HOW TO LIFT A LADY ON A HOT WATER BOTTLE
PUSH ONE END OF A 9ft. LENGTH OF GARDEN HOSE VERY FIRMLY INTO MOUTH OF A HOT WATER BOTTLE. ASK LADY TO STAND ON PLANK, RESTING ON BOTTLE. THEN STAND ON CHAIR & POUR WATER DOWN HOSE. LADY WILL SLOWLY RISE TILL BOTTLE IS FULL.

NEXT WEEK HOW TO BOIL WATER ON A VISITING CARD

☆ BATTERIES ☆
DEVICES FOR CREATING ELECTRICITY BY CHEMICAL ACTION

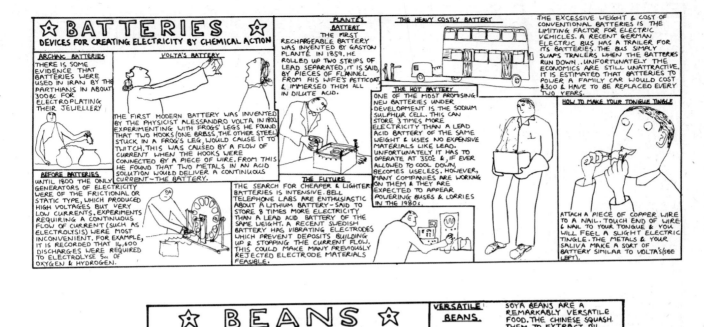

ARCHAIC BATTERIES
THERE IS SOME EVIDENCE THAT BATTERIES WERE USED IN IRAN BY THE PARTHIANS IN ABOUT 300BC FOR ELECTROPLATING THEIR JEWELLERY.

BEFORE BATTERIES
UNTIL 1800 THE ONLY GENERATORS OF ELECTRICITY WERE OF THE FRICTIONAL OR STATIC TYPE, WHICH PRODUCED HIGH VOLTAGES BUT VERY LOW CURRENTS. EXPERIMENTS REQUIRING A CONTINUOUS FLOW OF CURRENT (SUCH AS ELECTROLYSIS) WERE MOST INCONVENIENT. FOR EXAMPLE, IT IS RECORDED THAT 14,600 DISCHARGES WERE REQUIRED TO ELECTROLYSE 5cc OF OXYGEN & HYDROGEN.

VOLTA'S BATTERY
THE FIRST MODERN BATTERY WAS INVENTED BY THE PHYSICIST ALESSANDRO VOLTA IN 1800. EXPERIMENTING WITH FROGS' LEGS HE FOUND THAT TWO HOOKS (ONE BRASS, THE OTHER STEEL) STUCK IN A FROG'S LEG, WOULD CAUSE IT TO TWITCH. THIS WAS CAUSED BY A FLOW OF CURRENT WHEN THE HOOKS WERE CONNECTED BY A PIECE OF WIRE. FROM THIS HE FOUND THAT TWO METALS IN AN ACID SOLUTION WOULD DELIVER A CONTINUOUS CURRENT ~ THE BATTERY.

PLANTÉ'S BATTERY
THE FIRST RECHARGEABLE BATTERY WAS INVENTED BY GASTON PLANTÉ IN 1859. HE ROLLED UP TWO STRIPS OF LEAD SEPARATED, IT IS SAID, BY PIECES OF FLANNEL FROM HIS WIFE'S PETTICOAT & IMMERSED THEM ALL IN DILUTE ACID.

THE FUTURE
THE SEARCH FOR CHEAPER & LIGHTER BATTERIES IS INTENSIVE. BELL TELEPHONE LABS ARE ENTHUSIASTIC ABOUT A LITHIUM BATTERY – SAID TO STORE 8 TIMES MORE ELECTRICITY THAN A LEAD ACID BATTERY OF THE SAME WEIGHT. A RECENT SWEDISH BATTERY HAS VIBRATING ELECTRODES WHICH PREVENT DEPOSITS BUILDING UP & STOPPING THE CURRENT FLOW. THIS COULD MAKE MANY PREVIOUSLY REJECTED ELECTRODE MATERIALS FEASIBLE.

THE HEAVY COSTLY BATTERY
THE EXCESSIVE WEIGHT & COST OF CONVENTIONAL BATTERIES IS THE LIMITING FACTOR FOR ELECTRIC VEHICLES. A RECENT GERMAN ELECTRIC BUS HAS A TRAILER FOR ITS BATTERIES. THE BUS SIMPLY SWAPS TRAILERS WHEN THE BATTERIES RUN DOWN. UNFORTUNATELY THE ECONOMICS ARE STILL UNATTRACTIVE. IT IS ESTIMATED THAT BATTERIES TO POWER A FAMILY CAR WOULD COST £300 & HAVE TO BE REPLACED EVERY TWO YEARS.

THE HOT BATTERY
ONE OF THE MOST PROMISING NEW BATTERIES UNDER DEVELOPMENT IS THE SODIUM SULPHUR CELL. THIS CAN STORE 3 TIMES MORE ELECTRICITY THAN A LEAD ACID BATTERY OF THE SAME WEIGHT & USES NO EXPENSIVE MATERIALS LIKE LEAD. UNFORTUNATELY IT HAS TO OPERATE AT 350°C & IF EVER ALLOWED TO COOL DOWN, BECOMES USELESS. HOWEVER, MANY COMPANIES ARE WORKING ON THEM & THEY ARE EXPECTED TO APPEAR POWERING BUSES & LORRIES IN THE 1980s.

HOW TO MAKE YOUR TONGUE TINGLE
ATTACH A PIECE OF COPPER WIRE TO A NAIL. TOUCH END OF WIRE & NAIL TO YOUR TONGUE & YOU WILL FEEL A SLIGHT ELECTRIC TINGLE. THE METALS & YOUR SALIVA MAKE A SORT OF BATTERY SIMILAR TO VOLTA'S (SEE LEFT).

☆ BEANS ☆
THE SEEDS OR PODS OF CERTAIN LEGUMINOUS PLANTS

BEANS IN HISTORY
THE FIRST COUNTRY TO CULTIVATE BEANS WAS PROBABLY PERU, WHERE EVIDENCE DATES BACK TO 5860 BC. THE SOUTH AMERICAN DIET WAS QUITE VARIED & INCLUDED GUINEA PIGS & DOGS (SIMILAR TO CHIHUAHUAS) BRED FOR FOOD.

BEANS IN AMERICA
THE FIRST RECIPE FOR BAKED BEANS COMES FROM AN AMERICAN BOOK CALLED THE FRUGAL HOUSEWIFE (1829). THE BEANS WERE TO BE SOAKED OVERNIGHT, SEASONED WITH MUSTARD, BACON & MOLASSES, THEN TO BE TAKEN TO THE LOCAL BAKERY & COOKED IN THE BAKERY OVENS FOR 12 HOURS. CANNED BAKED BEANS FIRST APPEARED IN 1875, ORIGINALLY INTENDED FOR FISHERMEN TO EAT AT SEA.

BEANS IN BULK
A RECENT SURVEY SHOWED THAT 84% OF BRITISH SHOPPERS BUY BAKED BEANS REGULARLY, AND, WITH SALES EXCEEDING 1,000,000 CANS PER DAY, WE CONSUME TWICE AS MANY BAKED BEANS PER CAPITA AS THE AMERICANS. THIS COSTS BRITAIN £30,000,000 A YEAR IN IMPORTS AS THE RAW BEANS ARE IMPORTED FROM AMERICA. NO BRITISH BEAN HAS QUITE THE RIGHT FLAVOUR & THE AMERICAN BEANS BEHAVE UNPREDICTABLY IF GROWN IN OUR UNSETTLED CLIMATE. HOWEVER A FAST-GROWING STRAIN OF BEAN IS BEING DEVELOPED AT CAMBRIDGE. THIS WILL HOPEFULLY MAKE BRITISH BAKED BEANS POSSIBLE.

VERSATILE BEANS
SOYA BEANS ARE A REMARKABLY VERSATILE FOOD. THE CHINESE SQUASH THEM TO EXTRACT OIL, GRIND THEM FOR FLOUR & LEAVE THEM TO GERMINATE TO GIVE BEAN SPROUTS. THEY ARE ALSO BOILED WITH WATER TO YIELD A 'MILK' & A 'PUREE'. THE 'MILK' WHEN REBOILED LEAVES A SEDIMENT THAT IS DRIED TO GIVE BEAN CURD (A BLAND, NOURISHING SUBSTANCE FUNDAMENTAL TO CHINESE HOME COOKING). THE DRAINED, PRESSED PUREE IS LEFT TO FERMENT FOR SEVERAL WEEKS & THEN CLEANED OF SURFACE MOULD & SOAKED IN BRINE. THE BRINE BECOMES FLAVOURSOME & TURNS INTO SOY SAUCE.

BEANS & ASTRONAUTS
AMERICAN ASTRONAUTS ARE NOT ALLOWED TO EAT BAKED BEANS BEFORE A FLIGHT TO AVOID THE UNPLEASANT CONSEQUENCES OF BREAKING WIND (FARTING) INSIDE A SPACESUIT. A SYSTEM FOR QUANTIFYING THE FLATUS-PRODUCING EFFECT OF VARIOUS FOODS HAS BEEN DEVISED FOR N.A.S.A. TO ASSIST IN THE SEARCH FOR SUITABLE IN-FLIGHT FOODS.

BEANS & MEAT
MOST SOYA BEAN MEAT IS MADE BY TEXTILE COMPANIES BECAUSE REAL MEAT IS MADE UP OF FIBROUS STRANDS OF PROTEIN & SOYA BEAN MEAT IS MADE BY EXTRUDING A SOYA BEAN PULP IN A SIMILAR MACHINE AS THAT USED FOR MAKING NYLON. SOME ENTHUSIASTS BELIEVE IT IS ESSENTIAL TO THE WORLD'S FUTURE. THEY CLAIM THAT DEVELOPING COUNTRIES WILL INCREASINGLY DEMAND A WESTERN STYLE MEAT DIET & THAT SOYA BEAN MEAT WILL BE THE ONLY WAY TO SATISFY THE DEMAND. FEEDING & SLAUGHTERING ANIMALS IS VERY INEFFICIENT. AN INTENSIVELY REARED STEER EATS 1200lb RAW PROTEIN TO PRODUCE 75lb MEAT.

HOW TO REMOVE THE ROPE WITHOUT TAKING YOUR HAND OUT OF YOUR POCKET
STUFF ROPE UP SLEEVE WITH LEFT HAND, GET FRIEND TO REACH IN TOP OF JACKET & PULL ROPE OUT OF SLEEVE OVER HEAD & INTO LEFT SLEEVE. PULL ROPE OUT END OF SLEEVE, SLIP IT OVER LEFT HAND, THEN PULL BACK THROUGH FRONT OF JACKET. ROPE WILL THEN FALL ROUND YOUR FEET ENABLING YOU TO WALK OUT OF IT.

☆ BEARS ☆
LARGE CARNIVOROUS CANOIDAE

CRAFTY BEARS

BEARS ARE VERY CUNNING HUNTERS. POLAR BEARS WILL COVER THEIR UNCAMOUFLAGED BLACK NOSES WITH A PAW WHILE STALKING. RUSSIAN BROWN BEARS HAVE BEEN KNOWN TO IMITATE THE MATING CALL OF AN ELK. SOME GRIZZLY BEARS HAVE ADOPTED THE RUSE OF CATCHING CATTLE BY ROLLING & TUMBLING AROUND NEAR A HERD WAITING FOR A STUPID COW TO MAKE A RUSH AT THE DISTRACTING OBJECT.

GOURMET BEARS

BEARS WILL GO TO GREAT LENGTHS FOR MINUTE SNACKS OF THEIR FAVOURITE DELICACIES, DIGGING HOLES THE SIZE OF PIANOS TO CATCH GROUND SQUIRRELS & GETTING BADLY STUNG ON THE NOSE WHILE RAIDING BEEHIVES.

BEARS RECEIVE WRONG MESSAGE

SOME YUGOSLAVIAN BEARS HAVE RECENTLY BEEN OBSERVED CLIMBING TELEGRAPH POLES. IT IS THOUGHT THAT THE HUMMING OF THE WIRES CONVINCED THEM THAT THERE WERE BEEHIVES AT THE TOP.

SOME BEAR FACTS

FEMALE BEARS INVARIABLY HAVE 2 CUBS, ONE MALE & ONE FEMALE.

THE POLAR BEAR IS THE ONLY BEAR THAT HAS FUR ON THE SOLES OF ITS FEET.

THE SUN BEAR OF MALAYA HAS SUCH PRECISION CLAWS THAT IT CAN PICK UP SINGLE GRAINS OF RICE.

THE KODIAK BEAR IS THE WORLD'S HEAVIEST BEAR & WEIGHS UP TO ¾ TON.

ALL BEARS TEND TO HAVE AN IRRATIONAL FEAR OF DOGS.

A BEAR'S FAVOURITE FOOD

THE CANADIAN WILD LIFE SERVICE HAS FOUND THAT THE BEST BAIT FOR BEAR TRAPS IS A MIXTURE OF HONEY, BACON & PINEAPPLE JUICE.

A BEAR'S IDEAL HOME

BEARS SELDOM STRAY FROM AMERICA'S NATIONAL PARKS, HAVING BECOME DEPENDENT ON TOURISTS. THEY HAVE LEARNT TO ACT & CLOWN TO OBTAIN BUNS, SUGAR, BACON & BAKED BEANS & WILL EVEN BREAK INTO CARS & CABINS. YELLOWSTONE PARK HAS AN ADDITIONAL ATTRACTION: STEAM HEATED CAVES, IDEAL FOR HIBERNATING.

POLAR BEARS & WATER

POLAR BEARS ARE SURPRISINGLY HELPLESS IN WATER (MAX. SPEED 3 KNOTS). THEY WILL TRAVEL LONG DISTANCES OVERLAND TO AVOID SHORT SEA CROSSINGS. EVEN YOUNG SEALS CAN GANG UP ON A SWIMMING BEAR, NIPPING HIS FLANKS & FORCING HIM HURRIEDLY ASHORE.

SPYING ON BEARS

SPY SATELLITES ARE NOT ONLY MONITORING THE RUSSIANS. THE HUMIDITY & TEMPERATURE OF SOME MONTANA BEARS IS BEING CONTINUOUSLY RECORDED VIA THE NIMBUS 4 SATELLITE & MINIATURE TRANSMITTERS FIXED ON THE BEARS. IT IS HOPED TO FIND OUT DETAILS OF THEIR HIBERNATION CYCLE.

HOW TO GET AN APPLE INTO A BOTTLE

CHOOSE A STRONG BRANCH WITH A SMALL UNRIPE APPLE GROWING. PASS APPLE THROUGH NECK OF BOTTLE THEN TIE BOTTLE TO BRANCH & WAIT FOR APPLE TO GROW.

NEXT WEEK — HOW TO MAKE STEEL BURN

☆ BEASTS ☆
IRRATIONAL ANIMALS

CATCHING A UNICORN

THE UNICORN IS SAID TO HAVE BEEN VERY FAST & DIFFICULT TO HUNT. HOWEVER ONE STRATAGEM THAT NEVER FAILED WAS TO SEND A VIRGIN GIRL INTO A WOOD BY HERSELF. ANY UNICORN THERE WOULD SOON "LEAP INTO HER LAP & EMBRACE HER", WHEN IT MIGHT EASILY BE CAUGHT. UNFORTUNATELY, IF SOME AUTHORITIES ARE CORRECT IN THINKING THAT THE UNICORN AROSE FROM MISINTERPRETED DESCRIPTIONS OF THE RHINO, THE POOR GIRL WOULD CERTAINLY BE FATALLY CRUSHED.

THE ECHENIS

THE ECHENIS IS AN ODD CREATURE ONLY 6 INCHES LONG BUT REPUTED TO HOLD A SHIP MOTIONLESS BY CLINGING TO IT. THE CREATURE'S ORIGIN IS OBSCURE.

THE PHOENIX

MANY IDENTITIES HAVE BEEN SUGGESTED FOR THE PHOENIX, INCLUDING A BIRD OF PARADISE, A FLAMINGO, A STORK & AN EGRET. ONE LIKELY THEORY IS THAT IT WAS REALLY A PURPLE HERON, FROM THE WORD PHOENICUS MEANING PURPLE. ANOTHER THEORY IS THAT IT WAS NOT A BIRD BUT REFERRED TO THE SUN, AS THIS WOULD EXPLAIN HOW IT DIED IN ITS OWN FIRES & THEN ROSE AFRESH.

THE AMPHISBENA

THE AMPHISBENA WAS AN ENDEARING MEDIEVAL REPTILE WITH TWO HEADS. WITH ONE HEAD HOLDING THE OTHER IT WAS SAID TO BOWL ALONG IN EITHER DIRECTION LIKE A HOOP. THE STORY PROBABLY REFERS TO THE INDIAN SAND BOA WHICH HAS A LUMP IN ITS TAIL AND IS OFTEN CALLED THE TWO HEADED SNAKE.

CYCLOPS & MERMAIDS

TALES OF ONE EYED GIANTS & MERMAIDS MAY HAVE STEMMED FROM GENETICALLY DEFORMED BABIES. BOTH DEFORMITIES OCCUR OCCASIONALLY & HAVE THE MEDICAL NAMES CYCLOPIA AND SYMPODIA.

THE CALDRICUS

THIS BIRD IS SAID TO HAVE POSSESSED THE USEFUL ABILITY OF BEING ABLE TO TELL IF VERY ILL PEOPLE WERE GOING TO SURVIVE. IF THE BIRD FACES THE PATIENT, THE MAN WILL LIVE, BUT IF THE BIRD TURNS ITS BACK ON THE PATIENT, HE WILL DIE. THE DIFFICULTY IN IDENTIFYING THIS BIRD IS PARTLY DUE TO THE FACT THAT PEOPLE DID NOT ACTUALLY HAVE TO BUY ONE TO RECEIVE A DIAGNOSIS, SO DEALERS WERE RELUCTANT TO DISPLAY THEM.

THE BASILISK

THE BASILISK IS ONE OF THE MOST TERRIFYING MEDIEVAL BEASTS. IT WAS SAID TO KILL PEOPLE MERELY BY ITS BREATH AND A BIRD FLYING PAST ONE, ALTHOUGH IT MIGHT BE FAR FROM ITS MOUTH, GOT FRIZZLED UP & DEVOURED. FORTUNATELY THEY COULD BE CONQUERED BY WEASELS.

HOW TO GET AN ENEMY'S FEET WET

PUNCH LOTS OF HOLES IN BOTTOM OF A PLASTIC BLEACH BOTTLE WITH A SCREW TOP. FILL WITH WATER BY IMMERSING BOTTLE COMPLETELY & SCREW ON CAP WHILE STILL IMMERSED. REMOVE BOTTLE FROM WATER & BET YOUR ENEMY HE IS NOT STRONG ENOUGH TO UNSCREW TOP. WATER WILL NOT FALL THROUGH HOLES TILL TOP IS OFF.

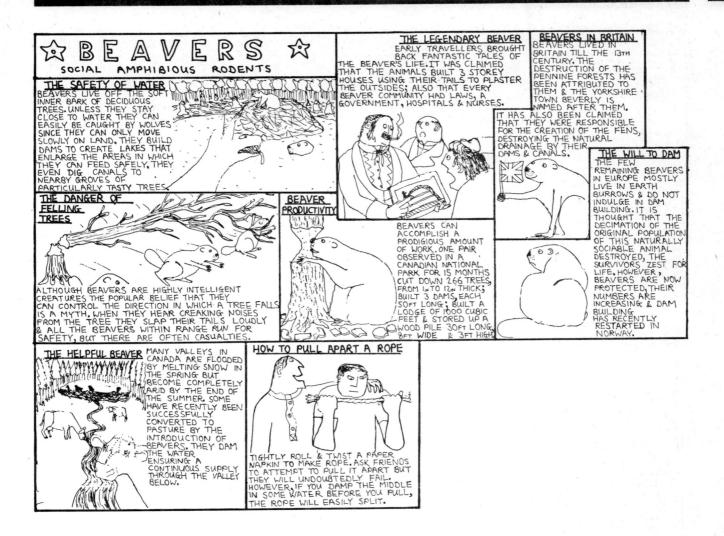

☆ BEAVERS ☆
SOCIAL AMPHIBIOUS RODENTS

THE SAFETY OF WATER
BEAVERS LIVE OFF THE SOFT INNER BARK OF DECIDUOUS TREES. UNLESS THEY STAY CLOSE TO WATER THEY CAN EASILY BE CAUGHT BY WOLVES SINCE THEY CAN ONLY MOVE SLOWLY ON LAND. THEY BUILD DAMS TO CREATE LAKES THAT ENLARGE THE AREAS IN WHICH THEY CAN FEED SAFELY. THEY EVEN DIG CANALS TO NEARBY GROVES OF PARTICULARLY TASTY TREES.

THE DANGER OF FELLING TREES
ALTHOUGH BEAVERS ARE HIGHLY INTELLIGENT CREATURES THE POPULAR BELIEF THAT THEY CAN CONTROL THE DIRECTION IN WHICH A TREE FALLS IS A MYTH. WHEN THEY HEAR CREAKING NOISES FROM THE TREE THEY SLAP THEIR TAILS LOUDLY & ALL THE BEAVERS WITHIN RANGE RUN FOR SAFETY, BUT THERE ARE OFTEN CASUALTIES.

THE HELPFUL BEAVER
MANY VALLEYS IN CANADA ARE FLOODED BY MELTING SNOW IN THE SPRING BUT BECOME COMPLETELY ARID BY THE END OF THE SUMMER. SOME HAVE RECENTLY BEEN SUCCESSFULLY CONVERTED TO PASTURE BY THE INTRODUCTION OF BEAVERS. THEY DAM THE WATER ENSURING A CONTINUOUS SUPPLY THROUGH THE VALLEY BELOW.

THE LEGENDARY BEAVER
EARLY TRAVELLERS BROUGHT BACK FANTASTIC TALES OF THE BEAVER'S LIFE. IT WAS CLAIMED THAT THE ANIMALS BUILT 3 STOREY HOUSES USING THEIR TAILS TO PLASTER THE OUTSIDES; ALSO THAT EVERY BEAVER COMMUNITY HAD LAWS, A GOVERNMENT, HOSPITALS & NURSES.

BEAVER PRODUCTIVITY
BEAVERS CAN ACCOMPLISH A PRODIGIOUS AMOUNT OF WORK. ONE PAIR OBSERVED IN A CANADIAN NATIONAL PARK FOR 15 MONTHS CUT DOWN 266 TREES FROM 1in TO 12in THICK; BUILT 3 DAMS, EACH 50FT LONG; BUILT A LODGE OF 1000 CUBIC FEET & STORED UP A WOOD PILE 30FT LONG, 8FT WIDE & 3FT HIGH.

BEAVERS IN BRITAIN
BEAVERS LIVED IN BRITAIN TILL THE 13TH CENTURY. THE DESTRUCTION OF THE PENNINE FORESTS HAS BEEN ATTRIBUTED TO THEM & THE YORKSHIRE TOWN BEVERLY IS NAMED AFTER THEM. IT HAS ALSO BEEN CLAIMED THAT THEY WERE RESPONSIBLE FOR THE CREATION OF THE FENS, DESTROYING THE NATURAL DRAINAGE BY THEIR DAMS & CANALS.

THE WILL TO DAM
THE FEW REMAINING BEAVERS IN EUROPE MOSTLY LIVE IN EARTH BURROWS & DO NOT INDULGE IN DAM BUILDING. IT IS THOUGHT THAT THE DECIMATION OF THE ORIGINAL POPULATION OF THIS NATURALLY SOCIABLE ANIMAL DESTROYED THE SURVIVORS' ZEST FOR LIFE. HOWEVER, BEAVERS ARE NOW PROTECTED, THEIR NUMBERS ARE INCREASING & DAM BUILDING HAS RECENTLY RESTARTED IN NORWAY.

HOW TO PULL APART A ROPE
TIGHTLY ROLL & TWIST A PAPER NAPKIN TO MAKE ROPE. ASK FRIENDS TO ATTEMPT TO PULL IT APART BUT THEY WILL UNDOUBTEDLY FAIL. HOWEVER, IF YOU DAMP THE MIDDLE IN SOME WATER BEFORE YOU PULL, THE ROPE WILL EASILY SPLIT.

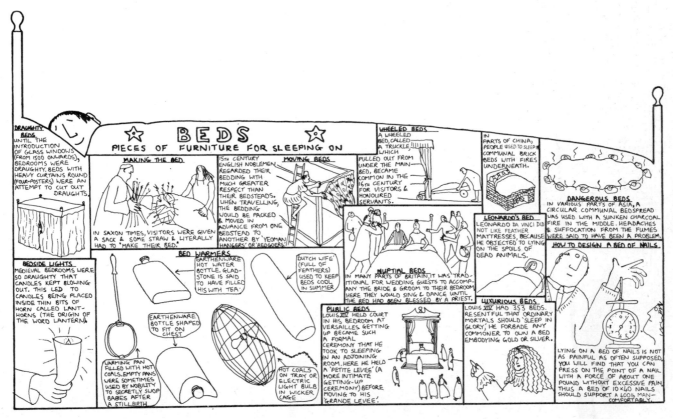

☆ BEDS ☆
PIECES OF FURNITURE FOR SLEEPING ON

DRAUGHTY BEDS
UNTIL THE INTRODUCTION OF GLASS WINDOWS (FROM 1500 ONWARDS), BEDROOMS WERE DRAUGHTY. BEDS WITH HEAVY CURTAINS ROUND (FOUR-POSTERS) WERE AN ATTEMPT TO CUT OUT DRAUGHTS.

MAKING THE BED
IN SAXON TIMES, VISITORS WERE GIVEN A SACK & SOME STRAW & LITERALLY HAD TO 'MAKE THEIR BED'.

MOVING BEDS
15TH CENTURY ENGLISH NOBLEMEN REGARDED THEIR BEDDING WITH MUCH GREATER RESPECT THAN THEIR BEDSTEADS. WHEN TRAVELLING, THE BEDDING WOULD BE PACKED IN ADVANCE FROM ONE BEDSTEAD TO ANOTHER BY YEOMAN HANGERS OR HANGERS.

WHEELED BEDS
A WHEELED BED, CALLED A TRUCKLE WHICH PULLED OUT FROM UNDER THE MAIN BED, BECAME COMMON IN THE 16TH CENTURY FOR VISITORS & HONOURED SERVANTS.

IN PARTS OF CHINA, PEOPLE USED TO SLEEP ON COMMUNAL BRICK BEDS WITH FIRES UNDERNEATH.

DANGEROUS BEDS
IN VARIOUS PARTS OF ASIA, A CIRCULAR COMMUNAL BEDSPREAD WAS USED WITH A SUNKEN CHARCOAL FIRE IN THE MIDDLE. HEADACHES & SUFFOCATION FROM THE FUMES WERE SAID TO HAVE BEEN A PROBLEM.

LEONARDO'S BED
LEONARDO DA VINCI DID NOT LIKE FEATHER MATTRESSES, BECAUSE HE OBJECTED TO LYING ON THE SPOILS OF DEAD ANIMALS.

BEDSIDE LIGHTS
MEDIEVAL BEDROOMS WERE SO DRAUGHTY THAT CANDLES KEPT BLOWING OUT. THIS LED TO CANDLES BEING PLACED INSIDE THIN BITS OF HORN CALLED LANT-HORN (THE ORIGIN OF THE WORD LANTERN).

BED WARMERS
EARTHENWARE HOT WATER BOTTLE. GLADSTONE IS SAID TO HAVE FILLED HIS WITH TEA.

EARTHENWARE BOTTLE SHAPED TO FIT ON CHEST

'DUTCH WIFE' (FULL OF FEATHERS) USED TO KEEP BEDS COOL IN SUMMER

WARMING PAN FILLED WITH HOT COALS. EMPTY PANS WERE SOMETIMES USED BY MIDWIFERY TO SECRETLY SWOP BABIES AFTER A STILLBIRTH

HOT COALS ON TRAY OR ELECTRIC LIGHT BULB IN WICKER CAGE

NUPTIAL BEDS
IN MANY PARTS OF BRITAIN, IT WAS TRADITIONAL FOR WEDDING GUESTS TO ACCOMPANY THE BRIDE & GROOM TO THEIR BEDROOM. HERE THEY WOULD SING & DANCE UNTIL THE BED HAD BEEN BLESSED BY A PRIEST.

PUBLIC BEDS
LOUIS XIV HELD COURT IN HIS BEDROOM AT VERSAILLES. GETTING UP BECAME SUCH A FORMAL CEREMONY THAT HE TOOK TO SLEEPING IN AN ADJOINING ROOM. HERE HE HELD A 'PETITE LEVEE' (A MORE INTIMATE GETTING-UP CEREMONY) BEFORE MOVING TO HIS 'GRANDE LEVEE'.

LUXURIOUS BEDS
LOUIS XIV HAD 353 BEDS. RESENTFUL THAT ORDINARY MORTALS SHOULD SLEEP IN GLORY, HE FORBADE ANY COMMONER TO OWN A BED EMBODYING GOLD OR SILVER.

HOW TO DESIGN A BED OF NAILS
LYING ON A BED OF NAILS IS NOT AS PAINFUL AS OFTEN SUPPOSED. YOU WILL FIND THAT YOU CAN PRESS ON THE POINT OF A NAIL WITH A FORCE OF ABOUT ONE POUND WITHOUT EXCESSIVE PAIN, THUS A BED OF 10×40 NAILS SHOULD SUPPORT A 400lb MAN COMFORTABLY.

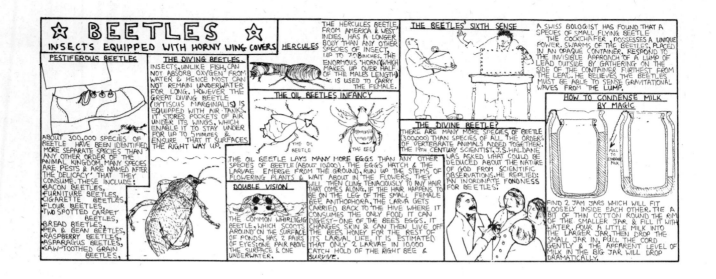

☆ BEETLES ☆
INSECTS EQUIPPED WITH HORNY WING COVERS

PESTIFEROUS BEETLES
ABOUT 300,000 SPECIES OF BEETLE HAVE BEEN IDENTIFIED, MORE SEPARATE SPECIES THAN ANY OTHER ORDER OF THE ANIMAL KINGDOM. MANY SPECIES ARE PESTS & ARE NAMED AFTER THE 'DELICACY' THAT THEY CONSUME. THESE INCLUDE:
- BACON BEETLES,
- FURNITURE BEETLES,
- CIGARETTE BEETLES,
- FLOUR BEETLES,
- TWO SPOTTED CARPET BEETLES,
- BREAD BEETLES,
- PEA & BEAN BEETLES,
- RASPBERRY BEETLES,
- ASPARAGUS BEETLES,
- SAW-TOOTHED GRAIN BEETLES,

THE DIVING BEETLES
INSECTS, UNLIKE FISH, CAN NOT ABSORB OXYGEN FROM WATER & HENCE MOST CAN NOT REMAIN UNDERWATER FOR LONG. HOWEVER THE GREAT DIVING BEETLE (DYTISCUS MARGINALIS) IS EQUIPPED WITH AIR-TANKS. IT STORES POCKETS OF AIR UNDER ITS WINGS, WHICH ENABLE IT TO STAY UNDER FOR UP TO 5 MINUTES & ENSURE THAT IT SURFACES THE RIGHT WAY UP.

DOUBLE VISION
THE COMMON WHIRLIGIG BEETLE, WHICH SCOOTS AROUND ON THE SURFACE OF PONDS, HAS 2 PAIRS OF EYES: ONE PAIR ABOVE THE SURFACE & ONE UNDERWATER.

HERCULES
THE HERCULES BEETLE, FROM AMERICA & WEST INDIES, HAS A LONGER BODY THAN ANY OTHER SPECIES OF INSECT, UP TO 7.08 INCHES. THE ENORMOUS 'HORN' (WHICH MAKES UP OVER HALF OF THE MALE'S LENGTH) IS USED TO CARRY THE FEMALE.

THE OIL BEETLES INFANCY
THE OIL BEETLE — THE BEE

THE OIL BEETLE LAYS MANY MORE EGGS THAN ANY OTHER SPECIES OF BEETLE (ABOUT 10,000). THE EGGS HATCH & THE LARVAE EMERGE FROM THE GROUND, RUN UP THE STEMS OF FLOWERING PLANTS & WAIT ABOUT IN THE FLOWERS. THEY WILL THEN CLING TENACIOUSLY TO ANY HAIR THAT COMES ALONG. IF THE HAIR HAPPENS TO BE ON THE LEG OF THE SMALL FEMALE BEE ANTHOPHORA, THE LARVA GETS CARRIED BACK TO THE HIVE WHERE IT CONSUMES THE ONLY FOOD IT CAN DIGEST — ONE OF THE BEE'S EGGS. IT CHANGES SKIN & CAN THEN LIVE OFF THE BEE'S HONEY FOR THE REST OF ITS LARVAL LIFE. IT IS ESTIMATED THAT ONLY 2 LARVAE IN 10,000 CATCH HOLD OF THE RIGHT BEE & SURVIVE.

THE BEETLES' SIXTH SENSE
A SWISS BIOLOGIST HAS FOUND THAT A SPECIES OF SMALL FLYING BEETLE, THE COCKCHAFER, POSSESSES A UNIQUE POWER. SWARMS OF THE BEETLES, PLACED IN AN OPAQUE CONTAINER, RESPOND TO THE INVISIBLE APPROACH OF A LUMP OF LEAD OUTSIDE BY GATHERING ON THE SIDE OF THE CONTAINER FURTHEST FROM THE LEAD. HE BELIEVES THE BEETLES MUST BE ABLE TO SENSE GRAVITATIONAL WAVES FROM THE LUMP.

THE DIVINE BEETLE?
THERE ARE MANY MORE SPECIES OF BEETLE (300,000) THAN SPECIES OF ALL THE ORDERS OF VERTEBRATE ANIMALS ADDED TOGETHER. THE 19TH CENTURY SCIENTIST, J.S. HALDANE WAS ASKED WHAT COULD BE DEDUCED ABOUT THE NATURE OF GOD FROM SCIENTIFIC OBSERVATIONS. HE REPLIED: 'AN INORDINATE FONDNESS FOR BEETLES.'

HOW TO CONDENSE MILK BY MAGIC
FULL TO CONDENSE MILK

FIND 2 JAM JARS WHICH WILL FIT LOOSELY INSIDE EACH OTHER. TIE A BIT OF THIN COTTON ROUND THE RIM OF THE SMALLER JAR & FILL IT WITH WATER. POUR A LITTLE MILK INTO THE LARGER JAR, THEN DROP THE SMALL JAR IN. PULL THE CORD GENTLY & THE APPARENT LEVEL OF MILK IN THE BIG JAR WILL DROP DRAMATICALLY.

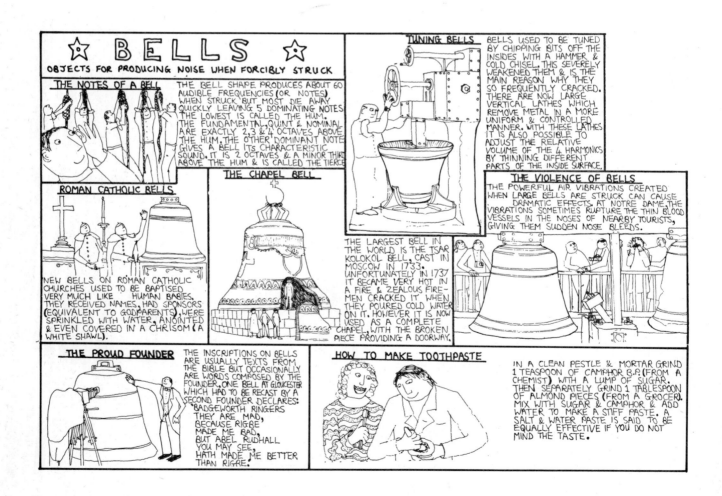

☆ BELLS ☆
OBJECTS FOR PRODUCING NOISE WHEN FORCIBLY STRUCK

THE NOTES OF A BELL
THE BELL SHAPE PRODUCES ABOUT 60 AUDIBLE FREQUENCIES (OR NOTES) WHEN STRUCK BUT MOST DIE AWAY QUICKLY LEAVING 5 DOMINATING NOTES. THE LOWEST IS CALLED THE HUM. THE FUNDAMENTAL, QUINT & NOMINAL ARE EXACTLY 2, 3 & 4 OCTAVES ABOVE THE HUM. THE OTHER DOMINANT NOTE GIVES A BELL ITS CHARACTERISTIC SOUND. IT IS 2 OCTAVES & A MINOR THIRD ABOVE THE HUM & IS CALLED THE TIERCE.

ROMAN CATHOLIC BELLS
NEW BELLS ON ROMAN CATHOLIC CHURCHES USED TO BE BAPTISED VERY MUCH LIKE HUMAN BABIES. THEY RECEIVED NAMES, HAD SPONSORS (EQUIVALENT TO GODPARENTS), WERE SPRINKLED WITH WATER, ANOINTED & EVEN COVERED IN A CHRISOM (A WHITE SHAWL).

THE CHAPEL BELL

TUNING BELLS
BELLS USED TO BE TUNED BY CHIPPING BITS OFF THE INSIDES WITH A HAMMER & COLD CHISEL. THIS SEVERELY WEAKENED THEM & IS THE MAIN REASON WHY THEY SO FREQUENTLY CRACKED. THERE ARE NOW LARGE VERTICAL LATHES WHICH REMOVE METAL IN A MORE UNIFORM & CONTROLLED MANNER. WITH THESE LATHES IT IS ALSO POSSIBLE TO ADJUST THE RELATIVE VOLUME OF THE 4 HARMONICS BY THINNING DIFFERENT PARTS OF THE INSIDE SURFACE.

THE VIOLENCE OF BELLS
THE POWERFUL AIR VIBRATIONS CREATED WHEN LARGE BELLS ARE STRUCK CAN CAUSE DRAMATIC EFFECTS. AT NOTRE DAME, THE VIBRATIONS SOMETIMES RUPTURE THE THIN BLOOD VESSELS IN THE NOSES OF NEARBY TOURISTS, GIVING THEM SUDDEN NOSE BLEEDS.

THE LARGEST BELL IN THE WORLD IS THE TSAR KOLOKOL BELL, CAST IN MOSCOW IN 1733. UNFORTUNATELY IN 1737 IT BECAME VERY HOT IN A FIRE & ZEALOUS FIREMEN CRACKED IT WHEN THEY POURED COLD WATER ON IT. HOWEVER IT IS NOW USED AS A COMPLETE CHAPEL, WITH THE BROKEN PIECE PROVIDING A DOORWAY.

THE PROUD FOUNDER
THE INSCRIPTIONS ON BELLS ARE USUALLY TEXTS FROM THE BIBLE BUT OCCASIONALLY ARE WORDS COMPOSED BY THE FOUNDER. ONE BELL AT GLOUCESTER WHICH HAD TO BE RECAST BY A SECOND FOUNDER DECLARES:
'BADGEWORTH RINGERS THEY ARE MAD, BECAUSE RIGBE MADE ME BAD, BUT ABEL RUDHALL YOU MAY SEE, HATH MADE ME BETTER THAN RIGBE.'

HOW TO MAKE TOOTHPASTE
IN A CLEAN PESTLE & MORTAR GRIND 1 TEASPOON OF CAMPHOR B.P. (FROM A CHEMIST) WITH A LUMP OF SUGAR. THEN SEPARATELY GRIND 1 TABLESPOON OF ALMOND PIECES (FROM A GROCER). MIX WITH SUGAR & CAMPHOR & ADD WATER TO MAKE A STIFF PASTE. A SALT & WATER PASTE IS SAID TO BE EQUALLY EFFECTIVE IF YOU DO NOT MIND THE TASTE.

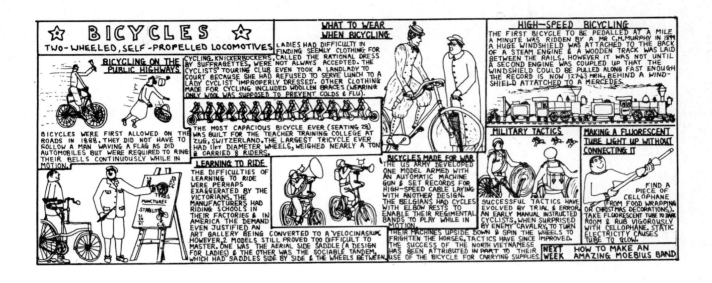

☆ BICYCLES ☆
TWO-WHEELED, SELF-PROPELLED LOCOMOTIVES

BICYCLING ON THE PUBLIC HIGHWAYS
BICYCLES WERE FIRST ALLOWED ON THE ROADS IN 1888. THEY DID NOT HAVE TO FOLLOW A MAN WAVING A FLAG AS DID AUTOMOBILES BUT WERE REQUIRED TO RING THEIR BELLS CONTINUOUSLY WHILE IN MOTION.

LEARNING TO RIDE
THE DIFFICULTIES OF LEARNING TO RIDE WERE PERHAPS EXAGGERATED BY THE VICTORIANS. THE MANUFACTURERS HAD RIDING SCHOOLS IN THEIR FACTORIES & IN AMERICA THE DEMAND EVEN JUSTIFIED AN ART GALLERY BEING CONVERTED TO A 'VELOCINASIUM'. HOWEVER, 2 MODELS STILL PROVED TOO DIFFICULT TO MASTER. ONE WAS THE AERIAL SIDE SADDLE (A DESIGN FOR LADIES) & THE OTHER WAS THE SOCIABLE TANDEM, WHICH HAD SADDLES SIDE BY SIDE & THE WHEELS BETWEEN.

WHAT TO WEAR WHEN BICYCLING
LADIES HAD DIFFICULTY IN FINDING SEEMLY CLOTHING FOR CYCLING. KNICKERBOCKERS, CALLED THE RATIONAL DRESS BY SUFFRAGETTES, WERE NOT ALWAYS ACCEPTED. THE CYCLISTS' TOURING CLUB EVEN TOOK A LANDLADY TO COURT BECAUSE SHE HAD REFUSED TO SERVE LUNCH TO A LADY CYCLIST 'IMPROPERLY DRESSED'. OTHER CLOTHING MADE FOR CYCLING INCLUDED WOOLLEN BRACES (WEARING ONLY WOOL WAS SUPPOSED TO PREVENT COLDS & FLU).

THE MOST CAPACIOUS BICYCLE EVER (SEATING 29) WAS BUILT FOR THE TEACHER TRAINING COLLEGE AT ZUG, SWITZERLAND. THE LARGEST TRICYCLE EVER HAD 11ft DIAMETER WHEELS, WEIGHED NEARLY A TON & CARRIED 8 RIDERS.

BICYCLES MADE FOR WAR
THE US ARMY DEVELOPED ONE MODEL ARMED WITH AN AUTOMATIC MACHINE GUN & SET RECORDS FOR HIGH-SPEED CABLE LAYING WITH ANOTHER DESIGN. THE BELGIANS HAD CYCLES WITH ELBOW RESTS TO ENABLE THEIR REGIMENTAL BANDS TO PLAY WHILE IN MOTION. THEIR MACHINES UPSIDE DOWN & SPIN THE WHEELS TO FRIGHTEN THE HORSES. TACTICS HAVE SINCE IMPROVED.

HIGH-SPEED BICYCLING
THE FIRST BICYCLE TO BE PEDALLED AT A MILE A MINUTE WAS RIDDEN BY A MR C.M. MURPHY IN 1899. A HUGE WINDSHIELD WAS ATTACHED TO THE BACK OF A STEAM ENGINE & A WOODEN TRACK WAS LAID BETWEEN THE RAILS. HOWEVER IT WAS NOT UNTIL A SECOND ENGINE WAS COUPLED UP THAT THE WINDSHIELD COULD BE PULLED ALONG FAST ENOUGH. THE RECORD IS NOW 127.43 MPH, BEHIND A WINDSHIELD ATTATCHED TO A MERCEDES.

MILITARY TACTICS
SUCCESSFUL TACTICS HAVE EVOLVED BY TRIAL & ERROR. AN EARLY MANUAL INSTRUCTED CYCLISTS, WHEN SURPRISED BY ENEMY CAVALRY, TO TURN THE SUCCESS OF THE NORTH VIETNAMESE HAS BEEN ATTRIBUTED IN PART TO THEIR USE OF THE BICYCLE FOR CARRYING SUPPLIES.

MAKING A FLUORESCENT TUBE LIGHT UP WITHOUT CONNECTING IT
FIND A PIECE OF CELLOPHANE (FROM FOOD WRAPPING OR CHRISTMAS DECORATIONS). TAKE FLUORESCENT TUBE TO DARK ROOM & RUB VIGOROUSLY WITH CELLOPHANE. STATIC ELECTRICITY CAUSES TUBE TO GLOW.

NEXT WEEK — HOW TO MAKE AN AMAZING MOEBIUS BAND

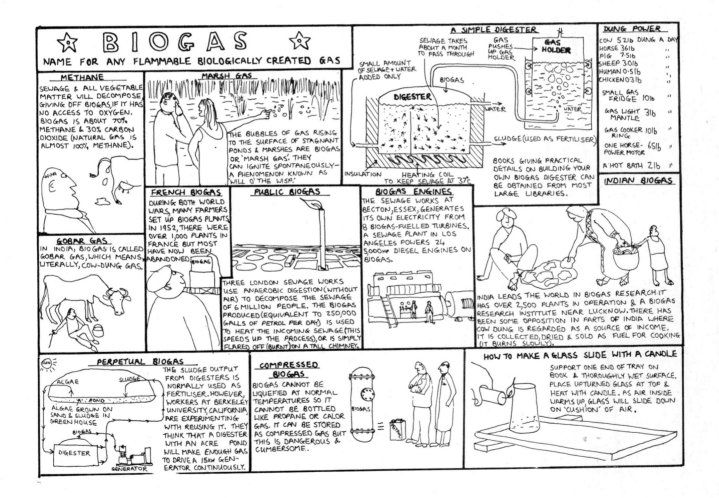

☆ BIOGAS ☆
NAME FOR ANY FLAMMABLE BIOLOGICALLY CREATED GAS

METHANE
SEWAGE & ALL VEGETABLE MATTER WILL DECOMPOSE, GIVING OFF BIOGAS, IF IT HAS NO ACCESS TO OXYGEN. BIOGAS IS ABOUT 70% METHANE & 30% CARBON DIOXIDE (NATURAL GAS IS ALMOST 100% METHANE).

GOBAR GAS
IN INDIA, BIOGAS IS CALLED GOBAR GAS, WHICH MEANS, LITERALLY, COW-DUNG GAS.

MARSH GAS
THE BUBBLES OF GAS RISING TO THE SURFACE OF STAGNANT PONDS & MARSHES ARE BIOGAS OR 'MARSH GAS.' THEY CAN IGNITE SPONTANEOUSLY - A PHENOMENON KNOWN AS 'WILL O' THE WISP.'

FRENCH BIOGAS
DURING BOTH WORLD WARS, MANY FARMERS SET UP BIOGAS PLANTS. IN 1952, THERE WERE OVER 1,000 PLANTS IN FRANCE BUT MOST HAVE NOW BEEN ABANDONED.

PUBLIC BIOGAS
THREE LONDON SEWAGE WORKS USE ANAEROBIC DIGESTION (WITHOUT AIR) TO DECOMPOSE THE SEWAGE OF 6 MILLION PEOPLE. THE BIOGAS PRODUCED (EQUIVALENT TO 250,000 GALLS OF PETROL PER DAY) IS USED TO HEAT THE INCOMING SEWAGE (THIS SPEEDS UP THE PROCESS), OR IS SIMPLY FLARED OFF (BURNT) ON A TALL CHIMNEY.

A SIMPLE DIGESTER
SEWAGE TAKES ABOUT A MONTH TO PASS THROUGH
SMALL AMOUNT OF SEWAGE + WATER ADDED ONLY
GAS PUSHES UP GAS HOLDER
GAS HOLDER
BIOGAS
DIGESTER
WATER
WATER
SLUDGE (USED AS FERTILISER)
INSULATION
HEATING COIL TO KEEP SEWAGE AT 37°C

BOOKS GIVING PRACTICAL DETAILS ON BUILDING YOUR OWN BIOGAS DIGESTER CAN BE OBTAINED FROM MOST LARGE LIBRARIES.

BIOGAS ENGINES
THE SEWAGE WORKS AT BECTON, ESSEX, GENERATES ITS OWN ELECTRICITY FROM 8 BIOGAS-FUELLED TURBINES. A SEWAGE PLANT IN LOS ANGELES POWERS 24 5,000HP DIESEL ENGINES ON BIOGAS.

DUNG POWER
COW	52lb DUNG A DAY
HORSE	36lb "
PIG	7.5lb "
SHEEP	3.0lb "
HUMAN	0.5lb "
CHICKEN	0.3lb "
SMALL GAS FRIDGE	10lb "
GAS LIGHT MANTLE	3lb "
GAS COOKER RING	10lb "
ONE HORSE-POWER MOTOR	65lb "
A HOT BATH	2lb "

INDIAN BIOGAS
INDIA LEADS THE WORLD IN BIOGAS RESEARCH. IT HAS OVER 2,500 PLANTS IN OPERATION & A BIOGAS RESEARCH INSTITUTE NEAR LUCKNOW. THERE HAS BEEN SOME OPPOSITION IN PARTS OF INDIA WHERE COW DUNG IS REGARDED AS A SOURCE OF INCOME. IT IS COLLECTED, DRIED & SOLD AS FUEL FOR COOKING (IT BURNS SLOWLY).

PERPETUAL BIOGAS
ALGAE   SLUDGE
'A' POND
ALGAE GROWN ON SAND & SLUDGE IN GREEN HOUSE
BIOGAS
DIGESTER
GENERATOR

THE SLUDGE OUTPUT FROM DIGESTERS IS NORMALLY USED AS FERTILISER. HOWEVER, WORKERS AT BERKELEY UNIVERSITY, CALIFORNIA, ARE EXPERIMENTING WITH REUSING IT. THEY THINK THAT A DIGESTER WITH AN ACRE POND WILL MAKE ENOUGH GAS TO DRIVE A 15kW GENERATOR CONTINUOUSLY.

COMPRESSED BIOGAS
BIOGAS CANNOT BE LIQUEFIED AT NORMAL TEMPERATURES SO IT CANNOT BE BOTTLED LIKE PROPANE OR CALOR GAS. IT CAN BE STORED AS COMPRESSED GAS BUT THIS IS DANGEROUS & CUMBERSOME.

HOW TO MAKE A GLASS SLIDE WITH A CANDLE
SUPPORT ONE END OF TRAY ON BOOK & THOROUGHLY WET SURFACE. PLACE UPTURNED GLASS AT TOP & HEAT WITH CANDLE. AS AIR INSIDE WARMS UP, GLASS WILL SLIDE DOWN ON 'CUSHION' OF AIR.

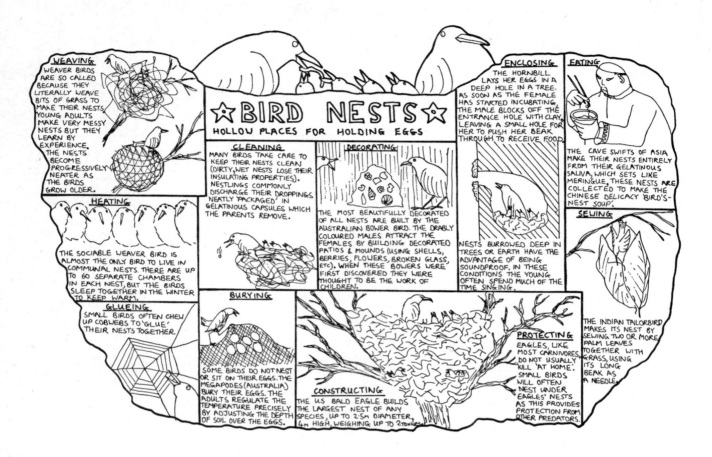

☆ BIRD NESTS ☆
HOLLOW PLACES FOR HOLDING EGGS

WEAVING
WEAVER BIRDS ARE SO CALLED BECAUSE THEY LITERALLY WEAVE BITS OF GRASS TO MAKE THEIR NESTS. YOUNG ADULTS MAKE VERY MESSY NESTS BUT THEY LEARN BY EXPERIENCE. THE NESTS BECOME PROGRESSIVELY NEATER AS THE BIRDS GROW OLDER.

HEATING
THE SOCIABLE WEAVER BIRD IS ALMOST THE ONLY BIRD TO LIVE IN COMMUNAL NESTS. THERE ARE UP TO 60 SEPARATE CHAMBERS IN EACH NEST, BUT THE BIRDS SLEEP TOGETHER IN THE WINTER TO KEEP WARM.

GLUEING
SMALL BIRDS OFTEN CHEW UP COBWEBS TO 'GLUE' THEIR NESTS TOGETHER.

CLEANING
MANY BIRDS TAKE CARE TO KEEP THEIR NESTS CLEAN (DIRTY, WET NESTS LOSE THEIR INSULATING PROPERTIES). NESTLINGS COMMONLY DISCHARGE THEIR DROPPINGS NEATLY 'PACKAGED' IN GELATINOUS CAPSULES WHICH THE PARENTS REMOVE.

DECORATING
THE MOST BEAUTIFULLY DECORATED OF ALL NESTS ARE BUILT BY THE AUSTRALIAN BOWER BIRD. THE DRABLY COLOURED MALES ATTRACT THE FEMALES BY BUILDING DECORATED PATIOS & MOUNDS (USING SHELLS, BERRIES, FLOWERS, BROKEN GLASS, ETC). WHEN THESE BOWERS WERE FIRST DISCOVERED THEY WERE THOUGHT TO BE THE WORK OF CHILDREN.

BURYING
SOME BIRDS DO NOT NEST OR SIT ON THEIR EGGS. THE MEGAPODES (AUSTRALIA) BURY THEIR EGGS. THE ADULTS REGULATE THE TEMPERATURE PRECISELY BY ADJUSTING THE DEPTH OF SOIL OVER THE EGGS.

CONSTRUCTING
THE US BALD EAGLE BUILDS THE LARGEST NEST OF ANY SPECIES, UP TO 2.5m DIAMETER, 4m HIGH, WEIGHING UP TO 2 TONNES.

ENCLOSING
THE HORNBILL LAYS HER EGGS IN A DEEP HOLE IN A TREE. AS SOON AS THE FEMALE HAS STARTED INCUBATING, THE MALE BLOCKS OFF THE ENTRANCE HOLE WITH CLAY, LEAVING A SMALL HOLE FOR HER TO PUSH HER BEAK THROUGH TO RECEIVE FOOD.

NESTS BURROWED DEEP IN TREES OR EARTH HAVE THE ADVANTAGE OF BEING SOUNDPROOF. IN THESE CONDITIONS THE YOUNG OFTEN SPEND MUCH OF THE TIME SINGING.

PROTECTING
EAGLES, LIKE MOST CARNIVORES, DO NOT USUALLY KILL 'AT HOME'. SMALL BIRDS WILL OFTEN NEST UNDER EAGLES' NESTS AS THIS PROVIDES PROTECTION FROM OTHER PREDATORS.

EATING
THE CAVE SWIFTS OF ASIA MAKE THEIR NESTS ENTIRELY FROM THEIR GELATINOUS SALIVA, WHICH SETS LIKE MERINGUE. THESE NESTS ARE COLLECTED TO MAKE THE CHINESE DELICACY 'BIRD'S-NEST SOUP'.

SEWING
THE INDIAN TAILORBIRD MAKES ITS NEST BY SEWING TWO OR MORE PALM LEAVES TOGETHER WITH GRASS, USING ITS LONG BEAK AS A NEEDLE.

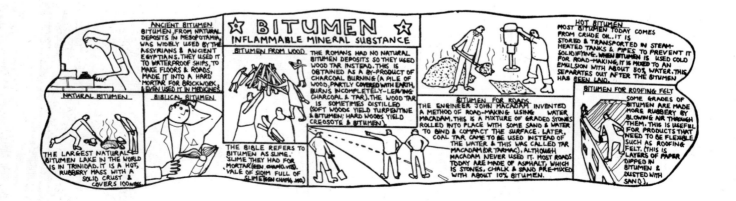

☆ BITUMEN ☆
INFLAMMABLE MINERAL SUBSTANCE

ANCIENT BITUMEN
BITUMEN, FROM NATURAL DEPOSITS IN MESOPOTAMIA, WAS WIDELY USED BY THE ASSYRIANS & ANCIENT EGYPTIANS. THEY USED IT TO WATERPROOF SHIPS, TO MAKE FLOORS & ROADS, MADE IT INTO A HARD MORTAR FOR BRICKWORK, & EVEN USED IT IN MEDICINES.

NATURAL BITUMEN
THE LARGEST NATURAL BITUMEN LAKE IN THE WORLD IS IN TRINIDAD. IT IS A HOT, RUBBERY MASS WITH A SOLID CRUST & COVERS 100ACRES.

BIBLICAL BITUMEN
THE BIBLE REFERS TO BITUMEN AS SLIME. 'SLIME THEY HAD FOR MORTAR (GEN CHAP.10. VII.3). VALE OF SIDIM FULL OF SLIME (GEN CHAP.14. XII).

BITUMEN FROM WOOD
THE ROMANS HAD NO NATURAL BITUMEN DEPOSITS SO THEY USED WOOD TAR INSTEAD. THIS IS OBTAINED AS A BY-PRODUCT OF CHARCOAL BURNING (A PILE OF WOOD, PARTLY COVERED WITH EARTH, BURNS INCOMPLETELY - LEAVING CHARCOAL & TAR). THE WOOD TAR IS SOMETIMES DISTILLED (SOFT WOODS YIELD TURPENTINE & BITUMEN; HARD WOODS YIELD CREOSOTE & BITUMEN).

BITUMEN FOR ROADS
THE ENGINEER JOHN MACADAM INVENTED A METHOD OF ROAD-MAKING USING WATER MACADAM. THIS IS A MIXTURE OF GRADED STONES ROLLED INTO PLACE WITH SOME SAND & WATER TO BIND & COMPACT THE SURFACE. LATER, COAL TAR CAME TO BE USED INSTEAD OF THE WATER & THIS WAS CALLED TAR MACADAM (OR TARMAC), ALTHOUGH MACADAM NEVER USED IT. MOST ROADS TODAY ARE MADE OF ASPHALT, WHICH IS STONES, CHALK & SAND PRE-MIXED WITH ABOUT 10% BITUMEN.

HOT BITUMEN
MOST BITUMEN TODAY COMES FROM CRUDE OIL. IT IS STORED & TRANSPORTED IN STEAM-HEATED TANKS & PIPES TO PREVENT IT SOLIDIFYING. WHEN BITUMEN IS USED COLD FOR ROAD-MAKING, IT IS MIXED TO AN EMULSION WITH ABOUT 50% WATER. THIS SEPARATES OUT AFTER THE BITUMEN HAS BEEN LAID.

BITUMEN FOR ROOFING FELT
SOME GRADES OF BITUMEN ARE MADE MORE RUBBERY BY BLOWING AIR THROUGH THEM. THIS IS USEFUL FOR PRODUCTS THAT NEED TO BE FLEXIBLE SUCH AS ROOFING FELT. (THIS IS LAYERS OF PAPER DIPPED IN BITUMEN & DUSTED WITH SAND).

BLOOD
THE BODY'S OXYGENATING FLUID

MULTICOLOURED BLOOD

THE BLOOD OF MAMMALS IS RED BECAUSE OF THE HAEMOGLOBIN IT CONTAINS. SOME WORMS HAVE GREEN BLOOD (FROM THE PIGMENT CHLOROCRUORIN), MOLLUSCS & CRUSTACEANS HAVE BLUE BLOOD (FROM THE PIGMENT HAEMOCYANIN).

CAMEL BLOOD

CAMELS HAVE SPECIAL BLOOD WHICH HELPS THEM TO TOLERATE EXTREME HEAT & DEHYDRATION. THE RED CELLS ARE OVAL IN SHAPE & HAVE VERY STRONG OUTER WALLS. THE CAMEL IS THE ONLY MAMMAL WHICH CAN VARY THE CONCENTRATION OF SALT IN ITS BLOOD WITHOUT THE RED CELLS BURSTING.

BLOOD FUNCTIONS

BLOOD IS THE BODY'S TRANSPORT SYSTEM, DELIVERING NUTRIENTS & CARRYING AWAY WASTE FROM EACH OF THE BODY'S CELLS. BLOOD IS COMPOSED OF A CLEAR LIQUID (PLASMA), RED CELLS, WHITE CELLS & PLATELETS. THE PLASMA CARRIES SUGAR & MANY ESSENTIAL SALTS DISSOLVED IN IT; THE RED CELLS ABSORB OXYGEN FROM THE LUNGS & FEED IT TO THE MUSCLES; THE WHITE CELLS FIGHT HARMFUL BACTERIA ENTERING THE SYSTEM; THE PLATELETS CAUSE THE BLOOD TO SOLIDIFY OR CLOT IF ANY ESCAPES FROM THE SYSTEM.

BLOODSTAINS

LATEST FORENSIC TECHNIQUES CAN IDENTIFY RACE & SEX FROM BLOOD STAINS. TESTS FOR AGE, ILLNESSES & EVENTUALLY INDIVIDUAL IDENTITY ARE BEING DEVELOPED.

BLOOD LETTING

BLOOD-LETTING & THE APPLICATION OF VORACIOUS LEECHES WERE POPULAR MEDICAL TREATMENTS IN THE 19th CENTURY. IN 1890, FRANCE IMPORTED 40 MILLION LEECHES A YEAR FOR THIS PURPOSE. RECENT RESEARCH HAS SHOWN THAT THERE MAY HAVE BEEN SOME VIRTUE IN THE PRACTICE AS IT REDUCED THE VISCOSITY OF THE BLOOD (A FACTOR IN MANY DISEASES INCLUDING CORONARIES, DIABETES & SOME CANCERS.)

BLOOD & STATURE

RECENT RESEARCH AT COLORADO UNIVERSITY SUGGESTS THAT SIZE & STATURE MAY BE A FUNCTION OF BLOOD GROUP. FOR EXAMPLE: MEN WITH GROUP O TEND TO HAVE LONGER FACES; WOMEN WITH GROUP A TEND TO BE HEAVIER.

VOLUNTEER BLOOD

IN THE USA ALL BLOOD SUPPLIES HAVE TO BE LABELLED AS COMING FROM EITHER A PAID OR VOLUNTEER DONOR. IT HAS BEEN FOUND THAT VIRAL HEPATITIS (A DISEASE TRANSMITTED BY BLOOD TRANSFUSIONS) IS UP TO 10 TIMES MORE LIKELY TO BE TRANSMITTED BY PAID DONORS.

HOW TO MAKE ORANGE PEEL FANGS

CUT ORANGE PEEL INTO SHAPES AS ABOVE. WEDGE ONE UNDER YOUR TOP LIP & OTHER UNDER BOTTOM LIP. KEEP MOUTH SHUT UNTIL SUITABLE DRAMATIC MOMENT.

FEEDING ON BLOOD

BLOOD ACTS AS AN IRRIGATION CHANNEL CARRYING LIQUID NOURISHMENT TO MOST OF OUR 100,000,000,000,000 CELLS & PROVIDES A GENERAL EXCHANGE POOL FOR RAW MATERIALS. EVEN BONES HAVE CENTRAL ARTERIES WHICH FEED THEIR CELLS. ONLY HAIR, NAIL, CARTILAGE & THE EYE'S CORNEA & LENS CELLS ARE NOT SUPPLIED WITH BLOOD.

A LACK OF BLOOD

FAINTING OCCURS WHEN THERE IS NOT ENOUGH BLOOD RETURNING TO THE HEART TO FILL IT UP AS IT PUMPS. IT IS A CLEVER SAFETY MECHANISM BECAUSE BY COLLAPSING THE BODY TAKES ON A HORIZONTAL POSITION WHICH AUTOMATICALLY INCREASES THE FLOW OF BLOOD TO THE HEART. IF A FAINTED PERSON IS HELD VERTICAL DEATH CAN RESULT (THIS IS HOW PEOPLE DIE BY CRUCIFIXION). TIGHT CORSETS CAN ALSO HINDER THE RETURN OF BLOOD TO THE HEART, WHICH PARTLY EXPLAINS WHY VICTORIAN LADIES WERE ALWAYS SWOONING. PEOPLE FAINT WHEN STARTLED BECAUSE THE ADRENALIN RELEASED STIMULATES THE HEART TO WORK FASTER SO IT IS MORE LIKELY TO RUN SHORT OF BLOOD.

HAEMOGLOBIN

DOING PHYSICAL WORK, OUR MUSCLES NEED ABOUT 2.5 OF OXYGEN GAS PER MINUTE. IF THERE WERE NO HAEMOGLOBIN IN OUR BLOOD, THIS AMOUNT OF GAS WOULD TAKE 300 GALLONS OF BLOOD TO DISSOLVE IT. HAEMOGLOBIN INCREASES THE CAPACITY OF OUR BLOOD TO ABSORB OXYGEN BY 40 TIMES, SO OUR HEARTS NEED ONLY PROVIDE ABOUT 8 GALL/MIN.

PELICAN BLOOD

THE EGYPTIANS THOUGHT THAT THE PELICAN FED HER OWN BLOOD TO HER YOUNG & HENCE REGARDED THE BIRD AS A SYMBOL OF FAMILY PIETY. THIS BELIEF PROBABLY STEMMED FROM OBSERVING ONE TYPE OF PELICAN THAT HAS A RED-TIPPED BEAK.

THE IRON IN RED BLOOD

IRON IS ESSENTIAL FOR THE MANUFACTURE OF RED BLOOD CELLS. THE FAMOUS SOURCE OF IRON IS SPINACH. HOWEVER, IT IS NOW KNOWN THAT OUR SYSTEM ONLY ABSORBS 3% OF THE IRON IN SPINACH, SO IF THIS WAS OUR SOLE SOURCE OF IRON WE WOULD NEED TO EAT OUR OWN WEIGHT OF SPINACH EVERY YEAR. THIS IS NOT ADVISABLE SINCE SPINACH ALSO CONTAINS OXALIC ACID, A POISON THAT CAN CAUSE KIDNEY STONES. FORTUNATELY OUR BODIES ARE MORE EFFICIENT AT ABSORBING IRON FROM OTHER FOODS (ESPECIALLY WHEN PRESENT AS A SUGAR-IRON COMPLEX — AS IN A SWEET RED WINE).

SWEATING BLOOD

THE HIPPO WAS THOUGHT TO SWEAT BLOOD. ACTUALLY THE BLOOD COMES FROM A REDDISH PIGMENT IN THE PORES OF THEIR SKINS WHICH MIXES WITH THEIR SWEAT.

SPITTING BLOOD

THE HORNED LIZARD'S EYES CAN SPIT BLOOD. BY CLOSING A VALVE IT CAN PREVENT THE RETURN OF BLOOD FROM ITS HEAD WHICH CAUSES THE PRESSURE TO BUILD UP TILL THE THIN BLOOD VESSELS IN THE EYELIDS BURST & SPRAY PREDATORS UP TO GET AWAY ITS BLOOD EVEN CONTAINS A SPECIAL IRRITANT TO DISCOURAGE PREDATORS.

HOW TO TURN ON A RADIO WITH AN ALARM CLOCK

ATTACH STRIP OF WOOD TO RADIO ON-OFF VOLUME CONTROL WITH 2 NUTS & BOLTS.

FIX ALARM CLOCK TO PLANK OF WOOD WITH 2 SCREWS & WASHERS.

SAW COTTON REEL IN HALF THEN SAW SLIT & GLUE OVER ALARM BELL WINDER.

LINK CLOCK TO RADIO WITH STRING. VARY DISTANCE X TO OBTAIN DESIRED VOLUME.

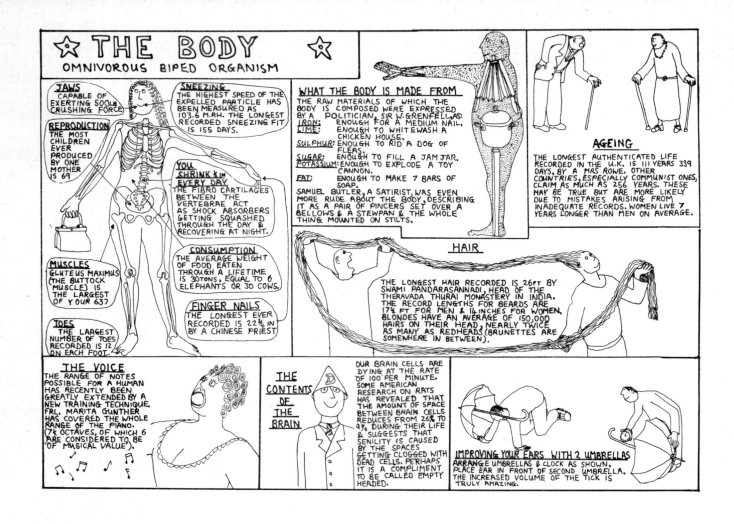

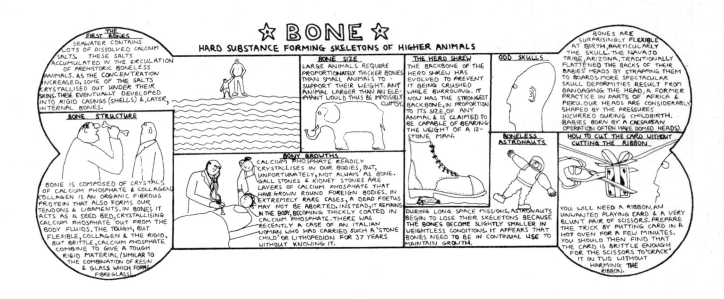

☆ BONE ☆
HARD SUBSTANCE FORMING SKELETONS OF HIGHER ANIMALS

THE FIRST BONES
SEAWATER CONTAINS LOTS OF DISSOLVED CALCIUM SALTS. THESE SALTS ACCUMULATED IN THE CIRCULATION OF PREHISTORIC BONELESS ANIMALS. AS THE CONCENTRATION INCREASED, SOME OF THE SALTS CRYSTALLISED OUT UNDER THEIR SKINS. THESE EVENTUALLY DEVELOPED INTO RIGID CASINGS (SHELLS) &, LATER, INTERNAL BONES.

BONE STRUCTURE
BONE IS COMPOSED OF CRYSTALS OF CALCIUM PHOSPHATE & COLLAGEN. COLLAGEN IS AN ORGANIC FIBROUS PROTEIN THAT ALSO FORMS OUR TENDONS & LIGAMENTS. IN BONES IT ACTS AS A SEED BED, CRYSTALLISING CALCIUM PHOSPHATE OUT FROM THE BODY FLUIDS. THE TOUGH, BUT FLEXIBLE, COLLAGEN & THE RIGID, BUT BRITTLE, CALCIUM PHOSPHATE COMBINE TO GIVE A TOUGH RIGID MATERIAL (SIMILAR TO THE COMBINATION OF RESIN & GLASS WHICH FORMS FIBREGLASS).

BONE SIZE
LARGE ANIMALS REQUIRE PROPORTIONALLY THICKER BONES THAN SMALL ANIMALS TO SUPPORT THEIR WEIGHT. ANY ANIMAL LARGER THAN AN ELEPHANT WOULD THUS BE IMPOSSIBLY CLUMSY.

BONY GROWTHS
CALCIUM PHOSPHATE READILY CRYSTALLISES IN OUR BODIES, BUT, UNFORTUNATELY, NOT ALWAYS AS BONE. GALL STONES & KIDNEY STONES ARE LAYERS OF CALCIUM PHOSPHATE THAT HAVE GROWN ROUND FOREIGN BODIES. IN EXTREMELY RARE CASES, A DEAD FOETUS MAY NOT BE ABORTED, INSTEAD, IT REMAINS IN THE BODY, BECOMING THICKLY COATED IN CALCIUM PHOSPHATE. THERE WAS RECENTLY A CASE OF AN ITALIAN WOMAN WHO HAD CARRIED SUCH A 'STONE CHILD' OR LITHOPEDION FOR 37 YEARS WITHOUT KNOWING IT.

THE HERO SHREW
THE BACKBONE OF THE HERO SHREW HAS EVOLVED TO PREVENT IT BEING CRUSHED WHILE BURROWING. IT NOW HAS THE STRONGEST BACKBONE, IN PROPORTION TO ITS SIZE, OF ANY ANIMAL & IS CLAIMED TO BE CAPABLE OF BEARING THE WEIGHT OF A 12-STONE MAN.

ODD SKULLS

BONELESS ASTRONAUTS
DURING LONG SPACE MISSIONS, ASTRONAUTS BEGIN TO LOSE THEIR SKELETONS BECAUSE THE BONES BECOME SLIGHTLY SMALLER IN WEIGHTLESS CONDITIONS. IT APPEARS THAT BONES NEED TO BE IN CONTINUAL USE TO MAINTAIN GROWTH.

BONES ARE SURPRISINGLY FLEXIBLE AT BIRTH, PARTICULARLY THE SKULL. THE NAVAJO TRIBE, ARIZONA, TRADITIONALLY FLATTENED THE BACKS OF THEIR BABIES' HEADS BY STRAPPING THEM TO BOARDS. MORE SPECTACULAR SKULL DEFORMITIES RESULT FROM BANDAGING THE HEAD, A FORMER PRACTICE IN PARTS OF AFRICA & PERU. OUR HEADS ARE CONSIDERABLY SHAPED BY THE PRESSURES INCURRED DURING CHILDBIRTH. (BABIES BORN BY A CAESAREAN OPERATION OFTEN HAVE DOMED HEADS).

HOW TO CUT THE CARD WITHOUT CUTTING THE RIBBON
YOU WILL NEED A RIBBON, AN UNWANTED PLAYING CARD & A VERY BLUNT PAIR OF SCISSORS. PREPARE THE TRICK BY PUTTING CARD IN A HOT OVEN FOR A FEW MINUTES. YOU SHOULD THEN FIND THAT THE CARD IS BRITTLE ENOUGH FOR THE SCISSORS TO 'CRACK' IT IN TWO WITHOUT HARMING THE RIBBON.

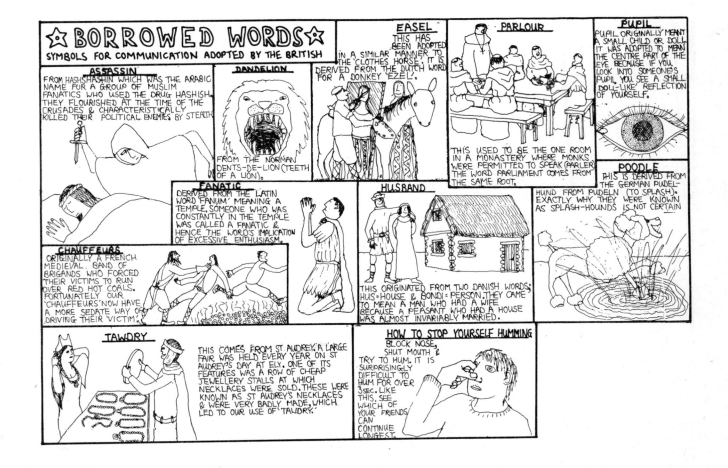

☆ BORROWED WORDS ☆
SYMBOLS FOR COMMUNICATION ADOPTED BY THE BRITISH

ASSASSIN
FROM HASHSHASHIN WHICH WAS THE ARABIC NAME FOR A GROUP OF MUSLIM FANATICS WHO USED THE DRUG HASHISH. THEY FLOURISHED AT THE TIME OF THE CRUSADES & CHARACTERISTICALLY KILLED THEIR POLITICAL ENEMIES BY STEALTH.

DANDELION
FROM THE NORMAN DENTS-DE-LION (TEETH OF A LION).

EASEL
THIS HAS BEEN ADOPTED IN A SIMILAR MANNER TO THE 'CLOTHES HORSE'. IT IS DERIVED FROM THE DUTCH WORD FOR A DONKEY 'EZEL'.

PARLOUR
THIS USED TO BE THE ONE ROOM IN A MONASTERY WHERE MONKS WERE PERMITTED TO SPEAK (PARLER) THE WORD PARLIAMENT COMES FROM THE SAME ROOT.

PUPIL
PUPIL ORIGINALLY MEANT A SMALL CHILD OR DOLL. IT WAS ADOPTED TO MEAN THE CENTRE PART OF THE EYE BECAUSE IF YOU LOOK INTO SOMEONE'S PUPIL YOU SEE A SMALL DOLL-LIKE REFLECTION OF YOURSELF.

FANATIC
DERIVED FROM THE LATIN WORD 'FANUM' MEANING A TEMPLE, SOMEONE WHO WAS CONSTANTLY IN THE TEMPLE WAS CALLED A FANATIC & HENCE THE WORD'S IMPLICATION OF EXCESSIVE ENTHUSIASM.

HUSBAND
THIS ORIGINATED FROM TWO DANISH WORDS; HUS = HOUSE & BONDI = PERSON. THEY CAME TO MEAN A MAN WHO HAD A WIFE BECAUSE A PEASANT WHO HAD A HOUSE WAS ALMOST INVARIABLY MARRIED.

POODLE
THIS IS DERIVED FROM THE GERMAN PUDEL. HUND FROM PUDELN (TO SPLASH). EXACTLY WHY THEY WERE KNOWN AS SPLASH-HOUNDS IS NOT CERTAIN

CHAUFFEURS
ORIGINALLY A FRENCH MEDIEVAL BAND OF BRIGANDS WHO FORCED THEIR VICTIMS TO RUN OVER RED HOT COALS. FORTUNATELY OUR 'CHAUFFEURS' NOW HAVE A MORE SEDATE WAY OF DRIVING THEIR 'VICTIM'.

TAWDRY
THIS COMES FROM ST AUDREY. A LARGE FAIR WAS HELD EVERY YEAR ON ST AUDREY'S DAY AT ELY. ONE OF ITS FEATURES WAS A ROW OF CHEAP JEWELLERY STALLS AT WHICH NECKLACES WERE SOLD. THESE WERE KNOWN AS ST AUDREY'S NECKLACES & WERE VERY BADLY MADE, WHICH LED TO OUR USE OF 'TAWDRY.'

HOW TO STOP YOURSELF HUMMING
BLOCK NOSE, SHUT MOUTH & TRY TO HUM. IT IS SURPRISINGLY DIFFICULT TO HUM FOR OVER 3 SEC. LIKE THIS. SEE WHICH OF YOUR FRIENDS CAN CONTINUE LONGEST.

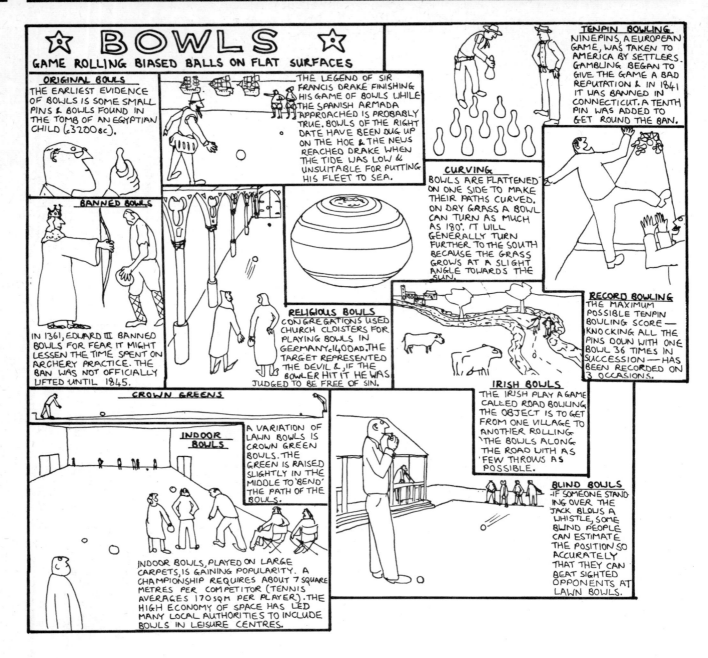

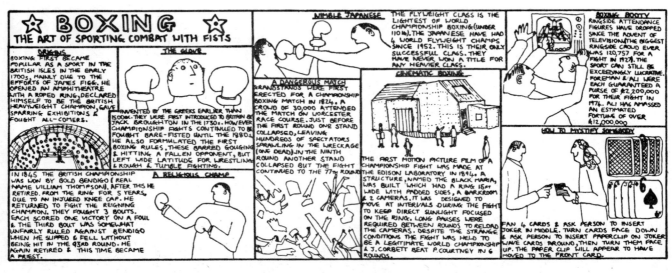

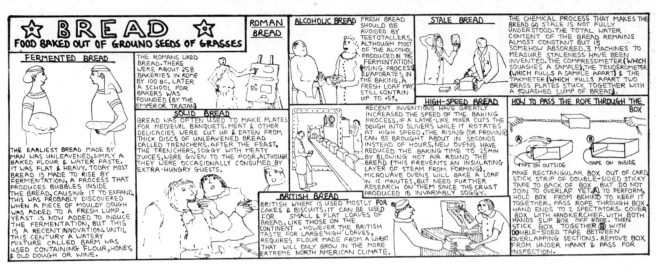

☆ BREAD ☆
FOOD BAKED OUT OF GROUND SEEDS OF GRASSES

ROMAN BREAD

FERMENTED BREAD

THE EARLIEST BREAD MADE BY MAN WAS UNLEAVENED, SIMPLY A BAKED FLOUR & WATER PASTE. IT WAS FLAT & HEAVY. TODAY MOST BREAD IS MADE TO RISE BY FERMENTATION, A PROCESS THAT PRODUCES BUBBLES INSIDE THE BREAD, CAUSING IT TO EXPAND. THIS WAS PROBABLY DISCOVERED WHEN A PIECE OF MOULDY DOUGH WAS ADDED TO A FRESH LUMP. YEAST IS NOW ADDED TO INDUCE THE FERMENTATION, BUT THIS IS A RECENT INNOVATION. UNTIL THIS CENTURY A WATERY MIXTURE CALLED BARM WAS USED CONTAINING FLOUR, HONEY, & OLD DOUGH OR WINE.

THE ROMANS LIKED BREAD. THERE WERE ABOUT 258 BAKERIES IN ROME BY 100 BC. LATER A SCHOOL FOR BAKERS WAS FOUNDED (BY THE EMPEROR TRAJAN)

SOLID BREAD

BREAD WAS OFTEN USED TO MAKE PLATES FOR MEDIEVAL BANQUETS. MEAT & OTHER DELICACIES WERE CUT UP & EATEN FROM THICK DISCS OF UNLEAVENED BREAD CALLED TRENCHERS. AFTER THE FEAST, THE TRENCHERS, SOGGY WITH MEATY JUICES, WERE GIVEN TO THE POOR, ALTHOUGH THEY WERE OCCASIONALLY CONSUMED BY EXTRA-HUNGRY GUESTS.

ALCOHOLIC BREAD

FRESH BREAD SHOULD BE AVOIDED BY TEETOTALLERS, ALTHOUGH MOST OF THE ALCOHOL PRODUCED IN THE FERMENTATION (RISING) PROCESS EVAPORATES IN THE BAKING. A FRESH LOAF MAY STILL CONTAIN UP TO ·5%.

BRITISH BREAD

BRITISH WHEAT IS USED MOSTLY FOR CAKES & BISCUITS. IT CAN BE USED FOR SMALL & FLAT LOAVES OF BREAD, LIKE THOSE ON THE CONTINENT. HOWEVER THE BRITISH TASTE FOR LARGE, HIGH LOAVES, REQUIRES FLOUR MADE FROM A WHEAT THAT WILL ONLY GROW IN THE MORE EXTREME NORTH AMERICAN CLIMATE.

HIGH-SPEED BREAD

RECENT INVENTIONS HAVE GREATLY INCREASED THE SPEED OF THE BAKING PROCESS. IF A LATHE-LIKE MIXER CUTS THE DOUGH INTO SLIVERS WHILE IT ROTATES AT HIGH SPEED, THE RISING (OR PROVING) CAN BE BROUGHT ABOUT IN SECONDS INSTEAD OF HOURS. NEW OVENS HAVE REDUCED THE BAKING TIME TO 25 MIN BY BLOWING HOT AIR ROUND THE BREAD (THIS PREVENTS AN INSULATING LAYER OF STEAM FROM FORMING). MICROWAVE OVENS WILL BAKE A LOAF IN 12 MINUTES, BUT NEED FURTHER RESEARCH ON THEM SINCE THE CRUST PRODUCED IS INVARIABLY SOGGY.

STALE BREAD

THE CHEMICAL PROCESS THAT MAKES THE BREAD GO STALE IS NOT FULLY UNDERSTOOD. THE TOTAL WATER CONTENT OF THE BREAD REMAINS ALMOST CONSTANT BUT IS SOMEHOW ABSORBED. 3 MACHINES TO MEASURE STALENESS HAVE BEEN INVENTED. THE COMPRESSIMETER (WHICH SQUASHES A SAMPLE), THE TENDEROMETER (WHICH PULLS A SAMPLE APART) & THE TAKMETER (WHICH PULLS APART TWO BRASS PLATES STUCK TOGETHER WITH A SQUASHED LUMP OF BREAD).

HOW TO PASS THE ROPE THROUGH THE BOX

TAPE ON OUTSIDE / TAPE ON INSIDE

MAKE RECTANGULAR BOX OUT OF CARD. STICK STRIP OF DOUBLE-SIDED STICKY TAPE TO BACK OF BOX, BUT DO NOT JOIN TO OVERLAP YET. A) TO PERFORM, HOLD BOX FROM BEHIND TO KEEP IT TOGETHER. PASS ROPE THROUGH BOX & HAND ENDS TO 2 SPECTATORS. COVER BOX WITH HANDKERCHIEF. WITH BOTH HANDS SLIP BOX OFF ROPE. THEN STICK BOX TOGETHER B) WITH DOUBLE-SIDED TAPE BETWEEN OVERLAPPING SECTIONS. REMOVE BOX FROM UNDER HANKY & PASS FOR INSPECTION.

☆ BREATHING ☆
A MECHANISM FOR ABSORBING OXYGEN

OXYGENATING

RIGHT LUNG / HEART / LEFT LUNG

WE HAVE 10-20 MILLION THIN TUBES IN OUR LUNGS WITH A TOTAL SURFACE AREA OF 1000 SQ M FOR ABSORBING OXYGEN INTO THE BLOOD.

THE VITAL PROCESS

BREATHING, OR RESPIRATION, IS VITAL TO LIFE. THUS EXPIRATION HAS COME TO MEAN THE END OF LIFE & INSPIRATION A TOUCH OF GENIUS.

INSPIRING / RESPIRING / EXPIRING

ARISTOTLE

ARISTOTLE (c350 BC) THOUGHT THAT WE BREATHED SO AS TO PROVIDE A COOLING CURRENT OF AIR FOR THE 'FIRE IN OUR HEARTS'.

GALEN

GALEN (c150 AD) THOUGHT THAT THE AIR FUELLED THE 'FIRE' IN OUR HEARTS - LIKE BELLOWS ON A FIRE.

COLOUR CHANGE

IN ABOUT 1650, IT WAS DISCOVERED THAT BLOOD ENTERING THE LUNGS WAS PURPLE, BLOOD LEAVING THE LUNGS WAS RED. THIS LED TO THE MODERN THEORY OF THE LUNGS 'FEEDING' THE BLOOD WITH OXYGEN.

INSECTS

THE ONLY SECTION OF THE ANIMAL KINGDOM WHICH DOES NOT BREATHE IS THE INSECT WORLD. THE AIR THEY TAKE IN IS PIPED DIRECTLY TO EVERY CELL THROUGH THIN TUBES FROM THE SURFACE OF THE SKIN. THESE TUBES CANNOT BE VERY LONG OR ELSE TOO LITTLE OXYGEN GETS THROUGH, THEREFORE ALL INSECTS TEND TO BE SMALL.

FISH

FISHES EXTRACT OXYGEN FROM WATER SUCKED THROUGH THEIR GILLS. MANY FISHES ALSO HAVE A FLOAT BLADDER WHICH THEY PARTLY FILL WITH AIR TO ADJUST THEIR BUOYANCY. IT IS THIS ORGAN WHICH HAS EVOLVED INTO THE LUNGS OF ANIMALS.

BIRDS

BIRDS HAVE SEVERAL AIR SACS LEADING OFF THEIR LUNGS. THEY ARE THOUGHT TO PROVIDE AN INTERNAL COOLING SYSTEM DURING FLIGHT.

MEN V WOMEN

MEN BREATHE PARTLY BY EXPANDING THEIR CHESTS & PARTLY BY LIFTING THEIR STOMACHS. WOMEN HAVE MORE FLEXIBLE RIBS & BREATHE ALMOST ENTIRELY WITH THEIR CHESTS.

PLASTIC BREATHING

THE JAPANESE HAVE RECENTLY PERFECTED A PLASTIC LUNG. BLOOD IS PUMPED THROUGH 30,000 THIN TUBES PUNCTURED WITH PINHOLES. THE OXYGEN CAN ENTER THROUGH THE HOLES BUT THE BLOOD CANNOT ESCAPE.

ENERGETIC EATING

WE BREATHE FASTER AFTER A MEAL BECAUSE OF THE ENERGY REQUIRED FOR DIGESTION.

DIAGNOSIS

DOCTORS TAP YOUR CHEST TO CHECK THAT THE LUNGS ARE HEALTHY. IF THEY ARE CLOGGED OR PARTLY COLLAPSED THEY MAKE A DULL SOUND. HEALTHY LUNGS ARE RESONANT.

HOW TO USE OLD CREDIT CARDS

CUT ONE EDGE WITH A PAIR OF PINKING SHEARS & USE AS A GLUE SPREADER.

CUT TO HEART SHAPE & USE AS A GUITAR PLECTRUM.

SEND YOUR OWN IDEAS FOR OLD CREDIT CARDS TO: THE RUDIMENTS OF WISDOM % YOUNG OBSERVER 8 ST ANDREWS HILL LONDON EC4V 5JA

CORN FLAKES

'CORNFLAKES' ARE MADE FROM CORN OR MAIZE, SIMILAR TO THE CORN YOU CAN BUY TO MAKE POP CORN. IT COMES FROM THE RIVER PLATE AREA OF SOUTH AMERICA.

INGREDIENTS IN HERE

MIXER

THE CORN IS BROKEN INTO SMALL PIECES & MIXED WITH SUGAR, SALT & MALT EXTRACT (THIS IS THE LIQUID OBTAINED BY SOAKING MALTED BARLEY IN WATER TO EXTRACT THE SOLUBLE PARTS.

THE GRAINS ARE COOKED & SOFTENED IN ROTATING PRESSURE COOKERS FOR 90 MIN.

OVEN

THE GRAINS ARE PARTLY DRIED IN OVENS UNTIL THEY REACH A RUBBERY CONSISTENCY.

ROLLERS SQUASH & STRETCH THE GRAINS INTO PAPER-THIN FLEXIBLE FLAKES. ONE ROLLER ROTATES AT TWICE THE SPEED OF THE OTHER TO STRETCH THE GRAINS.

THE FLAKES ARE TOASTED & CRISPENED IN LARGE ROTATING OVENS. THE ACTION IS LIKE LAUNDERETTE TUMBLE DRIERS.

THE FLAKES ARE THEN SPRAYED WITH VITAMINS, INSPECTED & PACKED.

Shredded wheat

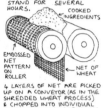

'SHREDDED WHEAT' IS MADE FROM GRAINS OF WHEAT WITH 'NOTHING ADDED AND NOTHING TAKEN AWAY'. THE GRAINS ARE WASHED, COOKED IN BOILING WATER & LEFT TO 'CURE' FOR 18 HOURS.

COOKED INGREDIENTS

15-20 SETS OF SIMILAR ROLLERS

GROOVED ROLLERS

CURTAINS OF WHEAT STRANDS

MAT OF 15-20 LAYERS

ROTATING KNIVES CUT MAT INTO SECTIONS

TO CRISPING OVEN

Rice Krispies

'RICE KRISPIES' ARE MADE FROM GRAINS OF RICE MIXED & BOILED IN MALT EXTRACT, SUGAR & SALT & WATER. AFTER PARTIAL DRYING, THE GRAINS ARE TOASTED & THE REMAINING MOISTURE SWELLS THE GRAINS TO THEIR FINISHED SIZE & SHAPE.

Special K

'SPECIAL K' IS MADE OF COOKED RICE COATED WITH A HIGH PROTEIN MIX OF WHEAT GLUCOSE, WHEAT GERM & DRIED MILK. THE COATED GRAINS ARE DRIED, FLATTENED BY ROLLERS & TOASTED (AS 'RICE KRISPIES').

ALL-BRAN

'ALL-BRAN' IS MADE FROM THE OUTER LAYERS OF WHEAT GRAINS, MIXED WITH MALT EXTRACT, SUGAR & SALT. THIS IS COOKED & DRIED IN A SIMILAR MANNER TO CORN-FLAKES. THE MIX IS THEN PASSED THROUGH GROOVED ROLLERS (SIMILAR TO THOSE USED FOR SHREDDED WHEAT), THESE PRODUCE AN END-LESS STREAM OF BRAN SPAGHETTI (ELASTIC & FLEXIBLE AT THIS STAGE). THIS IS THEN TOASTED & CRISPED.

BRITISH ANNUAL CONSUMPTION

GRAMS PER PERSON PER YEAR

630	1387	1982	7683				6/30
1925	1937	1947	1957	1967	1977		

THE SCALE OF BREAKFAST CEREAL PRODUCTION IS VAST. THE BRITISH EAT AN AVERAGE OF 4000 GMS OF BREAKFAST CEREAL PER PERSON PER YEAR & KELLOGG'S ALONE PRODUCE 12-15 MILLION PACKETS PER WEEK.

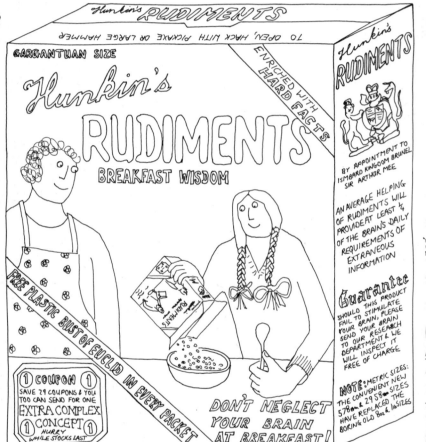

Hunkin's RUDIMENTS

TO OPEN, HACK WITH PICKAXE OR LARGE HAMMER

GARGANTUAN SIZE

Hunkin's RUDIMENTS BREAKFAST WISDOM

ENRICHED WITH HARD FACTS

FREE PLASTIC BUST OF EUCLID IN EVERY PACKET

① COUPON ①
SAVE 29 COUPONS & YOU TOO CAN SEND FOR ONE
EXTRA COMPLEX
① CONCEPT ①
HURRY WHILE STOCKS LAST

Hunkin's RUDIMENTS

BY APPOINTMENT TO ISMBARD KINGDOM BRUNEL SIR ARTHUR MEE

AN AVERAGE HELPING OF RUDIMENTS WILL PROVIDE AT LEAST ¼ OF THE BRAIN'S DAILY REQUIREMENTS OF EXTRANEOUS INFORMATION

Guarantee
SHOULD THIS PRODUCT FAIL TO STIMULATE YOUR BRAIN, PLEASE SEND YOUR BRAIN TO OUR RESEARCH DEPARTMENT & WE WILL INSPECT IT FREE OF CHARGE

NOTE: METRIC SIZES: THE CONVENIENT NEW 578 gm & 293 gm SIZES HAVE REPLACED THE BORING OLD 8oz & 11b SIZES

DON'T NEGLECT YOUR BRAIN AT BREAKFAST!

Shreddies

SHREDDIES ARE MADE OF WHEAT MIXED WITH A LITTLE MALT, SUGAR, SALT & VITAMINS, & COOKED IN ROTATING PRESSURE COOKERS. THE RESULTING STICKY MASS IS BROKEN INTO SMALL LUMPS & LEFT TO STAND FOR SEVERAL HOURS.

COOKED INGREDIENTS

EMBOSSED NET PATTERN ON ROLLER

NET OF WHEAT

4 LAYERS OF NET ARE PICKED UP ON A CONVEYOR (AS IN THE SHREDDED WHEAT PROCESS) & CHOPPED INTO INDIVIDUAL SHREDDIES, & CRISPED IN AN OVEN.

Weetabix

'WEETABIX' IS MADE BY MIXING WHEAT GRAIN WITH MALT EXTRACT, SUGAR & SALT & COOKING IN PRESSURE COOKERS UNTIL THE WHEAT HAS SOAKED UP THE LIQUID & BECOME SOFT. THE GRAIN IS THEN ROLLED INTO FLAKES –THE FLAKES ARE SQUASHED INTO THE BISCUIT SHAPES– & THE BISCUITS ARE BAKED IN AN OVEN.

INSTANT OATS

INSTANT HOT OAT CEREALS ARE A COMBINATION OF TWO TYPES OF OAT PROCESSED IN DIFFERENT WAYS. HALF THE OATS ARE MILLED TO A FLOUR, MIXED WITH WATER & FED ONTO THE SURFACE OF HEATED STEEL ROLLERS. THE WATER EVAPORATES, LEAV-ING A THIN WHITE FILM OF 'OAT' WHICH IS THEN BROKEN INTO FLAKES. THESE RECONSTITUTED FLAKES ARE THEN MIXED WITH SOME PRE-COOKED WHOLE OAT FLAKES.

Puffed wheat

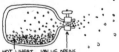

HOT WHEAT UNDER PRESSURE

VALVE OPENS & GRAINS SHOOT OUT

'PUFFED WHEAT' IS MADE BY HEATING GRAINS OF WHEAT & SHOOTING THEM OUT OF A VALVE IN A PRESSURISED CONTAINER (HENCE THE CLAIM 'SHOT FROM A GUN'). THE SUDDEN PRESSURE DROP CAUSES ALL THE MOISTURE IN THE GRAINS TO BOIL INSTANTLY. AS THE MOISTURE CHANGES TO STEAM, IT EXPANDS & PUFFS THE GRAINS OUT. (POP CORN 'EXPLODES' FOR THE SAME REASON) ONLY THE BEST QUALITY HARD WHEAT FROM THE US CAN BE USED IN THIS PROCESS, AS SOFT WHEATS DISINTEGRATE.

HARD WHEAT GRAINS ARE TRANSLUCENT IN THE MIDDLE LIKE UNCOOKED RICE GRAINS. SOFT WHEAT GRAINS ARE WHITE & POWDERY IN THE MIDDLE LIKE FLOUR.

HOW TO MAKE YOUR OWN CEREALS

⭐ PUFFED WHEAT SUITABLE VARIETIES OF WHEAT ARE NOT EASY TO FIND, BUT AN IMITATION CAN BE MADE FROM POPPING CORN WHICH CAN BE BOUGHT IN DELICATESSENS. TO 'POP' THE CORN, HEAT 2 TABLESPOONS OF OIL IN A SAUCEPAN. WHEN THIS STARTS TO SMOKE, DROP IN A GRAIN OF CORN & WAIT UNTIL IT POPS; THEN TIP IN HALF A CUP OF CORN. PUT LID ON PAN & WAIT FOR IT ALL TO POP, SHAKING PAN OCCASIONALLY

⭐ RICE KRISPIES A CRISPED RICE CEREAL CAN BE MADE AT HOME BUT IT WILL NOT SWELL OUT AS MUCH AS FACTORY MADE 'RICE KRISPIES' (THE MOISTURE CONTENT & TOASTING ACTION ARE CRITICAL IN CAUSING THE GRAINS TO SWELL). COOK 80 gm LONG-GRAIN RICE IN 1 LITRE OF WATER WITH A TEASPOONFUL OF SALT & A TABLESPOONFUL OF CONCENTRATED MALT EXTRACT. DRAIN & SPREAD COOKED RICE OUT IN A THIN LAYER ON A BAKING TRAY, THEN TOAST IN HOT OVEN (350) FOR 5-10 MIN.

SUGAR-COATED CEREALS

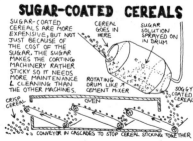

SUGAR-COATED CEREALS ARE MORE EXPENSIVE, BUT NOT JUST BECAUSE OF THE COST OF THE SUGAR. THE SUGAR MAKES THE COATING MACHINERY RATHER STICKY SO IT NEEDS MORE MAINTENANCE & CLEANING THAN THE OTHER MACHINES.

CEREAL GOES IN HERE

SUGAR SOLUTION SPRAYED ON IN DRUM

ROTATING DRUM LIKE A CEMENT MIXER

SOGGY COATED CEREAL

CRISP CEREAL

OVEN

CONVEYOR IN CASCADES TO STOP CEREAL STICKING TOGETHER

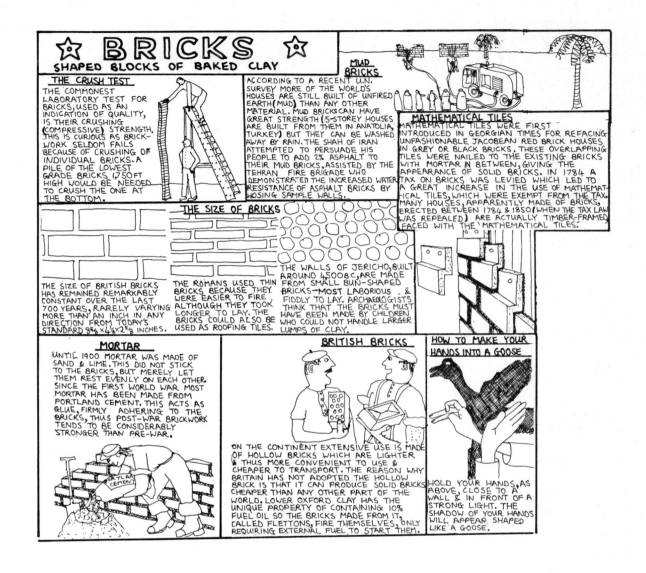

☆ BRICKS ☆
SHAPED BLOCKS OF BAKED CLAY

THE CRUSH TEST
THE COMMONEST LABORATORY TEST FOR BRICKS, USED AS AN INDICATION OF QUALITY, IS THEIR CRUSHING (COMPRESSIVE) STRENGTH. THIS IS CURIOUS AS BRICKWORK SELDOM FAILS BECAUSE OF CRUSHING OF INDIVIDUAL BRICKS. A PILE OF THE LOWEST GRADE BRICKS 1,750 FT HIGH WOULD BE NEEDED TO CRUSH THE ONE AT THE BOTTOM.

MUD BRICKS
ACCORDING TO A RECENT U.N. SURVEY MORE OF THE WORLD'S HOUSES ARE STILL BUILT OF UNFIRED EARTH (MUD) THAN ANY OTHER MATERIAL. MUD BRICKS CAN HAVE GREAT STRENGTH (5-STOREY HOUSES ARE BUILT FROM THEM IN ANATOLIA, TURKEY) BUT THEY CAN BE WASHED AWAY BY RAIN. THE SHAH OF IRAN ATTEMPTED TO PERSUADE HIS PEOPLE TO ADD 2% ASPHALT TO THEIR MUD BRICKS, ASSISTED BY THE TEHRAN FIRE BRIGADE WHO DEMONSTRATED THE INCREASED WATER RESISTANCE OF ASPHALT BRICKS BY HOSING SAMPLE WALLS.

MATHEMATICAL TILES
MATHEMATICAL TILES WERE FIRST INTRODUCED IN GEORGIAN TIMES FOR REFACING UNFASHIONABLE JACOBEAN RED BRICK HOUSES IN GREY OR BLACK BRICKS. THESE OVERLAPPING TILES WERE NAILED TO THE EXISTING BRICKS WITH MORTAR IN BETWEEN, GIVING THE APPEARANCE OF SOLID BRICKS. IN 1784 A TAX ON BRICKS WAS LEVIED WHICH LED TO A GREAT INCREASE IN THE USE OF MATHEMATICAL TILES, WHICH WERE EXEMPT FROM THE TAX. MANY HOUSES, APPARENTLY MADE OF BRICKS, ERECTED BETWEEN 1784 & 1850 (WHEN THE TAX LAW WAS REPEALED) ARE ACTUALLY TIMBER-FRAMED FACED WITH THE MATHEMATICAL TILES.

THE SIZE OF BRICKS
THE SIZE OF BRITISH BRICKS HAS REMAINED REMARKABLY CONSTANT OVER THE LAST 700 YEARS, RARELY VARYING MORE THAN AN INCH IN ANY DIRECTION FROM TODAY'S STANDARD $8\frac{5}{8} \times 4\frac{1}{8} \times 2\frac{5}{8}$ INCHES.

THE ROMANS USED THIN BRICKS BECAUSE THEY WERE EASIER TO FIRE ALTHOUGH THEY TOOK LONGER TO LAY. THE BRICKS COULD ALSO BE USED AS ROOFING TILES.

THE WALLS OF JERICHO, BUILT AROUND 4500 B.C., ARE MADE FROM SMALL BUN-SHAPED BRICKS—MOST LABORIOUS & FIDDLY TO LAY. ARCHAEOLOGISTS THINK THAT THE BRICKS MUST HAVE BEEN MADE BY CHILDREN WHO COULD NOT HANDLE LARGER LUMPS OF CLAY.

MORTAR
UNTIL 1900 MORTAR WAS MADE OF SAND & LIME. THIS DID NOT STICK TO THE BRICKS, BUT MERELY LET THEM REST EVENLY ON EACH OTHER. SINCE THE FIRST WORLD WAR MOST MORTAR HAS BEEN MADE FROM PORTLAND CEMENT. THIS ACTS AS GLUE, FIRMLY ADHERING TO THE BRICKS, THUS POST-WAR BRICKWORK TENDS TO BE CONSIDERABLY STRONGER THAN PRE-WAR.

BRITISH BRICKS
ON THE CONTINENT EXTENSIVE USE IS MADE OF HOLLOW BRICKS WHICH ARE LIGHTER & THUS MORE CONVENIENT TO USE & CHEAPER TO TRANSPORT. THE REASON WHY BRITAIN HAS NOT ADOPTED THE HOLLOW BRICK IS THAT IT CAN PRODUCE SOLID BRICKS CHEAPER THAN ANY OTHER PART OF THE WORLD. LOWER OXFORD CLAY HAS THE UNIQUE PROPERTY OF CONTAINING 10% FUEL OIL SO THE BRICKS MADE FROM IT, CALLED FLETTONS, FIRE THEMSELVES, ONLY REQUIRING EXTERNAL FUEL TO START THEM.

HOW TO MAKE YOUR HANDS INTO A GOOSE
HOLD YOUR HANDS, AS ABOVE, CLOSE TO A WALL & IN FRONT OF A STRONG LIGHT. THE SHADOW OF YOUR HANDS WILL APPEAR SHAPED LIKE A GOOSE.

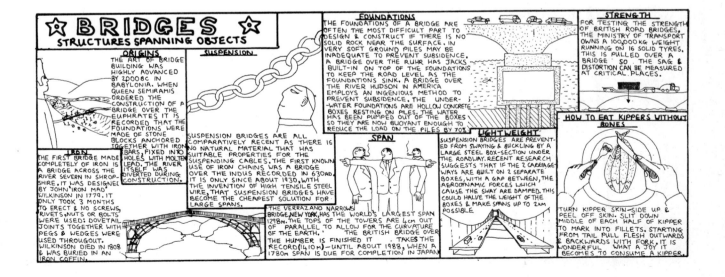

☆ BRIDGES ☆
STRUCTURES SPANNING OBJECTS

ORIGINS
THE ART OF BRIDGE BUILDING WAS HIGHLY ADVANCED BY 2000 B.C. IN BABYLONIA. WHEN QUEEN SEMIRAMIS ORDERED THE CONSTRUCTION OF A BRIDGE OVER THE EUPHRATES IT IS RECORDED THAT THE FOUNDATIONS WERE MADE OF STONE BLOCKS ANCHORED TOGETHER WITH IRON BARS, FIXED INTO HOLES WITH MOLTEN LEAD. THE RIVER ITSELF WAS DIVERTED DURING CONSTRUCTION.

IRON
THE FIRST BRIDGE MADE COMPLETELY OF IRON IS A BRIDGE ACROSS THE RIVER SEVERN IN SHROPSHIRE. IT WAS DESIGNED BY JOHN "IRON MAD" WILKINSON IN 1779. IT ONLY TOOK 3 MONTHS TO ERECT & NO SCREWS, RIVETS, NUTS OR BOLTS WERE USED: DOVETAIL JOINTS TOGETHER WITH PEGS & WEDGES WERE USED THROUGHOUT. WILKINSON DIED IN 1808 & WAS BURIED IN AN IRON COFFIN.

SUSPENSION
SUSPENSION BRIDGES ARE ALL COMPARATIVELY RECENT AS THERE IS NO NATURAL MATERIAL THAT HAS SUITABLE PROPERTIES FOR THE SUSPENDING CABLES. THE FIRST KNOWN USE OF IRON CHAINS WAS A BRIDGE OVER THE INDUS RECORDED IN 630 A.D. IT IS ONLY SINCE ABOUT 1930, WITH THE INVENTION OF HIGH TENSILE STEEL WIRE, THAT SUSPENSION BRIDGES HAVE BECOME THE CHEAPEST SOLUTION FOR LARGE SPANS.

FOUNDATIONS
THE FOUNDATIONS OF A BRIDGE ARE OFTEN THE MOST DIFFICULT PART TO DESIGN & CONSTRUCT. IF THERE IS NO SOLID ROCK NEAR THE SURFACE, IN VERY SOFT GROUND PILES MAY BE INADEQUATE TO PREVENT SUBSIDENCE. A BRIDGE OVER THE RUHR HAS JACKS BUILT-IN ON TOP OF THE FOUNDATIONS TO KEEP THE ROAD LEVEL AS THE FOUNDATIONS SINK. A BRIDGE OVER THE RIVER HUDSON IN AMERICA EMPLOYS AN INGENIOUS METHOD TO PREVENT SUBSIDENCE. THE UNDER-WATER FOUNDATIONS ARE HOLLOW CONCRETE BOXES RESTING ON PILES. THE WATER HAS BEEN PUMPED OUT OF THE BOXES SO THEY ARE NOW BUOYANT ENOUGH TO REDUCE THE LOAD ON THE PILES BY 70%.

STRENGTH
FOR TESTING THE STRENGTH OF BRITISH ROAD BRIDGES, THE MINISTRY OF TRANSPORT OWNS A 100,000 KG WEIGHT RUNNING ON 16 SOLID TYRES. THIS IS PULLED OVER A BRIDGE SO THE SAG & DISTORTION CAN BE MEASURED AT CRITICAL PLACES.

SPAN
THE VERRAZANO NARROWS BRIDGE, NEW YORK, HAS THE WORLD'S LARGEST SPAN 1298 m. THE TOPS OF THE TOWERS ARE 4 cm OUT OF PARALLEL TO ALLOW FOR THE CURVATURE OF THE EARTH. THE BRITISH BRIDGE OVER THE HUMBER IS FINISHED IT TAKES THE RECORD (1410 m) — UNTIL ABOUT 1988, WHEN A 1780 m SPAN IS DUE FOR COMPLETION IN JAPAN.

LIGHTWEIGHT
SUSPENSION BRIDGES ARE PREVENTED FROM SWAYING & BUCKLING BY A LARGE STEEL BOX-SECTION UNDER THE ROADWAY. RECENT RESEARCH SUGGESTS THAT IF THE 2 CARRIAGE WAYS ARE BUILT ON 2 SEPARATE BOXES, WITH A GAP BETWEEN, THE AERODYNAMIC FORCES WHICH CAUSE THE SWAY ARE DAMPED. THIS COULD HALVE THE WEIGHT OF THE BOXES & MAKE SPANS UP TO 2 km POSSIBLE.

HOW TO EAT KIPPERS WITHOUT BONES
TURN KIPPER SKIN-SIDE UP & PEEL OFF SKIN. SLIT DOWN MIDDLE OF EACH HALF OF KIPPER TO MARK INTO FILLETS. STARTING FROM TAIL PULL FLESH OUTWARDS & BACKWARDS WITH FORK. IT IS WONDERFUL. WHAT A JOY IT BECOMES TO CONSUME A KIPPER.

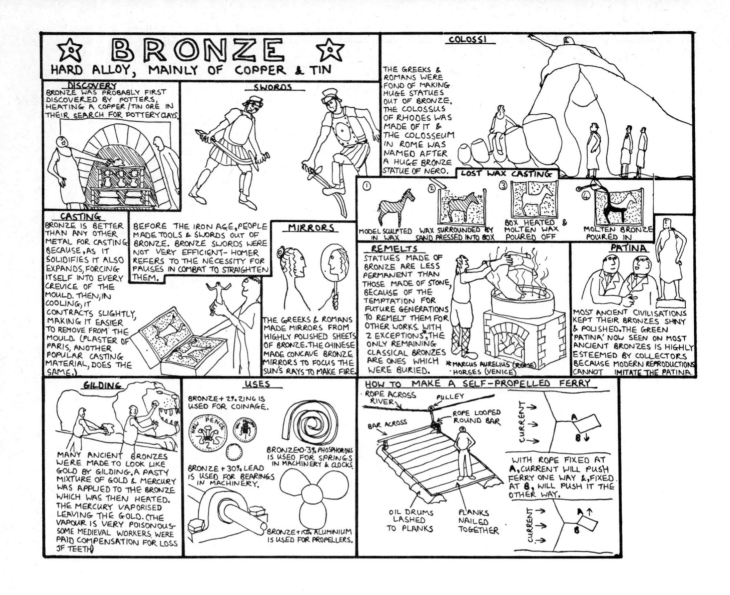

☆ BRONZE ☆
HARD ALLOY, MAINLY OF COPPER & TIN

DISCOVERY
BRONZE WAS PROBABLY FIRST DISCOVERED BY POTTERS, HEATING A COPPER/TIN ORE IN THEIR SEARCH FOR POTTERY CLAYS.

SWORDS

CASTING
BRONZE IS BETTER THAN ANY OTHER METAL FOR CASTING BECAUSE, AS IT SOLIDIFIES IT ALSO EXPANDS, FORCING ITSELF INTO EVERY CREVICE OF THE MOULD. THEN, IN COOLING, IT CONTRACTS SLIGHTLY, MAKING IT EASIER TO REMOVE FROM THE MOULD. (PLASTER OF PARIS, ANOTHER POPULAR CASTING MATERIAL, DOES THE SAME.)

BEFORE THE IRON AGE, PEOPLE MADE TOOLS & SWORDS OUT OF BRONZE. BRONZE SWORDS WERE NOT VERY EFFICIENT- HOMER REFERS TO THE NECESSITY FOR PAUSES IN COMBAT TO STRAIGHTEN THEM.

MIRRORS
THE GREEKS & ROMANS MADE MIRRORS FROM HIGHLY POLISHED SHEETS OF BRONZE. THE CHINESE MADE CONCAVE BRONZE MIRRORS TO FOCUS THE SUN'S RAYS TO MAKE FIRE.

COLOSSI
THE GREEKS & ROMANS WERE FOND OF MAKING HUGE STATUES OUT OF BRONZE. THE COLOSSUS OF RHODES WAS MADE OF IT & THE COLOSSEUM IN ROME WAS NAMED AFTER A HUGE BRONZE STATUE OF NERO.

LOST WAX CASTING
① MODEL SCULPTED IN WAX
② WAX SURROUNDED BY SAND PRESSED INTO BOX
③ BOX HEATED & MOLTEN WAX POURED OFF
④ MOLTEN BRONZE POURED IN

REMELTS
STATUES MADE OF BRONZE ARE LESS PERMANENT THAN THOSE MADE OF STONE, BECAUSE OF THE TEMPTATION FOR FUTURE GENERATIONS TO REMELT THEM FOR OTHER WORKS. WITH 2 EXCEPTIONS*, THE ONLY REMAINING CLASSICAL BRONZES ARE ONES WHICH WERE BURIED.

*MARCUS AURELIUS (ROME) · HORSES (VENICE)

PATINA
MOST ANCIENT CIVILISATIONS KEPT THEIR BRONZES SHINY & POLISHED. THE GREEN 'PATINA' NOW SEEN ON MOST ANCIENT BRONZES IS HIGHLY ESTEEMED BY COLLECTORS BECAUSE MODERN REPRODUCTIONS CANNOT IMITATE THE PATINA.

GILDING
MANY ANCIENT BRONZES WERE MADE TO LOOK LIKE GOLD BY GILDING. A PASTY MIXTURE OF GOLD & MERCURY WAS APPLIED TO THE BRONZE WHICH WAS THEN HEATED. THE MERCURY VAPORISED LEAVING THE GOLD. (THE VAPOUR IS VERY POISONOUS-SOME MEDIEVAL WORKERS WERE PAID COMPENSATION FOR LOSS OF TEETH.)

USES
BRONZE + 2% ZINC IS USED FOR COINAGE.

NEW PENCE

BRONZE + 30% LEAD IS USED FOR BEARINGS IN MACHINERY.

BRONZE + 3% PHOSPHORUS IS USED FOR SPRINGS IN MACHINERY & CLOCKS.

BRONZE + 10% ALUMINIUM IS USED FOR PROPELLERS.

HOW TO MAKE A SELF-PROPELLED FERRY
ROPE ACROSS RIVER
PULLEY
BAR ACROSS
ROPE LOOPED ROUND BAR
CURRENT
A B↓
OIL DRUMS LASHED TO PLANKS
PLANKS NAILED TOGETHER

WITH ROPE FIXED AT A, CURRENT WILL PUSH FERRY ONE WAY &, FIXED AT B, WILL PUSH IT THE OTHER WAY.

CURRENT
A↑ B

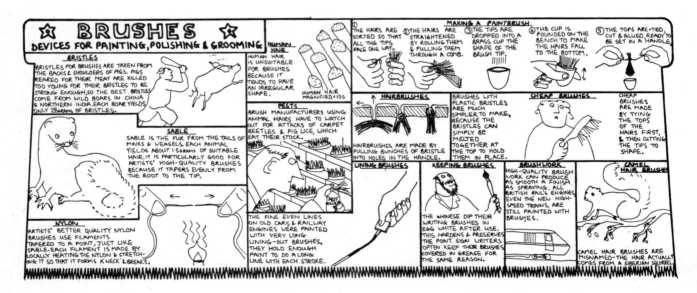

☆ BRUSHES ☆
DEVICES FOR PAINTING, POLISHING & GROOMING

BRISTLES
BRISTLES FOR BRUSHES ARE TAKEN FROM THE BACKS & SHOULDERS OF PIGS. PIGS REARED FOR THEIR MEAT ARE KILLED TOO YOUNG FOR THEIR BRISTLES TO BE STRONG ENOUGH, SO THE BEST BRISTLES COME FROM WILD BOARS IN CHINA & NORTHERN INDIA. EACH BOAR YIELDS ONLY 28 GRAMS OF BRISTLES.

SABLE
SABLE IS THE FUR FROM THE TAILS OF MINKS & WEASELS. EACH ANIMAL YIELDS ABOUT 1.5 GRAMS OF SUITABLE HAIR. IT IS PARTICULARLY GOOD FOR ARTISTS' HIGH-QUALITY BRUSHES BECAUSE IT TAPERS EVENLY FROM THE ROOT TO THE TIP.

NYLON
ARTISTS' BETTER QUALITY NYLON BRUSHES USE FILAMENTS TAPERED TO A POINT, JUST LIKE SABLE. EACH FILAMENT IS MADE BY LOCALLY HEATING THE NYLON & STRETCHING IT SO THAT IT FORMS A 'NECK' & BREAKS.

HUMAN HAIR
HUMAN HAIR IS UNSUITABLE FOR BRUSHES BECAUSE IT TENDS TO HAVE AN IRREGULAR SHAPE.

HUMAN HAIR MAGNIFIED x100

PESTS
BRUSH MANUFACTURERS USING ANIMAL HAIRS HAVE TO WATCH OUT FOR ATTACKS OF CARPET BEETLES & PIG LICE, WHICH EAT THEIR STOCK.

THE FINE EVEN LINES ON OLD CARS & RAILWAY ENGINES WERE PAINTED WITH VERY LONG LINING-OUT BRUSHES. THEY HOLD ENOUGH PAINT TO DO A LONG LINE WITH EACH STROKE.

MAKING A PAINTBRUSH
① THE HAIRS ARE SORTED SO THAT ALL THE TIPS FACE ONE WAY.
② THE HAIRS ARE STRAIGHTENED BY ROLLING THEM & PULLING THEM THROUGH A COMB.
③ THE TIPS ARE DROPPED INTO A BRASS CUP THE SHAPE OF THE BRUSH TIP.
④ THE CUP IS POUNDED ON THE BENCH TO MAKE THE HAIRS FALL TO THE BOTTOM.
⑤ THE TOPS ARE TIED, CUT & GLUED, READY TO BE SET IN A HANDLE.

HAIRBRUSHES
HAIRBRUSHES ARE MADE BY PULLING BUNCHES OF BRISTLE INTO HOLES IN THE HANDLE.

BRUSHES WITH PLASTIC BRISTLES ARE MUCH SIMPLER TO MAKE, BECAUSE THE BRISTLES CAN SIMPLY BE MELTED TOGETHER AT THE TOP TO HOLD THEM IN PLACE.

CHEAP BRUSHES
CHEAP BRUSHES ARE MADE BY TYING THE TOPS OF THE HAIRS FIRST, & THEN CUTTING THE TIPS TO SHAPE.

LINING BRUSHES

KEEPING BRUSHES
THE CHINESE DIP THEIR WRITING BRUSHES IN EGG WHITE AFTER USE. THIS HARDENS & PRESERVES THE POINT. SIGN WRITERS OFTEN KEEP THEIR BRUSHES COVERED IN GREASE FOR THE SAME REASON.

BRUSHWORK
HIGH-QUALITY BRUSH WORK CAN PRODUCE AS SMOOTH A FINISH AS SPRAYING. ALL BRITISH RAIL'S ENGINES EVEN THE NEW HIGH-SPEED TRAINS, ARE STILL PAINTED WITH BRUSHES.

CAMEL HAIR BRUSHES
CAMEL HAIR BRUSHES ARE MISNAMED—THE HAIR ACTUALLY COMES FROM A SIBERIAN SQUIRREL.

BUFFALO & BISON

MEMBERS OF THE CATTLE TRIBE

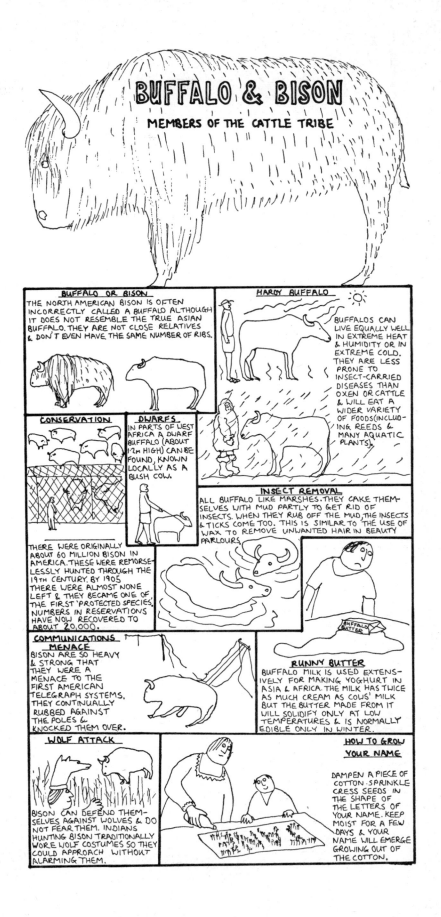

BUFFALO OR BISON

THE NORTH AMERICAN BISON IS OFTEN INCORRECTLY CALLED A BUFFALO ALTHOUGH IT DOES NOT RESEMBLE THE TRUE ASIAN BUFFALO. THEY ARE NOT CLOSE RELATIVES & DON'T EVEN HAVE THE SAME NUMBER OF RIBS.

HARDY BUFFALO

BUFFALOS CAN LIVE EQUALLY WELL IN EXTREME HEAT & HUMIDITY OR IN EXTREME COLD. THEY ARE LESS PRONE TO INSECT-CARRIED DISEASES THAN OXEN OR CATTLE & WILL EAT A WIDER VARIETY OF FOODS (INCLUDING REEDS & MANY AQUATIC PLANTS).

CONSERVATION

THERE WERE ORIGINALLY ABOUT 60 MILLION BISON IN AMERICA. THESE WERE REMORSELESSLY HUNTED THROUGH THE 19TH CENTURY. BY 1905 THERE WERE ALMOST NONE LEFT & THEY BECAME ONE OF THE FIRST 'PROTECTED SPECIES'. NUMBERS IN RESERVATIONS HAVE NOW RECOVERED TO ABOUT 20,000.

DWARFS

IN PARTS OF WEST AFRICA A DWARF BUFFALO (ABOUT 1.2m HIGH) CAN BE FOUND, KNOWN LOCALLY AS A BUSH COW.

INSECT REMOVAL

ALL BUFFALO LIKE MARSHES. THEY CAKE THEMSELVES WITH MUD PARTLY TO GET RID OF INSECTS. WHEN THEY RUB OFF THE MUD, THE INSECTS & TICKS COME TOO. THIS IS SIMILAR TO THE USE OF WAX TO REMOVE UNWANTED HAIR IN BEAUTY PARLOURS.

BUFFALO BUTTER

COMMUNICATIONS MENACE

BISON ARE SO HEAVY & STRONG THAT THEY WERE A MENACE TO THE FIRST AMERICAN TELEGRAPH SYSTEMS. THEY CONTINUALLY RUBBED AGAINST THE POLES & KNOCKED THEM OVER.

RUNNY BUTTER

BUFFALO MILK IS USED EXTENSIVELY FOR MAKING YOGHURT IN ASIA & AFRICA. THE MILK HAS TWICE AS MUCH CREAM AS COWS' MILK BUT THE BUTTER MADE FROM IT WILL SOLIDIFY ONLY AT LOW TEMPERATURES & IS NORMALLY EDIBLE ONLY IN WINTER.

WOLF ATTACK

BISON CAN DEFEND THEMSELVES AGAINST WOLVES & DO NOT FEAR THEM. INDIANS HUNTING BISON TRADITIONALLY WORE WOLF COSTUMES SO THEY COULD APPROACH WITHOUT ALARMING THEM.

HOW TO GROW YOUR NAME

DAMPEN A PIECE OF COTTON. SPRINKLE CRESS SEEDS IN THE SHAPE OF THE LETTERS OF YOUR NAME. KEEP MOIST FOR A FEW DAYS & YOUR NAME WILL EMERGE GROWING OUT OF THE COTTON.

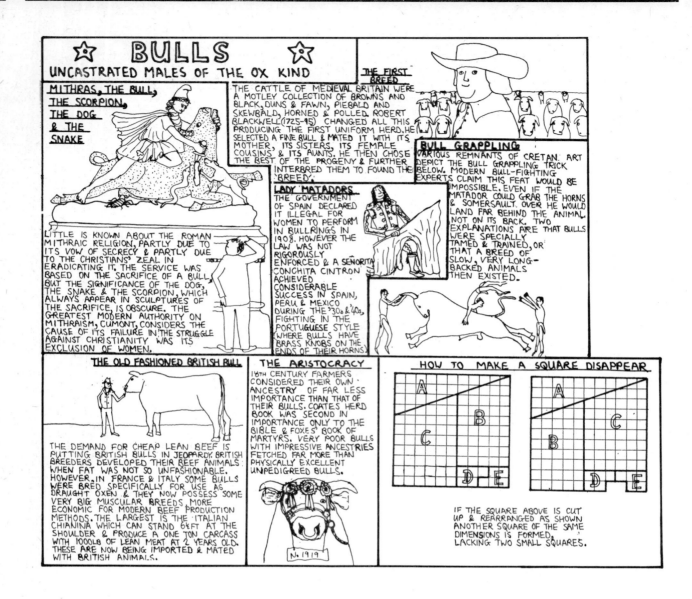

☆ BULLS ☆
UNCASTRATED MALES OF THE OX KIND

MITHRAS, THE BULL, THE SCORPION, THE DOG & THE SNAKE

LITTLE IS KNOWN ABOUT THE ROMAN MITHRAIC RELIGION, PARTLY DUE TO ITS VOW OF SECRECY & PARTLY DUE TO THE CHRISTIANS' ZEAL IN ERADICATING IT. THE SERVICE WAS BASED ON THE SACRIFICE OF A BULL, BUT THE SIGNIFICANCE OF THE DOG, THE SNAKE & THE SCORPION, WHICH ALWAYS APPEAR IN SCULPTURES OF THE SACRIFICE, IS OBSCURE. THE GREATEST MODERN AUTHORITY ON MITHRAISM, CUMONT, CONSIDERS THE CAUSE OF ITS FAILURE IN THE STRUGGLE AGAINST CHRISTIANITY WAS ITS EXCLUSION OF WOMEN.

THE FIRST BREED

THE CATTLE OF MEDIEVAL BRITAIN WERE A MOTLEY COLLECTION OF BROWNS AND BLACK, DUNS & FAWN, PIEBALD AND SKEWBALD, HORNED & POLLED. ROBERT BLACKWELL (1725-95) CHANGED ALL THIS PRODUCING THE FIRST UNIFORM HERD. HE SELECTED A FINE BULL & MATED IT WITH ITS MOTHER, ITS SISTERS, ITS FEMALE COUSINS, & ITS AUNTS. HE THEN CHOSE THE BEST OF THE PROGENY & FURTHER INTERBRED THEM TO FOUND THE 'BREED'.

LADY MATADORS

THE GOVERNMENT OF SPAIN DECLARED IT ILLEGAL FOR WOMEN TO PERFORM IN BULLRINGS IN 1908. HOWEVER THE LAW WAS NOT RIGOROUSLY ENFORCED & A SEÑORITA CONCHITA CINTRON ACHIEVED CONSIDERABLE SUCCESS IN SPAIN, PERU & MEXICO DURING THE '30s & '40s, FIGHTING IN THE PORTUGUESE STYLE WHERE BULLS HAVE BRASS KNOBS ON THE ENDS OF THEIR HORNS.

BULL GRAPPLING

VARIOUS REMNANTS OF CRETAN ART DEPICT THE BULL GRAPPLING TRICK BELOW. MODERN BULL-FIGHTING EXPERTS CLAIM THIS FEAT WOULD BE IMPOSSIBLE. EVEN IF THE MATADOR COULD GRAB THE HORNS & SOMERSAULT OVER HE WOULD LAND FAR BEHIND THE ANIMAL, NOT ON ITS BACK. TWO EXPLANATIONS ARE THAT BULLS WERE SPECIALLY TAMED & TRAINED, OR THAT A BREED OF SLOW, VERY LONG-BACKED ANIMALS THEN EXISTED.

THE OLD FASHIONED BRITISH BULL

THE DEMAND FOR CHEAP LEAN BEEF IS PUTTING BRITISH BULLS IN JEOPARDY. BRITISH BREEDERS DEVELOPED THEIR BEEF ANIMALS WHEN FAT WAS NOT SO UNFASHIONABLE. HOWEVER, IN FRANCE & ITALY SOME BULLS WERE BRED SPECIFICALLY FOR USE AS DRAUGHT OXEN & THEY NOW POSSESS SOME VERY BIG MUSCULAR BREEDS, MORE ECONOMIC FOR MODERN BEEF PRODUCTION METHODS. THE LARGEST IS THE ITALIAN CHIANINA WHICH CAN STAND 6½FT AT THE SHOULDER & PRODUCE A ONE TON CARCASS WITH 1000LB OF LEAN MEAT AT 2 YEARS OLD. THESE ARE NOW BEING IMPORTED & MATED WITH BRITISH ANIMALS.

THE ARISTOCRACY

18th CENTURY FARMERS CONSIDERED THEIR OWN ANCESTRY OF FAR LESS IMPORTANCE THAN THAT OF THEIR BULLS. COATES HERD BOOK WAS SECOND IN IMPORTANCE ONLY TO THE BIBLE & FOXES' BOOK OF MARTYRS. VERY POOR BULLS WITH IMPRESSIVE ANCESTRIES FETCHED FAR MORE THAN PHYSICALLY EXCELLENT UNPEDIGREED BULLS.

No. 1919

HOW TO MAKE A SQUARE DISAPPEAR

IF THE SQUARE ABOVE IS CUT UP & REARRANGED AS SHOWN ANOTHER SQUARE OF THE SAME DIMENSIONS IS FORMED, LACKING TWO SMALL SQUARES.

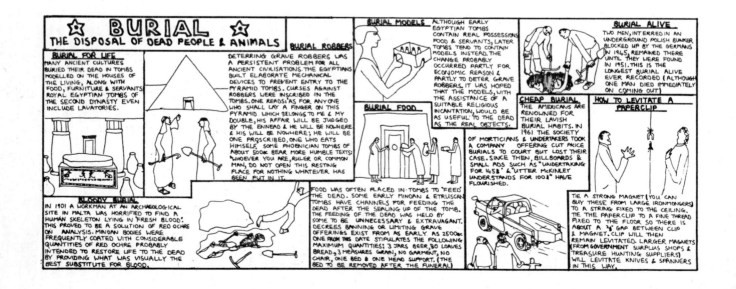

☆ BURIAL ☆
THE DISPOSAL OF DEAD PEOPLE & ANIMALS

BURIAL FOR LIFE

MANY ANCIENT CULTURES BURIED THEIR DEAD IN TOMBS MODELLED ON THE HOUSES OF THE LIVING, ALONG WITH FOOD, FURNITURE & SERVANTS. ROYAL EGYPTIAN TOMBS OF THE SECOND DYNASTY EVEN INCLUDE LAVATORIES.

BURIAL ROBBERS

DETERRING GRAVE ROBBERS WAS A PERSISTENT PROBLEM FOR ALL ANCIENT CIVILISATIONS. THE EGYPTIANS BUILT ELABORATE MECHANICAL DEVICES TO PREVENT ENTRY TO THE PYRAMID TOMBS. CURSES AGAINST ROBBERS WERE INSCRIBED IN THE TOMBS. ONE READS: 'AS FOR ANYONE WHO SHALL LAY A FINGER ON THIS PYRAMID WHICH BELONGS TO ME & MY DOUBLE, HIS AFFAIR WILL BE JUDGED BY THE ENNEAD & HE WILL BE NOWHERE & HIS WILL BE NOWHERE; HE WILL BE ONE PROSCRIBED, ONE WHO EATS HIMSELF.' SOME PHOENICIAN TOMBS OF ABOUT 500BC BEAR MORE HUMBLE TEXTS: 'WHOEVER YOU ARE, RULER OR COMMON MAN, DO NOT OPEN THIS RESTING PLACE FOR NOTHING WHATEVER HAS BEEN PUT IN IT.

BLOODY BURIAL

IN 1901 A WORKMAN AT AN ARCHAEOLOGICAL SITE IN MALTA WAS HORRIFIED TO FIND A HUMAN SKELETON LYING IN FRESH BLOOD'. THIS PROVED TO BE A SOLUTION OF RED OCHRE ON ANALYSIS. MINOAN BODIES WERE FREQUENTLY COATED WITH CONSIDERABLE QUANTITIES OF RED OCHRE PROBABLY INTENDED TO RESTORE LIFE TO THE DEAD BY PROVIDING WHAT WAS VISUALLY THE BEST SUBSTITUTE FOR BLOOD.

BURIAL MODELS

ALTHOUGH EARLY EGYPTIAN TOMBS CONTAIN REAL POSSESSIONS FOOD & SERVANTS, LATER TOMBS TEND TO CONTAIN MODELS INSTEAD. THE CHANGE PROBABLY OCCURRED PARTLY FOR ECONOMIC REASON & PARTLY TO DETER GRAVE ROBBERS. IT WAS HOPED THAT THE MODELS, WITH THE ASSISTANCE OF A SUITABLE RELIGIOUS INCANTATION, WOULD BE AS USEFUL TO THE DEAD AS THE REAL OBJECTS.

BURIAL FOOD

FOOD WAS OFTEN PLACED IN TOMBS TO 'FEED' THE DEAD. SOME EARLY MINOAN & ETRUSCAN TOMBS HAVE CHANNELS FOR FEEDING THE DEAD AFTER THE SEALING UP OF THE TOMB. THE FEEDING OF THE DEAD WAS HELD BY SOME TO BE UNNECESSARY & EXTRAVAGANT. DECREES BANNING OR LIMITING GRAVE OFFERINGS EXIST FROM AS EARLY AS 2500BC. ONE FROM THIS DATE STIPULATES THE FOLLOWING MAXIMUM QUANTITIES: 3 JARS BEER, 80 LOAVES BREAD, 3 MEASURES GRAIN, NO GARMENT, NO CHAIR, ONE BED & ONE HEAD SUPPORT. (THE BED TO BE REMOVED AFTER THE FUNERAL)

BURIAL ALIVE

TWO MEN, INTERRED IN AN UNDERGROUND POLISH BUNKER BLOCKED UP BY THE GERMANS IN 1945, REMAINED THERE UNTIL THEY WERE FOUND IN 1951. THIS IS THE LONGEST BURIAL ALIVE EVER RECORDED (ALTHOUGH ONE MAN DIED IMMEDIATELY ON COMING OUT)

CHEAP BURIAL

THE AMERICANS ARE RENOWNED FOR THEIR LAVISH BURIAL HABITS. IN 1961 THE SOCIETY OF MORTICIANS & UNDERTAKERS TOOK A COMPANY OFFERING CUT PRICE BURIALS TO COURT BUT LOST THEIR CASE. SINCE THEN, BILLBOARDS & SIGNS SUCH AS "UNDERTAKING FOR 45$" & "LITTLE McKINLEY UNDERSTANDS FOR 100$" HAVE FLOURISHED.

HOW TO LEVITATE A PAPERCLIP

TIE A STRONG MAGNET (YOU CAN BUY THESE FROM LARGE IRONMONGERS) TO A STRING FIXED TO THE CEILING. TIE THE PAPERCLIP TO A FINE THREAD FIXED TO THE FLOOR SO THERE IS ABOUT A ¾" GAP BETWEEN CLIP & MAGNET. CLIP WILL THEN REMAIN LEVITATED. LARGER MAGNETS (FROM GOVERNMENT SURPLUS SHOPS & TREASURE HUNTING SUPPLIERS) WILL LEVITATE KNIVES & SPANNERS IN THIS WAY.

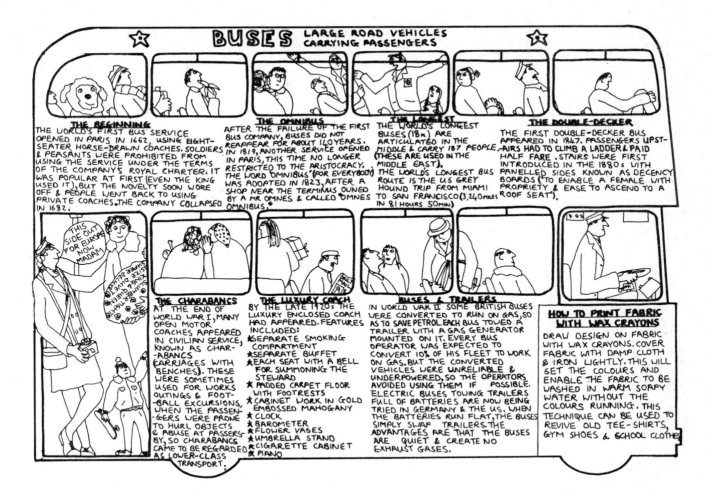

BUSES
LARGE ROAD VEHICLES CARRYING PASSENGERS

THE BEGINNING
THE WORLD'S FIRST BUS SERVICE OPENED IN PARIS IN 1662, USING EIGHT-SEATER HORSE-DRAWN COACHES. SOLDIERS & PEASANTS WERE PROHIBITED FROM USING THE SERVICE UNDER THE TERMS OF THE COMPANY'S ROYAL CHARTER. IT WAS POPULAR AT FIRST (EVEN THE KING USED IT), BUT THE NOVELTY SOON WORE OFF & PEOPLE WENT BACK TO USING PRIVATE COACHES. THE COMPANY COLLAPSED IN 1682.

THE OMNIBUS
AFTER THE FAILURE OF THE FIRST BUS COMPANY, BUSES DID NOT REAPPEAR FOR ABOUT 110 YEARS. IN 1819, ANOTHER SERVICE OPENED IN PARIS, THIS TIME NO LONGER RESTRICTED TO THE ARISTOCRACY. THE WORD "OMNIBUS" (FOR EVERYBODY) WAS ADOPTED IN 1823, AFTER A SHOP NEAR THE TERMINUS OWNED BY A MR OMNES & CALLED OMNES OMNIBUS.

THE LONGEST
THE WORLD'S LONGEST BUSES (18 m) ARE ARTICULATED IN THE MIDDLE & CARRY 187 PEOPLE (THESE ARE USED IN THE MIDDLE EAST). THE WORLD'S LONGEST BUS ROUTE IS THE US GREY HOUND TRIP FROM MIAMI TO SAN FRANCISCO (3,240 MILES IN 81 HOURS 50 MIN)

THE DOUBLE-DECKER
THE FIRST DOUBLE-DECKER BUS APPEARED IN 1847. PASSENGERS UPSTAIRS HAD TO CLIMB A LADDER & PAID HALF FARE. STAIRS WERE FIRST INTRODUCED IN THE 1880s WITH PANELLED SIDES KNOWN AS DECENCY BOARDS ("TO ENABLE A FEMALE WITH PROPRIETY & EASE TO ASCEND TO A ROOF SEAT").

THE CHARABANCS
AT THE END OF WORLD WAR I, MANY OPEN MOTOR COACHES APPEARED IN CIVILIAN SERVICE, KNOWN AS CHARABANCS (CARRIAGES WITH BENCHES). THESE WERE SOMETIMES USED FOR WORKS OUTINGS & FOOTBALL EXCURSIONS, WHEN THE PASSENGERS WERE PRONE TO HURL OBJECTS & ABUSE AT PASSERS-BY, SO CHARABANCS CAME TO BE REGARDED AS LOWER-CLASS TRANSPORT.

THE LUXURY COACH
BY THE LATE 1920s THE LUXURY ENCLOSED COACH HAD APPEARED. FEATURES INCLUDED:
* SEPARATE SMOKING COMPARTMENT
* SEPARATE BUFFET
* EACH SEAT WITH A BELL FOR SUMMONING THE STEWARD
* PADDED CARPET FLOOR WITH FOOTRESTS
* CABINET WORK IN GOLD EMBOSSED MAHOGANY
* CLOCK
* BAROMETER
* FLOWER VASES
* UMBRELLA STAND
* CIGARETTE CABINET
* PIANO

BUSES & TRAILERS
IN WORLD WAR II SOME BRITISH BUSES WERE CONVERTED TO RUN ON GAS, SO AS TO SAVE PETROL. EACH BUS TOWED A TRAILER WITH A GAS GENERATOR MOUNTED ON IT. EVERY BUS OPERATOR WAS EXPECTED TO CONVERT 10% OF HIS FLEET TO WORK ON GAS. BUT THE CONVERTED VEHICLES WERE UNRELIABLE & UNDERPOWERED, SO THE OPERATORS AVOIDED USING THEM IF POSSIBLE. ELECTRIC BUSES TOWING TRAILERS FULL OF BATTERIES ARE NOW BEING TRIED IN GERMANY & THE US. WHEN THE BATTERIES RUN FLAT, THE BUSES SIMPLY SWAP TRAILERS. THE ADVANTAGES ARE THAT THE BUSES ARE QUIET & CREATE NO EXHAUST GASES.

HOW TO PRINT FABRIC WITH WAX CRAYONS
DRAW DESIGN ON FABRIC WITH WAX CRAYONS. COVER FABRIC WITH DAMP CLOTH & IRON LIGHTLY. THIS WILL SET THE COLOURS AND ENABLE THE FABRIC TO BE WASHED IN WARM SOAPY WATER WITHOUT THE COLOURS RUNNING. THIS TECHNIQUE CAN BE USED TO REVIVE OLD TEE-SHIRTS, GYM SHOES & SCHOOL CLOTHES

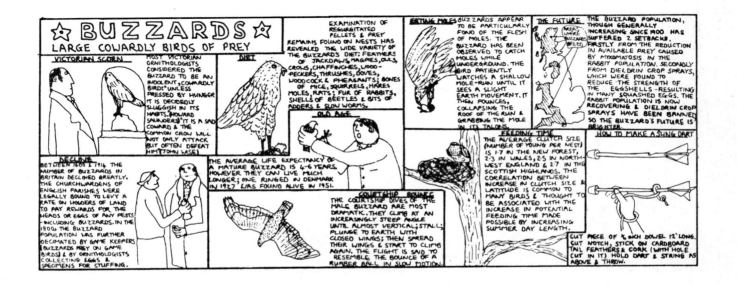

☆ BUZZARDS ☆
LARGE COWARDLY BIRDS OF PREY

VICTORIAN SCORN
MOST VICTORIAN ORNITHOLOGISTS CONSIDERED THE BUZZARD TO BE AN INDOLENT & COWARDLY BIRD: "UNLESS PRESSED BY HUNGER IT IS DECIDEDLY SLUGGISH IN ITS HABITS. (HOWARD SAUNDERS) "IT IS A SAD COWARD & THE COMMON CROW WILL NOT ONLY ATTACK BUT OFTEN DEFEAT HIM" (JOHN LEASE)

DECLINE
BETWEEN 1600 & 1914 THE NUMBER OF BUZZARDS IN BRITAIN DECLINED GREATLY. THE CHURCHWARDENS OF ENGLISH PARISHES WERE LEGALLY BOUND TO LEVY A RATE ON HOLDERS OF LAND TO PAY REWARDS FOR THE HEADS OR EGGS OF ANY PESTS – INCLUDING BUZZARDS. IN THE 1800s THE BUZZARD POPULATION WAS FURTHER DECIMATED BY GAME KEEPERS (BUZZARDS PREY ON GAME BIRDS) & BY ORNITHOLOGISTS COLLECTING EGGS & SPECIMENS FOR STUFFING.

DIET
EXAMINATION OF REGURGITATED PELLETS & PREY REMAINS FOUND ON NESTS HAS REVEALED THE WIDE VARIETY OF THE BUZZARD'S DIET: FEATHERS OF JACKDAWS, MAGPIES, OWLS, CROWS, CHAFFINCHES, WOODPECKERS, THRUSHES, DOVES, WOODCOCK & PHEASANTS; BONES OF MICE, SQUIRRELS, HARES, MOLES, RATS; FUR OF RABBITS, SHELLS OF BEETLES & BITS OF ADDERS & SLOW WORMS.

OLD AGE
THE AVERAGE LIFE EXPECTANCY OF A MATURE BUZZARD IS 4-6 YEARS, HOWEVER THEY CAN LIVE MUCH LONGER; ONE RINGED IN DENMARK IN 1927 WAS FOUND ALIVE IN 1951.

COURTSHIP BOUNCE
THE COURTSHIP DIVES OF THE MALE BUZZARD ARE MOST DRAMATIC. THEY CLIMB AT AN INCREASINGLY STEEP ANGLE UNTIL ALMOST VERTICAL; STALL; PLUNGE TO EARTH WITH CLOSED WINGS; THEN SPREAD THEIR WINGS & START TO CLIMB AGAIN. THE FLIGHT IS SAID TO RESEMBLE THE BOUNCE OF A RUBBER BALL IN SLOW MOTION.

EATING MOLES
BUZZARDS APPEAR TO BE PARTICULARLY FOND OF THE FLESH OF MOLES. THE BUZZARD HAS BEEN OBSERVED TO CATCH MOLES WHILE UNDERGROUND. THE BIRD PATIENTLY WATCHES A SHALLOW MOLE-RUN UNTIL IT SEES A SLIGHT EARTH MOVEMENT. IT THEN POUNCES, COLLAPSING THE ROOF OF THE RUN & GRABBING THE MOLE IN ITS TALONS.

FEEDING TIME
THE AVERAGE CLUTCH SIZE (NUMBER OF YOUNG PER NEST) IS 1.7 IN THE NEW FOREST, 2.3 IN WALES, 2.5 IN NORTH-WEST ENGLAND & 2.7 IN THE SCOTTISH HIGHLANDS. THE CORRELATION BETWEEN INCREASE IN CLUTCH SIZE & LATITUDE IS COMMON TO MANY BIRDS & THOUGHT TO BE ASSOCIATED WITH THE INCREASE IN POTENTIAL FEEDING TIME MADE POSSIBLE BY INCREASING SUMMER DAY LENGTH.

THE FUTURE
THE BUZZARD POPULATION, THOUGH GENERALLY INCREASING SINCE 1900 HAS SUFFERED 2 SETBACKS. FIRSTLY FROM THE REDUCTION IN AVAILABLE PREY CAUSED BY MIXOMATOSIS IN THE RABBIT POPULATION. SECONDLY FROM DIELDRIN CROP SPRAYS, WHICH WERE FOUND TO REDUCE THE STRENGTH OF THE EGGSHELLS – RESULTING IN MANY SQUASHED EGGS. THE RABBIT POPULATION IS NOW RECOVERING & DIELDRIN CROP SPRAYS HAVE BEEN BANNED SO THE BUZZARD'S FUTURE IS BRIGHTER

HOW TO MAKE A SLING DART
CUT PIECE OF ¼ INCH DOWEL 12" LONG. CUT NOTCH, STICK ON CARDBOARD TAIL FEATHERS & CORK (WITH HOLE CUT IN IT) HOLD DART & STRING AS ABOVE & THROW.

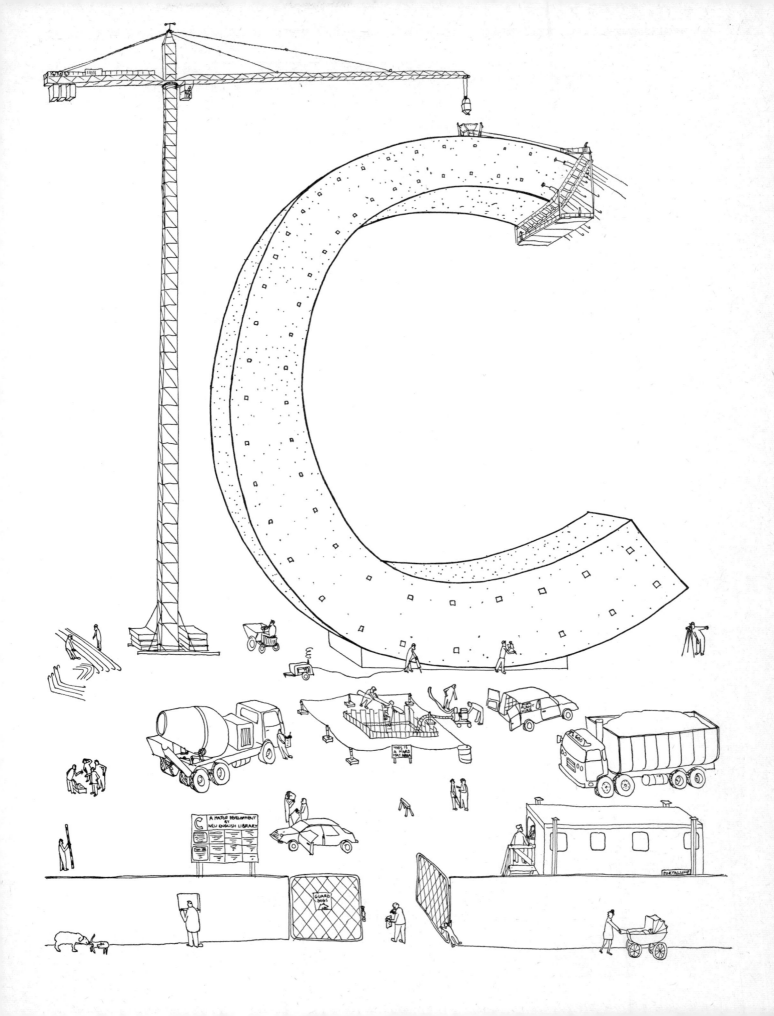

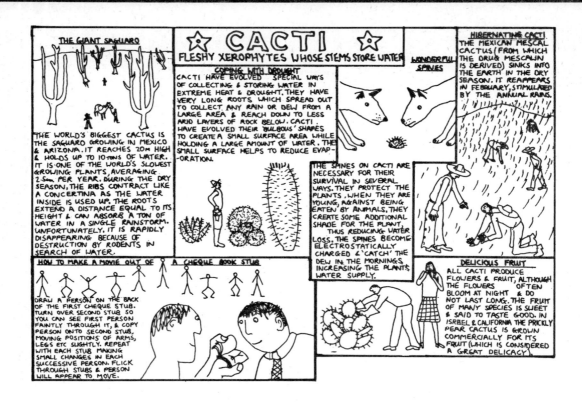

THE GIANT SAGUARO

THE WORLD'S BIGGEST CACTUS IS THE SAGUARO GROWING IN MEXICO & ARIZONA. IT REACHES 20m HIGH & HOLDS UP TO 10 TONS OF WATER. IT IS ONE OF THE WORLD'S SLOWEST GROWING PLANTS, AVERAGING 2.5cm PER YEAR. DURING THE DRY SEASON, THE RIBS CONTRACT LIKE A CONCERTINA AS THE WATER INSIDE IS USED UP. THE ROOTS EXTEND A DISTANCE EQUAL TO ITS HEIGHT & CAN ABSORB A TON OF WATER IN A SINGLE RAINSTORM. UNFORTUNATELY, IT IS RAPIDLY DISAPPEARING BECAUSE OF DESTRUCTION BY RODENTS IN SEARCH OF WATER.

☆ CACTI ☆
FLESHY XEROPHYTES WHOSE STEMS STORE WATER

WONDERFUL SPINES

COPING WITH DROUGHT
CACTI HAVE EVOLVED SPECIAL WAYS OF COLLECTING & STORING WATER IN EXTREME HEAT & DROUGHT. THEY HAVE VERY LONG ROOTS WHICH SPREAD OUT TO COLLECT ANY RAIN OR DEW FROM A LARGE AREA & REACH DOWN TO LESS ARID LAYERS OF ROCK BELOW. CACTI HAVE EVOLVED THEIR 'BULBOUS' SHAPES TO CREATE A SMALL SURFACE AREA WHILE HOLDING A LARGE AMOUNT OF WATER. THE SMALL SURFACE HELPS TO REDUCE EVAPORATION.

THE SPINES ON CACTI ARE NECESSARY FOR THEIR SURVIVAL IN SEVERAL WAYS. THEY PROTECT THE PLANTS, WHEN THEY ARE YOUNG, AGAINST BEING EATEN BY ANIMALS, THEY CREATE SOME ADDITIONAL SHADE FOR THE PLANT, THUS REDUCING WATER LOSS. THE SPINES BECOME ELECTROSTATICALLY CHARGED & 'CATCH' THE DEW IN THE MORNINGS, INCREASING THE PLANTS WATER SUPPLY.

HIBERNATING CACTI
THE MEXICAN MESCAL CACTUS (FROM WHICH THE DRUG MESCALIN IS DERIVED) SINKS INTO THE EARTH IN THE DRY SEASON. IT REAPPEARS IN FEBRUARY, STIMULATED BY THE ANNUAL RAINS.

DELICIOUS FRUIT
ALL CACTI PRODUCE FLOWERS & FRUIT, ALTHOUGH THE FLOWERS OFTEN BLOOM AT NIGHT & DO NOT LAST LONG. THE FRUIT OF MANY SPECIES IS SWEET & SAID TO TASTE GOOD. IN ISRAEL & CALIFORNIA THE PRICKLY PEAR CACTUS IS GROWN COMMERCIALLY FOR ITS FRUIT (WHICH IS CONSIDERED A GREAT DELICACY).

HOW TO MAKE A MOVIE OUT OF A CHEQUE BOOK STUB

DRAW A PERSON ON THE BACK OF THE FIRST CHEQUE STUB. TURN OVER SECOND STUB SO YOU CAN SEE FIRST PERSON FAINTLY THROUGH IT, & COPY PERSON ONTO SECOND STUB, MOVING POSITIONS OF ARMS, LEGS ETC SLIGHTLY. REPEAT WITH EACH STUB MAKING SMALL CHANGES IN EACH SUCCESSIVE PERSON. FLICK THROUGH STUBS & PERSON WILL APPEAR TO MOVE.

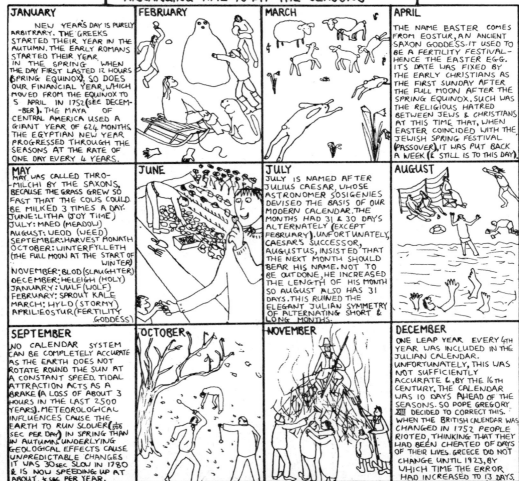

☆ THE CALENDAR ☆
ARRANGING TIME TO FIT THE SEASONS

JANUARY
NEW YEAR'S DAY IS PURELY ARBITRARY. THE GREEKS STARTED THEIR YEAR IN THE AUTUMN. THE EARLY ROMANS STARTED THEIR YEAR IN THE SPRING WHEN THE DAY FIRST LASTED 12 HOURS (SPRING EQUINOX), SO DOES OUR FINANCIAL YEAR, WHICH MOVED FROM THE EQUINOX TO 5 APRIL IN 1752 (SEE DECEMBER). THE MAYA OF CENTRAL AMERICA USED A GIANT YEAR OF 624 MONTHS. THE EGYPTIAN NEW YEAR PROGRESSED THROUGH THE SEASONS AT THE RATE OF ONE DAY EVERY 4 YEARS.

FEBRUARY

MARCH

APRIL
THE NAME EASTER COMES FROM EOSTUR, AN ANCIENT SAXON GODDESS. IT USED TO BE A FERTILITY FESTIVAL—HENCE THE EASTER EGG. ITS DATE WAS FIXED BY THE EARLY CHRISTIANS AS THE FIRST SUNDAY AFTER THE FULL MOON AFTER THE SPRING EQUINOX. SUCH WAS THE RELIGIOUS HATRED BETWEEN JEWS & CHRISTIANS AT THIS TIME THAT, WHEN EASTER COINCIDED WITH THE JEWISH SPRING FESTIVAL (PASSOVER), IT WAS PUT BACK A WEEK (& STILL IS TO THIS DAY).

MAY
MAY WAS CALLED THROMILCHI BY THE SAXONS, BECAUSE THE GRASS GREW SO FAST THAT THE COWS COULD BE MILKED 3 TIMES A DAY.
JUNE: LITHA (JOY TIME)
JULY: MAED (MEADOW)
AUGUST: WEOD (WEED)
SEPTEMBER: HARVEST MONATH
OCTOBER: WINTERFYLLETH (THE FULL MOON AT THE START OF WINTER)
NOVEMBER: BLOD (SLAUGHTER)
DECEMBER: HELEIGH (HOLY)
JANUARY: WULF (WOLF)
FEBRUARY: SPROUT KALE
MARCH: HYLD (STORMY)
APRIL: EOSTUR (FERTILITY GODDESS)

JUNE

JULY
JULY IS NAMED AFTER JULIUS CAESAR, WHOSE ASTRONOMER SOSIGENIES DEVISED THE BASIS OF OUR MODERN CALENDAR. THE MONTHS HAD 31 & 30 DAYS ALTERNATELY (EXCEPT FEBRUARY). UNFORTUNATELY, CAESAR'S SUCCESSOR, AUGUSTUS, INSISTED THAT THE NEXT MONTH SHOULD BEAR HIS NAME. NOT TO BE OUTDONE, HE INCREASED THE LENGTH OF HIS MONTH SO AUGUST ALSO HAS 31 DAYS. THIS RUINED THE ELEGANT JULIAN SYMMETRY OF ALTERNATING SHORT & LONG MONTHS.

AUGUST

SEPTEMBER
NO CALENDAR SYSTEM CAN BE COMPLETELY ACCURATE AS THE EARTH DOES NOT ROTATE ROUND THE SUN AT A CONSTANT SPEED. TIDAL ATTRACTION ACTS AS A BRAKE (A LOSS OF ABOUT 3 HOURS IN THE LAST 2500 YEARS). METEOROLOGICAL INFLUENCES CAUSE THE EARTH TO RUN SLOWER (1/500 SEC PER DAY) IN SPRING THAN IN AUTUMN. UNDERLYING GEOLOGICAL EFFECTS CAUSE UNPREDICTABLE CHANGES. IT WAS 30 SEC SLOW IN 1780 & IS NOW SPEEDING UP AT ABOUT 1/2 SEC PER YEAR.

OCTOBER

NOVEMBER

DECEMBER
ONE LEAP YEAR EVERY 4TH YEAR WAS INCLUDED IN THE JULIAN CALENDAR. UNFORTUNATELY, THIS WAS NOT SUFFICIENTLY ACCURATE & , BY THE 16TH CENTURY, THE CALENDAR WAS 10 DAYS AHEAD OF THE SEASONS. SO POPE GREGORY XIII DECIDED TO CORRECT THIS. WHEN THE BRITISH CALENDAR WAS CHANGED IN 1752 PEOPLE RIOTED, THINKING THAT THEY HAD BEEN CHEATED OF DAYS OF THEIR LIVES. GREECE DID NOT CHANGE UNTIL 1923, BY WHICH TIME THE ERROR HAD INCREASED TO 13 DAYS.

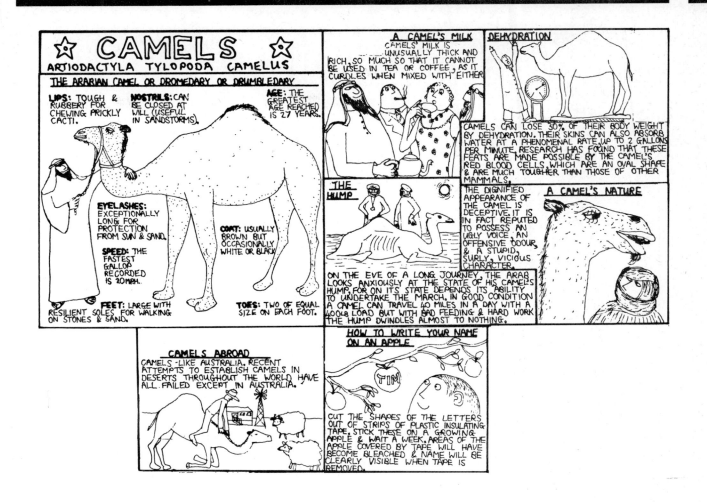

☆ CAMELS ☆
ARTIODACTYLA TYLOPODA CAMELUS

THE ARABIAN CAMEL OR DROMEDARY OR DRUMBLEDARY

LIPS: TOUGH & RUBBERY FOR CHEWING PRICKLY CACTI.

NOSTRILS: CAN BE CLOSED AT WILL (USEFUL IN SANDSTORMS).

AGE: THE GREATEST AGE REACHED IS 27 YEARS.

EYELASHES: EXCEPTIONALLY LONG FOR PROTECTION FROM SUN & SAND.

SPEED: THE FASTEST GALLOP RECORDED IS 20 M.P.H.

COAT: USUALLY BROWN BUT OCCASIONALLY WHITE OR BLACK.

FEET: LARGE WITH RESILIENT SOLES FOR WALKING ON STONES & SAND.

TOES: TWO OF EQUAL SIZE ON EACH FOOT.

A CAMEL'S MILK
CAMELS' MILK IS UNUSUALLY THICK AND RICH, SO MUCH SO THAT IT CANNOT BE USED IN TEA OR COFFEE, AS IT CURDLES WHEN MIXED WITH EITHER.

DEHYDRATION
CAMELS CAN LOSE 30% OF THEIR BODY WEIGHT BY DEHYDRATION. THEIR SKINS CAN ALSO ABSORB WATER AT A PHENOMENAL RATE, UP TO 2 GALLONS PER MINUTE. RESEARCH HAS FOUND THAT THESE FEATS ARE MADE POSSIBLE BY THE CAMEL'S RED BLOOD CELLS, WHICH ARE AN OVAL SHAPE & ARE MUCH TOUGHER THAN THOSE OF OTHER MAMMALS.

THE HUMP
ON THE EVE OF A LONG JOURNEY, THE ARAB LOOKS ANXIOUSLY AT THE STATE OF HIS CAMEL'S HUMP, FOR ON ITS STATE DEPENDS ITS ABILITY TO UNDERTAKE THE MARCH. IN GOOD CONDITION A CAMEL CAN TRAVEL 40 MILES IN A DAY WITH A 400LB LOAD BUT WITH BAD FEEDING & HARD WORK THE HUMP DWINDLES ALMOST TO NOTHING.

A CAMEL'S NATURE
THE DIGNIFIED APPEARANCE OF THE CAMEL IS DECEPTIVE. IT IS IN FACT REPUTED TO POSSESS AN UGLY VOICE, AN OFFENSIVE ODOUR, & A STUPID, SURLY, VICIOUS CHARACTER.

CAMELS ABROAD
CAMELS -LIKE AUSTRALIA. RECENT ATTEMPTS TO ESTABLISH CAMELS IN DESERTS THROUGHOUT THE WORLD HAVE ALL FAILED EXCEPT IN AUSTRALIA.

HOW TO WRITE YOUR NAME ON AN APPLE
CUT THE SHAPES OF THE LETTERS OUT OF STRIPS OF PLASTIC INSULATING TAPE. STICK THESE ON A GROWING APPLE & WAIT A WEEK. AREAS OF THE APPLE COVERED BY TAPE WILL HAVE BECOME BLEACHED & NAME WILL BE CLEARLY VISIBLE WHEN TAPE IS REMOVED.

☆ CAMOUFLAGE ☆
ANY DEVICE FOR CONFUSING ADVERSARIES

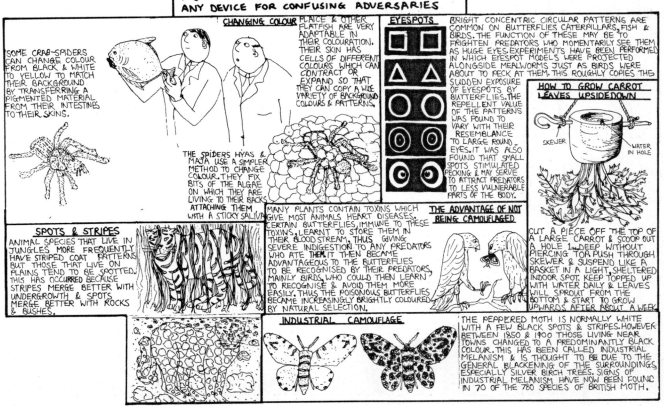

SOME CRAB-SPIDERS CAN CHANGE COLOUR FROM BLACK & WHITE TO YELLOW TO MATCH THEIR BACKGROUND BY TRANSFERRING A PIGMENTED MATERIAL FROM THEIR INTESTINES TO THEIR SKINS.

CHANGING COLOUR
PLAICE & OTHER FLATFISH ARE VERY ADAPTABLE IN THEIR COLOURATION. THEIR SKIN HAS CELLS OF DIFFERENT COLOURS WHICH CAN CONTRACT OR EXPAND SO THAT THEY CAN COPY A WIDE VARIETY OF BACKGROUND COLOURS & PATTERNS.

THE SPIDERS HYAS & MAJA USE A SIMPLER METHOD TO CHANGE COLOUR. THEY FIX BITS OF THE ALGAE ON WHICH THEY ARE LIVING TO THEIR BACKS ATTACHING THEM WITH A STICKY SALIVA.

EYESPOTS
BRIGHT CONCENTRIC CIRCULAR PATTERNS ARE COMMON ON BUTTERFLIES, CATERPILLARS, FISH & BIRDS. THE FUNCTION OF THESE MAY BE TO FRIGHTEN PREDATORS WHO MOMENTARILY SEE THEM AS HUGE EYES. EXPERIMENTS HAVE BEEN PERFORMED IN WHICH EYESPOT MODELS WERE PROJECTED ALONGSIDE MEALWORMS JUST AS BIRDS WERE ABOUT TO PECK AT THEM. THIS ROUGHLY COPIES THE SUDDEN EXPOSURE OF EYESPOTS BY BUTTERFLIES. THE REPELLENT VALUE OF THE PATTERNS WAS FOUND TO VARY WITH THEIR RESEMBLANCE TO LARGE ROUND EYES. IT WAS ALSO FOUND THAT SMALL SPOTS STIMULATED PECKING & MAY SERVE TO ATTRACT PREDATORS TO LESS VULNERABLE PARTS OF THE BODY.

HOW TO GROW CARROT LEAVES UPSIDEDOWN

SKEWER

WATER IN HOLE

CUT A PIECE OFF THE TOP OF A LARGE CARROT & SCOOP OUT A HOLE 1" DEEP WITHOUT PIERCING TOP. PUSH THROUGH SKEWER & SUSPEND LIKE A BASKET IN A LIGHT, SHELTERED INDOOR SPOT. KEEP TOPPED UP WITH WATER DAILY & LEAVES WILL SPROUT FROM THE BOTTOM & START TO GROW UPWARDS AFTER ABOUT A WEEK.

SPOTS & STRIPES
ANIMAL SPECIES THAT LIVE IN JUNGLES MORE FREQUENTLY HAVE STRIPED COAT PATTERNS BUT THOSE THAT LIVE ON PLAINS TEND TO BE SPOTTED. THIS HAS OCCURRED BECAUSE STRIPES MERGE BETTER WITH UNDERGROWTH & SPOTS MERGE BETTER WITH ROCKS & BUSHES.

MANY PLANTS CONTAIN TOXINS WHICH GIVE MOST ANIMALS HEART DISEASES. CERTAIN BUTTERFLIES, IMMUNE TO THESE TOXINS, LEARNT TO STORE THEM IN THEIR BLOOD STREAM, THUS GIVING SEVERE INDIGESTION TO ANY PREDATORS WHO ATE THEM. IT THEN BECAME ADVANTAGEOUS TO THE BUTTERFLIES TO BE RECOGNISED BY THEIR PREDATORS, MAINLY BIRDS, WHO COULD THEN LEARN TO RECOGNISE & AVOID THEM MORE EASILY. THUS THE POISONOUS BUTTERFLIES BECAME INCREASINGLY BRIGHTLY COLOURED BY NATURAL SELECTION.

THE ADVANTAGE OF NOT BEING CAMOUFLAGED

INDUSTRIAL CAMOUFLAGE
THE PEPPERED MOTH IS NORMALLY WHITE WITH A FEW BLACK SPOTS & STRIPES. HOWEVER BETWEEN 1850 & 1900 THOSE LIVING NEAR TOWNS CHANGED TO A PREDOMINANTLY BLACK COLOUR. THIS HAS BEEN CALLED INDUSTRIAL MELANISM & IS THOUGHT TO BE DUE TO THE GENERAL BLACKENING OF THE SURROUNDINGS, ESPECIALLY SILVER BIRCH TREES. SIGNS OF INDUSTRIAL MELANISM HAVE NOW BEEN FOUND IN 70 OF THE 780 SPECIES OF BRITISH MOTH.

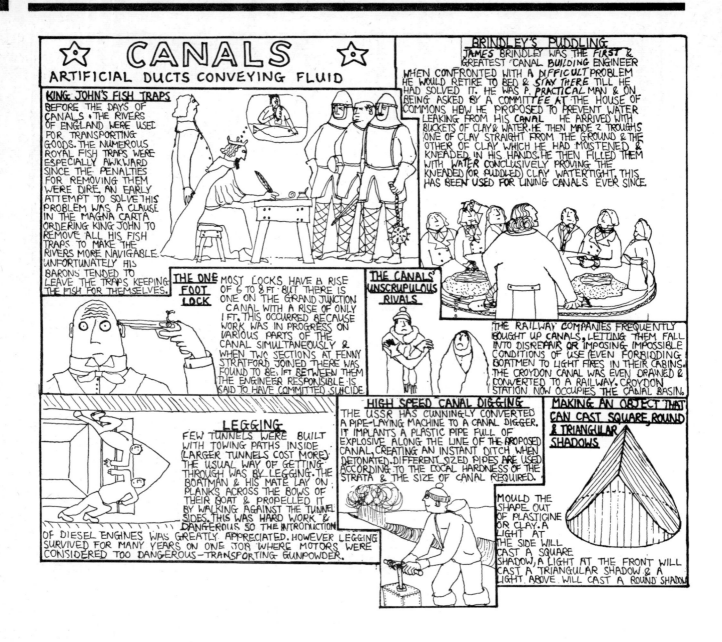

☆ CANALS ☆
ARTIFICIAL DUCTS CONVEYING FLUID

KING JOHN'S FISH TRAPS
BEFORE THE DAYS OF CANALS, THE RIVERS OF ENGLAND WERE USED FOR TRANSPORTING GOODS. THE NUMEROUS ROYAL FISH TRAPS WERE ESPECIALLY AWKWARD SINCE THE PENALTIES FOR REMOVING THEM WERE DIRE. AN EARLY ATTEMPT TO SOLVE THIS PROBLEM WAS A CLAUSE IN THE MAGNA CARTA ORDERING KING JOHN TO REMOVE ALL HIS FISH TRAPS TO MAKE THE RIVERS MORE NAVIGABLE. UNFORTUNATELY HIS BARONS TENDED TO LEAVE THE TRAPS KEEPING THE FISH FOR THEMSELVES.

BRINDLEY'S PUDDLING
JAMES BRINDLEY WAS THE FIRST & GREATEST CANAL BUILDING ENGINEER. WHEN CONFRONTED WITH A DIFFICULT PROBLEM HE WOULD RETIRE TO BED & STAY THERE TILL HE HAD SOLVED IT. HE WAS A PRACTICAL MAN & ON BEING ASKED BY A COMMITTEE AT THE HOUSE OF COMMONS HOW HE PROPOSED TO PREVENT WATER LEAKING FROM HIS CANAL HE ARRIVED WITH BUCKETS OF CLAY & WATER. HE THEN MADE 2 TROUGHS ONE OF CLAY STRAIGHT FROM THE GROUND & THE OTHER OF CLAY WHICH HE HAD MOISTENED & KNEADED IN HIS HANDS. HE THEN FILLED THEM WITH WATER CONCLUSIVELY PROVING THE KNEADED (OR PUDDLED) CLAY WATERTIGHT. THIS HAS BEEN USED FOR LINING CANALS EVER SINCE.

THE ONE FOOT LOCK
MOST LOCKS HAVE A RISE OF 6 TO 8 FT. BUT THERE IS ONE ON THE GRAND JUNCTION CANAL WITH A RISE OF ONLY 1 FT. THIS OCCURRED BECAUSE WORK WAS IN PROGRESS ON VARIOUS PARTS OF THE CANAL SIMULTANEOUSLY & WHEN TWO SECTIONS AT FENNY STRATFORD JOINED THERE WAS FOUND TO BE 1 FT BETWEEN THEM THE ENGINEER RESPONSIBLE IS SAID TO HAVE COMMITTED SUICIDE.

THE CANALS' UNSCRUPULOUS RIVALS
THE RAILWAY COMPANIES FREQUENTLY BOUGHT UP CANALS, LETTING THEM FALL INTO DISREPAIR OR IMPOSING IMPOSSIBLE CONDITIONS OF USE (EVEN FORBIDDING BOATMEN TO LIGHT FIRES IN THEIR CABINS). THE CROYDON CANAL WAS EVEN DRAINED & CONVERTED TO A RAILWAY. CROYDON STATION NOW OCCUPIES THE CANAL BASIN.

LEGGING
FEW TUNNELS WERE BUILT WITH TOWING PATHS INSIDE (LARGER TUNNELS COST MORE). THE USUAL WAY OF GETTING THROUGH WAS BY LEGGING. THE BOATMAN & HIS MATE LAY ON PLANKS ACROSS THE BOWS OF THEIR BOAT & PROPELLED IT BY WALKING AGAINST THE TUNNEL SIDES. THIS WAS HARD WORK & DANGEROUS SO THE INTRODUCTION OF DIESEL ENGINES WAS GREATLY APPRECIATED. HOWEVER LEGGING SURVIVED FOR MANY YEARS ON ONE JOB WHERE MOTORS WERE CONSIDERED TOO DANGEROUS – TRANSPORTING GUNPOWDER.

HIGH SPEED CANAL DIGGING
THE USSR HAS CUNNINGLY CONVERTED A PIPE-LAYING MACHINE TO A CANAL DIGGER. IT IMPLANTS A PLASTIC PIPE FULL OF EXPLOSIVE ALONG THE LINE OF THE PROPOSED CANAL, CREATING AN INSTANT DITCH WHEN DETONATED. DIFFERENT SIZED PIPES ARE USED ACCORDING TO THE LOCAL HARDNESS OF THE STRATA & THE SIZE OF CANAL REQUIRED.

MAKING AN OBJECT THAT CAN CAST SQUARE, ROUND & TRIANGULAR SHADOWS
MOULD THE SHAPE OUT OF PLASTICINE OR CLAY. A LIGHT AT THE SIDE WILL CAST A SQUARE SHADOW, A LIGHT AT THE FRONT WILL CAST A TRIANGULAR SHADOW & A LIGHT ABOVE WILL CAST A ROUND SHADOW.

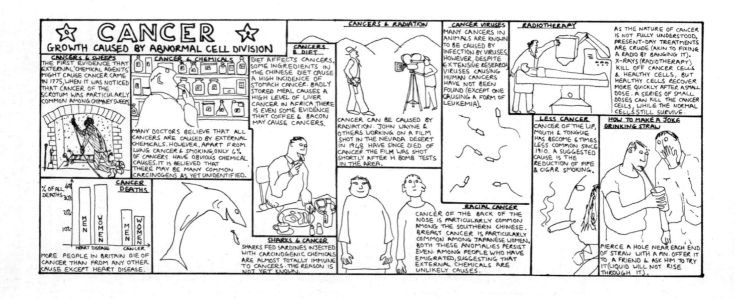

☆ CANCER ☆
GROWTH CAUSED BY ABNORMAL CELL DIVISION

CANCERS & SOOTS
THE FIRST EVIDENCE THAT EXTERNAL CHEMICAL AGENTS MIGHT CAUSE CANCER CAME IN 1775, WHEN IT WAS NOTICED THAT CANCER OF THE SCROTUM WAS PARTICULARLY COMMON AMONG CHIMNEY SWEEPS.

CANCER & CHEMICALS
MANY DOCTORS BELIEVE THAT ALL CANCERS ARE CAUSED BY EXTERNAL CHEMICALS. HOWEVER, APART FROM LUNG CANCER & SMOKING, ONLY 6% OF CANCERS HAVE OBVIOUS CHEMICAL CAUSES. IT IS BELIEVED THAT THERE MAY BE MANY COMMON CARCINOGENS AS YET UNIDENTIFIED.

CANCER & DIET
DIET AFFECTS CANCERS. SOME INGREDIENTS IN THE CHINESE DIET CAUSE A HIGH INCIDENCE OF STOMACH CANCER. BADLY STORED MEAL CAUSES A HIGH LEVEL OF LIVER CANCER IN AFRICA. THERE IS EVEN SOME EVIDENCE THAT COFFEE & BACON MAY CAUSE CANCERS.

CANCERS & RADIATION
CANCER CAN BE CAUSED BY RADIATION. JOHN WAYNE & OTHERS WORKING ON A FILM SHOT IN THE NEVADA DESERT IN 1948 HAVE SINCE DIED OF CANCER. THE FILM WAS SHOT SHORTLY AFTER H BOMB TESTS IN THE AREA.

CANCER VIRUSES
MANY CANCERS IN ANIMALS ARE KNOWN TO BE CAUSED BY INFECTION BY VIRUSES. HOWEVER, DESPITE EXTENSIVE RESEARCH VIRUSES CAUSING HUMAN CANCERS HAVE NOT BEEN FOUND (EXCEPT ONE CAUSING A FORM OF LEUKEMIA).

RADIOTHERAPY
AS THE NATURE OF CANCER IS NOT FULLY UNDERSTOOD, PRESENT-DAY TREATMENTS ARE CRUDE (AKIN TO FIXING A RADIO BY BANGING IT). X-RAYS (RADIOTHERAPY) KILL OFF CANCER CELLS & HEALTHY CELLS, BUT HEALTHY CELLS RECOVER MORE QUICKLY AFTER A SMALL DOSE. A SERIES OF SMALL DOSES CAN KILL THE CANCER CELLS, WHILE THE NORMAL CELLS STILL SURVIVE.

LESS CANCER
CANCER OF THE LIP, MOUTH & TONGUE HAS BECOME 6 TIMES LESS COMMON SINCE 1910. A SUGGESTED CAUSE IS THE REDUCTION OF PIPE & CIGAR SMOKING.

RACIAL CANCER
CANCER OF THE BACK OF THE NOSE IS PARTICULARLY COMMON AMONG THE SOUTHERN CHINESE. BREAST CANCER IS PARTICULARLY COMMON AMONG JAPANESE WOMEN. BOTH THESE ANOMALIES PERSIST EVEN AMONG PEOPLE WHO HAVE EMIGRATED, SUGGESTING THAT EXTERNAL CHEMICALS ARE UNLIKELY CAUSES.

SHARKS & CANCER
SHARKS FED SARDINES INJECTED WITH CARCINOGENIC CHEMICALS ARE ALMOST TOTALLY IMMUNE TO CANCERS. THE REASON IS NOT YET KNOWN.

CANCER DEATHS
% OF ALL DEATHS — MEN / WOMEN (HEART DISEASE), MEN / WOMEN (CANCER). MORE PEOPLE IN BRITAIN DIE OF CANCER THAN FROM ANY OTHER CAUSE EXCEPT HEART DISEASE.

HOW TO MAKE A JOKE DRINKING STRAW
PIERCE A HOLE NEAR EACH END OF STRAW WITH A PIN. OFFER IT TO A FRIEND & ASK HIM TO TRY IT (LIQUID WILL NOT RISE THROUGH IT).

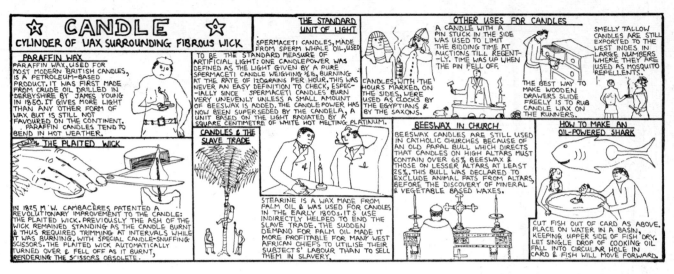

☆ CANDLE ☆
CYLINDER OF WAX SURROUNDING FIBROUS WICK

PARAFFIN WAX
PARAFFIN WAX, USED FOR MOST MODERN BRITISH CANDLES, IS A PETROLEUM-BASED PRODUCT. IT WAS FIRST MADE FROM CRUDE OIL DRILLED IN DERBYSHIRE BY JAMES YOUNG IN 1850. IT GIVES MORE LIGHT THAN ANY OTHER FORM OF WAX BUT IS STILL NOT FAVOURED ON THE CONTINENT. PARAFFIN CANDLES TEND TO BEND IN HOT WEATHER.

THE PLAITED WICK
IN 1825 M'W. CAMBACÈRES PATENTED A REVOLUTIONARY IMPROVEMENT TO THE CANDLE: THE PLAITED WICK. PREVIOUSLY THE ASH OF THE WICK REMAINED STANDING AS THE CANDLE BURNT & THUS REQUIRED TRIMMING AT INTERVALS WHILE IT WAS BURNING, WITH SPECIAL CANDLE-SNUFFING SCISSORS. THE PLAITED WICK AUTOMATICALLY TURNED OVER & FELL OFF AS IT BURNT, RENDERING THE SCISSORS OBSOLETE.

THE STANDARD UNIT OF LIGHT
SPERMACETI CANDLES, MADE FROM SPERM WHALE OIL, USED TO BE THE STANDARD MEASURE OF ARTIFICIAL LIGHT: ONE CANDLEPOWER WAS DEFINED AS THE LIGHT GIVEN BY A PURE SPERMACETI CANDLE WEIGHING ⅙lb, BURNING AT THE RATE OF 120 GRAINS PER HOUR. THIS WAS NEVER AN EASY DEFINITION TO CHECK, ESPECIALLY SINCE SPERMACETI CANDLES BURN VERY UNEVENLY UNLESS A SMALL AMOUNT OF BEESWAX IS ADDED. THE CANDLEPOWER HAS NOW BEEN SUPERSEDED BY THE CANDELA, A UNIT BASED ON THE LIGHT RADIATED BY A SQUARE CENTIMETRE OF WHITE HOT MELTING PLATINUM.

CANDLES & THE SLAVE TRADE
STEARINE IS A WAX MADE FROM PALM OIL & WAS USED FOR CANDLES IN THE EARLY 1800s. ITS USE INDIRECTLY HELPED TO END THE SLAVE TRADE. THE SUDDEN DEMAND FOR PALM OIL MADE IT MORE PROFITABLE FOR MANY WEST AFRICAN CHIEFS TO UTILISE THEIR SUBJECTS' LABOUR THAN TO SELL THEM IN SLAVERY.

OTHER USES FOR CANDLES
A CANDLE WITH A PIN STUCK IN THE SIDE WAS USED TO LIMIT THE BIDDING TIME AT AUCTIONS TILL RECENTLY. TIME WAS UP WHEN THE PIN FELL OFF.

CANDLES, WITH THE HOURS MARKED ON THE SIDES, WERE USED AS CLOCKS BY THE EGYPTIANS & BY THE SAXONS.

THE BEST WAY TO MAKE WOODEN DRAWERS SLIDE FREELY IS TO RUB CANDLE WAX ON THE RUNNERS.

SMELLY TALLOW CANDLES ARE STILL EXPORTED TO THE WEST INDIES IN LARGE NUMBERS WHERE THEY ARE USED AS MOSQUITO REPELLENTS.

BEESWAX IN CHURCH
BEESWAX CANDLES ARE STILL USED IN CATHOLIC CHURCHES BECAUSE OF AN OLD PAPAL BULL WHICH DIRECTS THAT CANDLES ON HIGH ALTARS MUST CONTAIN OVER 65% BEESWAX & THOSE ON LESSER ALTARS AT LEAST 25%. THIS BULL WAS DECLARED TO EXCLUDE ANIMAL FATS FROM ALTARS BEFORE THE DISCOVERY OF MINERAL & VEGETABLE BASED WAXES.

HOW TO MAKE AN OIL-POWERED SHARK
CUT FISH OUT OF CARD AS ABOVE. PLACE ON WATER IN A BASIN, KEEPING UPPER SIDE OF FISH DRY. LET SINGLE DROP OF COOKING OIL FALL INTO CIRCULAR HOLE IN CARD & FISH WILL MOVE FORWARD.

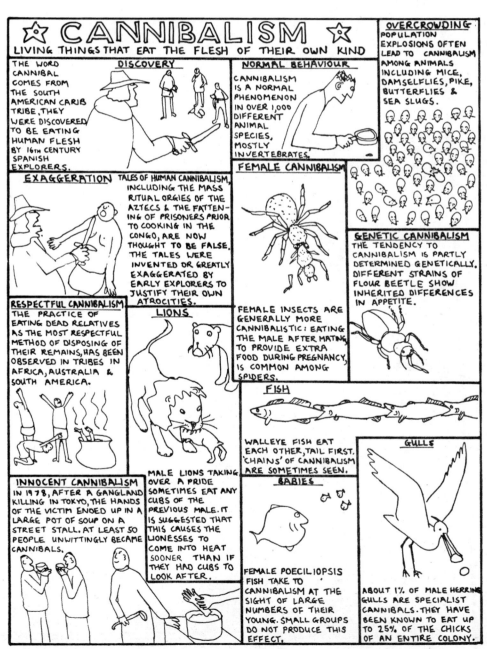

☆ CANNIBALISM ☆
LIVING THINGS THAT EAT THE FLESH OF THEIR OWN KIND

DISCOVERY
THE WORD CANNIBAL COMES FROM THE SOUTH AMERICAN CARIB TRIBE. THEY WERE DISCOVERED TO BE EATING HUMAN FLESH BY 16th CENTURY SPANISH EXPLORERS.

EXAGGERATION
TALES OF HUMAN CANNIBALISM, INCLUDING THE MASS RITUAL ORGIES OF THE AZTECS & THE FATTENING OF PRISONERS PRIOR TO COOKING IN THE CONGO, ARE NOW THOUGHT TO BE FALSE. THE TALES WERE INVENTED OR GREATLY EXAGGERATED BY EARLY EXPLORERS TO JUSTIFY THEIR OWN ATROCITIES.

RESPECTFUL CANNIBALISM
THE PRACTICE OF EATING DEAD RELATIVES AS THE MOST RESPECTFUL METHOD OF DISPOSING OF THEIR REMAINS, HAS BEEN OBSERVED IN TRIBES IN AFRICA, AUSTRALIA & SOUTH AMERICA.

INNOCENT CANNIBALISM
IN 1978, AFTER A GANGLAND KILLING IN TOKYO, THE HANDS OF THE VICTIM ENDED UP IN A LARGE POT OF SOUP ON A STREET STALL. AT LEAST 50 PEOPLE UNWITTINGLY BECAME CANNIBALS.

NORMAL BEHAVIOUR
CANNIBALISM IS A NORMAL PHENOMENON IN OVER 1,000 DIFFERENT ANIMAL SPECIES, MOSTLY INVERTEBRATES.

FEMALE CANNIBALISM
FEMALE INSECTS ARE GENERALLY MORE CANNIBALISTIC: EATING THE MALE AFTER MATING TO PROVIDE EXTRA FOOD DURING PREGNANCY, IS COMMON AMONG SPIDERS.

LIONS
MALE LIONS TAKING OVER A PRIDE SOMETIMES EAT ANY CUBS OF THE PREVIOUS MALE. IT IS SUGGESTED THAT THIS CAUSES THE LIONESSES TO COME INTO HEAT SOONER THAN IF THEY HAD CUBS TO LOOK AFTER.

OVERCROWDING
POPULATION EXPLOSIONS OFTEN LEAD TO CANNIBALISM AMONG ANIMALS INCLUDING MICE, DAMSELFLIES, PIKE, BUTTERFLIES & SEA SLUGS.

GENETIC CANNIBALISM
THE TENDENCY TO CANNIBALISM IS PARTLY DETERMINED GENETICALLY. DIFFERENT STRAINS OF FLOUR BEETLE SHOW INHERITED DIFFERENCES IN APPETITE.

FISH
WALLEYE FISH EAT EACH OTHER, TAIL FIRST. 'CHAINS' OF CANNIBALISM ARE SOMETIMES SEEN.

BABIES
FEMALE POECILIOPSIS FISH TAKE TO CANNIBALISM AT THE SIGHT OF LARGE NUMBERS OF THEIR YOUNG. SMALL GROUPS DO NOT PRODUCE THIS EFFECT.

GULLS
ABOUT 1% OF MALE HERRING GULLS ARE SPECIALIST CANNIBALS. THEY HAVE BEEN KNOWN TO EAT UP TO 25% OF THE CHICKS OF AN ENTIRE COLONY.

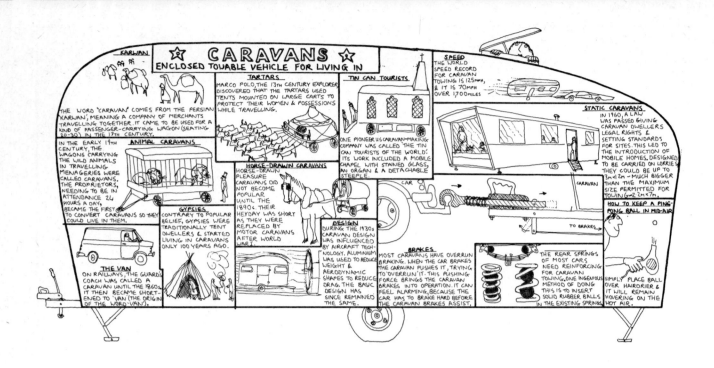

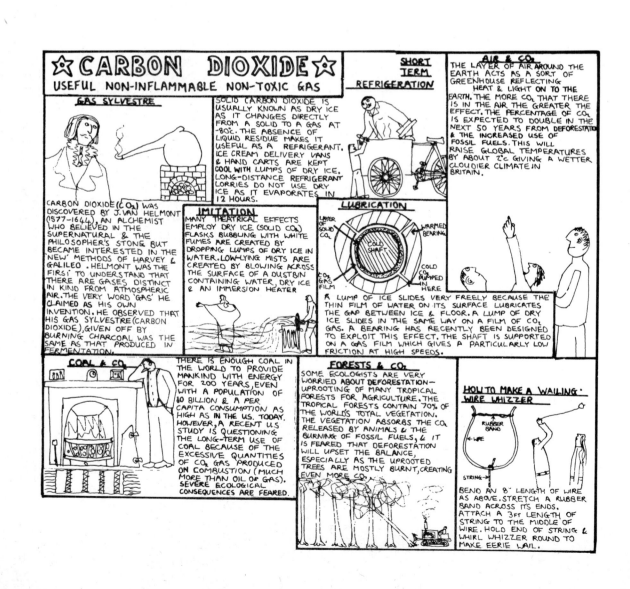

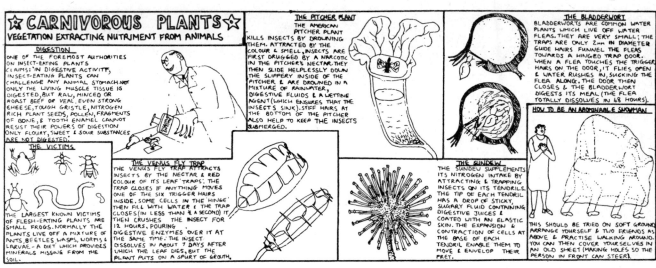

☆ CARNIVOROUS PLANTS ☆
VEGETATION EXTRACTING NUTRIMENT FROM ANIMALS

DIGESTION

ONE OF THE FOREMOST AUTHORITIES ON INSECT-EATING PLANTS CLAIMS: "IN DIGESTIVE ACTIVITY, INSECT-EATING PLANTS CAN CHALLENGE ANY ANIMAL STOMACH. NOT ONLY THE LIVING MUSCLE TISSUE IS DIGESTED, BUT RAW, MINCED OR ROAST BEEF OR VEAL. EVEN STRONG CHEESE, TOUGH GRISTLE, NITROGEN RICH PLANT SEEDS, POLLEN, FRAGMENTS OF BONE, & TOOTH ENAMEL CANNOT RESIST THEIR POWERS OF DIGESTION ONLY FLOURY, SWEET & SOUR SUBSTANCES ARE NOT DIGESTED.

THE VICTIMS

THE LARGEST KNOWN VICTIMS OF FLESH-EATING PLANTS ARE SMALL FROGS. NORMALLY THE PLANTS LIVE OFF A MIXTURE OF ANTS, BEETLES, WASPS, WORMS & LARVAE - A DIET WHICH PROVIDES MINERALS MISSING FROM THE SOIL.

THE VENUS FLY TRAP

THE VENUS FLY TRAP ATTRACTS INSECTS BY THE NECTAR & RED COLOUR OF ITS LEAF 'TRAPS'. THE TRAP CLOSES IF ANYTHING MOVES ONE OF THE SIX TRIGGER HAIRS INSIDE. SOME CELLS IN THE HINGE THEN FILL WITH WATER & THE TRAP CLOSES (IN LESS THAN ½ A SECOND) IT THEN CRUSHES THE INSECT FOR 12 HOURS, POURING DIGESTIVE ENZYMES OVER IT AT THE SAME TIME. THE INSECT DISSOLVES IN ABOUT 7 DAYS AFTER WHICH THE LEAF DIES, BUT THE PLANT PUTS ON A SPURT OF GROWTH.

THE PITCHER PLANT

THE AMERICAN PITCHER PLANT KILLS INSECTS BY DROWNING THEM. ATTRACTED BY THE COLOUR & SMELL, INSECTS ARE FIRST DRUGGED BY A NARCOTIC IN THE PITCHER'S NECTAR. THEY THEN SLIDE HELPLESSLY DOWN THE SLIPPERY INSIDE OF THE PITCHER & ARE DROWNED IN A MIXTURE OF RAINWATER, DIGESTIVE FLUIDS & A WETTING AGENT (WHICH ENSURES THAT THE INSECTS SINK). STIFF HAIRS AT THE BOTTOM OF THE PITCHER ALSO HELP TO KEEP THE INSECTS SUBMERGED.

THE SUNDEW

THE SUNDEW SUPPLEMENTS ITS NITROGEN INTAKE BY ATTRACTING & TRAPPING INSECTS ON ITS TENDRILS. THE TIP OF EACH TENDRIL HAS A DROP OF STICKY, SUGARY FLUID CONTAINING DIGESTIVE JUICES & COATED WITH AN ELASTIC SKIN. THE EXPANSION & CONTRACTION OF CELLS AT THE BASE OF EACH TENDRIL ENABLE THEM TO MOVE & ENVELOP THEIR PREY.

THE BLADDERWORT

BLADDERWORTS ARE COMMON WATER PLANTS WHICH LIVE OFF WATER FLEAS. THEY ARE VERY SMALL; THE TRAPS ARE ONLY 2mm IN DIAMETER GUIDE HAIRS FUNNEL THE FLEAS TOWARDS A HINGED TRAP DOOR. WHEN A FLEA TOUCHES THE TRIGGER HAIRS ON THE DOOR, IT FLIES OPEN & WATER RUSHES IN, SUCKING THE FLEA ALONG. THE DOOR THEN CLOSES & THE BLADDERWORT DIGESTS ITS MEAL (THE FLEA TOTALLY DISSOLVES IN 48 HOURS).

HOW TO BE AN ABOMINABLE SNOWMAN

THIS SHOULD BE TRIED ON SOFT GROUND. ARRANGE YOURSELF & TWO FRIENDS AS ABOVE & PRACTISE WALKING AROUND. YOU CAN THEN COVER YOURSELVES IN AN OLD SHEET (MAKING HOLES SO THE PERSON IN FRONT CAN STEER).

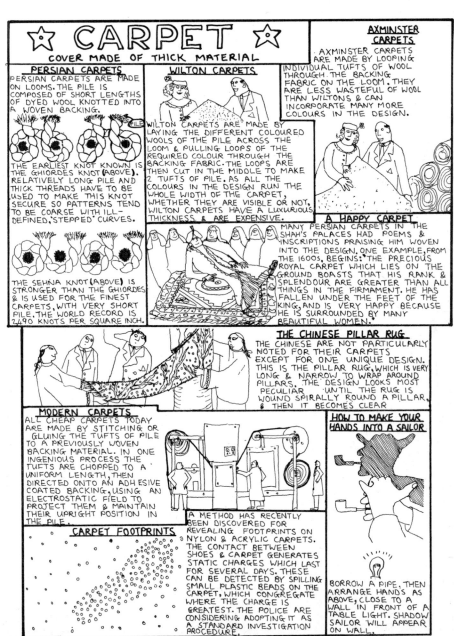

☆ CARPET ☆
COVER MADE OF THICK MATERIAL

PERSIAN CARPETS

PERSIAN CARPETS ARE MADE ON LOOMS. THE PILE IS COMPOSED OF SHORT LENGTHS OF DYED WOOL KNOTTED INTO A WOVEN BACKING.

THE EARLIEST KNOT KNOWN IS THE GHIORDES KNOT (ABOVE). RELATIVELY LONG PILE AND THICK THREADS HAVE TO BE USED TO MAKE THIS KNOT SECURE SO PATTERNS TEND TO BE COARSE WITH ILL-DEFINED 'STEPPED' CURVES.

THE SEHNA KNOT (ABOVE) IS STRONGER THAN THE GHIORDES & IS USED FOR THE FINEST CARPETS, WITH VERY SHORT PILE. THE WORLD RECORD IS 2,490 KNOTS PER SQUARE INCH.

WILTON CARPETS

WILTON CARPETS ARE MADE BY LAYING THE DIFFERENT COLOURED WOOLS OF THE PILE ACROSS THE LOOM & PULLING LOOPS OF THE REQUIRED COLOUR THROUGH THE BACKING FABRIC. THE LOOPS ARE THEN CUT IN THE MIDDLE TO MAKE 2 TUFTS OF PILE. AS ALL THE COLOURS IN THE DESIGN RUN THE WHOLE WIDTH OF THE CARPET, WHETHER THEY ARE VISIBLE OR NOT, WILTON CARPETS HAVE A LUXURIOUS THICKNESS & ARE EXPENSIVE.

AXMINSTER CARPETS

AXMINSTER CARPETS ARE MADE BY LOOPING INDIVIDUAL TUFTS OF WOOL THROUGH THE BACKING FABRIC ON THE LOOM. THEY ARE LESS WASTEFUL OF WOOL THAN WILTONS & CAN INCORPORATE MANY MORE COLOURS IN THE DESIGN.

A HAPPY CARPET

MANY PERSIAN CARPETS IN THE SHAH'S PALACES HAD POEMS & INSCRIPTIONS PRAISING HIM WOVEN INTO THE DESIGN. ONE EXAMPLE, FROM THE 1600s, BEGINS: "THE PRECIOUS ROYAL CARPET WHICH LIES ON THE GROUND BOASTS THAT HIS RANK & SPLENDOUR ARE GREATER THAN ALL THINGS IN THE FIRMAMENT. HE HAS FALLEN UNDER THE FEET OF THE KING, AND IS VERY HAPPY BECAUSE HE IS SURROUNDED BY MANY BEAUTIFUL WOMEN."

THE CHINESE PILLAR RUG

THE CHINESE ARE NOT PARTICULARLY NOTED FOR THEIR CARPETS EXCEPT FOR ONE UNIQUE DESIGN. THIS IS THE PILLAR RUG, WHICH IS VERY LONG & NARROW TO WRAP AROUND PILLARS. THE DESIGN LOOKS MOST PECULIAR UNTIL THE RUG IS WOUND SPIRALLY ROUND A PILLAR, & THEN IT BECOMES CLEAR.

MODERN CARPETS

ALL CHEAP CARPETS TODAY ARE MADE BY STITCHING OR GLUING THE TUFTS OF PILE TO A PREVIOUSLY WOVEN BACKING MATERIAL. IN ONE INGENIOUS PROCESS THE TUFTS ARE CHOPPED TO A UNIFORM LENGTH, THEN DIRECTED ONTO AN ADHESIVE COATED BACKING, USING AN ELECTROSTATIC FIELD TO PROJECT THEM & MAINTAIN THEIR UPRIGHT POSITION IN THE PILE.

CARPET FOOTPRINTS

A METHOD HAS RECENTLY BEEN DISCOVERED FOR REVEALING FOOTPRINTS ON NYLON & ACRYLIC CARPETS. THE CONTACT BETWEEN SHOES & CARPET GENERATES STATIC CHARGES WHICH LAST FOR SEVERAL DAYS. THESE CAN BE DETECTED BY SPILLING SMALL PLASTIC BEADS ON THE CARPET, WHICH CONGREGATE WHERE THE CHARGE IS GREATEST. THE POLICE ARE CONSIDERING ADOPTING IT AS A STANDARD INVESTIGATION PROCEDURE.

HOW TO MAKE YOUR HANDS INTO A SAILOR

BORROW A PIPE, THEN ARRANGE HANDS AS ABOVE, CLOSE TO A WALL IN FRONT OF A TABLE LIGHT. SHADOW SAILOR WILL APPEAR ON WALL.

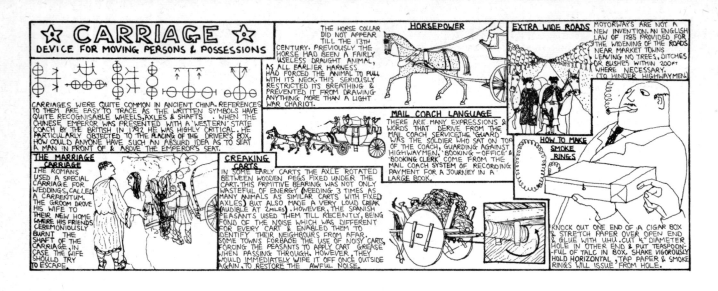

☆ CARRIAGE ☆
DEVICE FOR MOVING PERSONS & POSSESSIONS

CARRIAGES WERE QUITE COMMON IN ANCIENT CHINA. REFERENCES TO THEM ARE EASY TO TRACE AS THE WRITTEN SYMBOLS HAVE QUITE RECOGNISABLE WHEELS, AXLES & SHAFTS. WHEN THE CHINESE EMPEROR WAS PRESENTED WITH A WESTERN STATE COACH BY THE BRITISH IN 1912, HE WAS HIGHLY CRITICAL. HE PARTICULARLY OBJECTED TO THE PLACING OF THE DRIVER'S BOX. HOW COULD ANYONE HAVE SUCH AN ABSURD IDEA AS TO SEAT A MAN IN FRONT OF & ABOVE THE EMPEROR'S SEAT.

THE MARRIAGE CARRIAGE
THE ROMANS USED A SPECIAL CARRIAGE FOR WEDDINGS, CALLED A CARPENTUM. THE GROOM DROVE HIS WIFE TO THEIR NEW HOME WHERE HIS FRIENDS CEREMONIOUSLY BURNT THE SHAFT OF THE CARRIAGE, IN CASE THE WIFE SHOULD TRY TO ESCAPE.

CREAKING CARTS
IN SOME EARLY CARTS THE AXLE ROTATED BETWEEN WOODEN PEGS FIXED UNDER THE CART. THIS PRIMITIVE BEARING WAS NOT ONLY WASTEFUL OF ENERGY (NEEDING 3 TIMES AS MANY ANIMALS AS SIMILAR CARTS WITH FIXED AXLES) BUT ALSO MADE A VERY LOUD CREAK (AUDIBLE AT 2 MILES). HOWEVER, THE SPANISH PEASANTS USED THEM TILL RECENTLY, BEING FOND OF THE NOISE WHICH WAS DIFFERENT FOR EVERY CART & ENABLED THEM TO IDENTIFY THEIR NEIGHBOURS FROM AFAR. SOME TOWNS FORBADE THE USE OF NOISY CARTS, FORCING THE PEASANTS TO APPLY CART GREASE WHEN PASSING THROUGH. HOWEVER, THEY WOULD IMMEDIATELY WIPE IT OFF ONCE OUTSIDE AGAIN, TO RESTORE THE AWFUL NOISE.

HORSEPOWER
THE HORSE COLLAR DID NOT APPEAR TILL THE 13TH CENTURY. PREVIOUSLY THE HORSE HAD BEEN A FAIRLY USELESS DRAUGHT ANIMAL, AS ALL EARLIER HARNESS HAD FORCED THE ANIMAL TO PULL WITH ITS NECK. THIS SERIOUSLY RESTRICTED ITS BREATHING & PREVENTED IT FROM DRAWING ANYTHING MORE THAN A LIGHT WAR CHARIOT.

MAIL COACH LANGUAGE
THERE ARE MANY EXPRESSIONS & WORDS THAT DERIVE FROM THE MAIL COACH SERVICE. THE 'GUARD' WAS THE SOLDIER WHO SAT ON TOP OF THE COACH, GUARDING AGAINST HIGHWAYMEN. 'BOOKING-OFFICE' & 'BOOKING CLERK' COME FROM THE MAIL COACH SYSTEM OF RECORDING PAYMENT FOR A JOURNEY IN A LARGE BOOK.

EXTRA WIDE ROADS
MOTORWAYS ARE NOT A NEW INVENTION. AN ENGLISH LAW OF 1285 PROVIDED FOR THE WIDENING OF THE ROADS NEAR MARKET TOWNS LEAVING NO TREES, DITCHES OR BUSHES WITHIN 200FT WHERE NECESSARY. (TO HINDER HIGHWAYMEN)

HOW TO MAKE SMOKE RINGS
KNOCK OUT ONE END OF A CIGAR BOX & STRETCH PAPER OVER OPEN END & GLUE WITH UHU. CUT ½" DIAMETER HOLE IN OTHER END & PUT TEASPOONFUL OF TALC IN BOX. SHAKE VIGOROUSLY. HOLD HORIZONTAL, TAP PAPER & SMOKE RINGS WILL ISSUE FROM HOLE.

☆ CARTOON FILM ☆
SEQUENCES OF DRAWINGS GIVING ILLUSION OF MOVEMENT

MATCH APPEAL
THE FIRST BRITISH ANIMATED FILM WAS AN 1899 BOER WAR APPEAL MADE FOR BRYANT & MAY. IT DEPICTED A PLATOON OF MATCHSTICK MEN WHO CLIMB A WALL & FORM THEMSELVES INTO THE WORDS: 'SEND £1 & ENOUGH MATCHES WILL BE SENT TO SUPPLY A REGIMENT OF OUR FIGHTING SOLDIERS'

THE ENCHANTED DRAWING
THIS WAS THE FIRST FILM TO USE CARTOON DRAWINGS (1900). IT DEPICTED AN ARTIST SKETCHING A FACE. WHEN THE ARTIST STOPPED FOR A DRINK THE FACE LOOKED SAD – CHANGING TO HAPPINESS WHEN HE ADDED A DRINK TO THE DRAWING.

FIRST APPEARANCES

MICKEY MOUSE 'STEAMBOAT WILLIE', 1928. IN 1953 DISNEY SAID: 'MICKEY IS TOO SWEET TEMPERED FOR MODERN TASTE'. NO FURTHER FILMS WERE MADE.

DONALD DUCK 'THE WISE LITTLE HEN', 1934.

TOM & JERRY 'PUSS GETS THE BOOTS', 1939.

BUGS BUNNY 'PORKY'S HARE HUNT', 1938. APPEARED AS A HARE; BECAME A RABBIT IN 1940.

ROAD RUNNER 'FAST & FURRY-OUS', 1948.

COST
ANIMATION IS EXPENSIVE BECAUSE IT REQUIRES 12 DRAWINGS PER SECOND, SO IT TAKES A LONG TIME. WALT DISNEY'S 'SNOW WHITE' TOOK 750-2,000 PEOPLE 5 YEARS TO MAKE.

SOUND
MOST CARTOON FILMS ARE MADE BY RECORDING THE SOUND FIRST & THEN ADDING THE DRAWINGS TO FIT PRECISELY.

CELLS
FIGURES ARE USUALLY COPIED ONTO TRANSPARENT CELLS TO AVOID THE BACKGROUND HAVING TO BE REDRAWN ON EVERY FRAME OF THE FILM. WHEN ONLY PART OF A FIGURE MOVES IT IS OFTEN DRAWN ON A SEPARATE CELL SO THE REST OF THE FIGURE NEED NOT BE REDRAWN.

COMPUTERS
COMPUTERS ARE NOW WIDELY USED FOR CONTROLLING CAMERA MOVEMENTS & FOR ANIMATING SIMPLE SHAPES. THE FIRST & FINAL POSITIONS ARE DRAWN BY HAND & THE COMPUTER DOES THE INBETWEEN DRAWINGS. EVENTUALLY, COMPUTER VIDEO SYSTEMS WILL DO THESE DRAWINGS & IMMEDIATELY 'REPLAY' THE ACTION – ALLOWING ANIMATORS MORE FREEDOM TO EXPERIMENT.

LIGHT NEGATIVES
THE EFFECT OF A 'LUMINESCENT LINE' ON A BLACK BACKGROUND, COMMON IN MANY CURRENT ANIMATED ADVERTS IS ACHIEVED BY SHOOTING THE FILM AS ORDINARY DRAWINGS & THEN FILMING THE NEGATIVES WITH A LIGHT SHINING FROM BEHIND.

HOW TO MAKE A CARTOON FROM A CHEQUE BOOK STUB
DRAW A MATCHSTICK MAN ON THE BACK OF THE FIRST CHEQUE STUB. TURN OVER SECOND STUB SO YOU CAN SEE FIRST MAN FAINTLY THROUGH IT, & COPY MAN ONTO 2ND STUB, MOVING ARMS & LEGS SLIGHTLY. REPEAT WITH EACH STUB MAKING SMALL CHANGES IN EACH MAN. FLICK THROUGH STUBS & MAN WILL APPEAR TO MOVE.

☆ CASTLES ☆

RESIDENCES PROVIDING PROTECTION FROM UNWELCOME VISITORS

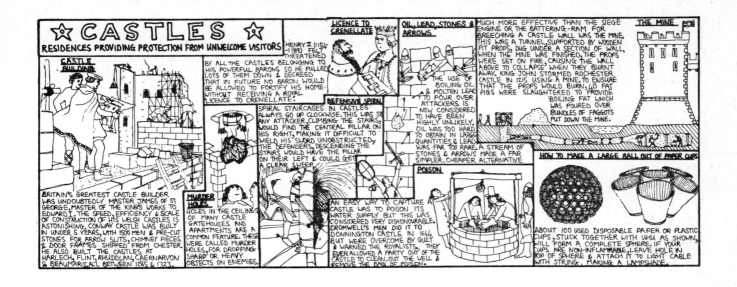

CASTLE BUILDING

BRITAIN'S GREATEST CASTLE BUILDER WAS UNDOUBTEDLY MASTER JAMES OF ST GEORGE, MASTER OF THE KING'S WORKS TO EDWARD I. THE SPEED, EFFICIENCY & SCALE OF CONSTRUCTION OF HIS WELSH CASTLES IS ASTONISHING. CONWAY CASTLE WAS BUILT IN UNDER 5 YEARS, WITH 1500 MEN & PRE-CUT STONES FOR ARROW SLITS, CHIMNEY PIECES & DOOR FRAMES SHIPPED FROM CHESTER. HE ALSO BUILT THE CASTLES AT HARLECH, FLINT, RHUDDLAN, CAERNARVON & BEAUMARIS, ALL BETWEEN 1285 & 1323.

LICENCE TO CRENELLATE

HENRY II (1154-1189) FELT THREATENED BY ALL THE CASTLES BELONGING TO HIS POWERFUL BARONS SO HE PULLED LOTS OF THEM DOWN & DECREED THAT IN FUTURE NO BARON WOULD BE ALLOWED TO FORTIFY HIS HOME WITHOUT RECEIVING A ROYAL LICENCE TO CRENELLATE.

DEFENSIVE SPIRAL

SPIRAL STAIRCASES IN CASTLES ALWAYS GO UP CLOCKWISE. THIS WAS SO ANY ATTACKER CLIMBING THE STAIRS WOULD FIND THE CENTRAL PILLAR ON HIS RIGHT, MAKING IT DIFFICULT TO WIELD HIS SWORD UNOBSTRUCTED. THE DEFENDERS, DESCENDING THE STAIRS WOULD HAVE THE PILLAR ON THEIR LEFT & COULD GET A CLEAR SWEEP.

MURDER HOLES

HOLES IN THE CEILINGS OF MANY CASTLE GATEHOUSES AND APARTMENTS ARE A COMMON FEATURE. THESE WERE CALLED MURDER HOLES, FOR DROPPING SHARP OR HEAVY OBJECTS ON ENEMIES.

OIL, LEAD, STONES & ARROWS

THE USE OF BOILING OIL & MOLTEN LEAD TO POUR OVER ATTACKERS IS NOW CONSIDERED TO HAVE BEEN HIGHLY UNLIKELY. OIL WAS TOO HARD TO OBTAIN IN LARGE QUANTITIES & LEAD WAS FAR TOO RARE. A STREAM OF STONES & ARROWS MADE A FAR SIMPLER, CHEAPER ALTERNATIVE.

POISON

AN EASY WAY TO CAPTURE A CASTLE WAS TO POISON ITS WATER SUPPLY BUT THIS WAS CONSIDERED VERY DISHONOURABLE. CROMWELL'S MEN DID IT TO DONNINGTON CASTLE IN 1644 BUT WERE OVERCOME BY GUILT & WARNED THE ROYALISTS. THEY EVEN ALLOWED A PARTY OUT OF THE CASTLE TO CLEAN OUT THE WELL & REMOVE THE BAGS OF POISON.

MUCH MORE EFFECTIVE THAN THE SIEGE ENGINE OR THE BATTERING-RAM FOR BREECHING A CASTLE WALL WAS THE MINE. THIS WAS A TUNNEL, SUPPORTED BY WOODEN PIT PROPS, DUG UNDER A SECTION OF WALL. WHEN THE MINE WAS FINISHED, THE PROPS WERE SET ON FIRE, CAUSING THE WALL ABOVE TO COLLAPSE WHEN THEY BURNT AWAY. KING JOHN STORMED ROCHESTER CASTLE IN 1215 USING A MINE. TO ENSURE THAT THE PROPS WOULD BURN, 40 FAT PIGS WERE SLAUGHTERED TO PROVIDE 'BOILING FAT' WHICH WAS POURED OVER BUNDLES OF FAGGOTS PUT DOWN THE MINE.

THE MINE

HOW TO MAKE A LARGE BALL OUT OF PAPER CUPS

ABOUT 100 USED DISPOSABLE PAPER OR PLASTIC CUPS, STUCK TOGETHER WITH UHU AS SHOWN, WILL FORM A COMPLETE SPHERE. IF YOUR CUPS ARE NON-INFLAMMABLE, LEAVE HOLE IN TOP OF SPHERE & ATTACH IT TO LIGHT CABLE WITH STRING, MAKING A LAMPSHADE.

☆ CATHEDRALS ☆

PRINCIPLE CHURCHES OF BISHOPS' DIOCESES

SUPPORTING THE ROOF

A MAJOR PROBLEM IN BUILDING ARCHED VAULTS IS THE OUTWARD FORCE THEY EXERT ON THEIR SUPPORTS. THIS CAN ONLY BE RESISTED BY MAKING THE SUPPORTS EXTREMELY HEAVY. MORTAR UNFORTUNATELY DOES NOT ACT AS A GLUE, IT ONLY HELPS THE STONES TO REST ON EACH OTHER WITHOUT WOBBLING. THE GOTHIC MASTER MASONS WERE HIGHLY INGENIOUS AT MAKING THEIR SUPPORTS APPEAR AS LIGHT AS POSSIBLE. THEY DEVELOPED POINTED ARCHES INSTEAD OF ROUND ARCHES, AS THESE PUSH OUTWARD LESS, & FLYING BUTTRESSES, PILLARS CONNECTED TO SUPPORTS, ADDING TO THEIR EFFECTIVE WEIGHT.

BUILDERS AT WORK

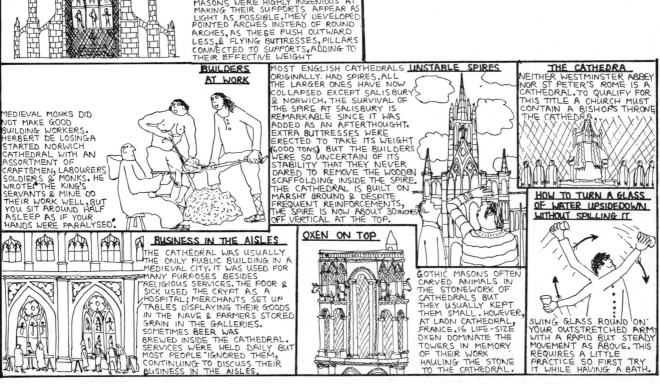

MEDIEVAL MONKS DID NOT MAKE GOOD BUILDING WORKERS. HERBERT DE LOSINGA STARTED NORWICH CATHEDRAL WITH AN ASSORTMENT OF CRAFTSMEN, LABOURERS SOLDIERS & MONKS. HE WROTE: "THE KING'S SERVANTS & MINE DO THEIR WORK WELL, BUT YOU SIT AROUND HALF ASLEEP AS IF YOUR HANDS WERE PARALYSED."

UNSTABLE SPIRES

MOST ENGLISH CATHEDRALS ORIGINALLY HAD SPIRES. ALL THE LARGER ONES HAVE NOW COLLAPSED EXCEPT SALISBURY & NORWICH. THE SURVIVAL OF THE SPIRE AT SALISBURY IS REMARKABLE SINCE IT WAS ADDED AS AN AFTERTHOUGHT. EXTRA BUTTRESSES WERE ERECTED TO TAKE ITS WEIGHT (6000 TONS) BUT THE BUILDERS WERE SO UNCERTAIN OF ITS STABILITY THAT THEY NEVER DARED TO REMOVE THE WOODEN SCAFFOLDING INSIDE THE SPIRE. THE CATHEDRAL IS BUILT ON MARSHY GROUND & DESPITE FREQUENT REINFORCEMENTS, THE SPIRE IS NOW ABOUT 30 INCHES OFF VERTICAL AT THE TOP.

THE CATHEDRA

NEITHER WESTMINSTER ABBEY NOR ST PETER'S ROME IS A CATHEDRAL. TO QUALIFY FOR THIS TITLE A CHURCH MUST CONTAIN A BISHOP'S THRONE, THE CATHEDRA.

HOW TO TURN A GLASS OF WATER UPSIDEDOWN WITHOUT SPILLING IT

SWING GLASS ROUND ON YOUR OUTSTRETCHED ARM WITH A RAPID BUT STEADY MOVEMENT AS ABOVE. THIS REQUIRES A LITTLE PRACTICE SO FIRST TRY IT WHILE HAVING A BATH.

BUSINESS IN THE AISLES

THE CATHEDRAL WAS USUALLY THE ONLY PUBLIC BUILDING IN A MEDIEVAL CITY. IT WAS USED FOR MANY PURPOSES BESIDES RELIGIOUS SERVICES. THE POOR & SICK USED THE CRYPT AS A HOSPITAL; MERCHANTS SET UP TABLES DISPLAYING THEIR GOODS IN THE NAVE & FARMERS STORED GRAIN IN THE GALLERIES. SOMETIMES BEER WAS BREWED INSIDE THE CATHEDRAL. SERVICES WERE HELD DAILY BUT MOST PEOPLE IGNORED THEM, CONTINUING TO DISCUSS THEIR BUSINESS IN THE AISLES.

OXEN ON TOP

GOTHIC MASONS OFTEN CARVED ANIMALS IN THE STONEWORK OF CATHEDRALS BUT THEY USUALLY KEPT THEM SMALL. HOWEVER, AT LAON CATHEDRAL, FRANCE, 16 LIFE-SIZE OXEN DOMINATE THE TOWERS IN MEMORY OF THEIR WORK HAULING THE STONE TO THE CATHEDRAL.

☆ CATS ☆
SMALL DOMESTICATED CARNIVORES

CAT ATTACK
THE ANCIENT EGYPTIAN VENERATION OF CATS WAS USED TO GOOD EFFECT BY THEIR ENEMIES, THE PERSIANS, IN 500BC. THE EGYPTIANS, BESIEGED IN THE TOWN OF PELUSIUM, RESISTED SUCCESSFULLY UNTIL THE PERSIANS ATTACKED, EACH CARRYING A CAT WITH HUNDREDS OF CATS RUNNING AHEAD. THE EGYPTIANS WOULD NOT THROW THEIR SPEARS FOR FEAR OF KILLING THE CATS & SURRENDERED.

CAT SCARES
DEAD CATS, WITH MICE IN THEIR TEETH, WERE BUILT INTO THE FOUNDATIONS OF SOME ENGLISH 14th–18thC HOUSES TO SCARE AWAY RATS.

AN ANCIENT SCOTTISH METHOD OF RAISING THE DEVIL WAS TO ROAST A SUCCESSION OF LIVE CATS FOR 4 DAYS. ONLY THE MOST CALLOUS COULD SURVIVE THE APPALLING SCREAMS.

CAT EXPORT
THE ANCIENT EGYPTIANS FORBADE THE EXPORT OF CATS SO THE GREEKS & ROMANS REMAINED WITHOUT THEM UNTIL ABOUT 100AD. MICE IN GRANARIES WERE CONTROLLED BY FERRETS & WEASELS WHICH OFTEN ATE CHICKENS & DUCKS AS WELL.

CAT POPULATION
6,000,000
BRITAIN'S CAT POPULATION IS ESTIMATED TO BE 6,000,000. 100,000 ARE USED ON GOVERNMENT PROPERTY, CONTROLLING MICE.

CAT PUNISHMENT
AN ANCIENT ICELANDIC PUNISHMENT CONSISTED OF DROPPING A WOMAN, TIED IN A SACK WITH A CAT, INTO A POND FOR SEVERAL MINUTES.

CAT SCREAMS

CAT FERTILISER
AN EGYPTIAN TEMPLE AT BENI-HASSAN EXCAVATED IN THE 19th CENTURY, YIELDED 300,000 MUMMIFIED CATS. THEY WERE SHIPPED TO LIVERPOOL & SOLD AS FERTILISER AT £4 A TONNE.

ISLAMIC CATS
THE ANCIENT EGYPTIAN FEELING FOR CATS HAS CONTINUED IN THE ISLAMIC WORLD. CATS ARE SAID TO HAVE BEEN MOHAMMED'S FAVOURITE ANIMALS. SOME TABBY CATS ARE BELIEVED TO BE HOLY: FOUR STRIPES BETWEEN THE EARS INDICATE WHERE THEY HAVE BEEN STROKED BY THE PROPHET.

CAT DIET
THE DIET OF FARM CATS IS HIGHLY VARIED. BESIDES MICE & YOUNG BIRDS, THEY EAT MOLES, SLOW WORMS, WEASELS & INSECTS (MAINLY GRASSHOPPERS).

CAT FALLS
CATS CAN FALL GREAT DISTANCES WITHOUT HARM. IN 1964 ONE FELL 11 STOREYS FROM A FLAT IN MAIDA VALE, LONDON.

CATS' EYES
CATS HAVE LIMITED COLOUR VISION. IT HAS RECENTLY BEEN FOUND THAT THEY CAN DISTINGUISH COLOUR ONLY OF VERY LARGE OR CLOSE OBJECTS (COVERING AN ANGLE OF OVER 45°).

☆ CAVES ☆
HOLLOW AREAS ENCLOSED BY ROCK

CAVE JARGON
ANIMALS WHO LIVE EXCLUSIVELY IN CAVES ARE CALLED TROGLODYTES. THOSE WHO SOMETIMES LIVE IN CAVES ARE CALLED TROGLOPHILES & THOSE WHO ARE JUST CASUAL VISITORS ARE CALLED TROGLOXENES. MEN WHO STUDY CAVES ARE CALLED SPELEOLOGISTS OR SPELUNKERS.

A CAPACIOUS CAVERN
EUROPE'S LARGEST CAVE CHAMBER, NEAR TRIESTE, IS CALLED, APPROPRIATELY THE GROTTA DEI GIGANTI. IT IS LARGE ENOUGH TO CONTAIN A CATHEDRAL.

ENDURANCE
MR VELJKOVIC, A YUGOSLAV SPELEOLOGIST, STAYED UNDERGROUND FOR 463 DAYS WITHOUT ANY COMMUNICATION WITH THE OUTSIDE WORLD. HE TOOK A NUMBER OF CATS, DOGS, HENS & DUCKS WITH HIM FOR COMPANY. HE REPORTED AFTERWARDS THAT HIS ANIMALS DID NOT SEEM GREATLY AFFECTED (THE HENS EVEN CONTINUED TO LAY NORMALLY). HE FOUND FLIES, WHICH PESTERED HIM RELENTLESSLY, THE WORST ASPECT OF HIS ORDEAL.

MOONMILK
A PALE POWDERY SUBSTANCE IS OFTEN FOUND COATING THE WALLS, FLOORS & ROOFS OF CAVES. THE BACTERIAL ACTION BY WHICH THIS IS FORMED IS NOT UNDERSTOOD. IT IS CALLED MOONMILK.

STALACTITES
STALACTITES ARE FORMED BY DRIPS OF CALCITE SOLUTION SLOWLY CRYSTALLISING. THE WORLD'S LONGEST, IN IRELAND, MEASURES 198FT LONG. THEY OFTEN SHOW CONCENTRIC GROWTH RINGS WHEN SECTIONED, SIMILAR TO TREES. IN CAVES THAT FREEZE UP IN WINTER, THE FLOW OF CALCITE SOLUTION HALTS ANNUALLY, LEAVING A RING. THE RINGS CAN THEN BE USED TO DATE THE STALACTITE.

A USEFUL TOOL
AN INGENIOUS DEVICE TO ASSIST CLIMBING ABOUT INSIDE CAVES IS MADE OF INTERLOCKING ALUMINIUM SCAFFOLD POLES. IT IS CALLED THE MAYPOLE.

CAVERNOUS PERPETUAL MOTION
A SEA MILL ON KEFALLINIA, A GREEK ISLAND, IS POWERED BY WATER WHICH CASCADES FROM THE SEA DOWN INTO SLITS IN THE ROCK. DYE, POURED THROUGH THE SLITS, HAS BEEN FOUND TO REAPPEAR ON THE FAR SIDE OF THE ISLAND 3FT ABOVE SEA LEVEL. THE EXPLANATION OF THIS UPHILL FLOW IS THAT FRESH WATER STREAMS FLOW INTO THE CAVE SYSTEM, WHICH DILUTES THE CONCENTRATION OF SALT IN THE CAVE SYSTEM. THE WEAKER BRINE IS LESS DENSE SO IT RISES, SIPHONING THE STRONGER BRINE THROUGH.

'THE BLIND CAVE NEWT'
THE BLIND CAVE NEWT IS A CURIOUS CREATURE FOUND ONLY IN CERTAIN POLISH CAVES. IT HAS EYES WHEN BORN BUT THESE DISAPPEAR AS IT DEVELOPS. ITS BODY IS SLIGHTLY PINK & RESEMBLES HUMAN FLESH (IT IS SOMETIMES CALLED THE HUMAN FISH). IF IT IS EXPOSED TO CONTINUOUS LIGHT, PIGMENT CELLS ARE ACTIVATED & IT TURNS BLACK.

HOW TO 'PROVE' 1 = 2
LET $X = Y$
$$X - Y = O$$
ALSO $2X - 2Y = O$
$$2X - 2Y = X - Y$$
$$2(X - Y) = (X - Y)$$
$\div X - Y$ EACH SIDE
$$2 = 1$$

THE FALLACY IN THE ABOVE 'PROOF' IS THAT NUMBERS CAN NOT BE DIVIDED BY O SO THE PROCESS $\div (X - Y)$ IS IMPOSSIBLE.

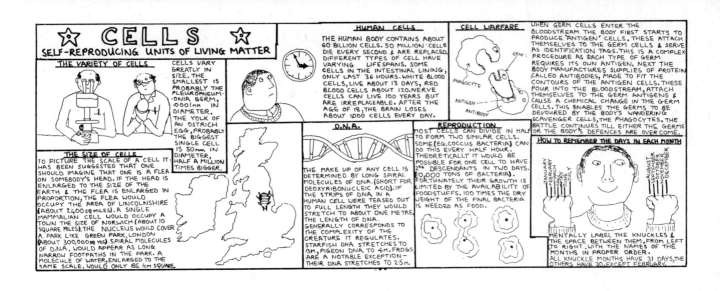

☆ CELLS ☆
SELF-REPRODUCING UNITS OF LIVING MATTER

THE VARIETY OF CELLS

CELLS VARY GREATLY IN SIZE. THE SMALLEST IS PROBABLY THE PLEUROPNEUM-ONIA GERM, .0001mm IN DIAMETER. THE YOLK OF AN OSTRICH EGG, PROBABLY THE BIGGEST SINGLE CELL IS 50mm IN DIAMETER, HALF A MILLION TIMES BIGGER.

THE SIZE OF CELLS

TO PICTURE THE SCALE OF A CELL IT HAS BEEN SUGGESTED THAT ONE SHOULD IMAGINE THAT ONE IS A FLEA ON SOMEBODY'S HEAD. IF THE HEAD IS ENLARGED TO THE SIZE OF THE EARTH & THE FLEA IS ENLARGED IN PROPORTION, THE FLEA WOULD OCCUPY THE AREA OF LINCOLNSHIRE (ABOUT 2400 SQ MILES). A SINGLE MAMMALIAN CELL WOULD OCCUPY A TOWN THE SIZE OF NORWICH (ABOUT 10 SQUARE MILES). THE NUCLEUS WOULD COVER A PARK LIKE GREEN PARK, LONDON (ABOUT 300,000 SQ YDS). SPIRAL MOLECULES OF D.N.A. WOULD APPEAR AS LONG NARROW FOOTPATHS IN THE PARK. A MOLECULE OF WATER, ENLARGED TO THE SAME SCALE, WOULD ONLY BE 1cm SQUARE.

HUMAN CELLS

THE HUMAN BODY CONTAINS ABOUT 60 BILLION CELLS. 50 MILLION CELLS DIE EVERY SECOND & ARE REPLACED. DIFFERENT TYPES OF CELL HAVE VARYING LIFESPANS. SOME CELLS IN THE INTESTINAL LINING, ONLY LAST 36 HOURS. WHITE BLOOD CELLS, LIVE ABOUT 13 DAYS, RED BLOOD CELLS ABOUT 120. NERVE CELLS CAN LIVE 100 YEARS BUT ARE IRREPLACEABLE. AFTER THE AGE OF 18, THE BRAIN LOSES ABOUT 1,000 CELLS EVERY DAY.

D.N.A.

THE MAKE UP OF ANY CELL IS DETERMINED BY LONG SPIRAL MOLECULES OF DNA. (SHORT FOR DEOXYRIBONUCLEIC ACID). IF THE STRIPS OF DNA IN A HUMAN CELL WERE TEASED OUT TO FULL LENGTH THEY WOULD STRETCH TO ABOUT ONE METRE. THE LENGTH OF DNA GENERALLY CORRESPONDS TO THE COMPLEXITY OF THE CREATURE IT REGULATES. STARFISH DNA STRETCHES TO 3M, PIGEON DNA TO 6M. FROGS ARE A NOTABLE EXCEPTION – THEIR DNA STRETCHES TO 2.5M.

REPRODUCTION

MOST CELLS CAN DIVIDE IN HALF TO FORM TWO SIMILAR CELLS. SOME (EG. COCCUS BACTERIA) CAN DO THIS EVERY HALF HOUR. THEORETICALLY IT WOULD BE POSSIBLE FOR ONE CELL TO HAVE 2^{96} DESCENDANTS IN TWO DAYS. (10,000 TONS OF BACTERIA). FORTUNATELY THEIR GROWTH IS LIMITED BY THE AVAILABILITY OF FOODSTUFFS. 100 TIMES THE DRY WEIGHT OF THE FINAL BACTERIA IS NEEDED AS FOOD.

CELL WARFARE

GERM
PHAGOCYTE
ANTIGEN
ANTIBODY

WHEN GERM CELLS ENTER THE BLOODSTREAM THE BODY FIRST STARTS TO PRODUCE 'ANTIGEN' CELLS. THESE ATTACH THEMSELVES TO THE GERM CELLS & SERVE AS IDENTIFICATION TAGS. THIS IS A COMPLEX PROCEDURE AS EACH TYPE OF GERM REQUIRES ITS OWN ANTIGEN. NEXT THE BODY MANUFACTURES SUPPLIES OF PROTEIN CALLED ANTIBODIES, MADE TO FIT THE CONTOURS OF THE ANTIGEN CELLS. THESE POUR INTO THE BLOODSTREAM, ATTACH THEMSELVES TO THE GERM ANTIGENS & CAUSE A CHEMICAL CHANGE IN THE GERM CELLS. THIS ENABLES THE GERMS TO BE DEVOURED BY THE BODY'S WANDERING SCAVENGER CELLS, THE PHAGOCYTES. THE BATTLE CONTINUES TILL EITHER THE GERMS OR THE BODY'S DEFENCES ARE OVERCOME.

HOW TO REMEMBER THE DAYS IN EACH MONTH

MENTALLY LABEL THE KNUCKLES & THE SPACE BETWEEN THEM, FROM LEFT TO RIGHT, WITH THE NAMES OF THE MONTHS IN PROPER ORDER. ALL KNUCKLE MONTHS HAVE 31 DAYS, THE OTHERS HAVE 30, EXCEPT FEBRUARY.

☆ CELLULOSE ☆
LONG UNBRANCHED CHAINS OF GLUCOSE MOLECULES

CELLULOID

THE AMERICANS STARTED EXPERIMENTS WITH PARKESINE INDUCED BY AN OFFER OF £10,000 FROM A BILLIARD BALL MANUF-ACTURER WHO WAS BADLY IN NEED OF A SUBSTITUTE FOR IVORY. IT WAS FOUND THAT CAMPHOR WORKED BETTER THAN VEGET-ABLE OILS & THE NEW VERSION WAS NAMED 'CELLULOID'.

CELLOPHANE IS MADE OF CELLULOSE MIXED WITH A SOLVENT WHICH IS EVAPORATED TO LEAVE A THIN, TRANSPARENT FILM. IT IS THINLY COATED WITH LACQUER (VARNISH), ON BOTH SIDES BECAUSE PURE CELLOPHANE IS SOLUBLE IN WATER.

FIRE

CELLULOID IS HIGHLY FLAMMABLE. EARLY DETACHABLE COLLARS MADE OF IT WERE SOMETIMES IGNITED BY CIG-ARETTES CAUSING SERIOUS BURNS. IT IS NOW ONLY USED FOR 'PING-PONG' BALLS, GUITAR PLECTRUMS & DRUM TRIM – FOR WHICH NO SUBSTITUTES HAVE BEEN FOUND.

RAYON

THE FIRST NON-FLAMMABLE PLASTIC WAS CELLULOSE ACETATE (MADE BY USING VINEGAR INSTEAD OF NITRIC ACID IN THE CELLULOID PROCESS). THIS WAS DRAWN INTO FILAMENTS & SPUN TO MAKE RAYON.

DRIP-DRY CLOTHES

CELLULOSE TRI-ACETATE WAS FIRST USED FOR WATER-PROOFING THE CANVAS ON WORLD WAR I AIRCRAFT. BY THE END OF THE WAR THERE WERE HUGE STOCKS OF IT. EXPERIMENTS WITH THE SURPLUS LED TO THE INVENTION OF 'CELANESE' FIBRES & THE FIRST 'DRIP-DRY' CLOTHING.

ENERGY

SOME EXPERTS BELIEVE THAT THE MOST PROMISING RENEWABLE ENERGY SOURCE IS CELLULOSE. IT CAN BE CONVERTED TO SUGAR OR METHANE OR BURNT AS FUEL. ACCORDING TO ONE ESTIMATE, A 250-MILE SQUARE OF HYBRID, FAST GROWING POPLAR TREES COULD PROVIDE ENOUGH FUEL TO POWER EVERY US ELECTRICITY GENERATING STATION.

HOW TO MAKE A PENCIL CHANGE COLOUR

WRAP COLOURED PIECE OF PAPER NEATLY ROUND PENCIL & SECURE WITH THIN STRIP OF SELLOTAPE. SHOW PENCIL TO AUDIENCE – THEN PULL IT THROUGH A HANKERCHIEF IN YOUR HAND, LEAVING PAPER COVER BEHIND.

SUGAR

CELLULOSE CONSISTS OF LONG CHAIN MOLECULES OF SUGAR (GLUCOSE). PLANTS CONVERT THE SUGARS IN THE SAP TO CELLULOSE. SOME ANIMALS, SUCH AS SHEEP & COWS CAN BREAK CELLULOSE DOWN AGAIN TO SUGARS IN THEIR STOMACHS.

PARKESINE

SAWDUST
ACID
CORN OIL

PARKESINE, THE EARLIEST PLASTIC (1860) WAS MADE BY DISSOLVING CELLULOSE (AS SAWDUST) IN NITRIC ACID & MIXING IT WITH VEGETABLE OILS. THIS MADE A DOUGH WHICH COULD BE PRESSED INTO MOULDS & HEATED TO SET IT.

ABUNDANCE

CELLULOSE IS THE MOST ABUNDANT BIOLOGICAL CHEMICAL IN THE WORLD. THE WALLS OF ALL PLANT CELLS ARE MADE OF IT. PLANTS & TREES MAKE 100 BILLION TONS OF IT A YEAR.

COTTON WOOL

NATURAL COTTON WOOL IS ONE OF THE PUREST FORMS OF CELLULOSE.

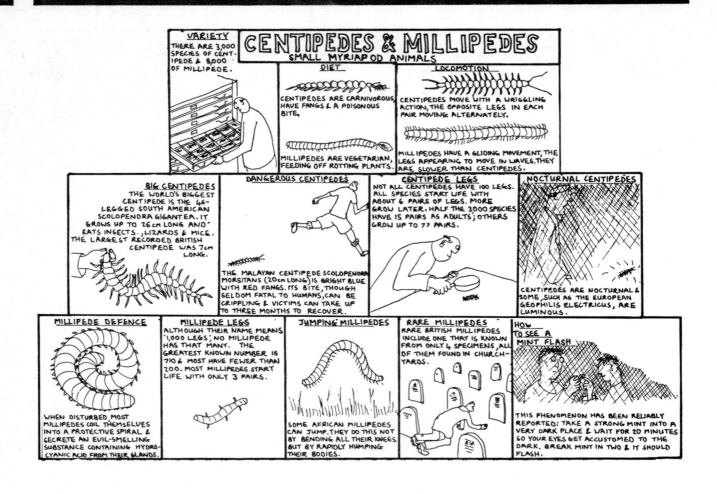

CENTIPEDES & MILLIPEDES
SMALL MYRIAPOD ANIMALS

VARIETY
THERE ARE 3,000 SPECIES OF CENTIPEDE & 8,000 OF MILLIPEDE.

DIET
CENTIPEDES ARE CARNIVOROUS, HAVE FANGS & A POISONOUS BITE.

MILLIPEDES ARE VEGETARIAN, FEEDING OFF ROTTING PLANTS.

LOCOMOTION
CENTIPEDES MOVE WITH A WRIGGLING ACTION, THE OPPOSITE LEGS IN EACH PAIR MOVING ALTERNATELY.

MILLIPEDES HAVE A GLIDING MOVEMENT, THE LEGS APPEARING TO MOVE IN WAVES. THEY ARE SLOWER THAN CENTIPEDES.

BIG CENTIPEDES
THE WORLD'S BIGGEST CENTIPEDE IS THE 46-LEGGED SOUTH AMERICAN SCOLOPENDRA GIGANTEA. IT GROWS UP TO 26cm LONG AND EATS INSECTS, LIZARDS & MICE. THE LARGEST RECORDED BRITISH CENTIPEDE WAS 7cm LONG.

DANGEROUS CENTIPEDES
THE MALAYAN CENTIPEDE SCOLOPENDRA MORSITANS (20cm LONG) IS BRIGHT BLUE WITH RED FANGS. ITS BITE, THOUGH SELDOM FATAL TO HUMANS, CAN BE CRIPPLING & VICTIMS CAN TAKE UP TO THREE MONTHS TO RECOVER.

CENTIPEDE LEGS
NOT ALL CENTIPEDES HAVE 100 LEGS. ALL SPECIES START LIFE WITH ABOUT 6 PAIRS OF LEGS. MORE GROW LATER. HALF THE 3,000 SPECIES HAVE 15 PAIRS AS ADULTS; OTHERS GROW UP TO 77 PAIRS.

NOCTURNAL CENTIPEDES
CENTIPEDES ARE NOCTURNAL & SOME, SUCH AS THE EUROPEAN GEOPHILIS ELECTRICUS, ARE LUMINOUS.

MILLIPEDE DEFENCE
WHEN DISTURBED, MOST MILLIPEDES COIL THEMSELVES INTO A PROTECTIVE SPIRAL & SECRETE AN EVIL-SMELLING SUBSTANCE CONTAINING HYDROCYANIC ACID FROM THEIR GLANDS.

MILLIPEDE LEGS
ALTHOUGH THEIR NAME MEANS '1,000 LEGS', NO MILLIPEDE HAS THAT MANY. THE GREATEST KNOWN NUMBER IS 710 & MOST HAVE FEWER THAN 200. MOST MILLIPEDES START LIFE WITH ONLY 3 PAIRS.

JUMPING MILLIPEDES
SOME AFRICAN MILLIPEDES CAN JUMP. THEY DO THIS NOT BY BENDING ALL THEIR KNEES BUT BY RAPIDLY HUMPING THEIR BODIES.

RARE MILLIPEDES
RARE BRITISH MILLIPEDES INCLUDE ONE THAT IS KNOWN FROM ONLY 4 SPECIMENS, ALL OF THEM FOUND IN CHURCHYARDS.

HOW TO SEE A MINT FLASH
THIS PHENOMENON HAS BEEN RELIABLY REPORTED: TAKE A STRONG MINT INTO A VERY DARK PLACE & WAIT FOR 20 MINUTES SO YOUR EYES GET ACCUSTOMED TO THE DARK. BREAK MINT IN TWO & IT SHOULD FLASH.

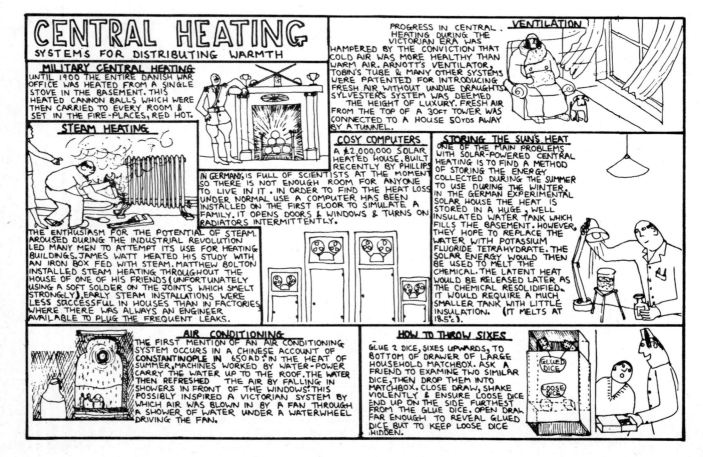

CENTRAL HEATING
SYSTEMS FOR DISTRIBUTING WARMTH

MILITARY CENTRAL HEATING
UNTIL 1900 THE ENTIRE DANISH WAR OFFICE WAS HEATED FROM A SINGLE STOVE IN THE BASEMENT. THIS HEATED CANNON BALLS WHICH WERE THEN CARRIED TO EVERY ROOM & SET IN THE FIRE-PLACES, RED HOT.

STEAM HEATING
THE ENTHUSIASM FOR THE POTENTIAL OF STEAM AROUSED DURING THE INDUSTRIAL REVOLUTION LED MANY MEN TO ATTEMPT ITS USE FOR HEATING BUILDINGS. JAMES WATT HEATED HIS STUDY WITH AN IRON BOX FED WITH STEAM. MATTHEW BOLTON INSTALLED STEAM HEATING THROUGHOUT THE HOUSE OF ONE OF HIS FRIENDS (UNFORTUNATELY USING A SOFT SOLDER ON THE JOINTS WHICH SMELT STRONGLY). EARLY STEAM INSTALLATIONS WERE LESS SUCCESSFUL IN HOUSES THAN IN FACTORIES WHERE THERE WAS ALWAYS AN ENGINEER AVAILABLE TO PLUG THE FREQUENT LEAKS.

VENTILATION
PROGRESS IN CENTRAL HEATING DURING THE VICTORIAN ERA WAS HAMPERED BY THE CONVICTION THAT COLD AIR WAS MORE HEALTHY THAN WARM AIR. ARNOTT'S VENTILATOR, TOBIN'S TUBE & MANY OTHER SYSTEMS WERE PATENTED FOR INTRODUCING FRESH AIR WITHOUT UNDUE DRAUGHTS. SYLVESTER'S SYSTEM WAS DEEMED THE HEIGHT OF LUXURY. FRESH AIR FROM THE TOP OF A 30FT TOWER WAS CONNECTED TO A HOUSE 50YDS AWAY BY A TUNNEL.

COSY COMPUTERS
A £2,000,000 SOLAR HEATED HOUSE, BUILT RECENTLY BY PHILLIPS IN GERMANY, IS FULL OF SCIENTISTS AT THE MOMENT SO THERE IS NOT ENOUGH ROOM FOR ANYONE TO LIVE IN IT. IN ORDER TO FIND THE HEAT LOSS UNDER NORMAL USE A COMPUTER HAS BEEN INSTALLED ON THE FIRST FLOOR TO SIMULATE A FAMILY. IT OPENS DOORS & WINDOWS & TURNS ON RADIATORS INTERMITTENTLY.

STORING THE SUN'S HEAT
ONE OF THE MAIN PROBLEMS WITH SOLAR-POWERED CENTRAL HEATING IS TO FIND A METHOD OF STORING THE ENERGY COLLECTED DURING THE SUMMER TO USE DURING THE WINTER. IN THE GERMAN EXPERIMENTAL SOLAR HOUSE THE HEAT IS STORED IN A HUGE, WELL INSULATED WATER TANK WHICH FILLS THE BASEMENT. HOWEVER, THEY HOPE TO REPLACE THE WATER WITH POTASSIUM FLUORIDE TETRAHYDRATE. THE SOLAR ENERGY WOULD THEN BE USED TO MELT THE CHEMICAL. THE LATENT HEAT WOULD BE RELEASED LATER AS THE CHEMICAL RESOLIDIFIED. IT WOULD REQUIRE A MUCH SMALLER TANK WITH LITTLE INSULATION. (IT MELTS AT 18.5°C).

AIR CONDITIONING
THE FIRST MENTION OF AN AIR CONDITIONING SYSTEM OCCURS IN A CHINESE ACCOUNT OF CONSTANTINOPLE IN 650AD. IN THE HEAT OF SUMMER, MACHINES WORKED BY WATER-POWER CARRY THE WATER UP TO THE ROOF. THE WATER THEN REFRESHED THE AIR BY FALLING IN SHOWERS IN FRONT OF THE WINDOWS. THIS POSSIBLY INSPIRED A VICTORIAN SYSTEM BY WHICH AIR WAS BLOWN IN BY A FAN THROUGH A SHOWER OF WATER UNDER A WATERWHEEL DRIVING THE FAN.

HOW TO THROW SIXES
GLUE 2 DICE, SIXES UPWARDS, TO BOTTOM OF DRAWER OF LARGE HOUSEHOLD MATCHBOX. ASK A FRIEND TO EXAMINE TWO SIMILAR DICE, THEN DROP THEM INTO MATCHBOX. CLOSE DRAW, SHAKE VIOLENTLY & ENSURE LOOSE DICE END UP ON THE SIDE FURTHEST FROM THE GLUE DICE. OPEN DRAW FAR ENOUGH TO REVEAL GLUED DICE BUT TO KEEP LOOSE DICE HIDDEN.

GLUED DICE

LOOSE DICE

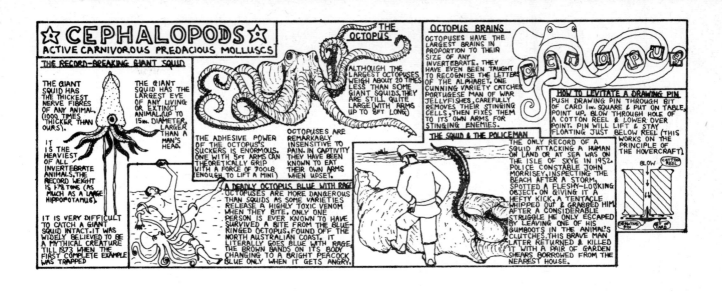

☆ CEPHALOPODS ☆
ACTIVE CARNIVOROUS PREDACIOUS MOLLUSCS

THE RECORD-BREAKING GIANT SQUID

THE GIANT SQUID HAS THE THICKEST NERVE FIBRES OF ANY ANIMAL (1000 TIMES THICKER THAN OURS).

IT IS THE HEAVIEST OF ALL INVERTEBRATE ANIMALS, THE RECORD WEIGHT IS 1.78 TONS (AS MUCH AS A LARGE HIPPOPOTAMUS).

IT IS VERY DIFFICULT TO CATCH A GIANT SQUID INTACT. IT WAS WIDELY BELIEVED TO BE A MYTHICAL CREATURE TILL 1873 WHEN THE FIRST COMPLETE EXAMPLE WAS TRAPPED

THE GIANT SQUID HAS THE LARGEST EYE OF ANY LIVING OR EXTINCT ANIMAL UP TO 15IN. DIAMETER, LARGER THAN A MAN'S HEAD.

THE OCTOPUS

ALTHOUGH THE LARGEST OCTOPUSES WEIGH ABOUT 20 TIMES LESS THAN SOME GIANT SQUIDS, THEY ARE STILL QUITE LARGE (WITH ARMS UP TO 8FT LONG)

THE ADHESIVE POWER OF THE OCTOPUS'S SUCKERS IS ENORMOUS. ONE WITH 5FT ARMS CAN THEORETICALLY GRIP WITH A FORCE OF 700LB (ENOUGH TO LIFT A MINI)

OCTOPUSES ARE REMARKABLY INSENSITIVE TO PAIN. IN CAPTIVITY THEY HAVE BEEN KNOWN TO EAT THEIR OWN ARMS WHEN UPSET.

A DEADLY OCTOPUS BLUE WITH RAGE

OCTOPUSES ARE MORE DANGEROUS THAN SQUIDS AS SOME VARIETIES RELEASE A HIGHLY TOXIC VENOM WHEN THEY BITE. ONLY ONE PERSON IS EVER KNOWN TO HAVE SURVIVED A BITE FROM THE BLUE-RINGED OCTOPUS, FOUND OFF THE NORTH AUSTRALIAN COAST. IT LITERALLY GOES BLUE WITH RAGE, THE BROWN BANDS ON ITS BODY CHANGING TO A BRIGHT PEACOCK BLUE ONLY WHEN IT GETS ANGRY.

OCTOPUS BRAINS

OCTOPUSES HAVE THE LARGEST BRAINS IN PROPORTION TO THEIR SIZE OF ANY INVERTEBRATE. THEY HAVE EVEN BEEN TAUGHT TO RECOGNISE THE LETTERS OF THE ALPHABET. ONE CUNNING VARIETY CATCHES PORTUGESE MAN OF WAR JELLYFISHES, CAREFULLY REMOVES THEIR STINGING CELLS, THEN FIXES THEM TO ITS OWN ARMS FOR STINGING ENEMIES.

THE SQUID & THE POLICEMAN

THE ONLY RECORD OF A SQUID ATTACKING A HUMAN ON LAND OR AT SEA WAS ON THE ISLE OF SKYE IN 1952. POLICE CONSTABLE JOHN MORRISEY, INSPECTING THE BEACH AFTER A STORM, SPOTTED A FLESHY-LOOKING OBJECT. ON GIVING IT A HEFTY KICK, A TENTACLE WHIPPED OUT & GRABBED HIM. AFTER A CONSIDERABLE STRUGGLE HE ONLY ESCAPED BY LEAVING ONE OF HIS GUMBOOTS IN THE ANIMAL'S CLUTCHES. THIS BRAVE MAN LATER RETURNED & KILLED IT WITH A PAIR OF GARDEN SHEARS BORROWED FROM THE NEAREST HOUSE.

HOW TO LEVITATE A DRAWING PIN

PUSH DRAWING PIN THROUGH BIT OF CARD 1IN. SQUARE & PUT ON TABLE, POINT UP. BLOW THROUGH HOLE OF A COTTON REEL & LOWER OVER POINT. PIN WILL LIFT & STAY FLOATING JUST BELOW REEL (THIS WORKS ON THE PRINCIPLE OF THE HOVERCRAFT).

BLOW / COTTON REEL / DRAWING PIN / CARD

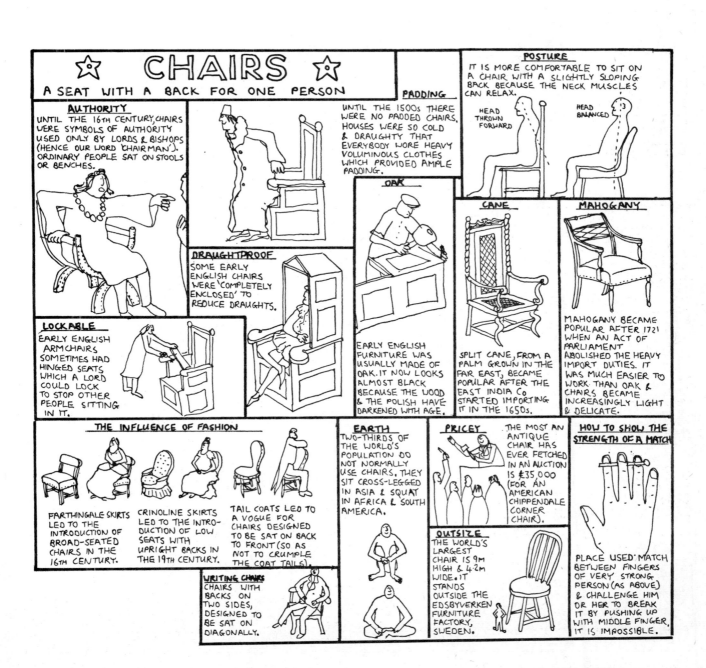

☆ CHAIRS ☆
A SEAT WITH A BACK FOR ONE PERSON

AUTHORITY

UNTIL THE 16TH CENTURY, CHAIRS WERE SYMBOLS OF AUTHORITY USED ONLY BY LORDS & BISHOPS (HENCE OUR WORD 'CHAIRMAN'). ORDINARY PEOPLE SAT ON STOOLS OR BENCHES.

LOCKABLE

EARLY ENGLISH ARMCHAIRS SOMETIMES HAD HINGED SEATS WHICH A LORD COULD LOCK TO STOP OTHER PEOPLE SITTING IN IT.

DRAUGHTPROOF

SOME EARLY ENGLISH CHAIRS WERE 'COMPLETELY ENCLOSED' TO REDUCE DRAUGHTS.

PADDING

UNTIL THE 1500s THERE WERE NO PADDED CHAIRS. HOUSES WERE SO COLD & DRAUGHTY THAT EVERYBODY WORE HEAVY VOLUMINOUS CLOTHES WHICH PROVIDED AMPLE PADDING.

OAK

EARLY ENGLISH FURNITURE WAS USUALLY MADE OF OAK. IT NOW LOOKS ALMOST BLACK BECAUSE THE WOOD & THE POLISH HAVE DARKENED WITH AGE.

POSTURE

IT IS MORE COMFORTABLE TO SIT ON A CHAIR WITH A SLIGHTLY SLOPING BACK BECAUSE THE NECK MUSCLES CAN RELAX.

HEAD THROWN FORWARD — HEAD BALANCED

CANE

SPLIT CANE, FROM A PALM GROWN IN THE FAR EAST, BECAME POPULAR AFTER THE EAST INDIA Co STARTED IMPORTING IT IN THE 1650s.

MAHOGANY

MAHOGANY BECAME POPULAR AFTER 1721 WHEN AN ACT OF PARLIAMENT ABOLISHED THE HEAVY IMPORT DUTIES. IT WAS MUCH EASIER TO WORK THAN OAK & CHAIRS BECAME INCREASINGLY LIGHT & DELICATE.

THE INFLUENCE OF FASHION

FARTHINGALE SKIRTS LED TO THE INTRODUCTION OF BROAD-SEATED CHAIRS IN THE 16TH CENTURY.

CRINOLINE SKIRTS LED TO THE INTRODUCTION OF LOW SEATS WITH UPRIGHT BACKS IN THE 19TH CENTURY.

TAIL COATS LED TO A VOGUE FOR CHAIRS DESIGNED TO BE SAT ON BACK TO FRONT (SO AS NOT TO CRUMPLE THE COAT TAILS).

WRITING CHAIRS

CHAIRS WITH BACKS ON TWO SIDES, DESIGNED TO BE SAT ON DIAGONALLY.

EARTH

TWO-THIRDS OF THE WORLD'S POPULATION DO NOT NORMALLY USE CHAIRS. THEY SIT CROSS-LEGGED IN ASIA & SQUAT IN AFRICA & SOUTH AMERICA.

OUTSIZE

THE WORLD'S LARGEST CHAIR IS 9M HIGH & 4.2M WIDE. IT STANDS OUTSIDE THE EDSBYVERKEN FURNITURE FACTORY, SWEDEN.

PRICEY

THE MOST AN ANTIQUE CHAIR HAS EVER FETCHED IN AN AUCTION IS £35,000 (FOR AN AMERICAN CHIPPENDALE CORNER CHAIR).

HOW TO SHOW THE STRENGTH OF A MATCH

PLACE USED MATCH BETWEEN FINGERS OF VERY STRONG PERSON (AS ABOVE) & CHALLENGE HIM OR HER TO BREAK IT BY PUSHING UP WITH MIDDLE FINGER. IT IS IMPOSSIBLE.

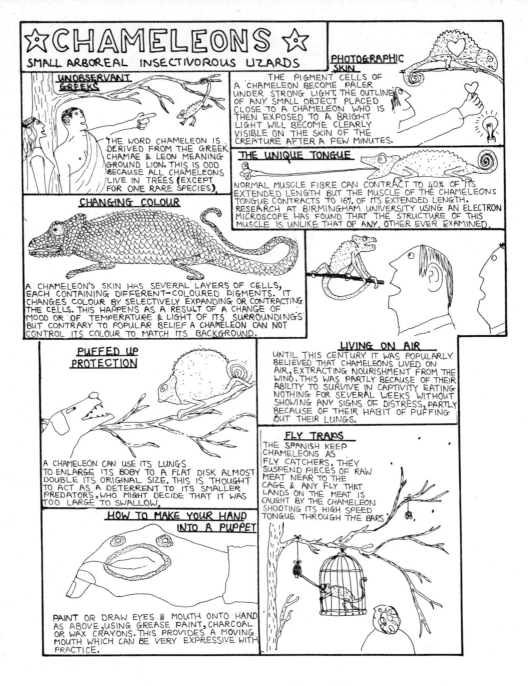

☆ CHAMELEONS ☆
SMALL ARBOREAL INSECTIVOROUS LIZARDS

UNOBSERVANT GREEKS

THE WORD CHAMELEON IS DERIVED FROM THE GREEK CHAMAE & LEON MEANING GROUND LION. THIS IS ODD BECAUSE ALL CHAMELEONS LIVE IN TREES (EXCEPT FOR ONE RARE SPECIES).

PHOTOGRAPHIC SKIN

THE PIGMENT CELLS OF A CHAMELEON BECOME PALER UNDER STRONG LIGHT. THE OUTLINE OF ANY SMALL OBJECT PLACED CLOSE TO A CHAMELEON WHO IS THEN EXPOSED TO A BRIGHT LIGHT WILL BECOME CLEARLY VISIBLE ON THE SKIN OF THE CREATURE AFTER A FEW MINUTES.

THE UNIQUE TONGUE

NORMAL MUSCLE FIBRE CAN CONTRACT TO 40% OF ITS EXTENDED LENGTH BUT THE MUSCLE OF THE CHAMELEONS TONGUE CONTRACTS TO 16% OF ITS EXTENDED LENGTH. RESEARCH AT BIRMINGHAM UNIVERSITY USING AN ELECTRON MICROSCOPE HAS FOUND THAT THE STRUCTURE OF THIS MUSCLE IS UNLIKE THAT OF ANY OTHER EVER EXAMINED.

CHANGING COLOUR

A CHAMELEON'S SKIN HAS SEVERAL LAYERS OF CELLS, EACH CONTAINING DIFFERENT-COLOURED PIGMENTS. IT CHANGES COLOUR BY SELECTIVELY EXPANDING OR CONTRACTING THE CELLS. THIS HAPPENS AS A RESULT OF A CHANGE OF MOOD OR OF TEMPERATURE & LIGHT OF ITS SURROUNDINGS BUT CONTRARY TO POPULAR BELIEF A CHAMELEON CAN NOT CONTROL ITS COLOUR TO MATCH ITS BACKGROUND.

PUFFED UP PROTECTION

A CHAMELEON CAN USE ITS LUNGS TO ENLARGE ITS BODY TO A FLAT DISK ALMOST DOUBLE ITS ORIGINAL SIZE. THIS IS THOUGHT TO ACT AS A DETERRENT TO ITS SMALLER PREDATORS, WHO MIGHT DECIDE THAT IT WAS TOO LARGE TO SWALLOW.

LIVING ON AIR

UNTIL THIS CENTURY IT WAS POPULARLY BELIEVED THAT CHAMELEONS LIVED ON AIR, EXTRACTING NOURISHMENT FROM THE WIND. THIS WAS PARTLY BECAUSE OF THEIR ABILITY TO SURVIVE IN CAPTIVITY EATING NOTHING FOR SEVERAL WEEKS WITHOUT SHOWING ANY SIGNS OF DISTRESS, PARTLY BECAUSE OF THEIR HABIT OF PUFFING OUT THEIR LUNGS.

FLY TRAPS

THE SPANISH KEEP CHAMELEONS AS FLY CATCHERS. THEY SUSPEND PIECES OF RAW MEAT NEAR TO THE CAGE & ANY FLY THAT LANDS ON THE MEAT IS CAUGHT BY THE CHAMELEON SHOOTING ITS HIGH SPEED TONGUE THROUGH THE BARS.

HOW TO MAKE YOUR HAND INTO A PUPPET

PAINT OR DRAW EYES & MOUTH ONTO HAND AS ABOVE, USING GREASE PAINT, CHARCOAL OR WAX CRAYONS. THIS PROVIDES A MOVING MOUTH WHICH CAN BE VERY EXPRESSIVE WITH PRACTICE.

☆ CHEESE ☆
FOOD MADE FROM COAGULATED MILK

MAKING CHEESE

TO MAKE CHEESE, MILK IS FIRST SEPARATED INTO CURDS & WHEY BY THE ADDITION OF RENNET, AN ENZYME EXTRACTED FROM THE FOURTH STOMACH OF RUMINANT ANIMALS. THE CURDS ARE THEN BROKEN UP TO ALLOW FURTHER DRAINING. NEXT, THE CURDS ARE PRESSED INTO MOULDS & LEFT TO AGE IN SURROUNDINGS OF CONSTANT HUMIDITY & TEMPERATURE, USUALLY CAVES. SOFT CHEESES RESULT FROM MOIST CURDS. A SOFT WHITE SURFACE MOULD GROWS WHICH PREVENTS THE FORMATION OF CRACKS & LOSS OF MOISTURE. HARD CHEESES RESULT FROM HEATED CURDS, REPEATEDLY DRAINED & BROKEN UP TO EXTRACT AS MUCH WHEY AS POSSIBLE. THEY ARE THEN DIPPED IN SALT WATER TO START THEIR PRESERVATIVE RIND.

A GREEK REMEDY

THE ANCIENT GREEKS REGARDED CHEESE AS A MEDICINE, AN ANTIDOTE FOR POISONS.

ROQUEFORT

ROQUEFORT IS A STRONG CHEESE MADE FROM SHEEP'S MILK. IT IS RIPENED IN CAVES ALONGSIDE SLICES OF DAMP BREAD, ON WHICH THE MOULD PENICILLIUM ROQUEFORTI FLOURISHES. IT THEN PERMEATES THE CHEESE.

FROMAGE FORT

STALE CHEESES NEED NOT ALWAYS BE THROWN AWAY. IN PARTS OF FRANCE STALE CHEESE IS CONVERTED TO 'FROMAGE FORT' BY BLENDING THE GRATED REMAINS WITH BRANDY, OLIVE OIL OR LEEK STOCK & RE-PRESSING. THE RESULTS ARE INVARIABLY SMELLY & TASTY.

CHINESE SUSPICION

THE ABSENCE OF DAIRY PRODUCTS FROM THE TRADITIONAL DIET OF THE CHINESE IS PUZZLING. FRESH MILK WAS THOUGHT TO BE INDIGESTIBLE & SOURED MILK PRODUCTS WERE SAID TO BE UNCLEAN, ALTHOUGH KNOWLEDGE OF DAIRY PRODUCE REACHED CHINA AS EARLY AS 2000 B.C.

CHEESE GOURMETS

CHEESE AROUSES THE PASSIONS OF MANY GOURMETS. BRILLAT SAVARIN WROTE: 'A MEAL WITHOUT CHEESE IS LIKE A BEAUTIFUL WOMAN WITH ONE EYE'. CONNOISSEURS CAN TASTE WHETHER SOME CHEESES HAVE BEEN MADE FROM PASTEURISED OR UNTREATED MILK & EVEN CLAIM TO DETECT WHETHER THE MILK CAME FROM A MORNING OR AN EVENING MILKING.

GRUYERE

THE SHAPE OF THE HOLES IN GRUYERE CHEESE IS MOST IMPORTANT. THEY SHOULD BE SPHERES THE SIZE OF WALNUTS. LARGE OR OVAL HOLES TEND TO INDICATE SHARP OR TASTELESS CHEESES. HOLES DAMP WITH SALT WATER ARE SAID TO BE WEEPING, A SIGN OF A GOOD GRUYERE.

HOW TO MAKE A WEATHER HOUSE

CORK   HAIR

TIE ONE END OF A HUMAN HAIR ROUND A SCREW EYE FIXED ON A SMALL WOODEN BATTEN. GLUE OTHER END OF HAIR TO A CORK. CUT OUT CARDBOARD HOUSE AS ABOVE & STICK TO OTHER SIDE OF CORK. GLUE FIGURES TO ENDS OF BATTEN. HUMAN HAIR TWISTS AS THE MOISTURE CONTENT OF THE AIR CHANGES. TURNING THE SCREW EYE SLIGHTLY IN OR OUT OF THE WOOD, THE HOUSE CAN BE SET SO THE MAN WITH THE UMBRELLA APPEARS IN WET WEATHER & RETREATS IN DRY WEATHER.

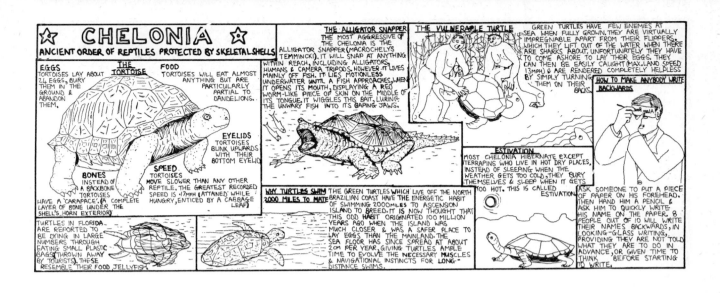

☆ CHELONIA ☆
ANCIENT ORDER OF REPTILES PROTECTED BY SKELETAL SHELLS

EGGS
TORTOISES LAY ABOUT 24 EGGS, BURY THEM IN THE GROUND & ABANDON THEM.

THE TORTOISE

FOOD
TORTOISES WILL EAT ALMOST ANYTHING BUT ARE PARTICULARLY PARTIAL TO DANDELIONS.

EYELIDS
TORTOISES BLINK UPWARDS WITH THEIR BOTTOM EYELID

BONES
INSTEAD OF A BACKBONE TORTOISES HAVE A CARAPACE, (A COMPLETE LAYER OF BONE UNDER THE SHELL'S HORN EXTERIOR)

SPEED
TORTOISES MOVE SLOWER THAN ANY OTHER REPTILE. THE GREATEST RECORDED SPEED IS 17MM (ATTAINED) WHILE HUNGRY, ENTICED BY A CABBAGE LEAF)

TURTLES IN FLORIDA ARE REPORTED TO BE DYING IN LARGE NUMBERS THROUGH EATING SMALL PLASTIC BAGS THROWN AWAY BY TOURISTS. THESE RESEMBLE THEIR FOOD JELLYFISH.

THE ALLIGATOR SNAPPER
THE MOST AGGRESSIVE OF THE CHELONIA IS THE ALLIGATOR SNAPPER (MACROCHELYS TEMMINCKI). IT WILL SNAP AT ANYTHING WITHIN REACH, INCLUDING ALLIGATORS, HUMANS & CAMERA TRIPODS. HOWEVER IT LIVES MAINLY OFF FISH. IT LIES MOTIONLESS UNDERWATER UNTIL A FISH APPROACHES, WHEN IT OPENS ITS MOUTH, DISPLAYING A RED WORM-LIKE PIECE OF SKIN ON THE MIDDLE OF ITS TONGUE. IT WIGGLES THIS BAIT, LURING THE UNWARY FISH INTO ITS GAPING JAWS.

WHY TURTLES SWIM 2000 MILES TO MATE
THE GREEN TURTLES WHICH LIVE OFF THE NORTH BRAZILIAN COAST HAVE THE ENERGETIC HABIT OF SWIMMING 2000MILES TO ASCENSION ISLAND TO BREED. IT IS NOW THOUGHT THAT THIS ODD HABIT ORIGINATED 100 MILLION YEARS AGO WHEN THE ISLAND WAS MUCH CLOSER & WAS A SAFER PLACE TO LAY EGGS THAN THE MAINLAND. THE SEA FLOOR HAS SINCE SPREAD AT ABOUT 2CM PER YEAR, GIVING TURTLES AMPLE TIME TO EVOLVE THE NECESSARY MUSCLES & NAVIGATIONAL INSTINCTS FOR LONG-DISTANCE SWIMS.

THE VULNERABLE TURTLE
GREEN TURTLES HAVE FEW ENEMIES AT SEA WHEN FULLY GROWN. THEY ARE VIRTUALLY IMPREGNABLE APART FROM THEIR FLIPPERS, WHICH THEY LIFT OUT OF THE WATER WHEN THERE ARE SHARKS ABOUT. UNFORTUNATELY THEY HAVE TO COME ASHORE TO LAY THEIR EGGS. THEY CAN THEN BE EASILY CAUGHT (MAX. LAND SPEED 13MPH) & ARE RENDERED COMPLETELY HELPLESS BY SIMPLY TURNING THEM ON THEIR BACKS.

ESTIVATION
MOST CHELONIA HIBERNATE EXCEPT TERRAPINS WHO LIVE IN HOT DRY PLACES. INSTEAD OF SLEEPING WHEN THE WEATHER GETS TOO COLD, THEY BURY THEMSELVES & SLEEP WHEN IT GETS TOO HOT. THIS IS CALLED ESTIVATION

HOW TO MAKE ANYBODY WRITE BACKWARDS
ASK SOMEONE TO PUT A PIECE OF PAPER ON HIS FOREHEAD, THEN HAND HIM A PENCIL & ASK HIM TO QUICKLY WRITE HIS NAME ON THE PAPER. 8 PEOPLE OUT OF 10 WILL WRITE THEIR NAMES BACKWARDS, IN LOOKING-GLASS WRITING, PROVIDING THEY ARE NOT TOLD WHAT THEY ARE TO DO IN ADVANCE, OR GIVEN TIME TO THINK BEFORE STARTING TO WRITE.

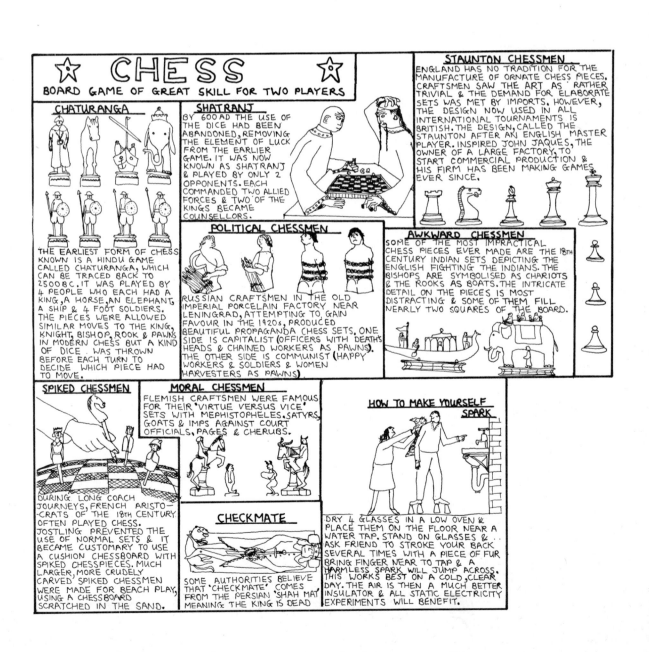

☆ CHESS ☆
BOARD GAME OF GREAT SKILL FOR TWO PLAYERS

CHATURANGA

THE EARLIEST FORM OF CHESS KNOWN IS A HINDU GAME CALLED CHATURANGA, WHICH CAN BE TRACED BACK TO 2500 BC. IT WAS PLAYED BY 4 PEOPLE WHO EACH HAD A KING, A HORSE, AN ELEPHANT, A SHIP & 4 FOOT SOLDIERS. THE PIECES WERE ALLOWED SIMILAR MOVES TO THE KING, KNIGHT, BISHOP, ROOK & PAWNS IN MODERN CHESS BUT A KIND OF DICE WAS THROWN BEFORE EACH TURN TO DECIDE WHICH PIECE HAD TO MOVE.

SHATRANJ
BY 600 AD THE USE OF THE DICE HAD BEEN ABANDONED, REMOVING THE ELEMENT OF LUCK FROM THE EARLIER GAME. IT WAS NOW KNOWN AS SHATRANJ & PLAYED BY ONLY 2 OPPONENTS. EACH COMMANDED TWO ALLIED FORCES & TWO OF THE KINGS BECAME COUNSELLORS.

STAUNTON CHESSMEN
ENGLAND HAS NO TRADITION FOR THE MANUFACTURE OF ORNATE CHESS PIECES. CRAFTSMEN SAW THE ART AS RATHER TRIVIAL & THE DEMAND FOR ELABORATE SETS WAS MET BY IMPORTS. HOWEVER, THE DESIGN NOW USED IN ALL INTERNATIONAL TOURNAMENTS IS BRITISH. THE DESIGN, CALLED THE STAUNTON AFTER AN ENGLISH MASTER PLAYER, INSPIRED JOHN JAQUES, THE OWNER OF A LARGE FACTORY, TO START COMMERCIAL PRODUCTION & HIS FIRM HAS BEEN MAKING GAMES EVER SINCE.

POLITICAL CHESSMEN
RUSSIAN CRAFTSMEN IN THE OLD IMPERIAL PORCELAIN FACTORY NEAR LENINGRAD, ATTEMPTING TO GAIN FAVOUR IN THE 1920s, PRODUCED BEAUTIFUL PROPAGANDA CHESS SETS. ONE SIDE IS CAPITALIST (OFFICERS WITH DEATH'S HEADS & CHAINED WORKERS AS PAWNS). THE OTHER SIDE IS COMMUNIST (HAPPY WORKERS & SOLDIERS & WOMEN HARVESTERS AS PAWNS)

AWKWARD CHESSMEN
SOME OF THE MOST IMPRACTICAL CHESS PIECES EVER MADE ARE THE 18TH CENTURY INDIAN SETS DEPICTING THE ENGLISH FIGHTING THE INDIANS. THE BISHOPS ARE SYMBOLISED AS CHARIOTS & THE ROOKS AS BOATS. THE INTRICATE DETAIL ON THE PIECES IS MOST DISTRACTING & SOME OF THEM FILL NEARLY TWO SQUARES OF THE BOARD.

SPIKED CHESSMEN
DURING LONG COACH JOURNEYS, FRENCH ARISTO-CRATS OF THE 18TH CENTURY OFTEN PLAYED CHESS. JOSTLING PREVENTED THE USE OF NORMAL SETS & IT BECAME CUSTOMARY TO USE A CUSHION CHESSBOARD WITH SPIKED CHESSPIECES. MUCH LARGER, MORE CRUDELY CARVED SPIKED CHESSMEN WERE MADE FOR BEACH PLAY, USING A CHESSBOARD SCRATCHED IN THE SAND.

MORAL CHESSMEN
FLEMISH CRAFTSMEN WERE FAMOUS FOR THEIR 'VIRTUE VERSUS VICE' SETS WITH MEPHISTOPHELES, SATYRS, GOATS & IMPS AGAINST COURT OFFICIALS, PAGES & CHERUBS.

CHECKMATE
SOME AUTHORITIES BELIEVE THAT 'CHECKMATE' COMES FROM THE PERSIAN 'SHAH MAT' MEANING THE KING IS DEAD

HOW TO MAKE YOURSELF SPARK
DRY 4 GLASSES IN A LOW OVEN & PLACE THEM ON THE FLOOR NEAR A WATER TAP. STAND ON GLASSES & ASK FRIEND TO STROKE YOUR BACK SEVERAL TIMES WITH A PIECE OF FUR. BRING FINGER NEAR TO TAP & A HARMLESS SPARK WILL JUMP ACROSS. THIS WORKS BEST ON A COLD, CLEAR DAY. THE AIR IS THEN A MUCH BETTER INSULATOR & ALL STATIC ELECTRICITY EXPERIMENTS WILL BENEFIT.

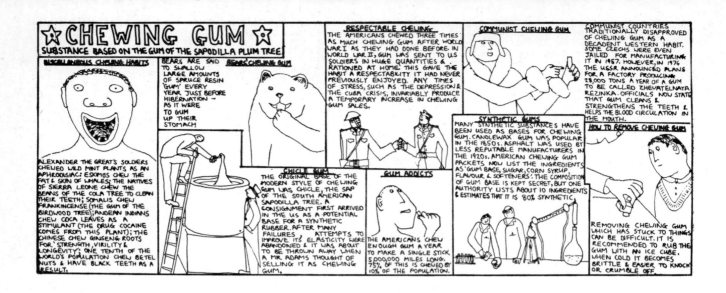

☆ CHEWING GUM ☆
SUBSTANCE BASED ON THE GUM OF THE SAPODILLA PLUM TREE

MISCELLANEOUS CHEWING HABITS

ALEXANDER THE GREAT'S SOLDIERS CHEWED WILD MINT PLANTS AS AN APHRODISIAC; ESKIMOS CHEW THE FAT & SKIN OF WHALES; THE NATIVES OF SIERRA LEONE CHEW THE BEANS OF THE COLA TREE TO CLEAN THEIR TEETH; SOMALIS CHEW FRANKINCENSE (THE GUM OF THE BIRDWOOD TREE); ANDEAN INDIANS CHEW COCA LEAVES AS A STIMULANT (THE DRUG COCAINE COMES FROM THIS PLANT); THE CHINESE CHEW GINSENG ROOTS FOR 'STRENGTH, VIRILITY & LONGEVITY'; ONE TENTH OF THE WORLD'S POPULATION CHEW BETEL NUTS & HAVE BLACK TEETH AS A RESULT.

BEARS ARE SAID TO SWALLOW LARGE AMOUNTS OF SPRUCE RESIN 'GUM' EVERY YEAR JUST BEFORE HIBERNATION – AS IT WERE TO GUM UP THEIR STOMACH

BEARS CHEWING GUM

CHICLE GUM
THE ORIGINAL BASE OF THE MODERN STYLE OF CHEWING GUM WAS CHICLE, THE SAP OF THE SOUTH AMERICAN SAPODILLA TREE. A CONSIGNMENT FIRST ARRIVED IN THE US AS A POTENTIAL BASE FOR A SYNTHETIC RUBBER. AFTER MANY FAILURES ATTEMPTS TO IMPROVE ITS ELASTICITY WERE ABANDONED & IT WAS ABOUT TO BE THROWN AWAY WHEN A MR ADAMS THOUGHT OF SELLING IT AS CHEWING GUM.

RESPECTABLE CHEWING
THE AMERICANS CHEWED THREE TIMES AS MUCH CHEWING GUM AFTER WORLD WAR I AS THEY HAD DONE BEFORE. IN WORLD WAR II, GUM WAS SENT TO US SOLDIERS IN HUGE QUANTITIES & RATIONED AT HOME. THIS GAVE THE HABIT A RESPECTABILITY IT HAD NEVER PREVIOUSLY ENJOYED. ANY TIMES OF STRESS, SUCH AS THE DEPRESSION & THE CUBA CRISIS, INVARIABLY PRODUCE A TEMPORARY INCREASE IN CHEWING GUM SALES.

GUM ADDICTS
THE AMERICANS CHEW ENOUGH GUM A YEAR TO MAKE A SINGLE STICK 5,000,000 MILES LONG. 75% OF THIS IS CHEWED BY 10% OF THE POPULATION.

COMMUNIST CHEWING GUM

COMMUNIST COUNTRIES TRADITIONALLY DISAPPROVED OF CHEWING GUM AS A DECADENT WESTERN HABIT. SOME CZECHS WERE EVEN JAILED FOR MANUFACTURING IT IN 1957. HOWEVER, IN 1976 THE USSR ANNOUNCED PLANS FOR A FACTORY PRODUCING 28,000 TONS A YEAR OF A GUM TO BE CALLED ZHEVATELNAYA REZINKA. OFFICIALS NOW STATE THAT GUM CLEANS & STRENGTHENS THE TEETH & HELPS THE BLOOD CIRCULATION IN THE MOUTH.

SYNTHETIC GUMS
MANY SYNTHETIC SUBSTANCES HAVE BEEN USED AS BASES FOR CHEWING GUM. CANDLEWAX GUM WAS POPULAR IN THE 1850s. ASPHALT WAS USED BY LESS REPUTABLE MANUFACTURERS IN THE 1920s. AMERICAN CHEWING GUM PACKETS NOW LIST THE INGREDIENTS AS 'GUM BASE, SUGAR, CORN SYRUP, FLAVOUR & SOFTENERS'. THE COMPOSITION OF GUM BASE IS KEPT SECRET, BUT ONE AUTHORITY LISTS ABOUT 10 INGREDIENTS & ESTIMATES THAT IT IS 80% SYNTHETIC.

HOW TO REMOVE CHEWING GUM
REMOVING CHEWING GUM WHICH HAS STUCK TO THINGS CAN BE DIFFICULT. IT IS RECOMMENDED TO RUB THE GUM WITH AN ICE CUBE. WHEN COLD IT BECOMES BRITTLE & EASIER TO KNOCK OR CRUMBLE OFF.

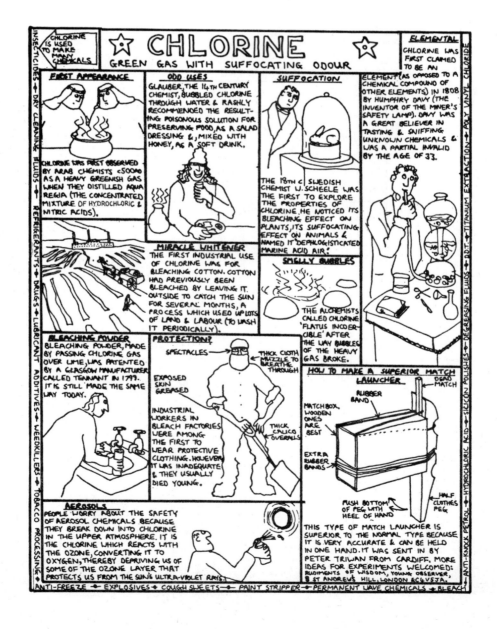

☆ CHLORINE ☆
GREEN GAS WITH SUFFOCATING ODOUR

CHLORINE IS USED TO MAKE MANY CHEMICALS

FIRST APPEARANCE
CHLORINE WAS FIRST OBSERVED BY ARAB CHEMISTS <500AD AS A HEAVY GREENISH GAS WHEN THEY DISTILLED AQUA REGIA (THE CONCENTRATED MIXTURE OF HYDROCHLORIC & NITRIC ACIDS).

ODD USES
GLAUBER, THE 14th CENTURY CHEMIST, BUBBLED CHLORINE THROUGH WATER & RASHLY RECOMMENDED THE RESULTING POISONOUS SOLUTION FOR PRESERVING FOOD, AS A SALAD DRESSING &, MIXED WITH HONEY, AS A SOFT DRINK.

MIRACLE WHITENER
THE FIRST INDUSTRIAL USE OF CHLORINE WAS FOR BLEACHING COTTON. COTTON HAD PREVIOUSLY BEEN BLEACHED BY LEAVING IT OUTSIDE TO CATCH THE SUN FOR SEVERAL MONTHS, A PROCESS WHICH USED UP LOTS OF LAND & LABOUR (TO WASH IT PERIODICALLY).

SUFFOCATION
THE 18th C. SWEDISH CHEMIST W. SCHEELE WAS THE FIRST TO EXPLORE THE PROPERTIES OF CHLORINE. HE NOTICED ITS BLEACHING EFFECT ON PLANTS, ITS SUFFOCATING EFFECT ON ANIMALS & NAMED IT 'DEPHLOGISTICATED MARINE ACID AIR'.

SMELLY BUBBLES
THE ALCHEMISTS CALLED CHLORINE 'FLATUS INCOERCIBLE' AFTER THE WAY BUBBLES OF THE HEAVY GAS BROKE.

ELEMENTAL
CHLORINE WAS FIRST CLAIMED TO BE AN ELEMENT (AS OPPOSED TO A CHEMICAL COMPOUND OR OTHER ELEMENTS) IN 1808 BY HUMPHRY DAVY (THE INVENTOR OF THE MINER'S SAFETY LAMP). DAVY WAS A GREAT BELIEVER IN TASTING & SNIFFING UNKNOWN CHEMICALS & WAS A PARTIAL INVALID BY THE AGE OF 33.

BLEACHING POWDER
BLEACHING POWDER, MADE BY PASSING CHLORINE GAS OVER LIME, WAS PATENTED BY A GLASGOW MANUFACTURER CALLED TENNANT IN 1799. IT IS STILL MADE THE SAME WAY TODAY.

PROTECTION?
SPECTACLES
EXPOSED SKIN GREASED
THICK CLOTH MUZZLE TO BREATHE THROUGH
THICK CALICO OVERALLS

INDUSTRIAL WORKERS IN BLEACH FACTORIES WERE AMONG THE FIRST TO WEAR PROTECTIVE CLOTHING. HOWEVER IT WAS INADEQUATE & THEY USUALLY DIED YOUNG.

HOW TO MAKE A SUPERIOR MATCH LAUNCHER
DEAD MATCH
RUBBER BAND
MATCHBOX WOODEN ONES ARE BEST
EXTRA RUBBER BANDS
PUSH BOTTOM OF PEG WITH HEEL OF HAND
HALF CLOTHES PEG

THIS TYPE OF MATCH LAUNCHER IS SUPERIOR TO THE NORMAL TYPE BECAUSE IT IS VERY ACCURATE & CAN BE HELD IN ONE HAND. IT WAS SENT IN BY PETER TRIWAN FROM CARDIFF. MORE IDEAS FOR EXPERIMENTS WELCOMED: RUDIMENTS OF WISDOM, YOUNG OBSERVER, 8 ST ANDREWS HILL, LONDON EC4V5JA.

AEROSOLS
PEOPLE WORRY ABOUT THE SAFETY OF AEROSOL CHEMICALS BECAUSE THEY BREAK DOWN INTO CHLORINE IN THE UPPER ATMOSPHERE. IT IS THE CHLORINE WHICH REACTS WITH THE OZONE, CONVERTING IT TO OXYGEN, THEREBY DEPRIVING US OF SOME OF THE OZONE LAYER THAT PROTECTS US FROM THE SUN'S ULTRA-VIOLET RAYS.

(left border) INSECTICIDES → DRY CLEANING FLUIDS → REFRIGERANTS → DRUGS → LUBRICANT ADDITIVES → WEEDKILLERS → TOBACCO PROCESSING →

(right border) POLY VINYL CHLORIDE → TITANIUM EXTRACTION → D.D.T. → DEGREASING FLUIDS → SILICON POLISHES → HYDROCHLORIC ACID → KNOCK PETROL → ANTI-

(bottom border) ANTI-FREEZE → EXPLOSIVES → COUGH SWEETS → PAINT STRIPPER → PERMANENT WAVE CHEMICALS → BLEACH

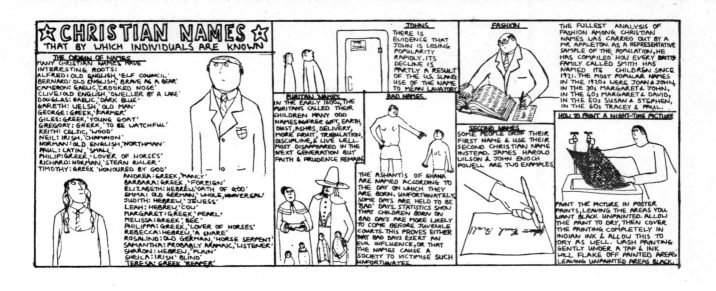

☆ CHRISTIAN NAMES ☆
THAT BY WHICH INDIVIDUALS ARE KNOWN

THE ORIGIN OF NAMES
MANY CHRISTIAN NAMES HAVE INTERESTING ROOTS:
ALFRED: OLD ENGLISH, 'ELF COUNCIL.'
BERNARD: OLD ENGLISH, 'BRAVE AS A BEAR'
CAMERON: GAELIC, 'CROOKED NOSE'
CLIVE: OLD ENGLISH, 'DWELLER BY A LAKE'
DOUGLAS: GAELIC, 'DARK BLUE'
GARETH: WELSH, 'OLD MAN'
GEORGE: GREEK, 'FARMER'
GILES: GREEK, 'YOUNG GOAT'
GREGORY: GREEK, 'TO BE WATCHFUL'
KEITH: CELTIC, 'WOOD'
NEIL: IRISH, 'CHAMPION'
NORMAN: OLD ENGLISH, 'NORTHMAN'
PAUL: LATIN, 'SMALL'
PHILIP: GREEK, 'LOVER OF HORSES'
RICHARD: NORMAN, 'STERN RULER'
TIMOTHY: GREEK, 'HONOURED BY GOD'

ANDREA: GREEK, 'MANLY'
BARBARA: GREEK, 'FOREIGN'
ELIZABETH: HEBREW, 'OATH OF GOD'
EMMA: OLD GERMAN, 'WHOLE, UNIVERSAL'
JUDITH: HEBREW, 'JEWESS'
LEAH: HEBREW, 'COW'
MARGARET: GREEK, 'PEARL'
MELISSA: GREEK, 'BEE'
PHILIPPA: GREEK, 'LOVER OF HORSES'
REBECCA: HEBREW, 'A SNARE'
ROSALIND: OLD GERMAN, 'HORSE SERPENT'
SAMANTHA: PROBABLY ARAMAIC, 'LISTENER'
SHARON: HEBREW, 'PLAIN'
SHEILA: IRISH, 'BLIND'
TERESA: GREEK, 'REAPER'

JOHNS
THERE IS EVIDENCE THAT JOHN IS LOSING POPULARITY. ITS DECLINE IS PARTLY A RESULT OF THE U.S. SLANG USE OF THE NAME TO MEAN LAVATORY.

PURITAN NAMES
IN THE EARLY 1600s, THE PURITANS CALLED THEIR CHILDREN MANY ODD NAMES &c FREE GIFT, EARTH, DUST, ASHES, DELIVERY, MORE FRUIT, TRIBULATION, DISCIPLINE, & LIVE WELL. MOST DISAPPEARED IN THE NEXT GENERATION BUT FAITH & PRUDENCE REMAIN.

BAD NAMES
THE ASHANTIS OF GHANA ARE NAMED ACCORDING TO THE DAY ON WHICH THEY ARE BORN. UNFORTUNATELY, SOME DAYS ARE HELD TO BE 'BAD' DAYS. STATISTICS SHOW THAT CHILDREN BORN ON BAD DAYS ARE MORE LIKELY TO COME BEFORE JUVENILE COURTS. THIS PROVES EITHER THAT BAD DAYS EXERT AN EVIL INFLUENCE, OR THAT THE NAMES CAUSE A SOCIETY TO VICTIMISE SUCH UNFORTUNATES.

FASHION
THE FULLEST ANALYSIS OF FASHION AMONG CHRISTIAN NAMES WAS CARRIED OUT BY A MR APPLETON. AS A REPRESENTATIVE SAMPLE OF THE POPULATION, HE HAS COMPILED HOW EVERY BRITISH FAMILY CALLED SMITH HAS NAMED ITS CHILDREN SINCE 1921. THE MOST POPULAR NAMES IN THE 1920s WERE JOAN & JOHN, IN THE 30s MARGARET & JOHN, IN THE 40s MARGARET & DAVID, IN THE 50s SUSAN & STEPHEN, IN THE 60s TRACEY & PAUL.

SECOND NAMES
SOME PEOPLE DROP THEIR FIRST NAME & USE THEIR SECOND CHRISTIAN NAME INSTEAD. JAMES HAROLD WILSON & JOHN ENOCH POWELL ARE TWO EXAMPLES.

HOW TO PAINT A NIGHT-TIME PICTURE
PAINT THE PICTURE IN POSTER PAINTS, LEAVING THE AREAS YOU WANT BLACK UNPAINTED. ALLOW THE PAINT TO DRY, THEN COVER THE PAINTING COMPLETELY IN INDIAN INK & ALLOW THIS TO DRY AS WELL. WASH PAINTING GENTLY UNDER A TAP & INK WILL FLAKE OFF PAINTED AREAS LEAVING UNPAINTED AREAS BLACK.

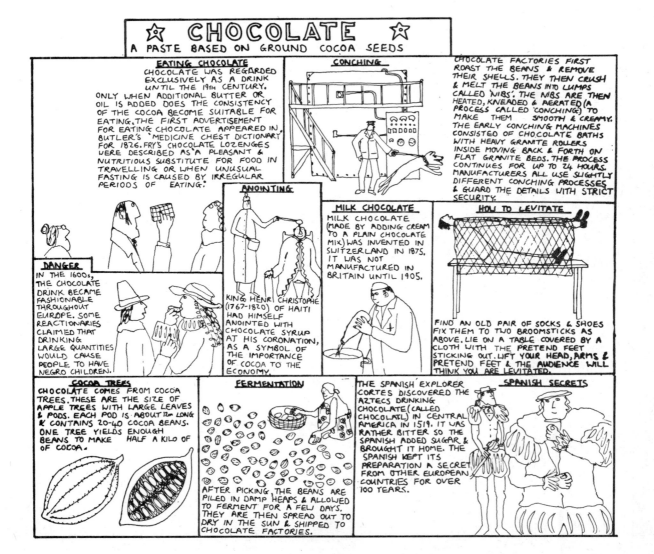

☆ CHOCOLATE ☆
A PASTE BASED ON GROUND COCOA SEEDS

EATING CHOCOLATE
CHOCOLATE WAS REGARDED EXCLUSIVELY AS A DRINK UNTIL THE 19th CENTURY. ONLY WHEN ADDITIONAL BUTTER OR OIL IS ADDED DOES THE CONSISTENCY OF THE COCOA BECOME SUITABLE FOR EATING. THE FIRST ADVERTISEMENT FOR EATING CHOCOLATE APPEARED IN BUTLER'S 'MEDICINE CHEST DICTIONARY' FOR 1826. FRY'S CHOCOLATE LOZENGES WERE DESCRIBED AS 'A PLEASANT & NUTRITIOUS SUBSTITUTE FOR FOOD IN TRAVELLING OR WHEN UNUSUAL FASTING IS CAUSED BY IRREGULAR PERIODS OF EATING.'

CONCHING

CHOCOLATE FACTORIES FIRST
ROAST THE BEANS & REMOVE THEIR SHELLS. THEY THEN CRUSH & MELT THE BEANS INTO LUMPS CALLED 'NIBS'. THE NIBS ARE THEN HEATED, KNEADED & AERATED (A PROCESS CALLED 'CONCHING') TO MAKE THEM SMOOTH & CREAMY. THE EARLY CONCHING MACHINES CONSISTED OF CHOCOLATE BATHS WITH HEAVY GRANITE ROLLERS INSIDE MOVING BACK & FORTH ON FLAT GRANITE BEDS. THE PROCESS CONTINUES FOR UP TO 24 HOURS. MANUFACTURERS ALL USE SLIGHTLY DIFFERENT CONCHING PROCESSES & GUARD THE DETAILS WITH STRICT SECURITY.

DANGER
IN THE 1600s, THE CHOCOLATE DRINK BECAME FASHIONABLE THROUGHOUT EUROPE. SOME REACTIONARIES CLAIMED THAT DRINKING LARGE QUANTITIES WOULD CAUSE PEOPLE TO HAVE NEGRO CHILDREN.

ANOINTING
KING HENRI CHRISTOPHE (1767-1820) OF HAITI HAD HIMSELF ANOINTED WITH CHOCOLATE SYRUP AT HIS CORONATION, AS A SYMBOL OF THE IMPORTANCE OF COCOA TO THE ECONOMY.

MILK CHOCOLATE
MILK CHOCOLATE (MADE BY ADDING CREAM TO A PLAIN CHOCOLATE MIX) WAS INVENTED IN SWITZERLAND IN 1875. IT WAS NOT MANUFACTURED IN BRITAIN UNTIL 1905.

HOW TO LEVITATE
FIND AN OLD PAIR OF SOCKS & SHOES FIX THEM TO TWO BROOMSTICKS AS ABOVE. LIE ON A TABLE COVERED BY A CLOTH WITH THE PRETEND FEET STICKING OUT. LIFT YOUR HEAD, ARMS & PRETEND FEET & THE AUDIENCE WILL THINK YOU ARE LEVITATED.

COCOA TREES
CHOCOLATE COMES FROM COCOA TREES. THESE ARE THE SIZE OF APPLE TREES WITH LARGE LEAVES & PODS. EACH POD IS ABOUT 12cm LONG & CONTAINS 20-40 COCOA BEANS. ONE TREE YIELDS ENOUGH BEANS TO MAKE HALF A KILO OF COCOA.

FERMENTATION
AFTER PICKING, THE BEANS ARE PILED IN DAMP HEAPS & ALLOWED TO FERMENT FOR A FEW DAYS. THEY ARE THEN SPREAD OUT TO DRY IN THE SUN & SHIPPED TO CHOCOLATE FACTORIES.

SPANISH SECRETS
THE SPANISH EXPLORER CORTES DISCOVERED THE AZTECS DRINKING CHOCOLATE (CALLED CHOCOLATL) IN CENTRAL AMERICA IN 1519. IT WAS RATHER BITTER SO THE SPANISH ADDED SUGAR & BROUGHT IT HOME. THE SPANISH KEPT ITS PREPARATION A SECRET FROM OTHER EUROPEAN COUNTRIES FOR OVER 100 YEARS.

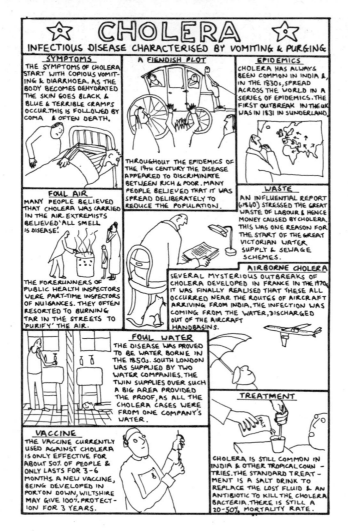

CHOLERA
INFECTIOUS DISEASE CHARACTERISED BY VOMITING & PURGING

SYMPTOMS
THE SYMPTOMS OF CHOLERA START WITH COPIOUS VOMITING & DIARRHOEA. AS THE BODY BECOMES DEHYDRATED THE SKIN GOES BLACK & BLUE & TERRIBLE CRAMPS OCCUR. THIS IS FOLLOWED BY COMA & OFTEN DEATH.

A FIENDISH PLOT
THROUGHOUT THE EPIDEMICS OF THE 19TH CENTURY THE DISEASE APPEARED TO DISCRIMINATE BETWEEN RICH & POOR. MANY PEOPLE BELIEVED THAT IT WAS SPREAD DELIBERATELY TO REDUCE THE POPULATION.

EPIDEMICS
CHOLERA HAS ALWAYS BEEN COMMON IN INDIA &, IN THE 1830s, SPREAD ACROSS THE WORLD IN A SERIES OF EPIDEMICS. THE FIRST OUTBREAK IN THE UK WAS IN 1831 IN SUNDERLAND.

FOUL AIR
MANY PEOPLE BELIEVED THAT CHOLERA WAS CARRIED IN THE AIR. EXTREMISTS BELIEVED 'ALL SMELL IS DISEASE'.

THE FORERUNNERS OF PUBLIC HEALTH INSPECTORS WERE PART-TIME INSPECTORS OF NUISANCES. THEY OFTEN RESORTED TO BURNING TAR IN THE STREETS TO 'PURIFY' THE AIR.

WASTE
AN INFLUENTIAL REPORT (c.1840) STRESSED THE GREAT WASTE OF LABOUR & HENCE MONEY CAUSED BY CHOLERA. THIS WAS ONE REASON FOR THE START OF THE GREAT VICTORIAN WATER SUPPLY & SEWAGE SCHEMES.

AIRBORNE CHOLERA
SEVERAL MYSTERIOUS OUTBREAKS OF CHOLERA DEVELOPED IN FRANCE IN THE 1970s. IT WAS FINALLY REALISED THAT THESE ALL OCCURRED NEAR THE ROUTES OF AIRCRAFT ARRIVING FROM INDIA. THE INFECTION WAS COMING FROM THE WATER, DISCHARGED OUT OF THE AIRCRAFT HANDBASINS.

FOUL WATER
THE DISEASE WAS PROVED TO BE WATER BORNE IN THE 1850s. SOUTH LONDON WAS SUPPLIED BY TWO WATER COMPANIES. THE TWIN SUPPLIES OVER SUCH A BIG AREA PROVIDED THE PROOF, AS ALL THE CHOLERA CASES WERE FROM ONE COMPANY'S WATER.

TREATMENT
CHOLERA IS STILL COMMON IN INDIA & OTHER TROPICAL COUNTRIES. THE STANDARD TREATMENT IS A SALT DRINK TO REPLACE THE LOST FLUID & AN ANTIBIOTIC TO KILL THE CHOLERA BACTERIA. THERE IS STILL A 20-50% MORTALITY RATE.

VACCINE
THE VACCINE CURRENTLY USED AGAINST CHOLERA IS ONLY EFFECTIVE FOR ABOUT 50% OF PEOPLE & ONLY LASTS FOR 3-6 MONTHS. A NEW VACCINE, BEING DEVELOPED IN PORTON DOWN, WILTSHIRE MAY GIVE 100% PROTECTION FOR 3 YEARS.

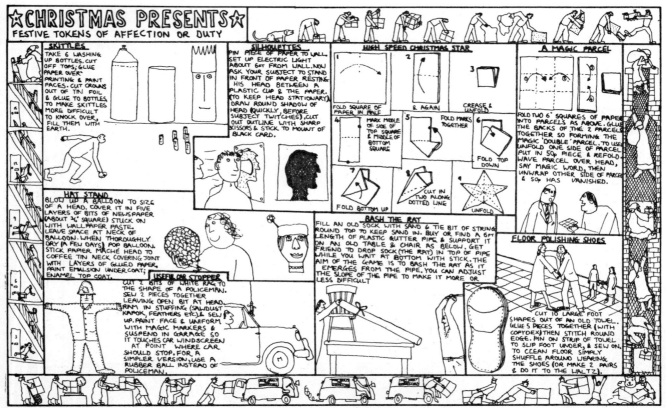

☆ CHRISTMAS PRESENTS ☆
FESTIVE TOKENS OF AFFECTION OR DUTY

SKITTLES
TAKE 6 WASHING UP BOTTLES. CUT OFF TOPS; GLUE PAPER OVER PRINTING & PAINT FACES. CUT CROWNS OUT OF TIN FOIL & GLUE TO BOTTLES TO MAKE SKITTLES MORE DIFFICULT TO KNOCK OVER, FILL THEM WITH EARTH.

HAT STAND
BLOW UP A BALLOON TO SIZE OF A HEAD. COVER IT IN FIVE LAYERS OF BITS OF NEWSPAPER (ABOUT 3/4" SQUARE) STUCK ON WITH WALLPAPER PASTE. LEAVE SPACE AT NECK OF BALLOON. WHEN THOROUGHLY DRY (A FEW DAYS) POP BALLOON. STICK PAPER MÂCHÉ HEAD TO COFFEE TIN NECK COVERING JOINT WITH LAYERS OF GLUED PAPER. PAINT EMULSION UNDERCOAT; ENAMEL TOP COAT.

USEFUL CAR STOPPER
CUT 2 BITS OF WHITE RAG TO THE SHAPE OF A POLICEMAN. SEW 2 PIECES TOGETHER LEAVING OPEN BIT AT HEAD. BRAM IN STUFFING (SAWDUST, KAPOK, FEATHERS ETC.) & SEW UP. PAINT FACE & UNIFORM WITH MAGIC MARKERS & SUSPEND IN GARAGE SO IT TOUCHES CAR WINDSCREEN AT POINT WHERE CAR SHOULD STOP. FOR A SIMPLER VERSION, USE A RUBBER BALL INSTEAD OF POLICEMAN.

SILHOUETTES
PIN PIECE OF PAPER TO WALL. SET UP ELECTRIC LIGHT ABOUT 6FT FROM WALL. NOW ASK YOUR SUBJECT TO STAND IN FRONT OF PAPER RESTING HIS HEAD BETWEEN A PLASTIC CUP & THE PAPER (TO KEEP HEAD STATIONARY). DRAW ROUND SHADOW OF HEAD (QUICKLY, BEFORE SUBJECT TWITCHES), CUT OUT OUTLINE WITH SHARP SCISSORS & STICK TO MOUNT OF BLACK CARD.

HIGH SPEED CHRISTMAS STAR
1. FOLD SQUARE OF PAPER IN HALF
2. & AGAIN
3. CREASE & UNFOLD
4. MARK MIDDLE OF SIDE OF TOP SQUARE & MIDDLE OF BOTTOM SQUARE
5. FOLD MARKS TOGETHER
6. FOLD TOP DOWN
7. FOLD BOTTOM UP
8. CUT IN TWO ALONG DOTTED LINE
9. UNFOLD

BASH THE RAT
FILL AN OLD SOCK WITH SAND & TIE BIT OF STRING ROUND TOP TO KEEP SAND IN. BUY OR FIND A 6FT LENGTH OF PLASTIC GUTTER PIPE & SUPPORT IT ON AN OLD TABLE & CHAIR AS BELOW. GET FRIEND TO DROP SOCK (THE RAT) IN TOP OF PIPE WHILE YOU WAIT AT BOTTOM WITH STICK. THE AIM OF THE GAME IS TO BASH THE RAT AS IT EMERGES FROM THE PIPE. YOU CAN ADJUST THE SLOPE OF THE PIPE TO MAKE IT MORE OR LESS DIFFICULT.

A MAGIC PARCEL
FOLD TWO 6" SQUARES OF PAPER INTO PARCELS AS ABOVE. GLUE THE BACKS OF THE 2 PARCELS TOGETHER SO FORMING THE MAGIC 'DOUBLE' PARCEL. TO USE, UNFOLD ONE SIDE OF PARCEL, PUT IN 50p PIECE & REFOLD. WAVE PARCEL OVER HEAD, SAY MAGIC WORD, THEN UNWRAP OTHER SIDE OF PARCEL & 50p HAS VANISHED.

FLOOR POLISHING SHOES
CUT 10 LARGE FOOT SHAPES OUT OF AN OLD TOWEL. GLUE 5 PIECES TOGETHER (WITH COPYDEX) THEN STITCH ROUND EDGE. PIN ON STRIP OF TOWEL TO SLIP FOOT UNDER, & SEW ON. TO CLEAN FLOOR SIMPLY SHUFFLE AROUND WEARING THE SHOES (OR MAKE 2 PAIRS & DO IT TO THE WALTZ).

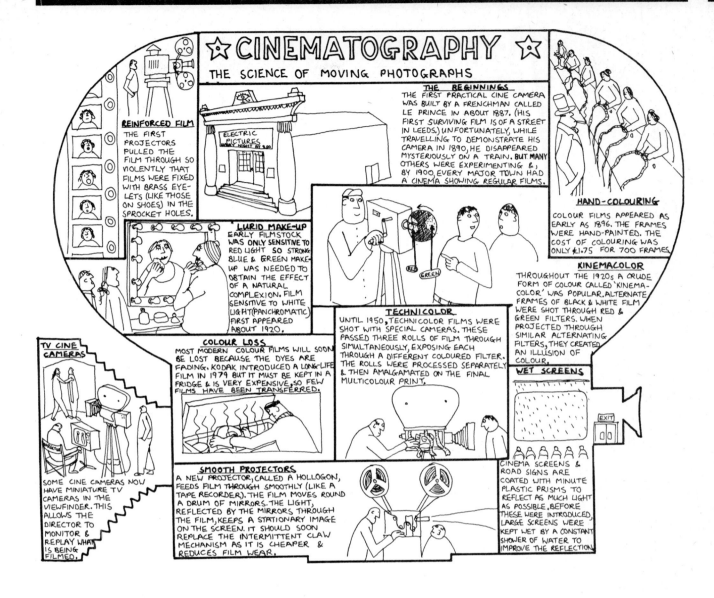

☆ CINEMATOGRAPHY ☆
THE SCIENCE OF MOVING PHOTOGRAPHS

REINFORCED FILM
THE FIRST PROJECTORS PULLED THE FILM THROUGH SO VIOLENTLY THAT FILMS WERE FIXED WITH BRASS EYELETS (LIKE THOSE ON SHOES) IN THE SPROCKET HOLES.

THE BEGINNINGS
THE FIRST PRACTICAL CINE CAMERA WAS BUILT BY A FRENCHMAN CALLED LE PRINCE IN ABOUT 1887. (HIS FIRST SURVIVING FILM IS OF A STREET IN LEEDS.) UNFORTUNATELY, WHILE TRAVELLING TO DEMONSTRATE HIS CAMERA IN 1890, HE DISAPPEARED MYSTERIOUSLY ON A TRAIN. BUT MANY OTHERS WERE EXPERIMENTING &, BY 1900, EVERY MAJOR TOWN HAD A CINEMA SHOWING REGULAR FILMS.

HAND-COLOURING
COLOUR FILMS APPEARED AS EARLY AS 1896. THE FRAMES WERE HAND-PAINTED. THE COST OF COLOURING WAS ONLY £1.75 FOR 700 FRAMES

LURID MAKE-UP
EARLY FILMSTOCK WAS ONLY SENSITIVE TO RED LIGHT SO STRONG BLUE & GREEN MAKE-UP WAS NEEDED TO OBTAIN THE EFFECT OF A NATURAL COMPLEXION. FILM SENSITIVE TO WHITE LIGHT (PANCHROMATIC) FIRST APPEARED ABOUT 1920.

KINEMACOLOR
THROUGHOUT THE 1920s A CRUDE FORM OF COLOUR CALLED 'KINEMA-COLOR' WAS POPULAR. ALTERNATE FRAMES OF BLACK & WHITE FILM WERE SHOT THROUGH RED & GREEN FILTERS. WHEN PROJECTED THROUGH SIMILAR ALTERNATING FILTERS, THEY CREATED AN ILLUSION OF COLOUR.

TECHNICOLOR
UNTIL 1950, TECHNICOLOR FILMS WERE SHOT WITH SPECIAL CAMERAS. THESE PASSED THREE ROLLS OF FILM THROUGH SIMULTANEOUSLY, EXPOSING EACH THROUGH A DIFFERENT COLOURED FILTER. THE ROLLS WERE PROCESSED SEPARATELY & THEN AMALGAMATED ON THE FINAL MULTICOLOUR PRINT.

TV CINE CAMERAS
SOME CINE CAMERAS NOW HAVE MINIATURE TV CAMERAS IN THE VIEWFINDER. THIS ALLOWS THE DIRECTOR TO MONITOR & REPLAY WHAT IS BEING FILMED.

COLOUR LOSS
MOST MODERN COLOUR FILMS WILL SOON BE LOST BECAUSE THE DYES ARE FADING. KODAK INTRODUCED A LONG-LIFE FILM IN 1979 BUT IT MUST BE KEPT IN A FRIDGE & IS VERY EXPENSIVE, SO FEW FILMS HAVE BEEN TRANSFERRED.

WET SCREENS
CINEMA SCREENS & ROAD SIGNS ARE COATED WITH MINUTE PLASTIC PRISMS TO REFLECT AS MUCH LIGHT AS POSSIBLE. BEFORE THESE WERE INTRODUCED, LARGE SCREENS WERE KEPT WET BY A CONSTANT SHOWER OF WATER TO IMPROVE THE REFLECTION.

SMOOTH PROJECTORS
A NEW PROJECTOR, CALLED A HOLLOGON, FEEDS FILM THROUGH SMOOTHLY (LIKE A TAPE RECORDER). THE FILM MOVES ROUND A DRUM OF MIRRORS. THE LIGHT, REFLECTED BY THE MIRRORS THROUGH THE FILM, KEEPS A STATIONARY IMAGE ON THE SCREEN. IT SHOULD SOON REPLACE THE INTERMITTENT CLAW MECHANISM AS IT IS CHEAPER & REDUCES FILM WEAR.

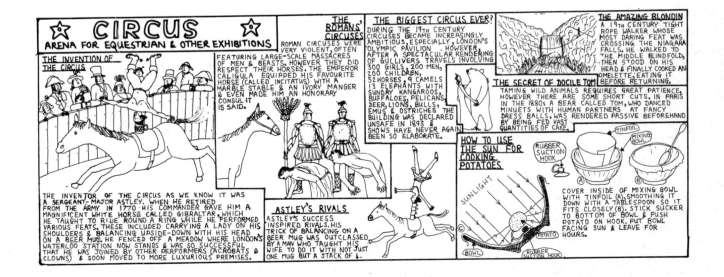

☆ CIRCUS ☆
ARENA FOR EQUESTRIAN & OTHER EXHIBITIONS

THE INVENTION OF THE CIRCUS
THE INVENTOR OF THE CIRCUS AS WE KNOW IT WAS A SERGEANT-MAJOR ASTLEY. WHEN HE RETIRED FROM THE ARMY IN 1770 HIS COMMANDER GAVE HIM A MAGNIFICENT WHITE HORSE CALLED GIBRALTAR, WHICH HE TAUGHT TO RIDE ROUND A RING WHILE HE PERFORMED VARIOUS FEATS. THESE INCLUDED CARRYING A LADY ON HIS SHOULDERS & BALANCING UPSIDE-DOWN WITH HIS HEAD ON A BEER MUG. HE FENCED OFF A MEADOW WHERE LONDON'S WATERLOO STATION NOW STANDS & WAS SO SUCCESSFUL THAT HE WAS JOINED BY OTHER PERFORMERS (ACROBATS & CLOWNS) & SOON MOVED TO MORE LUXURIOUS PREMISES.

THE ROMANS' CIRCUSES
ROMAN CIRCUSES WERE VERY VIOLENT, OFTEN FEATURING LARGE-SCALE MASSACRES OF MEN & BEASTS. HOWEVER THEY DID RESPECT THEIR HORSES. THE EMPEROR CALIGULA EQUIPPED HIS FAVOURITE HORSE (CALLED INCITATUS) WITH A MARBLE STABLE & AN IVORY MANGER & EVEN MADE HIM AN HONORARY CONSUL IT IS SAID.

THE BIGGEST CIRCUS EVER?
DURING THE 19TH CENTURY CIRCUSES BECAME INCREASINGLY AMBITIOUS, ESPECIALLY LONDON'S OLYMPIC PAVILION. HOWEVER, AFTER A SPECTACULAR RENDERING OF GULLIVERS TRAVELS INVOLVING 300 GIRLS, 200 MEN, 200 CHILDREN, 52 HORSES, 9 CAMELS 13 ELEPHANTS WITH SUNDRY KANGAROOS, BUFFALOES, PELICANS, DEER, LIONS, BULLS, EMUS & OSTRICHES THE BUILDING WAS DECLARED UNSAFE IN 1893 & SHOWS HAVE NEVER AGAIN BEEN SO ELABORATE.

ASTLEY'S RIVALS
ASTLEY'S SUCCESS INSPIRED RIVALS. HIS TRICK OF BALANCING ON A BEER MUG WAS OUTCLASSED BY A MAN WHO TAUGHT HIS WIFE TO DO IT WITH NOT JUST ONE MUG BUT A STACK OF 4.

THE AMAZING BLONDIN
A 19TH CENTURY TIGHT ROPE WALKER WHOSE MOST DARING FEAT WAS CROSSING THE NIAGARA FALLS. HE WALKED TO THE MIDDLE BLINDFOLD, THEN STOOD ON HIS HEAD & FINALLY COOKED AN OMELETTE, EATING IT BEFORE RETURNING.

THE SECRET OF DOCILE TOM
TAMING WILD ANIMALS REQUIRES GREAT PATIENCE, HOWEVER THERE ARE SOME SHORT CUTS. IN PARIS IN THE 1880s A BEAR CALLED TOM, WHO DANCED MINUETS WITH HUMAN PARTNERS AT FANCY DRESS BALLS, WAS RENDERED PASSIVE BEFOREHAND BY BEING FED VAST QUANTITIES OF CAKE.

HOW TO USE THE SUN FOR COOKING POTATOES
COVER INSIDE OF MIXING BOWL WITH TINFOIL (A) SMOOTHING IT DOWN WITH A TABLESPOON SO IT FITS CLOSELY (B). STICK SUCKER TO BOTTOM OF BOWL & PUSH POTATO ON HOOK, PUT BOWL FACING SUN & LEAVE FOR HOURS.

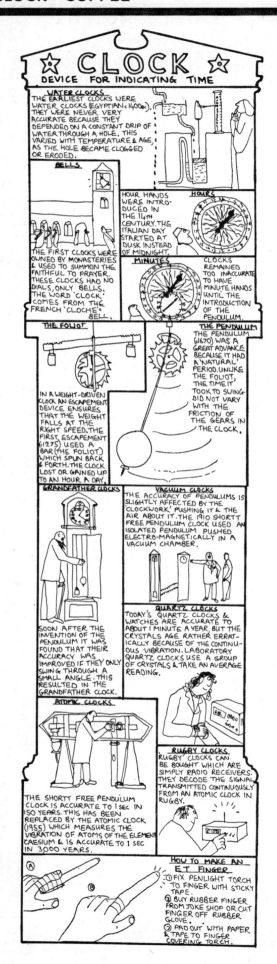

☆ CLOCK ☆
DEVICE FOR INDICATING TIME

WATER CLOCKS
THE EARLIEST CLOCKS WERE WATER CLOCKS (EGYPTIAN c.1400BC). THEY WERE NEVER VERY ACCURATE BECAUSE THEY DEPENDED ON A CONSTANT DRIP OF WATER THROUGH A HOLE. THIS VARIED WITH TEMPERATURE & AGE, AS THE HOLE BECAME CLOGGED OR ERODED.

BELLS
THE FIRST CLOCKS WERE OWNED BY MONASTERIES & USED TO SUMMON THE FAITHFUL TO PRAYER. THESE CLOCKS HAD NO DIALS, ONLY BELLS. THE WORD 'CLOCK' COMES FROM THE FRENCH 'CLOCHE'= BELL.

HOURS
HOUR HANDS WERE INTRODUCED IN THE 14th CENTURY. THE ITALIAN DAY STARTED AT DUSK INSTEAD OF MIDNIGHT.

MINUTES
CLOCKS REMAINED TOO INACCURATE TO HAVE MINUTE HANDS UNTIL THE INTRODUCTION OF THE PENDULUM.

THE FOLIOT
IN A WEIGHT-DRIVEN CLOCK AN ESCAPEMENT DEVICE ENSURES THAT THE WEIGHT FALLS AT THE RIGHT SPEED. THE FIRST ESCAPEMENT (c1275) USED A BAR (THE FOLIOT) WHICH SPUN BACK & FORTH. THE CLOCK LOST OR GAINED UP TO AN HOUR A DAY.

THE PENDULUM
THE PENDULUM (1670) WAS A GREAT ADVANCE BECAUSE IT HAD A 'NATURAL PERIOD'. UNLIKE THE FOLIOT, THE TIME IT TOOK TO SWING DID NOT VARY WITH THE FRICTION OF THE GEARS IN THE CLOCK.

GRANDFATHER CLOCKS
SOON AFTER THE INVENTION OF THE PENDULUM IT WAS FOUND THAT THEIR ACCURACY WAS IMPROVED IF THEY ONLY SWING THROUGH A SMALL ANGLE. THIS RESULTED IN THE GRANDFATHER CLOCK.

VACUUM CLOCKS
THE ACCURACY OF PENDULUMS IS SLIGHTLY AFFECTED BY THE 'CLOCKWORK' PUSHING IT & THE AIR ABOUT IT. THE 1910 SHORTT FREE PENDULUM CLOCK USED AN ISOLATED PENDULUM PUSHED ELECTRO-MAGNETICALLY IN A VACUUM CHAMBER.

QUARTZ CLOCKS
TODAY'S QUARTZ CLOCKS & WATCHES ARE ACCURATE TO ABOUT 1 MINUTE A YEAR, BUT THE CRYSTALS AGE RATHER ERRATICALLY BECAUSE OF THE CONTINUOUS VIBRATION. LABORATORY QUARTZ CLOCKS USE A GROUP OF CRYSTALS & TAKE AN AVERAGE READING.

ATOMIC CLOCKS
THE SHORTT FREE PENDULUM CLOCK IS ACCURATE TO 1 SEC IN 150 YEARS. THIS HAS BEEN REPLACED BY THE ATOMIC CLOCK (1955) WHICH MEASURES THE VIBRATION OF ATOMS OF THE ELEMENT CAESIUM & IS ACCURATE TO 1 SEC IN 3000 YEARS.

RUGBY CLOCKS
RUGBY CLOCKS CAN BE BOUGHT WHICH ARE SIMPLY RADIO RECEIVERS. THEY DECODE THE SIGNAL TRANSMITTED CONTINUOUSLY FROM AN ATOMIC CLOCK IN RUGBY.

HOW TO MAKE AN E.T. FINGER
① FIX PENLIGHT TORCH TO FINGER WITH STICKY TAPE.
② BUY RUBBER FINGER FROM JOKE SHOP OR CUT FINGER OFF RUBBER GLOVE.
③ PAD OUT WITH PAPER & TAPE TO FINGER COVERING TORCH.

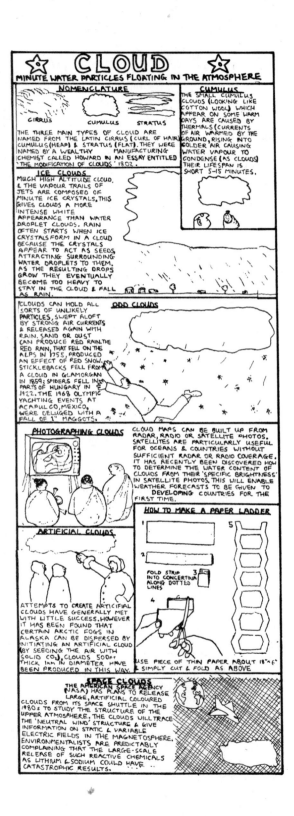

☆ CLOUD ☆
MINUTE WATER PARTICLES FLOATING IN THE ATMOSPHERE

NOMENCLATURE
CIRRUS   CUMULUS   STRATUS
THE THREE MAIN TYPES OF CLOUD ARE NAMED FROM THE LATIN CIRRUS (CURL OF HAIR), CUMULUS (HEAP) & STRATUS (FLAT). THEY WERE NAMED BY A WEALTHY MANUFACTURING CHEMIST CALLED HOWARD IN AN ESSAY ENTITLED 'THE MODIFICATION OF CLOUDS' 1802.

CUMULUS
THE SMALL CUMULUS CLOUDS (LOOKING LIKE COTTON WOOL) WHICH APPEAR ON SOME WARM DAYS ARE CAUSED BY THERMALS (CURRENTS OF AIR WARMED BY THE GROUND, RISING INTO COLDER AIR CAUSING WATER VAPOUR TO CONDENSE (AS CLOUDS). THEIR LIFESPAN IS SHORT 5-15 MINUTES.

ICE CLOUDS
MUCH HIGH ALTITUDE CLOUD & THE VAPOUR TRAILS OF JETS ARE COMPOSED OF MINUTE ICE CRYSTALS. THIS GIVES CLOUDS A MORE INTENSE WHITE APPEARANCE THAN WATER DROPLET CLOUDS. RAIN OFTEN STARTS WHEN ICE CRYSTALS FORM IN A CLOUD BECAUSE THE CRYSTALS APPEAR TO ACT AS SEEDS ATTRACTING SURROUNDING WATER DROPLETS TO THEM. AS THE RESULTING DROPS GROW THEY EVENTUALLY BECOME TOO HEAVY TO STAY IN THE CLOUD & FALL AS RAIN.

ODD CLOUDS
CLOUDS CAN HOLD ALL SORTS OF UNLIKELY PARTICLES, SWEPT ALOFT BY STRONG AIR CURRENTS & RELEASED AGAIN WITH RAIN. SAND OR DUST CAN PRODUCE RED RAIN. THE RED RAIN THAT FELL ON THE ALPS IN 1755, PRODUCED AN EFFECT OF RED SNOW. STICKLEBACKS FELL FROM A CLOUD IN GLAMORGAN IN 1859; SPIDERS FELL IN PARTS OF HUNGARY IN 1922. THE 1968 OLYMPIC YACHTING EVENTS AT ACAPULCO, MEXICO, WERE DELUGED WITH A FALL OF 1" MAGGOTS.

PHOTOGRAPHING CLOUDS
CLOUD MAPS CAN BE BUILT UP FROM RADAR, RADIO OR SATELLITE PHOTOS. SATELLITES ARE PARTICULARLY USEFUL FOR OCEANS & COUNTRIES WITHOUT SUFFICIENT RADAR OR RADIO COVERAGE. IT HAS RECENTLY BEEN DISCOVERED HOW TO DETERMINE THE WATER CONTENT OF CLOUDS FROM THEIR 'SPECIFIC BRIGHTNESS' IN SATELLITE PHOTOS. THIS WILL ENABLE WEATHER FORECASTS TO BE GIVEN TO DEVELOPING COUNTRIES FOR THE FIRST TIME.

ARTIFICIAL CLOUDS
ATTEMPTS TO CREATE ARTIFICIAL CLOUDS HAVE GENERALLY MET WITH LITTLE SUCCESS. HOWEVER IT HAS BEEN FOUND THAT CERTAIN ARCTIC FOGS IN ALASKA CAN BE DISPERSED BY INITIATING AN ARTIFICIAL CLOUD BY SEEDING THE AIR WITH SOLID CO_2. CLOUDS 500ft THICK 1km IN DIAMETER HAVE BEEN PRODUCED IN THIS WAY.

HOW TO MAKE A PAPER LADDER
FOLD STRIP INTO CONCERTINA ALONG DOTTED LINES
USE PIECE OF THIN PAPER ABOUT 18"x6" SIMPLY CUT & FOLD AS ABOVE

SPACE CLOUDS
THE AMERICAN SPACE AGENCY (NASA) HAS PLANS TO RELEASE LARGE, ARTIFICIAL COLOURED CLOUDS FROM ITS SPACE SHUTTLE IN THE 1980s TO STUDY THE STRUCTURE OF THE UPPER ATMOSPHERE. THE CLOUDS WILL TRACE THE 'NEUTRAL WIND' STRUCTURE & GIVE INFORMATION ON STATIC & VARIABLE ELECTRIC FIELDS IN THE MAGNETOSPHERE. ENVIRONMENTALISTS ARE PREDICTABLY COMPLAINING THAT THE LARGE-SCALE RELEASE OF SUCH REACTIVE CHEMICALS AS LITHIUM & SODIUM COULD HAVE CATASTROPHIC RESULTS.

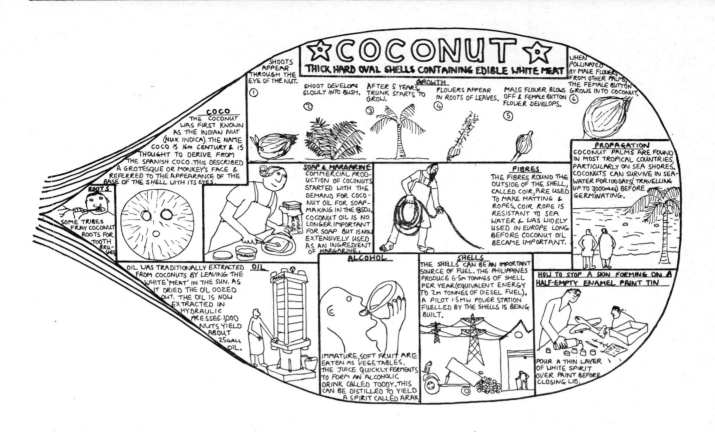

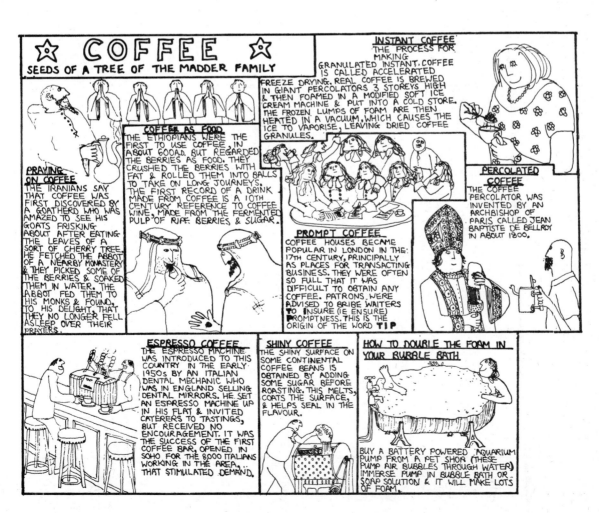

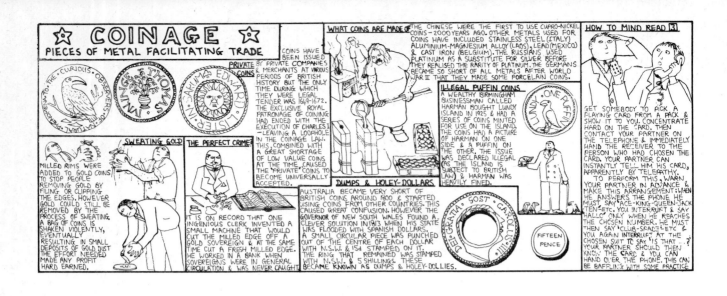

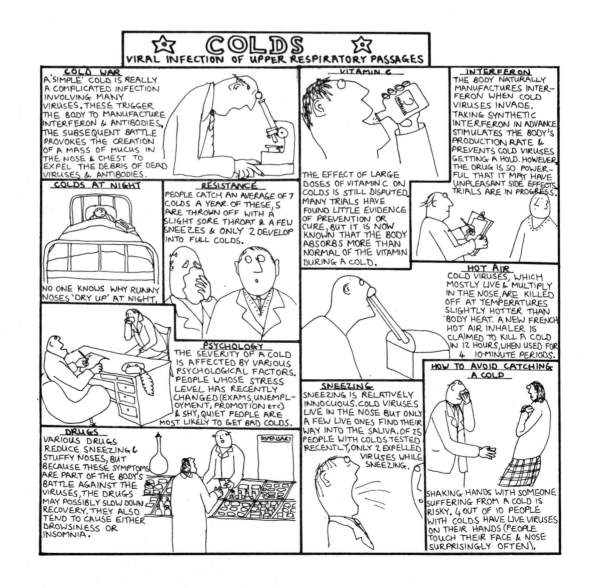

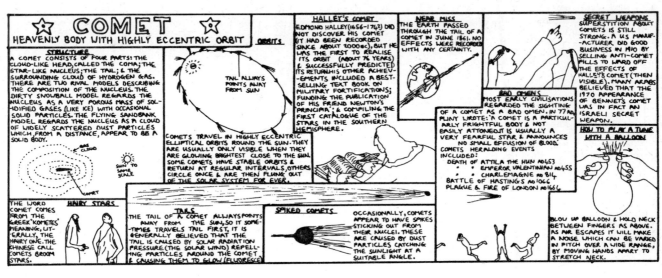

☆ COMET ☆
HEAVENLY BODY WITH HIGHLY ECCENTRIC ORBIT

STRUCTURE
A COMET CONSISTS OF FOUR PARTS: THE CLOUD-LIKE HEAD, CALLED THE COMA; THE STAR-LIKE NUCLEUS; THE TAIL; & THE SURROUNDING CLOUD OF HYDROGEN GAS. THERE ARE TWO RIVAL MODELS DESCRIBING THE COMPOSITION OF THE NUCLEUS. THE DIRTY SNOWBALL MODEL REGARDS THE NUCLEUS AS A VERY POROUS MASS OF SOLIDIFIED GASES (LIKE ICE) WITH OCCASIONAL SOLID PARTICLES. THE FLYING SANDBANK MODEL REGARDS THE NUCLEUS AS A CLOUD OF WIDELY SCATTERED DUST PARTICLES WHICH, FROM A DISTANCE, APPEAR TO BE A SOLID BODY.

ORBITS
TAIL ALWAYS POINTS AWAY FROM SUN

COMETS TRAVEL IN HIGHLY ECCENTRIC ELLIPTICAL ORBITS ROUND THE SUN. THEY ARE USUALLY ONLY VISIBLE WHEN THEY ARE GLOWING BRIGHTEST CLOSE TO THE SUN. SOME COMETS HAVE STABLE ORBITS & RETURN AT REGULAR INTERVALS, OTHERS CIRCLE ONCE & ARE THEN FLUNG OUT OF THE SOLAR SYSTEM FOR EVER.

HAIRY STARS
THE WORD COMET COMES FROM THE GREEK 'KOMETES' MEANING, LITERALLY, THE HAIRY ONE. THE CHINESE CALL COMETS BROOM STARS.

TAILS
THE TAIL OF A COMET ALWAYS POINTS AWAY FROM THE SUN, SO IT SOMETIMES TRAVELS TAIL FIRST. IT IS GENERALLY BELIEVED THAT THE TAIL IS CAUSED BY SOLAR RADIATION PRESSURE (THE SOLAR WIND) REPELLING PARTICLES AROUND THE COMET & CAUSING THEM TO GLOW (FLUORESCE).

SPIKED COMETS
OCCASIONALLY, COMETS APPEAR TO HAVE SPIKES STICKING OUT FROM THEIR NUCLEI. THESE ARE CAUSED BY DUST PARTICLES CATCHING THE SUNLIGHT AT A SUITABLE ANGLE.

HALLEY'S COMET
EDMOND HALLEY (1656-1742) DID NOT DISCOVER HIS COMET (IT HAD BEEN RECORDED SINCE ABOUT 2000BC), BUT HE WAS THE FIRST TO REALISE ITS ORBIT (ABOUT 76 YEARS) & SUCCESSFULLY PREDICTED ITS RETURN. HIS OTHER ACHIEVEMENTS INCLUDED A BESTSELLING TEXT BOOK ON MILITARY FORTIFICATIONS; FUNDING THE PUBLICATION OF HIS FRIEND NEWTON'S 'PRINCIPIA' & COMPILING THE FIRST CATALOGUE OF THE STARS IN THE SOUTHERN HEMISPHERE.

NEAR MISS
THE EARTH PASSED THROUGH THE TAIL OF A COMET IN JUNE 1861. NO EFFECTS WERE RECORDED WITH ANY CERTAINTY.

BAD OMENS
MOST EARLY CIVILISATIONS REGARDED THE SIGHTING OF A COMET AS A BAD OMEN. IN 77AD PLINY WROTE: 'A COMET IS A PARTICULARLY FRIGHTFUL BODY & NOT EASILY ATTONED. IT IS USUALLY A VERY FEARFUL STAR & ANNOUNCES NO SMALL EFFUSION OF BLOOD'. COMETS HERALDING EVENTS INCLUDED:
- DEATH OF ATTILA THE HUN AD453
- EMPEROR VALENTINIAN AD455
- CHARLEMAGNE AD814
- BATTLE OF HASTINGS AD1066
- PLAGUE & FIRE OF LONDON AD1666

SECRET WEAPONS
SUPERSTITION ABOUT COMETS IS STILL STRONG. A US MANUFACTURER DID GOOD BUSINESS IN 1910 BY SELLING ANTI-COMET PILLS TO WARD OFF THE EFFECTS OF HALLEY'S COMET (THEN VISIBLE). MANY ARABS BELIEVED THAT THE 1970 APPEARANCE OF BENNET'S COMET WAS IN FACT AN ISRAELI SECRET WEAPON.

HOW TO PLAY A TUNE WITH A BALLOON
BLOW UP BALLOON & HOLD NECK BETWEEN FINGERS AS ABOVE. AS AIR ESCAPES IT WILL MAKE A NOISE WHICH CAN BE VARIED IN PITCH OVER A WIDE RANGE, BY MOVING HANDS APART TO STRETCH NECK.

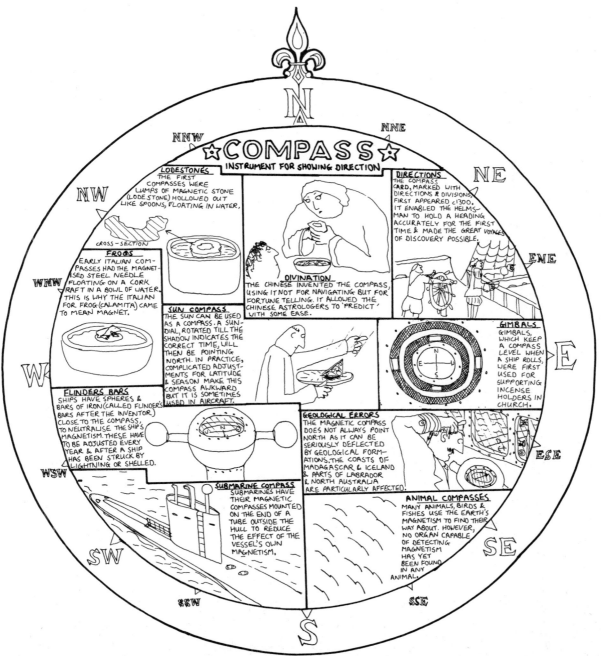

☆ COMPASS ☆
INSTRUMENT FOR SHOWING DIRECTION

LODESTONES
THE FIRST COMPASSES WERE LUMPS OF MAGNETIC STONE (LODESTONE) HOLLOWED OUT LIKE SPOONS, FLOATING IN WATER.

CROSS-SECTION

FROGS
EARLY ITALIAN COMPASSES HAD THE MAGNETISED STEEL NEEDLE FLOATING ON A CORK RAFT IN A BOWL OF WATER. THIS IS WHY THE ITALIAN FOR FROG (CALAMITA) CAME TO MEAN MAGNET.

SUN COMPASS
THE SUN CAN BE USED AS A COMPASS. A SUNDIAL, ROTATED TILL THE SHADOW INDICATES THE CORRECT TIME, WILL THEN BE POINTING NORTH. IN PRACTICE, COMPLICATED ADJUSTMENTS FOR LATITUDE & SEASON MAKE THIS COMPASS AWKWARD BUT IT IS SOMETIMES USED IN AIRCRAFT.

FLINDERS BARS
SHIPS HAVE SPHERES & BARS OF IRON (CALLED FLINDERS BARS AFTER THE INVENTOR) CLOSE TO THE COMPASS, TO NEUTRALISE THE SHIP'S MAGNETISM. THESE HAVE TO BE ADJUSTED EVERY YEAR & AFTER A SHIP HAS BEEN STRUCK BY LIGHTNING OR SHELLED.

SUBMARINE COMPASS
SUBMARINES HAVE THEIR MAGNETIC COMPASSES MOUNTED ON THE END OF A TUBE OUTSIDE THE HULL TO REDUCE THE EFFECT OF THE VESSEL'S OWN MAGNETISM.

DIVINATION
THE CHINESE INVENTED THE COMPASS, USING IT NOT FOR NAVIGATING BUT FOR FORTUNE TELLING. IT ALLOWED THE CHINESE ASTROLOGERS TO 'PREDICT' WITH SOME EASE.

DIRECTIONS
THE COMPASS CARD, MARKED WITH DIRECTIONS & DIVISIONS, FIRST APPEARED c1300. IT ENABLED THE HELMSMAN TO HOLD A HEADING ACCURATELY FOR THE FIRST TIME & MADE THE GREAT VOYAGES OF DISCOVERY POSSIBLE.

GIMBALS
GIMBALS, WHICH KEEP A COMPASS LEVEL WHEN A SHIP ROLLS, WERE FIRST USED FOR SUPPORTING INCENSE HOLDERS IN CHURCH.

GEOLOGICAL ERRORS
THE MAGNETIC COMPASS DOES NOT ALWAYS POINT NORTH AS IT CAN BE SERIOUSLY DEFLECTED BY GEOLOGICAL FORMATIONS. THE COASTS OF MADAGASCAR & ICELAND & PARTS OF LABRADOR & NORTH AUSTRALIA ARE PARTICULARLY AFFECTED.

ANIMAL COMPASSES
MANY ANIMALS, BIRDS & FISHES USE THE EARTH'S MAGNETISM TO FIND THEIR WAY ABOUT. HOWEVER, NO ORGAN CAPABLE OF DETECTING MAGNETISM HAS YET BEEN FOUND IN ANY ANIMAL.

N
NNW NNE
NW NE
WNW ENE
W E
WSW ESE
SW SE
SSW SSE
S

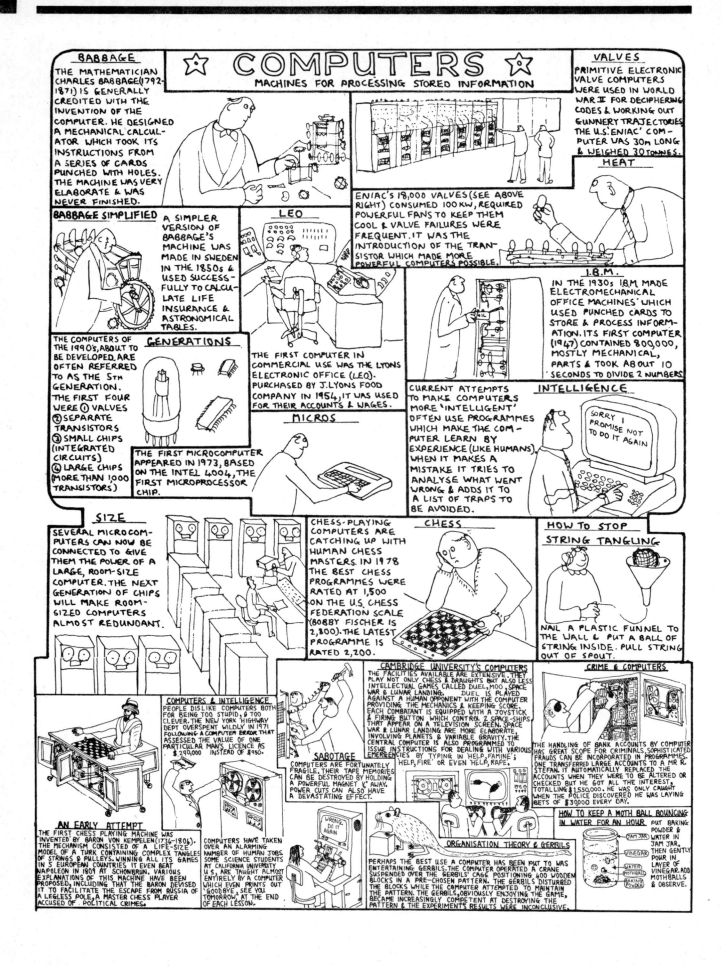

☆ COMPUTERS ☆
MACHINES FOR PROCESSING STORED INFORMATION

BABBAGE

THE MATHEMATICIAN CHARLES BABBAGE (1792-1871) IS GENERALLY CREDITED WITH THE INVENTION OF THE COMPUTER. HE DESIGNED A MECHANICAL CALCULATOR WHICH TOOK ITS INSTRUCTIONS FROM A SERIES OF CARDS PUNCHED WITH HOLES. THE MACHINE WAS VERY ELABORATE & WAS NEVER FINISHED.

BABBAGE SIMPLIFIED

A SIMPLER VERSION OF BABBAGE'S MACHINE WAS MADE IN SWEDEN IN THE 1850s & USED SUCCESSFULLY TO CALCULATE LIFE INSURANCE & ASTRONOMICAL TABLES.

VALVES

PRIMITIVE ELECTRONIC VALVE COMPUTERS WERE USED IN WORLD WAR II FOR DECIPHERING CODES & WORKING OUT GUNNERY TRAJECTORIES. THE U.S. 'ENIAC' COMPUTER WAS 30m LONG & WEIGHED 30 TONNES.

HEAT

ENIAC'S 18,000 VALVES (SEE ABOVE RIGHT) CONSUMED 100 KW, REQUIRED POWERFUL FANS TO KEEP THEM COOL & VALVE FAILURES WERE FREQUENT. IT WAS THE INTRODUCTION OF THE TRANSISTOR WHICH MADE MORE POWERFUL COMPUTERS POSSIBLE.

LEO

THE FIRST COMPUTER IN COMMERCIAL USE WAS THE LYONS ELECTRONIC OFFICE (LEO). PURCHASED BY J. LYONS FOOD COMPANY IN 1954, IT WAS USED FOR THEIR ACCOUNTS & WAGES.

GENERATIONS

THE COMPUTERS OF THE 1990's, ABOUT TO BE DEVELOPED, ARE OFTEN REFERRED TO AS THE 5TH GENERATION. THE FIRST FOUR WERE ① VALVES ② SEPARATE TRANSISTORS ③ SMALL CHIPS (INTEGRATED CIRCUITS) ④ LARGE CHIPS (MORE THAN 1000 TRANSISTORS)

I.B.M.

IN THE 1930s I.B.M. MADE ELECTROMECHANICAL OFFICE MACHINES WHICH USED PUNCHED CARDS TO STORE & PROCESS INFORMATION. ITS FIRST COMPUTER (1947) CONTAINED 800,000, MOSTLY MECHANICAL, PARTS & TOOK ABOUT 10 SECONDS TO DIVIDE 2 NUMBERS.

MICROS

THE FIRST MICROCOMPUTER APPEARED IN 1973, BASED ON THE INTEL 4004, THE FIRST MICROPROCESSOR CHIP.

INTELLIGENCE

CURRENT ATTEMPTS TO MAKE COMPUTERS MORE 'INTELLIGENT' OFTEN USE PROGRAMMES WHICH MAKE THE COMPUTER LEARN BY EXPERIENCE (LIKE HUMANS). WHEN IT MAKES A MISTAKE IT TRIES TO ANALYSE WHAT WENT WRONG & ADDS IT TO A LIST OF TRAPS TO BE AVOIDED.

SORRY I PROMISE NOT TO DO IT AGAIN

SIZE

SEVERAL MICROCOMPUTERS CAN NOW BE CONNECTED TO GIVE THEM THE POWER OF A LARGE, ROOM-SIZE COMPUTER. THE NEXT GENERATION OF CHIPS WILL MAKE ROOM-SIZED COMPUTERS ALMOST REDUNDANT.

CHESS

CHESS-PLAYING COMPUTERS ARE CATCHING UP WITH HUMAN CHESS MASTERS. IN 1978 THE BEST CHESS PROGRAMMES WERE RATED AT 1,500 ON THE U.S. CHESS FEDERATION SCALE (BOBBY FISCHER IS 2,800). THE LATEST PROGRAMME IS RATED 2,200.

HOW TO STOP STRING TANGLING

NAIL A PLASTIC FUNNEL TO THE WALL & PUT A BALL OF STRING INSIDE. PULL STRING OUT OF SPOUT.

CAMBRIDGE UNIVERSITY'S COMPUTERS

THE FACILITIES AVAILABLE ARE EXTENSIVE. THEY PLAY NOT ONLY CHESS & DRAUGHTS BUT ALSO LESS INTELLECTUAL GAMES CALLED DUEL, MOO, SPACE WAR & LUNAR LANDING. DUEL IS PLAYED AGAINST A HUMAN OPPONENT WITH THE COMPUTER PROVIDING THE MECHANICS & KEEPING SCORE. EACH COMBATANT IS EQUIPPED WITH A JOYSTICK & FIRING BUTTON WHICH CONTROL 2 SPACE-SHIPS THAT APPEAR ON A TELEVISION SCREEN. SPACE WAR & LUNAR LANDING ARE MORE ELABORATE, INVOLVING PLANETS & VARIABLE GRAVITY. THE CENTRAL COMPUTER IS ALSO PROGRAMMED TO ISSUE INSTRUCTIONS FOR DEALING WITH VARIOUS EMERGENCIES BY TYPING IN 'HELP, FAMINE', 'HELP, FIRE' OR EVEN 'HELP, RAPE'.

COMPUTERS & INTELLIGENCE

PEOPLE DISLIKE COMPUTERS BOTH FOR BEING TOO STUPID, & TOO CLEVER. THE NEW YORK HIGHWAY DEPT OVERSPENT WILDLY IN 1971 FOLLOWING A COMPUTER ERROR THAT ASSESSED THE VALUE OF ONE PARTICULAR MAN'S LICENCE AS $290,000 INSTEAD OF $950.

SABOTAGE

COMPUTERS ARE FORTUNATELY FRAGILE. THEIR TAPE MEMORIES CAN BE DESTROYED BY HOLDING A POWERFUL MAGNET 6' AWAY. POWER CUTS CAN ALSO HAVE A DEVASTATING EFFECT.

CRIME & COMPUTERS

THE HANDLING OF BANK ACCOUNTS BY COMPUTER HAS GREAT SCOPE FOR CRIMINALS. SOPHISTICATED FRAUDS CAN BE INCORPORATED IN PROGRAMMES. ONE TRANSFERRED LARGE ACCOUNTS TO A MR R. STEFAN. IT AUTOMATICALLY REPLACED THE ACCOUNTS WHEN THEY WERE TO BE ALTERED OR CHECKED BUT HE GOT ALL THE INTEREST, TOTALLING $1,550,000. HE WAS ONLY CAUGHT WHEN THE POLICE DISCOVERED HE WAS LAYING BETS OF $30000 EVERY DAY.

AN EARLY ATTEMPT

THE FIRST CHESS PLAYING MACHINE WAS INVENTED BY BARON VON KEMPELEN (1734-1804). THE MECHANISM CONSISTED OF A LIFE-SIZE MODEL OF A TURK CONTAINING COMPLEX TANGLES OF STRINGS & PULLEYS. WINNING ALL ITS GAMES IN 5 EUROPEAN COUNTRIES IT EVEN BEAT NAPOLEON IN 1809 AT SCHONBRUN. VARIOUS EXPLANATIONS OF THIS MACHINE HAVE BEEN PROPOSED, INCLUDING THAT THE BARON DEVISED IT TO FACILITATE THE ESCAPE FROM RUSSIA OF A LEGLESS POLE, A MASTER CHESS PLAYER ACCUSED OF POLITICAL CRIMES.

COMPUTERS HAVE TAKEN OVER AN ALARMING NUMBER OF HUMAN JOBS. SOME SCIENCE STUDENTS AT CALIFORNIA UNIVERSITY U.S. ARE TAUGHT ALMOST ENTIRELY BY A COMPUTER WHICH EVEN PRINTS OUT 'GOODBYE, SEE YOU TOMORROW' AT THE END OF EACH LESSON.

WRONG, DO IT AGAIN

ORGANISATION THEORY & GERBILS

PERHAPS THE BEST USE A COMPUTER HAS BEEN PUT TO WAS ENTERTAINING GERBILS. THE COMPUTER OPERATED A CRANE SUSPENDED OVER THE GERBILS' CAGE POSITIONING 400 WOODEN BLOCKS IN A PRE-CHOSEN PATTERN. THE GERBILS DISTURBED THE BLOCKS WHILE THE COMPUTER ATTEMPTED TO MAINTAIN THE PATTERN. THE GERBILS, OBVIOUSLY ENJOYING THE GAME, BECAME INCREASINGLY COMPETENT AT DESTROYING THE PATTERN & THE EXPERIMENT'S RESULTS WERE INCONCLUSIVE.

HOW TO KEEP A MOTH BALL BOUNCING IN WATER FOR AN HOUR

PUT BAKING POWDER & WATER IN JAM JAR, THEN GENTLY POUR IN LAYER OF VINEGAR. ADD MOTHBALLS & OBSERVE.

JAM JAR / VINEGAR / WATER / MOTHBALL / BAKING POWDER

☆ CONJURING ☆
APPEARING TO PERFORM THE IMPOSSIBLE

CHEOPS & DEDI

THE FIRST BOOK

THE FIRST ENGLISH BOOK DEVOTED COMPLETELY TO CONJURING WAS PUBLISHED IN 1612 "THE ART OF JUGGLING" (UNTIL THE 1800s JUGGLING WAS TAKEN TO MEAN CONJURING). IT WAS WRITTEN TO PROVE THAT NOT EVERYONE WHO WORKED WONDERS WAS A WITCH OR WARLOCK AND APOLOGISED FOR REVEALING "THE SECRETS TO THE HINDERANCE OF SUCH POOR MEN AS LIVE THEREBY."

FATAL FEATS

THE BULLET CATCHING TRICK (IN WHICH THE MAGICIAN CATCHES BULLETS FIRED AT HIM IN HIS TEETH) HAS CAUSED MORE FATAL ACCIDENTS THAN ANY OTHER TRICK. MAGICIANS WHO HAVE DIED FROM WOUNDS INCLUDE DE LINSKY (1820), DR EPSTEIN (1869), HATAL (1899), BLUENFELD (1906) DE LINE, H.T. SARTEL AND OTHERS.

ABRACADABRA

THE EARLIEST REFERENCE TO A CONJURER IS CONTAINED IN THE WESTCAR MANUSCRIPT OF 1,700BC. CHEOPS, THE BUILDER OF THE GREAT PYRAMID, IS SAID TO HAVE BEEN ENTERTAINED BY A CONJURER CALLED DEDI. HIS MOST FAMOUS FEAT WAS THE FASTENING ON OF SEVERED HEADS. HE SLICED THE HEAD OFF A GOOSE, PUT THE HEAD ON THE EAST SIDE OF THE HALL & THE TRUNK ON THE WEST, UTTERED THE MAGIC WORDS & THE GOOSE WAS RESTORED. HE PERFORMED THE TRICK WITH GEESE, PELICANS & OXEN BUT REFUSED TO USE HUMANS.

```
A B R A C A D A B R A
 A B R A C A D A B R
  A B R A C A D A B
   A B R A C A D A
    A B R A C A D
     A B R A C A
      A B R A C
       A B R A
        A B R
         A B
          A
```

THE WORD ABRACADABRA CAME FROM THE GNOSTICS OF BASILIDES (A SECT OF EARLY CHRISTIANS, c125AD). THEY CLAIMED THAT THE WORD WAS HIGHLY EFFECTIVE IN CURING ILLNESS & ENGRAVED IT IN TRIANGLES (AS ABOVE) ON STONES WORN ROUND THE NECK.

18 CENTURY FEATS

CONJURING WAS POPULAR BY THE 1700s & MANY CONJURERS, ALL WITH THEIR OWN SPECIALITIES, FLOURISHED.
★ DELISLE CONJURED UP HOT OMELETTES IN BORROWED HATS.
★ LANE NAILED GENTS' BREECHES TO CHAIRS & MAGICALLY EXTRACTED THEM WITHOUT DAMAGE.
★ INGLEBY CHANGED TWO FRESH EGGS INTO A CHILD & A SET OF BED LINEN.
★ CHABERT ENDED HIS ACT COOKING STEAKS BY BREATHING FIRE ON THEM.

POPULAR SAWING

THE "SAWING A WOMAN IN HALF" TRICK WAS FIRST PERFORMED IN 1920 BY A MAGICIAN CALLED P.T. SELBIT. DURING THE 1921-22 SEASON THERE WAS SUCH A CRAZE FOR THE ILLUSION THAT HE ORGANISED NINE ROAD COMPANIES TO PERFORM THE TRICK. AMBULANCES WERE ALWAYS IN ATTENDANCE TO ADD TO THE DRAMA.

HOW TO MAKE A COIN RISE THROUGH A CIGARETTE PACKET

PUT COIN IN BOTTOM OF FULL DRAWER-TYPE CIGARETTE PACKET (IF PACKET IS EMPTY FILL IT WITH PAPER). TAP PACKET HARD ON TOP & COIN WILL RISE.

SPOON BENDING

SOME AUTHORITIES NOW BELIEVE THAT URI GELLER BENT HIS SPOONS BY TRICKERY INSTEAD OF THE PARANORMAL POWERS HE CLAIMS. VARIOUS OTHER CLAIMANTS HAVE NOW BEEN PROVED TO BE MAGICIANS WHEN WATCHED THROUGH TWO WAY MIRRORS. THE ONLY GOVERNMENT MONEY FOR RESEARCH CONNECTED WITH PARANORMAL POWERS IS A £10,000 GRANT FOR THE STUDY OF SCIENTISTS INVESTIGATING THE SUBJECT.

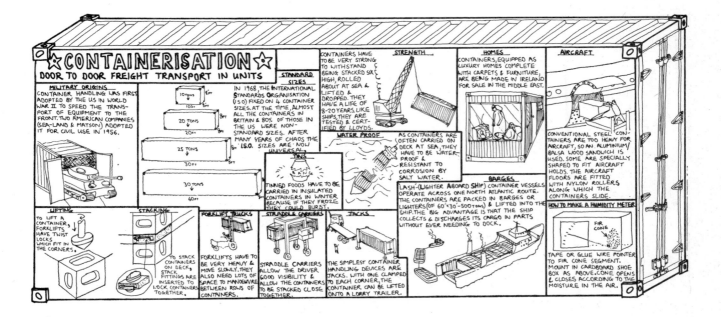

☆ CONTAINERISATION ☆
DOOR TO DOOR FREIGHT TRANSPORT IN UNITS

MILITARY ORIGINS

CONTAINER HANDLING WAS FIRST ADOPTED BY THE US IN WORLD WAR II TO SPEED THE TRANSPORT OF EQUIPMENT TO THE FRONT. TWO AMERICAN COMPANIES (SEA-LAND & MATSON) ADOPTED IT FOR CIVIL USE IN 1956.

STANDARD SIZES

IN 1968 THE INTERNATIONAL STANDARDS ORGANISATION (ISO) FIXED ON 4 CONTAINER SIZES. AT THE TIME, ALMOST ALL THE CONTAINERS IN BRITAIN & 80% OF THOSE IN THE US WERE NON-STANDARD SIZES. AFTER MANY YEARS OF CHAOS THE I.S.O. SIZES ARE NOW UNIVERSAL.

10 TONS — 6ft / 8ft
20 TONS — 20ft
25 TONS — 30ft / 8ft
30 TONS — 40ft

STRENGTH

CONTAINERS HAVE TO BE VERY STRONG TO WITHSTAND BEING STACKED SIX HIGH, ROLLED ABOUT AT SEA & LIFTED & DROPPED. THEY HAVE A LIFE OF 8-20 YEARS LIKE SHIPS. THEY ARE TESTED & CERTIFIED BY LLOYDS.

HOMES

CONTAINERS, EQUIPPED AS LUXURY HOMES COMPLETE WITH CARPETS & FURNITURE, ARE BEING MADE IN IRELAND FOR SALE IN THE MIDDLE EAST.

AIRCRAFT

CONVENTIONAL STEEL CONTAINERS ARE TOO HEAVY FOR AIRCRAFT, SO AN ALUMINIUM/BALSA WOOD SANDWICH IS USED. SOME ARE SPECIALLY SHAPED TO FIT AIRCRAFT HOLDS. THE AIRCRAFT FLOORS ARE FITTED WITH NYLON ROLLERS ALONG WHICH THE CONTAINERS SLIDE.

WATER PROOF

AS CONTAINERS ARE OFTEN CARRIED ON DECK AT SEA, THEY HAVE TO BE WATERPROOF & RESISTANT TO CORROSION BY SALT WATER.

TINS

TINNED FOODS HAVE TO BE CARRIED IN INSULATED CONTAINERS IN WINTER BECAUSE IF THEY FROZE THEY COULD BURST.

BARGES

LASH (LIGHTER ABOARD SHIP) CONTAINER VESSELS OPERATE ACROSS ONE NORTH ATLANTIC ROUTE. THE CONTAINERS ARE PACKED IN BARGES OR LIGHTERS (OF 60'×30'-500 TONS) & LIFTED INTO THE SHIP. THE BIG ADVANTAGE IS THAT THE SHIP COLLECTS & DISCHARGES ITS CARGO IN PARTS WITHOUT EVER NEEDING TO DOCK.

HOW TO MAKE A HUMIDITY METER

FIR CONE

TAPE OR GLUE WIRE POINTER TO FIR CONE SEGMENT. MOUNT IN CARDBOARD SHOE BOX AS ABOVE. CONE OPENS & CLOSES ACCORDING TO THE MOISTURE IN THE AIR.

LIFTING

TO LIFT A CONTAINER, FORKLIFTS HAVE TWIST LOCKS WHICH FIT IN THE CORNERS.

STACKING

TO STACK CONTAINERS ON DECK, STACK FITTINGS ARE INSERTED TO LOCK CONTAINERS TOGETHER.

FORKLIFT TRUCKS

FORKLIFTS HAVE TO BE VERY HEAVY & MOVE SLOWLY. THEY ALSO NEED LOTS OF SPACE TO MANOEUVRE BETWEEN ROWS OF CONTAINERS.

STRADDLE CARRIERS

STRADDLE CARRIERS ALLOW THE DRIVER GOOD VISIBILITY & ALLOW THE CONTAINERS TO BE STACKED CLOSE TOGETHER.

JACKS

THE SIMPLEST CONTAINER HANDLING DEVICES ARE JACKS. WITH ONE CLAMPED TO EACH CORNER, THE CONTAINER CAN BE LIFTED ONTO A LORRY TRAILER.

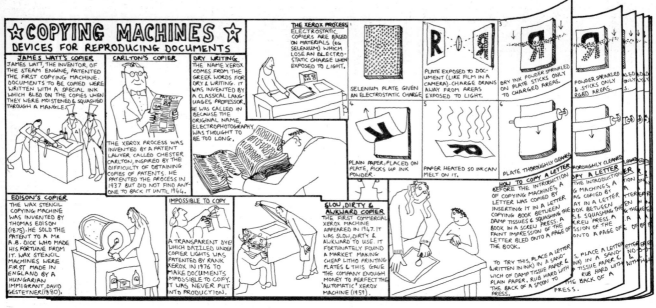

☆ COPYING MACHINES ☆
DEVICES FOR REPRODUCING DOCUMENTS

JAMES WATT'S COPIER
JAMES WATT, THE INVENTOR OF THE STEAM ENGINE, PATENTED THE FIRST COPYING MACHINE. DOCUMENTS TO BE COPIED WERE WRITTEN WITH A SPECIAL INK WHICH BLED ON THE COPIES WHEN THEY WERE MOISTENED & SQUASHED THROUGH A MANGLE.

CARLTON'S COPIER
THE XEROX PROCESS WAS INVENTED BY A PATENT LAWYER CALLED CHESTER CARLTON, INSPIRED BY THE DIFFICULTY OF OBTAINING COPIES OF PATENTS. HE PATENTED THE PROCESS IN 1937 BUT DID NOT FIND ANYONE TO BACK IT UNTIL 1944.

DRY WRITING
THE NAME XEROX COMES FROM THE GREEK WORDS FOR DRY & WRITING. IT WAS INVENTED BY A CLASSICAL LANGUAGES PROFESSOR. HE WAS CALLED IN BECAUSE THE ORIGINAL NAME, ELECTROPHOTOGRAPHY, WAS THOUGHT TO BE TOO LONG.

THE XEROX PROCESS
ELECTROSTATIC COPIERS ARE BASED ON MATERIALS (EG SELENIUM) WHICH LOSE AN ELECTROSTATIC CHARGE WHEN EXPOSED TO LIGHT.

SELENIUM PLATE GIVEN AN ELECTROSTATIC CHARGE

PLATE EXPOSED TO DOCUMENT (LIKE FILM IN A CAMERA). CHARGE DRAINS AWAY FROM AREAS EXPOSED TO LIGHT.

DRY INK POWDER SPRINKLED ON PLATE STICKS ONLY TO CHARGED AREAS.

POWDER SPRINKLED & STICKS ONLY...ARGED AREAS.

PLAIN PAPER, PLACED ON PLATE, PICKS UP INK POWDER.

PAPER HEATED SO INK CAN MELT ON IT.

PLATE THOROUGHLY CLEANED

EDISON'S COPIER
THE WAX STENCIL COPYING MACHINE WAS INVENTED BY THOMAS EDISON (1875). HE SOLD THE PATENT TO A MR A.B. DICK WHO MADE HIS FORTUNE FROM IT. WAX STENCIL MACHINES WERE FIRST MADE IN ENGLAND BY A HUNGARIAN IMMIGRANT, DAVID GESTETNER (1880).

IMPOSSIBLE TO COPY
A TRANSPARENT DYE WHICH DAZZLED UNDER COPIER LIGHTS WAS PATENTED BY RANK XEROX IN 1976 TO MAKE DOCUMENTS IMPOSSIBLE TO COPY. IT WAS NEVER PUT INTO PRODUCTION.

SLOW, DIRTY & AWKWARD COPIER
THE FIRST COMMERCIAL XEROX MACHINE APPEARED IN 1947. IT WAS SLOW, DIRTY & AWKWARD TO USE. IT FORTUNATELY FOUND A MARKET MAKING CHEAP LITHO PRINTING PLATES & THIS GAVE THE COMPANY ENOUGH MONEY TO PERFECT THE 'AUTOMATIC' XEROX MACHINE (1959).

HOW TO COPY A LETTER
BEFORE THE INTRODUCTION OF COPYING MACHINES, A LETTER WAS COPIED BY INSERTING IT IN A LETTER COPYING BOOK BETWEEN DAMP TISSUES & SQUASHING THE BOOK IN A SCREW PRESS. A FAINT IMPRESSION OF THE LETTER BLED ONTO A PAGE OF THE BOOK.

TO TRY THIS, PLACE A LETTER (WRITTEN IN INK) IN A SANDWICH OF DAMP TISSUE PAPER & PLAIN PAPER. RUB HARD WITH THE BACK OF A SPOON TO PRESS.

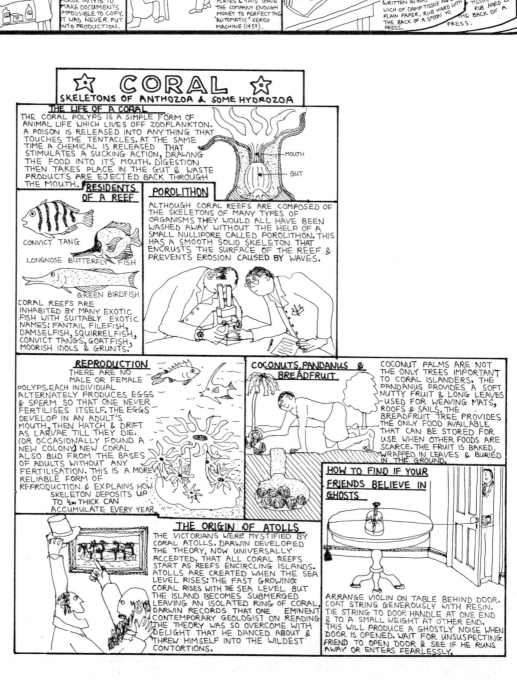

☆ CORAL ☆
SKELETONS OF ANTHOZOA & SOME HYDROZOA

THE LIFE OF A CORAL
THE CORAL POLYP IS A SIMPLE FORM OF ANIMAL LIFE WHICH LIVES OFF ZOOPLANKTON. A POISON IS RELEASED INTO ANYTHING THAT TOUCHES THE TENTACLES. AT THE SAME TIME A CHEMICAL IS RELEASED THAT STIMULATES A SUCKING ACTION, DRAWING THE FOOD INTO ITS MOUTH. DIGESTION THEN TAKES PLACE IN THE GUT & WASTE PRODUCTS ARE EJECTED BACK THROUGH THE MOUTH.

— MOUTH
— GUT

RESIDENTS OF A REEF
CONVICT TANG
LONGNOSE BUTTERFLY FISH
GREEN BIRDFISH

CORAL REEFS ARE INHABITED BY MANY EXOTIC FISH WITH SUITABLY EXOTIC NAMES: FANTAIL FILEFISH, DAMSELFISH, SQUIRRELFISH, CONVICT TANGS, GOATFISH, MOORISH IDOLS & GRUNTS.

POROLITHON
ALTHOUGH CORAL REEFS ARE COMPOSED OF THE SKELETONS OF MANY TYPES OF ORGANISMS THEY WOULD ALL HAVE BEEN WASHED AWAY WITHOUT THE HELP OF A SMALL NULLIPORE CALLED POROLITHON. THIS HAS A SMOOTH SOLID SKELETON THAT ENCRUSTS THE SURFACE OF THE REEF & PREVENTS EROSION CAUSED BY WAVES.

REPRODUCTION
THERE ARE NO MALE OR FEMALE POLYPS. EACH INDIVIDUAL ALTERNATELY PRODUCES EGGS & SPERM SO THAT ONE NEVER FERTILISES ITSELF. THE EGGS DEVELOP IN AN ADULT'S MOUTH, THEN HATCH & DRIFT AS LARVAE TILL THEY DIE. (OR OCCASIONALLY FOUND A NEW COLONY) NEW CORAL ALSO BUD FROM THE BASES OF ADULTS WITHOUT ANY FERTILISATION. THIS IS A MORE RELIABLE FORM OF REPRODUCTION. & EXPLAINS HOW SKELETON DEPOSITS UP TO ½IN THICK CAN ACCUMULATE EVERY YEAR.

COCONUTS, PANDANUS & BREADFRUIT
COCONUT PALMS ARE NOT THE ONLY TREES IMPORTANT TO CORAL ISLANDERS. THE PANDANUS PROVIDES A SOFT NUTTY FRUIT & LONG LEAVES USED FOR WEAVING MATS, ROOFS & SAILS. THE BREADFRUIT TREE PROVIDES THE ONLY FOOD AVAILABLE THAT CAN BE STORED FOR USE WHEN OTHER FOODS ARE SCARCE. THE FRUIT IS BAKED, WRAPPED IN LEAVES & BURIED IN THE GROUND.

THE ORIGIN OF ATOLLS
THE VICTORIANS WERE MYSTIFIED BY CORAL ATOLLS. DARWIN DEVELOPED THE THEORY, NOW UNIVERSALLY ACCEPTED, THAT ALL CORAL REEFS START AS REEFS ENCIRCLING ISLANDS. ATOLLS ARE CREATED WHEN THE SEA LEVEL RISES: THE FAST GROWING CORAL RISES WITH THE SEA LEVEL BUT THE ISLAND BECOMES SUBMERGED LEAVING AN ISOLATED RING OF CORAL. DARWIN RECORDS THAT ONE EMINENT CONTEMPORARY GEOLOGIST ON READING THE THEORY WAS SO OVERCOME WITH DELIGHT THAT HE DANCED ABOUT & THREW HIMSELF INTO THE WILDEST CONTORTIONS.

HOW TO FIND IF YOUR FRIENDS BELIEVE IN GHOSTS
ARRANGE VIOLIN ON TABLE BEHIND DOOR. COAT STRING GENEROUSLY WITH RESIN. TIE STRING TO DOOR HANDLE AT ONE END & TO A SMALL WEIGHT AT OTHER END. THIS WILL PRODUCE A GHOSTLY NOISE WHEN DOOR IS OPENED. WAIT FOR UNSUSPECTING FRIEND TO OPEN DOOR & SEE IF HE RUNS AWAY OR ENTERS FEARLESSLY.

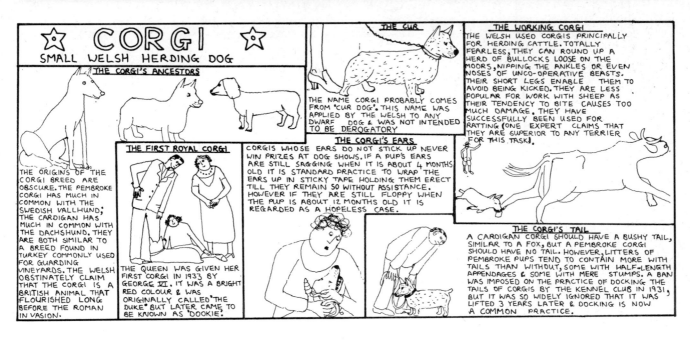

☆ CORGI ☆
SMALL WELSH HERDING DOG

THE CORGI'S ANCESTORS

THE CUR
THE NAME CORGI PROBABLY COMES FROM 'CUR DOG'. THIS NAME WAS APPLIED BY THE WELSH TO ANY DWARF DOG & WAS NOT INTENDED TO BE DEROGATORY.

THE WORKING CORGI
THE WELSH USED CORGIS PRINCIPALLY FOR HERDING CATTLE. TOTALLY FEARLESS, THEY CAN ROUND UP A HERD OF BULLOCKS LOOSE ON THE MOORS, NIPPING THE ANKLES OR EVEN NOSES OF UNCO-OPERATIVE BEASTS. THEIR SHORT LEGS ENABLE THEM TO AVOID BEING KICKED. THEY ARE LESS POPULAR FOR WORK WITH SHEEP AS THEIR TENDENCY TO BITE CAUSES TOO MUCH DAMAGE. THEY HAVE SUCCESSFULLY BEEN USED FOR RATTING (ONE EXPERT CLAIMS THAT THEY ARE SUPERIOR TO ANY TERRIER FOR THIS TASK).

THE ORIGINS OF THE CORGI BREED ARE OBSCURE. THE PEMBROKE CORGI HAS MUCH IN COMMON WITH THE SWEDISH VALLHUND; THE CARDIGAN HAS MUCH IN COMMON WITH THE DACHSHUND. THEY ARE BOTH SIMILAR TO A BREED FOUND IN TURKEY COMMONLY USED FOR GUARDING VINEYARDS. THE WELSH OBSTINATELY CLAIM THAT THE CORGI IS A BRITISH ANIMAL THAT FLOURISHED LONG BEFORE THE ROMAN INVASION.

THE FIRST ROYAL CORGI
THE QUEEN WAS GIVEN HER FIRST CORGI IN 1933 BY GEORGE VI. IT WAS A BRIGHT RED COLOUR & WAS ORIGINALLY CALLED 'THE DUKE' BUT LATER CAME TO BE KNOWN AS 'DOOKIE'.

THE CORGI'S EARS
CORGIS WHOSE EARS DO NOT STICK UP NEVER WIN PRIZES AT DOG SHOWS. IF A PUP'S EARS ARE STILL SAGGING WHEN IT IS ABOUT 4 MONTHS OLD IT IS STANDARD PRACTICE TO WRAP THE EARS UP IN STICKY TAPE HOLDING THEM ERECT TILL THEY REMAIN SO WITHOUT ASSISTANCE. HOWEVER IF THEY ARE STILL FLOPPY WHEN THE PUP IS ABOUT 12 MONTHS OLD IT IS REGARDED AS A HOPELESS CASE.

THE CORGI'S TAIL
A CARDIGAN CORGI SHOULD HAVE A BUSHY TAIL, SIMILAR TO A FOX, BUT A PEMBROKE CORGI SHOULD HAVE NO TAIL. HOWEVER, LITTERS OF PEMBROKE PUPS TEND TO CONTAIN MORE WITH TAILS THAN WITHOUT, SOME WITH HALF-LENGTH APPENDAGES & SOME WITH MERE STUMPS. A BAN WAS IMPOSED ON THE PRACTICE OF DOCKING THE TAILS OF CORGIS BY THE KENNEL CLUB IN 1931, BUT IT WAS SO WIDELY IGNORED THAT IT WAS LIFTED 3 YEARS LATER & DOCKING IS NOW A COMMON PRACTICE.

☆ COSMETICS ☆
BEAUTIFYING PREPARATIONS APPLIED TO THE BODY

KOHL
THE ANCIENT EGYPTIANS' MAIN FACIAL MAKE-UP WAS A HEAVY DARK LINE ROUND THE EYES MADE WITH A MIXTURE NOW CALLED KOHL. BESIDES BEING DECORATIVE, IT ALSO PROTECTED THE EYES AGAINST INFECTION & WAS OFTEN WORN BY CHILDREN.

THE WHITE FACE
THE MEDIEVAL IDEAL OF BEAUTY WAS A 'LILY-WHITE' FACE. THIS DISTINGUISHED THE ARISTOCRACY FROM THE PEASANTS, WHO WORKED OUTDOORS & DEVELOPED TANS. COSMETICS WERE NOT USED, BUT VEILS & GLOVES WERE ALWAYS WORN OUTDOORS BY UPPER-CLASS WOMEN TO PREVENT SUNBURN.

POWDER
BY THE 16TH CENTURY, THE APPLICATION OF POWDER (HELD IN PLACE BY A COAT OF EGG WHITE) TO KEEP THE FACE EXTRA PALE WAS SOCIALLY ACCEPTABLE. ELIZABETH I EVEN PAINTED SHADOWY VEINS ON HER FACE TO AUGMENT THE EFFECT OF 'TRANSLUCENT' SKIN.

NERO
THE ROMAN EMPEROR NERO'S MAKE-UP INCLUDED POWDER, ROUGE, KOHL & BLOND WIGS (IMPORTED FROM GAUL).

POISONOUS POWDER
THE MOST POPULAR FACE POWDER UNTIL THE 19TH CENTURY WAS MADE OF WHITE LEAD. THIS WAS POISONOUS & RUINED EVERY FASHIONABLE SKIN BY THE AGE OF 30-NECESSITATING EVER HEAVIER LAYERS.

PATCHES
DURING THE 1600s SMALL BLACK & RED SHAPES WERE POPULAR—MAINLY TO COVER SPOTS & SMALLPOX SCARS.

EYEBROWS
DURING THE 1700s MAKE-UP INCLUDED FALSE EYE-BROWS MADE OF MOUSE-SKIN (WHICH OFTEN FELL OFF) & CORK BALLS INSIDE THE MOUTH TO SWELL THE CHEEKS.

INHUMANE COSMETICS
SPERM WHALE OIL & BEAR FAT ARE STILL USED IN COSMETICS. MOST COSMETICS (EXCEPT NATURAL ONES FROM HEALTH FOOD SHOPS) ARE THOROUGHLY TESTED ON ANIMALS TO CHECK FOR HARMFUL EFFECTS.

WASHING
BY 1800, FREQUENT WASHING WAS FASHIONABLE & MOST MAKE-UP HAD BEEN DISCARDED. PREVIOUSLY, PEOPLE RARELY HAD MORE THAN ONE BATH A MONTH.

COSMETIC STOCKINGS
IN WORLD WAR II STOCKINGS WERE UNOBTAINABLE & ONE COSMETICS FIRM STARTED SELLING 'STOCKINGLESS' CREAM. WOMEN COLOURED THEIR LEGS WITH THIS & THEN DREW 'SEAMS' DOWN THE BACK OF EACH LEG WITH EYEBROW PENCIL.

HOW TO MAKE AN EGG FLY
MAKE HOLE AT EACH END OF AN EGG (WITH A PIN) & BLOW OUT CONTENTS.

PLACE EGG IN CUP, POINTED END DOWN, SO THERE IS A SMALL GAP ROUND RIM. BLOW DOWN TOWARDS THIS GAP & AIR WILL EJECT EGG.

WITH PRACTICE, EGG CAN BE MADE TO LAND IN 2ND CUP.

CINEMA COSMETICS
COSMETICS WERE TRADITIONALLY USED PRINCIPALLY BY OLDER WOMEN TO DISGUISE THE EFFECTS OF AGEING. IT WAS THE INFLUENCE OF SILENT FILMS THAT FIRST MADE 'THEATRICAL MAKE-UP':- SHINY LIPS, DARK EYES & NAIL VARNISH - POPULAR WITH THE YOUNG.

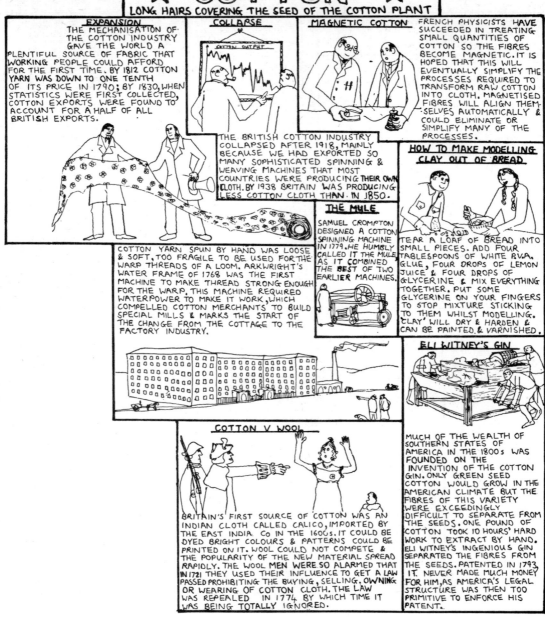

☆ COTTON ☆
LONG HAIRS COVERING THE SEED OF THE COTTON PLANT

EXPANSION
THE MECHANISATION OF THE COTTON INDUSTRY GAVE THE WORLD A PLENTIFUL SOURCE OF FABRIC THAT WORKING PEOPLE COULD AFFORD FOR THE FIRST TIME. BY 1812 COTTON YARN WAS DOWN TO ONE TENTH OF ITS PRICE IN 1790; BY 1830, WHEN STATISTICS WERE FIRST COLLECTED, COTTON EXPORTS WERE FOUND TO ACCOUNT FOR A HALF OF ALL BRITISH EXPORTS.

COLLAPSE
COTTON OUTPUT

THE BRITISH COTTON INDUSTRY COLLAPSED AFTER 1918, MAINLY BECAUSE WE HAD EXPORTED SO MANY SOPHISTICATED SPINNING & WEAVING MACHINES THAT MOST COUNTRIES WERE PRODUCING THEIR OWN CLOTH. BY 1938 BRITAIN WAS PRODUCING LESS COTTON CLOTH THAN IN 1850.

MAGNETIC COTTON
FRENCH PHYSICISTS HAVE SUCCEEDED IN TREATING SMALL QUANTITIES OF COTTON SO THE FIBRES BECOME MAGNETIC. IT IS HOPED THAT THIS WILL EVENTUALLY SIMPLIFY THE PROCESSES REQUIRED TO TRANSFORM RAW COTTON INTO CLOTH. MAGNETISED FIBRES WILL ALIGN THEMSELVES AUTOMATICALLY & COULD ELIMINATE OR SIMPLIFY MANY OF THE PROCESSES.

HOW TO MAKE MODELLING CLAY OUT OF BREAD
TEAR A LOAF OF BREAD INTO SMALL PIECES. ADD FOUR TABLESPOONS OF WHITE P.V.A. GLUE, FOUR DROPS OF LEMON JUICE & FOUR DROPS OF GLYCERINE & MIX EVERYTHING TOGETHER. PUT SOME GLYCERINE ON YOUR FINGERS TO STOP MIXTURE STICKING TO THEM WHILST MODELLING. 'CLAY' WILL DRY & HARDEN & CAN BE PAINTED & VARNISHED.

THE MULE
SAMUEL CROMPTON DESIGNED A COTTON SPINNING MACHINE IN 1779. HE HUMBLY CALLED IT THE MULE AS IT COMBINED THE BEST OF TWO EARLIER MACHINES.

COTTON YARN SPUN BY HAND WAS LOOSE & SOFT, TOO FRAGILE TO BE USED FOR THE WARP THREADS OF A LOOM. ARKWRIGHT'S WATER FRAME OF 1768 WAS THE FIRST MACHINE TO MAKE THREAD STRONG ENOUGH FOR THE WARP. THIS MACHINE REQUIRED WATERPOWER TO MAKE IT WORK, WHICH COMPELLED COTTON MERCHANTS TO BUILD SPECIAL MILLS & MARKS THE START OF THE CHANGE FROM THE COTTAGE TO THE FACTORY INDUSTRY.

ELI WITNEY'S GIN
MUCH OF THE WEALTH OF SOUTHERN STATES OF AMERICA IN THE 1800s WAS FOUNDED ON THE INVENTION OF THE COTTON GIN. ONLY GREEN SEED COTTON WOULD GROW IN THE AMERICAN CLIMATE BUT THE FIBRES OF THIS VARIETY WERE EXCEEDINGLY DIFFICULT TO SEPARATE FROM THE SEEDS. ONE POUND OF COTTON TOOK 10 HOURS' HARD WORK TO EXTRACT BY HAND. ELI WITNEY'S INGENIOUS GIN SEPARATED THE FIBRES FROM THE SEEDS. PATENTED IN 1793, IT NEVER MADE MUCH MONEY FOR HIM, AS AMERICA'S LEGAL STRUCTURE WAS THEN TOO PRIMITIVE TO ENFORCE HIS PATENT.

COTTON V WOOL
BRITAIN'S FIRST SOURCE OF COTTON WAS AN INDIAN CLOTH CALLED CALICO, IMPORTED BY THE EAST INDIA CO IN THE 1600s. IT COULD BE DYED BRIGHT COLOURS & PATTERNS COULD BE PRINTED ON IT. WOOL COULD NOT COMPETE & THE POPULARITY OF THE NEW MATERIAL SPREAD RAPIDLY. THE WOOL MEN WERE SO ALARMED THAT IN 1721 THEY USED THEIR INFLUENCE TO GET A LAW PASSED PROHIBITING THE BUYING, SELLING, OWNING OR WEARING OF COTTON CLOTH. THE LAW WAS REPEALED IN 1774 BY WHICH TIME IT WAS BEING TOTALLY IGNORED.

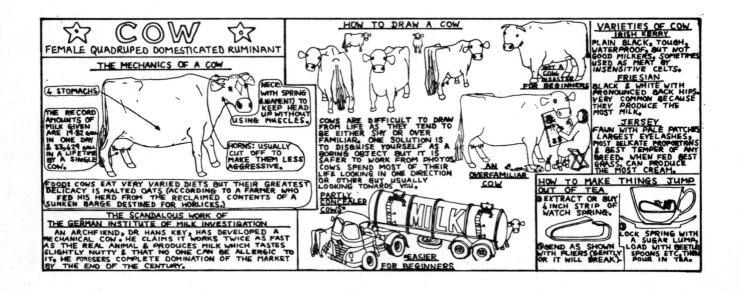

☆ COW ☆
FEMALE QUADRUPED DOMESTICATED RUMINANT

THE MECHANICS OF A COW
4 STOMACHS

NECK: WITH SPRING (LIGAMENT) TO KEEP HEAD UP WITHOUT USING MUSCLES.

THE RECORD AMOUNTS OF MILK GIVEN ARE 19.92 cu IN ONE DAY & 33,629 cu IN A LIFETIME BY A SINGLE COW.

HORNS: USUALLY CUT OFF TO MAKE THEM LESS AGGRESSIVE.

FOOD: COWS EAT VERY VARIED DIETS BUT THEIR GREATEST DELICACY IS MALTED OATS (ACCORDING TO A FARMER WHO FED HIS HERD FROM THE RECLAIMED CONTENTS OF A SUNKEN BARGE DESTINED FOR HORLICKS.)

THE SCANDALOUS WORK OF THE GERMAN INSTITUTE OF MILK INVESTIGATION
AN ARCHFIEND, DR HANS KEY, HAS DEVELOPED A MECHANICAL COW. HE CLAIMS IT WORKS TWICE AS FAST AS THE REAL ANIMAL & PRODUCES MILK WHICH TASTES SLIGHTLY NUTTY & THAT NO ONE CAN BE ALLERGIC TO IT. HE FORESEES COMPLETE DOMINATION OF THE MARKET BY THE END OF THE CENTURY.

HOW TO DRAW A COW
HOW A COW DISASTER FOR BEGINNERS

COWS ARE DIFFICULT TO DRAW FROM LIFE AS THEY TEND TO BE EITHER SHY OR OVER FAMILIAR. ONE SOLUTION IS TO DISGUISE YOURSELF AS A BORING OBJECT BUT IT IS SAFER TO WORK FROM PHOTOS. COWS SPEND MOST OF THEIR LIFE LOOKING IN ONE DIRECTION OR OTHER BUT USUALLY LOOKING TOWARDS YOU.

AN OVERFAMILIAR COW

PARTLY CONCEALED COWS

MILK

EASIER FOR BEGINNERS

VARIETIES OF COW
IRISH KERRY
PLAIN BLACK, TOUGH, WATERPROOF, BUT NOT GOOD MILKERS. SOMETIMES USED AS MEAT BY INSENSITIVE CELTS.

FRIESIAN
BLACK & WHITE WITH PRONOUNCED BACK HIPS. VERY COMMON BECAUSE THEY PRODUCE THE MOST MILK.

JERSEY
FAWN WITH PALE PATCHES. LARGEST EYELASHES, MOST DELICATE PROPORTIONS & BEST TEMPER OF ANY BREED. WHEN FED BEST GRASS, CAN PRODUCE THE MOST CREAM.

HOW TO MAKE THINGS JUMP OUT OF TEA
① EXTRACT OR BUY 4 INCH STRIP OF WATCH SPRING.

② BEND AS SHOWN WITH PLIERS (GENTLY OR IT WILL BREAK).

③ LOCK SPRING WITH A SUGAR LUMP. LOAD WITH BEETLE SPOONS ETC. THEN POUR IN TEA.

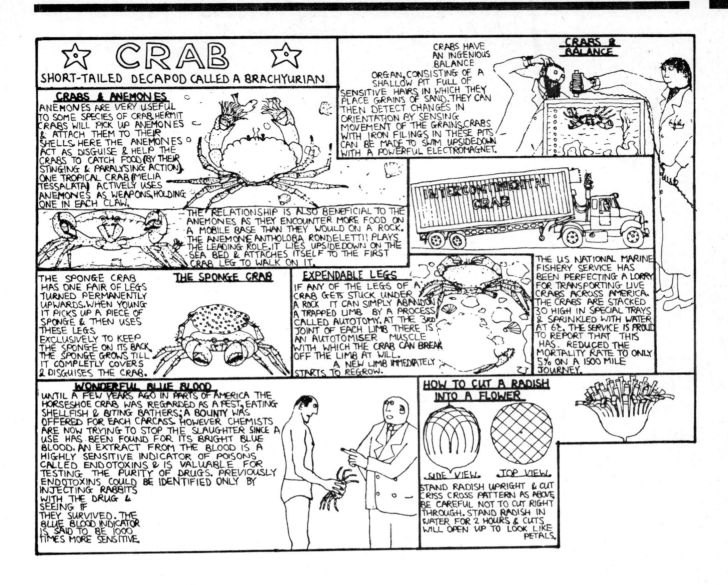

☆ CRAB ☆
SHORT-TAILED DECAPOD CALLED A BRACHYURIAN

CRABS & ANEMONES
ANEMONES ARE VERY USEFUL TO SOME SPECIES OF CRAB. HERMIT CRABS WILL PICK UP ANEMONES & ATTACH THEM TO THEIR SHELLS. HERE THE ANEMONES ACT AS DISGUISE & HELP THE CRABS TO CATCH FOOD (BY THEIR STINGING & PARALYSING ACTION). ONE TROPICAL CRAB (MELIA TESSALATA) ACTIVELY USES ANEMONES AS WEAPONS, HOLDING ONE IN EACH CLAW.

THE RELATIONSHIP IS ALSO BENEFICIAL TO THE ANEMONES AS THEY ENCOUNTER MORE FOOD ON A MOBILE BASE THAN THEY WOULD ON A ROCK. THE ANEMONE ANTHOLOBA RONDELETTII PLAYS THE LEADING ROLE. IT LIES UPSIDEDOWN ON THE SEA BED & ATTACHES ITSELF TO THE FIRST CRAB LEG TO WALK ON IT.

THE SPONGE CRAB
THE SPONGE CRAB HAS ONE PAIR OF LEGS TURNED PERMANENTLY UPWARDS. WHEN YOUNG IT PICKS UP A PIECE OF SPONGE & THEN USES THESE LEGS EXCLUSIVELY TO KEEP THE SPONGE ON ITS BACK. THE SPONGE GROWS TILL IT COMPLETLY COVERS & DISGUISES THE CRAB.

EXPENDABLE LEGS
IF ANY OF THE LEGS OF A CRAB GETS STUCK UNDER A ROCK IT CAN SIMPLY ABANDON A TRAPPED LIMB BY A PROCESS CALLED AUTOTOMY. AT THE 3RD JOINT OF EACH LIMB THERE IS AN AUTOTOMISER MUSCLE WITH WHICH THE CRAB CAN BREAK OFF THE LIMB AT WILL. A NEW LIMB IMMEDIATELY STARTS TO REGROW.

CRABS & BALANCE
CRABS HAVE AN INGENIOUS BALANCE ORGAN, CONSISTING OF A SHALLOW PIT FULL OF SENSITIVE HAIRS IN WHICH THEY PLACE GRAINS OF SAND. THEY CAN THEN DETECT CHANGES IN ORIENTATION BY SENSING MOVEMENT OF THE GRAINS. CRABS WITH IRON FILINGS IN THESE PITS CAN BE MADE TO SWIM UPSIDEDOWN WITH A POWERFUL ELECTROMAGNET.

INTERCONTINENTAL CRAB
THE US NATIONAL MARINE FISHERY SERVICE HAS BEEN PERFECTING A LORRY FOR TRANSPORTING LIVE CRABS ACROSS AMERICA. THE CRABS ARE STACKED 30 HIGH IN SPECIAL TRAYS & SPRINKLED WITH WATER AT 6C. THE SERVICE IS PROUD TO REPORT THAT THIS HAS REDUCED THE MORTALITY RATE TO ONLY 5% ON A 1500 MILE JOURNEY.

WONDERFUL BLUE BLOOD
UNTIL A FEW YEARS AGO IN PARTS OF AMERICA THE HORSESHOE CRAB WAS REGARDED AS A PEST, EATING SHELLFISH & BITING BATHERS; A BOUNTY WAS OFFERED FOR EACH CARCASS. HOWEVER CHEMISTS ARE NOW TRYING TO STOP THE SLAUGHTER SINCE A USE HAS BEEN FOUND FOR ITS BRIGHT BLUE BLOOD. AN EXTRACT FROM THE BLOOD IS A HIGHLY SENSITIVE INDICATOR OF POISONS CALLED ENDOTOXINS & IS VALUABLE FOR TESTING THE PURITY OF DRUGS. PREVIOUSLY ENDOTOXINS COULD BE IDENTIFIED ONLY BY INJECTING RABBITS WITH THE DRUG & SEEING IF THEY SURVIVED. THE BLUE BLOOD INDICATOR IS SAID TO BE 1000 TIMES MORE SENSITIVE.

HOW TO CUT A RADISH INTO A FLOWER
SIDE VIEW   TOP VIEW

STAND RADISH UPRIGHT & CUT CRISS CROSS PATTERN AS ABOVE. BE CAREFUL NOT TO CUT RIGHT THROUGH. STAND RADISH IN WATER FOR 2 HOURS & CUTS WILL OPEN UP TO LOOK LIKE PETALS.

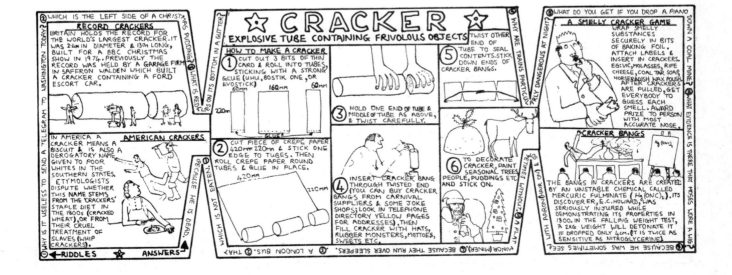

☆ CRACKER ☆
EXPLOSIVE TUBE CONTAINING FRIVOLOUS OBJECTS

RECORD CRACKERS
BRITAIN HOLDS THE RECORD FOR THE WORLD'S LARGEST CRACKER. IT WAS 2¼M IN DIAMETER & 13M LONG, BUILT FOR A BBC CHRISTMAS SHOW IN 1974. PREVIOUSLY THE RECORD WAS HELD BY A GARAGE FIRM IN SAFFRON WALDEN WHICH BUILT A CRACKER CONTAINING A FORD ESCORT CAR.

AMERICAN CRACKERS
IN AMERICA A CRACKER MEANS A BISCUIT & IS ALSO A DEROGATORY NAME GIVEN TO POOR WHITES IN THE SOUTHERN STATES. ETYMOLOGISTS DISPUTE WHETHER THIS NAME STEMS FROM THE CRACKERS' STAPLE DIET IN THE 1800S (CRACKED WHEAT), OR FROM THEIR CRUEL TREATMENT OF SLAVES (WHIP CRACKERS).

HOW TO MAKE A CRACKER
1. CUT OUT 3 BITS OF THIN CARD & ROLL INTO TUBES, STICKING WITH A STRONG GLUE (UHU, BOSTIK ONE, OR EVOSTICK). 60MM 160MM 60MM 220M / GLUE
2. CUT PIECE OF CREPE PAPER 420MM x 220MM & STICK ONE EDGE TO TUBES. THEN ROLL CREPE PAPER ROUND TUBES & GLUE IN PLACE. 420MM 220MM
3. HOLD ONE END OF TUBE & MIDDLE OF TUBE AS ABOVE, & TWIST CAREFULLY.
4. INSERT CRACKER BANG THROUGH TWISTED END (YOU CAN BUY CRACKER BANGS FROM CARNIVAL SUPPLIERS & SOME JOKE SHOPS; LOOK IN TELEPHONE DIRECTORY YELLOW PAGES FOR ADDRESSES). THEN FILL CRACKER WITH HATS, RUBBER MONSTERS, MOTTOES, SWEETS ETC.
5. TWIST OTHER END OF TUBE TO SEAL CONTENTS. STICK DOWN ENDS OF CRACKER BANGS.
6. TO DECORATE CRACKER, PAINT SEASONAL TREES PEOPLE, PUDDINGS ETC AND STICK ON.

A SMELLY CRACKER GAME
WRAP SMELLY SUBSTANCES SECURELY IN BITS OF BAKING FOIL. ATTACH LABELS & INSERT IN CRACKERS. EG UIC, MOLASSES, RIPE CHEESE, COAL TAR SOAP, HORSERADISH WAX POLISH. AFTER CRACKERS ARE PULLED, GET EVERYBODY TO GUESS EACH SMELL. AWARD PRIZE TO PERSON WITH MOST ACCURATE NOSE.

CRACKER BANGS
THE BANGS IN CRACKERS ARE CREATED BY AN UNSTABLE CHEMICAL CALLED MERCURIC FULMINATE ($Hg(ONC)_2$). ITS DISCOVERER, E.C. HOWARD, WAS SERIOUSLY INJURED WHILE DEMONSTRATING ITS PROPERTIES IN 1800. IN THE FALLING WEIGHT TEST, A 2KG WEIGHT WILL DETONATE IT IF DROPPED ONLY 4CM. IT IS TWICE AS SENSITIVE AS NITROGLYCERINE.

RIDDLES
- WHICH IS THE LEFT SIDE OF A CHRISTMAS PUDDING?
- WHAT IS RED & ON ITS BOTTOM IN A GUTTER?
- WHY ARE TRAINS PARTICULARLY DANGEROUS AT NIGHT?
- WHAT DO YOU GET IF YOU DROP A PIANO DOWN A COAL MINE?
- WHAT EVIDENCE IS THERE THAT MOSES WORE A WIG?
- WHY IS IT USELESS TO SEND A TELEGRAM TO WASHINGTON TODAY?

ANSWERS
- BECAUSE HE IS DEAD.
- A MINOR (MINER).
- A LONDON BUS.
- BECAUSE THEY RUN OVER SLEEPERS.
- THAT.
- BECAUSE HE WAS SOMETIMES SEEN WITH AARON (HAIR ON) & A...

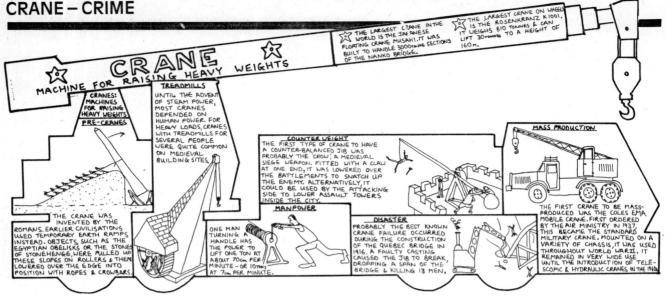

☆ CRANE ☆
MACHINE FOR RAISING HEAVY WEIGHTS

☆ THE LARGEST CRANE IN THE WORLD IS THE JAPANESE FLOATING CRANE MUSASHI. IT WAS BUILT TO HANDLE 3000 tonne SECTIONS OF THE NANKO BRIDGE.

☆ THE LARGEST CRANE ON WHEELS IS THE ROSENKRANZ K1001. IT WEIGHS 810 TONNES & CAN LIFT 30 tonnes TO A HEIGHT OF 160 m.

CRANES: MACHINES FOR RAISING HEAVY WEIGHTS

PRE-CRANES

THE CRANE WAS INVENTED BY THE ROMANS. EARLIER CIVILISATIONS USED TEMPORARY EARTH RAMPS INSTEAD. OBJECTS, SUCH AS THE EGYPTIAN OBELISKS OR THE STONES OF STONEHENGE, WERE PULLED UP THESE SLOPES ON ROLLERS & THEN LOWERED OVER THE EDGE INTO POSITION WITH ROPES & CROWBARS.

TREADMILLS

UNTIL THE ADVENT OF STEAM POWER, MOST CRANES DEPENDED ON HUMAN POWER. FOR HEAVY LOADS, CRANES WITH TREADMILLS FOR SEVERAL PEOPLE WERE QUITE COMMON ON MEDIEVAL BUILDING SITES.

MANPOWER

ONE MAN TURNING A HANDLE HAS THE POWER TO LIFT ONE TON AT ABOUT 70cm PER MINUTE — OR 10 tons AT 7cm PER MINUTE.

COUNTER WEIGHT

THE FIRST TYPE OF CRANE TO HAVE A COUNTER-BALANCED JIB WAS PROBABLY THE 'CROW', A MEDIEVAL SIEGE WEAPON. FITTED WITH A CLAW AT ONE END, IT WAS LOWERED OVER THE BATTLEMENTS TO SNATCH UP THE ENEMY. ALTERNATIVELY, IT COULD BE USED BY THE ATTACKING SIDE TO LOWER ASSAULT TOWERS INSIDE THE CITY.

DISASTER

PROBABLY THE BEST KNOWN CRANE FAILURE OCCURRED DURING THE CONSTRUCTION OF THE QUEBEC BRIDGE IN 1916. A FAULTY CASTING CAUSED THE JIB TO BREAK, DROPPING A SPAN OF THE BRIDGE & KILLING 13 MEN.

MASS PRODUCTION

THE FIRST CRANE TO BE MASS-PRODUCED WAS THE COLES EMA MOBILE CRANE. FIRST ORDERED BY THE AIR MINISTRY IN 1937, THIS BECAME THE STANDARD MILITARY CRANE. MOUNTED ON A VARIETY OF CHASSIS, IT WAS USED THROUGHOUT WORLD WAR II. IT REMAINED IN VERY WIDE USE UNTIL THE INTRODUCTION OF TELESCOPIC & HYDRAULIC CRANES IN THE 1960s.

☆ CREATION ☆
THE ORIGIN OF ALL THINGS ANIMAL, VEGETABLE & MINERAL

THE PHILOSOPHIC GREEKS

THE GREEKS THOUGHT THAT THE HEAVENS & THE EARTH WERE SPUN FROM CHAOS BY THE FORCE OF TIME. CHAOS WAS A FORMLESS MASS OF DISORDER: NIGHT, MIST & FIERY AIR DRIFTING IN AIMLESS ANARCHY. TIME IMPOSED ORDER; THE MASS BEGAN TO SPIN, EVENTUALLY ASSUMING AN EGG-SHAPE. THE MASS SPLIT & THE UNIVERSE CAME INTO BEING.

THE WILD NORSEMEN

ACCORDING TO SCANDINAVIAN MYTHOLOGY FIERY CLOUDS FROM THE SOUTH MET ICY ARCTIC GUSTS FROM THE NORTH, & FROM THE RESULTANT MISTS WERE CREATED YMIR, THE FIRST GIANT, & A BEVY OF BEAUTIFUL FROST MAIDENS. THEIR MATING EVENTUALLY LED TO THREE GRANDSONS WHO HACKED YMIR INTO SEVERAL CHUNKS. HIS BLOOD BECAME THE SEAS, HIS BODY THE EARTH, & HIS BATTERED SKULL THE HEAVENS.

NEWTON'S FAITH

NEWTON MADE EXPERIMENTS ON THE RATE OF COOLING OF RED-HOT SPHERES TO ESTABLISH THE AGE OF THE COOLING EARTH, BUT FINDING THAT HIS ANSWER DID NOT TALLY WITH THE BIBLE, HE ASSUMED IT TO BE WRONG. THE EXPERIMENTS WERE REPEATED IN ABOUT 1750 & THE CONCLUSION WAS REACHED THAT THE EARTH WAS 75,000 YEARS OLD. THIS UNDERESTIMATED THE EFFECT OF SOLAR RADIATION SO THE FIGURES WERE FAR TOO LOW, BUT THEY WERE A STAGGERING INCREASE ON THE BIBLE'S 4000 YEARS.

THE STRANGE MAYAS

THE CENTRAL AMERICAN MAYANS THOUGHT THAT THEIR FOREFATHER GODS, TEPEU & GUCUMATZ, BROUGHT FORTH THE EARTH FROM A WATERY VOID & ENDOWED IT WITH PLANTS & ANIMALS. ANXIOUS FOR PRAISE & VENERATION AFTER THE CREATION, THE DIVINE PROGENITORS FASHIONED MAN-LIKE CREATURES FROM MUD, BUT TO MUD THEY RETURNED. NEXT A RACE OF WOODEN FIGURES APPEARED, BUT THE MINDLESS MANNEQUINS WERE DESTROYED BY THE GODS, TO BE REPLACED BY MEN MADE OF FLESH. THESE, HOWEVER, TURNED TO WICKEDNESS & WERE ANNIHILATED AS BLACK RAINS FELL & FLOODED THE EARTH. FINALLY, TRUE MEN, THEIR ANCESTORS, WERE CREATED FROM MAIZE DOUGH.

SPONTANEOUS GENERATION

ALCHEMISTS BELIEVED THAT CERTAIN FORMS OF LIFE GENERATED SPONTANEOUSLY FROM DECOMPOSING MATTER. THIS WAS FIRST CHALLENGED BY A FLORENTINE DOCTOR, F. REDI, IN 1668. HE PUT MEAT INTO 2 JARS, COVERED ONE & WATCHED FLIES LAY EGGS IN THE OTHER. MEAT IN BOTH BOTTLES PUTREFIED BUT ONLY THE OPEN BOTTLE SPAWNED ANY FLIES.

HOW TO SEE CONCENTRIC CIRCLES IN THIS PATTERN

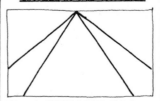

DRAW 4 THICK LINES ON A BIT OF CARD AS ABOVE. PUSH A PIN THROUGH THE CENTRE, & HOLDING THE PIN, SPIN THE CARD. 2 CONCENTRIC CIRCLES WILL MYSTERIOUSLY APPEAR.

CREATION 4004 BC

BY LITERAL INTERPRETATION OF THE BIBLE ARCHBISHOP USSHER (1581-1656) ESTIMATED THAT THE CREATION OCCURRED IN 4004 BC. KEPLER, THE GERMAN SCIENTIST, REACHED THE SAME DATE USING AN EARLIER BIBLICAL ESTIMATE OF 4000 BC. HE ADDED 4 YEARS BECAUSE HE WORKED OUT THAT THE BIRTH OF CHRIST HAPPENED IN 4 BC. HE DID THIS BY CORRELATING HIS ECLIPSE TABLES WITH THE CRUCIFIXION WHEN THERE HAD BEEN 'DARKNESS OVER ALL THE LAND'.

THE FIRST CELL

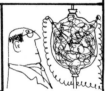

IN 1952 A U.S. CHEMIST MANAGED TO CREATE A RANGE OF ORGANIC COMPOUNDS, INCLUDING PROTEINS, FROM A MIXTURE OF GASES SIMILAR TO THE WORLD'S EARLY ATMOSPHERE. HOWEVER, THE MECHANISM BY WHICH THESE COMPOUNDS FORMED THEMSELVES INTO THE FIRST SELF-REPLICATING STRUCTURES, CELLS — CREATING ORDER OUT OF CHAOS — CAN STILL NOT BE SATISFACTORILY EXPLAINED SCIENTIFICALLY.

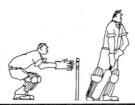

☆ CRICKET ☆
OUTDOOR GAME PLAYED WITH BATS, BALL & WICKETS

ORIGINS

THE EARLIEST RECORD OF A FORM OF CRICKET IS A MENTION OF IT IN THE WARDROBE ACCOUNTS OF EDWARD I IN 1300, IN A DRAWING DATED 1344. THERE WERE NO WICKETS; INSTEAD THE PLAYERS CUT CIRCULAR HOLES IN THE TURF. A BATSMAN WAS OUT WHEN HE MISSED THE BALL & IT LANDED IN THE HOLE.

PUZZLE

PEOPLE NOT FAMILIAR WITH CRICKET FIND IT A PARTICULARLY PUZZLING GAME TO FOLLOW. IT HAS BEEN DESCRIBED AS 'CASTING A BALL AT 3 STRAIGHT STICKS & DEFENDING THE SAME WITH A 4th'.

SHEPHERDS

SOME AUTHORITIES CLAIM THAT ENGLISH CRICKET ORIGINATED IN THE SHEEP COUNTRY OF SOUTH-EAST ENGLAND. A BALL OF WOOL WAS LITERALLY BOWLED ALONG THE GROUND AT THE WICKET GATE OF A SHEEPFOLD. THERE THE 'BATSMAN' STOOD HOLDING A SHEP-HERD'S CROOK UPSIDE DOWN WITH WHICH HE WOULD TRY TO HIT THE BALL.

RULES

THE BASIC RULES OF MODERN CRICKET WERE FIXED IN 1788 BY THE MARYLEBONE CRICKET CLUB THE ONLY MAJOR CHANGE EVER MADE WAS THE ACCEPTANCE OF OVER-ARM BOWLING IN 1864. THIS, WITH THE ADVENT OF PERFECTLY FLAT PITCHES HAS DOUBLED THE SPEED OF THE BALL IN THE AIR.

RULES

BATS

| 1750 | 1780 | 1800 | 1850 | 1950 |

CRICKET BATS USED TO BE CURVED. THIS IS SOMETIMES CLAIMED AS EVIDENCE THAT THEY EVOLVED FROM SHEPHERDS' CROOKS.

ASHES

THE ASHES ORIGINATED IN THE 'SPORTING TIMES' MAGAZINE ON 29 AUGUST 1882, AFTER ENGLAND HAD BEEN BEATEN BY AUSTRALIA FOR THE FIRST TIME AT HOME. THE MAGAZINE PRINTED A MOCK OBITUARY OF ENGLISH CRICKET, ENDING WITH: THE BODY WILL BE CREMATED & THE ASHES TAKEN TO AUSTRALIA.

RECORDS

★ THE PLAYER TO HAVE MADE THE MOST RUNS IN A SINGLE SEASON IS DENIS COMPTON, WHO SCORED 3,816 IN 50 INNINGS IN 1947.
★ THE PLAYER TO HAVE SCORED THE MOST RUNS IN A LIFETIME WAS SIR JACK HOBBS, WHO MADE 61,237 IN 1,315 INNINGS BETWEEN 1905 & 1934.

PACKER

AUSTRALIA HAS INTRO-DUCED NIGHT CRICKET UNDER FLOODLIGHTS & USING A WHITE BALL. THE PLAYERS WEAR YELLOW & PINK & THE SPECTATORS ARE FAR NOISIER THAN AT TRAD-ITIONAL TEST MATCHES. THERE ARE MANY MORE TEENAGERS & THE ATMOSPHERE IS SAID TO BE MORE LIKE BASEBALL THAN CRICKET.

HOW TO PAINT WITH A DRINKING STRAW

DROP A BLOB OF PAINT OR INK ON A BIT OF PAPER & BLOW AT IT THROUGH A DRINKING STRAW — FORCING IT TO SPREAD ACROSS THE PAPER. WEIRD LANDSCAPES, PLANTS & UNDERWATER SCENES CAN BE CREATED BY THIS TECHNIQUE. FLOWERS CAN BE ADDED BY DIPPING THE END OF THE STRAW INTO THE SELECTED COLOUR & THEN BLOWING THE PAINT OUT OVER THE AREA WHERE THE 'FLOWER' IS REQUIRED.

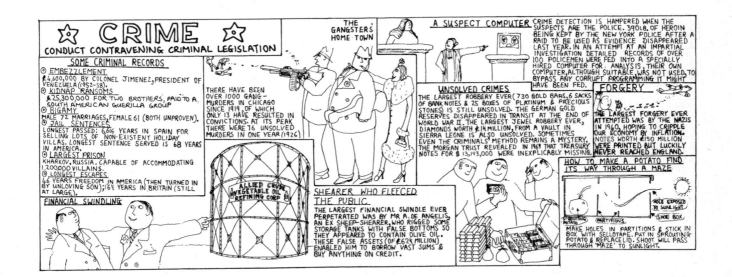

☆ CRIME ☆
CONDUCT CONTRAVENING CRIMINAL LEGISLATION

SOME CRIMINAL RECORDS
⊙ EMBEZZLEMENT
£4,600,000 BY COLONEL JIMENEZ, PRESIDENT OF VENEZUELA (1952-58).
⊙ KIDNAP RANSOMS
£25,300,000 FOR TWO BROTHERS, PAID TO A SOUTH AMERICAN GUERILLA GROUP
⊙ BIGAMY
MALE 72 MARRIAGES, FEMALE 61 (BOTH UNPROVEN).
⊙ JAIL SENTENCES
LONGEST PASSED: 6,816 YEARS IN SPAIN FOR SELLING LOTS OF NON-EXISTENT HOLIDAY VILLAS. LONGEST SENTENCE SERVED IS 68 YEARS IN AMERICA.
⊙ LARGEST PRISON
KHARKOV, RUSSIA. CAPABLE OF ACCOMMODATING 1,200,000 VILLAINS.
⊙ LONGEST ESCAPES
46 YEARS FREEDOM IN AMERICA (THEN TURNED IN BY UNLOVING SON) 16½ YEARS IN BRITAIN (STILL AT LARGE).

FINANCIAL SWINDLING

THE GANGSTERS HOME TOWN

THERE HAVE BEEN OVER 1000 GANG-MURDERS IN CHICAGO SINCE 1919, OF WHICH ONLY 13 HAVE RESULTED IN CONVICTIONS. AT ITS PEAK THERE WERE 76 UNSOLVED MURDERS IN ONE YEAR (1926)

SHEARER WHO FLEECED THE PUBLIC
THE LARGEST FINANCIAL SWINDLE EVER PERPETRATED WAS BY MR A. DE ANGELIS, AN EX SHEEP-SHEARER, WHO RIGGED SOME STORAGE TANKS WITH FALSE BOTTOMS SO THEY APPEARED TO CONTAIN OLIVE OIL. THESE FALSE ASSETS (OF £62½ MILLION) ENABLED HIM TO BORROW VAST SUMS & BUY ANYTHING ON CREDIT.

A SUSPECT COMPUTER
CRIME DETECTION IS HAMPERED WHEN THE SUSPECTS ARE THE POLICE. 390LB. OF HEROIN BEING KEPT BY THE NEW YORK POLICE AFTER A RAID TO BE USED AS EVIDENCE DISAPPEARED LAST YEAR. IN AN ATTEMPT AT AN IMPARTIAL INVESTIGATION DETAILED RECORDS OF OVER 100 POLICEMEN WERE FED INTO A SPECIALLY HIRED COMPUTER FOR ANALYSIS. THEIR OWN COMPUTER, ALTHOUGH SUITABLE, WAS NOT USED, TO BYPASS ANY CORRUPT PROGRAMMING IT MIGHT HAVE BEEN FED.

UNSOLVED CRIMES
THE LARGEST ROBBERY EVER (730 GOLD BARS, 6 SACKS OF BANK NOTES & 25 BOXES OF PLATINUM & PRECIOUS STONES) IS STILL UNSOLVED. THE GERMAN GOLD RESERVES DISAPPEARED IN TRANSIT AT THE END OF WORLD WAR II. THE LARGEST JEWEL ROBBERY EVER, DIAMONDS WORTH £1k MILLION, FROM A VAULT IN SIERRA LEONE IS ALSO UNSOLVED. SOMETIMES EVEN THE CRIMINALS' METHOD REMAINS A MYSTERY. THE MORGAN TRUST REVEALED IN 1969 THAT TREASURY NOTES FOR $13,193,000 WERE INEXPLICABLY MISSING.

FORGERY
THE LARGEST FORGERY EVER ATTEMPTED WAS BY THE NAZIS IN 1940, HOPING TO CRIPPLE OUR ECONOMY BY INFLATION. NOTES WORTH £150 MILLION WERE PRINTED BUT LUCKILY NEVER REACHED ENGLAND.

HOW TO MAKE A POTATO FIND ITS WAY THROUGH A MAZE
MAKE HOLES IN PARTITIONS & STICK IN BOX WITH SELLOTAPE. PUT IN SPROUTING POTATO & REPLACE LID. SHOOT WILL PASS THROUGH 'MAZE' TO SUNLIGHT.

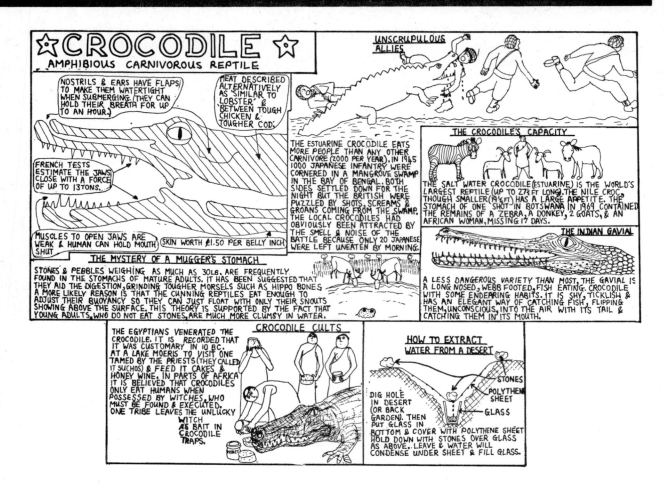

☆ CROCODILE ☆
AMPHIBIOUS CARNIVOROUS REPTILE

NOSTRILS & EARS HAVE FLAPS TO MAKE THEM WATERTIGHT WHEN SUBMERGING. (THEY CAN HOLD THEIR BREATH FOR UP TO AN HOUR.)

MEAT DESCRIBED ALTERNATIVELY AS 'SIMILAR TO LOBSTER' & 'BETWEEN TOUGH CHICKEN & TOUGHER COD.'

FRENCH TESTS ESTIMATE THE JAWS CLOSE WITH A FORCE OF UP TO 13 TONS.

MUSCLES TO OPEN JAWS ARE WEAK & HUMAN CAN HOLD MOUTH SHUT.

SKIN WORTH £1.50 PER BELLY INCH

UNSCRUPULOUS ALLIES

THE ESTUARINE CROCODILE EATS MORE PEOPLE THAN ANY OTHER CARNIVORE (2000 PER YEAR). IN 1945 1000 JAPANESE INFANTRY WERE CORNERED IN A MANGROVE SWAMP IN THE BAY OF BENGAL. BOTH SIDES SETTLED DOWN FOR THE NIGHT BUT THE BRITISH WERE PUZZLED BY SHOTS, SCREAMS & GROANS COMING FROM THE SWAMP. THE LOCAL CROCODILES HAD OBVIOUSLY BEEN ATTRACTED BY THE SMELL & NOISE OF THE BATTLE BECAUSE ONLY 20 JAPANESE WERE LEFT UNEATEN BY MORNING.

THE CROCODILE'S CAPACITY

THE SALT WATER CROCODILE (ESTUARINE) IS THE WORLD'S LARGEST REPTILE (UP TO 27 FT LONG). THE NILE CROC THOUGH SMALLER (19½ FT) HAS A LARGE APPETITE. THE STOMACH OF ONE SHOT IN BOTSWANA IN 1969 CONTAINED THE REMAINS OF A ZEBRA, A DONKEY, 2 GOATS, & AN AFRICAN WOMAN, MISSING 17 DAYS.

THE INDIAN GAVIAL

A LESS DANGEROUS VARIETY THAN MOST, THE GAVIAL IS A LONG NOSED, WEBB FOOTED, FISH EATING CROCODILE WITH SOME ENDEARING HABITS. IT IS SHY, TICKLISH & HAS AN ELEGANT WAY OF CATCHING FISH, FLIPPING THEM, UNCONSCIOUS, INTO THE AIR WITH ITS TAIL & CATCHING THEM IN ITS MOUTH.

THE MYSTERY OF A MUGGER'S STOMACH

STONES & PEBBLES WEIGHING AS MUCH AS 30LB. ARE FREQUENTLY FOUND IN THE STOMACHS OF MATURE ADULTS. IT HAS BEEN SUGGESTED THAT THEY AID THE DIGESTION, GRINDING TOUGHER MORSELS SUCH AS HIPPO BONES. A MORE LIKELY REASON IS THAT THE CUNNING REPTILES EAT ENOUGH TO ADJUST THEIR BUOYANCY SO THEY CAN JUST FLOAT WITH ONLY THEIR SNOUTS SHOWING ABOVE THE SURFACE. THIS THEORY IS SUPPORTED BY THE FACT THAT YOUNG ADULTS, WHO DO NOT EAT STONES, ARE MUCH MORE CLUMSY IN WATER.

CROCODILE CULTS

THE EGYPTIANS VENERATED THE CROCODILE. IT IS RECORDED THAT IT WAS CUSTOMARY IN 10 BC. AT A LAKE MOERIS TO VISIT ONE TAMED BY THE PRIESTS (THEY CALLED IT SUCHOS) & FEED IT CAKES & HONEY WINE. IN PARTS OF AFRICA IT IS BELIEVED THAT CROCODILES ONLY EAT HUMANS WHEN POSSESSED BY WITCHES, WHO MUST BE FOUND & EXECUTED. ONE TRIBE LEAVES THE UNLUCKY WITCH AS BAIT IN CROCODILE TRAPS.

HONEY

HOW TO EXTRACT WATER FROM A DESERT

DIG HOLE IN DESERT (OR BACK GARDEN). THEN PUT GLASS IN BOTTOM & COVER WITH POLYTHENE SHEET. HOLD DOWN WITH STONES OVER GLASS AS ABOVE. LEAVE & WATER WILL CONDENSE UNDER SHEET & FILL GLASS.

STONES — POLYTHENE SHEET — GLASS

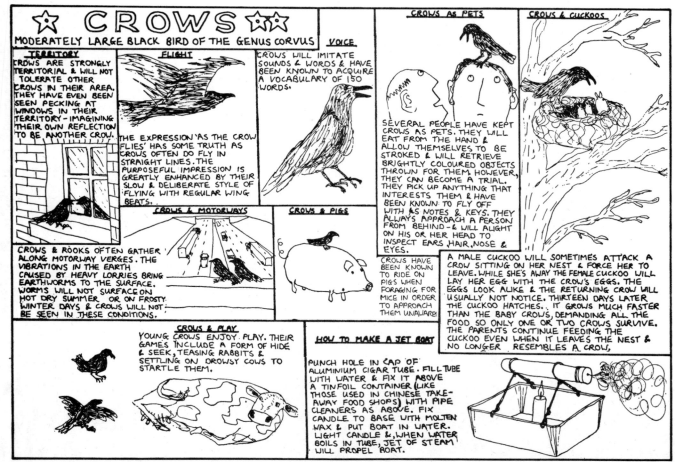

☆ CROWS ☆☆
MODERATELY LARGE BLACK BIRD OF THE GENUS CORVUS

TERRITORY

CROWS ARE STRONGLY TERRITORIAL & WILL NOT TOLERATE OTHER CROWS IN THEIR AREA. THEY HAVE EVEN BEEN SEEN PECKING AT WINDOWS IN THEIR TERRITORY - IMAGINING THEIR OWN REFLECTION TO BE ANOTHER CROW.

FLIGHT

THE EXPRESSION 'AS THE CROW FLIES' HAS SOME TRUTH AS CROWS OFTEN DO FLY IN STRAIGHT LINES. THE PURPOSEFUL IMPRESSION IS GREATLY ENHANCED BY THEIR SLOW & DELIBERATE STYLE OF FLYING WITH REGULAR WING BEATS.

VOICE

CROWS WILL IMITATE SOUNDS & WORDS & HAVE BEEN KNOWN TO ACQUIRE A VOCABULARY OF 150 WORDS.

CROWS AS PETS

SEVERAL PEOPLE HAVE KEPT CROWS AS PETS. THEY WILL EAT FROM THE HAND & ALLOW THEMSELVES TO BE STROKED & WILL RETRIEVE BRIGHTLY COLOURED OBJECTS THROWN FOR THEM. HOWEVER, THEY CAN BECOME A TRIAL. THEY PICK UP ANYTHING THAT INTERESTS THEM & HAVE BEEN KNOWN TO FLY OFF WITH £5 NOTES & KEYS. THEY ALWAYS APPROACH A PERSON FROM BEHIND - & WILL ALIGHT ON HIS OR HER HEAD TO INSPECT EARS, HAIR, NOSE & EYES.

CROWS & CUCKOOS

A MALE CUCKOO WILL SOMETIMES ATTACK A CROW SITTING ON HER NEST & FORCE HER TO LEAVE. WHILE SHE'S AWAY THE FEMALE CUCKOO WILL LAY HER EGG WITH THE CROW'S EGGS. THE EGGS LOOK ALIKE & THE RETURNING CROW WILL USUALLY NOT NOTICE. THIRTEEN DAYS LATER THE CUCKOO HATCHES. IT GROWS MUCH FASTER THAN THE BABY CROWS, DEMANDING ALL THE FOOD SO ONLY ONE OR TWO CROWS SURVIVE. THE PARENTS CONTINUE FEEDING THE CUCKOO EVEN WHEN IT LEAVES THE NEST & NO LONGER RESEMBLES A CROW.

CROWS & MOTORWAYS

CROWS & ROOKS OFTEN GATHER ALONG MOTORWAY VERGES. THE VIBRATIONS IN THE EARTH CAUSED BY HEAVY LORRIES BRING EARTHWORMS TO THE SURFACE. WORMS WILL NOT SURFACE ON HOT DRY SUMMER OR ON FROSTY WINTER DAYS & CROWS WILL NOT BE SEEN IN THESE CONDITIONS.

CROWS & PIGS

CROWS HAVE BEEN KNOWN TO RIDE ON PIGS WHEN FORAGING FOR MICE IN ORDER TO APPROACH THEM UNAWARES.

CROWS & PLAY

YOUNG CROWS ENJOY PLAY. THEIR GAMES INCLUDE A FORM OF HIDE & SEEK, TEASING RABBITS & SETTLING ON DROWSY COWS TO STARTLE THEM.

HOW TO MAKE A JET BOAT

PUNCH HOLE IN CAP OF ALUMINIUM CIGAR TUBE. FILL TUBE WITH WATER & FIX IT ABOVE A TINFOIL CONTAINER (LIKE THOSE USED IN CHINESE TAKE-AWAY FOOD SHOPS) WITH PIPE CLEANERS AS ABOVE. FIX CANDLE TO BASE WITH MOLTEN WAX & PUT BOAT IN WATER. LIGHT CANDLE & WHEN WATER BOILS IN TUBE, JET OF STEAM WILL PROPEL BOAT.

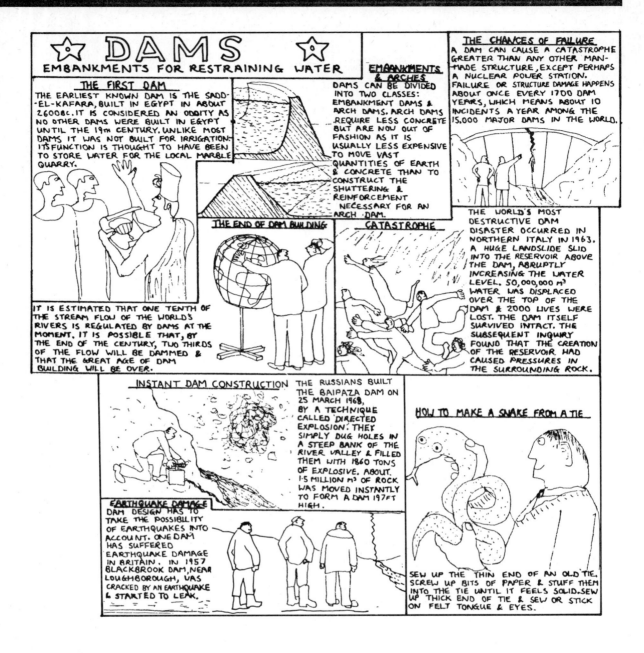

☆ DAMS ☆
EMBANKMENTS FOR RESTRAINING WATER

THE FIRST DAM
THE EARLIEST KNOWN DAM IS THE SADD-EL-KAFARA, BUILT IN EGYPT IN ABOUT 2600BC. IT IS CONSIDERED AN ODDITY AS NO OTHER DAMS WERE BUILT IN EGYPT UNTIL THE 19th CENTURY. UNLIKE MOST DAMS IT WAS NOT BUILT FOR IRRIGATION: ITS FUNCTION IS THOUGHT TO HAVE BEEN TO STORE WATER FOR THE LOCAL MARBLE QUARRY.

IT IS ESTIMATED THAT ONE TENTH OF THE STREAM FLOW OF THE WORLD'S RIVERS IS REGULATED BY DAMS AT THE MOMENT. IT IS POSSIBLE THAT, BY THE END OF THE CENTURY, TWO THIRDS OF THE FLOW WILL BE DAMMED & THAT THE GREAT AGE OF DAM BUILDING WILL BE OVER.

EMBANKMENTS & ARCHES
DAMS CAN BE DIVIDED INTO TWO CLASSES: EMBANKMENT DAMS & ARCH DAMS. ARCH DAMS REQUIRE LESS CONCRETE BUT ARE NOW OUT OF FASHION AS IT IS USUALLY LESS EXPENSIVE TO MOVE VAST QUANTITIES OF EARTH & CONCRETE THAN TO CONSTRUCT THE SHUTTERING & REINFORCEMENT NECESSARY FOR AN ARCH DAM.

THE END OF DAM BUILDING

CATASTROPHE

THE CHANCES OF FAILURE
A DAM CAN CAUSE A CATASTROPHE GREATER THAN ANY OTHER MAN-MADE STRUCTURE, EXCEPT PERHAPS A NUCLEAR POWER STATION. FAILURE OR STRUCTURE DAMAGE HAPPENS ABOUT ONCE EVERY 1700 DAM YEARS, WHICH MEANS ABOUT 10 INCIDENTS A YEAR AMONG THE 15,000 MAJOR DAMS IN THE WORLD.

THE WORLD'S MOST DESTRUCTIVE DAM DISASTER OCCURRED IN NORTHERN ITALY IN 1963. A HUGE LANDSLIDE SLID INTO THE RESERVOIR ABOVE THE DAM, ABRUPTLY INCREASING THE WATER LEVEL. 50,000,000 m³ WATER WAS DISPLACED OVER THE TOP OF THE DAM & 2000 LIVES WERE LOST. THE DAM ITSELF SURVIVED INTACT. THE SUBSEQUENT INQUIRY FOUND THAT THE CREATION OF THE RESERVOIR HAD CAUSED PRESSURES IN THE SURROUNDING ROCK.

INSTANT DAM CONSTRUCTION
THE RUSSIANS BUILT THE BAIPAZA DAM ON 25 MARCH 1968, BY A TECHNIQUE CALLED 'DIRECTED EXPLOSION'. THEY SIMPLY DUG HOLES IN A STEEP BANK OF THE RIVER VALLEY & FILLED THEM WITH 1860 TONS OF EXPLOSIVE. ABOUT 1·5 MILLION m³ OF ROCK WAS MOVED INSTANTLY TO FORM A DAM 197FT HIGH.

EARTHQUAKE DAMAGE
DAM DESIGN HAS TO TAKE THE POSSIBILITY OF EARTHQUAKES INTO ACCOUNT. ONE DAM HAS SUFFERED EARTHQUAKE DAMAGE IN BRITAIN. IN 1957 BLACKBROOK DAM, NEAR LOUGHBOROUGH, WAS CRACKED BY AN EARTHQUAKE & STARTED TO LEAK.

HOW TO MAKE A SNAKE FROM A TIE
SEW UP THE THIN END OF AN OLD TIE. SCREW UP BITS OF PAPER & STUFF THEM INTO THE TIE UNTIL IT FEELS SOLID. SEW UP THICK END OF TIE & SEW OR STICK ON FELT TONGUE & EYES.

☆ DANCING ☆
RHYTHMIC MOVEMENTS TO MUSIC

COUPLE DANCES
THERE ARE PRACTICALLY NO TRIBAL DANCES WHICH INVOLVE COUPLES DANCING TOGETHER. MEN & WOMEN SOMETIMES DANCE AT EACH OTHER, BUT NEVER WITH EACH OTHER. COUPLE DANCES DID NOT APPEAR UNTIL THE 15TH CENTURY IN EUROPEAN ROYAL COURTS. EVEN THEN, THE COUPLES REMAINED AT ARM'S LENGTH.

THE MORRIS DANCE
THE MORRIS DANCE STEMS FROM THE PRE-CHRISTIAN ERA WHEN IT WAS PRIMARILY A FERTILITY DANCE. IT WAS DISCOURAGED BY THE CHURCH & NEVER REGULARLY DANCED UNTIL IT WAS REDISCOVERED IN THE 1920s.

ST VITUS'S DANCE
A DANCING MANIA BROKE OUT ALL OVER EUROPE AFTER THE BLACK DEATH IN THE 14th CENTURY. PEOPLE SPONTANEOUSLY STARTED SINGING & DANCING IN THE MIDDLE OF CHURCH SERVICES & COULD NOT BE MADE TO STOP. THE WATER OF THE SHRINE OF ST VITUS WAS SUPPOSED TO CURE THE MANIA – HENCE THE NAME ST VITUS'S DANCE.

THE WALTZ
THE WALTZ ORIGINATES IN GERMAN FOLK DANCES. IT WAS ADOPTED BY THE GERMAN ARISTOCRACY IN THE 1780s & SPREAD TO THE REST OF EUROPE AFTER THE NAPOLEONIC WARS. THE PROXIMITY OF THE DANCERS WAS AT FIRST CONSIDERED HIGHLY SHOCKING. IN 1816 THE TIMES STATED: "IT IS QUITE SUFFICIENT TO CAST ONE'S EYES ON THE VOLUPTUOUS INTERTWINING OF THE LIMBS & CLOSE COMPRESSURE OF THE BODIES, IN THEIR DANCE, TO SEE THAT IT IS INDEED FAR REMOVED FROM THE MODEST RESERVE THAT HAS HITHERTO BEEN CONSIDERED DISTINCTIVE OF ENGLISH FEMALES."

THE TANGO
THE TANGO APPEARED IN BUENOS AIRES IN THE 1890s AS A POPULAR EROTIC DANCE IGNORED BY ANYONE WITH PRETENTIONS TO GENTILITY. IT WAS BROUGHT TO EUROPE BY A MUSICAL ENTREPRENEUR WHO REARRANGED IT TO GET RID OF THE RUDE BITS & MAKE IT SUITABLE FOR EUROPEAN BALLROOMS.

DANCE MARATHONS
DANCE MARATHONS WERE POPULAR IN AMERICA IN THE 1920s. THE RULES WERE STRICT: COUPLES WERE NOT ALLOWED TO SLEEP, SMOKE OR SPIT BUT WERE ALLOWED 10 MINUTES' REST PER HOUR, EIGHT HOT MEALS A DAY & A SHOWER EVERY 12 HOURS. THE REST PERIODS WERE OFTEN SHORTENED TO SPEED UP THE CLOSING STAGES OF A MARATHON. IN 1932 A MAN DROPPED DEAD AFTER 48 DAYS NON-STOP DANCING & IN 1933 DANCE MARATHONS WERE DECLARED ILLEGAL. THE RECORD STANDS AT 24 WEEKS & 5 DAYS.

THE CHARLESTON
THE CHARLESTON WAS DISCOVERED IN CHARLESTON SOUTH CAROLINA, IN 1923 BEING PERFORMED BY NEGRO DOCK WORKERS.

HOW TO MAKE A FLY TRAP
TWIST TWO BITS OF WIRE SO THEY FORM A CROSS FITTING OVER THE TOP OF A FUNNEL. EMBED A BIT OF NYLON FISHING LINE IN A LUMP OF PLASTICINE & PUSH THIS INTO THE CENTRE OF THE WIRE CROSS SO THE NYLON JUST REACHES THE NARROW PART OF THE FUNNEL. CUT A HOLE IN A CARDBOARD SHOE BOX, PUT SOME SMELLY FOOD INSIDE & PLACE SPOUT OF FUNNEL IN HOLE. FLIES CAN ENTER BOX THROUGH FUNNEL BY PUSHING NYLON ASIDE – BUT CAN'T GET OUT AGAIN.

DANGER
THE POSSIBILITY
OF HARM OR LOSS

DANGER AT HOME
STAYING AT HOME IS SURPRISINGLY DANGEROUS: NEARLY AS MANY PEOPLE ARE KILLED IN ACCIDENTS IN THE HOME AS ARE KILLED ON THE ROADS. (ABOUT 70% OF THE FATALITIES ARE OVER 65).

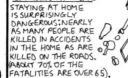

A VARIETY OF DANGERS

MOTORCYCLISTS	2000 (DEATHS PER 100,000 PEOPLE PER YEAR
SMOKERS	500 "
DEEP-SEA FISHERMEN	400 "
STEEL ERECTORS	134 "
CAR RACING DRIVERS	120 "
RAILWAY SHUNTERS	90 "
MINERS	24 "
FARM WORKERS	20 "
CAR DRIVERS	17 "
BUILDING WORKERS	16 "
ROCK CLIMBERS	14 "
INHABITANTS OF CANVEY ISLAND (DANGER OF CHEMICAL PLANT EXPLOSION)	16 "
ACCIDENTS AT HOME	8 "
INFLUENZA	6 "
BEING RUN OVER	6 "
FOOTBALL PLAYERS	4 "
TAKING CONTRACEPTIVE PILLS	2 "
BEING HIT BY LIGHTNING	.01 "
BEING HIT BY FALLING AIRCRAFT	.002 "
BEING BITTEN BY SNAKES	.02 "
BEING HIT BY METEORITES	.00006 "

THE LIST ABOVE GIVES THE AVERAGE DANGER OF DEATH FROM EACH CAUSE FOR A PERSON IN ANY ONE YEAR. THE FIGURES ARE APPROXIMATE BECAUSE THE RELATIVE DANGERS OBVIOUSLY VARY WITH A PERSON'S AGE (OLD PEOPLE ARE MORE LIKELY TO DIE FROM INFLUENZA: YOUNG PEOPLE ARE MORE LIKELY TO DIE IN MOTORCYCLE ACCIDENTS). ALSO THE FIGURE GIVEN BY DIFFERENT AUTHORITIES FOR EACH CAUSE OFTEN VARIES CONSIDERABLY.

DANGER TIME
ACCORDING TO THE SOVIET MINISTRY OF HEALTH, THE MAJORITY OF INDUSTRIAL ACCIDENTS IN THE USSR OCCUR BETWEEN 5 & 6 PM ON MONDAYS.

DANGER POWER
ADVOCATES OF NUCLEAR POWER CLAIM THAT SO FAR IT HAS BEEN LESS DANGEROUS THAN CONVENTIONAL ENERGY. ON AVERAGE, ONE MINER OR OIL RIG WORKER DIES FOR EACH 2 MEGAWATTS GENERATED PER YEAR.

DANGER PLAY
MORE THAN 20,000 CHILDREN A YEAR NEED HOSPITAL TREATMENT BECAUSE OF ACCIDENTS IN PLAYGROUNDS. THE MOST COMMON CAUSE IS CHILDREN BEING HIT BY SWINGS.

DANGER PRONE
A US PSYCHOLOGY PROFESSOR CLAIMS THAT SOME PEOPLE ARE ACCIDENT-PRONE BECAUSE THEIR ATTENTION WANDERS PARTICULARLY EASILY. HIS 'ATTENTION' TEST, TRIED ON 55 CRANE OPERATORS, PICKED 26 AS ACCIDENT-PRONE. 18 SUBSEQUENTLY HAD MORE THAN AVERAGE ACCIDENTS.

UNIT DANGER
LORD ROTHSCHILD HAS PROPOSED A UNIT OF DANGER (POSSIBLY THE CHANCE OF BEING KILLED ON THE ROADS) AGAINST WHICH OTHER DANGERS COULD BE RATED. HE ARGUES THAT IT WOULD HELP PEOPLE TO DECIDE WHAT LEVEL OF DANGER (FROM CHEMICAL PLANTS, NUCLEAR POWER ETC) IS ACCEPTABLE.

.00001 DANGER UNITS

☆ DEEP SEA FISH ☆
DRAMATIC DENIZENS OF THE DEEP

ANGLER FISHES
DEEP SEA ANGLER FISHES HAVE VARIOUS ODD SHAPES BUT ARE USUALLY LESS THAN ONE INCH LONG & ALL HAVE A FISHING LURE ATTACHED TO THE END OF THEIR LINES. MOST HAVE GLOWING CELLS (PHOTOPHORES) ON THE END OF THE LINE WHICH THEY CAN TURN ON OR FLASH AT WILL. THIS ATTRACTS PRAWNS & OTHER PREY INTO THE ANGLER'S JAWS.

THE DEPENDENT MALES
A MALE ANGLER FISH HAS NO LINE OR LIGHT. HE FINDS A FEMALE, DIGS HIS JAWS INTO HER SKIN & STAYS THERE. EVENTUALLY THEY BECOME FUSED TOGETHER & HE COMPLETELY DEPENDS ON HER FOR NOURISHMENT & TRANSPORT.

THE VAMPIRE OF THE INFERNO
8IN TALL, A CROSS BETWEEN AN OCTOPUS & A SQUID & HAS TWO GLOWING SEARCHLIGHTS. VERY LITTLE IS KNOWN ABOUT IT. EVEN ITS DIET IS A MYSTERY.

DEEP SEA SQUIDS
THE INK WITH WHICH MOST SQUIDS CREATE SCREEN TO ESCAPE FROM PREDATORS IS INEFFECTIVE AT GREAT DEPTHS AS THE SEA IS SO DARK TO START WITH. THE DEEP SEA SQUID HAS OVERCOME THIS PROBLEM BY THROWING OUT CLOUDS OF LUMINOUS SPARKS TO SCREEN ITS ESCAPE.

THE GULPER
THERE IS VERY LITTLE FOOD IN THE DEPTHS AS THERE IS INSUFFICIENT LIGHT FOR ANY VEGETATION TO SURVIVE. THIS HAS FORCED SOME FISH TO ADAPT TO EATING INFREQUENT MEALS OF FISH FATTER THAN THEMSELVES. THE GULPER ABOVE HAS DEVELOPED A HUGE MOUTH FOR THIS REASON.

THE VIPER FISH
THE VIPER FISH IS ONE OF THE MOST EXTRAORDINARY VARIETIES OF ANGLER FISHES. IT HAS AN EXTERNAL LOWER JAW WHICH ACTS AT HIGH SPEED AS A SORT OF MOUSE TRAP. IT ALSO HAS ROWS OF LUMINOUS 'PORTHOLES' ALONG ITS SIDES TO ATTRACT VICTIMS.

THE GIANT SWALLOWER
THE GIANT SWALLOWER HAS A VERY ELASTIC STOMACH THAT ENABLES IT TO SWALLOW FISH TWICE ITS OWN LENGTH. THE STOMACH IS SO THIN THAT THE OUTLINE OF ITS MOST RECENT PREY CAN EASILY BE SEEN INSIDE.

HOW TO DEMONSTRATE CONVECTION CURRENTS WITH GHOSTLY GLOWING GLOBULES
50% METHYLATED SPIRITS MIXED WITH 50% WATER. GLUE BULB SOCKET TO PLYWOOD WITH A HOLE FOR WIRES. REMOVE BOTTOM OF TIN WITH A CAN OPENER. STICK TIN ON THE PLYWOOD & PLACE BOTTLE ON TOP. WHEN THE BOTTLE IS FILLED WITH THE TWO IMMISCIBLE LIQUIDS OF THE SAME DENSITY THE HEAT OF THE BULB WILL MAKE THE GLOWING GLOBULES CIRCULATE. IF OIL IS HEAVIER THAN WATER-METHS MIXTURE ADD MORE WATER IF LIGHTER ADD MORE METHS.
LARGE WHITE WINE BOTTLE
COOKING OIL
EMPTY ½ GALL PAINT TIN
60 WATT BULB

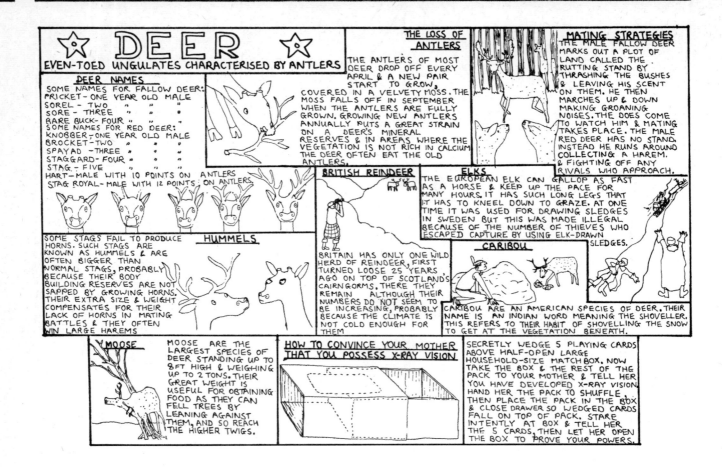

☆ DEER ☆
EVEN-TOED UNGULATES CHARACTERISED BY ANTLERS

DEER NAMES

SOME NAMES FOR FALLOW DEER:
PRICKET - ONE YEAR OLD MALE
SOREL - TWO " " "
SORE - THREE " " "
BARE BUCK - FOUR " " "
SOME NAMES FOR RED DEER:
KNOBBER - ONE YEAR OLD MALE
BROCKET - TWO " " "
SPAYAD - THREE " " "
STAGGARD - FOUR " " "
STAG - FIVE " " "
HART - MALE WITH 10 POINTS ON ANTLERS
STAG ROYAL - MALE WITH 12 POINTS ON ANTLERS

HUMMELS

SOME STAGS FAIL TO PRODUCE HORNS. SUCH STAGS ARE KNOWN AS HUMMELS & ARE OFTEN BIGGER THAN NORMAL STAGS, PROBABLY BECAUSE THEIR BODY BUILDING RESERVES ARE NOT SAPPED BY GROWING HORNS. THEIR EXTRA SIZE & WEIGHT COMPENSATES FOR THEIR LACK OF HORNS IN MATING BATTLES & THEY OFTEN WIN LARGE HAREMS.

THE LOSS OF ANTLERS

THE ANTLERS OF MOST DEER DROP OFF EVERY APRIL & A NEW PAIR START TO GROW, COVERED IN A VELVETY MOSS. THE MOSS FALLS OFF IN SEPTEMBER WHEN THE ANTLERS ARE FULLY GROWN. GROWING NEW ANTLERS ANNUALLY PUTS A GREAT STRAIN ON A DEER'S MINERAL RESERVES & IN AREAS WHERE THE VEGETATION IS NOT RICH IN CALCIUM THE DEER OFTEN EAT THE OLD ANTLERS.

BRITISH REINDEER

BRITAIN HAS ONLY ONE WILD HERD OF REINDEER, FIRST TURNED LOOSE 25 YEARS AGO ON TOP OF SCOTLAND'S CAIRNGORMS. THERE THEY REMAIN ALTHOUGH THEIR NUMBERS DO NOT SEEM TO BE INCREASING, PROBABLY BECAUSE THE CLIMATE IS NOT COLD ENOUGH FOR THEM

MATING STRATEGIES

THE MALE FALLOW DEER MARKS OUT A PLOT OF LAND CALLED THE RUTTING STAND BY THRASHING THE BUSHES & LEAVING HIS SCENT ON THEM. HE THEN MARCHES UP & DOWN MAKING GROANING NOISES. THE DOES COME TO WATCH HIM & MATING TAKES PLACE. THE MALE RED DEER HAS NO STAND INSTEAD HE RUNS AROUND COLLECTING A HAREM, & FIGHTING OFF ANY RIVALS WHO APPROACH.

ELKS

THE EUROPEAN ELK CAN GALLOP AS FAST AS A HORSE & KEEP UP THE PACE FOR MANY HOURS. IT HAS SUCH LONG LEGS THAT IT HAS TO KNEEL DOWN TO GRAZE. AT ONE TIME IT WAS USED FOR DRAWING SLEDGES IN SWEDEN BUT THIS WAS MADE ILLEGAL BECAUSE OF THE NUMBER OF THIEVES WHO ESCAPED CAPTURE BY USING ELK-DRAWN SLEDGES.

CARIBOU

CARIBOU ARE AN AMERICAN SPECIES OF DEER. THEIR NAME IS AN INDIAN WORD MEANING THE SHOVELLER. THIS REFERS TO THEIR HABIT OF SHOVELLING THE SNOW TO GET AT THE VEGETATION BENEATH.

MOOSE

MOOSE ARE THE LARGEST SPECIES OF DEER STANDING UP TO 8FT HIGH & WEIGHING UP TO 2 TONS. THEIR GREAT WEIGHT IS USEFUL FOR OBTAINING FOOD AS THEY CAN FELL TREES BY LEANING AGAINST THEM, AND SO REACH THE HIGHER TWIGS.

HOW TO CONVINCE YOUR MOTHER THAT YOU POSSESS X-RAY VISION

SECRETLY WEDGE 5 PLAYING CARDS ABOVE HALF-OPEN LARGE HOUSEHOLD-SIZE MATCH BOX. NOW TAKE THE BOX & THE REST OF THE PACK TO YOUR MOTHER & TELL HER YOU HAVE DEVELOPED X-RAY VISION. HAND HER THE PACK TO SHUFFLE THEN PLACE THE PACK IN THE BOX & CLOSE DRAWER SO WEDGED CARDS FALL ON TOP OF PACK. STARE INTENTLY AT BOX & TELL HER THE 5 CARDS, THEN LET HER OPEN THE BOX TO PROVE YOUR POWERS.

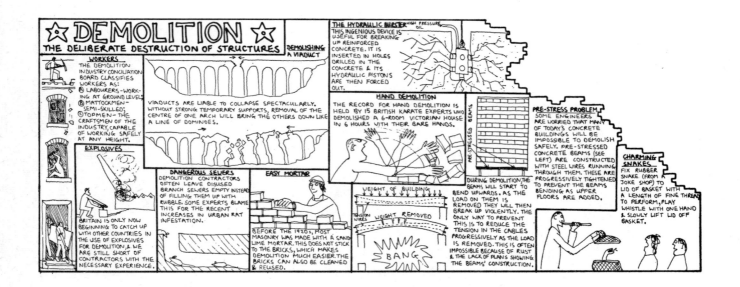

☆ DEMOLITION ☆
THE DELIBERATE DESTRUCTION OF STRUCTURES

WORKERS

THE DEMOLITION INDUSTRY CONCILIATION BOARD CLASSIFIES WORKERS AS:
Ⓐ LABOURERS - WORKING AT GROUND LEVEL;
Ⓑ MATTOCKMEN - SEMI-SKILLED;
Ⓒ TOPMEN - THE CRAFTSMEN OF THE INDUSTRY, CAPABLE OF WORKING SAFELY AT ANY HEIGHT.

EXPLOSIVES

BRITAIN IS ONLY NOW BEGINNING TO CATCH UP WITH OTHER COUNTRIES IN THE USE OF EXPLOSIVES FOR DEMOLITION, & WE ARE STILL SHORT OF CONTRACTORS WITH THE NECESSARY EXPERIENCE.

DEMOLISHING A VIADUCT

VIADUCTS ARE LIABLE TO COLLAPSE SPECTACULARLY. WITHOUT STRONG TEMPORARY SUPPORTS, REMOVAL OF THE CENTRE OF ONE ARCH WILL BRING THE OTHERS DOWN LIKE A LINE OF DOMINOES.

DANGEROUS SEWERS

DEMOLITION CONTRACTORS OFTEN LEAVE DISUSED BRANCH SEWERS EMPTY INSTEAD OF FILLING THEM UP WITH RUBBLE. SOME EXPERTS BLAME THIS FOR THE RECENT INCREASES IN URBAN RAT INFESTATION.

EASY MORTAR

BEFORE THE 1920s, MOST MASONRY WAS MADE WITH A SAND-LIME MORTAR. THIS DOES NOT STICK TO THE BRICKS, WHICH MAKES DEMOLITION MUCH EASIER. THE BRICKS CAN ALSO BE CLEANED & REUSED.

THE HYDRAULIC BURSTER

HIGH PRESSURE OIL

THIS INGENIOUS DEVICE IS USEFUL FOR BREAKING UP REINFORCED CONCRETE. IT IS INSERTED IN HOLES DRILLED IN THE CONCRETE & ITS HYDRAULIC PISTONS ARE THEN FORCED OUT.

HAND DEMOLITION

THE RECORD FOR HAND DEMOLITION IS HELD BY 15 BRITISH KARATE EXPERTS WHO DEMOLISHED A 6-ROOM VICTORIAN HOUSE IN 6 HOURS WITH THEIR BARE HANDS.

WEIGHT OF BUILDING

TENSION WIRES WEIGHT REMOVED

BANG

DURING DEMOLITION, THE BEAMS WILL START TO BEND UPWARDS. AS THE LOAD ON THEM IS REMOVED THEY WILL THEN BREAK UP VIOLENTLY. THE ONLY WAY TO PREVENT THIS IS TO REDUCE THE TENSION IN THE CABLES PROGRESSIVELY AS THE LOAD IS REMOVED. THIS IS OFTEN IMPOSSIBLE BECAUSE OF RUST & THE LACK OF PLANS SHOWING THE BEAMS' CONSTRUCTION.

PRE-STRESS PROBLEM

PRE-STRESSED BEAMS

SOME ENGINEERS ARE WORRIED THAT MANY OF TODAY'S CONCRETE BUILDINGS WILL BE IMPOSSIBLE TO DEMOLISH SAFELY. PRE-STRESSED CONCRETE BEAMS (SEE LEFT) ARE CONSTRUCTED WITH STEEL WIRES RUNNING THROUGH THEM. THESE ARE PROGRESSIVELY TIGHTENED TO PREVENT THE BEAMS BENDING AS UPPER FLOORS ARE ADDED.

CHARMING SNAKES

FIX RUBBER SNAKE (FROM JOKE SHOP) TO LID OF BASKET WITH A LENGTH OF FINE THREAD. TO PERFORM, PLAY WHISTLE WITH ONE HAND & SLOWLY LIFT LID OFF BASKET.

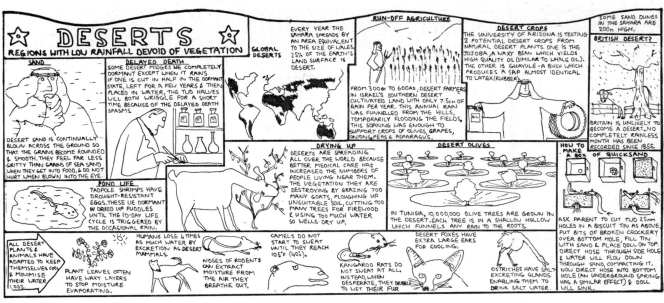

☆ DESERTS ☆
REGIONS WITH LOW RAINFALL DEVOID OF VEGETATION

GLOBAL DESERTS

SAND

DESERT SAND IS CONTINUALLY BLOWN ACROSS THE GROUND SO THAT THE GRAINS BECOME ROUNDED & SMOOTH. THEY FEEL FAR LESS GRITTY THAN GRAINS OF SEA SAND WHEN THEY GET INTO FOOD, & DO NOT HURT WHEN BLOWN INTO THE EYE.

DELAYED DEATH

SOME DESERT MIDGES LIE COMPLETELY DORMANT EXCEPT WHEN IT RAINS. IF ONE IS CUT IN HALF IN THE DORMANT STATE, LEFT FOR A FEW YEARS & THEN PLACED IN WATER, THE TWO HALVES WILL BOTH WRIGGLE FOR A SHORT TIME BECAUSE OF THE DELAYED DEATH SPASMS.

EVERY YEAR THE SAHARA SPREADS BY AN AREA EQUIVALENT TO THE SIZE OF WALES. 25% OF THE EARTH'S LAND SURFACE IS DESERT.

RUN-OFF AGRICULTURE

FROM 300BC TO 600AD, DESERT FARMERS IN ISRAEL'S SOUTHERN DESERT CULTIVATED LAND WITH ONLY 7.5CM OF RAIN PER YEAR. THIS ANNUAL RAIN WAS FUNNELLED FROM THE HILLS, TEMPORARILY FLOODING THE FIELDS, THIS SOAKING WAS ENOUGH TO SUPPORT CROPS OF OLIVES, GRAPES, ONIONS, PEAS & ASPARAGUS.

DESERT CROPS

THE UNIVERSITY OF ARIZONA IS TESTING 2 POTENTIAL DESERT CROPS FROM NATURAL DESERT PLANTS. ONE IS THE JOJOBA, A WAXY BEAN WHICH YIELDS HIGH QUALITY OIL (SIMILAR TO WHALE OIL). THE OTHER IS GUAYULE - A BUSH WHICH PRODUCES A SAP ALMOST IDENTICAL TO LATEX (RUBBER).

SOME SAND DUNES IN THE SAHARA ARE 200M HIGH.

BRITISH DESERT?

BRITAIN IS UNLIKELY TO BECOME A DESERT. NO COMPLETELY RAINLESS MONTH HAS BEEN RECORDED SINCE 1855.

POND LIFE

TADPOLE SHRIMPS HAVE DROUGHT-RESISTANT EGGS. THESE LIE DORMANT IN DRIED UP PUDDLES UNTIL THE 10-DAY LIFE CYCLE IS TRIGGERED BY THE OCCASIONAL RAIN.

DRYING UP

DESERTS ARE SPREADING ALL OVER THE WORLD BECAUSE BETTER MEDICAL CARE HAS INCREASED THE NUMBERS OF PEOPLE LIVING NEAR THEM. THE VEGETATION THEY ARE DESTROYING BY GRAZING TOO MANY GOATS, PLOUGHING UP UNSUITABLE SOIL, CUTTING TOO MANY TREES FOR FIREWOOD & USING TOO MUCH WATER SO WELLS DRY UP.

DESERT OLIVES

IN TUNISIA, 10,000,000 OLIVE TREES ARE GROWN IN THE DESERT. EACH TREE IS IN A SHALLOW HOLLOW WHICH FUNNELS ANY RAIN TO THE ROOTS.

HOW TO MAKE A BOX OF QUICKSAND

ASK PARENT TO CUT TWO 25MM HOLES IN A BISCUIT TIN AS ABOVE. PUT BITS OF BROKEN CROCKERY OVER BOTTOM HOLE, FILL TIN WITH SAND & PLACE DOLL ON TOP. DIRECT HOSE THROUGH SIDE HOLE & WATER WILL FLOW DOWN THROUGH SAND, COMPACTING IT. NOW DIRECT HOSE INTO BOTTOM HOLE (AN UNDERGROUND SPRING HAS A SIMILAR EFFECT) & DOLL WILL SINK.

ALL DESERT PLANTS & ANIMALS HAVE ADAPTED TO KEEP THEMSELVES COOL & MINIMISE THEIR WATER LOSS.

PLANT LEAVES OFTEN HAVE WAXY LAYERS TO STOP MOISTURE EVAPORATING.

HUMANS LOSE 4 TIMES AS MUCH WATER BY EXCRETION AS DESERT MAMMALS.

NOSES OF RODENTS CAN EXTRACT MOISTURE FROM THE AIR THEY BREATHE OUT.

CAMELS DO NOT START TO SWEAT UNTIL THEY REACH 105°F (40°C).

KANGAROO RATS DO NOT SWEAT AT ALL. INSTEAD, WHEN DESPERATE, THEY DRIBBLE TO WET THEIR FUR

DESERT FOXES HAVE EXTRA LARGE EARS FOR COOLING.

OSTRICHES HAVE SALT EXCRETING GLANDS ENABLING THEM TO DRINK SALT WATER.

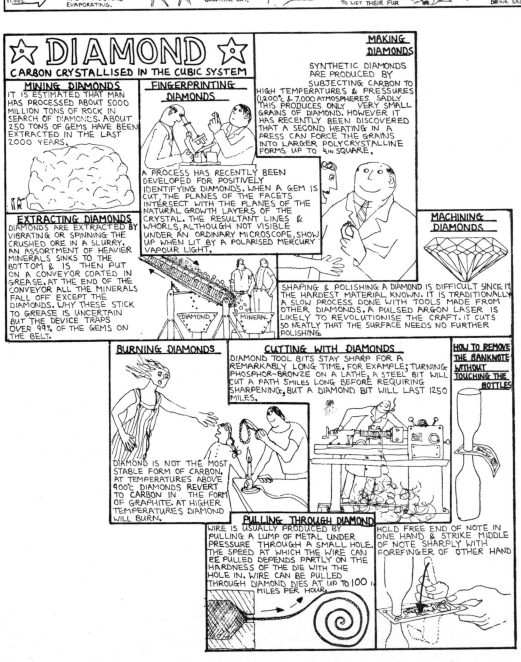

☆ DIAMOND ☆
CARBON CRYSTALLISED IN THE CUBIC SYSTEM

MINING DIAMONDS

IT IS ESTIMATED THAT MAN HAS PROCESSED ABOUT 5000 MILLION TONS OF ROCK IN SEARCH OF DIAMONDS. ABOUT 250 TONS OF GEMS HAVE BEEN EXTRACTED IN THE LAST 2000 YEARS.

FINGERPRINTING DIAMONDS

A PROCESS HAS RECENTLY BEEN DEVELOPED FOR POSITIVELY IDENTIFYING DIAMONDS. WHEN A GEM IS CUT, THE PLANES OF THE FACETS INTERSECT WITH THE PLANES OF THE NATURAL GROWTH LAYERS OF THE CRYSTAL. THE RESULTANT LINES & WHORLS, ALTHOUGH NOT VISIBLE UNDER AN ORDINARY MICROSCOPE, SHOW UP WHEN LIT BY A POLARISED MERCURY VAPOUR LIGHT.

MAKING DIAMONDS

SYNTHETIC DIAMONDS ARE PRODUCED BY SUBJECTING CARBON TO HIGH TEMPERATURES & PRESSURES (1,200°C & 7,000 ATMOSPHERES. SADLY THIS PRODUCES ONLY VERY SMALL GRAINS OF DIAMOND. HOWEVER IT HAS RECENTLY BEEN DISCOVERED THAT A SECOND HEATING IN A PRESS CAN FORCE THE GRAINS INTO LARGER POLYCRYSTALLINE FORMS UP TO ¼IN SQUARE.

EXTRACTING DIAMONDS

DIAMONDS ARE EXTRACTED BY VIBRATING OR SPINNING THE CRUSHED ORE IN A SLURRY. AN ASSORTMENT OF HEAVIER MINERALS SINKS TO THE BOTTOM & IS THEN PUT ON A CONVEYOR COATED IN GREASE. AT THE END OF THE CONVEYOR ALL THE MINERALS FALL OFF EXCEPT THE DIAMONDS. WHY THESE STICK TO GREASE IS UNCERTAIN BUT THE DEVICE TRAPS OVER 99% OF THE GEMS ON THE BELT.

DIAMOND · MINERAL

MACHINING DIAMONDS

SHAPING & POLISHING A DIAMOND IS DIFFICULT SINCE IT IS THE HARDEST MATERIAL KNOWN. IT IS TRADITIONALLY A SLOW PROCESS DONE WITH TOOLS MADE FROM OTHER DIAMONDS. A PULSED ARGON LASER IS LIKELY TO REVOLUTIONISE THE CRAFT. IT CUTS SO NEATLY THAT THE SURFACE NEEDS NO FURTHER POLISHING.

BURNING DIAMONDS

DIAMOND IS NOT THE MOST STABLE FORM OF CARBON. AT TEMPERATURES ABOVE 900°C DIAMONDS REVERT TO CARBON IN THE FORM OF GRAPHITE. AT HIGHER TEMPERATURES DIAMOND WILL BURN.

CUTTING WITH DIAMONDS

DIAMOND TOOL BITS STAY SHARP FOR A REMARKABLY LONG TIME. FOR EXAMPLE; TURNING PHOSPHOR-BRONZE ON A LATHE, A STEEL BIT WILL CUT A PATH 5 MILES LONG BEFORE REQUIRING SHARPENING, BUT A DIAMOND BIT WILL LAST 1250 MILES.

HOW TO REMOVE THE BANKNOTE WITHOUT TOUCHING THE BOTTLES

HOLD FREE END OF NOTE IN ONE HAND & STRIKE MIDDLE OF NOTE SHARPLY WITH FOREFINGER OF OTHER HAND

PULLING THROUGH DIAMOND

WIRE IS USUALLY PRODUCED BY PULLING A LUMP OF METAL UNDER PRESSURE THROUGH A SMALL HOLE. THE SPEED AT WHICH THE WIRE CAN BE PULLED DEPENDS PARTLY ON THE HARDNESS OF THE DIE WITH THE HOLE IN. WIRE CAN BE PULLED THROUGH DIAMOND DIES AT UP TO 100 MILES PER HOUR.

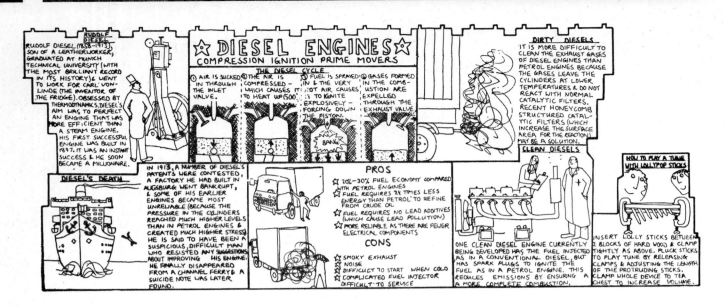

☆ DIESEL ENGINES ☆
COMPRESSION IGNITION PRIME MOVERS

RUDOLF DIESEL

RUDOLF DIESEL (1858–1913), SON OF A LEATHERWORKER, GRADUATED AT MUNICH TECHNICAL UNIVERSITY (WITH THE MOST BRILLIANT RECORD IN ITS HISTORY) & WENT TO WORK FOR CARL VON LINDE (THE INVENTOR OF THE FRIDGE). OBSESSED BY THERMODYNAMICS, DIESEL'S AIM WAS TO PERFECT AN ENGINE THAT WAS MORE EFFICIENT THAN A STEAM ENGINE. HIS FIRST SUCCESSFUL ENGINE WAS BUILT IN 1897. IT WAS AN INSTANT SUCCESS & HE SOON BECAME A MILLIONAIRE.

DIESEL'S DEATH

IN 1913, A NUMBER OF DIESEL'S PATENTS WERE CONTESTED, A FACTORY HE HAD BUILT IN AUGSBURG WENT BANKRUPT, & SOME OF HIS EARLIER ENGINES BECAME MOST UNRELIABLE (BECAUSE THE PRESSURE IN THE CYLINDERS REACHED MUCH HIGHER LEVELS THAN IN PETROL ENGINES & CREATED MUCH HIGHER STRESS). HE IS SAID TO HAVE BEEN A SUSPICIOUS, DIFFICULT MAN WHO RESISTED ANY SUGGESTIONS ABOUT IMPROVING HIS ENGINE. HE FINALLY DISAPPEARED FROM A CHANNEL FERRY & A SUICIDE NOTE WAS LATER FOUND.

THE DIESEL CYCLE

① AIR IS SUCKED IN THROUGH THE INLET VALVE.
② THE AIR IS COMPRESSED – WHICH CAUSES IT TO HEAT UP (500°).
③ FUEL IS SPRAYED IN & THE VERY HOT AIR CAUSES IT TO IGNITE EXPLOSIVELY – FORCING DOWN THE PISTON.
④ GASES FORMED IN THE COMBUSTION ARE EXPELLED THROUGH THE EXHAUST VALVE.

PROS
☆ 20%–30% FUEL ECONOMY COMPARED WITH PETROL ENGINES
☆ FUEL REQUIRES 2¼ TIMES LESS ENERGY THAN PETROL TO REFINE FROM CRUDE OIL
☆ FUEL REQUIRES NO LEAD ADDITIVES (WHICH CAUSE LEAD POLLUTION)
☆ MORE RELIABLE AS THERE ARE FEWER ELECTRICAL COMPONENTS

CONS
☆ SMOKY EXHAUST
☆ NOISE
☆ DIFFICULT TO START WHEN COLD
☆ COMPLICATED FUEL INJECTOR DIFFICULT TO SERVICE

DIRTY DIESELS

IT IS MORE DIFFICULT TO CLEAN THE EXHAUST GASES OF DIESEL ENGINES THAN PETROL ENGINES BECAUSE THE GASES LEAVE THE CYLINDERS AT LOWER TEMPERATURES & DO NOT REACT WITH NORMAL CATALYTIC FILTERS. RECENT HONEYCOMB STRUCTURED CATALYTIC FILTERS (WHICH INCREASE THE SURFACE AREA FOR THE REACTION) MAY BE A SOLUTION.

CLEAN DIESELS

ONE CLEAN DIESEL ENGINE CURRENTLY BEING DEVELOPED HAS THE FUEL INJECTED AS IN A CONVENTIONAL DIESEL, BUT HAS SPARK PLUGS TO IGNITE THE FUEL AS IN A PETROL ENGINE. THIS REDUCES EMISSIONS BY ENSURING A MORE COMPLETE COMBUSTION.

HOW TO PLAY A TUNE WITH LOLLYPOP STICKS

INSERT LOLLY STICKS BETWEEN 2 BLOCKS OF HARD WOOD & CLAMP TIGHTLY AS ABOVE. PLUCK STICKS TO PLAY TUNE BY RELEASING CLAMPS & ADJUSTING THE LENGTH OF THE PROTRUDING STICKS. CLAMP WHOLE DEVICE TO TEA CHEST TO INCREASE VOLUME.

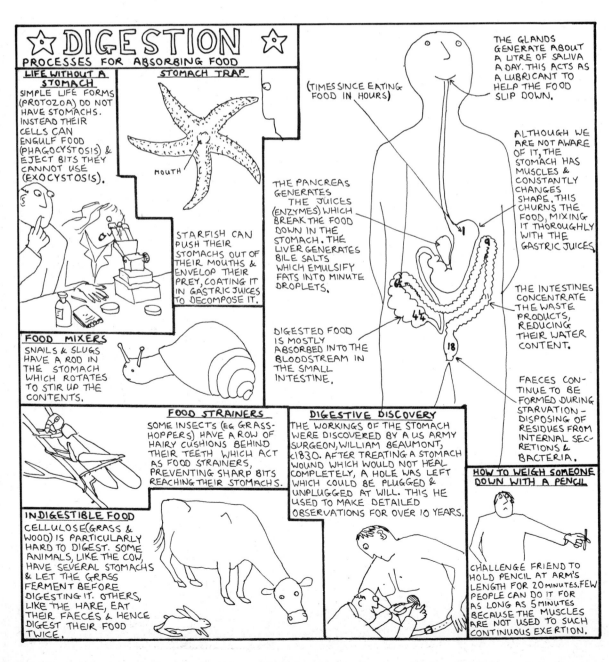

☆ DIGESTION ☆
PROCESSES FOR ABSORBING FOOD

LIFE WITHOUT A STOMACH

SIMPLE LIFE FORMS (PROTOZOA) DO NOT HAVE STOMACHS. INSTEAD THEIR CELLS CAN ENGULF FOOD (PHAGOCYSTOSIS) & EJECT BITS THEY CANNOT USE (EXOCYSTOSIS).

STOMACH TRAP

MOUTH

STARFISH CAN PUSH THEIR STOMACHS OUT OF THEIR MOUTHS & ENVELOP THEIR PREY, COATING IT IN GASTRIC JUICES TO DECOMPOSE IT.

FOOD MIXERS

SNAILS & SLUGS HAVE A ROD IN THE STOMACH WHICH ROTATES TO STIR UP THE CONTENTS.

FOOD STRAINERS

SOME INSECTS (EG GRASSHOPPERS) HAVE A ROW OF HAIRY CUSHIONS BEHIND THEIR TEETH WHICH ACT AS FOOD STRAINERS, PREVENTING SHARP BITS REACHING THEIR STOMACHS.

INDIGESTIBLE FOOD

CELLULOSE (GRASS & WOOD) IS PARTICULARLY HARD TO DIGEST. SOME ANIMALS, LIKE THE COW, HAVE SEVERAL STOMACHS & LET THE GRASS FERMENT BEFORE DIGESTING IT. OTHERS, LIKE THE HARE, EAT THEIR FAECES & HENCE DIGEST THEIR FOOD TWICE.

DIGESTIVE DISCOVERY

THE WORKINGS OF THE STOMACH WERE DISCOVERED BY A US ARMY SURGEON, WILLIAM BEAUMONT, c1830. AFTER TREATING A STOMACH WOUND WHICH WOULD NOT HEAL COMPLETELY, A HOLE WAS LEFT WHICH COULD BE PLUGGED & UNPLUGGED AT WILL. THIS HE USED TO MAKE DETAILED OBSERVATIONS FOR OVER 10 YEARS.

(TIMES SINCE EATING FOOD IN HOURS)

THE PANCREAS GENERATES THE JUICES (ENZYMES) WHICH BREAK THE FOOD DOWN IN THE STOMACH. THE LIVER GENERATES BILE SALTS WHICH EMULSIFY FATS INTO MINUTE DROPLETS.

DIGESTED FOOD IS MOSTLY ABSORBED INTO THE BLOODSTREAM IN THE SMALL INTESTINE.

THE GLANDS GENERATE ABOUT A LITRE OF SALIVA A DAY. THIS ACTS AS A LUBRICANT TO HELP THE FOOD SLIP DOWN.

ALTHOUGH WE ARE NOT AWARE OF IT, THE STOMACH HAS MUSCLES & CONSTANTLY CHANGES SHAPE. THIS CHURNS THE FOOD, MIXING IT THOROUGHLY WITH THE GASTRIC JUICES.

THE INTESTINES CONCENTRATE THE WASTE PRODUCTS, REDUCING THEIR WATER CONTENT.

FAECES CONTINUE TO BE FORMED DURING STARVATION - DISPOSING OF RESIDUES FROM INTERNAL SECRETIONS & BACTERIA.

HOW TO WEIGH SOMEONE DOWN WITH A PENCIL

CHALLENGE FRIEND TO HOLD PENCIL AT ARM'S LENGTH FOR 20 MINUTES. FEW PEOPLE CAN DO IT FOR AS LONG AS 5 MINUTES BECAUSE THE MUSCLES ARE NOT USED TO SUCH CONTINUOUS EXERTION.

DIVING

WORKING & EXPLORING UNDERWATER

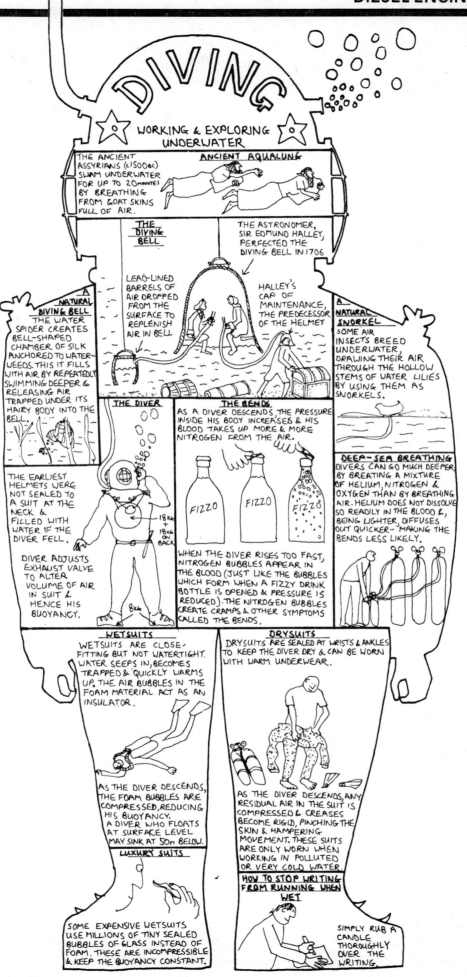

THE ANCIENT AQUALUNG

THE ANCIENT ASSYRIANS (c1500 BC) SWAM UNDERWATER FOR UP TO 20 minutes BY BREATHING FROM GOAT SKINS FULL OF AIR.

THE DIVING BELL

THE ASTRONOMER, SIR EDMUND HALLEY, PERFECTED THE DIVING BELL IN 1706

LEAD-LINED BARRELS OF AIR DROPPED FROM THE SURFACE TO REPLENISH AIR IN BELL

HALLEY'S CAP OF MAINTENANCE, THE PREDECESSOR OF THE HELMET

A NATURAL DIVING BELL

THE WATER SPIDER CREATES BELL-SHAPED CHAMBER OF SILK ANCHORED TO WATER WEEDS. THIS IT FILLS WITH AIR BY REPEATEDLY SWIMMING DEEPER & RELEASING AIR TRAPPED UNDER ITS HAIRY BODY INTO THE BELL.

A NATURAL SNORKEL

SOME AIR INSECTS BREED UNDERWATER, DRAWING THEIR AIR THROUGH THE HOLLOW STEMS OF WATER LILIES BY USING THEM AS SNORKELS.

THE DIVER

THE EARLIEST HELMETS WERE NOT SEALED TO A SUIT AT THE NECK & FILLED WITH WATER IF THE DIVER FELL.

DIVER ADJUSTS EXHAUST VALVE TO ALTER VOLUME OF AIR IN SUIT & HENCE HIS BUOYANCY.

18 KG + 18 KG ON BACK

8 KG

THE BENDS

AS A DIVER DESCENDS, THE PRESSURE INSIDE HIS BODY INCREASES & HIS BLOOD TAKES UP MORE & MORE NITROGEN FROM THE AIR.

FIZZO   FIZZO   FIZZO

WHEN THE DIVER RISES TOO FAST, NITROGEN BUBBLES APPEAR IN THE BLOOD (JUST LIKE THE BUBBLES WHICH FORM WHEN A FIZZY DRINK BOTTLE IS OPENED & PRESSURE IS REDUCED). THE NITROGEN BUBBLES CREATE CRAMPS & OTHER SYMPTOMS CALLED THE BENDS.

DEEP-SEA BREATHING

DIVERS CAN GO MUCH DEEPER BY BREATHING A MIXTURE OF HELIUM, NITROGEN & OXYGEN THAN BY BREATHING AIR. HELIUM DOES NOT DISSOLVE SO READILY IN THE BLOOD &, BEING LIGHTER, DIFFUSES OUT QUICKER - MAKING THE BENDS LESS LIKELY.

WETSUITS

WETSUITS ARE CLOSE-FITTING BUT NOT WATERTIGHT. WATER SEEPS IN, BECOMES TRAPPED & QUICKLY WARMS UP. THE AIR BUBBLES IN THE FOAM MATERIAL ACT AS AN INSULATOR.

AS THE DIVER DESCENDS, THE FOAM BUBBLES ARE COMPRESSED, REDUCING HIS BUOYANCY. A DIVER WHO FLOATS AT SURFACE LEVEL MAY SINK AT 50m BELOW.

LUXURY SUITS

SOME EXPENSIVE WETSUITS USE MILLIONS OF TINY SEALED BUBBLES OF GLASS INSTEAD OF FOAM. THESE ARE INCOMPRESSIBLE & KEEP THE BUOYANCY CONSTANT.

DRYSUITS

DRYSUITS ARE SEALED AT WRISTS & ANKLES TO KEEP THE DIVER DRY & CAN BE WORN WITH WARM UNDERWEAR.

AS THE DIVER DESCENDS, ANY RESIDUAL AIR IN THE SUIT IS COMPRESSED & CREASES BECOME RIGID, PINCHING THE SKIN & HAMPERING MOVEMENT. THESE SUITS ARE ONLY WORN WHEN WORKING IN POLLUTED OR VERY COLD WATER.

HOW TO STOP WRITING FROM RUNNING WHEN WET

SIMPLY RUB A CANDLE THOROUGHLY OVER THE WRITING.

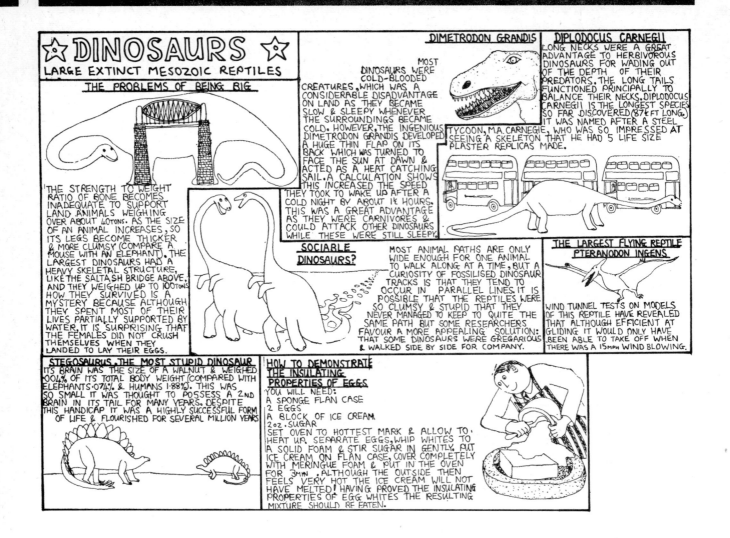

☆ DINOSAURS ☆
LARGE EXTINCT MESOZOIC REPTILES

THE PROBLEMS OF BEING BIG

THE STRENGTH TO WEIGHT RATIO OF BONE BECOMES INADEQUATE TO SUPPORT LAND ANIMALS WEIGHING OVER ABOUT 40 TONS. AS THE SIZE OF AN ANIMAL INCREASES, SO ITS LEGS BECOME THICKER & MORE CLUMSY (COMPARE A MOUSE WITH AN ELEPHANT). THE LARGEST DINOSAURS HAD A HEAVY SKELETAL STRUCTURE, LIKE THE SALTASH BRIDGE ABOVE, AND THEY WEIGHED UP TO 100 TONS. HOW THEY SURVIVED IS A MYSTERY BECAUSE ALTHOUGH THEY SPENT MOST OF THEIR LIVES PARTIALLY SUPPORTED BY WATER, IT IS SURPRISING THAT THE FEMALES DID NOT CRUSH THEMSELVES WHEN THEY LANDED TO LAY THEIR EGGS.

MOST DINOSAURS WERE COLD-BLOODED CREATURES, WHICH WAS A CONSIDERABLE DISADVANTAGE ON LAND AS THEY BECAME SLOW & SLEEPY WHENEVER THE SURROUNDINGS BECAME COLD. HOWEVER, THE INGENIOUS DIMETRODON GRANDIS DEVELOPED A HUGE THIN FLAP ON ITS BACK WHICH WAS TURNED TO FACE THE SUN AT DAWN & ACTED AS A HEAT CATCHING SAIL. A CALCULATION SHOWS THIS INCREASED THE SPEED THEY TOOK TO WAKE UP AFTER A COLD NIGHT BY ABOUT 1½ HOURS. THIS WAS A GREAT ADVANTAGE AS THEY WERE CARNIVORES & COULD ATTACK OTHER DINOSAURS WHILE THESE WERE STILL SLEEPY.

DIMETRODON GRANDIS

DIPLODOCUS CARNEGII

LONG NECKS WERE A GREAT ADVANTAGE TO HERBIVOROUS DINOSAURS FOR WADING OUT OF THE DEPTH OF THEIR PREDATORS. THE LONG TAILS FUNCTIONED PRINCIPALLY TO BALANCE THEIR NECKS. DIPLODOCUS CARNEGII IS THE LONGEST SPECIES SO FAR DISCOVERED (87 FT LONG) IT WAS NAMED AFTER A STEEL TYCOON, M.A. CARNEGIE, WHO WAS SO IMPRESSED AT SEEING A SKELETON THAT HE HAD 5 LIFE SIZE PLASTER REPLICAS MADE.

SOCIABLE DINOSAURS?

MOST ANIMAL PATHS ARE ONLY WIDE ENOUGH FOR ONE ANIMAL TO WALK ALONG AT A TIME, BUT A CURIOSITY OF FOSSILISED DINOSAUR TRACKS IS THAT THEY TEND TO OCCUR IN PARALLEL LINES. IT IS POSSIBLE THAT THE REPTILES WERE SO CLUMSY & STUPID THAT THEY NEVER MANAGED TO KEEP TO QUITE THE SAME PATH BUT SOME RESEARCHERS FAVOUR A MORE APPEALING SOLUTION: THAT SOME DINOSAURS WERE GREGARIOUS & WALKED SIDE BY SIDE FOR COMPANY.

THE LARGEST FLYING REPTILE PTERANODON INGENS

WIND TUNNEL TESTS ON MODELS OF THIS REPTILE HAVE REVEALED THAT ALTHOUGH EFFICIENT AT GLIDING IT WOULD ONLY HAVE BEEN ABLE TO TAKE OFF WHEN THERE WAS A 15 MPH WIND BLOWING.

STEGOSAURUS, THE MOST STUPID DINOSAUR

ITS BRAIN WAS THE SIZE OF A WALNUT & WEIGHED .0001% OF ITS TOTAL BODY WEIGHT (COMPARED WITH ELEPHANTS .0074% & HUMANS 1.88%). THIS WAS SO SMALL IT WAS THOUGHT TO POSSESS A 2ND BRAIN IN ITS TAIL FOR MANY YEARS. DESPITE THIS HANDICAP IT WAS A HIGHLY SUCCESSFUL FORM OF LIFE & FLOURISHED FOR SEVERAL MILLION YEARS.

HOW TO DEMONSTRATE THE INSULATING PROPERTIES OF EGGS

YOU WILL NEED:
A SPONGE FLAN CASE
2 EGGS
A BLOCK OF ICE CREAM
2 OZ. SUGAR

SET OVEN TO HOTTEST MARK & ALLOW TO HEAT UP. SEPARATE EGGS, WHIP WHITES TO A SOLID FOAM & STIR SUGAR IN GENTLY. PUT ICE CREAM ON FLAN CASE, COVER COMPLETELY WITH MERINGUE FOAM & PUT IN THE OVEN FOR 3 MIN. ALTHOUGH THE OUTSIDE THEN FEELS VERY HOT THE ICE CREAM WILL NOT HAVE MELTED! HAVING PROVED THE INSULATING PROPERTIES OF EGG WHITES THE RESULTING MIXTURE SHOULD BE EATEN.

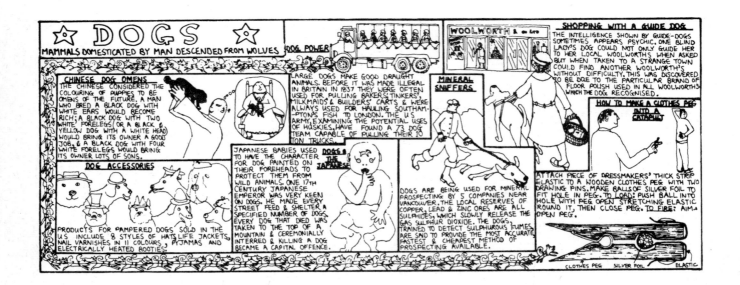

☆ DOGS ☆
MAMMALS DOMESTICATED BY MAN DESCENDED FROM WOLVES

CHINESE DOG OMENS

THE CHINESE CONSIDERED THE COLOURING OF PUPPIES TO BE OMENS OF THE FUTURE. A MAN WHO BRED A BLACK DOG WITH WHITE EARS WOULD BECOME RICH; A BLACK DOG WITH TWO WHITE FORELEGS (OR A BLACK & YELLOW DOG WITH A WHITE HEAD) WOULD BRING ITS OWNER A GOOD JOB, & A BLACK DOG WITH FOUR WHITE FORELEGS WOULD BRING ITS OWNER LOTS OF SONS.

DOG ACCESSORIES

PRODUCTS FOR PAMPERED DOGS SOLD IN THE U.S. INCLUDE 8 STYLES OF HATS, LIFE JACKETS, NAIL VARNISHES IN 11 COLOURS, PYJAMAS AND ELECTRICALLY HEATED BOOTIES.

DOG POWER

LARGE DOGS MAKE GOOD DRAUGHT ANIMALS. BEFORE IT WAS MADE ILLEGAL IN BRITAIN IN 1837 THEY WERE OFTEN USED FOR PULLING BAKERS', TINKERS', MILKMAIDS' & BUILDERS' CARTS & WERE ALWAYS USED FOR HAULING SOUTHAMPTON'S FISH TO LONDON. THE U.S. ARMY, EXAMINING THE POTENTIAL USES OF HUSKIES, HAVE FOUND A 73 DOG TEAM CAPABLE OF PULLING THEIR 10 TON TRUCKS.

DOGS & THE JAPANESE

JAPANESE BABIES USED TO HAVE THE CHARACTER FOR DOG PAINTED ON THEIR FOREHEADS TO PROTECT THEM FROM WILD ANIMALS. ONE 17TH CENTURY JAPANESE EMPEROR WAS VERY KEEN ON DOGS. HE MADE EVERY STREET FEED & SHELTER A SPECIFIED NUMBER OF DOGS. EVERY DOG THAT DIED WAS TAKEN TO THE TOP OF A MOUNTAIN & CEREMONIALLY INTERRED & KILLING A DOG BECAME A CAPITAL OFFENCE.

MINERAL SNIFFERS

DOGS ARE BEING USED FOR MINERAL PROSPECTING BY 5 COMPANIES NEAR VANCOUVER. THE LOCAL RESERVES OF COPPER, LEAD & ZINC ORES ARE ALL SULPHIDES, WHICH SLOWLY RELEASE THE GAS SULPHUR DIOXIDE. THE DOGS, TRAINED TO DETECT SULPHUROUS FUMES ARE SAID TO PROVIDE THE MOST ACCURATE, FASTEST & CHEAPEST METHOD OF PROSPECTING AVAILABLE.

SHOPPING WITH A GUIDE DOG

THE INTELLIGENCE SHOWN BY GUIDE-DOGS SOMETIMES APPEARS PSYCHIC. ONE BLIND LADY'S DOG COULD NOT ONLY GUIDE HER TO HER LOCAL WOOLWORTHS WHEN ASKED BUT WHEN TAKEN TO A STRANGE TOWN COULD FIND ANOTHER WOOLWORTH'S WITHOUT DIFFICULTY. THIS WAS DISCOVERED TO BE DUE TO THE PARTICULAR BRAND OF FLOOR POLISH USED IN ALL WOOLWORTHS WHICH THE DOG RECOGNISED.

HOW TO MAKE A CLOTHES PEG INTO A CATAPULT

ATTACH PIECE OF DRESSMAKERS' THICK STRIP ELASTIC TO A WOODEN CLOTHES PEG WITH TWO DRAWING PINS. MAKE BALLS OF SILVER FOIL TO FIT HOLE IN PEG. TO LOAD: PUSH BALL INTO HOLE WITH PEG OPEN, STRETCHING ELASTIC ROUND IT, THEN CLOSE PEG. TO FIRE: AIM & OPEN PEG.

CLOTHES PEG   SILVER FOIL   ELASTIC

☆ DOLPHINS ☆
AQUATIC MAMMALS OF THE DELPHINIDAE FAMILY

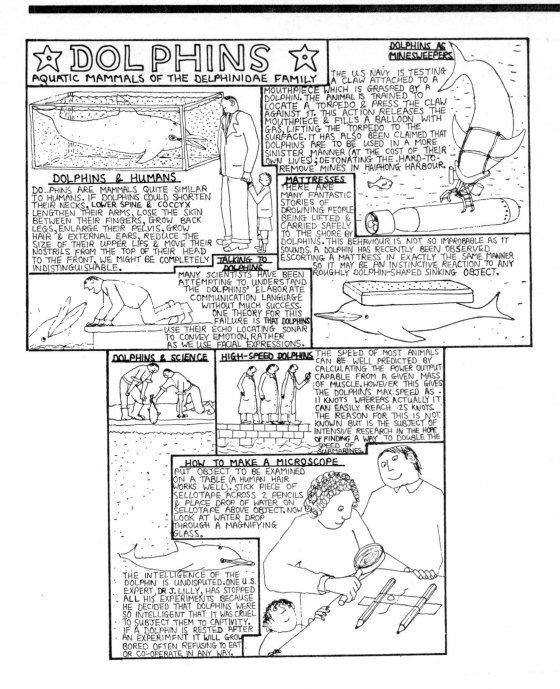

DOLPHINS & HUMANS
DOLPHINS ARE MAMMALS QUITE SIMILAR TO HUMANS. IF DOLPHINS COULD SHORTEN THEIR NECKS, LOWER SPINE & COCCYX LENGTHEN THEIR ARMS, LOSE THE SKIN BETWEEN THEIR FINGERS, GROW BACK LEGS, ENLARGE THEIR PELVIS, GROW HAIR & EXTERNAL EARS, REDUCE THE SIZE OF THEIR UPPER LIPS & MOVE THEIR NOSTRILS FROM THE TOP OF THEIR HEAD TO THE FRONT, WE MIGHT BE COMPLETELY INDISTINGUISHABLE.

TALKING TO DOLPHINS
MANY SCIENTISTS HAVE BEEN ATTEMPTING TO UNDERSTAND THE DOLPHINS' ELABORATE COMMUNICATION LANGUAGE WITHOUT MUCH SUCCESS. ONE THEORY FOR THIS FAILURE IS THAT DOLPHINS USE THEIR ECHO LOCATING SONAR TO CONVEY EMOTION, RATHER AS WE USE FACIAL EXPRESSIONS.

DOLPHINS AS MINESWEEPERS
THE U.S NAVY IS TESTING A CLAW ATTACHED TO A MOUTHPIECE WHICH IS GRASPED BY A DOLPHIN. THE ANIMAL IS TRAINED TO LOCATE A TORPEDO & PRESS THE CLAW AGAINST IT. THIS ACTION RELEASES THE MOUTHPIECE & FILLS A BALLOON WITH GAS, LIFTING THE TORPEDO TO THE SURFACE. IT HAS ALSO BEEN CLAIMED THAT DOLPHINS ARE TO BE USED IN A MORE SINISTER MANNER (AT THE COST OF THEIR OWN LIVES); DETONATING THE HARD-TO-REMOVE MINES IN HAIPHONG HARBOUR.

MATTRESSES
THERE ARE MANY FANTASTIC STORIES OF DROWNING PEOPLE BEING LIFTED & CARRIED SAFELY TO THE SHORE BY DOLPHINS. THIS BEHAVIOUR IS NOT SO IMPROBABLE AS IT SOUNDS. A DOLPHIN HAS RECENTLY BEEN OBSERVED ESCORTING A MATTRESS IN EXACTLY THE SAME MANNER SO IT MAY BE AN INSTINCTIVE REACTION TO ANY ROUGHLY DOLPHIN-SHAPED SINKING OBJECT.

DOLPHINS & SCIENCE

HIGH-SPEED DOLPHINS
THE SPEED OF MOST ANIMALS CAN BE WELL PREDICTED BY CALCULATING THE POWER OUTPUT CAPABLE FROM A GIVEN MASS OF MUSCLE. HOWEVER THIS GIVES THE DOLPHIN'S MAX. SPEED AS - 11 KNOTS WHEREAS ACTUALLY IT CAN EASILY REACH - 25 KNOTS. THE REASON FOR THIS IS NOT KNOWN BUT IS THE SUBJECT OF INTENSIVE RESEARCH IN THE HOPE OF FINDING A WAY TO DOUBLE THE SPEED OF SUBMARINES.

HOW TO MAKE A MICROSCOPE
PUT OBJECT TO BE EXAMINED ON A TABLE (A HUMAN HAIR WORKS WELL). STICK PIECE OF SELLOTAPE ACROSS 2 PENCILS & PLACE DROP OF WATER ON SELLOTAPE ABOVE OBJECT. NOW LOOK AT WATER DROP THROUGH A MAGNIFYING GLASS.

THE INTELLIGENCE OF THE DOLPHIN IS UNDISPUTED. ONE U.S. EXPERT, DR J. LILLY, HAS STOPPED ALL HIS EXPERIMENTS BECAUSE HE DECIDED THAT DOLPHINS WERE SO INTELLIGENT THAT IT WAS CRUEL TO SUBJECT THEM TO CAPTIVITY. IF A DOLPHIN IS RESTED AFTER AN EXPERIMENT IT WILL GROW BORED OFTEN REFUSING TO EAT OR CO-OPERATE IN ANY WAY.

☆ DOMES ☆
BUILDINGS MADE OF CURVED STRUCTURES

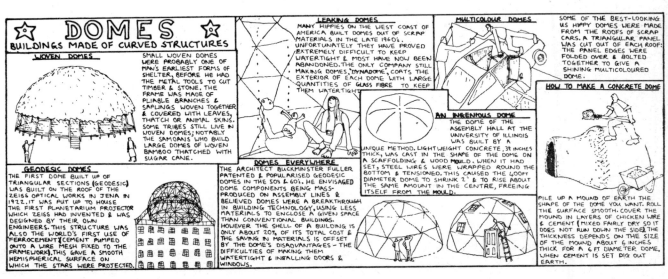

WOVEN DOMES
SMALL WOVEN DOMES WERE PROBABLY ONE OF MAN'S EARLIEST FORMS OF SHELTER, BEFORE HE HAD THE METAL TOOLS TO CUT TIMBER & STONE. THE FRAME WAS MADE OF PLIABLE BRANCHES & SAPLINGS WOVEN TOGETHER & COVERED WITH LEAVES, THATCH OR ANIMAL SKINS. SOME TRIBES STILL LIVE IN WOVEN DOMES; NOTABLY THE SAMOANS WHO BUILD LARGE DOMES OF WOVEN BAMBOO THATCHED WITH SUGAR CANE.

GEODESIC DOMES
THE FIRST DOME BUILT UP OF TRIANGULAR SECTIONS (GEODESIC) WAS BUILT ON THE ROOF OF THE ZEISS OPTICAL WORKS IN JENA IN 1922. IT WAS PUT UP TO HOUSE THE FIRST PLANETARIUM PROJECTOR WHICH ZEISS HAD INVENTED & WAS DESIGNED BY THEIR OWN ENGINEERS. THIS STRUCTURE WAS ALSO THE WORLD'S FIRST USE OF FERROCEMENT (CEMENT PUMPED ONTO A WIRE MESH FIXED TO THE FRAMEWORK). THIS GAVE A SMOOTH HEMISPHERICAL SURFACE ON WHICH THE STARS WERE PROJECTED.

LEAKING DOMES
MANY HIPPIES ON THE WEST COAST OF AMERICA BUILT DOMES OUT OF SCRAP MATERIALS IN THE LATE 1960s. UNFORTUNATELY THEY HAVE PROVED EXTREMELY DIFFICULT TO KEEP WATERTIGHT & MOST HAVE NOW BEEN ABANDONED. THE ONLY COMPANY STILL MAKING DOMES, 'DYNADOME', COATS THE EXTERIOR OF EACH DOME WITH LARGE QUANTITIES OF GLASS FIBRE TO KEEP THEM WATERTIGHT.

DOMES EVERYWHERE
THE ARCHITECT BUCKMINSTER FULLER PATENTED & POPULARISED GEODESIC DOMES IN THE 50s & 60s. HE ENVISAGED DOME COMPONENTS BEING MASS-PRODUCED ON ASSEMBLY LINES & BELIEVED DOMES WERE A BREAKTHROUGH IN BUILDING TECHNOLOGY, USING LESS MATERIALS TO ENCLOSE A GIVEN SPACE THAN CONVENTIONAL BUILDINGS. HOWEVER THE SHELL OF A BUILDING IS ONLY ABOUT 20% OF ITS TOTAL COST & THE SAVING IN MATERIALS IS OFFSET BY THE DOME'S DISADVANTAGES - THE DIFFICULTIES OF MAKING THEM WATERTIGHT & INSTALLING DOORS & WINDOWS.

AN INGENIOUS DOME
THE DOME OF THE ASSEMBLY HALL AT THE UNIVERSITY OF ILLINOIS WAS BUILT BY A UNIQUE METHOD. LIGHTWEIGHT CONCRETE, 3t INCHES THICK, WAS CAST IN THE SHAPE OF THE DOME ON A SCAFFOLDING & WOOD MOULD. WHEN IT HAD SET, STEEL WIRES WERE WRAPPED ROUND THE BOTTOM & TENSIONED. THIS CAUSED THE 400ft DIAMETER DOME TO SHRINK 2" & TO RISE ABOUT THE SAME AMOUNT IN THE CENTRE, FREEING ITSELF FROM THE MOULD.

MULTICOLOUR DOMES
SOME OF THE BEST-LOOKING US HIPPY DOMES WERE MADE FROM THE ROOFS OF SCRAP CARS. A TRIANGULAR PANEL WAS CUT OUT OF EACH ROOF; THE PANEL EDGES WERE FOLDED OVER & BOLTED TOGETHER TO GIVE A SHINING MULTICOLOURED DOME.

HOW TO MAKE A CONCRETE DOME
PILE UP A MOUND OF EARTH THE SHAPE OF THE DOME YOU WANT. ROLL THE SURFACE SMOOTH. COVER THE MOUND IN LAYERS OF CHICKEN WIRE & CEMENT (MIXED FAIRLY DRY SO IT DOES NOT RUN DOWN THE SIDE). THE THICKNESS DEPENDS ON THE SIZE OF THE MOUND ABOUT 6 INCHES THICK FOR A 6 FT DIAMETER DOME. WHEN CEMENT IS SET DIG OUT EARTH.

☆ DONKEYS ☆
SMALL, LONG-EARED MEMBERS OF THE HORSE GENUS

THE ECCLESIASTIC MULE

THE NATIVITY DONKEY

THE ORIGIN OF THE DONKEY'S ASSOCIATION WITH THE NATIVITY IS OBSCURE; THERE IS NO MENTION OF IT IN THE BIBLE. IT WAS PROBABLY INTRODUCED AS A MEDIEVAL SYMBOL OF HUMILITY, REFERRED TO AS 'THE SLAWE AS, DRUGAR BESTE OF PYNNE' (THE SLOW ASS, DRUDGING BEAST OF LABOUR,...

THE FEARLESS DONKEY

THE MULE & THE WILD DONKEY ARE BOTH BRAVER THAN THE WILD HORSE. IN THE ROCKIES, MOUNTAIN LIONS & PUMAS PREY ON THE HORSES, ESPECIALLY FOALS, BUT THE MULES & DONKEYS ARE NOT FRIGHTENED & SELDOM FALL VICTIM.

IN SOME PARTS OF PRE-CHRISTIAN EUROPE IT WAS TABOO FOR THE PAGAN PRIESTS TO RIDE HORSES. THIS PERSISTED INTO THE CHRISTIAN ERA, WHICH MAY ACCOUNT FOR THE USE BY HIGH RANKING ECCLESIASTICS OF MULES, ALTHOUGH SOME PRIESTS RODE STALLIONS IN DEFIANCE OF THE TABOO.

THE DAMP ENGLISH DONKEY

THE DONKEY'S COAT IS NOT WATERPROOF. UNLIKE THE SHAGGY PONY, ITS COAT LACKS A DOUBLE PILE OF INNER & OUTER HAIRS SO WATER EASILY PENETRATES TO ITS SKIN. DUE TO THE CLIMATE, ENGLISH DONKEYS HAVE, IN SUCCESSIVE GENERATIONS, BECOME INCREASINGLY UNHEALTHY & DWARFED, LACKING ANY CROSS BREEDING WITH HEALTHY DONKEYS FROM HOTTER, DRIER COUNTRIES.

THE DONKEY'S DECLINE

DONKEYS IN ENGLAND HAVE DECLINED IN STATUS & NUMBER DURING THE LAST 100 YEARS. THE DONKEY SHOW AT THE ROYAL AGRICULTURAL HALL DISAPPEARED DURING THE 1870s; THE INTERNATIONAL HORSE SHOW CEASED TO HAVE A SECTION FOR DONKEYS IN 1904. BY 1939 THERE WERE AN ESTIMATED 100 DONKEYS LEFT IN ENGLAND. SINCE THE WAR THERE HAS BEEN A RECOVERY DUE TO THE DEMAND FOR SEASIDE DONKEY RIDES & THE EFFORTS OF THE DONKEY BREED SOCIETY.

ENGLISH DONKEY POPULATION
1820 1940

HOW TO MAKE A 10p PIECE APPEAR TO BE A SPHERE

GRIP A 10p PIECE BETWEEN 2 PINS STICKING INTO OPPOSITE SIDES ON THE RIM. LIFT & BLOW AGAINST UPPER HALF OF COIN. THE COIN WILL REVOLVE AT GREAT SPEED & APPEAR TO BE A METALLIC SPHERE.

IRISH DONKEYS

DONKEYS WERE UNKNOWN IN IRELAND TILL THE 1600s. IT IS THOUGHT THAT THEY ARRIVED WITH THE WAGON TRAINS OF BRITISH ARMIES. THE REASON FOR THEIR WIDE-SPREAD ADOPTION WAS PRINCIPALLY BECAUSE DURING OUR MANY WARS WITH FRANCE OUR CAVALRY LOSSES WERE HIGH & IRELAND WAS THE CHIEF SOURCE OF REPLACEMENTS. BY 1815 IRELAND WAS VIRTUALLY DENUDED OF HORSES.

CORNISH DONKEYS

HENRY VIII PASSED A LAW EMPOWERING SHERIFFS TO CONFISCATE PONIES BELOW A CERTAIN HEIGHT FOUND GRAZING ON COMMON LAND. THIS WAS TO PREVENT THE DECLINE OF THE STOCK. ABOUT ⅘ OF THE PONIES IN ENGLAND WERE 'SUBSTANDARD' BUT MOST SHERIFFS DID NOT ENFORCE THE LAW. HOWEVER IN CORNWALL IT WAS RIGOROUSLY APPLIED, FORCING FARMERS TO ADOPT DONKEYS & MULES INSTEAD.

☆ DRAGONS ☆
MYTHICAL FIRE-BREATHING REPTILIAN MONSTERS

ANATOMY OF A DRAGON

THE CHINESE DESCRIBE A DRAGON AS BEING MADE UP OF 9 COMPONENTS OF OTHER ANIMALS (WITH A LUMP ON THE BACK OF ITS HEAD WITHOUT WHICH IT COULD NOT FLY).

HORNS OF A STAG
LUMP ON HEAD (WITHOUT WHICH IT CAN'T FLY)
EARS OF A COW
EYES OF A DEMON
HEAD OF A CAMEL
FEET OF A TIGER
NECK OF A SNAKE
BELLY OF A CLAM
SCALES OF A CARP
CLAWS OF AN EAGLE

HORSE DRAGONS

THE JAPANESE SAY THAT IN HEAVEN, A HORSE IS MADE INTO A DRAGON; AMONG MEN, A DRAGON IS MADE INTO A HORSE.

NICE DRAGONS

IN THE WESTERN WORLD, DRAGONS HAVE ALWAYS BEEN REGARDED AS EVIL. IN THE EAST, THIS IS NOT THE CASE. BUDDHA IS SAID TO HAVE TAMED ONE & CHINESE EMPERORS ARE SAID TO HAVE KEPT THEM AS PETS.

THE MOUTH OF HELL

THE ENTRANCE TO HELL WAS OFTEN DEPICTED AS A DRAGON'S MOUTH IN MEDIEVAL CHRISTIAN ART.

THE CAVERNOUS MOUTH

THE HINDU GOD, KRISHNA, RASHLY TOOK SHELTER IN A DRAGON'S MOUTH, MISTAKING IT FOR A MOUNTAIN CAVE. FORTUNATELY, HE ESCAPED BY MAKING HIMSELF VERY LARGE & BURSTING THE BEAST APART.

ST GEORGE'S DRAGON

ST GEORGE'S DRAGON CAN BE TRACED TO A GREEK LEGEND OF A SEA MONSTER AT JOPPA, ISRAEL, SLAIN BY PERSEUS. WITH THE SPREAD OF CHRISTIANITY, THE CREDIT FOR THE SLAYING WAS TRANSFERRED TO ST GEORGE.

HURRICANE DRAGON

THE WEST INDIANS BELIEVED THAT EARTHQUAKES & HURRICANES WERE CAUSED BY A DRAGON CALLED HURACAN. HE USUALLY WALKED ABOUT ON ONE LEG AS A TORNADO.

AERIAL DRAGONS

THE CHINESE BELIEVE THAT DRAGONS DIVIDE THE SKY INTO TERRITORIES. CLOUDS ARE THEIR BREATH, IN WHICH THEY HIDE.

DRAGON BOATS

THE JAPANESE STILL MAKE DRAGON BOATS AS PLEASURE CRUISERS.

ST MARGARET'S DRAGON

ST MARGARET BECAME THE PATRON SAINT OF CHILDBIRTH BECAUSE OF HER ENCOUNTER WITH A DRAGON. AFTER BEING DEVOURED, SHE MIRACULOUSLY REAPPEARED OUT OF ITS STOMACH.

HOW TO PULL A STRING THROUGH YOUR NECK

(A) BRING HANDS TOGETHER.
(B) MOVE LEFT LOOP FROM THUMB TO FIRST FINGER.
(C) SLIP LEFT THUMB INTO RIGHT LOOP.
(D) RELEASE LEFT LOOP & PULL HANDS APART.

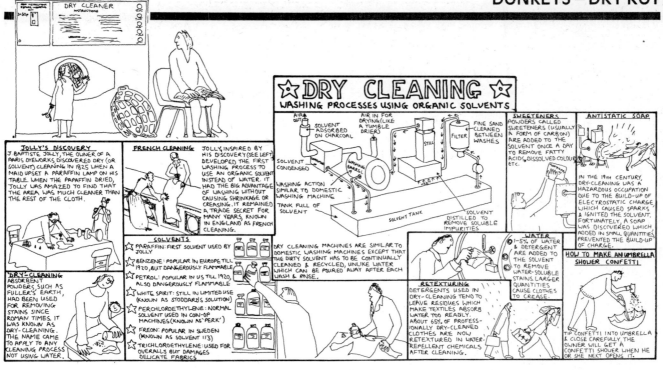

☆ DRY CLEANING ☆
WASHING PROCESSES USING ORGANIC SOLVENTS

JOLLY'S DISCOVERY
J BAPTISTE JOLLY, THE OWNER OF A PARIS DYEWORKS, DISCOVERED DRY (OR SOLVENT) CLEANING IN 1825 WHEN A MAID UPSET A PARAFFIN LAMP ON HIS TABLE. WHEN THE PARAFFIN DRIED, JOLLY WAS AMAZED TO FIND THAT THE AREA WAS MUCH CLEANER THAN THE REST OF THE CLOTH.

FRENCH CLEANING
JOLLY, INSPIRED BY HIS DISCOVERY (SEE LEFT) DEVELOPED THE FIRST WASHING PROCESS TO USE AN ORGANIC SOLVENT INSTEAD OF WATER. IT HAD THE BIG ADVANTAGE OF WASHING WITHOUT CAUSING SHRINKAGE OR CREASING. IT REMAINED A TRADE SECRET FOR MANY YEARS, KNOWN IN ENGLAND AS FRENCH CLEANING.

'DRY-CLEANING'
ABSORBENT POWDERS, SUCH AS FULLER'S EARTH, HAD BEEN USED FOR REMOVING STAINS SINCE ROMAN TIMES. IT WAS KNOWN AS DRY-CLEANING. THE NAME CAME TO APPLY TO ANY CLEANING PROCESS NOT USING WATER.

SOLVENTS
☆ PARAFFIN: FIRST SOLVENT USED BY JOLLY
☆ BENZENE: POPULAR IN EUROPE TILL 1920, BUT DANGEROUSLY FLAMMABLE
☆ PETROL: POPULAR IN US TILL 1920, ALSO DANGEROUSLY FLAMMABLE
☆ WHITE SPIRIT: STILL IN LIMITED USE (KNOWN AS STODDARD'S SOLUTION)
☆ PERCHLOROETHYLENE: NORMAL SOLVENT USED IN COIN-OP MACHINES (KNOWN AS 'PERK')
☆ FREON: POPULAR IN SWEDEN (KNOWN AS SOLVENT 113)
☆ TRICHLOROETHYLENE: USED FOR OVERALLS BUT DAMAGES DELICATE FABRICS

DRY CLEANING MACHINES ARE SIMILAR TO DOMESTIC WASHING MACHINES EXCEPT THAT THE DIRTY SOLVENT HAS TO BE CONTINUALLY CLEANED & RECYCLED, UNLIKE WATER WHICH CAN BE POURED AWAY AFTER EACH WASH & RINSE.

RETEXTURING
DETERGENTS USED IN DRY-CLEANING TEND TO LEAVE RESIDUES WHICH MAKE TEXTILES ABSORB WATER TOO READILY. ABOUT 65% OF PROFESSIONALLY DRY-CLEANED CLOTHES ARE NOW RETEXTURED IN WATER-REPELLENT CHEMICALS AFTER CLEANING.

SWEETENERS
POWDERS CALLED SWEETENERS (USUALLY A FORM OF CARBON) ARE ADDED TO THE SOLVENT ONCE A DAY TO REMOVE FATTY ACIDS, DISSOLVED COLOUR ETC.

WATER
1-5% OF WATER & DETERGENT ARE ADDED TO THE SOLVENT TO REMOVE WATER-SOLUBLE STAINS. LARGER QUANTITIES CAUSE CLOTHES TO CREASE.

ANTISTATIC SOAP
IN THE 19TH CENTURY, DRY-CLEANING WAS A HAZARDOUS OCCUPATION DUE TO THE BUILD-UP OF ELECTROSTATIC CHARGE WHICH CAUSED SPARKS & IGNITED THE SOLVENT. FORTUNATELY, A SOAP WAS DISCOVERED WHICH, ADDED IN SMALL QUANTITIES PREVENTED THE BUILD-UP OF CHARGE.

HOW TO MAKE AN UMBRELLA SHOWER CONFETTI
TIP CONFETTI INTO UMBRELLA & CLOSE CAREFULLY. THE OWNER WILL GET A CONFETTI SHOWER WHEN HE OR SHE NEXT OPENS IT.

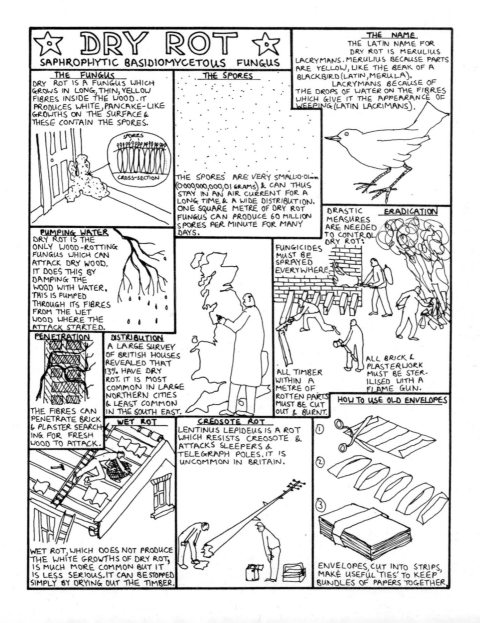

☆ DRY ROT ☆
SAPHROPHYTIC BASIDIOMYCETOUS FUNGUS

THE FUNGUS
DRY ROT IS A FUNGUS WHICH GROWS IN LONG, THIN, YELLOW FIBRES INSIDE THE WOOD. IT PRODUCES WHITE, PANCAKE-LIKE GROWTHS ON THE SURFACE & THESE CONTAIN THE SPORES.

THE SPORES
THE SPORES ARE VERY SMALL: 0.01mm (0.000,000,000,01 GRAMS) & CAN THUS STAY IN AN AIR CURRENT FOR A LONG TIME & A WIDE DISTRIBUTION. ONE SQUARE METRE OF DRY ROT FUNGUS CAN PRODUCE 60 MILLION SPORES PER MINUTE FOR MANY DAYS.

THE NAME
THE LATIN NAME FOR DRY ROT IS MERULIUS LACRYMANS. MERULIUS BECAUSE PARTS ARE YELLOW, LIKE THE BEAK OF A BLACKBIRD (LATIN, MERULA). LACRYMANS BECAUSE OF THE DROPS OF WATER ON THE FIBRES WHICH GIVE IT THE APPEARANCE OF WEEPING (LATIN LACRIMANS).

PUMPING WATER
DRY ROT IS THE ONLY WOOD-ROTTING FUNGUS WHICH CAN ATTACK DRY WOOD. IT DOES THIS BY DAMPING THE WOOD WITH WATER. THIS IS PUMPED THROUGH ITS FIBRES FROM THE WET WOOD WHERE THE ATTACK STARTED.

PENETRATION
THE FIBRES CAN PENETRATE BRICK & PLASTER SEARCHING FOR FRESH WOOD TO ATTACK.

DISTRIBUTION
A LARGE SURVEY OF BRITISH HOUSES REVEALED THAT 13% HAVE DRY ROT. IT IS MOST COMMON IN LARGE NORTHERN CITIES & LEAST COMMON IN THE SOUTH EAST.

ERADICATION
DRASTIC MEASURES ARE NEEDED TO CONTROL DRY ROT:
FUNGICIDES MUST BE SPRAYED EVERYWHERE.
ALL TIMBER WITHIN A METRE OF ROTTEN PARTS MUST BE CUT OUT & BURNT.
ALL BRICK & PLASTERWORK MUST BE STERILISED WITH A FLAME GUN.

WET ROT
WET ROT, WHICH DOES NOT PRODUCE THE WHITE GROWTHS OF DRY ROT, IS MUCH MORE COMMON BUT IT IS LESS SERIOUS. IT CAN BE STOPPED SIMPLY BY DRYING OUT THE TIMBER.

CREOSOTE ROT
LENTINUS LEPIDEUS IS A ROT WHICH RESISTS CREOSOTE & ATTACKS SLEEPERS & TELEGRAPH POLES. IT IS UNCOMMON IN BRITAIN.

HOW TO USE OLD ENVELOPES
1. 2. 3.
ENVELOPES, CUT INTO STRIPS, MAKE USEFUL 'TIES' TO KEEP BUNDLES OF PAPERS TOGETHER.

DYES

COLOURANTS ABSORBED BY MATERIALS

TYRIAN PURPLE

TYRIAN PURPLE COMES FROM A MEDITERRANEAN SHELLFISH. IT DOES NOT GIVE A BRIGHT COLOUR BY MODERN STANDARDS, BUT IT BECAME A SYMBOL OF WEALTH & POWER IN THE ANCIENT WORLD BECAUSE OF ITS PERMANENCE (MOST ANCIENT DYES FADED IN THE SUN). THE GREEKS BELIEVED THAT IT WAS DISCOVERED BY HERCULES, WHEN HE NOTICED THAT THE JAWS OF HIS DOG, WHO WAS EATING ONE OF THE SHELLFISH AT THE TIME, WERE BEING STAINED BRIGHT PURPLE.

WOAD

WOAD COMES FROM THE LEAVES OF ISATIS TINCTORA, A PLANT NOT INDIGENOUS TO BRITAIN. ITS ROTTEN LEAVES WERE USED AS A BODY PAINT BEFORE ROMAN TIMES, BUT THERE IS NO EVIDENCE THAT THE DYE WAS EXTRACTED & USED FOR COLOURING FABRICS TILL ANGLO-SAXON TIMES. THE LEAVES HAD TO BE CRUSHED, MOULDED INTO BALLS, DRIED, POWDERED, WETTED & FERMENTED TO LIBERATE THE DYE — A RELATIVELY COMPLEX PROCESS DEMANDING A DEGREE OF CIVILISATION.

MAUVE

MAUVE, THE FIRST SYNTHETIC DYE TO BE MANUFACTURED WAS DISCOVERED BY W.H. PERKIN, A CHEMISTRY STUDENT, IN 1856. DURING SOME UNSUCCESSFUL ATTEMPTS TO MAKE COAL TAR INTO THE DRUG QUININE, HE FOUND SOME BRILLIANT PURPLE CRYSTALS IN THE MIDDLE OF A BLACK SLUDGE. HE BORROWED MONEY FROM HIS FATHER & BROTHER, SET UP A DYE FACTORY &, BY THE AGE OF 35, HAD MADE HIS FORTUNE & RETIRED. MAUVE (OR ANILINE PURPLE) IS NO LONGER USED AS A DYE BUT ITS DISCOVERY WAS IMPORTANT AS IT QUICKLY LED TO A VAST RANGE OF ALL-COLOURED SYNTHETIC DYES.

MULTICOLOURED SHEEP

DYEING CAN BE PERFORMED AT ANY STAGE OF TEXTILE MANUFACTURE. IN MESOPOTAMIA (IRAQ) WHOLE SHEEP WERE TRADITIONALLY DYED BEFORE SHEARING.

INDIGO

INDIGO COMES FROM AN ASIATIC PLANT. IT WAS KNOWN TO THE ROMANS BUT NOT WIDELY USED IN THE WESTERN WORLD TILL THE 1600s WHEN IT WAS BROUGHT FROM INDIA. THE DYE EXTRACTED FROM INDIGO IS CHEMICALLY IDENTICAL TO THAT EXTRACTED FROM WOAD BUT INDIGO IS A MUCH MORE POTENT SOURCE. IT REPLACED WOAD VERY SLOWLY DUE TO BITTER RESISTANCE FROM THE ESTABLISHED WOAD DYERS, DESPITE THE FACT THAT THE FERMENTATION OF WOAD WAS ONE OF THE SMELLIEST & MOST REPULSIVE PROCESSES IN MEDIEVAL INDUSTRY. THE WORLD'S LAST TWO WOAD MILLS (IN LINCOLNSHIRE) DID NOT CLOSE TILL THE 1930s.

STRATEGIC DYEING

GERMANY HELD A MONOPOLY IN THE MANUFACTURE OF SYNTHETIC DYES IN 1914. ONLY 20% OF THE DYES USED IN BRITAIN WERE OF DOMESTIC MANUFACTURE. THIS WAS A GRAVE STRATEGIC DISADVANTAGE, & THE DYEING OF MILITARY UNIFORMS WAS A SERIOUS PROBLEM.

MAGENTA

MAGENTA IS A SYNTHETIC DYE DEVELOPED IN FRANCE IN 1859. IT WAS PATRIOTICALLY NAMED AFTER A TOWN IN NORTH ITALY WHERE THAT SUMMER NAPOLEON III DEFEATED THE AUSTRIANS.

HOW TO TRISECT AN ANGLE

① AC = CD = DE

②

IT IS IMPOSSIBLE TO DIVIDE AN ANGLE IN THREE USING ONLY A COMPASS & STRAIGHT EDGE. HOWEVER, IT CAN BE DONE WITH A BIT OF CARD CUT AS FIG 1. PLACE THE DEVICE ON THE ANGLE (SEE FIG 2). POINT **A** LIES ON ONE SIDE OF THE ANGLE, EDGE **B** INTERSECTS THE ANGLE'S VERTEX, & THE CURVED EDGE IS TANGENT TO THE OTHER SIDE. FINALLY MARK THE PAPER AT **C** & **D**, & DRAW LINES FROM THE ANGLE THROUGH THE MARKS.

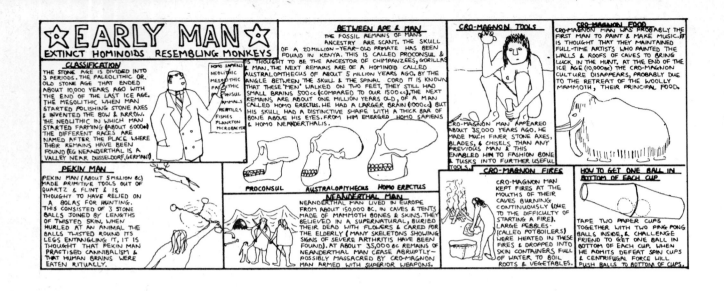

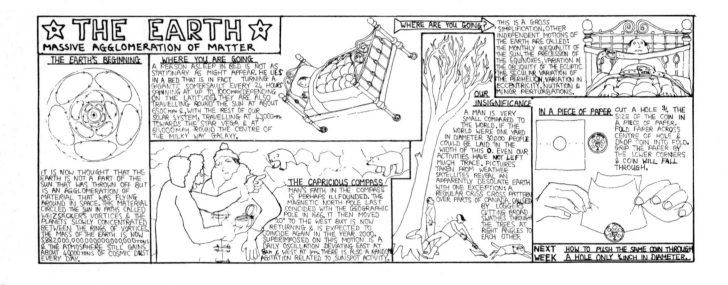

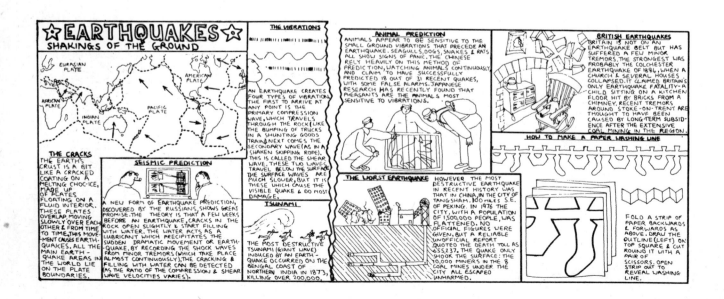

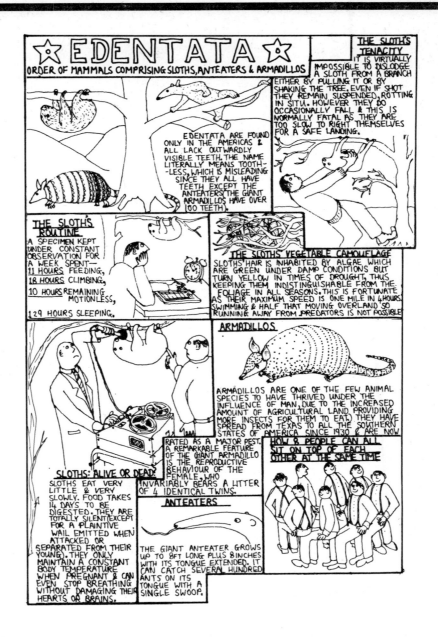

☆ EDENTATA ☆
ORDER OF MAMMALS COMPRISING SLOTHS, ANTEATERS & ARMADILLOS

EDENTATA ARE FOUND ONLY IN THE AMERICAS & ALL LACK OUTWARDLY VISIBLE TEETH. THE NAME LITERALLY MEANS TOOTH-LESS, WHICH IS MISLEADING SINCE THEY ALL HAVE TEETH EXCEPT THE ANTEATERS (THE GIANT ARMADILLOS HAVE OVER 100 TEETH).

THE SLOTH'S TENACITY
IT IS VIRTUALLY IMPOSSIBLE TO DISLODGE A SLOTH FROM A BRANCH EITHER BY PULLING IT OR BY SHAKING THE TREE. EVEN IF SHOT THEY REMAIN SUSPENDED, ROTTING IN SITU. HOWEVER THEY DO OCCASIONALLY FALL & THIS IS NORMALLY FATAL AS THEY ARE TOO SLOW TO RIGHT THEMSELVES FOR A SAFE LANDING.

THE SLOTH'S ROUTINE
A SPECIMEN KEPT UNDER CONSTANT OBSERVATION FOR A WEEK SPENT—
11 HOURS FEEDING,
18 HOURS CLIMBING,
10 HOURS REMAINING MOTIONLESS,
129 HOURS SLEEPING.

THE SLOTH'S VEGETABLE CAMOUFLAGE
SLOTHS' HAIR IS INHABITED BY ALGAE WHICH ARE GREEN UNDER DAMP CONDITIONS BUT TURN YELLOW IN TIMES OF DROUGHT, THUS KEEPING THEM INDISTINGUISHABLE FROM THE FOLIAGE IN ALL SEASONS. THIS IS FORTUNATE AS THEIR MAXIMUM SPEED IS ONE MILE IN 4 HOURS SWIMMING & HALF THAT MOVING OVERLAND SO RUNNING AWAY FROM PREDATORS IS NOT POSSIBLE.

ARMADILLOS
ARMADILLOS ARE ONE OF THE FEW ANIMAL SPECIES TO HAVE THRIVED UNDER THE INFLUENCE OF MAN, DUE TO THE INCREASED AMOUNT OF AGRICULTURAL LAND PROVIDING MORE INSECTS FOR THEM TO EAT. THEY HAVE SPREAD FROM TEXAS TO ALL THE SOUTHERN STATES OF AMERICA SINCE 1930 & ARE NOW RATED AS A MAJOR PEST. A REMARKABLE FEATURE OF THE GIANT ARMADILLO IS THE REPRODUCTIVE BEHAVIOUR OF THE FEMALE, WHO INVARIABLY BEARS A LITTER OF 4 IDENTICAL TWINS.

SLOTHS: ALIVE OR DEAD?
SLOTHS EAT VERY LITTLE & VERY SLOWLY. FOOD TAKES 14 DAYS TO BE DIGESTED. THEY ARE TOTALLY SILENT (EXCEPT FOR A PLAINTIVE WAIL EMITTED WHEN ATTACKED OR SEPARATED FROM THEIR YOUNG). THEY ONLY MAINTAIN A CONSTANT BODY TEMPERATURE WHEN PREGNANT & CAN EVEN STOP BREATHING WITHOUT DAMAGING THEIR HEARTS OR BRAINS.

ANTEATERS
THE GIANT ANTEATER GROWS UP TO 8FT LONG PLUS 8INCHES WITH ITS TONGUE EXTENDED. IT CAN CATCH SEVERAL HUNDRED ANTS ON ITS TONGUE WITH A SINGLE SWOOP.

HOW 8 PEOPLE CAN ALL SIT ON TOP OF EACH OTHER AT THE SAME TIME

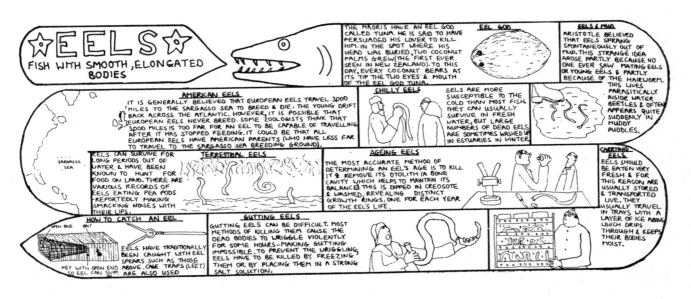

☆ EELS ☆
FISH WITH SMOOTH, ELONGATED BODIES

THE MAORIS HAVE AN EEL GOD CALLED TUNA. HE IS SAID TO HAVE PERSUADED HIS LOVER TO KILL HIM. IN THE SPOT WHERE HIS HEAD WAS BURIED, TWO COCONUT PALMS GREW (THE FIRST EVER SEEN IN NEW ZEALAND). TO THIS DAY, EVERY COCONUT BEARS AT ITS TIP THE TWO EYES & MOUTH OF THE EEL GOD TUNA.

EEL GOD

EELS & MUD
ARISTOTLE BELIEVED THAT EELS SPRANG SPONTANEOUSLY OUT OF MUD. THIS STRANGE IDEA AROSE PARTLY BECAUSE NO ONE EVER SAW MATING EELS OR YOUNG EELS & PARTLY BECAUSE OF THE HAIRWORM. THIS LIVES PARASITICALLY INSIDE WATER BEETLES & OFTEN APPEARS QUITE SUDDENLY IN MUDDY PUDDLES.

AMERICAN EELS
IT IS GENERALLY BELIEVED THAT EUROPEAN EELS TRAVEL 3000 MILES TO THE SARGASSO SEA TO BREED & DIE. THE YOUNG DRIFT BACK ACROSS THE ATLANTIC. HOWEVER, IT IS POSSIBLE THAT EUROPEAN EELS NEVER BREED. SOME ZOOLOGISTS THINK THAT 3000 MILES IS TOO FAR FOR AN EEL TO BE CAPABLE OF TRAVELLING AFTER IT HAS STOPPED FEEDING. IT COULD BE THAT ALL EUROPEAN EELS HAVE AMERICAN PARENTS (WHO HAVE LESS FAR TO TRAVEL TO THE SARGASSO SEA BREEDING GROUND).

CHILLY EELS
EELS ARE MORE SUSCEPTIBLE TO THE COLD THAN MOST FISH. THEY CAN USUALLY SURVIVE IN FRESH WATER, BUT LARGE NUMBERS OF DEAD EELS ARE SOMETIMES WASHED UP IN ESTUARIES IN WINTER.

SARGASSO SEA

TERRESTRIAL EELS
EELS CAN SURVIVE FOR LONG PERIODS OUT OF WATER & HAVE BEEN KNOWN TO HUNT FOR FOOD ON LAND. THERE ARE VARIOUS RECORDS OF EELS EATING PEA PODS REPORTEDLY MAKING SMACKING NOISES WITH THEIR LIPS.

AGEING EELS
THE MOST ACCURATE METHOD OF DETERMINING AN EEL'S AGE IS TO KILL IT & REMOVE ITS OTOLITH (A BONE CAVITY WHICH HELPS TO MAINTAIN ITS BALANCE). THIS IS DIPPED IN CREOSOTE & WASHED, REVEALING DISTINCT GROWTH RINGS, ONE FOR EACH YEAR OF THE EEL'S LIFE.

CARRYING EELS
EELS SHOULD BE EATEN VERY FRESH & FOR THIS REASON ARE USUALLY STORED & TRANSPORTED LIVE. THEY USUALLY TRAVEL IN TRAYS WITH A LAYER OF ICE ABOVE WHICH DRIPS THROUGH & KEEPS THEIR BODIES MOIST.

HOW TO CATCH AN EEL
OPEN END, OUT.
EELS HAVE TRADITIONALLY BEEN CAUGHT WITH EEL SPEARS SUCH AS THOSE ABOVE. CAGE TRAPS (LEFT) ARE ALSO USED.
NET WITH OPEN END SO EEL CAN SWIM IN

GUTTING EELS
GUTTING EELS CAN BE DIFFICULT. MOST METHODS OF KILLING CAUSE THE DEAD BODIES TO WRIGGLE VIOLENTLY FOR SOME HOURS—MAKING GUTTING IMPOSSIBLE. TO PREVENT THE WRIGGLING, EELS HAVE TO BE KILLED BY FREEZING THEM OR BY PLACING THEM IN A STRONG SALT SOLUTION.

EGGS
SPHERICAL BODIES CONTAINING NEW INDIVIDUALS
EXPERIMENTS WITH EGGS

EGG CONSUMPTION

THE RECORD NUMBER OF EGGS CONSUMED AT A SITTING IS 144 IN A ½ HOUR (SOFT BOILED) & THE GREATEST SPEED IS 14 IN 9.4 SECONDS (RAW). FOR MASOCHISTS THERE IS A RECORD FOR EATING RAW EGGS COMPLETE WITH SHELLS (16 IN 3min 20sec). POSSIBLY EVEN NASTIER IS A CHINESE FOOD DELICACY: EGGS DUG UP AFTER BEING BURIED FOR SEVERAL YEARS, THEY EMERGE WITH GREEN YOLKS & BROWN WHITES.

BREAKING EGGS

THE STRENGTH OF AN EGG SHELL IS TRULY AMAZING. THE DOMESTIC HEN'S EGG WILL SUPPORT A 50lb WEIGHT & HAS BEEN THROWN A DISTANCE OF 122FT WITHOUT BREAKING. AN OSTRICH EGG WILL SUPPORT AN 18 STONE MAN.

SOME USES FOR EGGS

BESIDES EATING EGGS, MEN HAVE ALSO USED THEM IN VARNISHES, GLUES, MEDICINES, PHOTOGRAPHIC FILMS, FACE PACKS, TEMPERA PAINTS, SHAMPOOS & EVEN IN CEMENT. EGG SHELLS ALSO HAVE USES. SOME CLOWNS HAVE THEIR OWN FACE MAKE-UP DESIGN AS A SORT OF TRADE MARK & TO PROTECT THEIR COPYRIGHT, THEY PAINT IT ON AN EGG SHELL, WHICH IS STORED IN THE VAULTS OF THE INTERNATIONAL CIRCUS CLUB, PARIS.

EGG PRODUCTION

AN AMERICAN BIRD 'THE BOBWHITE' HOLDS THE RECORD FOR THE MOST EGGS PRODUCED AT A TIME (UP TO 24) FOLLOWED CLOSELY BY THE COMMON PARTRIDGE (20). THESE NUMBERS CAN BE GREATLY INCREASED BY REMOVING MOST OF THE EGGS AS THEY APPEAR. THE BOBWHITE HAS LAID 128 BEFORE STOPPING. UNDER THESE CONDITIONS. IN SEVERAL SPECIES THE TOTAL WEIGHT OF THE EGGS IS AS MUCH AS 3 TIMES THE WEIGHT OF THE MOTHER. BIRDS LAY VERY FEW EGGS COMPARED WITH ANIMALS. (RECORD 25,650 BY A WOODHOUSES TOAD) WITH FISHES (RECORD 300,000,000 BY AN OCEAN SUNFISH) THE EGGS ARE OBVIOUSLY MUCH SMALLER, THE LAVAL SUNFISH IS TO ITS MOTHER AS A ISOLA ROWING BOAT IS TO 10 IS SUPER TANKERS (325,000 TONS EACH).

TO MAKE EGGS EXPAND

LOOK UP 'SOUFFLETTE' IN BIG COOKERY BOOK & FOLLOW DIRECTIONS CLOSELY WITH PERMISSION & PREFERABLY ASSISTANCE FROM THE FAMILY'S COOK. IF SUCCESSFUL, THE EXPANSION IS HIGHLY SPECTACULAR.

TO TEST YOUR STRENGTH

TRY TO BREAK AN EGG SQUEEZING IT IN THE PALM OF YOUR HAND WITHOUT USING FINGER TIPS. IT IS SAID TO BE IMPOSSIBLE.

TO DISTINGUISH A HARD BOILED EGG FROM A RAW EGG

SPIN EGG ON POINTED END, RAW EGGS TOPPLE OVER, IMMEDIATELY BUT BOILED EGGS SPIN EASILY.

TO PUT AN EGG IN A MILK BOTTLE

FIRST SOFTEN SHELL BY IMMERSING IN VINEGAR FOR ABOUT 2 DAYS, THEN HEAT BOTTLE IN BOILING WATER & HOLD SOFTENED EGG ON NECK. COOL BOTTLE & AIR INSIDE CONTRACTS, SUCKING IN EGG.

TO MAKE AN EGG RISE IN WATER

PUT EGG IN JUG OF WARM WATER, THEN POUR IN LOTS OF SALT. STIR GENTLY & EGG WILL RISE TO SURFACE. BAD EGGS CAN BE DETECTED IN THIS EXPERIMENT. THEY FLOAT WITHOUT ANY SALT.

HOW TO HIDE AN EGG

THE OSTRICH LAYS THE LARGEST EGG OF ANY SPECIES (EXCEPT THE WHALE SHARK) WITH A VOLUME OF 2½ PINTS. IT TAKES 40min TO BOIL & 42 DAYS TO INCUBATE. ALTHOUGH REPUTED TO BE VERY STUPID OSTRICHES HAVE A FIENDISHLY CUNNING METHOD OF CAMOUFLAGING THEIR NESTS. THE FEMALE, WHO MERGES WITH THE SANDY SOIL, LIES ON THE EGG WITH HER NECK FLAT ON THE GROUND DISGUISING HERSELF AS A HILLOCK, TO COMPLETE THE CAMOUFLAGE & THE BLACK MALE BIRD TAKES OVER AT NIGHT.

KIWIS & THEIR EGGS

THE KIWI IS A MOST UNFORTUNATE BIRD. IT LAYS THE LARGEST EGG IN PROPORTION TO ITS SIZE OF ANY SPECIES & THE HEN STAGGERS AROUND AS IF DRUNK BEFORE LAYING THE EGG, WHICH WEIGHS UP TO ⅓ AS MUCH AS SHE. SHE HOWEVER, UNLIKE ANY OTHER BIRD, DOES HAVE THE FATE OF THE MALE. HE DOES ALL THE INCUBATING, WHICH LASTS 75-80 DAYS, LONGER THAN WITH ANY OTHER EXCEPT THE ALBATROSS.

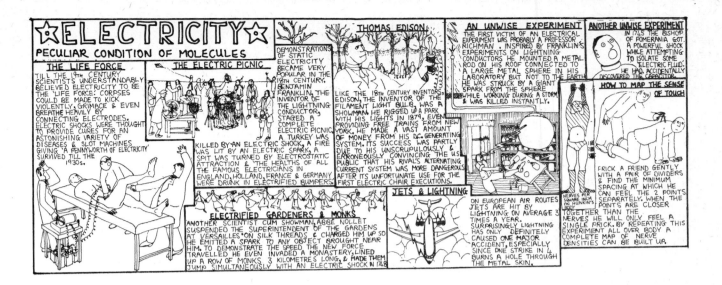

☆ELECTRICITY☆
PECULIAR CONDITION OF MOLECULES

THE LIFE FORCE
TILL THE 19TH CENTURY SCIENTISTS UNDERSTANDABLY BELIEVED ELECTRICITY TO BE THE 'LIFE FORCE'. CORPSES COULD BE MADE TO KICK VIOLENTLY, GRIMACE & EVEN BREATHE HEAVILY BY CONNECTING ELECTRODES. ELECTRIC SHOCKS WERE THOUGHT TO PROVIDE CURES FOR AN ASTONISHING VARIETY OF DISEASES & SLOT MACHINES GIVING 'A PENNYWORTH OF ELECTRICITY' SURVIVED TILL THE 1930s.

THE ELECTRIC PICNIC
DEMONSTRATIONS OF STATIC ELECTRICITY BECAME VERY POPULAR IN THE 18TH CENTURY. BENJAMIN FRANKLIN, THE INVENTOR OF THE LIGHTNING CONDUCTOR, STAGED A COMPLETE ELECTRIC PICNIC. A TURKEY WAS KILLED BY AN ELECTRIC SHOCK, A FIRE WAS LIT BY AN ELECTRIC SPARK, A SPIT WAS TURNED BY ELECTROSTATIC ATTRACTION & 'THE HEALTHS OF ALL THE FAMOUS ELECTRICIANS IN ENGLAND, HOLLAND, FRANCE & GERMANY WERE DRUNK IN ELECTRIFIED BUMPERS.'

THOMAS EDISON
LIKE THE 19TH CENTURY INVENTORS, EDISON, THE INVENTOR OF THE FILAMENT LIGHT BULB, WAS A SHOWMAN. HE RIGGED UP A PARK WITH HIS LIGHTS IN 1879, EVEN PROVIDING FREE TRAINS FROM NEW YORK. HE MADE A VAST AMOUNT OF MONEY FROM HIS DC GENERATING SYSTEM. ITS SUCCESS WAS PARTLY DUE TO HIS UNSCRUPULOUSLY & ERRONEOUSLY CONVINCING THE US PUBLIC THAT HIS RIVAL'S ALTERNATING CURRENT SYSTEM WAS MORE DANGEROUS AFTER ITS UNFORTUNATE USE FOR THE FIRST ELECTRIC CHAIR EXECUTIONS.

AN UNWISE EXPERIMENT
THE FIRST VICTIM OF AN ELECTRICAL EXPERIMENT WAS PROBABLY A PROFESSOR RICHMAN. INSPIRED BY FRANKLIN'S EXPERIMENTS ON LIGHTNING CONDUCTORS HE MOUNTED A METAL ROD ON HIS ROOF CONNECTED TO A LARGE METAL SPHERE IN HIS LABORATORY BUT NOT TO THE EARTH. HE WAS STRUCK BY A GIANT SPARK FROM THE SPHERE WHILE WORKING DURING A STORM & WAS KILLED INSTANTLY.

ANOTHER UNWISE EXPERIMENT
IN 1745 THE BISHOP OF POMERANIA GOT A POWERFUL SHOCK WHILE ATTEMPTING TO ISOLATE SOME 'ELECTRIC FLUID'. HE HAD ACCIDENTALLY DISCOVERED THE CAPACITOR.

HOW TO MAP THE SENSE OF TOUCH
PRICK A FRIEND GENTLY WITH A PAIR OF DIVIDERS & FIND THE MINIMUM SPACING AT WHICH HE CAN FEEL THE 2 POINTS SEPARATELY. WHEN THE POINTS ARE CLOSER TOGETHER THAN THE NERVES HE WILL ONLY FEEL A SINGLE PRICK. BY REPEATING THIS EXPERIMENT ALL OVER BODY A COMPLETE MAP OF NERVE DENSITIES CAN BE BUILT UP.

NERVES PER SQUARE INCH ON HUNKIN'S BODY

ELECTRIFIED GARDENERS & MONKS
ANOTHER SCIENTIST CUM SHOWMAN, ABBE NOLLET SUSPENDED THE SUPERINTENDENT OF THE GARDENS AT VERSAILLES 'ON SILK THREADS & CHARGED HIM UP SO HE EMITTED A SPARK TO ANY OBJECT BROUGHT NEAR HIM. TO DEMONSTRATE THE SPEED THE NEW FORCE TRAVELLED HE EVEN INVADED A MONASTERY, LINED UP A ROW OF MONKS 3 KILOMETRES LONG, & MADE THEM JUMP SIMULTANEOUSLY WITH AN ELECTRIC SHOCK IN 1748.

JETS & LIGHTNING
ON EUROPEAN AIR ROUTES JETS ARE HIT BY LIGHTNING ON AVERAGE 3 TIMES A YEAR. SURPRISINGLY LIGHTNING HAS ONLY DEFINITELY CAUSED ONE MAJOR ACCIDENT, ESPECIALLY SINCE ONE STRIKE IN 4 BURNS A HOLE THROUGH THE METAL SKIN.

☆ ELECTRIC SHOCKS ☆
THE EFFECTS OF ELECTRICITY ON THE HUMAN BODY

SHOCK TREATMENT
THE FIRST MEDICAL USE OF ELECTRIC SHOCK WAS PROBABLY IN 47 AD, WHEN THE HEADACHE OF THE ROMAN EMPEROR CLAUDIUS WAS TREATED WITH SHOCKS FROM AN ELECTRIC EEL.

SHOCK PANACEA
MANY VICTORIANS THOUGHT SMALL ELECTRIC SHOCKS COULD CURE ALMOST ANY AILMENT. SMALL GENERATORS, WITH ELECTRODES TO HOLD IN THE HAND, CAN STILL BE FOUND IN MANY JUNK SHOPS.

BRAIN SHOCKS
ELECTRIC SHOCK THERAPY (ECT) IS STILL USED FOR SOME MENTAL PATIENTS SUFFERING FROM DEPRESSION. CURRENT IS PASSED THROUGH THE BRAIN, CAUSING CONVULSIONS & UNCONSCIOUSNESS.

AMNESIA SHOCKS
E.C.T. CAN RELIEVE DEPRESSION BUT IT HAS SERIOUS SIDE-EFFECTS, PARTICULARLY LOSS OF MEMORY. MOST PATIENTS NEVER REMEMBER THE THERAPY. THE LAW HAS RECENTLY BEEN CHANGED SO THAT IT CAN NORMALLY BE DONE ONLY WITH THE PATIENT'S (OR A GUARDIAN'S) CONSENT.

ACCIDENTAL SHOCK
ELECTROCUTION ACCOUNTS FOR 60 OF THE 5000 FATAL ACCIDENTS IN THE HOME IN BRITAIN EVERY YEAR. OF THESE, 25% ARE DUE TO FAULTY APPLIANCES, 30% ARE DUE TO FAULTY WIRING, INCLUDING PLUGS, THE REST ARE THE RESULT OF INADEQUATE SAFETY CARE: USING FIRES IN BATHROOMS, MENDING THINGS WITHOUT SWITCHING OFF THE CURRENT, ETC.

BIRDS
BIRDS SIT ON LIVE TRANSMISSION LINES WITHOUT GETTING A SHOCK BECAUSE NO CURRENT FLOWS THROUGH THEM. CURRENT WILL ONLY FLOW WHEN A CIRCUIT FROM A LIVE WIRE TO EARTH IS COMPLETED.

GUMBOOTS
DRY RUBBER GUMBOOTS ACT AS INSULATORS REDUCING THE CURRENT THAT WILL FLOW THROUGH THE BODY TO EARTH.

BATHS
METAL BATHS ACT AS CONDUCTORS, INCREASING THE CURRENT THAT CAN FLOW.

SHOCKPROOF PLUGS
A NEW 'SAFE' 13 AMP PLUG HAS RECENTLY BEEN INTRODUCED. IT CONTAINS A MINIATURE CIRCUIT BREAKER WHICH SENSES ANY CURRENT LEAKED TO EARTH. IT IS SENSITIVE ENOUGH & FAST ENOUGH (·03 SEC) TO PREVENT A SERIOUS SHOCK.

EXECUTION
THE FIRST ELECTROCUTION (NEW YORK 1890) WAS A HORRIFYING SPECTACLE. THE VICTIM TOOK 8 MINUTES TO DIE.

PUBLICITY
THE ELECTRIC CHAIR HAD BEEN DEVELOPED AT THOMAS EDISON'S LABORATORIES IN THE 1880s. THE GENERATOR USED CAME FROM HIS RIVAL, WESTINGHOUSE. EDISON'S UNSCRUPULOUS PUBLICITY AFTER THE EVENT STRESSED THE DANGERS IN THE HOME OF HIS RIVAL'S 240v AC SYSTEM COMPARED TO HIS OWN 110v DC.

240v

SURVIVAL
EXCLUDING LIGHTNING, THE BIGGEST ELECTRIC SHOCK SO FAR SURVIVED WAS 230,000v BY A 17-YEAR-OLD BOY. (LOS ANGELES 1967).

HOW TO TEST IF AN ELECTRIC FENCE IS LIVE
PICK UP A BLADE OF GRASS & HOLD FAR END ON WIRE. IF YOU FEEL A SLIGHT TINGLE, THE FENCE IS LIVE. THE GRASS ACTS AS AN INSULATOR & REDUCES THE CURRENT FLOWING THROUGH YOU & THE SHOCK.

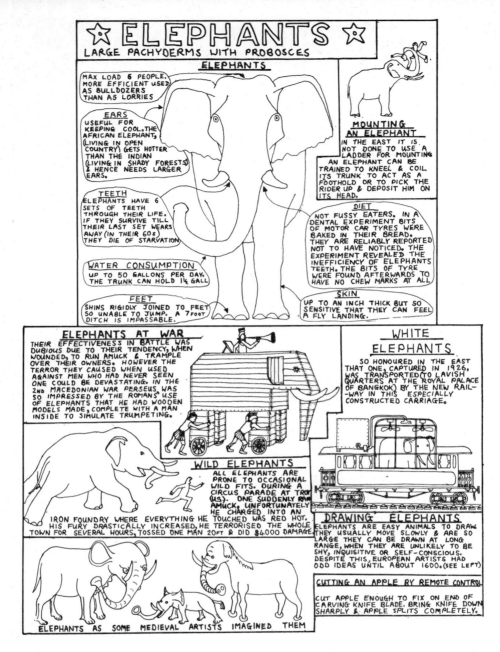

☆ ELEPHANTS ☆
LARGE PACHYDERMS WITH PROBOSCES

ELEPHANTS

MAX LOAD 6 PEOPLE. MORE EFFICIENT USED AS BULLDOZERS THAN AS LORRIES

EARS
USEFUL FOR KEEPING COOL. THE AFRICAN ELEPHANT, (LIVING IN OPEN COUNTRY) GETS HOTTER THAN THE INDIAN (LIVING IN SHADY FORESTS) & HENCE NEEDS LARGER EARS.

TEETH
ELEPHANTS HAVE 6 SETS OF TEETH THROUGH THEIR LIFE. IF THEY SURVIVE TILL THEIR LAST SET WEARS AWAY (IN THEIR 60s) THEY DIE OF STARVATION.

WATER CONSUMPTION
UP TO 50 GALLONS PER DAY. THE TRUNK CAN HOLD 1½ GALL

FEET
SHINS RIGIDLY JOINED TO FEET SO UNABLE TO JUMP. A 7 FOOT DITCH IS IMPASSABLE.

MOUNTING AN ELEPHANT
IN THE EAST IT IS NOT DONE TO USE A LADDER FOR MOUNTING AN ELEPHANT CAN BE TRAINED TO KNEEL & COIL ITS TRUNK TO ACT AS A FOOTHOLD OR TO PICK THE RIDER UP & DEPOSIT HIM ON ITS HEAD.

DIET
NOT FUSSY EATERS. IN A DENTAL EXPERIMENT BITS OF MOTOR CAR TYRES WERE BAKED IN THEIR BREAD. THEY ARE RELIABLY REPORTED NOT TO HAVE NOTICED. THE EXPERIMENT REVEALED THE INEFFICIENCY OF ELEPHANTS TEETH. THE BITS OF TYRE WERE FOUND AFTERWARDS TO HAVE NO CHEW MARKS AT ALL

SKIN
UP TO AN INCH THICK BUT SO SENSITIVE THAT THEY CAN FEEL A FLY LANDING.

ELEPHANTS AT WAR
THEIR EFFECTIVENESS IN BATTLE WAS DUBIOUS DUE TO THEIR TENDENCY, WHEN WOUNDED, TO RUN AMUCK & TRAMPLE OVER THEIR OWNERS. HOWEVER THE TERROR THEY CAUSED WHEN USED AGAINST MEN WHO HAD NEVER SEEN ONE COULD BE DEVASTATING. IN THE 2ND MACEDONIAN WAR PERSEUS WAS SO IMPRESSED BY THE ROMANS' USE OF ELEPHANTS THAT HE HAD WOODEN MODELS MADE, COMPLETE WITH A MAN INSIDE TO SIMULATE TRUMPETING.

WILD ELEPHANTS
ALL ELEPHANTS ARE PRONE TO OCCASIONAL WILD FITS. DURING A CIRCUS PARADE AT TROY (US). ONE SUDDENLY RAN AMUCK. UNFORTUNATELY HE CHARGED INTO AN IRON FOUNDRY WHERE EVERYTHING HE TOUCHED WAS RED HOT. HIS FURY DRASTICALLY INCREASED, HE TERRORISED THE WHOLE TOWN FOR SEVERAL HOURS, TOSSED ONE MAN 20FT & DID $4000 DAMAGE.

ELEPHANTS AS SOME MEDIEVAL ARTISTS IMAGINED THEM

WHITE ELEPHANTS
SO HONOURED IN THE EAST THAT ONE, CAPTURED IN 1926, WAS TRANSPORTED (TO LAVISH QUARTERS AT THE ROYAL PALACE OF BANGKOK) BY THE NEW RAILWAY IN THIS ESPECIALLY CONSTRUCTED CARRIAGE.

DRAWING ELEPHANTS
ELEPHANTS ARE EASY ANIMALS TO DRAW. THEY USUALLY MOVE SLOWLY & ARE SO LARGE THEY CAN BE DRAWN AT LONG RANGE, WHEN THEY ARE UNLIKELY TO BE SHY, INQUISITIVE OR SELF-CONSCIOUS. DESPITE THIS, EUROPEAN ARTISTS HAD ODD IDEAS UNTIL ABOUT 1600. (SEE LEFT)

CUTTING AN APPLE BY REMOTE CONTROL
CUT APPLE ENOUGH TO FIX ON END OF CARVING KNIFE BLADE. BRING KNIFE DOWN SHARPLY & APPLE SPLITS COMPLETELY.

ENCYCLOPEDIA ☆ ☆

WORK WITH INFORMATION ON EVERY AREA OF KNOWLEDGE

ROMAN
ROMAN ENCYCLOPEDIAS, PARTICULARLY PLINY'S HISTORIA NATURALIS, DID NOT DISCRIMINATE BETWEEN FACT & FANTASY. THE PLINY WAS, HOWEVER, VERY INFLUENTIAL, 43 EDITIONS HAD BEEN PUBLISHED BY 1543.

ARABIC
THE EARLIEST ARAB ENCYCLOPEDIA, c500AD, STARTED WITH POWER & WAR & ENDED WITH FOOD & WOMEN. A PERSIAN ENCYCLOPEDIA, 997AD, STARTED WITH LAW & PHILOSOPHY, PRACTICAL SUBJECTS (MEDICINE, MECHANICS etc) CAME UNDER THE TITLE 'FOREIGN KNOWLEDGE.'

CHINESE
THE LARGEST ENCYCLOPEDIA EVER IS THOUGHT TO HAVE BEEN THE CHINESE 'YUNG-LO TA-TIEN' (GREAT HANDBOOK), PUBLISHED c1400 WITH 22,937 CHAPTERS. UNFORTUNATELY, LITTLE HAS SURVIVED.

CLASSIFICATION
MANY SYSTEMS OF CLASSIFYING SUBJECTS HAVE BEEN TRIED, INCLUDING ELABORATE ALLEGORIES IN WHICH THE 7 BRIDESMAIDS REPRESENT THE 7 LIBERAL ARTS & 5 PARTS HONOUR CHRIST'S 5 WOUNDS. THE ALPHABETICAL ARRANGEMENT FIRST APPEARED c1000AD.

ODD NAMES
MANY EARLY ENCYCLOPEDIAS HAD FANCIFUL NAMES. 'HORTUS DELICARIUM' (GARDEN OF DELIGHTS); 'SPECULUM MAJOR' (THE GREAT MIRROR). LATIN REMAINED THE STANDARD LANGUAGE UNTIL THE 1600s.

HORTUS DELICARIUM

WHOLE EDUCATION
THE WORD ENCYCLOPEDIA COMES FROM THE GREEK ENKYKLIOS (CIRCLE OR WHOLE) PLUS PAIDEIA (EDUCATION). ITS FIRST RECORDED USE WAS IN 1559.

☆ ENERGY ☆
ACCUMULATED MECHANICAL WORK

DAZZLING ENERGY
ONE WAY OF SAVING ENERGY IS TO USE DIMMER LIGHTS. THE AMERICAN ILLUMINATING ENGINEERING SOCIETY HAVE RAISED THEIR MINIMUM STANDARDS SINCE 1945 FROM 30 TO 70 FOOT CANDLES INTENSITY IN SCHOOLS & FROM 35 TO 125 FT CANDLES IN OFFICES. HOWEVER THE OPHTHAMOLOGISTS CLAIM THAT 25 FT CANDLES ARE ENOUGH FOR READING WITHOUT STRAINING THE EYE.

FARMING ENERGY
THE ENERGY CONSUMED BY FARMERS HAS RISEN ALARMINGLY DUE TO INCREASED MECHANISATION & USE OF FERTILISER. SOME RECENT BRITISH ESTIMATES ARE 2·2 CALORIES OF WHEAT TAKES ONE CAL TO PRODUCE
- 1·1 " POTATOES
- ·3 " MILK
- ·16 " EGGS

AMERICAN FARMERS ARE WORSE USING ABOUT 5 TIMES THE TOTAL ENERGY VALUE OF THE FOOD THEY PRODUCE.

RUSTIC ENERGY
IN THE EARLY SIXTIES THE RUSSIANS EVOLVED A VERY HOMELY DEVICE FOR GENERATING ELECTRICITY TO POWER RADIOS, LIGHT BULBS & LOW POWER MOTORS. THE UNIT IS DESIGNED TO FIT OVER A PARAFFIN LAMP & CONVERTS THE HEAT GIVEN OUT TO ELECTRICITY. IT IS USED IN REMOTE SIBERIAN COTTAGES BUT ATTEMPTS TO SELL THEM TO CARAVAN OWNERS IN ENGLAND WERE UNSUCCESSFUL.

AIRSHIP ENERGY
THE AIRSHIP IS AN INVENTION THAT OUGHT TO BE ABLE TO SAVE LOTS OF ENERGY. NASA IS CONDUCTING ADVANCE FEASIBILITY STUDIES OF A 'HELIUM HORSE' BUT EXPRESS GRAVE DOUBTS: ONE PROBLEM IS THAT EVERY TIME A LOAD IS TRANSFERRED AN EQUAL AMOUNT OF BALLAST HAS TO BE TRANSFERRED IN THE OPPOSITE DIRECTION TO MAINTAIN THE CORRECT BUOYANCY. ANOTHER PROBLEM IS THAT MANOEUVRING A LARGE AIRSHIP IN A HIGH WIND WOULD REQUIRE NEAR UNIVERSAL CONSCRIPTION.

PIG ENERGY
IF THE EFFLUENT OF ALL THE PIGS IN BRITAIN WAS CONVERTED TO METHANE IT WOULD ONLY SUPPLY 50,000 OF OUR CURRENT ELECTRICITY CONSUMPTION.

HOW TO DRESS UP IN A GREEK CHITON
5'×8'
SAFETY PINS

LUMINOUS ENERGY
A NEW YORK SKY SCRAPER, THE 110 STOREY WORLD TRADE CENTRE, HAS NO LIGHT SWITCHES. ALL THE LIGHTS ARE CONTROLLED BY A CENTRAL COMPUTER WHICH ENSURES THAT NO LIGHT IS LEFT ON ALL NIGHT. UNFORTUNATELY THE SYSTEM IS SO COMPLEX & DELICATE THAT NO ONE DARES TO INTERFERE WITH IT TO TURN LIGHTS OFF ON BRIGHT DAYS.

NUCLEAR ENERGY & SPRATS
BRITAIN'S NEW BREEDER REACTOR AT DUNGENESS HAS HAD TO BE SHUT DOWN TWICE RECENTLY DUE TO THE COOLING WATER INTAKE SCREENS BECOMING JAMMED WITH SHOALS OF UNFORTUNATE SPRATS.

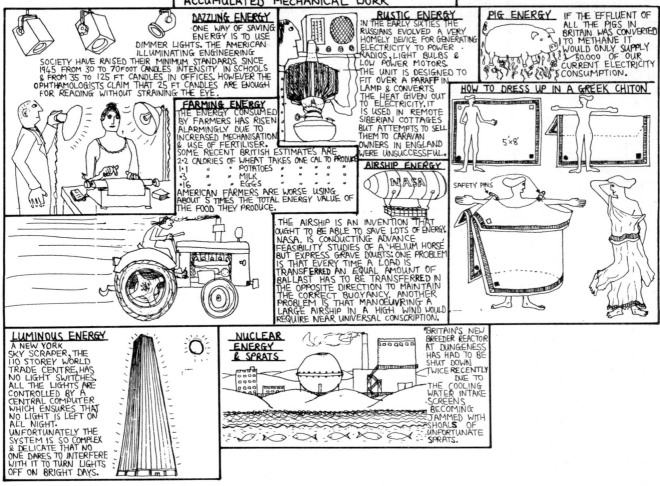

VERSE
VARIOUS ATTEMPTS HAVE BEEN MADE TO WRITE ENCYCLOPEDIAS IN VERSE – NOTABLY 'MAPPEMONDE' (1246) & THE UNCOMPLETED 'SCIENCE UNIVERSELLE' (1663).

SUBJECTS
17TH CENTURY ENCYCLOPEDIAS STILL CONTAINED MANY STRANGE ARTICLES. ALSTED'S (1630) INCLUDED: 'PARADOXOLOGIA' – THE ART OF EXPLAINING PARADOXES – AND 'DIPNOSOPHISTICA' – THE ART OF PHILOSOPHISING WHILE FEASTING.

INACCURACIES
THE FIRST EDITION OF THE BRITANNICA (1769) CONTAINED MANY INACCURACIES. CALIFORNIA WAS SAID TO BE A LARGE COUNTRY IN THE WEST INDIES. TOBACCO IN EXCESS WAS SAID TO REDUCE THE BRAIN TO 'A LITTLE BLACK LUMP OF MERE MEMBRANES'.

PICTURES
A PICTURE ENCYCLOPEDIA, CONTAINING A DRAWING OR PHOTO FOR EACH OF 10,000 ENTRIES, WAS PUBLISHED IN 1930 CALLED 'I SEE ALL'. IT ILLUSTRATED MANY VERBS EG 'LOAFING' – YOUTHS ON A STREET CORNER.

POLITICS
MODERN ENCYCLOPEDIAS ATTEMPT TO BE UNBIASED BUT DO NOT ALWAYS SUCCEED. THE 'ENCICLOPEDIA ITALIANA' (1929-39) CONTAINED A LONG ARTICLE ON FASCISM BY MUSSOLINI. THE 'GREAT SOVIET ENCYCLOPEDIA' OMITS A NUMBER OF POLITICIANS, VARYING FROM ONE EDITION TO THE NEXT.

HOW TO USE THE 'GREAT SOVIET ENCYCLOPEDIA'
THE 'GREAT SOVIET ENCYCLOPEDIA' (36 VOLUMES) HAS BEEN TRANSLATED INTO ENGLISH & CAN BE FOUND IN REFERENCE LIBRARIES. UNFORTUNATELY, SUBJECTS ARE ARRANGED IN THEIR RUSSIAN ALPHABETICAL ORDER. TO FIND A SUBJECT YOU NEED TO ASK FOR THE ENGLISH INDEX, WHICH IS PUBLISHED SEPARATELY.

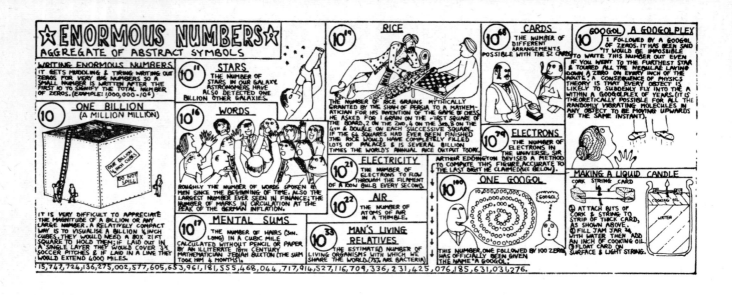

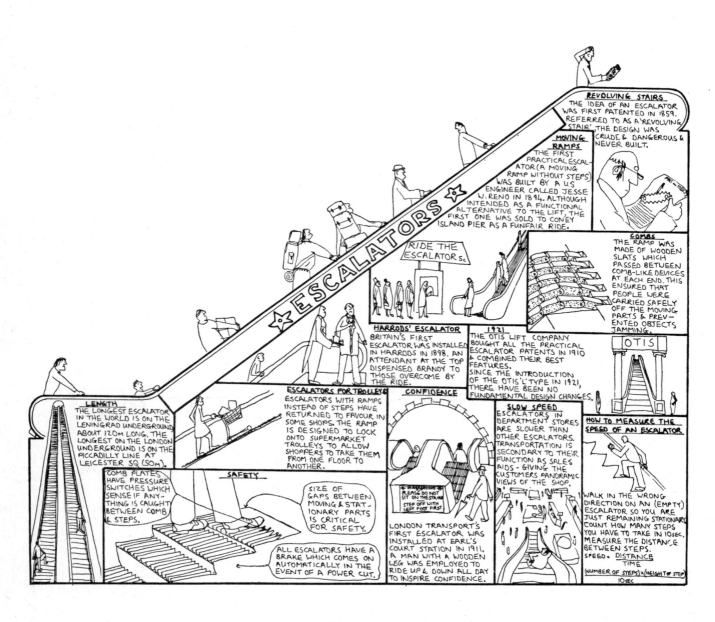

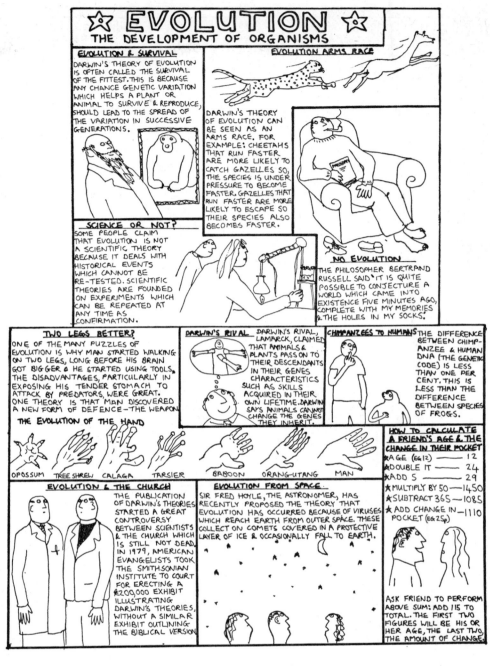

☆ EVOLUTION ☆
THE DEVELOPMENT OF ORGANISMS

EVOLUTION & SURVIVAL

DARWIN'S THEORY OF EVOLUTION IS OFTEN CALLED THE SURVIVAL OF THE FITTEST. THIS IS BECAUSE ANY CHANCE GENETIC VARIATION WHICH HELPS A PLANT OR ANIMAL TO SURVIVE & REPRODUCE, SHOULD LEAD TO THE SPREAD OF THE VARIATION IN SUCCESSIVE GENERATIONS.

EVOLUTION ARMS RACE

DARWIN'S THEORY OF EVOLUTION CAN BE SEEN AS AN ARMS RACE. FOR EXAMPLE: CHEETAHS THAT RUN FASTER ARE MORE LIKELY TO CATCH GAZELLES SO, THE SPECIES IS UNDER PRESSURE TO BECOME FASTER. GAZELLES THAT RUN FASTER ARE MORE LIKELY TO ESCAPE SO THEIR SPECIES ALSO BECOMES FASTER.

SCIENCE OR NOT?

SOME PEOPLE CLAIM THAT EVOLUTION IS NOT A SCIENTIFIC THEORY BECAUSE IT DEALS WITH HISTORICAL EVENTS WHICH CANNOT BE RE-TESTED. SCIENTIFIC THEORIES ARE FOUNDED ON EXPERIMENTS WHICH CAN BE REPEATED AT ANY TIME AS CONFIRMATION.

NO EVOLUTION

THE PHILOSOPHER BERTRAND RUSSELL SAID "IT IS QUITE POSSIBLE TO CONJECTURE A WORLD WHICH CAME INTO EXISTENCE FIVE MINUTES AGO, COMPLETE WITH MY MEMORIES & THE HOLES IN MY SOCKS."

TWO LEGS BETTER?

ONE OF THE MANY PUZZLES OF EVOLUTION IS WHY MAN STARTED WALKING ON TWO LEGS, LONG BEFORE HIS BRAIN GOT BIGGER & HE STARTED USING TOOLS. THE DISADVANTAGES, PARTICULARLY IN EXPOSING HIS TENDER STOMACH TO ATTACK BY PREDATORS, WERE GREAT. ONE THEORY IS THAT MAN DISCOVERED A NEW FORM OF DEFENCE – THE WEAPON

DARWIN'S RIVAL

DARWIN'S RIVAL, LAMARCK, CLAIMED THAT ANIMALS & PLANTS PASS ON TO THEIR DESCENDANTS IN THEIR GENES CHARACTERISTICS SUCH AS SKILLS ACQUIRED IN THEIR OWN LIFETIME. DARWIN SAYS ANIMALS CANNOT CHANGE THE GENES THEY INHERIT.

CHIMPANZEES TO HUMANS

THE DIFFERENCE BETWEEN CHIMPANZEE & HUMAN DNA (THE GENETIC CODE) IS LESS THAN ONE PER CENT. THIS IS LESS THAN THE DIFFERENCE BETWEEN SPECIES OF FROGS.

THE EVOLUTION OF THE HAND

OPOSSUM   TREE SHREW   CALAGA   TARSIER   BABOON   ORANG-UTANG   MAN

HOW TO CALCULATE A FRIEND'S AGE & THE CHANGE IN THEIR POCKET

★ AGE (EG 12)	12
★ DOUBLE IT	24
★ ADD 5	29
★ MULTIPLY BY 50	1450
★ SUBTRACT 365	1085
★ ADD CHANGE IN POCKET (EG 25p)	1110

ASK FRIEND TO PERFORM ABOVE SUM: ADD 115 TO TOTAL. THE FIRST TWO FIGURES WILL BE HIS OR HER AGE, THE LAST TWO, THE AMOUNT OF CHANGE.

EVOLUTION & THE CHURCH

THE PUBLICATION OF DARWIN'S THEORIES STARTED A GREAT CONTROVERSY BETWEEN SCIENTISTS & THE CHURCH WHICH IS STILL NOT DEAD. IN 1979, AMERICAN EVANGELISTS TOOK THE SMITHSONIAN INSTITUTE TO COURT FOR ERECTING A £200,000 EXHIBIT ILLUSTRATING DARWIN'S THEORIES, WITHOUT A SIMILAR EXHIBIT OUTLINING THE BIBLICAL VERSION.

EVOLUTION FROM SPACE

SIR FRED HOYLE, THE ASTRONOMER, HAS RECENTLY PROPOSED THE THEORY THAT EVOLUTION HAS OCCURRED BECAUSE OF VIRUSES WHICH REACH EARTH FROM OUTER SPACE. THESE COLLECT ON COMETS COVERED IN A PROTECTIVE LAYER OF ICE & OCCASIONALLY FALL TO EARTH.

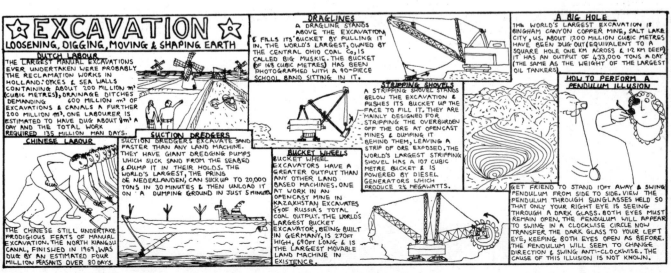

☆ EXCAVATION ☆
LOOSENING, DIGGING, MOVING & SHAPING EARTH

DUTCH LABOUR

THE LARGEST MANUAL EXCAVATIONS EVER UNDERTAKEN WERE PROBABLY THE RECLAMATION WORKS IN HOLLAND: DYKES & SEA WALLS CONTAINING ABOUT 200 MILLION m³ (CUBIC METRES), DRAINAGE DITCHES DEMANDING 600 MILLION m³ OF EXCAVATIONS & CANALS A FURTHER 200 MILLION m³. ONE LABOURER IS ESTIMATED TO HAVE DUG ABOUT 8m³ A DAY AND THE TOTAL WORK REQUIRED 135 MILLION MAN DAYS.

CHINESE LABOUR

THE CHINESE STILL UNDERTAKE PRODIGIOUS FEATS OF MANUAL EXCAVATION. THE NORTH KIANGSU CANAL, FINISHED IN 1969, WAS DUG BY AN ESTIMATED FOUR MILLION PEASANTS OVER 80 DAYS.

SUCTION DREDGERS

SUCTION DREDGERS EXCAVATE SAND FASTER THAN ANY LAND MACHINE. THEY HAVE GIANT DREDGING PUMPS WHICH SUCK SAND FROM THE SEABED & DUMP IT IN THEIR HOLDS. THE WORLD'S LARGEST, THE PRINS DE NEDERLANDEN, CAN SUCK UP TO 20,000 TONS IN 30 MINUTES & THEN UNLOAD IT ON A DUMPING GROUND IN JUST 5 MINUTES.

DRAGLINES

A DRAGLINE STANDS ABOVE THE EXCAVATION & FILLS ITS BUCKET BY PULLING IT IN. THE WORLD'S LARGEST, OWNED BY THE CENTRAL OHIO COAL Co, IS CALLED BIG MUSKIE. THE BUCKET OF 168 CUBIC METRES) HAS BEEN PHOTOGRAPHED WITH A 40-PIECE SCHOOL BAND SITTING IN IT.

STRIPPING SHOVELS

A STRIPPING SHOVEL STANDS BELOW THE EXCAVATION & PUSHES ITS BUCKET UP THE FACE TO FILL IT. THEY ARE MAINLY DESIGNED FOR STRIPPING THE OVERBURDEN OFF THE ORE AT OPENCAST MINES & DUMPING IT BEHIND THEM, LEAVING A STRIP OF ORE EXPOSED. THE WORLD'S LARGEST STRIPPING SHOVEL HAS A 107 CUBIC METRE BUCKET & IS POWERED BY DIESEL GENERATORS WHICH PRODUCE 2½ MEGAWATTS.

BUCKET WHEELS

BUCKET WHEEL EXCAVATORS HAVE A GREATER OUTPUT THAN ANY OTHER LAND BASED MACHINES. ONE AT WORK IN AN OPENCAST MINE IN KAZAKHSTAN EXCAVATES 150% OF RUSSIA'S TOTAL COAL OUTPUT. THE WORLDS LARGEST BUCKET EXCAVATOR, BEING BUILT IN GERMANY, IS 270ft HIGH, 690ft LONG & IS THE LARGEST MOVABLE LAND MACHINE IN EXISTENCE.

A BIG HOLE

THE WORLD'S LARGEST EXCAVATION IS BINGHAM CANYON COPPER MINE, SALT LAKE CITY, US. ABOUT 1200 MILLION CUBIC METRES HAVE BEEN DUG OUT (EQUIVALENT TO A SQUARE HOLE ONE KM ACROSS & 1.2 KM DEEP) IT HAS AN OUTPUT OF 433,000 TONS A DAY (THE SAME AS THE WEIGHT OF THE LARGEST OIL TANKERS).

HOW TO PERFORM A PENDULUM ILLUSION

GET FRIEND TO STAND 10ft AWAY & SWING PENDULUM FROM SIDE TO SIDE. VIEW THE PENDULUM THROUGH SUNGLASSES HELD SO THAT ONLY YOUR RIGHT EYE IS SEEING THROUGH A DARK GLASS. BOTH EYES MUST REMAIN OPEN. THE PENDULUM WILL APPEAR TO SWING IN A CLOCKWISE CIRCLE. NOW TRANSFER THE DARK GLASS TO YOUR LEFT EYE, KEEPING BOTH EYES OPEN AS BEFORE. THE PENDULUM WILL SEEM TO CHANGE DIRECTION & SWING ANTI-CLOCKWISE. THE CAUSE OF THIS ILLUSION IS NOT KNOWN.

☆ EXPLOSIVES ☆
SUBSTANCES CAPABLE OF RAPID VIOLENT REACTIONS

GUNPOWDER

THE GREATEST PROBLEM FACED BY THE MEDIEVAL MANUFACTURERS OF GUNPOWDER WAS OBTAINING THE SALTPETRE. THE USUAL SOURCE WAS THE EARTH FROM PIGSTIES & STABLES PRODUCED FROM BACTERIAL ACTION ON MANURE. ALL THE SOLUBLE SALTS WERE EXTRACTED WITH BOILING WATER & THE RESULTING SOLUTION WAS BOILED TILL THE MOST HARMFUL IMPURITY, COMMON SALT, SEPARATED OUT, ON COOLING, CRYSTALS OF FAIRLY PURE SALTPETRE FORMED. THE QUALITY OF THE PRODUCT WAS JUDGED BY LICKING IT, THE LESS SALTY THE BETTER.

THERE IS NO JUSTIFICATION FOR REGARDING ROGER BACON AS THE INVENTOR OF GUNPOWDER. HIS CLAIM WAS BASED ON A TRACT ENTITLED 'ON THE MARVELLOUS POWER OF NATURE & ART'. THIS CONTAINS AN ANAGRAM WHICH CAN BE DECIPHERED AS° OF SALTPETRE TAKE 7 PARTS, 5 OF YOUNG HAZEL TWIGS & 5 OF SULPHUR.' HOWEVER THERE IS ALSO MENTION OF GUNPOWDER IN OTHER CONTEMPORARY MANUSCRIPTS – INCLUDING THE LIBER IGNIUM (THE BOOK OF FIRES FOR BURNING ENEMIES), IT WAS CERTAINLY KNOWN IN CHINA (WHICH HAD THE ADVANTAGE OF NATURAL SUPPLIES OF SALTPETRE) BEFORE 900AD.

SALTPETRE

EXPLOSIVE VARIETY

DYNAMITE

ALFRED NOBEL'S FIRST EXPLOSIVE WAS CALLED NOBEL'S BLASTING OIL & CONSISTED OF PURE NITROGLYCERINE WHICH HE STARTED MAKING ON A BARGE IN THE MIDDLE OF A SWEDISH LAKE IN 1863. HIS FACTORY WAS DESTROYED TWICE BY EXPLOSIONS IN 5 YEARS; HIS YOUNGER BROTHER WAS KILLED & HIS FATHER WAS LEFT A PERMANENT INVALID. HOWEVER HE DISCOVERED THAT HE COULD USE A POROUS TYPE OF EARTH, CALLED KIESELGUHR, TO SOAK UP THE NITROGLYCERINE. THE RESULTING MIXTURE WAS MUCH MORE STABLE, BUT WORKED EQUALLY WELL AS AN EXPLOSIVE. HE PATENTED THIS IN 1867, CALLING IT DYNAMITE.

GELIGNITE CONSISTS OF NITROGLYCERINE IN AN ABSORBENT EXPLOSIVE SOLID MATERIAL CALLED COLLOIDON COTTON. **GUNCOTTON** IS ONE OF THE MOST STABLE EXPLOSIVES. IT IS A SOLID WHICH CAN SAFELY BE HANDLED, SAWN & FILED. **TNT** IS ALSO RELATIVELY STABLE, THE IMPACT OF A RIFLE BULLET WILL NOT DETONATE IT & WHEN HEATED IN SMALL QUANTITIES, IT BURNS QUIETLY & SLOWLY.

ENERGY

EXPLOSIVES ARE CHEMICALS WHICH WILL UNDERGO A VERY RAPID DECOMPOSITION BUT THEY DO NOT CONTAIN MORE ENERGY THAN OTHER SUBSTANCES. ONE KILO OF BUTTER RELEASES MORE ENERGY THAN A KILO OF T.N.T. WHEN BROKEN DOWN TO ITS CONSTITUENT ELEMENTS.

NITROGLYCERINE

THE MANUFACTURE OF NITROGLYCERINE HAS ALWAYS BEEN SOMEWHAT DANGEROUS. FACTORIES ARE ALWAYS SITED ON HILLSIDES SO ALL MOVEMENTS OF LIQUIDS CAN BE EFFECTED BY GRAVITY, THUS AVOIDING THE RISK OF EXPLOSIVE SOLUTIONS BEING TRAPPED IN PUMPS.

HOW TO MAKE AN EXPLOSIVE CLOCK

GOUGE A UNIFORM ZIG-ZAG CHANNEL IN A SLAB OF WET CLAY. ALLOW TO DRY. FILL CHANNEL WITH INCENSE POWDER, TIGHTLY PACKED. LIGHT ONE END & NOTE DOWN HOW MANY INCHES IT BURNS PER HOUR. THE CHANNEL CAN THEN BE MARKED AT INTERVALS INTO HOURS & MINUTES. CAPS CAN BE INSERTED IN THE CHANNEL SO THEY EXPLODE ON THE HOUR.

EXPLOSIVES OFTEN HAVE EXPRESSIVE TRADE NAMES: SAMSONITE, ATLAS POWDER, HERCULES POWDER, CHEDDITE, BOBBINITE, RACK-A-ROCK, TRITON, CYCLONITE, LYDDITE, RIPPITE.

☆ EXTINCT ANIMALS ☆
FRIENDS WHO COULD NOT STAY

THE QUAGGA

THE QUAGGA CAME FROM SOUTH AFRICA BUT WAS SHOT TO EXTINCTION BY THE BOERS. THE LAST ONE DIED AT AMSTERDAM ZOO IN 1883. ITS NAME IS AN IMITATION OF THE NOISE IT USED TO MAKE.

THE AUROCH

THE LAST AUROCH DIED IN 1627. THE ANCESTORS OF OUR DOMESTIC CATTLE, THEY WERE ONCE COMMON IN EUROPE BUT WERE HUNTED TOO HARD. HOWEVER THEIR EXTINCTION HELPED SAVE THE EUROPEAN BUFFALO BECAUSE IT MADE TSAR ALEXANDER I REALISE THE IMMINENT FATE OF THE BUFFALO. IN 1802 & HE TOOK DRASTIC ACTION. HE DECLARED 800 SQ. MILES OF THE BIALOWIEZA FOREST A PROTECTED AREA FOR BISON & EVEN FORCED ALL THE LOCAL PEASANTS TO MOVE TO PREVENT POACHING.

THE MOA

THE 24 SPECIES OF MOA LIVED IN NEW ZEALAND & RANGED FROM 3-12FT HIGH. THEY WERE HUNTED BY THE MAORIS UNTIL 1800 WHEN NONE WERE LEFT. CLUMSY BIRDS, UNABLE TO FLY OR RUN AWAY, THEY PROTECTED THEMSELVES BY KICKING VIOLENTLY. UNFORTUNATELY THEY HAD TO STAND ON ONE LEG WHILE KICKING WITH THE OTHER & THE MAORIS EASILY BROUGHT THEM TO THE GROUND BY AIMING THEIR BLOWS AGAINST THESE VULNERABLE SUPPORTS.

STELLA'S SEA COW

STELLA, A GERMAN DOCTOR, DISCOVERED HIS SEA COW WHEN HE WAS SHIPWRECKED ON BERING ISLAND, IN 1742. IT WAS ABOUT 30FT LONG & ATE SEAWEED CONTINUOUSLY. UNFORTUNATELY EACH COW YIELDED OVER 7000LB. OF MEAT WHICH TASTED DELICIOUS, 'RESEMBLING BEEF'. THE RUSSIAN FUR TRADERS TOOK TO VISITING THE ISLAND TO STOCK UP WITH FRESH & SALTED MEAT, TILL 1794 WHEN NO MORE COULD BE FOUND. SEA COWS WERE ASSUMED TO BE EXTINCT TILL A RUSSIAN WHALING SHIP REPORTED SEEING SIMILAR ANIMALS IN 1962, SO THERE IS STILL A POSSIBILITY THAT THEY SURVIVED.

THE GREAT AUK

THIS BIRD, THE PENGUIN OF THE NORTHERN HEMISPHERE, EXISTED IN VAST NUMBERS TILL THE 18TH CENTURY. ITS DOWNFALL WAS DUE PARTLY TO ITS INABILITY TO RUN AWAY ENABLING MEN TO KILL IT WITH ANY SHARP OR HEAVY OBJECT. BY 1821 THERE WAS ONLY ONE COLONY LEFT BUT UNFORTUNATELY THE WHOLE ISLAND ON WHICH THEY WERE SURVIVING SUDDENLY DISAPPEARED IN SOME VOLCANIC UPHEAVALS. 50 BIRDS ESCAPED BUT BY THIS TIME MUSEUM DIRECTORS WERE OFFERING A HIGH PRICE FOR SPECIMENS BY 1844 THE LAST 50 HAD BEEN KILLED & STUFFED.

HOW TO MAKE AN ENDLESS FOUNTAIN

BORROW FROM A CHEMISTRY LABORATORY:
1-GLASS NOZZLE
1-FUNNEL
2-GLASS BULBS
3-LENGTHS OF RUBBER TUBE
3-STANDS WITH CLAMPS.
ASSEMBLE PARTS WITH RELATIVE HEIGHTS AS IN DIAGRAM, THEN POUR SOME WATER DOWN FUNNEL & WATCH THE WATER CONTINUE FLOWING. FOUNTAINS LIKE THESE HAVE BEEN KNOWN TO FLOW FOR 12 HOURS BUT MY BEST LASTED TWO MINUTES.

THE DODO

FIRST OBSERVED & EATEN BY A DUTCH ADMIRAL CALLED VAN NEK IN 1601. HE NAMED THEM WALGHVOGELS (MEANING DISGUSTING BIRDS) BECAUSE HE REPORTED THAT THE LONGER THEY WERE COOKED THE LESS SOFT & MORE UNPALATABLE THEIR FLESH BECAME. HE BROUGHT 2 BACK TO EUROPE, WHERE THEY WERE ENTHUSIASTICALLY RECEIVED. A DUTCH PAINTER, ROELANDT SAVERY, EVEN MADE A CAREER PAINTING THEM. THEY COULD NOT FLY OR RUN & SOON BECAME EXTINCT BUT SAVERY CONTINUED TO PRODUCE PAINTINGS WHICH BECAME INCREASINGLY INACCURATE.

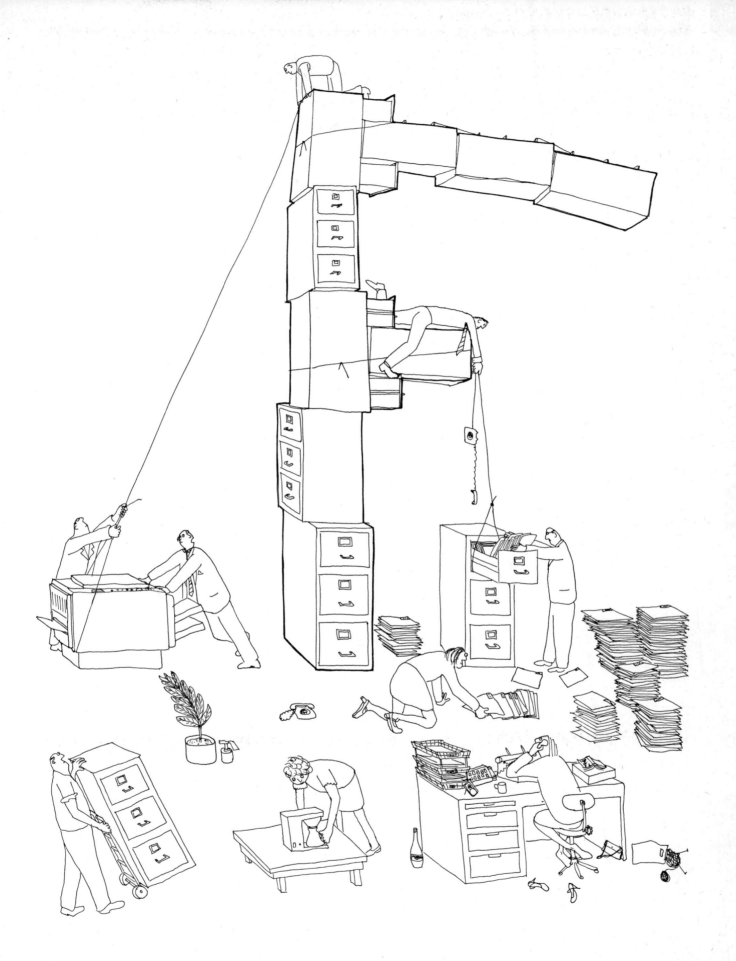

☆ FACES ☆
VITAL COMPONENTS OF HUMAN APPEARANCE

SUPPORT
THE FACE IS SUPPORTED BY 144 BONES & MORE THAN 100 MUSCLES.

SIZE
WOMEN'S FACES ARE, ON AVERAGE, ONE-FIFTH SMALLER THAN MEN'S FACES.

WRINKLES
THE FACE WRINKLES WITH AGE BECAUSE SKIN BECOMES LESS ELASTIC, ALTHOUGH THE SKIN CELLS ARE CONTINUALLY RENEWED. IT MAY BE BECAUSE THE CELLS ARE REPLACED LESS FREQUENTLY OR BECAUSE THE REPLACEMENT CELLS ARE WEAKER.

GREEK BEAUTY
THE GREEKS BELIEVED THAT THE PERFECT FACE HAD THE RATIO OF X TO Y EQUALLING 4 TO 3.

MEDIEVAL BEAUTY
MEDIEVAL ARTISTS THOUGHT THAT THE PERFECT FACE SHOULD DIVIDE INTO SEVENTHS.

BABY CHEEKS
BABIES HAVE PLUMP CHEEKS TO ACT AS SUCKING PADS. THEY ARE CLEARLY IMPORTANT, AS STARVING BABIES RETAIN THEIR CHEEK FAT.

PLUMPERS
A STRANGE DEVICE FOR CONCEALING FACIAL DEFECTS WAS THE PLUMPER: A PAD OF COTTON & CORK WORN INSIDE THE MOUTH TO SWELL THE CAVITIES LEFT BY LOSS OF TEETH. IT WAS POPULAR FROM ABOUT 1660 TO 1800.

FACE FLATTENING
FRENCH PEASANTS, NORTH AMERICAN INDIANS, AFRICANS, ARISTOCRATIC ANCIENT GREEKS & ROMANS HAVE ALL PRACTISED THE ART OF FLATTENING THE FOREHEADS OF THEIR CHILDREN. THE SKULL OF A NEWBORN BABY IS FLEXIBLE & PLATES, KEPT TIGHTLY TIED FOR THE FIRST 5 WEEKS, HAVE NO APPARENT ILL-EFFECTS.

AMERICAN EXPERIMENTS SUPPORT THE IDEA THAT WEARING SPECTACLES MAKES OTHERS THINK YOU ARE MORE INTELLIGENT.

SPECTACLES

FEMALE PERCEPTION
AMERICAN EXPERIMENTS HAVE SHOWN THAT WOMEN LOOK AT THE FACES OF PEOPLE THEY ARE TALKING TO MORE THAN MEN.

GUESSING FACES
PEOPLE ARE MUCH BETTER AT GUESSING 'SIMULATED' EXPRESSIONS OF ACTORS THAN GENUINE ONES OF ORDINARY PEOPLE. THIS IS PROBABLY BECAUSE ACTORS' EXPRESSIONS ARE LARGER THAN LIFE & MORE STEREOTYPED.

HOW TO TURN AN ORANGE INTO AN APPLE
CUT PEEL OF AN ORANGE INTO 4 SEGMENTS – LEAVING THEM JOINED AT THE TOP – & SCOOP OUT FLESH. ARRANGE 'HOLLOW' PEEL ON TABLE WITH APPLE INSIDE. PLACE HANKY OVER ORANGE & LIFT OFF CARRYING PEEL.

FACES & ILLNESS
EXOPHTHALMIC GOITRE CAUSES WILDLY STARING EYES.

ACROMEGALY CAUSES AN ENLARGEMENT OF NOSE & CHIN.

CONGENITAL SYPHILIS CAN CAUSE A SADDLE NOSE.

CUSHING'S DISEASE CAUSES A 'MOON-SHAPED FACE'.

☆ FACTORIES ☆
CONGERIES OF REPETITIVE PRODUCTION UNITS

WHEN FACTORIES WERE EXTRAORDINARY
THE EARLIEST FACTORY WAS PERHAPS THE LOMBE BROTHERS' SILK FACTORY, WHICH HAD 6 STOREYS & EMPLOYED 300 MEN BY 1719. DANIEL DEFOE DESCRIBED IT AS: "A CURIOSITY OF A VERY EXTRAORDINARY NATURE.... WITH 22,586 WHEELS THAT PRODUCE 73,726 YARDS OF SILK IN 24 HOURS."

KNITTING FACTORIES
ALTHOUGH KNITTING MACHINES CAPABLE OF PRODUCING MOST PATTERNS EXISTED BY 1840 FACTORIES CURIOUSLY DID NOT DEVELOP TILL THE TWENTIETH CENTURY. ONE EXPLANATION SUGGESTED IS THAT HAND KNITTERS WERE GIVEN ARTIFICIAL ENCOURAGE-MENT TO SURVIVE BY THE ARCHAIC & PECULIAR WAR OFFICE SPECIFICATION FOR ARMY UNDERWEAR (VIRTUALLY IMPOSS-IBLE TO KNIT BY MACHINE).

THE FIRST WORKS STUDY EXPERIMENTS WERE UNEXPECTEDLY SUCCESSFUL. A MR MAYO TRIED ALTERING LIGHTING, TEA BREAKS & WORKING HOURS AT A FACTORY IN CHICAGO IN 1924. EACH MODIFICATION PRODUCED AN INCREASED OUTPUT, BUT WHEN HE RETURNED THE WORKERS TO THEIR OLD ROUTINE, THEIR OUTPUT AGAIN WENT UP. VERY PUZZLED HE CONCLUDED THAT THE IMPROVEMENT WAS NOT DUE TO HIS ALTERATIONS, BUT TO THEIR ENJOYING THE EXPERIMENTS, GIVING THEM ADDED INTEREST IN THEIR JOBS.

HOW TO MAKE WORKERS WORK HARDER

SOME EARLY DISCIPLINE
BEFORE TRADE UNIONS SOME FACTORIES HAD FIERCE SYSTEMS OF FINES. A NOTORIOUS MILL NEAR MANCHESTER IMPOSED THE FOLLOWING TARIFF (TAKING THE AMOUNT DUE FROM THE 20p PER DAY WAGE):
★ LEAVING A WINDOW OPEN: 5p
★ FOUND DIRTY AT WORK: 5p
★ WASHING AT WORK: 5p
★ LEAVING GASLIGHT ON TOO LONG: 10p
★ WASTE LEFT ON SPINDLE: 5p
★ OFF SICK, IF NO REPLACEMENT AVAILABLE: 30p PER DAY TOWARDS COST OF STEAM ENGINE BEING KEPT GOING USELESSLY.

BISCUIT FACTORIES: THE FIRST MACHINE TO STAMP OUT BISCUITS WAS MADE BY MR CARR FROM AN OLD PRINTING PRESS. SOME MODERN STAMPING MACHINES ARE ENORMOUS TURNING OUT 6000 TONS OF BISCUITS PER DAY, ENOUGH FOR ABOUT 13 MILLION PACKETS.

CHOCOLATE FACTORIES: FOOD FACTORIES ARE AMAZINGLY LARGE. THE TOTAL ANNUAL TURNOVER OF AMERICA'S BIGGEST CHOCOLATE FACTORY, HERSHEY FOODS INC., IS £131,290,000. ONLY 7 TIMES SMALLER THAN THAT OF THE WORLD'S LARGEST COMPANY, GENERAL MOTORS.

COCA-COLA FACTORIES: ASTONISHINGLY HIGH SPEED & WIDESPREAD, THEY PRODUCE CANS & BOTTLES AT THE RATE OF 100 MILLION PER DAY IN 135 COUNTRIES.

HOW TO CUT TWO INTERLOCKING BANDS FROM THE MOEBIUS BAND
PIERCE BAND ⅓ OF THE WAY ACROSS & CUT ALL THE WAY ROUND TWICE, THEN CUT WILL JOIN UP & BAND WILL SEPARATE TO 2 LINKED BANDS, ONE TWICE AS LONG AS THE OTHER.

CUT ALONG DOTTED LINE

☆ FANS ☆
BROAD, FLAT INSTRUMENTS USED FOR COOLING

FANS & EDUCATION
LEARNING TO HANDLE & FLAP A FAN GRACEFULLY WAS CONSIDERED AN ESSENTIAL PART OF ANY YOUNG LADY'S EDUCATION IN THE 18TH CENTURY. ONE LONDON ACADEMY TRAINED ITS PUPILS TO PERFORM THE FOLLOWING COMMANDS TWICE DAILY:

HANDLE YOUR FANS
UNFURL YOUR FANS
DISCHARGE YOUR FANS
GROUND YOUR FANS
RECOVER YOUR FANS
FLUTTER YOUR FANS

FANS & DISGUISE
DOMINO & MASK FANS WERE HIGHLY EFFECTIVE FORMS OF DISGUISE. DOMINO FANS APPEARED PERFECTLY NORMAL, EXCEPT FOR TWO SMALL SECTIONS CUT OUT TO ENABLE ITS USER TO SEE WITHOUT BEING SEEN. THE MASK FAN WITH 2 EYEHOLES CUT IN A FACE PAINTED ON THE FABRIC WAS EVEN MORE EFFECTIVE AT CONCEALING THE WEARER'S IDENTITY.

FANS & VISION
THE LORGNETTE FAN HAD 2 SMALL LENSES BUILT INTO THE FABRIC. BY A GRACEFUL MOVEMENT OF HER FAN A SHORT-SIGHTED LADY COULD OBTAIN A CLEAR IMPRESSION OF A DISTANT ADMIRER.

FANS & COMMUNICATION
IN THE 19TH CENTURY VARIOUS FAN CODES WERE DEVISED TO ENABLE YOUNG LADIES TO CONVERSE SECRETLY WITH THEIR LOVERS. SPECIAL PHRASE BOOKS CONVERTED MESSAGES TO MOVEMENTS OF THE FAN. THESE BOOKS USUALLY INCLUDED ONLY AMOROUS PHRASES BUT FOR OTHER TOPICS THERE WAS ONE SYSTEM THAT USED A COMBINATION OF SIGNALS FOR EACH LETTER OF THE ALPHABET. THE FAN WAS FLAPPED VIGOROUSLY TO SIGNIFY THE END OF EACH WORD.

FANS & FIGHTING
JAPANESE MILITARY COMMANDERS CARRIED FANS, PRINCIPALLY FOR GESTICULATING DIRECTIONS. THEY ALSO SERVED AS WEAPONS IN EMERGENCIES BECAUSE THEY WERE MADE OF METAL & WERE VERY HEAVY.

HOW TO MAKE A FLY SOUND LIKE A GIANT MONSTER
TRAP A FLY IN A BAG OF GREASEPROOF PAPER (FROM AN EMPTY PACKET OF BREAKFAST CEREAL) HOLD BAG ON EAR & THE FLY'S FOOTSTEPS WILL SOUND TERRIFYING.

FANS & CHARIOTS
THE EARLIEST WRITTEN ACCOUNT OF THE USE OF FANS WAS BY THE WIFE OF THE EMPEROR TCHAO WONG OF CHINA 1052 B.C. THE MANUSCRIPT DESCRIBES HOW SHE KEPT A FAN IN HER CHARIOT TO BLOW DUST OFF THE WHEELS.

FANS & CHURCH
CHURCH & CHAPEL FANS WERE OFTEN PROVIDED FOR 18TH CENTURY CONGREGATIONS ON HOT SULTRY DAYS TO EQUIP THEM FOR THE LONG SERMONS THEN PREACHED. CHURCH FANS ARE INSCRIBED WITH THE CREED & THE 10 COMMANDMENTS, CHAPEL FANS WITH MORAL PICTURES & UPLIFTING CAPTIONS.

☆ FASHION ☆
EPHEMERAL CULTS OF ELEGANT APPAREL

WIGS
IN THE 1770s THERE WAS A BRIEF FEMALE CRAZE FOR HUGE WIGS, INCORPORATING UP TO 10 HEADS OF NATURAL HAIR. THEY OFTEN TOOK HALF A DAY TO MOUNT & ONCE ON WOULD BE MADE TO LAST A WEEK, WHICH FORCED THEIR OWNERS TO SLEEP WITH THEIR HEADS UPRIGHT & TO SQUAT ON THE FLOORS OF THEIR SEDAN CHAIRS. MOUSE-TRAPS WERE OFTEN ATTACHED TO THE INTERIOR & AFTER A FRENCH SEA VICTORY THERE WAS EVEN A SPELL WHEN MODEL BOATS WERE MOUNTED ON TOP. MEN'S 18TH CENTURY WIGS WERE HARDLY LESS SPECTACULAR, WITH NAMES SUCH AS:

ADONIS, ADORABLE, ARTICHOKE, APOTHECARY'S, GRIZZLED &...

CORSETS HAVE ALWAYS BEEN UNCOMFORTABLE, BUT THE REIGN OF QUEEN CATHERINE DE MEDICI (1519-89) MUST HAVE BEEN QUITE EXCRUCIATING FOR THE FRENCH NOBILITY. SHE DECREED A MAXIMUM WAIST OF 13in FOR LADIES AT COURT.

DOING UP BUTTONS
THE REASON WHY MEN & WOMEN HAVE BUTTONS ON DIFFERENT SIDES OF THEIR COATS IS OBSCURE. ONE SUGGESTION IS THAT A MAN'S PRIME NEED WAS TO BE ABLE TO REACH FOR HIS SWORD & THAT A WOMAN'S WAS TO SUCKLE HER OFFSPRING (THESE ACTIVITIES BEING MOST CONVENIENT FOR A RIGHT-HANDED PERSON WITH THE PRESENT ARRANGEMENT OF BUTTONS). MORE PROBABLY A MAN'S BUTTONS WERE ARRANGED SO THAT HE COULD DO THEM UP WITH HIS RIGHT HAND, BUT THAT A LADY WOULD NEVER NEED TO DO HERS UP, BEING ALWAYS DRESSED BY MAIDS.

DOING UP CORSETS

SPECS
SPECTACLES FIRST APPEARED IN THE 13TH CENTURY, WITH BIZARRE METHODS OF KEEPING THEM IN PLACE; INCLUDING ATTACHING THEM TO HATS & JACKETS & ELABORATE ARRANGEMENTS OF CHAINS & BALANCE WEIGHTS. THEY WERE VERY VALUABLE SO A MORE RELIABLE SOLUTION WAS EAGERLY SOUGHT. BY 1500 THEY WERE BEING HOOKED BEHIND THE EARS & POPE LEO X EVEN WENT HUNTING WEARING HIS IN 1520.

FALSE ECONOMIES
THE WHITE PLUMES OF THE HOUSEHOLD CAVALRY'S HELMETS, MADE OF WHALEBONE, WERE BECOMING ALARMINGLY EXPENSIVE SO NYLON WAS TRIED AS A SUBSTITUTE. HOWEVER IT WAS CONSIDERED TO BLOW ABOUT IN THE WIND TOO MUCH SO THEY REVERTED TO WHALEBONE. SOME ECONOMIES HAVE BEEN ACCEPTED BUT THEIR COMFORT HAS NOT BEEN COMPROMISED. THE LIFEGUARDS STILL SIT ON FUR RUGS; SHEEPSKINS FOR MEN, BEARSKINS FOR OFFICERS.

TROUSERS
INTRODUCED AT THE BEGINNING OF THE 19TH CENTURY, TROUSERS WERE AT FIRST CONSIDERED SHOCKING. ANY STUDENT AT TRINITY COLLEGE, CAMBRIDGE, FOUND WEARING TROUSERS IN CHAPEL OR HALL WAS DEEMED ABSENT & THE EDICT "UNDER NO CIRCUMSTANCES WHATSOEVER SHALL ANY PREACHER WHO WEARS TROUSERS BE ALLOWED TO OCCUPY A PULPIT" WAS ISSUED TO THE CLERGY OF SHEFFIELD. EVEN THE DUKE OF YORK WAS REFUSED ENTRY TO HIS CLUB FOR WEARING A PAIR IN 1814.

HOW TO SHOW STEEL IS LIGHTER THAN WATER
PLACE A STEEL PIN HORIZONTALLY ON THE SURFACE OF A BOWL OF WATER & IT WILL FLOAT (DUE TO SURFACE TENSION).

...CAULIFLOWER, ELEPHANT, GENTILLY, GRECIAN FLY, INCONSTANCE, IMPASSIANT, INDIFFERENCE, JALOUSIE, LUNATIQUE, MAW-WORM, NEGLIGENT, PHYSICAL, PIGEON'S WING, PRUDENCE PUFF, RAVIR, R...

...RHINOCEROS, SHE-DRAGON, SPINACH SEED, STAIRCASE, WILD BOAR'S BACK.

FEAR OF; BEING STARED AT – SCOPOPHOBIA; CROSSING A BRIDGE – GEPHYROPHOBIA; CERTAIN NAME – ONOMATOPHOBIA;

FEAR
PAINFUL EMOTION EXCITED BY DANGER

CHEMICAL FEAR

FEAR IS AN IMPORTANT PROTECTIVE INSTINCT. AT ANY HINT OF DANGER, NORADRENALIN IS RELEASED INTO THE BLOOD. THIS PREPARES THE BODY FOR ACTION.

SKIN GOES PALE AS BLOOD IS DIVERTED TO MUSCLES.

SWEATING INCREASES TO COOL MUSCLES.

FASTER BREATHING PROVIDES MORE OXYGEN FOR MUSCLES.

FAST HEARTBEATS PUSH MORE BLOOD TO THE MUSCLES.

GUT & BLADDER RELAX AS BLOOD IS DIVERTED FROM THEM TO MUSCLES.

INNATE FEAR
DUCKLINGS & GOSLINGS JUST AFTER HATCHING, SHOW FEAR WHEN THE SHAPE BELOW FLIES RIGHT (LOOKING LIKE A HAWK) BUT NOT WHEN IT FLIES LEFT (LOOKING LIKE A GOOSE). THIS SUGGESTS THAT THE FEAR IS INNATE, NOT LEARNT.

→ HAWK
← GOOSE

LEARNING & FEAR

DANGER KEEP OUT

YOUNG ANIMALS SHOW GREAT CURIOSITY & A DESIRE TO EXPLORE. THIS USUALLY DEVELOPS INTO A FEAR OF NOVELTY. THE INITIAL PERIOD FAMILIARISES THE ANIMAL WITH THE WORLD – THE LATER CAUTION HELPS IT TO AVOID DANGERS.

CURIOSITY & FEAR
MANY ANIMALS RETAIN THEIR CURIOSITY IN THE FACE OF MILD FEAR. GULLS, HEARING A DISTANT WARNING CRY, WILL FLY TO INVESTIGATE. GAZELLE, SPOTTING A CHEETAH, WILL APPROACH TO WITHIN 50M OF THE CAT.

REFUGE

THE YOUNG OF THE MOZAMBIQUE TILAPIA FISH SWIM INTO THEIR MOTHER'S MOUTH WHEN ALARMED.

APPETITE
NORADRENALIN AFFECTS APPETITE. INJECTIONS OF THE CHEMICAL DO NOT START RATS EATING BUT DO MAKE THEM EAT 3 TIMES AS MUCH AS NORMAL.

MEMORY
NORADRENALIN AFFECTS MEMORY. EXPERIMENTS HAVE SHOWN THAT SMALL DOSES IMPROVE MEMORY, BUT LARGE DOSES CAUSE MEMORY LOSS. THIS PARTLY EXPLAINS WHY PEOPLE MAKE MISTAKES UNDER EXTREME STRESS.

UNREASONABLE FEARS
THE CLASSIC METHOD OF CURING UNREASONABLE FEARS OR PHOBIAS IS 'DESENSITISATION'. THE PATIENT IS CONFRONTED WITH THE FEARED OBJECT IN EASY STAGES UNTIL IT BECOMES FAMILIAR.

REASONABLE FEARS

REASONABLE FEARS CAN ALSO BE DESENSITISED – MILITARY BATTLE TRAINING FAMILIARISES THE SOLDIER WITH DUMMY SHELL BURSTS ETC & REDUCES HIS FEAR WHEN CONFRONTED WITH THE REAL THING.

PARALYSIS

FEAR CAN INDUCE PARALYSIS IN MANY ANIMALS (LITERALLY FREEZING WITH TERROR). IT HAS BEEN FOUND THAT THIS IS CAUSED BY ANOTHER CHEMICAL RELEASED INTO THE BLOOD – CALLED SEROTONIN.

CALMING DRUGS
CHEMICALS HAVE BEEN DISCOVERED WHICH PREVENT NORADRENALIN INCREASING THE HEART RATE. THEY ARE CALLED BETA BLOCKERS & REDUCE THE SENSATION OF FEAR.

HOW TO FIND IF MATHS MAKES YOU FRIGHTENED

STRESS CAN PRODUCE THE SAME PHYSICAL REACTIONS AS FEAR. THE HEARTBEAT OF PEOPLE DOING MENTAL ARITHMETIC CAN RISE DRAMATICALLY. TRY COUNTING A FRIEND'S HEARTBEATS BEFORE, DURING & AFTER MENTAL ARITHMETIC.

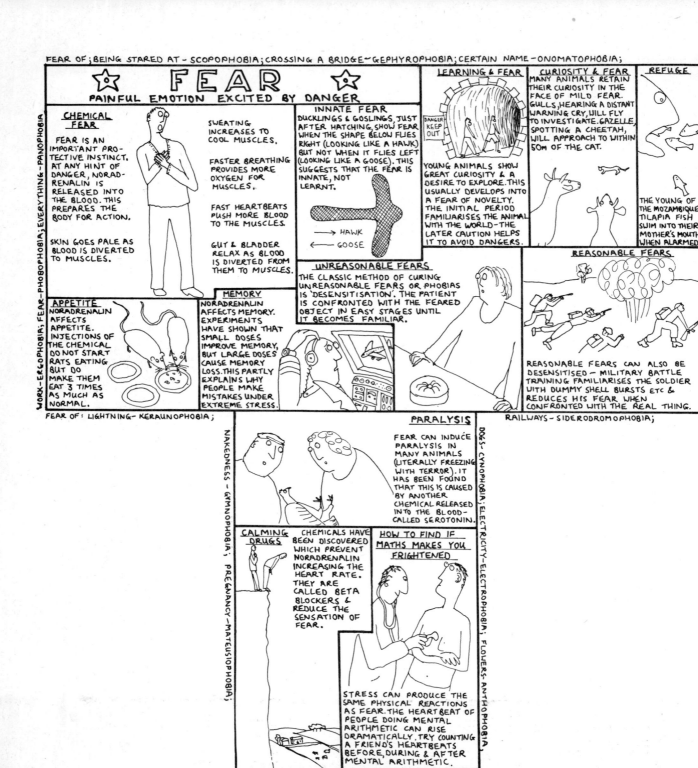

FEAR OF: LIGHTNING – KERAUNOPHOBIA;

RAILWAYS – SIDERODROMOPHOBIA;

FUR – DORAPHOBIA; FISH – ICHTHYOPHOBIA;

WORK – ERGOPHOBIA; FEAR – PHOBOPHOBIA; EVERYTHING – PANOPHOBIA;

ANIMALS – ZOOPHOBIA; BEING DIRTY – AUTOMYSOPHOBIA; BLOOD – HEMATOPHOBIA

NAKEDNESS – GYMNOPHOBIA; PREGNANCY – MATEUSIOPHOBIA;

DOGS – CYNOPHOBIA; ELECTRICITY – ELECTROPHOBIA; FLOWERS – ANTHOPHOBIA;

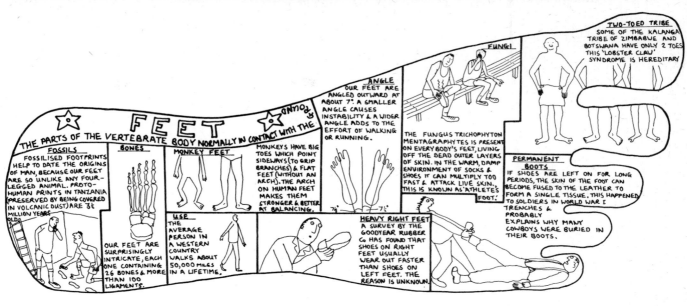

FEET (round)

THE PARTS OF THE VERTEBRATE BODY NORMALLY IN CONTACT WITH THE GROUND

FOSSILS
FOSSILISED FOOTPRINTS HELP TO DATE THE ORIGINS OF MAN, BECAUSE OUR FEET ARE SO UNLIKE ANY FOUR-LEGGED ANIMAL. PROTO-HUMAN PRINTS IN TANZANIA (PRESERVED BY BEING COVERED IN VOLCANIC DUST) ARE 3½ MILLION YEARS OLD.

BONES

MONKEY FEET
MONKEYS HAVE BIG TOES WHICH POINT SIDEWAYS (TO GRIP BRANCHES) & FLAT FEET (WITHOUT AN ARCH). THE ARCH ON HUMAN FEET MAKES THEM STRONGER & BETTER AT BALANCING.

USE
THE AVERAGE PERSON IN A WESTERN COUNTRY WALKS ABOUT 50,000 MILES IN A LIFETIME.

OUR FEET ARE SURPRISINGLY INTRICATE, EACH ONE CONTAINING 26 BONES & MORE THAN 100 LIGAMENTS.

ANGLE
OUR FEET ARE ANGLED OUTWARD AT ABOUT 7°. A SMALLER ANGLE CAUSES INSTABILITY & A WIDER ANGLE ADDS TO THE EFFORT OF WALKING OR RUNNING.

HEAVY RIGHT FEET
A SURVEY BY THE GOODYEAR RUBBER Co HAS FOUND THAT SHOES ON RIGHT FEET USUALLY WEAR OUT FASTER THAN SHOES ON LEFT FEET. THE REASON IS UNKNOWN.

FUNGI
THE FUNGUS TRICHOPHYTON MENTAGRAPHYTES IS PRESENT ON EVERYBODY'S FEET, LIVING OFF THE DEAD OUTER LAYERS OF SKIN. IN THE WARM, DAMP ENVIRONMENT OF SOCKS & SHOES IT CAN MULTIPLY TOO FAST & ATTACK LIVE SKIN. THIS IS KNOWN AS 'ATHLETE'S FOOT'.

TWO-TOED TRIBE
SOME OF THE KALANGA TRIBE OF ZIMBABWE AND BOTSWANA HAVE ONLY 2 TOES. THIS 'LOBSTER CLAW' SYNDROME IS HEREDITARY.

PERMANENT BOOTS
IF SHOES ARE LEFT ON FOR LONG PERIODS, THE SKIN OF THE FOOT CAN BECOME FUSED TO THE LEATHER TO FORM A SINGLE TISSUE. THIS HAPPENED TO SOLDIERS IN WORLD WAR I TRENCHES & PROBABLY EXPLAINS WHY MANY COWBOYS WERE BURIED IN THEIR BOOTS.

☆ FERTILISERS ☆

SUBSTANCES PROMOTING ABUNDANT GROWTH OF PLANTS

DISCOVERING FERTILISERS
VAN HELMONT'S FAMOUS EXPERIMENT WITH A WILLOW TREE (c1600) FIRST SHOWED THAT THE MATERIAL FOR PLANT GROWTH IS PRINCIPALLY EXTRACTED FROM THE AIR & WATER. HE DRIED SOME EARTH, WEIGHED IT & PLANTED A WILLOW TREE SHOOT. AFTER 5 YEARS, THE TREE HAD INCREASED IN WEIGHT FROM 5lb TO 169 lb. HE DRIED THE EARTH AGAIN & REWEIGHED IT. THIS HAD REDUCED BY ONLY 2 OUNCES, REPRESENTING THE ELEMENTS EXTRACTED FROM THE SOIL WHICH ARE ESSENTIAL TO GROWTH. FERTILISERS ARE CHEMICALS WHICH REPLENISH THESE NUTRIENT ELEMENTS.

FERTILISER INGREDIENTS
DIFFERENT ELEMENTS STIMULATE DIFFERENT ASPECTS OF GROWTH:
★ POTASSIUM STIMULATES FLOWERS & FRUITS
★ PHOSPHOROUS STIMULATES ROOTS (& THUS IS GOOD FOR POTATOES & ROOT CROPS)
★ NITROGEN STIMULATES LEAVES & SHOOTS (& THUS IS GOOD FOR CABBAGES, GRASSES, LETTUCES ETC).

HOME-MADE FERTILISER
IT WAS FIRST REALISED THAT SUBSTANCES OTHER THAN COMPOST & MANURE COULD STIMULATE PLANT GROWTH IN THE 16TH CENTURY. LIME, CHALK, ASHES, BONE-MEAL & DRIED BLOOD WERE USED, TOGETHER WITH A NUMBER OF LESS BENEFICIAL MATERIALS.

CEMENT FERTILISER
A SPRINKLING OF PORTLAND CEMENT PLOUGHED INTO THE GROUND A MONTH BEFORE PLANTING HAS INCREASED THE SUGAR CANE YIELDS IN QUEENSLAND, AUSTRALIA, BY 50%. THIS IS THOUGHT TO BE DUE TO A LACK OF SILICATE IN THE SOIL. IT WOULD NOT WORK IN DAMP CLIMATES, AS THE CEMENT IS LIABLE TO SET IN LUMPS. HOWEVER, A RECENT PATENT CLAIMS THAT ADDING 25% SUGAR TO THE CEMENT OVERCOMES THIS PROBLEM.

FACTORY FERTILISER
THE FIRST FACTORY-MADE FERTILISER WAS SUPERPHOSPHATE PATENTED IN 1842 & MADE BY TREATING BONES WITH SULPHURIC ACID. LARGE-SCALE FACTORY FERTILISER PRODUCTION STARTED AFTER WORLD WAR I, UTILISING THE NITRATE PRODUCTION CAPACITY DEVELOPED DURING THE WAR FOR MAKING EXPLOSIVES.

FERTILISER v CLOVER
CURRENT FARMING POLICY INVOLVES USING LARGE QUANTITIES OF NITROGEN FERTILISERS ON GRAZING LAND. THIS SUPPOSEDLY PAYS FOR ITSELF IN INCREASED GRASS YIELDS. HOWEVER, RECENT RESEARCH SHOWS THAT THE INCREASE IN YIELD IS LESS THAN IT SHOULD BE BECAUSE OF DAMAGE INFLICTED ON THE GRASS BY THE ANIMALS. ALSO, SOME AUTHORITIES BELIEVE THAT ADDING CLOVER TO THE SEEDING MIXTURE WOULD RAISE THE SOIL NITROGEN WITHOUT THE NEED FOR ANY FERTILISER.

FERTILISER v COMPOST
MANURE & COMPOST CONTAIN MOST OF THE ELEMENTS NEEDED FOR PLANT GROWTH, 'RECYCLED' FROM PREVIOUS PLANTS. THEY HAVE THE EXTRA ADVANTAGE THAT THEY IMPROVE THE SOIL TEXTURE (MAKING IT EASIER FOR PLANTS TO ABSORB WATER). THEIR DISADVANTAGE IS THAT SOME OF THE ESSENTIAL ELEMENTS TEND TO BE WASHED OUT BY RAIN.

GROW HUGE EXTRA SPECIAL FERT-ILISER

HOW TO EAT KNOTS
TIE A LOOP KNOT (SEE LEFT) WITH A VERY SMALL LOOP. HOLD ENDS OF STRING IN HANDS (SEE RIGHT) & PLACE KNOT IN MOUTH. CHEW VIGOROUSLY & TWIST WRISTS TO STRETCH STRING & PULL OUT KNOT. OPEN MOUTH TO REVEAL VANISHED 'EATEN' KNOT.

☆ FILMS ☆
SEQUENCES OF PHOTOGRAPHS GIVING ILLUSION OF MOVEMENT

BOAT RACE FIRST
THE FIRST COMMERCIAL FILM MADE IN BRITAIN WAS A NEWSREEL OF THE OXFORD & CAMBRIDGE BOAT RACE OF 1896.

IT WAS MADE BY A PHOTOGRAPHER (B. ACRES) & A SCIENTIFIC INSTRUMENT MAKER (R.W. PAUL), WHO ALSO BUILT THE CAMERA & PROJECTOR.

VANISHING KELLY
THE FIRST FEATURE FILM (LONGER THAN AN HOUR) WAS 'THE STORY OF THE KELLY GANG', MADE IN AUSTRALIA IN 1906. THE ACTOR PLAYING KELLY MYSTERIOUSLY DISAPPEARED BEFORE FILMING WAS COMPLETED. THE REMAINING SCENES WERE TAKEN IN LONG SHOT WITH AN EXTRA STANDING IN.

HOLLYWOOD
HOLLYWOOD BECAME THE CENTRE OF THE US FILM INDUSTRY BECAUSE IT HAD UNINTERRUPTED SUNSHINE & A WIDE VARIETY OF LOCAL SCENERY. THERE WERE SUITABLE LOCATIONS FOR TROPICAL ISLANDS, DESERTS, MOUNTAINS & ENGLISH COUNTRYSIDE. ONLY JUNGLES WERE MISSING, SO MOST STUDIOS BUILT THEIR OWN, COMPLETE WITH ZOOS.

CHINESE SUSPICION
THE INHABITANTS OF HONG KONG WERE SO SUSPICIOUS OF THE EVIL POWER OF THE 'MOVING SPIRITS' ON THEIR FIRST FILMS, THAT THE CINEMA PROPRIETOR HAD TO PAY AUDIENCES TO COME FOR THE FIRST THREE WEEKS.

UNUSUAL PUBLICITY
'RAJA HARISCHANDRA' (INDIA'S FIRST FEATURE FILM 1912) WAS ADVERTISED AS 'A PERFORMANCE WITH 57,000 PHOTOGRAPHS - A PICTURE 2 MILES LONG'.

'AFTER RAIN, CLEAR SKIES' (AN EARLY CHINESE SOUND FILM, 1931) WAS ADVERTISED WITH THE INFORMATION: 'ON THE 977 OCCASIONS FOR DIALOGUE, 6,935 SENTENCES ARE SPOKEN.'

THE EGYPTIAN (US, 1954) WAS ADVERTISED AS CONTAINING 10,965 PYRAMIDS, 5,337 DANCING GIRLS, A MILLION SWAYING BULRUSHES & 802 SACRED BULLS.

SHOCKING DIRECTION
DIRECTORS PANICKED WHEN SOUND WAS FIRST INTRODUCED BECAUSE THEY WERE ACCUSTOMED TO SHOUTING INSTRUCTIONS TO THE ACTORS DURING TAKES. ONE WENT SO FAR AS TO ATTACH ELECTRODES ALL OVER THE ACTORS' BODIES & SIGNALLING CODED INSTRUCTIONS BY MILD ELECTRIC SHOCKS.

LIVE SOUND
THAILAND LACKED THE EQUIPMENT TO MAKE FILMS WITH SOUND UNTIL THE 1970s. PREVIOUSLY, DIALOGUE WAS PROVIDED BY LIVE ACTORS SPEAKING THE FILM STARS' LINES FROM A BOOTH NEXT TO THE PROJECTIONIST.

ENTHUSIASM
PRESIDENT TITO WATCHED MORE THAN 200 FILMS A YEAR, ONE EVERY NIGHT HE WAS IN BELGRADE.

APPRECIATION
FILM APPRECIATION IS A COMPULSORY SUBJECT IN HUNGARIAN SECONDARY SCHOOLS.

LET'S GET OUT OF HERE
A RECENT SURVEY OF 150 US FEATURE FILMS MADE SINCE ... ED THAT THE PHRASE 'LET'S GET OUT OF HERE' APPEARED AT LEAST ONCE IN 84% OF THE FILMS.

EXTRAS
87,000 EXTRAS WERE USED IN THE FILM 'KOLBERG' - A RECORD, SHOT BY THE NAZIS 1943-4. THE FILM USED WHOLE ARMY DIVISIONS DIVERTED FROM THE FRONT TO DRESS UP AS NAPOLEONIC SOLDIERS.

FILMS MADE PER YEAR

INDIA	445
US	...
ITALY	204
FRANCE	191
JAPAN	367
BRITAIN	...

TOTAL CINEMA AUDIENCES PER YEAR

INDIA	3235×10^6
US	1130×10^6
ITALY	513740
FRANCE	172×10^6
JAPAN	166×10^6
BRITAIN	127×10^6

SMELLIES
THERE WAS A VOGUE FOR 'SMELLIES' (FILMS COMBINED WITH APPROPRIATE SMELLS PIPED TO EACH SEAT) IN AMERICA IN 1959-60. IN SMELLOVISION (OR AROMARAMA) A RANGE OF 72 SMELLS WERE CONTROLLED FROM THE SCENT TRACK OF THE FILM.

HOW TO MAKE CUSTARD PIES
REAL CUSTARD PIES FROM BAKERS DISINTEGRATE TOO EASILY IN MID-FLIGHT. THIS IS THE RECIPE FOR CINEMA CUSTARD PIES:

BASE: ORDINARY SHORT CRUST PASTRY, DOUBLE USUAL THICKNESS (ABOUT 6mm).

FILLING: FLOUR & WATER PASTE, THE CONSISTENCY OF THICK CUSTARD, WITH SOME WHIPPED CREAM.

ROLL OUT & BAKE PASTRY AS NORMAL RECIPE. SPREAD FILLING & LEAVE FOR AT LEAST AN HOUR.

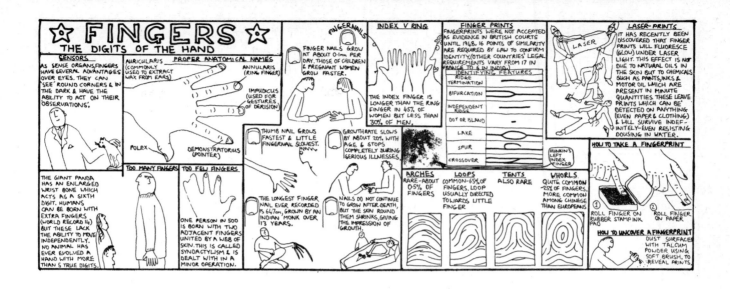

☆ FINGERS ☆
THE DIGITS OF THE HAND

SENSORS
AS SENSE ORGANS, FINGERS HAVE SEVERAL ADVANTAGES OVER EYES. THEY CAN 'SEE' ROUND CORNERS & IN THE DARK & HAVE THE ABILITY TO ACT ON THEIR OBSERVATIONS.

PROPER ANATOMICAL NAMES
AURICULARIS (COMMONLY USED TO EXTRACT WAX FROM EARS)
ANNULARIS (RING FINGER)
IMPUDICUS (USED FOR GESTURES OF DERISION)
POLEX
DEMONSTRATORIUS (POINTER)

TOO MANY FINGERS

TOO FEW FINGERS
ONE PERSON IN 500 IS BORN WITH TWO ADJACENT FINGERS UNITED BY A WEB OF SKIN. THIS IS CALLED SYNDACTYLISM & IS DEALT WITH IN A MINOR OPERATION.

THE GIANT PANDA HAS AN ENLARGED WRIST BONE WHICH ACTS AS A SIXTH DIGIT. HUMANS CAN BE BORN WITH EXTRA FINGERS (WORLD RECORD 14) BUT THESE LACK THE ABILITY TO MOVE INDEPENDENTLY. NO ANIMAL WAS EVER EVOLVED A HAND WITH MORE THAN 5 TRUE DIGITS.

FINGERNAILS
FINGER NAILS GROW AT ABOUT 0·1mm PER DAY. THOSE OF CHILDREN & PREGNANT WOMEN GROW FASTER.
THUMB NAIL GROWS FASTEST & LITTLE FINGERNAIL SLOWEST.
GROWTHRATE SLOWS BY ABOUT 20% WITH AGE & STOPS COMPLETELY DURING SERIOUS ILLNESSES.
THE LONGEST FINGER NAIL EVER RECORDED IS 64.7cm, GROWN BY AN INDIAN MONK OVER 13 YEARS.
NAILS DO NOT CONTINUE TO GROW AFTER DEATH, BUT THE SKIN ROUND THEM SHRINKS, GIVING THE IMPRESSION OF GROWTH.

INDEX V RING
THE INDEX FINGER IS LONGER THAN THE RING FINGER IN 45% OF WOMEN BUT LESS THAN 30% OF MEN.

FINGER PRINTS
FINGERPRINTS WERE NOT ACCEPTED AS EVIDENCE IN BRITISH COURTS UNTIL 1948. 16 POINTS OF SIMILARITY ARE REQUIRED BY LAW TO CONFIRM IDENTITY. (OTHER COUNTRIES' LEGAL REQUIREMENTS VARY FROM 17 IN FRANCE TO 6 IN INDIA).

IDENTIFYING FEATURES

RIDGE TERMINATION	
BIFURCATION	
INDEPENDENT RIDGE	
DOT OR ISLAND	
LAKE	
SPUR	
CROSSOVER	

ARCHES RARE-ABOUT 0·5% OF FINGERS

LOOPS COMMON-65% OF FINGERS. LOOP USUALLY DIRECTED TOWARDS LITTLE FINGER

TENTS ALSO RARE

WHORLS QUITE COMMON-25% OF FINGERS, MORE COMMON AMONG CHINESE THAN EUROPEANS

HUNKIN'S LEFT INDEX FINGER

LASER-PRINTS
IT HAS RECENTLY BEEN DISCOVERED THAT FINGER PRINTS WILL FLUORESCE (GLOW) UNDER LASER LIGHT. THIS EFFECT IS NOT DUE TO NATURAL OILS IN THE SKIN BUT TO CHEMICALS SUCH AS PAINTS, INKS & MOTOR OIL WHICH ARE PRESENT IN MINUTE QUANTITIES. THESE LEAVE PRINTS WHICH CAN BE DETECTED ON ANYTHING (EVEN PAPER & CLOTHING) & WILL SURVIVE INDEFINITELY - EVEN RESISTING DOUSING IN WATER.

HOW TO TAKE A FINGERPRINT
① ROLL FINGER ON RUBBER STAMP INK PAD
② ROLL FINGER ON PAPER

HOW TO UNCOVER A FINGERPRINT
DUST SURFACES WITH TALCUM POWDER USING SOFT BRUSH, TO REVEAL PRINTS.

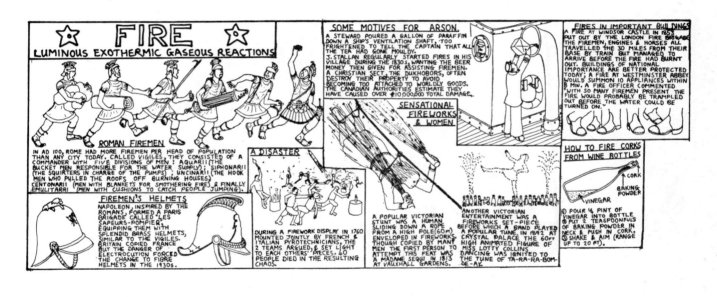

FIRE
LUMINOUS EXOTHERMIC GASEOUS REACTIONS

ROMAN FIREMEN
IN AD 100, ROME HAD MORE FIREMEN PER HEAD OF POPULATION THAN ANY CITY TODAY. CALLED VIGILES, THEY CONSISTED OF A COMMANDER WITH FIVE DIVISIONS OF MEN: AQUARII (THE BUCKET MEN RESPONSIBLE FOR THE WATER SUPPLY); SIPHONARII (THE SQUIRTERS IN CHARGE OF THE PUMPS); UNCINARII (THE HOOK MEN WHO PULLED THE ROOFS OFF BURNING HOUSES) CENTONARII (MEN WITH BLANKETS FOR SMOTHERING FIRE) & FINALLY EMULITARRI (MEN WITH CUSHIONS TO CATCH PEOPLE JUMPING).

FIREMEN'S HELMETS
NAPOLEON, INSPIRED BY THE ROMANS, FORMED A PARIS BRIGADE CALLED LES SAPEURS-POMPIER EQUIPPING THEM WITH SPLENDID BRASS HELMETS, SIMILAR TO THE VIGILES. BRITAIN COPIED FRANCE BUT THE DANGER OF ELECTROCUTION FORCED THE CHANGE TO FIBRE HELMETS IN THE 1930s.

A DISASTER
DURING A FIREWORK DISPLAY IN 1760 MOUNTED JOINTLY BY FRENCH & ITALIAN PYROTECHNICIANS, THE 2 TEAMS ARGUED, & SET LIGHT TO EACH OTHERS' PIECES. 40 PEOPLE DIED IN THE RESULTING CHAOS.

SOME MOTIVES FOR ARSON
A STEWARD POURED A GALLON OF PARAFFIN DOWN A SHIP'S VENTILATION SHAFT, 'TOO FRIGHTENED TO TELL THE CAPTAIN THAT ALL THE TEA HAD GONE MOULDY.
J. STALLAN REGULARLY STARTED FIRES IN HIS VILLAGE DURING THE 1830s, WANTING THE BEER MONEY THEN GIVEN FOR ASSISTING FIREMEN.
A CHRISTIAN SECT, THE DUKHOBORS, OFTEN DESTROY THEIR PROPERTY TO AVOID BECOMING TOO ATTACHED TO WORLDLY GOODS. THE CANADIAN AUTHORITIES ESTIMATE THEY HAVE CAUSED OVER £10,000,000 TOTAL DAMAGE.

SENSATIONAL FIREWORKS & WOMEN
A POPULAR VICTORIAN STUNT WAS A HUMAN SLIDING DOWN A ROPE FROM A HIGH POLE (60m) ENVELOPED IN FIREWORKS THOUGH COPIED BY MANY MEN, THE FIRST PERSON TO ATTEMPT THIS FEAT WAS A MADAME SEQUI IN 1813 AT VAUXHALL GARDENS.

ANOTHER VICTORIAN ENTERTAINMENT WAS A FIREWORKS SET-PIECE BEFORE WHICH A BAND PLAYED. A POPULAR TUNE, IN 1892 AT CRYSTAL PALACE, THE 60ft HIGH ANIMATED FIGURE OF MISS LOTTY COLLINS DANCING WAS IGNITED TO THE TUNE OF TA-RA-RA-BOM-DE-AY.

FIRES IN IMPORTANT BUILDINGS
A FIRE AT WINDSOR CASTLE IN 1853 WAS PUT OUT BY THE LONDON FIRE BRIGADE. THE FIREMEN, ENGINES & HORSES ALL TRAVELLED THE 30 MILES FROM THEIR BASE BY TRAIN BUT MANAGED TO ARRIVE BEFORE THE FIRE HAD BURNT OUT. BUILDINGS OF NATIONAL IMPORTANCE ARE BETTER PROTECTED TODAY; A FIRE AT WESTMINSTER ABBEY WOULD SUMMON 10 APPLIANCES WITHIN 8 MIN. A FIRE OFFICER COMMENTED WITH SO MANY FIREMEN PRESENT THE FIRE WOULD PROBABLY BE TRAMPLED OUT BEFORE THE WATER COULD BE TURNED ON.

HOW TO FIRE CORKS FROM WINE BOTTLES
A CORK
BAKING POWDER
VINEGAR
① POUR ¼ PINT OF VINEGAR INTO BOTTLE ② PUT 2 TEASPOONFULS OF BAKING POWDER IN NECK & PUSH CORK. ③ SHAKE & AIM (RANGE UP TO 20 FT).

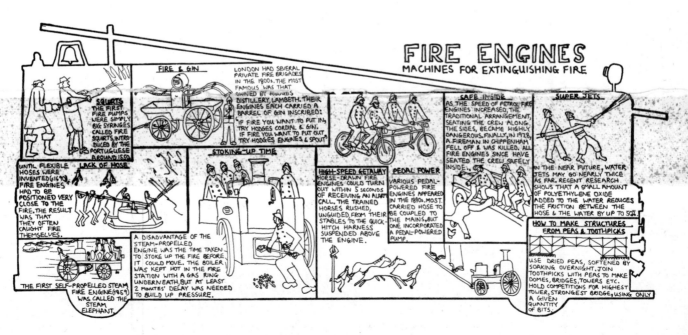

FIRE ENGINES
MACHINES FOR EXTINGUISHING FIRE

SQUIRTS
THE FIRST FIRE PUMPS WERE SIMPLY BIG SYRINGES CALLED FIRE SQUIRTS, INTRODUCED BY THE PORTUGUESE AROUND 1550.

LACK OF HOSE
UNTIL FLEXIBLE HOSES WERE INVENTED (c.1670) FIRE ENGINES HAD TO BE POSITIONED VERY CLOSE TO THE FIRE. THE RESULT WAS THAT THEY OFTEN CAUGHT FIRE THEMSELVES.

THE FIRST SELF-PROPELLED STEAM FIRE ENGINE (1859) WAS CALLED THE STEAM ELEPHANT.

FIRE & GIN
LONDON HAD SEVERAL PRIVATE FIRE BRIGADES IN THE 1800s. THE MOST FAMOUS WAS THAT OWNED BY HODGES DISTILLERY, LAMBETH. THEIR ENGINES EACH CARRIED A BARREL OF GIN INSCRIBED:
IF FIRE YOU WANT TO PUT IN, TRY HODGES CORDIAL & GIN. IF FIRE YOU WANT TO PUT OUT, TRY HODGES ENGINES & SPOUT.

STOKING-UP TIME
A DISADVANTAGE OF THE STEAM-PROPELLED ENGINE WAS THE TIME TAKEN TO STOKE UP THE FIRE BEFORE IT COULD MOVE. THE BOILER WAS KEPT HOT IN THE FIRE STATION WITH A GAS RING UNDERNEATH, BUT AT LEAST 2 MINUTES' DELAY WAS NEEDED TO BUILD UP PRESSURE.

HIGH-SPEED GETAWAY
HORSE-DRAWN FIRE ENGINES COULD TURN OUT WITHIN 5 SECONDS OF RECEIVING AN ALARM CALL. THE TRAINED HORSES RUSHED, UNGUIDED, FROM THEIR STABLES TO THE QUICK HITCH HARNESS SUSPENDED ABOVE THE ENGINE.

PEDAL POWER
VARIOUS PEDAL-POWERED FIRE ENGINES APPEARED IN THE 1890s. MOST CARRIED HOSE TO BE COUPLED TO THE MAINS, BUT ONE INCORPORATED A PEDAL-POWERED PUMP.

SAFE INSIDE
AS THE SPEED OF PETROL FIRE ENGINES INCREASED, THE TRADITIONAL ARRANGEMENT, SEATING THE CREW ALONG THE SIDES, BECAME HIGHLY DANGEROUS. FINALLY, IN 1928, A FIREMAN IN CHIPPENHAM FELL OFF & WAS KILLED. ALL FIRE ENGINES SINCE HAVE SEATED THE CREW SAFELY INSIDE.

SUPER JETS
IN THE NEAR FUTURE, WATER JETS MAY GO NEARLY TWICE AS FAR. REGENT RESEARCH SHOWS THAT A SMALL AMOUNT OF POLYETHYLENE OXIDE ADDED TO THE WATER REDUCES THE FRICTION BETWEEN THE HOSE & THE WATER BY UP TO 50%.

HOW TO MAKE STRUCTURES FROM PEAS & TOOTHPICKS
USE DRIED PEAS, SOFTENED BY SOAKING OVERNIGHT. JOIN TOOTHPICKS WITH PEAS TO MAKE DOMES, BRIDGES, TOWERS ETC. HOLD COMPETITIONS FOR HIGHEST TOWER, STRONGEST BRIDGE, USING ONLY A GIVEN QUANTITY OF BITS.

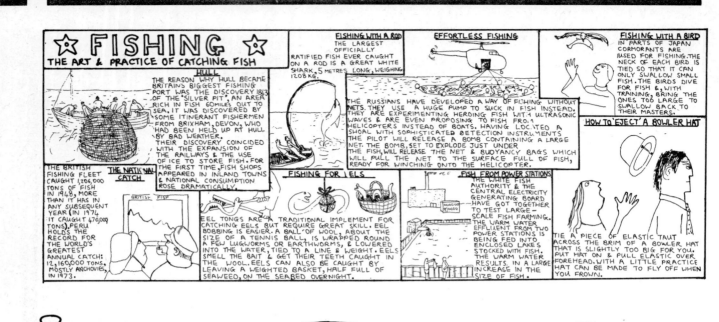

☆ FISHING ☆
THE ART & PRACTICE OF CATCHING FISH

HULL

THE REASON WHY HULL BECAME BRITAINS BIGGEST FISHING PORT WAS THE DISCOVERY 1843 OF THE 'SILVER PIT', AN AREA RICH IN FISH 60 MILES OUT TO SEA. IT WAS DISCOVERED BY SOME ITINERANT FISHERMEN FROM BRIXHAM, DEVON, WHO HAD BEEN HELD UP AT HULL BY BAD WEATHER.
THEIR DISCOVERY COINCIDED WITH THE EXPANSION OF THE RAILWAYS & THE USE OF ICE TO STORE FISH. FOR THE FIRST TIME, FISH SHOPS APPEARED IN INLAND TOWNS & NATIONAL CONSUMPTION ROSE DRAMATICALLY.

THE NATIONAL CATCH

THE BRITISH FISHING FLEET CAUGHT 1,206,000 TONS OF FISH IN 1948, MORE THAN IT HAS IN ANY SUBSEQUENT YEAR (IN 1974 IT CAUGHT 470,000 TONS). PERU HOLDS THE RECORD FOR THE WORLD'S GREATEST ANNUAL CATCH: 12,160,000 TONS, MOSTLY ANCHOVIES, IN 1973.

FISHING WITH A ROD

THE LARGEST OFFICIALLY RATIFIED FISH EVER CAUGHT ON A ROD IS A GREAT WHITE SHARK, 5 METRES LONG, WEIGHING 1208 KG.

EFFORTLESS FISHING

THE RUSSIANS HAVE DEVELOPED A WAY OF FISHING WITHOUT NETS. THEY USE A HUGE PUMP TO SUCK IN FISH INSTEAD. THEY ARE EXPERIMENTING HERDING FISH WITH ULTRASONIC WAVES & ARE EVEN PROPOSING TO FISH FROM HELICOPTERS. INSTEAD OF BOATS, HAVING LOCATED A SHOAL WITH SOPHISTICATED DETECTION INSTRUMENTS THE PILOT WILL RELEASE A BOMB CONTAINING A LARGE NET. THE BOMB, SET TO EXPLODE JUST UNDER THE FISH, WILL RELEASE THE NET & BUOYANCY BAGS WHICH WILL PULL THE NET TO THE SURFACE FULL OF FISH, READY FOR WINCHING ONTO THE HELICOPTER.

FISHING FOR EELS

EEL TONGS ARE A TRADITIONAL IMPLEMENT FOR CATCHING EELS BUT REQUIRE GREAT SKILL. EEL BOBBING IS EASIER. A BALL OF WOOL, ABOUT THE SIZE OF A TENNIS BALL, IS WRAPPED ROUND A FEW LUGWORMS OR EARTHWORMS, & LOWERED INTO THE WATER, TIED TO A LINE & WEIGHT. EELS SMELL THE BAIT & GET THEIR TEETH CAUGHT IN THE WOOL. EELS CAN ALSO BE CAUGHT BY LEAVING A WEIGHTED BASKET, HALF FULL OF SEAWEED, ON THE SEABED OVERNIGHT.

FISH FROM POWER STATIONS

THE WHITE FISH AUTHORITY & THE CENTRAL ELECTRICITY GENERATING BOARD HAVE GOT TOGETHER TO TEST LARGE-SCALE FISH FARMING. THE WARM WATER EFFLUENT FROM TWO POWER STATIONS IS BEING FED INTO ENCLOSED LAKES STOCKED WITH FISH. THE WARM WATER RESULTS, IN A LARGE INCREASE IN THE SIZE OF FISH.

FISHING WITH A BIRD

IN PARTS OF JAPAN CORMORANTS ARE USED FOR FISHING. THE NECK OF EACH BIRD IS TIED SO THAT IT CAN ONLY SWALLOW SMALL FISH. THE BIRDS DIVE FOR FISH &, WITH TRAINING, BRING THE ONES TOO LARGE TO SWALLOW BACK TO THEIR MASTERS.

HOW TO 'EJECT' A BOWLER HAT

TIE A PIECE OF ELASTIC TAUT ACROSS THE BRIM OF A BOWLER HAT THAT IS SLIGHTLY TOO BIG FOR YOU. PUT HAT ON & PULL ELASTIC OVER FOREHEAD. WITH A LITTLE PRACTICE THE HAT CAN BE MADE TO FLY OFF WHEN YOU FROWN.

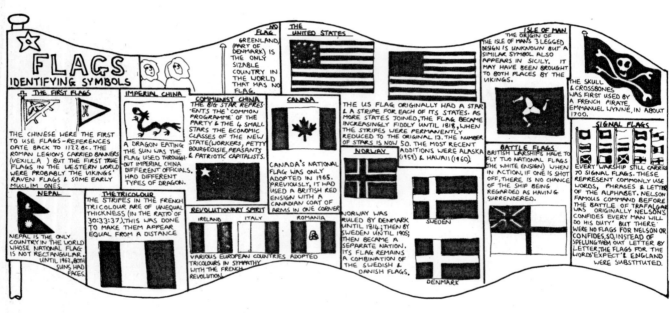

FLAGS
IDENTIFYING SYMBOLS

THE FIRST FLAGS

THE CHINESE WERE THE FIRST TO USE FLAGS – REFERENCES DATE BACK TO 1122 BC. THE ROMAN LEGIONS CARRIED BANNERS (VEXILLA.) BUT THE FIRST TRUE FLAGS IN THE WESTERN WORLD WERE PROBABLY THE VIKINGS' RAVEN FLAGS & SOME EARLY MUSLIM ONES.

IMPERIAL CHINA

A DRAGON EATING THE SUN WAS THE FLAG USED THROUGHOUT IMPERIAL CHINA. DIFFERENT OFFICIALS HAD DIFFERENT TYPES OF DRAGON.

COMMUNIST CHINA

THE BIG STAR REPRESENTS THE 'COMMON PROGRAMME' OF THE PARTY & THE 4 SMALL STARS THE ECONOMIC CLASSES OF THE NEW STATE (WORKERS, PETTY BOURGEOISIE, PEASANTS & PATRIOTIC CAPITALISTS.

NO FLAG

GREENLAND (PART OF DENMARK) IS THE ONLY SIZABLE COUNTRY IN THE WORLD THAT HAS NO FLAG.

THE UNITED STATES

THE US FLAG ORIGINALLY HAD A STAR & A STRIPE FOR EACH OF ITS STATES. AS MORE STATES JOINED, THE FLAG BECAME INCREASINGLY FIDDLY UNTIL 1818, WHEN THE STRIPES WERE PERMANENTLY REDUCED TO THE ORIGINAL 13. THE NUMBER OF STARS IS NOW 50. THE MOST RECENT ADDITIONS WERE ALASKA (1959) & HAWAII (1960).

CANADA

CANADA'S NATIONAL FLAG WAS ONLY ADOPTED IN 1965. PREVIOUSLY, IT HAD USED A BRITISH RED ENSIGN WITH A CANADIAN COAT OF ARMS IN ONE CORNER.

NORWAY

NORWAY WAS RULED BY DENMARK UNTIL 1814; THEN BY SWEDEN UNTIL 1905; THEN BECAME A SEPARATE NATION. ITS FLAG REMAINS A COMBINATION OF THE SWEDISH & DANISH FLAGS.

SWEDEN

DENMARK

ISLE OF MAN

THE ORIGIN OF THE ISLE OF MAN'S 3 LEGGED DESIGN IS UNKNOWN BUT A SIMILAR SYMBOL ALSO APPEARS IN SICILY. IT MAY HAVE BEEN BROUGHT TO BOTH PLACES BY THE VIKINGS.

THE SKULL & CROSSBONES WAS FIRST USED BY A FRENCH PIRATE, EMMANUEL WYNNE, IN ABOUT 1700.

BATTLE FLAGS

BRITISH WARSHIPS HAVE TO FLY TWO NATIONAL FLAGS (THE WHITE ENSIGN) WHEN IN ACTION. IF ONE IS SHOT OFF, THERE IS NO CHANCE OF THE SHIP BEING REGARDED AS HAVING SURRENDERED.

SIGNAL FLAGS

EVERY WARSHIP STILL CARRIES 70 SIGNAL FLAGS. THESE REPRESENT COMMONLY USED WORDS, PHRASES & LETTERS OF THE ALPHABET. NELSON FAMOUS COMMAND BEFORE THE BATTLE OF TRAFALGAR WAS ORIGINALLY NELSON'S CONFIDES EVERY MAN WILL DO HIS DUTY' BUT THERE WERE NO FLAGS FOR NELSON OR CONFIDES, SO, INSTEAD OF SPELLING THEM OUT LETTER BY LETTER, THE FLAGS FOR THE WORDS 'EXPECT' & ENGLAND WERE SUBSTITUTED.

NEPAL

NEPAL IS THE ONLY COUNTRY IN THE WORLD WHOSE NATIONAL FLAG IS NOT RECTANGULAR. UNTIL 1962, BOTH SUNS HAD FACES.

THE TRICOLOUR

THE STRIPES IN THE FRENCH TRICOLOUR ARE OF UNEQUAL THICKNESS (IN THE RATIO OF 30:33:37). THIS WAS DONE TO MAKE THEM APPEAR EQUAL FROM A DISTANCE

REVOLUTIONARY SPIRIT

IRELAND   ITALY   ROMANIA

VARIOUS EUROPEAN COUNTRIES ADOPTED TRICOLOURS IN SYMPATHY WITH THE FRENCH REVOLUTION.

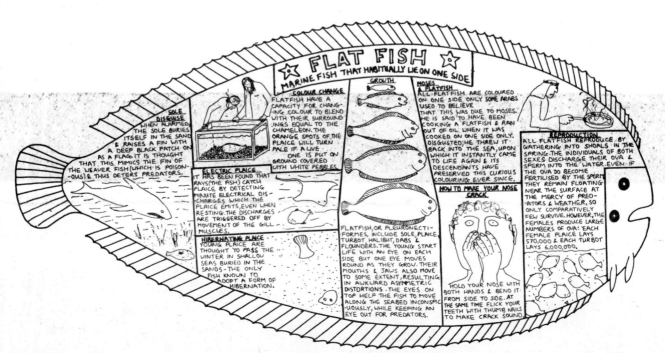

☆ FLAT FISH ☆
MARINE FISH THAT HABITUALLY LIE ON ONE SIDE

SOLE DISGUISE

WHEN ALARMED THE SOLE BURIES ITSELF IN THE SAND & RAISES A FIN WITH A DEEP BLACK PATCH ON IT. IT IS THOUGHT THAT THIS MIMICS THE FIN OF THE WEAVER FISH (WHICH IS POISONOUS) & THUS DETERS PREDATORS.

COLOUR CHANGE

FLATFISH HAVE A CAPACITY FOR CHANGING COLOUR TO BLEND WITH THEIR SURROUNDINGS EQUAL TO THE CHAMELEON. THE ORANGE SPOTS OF THE PLAICE WILL TURN PALE IF ALIVE ONE IS PUT ON GROUND COVERED WITH WHITE PEBBLES.

ELECTRIC PLAICE

IT HAS BEEN FOUND THAT RAYS (THE FISH) CATCH PLAICE BY DETECTING MINUTE ELECTRICAL DISCHARGES WHICH THE PLAICE EMITS, EVEN WHEN RESTING. THE DISCHARGES ARE TRIGGERED OFF BY MOVEMENT OF THE GILL MUSCLES.

HIBERNATING PLAICE

YOUNG PLAICE ARE THOUGHT TO PASS THE WINTER IN SHALLOW SEAS BURIED IN THE SANDS – THE ONLY FISH KNOWN TO ADOPT A FORM OF HIBERNATION.

GROWTH

FLATFISH, OR PLEURONECTIFORMES, INCLUDE SOLE, PLAICE, TURBOT, HALIBUT, DABS & FLOUNDERS. THE YOUNG START LIFE WITH AN EYE ON EACH SIDE BUT ONE EYE MOVES ROUND AS THEY GROW. THEIR MOUTHS & JAWS ALSO MOVE TO SOME EXTENT, RESULTING IN AWKWARD ASYMMETRIC DISTORTIONS. THE EYES ON TOP HELP THE FISH TO MOVE ALONG THE SEABED INCONSPICUOUSLY, WHILE KEEPING AN EYE OUT FOR PREDATORS.

MOSES & FLATFISH

ALL FLATFISH ARE COLOURED ON ONE SIDE ONLY. SOME ARABS USED TO BELIEVE THAT THIS WAS DUE TO MOSES. HE IS SAID TO HAVE BEEN COOKING A FLATFISH & RAN OUT OF OIL WHEN IT WAS COOKED ON ONE SIDE ONLY. DISGUSTED, HE THREW IT BACK INTO THE SEA, UPON WHICH IT INSTANTLY CAME TO LIFE AGAIN & ITS DESCENDANTS HAVE PRESERVED THIS CURIOUS COLOURING EVER SINCE.

HOW TO MAKE YOUR NOSE CRACK

HOLD YOUR NOSE WITH BOTH HANDS & BEND IT FROM SIDE TO SIDE. AT THE SAME TIME FLICK YOUR TEETH WITH THUMB NAILS TO MAKE CRACK SOUND.

REPRODUCTION

ALL FLATFISH REPRODUCE BY GATHERING INTO SHOALS IN THE SPRING. THE INDIVIDUALS OF BOTH SEXES DISCHARGE THEIR OVA & SPERM INTO THE WATER. EVEN IF THE OVA DO BECOME FERTILISED BY THE SPERM THEY REMAIN FLOATING NEAR THE SURFACE AT THE MERCY OF PREDATORS & WEATHER, SO ONLY COMPARATIVELY FEW SURVIVE. HOWEVER, THE FEMALES PRODUCE LARGE NUMBERS OF OVA: EACH FEMALE PLAICE LAYS 570,000 & EACH TURBOT LAYS 6,000,000.

☆ FLEAS ☆
WINGLESS BLOOD-SUCKING INSECT OF GREAT AGILITY

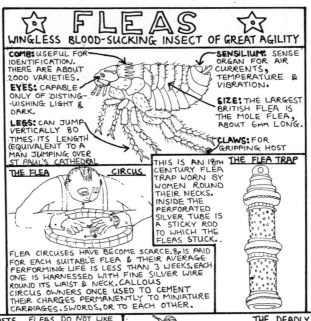

COMB: USEFUL FOR IDENTIFICATION. THERE ARE ABOUT 2000 VARIETIES.

EYES: CAPABLE ONLY OF DISTING-UISHING LIGHT & DARK.

LEGS: CAN JUMP VERTICALLY 80 TIMES ITS LENGTH (EQUIVALENT TO A MAN JUMPING OVER ST PAUL'S CATHEDRAL)

SENSILIUM: SENSE ORGAN FOR AIR CURRENTS, TEMPERATURE & VIBRATION.

SIZE: THE LARGEST BRITISH FLEA IS THE MOLE FLEA, ABOUT 6MM LONG.

CLAWS: FOR GRIPPING HOST

THE FLEA CIRCUS

FLEA CIRCUSES HAVE BECOME SCARCE. 8p IS PAID FOR EACH SUITABLE FLEA & THEIR AVERAGE PERFORMING LIFE IS LESS THAN 3 WEEKS. EACH ONE IS HARNESSED WITH FINE SILVER WIRE ROUND ITS WAIST & NECK. CALLOUS CIRCUS OWNERS ONCE USED TO CEMENT THEIR CHARGES PERMANENTLY TO MINIATURE CARRIAGES, SWORDS, OR TO EACH OTHER.

THE FLEA TRAP

THIS IS AN 18TH CENTURY FLEA TRAP WORN BY WOMEN ROUND THEIR NECKS. INSIDE THE PERFORATED SILVER TUBE IS A STICKY ROD TO WHICH THE FLEAS STUCK.

THE FLEAS' HOSTS

FLEAS DO NOT LIKE TO LIVE PERMANENTLY ON THEIR HOST; THEY PREFER TO HOP OFF TO SAFETY AFTER FEEDING. TO BE SURE OF FINDING THEIR HOST WHEN THEY NEXT FEEL HUNGRY THEY TEND TO AFFLICT ONLY ANIMALS THAT HAVE A PERMANENT HOME: BIRDS, HORSES & CATTLE RARELY ATTRACT FLEAS.

FLEAS, RATS & PLAGUE

BUBONIC PLAGUE IS TRANSMITTED TO HUMANS FROM INFECTED BLACK RATS BY THEIR FLEAS. BOTH RATS & FLEAS DIE IN THE PROCESS. EUROPE IS NOT LIKELY TO SUFFER ANOTHER PLAGUE BECAUSE BLACK RATS HAVE BEEN ALMOST WIPED OUT BY THE BIGGER BROWN RATS WHICH SPREAD FROM RUSSIA IN THE 1700s. BROWN RATS ARE NOT SO DOMESTICATED AS BLACK RATS (THEY PREFER DOCKS & SEWERS TO HOUSES) AND THEY CARRY A DIFFERENT TYPE OF FLEA, ONE WHICH IS NOT PARTIAL TO HUMAN BLOOD.

THE DEADLY JIGGER

THE JIGGER (TUNGA PENETRANS) IS A SPECIES OF FLEA WITH PARTICULARLY DISGUSTING HABITS, ABOUT 1mm LONG WHEN UNFED. THE MALES LEAVE THE HOST AFTER FEEDING, AS DO MOST FLEAS, BUT THE FEMALE BURROWS INTO THE SKIN (USUALLY BETWEEN THE HOST'S TOES) CONTINUING TO SUCK BLOOD TILL SHE IS AS LARGE AS A PEA. THEIR HOSTS, INCLUDING HUMANS, OFTEN DIE FROM BLOOD POISONING.

BEFORE / AFTER

PROVEN CULPRITS

FLEAS WERE NOT PROVED TO BE THE CARRIERS OF BUBONIC PLAGUE TILL THE EARLY 1900s. A CAGE OF GUINEA PIGS WAS THEN SUSPENDED ABOVE A NUMBER OF PLAGUE-RIDDEN ANIMALS. THE GUINEA PIGS REMAINED HEALTHY UNTIL THEY WERE LOWERED WITHIN JUMPING RANGE OF THE PLAGUE FLEAS.

HOW TO MAKE A MOUNTAINEER

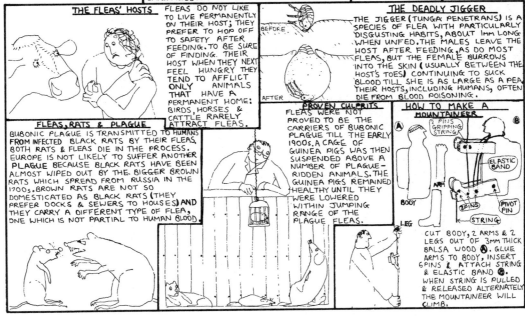

2 PINS GRIPPING STRING / ELASTIC BAND / BODY / ART / LEG / 3 PINS / PIVOT PIN / STRING

CUT BODY, 2 ARMS & 2 LEGS OUT OF 3MM THICK BALSA WOOD Ⓐ. GLUE ARMS TO BODY, INSERT 6 PINS & ATTACH STRING & ELASTIC BAND Ⓑ. WHEN STRING IS PULLED & RELEASED ALTERNATELY THE MOUNTAINEER WILL CLIMB.

☆ FLIES ☆
TWO-WINGED ADULT INSECTS OF THE ORDER DIPTERA

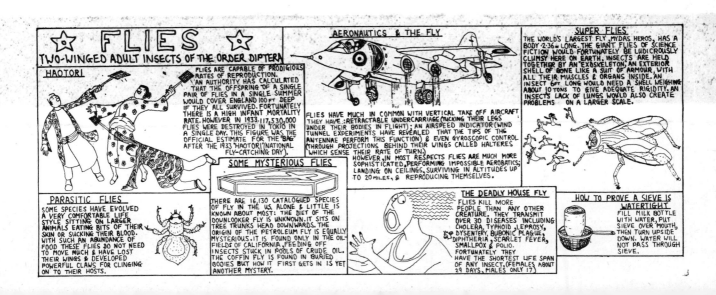

HAOTORI

FLIES ARE CAPABLE OF PRODIGIOUS RATES OF REPRODUCTION. AN AUTHORITY HAS CALCULATED THAT THE OFFSPRING OF A SINGLE PAIR OF FLIES IN A SINGLE SUMMER WOULD COVER ENGLAND 100 FT DEEP IF THEY ALL SURVIVED. FORTUNATELY THERE IS A HIGH INFANT MORTALITY RATE. HOWEVER IN 1933, 117,530,000 FLIES WERE DESTROYED IN TOKIO IN A SINGLE DAY. THIS FIGURE WAS THE OFFICIAL ESTIMATE FOR THE 'BAG' AFTER THE 1933 'HAOTORI' (NATIONAL FLY-CATCHING DAY).

AERONAUTICS & THE FLY

FLIES HAVE MUCH IN COMMON WITH VERTICAL TAKE OFF AIRCRAFT. THEY HAVE: RETRACTABLE UNDERCARRIAGE (TUCKING THEIR LEGS UNDER THEIR BODIES IN FLIGHT); AN AIRSPEED INDICATOR (WIND TUNNEL EXPERIMENTS HAVE REVEALED THAT THE TIPS OF THE ANTENNAE PERFORM THIS FUNCTION) & EVEN GYROSCOPIC CONTROL (THROUGH PROJECTIONS BEHIND THEIR WINGS CALLED HALTERES WHICH SENSE THEIR RATE OF TURN). HOWEVER IN MOST RESPECTS FLIES ARE MUCH MORE SOPHISTICATED, PERFORMING IMPOSSIBLE AEROBATICS; LANDING ON CEILINGS, SURVIVING IN ALTITUDES UP TO 20 MILES, & REPRODUCING THEMSELVES.

SUPER FLIES

THE WORLD'S LARGEST FLY, MYDAS HEROS, HAS A BODY 2·36" LONG. THE GIANT FLIES OF SCIENCE FICTION WOULD FORTUNATELY BE LUDICROUSLY CLUMSY HERE ON EARTH. INSECTS ARE HELD TOGETHER BY AN EXOSKELETON, AN EXTERIOR SHELL OF BONE LIKE A SUIT OF ARMOUR, WITH ALL THEIR MUSCLES & ORGANS INSIDE. AN INSECT 6FT LONG WOULD NEED A SHELL WEIGHING ABOUT 10 TONS TO GIVE ADEQUATE RIGIDITY. AN INSECTS LACK OF LUNGS WOULD ALSO CREATE PROBLEMS ON A LARGER SCALE.

PARASITIC FLIES

SOME SPECIES HAVE EVOLVED A VERY COMFORTABLE LIFE STYLE SITTING ON LARGER ANIMALS EATING BITS OF THEIR SKIN OR SUCKING THEIR BLOOD. WITH SUCH AN ABUNDANCE OF FOOD THESE FLIES DO NOT NEED TO MOVE MUCH & HAVE LOST THEIR WINGS & DEVELOPED POWERFUL CLAWS FOR CLINGING ON TO THEIR HOSTS.

SOME MYSTERIOUS FLIES

THERE ARE 16,130 CATALOGUED SPECIES OF FLY IN THE U.S. ALONE & LITTLE IS KNOWN ABOUT MOST: THE DIET OF THE DOWNLOOKER FLY IS UNKNOWN. IT SITS ON TREE TRUNKS HEAD DOWNWARDS. THE ORIGIN OF THE PETROLEUM FLY IS EQUALLY MYSTERIOUS. IT IS FOUND ONLY IN THE OIL-FIELDS OF CALIFORNIA, FEEDING OFF INSECTS STUCK IN POOLS OF CRUDE OIL. THE COFFIN FLY IS FOUND IN BURIED BODIES BUT HOW IT FIRST GETS IN IS YET ANOTHER MYSTERY.

THE DEADLY HOUSE FLY

FLIES KILL MORE PEOPLE THAN ANY OTHER CREATURE. THEY TRANSMIT OVER 30 DISEASES INCLUDING CHOLERA, TYPHOID, LEPROSY, DYSENTERY, BUBONIC PLAGUE, DIPHTHERIA, SCARLET FEVER, SMALLPOX & POLIO. FORTUNATELY THEY HAVE THE SHORTEST LIFE SPAN OF ANY INSECT. (FEMALES ABOUT 29 DAYS, MALES ONLY 17)

HOW TO PROVE A SIEVE IS WATERTIGHT

FILL MILK BOTTLE WITH WATER, PUT SIEVE OVER MOUTH, THEN TURN UPSIDE DOWN. WATER WILL NOT PASS THROUGH SIEVE.

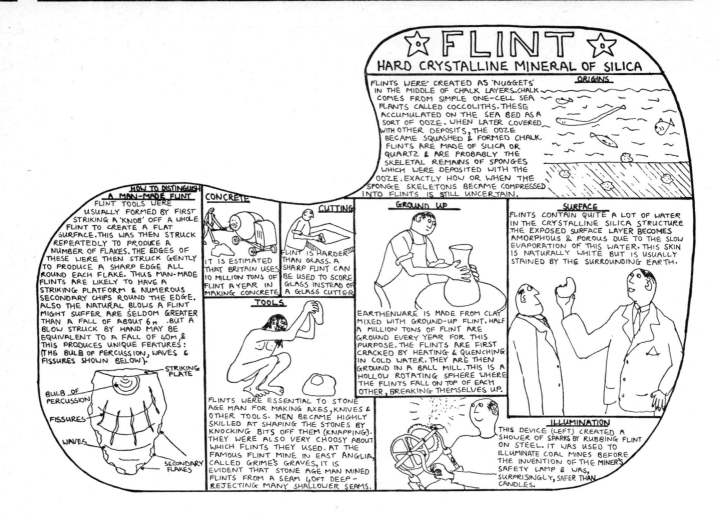

☆ FLINT ☆
HARD CRYSTALLINE MINERAL OF SILICA

ORIGINS
FLINTS WERE CREATED AS 'NUGGETS' IN THE MIDDLE OF CHALK LAYERS. CHALK COMES FROM SIMPLE ONE-CELL SEA PLANTS CALLED COCCOLITHS. THESE ACCUMULATED ON THE SEA BED AS A SORT OF OOZE. WHEN LATER COVERED WITH OTHER DEPOSITS, THE OOZE BECAME SQUASHED & FORMED CHALK. FLINTS ARE MADE OF SILICA OR QUARTZ & ARE PROBABLY THE SKELETAL REMAINS OF SPONGES WHICH WERE DEPOSITED WITH THE OOZE. EXACTLY HOW OR WHEN THE SPONGE SKELETONS BECAME COMPRESSED INTO FLINTS IS STILL UNCERTAIN.

HOW TO DISTINGUISH A MAN-MADE FLINT
FLINT TOOLS WERE USUALLY FORMED BY FIRST STRIKING A 'KNOB' OFF A WHOLE FLINT TO CREATE A FLAT SURFACE. THIS WAS THEN STRUCK REPEATEDLY TO PRODUCE A NUMBER OF FLAKES. THE EDGES OF THESE WERE THEN STRUCK GENTLY TO PRODUCE A SHARP EDGE ALL ROUND EACH FLAKE. THUS MAN-MADE FLINTS ARE LIKELY TO HAVE A STRIKING PLATFORM & NUMEROUS SECONDARY CHIPS ROUND THE EDGE. ALSO THE NATURAL BLOWS A FLINT MIGHT SUFFER ARE SELDOM GREATER THAN A FALL OF ABOUT 6M. BUT A BLOW STRUCK BY HAND MAY BE EQUIVALENT TO A FALL OF 40M, & THIS PRODUCES UNIQUE FEATURES (THE BULB OF PERCUSSION, WAVES & FISSURES SHOWN BELOW).

STRIKING PLATE
BULB OF PERCUSSION
FISSURES
WAVES
SECONDARY FLAKES

CONCRETE
IT IS ESTIMATED THAT BRITAIN USES 10 MILLION TONS OF FLINT A YEAR IN MAKING CONCRETE.

CUTTING
FLINT IS HARDER THAN GLASS. A SHARP FLINT CAN BE USED TO SCORE GLASS INSTEAD OF A GLASS CUTTER.

TOOLS
FLINTS WERE ESSENTIAL TO STONE AGE MAN FOR MAKING AXES, KNIVES & OTHER TOOLS. MEN BECAME HIGHLY SKILLED AT SHAPING THE STONES BY KNOCKING BITS OFF THEM (KNAPPING). THEY WERE ALSO VERY CHOOSY ABOUT WHICH FLINTS THEY USED. AT THE FAMOUS FLINT MINE IN EAST ANGLIA, CALLED GRIME'S GRAVES, IT IS EVIDENT THAT STONE AGE MAN MINED FLINTS FROM A SEAM 40FT DEEP – REJECTING MANY SHALLOWER SEAMS.

GROUND UP
EARTHENWARE IS MADE FROM CLAY MIXED WITH GROUND-UP FLINT. HALF A MILLION TONS OF FLINT ARE GROUND EVERY YEAR FOR THIS PURPOSE. THE FLINTS ARE FIRST CRACKED BY HEATING & QUENCHING IN COLD WATER. THEY ARE THEN GROUND IN A BALL MILL. THIS IS A HOLLOW ROTATING SPHERE WHERE THE FLINTS FALL ON TOP OF EACH OTHER, BREAKING THEMSELVES UP.

SURFACE
FLINTS CONTAIN QUITE A LOT OF WATER IN THE CRYSTALLINE SILICA STRUCTURE. THE EXPOSED SURFACE LAYER BECOMES AMORPHOUS & POROUS DUE TO THE SLOW EVAPORATION OF THIS WATER. THIS SKIN IS NATURALLY WHITE BUT IS USUALLY STAINED BY THE SURROUNDING EARTH.

ILLUMINATION
THIS DEVICE (LEFT) CREATED A SHOWER OF SPARKS BY RUBBING FLINT ON STEEL. IT WAS USED TO ILLUMINATE COAL MINES BEFORE THE INVENTION OF THE MINER'S SAFETY LAMP & WAS, SURPRISINGLY, SAFER THAN CANDLES.

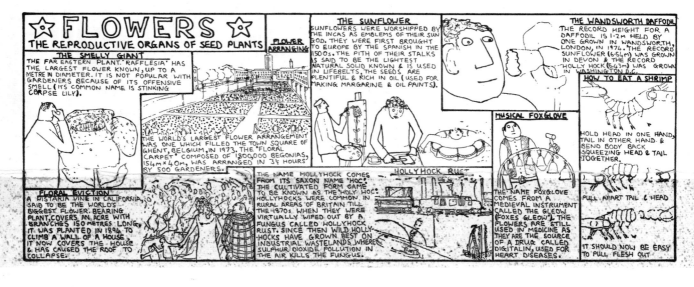

☆ FLOWERS ☆
THE REPRODUCTIVE ORGANS OF SEED PLANTS

THE SMELLY GIANT
THE FAR EASTERN PLANT 'RAFFLESIA' HAS THE LARGEST FLOWER KNOWN, UP TO A METRE IN DIAMETER. IT IS NOT POPULAR WITH GARDENERS BECAUSE OF ITS OFFENSIVE SMELL (ITS COMMON NAME IS STINKING CORPSE LILY).

FLOWER ARRANGING
THE WORLD'S LARGEST FLOWER ARRANGEMENT WAS ONE WHICH FILLED THE TOWN SQUARE OF GHENT, BELGIUM, IN 1973. THE 'FLORAL CARPET' COMPOSED OF 1,800,000 BEGONIAS, 154M x 40M, WAS ARRANGED IN 3½ HOURS BY 500 GARDENERS.

FLORAL EVICTION
A WISTARIA VINE IN CALIFORNIA, SAID TO BE THE WORLD'S BIGGEST FLOWER-BEARING PLANT, COVERS AN ACRE WITH BRANCHES 150 METRES LONG. IT WAS PLANTED IN 1894 TO CLIMB A WALL OF A HOUSE. IT NOW COVERS THE HOUSE & HAS CAUSED THE ROOF TO COLLAPSE.

THE SUNFLOWER
SUNFLOWERS WERE WORSHIPPED BY THE INCAS AS EMBLEMS OF THEIR SUN GOD. THEY WERE FIRST BROUGHT TO EUROPE BY THE SPANISH IN THE 1500s. THE PITH OF THEIR STALKS IS SAID TO BE THE LIGHTEST NATURAL SOLID KNOWN & IS USED IN LIFEBELTS. THE SEEDS ARE PLENTIFUL & RICH IN OIL (USED FOR MAKING MARGARINE & OIL PAINTS).

HOLLYHOCK RUST

THE NAME HOLLYHOCK COMES FROM ITS SAXON NAME 'HOC'. THE CULTIVATED FORM CAME TO BE KNOWN AS THE 'HOLY HOC'. HOLLYHOCKS WERE COMMON IN RURAL AREAS OF BRITAIN TILL THE 1870s WHEN THEY WERE VIRTUALLY WIPED OUT BY A FUNGUS CALLED HOLLYHOCK RUST. SINCE THEN WILD HOLLYHOCKS HAVE GROWN BEST ON INDUSTRIAL WASTELANDS WHERE SULPHUR DIOXIDE POLLUTION IN THE AIR KILLS THE FUNGUS.

MUSICAL FOXGLOVE
THE NAME FOXGLOVE COMES FROM A MEDIEVAL INSTRUMENT CALLED THE GLEOW (FOXES GLEOW). THE FLOWERS ARE STILL USED IN MEDICINE AS THEY ARE THE SOURCE OF A DRUG CALLED DIGITALIN, USED FOR HEART DISEASES.

THE WANDSWORTH DAFFODIL
THE RECORD HEIGHT FOR A DAFFODIL IS 1.2M HELD BY ONE GROWN IN WANDSWORTH, LONDON, IN 1974. THE RECORD SUNFLOWER (6.54M) WAS GROWN IN DEVON & THE RECORD HOLLYHOCK (5.43M) WAS GROWN IN WASHINGTON D.C.

HOW TO EAT A SHRIMP
HOLD HEAD IN ONE HAND, TAIL IN OTHER HAND & BEND BODY BACK SQUEEZING HEAD & TAIL TOGETHER.

PULL APART TAIL & HEAD

IT SHOULD NOW BE EASY TO PULL FLESH OUT

FLUORESCENCE
THE DEVELOPMENT OF THE FLUORESCENT LIGHT WAS LARGELY INSPIRED BY THE WORK OF THE PHYSICIST HENRI BEQUEREL (1852–1908), WHO TESTED MANY SUBSTANCES FOR FLUORESCENCE. HE IS BEST KNOWN FOR HIS DISCOVERY THAT URANIUM COMPOUNDS EMIT RADIATION WITHOUT ANY ELECTRICAL EXCITATION – THIS IS RADIOACTIVITY.

THE LUMILINE
THE FIRST PRACTICAL FLUORESCENT TUBE WAS UNVEILED BY GENERAL ELECTRIC IN AMERICA IN 1935. IT WAS BRIGHT GREEN & CALLED A LUMILINE LAMP.

FLUORESCENT DINNER
THE TUBE WAS FIRST USED AT A DINNER TO CELEBRATE THE CENTENARY OF THE US PATENT OFFICE IN 1936.

FLUORESCENT STATION
THE FIRST FLUORESCENT LIGHT IN BRITAIN WAS INSTALLED AT PICCADILLY TUBE STATION IN 1945.

QUARTZ-HALOGEN LIGHTS
QUARTZ-HALOGEN LAMPS HAVE TUNGSTEN FILAMENTS LIKE ORDINARY INCANDESCENT LAMPS. HOWEVER THE QUARTZ GLASS & THE IODINE VAPOUR (HALOGEN) INSIDE ALLOW IT TO WORK AT HIGHER TEMPERATURES (& BRIGHTER LIGHT).

NEON LIGHTS
neon
NEON LIGHTS HAVE NO FLUORESCENT COATING. THE GAS ITSELF GLOWS AT LOW PRESSURE. THEY HAVE NO STARTERS OR HEATERS BUT NEED CONSTANT HIGH VOLTAGES (2–15,000V) TO MAKE THE NEON BRIGHT ENOUGH.

FLUORESCENT
GLOWING SUBSTANCES

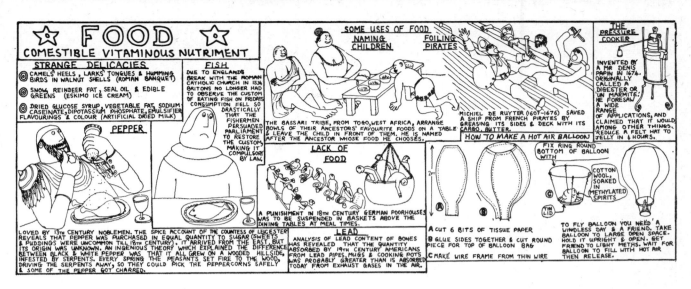

☆ FOOD ☆
COMESTIBLE VITAMINOUS NUTRIMENT

STRANGE DELICACIES
- CAMELS' HEELS, LARKS' TONGUES & HUMMING BIRDS IN WALNUT SHELLS (ROMAN BANQUET)
- SNOW, REINDEER FAT, SEAL OIL & EDIBLE GREENS (ESKIMO ICE CREAM)
- DRIED GLUCOSE SYRUP, VEGETABLE FAT, SODIUM CASEINATE, DIPOTASSIUM PHOSPHATE, EMULSIFIER FLAVOURINGS & COLOUR (ARTIFICIAL DRIED MILK)

FISH
DUE TO ENGLANDS BREAK WITH THE ROMAN CATHOLIC CHURCH IN 1534 BRITONS NO LONGER HAD TO OBSERVE THE CUSTOM OF EATING FISH ON FRIDAYS. CONSUMPTION FELL SO DRASTICALLY THAT THE FISHERMEN PERSUADED PARLIAMENT TO RESTORE THE CUSTOM MAKING IT COMPULSORY BY LAW.

PEPPER
LOVED BY 13TH CENTURY NOBLEMEN. THE SPICE ACCOUNT OF THE COUNTESS OF LEICESTER REVEALS THAT PEPPER WAS PURCHASED IN EQUAL QUANTITY TO SUGAR. SWEETS & PUDDINGS WERE UNCOMMON TILL 18TH CENTURY. IT ARRIVED FROM THE EAST, BUT ITS ORIGIN WAS UNKNOWN. AN INGENIOUS THEORY WHICH EXPLAINED THE DIFFERENCE BETWEEN BLACK & WHITE PEPPER WAS THAT IT ALL GREW ON A WOODED HILLSIDE INFESTED BY SERPENTS. EVERY SPRING THE PEASANTS SET FIRE TO THE WOOD, DRIVING THE SERPENTS AWAY SO THEY COULD PICK THE PEPPERCORNS SAFELY & SOME OF THE PEPPER GOT CHARRED.

SOME USES OF FOOD
NAMING CHILDREN
THE BASSARI TRIBE, FROM TOGO, WEST AFRICA, ARRANGE BOWLS OF THEIR ANCESTORS' FAVOURITE FOODS ON A TABLE & LEAVE THE CHILD IN FRONT OF THEM. HE IS NAMED AFTER THE ANCESTOR WHOSE FOOD HE CHOOSES.

FOILING PIRATES
MICHIEL DE RUYTER (1607-1676) SAVED A SHIP FROM FRENCH PIRATES BY GREASING ITS SIDES & DECK WITH ITS CARGO, BUTTER.

LACK OF FOOD
A PUNISHMENT IN 18TH CENTURY GERMAN POORHOUSES WAS TO BE SUSPENDED IN BASKETS ABOVE THE DINING TABLES AT MEAL TIMES.

LEAD
ANALYSIS OF LEAD CONTENT OF BONES HAS REVEALED THAT THE QUANTITY ABSORBED BY 19TH CENTURY AMERICANS FROM LEAD PIPES, MUGS & COOKING POTS WAS PROBABLY GREATER THAN IS ABSORBED TODAY FROM EXHAUST GASES IN THE AIR.

THE PRESSURE COOKER
INVENTED BY A MR DENIS PAPIN IN 1674. ORIGINALLY CALLED A DIGESTER OR UN MARMITE; HE FORESAW A WIDE RANGE OF APPLICATIONS, AND CLAIMED THAT IT WOULD AMONG OTHER THINGS, REDUCE A FELT HAT TO JELLY IN 4 HOURS.

HOW TO MAKE A HOT AIR BALLOON
A. CUT 6 BITS OF TISSUE PAPER
B. GLUE SIDES TOGETHER & CUT ROUND PIECE FOR TOP OF BALLOON BAG
C. MAKE WIRE FRAME FROM THIN WIRE
FIX RING ROUND BOTTOM OF BALLOON WITH COTTON WOOL, SOAKED IN METHYLATED SPIRITS. TIN LID.
TO FLY BALLOON YOU NEED A WINDLESS DAY & A FRIEND. TAKE BALLOON TO LARGE OPEN SPACE. HOLD IT UPRIGHT & OPEN; GET FRIEND TO LIGHT METHS. WAIT FOR BALLOON TO FILL WITH HOT AIR THEN RELEASE.

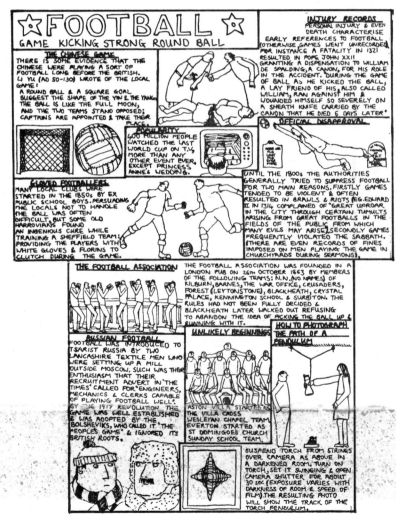

☆ FOOTBALL ☆
GAME KICKING STRONG ROUND BALL

THE CHINESE GAME
THERE IS SOME EVIDENCE THAT THE CHINESE WERE PLAYING A SORT OF FOOTBALL LONG BEFORE THE BRITISH. LI YU (AD 50-130) WROTE OF THE LOCAL GAME:
A ROUND BALL & A SQUARE GOAL SUGGEST THE SHAPE OF THE YIN & THE YANG. THE BALL IS LIKE THE FULL MOON, AND THE TWO TEAMS STAND OPPOSED; CAPTAINS ARE APPOINTED & TAKE THEIR PLACE.

POPULARITY
400 MILLION PEOPLE WATCHED THE LAST WORLD CUP ON T.V., MORE THAN ANY OTHER EVENT EVER, EXCEPT PRINCESS ANNE'S WEDDING.

GLOVED FOOTBALLERS
MANY LOCAL CLUBS WERE STARTED IN THE 1850s BY EX PUBLIC SCHOOL BOYS. PERSUADING THE LOCALS NOT TO HANDLE THE BALL WAS OFTEN DIFFICULT, BUT SOME OLD HARROVIANS FOUND AN INGENIOUS CURE WHILE TRAINING A SHEFFIELD TEAM; PROVIDING THE PLAYERS WITH WHITE GLOVES & FLORINS TO CLUTCH DURING THE GAME.

INJURY RECORDS
PERSONAL INJURY & EVEN DEATH CHARACTERISE EARLY REFERENCES TO FOOTBALL (OTHERWISE, GAMES WENT UNRECORDED). FOR INSTANCE A FATALITY IN 1321 RESULTED IN POPE JOHN XXII GRANTING A DISPENSATION TO WILLIAM DE SPALDING, A CANON, FOR HIS ROLE IN THE ACCIDENT. DURING THE GAME OF BALL AS HE KICKED THE BALL, A LAY FRIEND OF HIS, ALSO CALLED WILLIAM, RAN AGAINST HIM & WOUNDED HIMSELF SO SEVERELY ON A SHEATH KNIFE CARRIED BY THE CANON THAT HE DIED 6 DAYS LATER.

OFFICIAL DISAPPROVAL
UNTIL THE 1800s THE AUTHORITIES GENERALLY TRIED TO SUPPRESS FOOTBALL FOR TWO MAIN REASONS. FIRSTLY GAMES TENDED TO BE VIOLENT & OFTEN RESULTED IN BRAWLS & RIOTS (EG. EDWARD II IN 1314 COMPLAINED OF "GREAT UPROAR IN THE CITY THROUGH CERTAIN TUMULTS ARISING FROM GREAT FOOTBALLS IN THE FIELDS OF THE PUBLIC FROM WHICH MANY EVILS MAY ARISE.) SECONDLY GAMES FREQUENTLY VIOLATED THE SABBATH. THERE ARE EVEN RECORDS OF FINES IMPOSED ON MEN PLAYING THE GAME IN CHURCHYARDS DURING SERMONS.

THE FOOTBALL ASSOCIATION
THE FOOTBALL ASSOCIATION WAS FOUNDED IN A LONDON PUB ON 26TH OCTOBER 1863 BY MEMBERS OF THE FOLLOWING TEAMS: N.N. (NO NAMES) OF KILBURN, BARNES, THE WAR OFFICE, CRUSADERS, FOREST (LEYTONSTONE), BLACKHEATH, CRYSTAL PALACE, KENNINGTON SCHOOL & SURBITON. THE RULES HAD NOT BEEN FULLY DECIDED & BLACKHEATH LATER WALKED OUT REFUSING TO ABANDON THE IDEA OF PICKING THE BALL UP & RUNNING WITH IT.

RUSSIAN FOOTBALL
FOOTBALL WAS INTRODUCED TO TSARIST RUSSIA BY TWO LANCASHIRE TEXTILE MEN WHO WERE SETTING UP A MILL OUTSIDE MOSCOW. SUCH WAS THEIR ENTHUSIASM THAT THEIR RECRUITMENT ADVERT IN 'THE TIMES' CALLED FOR "ENGINEERS, MECHANICS & CLERKS CAPABLE OF PLAYING FOOTBALL WELL". BY THE 1917 REVOLUTION THE GAME WAS WELL ESTABLISHED & WAS ADOPTED BY THE BOLSHEVIKS, WHO CALLED IT 'THE PEOPLE'S GAME' & IGNORED ITS BRITISH ROOTS.

UNLIKELY BEGINNINGS
ASTON VILLA STARTED AS THE VILLA CROSS WESLEYAN CHAPEL TEAM. EVERTON STARTED AS ST DOMINGOES CHURCH SUNDAY SCHOOL TEAM.

HOW TO PHOTOGRAPH THE PATH OF A PENDULUM
SUSPEND TORCH FROM STRINGS OVER CAMERA AS ABOVE IN A DARKENED ROOM. TURN ON TORCH, SET IT SWINGING & OPEN CAMERA SHUTTER FOR ABOUT 30 SEC (EXPOSURE VARIES WITH DARKNESS OF ROOM & SPEED OF FILM). THE RESULTING PHOTO WILL SHOW THE TRACK OF THE TORCH PENDULUM.

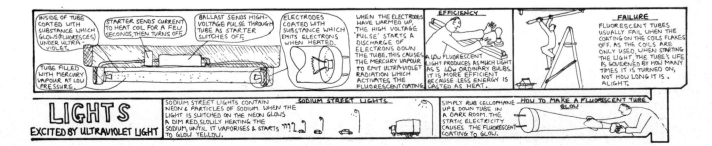

INSIDE OF TUBE COATED WITH SUBSTANCE WHICH GLOWS (FLUORESCES) UNDER ULTRA VIOLET.

TUBE FILLED WITH MERCURY VAPOUR AT LOW PRESSURE.

STARTER SENDS CURRENT TO HEAT COIL FOR A FEW SECONDS, THEN TURNS OFF.

BALLAST SENDS HIGH-VOLTAGE PULSE THROUGH TUBE AS STARTER SWITCHES OFF.

ELECTRODES COATED WITH SUBSTANCE WHICH EMITS ELECTRONS WHEN HEATED.

WHEN THE ELECTRODES HAVE WARMED UP, THE HIGH VOLTAGE 'PULSE' STARTS A DISCHARGE OF ELECTRONS DOWN THE TUBE. THIS CAUSES THE MERCURY VAPOUR TO EMIT ULTRAVIOLET RADIATION WHICH ACTIVATES THE FLUORESCENT COATING.

EFFICIENCY
A LOW FLUORESCENT LIGHT PRODUCES AS MUCH LIGHT AS 5 LOW ORDINARY BULBS. IT IS MORE EFFICIENT BECAUSE LESS ENERGY IS WASTED AS HEAT.

FAILURE
FLUORESCENT TUBES USUALLY FAIL WHEN THE COATING ON THE COILS FLAKES OFF. AS THE COILS ARE ONLY USED, WHEN STARTING THE LIGHT, THE TUBE'S LIFE IS GOVERNED BY HOW MANY TIMES IT IS TURNED ON, NOT HOW LONG IT IS ALIGHT.

LIGHTS
EXCITED BY ULTRAVIOLET LIGHT

SODIUM STREET LIGHTS
SODIUM STREET LIGHTS CONTAIN NEON & PARTICLES OF SODIUM. WHEN THE LIGHT IS SWITCHED ON THE NEON GLOWS A DIM RED, SLOWLY HEATING THE SODIUM, UNTIL IT VAPORISES & STARTS TO GLOW YELLOW.

HOW TO MAKE A FLUORESCENT TUBE GLOW
SIMPLY RUB CELLOPHANE UP & DOWN TUBE IN A DARK ROOM. THE STATIC ELECTRICITY CAUSES THE FLUORESCENT COATING TO GLOW.

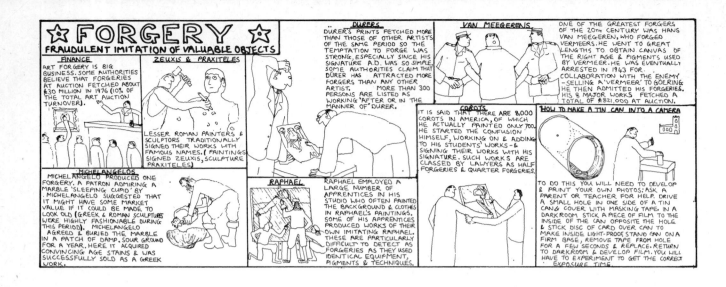

☆ FORGERY ☆
FRAUDULENT IMITATION OF VALUABLE OBJECTS

FINANCE
ART FORGERY IS BIG BUSINESS. SOME AUTHORITIES BELIEVE THAT FORGERIES AT AUCTION FETCHED ABOUT £30 MILLION IN 1976 (10% OF THE TOTAL ART AUCTION TURNOVER).

ZEUXIS & PRAXITELES
LESSER ROMAN PAINTERS & SCULPTORS TRADITIONALLY SIGNED THEIR WORKS WITH FAMOUS NAMES. (PAINTINGS SIGNED ZEUXIS, SCULPTURE PRAXITELES.)

MICHELANGELOS
MICHELANGELO PRODUCED ONE FORGERY. A PATRON ADMIRING A MARBLE 'SLEEPING CUPID' BY MICHELANGELO SUGGESTED THAT IT MIGHT HAVE SOME MARKET VALUE IF IT COULD BE MADE TO LOOK OLD (GREEK & ROMAN SCULPTURES WERE HIGHLY FASHIONABLE DURING THIS PERIOD). MICHELANGELO AGREED & BURIED THE MARBLE IN A PATCH OF DAMP, SOUR GROUND FOR A YEAR. HERE IT ACQUIRED CONVINCING AGE STAINS & WAS SUCCESSFULLY SOLD AS A GREEK WORK.

DURERS
DURER'S PRINTS FETCHED MORE THAN THOSE OF OTHER ARTISTS OF THE SAME PERIOD SO THE TEMPTATION TO FORGE WAS STRONG, ESPECIALLY SINCE HIS SIGNATURE A.D. WAS SO SIMPLE. SOME AUTHORITIES CLAIM THAT DURER HAS ATTRACTED MORE FORGERS THAN ANY OTHER ARTIST. MORE THAN 300 PERSONS ARE LISTED AS WORKING 'AFTER OR IN THE MANNER OF' DURER.

RAPHAEL
RAPHAEL EMPLOYED A LARGE NUMBER OF APPRENTICES IN HIS STUDIO WHO OFTEN PAINTED THE BACKGROUND & CLOTHES IN RAPHAEL'S PAINTINGS. SOME OF HIS APPRENTICES PRODUCED WORKS OF THEIR OWN IMITATING RAPHAEL. THESE ARE PARTICULARLY DIFFICULT TO DETECT AS FORGERIES AS THEY USED IDENTICAL EQUIPMENT, PIGMENTS & TECHNIQUES.

COROTS
IT IS SAID THAT THERE ARE 8,000 COROTS IN AMERICA, OF WHICH HE ACTUALLY PAINTED ONLY 700. HE STARTED THE CONFUSION HIMSELF, WORKING ON & ADDING TO HIS STUDENTS' WORKS - & SIGNING THEIR WORKS WITH HIS SIGNATURE. SUCH WORKS ARE CLASSED BY LAWYERS AS HALF FORGERIES & QUARTER FORGERIES.

VAN MEEGERENS
ONE OF THE GREATEST FORGERS OF THE 20TH CENTURY WAS HANS VAN MEEGEREN, WHO FORGED VERMEERS. HE WENT TO GREAT LENGTHS TO OBTAIN CANVAS OF THE RIGHT AGE & PIGMENTS USED BY VERMEER. HE WAS EVENTUALLY ARRESTED IN 1943 FOR COLLABORATION WITH THE ENEMY - SELLING A 'VERMEER' TO GOERING. HE THEN ADMITTED HIS FORGERIES. HIS 8 MAJOR WORKS FETCHED A TOTAL OF £821,000 AT AUCTION.

HOW TO MAKE A TIN CAN INTO A CAMERA
TO DO THIS YOU WILL NEED TO DEVELOP & PRINT YOUR OWN PHOTOS: ASK A PARENT OR TEACHER FOR HELP. DRIVE A SMALL HOLE IN ONE SIDE OF A TIN CAN & COVER WITH MASKING TAPE. IN A DARKROOM STICK A PIECE OF FILM TO THE INSIDE OF THE CAN OPPOSITE THE HOLE & STICK DISC OF CARD OVER CAN TO MAKE INSIDE LIGHT-PROOF. STAND CAN ON A FIRM BASE, REMOVE TAPE FROM HOLE FOR A FEW SECONDS & REPLACE. RETURN TO DARKROOM & DEVELOP FILM. YOU WILL HAVE TO EXPERIMENT TO GET THE CORRECT EXPOSURE TIME.

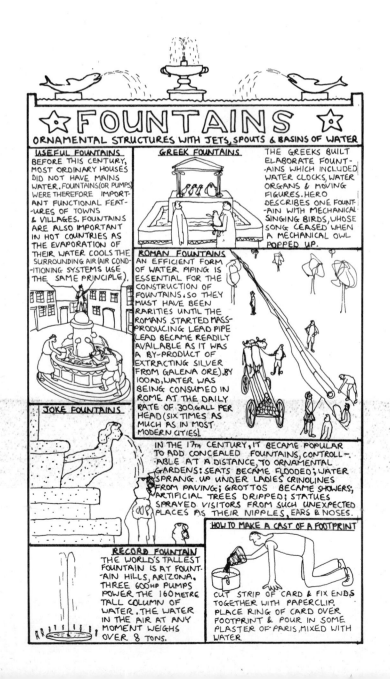

☆ FOUNTAINS ☆
ORNAMENTAL STRUCTURES WITH JETS, SPOUTS & BASINS OF WATER

USEFUL FOUNTAINS
BEFORE THIS CENTURY, MOST ORDINARY HOUSES DID NOT HAVE MAINS WATER. FOUNTAINS (OR PUMPS) WERE THEREFORE IMPORTANT FUNCTIONAL FEATURES OF TOWNS & VILLAGES. FOUNTAINS ARE ALSO IMPORTANT IN HOT COUNTRIES AS THE EVAPORATION OF THEIR WATER COOLS THE SURROUNDING AIR (AIR CONDITIONING SYSTEMS USE THE SAME PRINCIPLE).

GREEK FOUNTAINS
THE GREEKS BUILT ELABORATE FOUNTAINS WHICH INCLUDED WATER CLOCKS, WATER ORGANS & MOVING FIGURES. HERO DESCRIBES ONE FOUNTAIN WITH MECHANICAL SINGING BIRDS, WHOSE SONG CEASED WHEN A MECHANICAL OWL POPPED UP.

ROMAN FOUNTAINS
AN EFFICIENT FORM OF WATER PIPING IS ESSENTIAL FOR THE CONSTRUCTION OF FOUNTAINS, SO THEY MUST HAVE BEEN RARITIES UNTIL THE ROMANS STARTED MASS-PRODUCING LEAD PIPE. LEAD BECAME READILY AVAILABLE AS IT WAS A BY-PRODUCT OF EXTRACTING SILVER FROM GALENA ORE). BY 100AD, WATER WAS BEING CONSUMED IN ROME AT THE DAILY RATE OF 300 GALL PER HEAD (SIX TIMES AS MUCH AS IN MOST MODERN CITIES).

JOKE FOUNTAINS
IN THE 17TH CENTURY, IT BECAME POPULAR TO ADD CONCEALED FOUNTAINS, CONTROLLABLE AT A DISTANCE, TO ORNAMENTAL GARDENS: SEATS BECAME FLOODED; WATER SPRANG UP UNDER LADIES CRINOLINES FROM PAVING; GROTTOS BECAME SHOWERS; ARTIFICIAL TREES DRIPPED; STATUES SPRAYED VISITORS FROM SUCH UNEXPECTED PLACES AS THEIR NIPPLES, EARS & NOSES.

RECORD FOUNTAIN
THE WORLD'S TALLEST FOUNTAIN IS AT FOUNTAIN HILLS, ARIZONA. THREE 600HP PUMPS POWER THE 160 METRE TALL COLUMN OF WATER. THE WATER IN THE AIR AT ANY MOMENT WEIGHS OVER 8 TONS.

HOW TO MAKE A CAST OF A FOOTPRINT
CUT STRIP OF CARD & FIX ENDS TOGETHER WITH PAPERCLIP. PLACE RING OF CARD OVER FOOTPRINT & POUR IN SOME PLASTER OF PARIS, MIXED WITH WATER.

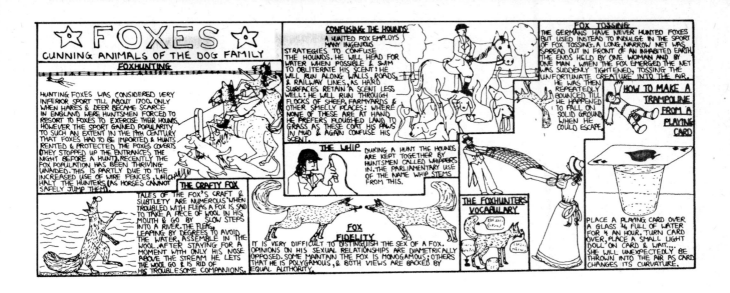

☆ FOXES ☆
CUNNING ANIMALS OF THE DOG FAMILY

FOXHUNTING

HUNTING FOXES WAS CONSIDERED VERY INFERIOR SPORT TILL ABOUT 1700. ONLY WHEN HARES & DEER BECAME SCARCE IN ENGLAND WERE HUNTSMEN FORCED TO RESORT TO FOXES TO EXERCISE THEIR HOUNDS. HOWEVER THE SPORT GAINED POPULARITY TO SUCH AN EXTENT IN THE 19TH CENTURY THAT FOXES HAD TO BE IMPORTED & HUNTS RENTED & PROTECTED THE FOXES COVERTS (THEY STOPPED UP THE ENTRANCES THE NIGHT BEFORE A HUNT). RECENTLY THE FOX POPULATION HAS BEEN THRIVING UNAIDED. THIS IS PARTLY DUE TO THE INCREASED USE OF WIRE FENCES, WHICH HALT THE HUNTERS (AS HORSES CANNOT SAFELY JUMP THEM).

THE CRAFTY FOX

TALES OF THE FOX'S CRAFT & SUBTLETY ARE NUMEROUS. WHEN TROUBLED WITH FLEAS A FOX IS SAID TO TAKE A PIECE OF WOOL IN HIS MOUTH & GO BY SLOW STEPS INTO A RIVER. THE FLEAS, LEAPING BY DEGREES TO AVOID THE WATER, ASSEMBLE IN THE WOOL. AFTER STAYING FOR A MOMENT WITH ONLY HIS NOSE ABOVE THE STREAM HE LETS THE WOOL GO & IS RID OF HIS TROUBLESOME COMPANIONS.

CONFUSING THE HOUNDS

A HUNTED FOX EMPLOYS MANY INGENIOUS STRATEGIES TO CONFUSE THE HOUNDS. HE WILL HEAD FOR WATER WHEN POSSIBLE & SWIM TO OBLITERATE HIS SCENT; HE WILL RUN ALONG WALLS, ROADS, & RAILWAY LINES, AS HARD SURFACES RETAIN A SCENT LESS WELL; HE WILL RUN THROUGH FLOCKS OF SHEEP, FARMYARDS & OTHER SMELLY PLACES; WHERE NONE OF THESE ARE AT HAND HE PREFERS PLOUGHED LAND TO GRASS AS THESE COAT HIS PAWS IN MUD & AGAIN CONFUSE HIS SCENT.

THE WHIP

DURING A HUNT THE HOUNDS ARE KEPT TOGETHER BY HUNTSMEN CALLED WHIPPERS IN. THE PARLIAMENTARY USE OF THE NAME WHIP STEMS FROM THIS.

FOX FIDELITY

IT IS VERY DIFFICULT TO DISTINGUISH THE SEX OF A FOX. OPINIONS ON HIS SEXUAL RELATIONSHIPS ARE DIAMETRICALLY OPPOSED. SOME MAINTAIN THE FOX IS MONOGAMOUS; OTHERS THAT HE IS POLYGAMOUS, & BOTH VIEWS ARE BACKED BY EQUAL AUTHORITY.

THE FOXHUNTERS VOCABULARY

FOX TOSSING

THE GERMANS HAVE NEVER HUNTED FOXES BUT USED INSTEAD TO INDULGE IN THE SPORT OF FOX TOSSING. A LONG, NARROW NET WAS SPREAD OUT IN FRONT OF AN INHABITED EARTH, THE ENDS HELD BY ONE WOMAN AND BY ONE MAN. WHEN THE FOX EMERGED THE NET WAS SUDDENLY TIGHTENED, TOSSING THE UNFORTUNATE CREATURE INTO THE AIR. HE WAS THEN REPEATEDLY BOUNCED TILL HE HAPPENED TO FALL ON SOLID GROUND WHEN HE COULD ESCAPE.

HOW TO MAKE A TRAMPOLINE FROM A PLAYING CARD

PLACE A PLAYING CARD OVER A GLASS ¾ FULL OF WATER FOR ¼ AN HOUR. TURN CARD OVER, PLACE A SMALL LIGHT DOLL ON CARD & WAIT... SHE WILL UNEXPECTEDLY BE THROWN INTO THE AIR AS CARD CHANGES ITS CURVATURE.

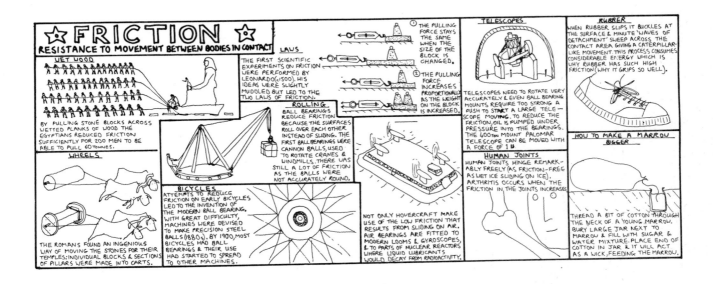

☆ FRICTION ☆
RESISTANCE TO MOVEMENT BETWEEN BODIES IN CONTACT

WET WOOD

BY PULLING STONE BLOCKS ACROSS WETTED PLANKS OF WOOD THE EGYPTIANS REDUCED FRICTION SUFFICIENTLY FOR 200 MEN TO BE ABLE TO PULL 60 TONNES.

WHEELS

THE ROMANS FOUND AN INGENIOUS WAY OF MOVING THE STONES FOR THEIR TEMPLES: INDIVIDUAL BLOCKS & SECTIONS OF PILLARS WERE MADE INTO CARTS.

LAWS

THE FIRST SCIENTIFIC EXPERIMENTS ON FRICTION WERE PERFORMED BY LEONARDO (c1500). HIS IDEAS WERE SLIGHTLY MUDDLED BUT LED TO THE TWO LAWS OF FRICTION.

① THE PULLING FORCE STAYS THE SAME WHEN THE SIZE OF THE BLOCK IS CHANGED.

② THE PULLING FORCE INCREASES PROPORTIONALLY AS THE WEIGHT ON THE BLOCK IS INCREASED.

ROLLING

BALL BEARINGS REDUCE FRICTION BECAUSE THE SURFACES ROLL OVER EACH OTHER INSTEAD OF SLIDING. THE FIRST BALL BEARINGS WERE CANNON BALLS, USED TO ROTATE CRANES & WINDMILLS. THERE WAS STILL A LOT OF FRICTION AS THE BALLS WERE NOT ACCURATELY ROUND.

BICYCLES

ATTEMPTS TO REDUCE FRICTION ON EARLY BICYCLES LED TO THE INVENTION OF THE MODERN BALL BEARING. WITH GREAT DIFFICULTY, MACHINES WERE DEVISED TO MAKE PRECISION STEEL BALLS (1880s). BY 1900, MOST BICYCLES HAD BALL BEARINGS & THEIR USE HAD STARTED TO SPREAD TO OTHER MACHINES.

NOT ONLY HOVERCRAFT MAKE USE OF THE LOW FRICTION THAT RESULTS FROM SLIDING ON AIR. AIR BEARINGS ARE FITTED TO MODERN LOOMS & GYROSCOPES & TO PARTS OF NUCLEAR REACTORS WHERE LIQUID LUBRICANTS WOULD DECAY FROM RADIOACTIVITY.

TELESCOPES

TELESCOPES NEED TO ROTATE VERY ACCURATELY & EVEN BALL BEARING MOUNTS REQUIRE TOO STRONG A PUSH TO START A LARGE TELE-SCOPE MOVING. TO REDUCE THE FRICTION, OIL IS PUMPED UNDER PRESSURE INTO THE BEARINGS. THE 400 TON MOUNT PALOMAR TELESCOPE CAN BE MOVED WITH A FORCE OF 1 lb.

HUMAN JOINTS

HUMAN JOINTS HINGE REMARK-ABLY FREELY (AS FRICTION-FREE AS WET ICE SLIDING ON ICE). ARTHRITIS OCCURS WHEN THE FRICTION IN THE JOINTS INCREASES.

RUBBER

WHEN RUBBER SLIPS IT BUCKLES AT THE SURFACE & MINUTE 'WAVES OF DETACHMENT' SWEEP ACROSS THE CONTACT AREA GIVING A CATERPILLAR-LIKE MOVEMENT. THIS PROCESS CONSUMES CONSIDERABLE ENERGY WHICH IS WHY RUBBER HAS SUCH HIGH FRICTION (WHY IT GRIPS SO WELL).

HOW TO MAKE A MARROW BIGGER

THREAD A BIT OF COTTON THROUGH THE NECK OF A YOUNG MARROW. BURY LARGE JAR NEXT TO MARROW & FILL WITH SUGAR & WATER MIXTURE. PLACE END OF COTTON IN JAR & IT WILL ACT AS A WICK, FEEDING THE MARROW.

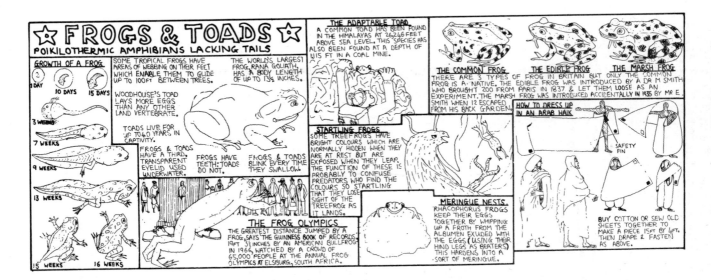

☆ FROGS & TOADS ☆
POIKILOTHERMIC AMPHIBIANS LACKING TAILS

GROWTH OF A FROG

1 DAY · 10 DAYS · 15 DAYS
3 WEEKS
7 WEEKS
9 WEEKS
13 WEEKS
15 WEEKS · 16 WEEKS

SOME TROPICAL FROGS HAVE AREAS OF WEBBING ON THEIR FEET WHICH ENABLE THEM TO GLIDE UP TO 100FT BETWEEN TREES.

WOODHOUSE'S TOAD LAYS MORE EGGS THAN ANY OTHER LAND VERTEBRATE.

TOADS LIVE FOR UP TO 40 YEARS IN CAPTIVITY.

FROGS & TOADS HAVE A THIRD TRANSPARENT EYELID USED UNDERWATER.

FROGS HAVE TEETH: TOADS DO NOT.

FROGS & TOADS BLINK EVERY TIME THEY SWALLOW.

THE WORLD'S LARGEST FROG, RANA GOLIATH, HAS A BODY LENGTH OF UP TO 13¾ INCHES.

THE FROG OLYMPICS

THE GREATEST DISTANCE JUMPED BY A FROG, SAYS 'THE GUINNESS BOOK OF RECORDS' IS 19FT 3½ INCHES BY AN AMERICAN BULLFROG IN 1966, WATCHED BY A CROWD OF 65,000 PEOPLE AT THE ANNUAL FROG OLYMPICS AT ELSBURG, SOUTH AFRICA.

THE ADAPTABLE TOAD

A COMMON TOAD HAS BEEN FOUND IN THE HIMALAYAS AT 26,246 FEET ABOVE SEA LEVEL. THIS SPECIES HAS ALSO BEEN FOUND AT A DEPTH OF 1115 FT IN A COAL MINE.

STARTLING FROGS

SOME TREEFROGS HAVE BRIGHT COLOURS WHICH ARE NORMALLY HIDDEN WHEN THEY ARE AT REST BUT ARE EXPOSED WHEN THEY LEAP. THE FUNCTION OF THESE IS PROBABLY TO CONFUSE PREDATORS WHO FIND THE COLOURS SO STARTLING THAT THEY LOSE SIGHT OF THE TREEFROG AS IT LANDS.

MERINGUE NESTS

RHACOPHORUS FROGS KEEP THEIR EGGS TOGETHER BY WHIPPING UP A FROTH FROM THE ALBUMEN EXUDED WITH THE EGGS (USING THEIR HIND LEGS AS BEATERS) THIS HARDENS INTO A SORT OF MERINGUE.

THE COMMON FROG · THE EDIBLE FROG · THE MARSH FROG

THERE ARE 3 TYPES OF FROG IN BRITAIN BUT ONLY THE COMMON FROG IS A NATIVE. THE EDIBLE FROG WAS INTRODUCED BY A DR M SMITH WHO BROUGHT 200 FROM PARIS IN 1837 & LET THEM LOOSE AS AN EXPERIMENT. THE MARSH FROG WAS INTRODUCED ACCIDENTALLY IN 1935 BY MR E. SMITH WHEN 12 ESCAPED FROM HIS BACK GARDEN.

HOW TO DRESS UP IN AN ARAB HAIK

SAFETY PIN

BUY COTTON OR SEW OLD SHEETS TOGETHER TO MAKE A PIECE 15FT BY 4FT, THEN DRAPE & FASTEN AS ABOVE.

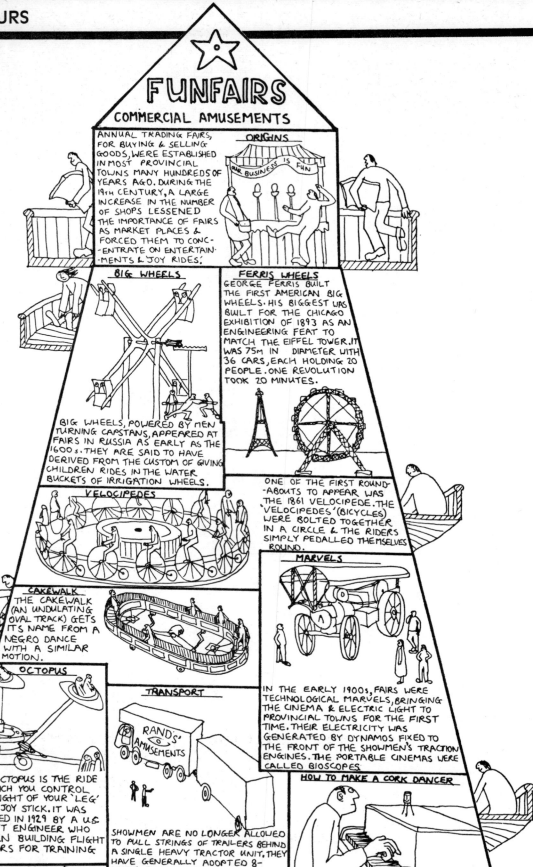

FUNFAIRS
COMMERCIAL AMUSEMENTS

ANNUAL TRADING FAIRS, FOR BUYING & SELLING GOODS, WERE ESTABLISHED IN MOST PROVINCIAL TOWNS MANY HUNDREDS OF YEARS AGO. DURING THE 19th CENTURY, A LARGE INCREASE IN THE NUMBER OF SHOPS LESSENED THE IMPORTANCE OF FAIRS AS MARKET PLACES & FORCED THEM TO CONCENTRATE ON ENTERTAINMENTS & JOY RIDES.

ORIGINS

OUR BUSINESS IS FUN

BIG WHEELS

BIG WHEELS, POWERED BY MEN TURNING CAPSTANS, APPEARED AT FAIRS IN RUSSIA AS EARLY AS THE 1600s. THEY ARE SAID TO HAVE DERIVED FROM THE CUSTOM OF GIVING CHILDREN RIDES IN THE WATER BUCKETS OF IRRIGATION WHEELS.

FERRIS WHEELS

GEORGE FERRIS BUILT THE FIRST AMERICAN BIG WHEELS. HIS BIGGEST WAS BUILT FOR THE CHICAGO EXHIBITION OF 1893 AS AN ENGINEERING FEAT TO MATCH THE EIFFEL TOWER. IT WAS 75m IN DIAMETER WITH 36 CARS, EACH HOLDING 20 PEOPLE. ONE REVOLUTION TOOK 20 MINUTES.

VELOCIPEDES

ONE OF THE FIRST ROUNDABOUTS TO APPEAR WAS THE 1861 VELOCIPEDE. THE 'VELOCIPEDES' (BICYCLES) WERE BOLTED TOGETHER IN A CIRCLE & THE RIDERS SIMPLY PEDALLED THEMSELVES ROUND.

CAKEWALK

THE CAKEWALK (AN UNDULATING OVAL TRACK) GETS ITS NAME FROM A NEGRO DANCE WITH A SIMILAR MOTION.

MARVELS

IN THE EARLY 1900s, FAIRS WERE TECHNOLOGICAL MARVELS, BRINGING THE CINEMA & ELECTRIC LIGHT TO PROVINCIAL TOWNS FOR THE FIRST TIME. THEIR ELECTRICITY WAS GENERATED BY DYNAMOS FIXED TO THE FRONT OF THE SHOWMEN'S TRACTION ENGINES. THE PORTABLE CINEMAS WERE CALLED BIOSCOPES.

OCTOPUS

THE OCTOPUS IS THE RIDE ON WHICH YOU CONTROL THE HEIGHT OF YOUR 'LEG' WITH A JOY STICK. IT WAS PATENTED IN 1929 BY A U.S. AIRCRAFT ENGINEER WHO HAD BEEN BUILDING FLIGHT SIMULATORS FOR TRAINING PILOTS.

TRANSPORT

RAND'S AMUSEMENTS

SHOWMEN ARE NO LONGER ALLOWED TO PULL STRINGS OF TRAILERS BEHIND A SINGLE HEAVY TRACTOR UNIT, THEY HAVE GENERALLY ADOPTED 8-WHEELED LORRIES PULLING SINGLE LARGE TRAILERS INSTEAD. IT HAS ALSO LED TO AN INCREASED POPULARITY FOR LIGHTER & LESS BULKY RIDES. SOME OF THE LATEST RIDES ARE DESIGNED ROUND STANDARD 6.5m STEEL CONTAINERS. THESE ACT AS BASES FOR THE RIDES & AS CONTAINERS FOR TRANSPORT.

HOW TO MAKE A CORK DANCER

MAKE 3 HOLES IN A CORK WITH A LARGE NEEDLE & INSERT A BRISTLE FROM A STIFF BRUSH IN EACH HOLE. PAINT A FACE ON THE CORK & STAND IT ON A PIANO. WHEN YOU PLAY THE VIBRATIONS WILL MAKE THE CORK 'DANCER' LEAP ABOUT.

POPULARITY

BRITAIN HAS MORE THAN 5000 FUNFAIRS EVERY YEAR

☆ FUNGI ☆
THALLOPHYTES LACKING CHLOROPHYLL

DEADLY FUNGI
90% OF DEATHS FROM FUNGI ARE DUE TO THE DEATH CAP TOADSTOOL (AMANITA PHALLOIDES). ITS VICTIMS INCLUDE POPE CLEMENT VII (1523-1534). THE CLOSELY RELATED FLY AGARIC IS SAID NOT TO KILL BUT CAUSES INTOXICATION & DELIRIUM. ITS NAME COMES FROM ITS FORMER USE AS A POISONOUS FLY BAIT, CHOPPED UP IN MILK. THE VIKINGS USED TO CHEW IT BEFORE BATTLE TO DRIVE THEMSELVES BERSERK.

THE MYSTERIOUS PREDACIOUS GOOPAGALES
THE MOST MYSTERIOUS OF THE ANIMAL EATING FUNGI IS THE GOOPAGALES, WHICH LIVES OFF EELWORMS. THE FUNGUS TRAPS THE WORMS ON A STICKY FLUID BUT IT IS UNKNOWN HOW IT CAUSES THEIR DEATH. THEY CEASE STRUGGLING TOO SOON TO HAVE DIED OF EXHAUSTION OR STARVATION & THEIR IS NO EVIDENCE THAT THE FUNGUS PRODUCES ANY POISONS. IT IS CONSIDERED A SERIOUS POSSIBILITY THAT THE WORMS DIE OF FRIGHT.

TRUFFLES
MOST FUNGI RELY ON THE WIND TO CARRY THEIR SPORES TO START COLONIES. HOWEVER THE TRUFFLE FUNGUS GROWS UNDERGROUND & CAN ONLY SPREAD BY BEING EATEN & HENCE DEPOSITING SPORES IN ANIMALS' FAECES. IT HAS EVOLVED ITS DELICATE TASTE TO MAKE ITS CONSUMPTION AS IRRESISTIBLE AS POSSIBLE.

FAIRY RINGS
FAIRY RINGS, CIRCLES OF LUSH GRASS, FOUND IN SOME FIELDS, ARE DUE TO FUNGI. THE ROOTS GROW SLOWLY OUTWARDS FROM AN ORIGINAL SPORE & LATER DIE OFF IN THE CENTRE. THEY DEPOSIT NITRATES IN THE SOIL WHICH ENHANCES THE GROWTH OF THE GRASS. THE OUTSIDE DIAMETER OF A RING IS A MEASURE OF ITS AGE AS THE FUNGI SPREAD 10-30 CENTIMETRES A YEAR. THE OLDEST IN ENGLAND IS 700 YEARS OLD.

TEETOTALERS & BREAD
BAKER'S YEAST IS SELECTED TO GIVE OFF THE MAXIMUM CO₂ TO MAKE THE BREAD RISE. HOWEVER THE FERMENTATION OF YEAST PRODUCES ALCOHOL & SOME IS ALWAYS PRESENT IN FRESHLY BAKED LOAVES (UP TO .5%)

USEFUL YEAST
THE MANUFACTURE OF CHOCOLATE CREAMS DEPENDS ON YEAST. THE CENTRES ARE MUCH TOO LIQUID TO HOLD THEIR SHAPE WHILE BEING COATED WITH CHOCOLATE SO AN EXTRACT OF YEAST IS ADDED WHICH TEMPORARILY CONVERTS THE SUCROSE TO A SOLID INVERT SUGAR.

DRY ROT
MANY FORMS OF FUNGUS ATTACK DAMP WOOD BUT MERULIUS LACRYMANS DOES THE MOST DAMAGE AS IT IS SO EFFICIENT AT SPREADING. THE PARENT MYCELIUM SENDS OUT ROOTS CALLED RHIZOMORPHS SEVERAL YARDS LONG, THAT CAN PENETRATE ANY POROUS SOLID. THESE CONDUCT WATER SO A NEW COLONY CAN BE STARTED ON ANY TIMBER THEY REACH. HOWEVER DRY IT MAY BE. SPORES OF M. LACRYMANS ARE SO NUMEROUS THERE ARE PROBABLY A FEW IN EVERY ROOM IN THE COUNTRY.

LIFTING A CUP WITH A RUBBER BAND & A CANDLE
BREAK A LONG RUBBER BAND & TIE THE ONE END TO A CUP HANDLE, LIGHT CANDLE & HOLD CUP SUSPENDED. GENTLY WARM RUBBER & CUP WILL RISE.

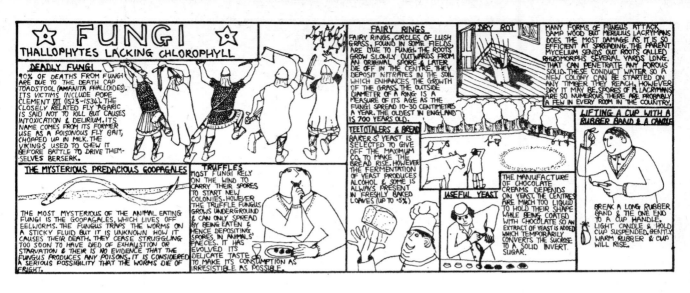

☆ FURS ☆
SOFT DENSE GROWTH COVERING CERTAIN ANIMALS

STOATS, HARES, SHEEP & RABBITS
FURS WITH EXOTIC NAMES OFTEN COME FROM QUITE ORDINARY ANIMALS. CANADIAN ERMINE COMES FROM STOATS; FOXALINE COMES FROM HARES; SUEDED SHEARLING FROM SHEEP; BEAVER FROM LAMBS & CONEY FROM RABBITS. COMPOUND NAMES SIMPLY REFER TO THE COLOUR WHICH THE FUR HAS BEEN DYED. FOR EXAMPLE MINK CONEY IS RABBIT (CONEY) FUR DYED DARK BROWN TO LOOK LIKE MINK.

MINK SABLE
THE MOST EXPENSIVE FUR COAT EVER IS PROBABLY THE £52000 MINK-SABLE COAT PURCHASED BY RICHARD BURTON FOR LIZ TAYLOR.

ERMINE
ERMINE COMES FROM THE WHITE STOAT. THIS ANIMAL HAS A TAN BROWN FUR IN SUMMER WHICH MOULTS & IS REPLACED BY A WHITE COAT (EXCEPT FOR A BLACK TIP ON THE END OF THE TAIL) IN WINTER.

DOMESTIC CAT
AMERICAN FUR TRADERS HAVE RECENTLY BEEN BUYING DOMESTIC CAT FURS FROM THE RUSSIANS. ACCORDING TO A U.P.I. REPORT 5000 PELTS HAVE BEEN SOLD AT A LENINGRAD AUCTION FOR ABOUT 35p EACH.

MINK
TRIALS WITH 1000WATT SODIUM STREET LIGHTS, AMONG THE MOST POWERFUL IN THE WORLD, HAVE BEEN ABANDONED BECAUSE OF A MINK FARM ALONGSIDE THE ROAD IN CALGARY, CANADA. BREEDING & THE GROWTH OF WINTER FUR BEGIN WHEN DAYLIGHT HOURS DECREASE. THE STREET LIGHTS STOPPED THE GROWTH OF WINTER FUR, & KITTENS WHELPED OUT OF SEASON HAVE NOT SURVIVED THE WINTER.

SEA OTTER
THE MOST EXPENSIVE FUR IS THAT OF THE SEA OTTER. THIS ANIMAL WAS ALMOST HUNTED TO EXTINCTION IN THE 1800s UNTIL TRAPPING WAS MADE ILLEGAL IN 1912. NUMBERS HAVE SINCE INCREASED & LIMITED TRAPPING BEGAN AGAIN IN 1967. AT AUCTION, THE PELTS FIRST FETCHED ABOUT £1000 EACH. THE PRICE HAS NOW FALLEN TO ABOUT £150 BUT IT IS STILL THE MOST EXPENSIVE FUR.

DUCKBILL
THE AUSTRALIAN DUCKBILL PLATYPUS HAS PROBABLY THE MOST EXTRAORDINARY FUR IN THE ANIMAL KINGDOM. THE LOWER PART OF EACH HAIR IS THIN & WOOL-LIKE, WHILE THE FREE END TERMINATES AS A FLATTENED SPEAR-SHAPED DARK NEEDLE.

WOLVERINE
ESKIMOS PARTICULARLY VALUE THE FUR OF THE WOLVERINE. THOUGH SLOW & CLUMSY IT IS A PATIENT & CUNNING ANIMAL. IT IS KNOWN TO INSPECT SNARES SET FOR IT & DEFTLY REMOVE THE BAIT. IT IS ALSO CALLED 'THE GLUTTON' AS IT WILL ATTACK & EAT ALMOST ANYTHING IT MEETS.

HOW TO CUT STRING WITHOUT A KNIFE OR SCISSORS
WRAP ONE END OF THE STRING AROUND YOUR LEFT FOREFINGER, THEN LOOP IT ROUND YOUR HAND, AS ABOVE. WITH OTHER HAND, GRIP STRING ABOUT 30cm BELOW, & WRAP IT ROUND RIGHT HAND SEVERAL TIMES. CLENCH BOTH HANDS & HOLD BOTH FISTS CLOSE TOGETHER THEN QUICKLY YANK YOUR RIGHT FIST DOWN & YOUR LEFT FIST UP. THE STRING WILL SNAP INSIDE YOUR LEFT FIST AT POINT **A**.

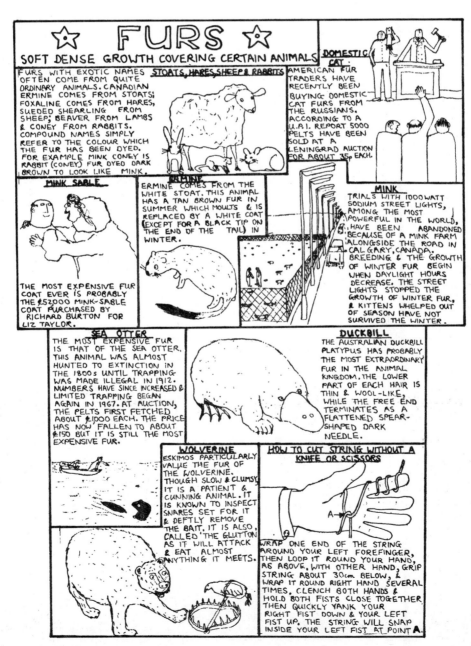

☆ FURNITURE ☆
CONTAINERS FOR POSSESSIONS & PEOPLE

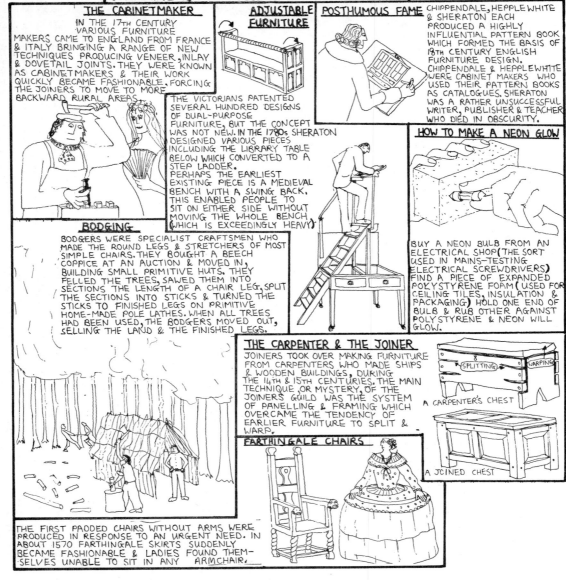

THE CABINETMAKER

IN THE 17TH CENTURY VARIOUS FURNITURE MAKERS CAME TO ENGLAND FROM FRANCE & ITALY BRINGING A RANGE OF NEW TECHNIQUES PRODUCING VENEER, INLAY & DOVETAIL JOINTS. THEY WERE KNOWN AS CABINETMAKERS & THEIR WORK QUICKLY BECAME FASHIONABLE, FORCING THE JOINERS TO MOVE TO MORE BACKWARD RURAL AREAS.

ADJUSTABLE FURNITURE

THE VICTORIANS PATENTED SEVERAL HUNDRED DESIGNS OF DUAL-PURPOSE FURNITURE, BUT THE CONCEPT WAS NOT NEW. IN THE 1780s SHERATON DESIGNED VARIOUS PIECES INCLUDING THE LIBRARY TABLE BELOW WHICH CONVERTED TO A STEP LADDER.
PERHAPS THE EARLIEST EXISTING PIECE IS A MEDIEVAL BENCH WITH A SWING BACK. THIS ENABLED PEOPLE TO SIT ON EITHER SIDE WITHOUT MOVING THE WHOLE BENCH (WHICH IS EXCEEDINGLY HEAVY).

POSTHUMOUS FAME

CHIPPENDALE, HEPPLEWHITE & SHERATON EACH PRODUCED A HIGHLY INFLUENTIAL PATTERN BOOK WHICH FORMED THE BASIS OF 18TH CENTURY ENGLISH FURNITURE DESIGN. CHIPPENDALE & HEPPLEWHITE WERE CABINET MAKERS WHO USED THEIR PATTERN BOOKS AS CATALOGUES. SHERATON WAS A RATHER UNSUCCESSFUL WRITER, PUBLISHER & TEACHER WHO DIED IN OBSCURITY.

HOW TO MAKE A NEON GLOW

BUY A NEON BULB FROM AN ELECTRICAL SHOP (THE SORT USED IN MAINS-TESTING ELECTRICAL SCREWDRIVERS) FIND A PIECE OF EXPANDED POLYSTYRENE FOAM (USED FOR CEILING TILES, INSULATION & PACKAGING) HOLD ONE END OF BULB & RUB OTHER AGAINST POLYSTYRENE & NEON WILL GLOW.

BODGING

BODGERS WERE SPECIALIST CRAFTSMEN WHO MADE THE ROUND LEGS & STRETCHERS OF MOST SIMPLE CHAIRS. THEY BOUGHT A BEECH COPPICE AT AN AUCTION & MOVED IN, BUILDING SMALL PRIMITIVE HUTS. THEY FELLED THE TREES, SAWED THEM INTO SECTIONS THE LENGTH OF A CHAIR LEG, SPLIT THE SECTIONS INTO STICKS & TURNED THE STICKS TO FINISHED LEGS ON PRIMITIVE HOME-MADE POLE LATHES. WHEN ALL TREES HAD BEEN USED, THE BODGERS MOVED OUT, SELLING THE LAND & THE FINISHED LEGS.

THE CARPENTER & THE JOINER

JOINERS TOOK OVER MAKING FURNITURE FROM CARPENTERS WHO MADE SHIPS & WOODEN BUILDINGS. DURING THE 14TH & 15TH CENTURIES, THE MAIN TECHNIQUE, OR MYSTERY, OF THE JOINERS GUILD WAS THE SYSTEM OF PANELLING & FRAMING WHICH OVERCAME THE TENDENCY OF EARLIER FURNITURE TO SPLIT & WARP.

SPLITTING — WARPING

A CARPENTER'S CHEST

A JOINED CHEST

FARTHINGALE CHAIRS

THE FIRST PADDED CHAIRS WITHOUT ARMS WERE PRODUCED IN RESPONSE TO AN URGENT NEED. IN ABOUT 1570 FARTHINGALE SKIRTS SUDDENLY BECAME FASHIONABLE & LADIES FOUND THEM-SELVES UNABLE TO SIT IN ANY ARMCHAIR.

☆ FUSION ☆
COMBINATION OF NUCLEII WITH RELEASE OF ENERGY

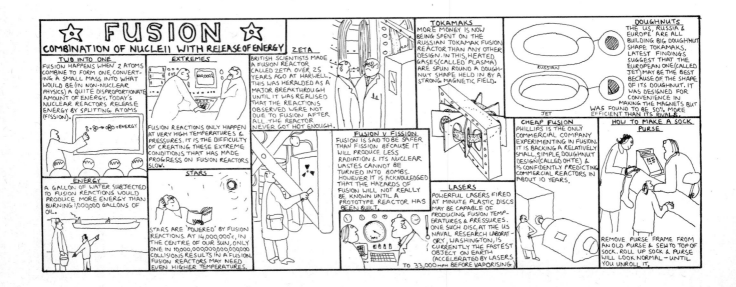

TWO INTO ONE

FUSION HAPPENS WHEN 2 ATOMS COMBINE TO FORM ONE, CONVERTING A SMALL MASS INTO WHAT WOULD BE (IN NON-NUCLEAR PHYSICS) A QUITE DISPROPORTIONATE AMOUNT OF ENERGY. TODAY'S NUCLEAR REACTORS RELEASE ENERGY BY SPLITTING ATOMS (FISSION).

EXTREMES

FUSION REACTIONS ONLY HAPPEN AT VERY HIGH TEMPERATURES & PRESSURES. IT IS THE DIFFICULTY OF CREATING THESE EXTREME CONDITIONS THAT HAS MADE PROGRESS ON FUSION REACTORS SLOW.

ENERGY

A GALLON OF WATER SUBJECTED TO FUSION REACTIONS WOULD PRODUCE MORE ENERGY THAN BURNING 1,000,000 GALLONS OF OIL.

STARS

STARS ARE 'POWERED' BY FUSION REACTIONS. AT 14,000,000°C, IN THE CENTRE OF OUR SUN, ONLY ONE IN 10,000,000,000,000,000,000 COLLISIONS RESULTS IN A FUSION. FUSION REACTORS MAY NEED EVEN HIGHER TEMPERATURES.

ZETA

BRITISH SCIENTISTS MADE A FUSION REACTOR CALLED ZETA OVER 25 YEARS AGO AT HARWELL. THIS WAS HERALDED AS A MAJOR BREAKTHROUGH UNTIL IT WAS REALISED THAT THE REACTIONS OBSERVED WERE NOT DUE TO FUSION AFTER ALL. THE REACTOR NEVER GOT HOT ENOUGH.

FUSION V FISSION

FUSION IS SAID TO BE SAFER THAN FISSION BECAUSE IT WILL PRODUCE LESS RADIATION & ITS NUCLEAR WASTES CANNOT BE TURNED INTO BOMBS. HOWEVER IT IS ACKNOWLEDGED THAT THE HAZARDS OF FUSION WILL NOT REALLY BE KNOWN UNTIL A PROTOTYPE REACTOR HAS BEEN BUILT.

TOKAMAKS

MORE MONEY IS NOW BEING SPENT ON THE RUSSIAN TOKAMAK FUSION REACTOR THAN ANY OTHER DESIGN. IN THIS, HEATED GASES (CALLED PLASMA) ARE SPUN ROUND A DOUGHNUT SHAPE HELD IN BY A STRONG MAGNETIC FIELD.

LASERS

POWERFUL LASERS FIRED AT MINUTE PLASTIC DISCS MAY BE CAPABLE OF PRODUCING FUSION TEMPERATURES & PRESSURES. ONE SUCH DISC, AT THE US NAVAL RESEARCH LABORATORY, WASHINGTON, IS CURRENTLY THE FASTEST OBJECT ON EARTH (ACCELERATED BY LASERS TO 33,000 mph BEFORE VAPORISING)

DOUGHNUTS

THE US, RUSSIA & EUROPE ARE ALL BUILDING BIG DOUGHNUT SHAPE TOKAMAKS. LATEST FINDINGS SUGGEST THAT THE EUROPEAN ONE (CALLED JET) MAY BE THE BEST BECAUSE OF THE SHAPE OF ITS DOUGHNUT. IT WAS DESIGNED FOR CONVENIENCE IN MAKING THE MAGNETS BUT WAS FOUND TO BE 50% MORE EFFICIENT THAN ITS RIVALS.

RUSSIAN

JET

CHEAP FUSION

PHILLIPS IS THE ONLY COMMERCIAL COMPANY EXPERIMENTING IN FUSION. IT IS BACKING A RELATIVELY SMALL, SIMPLE DOUGHNUT DESIGN (CALLED OHTE) & IS CONFIDENTLY PREDICTING COMMERCIAL REACTORS IN ABOUT 10 YEARS.

HOW TO MAKE A SOCK PURSE

REMOVE PURSE FRAME FROM AN OLD PURSE & SEW TO TOP OF SOCK. ROLL UP SOCK & PURSE WILL LOOK NORMAL – UNTIL YOU UNROLL IT.

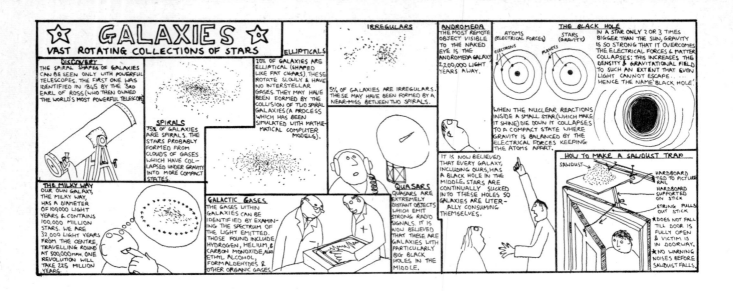

☆ GALAXIES ☆
VAST ROTATING COLLECTIONS OF STARS

DISCOVERY
THE SPIRAL SHAPES OF GALAXIES CAN BE SEEN ONLY WITH POWERFUL TELESCOPES. THE FIRST ONE WAS IDENTIFIED IN 1845 BY THE 3RD EARL OF ROSS (WHO THEN OWNED THE WORLD'S MOST POWERFUL TELESCOPE).

SPIRALS
75% OF GALAXIES ARE SPIRALS. THE STARS PROBABLY FORMED FROM CLOUDS OF GASES WHICH HAVE COLLAPSED UNDER GRAVITY INTO MORE COMPACT STATES.

THE MILKY WAY
OUR OWN GALAXY, THE MILKY WAY, HAS A DIAMETER OF 100000 LIGHT YEARS & CONTAINS 100,000 MILLION STARS. WE ARE 32,000 LIGHT YEARS FROM THE CENTRE, TRAVELLING ROUND AT 500,000 MPH. ONE REVOLUTION WILL TAKE 225 MILLION YEARS.

GALACTIC GASES
THE GASES WITHIN GALAXIES CAN BE IDENTIFIED BY EXAMINING THE SPECTRUM OF THE LIGHT EMITTED. THOSE FOUND INCLUDE HYDROGEN, HELIUM, & CARBON MONOXIDE, ALSO ETHYL ALCOHOL, FORMALDEHYDE & OTHER ORGANIC GASES.

ELLIPTICALS
20% OF GALAXIES ARE ELLIPTICAL (SHAPED LIKE FAT CIGARS). THESE ROTATE SLOWLY & HAVE NO INTERSTELLAR GASES. THEY MAY HAVE BEEN FORMED BY THE COLLISION OF TWO SPIRAL GALAXIES (A PROCESS WHICH HAS BEEN SIMULATED WITH MATHEMATICAL COMPUTER MODELS).

IRREGULARS
5% OF GALAXIES ARE IRREGULARS. THESE MAY HAVE BEEN FORMED BY A NEAR-MISS BETWEEN TWO SPIRALS.

QUASARS
QUASARS ARE EXTREMELY DISTANT OBJECTS WHICH EMIT STRONG RADIO SIGNALS. IT IS NOW BELIEVED THAT THESE ARE GALAXIES WITH PARTICULARLY BIG BLACK HOLES IN THE MIDDLE.

ANDROMEDA
THE MOST REMOTE OBJECT VISIBLE TO THE NAKED EYE IS THE ANDROMEDA GALAXY 2,200,000 LIGHT YEARS AWAY.

IT IS NOW BELIEVED THAT EVERY GALAXY, INCLUDING OURS, HAS A BLACK HOLE IN THE MIDDLE. STARS ARE CONTINUALLY SUCKED INTO THESE HOLES SO GALAXIES ARE LITERALLY CONSUMING THEMSELVES.

THE BLACK HOLE
ATOMS (ELECTRICAL FORCES) — ELECTRONS / PLANETS
STARS (GRAVITY)

IN A STAR ONLY 2 OR 3 TIMES BIGGER THAN THE SUN, GRAVITY IS SO STRONG THAT IT OVERCOMES THE ELECTRICAL FORCES & MATTER COLLAPSES; THIS INCREASES THE DENSITY & GRAVITATIONAL FIELD TO SUCH AN EXTENT THAT EVEN LIGHT CANNOT ESCAPE ..... HENCE THE NAME 'BLACK HOLE'.

WHEN THE NUCLEAR REACTIONS INSIDE A SMALL STAR (WHICH MAKE IT SHINE) DIE DOWN IT COLLAPSES TO A COMPACT STATE WHERE GRAVITY IS BALANCED BY THE ELECTRICAL FORCES KEEPING THE ATOMS APART.

HOW TO MAKE A SAWDUST TRAP
SAWDUST — HARDBOARD TIED TO PICTURE RAIL / HARDBOARD SUPPORTED ON STICK / STRING PULLS OUT STICK
* DOES NOT FALL TILL DOOR IS FULLY OPEN & VICTIM IS IN DOORWAY.
* NO WARNING NOISES BEFORE SAWDUST FALLS.

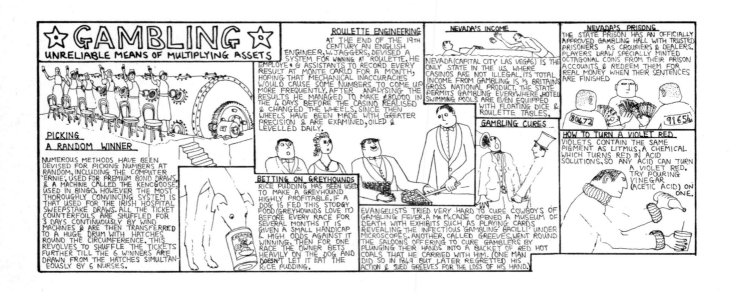

☆ GAMBLING ☆
UNRELIABLE MEANS OF MULTIPLYING ASSETS

PICKING A RANDOM WINNER
NUMEROUS METHODS HAVE BEEN DEVISED FOR PICKING NUMBERS AT RANDOM, INCLUDING THE COMPUTER 'ERNIE', USED FOR PREMIUM BOND DRAWS, & A MACHINE CALLED THE KENGOOSE USED IN BINGO. HOWEVER THE MOST THOROUGHLY CONVINCING SYSTEM IS THAT USED FOR THE IRISH HOSPITAL SWEEPSTAKE DRAWS. ALL THE TICKET COUNTERFOILS ARE SHUFFLED FOR 3 DAYS CONTINUOUSLY BY WIND MACHINES & ARE THEN TRANSFERRED TO A HUGE DRUM WITH HATCHES ROUND THE CIRCUMFERENCE. THIS REVOLVES TO SHUFFLE THE TICKETS FURTHER TILL THE 6 WINNERS ARE DRAWN FROM THE HATCHES SIMULTANEOUSLY BY 6 NURSES.

ROULETTE ENGINEERING
AT THE END OF THE 19TH CENTURY AN ENGLISH ENGINEER, W. JAGGERS, DEVISED A SYSTEM FOR WINNING AT ROULETTE. HE EMPLOYED 6 ASSISTANTS TO RECORD EVERY RESULT AT MONTE CARLO FOR A MONTH, HOPING THAT MECHANICAL INACCURACIES WOULD CAUSE SOME NUMBERS TO COME UP MORE FREQUENTLY. AFTER ANALYSING THE RESULTS HE MANAGED TO MAKE £80000 IN THE 4 DAYS BEFORE THE CASINO REALISED & CHANGED THE WHEELS. SINCE THEN WHEELS HAVE BEEN MADE WITH GREATER PRECISION & ARE EXAMINED, OILED & LEVELLED DAILY.

BETTING ON GREYHOUNDS
RICE PUDDING HAS BEEN USED TO MAKE A GREYHOUND HIGHLY PROFITABLE. IF A DOG IS FED THIS STODGY FOOD (GREYHOUNDS LOVE IT) BEFORE EVERY RACE FOR SEVERAL MONTHS IT IS GIVEN A SMALL HANDICAP & HIGH ODDS AGAINST IT WINNING. THEN FOR ONE RACE THE OWNER BETS HEAVILY ON THE DOG AND DOESN'T LET IT EAT THE RICE PUDDING.

NEVADA'S INCOME
NEVADA (CAPITAL CITY LAS VEGAS) IS THE ONLY STATE IN THE US WHERE CASINOS ARE NOT ILLEGAL. ITS TOTAL INCOME FROM GAMBLING IS ⅓ BRITAIN'S GROSS NATIONAL PRODUCT. THE STATE PERMITS GAMBLING EVERYWHERE. HOTEL SWIMMING POOLS ARE EVEN EQUIPPED WITH FLOATING DICE & ROULETTE TABLES.

GAMBLING CURES
EVANGELISTS TRIED VERY HARD TO CURE COWBOYS OF GAMBLING FEVER. A Mr McCADE OPENED A MUSEUM OF DEATH WITH EXHIBITS SUCH AS PLAYING CARDS REVEALING THE INFECTIOUS GAMBLING BACILLI UNDER MICROSCOPES. ANOTHER, CALLED GREEVES, WENT ROUND THE SALOONS OFFERING TO CURE GAMBLERS BY PLUNGING THEIR HANDS INTO A BUCKET OF RED HOT COALS THAT HE CARRIED WITH HIM. (ONE MAN DID SO IN 1849 BUT LATER REGRETTED HIS ACTION & SUED GREEVES FOR THE LOSS OF HIS HAND.)

NEVADA'S PRISONS
THE STATE PRISON HAS AN OFFICIALLY APPROVED GAMBLING HALL WITH TRUSTED PRISONERS AS CROUPIERS & DEALERS. PLAYERS DRAW SPECIALLY MINTED OCTAGONAL COINS FROM THEIR PRISON ACCOUNTS & REDEEM THEM FOR REAL MONEY WHEN THEIR SENTENCES ARE FINISHED.

80472   91656

HOW TO TURN A VIOLET RED
VIOLETS CONTAIN THE SAME PIGMENT AS LITMUS, A CHEMICAL WHICH TURNS RED IN ACID SOLUTIONS. SO ANY ACID CAN TURN A VIOLET RED. TRY POURING VINEGAR (ACETIC ACID) ON ONE.

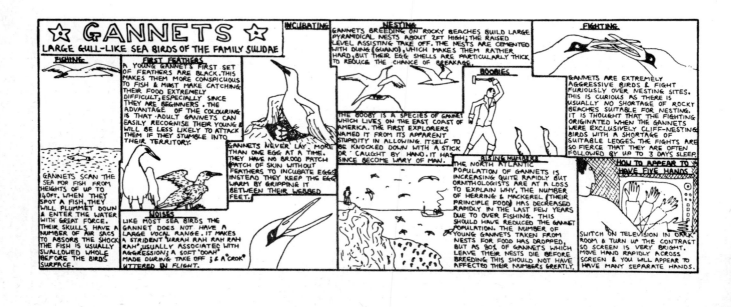

☆ GANNETS ☆
LARGE GULL-LIKE SEA BIRDS OF THE FAMILY SULIDAE

FISHING
GANNETS SCAN THE SEA FOR FISH FROM HEIGHTS OF UP TO 100FT. WHEN THEY SPOT A FISH, THEY WILL PLUMMET DOWN & ENTER THE WATER WITH GREAT FORCE. THEIR SKULLS HAVE A NUMBER OF AIR SACS TO ABSORB THE SHOCK. THE FISH IS USUALLY SWALLOWED WHOLE BEFORE THE BIRDS SURFACE.

FIRST FEATHERS
A YOUNG GANNET'S FIRST SET OF FEATHERS ARE BLACK. THIS MAKES THEM MORE CONSPICUOUS TO FISH & MUST MAKE CATCHING THEIR FOOD EXTREMELY DIFFICULT, ESPECIALLY SINCE THEY ARE BEGINNERS. THE ADVANTAGE OF THE COLOURING IS THAT ADULT GANNETS CAN EASILY RECOGNISE THEIR YOUNG & WILL BE LESS LIKELY TO ATTACK THEM IF THEY STUMBLE INTO THEIR TERRITORY.

GANNETS NEVER LAY MORE THAN ONE EGG AT A TIME. THEY HAVE NO BROOD PATCH (PATCH OF SKIN WITHOUT FEATHERS TO INCUBATE EGGS) INSTEAD THEY KEEP THE EGG WARM BY GRIPPING IT BETWEEN THEIR WEBBED FEET.

NOISES
LIKE MOST SEA BIRDS THE GANNET DOES NOT HAVE A LARGE VOCAL RANGE. IT MAKES A STRIDENT 'URRAH RAH RAH RAH RAH' USUALLY ASSOCIATED WITH AGGRESSION; A SOFT 'OOAH' MADE DURING TAKE OFF & A 'CROK' UTTERED IN FLIGHT.

INCUBATING
NESTING
GANNETS BREEDING ON ROCKY BEACHES BUILD LARGE PYRAMIDAL NESTS ABOUT 2FT HIGH; THE RAISED LEVEL ASSISTING TAKE OFF. THE NESTS ARE CEMENTED WITH DUNG (GUANO), WHICH MAKES THEM RATHER HARD, BUT THEIR EGG SHELLS ARE PARTICULARLY THICK TO REDUCE THE CHANCE OF BREAKAGE.

BOOBIES
THE BOOBY IS A SPECIES OF GANNET WHICH LIVES ON THE EAST COAST OF AMERICA. THE FIRST EXPLORERS NAMED IT FROM ITS APPARENT STUPIDITY IN ALLOWING ITSELF TO BE KNOCKED DOWN WITH A STICK OR CAUGHT BY HAND. IT HAS SINCE BECOME WARY OF MAN.

RISING NUMBERS
THE NORTH ATLANTIC POPULATION OF GANNETS IS INCREASING QUITE RAPIDLY BUT ORNITHOLOGISTS ARE AT A LOSS TO EXPLAIN WHY. THE NUMBER OF HERRING & MACKEREL (THEIR PRINCIPLE FOOD) HAS DECREASED RAPIDLY IN THE LAST FEW YEARS DUE TO OVER FISHING. THIS SHOULD HAVE REDUCED THE GANNET POPULATION. THE NUMBER OF YOUNG GANNETS TAKEN FROM NESTS FOR FOOD HAS DROPPED, BUT AS 80% OF GANNETS WHICH LEAVE THEIR NESTS DIE BEFORE BREEDING THIS SHOULD NOT HAVE AFFECTED THEIR NUMBERS GREATLY.

FIGHTING
GANNETS ARE EXTREMELY AGGRESSIVE BIRDS & FIGHT FURIOUSLY OVER NESTING SITES. THIS IS CURIOUS AS THERE IS USUALLY NO SHORTAGE OF ROCKY BEACHES SUITABLE FOR NESTING. IT IS THOUGHT THAT THE FIGHTING ORIGINATED WHEN THE GANNETS WERE EXCLUSIVELY CLIFF-NESTING BIRDS WITH A SHORTAGE OF SUITABLE LEDGES. THE FIGHTS ARE SO FIERCE THAT THEY ARE OFTEN FOLLOWED BY UP TO 3 DAYS SLEEP.

HOW TO APPEAR TO HAVE FIVE HANDS
SWITCH ON TELEVISION IN DARK ROOM & TURN UP THE CONTRAST SO SCREEN IS VERY BRIGHT. MOVE HAND RAPIDLY ACROSS SCREEN & YOU WILL APPEAR TO HAVE MANY SEPARATE HANDS.

☆ GARDENING ☆
CULTIVATION OF PLANTS FOR PLEASURE

UNTIL THE MIDDLE AGES, FLOWER GARDENS WERE PRACTICALLY UNKNOWN IN EUROPE. MONASTERIES KEPT HERB & VEGETABLE GARDENS WITH A FEW FLOWERS FOR DECORATING THE CHAPELS. THE MOST ELABORATE GARDENS WERE THOSE OF THE APOTHECARIES, GROWING A WIDE VARIETY OF MEDICINAL PLANTS. TOWN HOUSES WERE NOT BUILT WITH GARDENS UNTIL THE 17TH CENTURY. TURIN IS SAID TO BE THE FIRST GARDEN CITY. AFTER A FIRE IT WAS REBUILT IN 1659 WITH A GARDEN TO EACH HOUSE.

GARDENS & MEDICINE

FLOATING

THE AZTECS HAD FLOATING GARDENS CONSISTING OF RAFTS FULL OF SOIL LASHED TOGETHER. THE SPANIARDS WERE AMAZED BY THE HUGE GREEN 'ISLANDS' MOVING AROUND THE CITY OF TENOCHTITLAN AS THE AZTECS PUNTED FROM THEIR HOMES TO THE MARKET. SIMILAR FLOATING GARDENS ARE STILL USED IN THE LAKES OF KASHMIR.

GARDENS & PARADISE

SOME OF THE EARLIEST GARDENS WERE THE PARKS OF ANCIENT MESOPOTAMIA. THEY WERE CALLED 'PARDES', THE WORD FROM WHICH PARADISE IS DERIVED, VIA THE GREEK 'PARADISOS'.

TEMPORARY GARDENS

THE ANCIENT CHINESE ARE BELIEVED NOT TO HAVE DEVELOPED ANY SOPHISTICATED GARDENING METHODS. THIS IS PARTLY BECAUSE OF THE CUSTOM THAT A SON WOULD NOT CONTINUE LIVING IN A PROPERTY WHEN HIS FATHER DIED, SO GARDENS RARELY BECAME WELL ESTABLISHED.

TREE - MOVING

THE 18TH CENTURY VOGUE FOR LANDSCAPE GARDENING LED TO A VARIETY OF TREE-MOVING TECHNIQUES. THE DESIGNER, CAPABILITY BROWN, USED A SORT OF CART (SEE LEFT) FOR MOVING FULLY GROWN TREES. IT IS REPORTED THAT MUCH OF THE EARTH FELL OFF THE ROOTS IN TRANSIT & THAT, FOR SEVERAL YEARS AFTER, THE TREES GREW SO SLOWLY 'AS TO REMIND ONE OF STRICKEN DEER'.

HOW TO TURN A COUPLE TO FACE EACH OTHER

HOLD A KING IN ONE HAND & A QUEEN IN THE OTHER FACING OUTWARDS (SEE A). BRING THE CARDS TOGETHER, SWAP THE GRIP SO THE LEFT HAND HOLDS THE RIGHT HAND-CARD & VICE VERSA, AND PULL THE HANDS APART SLIDING ONE CARD OVER THE OTHER. ALTHOUGH IT MAY SEEM SURPRISING, AFTER ABOUT HALF AN HOUR'S PRACTICE THIS CAN BE DONE SO FAST THAT THE 'SWAP' CANNOT BE SEEN.

SEEDING

MODERN PROPAGATORS FOR GROWING SEEDLINGS HAVE HEATERS TO KEEP THE SOIL WARM & HUMIDIFIERS TO KEEP THE AIR MOIST. A GARDENING MANUAL OF 1650 SUGGESTED USING AN OLD FOUR-POSTER BED, PLACED IN A GARDEN WITH A LAYER OF SOIL ON THE MATTRESS. THE CURTAINS KEPT THE SEEDLINGS SHELTERED & THE AIR MOIST & THE MATTRESS INSULATED THE SOIL.

DIGGING

ACCORDING TO A. HUXLEY'S 'HISTORY OF GARDENING,' T HANDLED SPADES WERE TRADITIONALLY USED IN THE NORTH OF ENGLAND & D HANDLED SPADES IN THE SOUTH. MOST EUROPEAN COUNTRIES USE LONG HANDLED SPADES WITHOUT GRIPS & THINK THAT THE BRITISH ARE MAD, BENDING DOWN TO DIG.

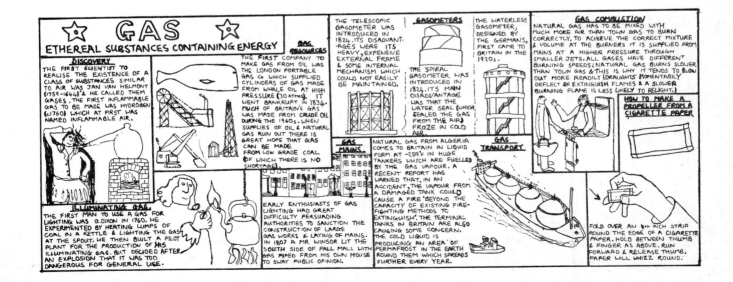

☆ GAS ☆
ETHEREAL SUBSTANCES CONTAINING ENERGY

DISCOVERY

THE FIRST SCIENTIST TO REALISE THE EXISTENCE OF A CLASS OF SUBSTANCES SIMILAR TO AIR WAS JAN VAN HELMONT (1759-1644). HE CALLED THEM GASES. THE FIRST INFLAMMABLE GAS TO BE MADE WAS HYDROGEN (c.1760) WHICH AT FIRST WAS NAMED INFLAMMABLE AIR.

ILLUMINATING GAS

THE FIRST MAN TO USE A GAS FOR LIGHTING WAS G. DIXON IN 1760. HE EXPERIMENTED BY HEATING LUMPS OF COAL IN A KETTLE & LIGHTING THE GAS AT THE SPOUT. HE THEN BUILT A PILOT PLANT FOR THE PRODUCTION OF HIS ILLUMINATING GAS. BUT DECIDED AFTER AN EXPLOSION THAT IT WAS TOO DANGEROUS FOR GENERAL USE.

GAS RESOURCES

THE FIRST COMPANY TO MAKE GAS FROM OIL WAS THE LONDON PORTABLE GAS Co WHICH SUPPLIED CYLINDERS OF GAS MADE FROM WHALE OIL AT HIGH PRESSURE (30 ATMOS). IT WENT BANKRUPT IN 1834. MUCH OF BRITAIN'S GAS WAS MADE FROM CRUDE OIL DURING THE 1960s. WHEN SUPPLIES OF OIL & NATURAL GAS RUN OUT THERE IS GREAT HOPE THAT GAS CAN BE MADE FROM LOW GRADE COAL (OF WHICH THERE IS NO SHORTAGE).

GAS MAINS

EARLY ENTHUSIASTS OF GAS LIGHTING HAD GREAT DIFFICULTY PERSUADING AUTHORITIES TO SANCTION THE CONSTRUCTION OF LARGE GAS WORKS & LAYING OF MAINS. IN 1807 A MR WINSOR LIT THE SOUTH SIDE OF PALL MALL WITH GAS PIPED FROM HIS OWN HOUSE TO SWAY PUBLIC OPINION.

GASOMETERS

THE TELESCOPIC GASOMETER WAS INTRODUCED IN 1824. ITS DISADVANTAGES WERE ITS HEAVY, EXPENSIVE EXTERNAL FRAME & SOME INTERNAL MECHANISM WHICH COULD NOT EASILY BE MAINTAINED.

THE SPIRAL GASOMETER WAS INTRODUCED IN 1824. ITS MAIN DISADVANTAGE WAS THAT THE WATER SEAL (WHICH SEALED THE GAS FROM THE AIR) FROZE IN COLD AIR.

THE WATERLESS GASOMETER, DESIGNED BY THE GERMANS, FIRST CAME TO BRITAIN IN THE 1920s.

NATURAL GAS FROM ALGERIA COMES TO BRITAIN IN LIQUID FORM AT -259° IN HUGE TANKERS WHICH ARE FUELLED BY THE GAS VAPOUR. A RECENT REPORT HAS WARNED THAT, IN AN ACCIDENT, THE VAPOUR FROM A DAMAGED TANK COULD CAUSE A FIRE 'BEYOND THE CAPACITY OF EXISTING FIRE-FIGHTING METHODS TO EXTINGUISH'. THE TERMINAL TANKS IN BRITAIN ARE ALSO CAUSING SOME CONCERN. THE COLD LIQUID IS PRODUCING AN AREA OF PERMAFROST IN THE EARTH ROUND THEM WHICH SPREADS FURTHER EVERY YEAR.

GAS TRANSPORT

GAS COMBUSTION

NATURAL GAS HAS TO BE MIXED WITH MUCH MORE AIR THAN TOWN GAS TO BURN CORRECTLY. TO ACHIEVE THE CORRECT MIXTURE & VOLUME AT THE BURNERS IT IS SUPPLIED FROM MAINS AT A HIGHER PRESSURE THROUGH SMALLER JETS. ALL GASES HAVE DIFFERENT BURNING SPEEDS; NATURAL GAS BURNS SLOWER THAN TOWN GAS & THIS IS WHY IT TENDS TO BLOW OUT MORE READILY (DRAUGHTS MOMENTARILY DEFLECT OR EXTINGUISH FLAMES) & A SLOWER BURNING FLAME IS LESS LIKELY TO RELIGHT.

HOW TO MAKE A PROPELLER FROM A CIGARETTE PAPER

FOLD OVER AN ⅛TH INCH STRIP ROUND THE EDGE OF A CIGARETTE PAPER. HOLD BETWEEN THUMB & FINGER AS ABOVE. RUN FORWARD & RELEASE THUMB. PAPER WILL WHIZZ ROUND.

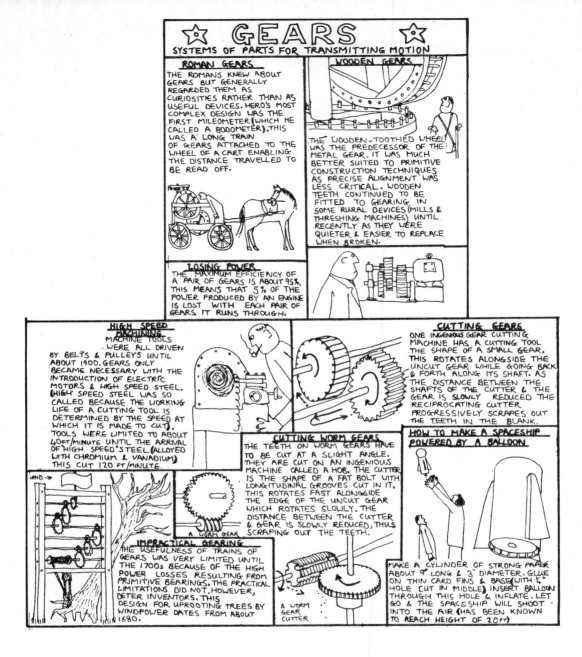

☆ GEARS ☆

SYSTEMS OF PARTS FOR TRANSMITTING MOTION

ROMAN GEARS

THE ROMANS KNEW ABOUT GEARS BUT GENERALLY REGARDED THEM AS CURIOSITIES RATHER THAN AS USEFUL DEVICES. HERO'S MOST COMPLEX DESIGN WAS THE FIRST MILEOMETER (WHICH HE CALLED A BODOMETER). THIS WAS A LONG TRAIN OF GEARS ATTACHED TO THE WHEEL OF A CART ENABLING THE DISTANCE TRAVELLED TO BE READ OFF.

WOODEN GEARS

THE WOODEN-TOOTHED WHEEL WAS THE PREDECESSOR OF THE METAL GEAR. IT WAS MUCH BETTER SUITED TO PRIMITIVE CONSTRUCTION TECHNIQUES AS PRECISE ALIGNMENT WAS LESS CRITICAL. WOODEN TEETH CONTINUED TO BE FITTED TO GEARING IN SOME RURAL DEVICES (MILLS & THRESHING MACHINES) UNTIL RECENTLY AS THEY WERE QUIETER & EASIER TO REPLACE WHEN BROKEN.

LOSING POWER

THE MAXIMUM EFFICIENCY OF A PAIR OF GEARS IS ABOUT 95%. THIS MEANS THAT 5% OF THE POWER PRODUCED BY AN ENGINE IS LOST WITH EACH PAIR OF GEARS IT RUNS THROUGH.

HIGH SPEED MACHINING

MACHINE TOOLS WERE ALL DRIVEN BY BELTS & PULLEYS UNTIL ABOUT 1900. GEARS ONLY BECAME NECESSARY WITH THE INTRODUCTION OF ELECTRIC MOTORS & HIGH SPEED STEEL. (HIGH SPEED STEEL WAS SO CALLED BECAUSE THE WORKING LIFE OF A CUTTING TOOL IS DETERMINED BY THE SPEED AT WHICH IT IS MADE TO CUT). TOOLS WERE LIMITED TO ABOUT 40FT/MINUTE UNTIL THE ARRIVAL OF HIGH SPEED STEEL (ALLOYED WITH CHROMIUM & VANADIUM) THIS CUT 120 FT/MINUTE.

CUTTING GEARS

ONE INGENIOUS GEAR CUTTING MACHINE HAS A CUTTING TOOL THE SHAPE OF A SMALL GEAR. THIS ROTATES ALONGSIDE THE UNCUT GEAR WHILE GOING BACK & FORTH ALONG ITS SHAFT. AS THE DISTANCE BETWEEN THE SHAFTS OF THE CUTTER & THE GEAR IS SLOWLY REDUCED THE RECIPROCATING CUTTER PROGRESSIVELY SCRAPES OUT THE TEETH IN THE BLANK.

CUTTING WORM GEARS

THE TEETH ON WORM GEARS HAVE TO BE CUT AT A SLIGHT ANGLE. THEY ARE CUT ON AN INGENIOUS MACHINE CALLED A HOB. THE CUTTER IS THE SHAPE OF A FAT BOLT WITH LONGITUDINAL GROOVES CUT IN IT. THIS ROTATES FAST ALONGSIDE THE EDGE OF THE UNCUT GEAR WHICH ROTATES SLOWLY. THE DISTANCE BETWEEN THE CUTTER & GEAR IS SLOWLY REDUCED, THUS SCRAPING OUT THE TEETH.

A WORM GEAR

A WORM GEAR CUTTER

IMPRACTICAL GEARING

THE USEFULNESS OF TRAINS OF GEARS WAS VERY LIMITED UNTIL THE 1700s BECAUSE OF THE HIGH POWER LOSSES RESULTING FROM PRIMITIVE BEARINGS. THE PRACTICAL LIMITATIONS DID NOT, HOWEVER, DETER INVENTORS. THIS DESIGN FOR UPROOTING TREES BY WINDPOWER DATES FROM ABOUT 1680.

WIND →

HOW TO MAKE A SPACESHIP POWERED BY A BALLOON

MAKE A CYLINDER OF STRONG PAPER ABOUT 9" LONG & 3" DIAMETER. GLUE ON THIN CARD FINS & BASE (WITH ½" HOLE CUT IN MIDDLE) INSERT BALLOON THROUGH THIS HOLE & INFLATE. LET GO & THE SPACESHIP WILL SHOOT INTO THE AIR (HAS BEEN KNOWN TO REACH HEIGHT OF 20FT)

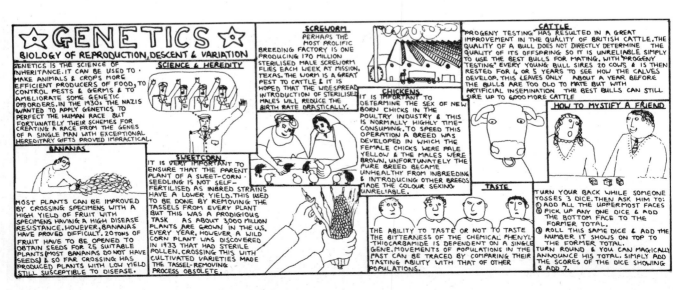

☆ GENETICS ☆

BIOLOGY OF REPRODUCTION, DESCENT & VARIATION

GENETICS IS THE SCIENCE OF INHERITANCE. IT CAN BE USED TO MAKE ANIMALS & CROPS MORE EFFICIENT PRODUCERS OF FOOD, TO CONTROL PESTS & GERMS & TO AMELIORATE SOME GENETIC DISORDERS. IN THE 1930s THE NAZIS WANTED TO APPLY GENETICS TO PERFECT THE HUMAN RACE BUT FORTUNATELY THEIR SCHEMES FOR CREATING A RACE FROM THE GENES OF A SINGLE MAN WITH EXCEPTIONAL HEREDITARY GIFTS PROVED IMPRACTICAL.

SCIENCE & HEREDITY

BANANAS

MOST PLANTS CAN BE IMPROVED BY CROSSING SPECIMENS WITH A HIGH YIELD OF FRUIT WITH SPECIMENS HAVING A HIGH DISEASE RESISTANCE. HOWEVER, BANANAS HAVE PROVED DIFFICULT. 20 TONS OF FRUIT HAVE TO BE OPENED TO OBTAIN SEEDS FOR 25 SUITABLE PLANTS (MOST BANANAS DO NOT HAVE SEEDS) & SO FAR CROSSING HAS PRODUCED PLANTS WITH LOW YIELD STILL SUSCEPTIBLE TO DISEASE.

SWEETCORN

IT IS VERY IMPORTANT TO ENSURE THAT THE PARENT PLANT OF A SWEET-CORN SEEDLING IS NOT SELF-FERTILISED AS INBRED STRAINS HAVE A LOWER YIELD. THIS USED TO BE DONE BY REMOVING THE TASSELS FROM EVERY PLANT BUT THIS WAS A PRODIGIOUS TASK AS ABOUT 3000 MILLION PLANTS ARE GROWN IN THE U.S. EVERY YEAR. HOWEVER A WILD CORN PLANT WAS DISCOVERED IN 1933 THAT HAD STERILE POLLEN. CROSSING THIS WITH CULTIVATED VARIETIES MADE THE TASSEL-REMOVING PROCESS OBSOLETE.

SCREWORM

PERHAPS THE MOST PROLIFIC BREEDING FACTORY IS ONE PRODUCING 170 MILLION STERILISED MALE SCREWORM FLIES EACH WEEK AT MISSION, TEXAS. THE WORM IS A GREAT PEST TO CATTLE & IT IS HOPED THAT THE WIDESPREAD INTRODUCTION OF STERILISED MALES WILL REDUCE THE BIRTH RATE DRASTICALLY.

CHICKENS

IT IS IMPORTANT TO DETERMINE THE SEX OF NEW BORN CHICKS IN THE POULTRY INDUSTRY & THIS IS NORMALLY HIGHLY TIME-CONSUMING. TO SPEED THIS OPERATION A BREED WAS DEVELOPED IN WHICH THE FEMALE CHICKS WERE PALE YELLOW & THE MALES WERE BROWN. UNFORTUNATELY THE PURE BREED BECAME UNHEALTHY FROM INBREEDING & INTRODUCING OTHER BREEDS MADE THE COLOUR SEXING UNRELIABLE.

TASTE

THE ABILITY TO TASTE OR NOT TO TASTE THE BITTERNESS OF THE CHEMICAL PHENYL THIOCARBAMIDE IS DEPENDENT ON A SINGLE GENE. MOVEMENTS OF POPULATIONS IN THE PAST CAN BE TRACED BY COMPARING THEIR TASTING ABILITY WITH THAT OF OTHER POPULATIONS.

CATTLE

PROGENY TESTING HAS RESULTED IN A GREAT IMPROVEMENT IN THE QUALITY OF BRITISH CATTLE. THE QUALITY OF A BULL DOES NOT DIRECTLY DETERMINE THE QUALITY OF ITS OFFSPRING SO IT IS UNRELIABLE SIMPLY TO USE THE BEST BULLS FOR MATING. WITH PROGENY TESTING EVERY YOUNG BULL SIRES 20 COWS & IS THEN RESTED FOR 4 OR 5 YEARS TO SEE HOW THE CALVES DEVELOP. THIS LEAVES ONLY ABOUT A YEAR BEFORE THE BULLS ARE TOO OLD TO MATE BUT WITH ARTIFICIAL INSEMINATION THE BEST BULLS CAN STILL SIRE UP 6 6000 MORE CATTLE

HOW TO MYSTIFY A FRIEND

TURN YOUR BACK WHILE SOMEONE TOSSES 3 DICE. THEN ASK HIM TO:
① ADD ALL THE UPPERMOST FACES
② PICK UP ANY ONE DICE & ADD THE BOTTOM FACE TO THE FORMER TOTAL.
③ ROLL THIS SAME DICE & ADD THE NUMBER IT SHOWS ON TOP TO THE FORMER TOTAL.
TURN ROUND & YOU CAN MAGICALLY ANNOUNCE HIS TOTAL. SIMPLY ADD THE SCORES OF THE DICE SHOWING & ADD 7.

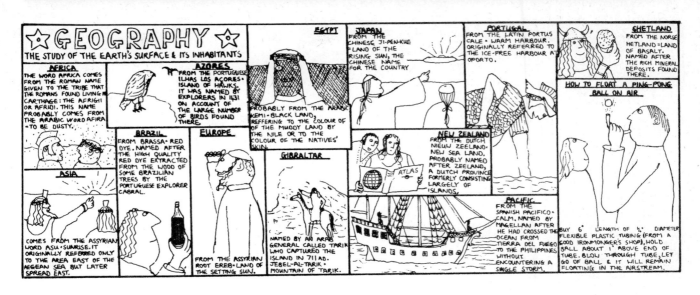

☆ GEOGRAPHY ☆
THE STUDY OF THE EARTH'S SURFACE & ITS INHABITANTS

AFRICA — THE WORD AFRICA COMES FROM THE ROMAN NAME GIVEN TO THE TRIBE THAT THE ROMANS FOUND LIVING AT CARTHAGE: THE AFRIGII OR AFRIDI. THIS NAME PROBABLY COMES FROM THE ARABIC WORD AFIRA - TO BE DUSTY.

AZORES — FROM THE PORTUGUESE ILHAS LOS AÇORES - ISLAND OF HAWKS. IT WAS NAMED BY EXPLORERS IN 1431 ON ACCOUNT OF THE LARGE NUMBER OF BIRDS FOUND THERE.

BRAZIL — FROM BRASSA - RED DYE. NAMED AFTER THE HIGH QUALITY RED DYE EXTRACTED FROM THE WOOD OF SOME BRAZILIAN TREES BY THE PORTUGUESE EXPLORER CABRAL.

EUROPE — FROM THE ASSYRIAN ROOT EREB - LAND OF THE SETTING SUN.

ASIA — COMES FROM THE ASSYRIAN WORD ASU - SUNRISE. IT ORIGINALLY REFERRED ONLY TO THE AREA EAST OF THE AEGEAN SEA BUT LATER SPREAD EAST.

EGYPT — PROBABLY FROM THE ARABIC KEMI - BLACK LAND, REFERRING TO THE COLOUR OF THE MUDDY LAND BY THE NILE OR TO THE COLOUR OF THE NATIVES' SKIN.

GIBRALTAR — NAMED BY AN ARAB GENERAL CALLED TARIK WHO CAPTURED THE ISLAND IN 711 AD. JEBEL-AL-TARIK - MOUNTAIN OF TARIK.

JAPAN — FROM THE CHINESE JI-PEN-KUE - LAND OF THE RISING SUN, THE CHINESE NAME FOR THE COUNTRY

NEW ZEALAND — FROM THE DUTCH NIEUW ZEELAND - NEW SEA LAND. PROBABLY NAMED AFTER ZEELAND, A DUTCH PROVINCE FORMERLY CONSISTING LARGELY OF ISLANDS.

PACIFIC — FROM THE SPANISH PACIFICO - CALM. NAMED BY MAGELLAN AFTER HE HAD CROSSED THE OCEAN FROM TIERRA DEL FUEGO TO THE PHILIPPINES WITHOUT ENCOUNTERING A SINGLE STORM.

PORTUGAL — FROM THE LATIN PORTUS CALE - WARM HARBOUR. ORIGINALLY REFERRED TO THE ICE-FREE HARBOUR AT OPORTO.

SHETLAND — FROM THE NORSE HETLAND - LAND OF BASALT. NAMED AFTER THE RICH MINERAL DEPOSITS FOUND THERE.

HOW TO FLOAT A PING-PONG BALL ON AIR — BUY 6" LENGTH OF ½" DIAMETER FLEXIBLE PLASTIC TUBING (FROM A GOOD IRONMONGER'S SHOP), HOLD BALL ABOUT 1" ABOVE END OF TUBE. BLOW THROUGH TUBE, LET GO OF BALL & IT WILL REMAIN FLOATING IN THE AIRSTREAM.

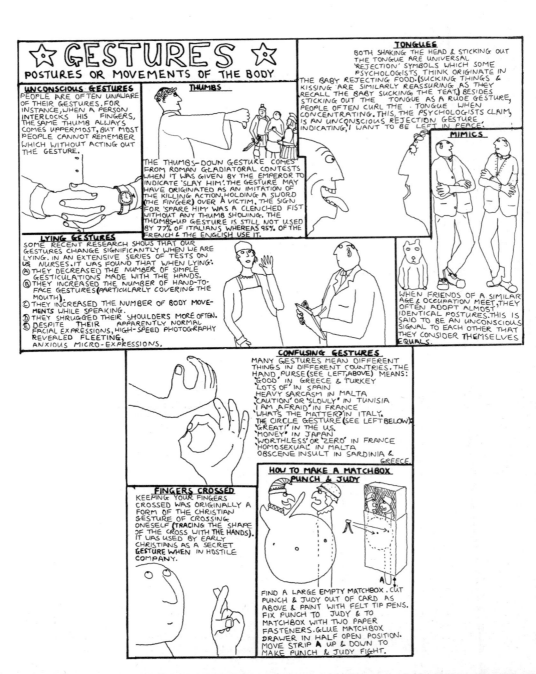

☆ GESTURES ☆
POSTURES OR MOVEMENTS OF THE BODY

UNCONSCIOUS GESTURES — PEOPLE ARE OFTEN UNAWARE OF THEIR GESTURES. FOR INSTANCE, WHEN A PERSON INTERLOCKS HIS FINGERS, THE SAME THUMB ALWAYS COMES UPPERMOST, BUT MOST PEOPLE CANNOT REMEMBER WHICH WITHOUT ACTING OUT THE GESTURE.

THUMBS — THE THUMBS-DOWN GESTURE COMES FROM ROMAN GLADIATORIAL CONTESTS WHEN IT WAS GIVEN BY THE EMPEROR TO INDICATE 'SLAY HIM'. THE GESTURE MAY HAVE ORIGINATED AS AN IMITATION OF THE KILLING ACTION, HOLDING A SWORD (THE FINGER) OVER A VICTIM. THE SIGN FOR 'SPARE HIM' WAS A CLENCHED FIST WITHOUT ANY THUMB SHOWING. THE THUMBS-UP GESTURE IS STILL NOT USED BY 77% OF ITALIANS WHEREAS 95% OF THE FRENCH & THE ENGLISH USE IT.

TONGUES — BOTH SHAKING THE HEAD & STICKING OUT THE TONGUE ARE UNIVERSAL 'REJECTION' SYMBOLS WHICH SOME PSYCHOLOGISTS THINK ORIGINATE IN THE BABY REJECTING FOOD. (SUCKING THINGS & KISSING ARE SIMILARLY REASSURING AS THEY RECALL THE BABY SUCKING THE TEAT.) BESIDES STICKING OUT THE TONGUE AS A RUDE GESTURE, PEOPLE OFTEN CURL THE TONGUE WHEN CONCENTRATING. THIS, THE PSYCHOLOGISTS CLAIM, IS AN UNCONSCIOUS REJECTION GESTURE INDICATING, 'I WANT TO BE LEFT IN PEACE.'

LYING GESTURES — SOME RECENT RESEARCH SHOWS THAT OUR GESTURES CHANGE SIGNIFICANTLY WHEN WE ARE LYING. IN AN EXTENSIVE SERIES OF TESTS ON US NURSES, IT WAS FOUND THAT WHEN LYING:
Ⓐ THEY DECREASED THE NUMBER OF SIMPLE GESTICULATIONS MADE WITH THE HANDS.
Ⓑ THEY INCREASED THE NUMBER OF HAND-TO-FACE GESTURES (PARTICULARLY COVERING THE MOUTH)
Ⓒ THEY INCREASED THE NUMBER OF BODY MOVE-MENTS WHILE SPEAKING.
Ⓓ THEY SHRUGGED THEIR SHOULDERS MORE OFTEN.
Ⓔ DESPITE THEIR APPARENTLY NORMAL FACIAL EXPRESSIONS, HIGH-SPEED PHOTOGRAPHY REVEALED FLEETING, ANXIOUS MICRO-EXPRESSIONS.

MIMICS — WHEN FRIENDS OF A SIMILAR AGE & OCCUPATION MEET, THEY OFTEN ADOPT ALMOST IDENTICAL POSTURES. THIS IS SAID TO BE AN UNCONSCIOUS SIGNAL TO EACH OTHER THAT THEY CONSIDER THEMSELVES EQUALS.

CONFUSING GESTURES — MANY GESTURES MEAN DIFFERENT THINGS IN DIFFERENT COUNTRIES. THE HAND PURSE (SEE LEFT, ABOVE) MEANS:
'GOOD' IN GREECE & TURKEY
'LOTS OF' IN SPAIN
HEAVY SARCASM IN MALTA
'CAUTION' OR 'SLOWLY' IN TUNISIA
'I AM AFRAID' IN FRANCE
'WHAT'S THE MATTER?' IN ITALY.
THE CIRCLE GESTURE (SEE LEFT, BELOW)
'GREAT!' IN THE US.
'MONEY' IN JAPAN
'WORTHLESS' OR 'ZERO' IN FRANCE
'HOMOSEXUAL' IN MALTA
OBSCENE INSULT IN SARDINIA & GREECE.

FINGERS CROSSED — KEEPING YOUR FINGERS CROSSED WAS ORIGINALLY A FORM OF THE CHRISTIAN GESTURE OF CROSSING ONESELF (TRACING THE SHAPE OF THE CROSS WITH THE HANDS). IT WAS USED BY EARLY CHRISTIANS AS A SECRET GESTURE WHEN IN HOSTILE COMPANY.

HOW TO MAKE A MATCHBOX PUNCH & JUDY — FIND A LARGE EMPTY MATCHBOX. CUT PUNCH & JUDY OUT OF CARD AS ABOVE & PAINT WITH FELT TIP PENS. FIX PUNCH TO JUDY & TO MATCHBOX WITH TWO PAPER FASTENERS. GLUE MATCHBOX DRAWER IN HALF OPEN POSITION. MOVE STRIP A UP & DOWN TO MAKE PUNCH & JUDY FIGHT.

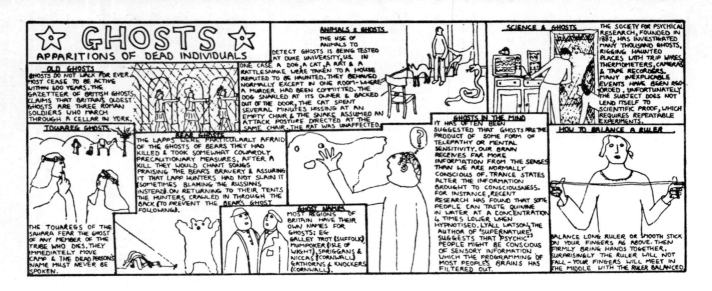

☆ GINSENG ☆
ARALIACEOUS PLANTS WITH FORKED AROMATIC ROOTS

CHINESE PANACEA
FOR 3,000 YEARS THE ROOT OF THE PLANT GINSENG HAS BEEN A KEY MEDICINE IN CHINA. FOR PREVENTING DISEASE & SPEEDING RECOVERY. (DOCTORS WERE PAID ONLY WHEN THEIR PATIENTS WERE HEALTHY.)

WESTERN SCEPTICISM
THE ENCYCLOPEDIA BRITANNICA DESCRIBES GINSENG AS A WORTHLESS PLANT, BUT THERE HAS RECENTLY BEEN INCREASED INTEREST IN THE WEST. VARIOUS DOCTORS HAVE WRITTEN ABOUT IT & HEALTH FOOD SHOPS NOW STOCK IT.

EATING
GINSENG ROOTS CAN BE CHEWED WHOLE (THE OLDER THE BETTER) OR GROUND UP & TAKEN AS PILLS OR IN SOLUTION SEVERAL TIMES DAILY. ITS EFFECTS ARE CUMULATIVE SO IT HAS TO BE TAKEN FOR AT LEAST A MONTH.

GROWING
GINSENG IS RELATED TO IVY. IT IS EXPENSIVE BECAUSE IT IS DIFFICULT TO GROW. IT ONLY GROWS EFFECTIVELY IN REMOTE PARTS OF CHINA & KOREA & THE GROUND HAS TO REMAIN FALLOW FOR SEVERAL YEARS AFTER HARVESTING (TO KILL OFF A FUNGUS WHICH ROTS THE ROOTS).

CONFISCATION
SOVIET INTEREST IN GINSENG WAS STIMULATED BY THE LARGE AMOUNT THE RUSSIANS FOUND UNDER CULTIVATION IN NORTH KOREA IN 1945. ONE ENTIRE CROP WAS CONFISCATED FOR THEIR EXPERIMENTS.

TRIALS
RUSSIAN TRIALS FOUND THAT GINSENG INCREASED THE AVERAGE RUNNING SPEED OF SOLDIERS BY 8%, REDUCED THE ERRORS MADE BY RADIO OPERATORS SENDING MORSE CODE BY OVER 10% & REDUCED WINTER COLDS & FLU IN A GROUP OF FACTORY WORKERS BY 70%.

HEALTH
THE RUSSIAN BELIEF IN GINSENG IS STILL STRONG. IT IS SOLD IN ALL USSR CHEMISTS & GIVEN TO ATHLETES & COSMONAUTS.

MODERN PRODUCTION TECHNIQUES HAVE REDUCED THE FALLOW PERIOD TO TWO YEARS THOUGH THIS DOES NOT KILL THE FUNGI, & ROOT ROT IS COMMON.

SIBERIAN GINSENG
HEALTH FOOD SHOPS ALSO SELL SIBERIAN GINSENG. THIS THORNY PLANT (ELEUTHEROCOCCUS) WAS FOUND TO POSSESS GINSENG'S MEDICINAL PROPERTIES. IT IS MUCH CHEAPER & PROBABLY JUST AS EFFECTIVE.

STRESS
SOME U.S. RESEARCH SUGGESTS THAT GINSENG ACTS ON THE HORMONES WHICH CONTROL OUR RESPONSE TO STRESS. IT FIRST EXAGGERATES THE RESPONSE BUT THEN QUICKLY RETURNS THE BODY TO NORMAL. ALL ITS CURATIVE POWERS RESULT FROM THIS REDUCTION IN RESIDUAL STRESS.

BEFORE   AFTER

HOW TO MAKE A BALANCING CHAIN
MAKE SLITS IN POTATOES (WITH A KNIFE) TO TAKE FORK HANDLES & ASSEMBLE AS IN DRAWING.

KOREAN VINTAGE GINSENG ROOT

U.S. CULTIVATED GINSENG

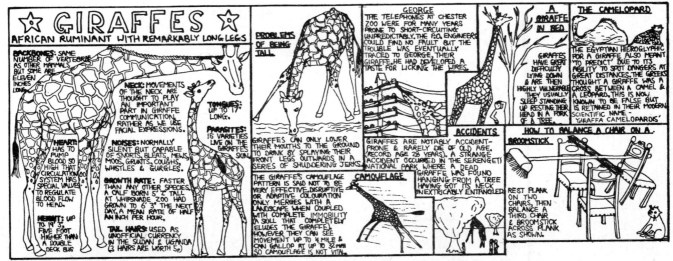

☆ GIRAFFES ☆
AFRICAN RUMINANT WITH REMARKABLY LONG LEGS

BACKBONES: SAME NUMBER OF VERTEBRAE AS OTHER MAMMALS BUT SOME ARE ELEVEN INCHES LONG.

NECK: MOVEMENTS OF THE NECK ARE THOUGHT TO PLAY AN IMPORTANT PART IN GIRAFFE COMMUNICATION RATHER AS WE USE FACIAL EXPRESSIONS.

TONGUES: UP TO 17" LONG.

PARASITES: 15 VARIETIES LIVE ON THE GIRAFFES SKIN.

HEART: HAS TO PUMP BLOOD SO HIGH THAT CIRCULATION SYSTEM HAS SPECIAL VALVES TO REGULATE BLOOD FLOW TO HEAD.

NOISES: NORMALLY SILENT BUT CAPABLE OF SNORTS, BLEATS, MEWS, MOOS, GRUNTS, COUGHS, WHISTLES & GURGLES.

GROWTH RATE: FASTER THAN ANY OTHER SPECIES. A CALF BORN 5'2" TALL AT WHIPSNADE ZOO HAD GROWN TO 6'3" THE NEXT DAY, A MEAN RATE OF HALF AN INCH PER HOUR.

HEIGHT: UP TO 19'3", FIVE FOOT HIGHER THAN A DOUBLE DECK BUS.

TAIL HAIRS: USED AS UNOFFICIAL CURRENCY IN THE SUDAN & UGANDA (3 HAIRS ARE WORTH 5p).

PROBLEMS OF BEING TALL
GIRAFFES CAN ONLY LOWER THEIR MOUTHS TO THE GROUND TO DRINK BY SPLAYING THEIR FRONT LEGS OUTWARDS IN A SERIES OF SHUDDERING JERKS.

GEORGE
THE TELEPHONES AT CHESTER ZOO WERE FOR MANY YEARS PRONE TO SHORT-CIRCUITING UNPREDICTABLY. THE P.O. ENGINEERS COULD FIND NO FAULT BUT THE TROUBLE WAS EVENTUALLY TRACED TO GEORGE, THEIR GIRAFFE. HE HAD DEVELOPED A TASTE FOR LICKING THE WIRES.

A GIRAFFE IN BED
GIRAFFES HAVE GREAT DIFFICULTY LYING DOWN & ARE THEN HIGHLY VULNERABLE. THEY USUALLY SLEEP STANDING UP RESTING THEIR HEAD IN A FORK OF A TREE.

THE CAMELOPARD
THE EGYPTIAN HIEROGLYPHIC FOR A GIRAFFE ALSO MEANT "TO PREDICT" DUE TO ITS ABILITY TO SPOT DANGERS AT GREAT DISTANCES. THE GREEKS THOUGHT A GIRAFFE WAS A CROSS BETWEEN A CAMEL & A LEOPARD. THIS IS NOW KNOWN TO BE FALSE BUT IS RETAINED IN THEIR MODERN SCIENTIFIC NAME - "GIRAFFA CAMELOPARDIS".

CAMOUFLAGE
THE GIRAFFE'S CAMOUFLAGE PATTERN IS SAID NOT TO BE VERY EFFECTIVE. DISRUPTIVE OR ADAPTIVE COLOURATION ONLY MERGES WITH A LANDSCAPE WHEN COUPLED WITH COMPLETE IMMOBILITY, A SKILL THAT COMPLETELY ELUDES THE GIRAFFE. HOWEVER THEY CAN SEE MOVEMENT UP TO 4 MILE & CAN GALLOP AT UP TO 32 mph SO CAMOUFLAGE IS NOT VITAL.

ACCIDENTS
GIRAFFES ARE NOTABLY ACCIDENT-PRONE & RARELY DIE OF OLD AGE (RECORD AGE 28 YEARS). A STRANGE ACCIDENT OCCURRED IN THE SERENGETI NATIONAL PARK WHERE A DEAD GIRAFFE WAS FOUND HANGING FROM A TREE HAVING GOT ITS NECK INEXTRICABLY ENTANGLED.

HOW TO BALANCE A CHAIR ON A BROOMSTICK
REST PLANK ON TWO CHAIRS, THEN BALANCE A THIRD CHAIR & BROOMSTICK ACROSS PLANK AS SHOWN.

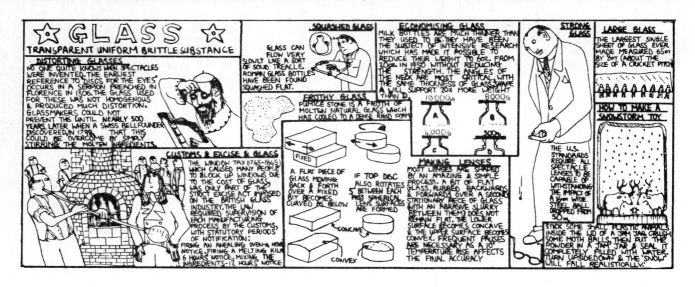

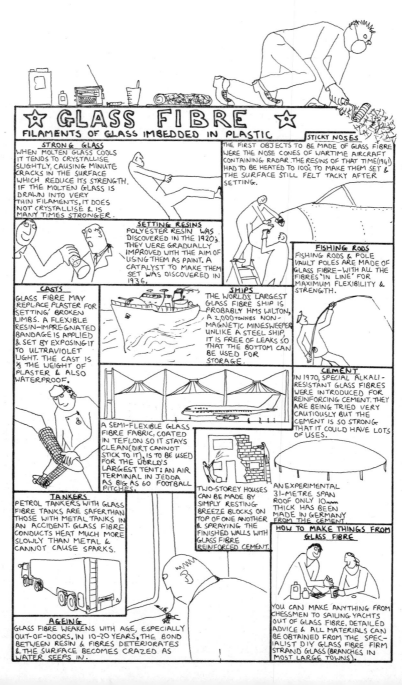

☆ GLUES ☆
SUBSTANCES USED FOR JOINING MATERIALS

NATURAL GLUES

UNTIL THE 1930s ALL ADHESIVES WERE BASED ON NATURAL PRODUCTS:
- **PASTE** WAS A STICKY MIX OF FLOUR AND WATER.
- **GUM** OOZED FROM TREES.
- **CEMENT** WAS RUBBER DISSOLVED IN A SOLVENT.
- **GLUE** WAS A STICKY SOLID MADE BY BOILING BONES.

ANIMAL GLUE

GLUES BASED ON GELATIN, AN ANIMAL PROTEIN DERIVATIVE, ARE OBTAINED BY BOILING BONES & HIDES. THE SPHERE OF YARDLEY'S EXTRACTOR (RIGHT) IS FILLED WITH BONES & IS ROTATED WHILE STEAM IS PASSED THROUGH IT.
EVENTUALLY GELATIN SEPARATES AS A LIQUID & IS POURED OFF. IF IT COMES OUT PURE IT IS TRANSPARENT & IS SOLD TO JAM-MAKERS & CONFECTIONERS (IT IS A PRINCIPAL INGREDIENT OF MARSHMALLOWS & OTHER SWEETS). ONLY THE MURKY SECOND-GRADE GELATIN IS USED FOR GLUE. THE LOWEST GRADE IS VERY SMELLY & KNOWN AS FISH GLUE.

CHEESE GLUE

THE STRONGEST NATURAL GLUE IS CASEIN (THE WHEY FROM MILK MIXED WITH LIME). THIS WAS USED BY THE EGYPTIANS FOR STICKING FURNITURE TOGETHER BUT THEN WAS FORGOTTEN UNTIL THE 1900s. IT COMES AS A WHITE POWDER, IT IS MIXED WITH WATER & IS STILL EXTENSIVELY USED IN WOODWORK. ITS ONLY DEFECT IS THAT, BEING BASICALLY CHEESE, UNDER PROLONGED DAMP CONDITIONS IT BECOMES VERY LIKE RIPE CAMEMBERT—A LIQUID SMELLY MESS THAT RUNS OUT OF THE JOINTS.

BAKELITE GLUE

SCIENTISTS EXPERIMENTING WITH BAKELITE IN THE 1930s FOUND THAT WHEN IT WAS HEATED TO 150°C IT COULD BE USED AS A WATERPROOF WOOD GLUE. THIS WAS INCONVENIENT FOR GLUEING JOINTS BUT IDEAL FOR BONDING THE LAYERS OF PLYWOOD. FOR THE FIRST TIME IT ENABLED PLYWOOD TO BE USED IN BOAT-BUILDING & IT HAS BEEN USED FOR MARINE PLY EVER SINCE.

HOW A GLUE GLUES

UNTIL RECENTLY IT WAS THOUGHT THAT ANY SUBSTANCE THAT WOULD FLOW INTO THE MICROSCOPIC PORES & CAVITIES OF THE SURFACES TO BE STUCK & THEN HARDENED WOULD ACT AS AN ADHESIVE. THIS MECHANICAL EXPLANATION IS NOW CONSIDERED TO BE A GROSS SIMPLIFICATION AS MOLECULAR & ATOMIC BONDING FORCES ARE THOUGHT TO PLAY AN IMPORTANT ROLE, ALTHOUGH PHYSICAL CHEMISTS ARE UNCERTAIN OF THEIR NATURE.

COW GUM

NO PART OF THE COW IS USED IN THE MANUFACTURE OF COW GUM. IT IS AN ENTIRELY SYNTHETIC PRODUCT INVENTED BY A MR COW.

ELECTRIC GLUE

AN INGENIOUS NEW ADHESIVE TAPE HAS RECENTLY BEEN INVENTED FOR LAYING CARPETS. THE STRONGEST BOND IS OBTAINED WITH A GLUE THAT WILL ONLY STICK WHEN HEATED—WHICH WAS PREVIOUSLY VERY INCONVENIENT. HOWEVER THIS TAPE, COATED IN THE HOT-MELT GLUE, HAS AN ALUMINIUM FOIL BACKING. WHEN THE TAPE IS IN PLACE ELECTRICITY IS PASSED THROUGH THE FOIL. THIS HEATS THE FOIL & MELTS THE GLUE.

HOW TO MAKE PIPES OF PAN

ARRANGE ABOUT 30 PLASTIC DRINKING STRAWS IN A ROW. STICK SELLOTAPE ACROSS STRAWS. CUT STRAWS DIAGONALLY. BLOW ACROSS TOP OF STRAWS TO PLAY.

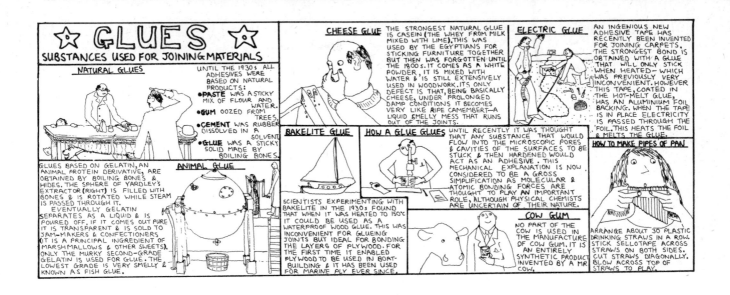

☆ GOATS ☆
HOLLOW-HORNED RUMINANTS OF THE BOVIDAE FAMILY

SCOTTISH WILD GOATS

SOME SCOTSMEN CLAIM THAT THE WILD GOATS ON THE WESTERN ISLES ARE DESCENDED FROM ONES THAT ESCAPED THE WRECKS OF THE SPANISH ARMADA. IT IS KNOWN THAT THE SPANISH CARRIED GOATS ON THEIR SHIPS (TO PROVIDE FRESH MILK FOR THE OFFICERS) BUT IT IS DOUBTFUL THAT ANY GOATS COULD HAVE SURVIVED SINCE THEY HAVE A STRONG AVERSION TO WATER. IT IS MORE PROBABLE THAT GOATS WERE ORIGINALLY IMPORTED BY THE VIKINGS, WHO WANTED TO USE THE ISLANDS AS REVICTUALLING STATIONS.

GOATS & ECOLOGY

GOATS CAN CAUSE DISASTROUS CHANGES TO THE ECOLOGY OF A REGION BECAUSE THEY 'BROWSE' (EAT FOOD AT EYE LEVEL) INSTEAD OF GRAZING LIKE OTHER HERBIVORES. THEY CHEW YOUNG TREES TO BITS & STRIP THE BARK OFF LARGER TREES. WITHOUT TREE ROOTS ARID LAND IS VERY LIABLE TO EROSION & THIS HAS CAUSED THE DEFOLIATION OF ST HELENA'S ISLAND & MAY HAVE PLAYED A MAJOR ROLE IN THE CREATION OF THE SAHARA DESERT.

GOATS & DEER

DEER HAVE AN AVERSION TO GOATS POSSIBLY BECAUSE THE SMELL OF A GOAT IS SO STRONG THAT IT OVERPOWERS ALL OTHER SCENTS & CAUSES THE SENSITIVE DEER TO FEEL INSECURE.

GOATS?

THE PLURAL OF GOAT HAS NOT ALWAYS BEEN GOATS. THE OXFORD ENGLISH DICTIONARY RECORDS THE USE OF: GETE, GEET, GEETE, GEATES, GOATES, GAIT, GOETE, GOTES & GAYTE.

GOATS & COWS

FARMERS HAVE ALWAYS CLAIMED THAT IT IMPROVES THE HEALTH OF CATTLE TO KEEP A GOAT WITH EACH HERD. THIS IS NOW BELIEVED BY SCIENTISTS AS THEY HAVE FOUND THAT ERGOT & RYE CAN CAUSE VARIOUS DISEASES AMONG CATTLE BUT GOATS EAT THEM EAGERLY & SAFELY.

GOATS & HORSES

GOATS ARE OFTEN KEPT WITH HORSES. THEY HELP TO CALM HIGHLY STRUNG RACE HORSES & ARE SAID TO STOP ANY HORSE PANICKING IN THE EVENT OF FIRE. THIS CLAIM IS SOMEWHAT SUSPECT. WHEN WATNEYS BREWERY WAS BOMBED IN 1943 THE 85 HORSES WERE LED AWAY CALMLY BUT THEIR GOATS PANICKED & COULD BE RESCUED ONLY WITH GREAT DIFFICULTY.

GOATS & MOUNTAINS

GOATS CAN SEPARATE THE TWO TOES ON EACH HOOF & PRESS THEM STRONGLY TOGETHER, ENABLING THEM TO GRIP SMALL PROJECTIONS & ASCEND ALMOST VERTICAL ROCK FACES. IN PARTS OF NORTH AMERICA SOME LIVE A LARGELY ARBOREAL EXISTENCE 10-20FT ABOVE THE GROUND IN ACACIA SHRUBS.

JUDAS GOATS

ONE GRISLY USE OF GOATS IS TO LEAD RELUCTANT CATTLE & LIVESTOCK INTO THE SLAUGHTERHOUSE.

HOW TO FIND YOUR WALKING SPEED

WIND A BALL OF STRING ROUND A CARDBOARD TUBE, TIEING A KNOT EVERY 11FT & TIE END OF STRING TO A STONE. WITH A FRIEND WHO OWNS A GOOD WATCH, START WALKING; THEN DROP THE STONE & COUNT THE NUMBER OF KNOTS YOU UNREEL IN 30 SECONDS. DIVIDE THIS NUMBER BY 4 TO FIND YOUR WALKING SPEED IN M.P.H.

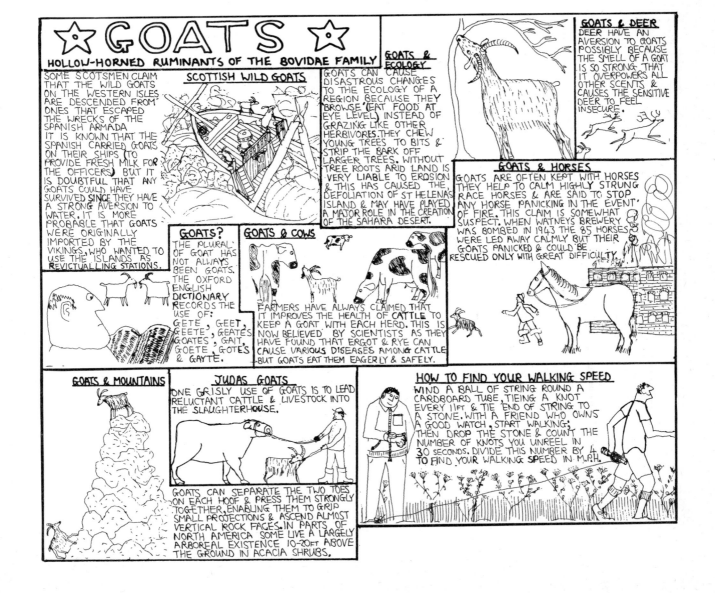

☆ GOLD ☆
HEAVY PRECIOUS YELLOW ELEMENT

BRITISH GOLD
BRITAIN'S GREATEST GOLD MINE WAS CLOGAN ST DAVID'S IN MERIONETHSHIRE. IT OPERATED FROM 1854 TO 1914 YIELDING A TOTAL OF 3 TONS OF GOLD. THIS IS RATHER PATHETIC COMPARED TO SOUTH AFRICA'S OUTPUT (UP TO 984 TONS A YEAR)

S. AFRICAN GOLD
THE SOUTH AFRICANS GO TO GREAT LENGTHS TO EXTRACT THEIR GOLD. THEY HAVE BORED THE WORLD'S DEEPEST MINE (11,626FT) WHICH GETS SO HOT (UP TO 126°F) THAT IT NEEDS THE WORLD'S LARGEST REFRIGERATION PLANT TO KEEP IT WORKABLE. ON AVERAGE 70 TONS OF ORE MUST BE EXTRACTED TO YIELD 1LB OF GOLD.

GOLD TEETH
GOLD USED IN DENTISTRY MUST BE VERY DUCTILE. EARLY AMERICAN DENTISTS USED GOLD COINS, SOFTENED BY PLACING THEM ON A RAIL & WAITING FOR A TRAIN TO RUN OVER THEM.

THE JAPANESE USE 20% OF THEIR FABRICATION GOLD IN DENTISTRY, DOUBLE THE PERCENTAGE USED ANYWHERE ELSE.

JASON'S GOLDEN FLEECE
THE LEGEND OF JASON & THE GOLDEN FLEECE PROBABLY STEMMED FROM AN ANCIENT METHOD OF REFINING GOLD FROM COARSE SEDIMENTARY DEPOSITS. SHEEPSKINS WERE PLACED IN A SHALLOW DITCH & THE DEPOSITS, MIXED WITH WATER, WERE POURED DOWN THE DITCH. THE FORCE OF THE WATER CARRIED THE GRAVEL ALONG BUT THE GOLD WAS SO MUCH HEAVIER THAT IT SANK TO THE BOTTOM, GETTING CAUGHT UP IN THE FIBRES, THUS PRODUCING A GOLDEN FLEECE. THE FLEECE WAS FINALLY BURNT UP TO EXTRACT THE GOLD FROM IT.

ASSAYING A NUGGET
THE PURITY OF ANY GOLD CAN BE FOUND VERY SIMPLY WITH A FLINTY BLACK ROCK CALLED A TOUCHSTONE. WHEN RUBBED AGAINST THE ROCK, A NUGGET LEAVES A YELLOW STREAK WHICH IS COMPARED IN COLOUR WITH STREAKS PRODUCED BY SAMPLE GOLD NEEDLES OF KNOWN PURITY.

GOLDEN MEDICINES
GOLD HAS BEEN ADVOCATED AS A CURE FOR MOST DISEASES AT SOME TIME IN THE PAST. SOME MEN, SUCH AS MOUSSA THE WISE (A PERSIAN PHYSICIAN OF ABOUT 800AD) HAVE EVEN RECOMMENDED IT AS THE CURE FOR EVERY DISEASE. IT IS STILL USED IN THE WEST IN THE TREATMENT OF ARTHRITIS & CANCER; INJECTED IN THE FORM OF A SOLUBLE SALT.

HOW TO BORE A HOLE THROUGH A NAIL
CORK
NAIL
NEEDLE
CORK
BOTTLE
PENKNIFE

FIX NEEDLE, POINT UPWARDS, INTO CORK IN TOP OF BOTTLE. FIX NAIL (1½" PANEL PIN WORKS BEST) & 2 IDENTICAL PENKNIVES INTO SECOND CORK & BALANCE NAIL ON NEEDLE POINT AS SHOWN. HOLD BOTTLE THEN GENTLY SPIN NAIL ASSEMBLY TILL NEEDLE BORES THROUGH.

GOLDEN RAILINGS
THE GOLD LEAF ON THE RAILINGS OF BUCKINGHAM PALACE IS WORTH OVER £2,000. HOWEVER IT WORKS OUT CHEAPER THAN GOLD PAINT AS IT LASTS 30 YEARS. GOLD PAINT ONLY LASTS ONE YEAR.

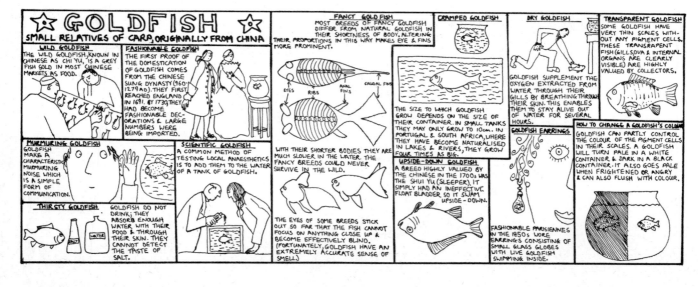

☆ GOLDFISH ☆
SMALL RELATIVES OF CARP, ORIGINALLY FROM CHINA

WILD GOLDFISH
THE WILD GOLDFISH, KNOWN IN CHINESE AS CHI YU, IS A GREY FISH SOLD IN MOST CHINESE MARKETS AS FOOD.

FASHIONABLE GOLDFISH
THE FIRST PROOF OF THE DOMESTICATION OF GOLDFISH COMES FROM THE CHINESE SUNG DYNASTY (960-1279AD). THEY FIRST REACHED ENGLAND IN 1691. BY 1730 THEY HAD BECOME FASHIONABLE DECORATIONS & LARGE NUMBERS WERE BEING IMPORTED.

MURMURING GOLDFISH
GOLDFISH MAKE A CHARACTERISTIC MURMURING NOISE WHICH IS A SIMPLE FORM OF COMMUNICATION.

THIRSTY GOLDFISH
GOLDFISH DO NOT DRINK; THEY ABSORB ENOUGH WATER WITH THEIR FOOD & THROUGH THEIR SKIN. THEY CANNOT DETECT THE TASTE OF SALT.

SCIENTIFIC GOLDFISH
A COMMON METHOD OF TESTING LOCAL ANAESTHETICS IS TO ADD THEM TO THE WATER OF A TANK OF GOLDFISH.

FANCY GOLD FISH
MOST BREEDS OF FANCY GOLDFISH DIFFER FROM NATURAL GOLDFISH IN THEIR SHORTNESS OF BODY. ALTERING THEIR PROPORTIONS IN THIS WAY MAKES EYE & FINS MORE PROMINENT.

EYES
RIBS
ANAL FINS
CAUDAL FINS

WITH THEIR SHORTER BODIES THEY ARE MUCH SLOWER IN THE WATER. THE FANCY BREEDS COULD NEVER SURVIVE IN THE WILD.

THE EYES OF SOME BREEDS STICK OUT SO FAR THAT THE FISH CANNOT FOCUS ON ANYTHING CLOSE UP & BECOME EFFECTIVELY BLIND. (FORTUNATELY, GOLDFISH HAVE AN EXTREMELY ACCURATE SENSE OF SMELL.)

CRAMPED GOLDFISH
THE SIZE TO WHICH GOLDFISH GROW DEPENDS ON THE SIZE OF THEIR CONTAINER. IN SMALL TANKS THEY MAY ONLY GROW TO 10cm. IN PORTUGAL & SOUTH AFRICA, WHERE THEY HAVE BECOME NATURALISED IN LAKES & RIVERS, THEY GROW FOUR TIMES AS BIG.

UPSIDE-DOWN GOLDFISH
A BREED HIGHLY VALUED BY THE CHINESE IN THE 1700s WAS THE SHUI YU (SLEEPER), IT SIMPLY HAD AN INEFFECTIVE FLOAT BLADDER SO IT SWAM UPSIDE-DOWN.

DRY GOLDFISH
GOLDFISH SUPPLEMENT THE OXYGEN EXTRACTED FROM WATER THROUGH THEIR GILLS BY BREATHING THROUGH THEIR SKIN. THIS ENABLES THEM TO STAY ALIVE OUT OF WATER FOR SEVERAL HOURS.

GOLDFISH EARRINGS
FASHIONABLE PARISIENNES IN THE 1850s WORE EARRINGS CONSISTING OF SMALL GLASS GLOBES WITH LIVE GOLDFISH SWIMMING INSIDE.

TRANSPARENT GOLDFISH
SOME GOLDFISH HAVE VERY THIN SCALES WITHOUT ANY PIGMENT CELLS. THESE TRANSPARENT FISH (GILLS, OVA & INTERNAL ORGANS ARE CLEARLY VISIBLE) ARE HIGHLY VALUED BY COLLECTORS.

HOW TO CHANGE A GOLDFISH'S COLOUR
GOLDFISH CAN PARTLY CONTROL THE COLOUR OF THE PIGMENT CELLS IN THEIR SCALES. A GOLDFISH WILL TURN PALE IN A WHITE CONTAINER & DARK IN A BLACK CONTAINER. IT ALSO GOES PALE WHEN FRIGHTENED OR ANGRY & CAN ALSO FLUSH WITH COLOUR.

☆ GOLF ☆
GAME HITTING SMALL HARD BALLS INTO HOLES WITH CLUBS

FEATHERIES & GUTTIES
THE FIRST GOLF BALLS WERE CALLED FEATHERIES & MADE FROM 3 BITS OF LEATHER STITCHED TOGETHER & STUFFED WITH BOILED CHICKEN FEATHERS, WHICH EXPANDED AS THEY DRIED. BALLS MADE OF GUTTAPERCHA (THE SOLIDIFIED SAP OF TROPICAL TREES) WERE INTRODUCED IN THE 1970s. THESE FLEW ERRATICALLY UNTIL IT WAS FOUND THAT ROUGHENING THEIR SURFACE IMPROVED THEIR AERODYNAMICS.

ORIGINS
GOLF IS GENERALLY CONSIDERED TO BE A SCOTTISH INVENTION THOUGH OTHER COUNTRIES HAD SIMILAR GAMES. THE ROMANS PLAYED PAGANICA (A MIXTURE OF GOLF & HOCKEY) THE FRENCH PLAYED JEU DE MAIL (PUTTING IN AN ENCLOSED COURT) THE DUTCH PLAYED HET KOLVEN (SIMILAR TO JEU DE MAIL BUT USING A LARGE SPONGY BALL THE SIZE OF A GRAPEFRUIT) & THE FLEMISH PLAYED CHOLE (A JOLLY GAMBLING GAME. PLAYERS BET HOW MANY SHOTS IT WOULD TAKE THEM TO GET A BALL TO SOME DISTANT HOUSE OR LANDMARK. AFTER EVERY THIRD SHOT AN OPPONENT HAD A SHOT TO HIT THE BALL AWAY FROM THE GOAL.

WHIPPY HICKORY
THE FIRST GOLF CLUBS HAD HICKORY SHAFTS. STEEL SHAFTS WERE PERFECTED IN THE 1930s. THEY DID NOT SEND THE BALL ANY FURTHER BUT WERE MORE PREDICTABLE AS HICKORY SHAFTS TWISTED SLIGHTLY WHEN SWUNG FAST.

GOLF
THE WORD GOLF COMES FROM THE TEUTONIC KOLBEN MEANING CLUB. CADDIE COMES FROM THE FRENCH CADET MEANING SERVANT.

RUBBER BALLS
THE RUBBER WOUND BALL WAS PATENTED IN 1898. THIS CONSISTED OF AN ELASTIC CENTRE SURROUNDED BY LAYERS OF STRETCHED RUBBER STRIPS, THE WHOLE THING COVERED IN A HARD RUBBER CASING. LIKE THE 'GUTTY' IT WAS NOT SUCCESSFUL AT FIRST, REQUIRING MOULDED IMPRESSIONS ON THE SURFACE TO MAKE IT FLY TRUE. WHEN PERFECTED IT FLEW 10% FURTHER THAN A 'GUTTY' & BECAME UNIVERSALLY ACCEPTED.

THROWING GOLF BALLS
SOME AMERICANS HOLD CONTESTS FOR THROWING GOLF BALLS INTO HOLES. THE RECORD FOR THROWING A BALL ROUND A FULL 18 HOLE COURSE IS 82 THROWS.

HIGH SPEED GOLF
THE RECORD FOR THE FASTEST 18 HOLE ROUND OF GOLF IS 28 MIN 18 SEC, HELD BY AN AUSTRALIAN

THE TEE
GOLFERS USED TO PILE SMALL MOUNDS OF EARTH UNDER THEIR BALLS WHEN STARTING A HOLE TO PREVENT THEIR CLUBS HITTING THE GROUND. THE WOODEN TEE WAS INVENTED IN 1920 BY A DENTIST WHO DISLIKED GETTING HIS HANDS DIRTY. IT BECAME POPULAR AFTER ONE 'PRO' STARTED CARRYING ONE AROUND BEHIND HIS EAR.

HOW TO DRY LEATHER BOOTS WITHOUT MAKING THEM SHRINK & HARDEN
SIMPLY FILL BOOTS WITH DRY PORRIDGE OATS & LEAVE IN A WARM PLACE. THE OATS CAN BE USED AGAIN & AGAIN IF DRIED AFTER USE.

LONG DISTANCE GOLF
A MR FLOYD SATTERLEE ROOD PLAYED A GOLF BALL FROM THE EAST COAST OF AMERICA TO THE WEST COAST, HE COVERED 3,400 MILES IN 390 DAYS MAKING 114,737 STROKES & LOSING 3511 BALLS.

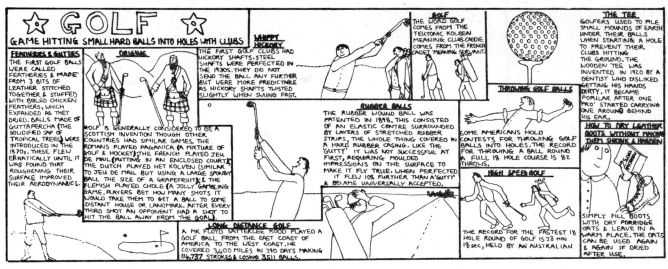

☆ GORILLAS ☆
LARGE AFRICAN ANTHROPOID APES

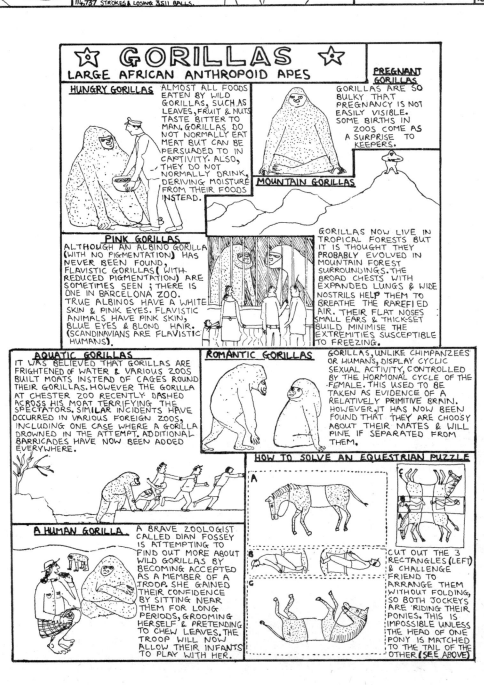

HUNGRY GORILLAS
ALMOST ALL FOODS EATEN BY WILD GORILLAS, SUCH AS LEAVES, FRUIT & NUTS TASTE BITTER TO MAN. GORILLAS DO NOT NORMALLY EAT MEAT BUT CAN BE PERSUADED TO IN CAPTIVITY. ALSO, THEY DO NOT NORMALLY DRINK, DERIVING MOISTURE FROM THEIR FOODS INSTEAD.

PREGNANT GORILLAS
GORILLAS ARE SO BULKY THAT PREGNANCY IS NOT EASILY VISIBLE. SOME BIRTHS IN ZOOS COME AS A SURPRISE TO KEEPERS.

MOUNTAIN GORILLAS
GORILLAS NOW LIVE IN TROPICAL FORESTS BUT IT IS THOUGHT THEY PROBABLY EVOLVED IN MOUNTAIN FOREST SURROUNDINGS. THE BROAD CHESTS WITH EXPANDED LUNGS & WIDE NOSTRILS HELP THEM TO BREATHE THE RAREFIED AIR. THEIR FLAT NOSES SMALL EARS & THICK-SET BUILD MINIMISE THE EXTREMITIES SUSCEPTIBLE TO FREEZING.

PINK GORILLAS
ALTHOUGH AN ALBINO GORILLA (WITH NO PIGMENTATION) HAS NEVER BEEN FOUND, FLAVISTIC GORILLAS (WITH REDUCED PIGMENTATION) ARE SOMETIMES SEEN ; THERE IS ONE IN BARCELONA ZOO. TRUE ALBINOS HAVE A WHITE SKIN & PINK EYES. FLAVISTIC ANIMALS HAVE PINK SKIN, BLUE EYES & BLOND HAIR. (SCANDINAVIANS ARE FLAVISTIC HUMANS).

AQUATIC GORILLAS
IT WAS BELIEVED THAT GORILLAS ARE FRIGHTENED OF WATER & VARIOUS ZOOS BUILT MOATS INSTEAD OF CAGES ROUND THEIR GORILLAS. HOWEVER THE GORILLA AT CHESTER ZOO RECENTLY DASHED ACROSS HIS MOAT TERRIFYING THE SPECTATORS. SIMILAR INCIDENTS HAVE OCCURRED IN VARIOUS FOREIGN ZOOS, INCLUDING ONE CASE WHERE A GORILLA DROWNED IN THE ATTEMPT. ADDITIONAL BARRICADES HAVE NOW BEEN ADDED EVERYWHERE.

ROMANTIC GORILLAS
GORILLAS, UNLIKE CHIMPANZEES OR HUMANS, DISPLAY CYCLIC SEXUAL ACTIVITY, CONTROLLED BY THE HORMONAL CYCLE OF THE FEMALE. THIS USED TO BE TAKEN AS EVIDENCE OF A RELATIVELY PRIMITIVE BRAIN. HOWEVER, IT HAS NOW BEEN FOUND THAT THEY ARE CHOOSY ABOUT THEIR MATES & WILL PINE IF SEPARATED FROM THEM.

A HUMAN GORILLA
A BRAVE ZOOLOGIST CALLED DIAN FOSSEY IS ATTEMPTING TO FIND OUT MORE ABOUT WILD GORILLAS BY BECOMING ACCEPTED AS A MEMBER OF A TROOP. SHE GAINED THEIR CONFIDENCE BY SITTING NEAR THEM FOR LONG PERIODS, GROOMING HERSELF & PRETENDING TO CHEW LEAVES. THE TROOP WILL NOW ALLOW THEIR INFANTS TO PLAY WITH HER.

HOW TO SOLVE AN EQUESTRIAN PUZZLE
CUT OUT THE 3 RECTANGLES (LEFT) & CHALLENGE FRIEND TO ARRANGE THEM WITHOUT FOLDING, SO BOTH JOCKEYS ARE 'RIDING' THEIR PONIES. THIS IS IMPOSSIBLE UNLESS THE HEAD OF ONE PONY IS MATCHED TO THE TAIL OF THE OTHER (SEE ABOVE)

☆ GRAMMAR ☆
RULES DEFINING THE CORRECT USE OF LANGUAGE

ORIGIN
THE WORD 'GRAMMAR' COMES FROM THE GREEK WORD MEANING 'TO WRITE'. THIS ASSOCIATION HAS REMAINED IN THE NAME GRAMMAR SCHOOL.

ENGLISH GRAMMAR
THE RULES OF ENGLISH GRAMMAR COME FROM 18TH CENTURY GRAMMAR BOOKS, WHICH ATTEMPTED TO ESTABLISH 'CORRECT' ENGLISH, BASED ON THE RULES OF LATIN GRAMMAR.

FRENCH GRAMMAR
IN FRANCE THERE IS AN AUTHORITY, THE FRENCH ACADEMY, WHICH, SINCE 1636, HAS DECIDED WHAT IS & WHAT IS NOT PERMISSIBLE IN THE FRENCH GRAMMAR.

ACCUSATIVES
THE CORRECTNESS OF 'IT IS I' INSTEAD OF THE USUAL 'IT IS ME' DERIVES FROM A LATIN RULE TAKEN OVER FOR ENGLISH. IN MANY OTHER LANGUAGES, INCLUDING ARABIC, THE VERB 'TO BE' REQUIRES AN ACCUSATIVE & 'IT IS I' IS INCORRECT.

NEGATIVES
DOUBLE NEGATIVES ARE NOT GOOD ENGLISH BECAUSE THE NEGATIVES CANCEL EACH OTHER OUT. 'I DIDN'T SEE NOTHING' = 'I SAW SOMETHING'. IN MANY LANGUAGES INCLUDING SPANISH & RUSSIAN, THE NEGATIVES REINFORCE EACH OTHER.

PLURALS
SOME LANGUAGES (EG FIJIAN & TIGRE) HAVE A 'LITTLE PLURAL' & A 'BIG PLURAL'. IN TIGRE A HORSE = FARÄS: A FEW HORSES = ÄFRÈSAM: HORSES = AFRAS.

CASES
FINNISH NOUNS HAVE MORE CASES THAN ALMOST ANY OTHER LANGUAGE.

NOMINATIVE (SUBJECT)
GENITIVE (OF)
ACCUSATIVE (OBJECT)
INESSIVE (IN)
ELATIVE (OUT OF)
ILLATIVE (INTO)
ADESSIVE (ON)
ABLATIVE (FROM)
COMITATIVE (ACCOMPANIED BY)
ALLATIVE (ON TO)
PARTITIVE (INVOLVING PART OF SUBJECT OR OBJECT)
ABESSIVE (WITHOUT)
INSTRUCTIVE (BY)
TRANSLATIVE (INVOLVING CHANGES TO)

DESCRIPTIVE GRAMMAR
RECENTLY CONCEPTS OF GRAMMAR USING DESCRIPTIVE RULES (RULES THAT DESCRIBE LANGUAGES) RATHER THAN PRESCRIPTIVE RULES (WHICH DICTATE HOW LANGUAGE SHOULD BE USED) HAVE GAINED FAVOUR WITH LINGUISTS.

STRUCTURAL GRAMMAR
ATTEMPTS TO WORK OUT FUNDAMENTAL RULES OF GRAMMAR HAVE PROVED DIFFICULT. LINGUISTS CAN'T EVEN AGREE WHAT THE WORD 'WORD' MEANS. THERE ARE NO PAUSES BETWEEN WORDS IN SPEECH & EVEN IN WRITTEN LANGUAGE WORDS LINKED WITH HYPHENS MAKE A DEFINITION DIFFICULT.

HOW TO TAKE NASTY TASTING MEDICINE
A STRONG SENSATION NUMBS THE TASTE CELLS. TRY SUCKING A STRONG PEPPERMINT OR AN ICE-CUBE BEFORE TAKING MEDICINE.

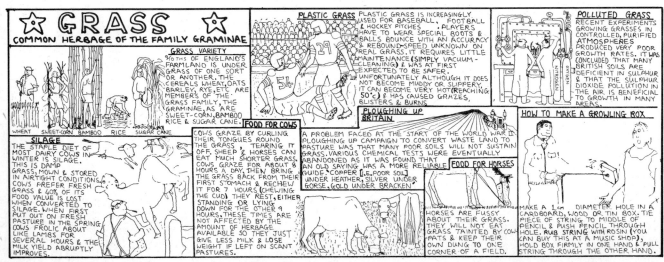

☆ GRASS ☆
COMMON HERBAGE OF THE FAMILY GRAMINAE

GRASS VARIETY
9/10THS OF ENGLAND'S FARMLAND IS UNDER GRASS OF ONE SORT OR ANOTHER. THE CEREALS WHEAT, OATS, BARLEY, RYE, ETC ARE MEMBERS OF THE GRASS FAMILY, THE GRAMINAE, AS ARE SWEET-CORN, BAMBOO, RICE & SUGAR CANE.

WHEAT SWEET-CORN BAMBOO RICE SUGAR CANE

SILAGE
THE STAPLE DIET OF MOST DAIRY COWS IN WINTER IS SILAGE. THIS IS DAMP GRASS, MOWN & STORED IN AIRTIGHT CONDITIONS. COWS PREFER FRESH GRASS & 40% OF ITS FOOD VALUE IS LOST WHEN CONVERTED TO SILAGE. WHEN FIRST PUT OUT ON FRESH PASTURE IN THE SPRING COWS FROLIC ABOUT LIKE LAMBS FOR SEVERAL HOURS & THE MILK YIELD ABRUPTLY IMPROVES.

FOOD FOR COWS
COWS GRAZE BY CURLING THEIR TONGUES ROUND THE GRASS, TEARING IT OFF. SHEEP & HORSES CAN EAT MUCH SHORTER GRASS. COWS GRAZE FOR ABOUT 8 HOURS A DAY, THEN BRING THE GRASS BACK FROM THEIR FIRST STOMACH & RECHEW IT FOR 7 HOURS (CHEWING THE CUD). THEY REST, EITHER STANDING OR LYING DOWN FOR THE OTHER 9 HOURS. THESE TIMES ARE NOT AFFECTED BY THE AMOUNT OF HERBAGE AVAILABLE SO THEY JUST GIVE LESS MILK & LOSE WEIGHT IF LEFT ON SCANT PASTURES.

PLASTIC GRASS
PLASTIC GRASS IS INCREASINGLY USED FOR BASEBALL, FOOTBALL & HOCKEY PITCHES. PLAYERS HAVE TO WEAR SPECIAL BOOTS & BALLS BOUNCE WITH AN ACCURACY & REBOUND-SPEED UNKNOWN ON REAL GRASS. IT REQUIRES LITTLE MAINTENANCE (SIMPLY VACUUM-CLEANING) & WAS AT FIRST EXPECTED TO BE SAFER. UNFORTUNATELY ALTHOUGH IT DOES NOT BECOME MUDDY OR SLIPPERY, IT CAN BECOME VERY HOT (REACHING 50°C) & HAS CAUSED GRAZES, BLISTERS & BURNS.

PLOUGHING UP BRITAIN
A PROBLEM FACED AT THE START OF THE WORLD WAR II PLOUGHING UP CAMPAIGN TO CONVERT WASTE LAND TO PASTURE WAS THAT MANY POOR SOILS WILL NOT SUSTAIN GRASS. VARIOUS CHEMICAL TESTS WERE EVENTUALLY ABANDONED AS IT WAS FOUND THAT AN OLD SAYING WAS A MORE RELIABLE GUIDE: COPPER (I.E. POOR SOIL) UNDER HEATHER, SILVER UNDER GORSE, GOLD UNDER BRACKEN.

FOOD FOR HORSES
HORSES ARE FUSSY ABOUT THEIR GRASS. THEY WILL NOT EAT GRASS TAINTED BY COWPATS & KEEP THEIR OWN DUNG TO ONE CORNER OF A FIELD.

POLLUTED GRASS
RECENT EXPERIMENTS GROWING GRASSES IN CONTROLLED, PURIFIED ATMOSPHERES PRODUCED VERY POOR GROWTH RATES. IT WAS CONCLUDED THAT MANY BRITISH SOILS ARE DEFICIENT IN SULPHUR & THAT THE SULPHUR DIOXIDE POLLUTION IN THE AIR IS BENEFICIAL TO GROWTH IN MANY AREAS.

HOW TO MAKE A GROWLING BOX
MAKE A 1 CM DIAMETER HOLE IN A CARDBOARD, WOOD OR TIN BOX. TIE PIECE OF STRING TO MIDDLE OF PENCIL & PUSH PENCIL THROUGH HOLE. RUB STRING WITH ROSIN (YOU CAN BUY THIS AT A MUSIC SHOP). HOLD BOX FIRMLY IN ONE HAND & PULL STRING THROUGH THE OTHER HAND.

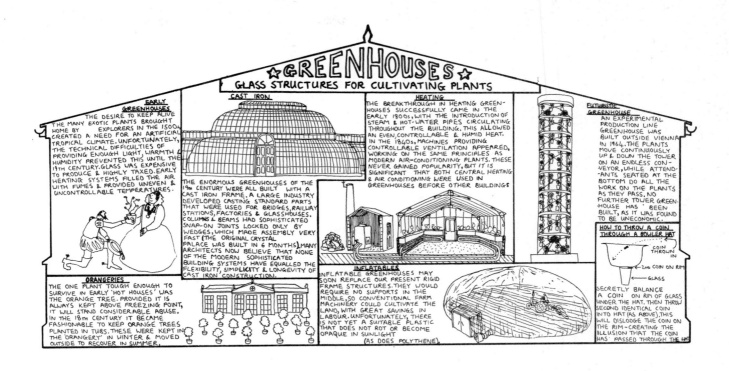

☆ GREENHOUSES ☆
GLASS STRUCTURES FOR CULTIVATING PLANTS

EARLY GREENHOUSES
THE DESIRE TO KEEP ALIVE THE MANY EXOTIC PLANTS BROUGHT HOME BY EXPLORERS IN THE 1500s CREATED A NEED FOR AN ARTIFICIAL TROPICAL CLIMATE. UNFORTUNATELY, THE TECHNICAL DIFFICULTIES OF PROVIDING ENOUGH LIGHT, WARMTH & HUMIDITY PREVENTED THIS UNTIL THE 19TH CENTURY. GLASS WAS EXPENSIVE TO PRODUCE & HIGHLY TAXED. EARLY HEATING SYSTEMS FILLED THE AIR WITH FUMES & PROVIDED UNEVEN & UNCONTROLLABLE TEMPERATURES.

ORANGERIES
THE ONE PLANT TOUGH ENOUGH TO SURVIVE IN EARLY 'HOT HOUSES' WAS THE ORANGE TREE. PROVIDED IT IS ALWAYS KEPT ABOVE FREEZING POINT, IT WILL STAND CONSIDERABLE ABUSE. IN THE 18TH CENTURY IT BECAME FASHIONABLE TO KEEP ORANGE TREES PLANTED IN TUBS. THESE WERE KEPT IN THE ORANGERY IN WINTER & MOVED OUTSIDE TO RECOVER IN SUMMER.

CAST IRON
THE ENORMOUS GREENHOUSES OF THE 19TH CENTURY WERE ALL BUILT WITH A CAST IRON FRAME. A LARGE INDUSTRY DEVELOPED CASTING STANDARD PARTS THAT WERE USED FOR BRIDGES, RAILWAY STATIONS, FACTORIES & GLASSHOUSES. COLUMNS & BEAMS HAD SOPHISTICATED SNAP-ON JOINTS LOCKED ONLY BY WEDGES, WHICH MADE ASSEMBLY VERY FAST (THE ORIGINAL CRYSTAL PALACE WAS BUILT IN 6 MONTHS). MANY ARCHITECTS NOW BELIEVE THAT NONE OF THE MODERN SOPHISTICATED BUILDING SYSTEMS HAVE EQUALLED THE FLEXIBILITY, SIMPLICITY & LONGEVITY OF CAST IRON CONSTRUCTION.

HEATING
THE BREAKTHROUGH IN HEATING GREENHOUSES SUCCESSFULLY CAME IN THE EARLY 1800s, WITH THE INTRODUCTION OF STEAM & HOT-WATER PIPES CIRCULATING THROUGHOUT THE BUILDING. THIS ALLOWED AN EVEN, CONTROLLABLE & HUMID HEAT. IN THE 1840s, MACHINES PROVIDING CONTROLLABLE VENTILATION APPEARED, WORKING ON THE SAME PRINCIPLES AS MODERN AIR-CONDITIONING PLANTS. THESE NEVER GAINED POPULARITY, BUT IT IS SIGNIFICANT THAT BOTH CENTRAL HEATING & AIR CONDITIONING WERE USED IN GREENHOUSES BEFORE OTHER BUILDINGS.

INFLATABLES
INFLATABLE GREENHOUSES MAY SOON REPLACE OUR PRESENT RIGID FRAME STRUCTURES. THEY WOULD REQUIRE NO SUPPORTS IN THE MIDDLE, SO CONVENTIONAL FARM MACHINERY COULD CULTIVATE THE LAND, WITH GREAT SAVINGS IN LABOUR. UNFORTUNATELY, THERE IS NOT YET A SUITABLE PLASTIC THAT DOES NOT ROT OR BECOME OPAQUE IN SUNLIGHT (AS DOES POLYTHENE).

FUTURISTIC GREENHOUSE
AN EXPERIMENTAL PRODUCTION LINE GREENHOUSE WAS BUILT OUTSIDE VIENNA IN 1964. THE PLANTS MOVE CONTINUOUSLY UP & DOWN THE TOWER ON AN ENDLESS CONVEYOR, WHILE ATTENDANTS SEATED AT THE BOTTOM DO ALL THE WORK ON THE PLANTS AS THEY PASS. NO FURTHER TOWER GREENHOUSE HAS BEEN BUILT, AS IT WAS FOUND TO BE UNECONOMIC.

HOW TO THROW A COIN THROUGH A BOWLER HAT
SECRETLY BALANCE A COIN ON RIM OF GLASS UNDER THE HAT. THEN THROW SECOND IDENTICAL COIN INTO HAT (AS ABOVE). THIS WILL DISLODGE THE COIN ON THE RIM - CREATING THE ILLUSION THAT THE COIN HAS PASSED THROUGH THE HAT.
COIN THROWN IN / 2ND COIN ON RIM / GLASS

☆ GREYHOUNDS ☆

☆ GREYHOUNDS: TALL SLENDER DOGS WITH GREAT SPEED & KEEN SIGHT

ORIGINS
THE GREYHOUND FAMILY IS VERY ANCIENT & IS DEPICTED ON TOMBS OF THE EGYPTIAN PHARAOHS & VASES OF THE ANCIENT GREEKS. THESE DOGS ARE THOUGHT TO HAVE HAD ROUGH COATS & PROBABLY WERE MORE LIKE SALUKIS THAN TODAYS GREYHOUNDS. THE NAME 'GREY HOUND' IS THOUGHT TO HAVE COME FROM THE OLD LATIN 'GRAE' MEANING 'GREEK'.

STATUS
GREYHOUNDS WERE CONSIDERED A SYMBOL OF NOBILITY BY THE SAXONS & NORMANS - SO MUCH SO THAT PEASANTS & SERFS WERE FORBIDDEN BY LAW TO OWN ONE.

COURSING
THE EARLIEST FORM OF GREYHOUND RACING WAS COURSING. TWO DOGS ON LEADS WERE TAKEN TO THE MIDDLE OF A LARGE FIELD WHILE SERVANTS (BEATERS) ATTEMPTED TO DISTURB ANY HARE IN THE VICINITY. WHEN A RUNNING HARE APPEARED, THE DOGS WOULD BE RELEASED TO GIVE CHASE. THE JUDGE, ON HORSEBACK, RODE AFTER THEM AWARDING POINTS (A) FOR SPEED (WHEN ONE DOG OVERTOOK THE OTHER) (B) FOR EACH OCCASION A DOG FORCED THE HARE TO CHANGE DIRECTION (C) FOR THE KILL (ALTHOUGH ENTHUSIASTS CLAIMED THAT 90% OF THE HARES ESCAPED).

AUSTRALIAN COURSING
THE AUSTRALIANS BEGAN COURSING IN THE 1860s, USING WALLABIES INSTEAD OF HARES AS QUARRY.

RACING
RACING GREYHOUNDS, BY INDUCING THEM TO CHASE AFTER AN IMITATION MECHANICAL HARE, WAS FIRST TRIED IN BRITAIN IN 1876 AT HENDON. THE TIMES REPORTED THAT THE EXPERIMENT WAS A SUCCESS, HEADING ITS REPORT 'COURSING BY PROXY'. HOWEVER THE IDEA DID NOT GAIN POPULARITY UNTIL THE 1920s, WHEN FLOODLIGHTING & EVENING MEETINGS WERE FIRST INTRODUCED IN AMERICA. BRITAIN'S FIRST PURPOSE-BUILT TRACK OPENED IN MANCHESTER IN 1926.

THE ELECTRIC HARE
THE MECHANICAL HARE (WHICH THE DOGS CHASE) IS KNOWN AS AN ALDRITT BUNNY AFTER ITS MANUFACTURER & IS USUALLY MADE OF PLASTIC FOAM. IT IS CONNECTED TO AN ELECTRIC MOTOR WHICH RUNS ON RAILS ROUND THE INSIDE (OR OUTSIDE) OF THE TRACK. IT CAN TRAVEL AT UP TO 100 MPH.

TRAINING
ONE OF THE MOST IMPORTANT ASPECTS OF TRAINING A GREYHOUND IS TO INDUCE IT TO START WELL. THE STARTING TRAPS ARE TOO NARROW TO ALLOW A DOG TO TURN ROUND, BUT SOME DOGS CAN NEVER BE MADE TO COME OUT FAST & RELIABLY. THE TRAPDOORS ARE CLEVERLY DESIGNED SO THE DOG HAS TO CROUCH (LIKE A RUNNER ON A STARTING GRID) TO SEE OUT.

DIET
CHAMPION GREYHOUNDS ARE FED LAVISH DIETS & ARE PROVIDED WITH A DIFFERENT DISH EVERY NIGHT. SOME TOP TRAINERS GIVE THEIR DOGS AN EGG CUP-FULL OF PORT THE MORNING BEFORE EACH RACE.

HOW TO SUSPEND A BOTTLE ON A PIECE OF ROPE WITHOUT ANY KNOTS
FIND A MARBLE OR RUBBER BALL WHICH JUST FITS IN THE NECK OF A DARK WINE BOTTLE. LOWER END OF ROPE INTO BOTTLE, TURN BOTTLE OVER & PULL ROPE SLIGHTLY SO BALL WEDGES ITSELF BETWEEN ROPE & BOTTLE. RELEASE BOTTLE & IT WILL STAY SUSPENDED BY THE ROPE.

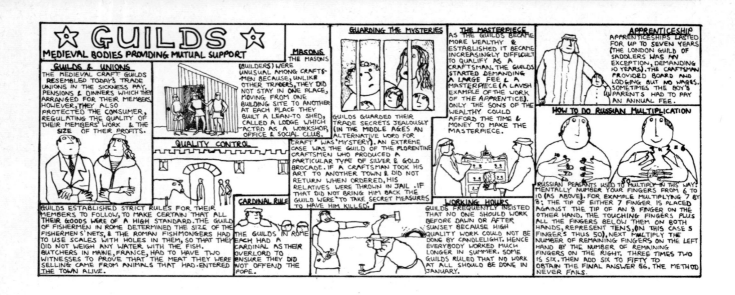

☆ GUILDS ☆
MEDIEVAL BODIES PROVIDING MUTUAL SUPPORT

GUILDS & UNIONS
THE MEDIEVAL CRAFT GUILDS RESEMBLED TODAY'S TRADE UNIONS IN THE SICKNESS PAY, PENSIONS & DINNERS WHICH THEY ARRANGED FOR THEIR MEMBERS. HOWEVER, THEY ALSO PROTECTED THE CONSUMER, REGULATING THE QUALITY OF THEIR MEMBERS' WORK & THE SIZE OF THEIR PROFITS.

QUALITY CONTROL
GUILDS ESTABLISHED STRICT RULES FOR THEIR MEMBERS TO FOLLOW, TO MAKE CERTAIN THAT ALL THEIR GOODS WERE OF A HIGH STANDARD. THE GUILD OF FISHERMEN IN ROME DETERMINED THE SIZE OF THE FISHERMENS' NETS, & THE ROMAN FISHMONGERS HAD TO USE SCALES WITH HOLES IN THEM, SO THAT THEY DID NOT WEIGH ANY WATER WITH THE FISH. BUTCHERS IN MAINE, FRANCE, HAD TO HAVE TWO WITNESSES TO PROVE THAT THE MEAT THEY WERE SELLING CAME FROM ANIMALS THAT HAD ENTERED THE TOWN ALIVE.

MASONS
THE MASONS (BUILDERS) WERE UNUSUAL AMONG CRAFTSMEN BECAUSE, UNLIKE OTHER TRADERS, THEY DID NOT STAY IN ONE PLACE, MOVING FROM ONE BUILDING SITE TO ANOTHER. AT EACH PLACE THEY BUILT A LEAN-TO SHED, CALLED A LODGE WHICH ACTED AS A WORKSHOP, OFFICE & SOCIAL CLUB.

GUARDING THE MYSTERIES
GUILDS GUARDED THEIR TRADE SECRETS JEALOUSLY (IN THE MIDDLE AGES AN ALTERNATIVE WORD FOR "CRAFT" WAS "MYSTERY"). AN EXTREME CASE WAS THE GUILD OF THE FLORENTINE CRAFTSMEN WHO PRODUCED A PARTICULAR TYPE OF SILVER & GOLD BROCADE. IF A CRAFTSMAN TOOK HIS ART TO ANOTHER TOWN & DID NOT RETURN WHEN ORDERED, HIS RELATIVES WERE THROWN IN JAIL. IF THAT DID NOT BRING HIM BACK THE GUILD WORE TO TAKE SECRET MEASURES TO HAVE HIM KILLED!

CARDINAL RULE
THE GUILDS IN ROME EACH HAD A CARDINAL AS THEIR OVERLORD TO ENSURE THEY DID NOT OFFEND THE POPE.

THE MASTERPIECE
AS THE GUILDS BECAME MORE WEALTHY & ESTABLISHED IT BECAME INCREASINGLY DIFFICULT TO QUALIFY AS A CRAFTSMAN. THE GUILDS STARTED DEMANDING A LARGE FEE & A MASTERPIECE (A LAVISH EXAMPLE OF THE WORK OF THE APPRENTICE). ONLY THE SONS OF THE WEALTHY COULD AFFORD THE TIME & MONEY TO MAKE THE MASTERPIECE.

WORKING HOURS
GUILDS FREQUENTLY INSISTED THAT NO ONE SHOULD WORK BEFORE DAWN OR AFTER SUNSET BECAUSE HIGH QUALITY WORK COULD NOT BE DONE BY CANDLELIGHT. HENCE EVERYBODY WORKED MUCH LONGER IN SUMMER. SOME GUILDS RULED THAT NO WORK AT ALL SHOULD BE DONE IN JANUARY.

APPRENTICESHIP
APPRENTICESHIPS LASTED FOR UP TO SEVEN YEARS (THE LONDON GUILD OF SADDLERS WAS AN EXCEPTION, DEMANDING 10 YEARS). THE CRAFTSMAN PROVIDED BOARD AND LODGING BUT NO WAGES. SOMETIMES THE BOY'S PARENTS HAD TO PAY AN ANNUAL FEE.

HOW TO DO RUSSIAN MULTIPLICATION
RUSSIAN PEASANTS USED TO MULTIPLY IN THIS WAY: MENTALLY NUMBER YOUR FINGERS FROM 6 TO 10 (AS ABOVE). FOR EXAMPLE MULTIPLYING 7 BY 8: THE TIP OF EITHER 7 FINGER IS PLACED AGAINST THE TIP OF AN 8 FINGER ON THE OTHER HAND. THE TOUCHING FINGERS PLUS ALL THE FINGERS BELOW THEM ON BOTH HANDS, REPRESENT TENS, (IN THIS CASE 5 FINGERS THUS 50). NEXT MULTIPLY THE NUMBER OF REMAINING FINGERS ON THE LEFT HAND BY THE NUMBER OF REMAINING FINGERS ON THE RIGHT. THREE TIMES TWO IS SIX. THEN ADD SIX TO FIFTY TO OBTAIN THE FINAL ANSWER 56. THE METHOD NEVER FAILS.

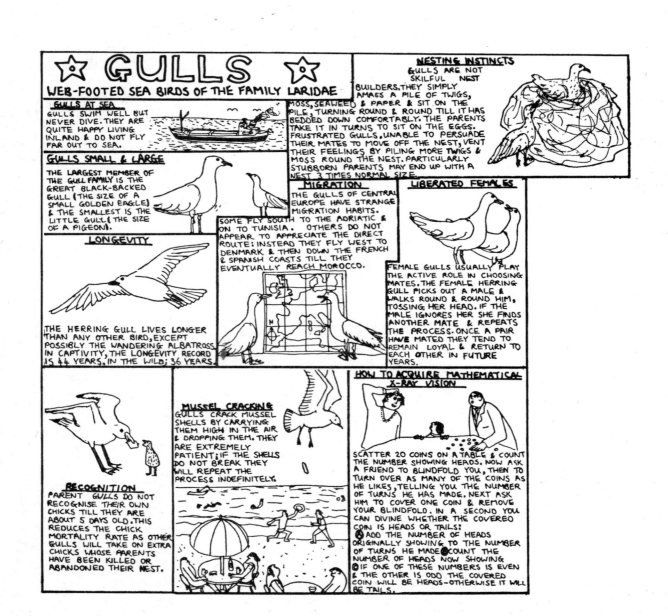

☆ GULLS ☆
WEB-FOOTED SEA BIRDS OF THE FAMILY LARIDAE

GULLS AT SEA
GULLS SWIM WELL BUT NEVER DIVE. THEY ARE QUITE HAPPY LIVING INLAND & DO NOT FLY FAR OUT TO SEA.

GULLS SMALL & LARGE
THE LARGEST MEMBER OF THE GULL FAMILY IS THE GREAT BLACK-BACKED GULL (THE SIZE OF A SMALL GOLDEN EAGLE) & THE SMALLEST IS THE LITTLE GULL (THE SIZE OF A PIGEON).

LONGEVITY
THE HERRING GULL LIVES LONGER THAN ANY OTHER BIRD, EXCEPT POSSIBLY THE WANDERING ALBATROSS. IN CAPTIVITY, THE LONGEVITY RECORD IS 44 YEARS. IN THE WILD: 36 YEARS.

NESTING INSTINCTS
GULLS ARE NOT SKILFUL NEST BUILDERS. THEY SIMPLY AMASS A PILE OF TWIGS, MOSS, SEAWEED & PAPER & SIT ON THE PILE, TURNING ROUND & ROUND TILL IT HAS BEDDED DOWN COMFORTABLY. THE PARENTS TAKE IT IN TURNS TO SIT ON THE EGGS. FRUSTRATED GULLS, UNABLE TO PERSUADE THEIR MATES TO MOVE OFF THE NEST, VENT THEIR FEELINGS BY PILING MORE TWIGS & MOSS ROUND THE NEST. PARTICULARLY STUBBORN PARENTS MAY END UP WITH A NEST 3 TIMES NORMAL SIZE.

MIGRATION
THE GULLS OF CENTRAL EUROPE HAVE STRANGE MIGRATION HABITS. SOME FLY SOUTH TO THE ADRIATIC & ON TO TUNISIA. OTHERS DO NOT APPEAR TO APPRECIATE THE DIRECT ROUTE: INSTEAD THEY FLY WEST TO DENMARK & THEN DOWN THE FRENCH & SPANISH COASTS TILL THEY EVENTUALLY REACH MOROCCO.

LIBERATED FEMALES
FEMALE GULLS USUALLY PLAY THE ACTIVE ROLE IN CHOOSING MATES. THE FEMALE HERRING GULL PICKS OUT A MALE & WALKS ROUND & ROUND HIM, TOSSING HER HEAD. IF THE MALE IGNORES HER SHE FINDS ANOTHER MATE & REPEATS THE PROCESS. ONCE A PAIR HAVE MATED THEY TEND TO REMAIN LOYAL & RETURN TO EACH OTHER IN FUTURE YEARS.

RECOGNITION
PARENT GULLS DO NOT RECOGNISE THEIR OWN CHICKS TILL THEY ARE ABOUT 5 DAYS OLD. THIS REDUCES THE CHICK MORTALITY RATE AS OTHER GULLS WILL TAKE ON EXTRA CHICKS WHOSE PARENTS HAVE BEEN KILLED OR ABANDONED THEIR NEST.

MUSSEL CRACKING
GULLS CRACK MUSSEL SHELLS BY CARRYING THEM HIGH IN THE AIR & DROPPING THEM. THEY ARE EXTREMELY PATIENT; IF THE SHELLS DO NOT BREAK THEY WILL REPEAT THE PROCESS INDEFINITELY.

HOW TO ACQUIRE MATHEMATICAL X-RAY VISION
SCATTER 20 COINS ON A TABLE & COUNT THE NUMBER SHOWING HEADS. NOW ASK A FRIEND TO BLINDFOLD YOU, THEN TO TURN OVER AS MANY OF THE COINS AS HE LIKES, TELLING YOU THE NUMBER OF TURNS HE HAS MADE. NEXT ASK HIM TO COVER ONE COIN & REMOVE YOUR BLINDFOLD. IN A SECOND YOU CAN DIVINE WHETHER THE COVERED COIN IS HEADS OR TAILS:
ⓐ ADD THE NUMBER OF HEADS ORIGINALLY SHOWING TO THE NUMBER OF TURNS HE MADE ⓑ COUNT THE NUMBER OF HEADS NOW SHOWING ⓒ IF ONE OF THESE NUMBERS IS EVEN & THE OTHER IS ODD THE COVERED COIN WILL BE HEADS—OTHERWISE IT WILL BE TAILS.

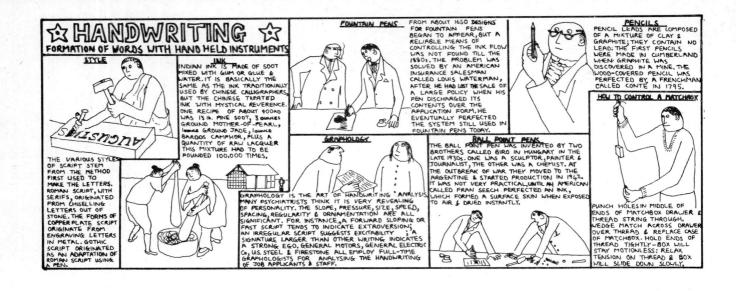

☆ HANDWRITING ☆
FORMATION OF WORDS WITH HAND HELD INSTRUMENTS

STYLE

THE VARIOUS STYLES OF SCRIPT STEM FROM THE METHOD FIRST USED TO MAKE THE LETTERS. ROMAN SCRIPT, WITH SERIFS, ORIGINATED FROM CHISELLING LETTERS OUT OF STONE. THE FORMS OF COPPERPLATE SCRIPT ORIGINATE FROM ENGRAVING LETTERS IN METAL. GOTHIC SCRIPT ORIGINATED AS AN ADAPTATION OF ROMAN SCRIPT USING A PEN.

INK

INDIAN INK IS MADE OF SOOT MIXED WITH GUM OR GLUE & WATER. IT IS BASICALLY THE SAME AS THE INK TRADITIONALLY USED BY CHINESE CALLIGRAPHERS, BUT THE CHINESE TREATED INK WITH MYSTICAL REVERENCE. ONE RECIPE OF ABOUT 400AD WAS 13LB. PINE SOOT, 3 OUNCES GROUND MOTHER-OF-PEARL, 1 OUNCE GROUND JADE, 1 OUNCE BAROOS CAMPHOR, PLUS A QUANTITY OF RAW LACQUER. THIS MIXTURE HAD TO BE POUNDED 100,000 TIMES.

FOUNTAIN PENS

FROM ABOUT 1650 DESIGNS FOR FOUNTAIN PENS BEGAN TO APPEAR, BUT A RELIABLE MEANS OF CONTROLLING THE INK FLOW WAS NOT FOUND TILL THE 1880s. THE PROBLEM WAS SOLVED BY AN AMERICAN INSURANCE SALESMAN CALLED LOUIS WATERMAN, AFTER HE HAD LOST THE SALE OF A LARGE POLICY WHEN HIS PEN DISCHARGED ITS CONTENTS OVER THE APPLICATION FORM. HE EVENTUALLY PERFECTED THE SYSTEM STILL USED IN FOUNTAIN PENS TODAY.

PENCILS

PENCIL LEADS ARE COMPOSED OF A MIXTURE OF CLAY & GRAPHITE; THEY CONTAIN NO LEAD. THE FIRST PENCILS WERE MADE IN CUMBERLAND WHEN GRAPHITE WAS DISCOVERED IN A MINE. THE WOOD-COVERED PENCIL WAS PERFECTED BY A FRENCHMAN CALLED CONTE IN 1795.

GRAPHOLOGY

GRAPHOLOGY IS THE ART OF HANDWRITING ANALYSIS. MANY PSYCHIATRISTS THINK IT IS VERY REVEALING OF PERSONALITY. THE SLOPE, PRESSURE, SIZE, SPEED, SPACING, REGULARITY & ORNAMENTATION ARE ALL SIGNIFICANT. FOR INSTANCE, A FORWARD SLOPING OR FAST SCRIPT TENDS TO INDICATE EXTROVERSION; AN IRREGULAR SCRIPT SUGGESTS EXCITABILITY; A SIGNATURE LARGER THAN OTHER WRITING INDICATES A STRONG EGO. GENERAL MOTORS, GENERAL ELECTRIC CO, US. STEEL & FIRESTONE ALL EMPLOY FULL-TIME GRAPHOLOGISTS FOR ANALYSING THE HANDWRITING OF JOB APPLICANTS & STAFF.

BALL POINT PENS

THE BALL POINT PEN WAS INVENTED BY TWO BROTHERS CALLED BIRO IN HUNGARY IN THE LATE 1930s. ONE WAS A SCULPTOR, PAINTER & JOURNALIST, THE OTHER WAS A CHEMIST. AT THE OUTBREAK OF WAR THEY MOVED TO THE ARGENTINE & STARTED PRODUCTION IN 1942. IT WAS NOT VERY PRACTICAL, UNTIL AN AMERICAN CALLED FRAN SEECH PERFECTED AN INK, WHICH FORMED A SURFACE SKIN WHEN EXPOSED TO AIR & DRIED INSTANTLY.

HOW TO CONTROL A MATCHBOX

PUNCH HOLES IN MIDDLE OF ENDS OF MATCHBOX DRAWER & THREAD STRING THROUGH. WEDGE MATCH ACROSS DRAWER OVER THREAD & REPLACE CASE OF MATCHBOX. HOLD ENDS OF THREAD TIGHTLY – BOX WILL STAY MOTIONLESS; RELAX TENSION ON THREAD & BOX WILL SLIDE DOWN SLOWLY.

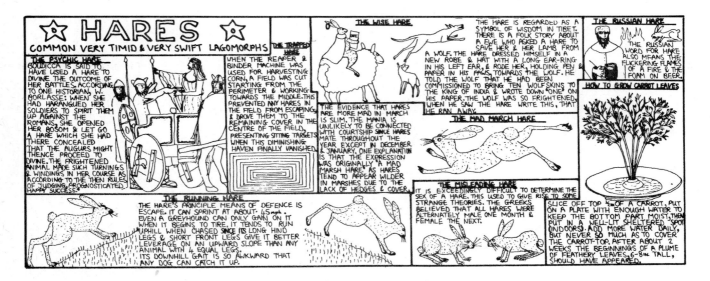

☆ HARES ☆
COMMON VERY TIMID & VERY SWIFT LAGOMORPHS

THE PSYCHIC HARE

BOUDICCA IS SAID TO HAVE USED A HARE TO DIVINE THE OUTCOME OF HER BATTLES. ACCORDING TO ONE HISTORIAN, W. BORLASE: WHEN SHE HAD HARANGUED HER SOLDIERS TO SPIRIT THEM UP AGAINST THE ROMANS, SHE OPENED HER BOSOM & LET GO A HARE WHICH SHE HAD THERE CONCEALED THAT THE AUGURS MIGHT THENCE PROCEED TO DIVINE. THE FRIGHTENED ANIMAL MADE SUCH TURNINGS & WINDINGS IN HER COURSE AS, ACCORDING TO THE THEN RULES OF JUDGING, PROGNOSTICATED HAPPY SUCCESS.

THE TRAPPED HARE

WHEN THE REAPER & BINDER MACHINE WAS USED FOR HARVESTING CORN, A FIELD WAS CUT STARTING FROM THE PERIMETER & WORKING TOWARDS THE MIDDLE. THIS PREVENTED ANY HARES IN THE FIELD FROM ESCAPING & DROVE THEM TO THE REMAINING COVER IN THE CENTRE OF THE FIELD, PRESENTING SITTING TARGETS WHEN THIS DIMINISHING HAVEN FINALLY VANISHED.

THE WISE HARE

THE HARE IS REGARDED AS A SYMBOL OF WISDOM IN TIBET. THERE IS A FOLK STORY ABOUT A EWE WHO ASKED A HARE TO SAVE HER & HER LAMB FROM A WOLF. THE HARE DRESSED HIMSELF IN A NEW ROBE & HAT WITH A LONG EAR-RING IN HIS LEFT EAR, & RODE HER, HOLDING PEN & PAPER IN HIS PAWS, TOWARDS THE WOLF. HE TOLD THE WOLF THAT HE HAD BEEN COMMISSIONED TO BRING TEN WOLF SKINS TO THE KING OF INDIA & WROTE DOWN "ONE" ON HIS PAPER. THE WOLF WAS SO FRIGHTENED, WHEN HE SAW THE HARE WRITE THIS, THAT HE RAN AWAY.

THE RUSSIAN HARE

THE RUSSIAN WORD FOR HARE ALSO MEANS THE FLICKERING FLAMES OF A FIRE & THE FOAM ON BEER.

THE MAD MARCH HARE

THE EVIDENCE THAT HARES ARE MORE MAD IN MARCH IS SLIM. THE MANIA IS UNLIKELY TO BE CONNECTED WITH COURTSHIP SINCE HARES MATE THROUGHOUT THE YEAR EXCEPT IN DECEMBER & JANUARY. ONE EXPLANATION IS THAT THE EXPRESSION WAS ORIGINALLY 'A MAD MARSH HARE' AS HARES TEND TO APPEAR WILDER IN MARSHES DUE TO THE LACK OF HEDGES & COVER.

THE MISLEADING HARE

IT IS EXCEEDINGLY DIFFICULT TO DETERMINE THE SEX OF A HARE. THIS USED TO GIVE RISE TO SOME STRANGE THEORIES. THE GREEKS BELIEVED THAT ALL HARES WERE ALTERNATELY MALE ONE MONTH & FEMALE THE NEXT.

HOW TO GROW CARROT LEAVES

SLICE OFF TOP ½ OF A CARROT, PUT ON A PLATE WITH ENOUGH WATER TO KEEP THE BOTTOM PART MOIST, THEN PUT IN A WELL-LIT SHELTERED SPOT (INDOORS). ADD MORE WATER DAILY, BUT NEVER SO MUCH AS TO COVER THE CARROT-TOP. AFTER ABOUT 2 WEEKS THE BEGINNINGS OF A PLUME OF FEATHERY LEAVES, 6-8IN. TALL, SHOULD HAVE APPEARED.

THE RUNNING HARE

THE HARE'S PRINCIPLE MEANS OF DEFENCE IS ESCAPE. IT CAN SPRINT AT ABOUT 45 mph. EVEN A GREYHOUND CAN ONLY GAIN ON IT WHEN IT BEGINS TO TIRE. IT TENDS TO RUN UPHILL WHEN CHASED SINCE ITS LONG HIND LEGS & SHORT FRONT LEGS GIVE IT BETTER LEVERAGE ON AN UPWARD SLOPE THAN ANY ANIMAL WITH 4 EQUAL LEGS. ITS DOWNHILL GAIT IS SO AWKWARD THAT ANY DOG CAN CATCH IT UP.

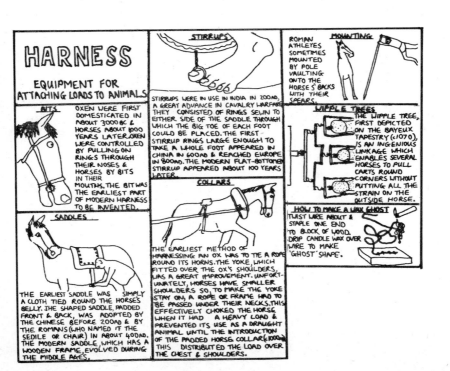

HARNESS
EQUIPMENT FOR ATTACHING LOADS TO ANIMALS

BITS

OXEN WERE FIRST DOMESTICATED IN ABOUT 3000 BC & HORSES ABOUT 1000 YEARS LATER. OXEN WERE CONTROLLED BY PULLING ON RINGS THROUGH THEIR NOSES & HORSES BY BITS IN THEIR MOUTHS. THE BIT WAS THE EARLIEST PART OF MODERN HARNESS TO BE INVENTED.

SADDLES

THE EARLIEST SADDLE WAS SIMPLY A CLOTH TIED ROUND THE HORSE'S BELLY. THE SHAPED SADDLE, PADDED FRONT & BACK, WAS ADOPTED BY THE CHINESE BEFORE 200AD & BY THE ROMANS (WHO NAMED IT THE SEDILE OR CHAIR) IN ABOUT 400AD. THE MODERN SADDLE, WHICH HAS A WOODEN FRAME, EVOLVED DURING THE MIDDLE AGES.

STIRRUPS

STIRRUPS WERE IN USE IN INDIA IN 200AD, A GREAT ADVANCE IN CAVALRY WARFARE. THEY CONSISTED OF RINGS SEWN TO EITHER SIDE OF THE SADDLE THROUGH WHICH THE BIG TOE OF EACH FOOT COULD BE PLACED. THE FIRST STIRRUP RINGS LARGE ENOUGH TO TAKE A WHOLE FOOT APPEARED IN CHINA IN 600AD & REACHED EUROPE IN 800AD. THE MODERN FLAT-BOTTOMED STIRRUP APPEARED ABOUT 100 YEARS LATER.

COLLARS

THE EARLIEST METHOD OF HARNESSING AN OX WAS TO TIE A ROPE ROUND ITS HORNS. THE YOKE, WHICH FITTED OVER THE OX'S SHOULDERS, WAS A GREAT IMPROVEMENT. UNFORTUNATELY, HORSES HAVE SMALLER SHOULDERS SO, TO MAKE THE YOKE STAY ON, A ROPE OR FRAME HAD TO BE PASSED UNDER THEIR NECKS. THIS EFFECTIVELY CHOKED THE HORSE WHEN IT HAD A HEAVY LOAD & PREVENTED ITS USE AS A DRAUGHT ANIMAL UNTIL THE INTRODUCTION OF THE PADDED HORSE COLLAR (1000AD). THIS DISTRIBUTED THE LOAD OVER THE CHEST & SHOULDERS.

MOUNTING

ROMAN ATHLETES SOMETIMES MOUNTED BY POLE VAULTING ONTO THE HORSE'S BACKS WITH THEIR SPEARS.

WIPPLE TREES

THE WIPPLE TREE, FIRST DEPICTED ON THE BAYEUX TAPESTRY (c.1070), IS AN INGENIOUS LINKAGE WHICH ENABLES SEVERAL HORSES TO PULL CARTS ROUND CORNERS WITHOUT PUTTING ALL THE STRAIN ON THE OUTSIDE HORSE.

HOW TO MAKE A WAX GHOST

TWIST WIRE ABOUT & STAPLE ONE END TO BLOCK OF WOOD. DRIP CANDLE WAX OVER WIRE TO MAKE GHOST SHAPE.

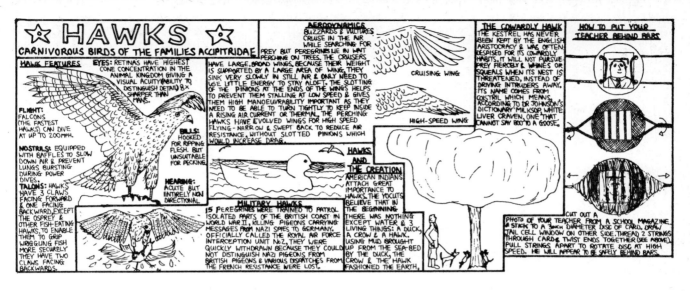

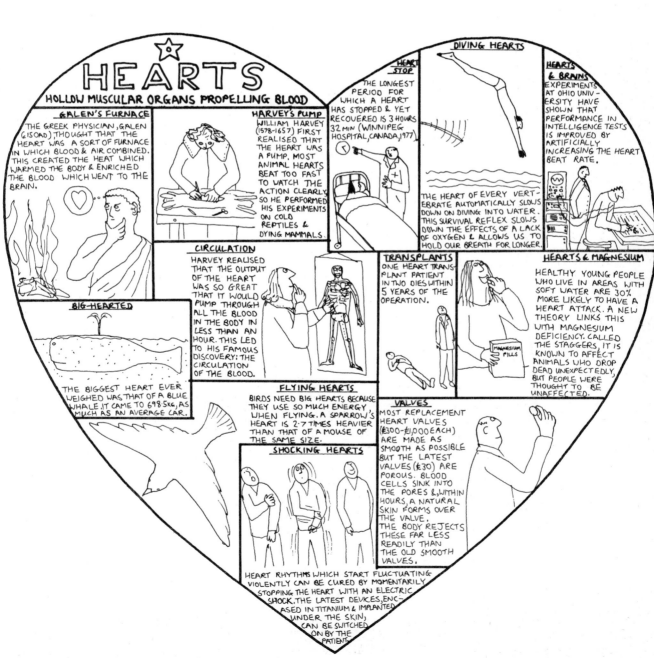

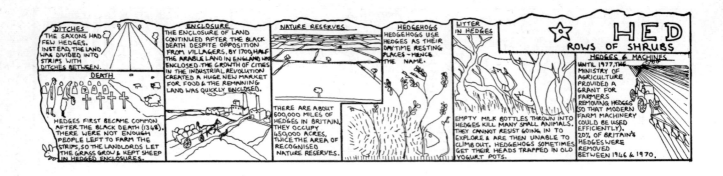

DITCHES
THE SAXONS HAD FEW HEDGES. INSTEAD, THE LAND WAS DIVIDED INTO STRIPS WITH DITCHES BETWEEN.

DEATH
HEDGES FIRST BECAME COMMON AFTER THE BLACK DEATH (1348). THERE WERE NOT ENOUGH PEOPLE LEFT TO FARM THE STRIPS, SO THE LANDLORDS LET THE GRASS GROW & KEPT SHEEP IN HEDGED ENCLOSURES.

ENCLOSURE
THE ENCLOSURE OF LAND CONTINUED AFTER THE BLACK DEATH DESPITE OPPOSITION FROM VILLAGERS. BY 1700 HALF THE ARABLE LAND IN ENGLAND WAS ENCLOSED. THE GROWTH OF CITIES IN THE INDUSTRIAL REVOLUTION CREATED A HUGE NEW MARKET FOR FOOD & THE REMAINING LAND WAS QUICKLY ENCLOSED.

NATURE RESERVES
THERE ARE ABOUT 600,000 MILES OF HEDGES IN BRITAIN. THEY OCCUPY 450,000 ACRES, TWICE THE AREA OF RECOGNISED NATURE RESERVES.

HEDGEHOGS
HEDGEHOGS USE HEDGES AS THEIR DAYTIME RESTING PLACES - HENCE THE NAME.

LITTER IN HEDGES
EMPTY MILK BOTTLES THROWN INTO HEDGES KILL MANY SMALL ANIMALS. THEY CANNOT RESIST GOING IN TO EXPLORE & ARE THEN UNABLE TO CLIMB OUT. HEDGEHOGS SOMETIMES GET THEIR HEADS TRAPPED IN OLD YOGURT POTS.

HED
ROWS OF SHRUBS

HEDGES & MACHINES
UNTIL 1977, THE MINISTRY OF AGRICULTURE PROVIDED A GRANT FOR FARMERS REMOVING HEDGES SO THAT MODERN FARM MACHINERY COULD BE USED EFFICIENTLY. 20% OF BRITAIN'S HEDGES WERE REMOVED BETWEEN 1946 & 1970.

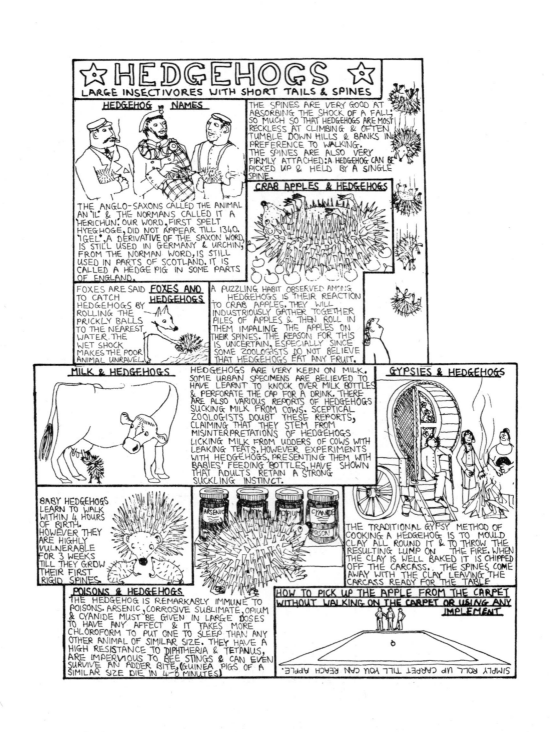

☆ HEDGEHOGS ☆
LARGE INSECTIVORES WITH SHORT TAILS & SPINES

HEDGEHOG NAMES
THE ANGLO-SAXONS CALLED THE ANIMAL AN 'IL' & THE NORMANS CALLED IT A HERICHUN. OUR WORD, FIRST SPELT HYEGHOGE, DID NOT APPEAR TILL 1340. 'IGEL', A DERIVATIVE OF THE SAXON WORD, IS STILL USED IN GERMANY & URCHIN, FROM THE NORMAN WORD, IS STILL USED IN PARTS OF SCOTLAND. IT IS CALLED A HEDGE PIG IN SOME PARTS OF ENGLAND.

THE SPINES ARE VERY GOOD AT ABSORBING THE SHOCK OF A FALL, SO MUCH SO THAT HEDGEHOGS ARE MOST RECKLESS AT CLIMBING & OFTEN TUMBLE DOWN HILLS & BANKS IN PREFERENCE TO WALKING. THE SPINES ARE ALSO VERY FIRMLY ATTACHED: A HEDGEHOG CAN BE PICKED UP & HELD BY A SINGLE SPINE.

CRAB APPLES & HEDGEHOGS

FOXES AND HEDGEHOGS
FOXES ARE SAID TO CATCH HEDGEHOGS BY ROLLING THE PRICKLY BALLS TO THE NEAREST WATER. THE WET SHOCK MAKES THE POOR ANIMAL UNRAVEL.

A PUZZLING HABIT OBSERVED AMONG HEDGEHOGS IS THEIR REACTION TO CRAB APPLES. THEY WILL INDUSTRIOUSLY GATHER TOGETHER PILES OF APPLES & THEN ROLL IN THEM IMPALING THE APPLES ON THEIR SPINES. THE REASON FOR THIS IS UNCERTAIN, ESPECIALLY SINCE SOME ZOOLOGISTS DO NOT BELIEVE THAT HEDGEHOGS EAT ANY FRUIT.

MILK & HEDGEHOGS
HEDGEHOGS ARE VERY KEEN ON MILK. SOME URBAN SPECIMENS ARE BELIEVED TO HAVE LEARNT TO KNOCK OVER MILK BOTTLES & PERFORATE THE CAP FOR A DRINK. THERE ARE ALSO VARIOUS REPORTS OF HEDGEHOGS SUCKING MILK FROM COWS. SCEPTICAL ZOOLOGISTS DOUBT THESE REPORTS, CLAIMING THAT THEY STEM FROM MISINTERPRETATIONS OF HEDGEHOGS LICKING MILK FROM UDDERS OF COWS WITH LEAKING TEATS. HOWEVER EXPERIMENTS WITH HEDGEHOGS, PRESENTING THEM WITH BABIES' FEEDING BOTTLES, HAVE SHOWN THAT ADULTS RETAIN A STRONG SUCKLING INSTINCT.

GYPSIES & HEDGEHOGS
THE TRADITIONAL GYPSY METHOD OF COOKING A HEDGEHOG IS TO MOULD CLAY ALL ROUND IT & TO THROW THE RESULTING LUMP ON THE FIRE. WHEN THE CLAY IS WELL BAKED IT IS CHIPPED OFF THE CARCASS. THE SPINES COME AWAY WITH THE CLAY LEAVING THE CARCASS READY FOR THE TABLE.

BABY HEDGEHOGS LEARN TO WALK WITHIN 4 HOURS OF BIRTH. HOWEVER THEY ARE HIGHLY VULNERABLE FOR 3 WEEKS TILL THEY GROW THEIR FIRST RIGID SPINES.

POISONS & HEDGEHOGS
THE HEDGEHOG IS REMARKABLY IMMUNE TO POISONS. ARSENIC, CORROSIVE SUBLIMATE, OPIUM & CYANIDE MUST BE GIVEN IN LARGE DOSES TO HAVE ANY AFFECT & IT TAKES MORE CHLOROFORM TO PUT ONE TO SLEEP THAN ANY OTHER ANIMAL OF SIMILAR SIZE. THEY HAVE A HIGH RESISTANCE TO DIPHTHERIA & TETANUS, ARE IMPERVIOUS TO BEE STINGS & CAN EVEN SURVIVE AN ADDER BITE. (GUINEA PIGS OF A SIMILAR SIZE DIE IN 4-8 MINUTES)

HOW TO PICK UP THE APPLE FROM THE CARPET WITHOUT WALKING ON THE CARPET OR USING ANY IMPLEMENT
SIMPLY ROLL UP CARPET TILL YOU CAN REACH APPLE.

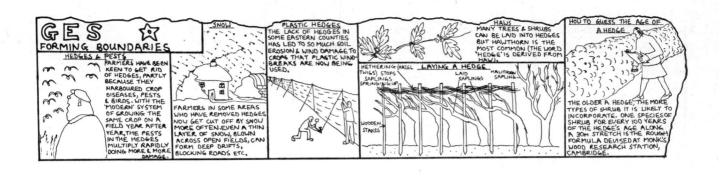

GES ☆
FORMING BOUNDARIES

HEDGES & PESTS

FARMERS HAVE BEEN KEEN TO GET RID OF HEDGES, PARTLY BECAUSE THEY HARBOURED CROP DISEASES, PESTS & BIRDS. WITH THE 'MODERN' SYSTEM OF GROWING THE SAME CROP ON A FIELD YEAR AFTER YEAR, THE PESTS IN THE HEDGES MULTIPLY RAPIDLY DOING MORE & MORE DAMAGE.

SNOW

FARMERS IN SOME AREAS WHO HAVE REMOVED HEDGES NOW GET CUT OFF BY SNOW MORE OFTEN. EVEN A THIN LAYER OF SNOW, BLOWN ACROSS OPEN FIELDS, CAN FORM DEEP DRIFTS, BLOCKING ROADS ETC.

PLASTIC HEDGES

THE LACK OF HEDGES IN SOME EASTERN COUNTIES HAS LED TO SO MUCH SOIL EROSION & WIND DAMAGE TO CROPS THAT PLASTIC WIND-BREAKS ARE NOW BEING USED.

LAYING A HEDGE

MANY TREES & SHRUBS CAN BE LAID INTO HEDGES BUT HAWTHORN IS THE MOST COMMON (THE WORD 'HEDGE' IS DERIVED FROM HAW).

HETHERING (HAZEL TWIGS) STOPS SAPLINGS SPRINGING UP. LAID SAPLINGS. HAWTHORN SAPLING. WOODEN STAKES

HOW TO GUESS THE AGE OF A HEDGE

THE OLDER A HEDGE, THE MORE TYPES OF SHRUB IT IS LIKELY TO INCORPORATE. ONE SPECIES OF SHRUB FOR EVERY 100 YEARS OF THE HEDGE'S AGE ALONG A 30m STRETCH IS THE ROUGH FORMULA DEVISED AT MONK'S WOOD RESEARCH STATION, CAMBRIDGE.

☆ HELICOPTERS ☆
FLYING MACHINES WITH POWERED HORIZONTAL ROTORS

THE CLOCKWORK HELICOPTER

THE FIRST SELF-PROPELLED LIFTING AIRSCREW WAS A SPRING DRIVEN MODEL CONSTRUCTED BY M. LOMONOSOV & DEMONSTRATED TO THE RUSSIAN ACADEMY OF SCIENCES IN 1754.

FREE FLIGHT OR LIFT OFF

TILL THE 1930s MOST EXPERIMENTAL HELICOPTERS SEEMED INCAPABLE OF RISING MORE THAN A FEW FEET OFF THE GROUND. THE REASON WHY IT IS EASIER TO RISE A LITTLE WAY IS THAT A CUSHION OF AIR BUILDS UP BETWEEN THE ROTOR & THE GROUND. IN FREE FLIGHT THERE IS NO AIR CUSHION & MORE POWER IS NEEDED.

THE SPINNING ENGINE

A HELICOPTER NEEDS MUCH MORE POWER TO LIFT IT OFF THE GROUND THAN A FIXED-WING AEROPLANE OF THE SAME WEIGHT. THE AIR-COOLED ROTARY ENGINE, DEVELOPED DURING THE FIRST WORLD WAR, WAS THE FIRST ENGINE LIGHT & POWERFUL ENOUGH TO MAKE A PRACTICAL HELICOPTER. THE SHAFT OF THIS ENGINE IS FIXED RIGIDLY TO THE FRAME, WHILE THE REST OF THE ENGINE, FIXED TO THE PROPELLER, ROTATES. THIS UNORTHODOX ARRANGEMENT ENSURED GOOD COOLING OF THE SPINNING CYLINDERS & GAVE A MUCH HIGHER POWER-TO-WEIGHT RATIO THAN ITS WATER-COOLED RIVALS

EDISON'S GUNPOWDER HELICOPTER

EDISON TESTED THE IDEA OF A HELICOPTER BY TYING AN ELECTRIC FAN TO A SPRING BALANCE TO DETERMINE ITS LIFTING CAPACITY. CONCLUDING THAT THERE WAS NO SUITABLE ENGINE HE STARTED TO BUILD A GUNPOWDER ENGINE. A GUNCOTTON TAPE WAS FED AUTOMATICALLY INTO THE CYLINDER & IGNITED BY A SPARK. WORK CEASED WHEN THE LABORATORY EXPLODED.

THE WONDERFUL NEW BRITISH ROTOR

HELICOPTER ROTOR-HEADS ARE HIGHLY COMPLEX. EACH BLADE MUST HAVE ADJUSTABLE PITCH & SOMETHING TO ENABLE IT TO MOVE A SMALL DISTANCE UP & DOWN & BACKWARDS & FORWARDS. NORMALLY HINGES COMPENSATE FOR THE UNEQUAL SPEEDS OF ROTOR BLADES MOVING WITH AND AGAINST THE DIRECTION OF FLIGHT & HELP REDUCE THE MECHANICAL STRESS AT THE BLADE ROOTS. HOWEVER A RECENT BRITISH ROTOR HAS A BETTER ARRANGEMENT. THE BLADES ARE JOINED FIRMLY TO THE HEAD BY TITANIUM CASTINGS WHICH ARE SUFFICIENTLY FLEXIBLE & STRONG TO ELIMINATE THE NEED FOR HINGES.

TAIL ROTORS

ONE PROBLEM FACED BY EARLY HELICOPTER DESIGNERS WAS THE TENDENCY FOR THE MACHINE TO START SPINNING IN THE OPPOSITE DIRECTION TO THE BLADES WHEN IT LEAVES THE GROUND. THE SMALL PROPELLOR ON THE TAIL OF TODAY'S MACHINES PREVENTS THIS OCCURRING.

FLEXIBLE ROTORS

ANOTHER PROBLEM WAS THE TENDENCY OF THE SPINNING ROTOR TO ACT AS A GIANT GYROSCOPE, MAKING THE CRAFT IMPOSSIBLE TO HANDLE. THIS WAS SOLVED BY MAKING THE BLADES SUFFIC-ENTLY FLEXIBLE.

HOW TO MAKE A MAGIC FACE

WITH A LENGTH OF THIN ELECTRIC WIRE, OUTLINE A HUMAN PROFILE STICKING IT DOWN TO A PIECE OF CARD WITH BITS OF SELLOTAPE. STICK SECOND PIECE OF CARD ON TOP TO COVER UP WIRE. SPRINKLE SOME IRON FILINGS OVER THE CARD & CONNECT THE ENDS OF THE WIRE TO THE BATTERY. TAP THE CARD GENTLY, THE WIRE WILL ATTRACT THE IRON & THE FACE WILL APPEAR.

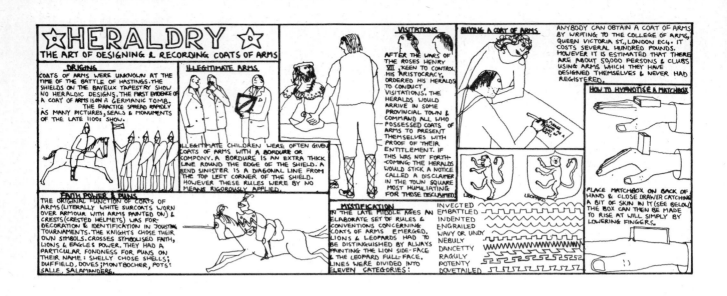

☆ HERALDRY ☆
THE ART OF DESIGNING & RECORDING COATS OF ARMS

ORIGINS
COATS OF ARMS WERE UNKNOWN AT THE TIME OF THE BATTLE OF HASTINGS. THE SHIELDS ON THE BAYEUX TAPESTRY SHOW NO HERALDIC DESIGNS. THE FIRST EVIDENCE OF A COAT OF ARMS IS ON A GERMANIC TOMB. THE PRACTICE SPREAD RAPIDLY AS MANY PICTURES, SEALS & MONUMENTS OF THE LATE 1100s SHOW.

ILLEGITIMATE ARMS
ILLEGITIMATE CHILDREN WERE OFTEN GIVEN COATS OF ARMS WITH A BORDURE OR COMPONY. A BORDURE IS AN EXTRA THICK LINE ROUND THE EDGE OF THE SHIELD. A BEND SINISTER IS A DIAGONAL LINE FROM THE TOP LEFT CORNER OF THE SHIELD. HOWEVER THESE RULES WERE BY NO MEANS RIGOROUSLY APPLIED.

FAITH POWER & PUNS
THE ORIGINAL FUNCTION OF COATS OF ARMS (LITERALLY WHITE SURCOATS WORN OVER ARMOUR WITH ARMS PAINTED ON) & CRESTS (CRESTED HELMETS) WAS FOR DECORATION & IDENTIFICATION IN JOUSTING TOURNAMENTS. THE KNIGHTS CHOSE THEIR OWN SYMBOLS. CROSSES SYMBOLISED FAITH, LIONS & EAGLES POWER. THEY HAD A PARTICULAR FONDNESS FOR PUNS ON THEIR NAME: SHELLY CHOSE SHELLS; DUFFIELD, DOVES; MONTBOCHER, POTS: SALLE, SALAMANDERS.

VISITATIONS
AFTER THE WARS OF THE ROSES HENRY VII, KEEN TO CONTROL HIS ARISTOCRACY, ORDERED HIS HERALDS TO CONDUCT VISITATIONS. THE HERALDS WOULD ARRIVE IN SOME PROVINCIAL TOWN & COMMAND ALL WHO POSSESSED COATS OF ARMS TO PRESENT THEMSELVES & PROOF OF THEIR ENTITLEMENT. IF THIS WAS NOT FORTHCOMING THE HERALDS WOULD STICK A NOTICE CALLED A DISCLAIMER IN THE TOWN SQUARE MOST HUMILIATING FOR THOSE DISCLAIMED.

MYSTIFICATION
IN THE LATE MIDDLE AGES AN ELABORATE SET OF RULES & CONVENTIONS CONCERNING COATS OF ARMS EMERGED. LIONS & LEOPARDS HAD TO BE DISTINGUISHED BY ALWAYS PAINTING THE LION SIDE-FACE & THE LEOPARD FULL-FACE. LINES WERE DIVIDED INTO ELEVEN CATEGORIES:

INVECTED
EMBATTLED
INDENTED
ENGRAILED
WAVY OR UNDY
NEBULY
DANCETTY
RAGULY
POTENTY
DOVETAILED

BUYING A COAT OF ARMS
ANYBODY CAN OBTAIN A COAT OF ARMS BY WRITING TO THE COLLEGE OF ARMS, QUEEN VICTORIA ST., LONDON EC4. IT COSTS SEVERAL HUNDRED POUNDS. HOWEVER IT IS ESTIMATED THAT THERE ARE ABOUT 50,000 PERSONS & CLUBS USING ARMS WHICH THEY HAVE DESIGNED THEMSELVES & NEVER HAD REGISTERED.

LION   LEOPARD

HOW TO HYPNOTISE A MATCHBOX
PLACE MATCHBOX ON BACK OF HAND & CLOSE DRAWER CATCHING A BIT OF SKIN IN IT (SEE BELOW) THE BOX CAN THEN BE MADE TO RISE AT WILL SIMPLY BY LOWERING FINGERS.

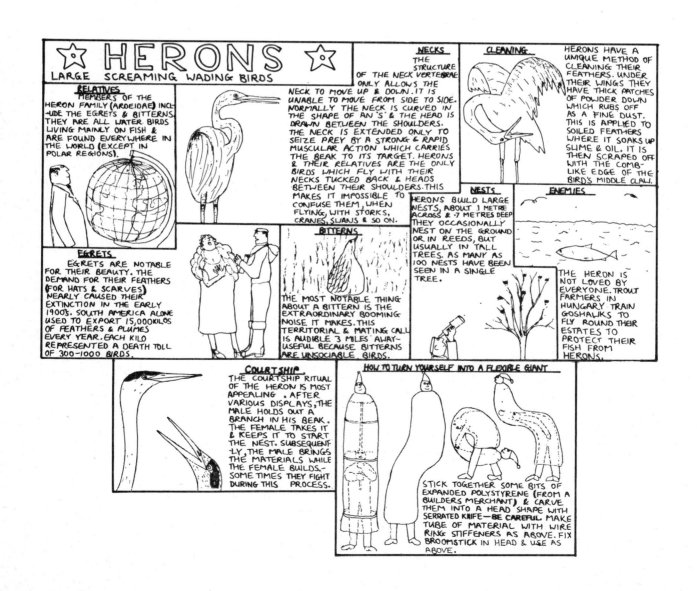

☆ HERONS ☆
LARGE SCREAMING WADING BIRDS

RELATIVES
MEMBERS OF THE HERON FAMILY (ARDEIDAE) INCLUDE THE EGRETS & BITTERNS. THEY ARE ALL WATER BIRDS LIVING MAINLY ON FISH & ARE FOUND EVERYWHERE IN THE WORLD (EXCEPT IN POLAR REGIONS).

EGRETS
EGRETS ARE NOTABLE FOR THEIR BEAUTY. THE DEMAND FOR THEIR FEATHERS (FOR HATS & SCARVES) NEARLY CAUSED THEIR EXTINCTION IN THE EARLY 1900s. SOUTH AMERICA ALONE USED TO EXPORT 15,000 KILOS OF FEATHERS & PLUMES EVERY YEAR. EACH KILO REPRESENTED A DEATH TOLL OF 300-1000 BIRDS.

NECKS
THE STRUCTURE OF THE NECK VERTEBRAE ONLY ALLOWS THE NECK TO MOVE UP & DOWN. IT IS UNABLE TO MOVE FROM SIDE TO SIDE. NORMALLY THE NECK IS CURVED IN THE SHAPE OF AN 'S' & THE HEAD IS DRAWN BETWEEN THE SHOULDERS. THE NECK IS EXTENDED ONLY TO SEIZE PREY BY A STRONG & RAPID MUSCULAR ACTION WHICH CARRIES THE BEAK TO ITS TARGET. HERONS & THEIR RELATIVES ARE THE ONLY BIRDS WHICH FLY WITH THEIR NECKS TUCKED BACK & HEADS BETWEEN THEIR SHOULDERS. THIS MAKES IT IMPOSSIBLE TO CONFUSE THEM, WHEN FLYING, WITH STORKS, CRANES, SWANS & SO ON.

BITTERNS
THE MOST NOTABLE THING ABOUT A BITTERN IS THE EXTRAORDINARY BOOMING NOISE IT MAKES. THIS TERRITORIAL & MATING CALL IS AUDIBLE 3 MILES AWAY - USEFUL BECAUSE BITTERNS ARE UNSOCIABLE BIRDS.

CLEANING
HERONS HAVE A UNIQUE METHOD OF CLEANING THEIR FEATHERS. UNDER THEIR WINGS THEY HAVE THICK PATCHES OF POWDER DOWN WHICH RUBS OFF AS A FINE DUST. THIS IS APPLIED TO SOILED FEATHERS WHERE IT SOAKS UP SLIME & OIL. IT IS THEN SCRAPED OFF WITH THE COMB-LIKE EDGE OF THE BIRD'S MIDDLE CLAW.

NESTS
HERONS BUILD LARGE NESTS, ABOUT 1 METRE ACROSS & .7 METRES DEEP. THEY OCCASIONALLY NEST ON THE GROUND OR IN REEDS, BUT USUALLY IN TALL TREES. AS MANY AS 100 NESTS HAVE BEEN SEEN IN A SINGLE TREE.

ENEMIES
THE HERON IS NOT LOVED BY EVERYONE. TROUT FARMERS IN HUNGARY TRAIN GOSHAWKS TO FLY ROUND THEIR ESTATES TO PROTECT THEIR FISH FROM HERONS.

COURTSHIP
THE COURTSHIP RITUAL OF THE HERON IS MOST APPEALING. AFTER VARIOUS DISPLAYS, THE MALE HOLDS OUT A BRANCH IN HIS BEAK. THE FEMALE TAKES IT & KEEPS IT TO START THE NEST. SUBSEQUENTLY, THE MALE BRINGS THE MATERIALS WHILE THE FEMALE BUILDS. SOMETIMES THEY FIGHT DURING THIS PROCESS.

HOW TO TURN YOURSELF INTO A FLEXIBLE GIANT
STICK TOGETHER SOME BITS OF EXPANDED POLYSTYRENE (FROM A BUILDERS MERCHANT) & CARVE THEM INTO A HEAD SHAPE WITH SERRATED KNIFE – BE CAREFUL. MAKE TUBE OF MATERIAL WITH WIRE RING STIFFENERS AS ABOVE. FIX BROOMSTICK IN HEAD & USE AS ABOVE.

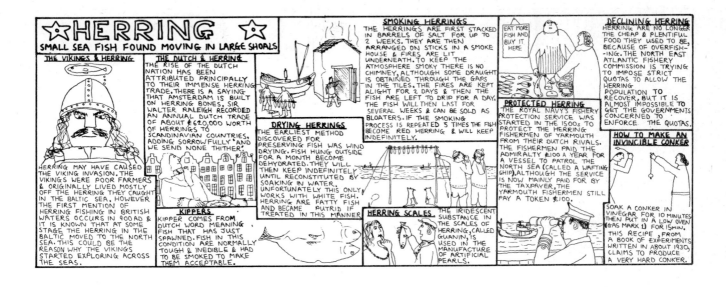

☆ HERRING ☆
SMALL SEA FISH FOUND MOVING IN LARGE SHOALS

THE VIKINGS & HERRING
HERRING MAY HAVE CAUSED THE VIKING INVASION. THE VIKINGS WERE POOR FARMERS & ORIGINALLY LIVED MOSTLY OFF THE HERRING THEY CAUGHT IN THE BALTIC SEA. HOWEVER THE FIRST MENTION OF HERRING FISHING IN BRITISH WATERS OCCURS IN 900AD & IT IS KNOWN THAT AT SOME STAGE THE HERRING IN THE BALTIC MOVED TO THE NORTH SEA. THIS COULD BE THE REASON WHY THE VIKINGS STARTED EXPLORING ACROSS THE SEAS.

THE DUTCH & HERRING
THE RISE OF THE DUTCH NATION HAS BEEN ATTRIBUTED PRINCIPALLY TO THEIR IMMENSE HERRING TRADE. THERE IS A SAYING THAT AMSTERDAM IS BUILT ON HERRING BONES. SIR WALTER RALEIGH RECORDED AN ANNUAL DUTCH TRADE OF ABOUT £620,000 WORTH OF HERRINGS TO SCANDINAVIAN COUNTRIES, ADDING SORROWFULLY 'AND WE SEND NONE THITHER.'

KIPPERS
KIPPER COMES FROM DUTCH WORD MEANING FISH THAT HAS JUST SPAWNED. FISH IN THIS CONDITION ARE NORMALLY TOUGH & INEDIBLE & HAD TO BE SMOKED TO MAKE THEM ACCEPTABLE.

SMOKING HERRINGS
THE HERRINGS ARE FIRST STACKED IN BARRELS OF SALT FOR UP TO 2 WEEKS. THEY ARE THEN ARRANGED ON STICKS IN A SMOKE HOUSE & FIRES ARE LIT UNDERNEATH. TO KEEP THE ATMOSPHERE SMOKY THERE IS NO CHIMNEY, ALTHOUGH SOME DRAUGHT IS OBTAINED THROUGH THE GAPS IN THE TILES. THE FIRES ARE KEPT ALIGHT FOR 2 DAYS & THEN THE FISH ARE LEFT TO DRIP FOR A DAY. THE FISH WILL THEN LAST FOR SEVERAL WEEKS & CAN BE SOLD AS BLOATERS. IF THE SMOKING PROCESS IS REPEATED 5 TIMES THE FISH BECOME RED HERRING & WILL KEEP INDEFINITELY.

DRYING HERRINGS
THE EARLIEST METHOD DISCOVERED FOR PRESERVING FISH WAS WIND DRYING. FISH HUNG OUTSIDE FOR A MONTH BECOME DEHYDRATED. THEY WILL THEN KEEP INDEFINITELY UNTIL RECONSTITUTED BY SOAKING IN WATER. UNFORTUNATELY THIS ONLY WORKS WITH WHITE FISH. HERRING ARE FATTY FISH AND BECAME PUTRID IF TREATED IN THIS MANNER.

HERRING SCALES
THE IRIDESCENT SUBSTANCE IN THE SCALES OF HERRING, CALLED GUANIN, IS USED IN THE MANUFACTURE OF ARTIFICIAL PEARLS.

DECLINING HERRING
HERRING ARE NO LONGER THE CHEAP & PLENTIFUL FOOD THEY USED TO BE, BECAUSE OF OVERFISH-ING. THE NORTH EAST ATLANTIC FISHERY COMMISSION IS TRYING TO IMPOSE STRICT QUOTAS TO ALLOW THE HERRING POPULATION TO RECOVER, BUT IT IS ALMOST IMPOSSIBLE TO GET THE GOVERNMENTS CONCERNED TO ENFORCE THE QUOTAS.

PROTECTED HERRING
THE ROYAL NAVY'S FISHERY PROTECTION SERVICE WAS STARTED IN THE 1500s TO PROTECT THE HERRING FISHERMEN OF YARMOUTH FROM THEIR DUTCH RIVALS. THE FISHERMEN PAID THE ADMIRALTY £100 A YEAR FOR A VESSEL TO PATROL THE NORTH SEA (CALLED A WAFTING SHIP), ALTHOUGH THE SERVICE IS NOW MAINLY PAID FOR BY THE TAXPAYER, THE YARMOUTH FISHERMEN STILL PAY A TOKEN £100.

HOW TO MAKE AN INVINCIBLE CONKER
SOAK A CONKER IN VINEGAR FOR 10 MINUTES THEN PUT IN A LOW OVEN (GAS MARK 1) FOR 15MIN. THIS RECIPE, FROM A BOOK OF EXPERIMENTS WRITTEN IN ABOUT 1930, CLAIMS TO PRODUCE A VERY HARD CONKER.

EAT MORE FISH AND BUY IT HERE

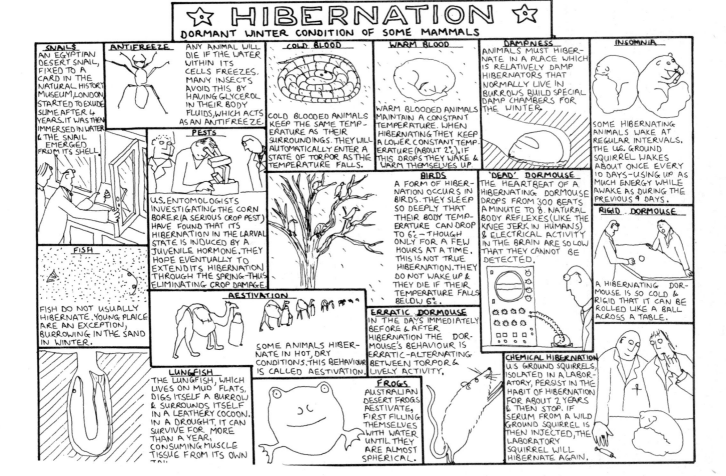

☆ HIBERNATION ☆
DORMANT WINTER CONDITION OF SOME MAMMALS

SNAILS
AN EGYPTIAN DESERT SNAIL, FIXED TO A CARD IN THE NATURAL HISTORY MUSEUM, LONDON, STARTED TO EXUDE SLIME AFTER 4 YEARS. IT WAS THEN IMMERSED IN WATER & THE SNAIL EMERGED FROM ITS SHELL.

ANTIFREEZE
ANY ANIMAL WILL DIE IF THE WATER WITHIN ITS CELLS FREEZES. MANY INSECTS AVOID THIS BY HAVING GLYCEROL IN THEIR BODY FLUIDS, WHICH ACTS AS AN ANTIFREEZE.

PESTS
US. ENTOMOLOGISTS INVESTIGATING THE CORN BORER (A SERIOUS CROP PEST) HAVE FOUND THAT ITS HIBERNATION IN THE LARVAL STATE IS INDUCED BY A JUVENILE HORMONE. THEY HOPE EVENTUALLY TO EXTEND ITS HIBERNATION THROUGH THE SPRING—THUS ELIMINATING CROP DAMAGE.

FISH
FISH DO NOT USUALLY HIBERNATE. YOUNG PLAICE ARE AN EXCEPTION, BURROWING IN THE SAND IN WINTER.

LUNGFISH
THE LUNGFISH, WHICH LIVES ON MUD FLATS, DIGS ITSELF A BURROW & SURROUNDS ITSELF IN A LEATHERY COCOON. IN A DROUGHT, IT CAN SURVIVE FOR MORE THAN A YEAR, CONSUMING MUSCLE TISSUE FROM ITS OWN TAIL.

COLD BLOOD
COLD BLOODED ANIMALS KEEP THE SAME TEMP-ERATURE AS THEIR SURROUNDINGS. THEY WILL AUTOMATICALLY ENTER A STATE OF TORPOR AS THE TEMPERATURE FALLS.

AESTIVATION
SOME ANIMALS HIBER-NATE IN HOT, DRY CONDITIONS. THIS BEHAVIOUR IS CALLED AESTIVATION.

WARM BLOOD
WARM BLOODED ANIMALS MAINTAIN A CONSTANT TEMPERATURE. WHEN HIBERNATING THEY KEEP A LOWER CONSTANT TEMP-ERATURE (ABOUT 2°C). IF THIS DROPS THEY WAKE & WARM THEMSELVES UP.

BIRDS
A FORM OF HIBER-NATION OCCURS IN BIRDS. THEY SLEEP SO DEEPLY THAT THEIR BODY TEMP-ERATURE CAN DROP TO 6°C – THOUGH ONLY FOR A FEW HOURS AT A TIME. THIS IS NOT TRUE HIBERNATION. THEY DO NOT WAKE UP & THEY DIE IF THEIR TEMPERATURE FALLS BELOW 6°C.

ERRATIC DORMOUSE
IN THE DAYS IMMEDIATELY BEFORE & AFTER HIBERNATION THE DOR-MOUSE'S BEHAVIOUR IS ERRATIC-ALTERNATING BETWEEN TORPOR & LIVELY ACTIVITY.

FROGS
AUSTRALIAN DESERT FROGS AESTIVATE, FIRST FILLING THEMSELVES WITH WATER UNTIL THEY ARE ALMOST SPHERICAL.

DAMPNESS
ANIMALS MUST HIBER-NATE IN A PLACE WHICH IS RELATIVELY DAMP. HIBERNATORS THAT NORMALLY LIVE IN BURROWS BUILD SPECIAL DAMP CHAMBERS FOR THE WINTER.

'DEAD' DORMOUSE
THE HEARTBEAT OF A HIBERNATING DORMOUSE DROPS FROM 300 BEATS A MINUTE TO 8. NATURAL BODY REFLEXES (LIKE THE KNEE JERK IN HUMANS) & ELECTRICAL ACTIVITY IN THE BRAIN ARE SO LOW THAT THEY CANNOT BE DETECTED.

CHEMICAL HIBERNATION
US GROUND SQUIRRELS, ISOLATED IN A LABOR-ATORY, PERSIST IN THE HABIT OF HIBERNATION FOR ABOUT 2 YEARS & THEN STOP. IF SERUM FROM A WILD GROUND SQUIRREL IS THEN INJECTED, THE LABORATORY SQUIRREL WILL HIBERNATE AGAIN.

INSOMNIA
SOME HIBERNATING ANIMALS WAKE AT REGULAR INTERVALS. THE U.S. GROUND SQUIRREL WAKES ABOUT ONCE EVERY 10 DAYS—USING UP AS MUCH ENERGY WHILE AWAKE AS DURING THE PREVIOUS 9 DAYS.

RIGID DORMOUSE
A HIBERNATING DOR-MOUSE IS SO COLD & RIGID THAT IT CAN BE ROLLED LIKE A BALL ACROSS A TABLE.

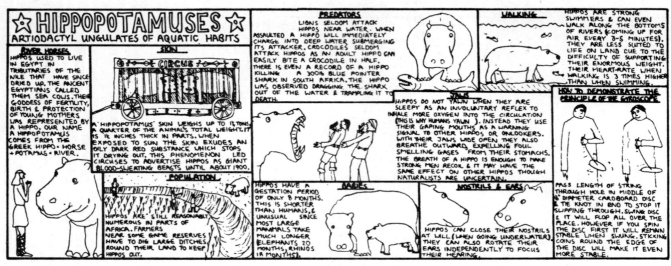

☆ HIPPOPOTAMUSES ☆
ARTIODACTYL UNGULATES OF AQUATIC HABITS

RIVER HORSES
HIPPOS USED TO LIVE IN EGYPT IN TRIBUTARIES OF THE NILE THAT HAVE SINCE DRIED UP. THE ANCIENT EGYPTIANS CALLED THEM SEA COWS. THEIR GODDESS OF FERTILITY, BIRTH & PROTECTION OF YOUNG MOTHERS WAS REPRESENTED BY A HIPPO. OUR NAME A HIPPOPOTAMUS COMES FROM THE GREEK HIPPO = HORSE + POTAMUS = RIVER.

SKIN
A 'HIPPOPOTAMUS' SKIN WEIGHS UP TO 1½ TONS A QUARTER OF THE ANIMAL'S TOTAL WEIGHT. IT IS 1½ INCHES THICK IN PARTS. WHEN EXPOSED TO SUN THE SKIN EXUDES AN OILY DARK RED SUBSTANCE WHICH STOPS IT DRYING OUT. THIS PHENOMENON LED CIRCUSES TO ADVERTISE HIPPOS AS GIANT BLOOD-SWEATING BEASTS UNTIL ABOUT 1900.

POPULATION
HIPPOS ARE STILL REASONABLY NUMEROUS IN PARTS OF AFRICA. FARMERS NEAR SOME GAME RESERVES HAVE TO DIG LARGE DITCHES ROUND THEIR LAND TO KEEP HIPPOS OUT.

PREDATORS
LIONS SELDOM ATTACK HIPPOS NEAR WATER. WHEN ASSAULTED A HIPPO WILL IMMEDIATELY CHARGE INTO DEEP WATER SUBMERGING ITS ATTACKER. CROCODILES SELDOM ATTACK HIPPOS AS AN ADULT HIPPO CAN EASILY BITE A CROCODILE IN HALF. THERE IS EVEN A RECORD OF A HIPPO KILLING A 300lb BLUE POINTER SHARK IN SOUTH AFRICA. THE HIPPO WAS OBSERVED DRAGGING THE SHARK OUT OF THE WATER & TRAMPLING IT TO DEATH.

YAWNS
HIPPOS DO NOT YAWN WHEN THEY ARE SLEEPY AS AN INVOLUNTARY REFLEX TO INHALE MORE OXYGEN INTO THE CIRCULATION (THIS IS WHY HUMANS YAWN). INSTEAD THEY USE THEIR GAPING MOUTHS AS A WARNING SIGNAL TO OTHER HIPPOS OR ONLOOKERS. WITH THEIR JAWS WIDE OPEN THEY ALSO BREATHE OUTWARD, EXPELLING FOUL SMELLING GASES FROM THEIR STOMACHS. THE BREATH OF A HIPPO IS ENOUGH TO MAKE STRONG MEN RECOIL & IT MAY HAVE THE SAME EFFECT ON OTHER HIPPOS THOUGH NATURALISTS ARE UNCERTAIN.

BABIES
HIPPOS HAVE A GESTATION PERIOD OF ONLY 8 MONTHS. THIS IS SHORTER THAN HUMANS, & UNUSUAL SINCE MOST LARGE MAMMALS TAKE MUCH LONGER (ELEPHANTS 20 MONTHS, RHINOS 18 MONTHS).

NOSTRILS & EARS
HIPPOS CAN CLOSE THEIR NOSTRILS AT WILL (WHEN GOING UNDERWATER). THEY CAN ALSO ROTATE THEIR EARS INDEPENDENTLY TO FOCUS THEIR HEARING.

WALKING
HIPPOS ARE STRONG SWIMMERS & CAN EVEN WALK ALONG THE BOTTOMS OF RIVERS (COMING UP FOR AIR EVERY 3-5 MINUTES). THEY ARE LESS SUITED TO LIFE ON LAND DUE TO THE DIFFICULTY OF SUPPORTING THEIR ENORMOUS WEIGHT. THEIR HEART-RATE WHEN WALKING IS 3 TIMES HIGHER THAN WHEN SWIMMING.

HOW TO DEMONSTRATE THE PRINCIPLE OF THE GYROSCOPE
PASS LENGTH OF STRING THROUGH HOLE IN MIDDLE OF 8" DIAMETER CARDBOARD DISC & TIE THE KNOT IN END TO STOP IT SLIPPING THROUGH. SWING DISC & IT WILL FLOP ALL OVER THE PLACE. HOWEVER IF YOU SPIN THE DISC FIRST IT WILL REMAIN STABLE WHEN SWUNG. STICKING COINS ROUND THE EDGE OF THE DISC WILL MAKE IT EVEN MORE STABLE.

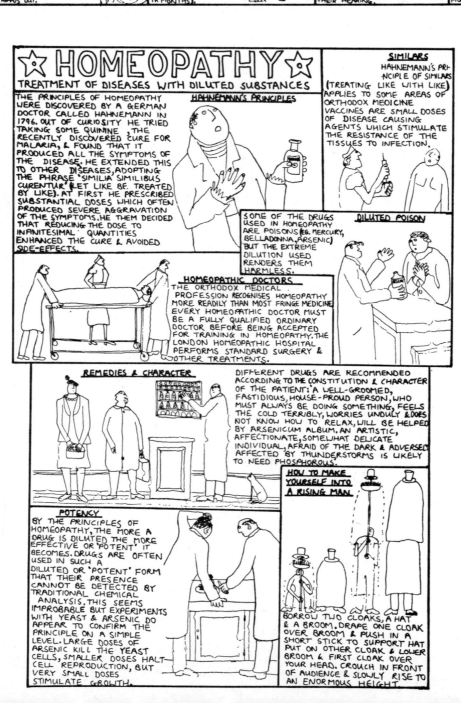

☆ HOMEOPATHY ☆
TREATMENT OF DISEASES WITH DILUTED SUBSTANCES

THE PRINCIPLES OF HOMEOPATHY WERE DISCOVERED BY A GERMAN DOCTOR CALLED HAHNEMANN IN 1796. OUT OF CURIOSITY HE TRIED TAKING SOME QUININE, THE RECENTLY DISCOVERED CURE FOR MALARIA, & FOUND THAT IT PRODUCED ALL THE SYMPTOMS OF THE DISEASE. HE EXTENDED THIS TO OTHER DISEASES, ADOPTING THE PHRASE 'SIMILIA SIMILIBUS CURENTUR' (LET LIKE BE TREATED BY LIKE). AT FIRST HE PRESCRIBED SUBSTANTIAL DOSES WHICH OFTEN PRODUCED SEVERE AGGRAVATION OF THE SYMPTOMS. HE THEN DECIDED THAT REDUCING THE DOSE TO INFINITESIMAL QUANTITIES ENHANCED THE CURE & AVOIDED SIDE-EFFECTS.

HAHNEMANN'S PRINCIPLES

SIMILARS
HAHNEMANN'S PRINCIPLE OF SIMILARS (TREATING LIKE WITH LIKE) APPLIES TO SOME AREAS OF ORTHODOX MEDICINE. VACCINES ARE SMALL DOSES OF DISEASE CAUSING AGENTS WHICH STIMULATE THE RESISTANCE OF THE TISSUES TO INFECTION.

DILUTED POISON
SOME OF THE DRUGS USED IN HOMEOPATHY ARE POISONS (E.G. MERCURY, BELLADONNA, ARSENIC) BUT THE EXTREME DILUTION USED RENDERS THEM HARMLESS.

HOMEOPATHIC DOCTORS
THE ORTHODOX MEDICAL PROFESSION RECOGNISES HOMEOPATHY MORE READILY THAN MOST FRINGE MEDICINE. EVERY HOMEOPATHIC DOCTOR MUST BE A FULLY QUALIFIED ORDINARY DOCTOR BEFORE BEING ACCEPTED FOR TRAINING IN HOMEOPATHY. THE LONDON HOMEOPATHIC HOSPITAL PERFORMS STANDARD SURGERY & OTHER TREATMENTS.

REMEDIES & CHARACTER
DIFFERENT DRUGS ARE RECOMMENDED ACCORDING TO THE CONSTITUTION & CHARACTER OF THE PATIENT: A WELL-GROOMED, FASTIDIOUS, HOUSE-PROUD PERSON, WHO MUST ALWAYS BE DOING SOMETHING, FEELS THE COLD TERRIBLY, WORRIES UNDULY & DOES NOT KNOW HOW TO RELAX, WILL BE HELPED BY ARSENICUM ALBUM. AN ARTISTIC, AFFECTIONATE, SOMEWHAT DELICATE INDIVIDUAL, AFRAID OF THE DARK & ADVERSELY AFFECTED BY THUNDERSTORMS IS LIKELY TO NEED PHOSPHOROUS.

POTENCY
BY THE PRINCIPLES OF HOMEOPATHY, THE MORE A DRUG IS DILUTED THE MORE EFFECTIVE OR 'POTENT' IT BECOMES. DRUGS ARE OFTEN USED IN SUCH A DILUTED OR 'POTENT' FORM THAT THEIR PRESENCE CANNOT BE DETECTED BY TRADITIONAL CHEMICAL ANALYSIS. THIS SEEMS IMPROBABLE BUT EXPERIMENTS WITH YEAST & ARSENIC DO APPEAR TO CONFIRM THE PRINCIPLE ON A SIMPLE LEVEL. LARGE DOSES OF ARSENIC KILL THE YEAST CELLS, SMALLER DOSES HALT CELL REPRODUCTION, BUT VERY SMALL DOSES STIMULATE GROWTH.

HOW TO MAKE YOURSELF INTO A RISING MAN
BORROW TWO CLOAKS, A HAT & A BROOM. DRAPE ONE CLOAK OVER BROOM & PUSH IN A SHORT STICK TO SUPPORT HAT. PUT ON OTHER CLOAK & LOWER BROOM & FIRST CLOAK OVER YOUR HEAD. CROUCH IN FRONT OF AUDIENCE & SLOWLY RISE TO AN ENORMOUS HEIGHT.

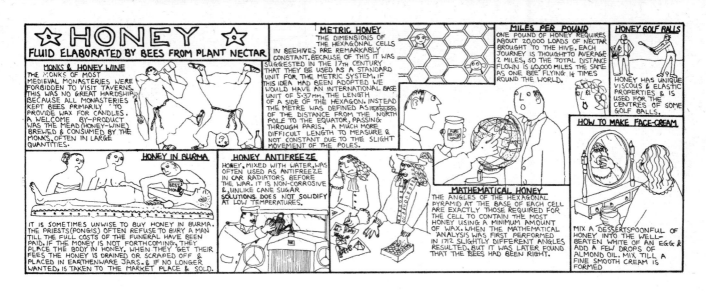

☆ HONEY ☆
FLUID ELABORATED BY BEES FROM PLANT NECTAR

MONKS & HONEY WINE
THE MONKS OF MOST MEDIEVAL MONASTERIES WERE FORBIDDEN TO VISIT TAVERNS. THIS WAS NO GREAT HARDSHIP BECAUSE ALL MONASTERIES KEPT BEES PRIMARILY TO PROVIDE WAX FOR CANDLES. A WELCOME BY-PRODUCT WAS THE MEAD (HONEY-WINE) BREWED & CONSUMED BY THE MONKS, OFTEN IN LARGE QUANTITIES.

HONEY IN BURMA
IT IS SOMETIMES UNWISE TO BUY HONEY IN BURMA. THE PRIESTS (PONGIS) OFTEN REFUSE TO BURY A MAN TILL THE FULL COSTS OF THE FUNERAL HAVE BEEN PAID. IF THE MONEY IS NOT FORTHCOMING, THEY PLACE THE BODY IN HONEY. WHEN THEY GET THEIR FEES THE HONEY IS DRAINED OR SCRAPED OFF & PLACED IN EARTHENWARE JARS. & IF NO LONGER WANTED, IS TAKEN TO THE MARKET PLACE & SOLD.

HONEY ANTIFREEZE
HONEY, MIXED WITH WATER, WAS OFTEN USED AS ANTIFREEZE IN CAR RADIATORS BEFORE THE WAR. IT IS NON-CORROSIVE &, UNLIKE CANE SUGAR SOLUTIONS, DOES NOT SOLIDIFY AT LOW TEMPERATURES.

METRIC HONEY
THE DIMENSIONS OF THE HEXAGONAL CELLS IN BEEHIVES ARE REMARKABLY CONSTANT. BECAUSE OF THIS IT WAS SUGGESTED IN THE 17th CENTURY THAT THEY BE USED AS A STANDARD UNIT FOR THE METRIC SYSTEM. IF THIS IDEA HAD BEEN ADOPTED WE WOULD HAVE AN INTERNATIONAL BASE UNIT OF 5·37mm, THE LENGTH OF A SIDE OF THE HEXAGON. INSTEAD THE METRE WAS DEFINED AS 1/10,000,000 OF THE DISTANCE FROM THE NORTH POLE TO THE EQUATOR, PASSING THROUGH PARIS, A MUCH MORE DIFFICULT LENGTH TO MEASURE & NOT CONSTANT DUE TO THE SLIGHT MOVEMENT OF THE POLES.

MATHEMATICAL HONEY
THE ANGLES OF THE HEXAGONAL PYRAMID AT THE BASE OF EACH CELL ARE EXACTLY THOSE REQUIRED FOR THE CELL TO CONTAIN THE MOST HONEY USING A MINIMUM AMOUNT OF WAX. WHEN THE MATHEMATICAL ANALYSIS WAS FIRST PERFORMED IN 1712 SLIGHTLY DIFFERENT ANGLES RESULTED, BUT IT WAS LATER FOUND THAT THE BEES HAD BEEN RIGHT.

MILES PER POUND
ONE POUND OF HONEY REQUIRES ABOUT 20,000 LOADS OF NECTAR BROUGHT TO THE HIVE. EACH JOURNEY IS THOUGHT TO AVERAGE 2 MILES, SO THE TOTAL DISTANCE FLOWN IS 40,000 MILES THE SAME AS ONE BEE FLYING 1½ TIMES ROUND THE WORLD.

HONEY GOLF BALLS
HONEY HAS UNIQUE VISCOUS & ELASTIC PROPERTIES & IS USED FOR THE CENTRES OF SOME GOLF BALLS.

HOW TO MAKE FACE-CREAM
MIX A DESSERTSPOONFUL OF HONEY INTO THE WELL-BEATEN WHITE OF AN EGG & ADD A FEW DROPS OF ALMOND OIL. MIX TILL A FINE SMOOTH CREAM IS FORMED

☆ HOTELS ☆
SUPERIOR HOUSES FOR ACCOMODATION OF STRANGERS

THE FIRST HOTEL
THE AMERICANS CLAIM THAT THE WORLD'S FIRST HOTEL WAS THE TREMONT, OPENED IN BOSTON IN 1829. ITS STANDARDS OF 'COMMERCIAL HOSPITALITY' WERE SO RADICALLY DIFFERENT FROM ANY PREVIOUS INSTITUTION THAT THE HOTEL CAN BE SAID TO BE AN AMERICAN INVENTION. THE TREMONT HAD A DINING ROOM FOR 200 PEOPLE, 12 PUBLIC ROOMS & 170 BEDROOMS, WITH A BAR OF SOAP PROVIDED FREE IN EACH. IT HAD NO INN SIGN WHICH HELPED DISCOURAGE ILLITERATE TRAVELLERS.

HOTELS WERE AMONG THE FIRST BUILDINGS TO BE FITTED WITH GAS LIGHTING. INITIALLY IT WAS A CONSTANT PROBLEM FOR PROPRIETORS BECAUSE UNSOPHISTICATED GUESTS KEPT BLOWING OUT THE GASLIGHTS IN THEIR ROOM AS THEY MIGHT BLOW OUT A CANDLE. A WIT REMARKED THAT THE MOST STRIKING FEATURE OF GASLIT HOTELS WAS THE BATTERED DOORS DUE TO THE NECESSITY OF FREQUENT FORCED ENTRIES

THE ELECTRIC HOTEL
HOTELS WERE ALSO AMONG THE FIRST BUILDINGS TO USE ELECTRICITY. THE SAVOY, LONDON, INSTALLED ITS OWN GENERATOR IN THE BASEMENT, A MODIFIED FAIRGROUND ENGINE, IN 1889. THE SAVOY STILL GENERATES ITS OWN ELECTRICITY & THE INSTALLATION IS NOW THE OLDEST OPERATING POWER STATION IN BRITAIN. IT IS STILL HIGHLY EFFICIENT & THE COOLING WATER IS CONNECTED TO THE CENTRAL HEATING SYSTEM.

RITZ
M. RITZ STARTED LIFE AS A WAITER BUT ROSE TO FOUND LUXURY HOTELS IN LONDON, PARIS & GENEVA. HIS ATTENTION TO DETAIL WAS EXTRAORDINARY. WORRIED BY THE HARSH LIGHT CAST BY THE FIRST ELECTRIC LAMPS, HE PERFORMED ENDLESS EXPERIMENTS, USING HIS WIFE TO POSE TO FIND A LIGHT FLATTERING TO HER COMPLEXION. HIS SOLUTION WAS INDIRECT LIGHTING WITH ALABASTER URNS THROWING LIGHT ONTO A TINTED CEILING.

THE BIGGEST HOTEL
THE LARGEST HOTEL IN THE WORLD IS NEW YORK'S WALDORF ASTORIA. THE KITCHEN BREWS AN AVERAGE OF 1000 GALLONS OF COFFEE EVERY DAY & THE STAFF INCLUDES A RESIDENT GYNAECOLOGIST & AN UNDERTAKER. HOWEVER IT HAS MANY FEWER BEDROOMS (1900) THAN MOSCOW'S LARGEST HOTEL, THE ROSSIYA (3200).

THE MOTEL
THE FIRST MOTORISTS' HOTEL WITH EVERY BEDROOM CONNECTED TO A GARAGE OPENED IN 1924 IN THE U.S. IT HAD AN ELECTRIC SIGN WITH AN ALTERNATELY FLASHING H & M FOLLOWED BY THE LETTERS ...'OTEL'. THIS WAS THE ORIGIN OF THE WORD 'MOTEL'.

HOW TO MAKE YOUR HANDS INTO A RABBIT
ARRANGE HANDS AS ABOVE, CLOSE TO A WALL IN FRONT OF A LIGHT. RABBIT WILL APPEAR ON WALL.

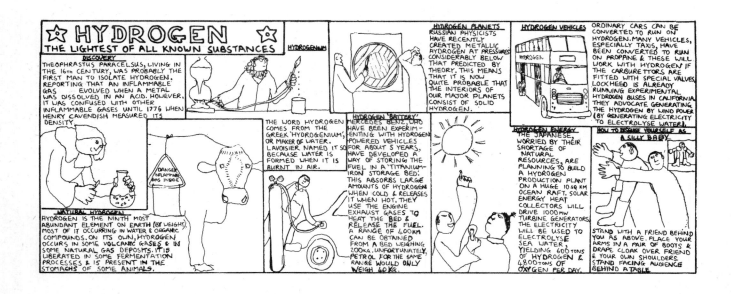

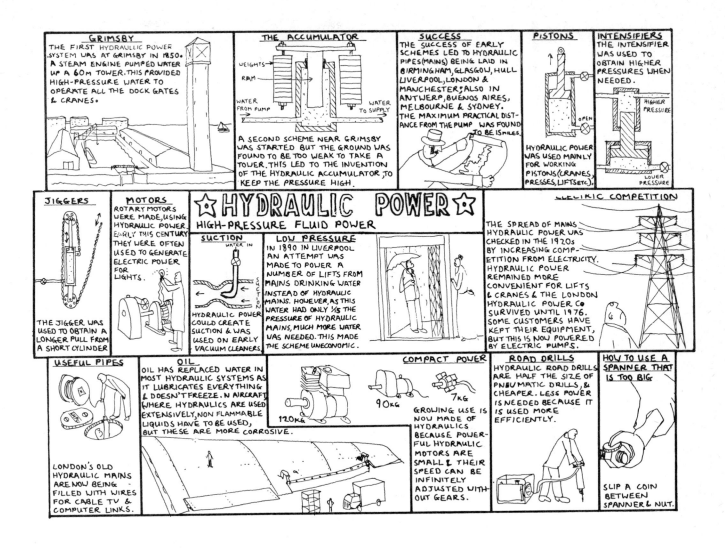

☆ HYDRAULIC POWER ☆
HIGH-PRESSURE FLUID POWER

GRIMSBY
THE FIRST HYDRAULIC POWER SYSTEM WAS AT GRIMSBY IN 1850. A STEAM ENGINE PUMPED WATER UP A 60m TOWER. THIS PROVIDED HIGH-PRESSURE WATER TO OPERATE ALL THE DOCK GATES & CRANES.

THE ACCUMULATOR
WEIGHTS · RAM · WATER FROM PUMP · WATER TO SUPPLY
A SECOND SCHEME NEAR GRIMSBY WAS STARTED BUT THE GROUND WAS FOUND TO BE TOO WEAK TO TAKE A TOWER. THIS LED TO THE INVENTION OF THE HYDRAULIC ACCUMULATOR, TO KEEP THE PRESSURE HIGH.

SUCCESS
THE SUCCESS OF EARLY SCHEMES LED TO HYDRAULIC PIPES (MAINS) BEING LAID IN BIRMINGHAM, GLASGOW, HULL, LIVERPOOL, LONDON & MANCHESTER; ALSO IN ANTWERP, BUENOS AIRES, MELBOURNE & SYDNEY. THE MAXIMUM PRACTICAL DISTANCE FROM THE PUMP WAS FOUND TO BE 15 miles.

PISTONS
HYDRAULIC POWER WAS USED MAINLY FOR WORKING PISTONS (CRANES, PRESSES, LIFTS etc).

INTENSIFIERS
THE INTENSIFIER WAS USED TO OBTAIN HIGHER PRESSURES WHEN NEEDED.
HIGHER PRESSURE · OPEN · LOWER PRESSURE

JIGGERS
THE JIGGER WAS USED TO OBTAIN A LONGER PULL FROM A SHORT CYLINDER

MOTORS
ROTARY MOTORS WERE MADE, USING HYDRAULIC POWER. EARLY THIS CENTURY THEY WERE OFTEN USED TO GENERATE ELECTRIC POWER FOR LIGHTS.

SUCTION
WATER IN
HYDRAULIC POWER COULD CREATE SUCTION & WAS USED ON EARLY VACUUM CLEANERS

LOW PRESSURE
IN 1890 IN LIVERPOOL AN ATTEMPT WAS MADE TO POWER A NUMBER OF LIFTS FROM MAINS DRINKING WATER INSTEAD OF HYDRAULIC MAINS. HOWEVER, AS THIS WATER HAD ONLY 1/5 THE PRESSURE OF HYDRAULIC MAINS, MUCH MORE WATER WAS NEEDED. THIS MADE THE SCHEME UNECONOMIC.

ELECTRIC COMPETITION
THE SPREAD OF MAINS HYDRAULIC POWER WAS CHECKED IN THE 1920s BY INCREASING COMPETITION FROM ELECTRICITY. HYDRAULIC POWER REMAINED MORE CONVENIENT FOR LIFTS & CRANES & THE LONDON HYDRAULIC POWER Co SURVIVED UNTIL 1976. SOME CUSTOMERS HAVE KEPT THEIR EQUIPMENT, BUT THIS IS NOW POWERED BY ELECTRIC PUMPS.

USEFUL PIPES
LONDON'S OLD HYDRAULIC MAINS ARE NOW BEING FILLED WITH WIRES FOR CABLE TV & COMPUTER LINKS.

OIL
OIL HAS REPLACED WATER IN MOST HYDRAULIC SYSTEMS AS IT LUBRICATES EVERYTHING & DOESN'T FREEZE. IN AIRCRAFT WHERE HYDRAULICS ARE USED EXTENSIVELY, NON FLAMMABLE LIQUIDS HAVE TO BE USED, BUT THESE ARE MORE CORROSIVE.

COMPACT POWER
120kg · 90kg · 7kg
GROWING USE IS NOW MADE OF HYDRAULICS BECAUSE POWERFUL HYDRAULIC MOTORS ARE SMALL & THEIR SPEED CAN BE INFINITELY ADJUSTED WITHOUT GEARS.

ROAD DRILLS
HYDRAULIC ROAD DRILLS ARE HALF THE SIZE OF PNEUMATIC DRILLS, & CHEAPER. LESS POWER IS NEEDED BECAUSE IT IS USED MORE EFFICIENTLY.

HOW TO USE A SPANNER THAT IS TOO BIG
SLIP A COIN BETWEEN SPANNER & NUT.

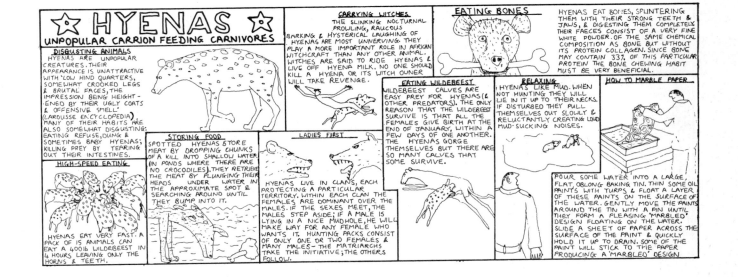

☆ HYENAS ☆
UNPOPULAR CARRION FEEDING CARNIVORES

DISGUSTING ANIMALS
HYENAS ARE UNPOPULAR CREATURES. THEIR APPEARANCE IS UNATTRACTIVE WITH 'LOW HIND QUARTERS, SOMEWHAT CROOKED LEGS & BRUTAL FACES, THE IMPRESSION BEING HEIGHTENED BY THEIR UGLY COATS & OFFENSIVE SMELL' (LAROUSSE ENCYCLOPEDIA). MANY OF THEIR HABITS ARE ALSO SOMEWHAT DISGUSTING: EATING REFUSE, DUNG & SOMETIMES BABY HYENAS; KILLING PREY BY TEARING OUT THEIR INTESTINES.

HIGH-SPEED EATING
HYENAS EAT VERY FAST. A PACK OF 15 ANIMALS CAN EAT A 400lb WILDEBEEST IN 4 HOURS LEAVING ONLY THE HORNS & TEETH.

STORING FOOD
SPOTTED HYENAS STORE MEAT BY DROPPING CHUNKS OF A KILL INTO SHALLOW WATER (IN PONDS WHERE THERE ARE NO CROCODILES). THEY RETRIEVE THE MEAT BY PLUNGING THEIR HEADS UNDER WATER IN THE APPROXIMATE SPOT & SEARCHING AROUND UNTIL THEY BUMP INTO IT.

CARRYING WITCHES
THE SLINKING NOCTURNAL PROWLING, RAUCOUS BARKING & HYSTERICAL LAUGHING OF HYENAS ARE MOST UNNERVING. THEY PLAY A MORE IMPORTANT ROLE IN AFRICAN WITCHCRAFT THAN ANY OTHER ANIMAL. WITCHES ARE SAID TO RIDE HYENAS & LIVE OFF HYENA MILK. NO ONE SHOULD KILL A HYENA OR ITS WITCH OWNER WILL TAKE REVENGE.

LADIES FIRST
HYENAS LIVE IN CLANS, EACH PROTECTING A PARTICULAR TERRITORY. WITHIN EACH CLAN THE FEMALES ARE DOMINANT OVER THE MALES. IF THE SEXES MEET, THE MALES STEP ASIDE; IF A MALE IS LYING IN A NICE MUDHOLE, HE WILL MAKE WAY FOR ANY FEMALE WHO WANTS IT. HUNTING PACKS CONSIST OF ONLY ONE OR TWO FEMALES & MANY MALES – THE MATRIARCHS TAKE THE INITIATIVE; THE OTHERS FOLLOW.

EATING BONES
HYENAS EAT BONES, SPLINTERING THEM WITH THEIR STRONG TEETH & JAWS, & DIGESTING THEM COMPLETELY. THEIR FAECES CONSIST OF A VERY FINE WHITE POWDER, OF THE SAME CHEMICAL COMPOSITION AS BONE BUT WITHOUT ITS PROTEIN COLLAGEN. SINCE BONE MAY CONTAIN 33% OF THIS PARTICULAR PROTEIN THE BONE CHEWING HABIT MUST BE VERY BENEFICIAL.

EATING WILDEBEEST
WILDEBEEST CALVES ARE EASY PREY FOR HYENAS (& OTHER PREDATORS). THE ONLY REASON THAT THE WILDEBEEST SURVIVE IS THAT ALL THE FEMALES GIVE BIRTH AT THE END OF JANUARY, WITHIN A FEW DAYS OF ONE ANOTHER. THE HYENAS GORGE THEMSELVES BUT THERE ARE SO MANY CALVES THAT SOME SURVIVE.

RELAXING
HYENAS LIKE MUD. WHEN NOT HUNTING THEY WILL LIE IN IT UP TO THEIR NECKS. IF DISTURBED THEY PULL THEMSELVES OUT SLOWLY & RELUCTANTLY CREATING LOUD MUD-SUCKING NOISES.

HOW TO MARBLE PAPER
POUR SOME WATER INTO A LARGE, FLAT OBLONG BAKING TIN. THIN SOME OIL PAINTS WITH TURPS & FLOAT A LAYER OF THESE PAINTS ON THE SURFACE OF THE WATER. GENTLY MOVE THE PAINTS AROUND THE TIN WITH A PIN UNTIL THEY FORM A PLEASING 'MARBLED' DESIGN FLOATING ON THE WATER. SLIDE A SHEET OF PAPER ACROSS THE SURFACE OF THE PAINT & QUICKLY HOLD IT UP TO DRAIN. SOME OF THE PAINT WILL STICK TO THE PAPER PRODUCING A 'MARBLED' DESIGN.

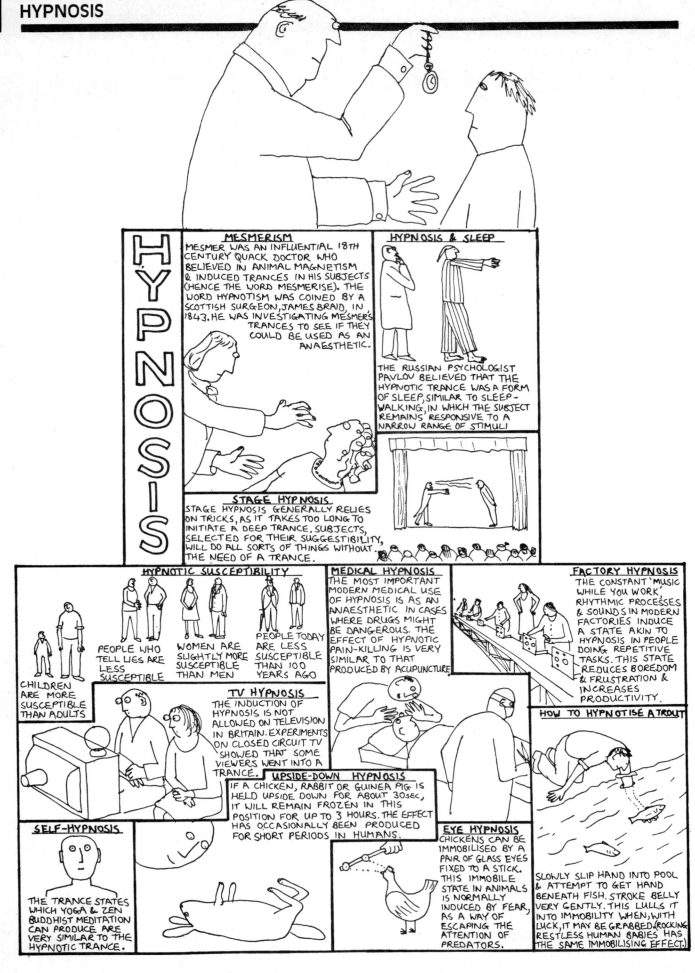

HYPNOSIS

MESMERISM
MESMER WAS AN INFLUENTIAL 18TH CENTURY QUACK DOCTOR WHO BELIEVED IN ANIMAL MAGNETISM & INDUCED TRANCES IN HIS SUBJECTS (HENCE THE WORD MESMERISE). THE WORD HYPNOTISM WAS COINED BY A SCOTTISH SURGEON, JAMES BRAID, IN 1843. HE WAS INVESTIGATING MESMER'S TRANCES TO SEE IF THEY COULD BE USED AS AN ANAESTHETIC.

HYPNOSIS & SLEEP
THE RUSSIAN PSYCHOLOGIST PAVLOV BELIEVED THAT THE HYPNOTIC TRANCE WAS A FORM OF SLEEP, SIMILAR TO SLEEP-WALKING, IN WHICH THE SUBJECT REMAINS RESPONSIVE TO A NARROW RANGE OF STIMULI

STAGE HYPNOSIS
STAGE HYPNOSIS GENERALLY RELIES ON TRICKS, AS IT TAKES TOO LONG TO INITIATE A DEEP TRANCE. SUBJECTS, SELECTED FOR THEIR SUGGESTIBILITY, WILL DO ALL SORTS OF THINGS WITHOUT THE NEED OF A TRANCE.

HYPNOTIC SUSCEPTIBILITY
CHILDREN ARE MORE SUSCEPTIBLE THAN ADULTS

PEOPLE WHO TELL LIES ARE LESS SUSCEPTIBLE

WOMEN ARE SLIGHTLY MORE SUSCEPTIBLE THAN MEN

PEOPLE TODAY ARE LESS SUSCEPTIBLE THAN 100 YEARS AGO

TV HYPNOSIS
THE INDUCTION OF HYPNOSIS IS NOT ALLOWED ON TELEVISION IN BRITAIN. EXPERIMENTS ON CLOSED CIRCUIT TV SHOWED THAT SOME VIEWERS WENT INTO A TRANCE.

MEDICAL HYPNOSIS
THE MOST IMPORTANT MODERN MEDICAL USE OF HYPNOSIS IS AS AN ANAESTHETIC IN CASES WHERE DRUGS MIGHT BE DANGEROUS. THE EFFECT OF HYPNOTIC PAIN-KILLING IS VERY SIMILAR TO THAT PRODUCED BY ACUPUNCTURE

FACTORY HYPNOSIS
THE CONSTANT 'MUSIC WHILE YOU WORK', RHYTHMIC PROCESSES & SOUNDS IN MODERN FACTORIES INDUCE A STATE AKIN TO HYPNOSIS IN PEOPLE DOING REPETITIVE TASKS. THIS STATE REDUCES BOREDOM & FRUSTRATION & INCREASES PRODUCTIVITY.

UPSIDE-DOWN HYPNOSIS
IF A CHICKEN, RABBIT OR GUINEA PIG IS HELD UPSIDE DOWN FOR ABOUT 30sec, IT WILL REMAIN FROZEN IN THIS POSITION FOR UP TO 3 HOURS. THE EFFECT HAS OCCASIONALLY BEEN PRODUCED FOR SHORT PERIODS IN HUMANS.

SELF-HYPNOSIS
THE TRANCE STATES WHICH YOGA & ZEN BUDDHIST MEDITATION CAN PRODUCE ARE VERY SIMILAR TO THE HYPNOTIC TRANCE.

EYE HYPNOSIS
CHICKENS CAN BE IMMOBILISED BY A PAIR OF GLASS EYES FIXED TO A STICK. THIS IMMOBILE STATE IN ANIMALS IS NORMALLY INDUCED BY FEAR, AS A WAY OF ESCAPING THE ATTENTION OF PREDATORS.

HOW TO HYPNOTISE A TROUT
SLOWLY SLIP HAND INTO POOL & ATTEMPT TO GET HAND BENEATH FISH. STROKE BELLY VERY GENTLY. THIS LULLS IT INTO IMMOBILITY WHEN, WITH LUCK, IT MAY BE GRABBED (ROCKING RESTLESS HUMAN BABIES HAS THE SAME IMMOBILISING EFFECT.)

☆ ICE ☆

ABUNDANT SOLID COMPOUND OF HYDROGEN & OXYGEN

SNOW

ICE CRYSTALS

IN SUB-ARCTIC INLAND LAKES FREEZING SOMETIMES TAKES PLACE ROUND A SINGLE NUCLEUS. THE WHOLE LAKE FREEZES INTO JUST ONE CRYSTAL, THOUGHT TO BE THE LARGEST SINGLE CRYSTAL OF ANY MATERIAL IN THE WORLD.

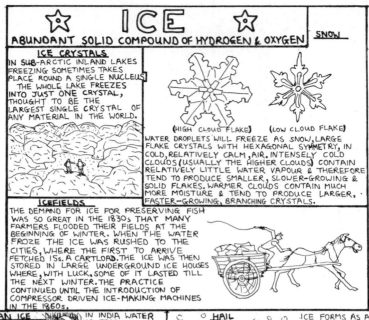

(HIGH CLOUD FLAKE)   (LOW CLOUD FLAKE)

WATER DROPLETS WILL FREEZE AS SNOW, LARGE FLAKE CRYSTALS WITH HEXAGONAL SYMMETRY, IN COLD, RELATIVELY CALM, AIR. INTENSELY COLD CLOUDS (USUALLY THE HIGHER CLOUDS) CONTAIN RELATIVELY LITTLE WATER VAPOUR & THEREFORE TEND TO PRODUCE SMALLER, SLOWER-GROWING & SOLID FLAKES. WARMER CLOUDS CONTAIN MUCH MORE MOISTURE & TEND TO PRODUCE LARGER, FASTER-GROWING, BRANCHING CRYSTALS.

ICEFIELDS

THE DEMAND FOR ICE FOR PRESERVING FISH WAS SO GREAT IN THE 1830s THAT MANY FARMERS FLOODED THEIR FIELDS AT THE BEGINNING OF WINTER. WHEN THE WATER FROZE THE ICE WAS RUSHED TO THE CITIES, WHERE THE FIRST TO ARRIVE FETCHED 15s. A CARTLOAD. THE ICE WAS THEN STORED IN LARGE UNDERGROUND ICE HOUSES WHERE, WITH LUCK, SOME OF IT LASTED TILL THE NEXT WINTER. THE PRACTICE CONTINUED UNTIL THE INTRODUCTION OF COMPRESSOR DRIVEN ICE-MAKING MACHINES IN THE 1860s.

INDIAN ICE

IN INDIA WATER IS FROZEN BY LEAVING IT IN POROUS VESSELS (CHATTI) ON CLEAR WINTER NIGHTS. THE EVAPORATION THROUGH THE PORES OF THE VESSEL ABSORBS SUFFICIENT HEAT FROM THE WATER ALTHOUGH THE AIR TEMPERATURE NEVER FALLS TO 0°C.

HAIL

ICE FORMS AS A HAIL STONE WHEN WATER DROPLETS COLLIDE WITH AN EXISTING ICE CRYSTAL. THIS REQUIRES THE TURBULENT ATMOSPHERIC CONDITIONS NORMALLY ASSOCIATED WITH THUNDERSTORMS. THE WORLD'S BIGGEST, OFFICIALLY RECORDED, HAILSTONE WAS 19cm IN DIAMETER, FOUND IN KANSAS U.S. IN 1970 BRITAIN'S RECORD WAS AN 11cm STONE WHICH FELL IN SUSSEX.

ICEBERGS

THREE QUARTERS OF THE WORLD'S TOTAL FRESH WATER SUPPLY IS LOCKED UP IN THE ICE SHEETS ROUND THE SOUTH POLE. SCHEMES TO LIBERATE THIS RESOURCE ARE UNDER DEVELOPMENT BY THE RAND CORPORATION IN AMERICA. THEY PROPOSE TOWING A TRAIN OF ICE-BERGS 80km LONG, 600m WIDE & 300m DEEP (FIRST CUTTING OFF ANY SHARP PROJECTIONS WITH A HUGE SAW) AT A SPEED OF ONE KNOT, BEHIND GIANT TUGS WITH AN OIL TANKER TO KEEP THEM FUELLED. THE JOURNEY WOULD TAKE OVER A YEAR & EACH ICEBERG WOULD HAVE TO BE WRAPPED IN POLYTHENE TO PRESERVE THE FRESH WATER AS IT MELTS. DESPITE THE COMPLEXITY OF THE SYSTEM, RAND ESTIMATE THE WATER WILL COST TWO THIRDS LESS THAN WATER FROM CONVENTIONAL DESALINATION PLANTS (THOUGH OTHER, MORE RECENT, ESTIMATES HAVE BEEN MUCH LESS OPTIMISTIC).

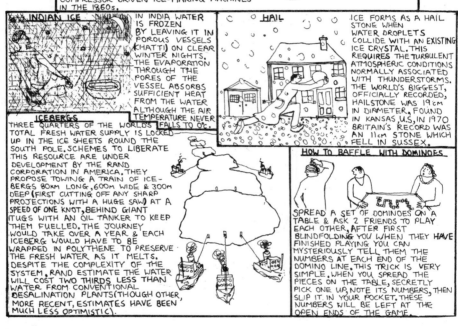

HOW TO BAFFLE WITH DOMINOES

SPREAD A SET OF DOMINOES ON A TABLE & ASK 2 FRIENDS TO PLAY EACH OTHER, AFTER FIRST BLINDFOLDING YOU. WHEN THEY HAVE FINISHED PLAYING YOU CAN MYSTERIOUSLY TELL THEM THE NUMBERS AT EACH END OF THE DOMINO LINE. THIS TRICK IS VERY SIMPLE. WHEN YOU SPREAD THE PIECES ON THE TABLE, SECRETLY PICK ONE UP, NOTE ITS NUMBERS, THEN SLIP IT IN YOUR POCKET. THESE NUMBERS WILL BE LEFT AT THE OPEN ENDS OF THE GAME.

☆ ICE CREAM ☆

SWEET FROZEN GASTRONOMIC DELICACIES

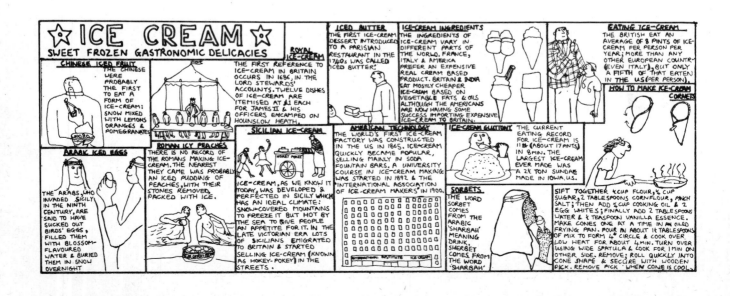

CHINESE ICED FRUIT

THE CHINESE WERE PROBABLY THE FIRST TO EAT A FORM OF ICE-CREAM: SNOW MIXED WITH LEMONS, ORANGES & POMEGRANATES.

ROYAL ICE-CREAM

THE FIRST REFERENCE TO ICE-CREAM IN BRITAIN OCCURS IN 1686, IN THE LORD STEWARDS' ACCOUNTS. TWELVE DISHES OF ICE-CREAM ARE ITEMISED AT £1 EACH FOR JAMES II & HIS OFFICERS ENCAMPED ON HOUNSLOW HEATH.

ARAB ICED EGGS

THE ARABS, WHO INVADED SICILY IN THE NINTH CENTURY, ARE SAID TO HAVE SUCKED OUT BIRDS' EGGS, FILLED THEM WITH BLOSSOM-FLAVOURED WATER & BURIED THEM IN SNOW OVERNIGHT.

ROMAN ICY PEACHES

THERE IS NO RECORD OF THE ROMANS MAKING ICE-CREAM. THE NEAREST THEY CAME WAS PROBABLY AN ICED PUDDING OF PEACHES, WITH THEIR STONES REMOVED, PACKED WITH ICE.

SICILIAN ICE-CREAM

ICE-CREAM, AS WE KNOW IT TODAY, WAS DEVELOPED & PERFECTED IN SICILY WHICH HAS AN IDEAL CLIMATE: SNOW-COVERED MOUNTAINS TO FREEZE IT BUT HOT BY THE SEA TO GIVE PEOPLE AN APPETITE FOR IT. IN THE LATE VICTORIAN ERA LOTS OF SICILIANS EMIGRATED TO BRITAIN & STARTED SELLING ICE-CREAM (KNOWN AS HOKEY-POKEY) IN THE STREETS.

ICED BUTTER

THE FIRST ICE-CREAM DESSERT INTRODUCED TO A PARISIAN RESTAURANT IN THE 1740s WAS CALLED 'ICED BUTTER'.

AMERICAN TECHNOLOGY

THE WORLD'S FIRST ICE-CREAM FACTORY WAS CONSTRUCTED IN THE US IN 1865. IT QUICKLY BECAME POPULAR, SELLING MAINLY IN SODA FOUNTAIN BARS. A UNIVERSITY COURSE IN ICE-CREAM MAKING WAS STARTED IN 1892 & THE INTERNATIONAL ASSOCIATION OF ICE-CREAM MAKERS' IN 1900.

INTERNATIONAL INSTITUTE ICE CREAM

ICE-CREAM INGREDIENTS

THE INGREDIENTS OF ICE-CREAM VARY IN DIFFERENT PARTS OF THE WORLD. FRANCE, ITALY & AMERICA PREFER AN EXPENSIVE REAL CREAM BASED PRODUCT. BRITAIN & INDIA EAT MOSTLY CHEAPER ICE-CREAM BASED ON VEGETABLE FATS & OILS ALTHOUGH THE AMERICANS ARE NOW HAVING SOME SUCCESS IMPORTING EXPENSIVE ICE-CREAM TO BRITAIN.

ICE-CREAM GLUTTONS

THE CURRENT EATING RECORD FOR ICE-CREAM IS 11lb (ABOUT 17 PINTS) IN 8min. THE LARGEST ICE-CREAM EVER MADE WAS A 2½ TON SUNDAE MADE IN IOWA, U.S.

SORBETS

THE WORD SORBET COMES FROM THE ARABIC 'SHARBAH' MEANING DRINK. SHERBET COMES FROM THE WORD 'SHARBAH'.

EATING ICE-CREAM

THE BRITISH EAT AN AVERAGE OF 8 PINTS OF ICE-CREAM PER PERSON PER YEAR; MORE THAN ANY OTHER EUROPEAN COUNTRY (EVEN ITALY), BUT ONLY A FIFTH OF THAT EATEN IN THE US (PER PERSON).

HOW TO MAKE ICE-CREAM CORNETS

SIFT TOGETHER ½ CUP FLOUR, ¼ CUP SUGAR, 2 TABLESPOONS CORNFLOUR, PINCH SALT; THEN ADD ¼ CUP COOKING OIL & 2 EGG WHITES; FINALLY ADD 2 TABLESPOONS WATER & ½ TEASPOON VANILLA ESSENCE. MAKE CONES ONE AT A TIME IN AN OILED FRYING PAN. POUR IN ABOUT 1½ TABLESPOONS OF MIX TO FORM 4" CIRCLE & COOK OVER LOW HEAT FOR ABOUT 4min. TURN OVER USING WIDE SPATULA & COOK FOR 1 min ON OTHER SIDE. REMOVE; ROLL QUICKLY INTO CONE SHAPE & SECURE WITH WOODEN PICK. REMOVE PICK WHEN CONE IS COOL.

☆ ILLUSIONS ☆
FALSE SENSE-IMPRESSIONS OF OUR SURROUNDINGS

MYSTERY OBJECT

THE BRAIN IS THOUGHT TO INTERPRET THE INFORMATION FROM THE EYE BY MATCHING IT WITH ITS MEMORIES OF OBJECTS & SCENES. WHEN PEOPLE ARE PRESENTED WITH AN OBJECT THAT THEY HAVE NEVER SEEN OR HEARD OF BEFORE THE BRAIN CAN EASILY BE TRICKED IF THERE ARE NO BACKGROUND CLUES. THIS HAPPENED WHEN HUYGENS BECAME THE FIRST MAN TO LOOK AT SATURN'S RINGS THROUGH HIS TELESCOPE. HE COULD NOT SEE OR INTERPRET THE OBJECT AS A RING. BELOW ARE SOME OF THE SHAPES HE DREW.

A REAL ELEPHANT

RECENT RESEARCH HAS BEEN INVESTIGATING HOW OUR CULTURE AFFECTS OUR PICTURE OF REALITY. WHEN SHOWN THE TWO ELEPHANT DRAWINGS, EUROPEANS PREDICTABLY THOUGHT THE LOWER DRAWING WAS MORE REALISTIC, BUT SOME ISOLATED AFRICANS, NOT USED TO PERSPECTIVE DRAWINGS, PREFERRED THE UPPER DRAWING.

THE GROWING MAN ILLUSION

THE PEOPLE ABOVE ARE ACTUALLY ALL THE SAME SIZE. THE REASON FOR THE ILLUSION IS THOUGHT TO BE THAT WE IMAGINE THE PEOPLE ON THE LEFT SIDE TO BE NEARER SO OUR BRAIN ENLARGES THE IMAGE OF THE MORE DISTANT FIGURES DUE TO ITS DEPTH COMPENSATION MECHANISM. (SEE ABOVE)

JUST DOTS?

THE BRAIN CAN SOMETIMES PICTURE OBJECTS WITH VERY LITTLE INFORMATION FROM THE EYE. TRY LOOKING AT THE DOTS BELOW FROM A DISTANCE & THEY WILL FORM AN EYE.

DEPTH COMPENSATION

ONE OF THE MOST STRIKING DISTORTIONS OF THE WORLD WE LOOK OUT ONTO IS CALLED 'DEPTH COMPENSATION' OR CONSTANCY SCALING). OUR BRAINS MAKE MORE DISTANT OBJECTS APPEAR LARGER IN RELATION TO NEARER OBJECTS. THE IMAGE OF AN OBJECT ON OUR RETINAS HALVES IN SIZE WITH EACH DOUBLING OF THE OBJECT'S DISTANCE, BUT THE OBJECT WILL NOT APPEAR TO SHRINK TO THIS EXTENT. TRY LOOKING AT YOUR TWO FOREFINGERS, ONE 9cm FROM YOUR EYES & THE OTHER TWICE AS FAR. IT IS VERY HARD TO BELIEVE THAT YOUR EYE IS RECEIVING AN IMAGE OF ONE FINGER TWICE AS LARGE AS THE OTHER.

ENTASIS

COLUMNS ARE OFTEN BUILT WITH A SLIGHT BULGE IN THE MIDDLE CALLED ENTASIS. TRUE CYLINDRICAL COLUMNS TEND TO APPEAR WIDER AT THE TOP DUE TO OUR DEPTH-COMPENSATION MECHANISM.

THE ENLARGED MOON

THE REASON WHY THE MOON OFTEN LOOKS VERY LARGE WHEN LOW IN THE SKY IS BECAUSE IT IS THEN SEEN BEHIND TERRESTRIAL OBJECTS. ON THE HORIZON & AS IT APPEARS TO BE FURTHER AWAY THE BRAIN ENLARGES ITS IMAGE DUE TO THE DEPTH COMPENSATION MECHANISM.

HOW TO REMOVE THE COIN WITHOUT TOUCHING THE BOTTLE

WINE BOTTLE
TOP PIECE
GENTLY TAP SIDE OF TABLE A FEW TIMES & BOTTLE WILL JOG OFF COIN.

☆ INVENTIONS ☆
NOVEL, ORIGINAL DEVICES & PROCESSES

EXOTIC BEGINNINGS

MOST INVENTIONS WHICH ARE NOW COMMON WERE AT FIRST EXOTIC:
ALUMINIUM WAS FIRST USED FOR A SET OF CUTLERY FOR QUEEN VICTORIA; BAKELITE WAS FIRST USED FOR THE GEAR KNOBS OF ROLLS ROYCES; BIROS WERE FIRST PUBLICISED AS HIGH-ALTITUDE & UNDERWATER PENS.

CHANCE & INVENTION

MANY INVENTIONS WERE ACCIDENTAL. F.P. SMITH'S 1834 PROPELLOR STARTED AS AN ARCHIMEDES SCREW. THIS BROKE IN TWO DURING TRIALS & THE BOAT SHOT FORWARD. FROM THIS OBSERVATION HE DEVELOPED THE MODERN BLADED PROPELLOR.

DIVERSIONS

INVENTORS ARE OFTEN DIVERTED FROM THEIR ORIGINAL IDEA:
CHEWING GUM CAME FROM AN ATTEMPT TO MAKE A SUBSTITUTE FOR RUBBER;
SYNTHETIC DYES CAME FROM AN ATTEMPT TO MAKE QUININE FROM TAR;
RADAR CAME FROM AN ATTEMPT TO MAKE A DEATH RAY.

IMPOSSIBILITIES

THE FIRST RAILWAYS (1830) WERE WIDELY CONDEMNED BECAUSE OF THE POPULAR BELIEF THAT IT WAS PHYSICALLY IMPOSSIBLE FOR HUMANS TO TRAVEL FASTER THAN 20mph.

THE US PATENT OFFICE REFUSED TO ACCEPT PATENTS FOR 'HEAVIER THAN AIR' FLYING MACHINES BEFORE THE 1890s BECAUSE IT CLAIMED THAT SUCH DEVICES WERE PHYSICALLY IMPOSSIBLE.

WRONG ORDERS

THE PROCESS OF SEALING FOOD IN TINS WAS INVENTED IN 1830, LONG BEFORE THE REASON FOR ITS PRESERVATIVE EFFECT WAS KNOWN. THE INSTRUCTIONS ADVISED OPENING WITH HAMMER & CHISEL— THE TIN OPENER WAS A MUCH LATER INVENTION. THE SCREWDRIVER, USED FOR EXTRACTING BENT NAILS, WAS INVENTED BEFORE THE SCREW.

CORNED BEEF

SECOND INVENTIONS

CHARLES PARSONS, FAMOUS FOR HIS STEAM TURBINES, INVENTED A STEAM PRAM AT THE AGE OF 14.

JOSEPH BRAHMAR, WHO INVENTED THE MODERN WATER CLOSET, ALSO INVENTED THE HYDRAULIC PRESS (USED IN STEEL FOUNDRIES).

BESSEMER, THE INVENTOR OF THE FIRST PROCESS FOR MASS-PRODUCING STEEL, SPENT HALF HIS LIFE TRYING TO MAKE A SHIP WITH A CABIN THAT DIDN'T SWAY.

CHARLES BABBAGE, FAMOUS FOR HIS 'COMPUTERS', ALSO INVENTED A STETHOSCOPE.

HALLEY THE FAMOUS ASTRONOMER, INVENTED THE DIVING BELL.

FRITZ HABER, THE CHEMIST WHO INVENTED SYNTHETIC FERTILISERS, SPENT YEARS TRYING TO FIND A METHOD TO EXTRACT GOLD FROM SEA WATER.

EDISON, THE INVENTOR OF THE GRAMOPHONE & ELECTRIC LIGHT BULB, SPENT 10 YEARS WORKING ON AN UNSUCCESSFUL BATTERY.

EDISON'S CUPBOARD

EDISON HID HIMSELF IN A CUPBOARD UNDER THE STAIRS WHEN HE WANTED TO SOLVE A PROBLEM.

SOLUTIONS WITHOUT PROBLEMS

IT WAS 17 YEARS AFTER THE INVENTION OF TEFLON BEFORE ANYONE THOUGHT OF USING IT ON FRYING PANS. SOME SUBSTANCES, LIKE POTTY PUTTY, STILL DON'T HAVE A SERIOUS USE.

☆ IRON ☆
METALLIC ELEMENT OF ATOMIC NUMBER 56

HEAVENLY IRON

THE FIRST IRON USED BY MAN WAS LITERALLY HEAVEN-SENT, IN THE FORM OF METEORS. IRON ORES WERE NOT EXPLOITED UNTIL AFTER 2000BC PROBABLY BECAUSE EXPERIMENTAL SMELTINGS TO SEE IF IT WOULD BEHAVE LIKE ORES OF COPPER OR OTHER KNOWN METALS WOULD HAVE BEEN DISCOURAGING: A MASS OF SLAG & CINDERS CONCEALING UNMELTED GLOBULES OF IRON. ONLY WHEN PEOPLE STARTED BLOWING AIR THROUGH THE CHARCOAL FIRE DID THE FURNACE TEMPERATURE RISE SUFFICIENTLY TO MAKE THE MASS SOFT ENOUGH TO BE WORKABLE.

THE CRUDE IRON (PIG IRON) THAT EMERGED FROM THE EARLY FURNACES WAS VERY BRITTLE. HOWEVER, REPEATEDLY BEATING IT OUT & DOUBLING IT OVER - MUCH AS IN MAKING FLAKY PASTRY- PRODUCED A VERY PURE & STRONG FORM OF IRON CALLED WROUGHT IRON. THE BEATING OUT TOOK A LONG TIME SO IT WAS VERY EXPENSIVE. EVEN SILVER WAS OFTEN CHEAPER.

CAST IRON

THE GREEKS WERE THE FIRST TO MELT IRON COMPLETELY. THEY TRIED POURING IT INTO MOULDS, BUT THE RESULTING CAST IRON WAS AS BRITTLE AS THEIR LUMPS OF PARTIALLY MELTED PIG IRON. THE INVENTION OF THE CANNON IN THE 1200s LED TO ITS REINTRODUCTION. CAST IRON BARRELS FREQUENTLY BURST, BUT NO ECONOMIC ALTERNATIVE WAS FOUND UNTIL THE INTRODUCTION OF STEEL IN 1860.

WROUGHT IRON

COKE

PUDDLING

PUDDLED WROUGHT IRON IS CONSIDERED BY MANY HISTORIANS TO BE THE KEY MATERIAL OF THE INDUSTRIAL REVOLUTION. FOR THE FIRST TIME WROUGHT IRON, ESSENTIAL FOR RELIABLE RAILS & STEAM ENGINES, COULD BE MADE CHEAPLY. THE PROCESS WAS INVENTED BY HENRY CORT IN 1784. THE PUDDLING, STIRRING PUDDLES OF MOLTEN PIG IRON WITH IRON OXIDE, WAS VERY HARD & SKILLED WORK. AFTER THE NAPOLEONIC WARS MANY ENGLISH PUDDLERS EARNED THEIR FORTUNE TRAVELLING ROUND EUROPE GIVING INSTRUCTION IN PUDDLING.

COAL CANNOT BE USED AS A FUEL FOR SMELTING IRON ORES BECAUSE IT CONTAINS SULPHUR. HOWEVER, IF THE COAL IS FIRST PARTIALLY BURNT, JUST AS WOOD IS CHARRED TO MAKE CHARCOAL, THE RESULTING COKE CAN BE USED. COKE WAS DISCOVERED IN ABOUT 1650 BY THE BREWERS OF DERBYSHIRE. THEY USED IT AS A FUEL FOR DRYING THE MALT SINCE COAL GAVE THE BEER A SULPHUROUS TASTE. COKE WAS NOT INTRODUCED AS A BLAST FURNACE FUEL UNTIL 1709 (BY ABRAHAM DARBY).

IRON OR STEEL

CAST IRON IS STILL WIDELY USED. IT IS CHEAPER THAN STEEL & MODERN TECHNOLOGY HAS GREATLY IMPROVED ITS MECHANICAL PROPERTIES IT IS EVEN REPLACING STEEL IN MANY APPLICATIONS.

WROUGHT IRON IS NO LONGER MADE, SINCE STEEL (IRON WITH A SMALL ADDITION OF CARBON) IS CHEAPER & EQUALLY STRONG. HOWEVER WROUGHT IRON HAD A RESISTANCE TO RUST UNEQUALLED BY STEEL.

IRON OR STEEL

HOW TO MAKE YOURSELF INTO A SILLY LADY

FOLD PIECE OF CARD, 14 IN. SQUARE IN HALF, THEN CUT SHAPE Ⓐ FOLD OVER NOSE & ATTACH ELASTIC Ⓑ, THEN PAINT MASK & PUT IT ON Ⓒ

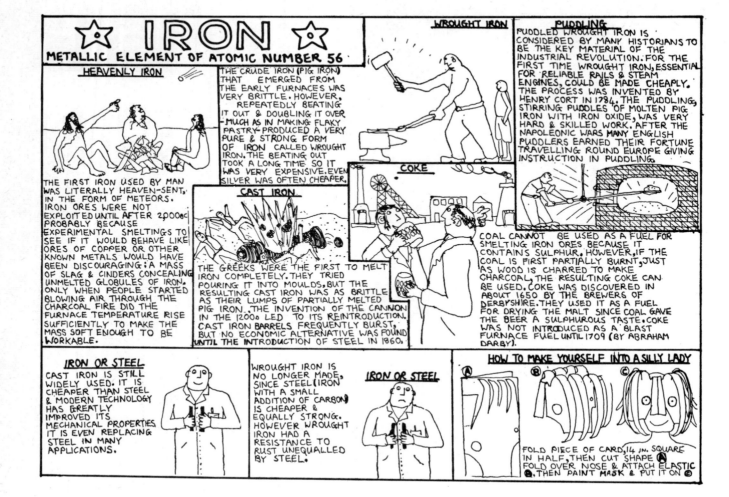

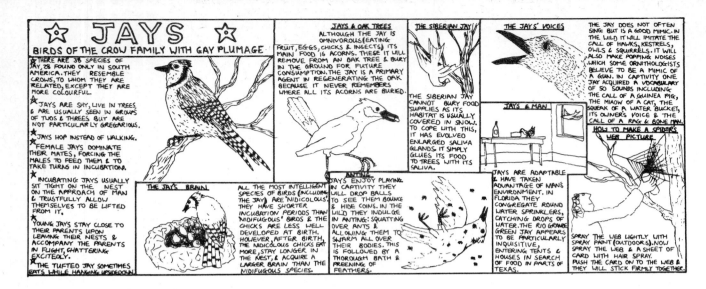

☆ JAYS ☆
BIRDS OF THE CROW FAMILY WITH GAY PLUMAGE

☆ THERE ARE 38 SPECIES OF JAY, 28 FOUND ONLY IN SOUTH AMERICA. THEY RESEMBLE CROWS, TO WHOM THEY ARE RELATED, EXCEPT THEY ARE MORE COLOURFUL.

☆ JAYS ARE SHY, LIVE IN TREES & ARE USUALLY SEEN IN GROUPS OF TWOS & THREES BUT ARE NOT PARTICULARLY GREGARIOUS.

☆ JAYS HOP INSTEAD OF WALKING.

☆ FEMALE JAYS DOMINATE THEIR MATES, FORCING THE MALES TO FEED THEM & TO TAKE TURNS IN INCUBATION.

☆ INCUBATING JAYS USUALLY SIT TIGHT ON THE NEST ON THE APPROACH OF MAN & TRUSTFULLY ALLOW THEMSELVES TO BE LIFTED FROM IT.

☆ YOUNG JAYS STAY CLOSE TO THEIR PARENTS UPON LEAVING THEIR NESTS & ACCOMPANY THE PARENTS IN FLIGHT, CHATTERING EXCITEDLY.

☆ THE TUFTED JAY SOMETIMES EATS WHILE HANGING UPSIDEDOWN.

JAYS & OAK TREES
ALTHOUGH THE JAY IS OMNIVOROUS (EATING FRUIT, EGGS, CHICKS & INSECTS) ITS MAIN FOOD IS ACORNS. THESE IT WILL REMOVE FROM AN OAK TREE & BURY IN THE GROUND FOR FUTURE CONSUMPTION. THE JAY IS A PRIMARY AGENT IN REGENERATING THE OAK BECAUSE IT NEVER REMEMBERS WHERE ALL ITS ACORNS ARE BURIED.

THE SIBERIAN JAY
THE SIBERIAN JAY CANNOT BURY FOOD SUPPLIES AS ITS HABITAT IS USUALLY COVERED IN SNOW. TO COPE WITH THIS, IT HAS EVOLVED ENLARGED SALIVA GLANDS. IT SIMPLY GLUES ITS FOOD TO TREES WITH ITS SALIVA.

THE JAY'S BRAIN
ALL THE MOST INTELLIGENT SPECIES OF BIRDS (INCLUDING THE JAY) ARE 'NIDICOLOUS.' THEY HAVE SHORTER INCUBATION PERIODS THAN 'NIDIFUGOUS' BIRDS & THE CHICKS ARE LESS WELL DEVELOPED AT BIRTH. HOWEVER AFTER BIRTH, THE NIDICOLOUS CHICKS EAT MORE, STAY LONGER IN THE NEST, & ACQUIRE A LARGER BRAIN THAN THE NIDIFUGOUS SPECIES.

ANTING
JAYS ENJOY PLAYING. IN CAPTIVITY THEY WILL DROP BALLS TO SEE THEM BOUNCE & HIDE COINS. IN THE WILD THEY INDULGE IN ANTING: SQUATTING OVER ANTS & ALLOWING THEM TO SWARM ALL OVER THEIR BODIES. THIS IS FOLLOWED BY A THOROUGH BATH & PREENING OF FEATHERS.

JAYS & MAN
JAYS ARE ADAPTABLE & HAVE TAKEN ADVANTAGE OF MAN'S ENVIRONMENT. IN FLORIDA THEY CONGREGATE ROUND WATER SPRINKLERS, CATCHING DROPS OF WATER. THE RIO GRANDE GREEN JAY APPEARS TO BE PARTICULARLY INQUISITIVE, ENTERING TENTS & HOUSES IN SEARCH OF FOOD IN PARTS OF TEXAS.

THE JAYS' VOICES
THE JAY DOES NOT OFTEN SING, BUT IS A GOOD MIMIC. IN THE WILD IT WILL IMITATE THE CALLS OF HAWKS, KESTRELS, OWLS & SQUIRRELS. IT WILL ALSO MAKE POPPING NOISES WHICH SOME ORNITHOLOGISTS BELIEVE TO BE A MIMIC OF A GUN. IN CAPTIVITY ONE JAY ACQUIRED A VOCABULARY OF 50 SOUNDS INCLUDING THE CALL OF A GUINEA PIG, THE MIAOW OF A CAT, THE SQUEAK OF A WATER BUCKET, ITS OWNER'S VOICE & THE CALL OF A RAG & BONE MAN.

HOW TO MAKE A SPIDERS' WEB PICTURE
SPRAY THE WEB LIGHTLY WITH SPRAY PAINT (OUTDOORS). NOW SPRAY THE WEB & A SHEET OF CARD WITH HAIR SPRAY. PUSH THE CARD ON TO THE WEB & THEY WILL STICK FIRMLY TOGETHER.

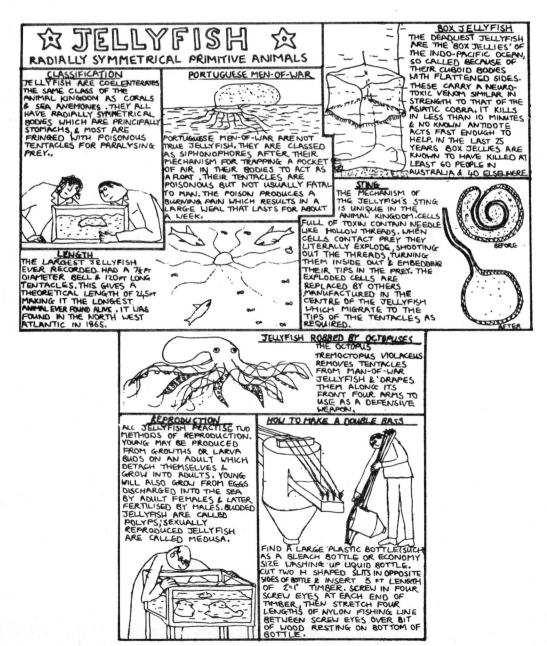

☆ JELLYFISH ☆
RADIALLY SYMMETRICAL PRIMITIVE ANIMALS

CLASSIFICATION
JELLYFISH ARE COELENTERATES, THE SAME CLASS OF THE ANIMAL KINGDOM AS CORALS & SEA ANEMONES. THEY ALL HAVE RADIALLY SYMMETRICAL BODIES WHICH ARE PRINCIPALLY STOMACHS, & MOST ARE FRINGED WITH POISONOUS TENTACLES FOR PARALYSING PREY.

LENGTH
THE LARGEST JELLYFISH EVER RECORDED HAD A 7½ FT DIAMETER BELL & 120 FT LONG TENTACLES. THIS GIVES A THEORETICAL LENGTH OF 245 FT MAKING IT THE LONGEST ANIMAL EVER FOUND ALIVE. IT WAS FOUND IN THE NORTH WEST ATLANTIC IN 1865.

PORTUGUESE MEN-OF-WAR
PORTUGUESE MEN-OF-WAR ARE NOT TRUE JELLYFISH. THEY ARE CLASSED AS SIPHONOPHORES AFTER THEIR MECHANISM FOR TRAPPING A POCKET OF AIR IN THEIR BODIES TO ACT AS A FLOAT. THEIR TENTACLES ARE POISONOUS BUT NOT USUALLY FATAL TO MAN. THE POISON PRODUCES A BURNING PAIN WHICH RESULTS IN A LARGE WEAL THAT LASTS FOR ABOUT A WEEK.

BOX JELLYFISH
THE DEADLIEST JELLYFISH ARE THE 'BOX JELLIES' OF THE INDO-PACIFIC OCEAN, SO CALLED BECAUSE OF THEIR CUBOID BODIES WITH FLATTENED SIDES. THESE CARRY A NEURO-TOXIC VENOM SIMILAR IN STRENGTH TO THAT OF THE ASIATIC COBRA. IT KILLS IN LESS THAN 10 MINUTES & NO KNOWN ANTIDOTE ACTS FAST ENOUGH TO HELP. IN THE LAST 25 YEARS BOX JELLIES ARE KNOWN TO HAVE KILLED AT LEAST 60 PEOPLE IN AUSTRALIA & 40 ELSEWHERE.

STING
THE MECHANISM OF THE JELLYFISH'S STING IS UNIQUE IN THE ANIMAL KINGDOM. CELLS FULL OF TOXIN CONTAIN NEEDLE-LIKE HOLLOW THREADS. WHEN CELLS CONTACT PREY THEY LITERALLY EXPLODE, SHOOTING OUT THE THREADS, TURNING THEM INSIDE OUT & EMBEDDING THEIR TIPS IN THE PREY. THE EXPLODED CELLS ARE REPLACED BY OTHERS MANUFACTURED IN THE CENTRE OF THE JELLYFISH WHICH MIGRATE TO THE TIPS OF THE TENTACLES AS REQUIRED.

BEFORE

AFTER

JELLYFISH ROBBED BY OCTOPUSES
THE OCTOPUS TREMOCTOPUS VIOLACEUS REMOVES TENTACLES FROM MAN-OF-WAR JELLYFISH & DRAPES THEM ALONG ITS FRONT FOUR ARMS TO USE AS A DEFENSIVE WEAPON.

REPRODUCTION
ALL JELLYFISH PRACTISE TWO METHODS OF REPRODUCTION. YOUNG MAY BE PRODUCED FROM GROWTHS OR LARVA BUDS ON AN ADULT WHICH DETACH THEMSELVES & GROW INTO ADULTS. YOUNG WILL ALSO GROW FROM EGGS DISCHARGED INTO THE SEA BY ADULT FEMALES & LATER FERTILISED BY MALES. BUDDED JELLYFISH ARE CALLED POLYPS, SEXUALLY REPRODUCED JELLYFISH ARE CALLED MEDUSA.

HOW TO MAKE A DOUBLE BASS
FIND A LARGE PLASTIC BOTTLE (SUCH AS A BLEACH BOTTLE OR ECONOMY SIZE WASHING UP LIQUID BOTTLE. CUT TWO H SHAPED SLITS IN OPPOSITE SIDES OF BOTTLE & INSERT 5 FT LENGTH OF 2"x1" TIMBER. SCREW IN FOUR SCREW EYES AT EACH END OF TIMBER, THEN STRETCH FOUR LENGTHS OF NYLON FISHING LINE BETWEEN SCREW EYES OVER BIT OF WOOD RESTING ON BOTTOM OF BOTTLE.

JET ENGINES
DEVICES PRODUCING THRUST BY ACCELERATING MASSES OF AIR

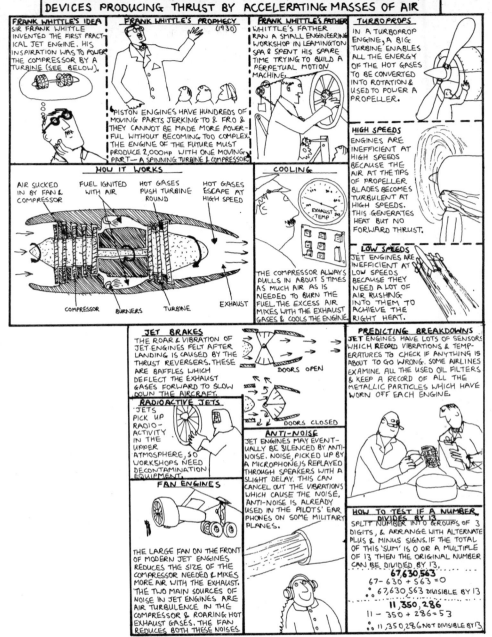

FRANK WHITTLE'S IDEA
SIR FRANK WHITTLE INVENTED THE FIRST PRACTICAL JET ENGINE. HIS INSPIRATION WAS TO POWER THE COMPRESSOR BY A TURBINE (SEE BELOW).

FRANK WHITTLE'S PROPHECY (1930)
PISTON ENGINES HAVE HUNDREDS OF MOVING PARTS JERKING TO & FRO & THEY CANNOT BE MADE MORE POWERFUL WITHOUT BECOMING TOO COMPLEX. THE ENGINE OF THE FUTURE MUST PRODUCE 2,000hp WITH ONE MOVING PART — A SPINNING TURBINE & COMPRESSOR.

FRANK WHITTLE'S FATHER
WHITTLE'S FATHER RAN A SMALL ENGINEERING WORKSHOP IN LEAMINGTON SPA & SPENT HIS SPARE TIME TRYING TO BUILD A PERPETUAL MOTION MACHINE.

TURBOPROPS
IN A TURBOPROP ENGINE, A BIG TURBINE ENABLES ALL THE ENERGY OF THE HOT GASES TO BE CONVERTED INTO ROTATION & USED TO POWER A PROPELLER.

HOW IT WORKS
AIR SUCKED IN BY FAN & COMPRESSOR
FUEL IGNITED WITH AIR
HOT GASES PUSH TURBINE ROUND
HOT GASES ESCAPE AT HIGH SPEED
COMPRESSOR   BURNERS   TURBINE   EXHAUST

COOLING
EXHAUST TEMP
THE COMPRESSOR ALWAYS PULLS IN ABOUT 5 TIMES AS MUCH AIR AS IS NEEDED TO BURN THE FUEL. THE EXCESS AIR MIXES WITH THE EXHAUST GASES & COOLS THE ENGINE.

HIGH SPEEDS
ENGINES ARE INEFFICIENT AT HIGH SPEEDS BECAUSE THE AIR AT THE TIPS OF PROPELLER BLADES BECOMES TURBULENT AT HIGH SPEEDS. THIS GENERATES HEAT BUT NO FORWARD THRUST.

LOW SPEEDS
JET ENGINES ARE INEFFICIENT AT LOW SPEEDS BECAUSE THEY NEED A LOT OF AIR RUSHING INTO THEM TO ACHIEVE THE RIGHT HEAT.

JET BRAKES
THE ROAR & VIBRATION OF JET ENGINES FELT AFTER LANDING IS CAUSED BY THE THRUST REVERSERS. THESE ARE BAFFLES WHICH DEFLECT THE EXHAUST GASES FORWARD TO SLOW DOWN THE AIRCRAFT.
DOORS OPEN
DOORS CLOSED

RADIOACTIVE JETS
JETS PICK UP RADIOACTIVITY IN THE UPPER ATMOSPHERE, SO WORKSHOPS NEED DECONTAMINATION EQUIPMENT.

FAN ENGINES
THE LARGE FAN ON THE FRONT OF MODERN JET ENGINES REDUCES THE SIZE OF THE COMPRESSOR NEEDED & MIXES MORE AIR WITH THE EXHAUST. THE TWO MAIN SOURCES OF NOISE IN JET ENGINES ARE AIR TURBULENCE IN THE COMPRESSOR & ROARING HOT EXHAUST GASES. THE FAN REDUCES BOTH THESE NOISES.

ANTI-NOISE
JET ENGINES MAY EVENTUALLY BE SILENCED BY ANTINOISE. NOISE, PICKED UP BY A MICROPHONE, IS REPLAYED THROUGH SPEAKERS WITH A SLIGHT DELAY. THIS CAN CANCEL OUT THE VIBRATIONS WHICH CAUSE THE NOISE. ANTI-NOISE IS ALREADY USED IN THE PILOTS' EAR PHONES ON SOME MILITARY PLANES.

PREDICTING BREAKDOWNS
JET ENGINES HAVE LOTS OF SENSORS WHICH RECORD VIBRATIONS & TEMPERATURES TO CHECK IF ANYTHING IS ABOUT TO GO WRONG. SOME AIRLINES EXAMINE ALL THE USED OIL FILTERS & KEEP A RECORD OF ALL THE METALLIC PARTICLES WHICH HAVE WORN OFF EACH ENGINE.

HOW TO TEST IF A NUMBER DIVIDES BY 13
SPLIT NUMBER INTO GROUPS OF 3 DIGITS, & ARRANGE WITH ALTERNATE PLUS & MINUS SIGNS. IF THE TOTAL OF THIS 'SUM' IS 0 OR A MULTIPLE OF 13 THEN THE ORIGINAL NUMBER CAN BE DIVIDED BY 13.

$$67,630,563$$
$$67 - 630 + 563 = 0$$
∴ 67,630,563 DIVISIBLE BY 13

$$11,350,286$$
$$11 - 350 + 286 = 53$$
∴ 11,350,286 NOT DIVISIBLE BY 13

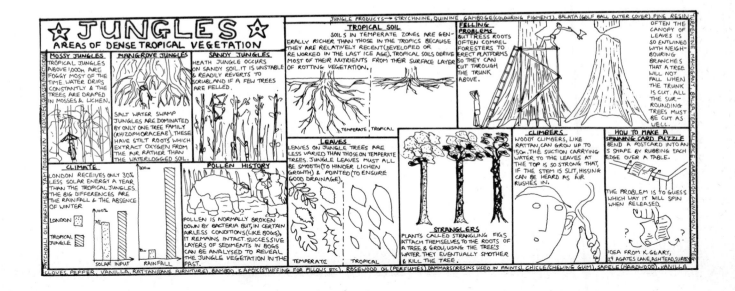

☆ JUNGLES ☆
AREAS OF DENSE TROPICAL VEGETATION

JUNGLE PRODUCTS → STRYCHNINE, QUININE, GAMBOGE (COLOURING PIGMENT), BALATA (GOLF BALL OUTER COVER), PINE RESIN,

MOSSY JUNGLES
TROPICAL JUNGLES ABOVE 1,000m ARE FOGGY MOST OF THE TIME. WATER DRIPS CONSTANTLY & THE TREES ARE DRAPED IN MOSSES & LICHEN.

MANGROVE JUNGLES
SALT WATER SWAMP JUNGLES ARE DOMINATED BY ONLY ONE TREE FAMILY (RHIZOPHORACEAE). THESE HAVE STILT ROOTS WHICH EXTRACT OXYGEN FROM THE AIR RATHER THAN THE WATERLOGGED SOIL.

SANDY JUNGLES
HEATH JUNGLE OCCURS ON SANDY SOIL. IT IS UNSTABLE & READILY REVERTS TO SCRUBLAND IF A FEW TREES ARE FELLED.

TROPICAL SOIL
SOILS IN TEMPERATE ZONES ARE GENERALLY RICHER THAN THOSE IN THE TROPICS BECAUSE THEY ARE RELATIVELY RECENT (DEVELOPED OR RE-WORKED IN THE LAST ICE AGE). TROPICAL SOILS DERIVE MOST OF THEIR NUTRIENTS FROM THEIR SURFACE LAYER OF ROTTING VEGETATION.
TEMPERATE   TROPICAL

FELLING PROBLEMS
BUTTRESS ROOTS OFTEN COMPEL FORESTERS TO ERECT PLATFORMS SO THEY CAN CUT THROUGH THE TRUNK ABOVE.

OFTEN THE CANOPY OF LEAVES IS SO ENTWINED WITH NEIGHBOURING BRANCHES THAT A TREE WILL NOT FALL WHEN THE TRUNK IS CUT. ALL THE SURROUNDING TREES MUST BE CUT AS WELL.

CLIMATE
LONDON RECEIVES ONLY 30% LESS SOLAR ENERGY A YEAR THAN THE TROPICAL JUNGLES. THE BIG DIFFERENCES ARE THE RAINFALL & THE ABSENCE OF WINTER.
(LONDON ☐)
(TROPICAL JUNGLE ▨)
100%
SOLAR INPUT   RAINFALL

POLLEN HISTORY
POLLEN IS NORMALLY BROKEN DOWN BY BACTERIA BUT, IN CERTAIN AIRLESS CONDITIONS (LIKE BOGS), IT REMAINS INTACT. SUCCESSIVE LAYERS OF SEDIMENTS IN BOGS CAN BE ANALYSED TO REVEAL THE JUNGLE VEGETATION IN THE PAST.

LEAVES
LEAVES ON JUNGLE TREES ARE LESS VARIED THAN THOSE ON TEMPERATE TREES. JUNGLE LEAVES MUST ALL BE SMOOTH (TO HINDER LICHEN GROWTH) & POINTED (TO ENSURE GOOD DRAINAGE).
TEMPERATE   TROPICAL

CLIMBERS
WOODY CLIMBERS, LIKE RATTAN, CAN GROW UP TO 150m. THE SUCTION CARRYING WATER TO THE TOP IS SO STRONG THAT, IF THE STEM IS SLIT, HISSING CAN BE HEARD AS AIR RUSHES IN.

STRANGLERS
PLANTS CALLED STRANGLING FIGS ATTACH THEMSELVES TO THE ROOTS OF A TREE & GROW, USING THE TREE'S WATER. THEY EVENTUALLY SMOTHER & KILL THE TREE.

HOW TO MAKE A SPINNING CARD PUZZLE
BEND A POSTCARD INTO AN S SHAPE BY RUBBING EACH EDGE OVER A TABLE.
THE PROBLEM IS TO GUESS WHICH WAY IT WILL SPIN WHEN RELEASED.
IDEA FROM K. GEARY, 29 AGATES LANE, ASHTEAD, SURREY.

CLOVES, PEPPER, VANILLA, RATTAN (CANE FURNITURE), BAMBOO, KAPOK (STUFFING FOR PILLOWS ETC), ROSEWOOD OIL (PERFUMES), DAMMARS (RESINS USED IN PAINTS), CHICLE (CHEWING GUM), SAPELE (HARDWOOD), VANILLA

☆ KANGAROOS ☆
POUCHED MAMMALS WITH ENLARGED HIND LIMBS

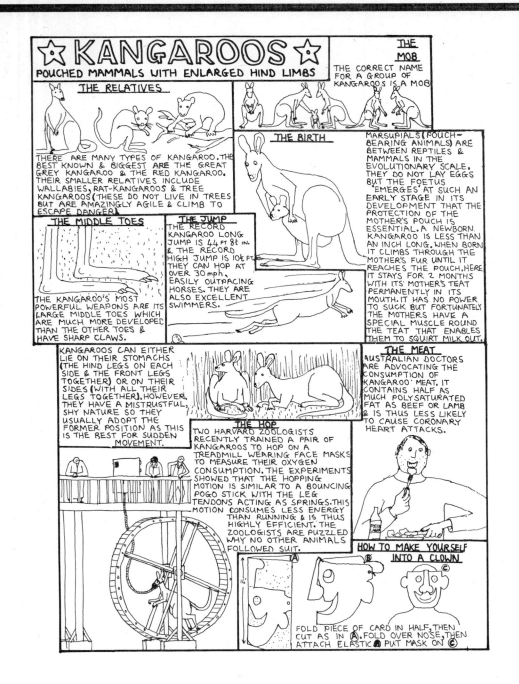

THE RELATIVES

THERE ARE MANY TYPES OF KANGAROO. THE BEST KNOWN & BIGGEST ARE THE GREAT GREY KANGAROO & THE RED KANGAROO. THEIR SMALLER RELATIVES INCLUDE WALLABIES, RAT-KANGAROOS & TREE KANGAROOS (THESE DO NOT LIVE IN TREES BUT ARE AMAZINGLY AGILE & CLIMB TO ESCAPE DANGER).

THE MOB

THE CORRECT NAME FOR A GROUP OF KANGAROOS IS A MOB

THE BIRTH

MARSUPIALS (POUCH-BEARING ANIMALS) ARE BETWEEN REPTILES & MAMMALS IN THE EVOLUTIONARY SCALE. THEY DO NOT LAY EGGS BUT THE FOETUS 'EMERGES' AT SUCH AN EARLY STAGE IN ITS DEVELOPMENT THAT THE PROTECTION OF THE MOTHER'S POUCH IS ESSENTIAL. A NEWBORN KANGAROO IS LESS THAN AN INCH LONG. WHEN BORN IT CLIMBS THROUGH THE MOTHER'S FUR UNTIL IT REACHES THE POUCH. HERE IT STAYS FOR 2 MONTHS WITH ITS MOTHER'S TEAT PERMANENTLY IN ITS MOUTH. IT HAS NO POWER TO SUCK BUT FORTUNATELY THE MOTHERS HAVE A SPECIAL MUSCLE ROUND THE TEAT THAT ENABLES THEM TO SQUIRT MILK OUT.

THE MIDDLE TOES

THE KANGAROO'S MOST POWERFUL WEAPONS ARE ITS LARGE MIDDLE TOES WHICH ARE MUCH MORE DEVELOPED THAN THE OTHER TOES & HAVE SHARP CLAWS.

THE JUMP

THE RECORD KANGAROO LONG JUMP IS 44 FT 8½ IN. & THE RECORD HIGH JUMP IS 10½ FT. THEY CAN HOP AT OVER 30 mph, EASILY OUTPACING HORSES. THEY ARE ALSO EXCELLENT SWIMMERS.

KANGAROOS CAN EITHER LIE ON THEIR STOMACHS (THE HIND LEGS ON EACH SIDE & THE FRONT LEGS TOGETHER) OR ON THEIR SIDES (WITH ALL THEIR LEGS TOGETHER). HOWEVER, THEY HAVE A MISTRUSTFUL, SHY NATURE SO THEY USUALLY ADOPT THE FORMER POSITION AS THIS IS THE BEST FOR SUDDEN MOVEMENT.

THE MEAT

AUSTRALIAN DOCTORS ARE ADVOCATING THE CONSUMPTION OF KANGAROO MEAT. IT CONTAINS HALF AS MUCH POLYSATURATED FAT AS BEEF OR LAMB & IS THUS LESS LIKELY TO CAUSE CORONARY HEART ATTACKS.

THE HOP

TWO HARVARD ZOOLOGISTS RECENTLY TRAINED A PAIR OF KANGAROOS TO HOP ON A TREADMILL WEARING FACE MASKS TO MEASURE THEIR OXYGEN CONSUMPTION. THE EXPERIMENTS SHOWED THAT THE HOPPING MOTION IS SIMILAR TO A BOUNCING POGO STICK WITH THE LEG TENDONS ACTING AS SPRINGS. THIS MOTION CONSUMES LESS ENERGY THAN RUNNING & IS THUS HIGHLY EFFICIENT. THE ZOOLOGISTS ARE PUZZLED WHY NO OTHER ANIMALS FOLLOWED SUIT.

HOW TO MAKE YOURSELF INTO A CLOWN

FOLD PIECE OF CARD IN HALF, THEN CUT AS IN Ⓐ. FOLD OVER NOSE, THEN ATTACH ELASTIC Ⓑ PUT MASK ON Ⓒ

☆ KITES ☆
LIGHT CLOTH-COVERED FRAMES FOR FLYING

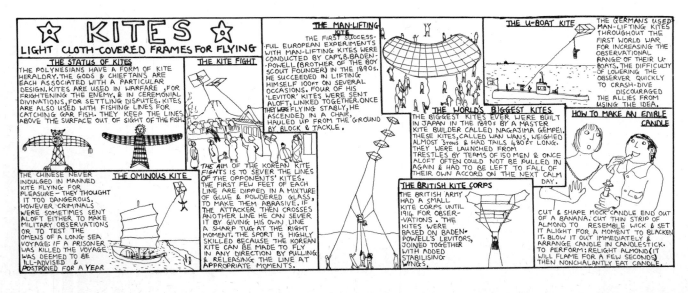

THE STATUS OF KITES

THE POLYNESIANS HAVE A FORM OF KITE HERALDRY. THE GODS & CHIEFTAINS ARE EACH ASSOCIATED WITH A PARTICULAR DESIGN. KITES ARE USED IN WARFARE, FOR FRIGHTENING THE ENEMY, & IN CEREMONIAL DIVINATIONS, FOR SETTLING DISPUTES. KITES ARE ALSO USED WITH FISHING LINES FOR CATCHING GAR FISH. THEY KEEP THE LINES ABOVE THE SURFACE OUT OF SIGHT OF THE FISH.

THE OMINOUS KITE

THE CHINESE NEVER INDULGED IN MANNED KITE FLYING FOR PLEASURE – THEY THOUGHT IT TOO DANGEROUS. HOWEVER CRIMINALS WERE SOMETIMES SENT ALOFT EITHER TO MAKE MILITARY OBSERVATIONS OR TO TEST THE OMENS OF A LONG SEA VOYAGE: IF A PRISONER WAS KILLED THE VOYAGE WAS DEEMED TO BE ILL-ADVISED & POSTPONED FOR A YEAR

THE KITE FIGHT

THE AIM OF THE KOREAN KITE FIGHTS IS TO SEVER THE LINES OF THE OPPONENTS' KITES. THE FIRST FEW FEET OF EACH LINE ARE DIPPED IN A MIXTURE OF GLUE & POWDERED GLASS, TO MAKE THEM ABRASIVE. IF THE ATTACKER THEN CROSSES ANOTHER LINE HE CAN SEVER IT BY GIVING HIS OWN LINE A SHARP TUG AT THE RIGHT MOMENT. THE SPORT IS HIGHLY SKILLED BECAUSE THE KOREAN KITE CAN BE MADE TO FLY IN ANY DIRECTION BY PULLING IN & RELEASING THE LINE AT APPROPRIATE MOMENTS.

THE MAN-LIFTING KITE

THE FIRST SUCCESSFUL EUROPEAN EXPERIMENTS WITH MAN-LIFTING KITES WERE CONDUCTED BY CAPT. B. BADEN-POWELL (BROTHER OF THE BOY SCOUT FOUNDER) IN THE 1890s. HE SUCCEEDED IN LIFTING HIMSELF 100 FT ON SEVERAL OCCASIONS. FOUR OF HIS 'LEVITOR' KITES WERE SENT ALOFT, LINKED TOGETHER. ONCE THEY WERE FLYING STABLY, HE ASCENDED IN A CHAIR, HAULED UP FROM THE GROUND BY BLOCK & TACKLE.

THE WORLD'S BIGGEST KITES

THE BIGGEST KITES EVER WERE BUILT IN JAPAN IN THE 1890s BY A MASTER KITE BUILDER CALLED NAGAJIMA GEMPEI. THESE KITES, CALLED WAN WANS, WEIGHED ALMOST 3 TONS & HAD TAILS 480 FT LONG. THEY WERE LAUNCHED FROM TRESTLES BY TEAMS OF 150 MEN & ONCE ALOFT OFTEN COULD NOT BE PULLED IN AGAIN & HAD TO BE LEFT TO FALL OF THEIR OWN ACCORD ON THE NEXT CALM DAY.

THE BRITISH KITE CORPS

THE BRITISH ARMY HAD A SMALL KITE CORPS UNTIL 1914 FOR OBSERVATIONS. THE KITES WERE BASED ON BADEN-POWELL'S LEVITORS, JOINED TOGETHER WITH ADDED STABILISING WINGS.

THE U-BOAT KITE

THE GERMANS USED MAN-LIFTING KITES THROUGHOUT THE FIRST WORLD WAR FOR INCREASING THE OBSERVATIONAL RANGE OF THEIR U-BOATS. THE DIFFICULTY OF LOWERING THE OBSERVER QUICKLY TO CRASH-DIVE DISCOURAGED THE ALLIES FROM USING THE IDEA.

HOW TO MAKE AN EDIBLE CANDLE

CUT & SHAPE MOCK CANDLE END OUT OF A BANANA. CUT THIN STRIP OF ALMOND TO RESEMBLE WICK & SET IT ALIGHT FOR A MOMENT TO BLACKEN IT. BLOW IT OUT IMMEDIATELY & ARRANGE CANDLE IN CANDLESTICK. TO PERFORM: RELIGHT ALMOND (IT WILL FLAME FOR A FEW SECONDS) THEN NONCHALANTLY EAT CANDLE.

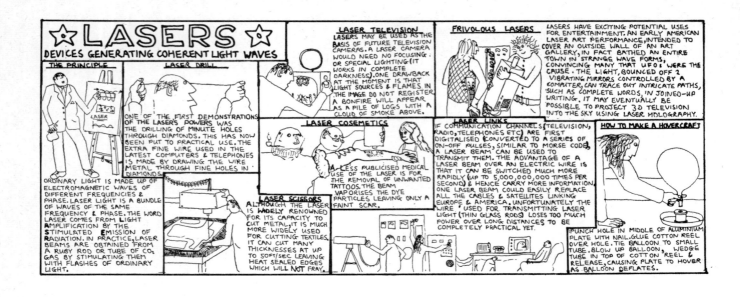

☆ LASERS ☆
DEVICES GENERATING COHERENT LIGHT WAVES

THE PRINCIPLE

LASER DRILL
ONE OF THE FIRST DEMONSTRATIONS OF THE LASER'S POWERS WAS THE DRILLING OF MINUTE HOLES THROUGH DIAMONDS. THIS HAS NOW BEEN PUT TO PRACTICAL USE. THE EXTRA FINE WIRE USED IN THE LATEST COMPUTERS & TELEPHONES IS MADE BY DRAWING THE WIRE METAL THROUGH FINE HOLES IN DIAMONDS.

ORDINARY LIGHT IS MADE UP OF ELECTROMAGNETIC WAVES OF DIFFERENT FREQUENCIES & PHASE. LASER LIGHT IS A BUNDLE OF WAVES OF THE SAME FREQUENCY & PHASE. THE WORD LASER COMES FROM LIGHT AMPLIFICATION BY THE STIMULATED EMISSION OF RADIATION. IN PRACTICE, LASER BEAMS ARE OBTAINED FROM A RUBY ROD OR TUBE OF CO_2 GAS BY STIMULATING THEM WITH FLASHES OF ORDINARY LIGHT.

LASER TELEVISION
LASERS MAY BE USED AS THE BASIS OF FUTURE TELEVISION CAMERAS. A LASER CAMERA WOULD NEED NO FOCUSING OR SPECIAL LIGHTING (IT WORKS IN COMPLETE DARKNESS). ONE DRAWBACK AT THE MOMENT IS THAT LIGHT SOURCES & FLAMES IN THE IMAGE DO NOT REGISTER. A BONFIRE WILL APPEAR AS A PILE OF LOGS WITH A CLOUD OF SMOKE ABOVE.

LASER COSEMETICS
A LESS PUBLICISED MEDICAL USE OF THE LASER IS FOR THE REMOVAL OF UNWANTED TATTOOS. THE BEAM VAPORISES THE DYE PARTICLES LEAVING ONLY A FAINT SCAR.

LASER SCISSORS
ALTHOUGH THE LASER IS WIDELY RENOWNED FOR ITS CAPACITY TO CUT METAL, IT IS MUCH MORE WIDELY USED FOR CUTTING TEXTILES. IT CAN CUT MANY THICKNESSES AT UP TO SOFT/SEC LEAVING HEAT SEALED EDGES WHICH WILL NOT FRAY.

FRIVOLOUS LASERS
LASERS HAVE EXCITING POTENTIAL USES FOR ENTERTAINMENT. AN EARLY AMERICAN LASER ART PERFORMANCE, INTENDED TO COVER AN OUTSIDE WALL OF AN ART GALLERY, IN FACT BATHED AN ENTIRE TOWN IN STRANGE WAVE FORMS, CONVINCING MANY THAT UFO's WERE THE CAUSE. THE LIGHT, BOUNCED OFF 2 VIBRATING MIRRORS CONTROLLED BY A COMPUTER, CAN TRACE OUT INTRICATE PATHS, SUCH AS COMPLETE WORDS, IN JOINED-UP WRITING. IT MAY EVENTUALLY BE POSSIBLE TO PROJECT 3D TELEVISION INTO THE SKY USING LASER HOLOGRAPHY.

LASER LINKS
IF COMMUNICATION CHANNELS (TELEVISION, RADIO, TELEPHONES ETC) ARE FIRST DIGITALISED (CONVERTED TO A SERIES OF ON-OFF PULSES, SIMILAR TO MORSE CODE) A LASER BEAM CAN BE USED TO TRANSMIT THEM. THE ADVANTAGE OF A LASER BEAM OVER AN ELECTRIC WIRE IS THAT IT CAN BE SWITCHED MUCH MORE RAPIDLY (UP TO 5,000,000,000 TIMES PER SECOND) & HENCE CARRY MORE INFORMATION. ONE LASER BEAM COULD EASILY REPLACE ALL THE CABLES & SATELLITES LINKING EUROPE & AMERICA. UNFORTUNATELY THE WIRE USED FOR TRANSMITTING LASER LIGHT (THIN GLASS RODS) LOSES TOO MUCH POWER OVER LONG DISTANCES TO BE COMPLETELY PRACTICAL YET.

HOW TO MAKE A HOVERCRAFT
PUNCH HOLE IN MIDDLE OF ALUMINIUM PLATE WITH NAIL. GLUE COTTON REEL OVER HOLE. TIE BALLOON TO SMALL TUBE. BLOW UP BALLOON, WEDGE TUBE IN TOP OF COTTON REEL & RELEASE, CAUSING PLATE TO HOVER AS BALLOON DEFLATES.

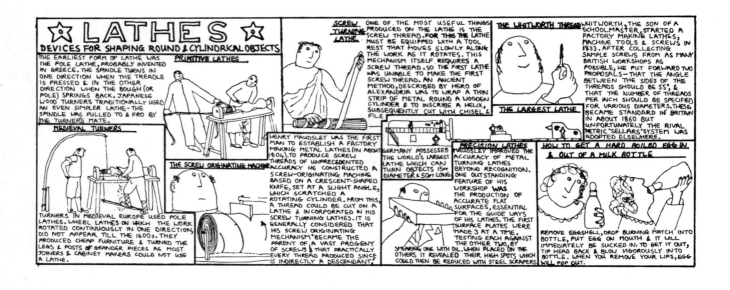

☆ LATHES ☆
DEVICES FOR SHAPING ROUND & CYLINDRICAL OBJECTS

THE EARLIEST FORM OF LATHE WAS THE POLE LATHE, PROBABLY INVENTED IN GREECE. THE SPINDLE TURNS IN ONE DIRECTION WHEN THE TREADLE IS PRESSED & IN THE OTHER DIRECTION WHEN THE BOUGH (OR POLE) SPRINGS BACK. JAPANESE WOOD TURNERS TRADITIONALLY USED AN EVEN SIMPLER LATHE—THE SPINDLE WAS PULLED TO & FRO BY THE TURNER'S MATE.

PRIMITIVE LATHES

MEDIEVAL TURNERS
TURNERS IN MEDIEVAL EUROPE USED POLE LATHES. WHEEL LATHES ON WHICH THE WORK ROTATED CONTINUOUSLY IN ONE DIRECTION, DID NOT APPEAR TILL THE 1600s. THEY PRODUCED CHEAP FURNITURE & TURNED THE LEGS & POSTS OF GRANDER PIECES AS MOST JOINERS & CABINET MAKERS COULD NOT USE A LATHE.

THE SCREW ORIGINATING MACHINE
HENRY MAUDSLEY WAS THE FIRST MAN TO ESTABLISH A FACTORY MAKING METAL LATHES (IN ABOUT 1804). TO PRODUCE SCREW THREADS OF UNPRECEDENTED ACCURACY HE CONSTRUCTED A SCREW-ORIGINATING MACHINE BASED ON A CRESCENT-SHAPED KNIFE, SET AT A SLIGHT ANGLE, WHICH SCRATCHED A ROTATING CYLINDER. FROM THIS, A THREAD COULD BE CUT ON A LATHE & INCORPORATED IN HIS SCREW TURNING LATHES. IT IS GENERALLY CONSIDERED THAT HIS SCREW ORIGINATING MECHANISM BECAME THE PARENT OF A VAST PROGENY OF SCREWS & THAT PRACTICALLY EVERY THREAD PRODUCED SINCE IS INDIRECTLY A DESCENDANT.

SCREW TURNING LATHE
ONE OF THE MOST USEFUL THINGS PRODUCED ON THE LATHE IS THE SCREW THREAD. FOR THIS THE LATHE MUST BE EQUIPPED WITH A TOOL REST THAT MOVES SLOWLY ALONG THE WORK AS IT ROTATES. THIS MECHANISM ITSELF REQUIRES A SCREW THREAD, SO THE FIRST LATHE WAS UNABLE TO MAKE THE FIRST SCREW THREAD. AN ANCIENT METHOD, DESCRIBED BY HERO OF ALEXANDRIA WAS TO WRAP A THIN STRIP OF METAL ROUND A WOODEN CYLINDER & TO INSCRIBE A HELIX, SUBSEQUENTLY CUT WITH CHISEL & FILE.

THE WHITWORTH THREAD
WHITWORTH, THE SON OF A SCHOOLMASTER, STARTED A FACTORY MAKING LATHES, MACHINE TOOLS & SCREWS IN 1833. AFTER COLLECTING SAMPLE SCREWS FROM AS MANY BRITISH WORKSHOPS AS POSSIBLE, HE PUT FORWARD TWO PROPOSALS—THAT THE ANGLE BETWEEN THE SIDES OF THE THREADS SHOULD BE 55°, & THAT THE NUMBER OF THREADS PER INCH SHOULD BE SPECIFIED FOR VARIOUS DIAMETERS. THESE BECAME STANDARD IN BRITAIN IN ABOUT 1860 BUT UNFORTUNATELY THE RIVAL METRIC 'SELLARS' SYSTEM WAS ADOPTED ELSEWHERE.

THE LARGEST LATHE
GERMANY POSSESSES THE WORLD'S LARGEST LATHE WHICH CAN TURN OBJECTS 15FT DIAMETER & 50FT LONG.

PRECISION LATHES
MAUDSLEY IMPROVED THE ACCURACY OF METAL TURNING LATHES BEYOND RECOGNITION. ONE OUTSTANDING FEATURE OF HIS WORKSHOP WAS THE PRODUCTION OF ACCURATE FLAT SURFACES, ESSENTIAL FOR THE GUIDE WAYS OF HIS LATHES. THE FIRST SURFACE PLATES WERE MADE 3 AT A TIME, TESTING EACH AGAINST THE OTHER TWO, BY SMEARING ONE WITH OIL. WHEN PLACED ON THE OTHERS IT REVEALED THEIR HIGH SPOTS WHICH COULD THEN BE REDUCED WITH STEEL SCRAPERS.

HOW TO GET A HARD BOILED EGG IN & OUT OF A MILK BOTTLE
REMOVE EGGSHELL, DROP BURNING MATCH INTO BOTTLE, PUT EGG ON MOUTH & IT WILL IMMEDIATELY BE SUCKED IN. TO GET IT OUT, TIP HEAD BACK & BLOW VIGOROUSLY INTO BOTTLE. WHEN YOU REMOVE YOUR LIPS, EGG WILL POP OUT.

☆ LAUGHTER ☆
CONVULSIVE MUSCULAR MOVEMENTS PRODUCING EXPLOSIVE SOUNDS

ELEMENTS OF LAUGHTER
1. HOOTING, BARKING NOISE
2. WIDE OPEN MOUTH
3. MOUTH CORNERS PULLED BACK
4. NOSE WRINKLED
5. EYES CLOSED
6. CREASE LINES ROUND EYES
7. TEARS
8. HEAD THROWN BACK
9. SHOULDERS RAISED
10. TRUNK ROLLED
11. BODY CLASPED
12. FOOT STAMPED

THE PSYCHOLOGIST DESMOND MORRIS HAS ISOLATED 12 ELEMENTS OF THE 'LAUGH'. THE INTENSITY OF A LAUGH CAN BE JUDGED BY HOW MANY OF THE ELEMENTS ARE ADOPTED.

CRYING & LAUGHING
THE GESTURES & EXPRESSIONS OF CRYING ARE VERY SIMILAR TO THOSE OF LAUGHING. LAUGHING IS GENERALLY THOUGHT TO HAVE EVOLVED FROM CRYING.

BABIES START CRYING AT BIRTH BUT DO NOT START LAUGHING UNTIL THEY RECOGNISE THEIR MOTHER (4-5 MONTHS). WHEN A MOTHER STARTLES A BABY (BY BOUNCING IT OR MAKING FACES) IT GIVES A RESPONSE THAT IS HALF ALARM & HALF A CONTENTED GURGLE — A LAUGH.

SMILING
WE SMILE IN SYMPATHY, IN GREETING, IN APOLOGY & OTHER SITUATIONS WHERE A LAUGH WOULD BE INAPPROPRIATE. SMILING PROBABLY ORIGINATED AS AN APPEASEMENT SIGNAL. A BABY CRIES TO ATTRACT ITS MOTHER'S ATTENTION BUT NEEDS TO SMILE TO KEEP HER NEAR.

FREUD'S THEORY
FREUD & OTHERS ARGUED THAT WE LAUGH TO RID OURSELVES OF TENSION & SEXUAL AROUSAL. THIS THEORY HAS RECENTLY BEEN TESTED BY SHOWING PEOPLE A SERIES OF PLAYBOY CARTOONS. BY FREUD'S THEORY, TENSION & AROUSAL SHOULD BE PROGRESSIVELY RELEASED & THE CARTOONS SHOULD PROVOKE LESS & LESS LAUGHTER. HOWEVER, PEOPLE IN FACT REACHED A STATE OF 'HUMOROUS AROUSAL' & WOULD THEN LAUGH AT ANYTHING.

TICKLING
TICKLISHNESS IS A FORM OF REFLEX ACTION BUT IT IS NOT KNOWN WHY TICKLING ONESELF DOES NOT WORK. VARIOUS TICKLING MACHINES HAVE RECENTLY BEEN CONSTRUCTED FOR EXPERIMENTS ON THIS SUBJECT.

HOW TO RAISE SOMEONE'S HAIR (ON STAGE)
ASSISTANTS HIDDEN OFF-STAGE HOLDING 'INVISIBLE' BLACK THREAD.

TAUT THREAD LINED UP BEHIND HEAD 'LIFTS' HAIR.

BLACK BACKGROUND

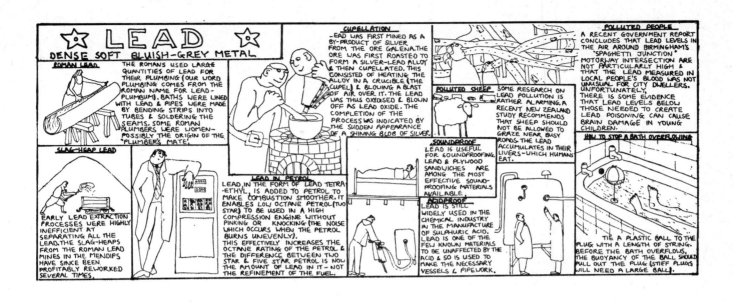

☆ LEAD ☆
DENSE SOFT BLUISH-GREY METAL

ROMAN LEAD

THE ROMANS USED LARGE QUANTITIES OF LEAD FOR THEIR PLUMBING (OUR WORD PLUMBING COMES FROM THE ROMAN NAME FOR LEAD – PLUMBUM). BATHS WERE LINED WITH LEAD & PIPES WERE MADE BY BENDING STRIPS INTO TUBES & SOLDERING THE SEAMS. SOME ROMAN PLUMBERS WERE WOMEN – POSSIBLY THE ORIGIN OF THE 'PLUMBER'S MATE'.

SLAG-HEAP LEAD

EARLY LEAD EXTRACTION PROCESSES WERE HIGHLY INEFFICIENT AT SEPARATING ALL THE LEAD. THE SLAG-HEAPS FROM THE ROMAN LEAD MINES IN THE MENDIPS HAVE SINCE BEEN PROFITABLY REWORKED SEVERAL TIMES.

CUPELLATION

LEAD WAS FIRST MINED AS A BY-PRODUCT OF SILVER FROM THE ORE GALENA. THE ORE WAS FIRST ROASTED TO FORM A SILVER-LEAD ALLOY & THEN CUPELLATED. THIS CONSISTED OF HEATING THE ALLOY IN A CRUCIBLE (THE CUPEL) & BLOWING A BLAST OF AIR OVER IT. THE LEAD WAS THUS OXIDISED & BLOWN OFF AS LEAD OXIDE. THE COMPLETION OF THE PROCESS WAS INDICATED BY THE SUDDEN APPEARANCE OF A SHINING BLOB OF SILVER.

LEAD IN PETROL

LEAD, IN THE FORM OF LEAD TETRA-ETHYL, IS ADDED TO PETROL TO MAKE COMBUSTION SMOOTHER. IT ENABLES LOW OCTANE PETROL (TWO STAR) TO BE USED IN A HIGH COMPRESSION ENGINE WITHOUT PINKING OR KNOCKING (THE NOISE WHICH OCCURS WHEN THE PETROL BURNS UNEVENLY). THIS EFFECTIVELY INCREASES THE OCTANE RATING OF THE PETROL & THE DIFFERENCE BETWEEN TWO STAR & FIVE STAR PETROL IS NOW THE AMOUNT OF LEAD IN IT – NOT THE REFINEMENT OF THE FUEL.

POLLUTED SHEEP

SOME RESEARCH ON LEAD POLLUTION IS RATHER ALARMING. A RECENT NEW ZEALAND STUDY RECOMMENDS THAT SHEEP SHOULD NOT BE ALLOWED TO GRAZE NEAR BUSY ROADS. THE LEAD ACCUMULATES IN THEIR LIVERS – WHICH HUMANS EAT.

SOUNDPROOF

LEAD IS USEFUL FOR SOUNDPROOFING. LEAD & PLYWOOD SANDWICHES ARE AMONG THE MOST EFFECTIVE SOUND-PROOFING MATERIALS AVAILABLE.

ACIDPROOF

LEAD IS STILL WIDELY USED IN THE CHEMICAL INDUSTRY IN THE MANUFACTURE OF SULPHURIC ACID. LEAD IS ONE OF THE FEW KNOWN MATERIALS TO BE UNAFFECTED BY THE ACID & SO IS USED TO MAKE THE NECESSARY VESSELS & PIPEWORK.

POLLUTED PEOPLE

A RECENT GOVERNMENT REPORT CONCLUDES THAT LEAD LEVELS IN THE AIR AROUND BIRMINGHAM'S 'SPAGHETTI JUNCTION' MOTORWAY INTERSECTION ARE NOT PARTICULARLY HIGH & THAT THE LEAD MEASURED IN LOCAL PEOPLE'S BLOOD WAS NOT UNUSUAL FOR CITY DWELLERS. UNFORTUNATELY, THERE IS SOME EVIDENCE THAT LEAD LEVELS BELOW THOSE NEEDED TO CREATE LEAD POISONING CAN CAUSE BRAIN DAMAGE IN YOUNG CHILDREN.

HOW TO STOP A BATH OVERFLOWING

TIE A PLASTIC BALL TO THE PLUG WITH A LENGTH OF STRING. BEFORE THE BATH OVERFLOWS, THE BUOYANCY OF THE BALL SHOULD PULL OUT THE PLUG (STIFF PLUGS WILL NEED A LARGE BALL).

☆ LEATHER ☆
PRESERVED ANIMAL SKIN

SKINNING

LEATHER IS MADE FROM ANIMAL SKINS. THE OUTER HAIRY LAYER & THE INNER FATTY LAYER ARE SCRAPED OFF. THE TOUGH REMAINING 'LEATHER' MUST THEN BE PREVENTED FROM ROTTING. SALTING, SMOKING, CHEWING, TREATING WITH URINE & ANIMAL DUNG HAVE ALL BEEN PRACTISED. HOWEVER, THE MOST EFFECTIVE TECHNIQUE HAS PROVED TO BE TANNING (SEE BELOW LEFT).

TANNING

TANNING IS TRADITIONALLY PERFORMED BY SOAKING LEATHER IN VATS OF TANNIC ACID (MADE FROM ACORNS & VARIOUS VEGETABLES & BARKS) FOR SEVERAL WEEKS. IN THE 1860s, CHROME TANNING (USING CHROMIUM SALTS INSTEAD OF TANNIC ACID) WAS INTRODUCED, WHICH TAKES ONLY A FEW DAYS. AFTER THIS PROCESS THE LEATHER IS WASHED & DRIED. TO KEEP IT FLAT WHILE DRYING, IT IS PASTED TO SHEETS OF PLATE GLASS.

ESKIMOS

UNTIL RECENTLY, ESKIMOS TREATED LEATHER BY CHEWING THE SKINS. THIS HAD A SOFTENING EFFECT & SQUEEZED OUT SOME OF THE FAT (THE TEETH OF ESKIMO WOMEN WERE OFTEN WORN TO THE GUMS BY THIS PROCESS). THE SKINS WERE THEN SMOKED (BY HANGING THEM OVER A SMOKY FIRE FOR A FEW WEEKS).

TANNING WAS ONE OF THE MOST UNPLEASANT MEDIEVAL INDUSTRIES. IT WAS VERY HARD WORK, NECESSITATING CONTINUOUS BEATING & SCRUBBING OF THE SKINS, & CREATING VILE SMELLS & DISEASES AMONG THE WORKERS.

POROMERICS

SYNTHETIC LEATHERS, CALLED POROMERICS, WERE INTRODUCED IN THE 1960s, IN AN ATTEMPT TO REPRODUCE THE POROUS QUALITIES OF NATURAL LEATHER. SOME ARE 'FELTS' OF COMPRESSED NON-WOVEN PLASTIC FIBRES & OTHERS ARE PLASTIC FOAMS. ALL HAVE A THIN LAYER OF POLYTHENE FILM ON ONE SIDE TO GIVE THEM A SHINY 'LEATHER' FINISH.

PIPES

THE FIRST FIRE ENGINES, INTRODUCED AFTER THE FIRE OF LONDON, HAD LEATHER HOSES.

TANNERIES

CHAMOIS

CHAMOIS LEATHER IS PRESERVED BY RUBBING & BEATING OIL INTO THE SKIN (TANNING ALWAYS REDUCES THE SOFTNESS & PLIABILITY OF A SKIN). THE OIL GRADUALLY PUSHES OUT ALL THE NATURAL MOISTURE IN THE SKIN, WHICH MUST FINALLY BE HEATED TO EVAPORATE EXCESS OIL.

HOW TO PLAY SHOVEL BALL

CUT 2 SHOE BOXES INTO SHOVELS AS ABOVE & GLUE OLD RULERS UNDERNEATH WITH EXTRA CARD REINFORCEMENTS BELOW. PLAY AS TENNIS USING SHOVELS AS RACKETS.

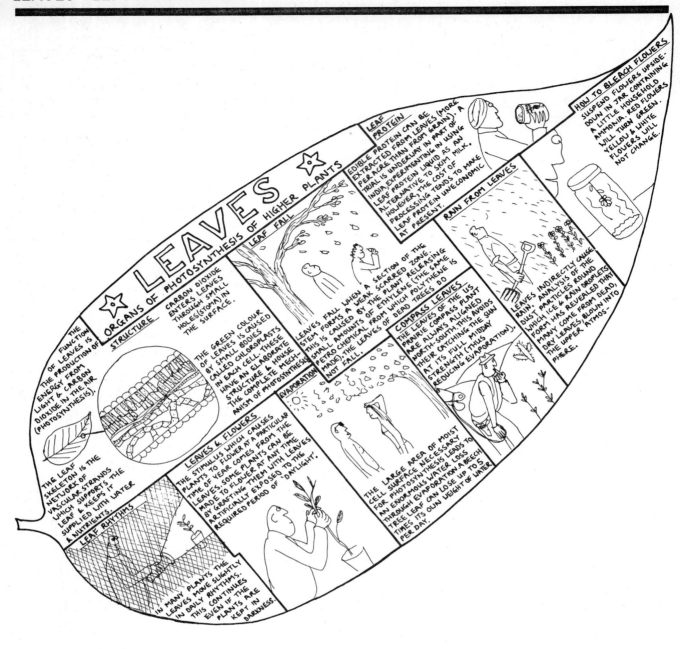

☆ LEAVES ☆
ORGANS OF PHOTOSYNTHESIS OF HIGHER PLANTS

STRUCTURE

THE FUNCTION OF LEAVES IS THE PRODUCTION OF ENERGY FROM LIGHT & CARBON DIOXIDE IN THE AIR (PHOTOSYNTHESIS).

THE LEAF IS THE SKELETON OF THE NETWORK OF VASCULAR STRANDS WHICH SUPPORTS THE LEAF & KEEPS IT SUPPLIED WITH WATER & NUTRIENTS.

CARBON DIOXIDE ENTERS LEAVES THROUGH SMALL HOLES (STOMA) IN THE SURFACE.

THE GREEN COLOUR OF LEAVES IS CAUSED BY SMALL BODIES CALLED CHLOROPLASTS IN EACH CELL. THESE HAVE AN ELABORATE STRUCTURE & HOUSE THE COMPLETE MECHANISM OF PHOTOSYNTHESIS.

LEAF FALL

LEAVES FALL WHEN A SECTION OF THE STEM FORMS A WEAK SCARRED ZONE. THIS IS CAUSED BY THE PLANT RELEASING SMALL AMOUNTS OF ETHYLENE (THE SAME PETRO CHEMICAL FROM WHICH POLYTHENE IS MADE). THE LEAVES OF DEAD TREES DO NOT FALL.

LEAVES & FLOWERS

THE STIMULUS WHICH CAUSES PLANTS TO FLOWER AT A PARTICULAR TIME OF YEAR COMES FROM THE LEAVES. SOME PLANTS CAN BE MADE TO FLOWER AT ANY TIME BY GRAFTING THEM WITH LEAVES ARTIFICIALLY EXPOSED TO THE REQUIRED PERIOD OF "DAYLIGHT".

LEAF RHYTHMS

IN MANY PLANTS THE LEAVES MOVE SLIGHTLY IN DAILY RHYTHMS. THIS CONTINUES EVEN IF THE PLANTS ARE KEPT IN DARKNESS.

EVAPORATION

THE LARGE AREA OF MOIST CELL SURFACE NECESSARY FOR PHOTOSYNTHESIS LEADS TO AN ENORMOUS WATER LOSS THROUGH EVAPORATION. A BEECH TREE LEAF CAN LOSE UP TO 5 TIMES ITS OWN WEIGHT OF WATER PER DAY.

COMPASS LEAVES

THE LEAVES OF THE US PRAIRIE COMPASS PLANT ARE ALWAYS ALIGNED NORTH-SOUTH. THIS AVOIDS THEIR CATCHING THE SUN AT ITS FULL MIDDAY STRENGTH (THUS REDUCING EVAPORATION).

LEAF PROTEIN

EDIBLE PROTEIN CAN BE EXTRACTED FROM LEAVES (MORE PER ACRE THAN FROM GRAIN). A TRIAL IS UNDERWAY IN PART OF INDIA EXPERIMENTING IN USING LEAF PROTEIN LIQUID AS AN ALTERNATIVE TO SKIM MILK. HOWEVER THE COST OF PROCESSING TENDS TO MAKE LEAF PROTEIN UNECONOMIC AT PRESENT.

RAIN FROM LEAVES

LEAVES INDIRECTLY CAUSE RAIN. ANALYSIS OF THE DUST PARTICLES FOUND IN ICE & RAIN DROPLETS WHICH FORM HAS REVEALED THAT MANY COME FROM DEAD, DRY LEAVES BLOWN INTO THE UPPER ATMOSPHERE.

HOW TO BLEACH FLOWERS

SUSPEND FLOWERS UPSIDE-DOWN IN JAR CONTAINING A LITTLE HOUSEHOLD AMMONIA. RED FLOWERS WILL TURN GREEN. YELLOW & WHITE FLOWERS WILL NOT CHANGE.

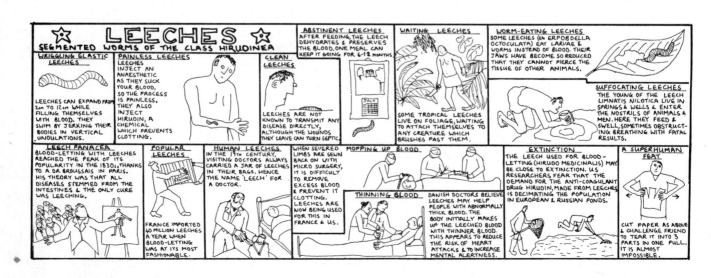

☆ LEECHES ☆
SEGMENTED WORMS OF THE CLASS HIRUDINEA

WRIGGLING ELASTIC LEECHES

LEECHES CAN EXPAND FROM 2cm TO 12cm WHILE FILLING THEMSELVES WITH BLOOD. THEY SWIM BY JERKING THEIR BODIES IN VERTICAL UNDULATIONS.

PAINLESS LEECHES

LEECHES INJECT AN ANAESTHETIC AS THEY SUCK YOUR BLOOD, SO THE PROCESS IS PAINLESS. THEY ALSO INJECT HIRUDIN, A CHEMICAL WHICH PREVENTS CLOTTING.

CLEAN LEECHES

LEECHES ARE NOT KNOWN TO TRANSMIT ANY DISEASE DIRECTLY, ALTHOUGH THE WOUNDS THEY LEAVE CAN TURN SEPTIC.

ABSTINENT LEECHES

AFTER FEEDING, THE LEECH DEHYDRATES & PRESERVES THE BLOOD. ONE MEAL CAN KEEP IT GOING FOR 6-12 MONTHS.

WAITING LEECHES

SOME TROPICAL LEECHES LIVE ON FOLIAGE, WAITING TO ATTACH THEMSELVES TO ANY CREATURE WHICH BRUSHES PAST THEM.

WORM-EATING LEECHES

SOME LEECHES (e.g. ERPOBDELLA OCTOCULATA) EAT LARVAE & WORMS INSTEAD OF BLOOD. THEIR JAWS HAVE BECOME SO REDUCED THAT THEY CANNOT PIERCE THE TISSUE OF OTHER ANIMALS.

SUFFOCATING LEECHES

THE YOUNG OF THE LEECH LIMNATIS NILOTICA LIVE IN SPRINGS & WELLS & ENTER THE NOSTRILS OF ANIMALS & MEN. HERE THEY FEED & SWELL, SOMETIMES OBSTRUCTING BREATHING WITH FATAL RESULTS.

LEECH PANACEA

BLOOD-LETTING WITH LEECHES REACHED THE PEAK OF ITS POPULARITY IN THE 1830s, THANKS TO A DR BROUSSAIS IN PARIS. HIS THEORY WAS THAT ALL DISEASES STEMMED FROM THE INTESTINES & THE ONLY CURE WAS LEECHING.

POPULAR LEECHES

FRANCE IMPORTED 40 MILLION LEECHES A YEAR WHEN BLOOD-LETTING WAS AT ITS MOST FASHIONABLE.

HUMAN LEECHES

IN THE 19TH CENTURY, VISITING DOCTORS ALWAYS CARRIED A JAR OF LEECHES IN THEIR BAGS. HENCE THE NAME 'LEECH' FOR A DOCTOR.

WHEN SEVERED LIMBS ARE SEWN BACK ON WITH MICRO SURGERY, IT IS DIFFICULT TO REMOVE EXCESS BLOOD & PREVENT IT CLOTTING. LEECHES ARE NOW BEING USED FOR THIS IN FRANCE & US.

MOPPING UP BLOOD

THINNING BLOOD

DANISH DOCTORS BELIEVE LEECHES MAY HELP PEOPLE WITH ABNORMALLY THICK BLOOD. THE BODY INITIALLY MAKES UP THE LEECHED BLOOD WITH THINNER BLOOD. THIS APPEARS TO REDUCE THE RISK OF HEART ATTACKS & TO INCREASE MENTAL ALERTNESS.

EXTINCTION

THE LEECH USED FOR BLOOD-LETTING (HIRUDO MEDICINALIS) MAY BE CLOSE TO EXTINCTION. US RESEARCHERS FEAR THAT THE DEMAND FOR THE ANTI-COAGULANT DRUG HIRUDIN, MADE FROM LEECHES IS DECIMATING THE POPULATION IN EUROPEAN & RUSSIAN PONDS.

A SUPERHUMAN FEAT

CUT PAPER AS ABOVE & CHALLENGE FRIEND TO TEAR IT INTO 3 PARTS IN ONE PULL. IT IS ALMOST IMPOSSIBLE.

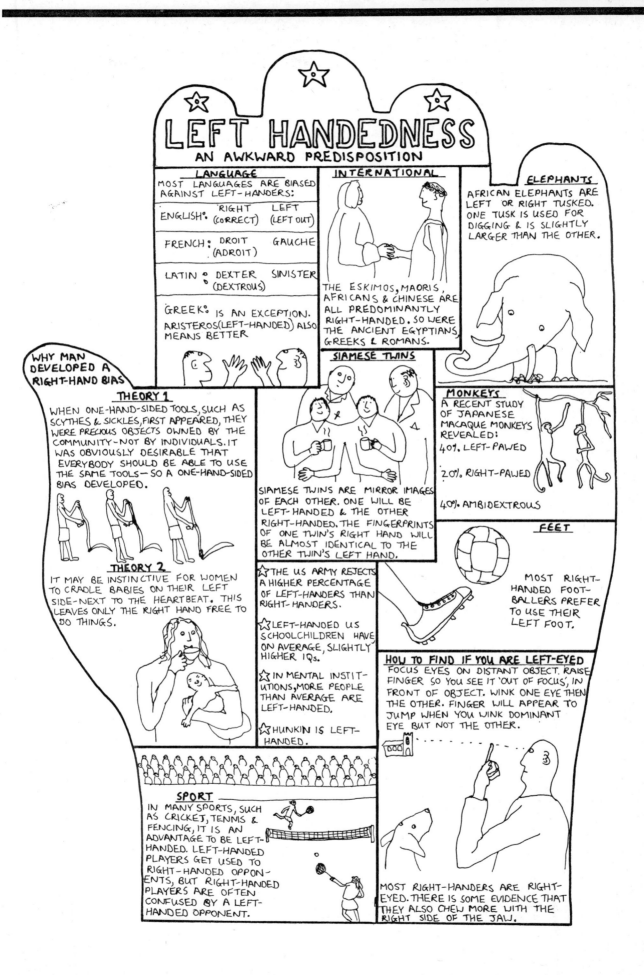

LEFT HANDEDNESS
AN AWKWARD PREDISPOSITION

LANGUAGE
MOST LANGUAGES ARE BIASED AGAINST LEFT-HANDERS:

ENGLISH: "RIGHT (CORRECT) LEFT (LEFT OUT)

FRENCH: DROIT (ADROIT) GAUCHE

LATIN: DEXTER (DEXTROUS) SINISTER

GREEK: IS AN EXCEPTION. ARISTEROS (LEFT-HANDED) ALSO MEANS BETTER

INTERNATIONAL
THE ESKIMOS, MAORIS, AFRICANS & CHINESE ARE ALL PREDOMINANTLY RIGHT-HANDED. SO WERE THE ANCIENT EGYPTIANS, GREEKS & ROMANS.

ELEPHANTS
AFRICAN ELEPHANTS ARE LEFT OR RIGHT TUSKED. ONE TUSK IS USED FOR DIGGING & IS SLIGHTLY LARGER THAN THE OTHER.

WHY MAN DEVELOPED A RIGHT-HAND BIAS

THEORY 1
WHEN ONE-HAND-SIDED TOOLS, SUCH AS SCYTHES & SICKLES, FIRST APPEARED, THEY WERE PRECIOUS OBJECTS OWNED BY THE COMMUNITY – NOT BY INDIVIDUALS. IT WAS OBVIOUSLY DESIRABLE THAT EVERYBODY SHOULD BE ABLE TO USE THE SAME TOOLS – SO A ONE-HAND-SIDED BIAS DEVELOPED.

THEORY 2
IT MAY BE INSTINCTIVE FOR WOMEN TO CRADLE BABIES ON THEIR LEFT SIDE – NEXT TO THE HEARTBEAT. THIS LEAVES ONLY THE RIGHT HAND FREE TO DO THINGS.

SIAMESE TWINS
SIAMESE TWINS ARE MIRROR IMAGES OF EACH OTHER. ONE WILL BE LEFT-HANDED & THE OTHER RIGHT-HANDED. THE FINGERPRINTS OF ONE TWIN'S RIGHT HAND WILL BE ALMOST IDENTICAL TO THE OTHER TWIN'S LEFT HAND.

☆ THE US ARMY REJECTS A HIGHER PERCENTAGE OF LEFT-HANDERS THAN RIGHT-HANDERS.

☆ LEFT-HANDED US SCHOOLCHILDREN HAVE ON AVERAGE, SLIGHTLY HIGHER IQs.

☆ IN MENTAL INSTITUTIONS, MORE PEOPLE THAN AVERAGE ARE LEFT-HANDED.

☆ HUNKIN IS LEFT-HANDED.

MONKEYS
A RECENT STUDY OF JAPANESE MACAQUE MONKEYS REVEALED:

40% LEFT-PAWED

20% RIGHT-PAWED

40% AMBIDEXTROUS

FEET
MOST RIGHT-HANDED FOOTBALLERS PREFER TO USE THEIR LEFT FOOT.

HOW TO FIND IF YOU ARE LEFT-EYED
FOCUS EYES ON DISTANT OBJECT. RAISE FINGER SO YOU SEE IT 'OUT OF FOCUS', IN FRONT OF OBJECT. WINK ONE EYE THEN THE OTHER. FINGER WILL APPEAR TO JUMP WHEN YOU WINK DOMINANT EYE BUT NOT THE OTHER.

MOST RIGHT-HANDERS ARE RIGHT-EYED. THERE IS SOME EVIDENCE THAT THEY ALSO CHEW MORE WITH THE RIGHT SIDE OF THE JAW.

SPORT
IN MANY SPORTS, SUCH AS CRICKET, TENNIS & FENCING, IT IS AN ADVANTAGE TO BE LEFT-HANDED. LEFT-HANDED PLAYERS GET USED TO RIGHT-HANDED OPPONENTS, BUT RIGHT-HANDED PLAYERS ARE OFTEN CONFUSED BY A LEFT-HANDED OPPONENT.

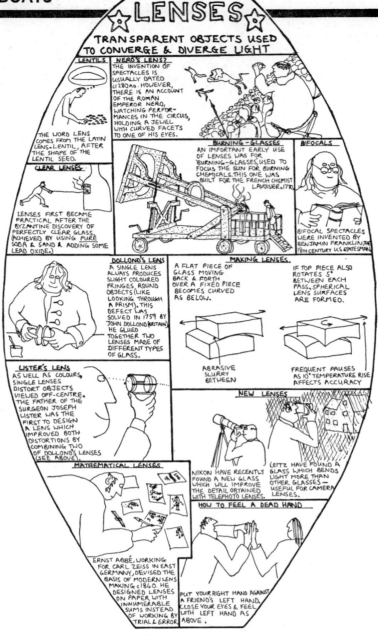

☆ LENSES ☆
TRANSPARENT OBJECTS USED TO CONVERGE & DIVERGE LIGHT

LENTILS
THE WORD LENS COMES FROM THE LATIN LENS-LENTIL, AFTER THE SHAPE OF THE LENTIL SEED.

NERO'S LENS?
THE INVENTION OF SPECTACLES IS USUALLY DATED c1280AD. HOWEVER, THERE IS AN ACCOUNT OF THE ROMAN EMPEROR NERO, WATCHING PERFORMANCES IN THE CIRCUS, HOLDING A JEWEL WITH CURVED FACETS TO ONE OF HIS EYES.

CLEAR LENSES
LENSES FIRST BECAME PRACTICAL AFTER THE BYZANTINE DISCOVERY OF PERFECTLY CLEAR GLASS (ACHIEVED BY USING PURE SODA & SAND & ADDING SOME LEAD OXIDE.)

BURNING-GLASSES
AN IMPORTANT EARLY USE OF LENSES WAS FOR 'BURNING-GLASSES' USED TO FOCUS THE SUN FOR BURNING CHEMICALS. THIS ONE WAS BUILT FOR THE FRENCH CHEMIST LAVOISIER, 1772.

BIFOCALS
BIFOCAL SPECTACLES WERE INVENTED BY BENJAMIN FRANKLIN, THE 18TH CENTURY US STATESMAN

DOLLOND'S LENS
A SINGLE LENS ALWAYS PRODUCES SLIGHT COLOURED FRINGES ROUND OBJECTS (LIKE LOOKING THROUGH A PRISM). THIS DEFECT WAS SOLVED IN 1759 BY JOHN DOLLOND (BRITAIN) HE GLUED TOGETHER TWO LENSES MADE OF DIFFERENT TYPES OF GLASS.

MAKING LENSES
A FLAT PIECE OF GLASS MOVING BACK & FORTH OVER A FIXED PIECE BECOMES CURVED AS BELOW.

IF TOP PIECE ALSO ROTATES 5° BETWEEN EACH PASS, SPHERICAL LENS SURFACES ARE FORMED.

ABRASIVE SLURRY BETWEEN

FREQUENT PAUSES AS 10° TEMPERATURE RISE AFFECTS ACCURACY

LISTER'S LENS
AS WELL AS COLOURS, SINGLE LENSES DISTORT OBJECTS VIEWED OFF-CENTRE. THE FATHER OF THE SURGEON JOSEPH LISTER WAS THE FIRST TO DESIGN A LENS WHICH IMPROVED BOTH DISTORTIONS BY COMBINING TWO OF DOLLOND'S LENSES (SEE ABOVE).

NEW LENSES
NIKON HAVE RECENTLY FOUND A NEW GLASS WHICH WILL IMPROVE THE DETAIL OBTAINED WITH TELEPHOTO LENSES.

LEITZ HAVE FOUND A GLASS WHICH BENDS LIGHT MORE THAN OTHER GLASSES — USEFUL FOR CAMERA LENSES.

MATHEMATICAL LENSES
ERNST ABBÉ, WORKING FOR CARL ZEISS IN EAST GERMANY, DEVISED THE BASIS OF MODERN LENS MAKING c1840. HE DESIGNED LENSES ON PAPER WITH INNUMERABLE SUMS INSTEAD OF WORKING BY TRIAL & ERROR.

HOW TO FEEL A DEAD HAND
PUT YOUR RIGHT HAND AGAINST A FRIEND'S LEFT HAND. CLOSE YOUR EYES & FEEL WITH LEFT HAND AS ABOVE.

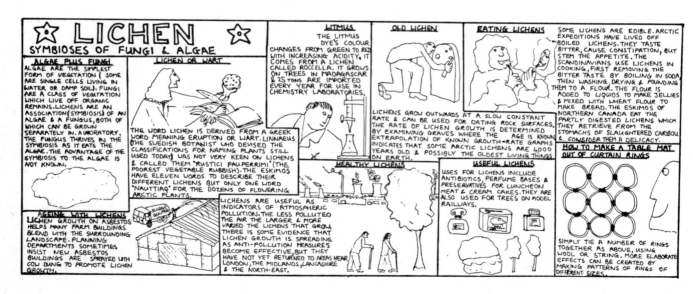

☆ LICHEN ☆
SYMBIOSES OF FUNGI & ALGAE

ALGAE PLUS FUNGI
ALGAE ARE THE SIMPLEST FORM OF VEGETATION (SOME ARE SINGLE CELLS LIVING IN WATER OR DAMP SOIL). FUNGI ARE A CLASS OF VEGETATION WHICH LIVE OFF ORGANIC REMAINS. LICHENS ARE AN ASSOCIATION (SYMBIOSIS) OF AN ALGAE & A FUNGUS, BOTH OF WHICH CAN BE GROWN SEPARATELY IN A LABORATORY. THE FUNGUS THRIVES IN THE SYMBIOSIS AS IT EATS THE ALGAE. THE ADVANTAGE OF THE SYMBIOSIS TO THE ALGAE IS NOT KNOWN.

AGEING WITH LICHENS
LICHEN GROWTH ON ASBESTOS HELPS MANY FARM BUILDINGS BLEND WITH THE SURROUNDING LANDSCAPE. PLANNING DEPARTMENTS SOMETIMES INSIST NEW ASBESTOS BUILDINGS ARE SPRAYED WITH COW DUNG TO PROMOTE LICHEN GROWTH.

LICHEN OR WART
THE WORD LICHEN IS DERIVED FROM A GREEK WORD MEANING ERUPTION OR WART. LINNAEUS (THE SWEDISH BOTANIST WHO DEVISED THE CLASSIFICATIONS FOR NAMING PLANTS STILL USED TODAY) WAS NOT VERY KEEN ON LICHENS & CALLED THEM "RUSTICI PAUPERRIMI" (THE POOREST VEGETABLE RUBBISH). THE ESKIMOS HAVE ELEVEN WORDS TO DESCRIBE THEIR DIFFERENT LICHENS BUT ONLY ONE WORD "NAUTTIAQ" FOR THE DOZENS OF FLOWERING ARCTIC PLANTS.

HEALTHY LICHENS
LICHENS ARE USEFUL AS INDICATORS OF ATMOSPHERIC POLLUTION. THE LESS POLLUTED THE AIR THE LARGER & MORE VARIED THE LICHENS THAT GROW. THERE IS SOME EVIDENCE THAT LICHEN GROWTH IS SPREADING AS ANTI-POLLUTION MEASURES BECOME EFFECTIVE, BUT THEY HAVE NOT YET RETURNED TO AREAS NEAR LONDON, THE MIDLANDS, LANCASHIRE & THE NORTH-EAST.

LITMUS
THE LITMUS DYE'S COLOUR CHANGES FROM GREEN TO RED WITH INCREASING ACIDITY. IT COMES FROM A LICHEN CALLED ROCCELLA. IT GROWS ON TREES IN MADAGASCAR & 25 TONS ARE IMPORTED EVERY YEAR FOR USE IN CHEMISTRY LABORATORIES.

OLD LICHEN
LICHENS GROW OUTWARDS AT A SLOW CONSTANT RATE & CAN BE USED FOR DATING ROCK SURFACES. THE RATE OF LICHEN GROWTH IS DETERMINED BY EXAMINING GRAVES WHERE THE AGE IS KNOWN. EXTRAPOLATION OF KNOWN GROWTH-RATE GRAPHS INDICATES THAT SOME ARCTIC LICHENS ARE 4000 YEARS OLD & POSSIBLY THE OLDEST LIVING THINGS ON EARTH.

USEFUL LICHENS
USES FOR LICHENS INCLUDE ANTIBIOTICS, PERFUME BASES & PRESERVATIVES FOR LUNCHEON MEAT & CREAM CAKES. THEY ARE ALSO USED FOR TREES ON MODEL RAILWAYS.

EATING LICHENS
SOME LICHENS ARE EDIBLE. ARCTIC EXPEDITIONS HAVE LIVED OFF BOILED LICHENS. THEY TASTE BITTER, CAUSE CONSTIPATION, BUT STEM THE APPETITE. THE SCANDINAVIANS USE LICHENS IN COOKING, FIRST REMOVING THE BITTER TASTE BY BOILING IN SODA, THEN WASHING, DRYING & POUNDING THEM TO A FLOUR. THE FLOUR IS ADDED TO LIQUIDS TO MAKE JELLIES & MIXED WITH WHEAT FLOUR TO MAKE BREAD. THE ESKIMOS OF NORTHERN CANADA EAT THE PARTLY DIGESTED LICHENS WHICH THEY RETRIEVE FROM THE STOMACHS OF SLAUGHTERED CARIBOU & CONSIDER THEM A DELICACY.

HOW TO MAKE A TABLE MAT OUT OF CURTAIN RINGS
SIMPLY TIE A NUMBER OF RINGS TOGETHER AS ABOVE, USING WOOL OR STRING. MORE ELABORATE EFFECTS CAN BE CREATED BY MAKING PATTERNS OF RINGS OF DIFFERENT SIZES.

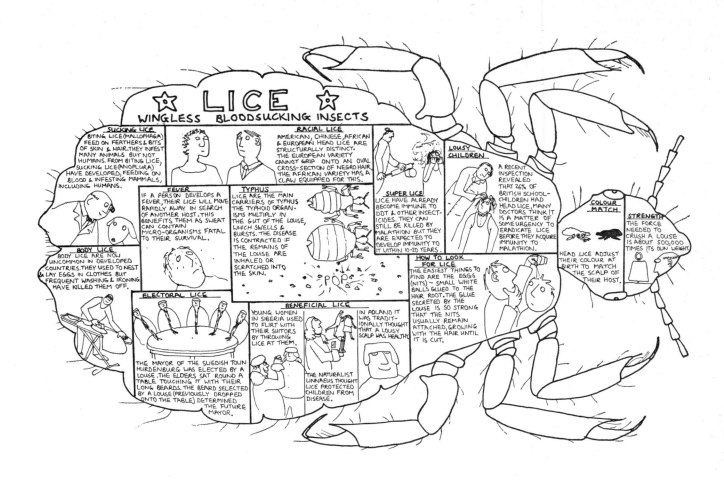

☆ LICE ☆
WINGLESS BLOODSUCKING INSECTS

SUCKING LICE — Biting lice (Mallophaga) feed on feathers & bits of skin & hair. They infest many animals but not humans. From biting lice, sucking lice (Anoplura) have developed, feeding on blood & infesting mammals, including humans.

RACIAL LICE — American, Chinese, African & European head lice are structurally distinct. The European variety cannot grip onto an oval cross-section of negro hair. The African variety has a claw equipped for this.

LOUSY CHILDREN — A recent inspection revealed that 26% of British school-children had head lice. Many doctors think it is a matter of some urgency to eradicate lice before they acquire immunity to malathion.

COLOUR MATCH — Head lice adjust their colour at birth to match the scalp of their host.

STRENGTH — The force needed to crush a louse is about 500,000 times its own weight.

FEVER — If a person develops a fever, their lice will move rapidly away in search of another host. This benefits them as sweat can contain micro-organisms fatal to their survival.

TYPHUS — Lice are the main carriers of typhus. The typhoid organisms multiply in the gut of the louse, which swells & bursts. The disease is contracted if the remains of the louse are inhaled or scratched into the skin. POP!

SUPER LICE — Lice have already become immune to DDT & other insecticides. They can still be killed by malathion but they are expected to develop immunity to it within 10-20 years.

BODY LICE — Body lice are now uncommon in developed countries. They used to nest & lay eggs in clothes but frequent washing & ironing have killed them off.

ELECTORAL LICE — The mayor of the Swedish town Hurdenburg was elected by a louse. The elders sat round a table touching it with their long beards. The beard selected by a louse (previously dropped onto the table) determined the future mayor.

BENEFICIAL LICE — Young women in Siberia used to flirt with their suitors by throwing lice at them. In Poland it was traditionally thought that a lousy scalp was healthy. The naturalist Linnaeus thought lice protected children from disease.

HOW TO LOOK FOR LICE — The easiest things to find are the eggs (nits) - small white balls glued to the hair root. The glue secreted by the louse is so strong that the nits usually remain attached, growing with the hair until it is cut.

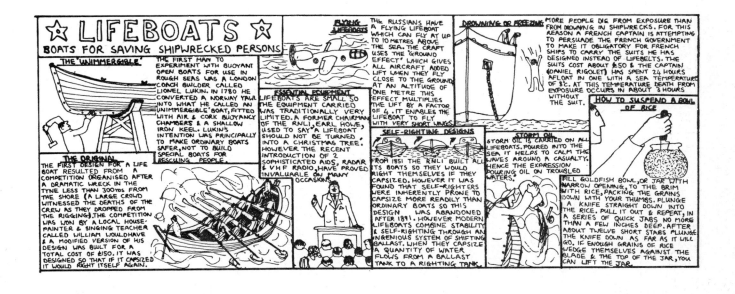

☆ LIFEBOATS ☆
BOATS FOR SAVING SHIPWRECKED PERSONS

THE 'UNIMMERGIBLE' — The first man to experiment with buoyant open boats for use in rough seas was a London coach builder called Lionel Lukin. In 1780 he converted a Norway yawl into what he called an 'unimmergible' boat, fitted with air & cork buoyancy chambers & a shallow iron keel. Lukin's intention was principally to make ordinary boats safer, not to build special boats for rescuing people.

THE ORIGINAL — The first design for a lifeboat resulted from a competition organised after a dramatic wreck in the Tyne less than 300 yds from the shore (a large crowd witnessed the deaths of the crew as they dropped from the rigging). The competition was won by a local house-painter & singing teacher called William Wouldhave & a modified version of his design was built for a total cost of £150. It was designed so that if it capsized it would right itself again.

FLYING LIFEBOATS — The Russians have a flying lifeboat which can fly at up to 10 metres above the sea. The craft uses the 'ground effect' which gives all aircraft added lift when they fly close to the ground. At an altitude of one metre this effect multiplies the lift by a factor of 4. It enables the lifeboat to fly with very short wings.

ESSENTIAL EQUIPMENT — Lifeboats are small so the equipment carried was traditionally very limited. A former chairman of the RNLI, Earl Howe, used to say 'a lifeboat should not be turned into a Christmas tree.' However the recent introduction of 2 sophisticated aids, radar & VHF radio, have proved invaluable on many occasions.

SELF-RIGHTING DESIGNS — From 1851 the RNLI built all its boats so they would right themselves if they capsized. However it was found that self-righters were inherently prone to capsize more readily than ordinary boats so this design was abandoned after 1891. However modern lifeboats combine stability & self-righting through an ingenious system of shifting ballast. When they capsize a quantity of water flows from a ballast tank to a righting tank.

DROWNING OR FREEZING — More people die from exposure than from drowning in shipwrecks. For this reason a French captain is attempting to persuade the French government to make it obligatory for French ships to carry the suits he has designed instead of lifebelts. The suits cost about £50 & the captain (Daniel Rigolet) has spent 24 hours afloat in one with a sea temperature of 8°C. At this temperature death from exposure occurs in about 3 hours without the suit.

STORM OIL — Storm oil is carried on all lifeboats. Poured into the sea it helps to calm the waves around a casualty, hence the expression 'pouring oil on troubled waters.'

HOW TO SUSPEND A BOWL OF RICE — Fill goldfish bowl, or jar with narrow opening, to the brim with rice, packing the grains down with your thumbs. Plunge a knife straight down into the rice. Pull it out & repeat, in a series of quick jabs no more than a few inches deep. After about twelve short stabs plunge the knife down as far as it will go. If enough grains of rice wedge themselves against the blade & the top of the jar, you can lift the jar.

☆LIFTS☆
DEVICES FOR EFFORTLESS ELEVATION

PRIVATE LIFTS

THE EARLIEST KNOWN LIFT WAS INSTALLED IN THE PALACE OF VERSAILLES IN 1743. IT CONNECTED THE PRIVATE APARTMENT OF LOUIS XV WITH THAT OF HIS MISTRESS MME DE CHATEAUROUX. IT RAN DOWN THE OUTSIDE OF THE BUILDING, WITH COUNTERWEIGHTS RUNNING INSIDE THE CHIMNEYS, & WAS OPERATED PULLING A ROPE.

SAFETY LIFTS

PASSENGER LIFTS BECAME POPULAR LARGELY THANKS TO THE EFFORTS OF ELISHA GRAVES OTIS. WORKING IN A NEW YORK BED FACTORY, HE DEVISED VARIOUS 'ELEVATORS' TO MOVE THE BEDS FROM FLOOR TO FLOOR. THIS LED TO HIS INVENTION OF A SAFETY MECHANISM WHICH INSTANTLY HALTED THE CAR IF THE SUSPENDING ROPE BROKE (TEETH ON THE CAR SPRANG OUT TO GRIP THE SHAFT). HE DEMONSTRATED HIS DEVICE AT A NEW YORK EXHIBITION IN 1853 BY INVITING SPECTATORS TO CUT THROUGH THE ROPE WITH AN AXE WHILE HE STOOD IN THE LIFT. HE EFFECTIVELY CONQUERED PUBLIC DISTRUST OF LIFTS. THIS EASE OF TRAVEL MADE IT FEASIBLE TO BUILD MORE THAN 10 STORIES HIGH. THE FIRST SKYSCRAPERS SOON FOLLOWED.

HIGH-SPEED LIFTS

THE WORLD'S FASTEST PASSENGER LIFT IS IN THE SEARS BUILDING, CHICAGO, TRAVELLING AT 20 MPH. MINESHAFT LIFTS GO MUCH QUICKER. THE FASTEST (IN A SOUTH AFRICAN DIAMOND MINE) REACHES 40 MPH.

THE LIMITING FACTOR IN THE SIZE & SPEED OF MOST LIFT INSTALLATIONS IS THE WEIGHT OF THE MOTORS (WHICH HAVE TO BE INSTALLED ON TOP OF THE LIFT SHAFT). IN THE LONDON POST OFFICE TOWER, THE 2 MOTORS WEIGH 8 TONS EACH.

AUTOMATIC LIFTS

AUTOMATICALLY CONTROLLED LIFTS, REQUIRING NO ATTENDANT, WERE FIRST INTRODUCED IN 1927. THE COMPLEXITY OF THE CONTROLS HAS INCREASED GREATLY SINCE THEN & A TYPICAL MODERN LIFT REQUIRES 200–300 WIRES CONNECTING EACH CAR TO THE CENTRAL CONTROLLER. MICROPROCESSOR CONTROLLERS ARE NOW BEING INTRODUCED, WHICH REQUIRE ONLY 10 WIRES TO EACH CAR & SAVE SEVERAL THOUSAND POUNDS PER LIFT.

MODERN LIFTS

SAFETY DEVICES ON MODERN LIFTS INCLUDE:
☆ A SENSOR WHICH READS THE WEIGHT OF THE CAR & STOPS IT FROM MOVING IF OVERLOADED.
☆ BRAKING ARMS WHICH ACT AUTOMATICALLY IF THE CAR EXCEEDS A CERTAIN SPEED
☆ DEVICES WHICH CUT OUT CALL BUTTONS IN CASE OF FIRE (HEAT HAS BEEN KNOWN TO ACTIVATE TOUCH-SENSITIVE CALL BUTTONS, SENDING THE LIFT TO THE FLOOR OF THE BLAZE)
☆ IN CASE ALL FAILS, A BUFFER IS STILL FITTED AT THE BOTTOM OF EVERY LIFT SHAFT.

☆LIGHTHOUSES☆
MACHINES MINISTERIAL TO THE MORE CONSPICUOUS EXHIBITION OF LIGHT

LIGHTHOUSE KEEPING

KEEPERS USED TO SPEND THEIR TIME CLEANING OIL LIGHTS & EQUIPMENT ON DUTY, DOING LOTS OF HOBBIES OFF DUTY & THEY WASHED IN TIN BATHS. THE INTRODUCTION OF CLEAN ELECTRIC LIGHTS, THE TELEVISION & HOT SHOWERS HAS MADE THEIR LIFE MUCH LESS ROMANTIC. THE INTRODUCTION OF THE DEEP-FREEZE HAS MEANT THEY DO NOT HAVE TO BAKE THEIR OWN BREAD & CAN EVEN EAT COMPLETE PRE-PREPARED MEALS.

BRIGHTEST LIGHTHOUSE OF THEM ALL

A HUGE LIGHTHOUSE WAS BUILT ON MONT AFRIQUE (IN FRANCE) TO GUIDE AIRSHIPS & PLANES ON THE PARIS-ALGIERS ROUTE. IT COULD BE SEEN UP TO 300 MILES WITH INTENSITY EQUAL TO 146 MILLION FIRST EDDYSTONE LIGHTHOUSES.

THE FIRST EDDYSTONE LIGHTHOUSE

DISADVANTAGES OF A LIGHTHOUSE

CORNISHMEN REGARDED THEIR DANGEROUS COAST AS A GIFT FROM GOD, PROVIDING OCCASIONAL WINDFALLS FROM THE WRECKS. THEY NATURALLY DID NOT ENTIRELY WELCOME THE ADVENT OF THE LIGHTHOUSE. JOHN WESLEY, SHOCKED BY THE PLUNDERING, WROTE IN 1776 "ONLY THE METHODISTS WILL HAVE NOTHING TO DO WITH IT."

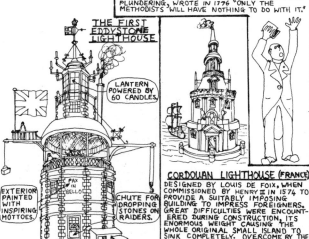

THE FIRST EDDYSTONE LIGHTHOUSE

LANTERN POWERED BY 60 CANDLES

EXTERIOR PAINTED WITH INSPIRING MOTTOES.

PAX IN BELLO

CHUTE FOR DROPPING STONES ON RAIDERS.

CORDOUAN LIGHTHOUSE (FRANCE)

DESIGNED BY LOUIS DE FOIX, WHEN COMMISSIONED BY HENRY III IN 1574 TO PROVIDE A SUITABLY IMPOSING BUILDING TO IMPRESS FOREIGNERS. GREAT DIFFICULTIES WERE ENCOUNTERED DURING CONSTRUCTION, ITS ENORMOUS WEIGHT CAUSING THE WHOLE ORIGINAL SMALL ISLAND TO SINK COMPLETELY. OVERCOME BY THE TASK, DE FOIX DISAPPEARED IN 1602 LEAVING HIS SON TO FINISH IT.

AFTER LOSING MONEY DUE TO A CARGO BEING LOST IN A WRECK ON THE EDDYSTONE ROCK, MR WINSTANLEY OBTAINED THE RIGHTS TO ERECT A LIGHTHOUSE & COLLECT DUES. DURING 1696 WHILE WORKING ON THE ROCK HE WAS CAPTURED BY FRENCH RAIDERS. RELEASED THE NEXT YEAR IN AN EXCHANGE OF PRISONERS AND CONTINUED WORK WITH FULL NAVAL PROTECTION. HIS SECOND ATTEMPT STOOD 5 WINTERS BUT ONE NIGHT IN 1703, WHILE HE WAS IN RESIDENCE, THERE WAS A HUGE STORM & IN THE MORNING THERE WAS NO TRACE OF HIM OR HIS LIGHTHOUSE.

EARLY AUTOMATIC FOG SIGNAL. THE ABSENCE OF WIND THAT USUALLY ACCOMPANIES FOG MADE IT UNRELIABLE

HALF INFLATE BALLOON, PLACE OVER MUG, THEN INFLATE FURTHER. IT IS NOW POSSIBLE TO LIFT & MOVE MUG BY BALLOON AS SHOWN.

MOVING A MUG OF WATER BY BALLOON

☆ LIGHTNING ☆
LARGE ELECTRIC SPARKS ISSUING FROM CLOUDS

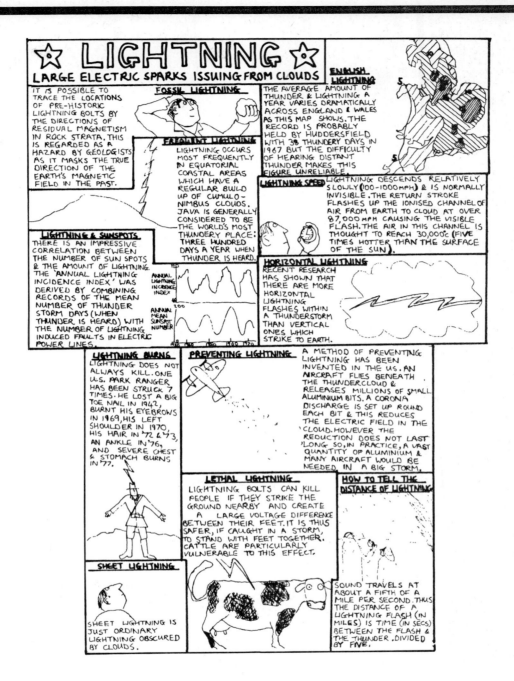

IT IS POSSIBLE TO TRACE THE LOCATIONS OF PRE-HISTORIC LIGHTNING BOLTS BY THE DIRECTIONS OF RESIDUAL MAGNETISM IN ROCK STRATA. THIS IS REGARDED AS A HAZARD BY GEOLOGISTS AS IT MASKS THE TRUE DIRECTION OF THE EARTH'S MAGNETIC FIELD IN THE PAST.

FOSSIL LIGHTNING

FREQUENT LIGHTNING
LIGHTNING OCCURS MOST FREQUENTLY IN EQUATORIAL COASTAL AREAS WHICH HAVE A REGULAR BUILD UP OF CUMULO-NIMBUS CLOUDS. JAVA IS GENERALLY CONSIDERED TO BE THE WORLD'S MOST THUNDERY PLACE: THREE HUNDRED DAYS A YEAR WHEN THUNDER IS HEARD.

LIGHTNING & SUNSPOTS
THERE IS AN IMPRESSIVE CORRELATION BETWEEN THE NUMBER OF SUN SPOTS & THE AMOUNT OF LIGHTNING. THE 'ANNUAL LIGHTNING INCIDENCE INDEX' WAS DERIVED BY COMBINING RECORDS OF THE MEAN NUMBER OF THUNDER STORM DAYS (WHEN THUNDER IS HEARD) WITH THE NUMBER OF LIGHTNING INDUCED FAULTS IN ELECTRIC POWER LINES.

ENGLISH LIGHTNING
THE AVERAGE AMOUNT OF THUNDER & LIGHTNING A YEAR VARIES DRAMATICALLY ACROSS ENGLAND & WALES AS THIS MAP SHOWS. THE RECORD IS PROBABLY HELD BY HUDDERSFIELD WITH 38 THUNDERY DAYS IN 1967 BUT THE DIFFICULTY OF HEARING DISTANT THUNDER MAKES THIS FIGURE UNRELIABLE.

LIGHTNING SPEED
LIGHTNING DESCENDS RELATIVELY SLOWLY (100-1000MPH) & IS NORMALLY INVISIBLE. THE RETURN STROKE FLASHES UP THE IONISED CHANNEL OF AIR FROM EARTH TO CLOUD AT OVER 87,000 MPH CAUSING THE VISIBLE FLASH. THE AIR IN THIS CHANNEL IS THOUGHT TO REACH 30,000°C (FIVE TIMES HOTTER THAN THE SURFACE OF THE SUN).

HORIZONTAL LIGHTNING
RECENT RESEARCH HAS SHOWN THAT THERE ARE MORE HORIZONTAL LIGHTNING FLASHES WITHIN A THUNDERSTORM THAN VERTICAL ONES WHICH STRIKE TO EARTH.

LIGHTNING BURNS
LIGHTNING DOES NOT ALWAYS KILL. ONE U.S. PARK RANGER HAS BEEN STRUCK 7 TIMES. HE LOST A BIG TOE NAIL IN 1942, BURNT HIS EYEBROWS IN 1969, HIS LEFT SHOULDER IN 1970, HIS HAIR IN '72 & '73, AN ANKLE IN '76, AND SEVERE CHEST & STOMACH BURNS IN '77.

PREVENTING LIGHTNING
A METHOD OF PREVENTING LIGHTNING HAS BEEN INVENTED IN THE US. AN AIRCRAFT FLIES BENEATH THE THUNDERCLOUD & RELEASES MILLIONS OF SMALL ALUMINIUM BITS. A CORONA DISCHARGE IS SET UP ROUND EACH BIT & THIS REDUCES THE ELECTRIC FIELD IN THE CLOUD. HOWEVER THE REDUCTION DOES NOT LAST LONG SO, IN PRACTICE, A VAST QUANTITY OF ALUMINIUM & MANY AIRCRAFT WOULD BE NEEDED IN A BIG STORM.

LETHAL LIGHTNING
LIGHTNING BOLTS CAN KILL PEOPLE IF THEY STRIKE THE GROUND NEARBY AND CREATE A LARGE VOLTAGE DIFFERENCE BETWEEN THEIR FEET. IT IS THUS SAFER, IF CAUGHT IN A STORM, TO STAND WITH FEET TOGETHER. CATTLE ARE PARTICULARLY VULNERABLE TO THIS EFFECT.

HOW TO TELL THE DISTANCE OF LIGHTNING
SOUND TRAVELS AT ABOUT A FIFTH OF A MILE PER SECOND. THUS THE DISTANCE OF A LIGHTNING FLASH (IN MILES) IS TIME (IN SECS) BETWEEN THE FLASH & THE THUNDER, DIVIDED BY FIVE.

SHEET LIGHTNING
SHEET LIGHTNING IS JUST ORDINARY LIGHTNING OBSCURED BY CLOUDS.

☆ LINEN ☆
CLOTH WOVEN FROM FLAX STALKS

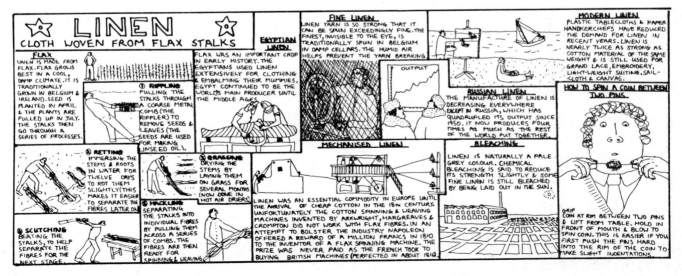

FLAX
LINEN IS MADE FROM FLAX. FLAX GROWS BEST IN A COOL, DAMP CLIMATE. IT IS TRADITIONALLY GROWN IN BELGIUM & IRELAND. SEED IS PLANTED IN APRIL & THE PLANTS ARE PULLED UP IN JULY. THE STALKS THEN GO THROUGH A SERIES OF PROCESSES.

① RIPPLING
PULLING THE STALKS THROUGH A COARSE METAL COMB (THE RIPPLER) TO REMOVE SEEDS & LEAVES (THE SEEDS ARE USED FOR MAKING LINSEED OIL).

② RETTING
IMMERSING THE STEMS & ROOTS IN WATER FOR TWELVE DAYS TO ROT THEM SLIGHTLY (THIS MAKES IT EASIER TO SEPARATE THE FIBRES LATER ON).

③ GRASSING
DRYING THE STEMS BY LAYING THEM ON GRASS FOR SEVERAL MONTHS (NOW DONE IN HOT AIR DRIERS).

④ SCUTCHING
BEATING THE STALKS, TO HELP SEPARATE THE FIBRES FOR THE NEXT STAGE.

⑤ HACKLING
SEPARATING THE STALKS INTO INDIVIDUAL FIBRES BY PULLING THEM ACROSS A SERIES OF COMBS. THE FIBRES ARE THEN READY FOR SPINNING & WEAVING.

EGYPTIAN LINEN
FLAX WAS AN IMPORTANT CROP IN EARLY HISTORY. THE EGYPTIANS USED LINEN EXTENSIVELY FOR CLOTHING & EMBALMING THEIR MUMMIES. EGYPT CONTINUED TO BE THE WORLD'S MAIN PRODUCER UNTIL THE MIDDLE AGES.

FINE LINEN
LINEN YARN IS SO STRONG THAT IT CAN BE SPUN EXCEEDINGLY FINE. THE FINEST, INVISIBLE TO THE EYE, IS TRADITIONALLY SPUN IN BELGIUM IN DAMP CELLARS. THE HUMID AIR HELPS PREVENT THE YARN BREAKING.

MECHANISED LINEN
LINEN WAS AN ESSENTIAL COMMODITY IN EUROPE UNTIL THE ARRIVAL OF CHEAP COTTON IN THE 18th CENTURY. UNFORTUNATELY THE COTTON SPINNING & WEAVING MACHINES INVENTED BY ARKWRIGHT, HARGREAVES & CROMPTON DID NOT WORK WITH FLAX FIBRES. IN AN ATTEMPT TO BOLSTER THE INDUSTRY NAPOLEON OFFERED A REWARD OF A MILLION FRANCS IN 1810 TO THE INVENTOR OF A FLAX SPINNING MACHINE. THE PRIZE WAS NEVER PAID AS THE FRENCH TOOK TO BUYING BRITISH MACHINES (PERFECTED IN ABOUT 1814).

RUSSIAN LINEN
THE MANUFACTURE OF LINEN IS DECREASING EVERYWHERE EXCEPT IN RUSSIA, WHICH HAS QUADRUPLED ITS OUTPUT SINCE 1950. IT NOW PRODUCES FOUR TIMES AS MUCH AS THE REST OF THE WORLD PUT TOGETHER.

BLEACHING
LINEN IS NATURALLY A PALE GREY COLOUR. CHEMICAL BLEACHING IS SAID TO REDUCE ITS STRENGTH SLIGHTLY & SOME FINE LINEN IS STILL BLEACHED BY BEING LAID OUT IN THE SUN.

MODERN LINEN
PLASTIC TABLECLOTHS & PAPER HANDKERCHIEFS HAVE REDUCED THE DEMAND FOR LINEN IN RECENT YEARS. LINEN IS NEARLY TWICE AS STRONG AS COTTON MATERIAL OF THE SAME WEIGHT & IS STILL USED FOR GRAND LACE, EMBROIDERY, LIGHT-WEIGHT SUITING, SAIL-CLOTH & CANVAS.

HOW TO SPIN A COIN BETWEEN TWO PINS
GRIP COIN AT RIM BETWEEN TWO PINS & LIFT FROM TABLE. HOLD IN FRONT OF MOUTH & BLOW TO SPIN COIN. THIS IS EASIER IF YOU FIRST PUSH THE PINS HARD INTO THE RIM OF THE COIN TO MAKE SLIGHT INDENTATIONS.

☆ LIONS ☆
COURAGEOUS ROARING CARNIVOROUS QUADRUPEDS

SOME PARTS OF A LION

THE FUNCTION OF THE MANE IS OBSCURE. THEORIES INCLUDE PROTECTING THE NECK & ATTRACTING FEMALES.

TONGUES FEEL LIKE COARSE SANDPAPER, USEFUL FOR SCRAPING BONES CLEAN OF FLESH.

ANOTHER MYSTERY IS THE ORIGIN & FUNCTION OF A HORNY SCALE IN THE SHAPE OF A CLAW ATTACHED TO THE END VERTEBRA OF ITS TAIL.

CLAWS ARE RETRACTABLE TO KEEP THEM SHARP. THIS IS SO IN ALL MEMBERS OF THE CAT FAMILY EXCEPT, MYSTERIOUSLY, THE CHEETAH.

THEIR SPRINGY STEALTHY WALK COMES FROM WALKING ON THEIR TOES WITH THEIR HEELS OFF THE GROUND.

LIONS IN CAPTIVITY

THE SEDENTARY LIFE LED BY CAPTIVE LIONS APPEARS TO SUIT THEIR TEMPERAMENT SINCE THEY HOLD THE RECORDS FOR BOTH THE LARGEST (825 lb) & LONGEST LIVED (29 YEARS) LIONS (THE RECORDS FOR WILD LIONS ARE ONLY 690 lb. & 12 YEARS)

MAN-EATING LIONS

LIONS ARE LESS DANGEROUS THAN IS GENERALLY BELIEVED. THE MAN-EATERS OF THE CAT FAMILY, LIONS, TIGERS & LEOPARDS ACCOUNT FOR ABOUT 1000 DEATHS EVERY YEAR (CROCODILES ACCOUNT FOR OVER 2000) & LIONS ARE THE LEAST DANGEROUS OF THE THREE. THE RECORD NUMBER OF PEOPLE KILLED BY A SINGLE MAN-EATER IS 40 FOR A LION COMPARED WITH 400 FOR A LEOPARD & 500 FOR A TIGER.

THE CAT FAMILY OWE THEIR HIGH RUNNING SPEED TO THE FLEXIBILITY OF THEIR BACK BONES & SHOULDER BLADES. THE STRIDE OF A RUNNING CHEETAH IS LONGER THAN THAT OF A GALLOPING HORSE.

HOW CATS RUN SO FAST

A FAMOUS LION

THE LION THAT ROARS AT THE START OF M.G.M. FILMS WAS CALLED LEO. HE HAD A LONG LIFE & STARRED IN MANY FILMS. TRAINED BY A CAPTAIN PHIFER HE NOT ONLY CRASHED THROUGH WALLS RIDING A MOTORCYCLE, SWAM FROM SINKING SHIP IN ROUGH SEAS BUT EVEN PARACHUTED FROM AN AEROPLANE. FOR THIS LAST FEAT HE HAD TO BE STRAPPED TO THE CAPTAIN WITH A SPECIAL RIGGING SO HE COULD CONTROL LEO'S BODY TO ENSURE THEY WOULD LAND SAFELY.

HOW TO MAKE A MOEBIUS BAND

CUT STRIP OF PAPER ABOUT 8in. LONG & TWIST IT ONCE.

NOW STICK ENDS TOGETHER FORMING A BAND. THIS MAY LOOK BORING BUT IT HAS MANY STRANGE PROPERTIES.

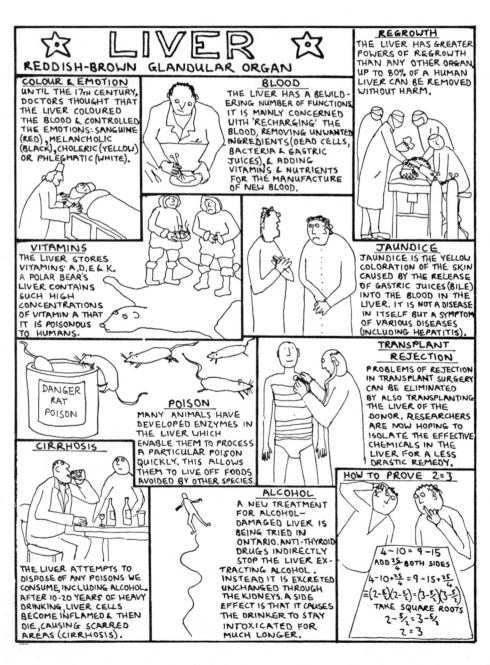

☆ LIVER ☆
REDDISH-BROWN GLANDULAR ORGAN

COLOUR & EMOTION

UNTIL THE 17TH CENTURY, DOCTORS THOUGHT THAT THE LIVER COLOURED THE BLOOD & CONTROLLED THE EMOTIONS: SANGUINE (RED), MELANCHOLIC (BLACK), CHOLERIC (YELLOW) OR PHLEGMATIC (WHITE).

BLOOD

THE LIVER HAS A BEWILDERING NUMBER OF FUNCTIONS. IT IS MAINLY CONCERNED WITH 'RECHARGING' THE BLOOD, REMOVING UNWANTED INGREDIENTS (DEAD CELLS, BACTERIA & GASTRIC JUICES), & ADDING VITAMINS & NUTRIENTS FOR THE MANUFACTURE OF NEW BLOOD.

REGROWTH

THE LIVER HAS GREATER POWERS OF REGROWTH THAN ANY OTHER ORGAN, UP TO 80% OF A HUMAN LIVER CAN BE REMOVED WITHOUT HARM.

VITAMINS

THE LIVER STORES VITAMINS A, D, E & K. A POLAR BEAR'S LIVER CONTAINS SUCH HIGH CONCENTRATIONS OF VITAMIN A THAT IT IS POISONOUS TO HUMANS.

JAUNDICE

JAUNDICE IS THE YELLOW COLORATION OF THE SKIN CAUSED BY THE RELEASE OF GASTRIC JUICES (BILE) INTO THE BLOOD IN THE LIVER. IT IS NOT A DISEASE IN ITSELF BUT A SYMPTOM OF VARIOUS DISEASES (INCLUDING HEPATITIS).

POISON

MANY ANIMALS HAVE DEVELOPED ENZYMES IN THE LIVER WHICH ENABLE THEM TO PROCESS A PARTICULAR POISON QUICKLY. THIS ALLOWS THEM TO LIVE OFF FOODS AVOIDED BY OTHER SPECIES.

DANGER RAT POISON

TRANSPLANT REJECTION

PROBLEMS OF REJECTION IN TRANSPLANT SURGERY CAN BE ELIMINATED BY ALSO TRANSPLANTING THE LIVER OF THE DONOR. RESEARCHERS ARE NOW HOPING TO ISOLATE THE EFFECTIVE CHEMICALS IN THE LIVER FOR A LESS DRASTIC REMEDY.

CIRRHOSIS

THE LIVER ATTEMPTS TO DISPOSE OF ANY POISONS WE CONSUME, INCLUDING ALCOHOL. AFTER 10-20 YEARS OF HEAVY DRINKING LIVER CELLS BECOME INFLAMED & THEN DIE, CAUSING SCARRED AREAS (CIRRHOSIS).

ALCOHOL

A NEW TREATMENT FOR ALCOHOL-DAMAGED LIVER IS BEING TRIED IN ONTARIO. ANTI-THYROID DRUGS INDIRECTLY STOP THE LIVER EXTRACTING ALCOHOL. INSTEAD IT IS EXCRETED UNCHANGED THROUGH THE KIDNEYS. A SIDE EFFECT IS THAT IT CAUSES THE DRINKER TO STAY INTOXICATED FOR MUCH LONGER.

HOW TO PROVE 2 = 3

$$4 - 10 = 9 - 15$$

ADD $\frac{25}{4}$ TO BOTH SIDES

$$4 - 10 + \frac{25}{4} = 9 - 15 + \frac{25}{4}$$

$$= \left(2 - \frac{5}{2}\right)\left(2 - \frac{5}{2}\right) = \left(3 - \frac{5}{2}\right)\left(3 - \frac{5}{2}\right)$$

TAKE SQUARE ROOTS

$$2 - \frac{5}{2} = 3 - \frac{5}{2}$$

$$2 = 3$$

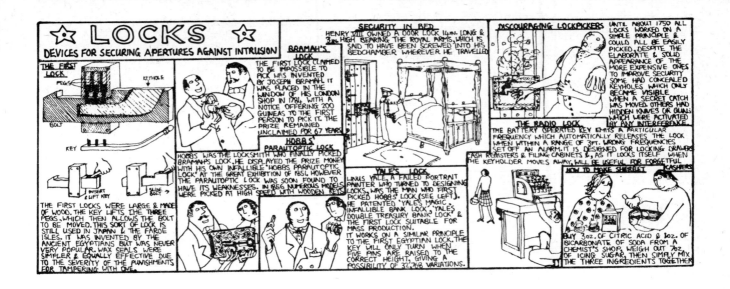

☆ LOCKS ☆
DEVICES FOR SECURING APERTURES AGAINST INTRUSION

THE FIRST LOCK

The first locks were large & made of wood. The key lifts the three pegs, which then allows the bolt to be moved. This sort of lock is still used in Japan & the Faroe Isles. It was invented by the Ancient Egyptians but was never very popular. Wax seals were simpler & equally effective due to the severity of the punishments for tampering with one.

BRAMAH'S LOCK

The first lock claimed to be impossible to pick was invented by Joseph Bramah. It was placed in the window of his London shop in 1784, with a notice offering 200 guineas to the first person to pick it. The prize remained unclaimed for 67 years.

HOBBS' PARAUTOPTIC LOCK

Hobbs was the locksmith who finally picked Bramah's lock. He displayed the prize money with his own infallible 'Hobbs parautoptic lock' at the great exhibition of 1851. However the parautoptic lock was soon found to have its weaknesses. In 1856 numerous models were picked at high speed with wooden keys.

SECURITY IN BED

Henry VIII owned a door lock 14 in. long & 3 in. high bearing the royal arms, which is said to have been screwed into his bedchamber wherever he travelled.

YALE'S LOCK

Linus Yale, a failed portrait painter who turned to designing locks, was the man who first picked Hobbs' lock (see left). He patented 'Yale's magic infallible bank lock', 'Yale's double treasury bank lock' & the first lock suitable for mass production. It works on a similar principle to the first Egyptian lock. The key will only turn when five pins are raised to the correct height, giving a possibility of 32,768 variations.

DISCOURAGING LOCKPICKERS

Until about 1750 all locks worked on a simple principle & could all be easily picked, despite the elaborate & solid appearance of the more expensive ones. To improve security some had concealed keyholes which only became visible when a secret catch was moved, others had hidden knives or guns which were activated by any interference.

THE RADIO LOCK

The battery operated key emits a particular frequency which automatically releases the lock when within a range of 3 ft. Wrong frequencies set off an alarm. It is designed for locking drawers, cash registers & filing cabinets &, as it locks itself when the keyholder moves away, will be useful for forgetful cashiers.

HOW TO MAKE SHERBET

Buy 3 oz. of citric acid & 2 oz. of bicarbonate of soda from a chemist's shop, weigh out 7 oz of icing sugar, then simply mix the three ingredients together.

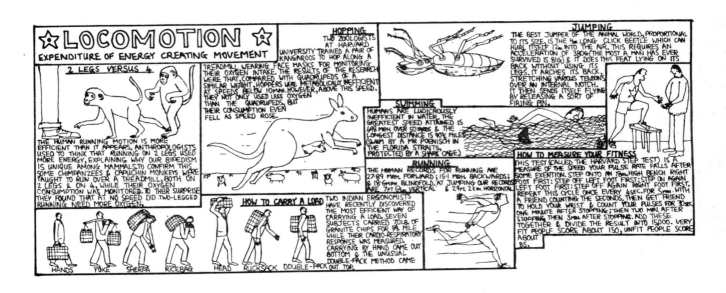

☆ LOCOMOTION ☆
EXPENDITURE OF ENERGY CREATING MOVEMENT

2 LEGS VERSUS 4

The human running motion is more efficient than it appears. Anthropologists used to think that running on 2 legs used more energy, explaining why our bipedism is unique among mammals. To confirm this some chimpanzees & capuchin monkeys were taught to run over a treadmill, both on 2 legs & on 4, while their oxygen consumption was monitored. To their surprise they found that at no speed did two-legged running need more oxygen.

HOPPING

Two zoologists at Harvard University trained a pair of kangaroos to hop along a treadmill wearing face masks for monitoring their oxygen intake. The results of the research were that, compared with quadrupeds of a similar weight, hoppers were metabolically inefficient at speeds below 10 m.p.h. However, above this speed they not only used less oxygen than the quadrupeds, but their consumption even fell as speed rose.

JUMPING

The best jumper of the animal world, proportional to its size, is the 1/16 in. long click beetle which can hurl itself 12 in. into the air. This requires an acceleration of 380 g. The most a man has ever survived is 80 g & it does this feat lying on its back without using its legs. It arches its back, stretching various tendons over an internal notch. It then sends itself flying by releasing a sort of firing pin.

SWIMMING

Humans are ludicrously inefficient in water. The greatest speed attained is 1.48 m.p.h. over 50 yards & the longest distance is 90% miles, swum by a Mr Poenisch in the Florida straits, protected by a shark cage.

RUNNING

The human records for running are 27.89 m.p.h. forward; 15.1 m.p.h. backwards; & 18.6 m.p.h. blindfold. At jumping our records are 7 ft 6 in. vertical & 29 ft 2 in. horizontal.

HOW TO CARRY A LOAD

Two Indian ergonomists have recently discovered the most efficient way of carrying a load. Seven subjects carried 70 lb of granite chips for 1/2 mile while their cardio-respiratory response was measured. Carrying by hand came out bottom & the unusual double-pack method came out top.

HANDS · YOKE · SHERPA · RICEBAG · HEAD · RUCKSACK · DOUBLE-PACK

HOW TO MEASURE YOUR FITNESS

This test (called the Harvard step test) is a measure of the speed your pulse rate falls after some exertion. Step onto an 18 in. high bench right foot first: step off left foot first: step on again left foot first: step off again right foot first. Repeat this cycle once every 4 sec. for 5 min. with a friend counting the seconds. Then get a friend to hold your wrist & count your pulses for 30 sec one minute after stopping; then two min. after stopping; then 3 min. after stopping. Add these together & divide the result into 15000. Very fit people score about 150, unfit people score about 85.

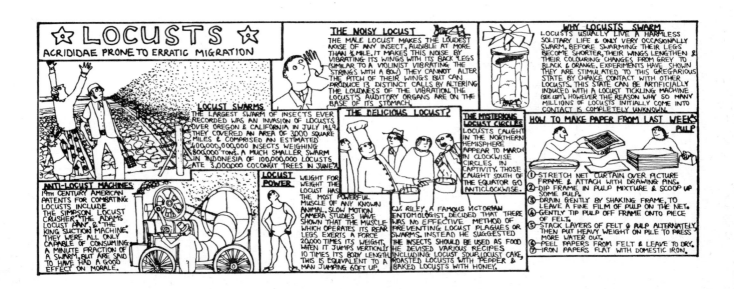

☆ LOCUSTS ☆
ACRIDIDAE PRONE TO ERRATIC MIGRATION

LOCUST SWARMS

The largest swarm of insects ever recorded was an invasion of locusts over Oregon & California in July 1949. They covered an area of 3000 square miles & comprised an estimated 400,000,000,000 insects weighing 800,000 tons. A much smaller swarm in Indonesia of 100,000,000 locusts ate 3,000,000 coconut trees in June.

ANTI-LOCUST MACHINES

19th century American patents for combating locusts include the Simpson locust crusher, the Adams locust pan & the King suction machine. They were all only capable of consuming a minute fraction of a swarm, but are said to have had a good effect on morale.

LOCUST POWER

Weight for weight the locust has the most powerful muscle of any known animal. Slow motion camera studies have shown that the muscle which operates its rear legs exerts a force 20,000 times its weight. When it jumps vertically 10 times its body length, this is equivalent to a man jumping 60 ft up.

THE NOISY LOCUST

The male locust makes the loudest noise of any insect, audible at more than 1/2 mile. It makes this noise by vibrating its wings with its back legs (similar to a violinist vibrating the strings with a bow). They cannot alter the pitch of their wings but can produce 13 distinct calls by altering the loudness of the vibration. The locust's auditory organs are on the base of its stomach.

THE DELICIOUS LOCUST?

C.V. Riley, a famous Victorian entomologist, decided that there was no effective method of preventing locust plagues or swarms. Instead he suggested the insects should be used as food, including locust soup, locust cake, roasted locusts with pepper & baked locusts with honey.

THE MYSTERIOUS LOCUST CIRCLE

Locusts caught in the northern hemisphere appear to march in clockwise circles in captivity. Those caught south of the equator go anticlockwise.

WHY LOCUSTS SWARM

Locusts usually live a harmless solitary life & only very occasionally swarm. Before swarming their legs become shorter, their wings lengthen & their colouring changes from grey to black & orange. Experiments have shown they are stimulated to this gregarious state by chance contact with other locusts. This state can be artificially induced with a locust tickling machine (see left). However the reason why so many millions of locusts initially come into contact is completely unknown.

HOW TO MAKE PAPER FROM LAST WEEK'S PULP

1. Stretch net curtain over picture frame & attach with drawing pins.
2. Dip frame in pulp mixture & scoop up some pulp.
3. Drain gently by shaking frame, to leave a fine film of pulp on the net.
4. Gently tip pulp off frame onto piece of felt.
5. Stack layers of felt & pulp alternately then put heavy weight on pile to press more water out.
6. Peel papers from felt & leave to dry.
7. Iron papers flat with domestic iron.

☆ LORRIES ☆
WHEELED MACHINES FOR TRANSPORTING OBJECTS

LORRIES v HORSES
THE HORSE WAS THE MAIN COMPETITION FOR THE EARLY LORRY MANUFACTURER. THE FORD SLOGAN 'IT DOESN'T NEED FEEDING WHEN STANDING STILL' WAS USED UNTIL THE 1920s.

TRUCKERS' SLANG
BRAKES: 'ANCHORS' OR 'BINDERS'. LOADING HANDS: 'DOCK WALLOPERS'. MECHANICS: 'HOOD LIFTERS' OR 'MANIACS'. TYRES 'DOUGHNUTS' OR IF IN POOR CONDITION, 'RAGS'. SLEEPER CABS: 'SUICIDE BOXES'.

LUXURY LORRIES
FEATURES OF SOME MODERN SLEEPER CABS: TWO-RING COOKERS WITH GRILLS; STAINLESS STEEL SINKS WITH RUNNING WATER; FRIDGES; SMALL WARDROBES; COOKING SEATS (INSTEAD OF PASSENGER SEATS).

LORRIES & ROADS
LONG VEHICLE

RECENT RESEARCH AT BRITAIN'S ROAD RESEARCH LABORATORY SUGGESTS THAT WEAR ON A ROAD IS PROPORTIONAL TO THE SIXTH POWER OF THE WEIGHT ON EACH AXLE. THIS MEANS THAT ONE LORRY AXLE CARRYING THE MAXIMUM PERMITTED LOAD OF 10 TONS CAN WEAR DOWN A ROAD THE SAME AMOUNT AS 66,000,000 SMALL CARS. SO CAR REGISTRATION TAX IS PAYING A CONSIDERABLE AMOUNT FOR ROAD WEAR CAUSED BY LORRIES. IT ALSO MEANS THAT ANY SMALL INCREASE IN MAXIMUM LEGAL AXLE LOAD WILL GREATLY INCREASE ROAD WEAR. UNFORTUNATELY, MOST EEC COUNTRIES HAVE HIGHER LIMITS THAN BRITAIN & SO THERE IS PRESSURE TO INCREASE THEM.

QUIET LORRIES
A PROTOTYPE ROLLS ROYCE FODEN LORRY HAS RECENTLY BEEN MADE WHICH IS QUIETER THAN AN AVERAGE CAR. SOUND REDUCTION IS ACHIEVED BY A NEW LOW-SPEED ENGINE FAN, SPECIAL LUBRICATION CHANNELS & SILENCERS — & SOUND-DEADENING PANELS. UNFORTUNATELY, THE IMPROVEMENTS WOULD ADD £2000 TO THE COST OF A PRODUCTION LORRY & THEY ARE NOT LIKELY TO BE ADOPTED UNTIL STRICTER NOISE STANDARDS BECOME STATUTORY.

WOMEN TRUCKERS
WOMEN TRUCK DRIVERS ARE MORE ACCEPTED IN THE US THAN IN EUROPE. MANY US TRANSPORT CAFES ARE NOW EQUIPPED WITH SEPARATE SHOWERS & POWDER ROOMS.

THE TACHOGRAPH
BRITISH DRIVERS DISLIKE THE LEGISLATION WHICH FORCES THEM TO CARRY A DEVICE TO RECORD TIME & MILEAGE (THE TACHOGRAPH). BY EEC STANDARDS A DRIVER'S DAILY MILEAGE IS LIMITED TO 281 MILES. DRIVERS CLAIM THAT THIS FIGURE WAS SET BEFORE THE ERA OF MOTORWAYS & HIGH EFFICIENCY BRAKING. THESE NOW MAKE IT POSSIBLE TO DRIVE MUCH GREATER DISTANCES SAFELY.

HOW TO TEST DOGS' NOSES
ASK YOUR FRIENDS TO REMOVE THEIR SHOES. ARRANGE THE SHOES IN A GROUP WITH A TASTY BIT OF FOOD IN ONE. LET THEIR DOGS LOOSE ONE AT A TIME. THE WINNER IS THE DOG THAT FINDS THE FOOD FASTEST.

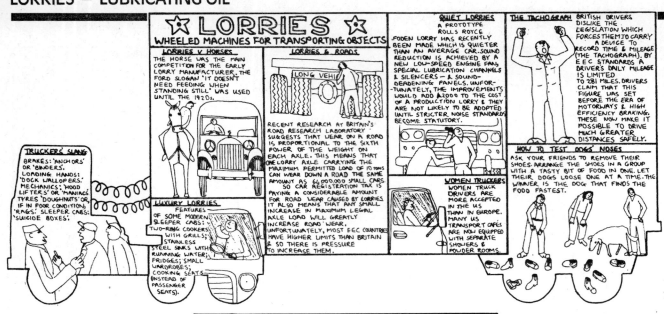

☆ LUBRICATING OIL ☆
LIQUIDS CREATING REDUCTION IN FRICTION

PRIMITIVE LUBRICATION
THE EARLIEST RECORD OF LUBRICATION IS A CARVING ON THE EGYPTIAN TOMB OF RA EM KA 2600-1700 BC. IN THE CARVING A MAN IS POURING LIQUID TO OIL THE ROLLERS.

OILED AXLES
TRACES OF ANIMAL FAT HAVE BEEN FOUND ON AXLES OF CHARIOTS OF ABOUT 1400 BC.

BETTON'S BRITISH OIL
THE FIRST MINERAL OIL TO BE SOLD IN BRITAIN WAS DISTILLED FROM SHALE OIL & SOLD AS BETTON'S BRITISH OIL (TO CURE RHEUMATISM) IN THE 1690s.

SPERM OIL
SPERM WHALE OIL IS SAID TO BE A PARTICULARLY CLEAN OIL, TRADITIONALLY USED FOR TEXTILE MACHINERY BECAUSE IT WOULD WASH OFF A FABRIC WITHOUT STAINING. SUBSTITUTES INTRODUCED SINCE THE CURB ON WHALING — ARE INFERIOR.

FRICTION
ANY TWO BITS OF METAL IN CONTACT TOUCH ONLY ON A FEW MICROSCOPIC HIGH POINTS. WHEN ONE BIT SLIDES OVER THE OTHER, A RISE IN TEMPERATURE OCCURS AT THE HIGH POINTS. MINUTE LOCAL WELDS ARE FORMED & TORN APART. THIS IS THE CAUSE OF FRICTION.

METAL INTERFACE X1000

OIL FILM

LUBRICATING OILS CREATE A FILM BETWEEN THE SURFACES, REDUCING THE NUMBER OF CONTACT POINTS.

GREASE V OIL
GREASE IS ONLY USED FOR LOW SPEED BEARINGS. HIGH SPEED BEARINGS GET MUCH HOTTER & THE ADVANTAGE OF OIL IS THAT IT CAN BE CIRCULATED & USED TO COOL THE BEARING.

SLIP WAYS
SHIPYARD SLIPWAYS ARE TRADITIONALLY LUBRICATED WITH A LAYER OF GREASE & A LAYER OF OIL. OVER 15 TONNES OF GREASE & OIL ARE NEEDED TO LAUNCH A 50,000 TONNE SHIP.

SOUTH AMERICAN CRUDE
THE WORLD'S OILIEST OIL

THE COMPOSITION OF SOME CRUDE OILS ARE MORE SUITABLE FOR LUBRICANTS THAN OTHERS. SOUTH AMERICAN CRUDE IS BEST.

VEGETABLE ENGINE OIL
COCONUT & PEANUT OIL USED TO BE INGREDIENTS OF CAR ENGINE OIL. THEY WERE ABANDONED AS COCONUT OIL PARTLY SOLIDIFIED IN COLD WEATHER & PEANUT OIL TENDED TO LEAVE GUMMY DEPOSITS. SOME RAPE OIL & FISH OIL ARE STILL USED.

HOW TO SHRINK PLASTIC
PLACE EMPTY PEANUT OR CRISP PACKET ON FLAT SURFACE IN MEDIUM OVEN FOR 2 MIN (IT SHRINKS UP TO ⅙ TH)

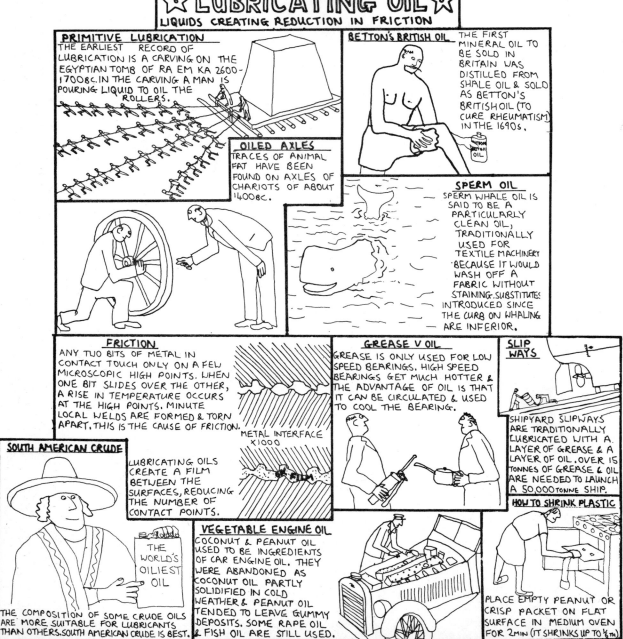

☆ MACHINE GUNS ☆
RAPID-FIRING WEAPONS DISCHARGING BULLETS

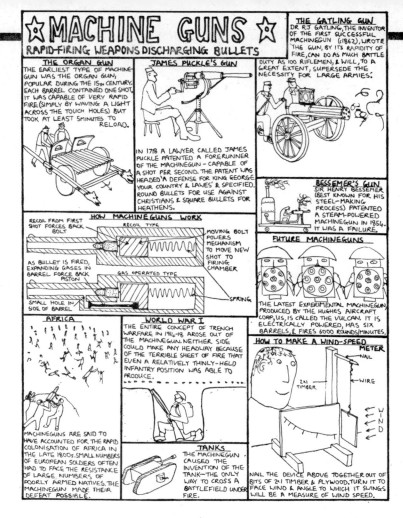

THE ORGAN GUN
THE EARLIEST TYPE OF MACHINE GUN WAS THE ORGAN GUN, POPULAR DURING THE 15TH CENTURY. EACH BARREL CONTAINED ONE SHOT. IT WAS CAPABLE OF VERY RAPID FIRE (SIMPLY BY WAVING A LIGHT ACROSS THE TOUCH HOLES) BUT TOOK AT LEAST 5 MINUTES TO RELOAD.

JAMES PUCKLE'S GUN
IN 1718 A LAWYER CALLED JAMES PUCKLE PATENTED A FORERUNNER OF THE MACHINEGUN – CAPABLE OF A SHOT PER SECOND. THE PATENT WAS HEADED 'A DEFENSE FOR KING GEORGE YOUR COUNTRY & LAWES' & SPECIFIED ROUND BULLETS FOR USE AGAINST CHRISTIANS & SQUARE BULLETS FOR HEATHENS.

THE GATLING GUN
DR. RJ GATLING, THE INVENTOR OF THE FIRST SUCCESSFUL MACHINEGUN (1862), WROTE 'THE GUN, BY ITS RAPIDITY OF FIRE, CAN DO AS MUCH BATTLE DUTY AS 100 RIFLEMEN, & WILL, TO A GREAT EXTENT, SUPERSEDE THE NECESSITY FOR LARGE ARMIES.'

BESSEMER'S GUN
SIR HENRY BESSEMER (BEST KNOWN FOR HIS STEEL-MAKING PROCESS) PATENTED A STEAM-POWERED MACHINEGUN IN 1854. IT WAS A FAILURE.

HOW MACHINEGUNS WORK
RECOIL FROM FIRST SHOT FORCES BACK BOLT

RECOIL TYPE

MOVING BOLT POWERS MECHANISM TO MOVE NEW SHOT TO FIRING CHAMBER

AS BULLET IS FIRED, EXPANDING GASES IN BARREL FORCE BACK PISTON

GAS OPERATED TYPE

SMALL HOLE IN SIDE OF BARREL

SPRING

FUTURE MACHINEGUNS
THE LATEST EXPERIMENTAL MACHINEGUN, PRODUCED BY THE HUGHES AIRCRAFT CORP, US, IS CALLED THE VULCAN. IT IS ELECTRICALLY POWERED, HAS SIX BARRELS, & FIRES 6000 ROUNDS/MINUTES.

AFRICA
MACHINEGUNS ARE SAID TO HAVE ACCOUNTED FOR THE RAPID COLONISATION OF AFRICA IN THE LATE 1800s. SMALL NUMBERS OF EUROPEAN SOLDIERS OFTEN HAD TO FACE THE RESISTANCE OF LARGE NUMBERS OF POORLY ARMED NATIVES. THE MACHINEGUN MADE THEIR DEFEAT POSSIBLE.

WORLD WAR I
THE ENTIRE CONCEPT OF TRENCH WARFARE IN 1914-18 AROSE OUT OF THE MACHINEGUN. NEITHER SIDE COULD MAKE ANY HEADWAY BECAUSE OF THE TERRIBLE SHEET OF FIRE THAT EVEN A RELATIVELY THINLY-HELD INFANTRY POSITION WAS ABLE TO PRODUCE.

TANKS
THE MACHINEGUN CAUSED THE INVENTION OF THE TANK—THE ONLY WAY TO CROSS A BATTLEFIELD UNDER FIRE.

HOW TO MAKE A WIND-SPEED METER
NAIL

WIRE

2×1 TIMBER

WIND

NAIL THE DEVICE ABOVE TOGETHER OUT OF BITS OF 2×1 TIMBER & PLYWOOD. TURN IT TO FACE WIND & ANGLE TO WHICH IT SWINGS WILL BE A MEASURE OF WIND SPEED.

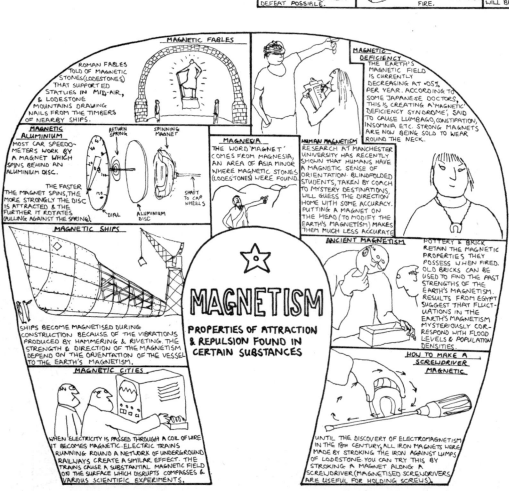

MAGNETIC FABLES
ROMAN FABLES TOLD OF MAGNETIC STONES (LODESTONES) THAT SUPPORTED STATUES IN MID-AIR, & LODESTONE MOUNTAINS DRAWING NAILS FROM THE TIMBERS OF NEARBY SHIPS.

MAGNETIC DEFICIENCY
THE EARTH'S MAGNETIC FIELD IS CURRENTLY DECREASING AT .05% PER YEAR. ACCORDING TO SOME JAPANESE DOCTORS, THIS IS CREATING A 'MAGNETIC' DEFICIENCY SYNDROME', SAID TO CAUSE LUMBAGO, CONSTIPATION, INSOMNIA ETC. STRONG MAGNETS ARE NOW BEING SOLD TO WEAR ROUND THE NECK.

MAGNETIC ALUMINIUM
RETURN SPRING

SPINNING MAGNET

SHAFT TO CAR WHEELS

DIAL

ALUMINIUM DISC

MOST CAR SPEEDO-METERS WORK BY A MAGNET WHICH SPINS BEHIND AN ALUMINIUM DISC.

THE FASTER THE MAGNET SPINS, THE MORE STRONGLY THE DISC IS ATTRACTED & THE FURTHER IT ROTATES (PULLING AGAINST THE SPRING).

MAGNESIA
THE WORD 'MAGNET' COMES FROM MAGNESIA, AN AREA OF ASIA MINOR WHERE MAGNETIC STONES (LODESTONES) WERE FOUND.

HUMAN MAGNETISM
RESEARCH AT MANCHESTER UNIVERSITY HAS RECENTLY SHOWN THAT HUMANS HAVE A MAGNETIC SENSE OF ORIENTATION. BLINDFOLDED STUDENTS, TAKEN BY COACH TO MYSTERY DESTINATIONS, WILL GUESS THE DIRECTION HOME WITH SOME ACCURACY. PUTTING A MAGNET ON THE HEAD (TO MODIFY THE EARTH'S MAGNETISM) MAKES THEM MUCH LESS ACCURATE

MAGNETIC SHIPS
SHIPS BECOME MAGNETISED DURING CONSTRUCTION BECAUSE OF THE VIBRATIONS PRODUCED BY HAMMERING & RIVETING. THE STRENGTH & DIRECTION OF THE MAGNETISM DEPEND ON THE ORIENTATION OF THE VESSEL TO THE EARTH'S MAGNETISM.

☆ MAGNETISM
PROPERTIES OF ATTRACTION & REPULSION FOUND IN CERTAIN SUBSTANCES

ANCIENT MAGNETISM
POTTERY & BRICK RETAIN THE MAGNETIC PROPERTIES THEY POSSESS WHEN FIRED. OLD BRICKS CAN BE USED TO FIND THE PAST STRENGTHS OF THE EARTH'S MAGNETISM. RESULTS FROM EGYPT SUGGEST THAT FLUCT-UATIONS IN THE EARTH'S MAGNETISM MYSTERIOUSLY COR-RESPOND WITH FLOOD LEVELS & POPULATION DENSITIES.

HOW TO MAKE A SCREWDRIVER MAGNETIC
UNTIL THE DISCOVERY OF ELECTROMAGNETISM IN THE 19TH CENTURY, ALL IRON MAGNETS WERE MADE BY STROKING THE IRON AGAINST LUMPS OF LODESTONE. YOU CAN TRY THIS BY STROKING A MAGNET ALONG A SCREWDRIVER (MAGNETISED SCREWDRIVERS ARE USEFUL FOR HOLDING SCREWS).

MAGNETIC CITIES
WHEN ELECTRICITY IS PASSED THROUGH A COIL OF WIRE IT BECOMES MAGNETIC. ELECTRIC TRAINS RUNNING ROUND A NETWORK OF UNDERGROUND RAILWAYS CREATE A SIMILAR EFFECT. THE TRAINS CAUSE A SUBSTANTIAL MAGNETIC FIELD ON THE SURFACE WHICH DISRUPTS COMPASSES & VARIOUS SCIENTIFIC EXPERIMENTS.

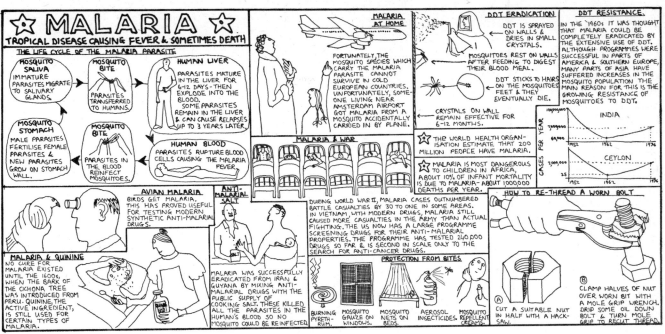

☆ MALARIA ☆
TROPICAL DISEASE CAUSING FEVER & SOMETIMES DEATH

THE LIFE CYCLE OF THE MALARIA PARASITE

MOSQUITO SALIVA — IMMATURE PARASITES MIGRATE TO SALIVARY GLANDS.

MOSQUITO BITE — PARASITES TRANSFERRED TO HUMANS.

HUMAN LIVER — PARASITES MATURE IN THE LIVER FOR 6–12 DAYS – THEN EXPLODE INTO THE BLOOD. SOME PARASITES REMAIN IN THE LIVER & CAN CAUSE RELAPSES UP TO 3 YEARS LATER.

MOSQUITO STOMACH — MALE PARASITES FERTILISE FEMALE PARASITES & NEW PARASITES GROW ON STOMACH WALL.

MOSQUITO BITE — PARASITES IN THE BLOOD REINFECT MOSQUITOES.

HUMAN BLOOD — PARASITES RUPTURE BLOOD CELLS CAUSING THE MALARIA FEVER.

AVIAN MALARIA — BIRDS GET MALARIA. THIS HAS PROVED USEFUL FOR TESTING MODERN SYNTHETIC ANTI-MALARIA DRUGS.

ANTI-MALARIAL SALT — MALARIA WAS SUCCESSFULLY ERADICATED FROM IRAN & GUYANA BY MIXING ANTI-MALARIAL DRUGS WITH THE PUBLIC SUPPLY OF COOKING SALT. THESE KILLED ALL THE PARASITES IN THE HUMAN'S BLOOD SO NO MOSQUITO COULD BE REINFECTED.

MALARIA & QUININE — NO CURE FOR MALARIA EXISTED UNTIL THE 1600s, WHEN THE BARK OF THE CICHONA TREE WAS INTRODUCED FROM PERU. QUININE, THE ACTIVE INGREDIENT, IS STILL USED FOR CERTAIN TYPES OF MALARIA.

MALARIA AT HOME — FORTUNATELY, THE MOSQUITO SPECIES WHICH CARRY THE MALARIA PARASITE CANNOT SURVIVE IN COLD EUROPEAN COUNTRIES. UNFORTUNATELY, SOMEONE LIVING NEAR AMSTERDAM AIRPORT GOT MALARIA FROM A MOSQUITO ACCIDENTALLY CARRIED IN BY PLANE.

MALARIA & WAR — DURING WORLD WAR II, MALARIA CASES OUTNUMBERED BATTLE CASUALTIES BY 30 TO ONE IN SOME AREAS. IN VIETNAM, WITH MODERN DRUGS, MALARIA STILL CAUSED MORE CASUALTIES IN THE ARMY THAN ACTUAL FIGHTING. THE US NOW HAS A LARGE PROGRAMME SCREENING DRUGS FOR THEIR ANTI-MALARIAL PROPERTIES. THE PROGRAMME HAS TESTED 240,000 DRUGS SO FAR & IS SECOND IN SCALE ONLY TO THE SEARCH FOR ANTI-CANCER DRUGS.

PROTECTION FROM BITES — BURNING PYRETHRUM. MOSQUITO GAUZE ON WINDOWS. MOSQUITO NETS ON BEDS. AEROSOL INSECTICIDES. MOSQUITO REPELLENT CREAMS.

DDT ERADICATION — DDT IS SPRAYED ON WALLS & DRIES IN SMALL CRYSTALS. MOSQUITOES REST ON WALLS AFTER FEEDING TO DIGEST THEIR BLOOD MEAL. DDT STICKS TO HAIRS ON THE MOSQUITOES FEET & THEY EVENTUALLY DIE. CRYSTALS ON WALL REMAIN EFFECTIVE FOR 6–12 MONTHS.

☆ THE WORLD HEALTH ORGANISATION ESTIMATE THAT 200 MILLION PEOPLE HAVE MALARIA.

☆ MALARIA IS MOST DANGEROUS TO CHILDREN IN AFRICA, ABOUT 10% OF INFANT MORTALITY IS DUE TO MALARIA – ABOUT 1,000,000 DEATHS PER YEAR.

DDT RESISTANCE — IN THE 1960s IT WAS THOUGHT THAT MALARIA COULD BE COMPLETELY ERADICATED BY THE EXTENSIVE USE OF DDT. ALTHOUGH PROGRAMMES WERE SUCCESSFUL IN PARTS OF AMERICA & SOUTHERN EUROPE, MANY PARTS OF ASIA HAVE SUFFERED INCREASES IN THE MOSQUITO POPULATION. THE MAIN REASON FOR THIS IS THE GROWING RESISTANCE OF MOSQUITOES TO DDT.

(Graphs: CASES PER YEAR — INDIA 1952, 1962, 1976; CEYLON 1952, 1962, 1976)

HOW TO RE-THREAD A WORN BOLT — (A) CUT A SUITABLE NUT IN HALF WITH A HACKSAW. (B) CLAMP HALVES OF NUT OVER WORN BIT WITH A MOLE GRIP WRENCH. DRIP SOME OIL DOWN BOLT & TURN MOLE GRIP TO RECUT THREAD.

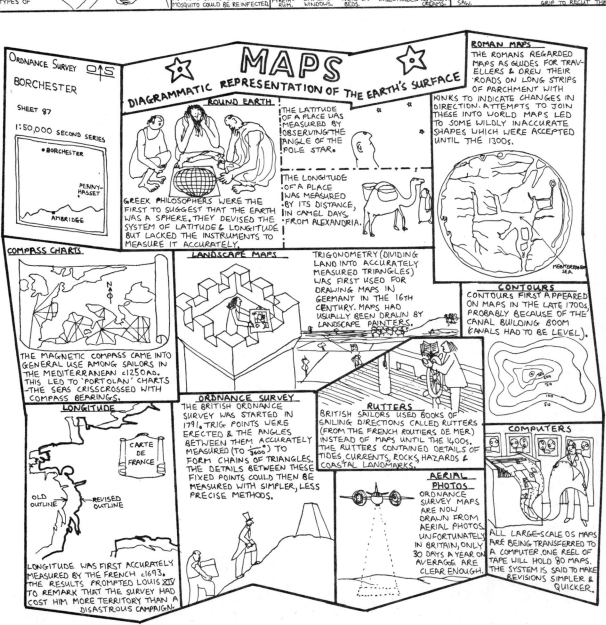

☆ MAPS ☆
DIAGRAMMATIC REPRESENTATION OF THE EARTH'S SURFACE

ORDNANCE SURVEY — O↑S — BORCHESTER — SHEET 87 — 1:50,000 SECOND SERIES — (map: BORCHESTER, PENNY-HASSET, AMBRIDGE)

ROUND EARTH — GREEK PHILOSOPHERS WERE THE FIRST TO SUGGEST THAT THE EARTH WAS A SPHERE. THEY DEVISED THE SYSTEM OF LATITUDE & LONGITUDE BUT LACKED THE INSTRUMENTS TO MEASURE IT ACCURATELY.

THE LATITUDE OF A PLACE WAS MEASURED BY OBSERVING THE ANGLE OF THE POLE STAR.

THE LONGITUDE OF A PLACE WAS MEASURED BY ITS DISTANCE, IN CAMEL DAYS, FROM ALEXANDRIA.

ROMAN MAPS — THE ROMANS REGARDED MAPS AS GUIDES FOR TRAVELLERS & DREW THEIR ROADS ON LONG STRIPS OF PARCHMENT WITH KINKS TO INDICATE CHANGES IN DIRECTION. ATTEMPTS TO JOIN THESE INTO WORLD MAPS LED TO SOME WILDLY INACCURATE SHAPES WHICH WERE ACCEPTED UNTIL THE 1300s. (MEDITERRANEAN SEA)

COMPASS CHARTS — THE MAGNETIC COMPASS CAME INTO GENERAL USE AMONG SAILORS IN THE MEDITERRANEAN c1250 AD. THIS LED TO 'PORTOLAN' CHARTS – THE SEAS CRISSCROSSED WITH COMPASS BEARINGS.

LANDSCAPE MAPS — TRIGONOMETRY (DIVIDING LAND INTO ACCURATELY MEASURED TRIANGLES) WAS FIRST USED FOR DRAWING MAPS IN GERMANY IN THE 16TH CENTURY. MAPS HAD USUALLY BEEN DRAWN BY LANDSCAPE PAINTERS.

CONTOURS — CONTOURS FIRST APPEARED ON MAPS IN THE LATE 1700s, PROBABLY BECAUSE OF THE CANAL BUILDING BOOM (CANALS HAD TO BE LEVEL).

LONGITUDE — LONGITUDE WAS FIRST ACCURATELY MEASURED BY THE FRENCH c1693. THE RESULTS PROMPTED LOUIS XIV TO REMARK THAT THE SURVEY HAD COST HIM MORE TERRITORY THAN A DISASTROUS CAMPAIGN. (CARTE DE FRANCE — OLD OUTLINE — REVISED OUTLINE)

ORDNANCE SURVEY — THE BRITISH ORDNANCE SURVEY WAS STARTED IN 1791. TRIG POINTS WERE ERECTED & THE ANGLES BETWEEN THEM ACCURATELY MEASURED (TO $\frac{1}{3600}$°) TO FORM CHAINS OF TRIANGLES. THE DETAILS BETWEEN THESE FIXED POINTS COULD THEN BE MEASURED WITH SIMPLER, LESS PRECISE METHODS.

RUTTERS — BRITISH SAILORS USED BOOKS OF SAILING DIRECTIONS CALLED RUTTERS (FROM THE FRENCH ROUTIERS DE MER) INSTEAD OF MAPS UNTIL THE 1600s. THE RUTTERS CONTAINED DETAILS OF TIDES, CURRENTS, ROCKS, HAZARDS & COASTAL LANDMARKS.

AERIAL PHOTOS — ORDNANCE SURVEY MAPS ARE NOW DRAWN FROM AERIAL PHOTOS. UNFORTUNATELY, IN BRITAIN, ONLY 30 DAYS A YEAR ON AVERAGE ARE CLEAR ENOUGH.

COMPUTERS — ALL LARGE-SCALE OS MAPS ARE BEING TRANSFERRED TO A COMPUTER. ONE REEL OF TAPE WILL HOLD 80 MAPS. THE SYSTEM IS SAID TO MAKE REVISIONS SIMPLER & QUICKER.

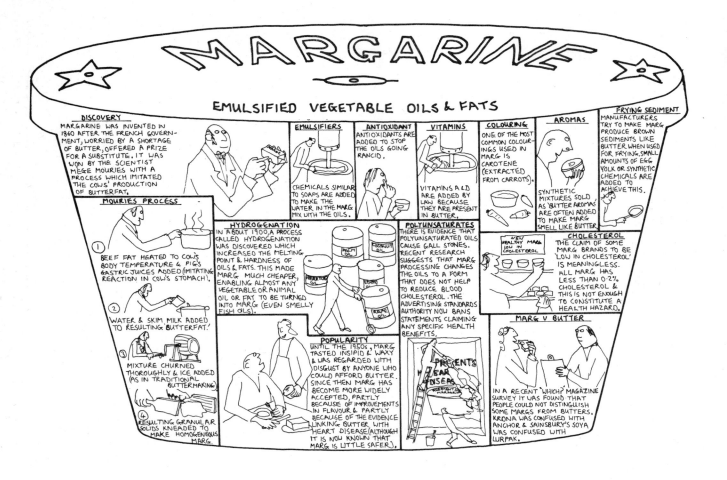

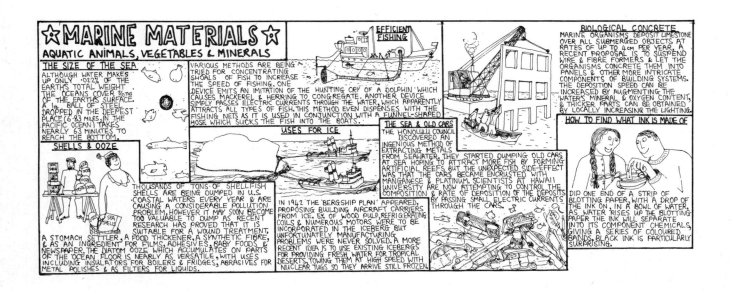

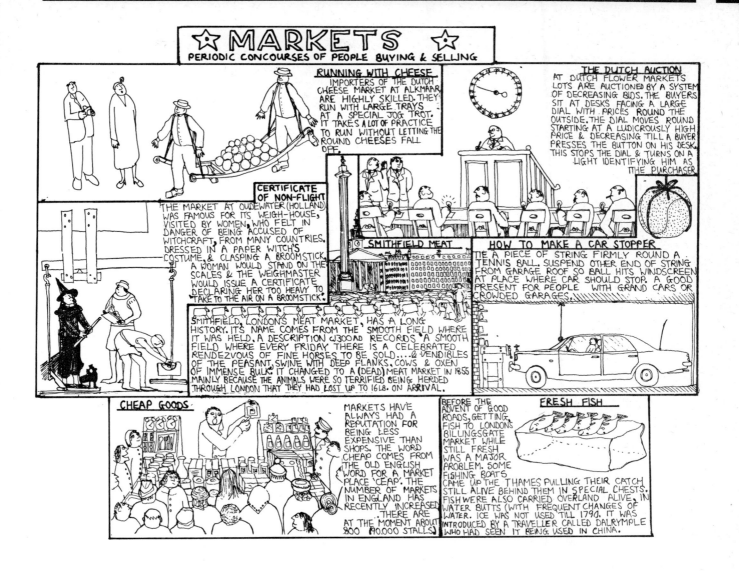

☆ MARKETS ☆
PERIODIC CONCOURSES OF PEOPLE BUYING & SELLING

RUNNING WITH CHEESE
IMPORTERS OF THE DUTCH CHEESE MARKET AT ALKMAAR ARE HIGHLY SKILLED. THEY RUN WITH LARGE TRAYS AT A SPECIAL JOG TROT. IT TAKES A LOT OF PRACTICE TO RUN WITHOUT LETTING THE ROUND CHEESES FALL OFF.

THE DUTCH AUCTION
AT DUTCH FLOWER MARKETS LOTS ARE AUCTIONED BY A SYSTEM OF DECREASING BIDS. THE BUYERS SIT AT DESKS FACING A LARGE DIAL WITH PRICES ROUND THE OUTSIDE. THE DIAL MOVES ROUND STARTING AT A LUDICROUSLY HIGH PRICE & DECREASING TILL A BUYER PRESSES THE BUTTON ON HIS DESK. THIS STOPS THE DIAL & TURNS ON A LIGHT IDENTIFYING HIM AS THE PURCHASER.

CERTIFICATE OF NON-FLIGHT
THE MARKET AT OUDEWATER (HOLLAND) WAS FAMOUS FOR ITS WEIGH-HOUSE, VISITED BY WOMEN, WHO FELT IN DANGER OF BEING ACCUSED OF WITCHCRAFT, FROM MANY COUNTRIES. DRESSED IN A PAPER WITCH'S COSTUME, & CLASPING A BROOMSTICK, A WOMAN WOULD STAND ON THE SCALES & THE WEIGHMASTER WOULD ISSUE A CERTIFICATE DECLARING HER TOO HEAVY TO TAKE TO THE AIR ON A BROOMSTICK.

SMITHFIELD MEAT
SMITHFIELD, LONDON'S MEAT MARKET, HAS A LONG HISTORY. ITS NAME COMES FROM THE SMOOTH FIELD WHERE IT WAS HELD. A DESCRIPTION C1300 AD RECORDS 'A SMOOTH FIELD WHERE EVERY FRIDAY THERE IS A CELEBRATED RENDEZVOUS OF FINE HORSES TO BE SOLD.... & VENDIBLES OF THE PEASANT, SWINE WITH DEEP FLANKS, COWS & OXEN OF IMMENSE BULK'. IT CHANGED TO A (DEAD) MEAT MARKET IN 1855 MAINLY BECAUSE THE ANIMALS WERE SO TERRIFIED BEING HERDED THROUGH LONDON THAT THEY HAD LOST UP TO 16LB. ON ARRIVAL.

HOW TO MAKE A CAR STOPPER
TIE A PIECE OF STRING FIRMLY ROUND A TENNIS BALL. SUSPEND OTHER END OF STRING FROM GARAGE ROOF SO BALL HITS WINDSCREEN AT PLACE WHERE CAR SHOULD STOP. A GOOD PRESENT FOR PEOPLE WITH GRAND CARS OR CROWDED GARAGES.

CHEAP GOODS

MARKETS HAVE ALWAYS HAD A REPUTATION FOR BEING LESS EXPENSIVE THAN SHOPS. THE WORD CHEAP COMES FROM THE OLD ENGLISH WORD FOR A MARKET PLACE 'CEAP'. THE NUMBER OF MARKETS IN ENGLAND HAS RECENTLY INCREASED. THERE ARE AT THE MOMENT ABOUT 800 (90,000 STALLS)

FRESH FISH
BEFORE THE ADVENT OF GOOD ROADS, GETTING FISH TO LONDONS BILLINGSGATE MARKET WHILE STILL FRESH WAS A MAJOR PROBLEM. SOME FISHING BOATS CAME UP THE THAMES PULLING THEIR CATCH STILL ALIVE BEHIND THEM IN SPECIAL CHESTS. FISH WERE ALSO CARRIED OVERLAND ALIVE, IN WATER BUTTS (WITH FREQUENT CHANGES OF WATER. ICE WAS NOT USED TILL 1790. IT WAS INTRODUCED BY A TRAVELLER CALLED DALRYMPLE WHO HAD SEEN IT BEING USED IN CHINA.

☆ MARRIAGE ☆
COHABITATION 'TILL DEATH DO US PART'

THE WEDDING CAKE
THE ROMANS MADE A WEDDING CAKE OF FLOUR, SALT & WATER. THE BRIDE & GROOM EACH NIBBLED A PIECE; THE REST WAS BROKEN OVER THEIR HEADS & THE GUESTS SCRAMBLED FOR THE FRAGMENTS. IN MEDIEVAL ENGLAND THE GUESTS EACH BROUGHT SMALL BUNS WHICH WERE PILED INTO ONE ENORMOUS HEAP. A FRENCH CHEF VISITING ENGLAND IN THE REIGN OF CHARLES II IS SAID TO HAVE FIRST THOUGHT OF AMALGAMATING THE BUNS & ICING THE RESULT.

THE HOURS OF MARRIAGE
ENGLISH LAW USED TO REQUIRE THAT THE MARRIAGE CEREMONY BE PERFORMED BETWEEN 8AM & NOON. IN 1886 THIS WAS GENEROUSLY EXTENDED TO 3PM.

NO ESCAPE
MEN WERE SOMETIMES FORCIBLY PREVENTED FROM CHANGING THEIR MINDS AT THE LAST MINUTE. IN PARTS OF ENGLAND THE PARISH ACCOUNTS OF GREAT STAUGHTON RECORD FOR DECEMBER 16L7. 'ITEM PAID FOR WAGES SPENT UPON MAN THAT WATCHED JOHN PICKLE ALL NIGHT TILL HE WAS MARRIED 1s 0d.

IMPOSTORS
A MARRIAGE CELEBRATED IN CHURCH BY A PERSON PROFESSING TO BE IN HOLY ORDERS, & NOT KNOWN TO BOTH PARTIES TO BE AN IMPOSTOR IS VALID. ONLY IF BOTH PARTIES KNOW THE PRIEST TO BE AN IMPOSTOR IS THE CEREMONY VOID.

INSTANT WEDLOCK
IN SCOTLAND, UNTIL THE 20TH CENTURY, A COUPLE WERE DEEMED TO BE LEGALLY MARRIED SIMPLY BY DECLARING THAT THEY CONSENT TO MARRY WITHOUT WITNESSES & ACTING ON THEIR DECLARATION. HOWEVER THEY COULD THEN BE PROSECUTED FOR CONDUCTING AN IRREGULAR MARRIAGE.

THE END OF THE WEDDING RECEPTION

MARRIAGE AND DEATH
SOME OLD ENGLISH MARRIAGE SUPERSTITIONS WERE DECIDEDLY MORBID. SOME BELIEVED THAT THE PARTNER WHO ANSWERED THE LOUDEST TO THE MARRIAGE QUESTIONS WOULD DIE FIRST. OTHERS THOUGHT THAT THE FIRST TO DIE WAS ALWAYS THE FIRST PARTNER TO GO TO SLEEP ON THE WEDDING NIGHT.

IN PARTS OF NORTHERN ENGLAND A FLAT CAKE OF FLOUR & WATER WITH A RING & A 6d INSIDE WAS DISTRIBUTED AMONG THE UNMARRIED FEMALE GUESTS AT THE END OF THE RECEPTION. THE ONE WHO FOUND THE RING WAS BELIEVED TO BE THE NEXT TO MARRY & THE ONE WHO FOUND THE 6d WAS TO DIE A SPINSTER.

HOW TO TEST WHETHER YOUR FATHER IS AN ADULT
DRAW THE 2 SHAPES ABOVE ON SQUARE BITS OF PAPER & ASK HIM TO ROTATE SQUARES TILL HE THINKS THAT THE SHAPES ARE UPRIGHT. ACCORDING TO RESEARCH AT MICHIGAN UNIVERSITY ADULTS TEND TO PLACE THE LONG AXIS OF THE DUMBELL HORIZONTALLY & THE DARK HALF OF THE SQUARE UNDER THE WHITE HALF. CHILDREN TEND TO DO THE OPPOSITE (DUMBELL VERTICAL & SQUARE DARK UPPERMOST).

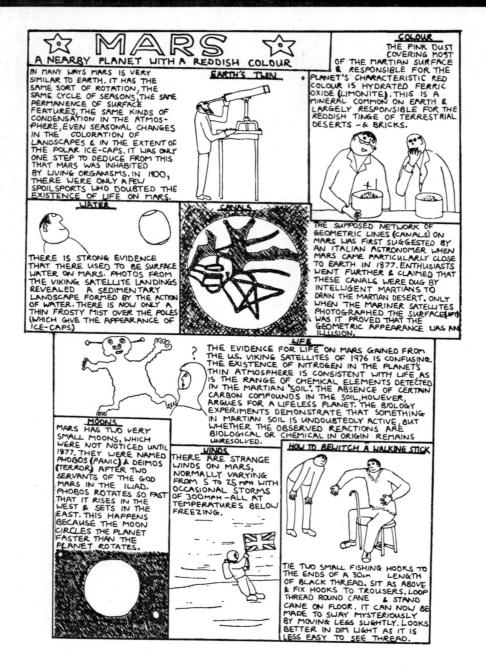

☆ MARS ☆
A NEARBY PLANET WITH A REDDISH COLOUR

IN MANY WAYS MARS IS VERY SIMILAR TO EARTH. IT HAS THE SAME SORT OF ROTATION, THE SAME CYCLE OF SEASONS, THE SAME PERMANENCE OF SURFACE FEATURES, THE SAME KINDS OF CONDENSATION IN THE ATMOSPHERE, EVEN SEASONAL CHANGES IN THE COLORATION OF LANDSCAPES & IN THE EXTENT OF THE POLAR ICE-CAPS. IT WAS ONLY ONE STEP TO DEDUCE FROM THIS THAT MARS WAS INHABITED BY LIVING ORGANISMS. IN 1900, THERE WERE ONLY A FEW SPOILSPORTS WHO DOUBTED THE EXISTENCE OF LIFE ON MARS.

EARTH'S THIN

COLOUR
THE PINK DUST COVERING MOST OF THE MARTIAN SURFACE & RESPONSIBLE FOR THE PLANET'S CHARACTERISTIC RED COLOUR IS HYDRATED FERRIC OXIDE (LIMONITE). THIS IS A MINERAL COMMON ON EARTH & LARGELY RESPONSIBLE FOR THE REDDISH TINGE OF TERRESTRIAL DESERTS – & BRICKS.

WATER
THERE IS STRONG EVIDENCE THAT THERE USED TO BE SURFACE WATER ON MARS. PHOTOS FROM THE VIKING SATELLITE LANDINGS REVEALED A SEDIMENTARY LANDSCAPE FORMED BY THE ACTION OF WATER. THERE IS NOW ONLY A THIN FROSTY MIST OVER THE POLES (WHICH GIVE THE APPEARANCE OF ICE-CAPS)

CANALS
THE SUPPOSED NETWORK OF GEOMETRIC LINES (CANALS) ON MARS WAS FIRST SUGGESTED BY AN ITALIAN ASTRONOMER WHEN MARS CAME PARTICULARLY CLOSE TO EARTH IN 1877. ENTHUSIASTS WENT FURTHER & CLAIMED THAT THESE CANALS WERE DUG BY INTELLIGENT MARTIANS TO DRAIN THE MARTIAN DESERT. ONLY WHEN THE MARINER SATELLITES PHOTOGRAPHED THE SURFACE (LEFT) WAS IT PROVED THAT THE GEOMETRIC APPEARANCE WAS AN ILLUSION.

LIFE
THE EVIDENCE FOR LIFE ON MARS GAINED FROM THE U.S. VIKING SATELLITES OF 1976 IS CONFUSING. THE EXISTENCE OF NITROGEN IN THE PLANET'S THIN ATMOSPHERE IS CONSISTENT WITH LIFE, AS IS THE RANGE OF CHEMICAL ELEMENTS DETECTED IN THE MARTIAN 'SOIL'. THE ABSENCE OF CERTAIN CARBON COMPOUNDS IN THE SOIL, HOWEVER, ARGUES FOR A LIFELESS PLANET. THE BIOLOGY EXPERIMENTS DEMONSTRATE THAT SOMETHING IN MARTIAN SOIL IS UNDOUBTEDLY ACTIVE, BUT WHETHER THE OBSERVED REACTIONS ARE BIOLOGICAL OR CHEMICAL IN ORIGIN REMAINS UNRESOLVED.

MOONS
MARS HAS TWO VERY SMALL MOONS, WHICH WERE NOT NOTICED UNTIL 1877. THEY WERE NAMED PHOBOS (PANIC) & DEIMOS (TERROR) AFTER TWO SERVANTS OF THE GOD MARS IN THE ILIAD. PHOBOS ROTATES SO FAST THAT IT RISES IN THE WEST & SETS IN THE EAST. THIS HAPPENS BECAUSE THE MOON CIRCLES THE PLANET FASTER THAN THE PLANET ROTATES.

WINDS
THERE ARE STRANGE WINDS ON MARS, NORMALLY VARYING FROM 5 TO 25 MPH WITH OCCASIONAL STORMS OF 300MPH – ALL AT TEMPERATURES BELOW FREEZING.

HOW TO BEWITCH A WALKING STICK
TIE TWO SMALL FISHING HOOKS TO THE ENDS OF A 30cm LENGTH OF BLACK THREAD. SIT AS ABOVE & FIX HOOKS TO TROUSERS. LOOP THREAD ROUND CANE & STAND CANE ON FLOOR. IT CAN NOW BE MADE TO SWAY MYSTERIOUSLY BY MOVING LEGS SLIGHTLY. LOOKS BETTER IN DIM LIGHT AS IT IS LESS EASY TO SEE THREAD.

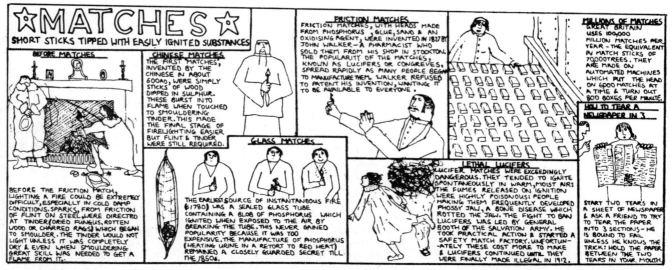

☆ MATCHES ☆
SHORT STICKS TIPPED WITH EASILY IGNITED SUBSTANCES

BEFORE MATCHES
BEFORE THE FRICTION MATCH, LIGHTING A FIRE COULD BE EXTREMELY DIFFICULT, ESPECIALLY IN COLD DAMP CONDITIONS. SPARKS, FROM FRICTION OF FLINT ON STEEL, WERE DIRECTED AT TINDER (DRIED FUNGUS, ROTTEN WOOD OR CHARRED RAGS) WHICH BEGAN TO SMOULDER. THE TINDER WOULD NOT LIGHT UNLESS IT WAS COMPLETELY DRY & EVEN WHEN SMOULDERING GREAT SKILL WAS NEEDED TO GET A FLAME FROM IT.

CHINESE MATCHES
THE FIRST MATCHES, INVENTED BY THE CHINESE IN ABOUT 600AD, WERE SIMPLY STICKS OF WOOD DIPPED IN SULPHUR. THESE BURST INTO FLAME WHEN TOUCHED TO SMOULDERING TINDER. THIS MADE THE FINAL STAGE OF FIRELIGHTING EASIER BUT FLINT & TINDER WERE STILL REQUIRED.

GLASS MATCHES
THE EARLIEST SOURCE OF INSTANTANEOUS FIRE (1780) WAS A SEALED GLASS TUBE CONTAINING A BLOB OF PHOSPHORUS WHICH IGNITED WHEN EXPOSED TO THE AIR BY BREAKING THE TUBE. THIS NEVER GAINED POPULARITY BECAUSE IT WAS TOO EXPENSIVE. THE MANUFACTURE OF PHOSPHORUS (HEATING URINE IN A RETORT TO RED HEAT) REMAINED A CLOSELY GUARDED SECRET TILL THE 1850s.

FRICTION MATCHES
FRICTION MATCHES, WITH HEADS MADE FROM PHOSPHORUS, GLUE, SAND & AN OXIDISING AGENT, WERE INVENTED IN 1827 BY JOHN WALKER – A PHARMACIST WHO SOLD THEM FROM HIS SHOP IN STOCKTON. THE POPULARITY OF THE MATCHES, KNOWN AS LUCIFERS OR CONGREVES, SPREAD RAPIDLY AS MANY PEOPLE BEGAN TO MANUFACTURE THEM. WALKER REFUSED TO PATENT HIS INVENTION, WANTING IT TO BE AVAILABLE TO EVERYONE.

LETHAL LUCIFERS
LUCIFER MATCHES WERE EXCEEDINGLY DANGEROUS. THEY TENDED TO IGNITE SPONTANEOUSLY IN WARM, MOIST AIR; THE FUMES RELEASED ON IGNITION WERE HIGHLY POISONOUS: PEOPLE MAKING THEM FREQUENTLY DEVELOPED PHOSSY JAW, A BONE DISEASE WHICH ROTTED THE JAW. THE FIGHT TO BAN LUCIFERS WAS LED BY GENERAL BOOTH OF THE SALVATION ARMY. HE TOOK PRACTICAL ACTION & STARTED A SAFETY MATCH FACTORY. UNFORTUNATELY THESE COST MORE TO MAKE & LUCIFERS CONTINUED UNTIL THEY WERE FINALLY MADE ILLEGAL IN 1912.

MILLIONS OF MATCHES
GREAT BRITAIN USES 100,000 MILLION MATCHES PER YEAR – THE EQUIVALENT IN MATCH STICKS OF 70,000 TREES. THEY ARE MADE ON AUTOMATED MACHINES WHICH PUT THE HEAD ON 6,900 MATCHES AT A TIME & TURN OUT 800 BOXES PER MINUTE.

HOW TO TEAR A NEWSPAPER IN 3
START TWO TEARS IN A SHEET OF NEWSPAPER & ASK A FRIEND TO TRY TO TEAR THE PAPER INTO 3 SECTIONS – HE IS BOUND TO FAIL UNLESS HE KNOWS THE TRICK: HOLD THE PAPER BETWEEN THE TWO TEARS IN YOUR MOUTH

☆ MATERIALS (MAN-MADE)
SUBSTANCES CONTRIVED FOR HUMAN EXPLOITS

EDIBLE STRUCTURAL MATERIAL
DEVELOPED BY THE GRUMMAN AIRCRAFT CORP. FOR SPACEMEN TO EAT IF FORCED TO REMAIN ALOFT LONGER THAN PLANNED. THE MATERIAL IS COMPOSED OF POWDERED MILK, MAIZE GRITS, CORNFLOUR & DRIED BANANA FLAKES. IT LOOKS SIMILAR TO FIBREBOARD & WILL BE MADE INTO SHELVES, PARTITIONS & INSTRUMENT PANELS.

RIGID FOAM & THE INSTANT IGLOO
POLYURETHANE FOAM IS MADE FROM 2 CHEMICALS WHICH, WHEN MIXED & WARMED, EXPAND 30 TIMES TO A FOAM WHICH SETS RIGID. THE INSTANT IGLOO, DEVELOPED FOR AN ARCTIC SURVIVAL PACK, COMES AS A PORTABLE PACK OF THE CHEMICALS, A HEMISPHERICAL PLASTIC BAG & A HEATING FUEL. THE PACK AUTOMATICALLY EXPANDS TO A 5FT DIAMETER 3IN. THICK SHELL WHEN THE FUEL IS LIT.

THE SMELLIEST MATERIAL
CALLED VANILLALDEHYDE 1/10,000 OF AN OUNCE WOULD BE DETECTABLE IN AN ENCLOSED SPACE WITH THE AREA OF A FOOTBALL PITCH 45FT HIGH. THE MOST EXPENSIVE MATERIAL IS AN ELEMENT CALLED CALIFORNIUM 252, OFFERED FOR SALE AT £40 FOR 1/10,000 GRAM. A 1LB. INGOT WOULD BE WORTH TWICE BRITAIN'S G.N.P.

NEW CONCRETES
VARIOUS NEW MATERIALS ARE REPLACING THE GRAVEL EMBEDDED IN CEMENT. GLASS FIBRES PRODUCE A STRONG MATERIAL CALLED G.R.C. WHICH IS BEING TRIED FOR COMPLETE SHIP'S HULLS. CARBONISED PUFFED WHEAT (MADE BY THE SAME PROCESS AS THE BREAKFAST CEREAL WITH SLIGHTLY DIFFERENT INGREDIENTS WHICH MAKE THE PRODUCT RIGID) PRODUCES A LIGHT MATERIAL THAT WILL MAKE STRUCTURES USING VAST VOLUMES OF CONCRETE POSSIBLE.

PLASTICS
A FIRST USE OF BAKELITE WAS FOR THE ROLLS-ROYCES GEAR KNOB. PLASTICS HAVE SINCE DECLINED IN STATUS, PARTLY DUE TO THEIR ADOPTION FOR UNSUITED APPLICATIONS. SOME PALM TREES IN LOS ANGELES WERE RECENTLY REPLACED BY PLASTIC IMITATIONS. THE AUTHORITIES CLAIM THE ONLY MAINTENANCE NEEDED IS AN ANNUAL SCRUB.

POLLUTION
MAN-MADE MATERIALS THAT DO NOT DECOMPOSE CAN CAUSE DISASTERS WHEN DUMPED AT SEA. TURTLES ARE DYING BY THE THOUSAND IN FLORIDA THROUGH EATING PLASTIC BAGS WHICH RESEMBLE THEIR FAVOURITE FOOD, JELLYFISH. DISCARDED NYLON FISHING NETS OFF NEWFOUNDLAND TRAP HUGE VOLUMES OF FISH & SINK TO THE BOTTOM. HERE THE FISH DECAY & THE NETS, EMPTY AGAIN, RISE TO TRAP MORE FISH.

ICE CREAM
THE LARGEST ICE CREAM SUNDAE EVER MADE (FOR AN AMERICAN TV SHOW) COMPRISED 600LB ICE CREAM, 68 PINTS CHOCOLATE SAUCE & £300 WORTH CHOPPED NUTS.

SYNTHETIC MEAT
CALLED KESP. IT COMES IN 2 FLAVOURS (CHICKEN & BEEF). TO GET THE CONSISTENCY OF REAL MEAT, WHICH IS COMPOSED OF FIBRES, IT IS SPUN BY THE SAME PROCESS AS SYNTHETIC TEXTILE YARNS.

HOW TO MAKE A NOISE FROM DRIED PEAS THAT LASTS ¼ HOUR
ARRANGE TUMBLERS, PEAS & TIN LID AS SHOWN. FILL TOP TUMBLER WITH WATER. PEAS OVERFLOW & DROP ON TIN LID AS THEY EXPAND.

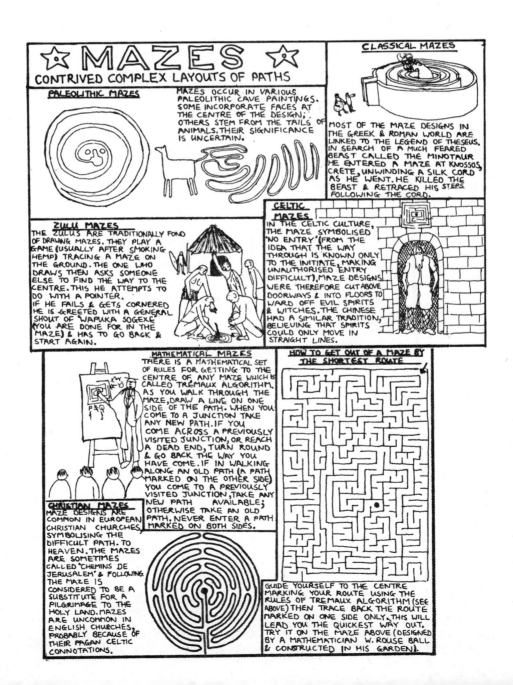

☆ MAZES ☆
CONTRIVED COMPLEX LAYOUTS OF PATHS

MAZES OCCUR IN VARIOUS PALEOLITHIC CAVE PAINTINGS. SOME INCORPORATE FACES AT THE CENTRE OF THE DESIGN; OTHERS STEM FROM THE TAILS OF ANIMALS. THEIR SIGNIFICANCE IS UNCERTAIN.

PALEOLITHIC MAZES

CLASSICAL MAZES
MOST OF THE MAZE DESIGNS IN THE GREEK & ROMAN WORLD ARE LINKED TO THE LEGEND OF THESEUS. IN SEARCH OF A MUCH FEARED BEAST CALLED THE MINOTAUR HE ENTERED A MAZE AT KNOSSOS, CRETE, UNWINDING A SILK CORD AS HE WENT. HE KILLED THE BEAST & RETRACED HIS STEPS FOLLOWING THE CORD.

ZULU MAZES
THE ZULUS ARE TRADITIONALLY FOND OF DRAWING MAZES. THEY PLAY A GAME (USUALLY AFTER SMOKING HEMP) TRACING A MAZE ON THE GROUND. THE ONE WHO DRAWS THEN ASKS SOMEONE ELSE TO FIND THE WAY TO THE CENTRE. THIS HE ATTEMPTS TO DO WITH A POINTER.
IF HE FAILS & GETS CORNERED HE IS GREETED WITH A GENERAL SHOUT OF 'WAPUKA SOGEXE' (YOU ARE DONE FOR IN THE MAZE) & HAS TO GO BACK & START AGAIN.

CELTIC MAZES
IN THE CELTIC CULTURE, THE MAZE SYMBOLISED 'NO ENTRY' (FROM THE IDEA THAT THE WAY THROUGH IS KNOWN ONLY TO THE INITIATE, MAKING UNAUTHORISED ENTRY DIFFICULT). MAZE DESIGNS WERE THEREFORE CUT ABOVE DOORWAYS & INTO FLOORS TO WARD OFF EVIL SPIRITS & WITCHES. THE CHINESE HAD A SIMILAR TRADITION, BELIEVING THAT SPIRITS COULD ONLY MOVE IN STRAIGHT LINES.

MATHEMATICAL MAZES
THERE IS A MATHEMATICAL SET OF RULES FOR GETTING TO THE CENTRE OF ANY MAZE WHICH IS CALLED TREMAUX ALGORITHM. AS YOU WALK THROUGH THE MAZE, DRAW A LINE ON ONE SIDE OF THE PATH. WHEN YOU COME TO A JUNCTION TAKE ANY NEW PATH. IF YOU COME ACROSS A PREVIOUSLY VISITED JUNCTION, OR REACH A DEAD END, TURN ROUND & GO BACK THE WAY YOU HAVE COME. IF IN WALKING ALONG AN OLD PATH (A PATH MARKED ON THE OTHER SIDE) YOU COME TO A PREVIOUSLY VISITED JUNCTION, TAKE ANY NEW PATH AVAILABLE; OTHERWISE TAKE AN OLD PATH. NEVER ENTER A PATH MARKED ON BOTH SIDES.

CHRISTIAN MAZES
MAZE DESIGNS ARE COMMON IN EUROPEAN CHRISTIAN CHURCHES, SYMBOLISING THE DIFFICULT PATH TO HEAVEN. THE MAZES ARE SOMETIMES CALLED 'CHEMINS DE JERUSALEM' & FOLLOWING THE MAZE IS CONSIDERED TO BE A SUBSTITUTE FOR A PILGRIMAGE TO THE HOLY LAND. MAZES ARE UNCOMMON IN ENGLISH CHURCHES, PROBABLY BECAUSE OF THEIR PAGAN CELTIC CONNOTATIONS.

HOW TO GET OUT OF A MAZE BY THE SHORTEST ROUTE
GUIDE YOURSELF TO THE CENTRE MARKING YOUR ROUTE USING THE RULES OF TREMAUX ALGORITHM (SEE ABOVE) THEN TRACE BACK THE ROUTE MARKED ON ONE SIDE ONLY. THIS WILL LEAD YOU THE QUICKEST WAY OUT. TRY IT ON THE MAZE ABOVE (DESIGNED BY A MATHEMATICIAN W. ROUSE BALL & CONSTRUCTED IN HIS GARDEN).

☆ MEAT ☆
FLESH OF ANIMALS USED AS FOOD

PORK

IT IS OFTEN CLAIMED THAT THE PROHIBITION ON EATING PORK IN THE JEWISH & MUSLIM RELIGIONS HAD ITS ORIGIN IN MEDICAL DOCTRINE. HOWEVER, PORK WAS EATEN BY THE PEOPLES OF THE NEAR EAST UNTIL ABOUT 1800 BC. IT CAN BE A DANGEROUS MEAT IN A HOT CLIMATE BUT ITS DANGERS WERE WELL KNOWN TO THE EGYPTIANS WHO ATE IT WITHOUT TABOOS. A MORE LIKELY EXPLANATION IS AN INTENSE DISLIKE OF THE PIG BY THE NOMADIC TRIBES DUE TO ITS LACK OF STAMINA & UNSUITABILITY FOR HERDING.

CHINESE MEAT

THE CHINESE HAVE PROBABLY EATEN THE MEAT OF A GREATER VARIETY OF BEASTS THAN ANY OTHER CULTURE: LOCUSTS, SILKWORMS, GRUBS, SNAKES, CAMELS, TIGERS, WOLVES & BEARS. THEIR CUISINE WAS INFLUENCED BY A PERSISTENT SHORTAGE OF TIMBER. THIS LED TO DISHES REQUIRING A SHORT COOKING TIME (AS AGAINST OUR PRACTICE OF SLOW ROASTING LARGE CUTS OF MEAT)

STEAK

THE MODERN LIKING FOR LEAN FLESH IS ALMOST WITHOUT PRECEDENT AMONG HUMANS OR ANIMALS. MOST CARNIVOROUS SPECIES CONSUME THEIR PREYS' INTESTINES & GUT BEFORE BOTHERING WITH THE RUMP OR FILLET STEAKS. IT HAS RECENTLY BEEN FOUND THAT A DIET EXCLUSIVELY OF LEAN FLESH HAS CAUSED THE DEATH OF MANY TAME FALCONS (FROM A DIETARY BONE DISEASE)

PRESERVED MEAT

UNTIL ABOUT 1840 PASSENGER SHIPS HAD TO CARRY LIVE ANIMALS TO PROVIDE FRESH MEAT FOR THE MENU. THE INTRODUCTION OF CANNED MEAT WAS SEEN AS A GREAT ADVANCE. MEAT THUS PRESERVED EATS NOTHING, NOR DRINKS – IT IS NOT APT TO DIE, DOES NOT TUMBLE OVERBOARD OR GET ITS LEGS BROKEN OR ITS FLESH WORN OFF ITS BONES BY TUMBLING ABOUT THE SHIP IN BAD WEATHER.

AUTOMATIC BUTCHERY

THE FRENCH HAVE INVENTED AN AUTOMATIC BUTCHERING MACHINE. CARCASSES ENTER IT WHILE STILL WARM; THEY ARE SAWN IN TWO; THEN CIRCULAR KNIVES REMOVE THE FILLET, SHOULDER & THE NECK. THE REMAINING MEAT IS THEN CUT OFF THE BACKBONE. THE MACHINE CAN BE ADJUSTED FOR BEEF, MUTTON OR VEAL, & PROCESSES 60 CARCASSES PER HOUR QUICKLY & HYGIENICALLY.

MEAT & PROTEIN

THE PERCENTAGE OF PROTEIN NECESSARY IN ONE'S DIET FOR HEALTH IS UNCERTAIN. PUBLISHED PROTEIN REQUIREMENT TABLES USED TO BE BASED ON THE INCIDENCE OF KWASHIORKOR AMONG CERTAIN AFRICAN TRIBES. THIS DISEASE WAS THOUGHT TO BE CAUSED BY PROTEIN DEFICIENCY. HOWEVER, IT HAS NOW BEEN SHOWN THAT THIS DISEASE ONLY RESULTS FROM THE COMBINATION OF LACK OF PROTEIN & LACK OF CALORIES. CULTURES EATING SUFFICIENT CALORIES NEED FAR LESS PROTEIN (THE LATEST FIGURE IS ABOUT 2 oz MEAT PER PERSON PER DAY).

INEFFICIENT MEAT

ACCORDING TO WORLD MEDICINE MAGAZINE THE WEST FEEDS MORE GRAIN TO LIVESTOCK THAN THE THIRD WORLD CONSUMES. FATTENING ANIMALS IS A GROSSLY INEFFICIENT METHOD OF FOOD PRODUCTION: CATTLE MUST BE FED ABOUT 10lb OF GRAIN FOR EVERY 1lb OF MEAT THEY PRODUCE.

HOW TO PASS A SWEET THROUGH A POSTCARD

INSERT SMALL MAGNETIC BITS OF STEEL UNDER THE WRAPPERS OF TWO SWEETS. ARRANGE ON TABLE AS ABOVE ENSURING THAT AUDIENCE ARE STANDING SO THEY CAN'T SEE SWEET UNDER POSTCARD. PLACE HAND OVER TOP SWEET & PALM IT. AS YOU LIFT IT OFF, THE SWEET BELOW WILL FALL INTO GLASS, APPEARING TO HAVE PASSED THROUGH POSTCARD.

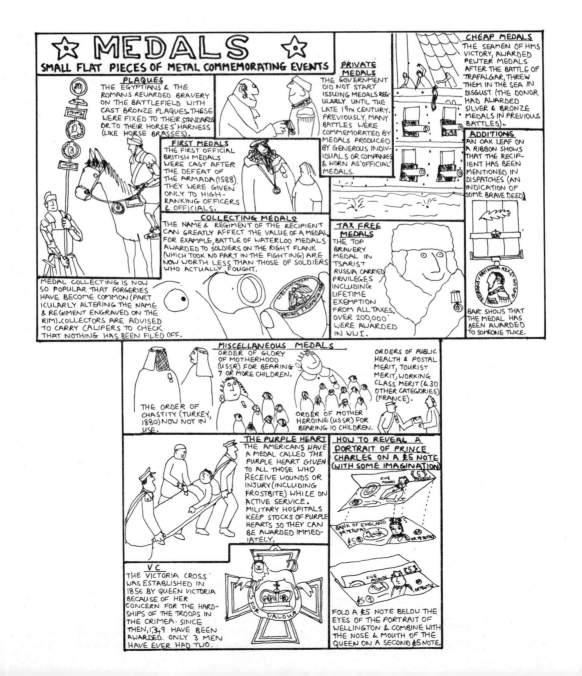

☆ MEDALS ☆
SMALL FLAT PIECES OF METAL COMMEMORATING EVENTS

PLAQUES

THE EGYPTIANS & THE ROMANS REWARDED BRAVERY ON THE BATTLEFIELD WITH CAST BRONZE PLAQUES. THESE WERE FIXED TO THEIR STANDARDS OR TO THEIR HORSES' HARNESS (LIKE HORSE BRASSES).

FIRST MEDALS

THE FIRST OFFICIAL BRITISH MEDALS WERE CAST AFTER THE DEFEAT OF THE ARMADA (1588). THEY WERE GIVEN ONLY TO HIGH-RANKING OFFICERS & OFFICIALS.

COLLECTING MEDALS

THE NAME & REGIMENT OF THE RECIPIENT CAN GREATLY AFFECT THE VALUE OF A MEDAL. FOR EXAMPLE, BATTLE OF WATERLOO MEDALS AWARDED TO SOLDIERS ON THE RIGHT FLANK (WHICH TOOK NO PART IN THE FIGHTING) ARE NOW WORTH LESS THAN THOSE OF SOLDIERS WHO ACTUALLY FOUGHT.

MEDAL COLLECTING IS NOW SO POPULAR THAT FORGERIES HAVE BECOME COMMON (PARTICULARLY ALTERING THE NAME & REGIMENT ENGRAVED ON THE RIM). COLLECTORS ARE ADVISED TO CARRY CALIPERS TO CHECK THAT NOTHING HAS BEEN FILED OFF.

PRIVATE MEDALS

THE GOVERNMENT DID NOT START ISSUING MEDALS REGULARLY UNTIL THE LATE 19th CENTURY. PREVIOUSLY, MANY BATTLES WERE COMMEMORATED BY MEDALS PRODUCED BY GENEROUS INDIVIDUALS OR COMPANIES & WORN AS 'OFFICIAL' MEDALS.

TAX FREE MEDALS

THE TOP BRAVERY MEDAL IN TSARIST RUSSIA CARRIED PRIVILEGES INCLUDING LIFETIME EXEMPTION FROM ALL TAXES. OVER 200,000 WERE AWARDED IN WWI.

CHEAP MEDALS

THE SEAMEN OF HMS VICTORY, AWARDED PEWTER MEDALS AFTER THE BATTLE OF TRAFALGAR, THREW THEM IN THE SEA IN DISGUST (THE DONOR HAD AWARDED SILVER & BRONZE MEDALS IN PREVIOUS BATTLES).

ADDITIONS

AN OAK LEAF ON A RIBBON SHOWS THAT THE RECIPIENT HAS BEEN MENTIONED IN DISPATCHES (AN INDICATION OF SOME BRAVE DEED)

BAR SHOWS THAT THE MEDAL HAS BEEN AWARDED TO SOMEONE TWICE.

MISCELLANEOUS MEDALS

ORDER OF GLORY OF MOTHERHOOD (USSR) FOR BEARING 7 OR MORE CHILDREN.

ORDER OF MOTHER HEROINE (USSR) FOR BEARING 10 CHILDREN.

THE ORDER OF CHASTITY (TURKEY, 1880) NOW NOT IN USE.

ORDERS OF PUBLIC HEALTH & POSTAL MERIT, TOURIST MERIT, WORKING CLASS MERIT (& 30 OTHER CATEGORIES) (FRANCE).

THE PURPLE HEART

THE AMERICANS HAVE A MEDAL CALLED *THE PURPLE HEART* GIVEN TO ALL THOSE WHO RECEIVE WOUNDS OR INJURY (INCLUDING FROSTBITE) WHILE ON ACTIVE SERVICE. MILITARY HOSPITALS KEEP STOCKS OF PURPLE HEARTS SO THEY CAN BE AWARDED IMMEDIATELY.

HOW TO REVEAL A PORTRAIT OF PRINCE CHARLES ON A £5 NOTE (WITH SOME IMAGINATION)

FOLD A £5 NOTE BELOW THE EYES OF THE PORTRAIT OF WELLINGTON & COMBINE WITH THE NOSE & MOUTH OF THE QUEEN ON A SECOND £5 NOTE.

VC

THE VICTORIA CROSS WAS ESTABLISHED IN 1856 BY QUEEN VICTORIA BECAUSE OF HER CONCERN FOR THE HARDSHIPS OF THE TROOPS IN THE CRIMEA. SINCE THEN, 1,3,9 HAVE BEEN AWARDED. ONLY 3 MEN HAVE EVER HAD TWO.

☆ MEDICAL HISTORY ☆
ATTEMPTS TO PREVENT THE BODY MALFUNCTIONING

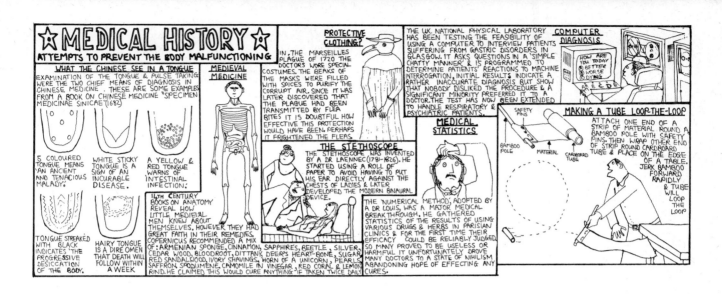

WHAT THE CHINESE SEE IN A TONGUE
EXAMINATION OF THE TONGUE & PULSE TAKING WERE THE TWO CHIEF MEANS OF DIAGNOSIS IN CHINESE MEDICINE. THESE ARE SOME EXAMPLES FROM A BOOK ON CHINESE MEDICINE 'SPECIMEN MEDICINAE SINICAE' (1682)

5 COLOURED TONGUE MEANS 'AN ANCIENT AND TENACIOUS MALADY.'

WHITE STICKY TONGUE IS A SIGN OF AN INCURABLE DISEASE.

A YELLOW & RED TONGUE WARNS OF INTESTINAL INFECTION.

TONGUE STREAKED WITH BLACK INDICATES 'THE PROGRESSIVE DESICCATION OF THE BODY.'

HAIRY TONGUE IS A DIRE OMEN THAT DEATH WILL FOLLOW WITHIN A WEEK

MEDIEVAL MEDICINE
11TH CENTURY BOOKS ON ANATOMY REVEAL HOW LITTLE MEDIEVAL MEN KNEW ABOUT THEMSELVES. HOWEVER THEY HAD GREAT FAITH IN THEIR REMEDIES. COPERNICUS RECOMMENDED A MIX OF: ARMENIAN SPONGE, CINNAMON, SAPPHIRES, BEETLE, SILVER, CEDAR WOOD, BLOODROOT, DITTANY, DEER'S HEART-BONE, SUGAR, RED SANDALWOOD, IVORY SHAVINGS, HORN OF A UNICORN, PEARLS, SAFFRON SPODIUM ENE, CAMOMILE IN VINEGAR, RED CORAL & LEMON RIND. HE CLAIMED THIS WOULD CURE ANYTHING IF TAKEN TWICE DAILY

PROTECTIVE CLOTHING?
IN THE MARSEILLES PLAGUE OF 1720 THE DOCTORS WORE SPECIAL COSTUMES. THE BEAKS OF THE MASKS WERE FILLED WITH SPICES TO PURIFY THE CORRUPT AIR. SINCE IT WAS LATER DISCOVERED THAT THE PLAGUE HAD BEEN TRANSMITTED BY FLEA BITES IT IS DOUBTFUL HOW EFFECTIVE THIS PROTECTION WOULD HAVE BEEN. PERHAPS IT FRIGHTENED THE FLEAS

THE STETHOSCOPE
THE STETHOSCOPE WAS INVENTED BY A DR LAENNEC (1781-1826). HE STARTED USING A ROLL OF PAPER TO AVOID HAVING TO PUT HIS EAR DIRECTLY AGAINST THE CHESTS OF LADIES & LATER DEVELOPED THE MODERN BINAURAL DEVICE.

MEDICAL STATISTICS
THE 'NUMERICAL METHOD' ADOPTED BY A DR LOUIS, WAS A MAJOR MEDICAL BREAKTHROUGH. HE GATHERED STATISTICS OF THE RESULTS OF USING VARIOUS DRUGS & HERBS IN PARISIAN CLINICS & FOR THE FIRST TIME THEIR EFFICACY COULD BE RELIABLY JUDGED. SO MANY PROVED TO BE USELESS OR HARMFUL IT UNFORTUNATELY DROVE MANY DOCTORS TO A STATE OF NIHILISM ABANDONING HOPE OF EFFECTING ANY CURES.

COMPUTER DIAGNOSIS
THE U.K. NATIONAL PHYSICAL LABORATORY HAS BEEN TESTING THE FEASIBILITY OF USING A COMPUTER TO INTERVIEW PATIENTS SUFFERING FROM GASTRIC DISORDERS IN GLASGOW. IT ASKS QUESTIONS IN A 'SIMPLE CHATTY MANNER' & IS PROGRAMMED TO DETERMINE PATIENTS' REACTIONS TO MACHINE INTERROGATION. INITIAL RESULTS INDICATE A RATHER INACCURATE DIAGNOSIS BUT SHOW THAT NOBODY DISLIKED THE PROCEDURE & A SIGNIFICANT MINORITY PREFERRED IT TO A DOCTOR. THE TEST HAS NOW BEEN EXTENDED TO HANDLE RESPIRATORY & PSYCHIATRIC PATIENTS.

MAKING A TUBE LOOP-THE-LOOP
ATTACH ONE END OF A STRIP OF MATERIAL ROUND A BAMBOO POLE WITH SAFETY PINS. THEN WRAP OTHER END OF STRIP ROUND CARDBOARD TUBE & PLACE ON THE EDGE OF A TABLE. JERK BAMBOO FORWARD RAPIDLY & TUBE WILL LOOP THE LOOP

☆ MEMORY ☆
THE ABILITY TO REMEMBER EXPERIENCE

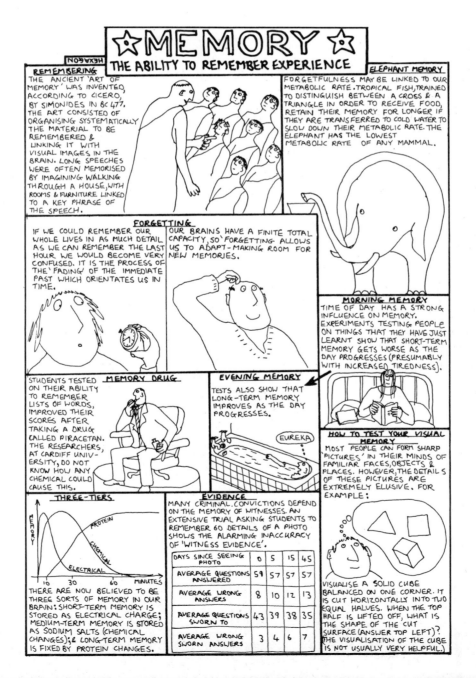

REMEMBERING
THE ANCIENT 'ART OF MEMORY' WAS INVENTED ACCORDING TO CICERO, BY SIMONIDES IN BC 477. THE ART CONSISTED OF ORGANISING SYSTEMATICALLY THE MATERIAL TO BE REMEMBERED & LINKING IT WITH VISUAL IMAGES IN THE BRAIN. LONG SPEECHES WERE OFTEN MEMORISED BY IMAGINING WALKING THROUGH A HOUSE, WITH ROOMS & FURNITURE LINKED TO A KEY PHRASE OF THE SPEECH.

FORGETTING
IF WE COULD REMEMBER OUR WHOLE LIVES IN AS MUCH DETAIL AS WE CAN REMEMBER THE LAST HOUR WE WOULD BECOME VERY CONFUSED. IT IS THE PROCESS OF THE 'FADING' OF THE IMMEDIATE PAST WHICH ORIENTATES US IN TIME.

OUR BRAINS HAVE A FINITE TOTAL CAPACITY, SO FORGETTING ALLOWS US TO ADAPT-MAKING ROOM FOR NEW MEMORIES.

MEMORY DRUG
STUDENTS TESTED ON THEIR ABILITY TO REMEMBER LISTS OF WORDS, IMPROVED THEIR SCORES AFTER TAKING A DRUG CALLED PIRACETAN. THE RESEARCHERS, AT CARDIFF UNIVERSITY, DO NOT KNOW HOW ANY CHEMICAL COULD CAUSE THIS.

EVENING MEMORY
TESTS ALSO SHOW THAT LONG-TERM MEMORY IMPROVES AS THE DAY PROGRESSES.

EUREKA

THREE-TIERS
THERE ARE NOW BELIEVED TO BE THREE SORTS OF MEMORY IN OUR BRAIN: SHORT-TERM MEMORY IS STORED AS ELECTRICAL CHARGE; MEDIUM-TERM MEMORY IS STORED AS SODIUM SALTS (CHEMICAL CHANGES); & LONG-TERM MEMORY IS FIXED BY PROTEIN CHANGES.

(graph axes: MEMORY vs MINUTES; 10, 30, 60; curves labelled PROTEIN, CHEMICAL, ELECTRICAL)

ELEPHANT MEMORY
FORGETFULNESS MAY BE LINKED TO OUR METABOLIC RATE. TROPICAL FISH, TRAINED TO DISTINGUISH BETWEEN A CROSS & A TRIANGLE IN ORDER TO RECEIVE FOOD, RETAIN THEIR MEMORY FOR LONGER IF THEY ARE TRANSFERRED TO COLD WATER TO SLOW DOWN THEIR METABOLIC RATE. THE ELEPHANT HAS THE LOWEST METABOLIC RATE OF ANY MAMMAL.

MORNING MEMORY
TIME OF DAY HAS A STRONG INFLUENCE ON MEMORY. EXPERIMENTS TESTING PEOPLE ON THINGS THAT THEY HAVE JUST LEARNT SHOW THAT SHORT-TERM MEMORY GETS WORSE AS THE DAY PROGRESSES (PRESUMABLY WITH INCREASED TIREDNESS).

HOW TO TEST YOUR VISUAL MEMORY
MOST PEOPLE CAN FORM SHARP 'PICTURES' IN THEIR MINDS OF FAMILIAR FACES, OBJECTS & PLACES. HOWEVER, THE DETAILS OF THESE PICTURES ARE EXTREMELY ELUSIVE. FOR EXAMPLE:

VISUALISE A SOLID CUBE BALANCED ON ONE CORNER. IT IS CUT HORIZONTALLY INTO TWO EQUAL HALVES. WHEN THE TOP HALF IS LIFTED OFF, WHAT IS THE SHAPE OF THE CUT SURFACE (ANSWER TOP LEFT)? THE VISUALISATION OF THE CUBE IS NOT USUALLY VERY HELPFUL.

EVIDENCE
MANY CRIMINAL CONVICTIONS DEPEND ON THE MEMORY OF WITNESSES. AN EXTENSIVE TRIAL ASKING STUDENTS TO REMEMBER 60 DETAILS OF A PHOTO SHOWS THE ALARMING INACCURACY OF 'WITNESS EVIDENCE'.

DAYS SINCE SEEING PHOTO	0	5	15	45
AVERAGE QUESTIONS ANSWERED	59	57	57	57
AVERAGE WRONG ANSWERS	8	10	12	13
AVERAGE QUESTIONS SWORN TO	43	39	38	35
AVERAGE WRONG SWORN ANSWERS	3	4	6	7

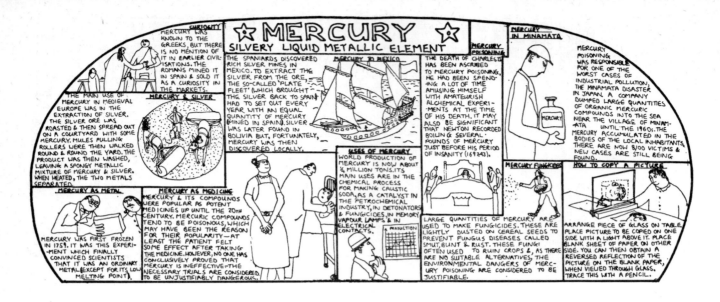

☆ MERCURY ☆
SILVERY LIQUID METALLIC ELEMENT

MERCURY & CURIOSITY

MERCURY WAS KNOWN TO THE GREEKS, BUT THERE IS NO MENTION OF IT IN EARLIER CIVILISATIONS. THE ROMANS MINED IT IN SPAIN & SOLD IT AS A CURIOSITY IN THE MARKETS.

MERCURY & SILVER

THE MAIN USE OF MERCURY IN MEDIEVAL EUROPE WAS IN THE EXTRACTION OF SILVER. THE SILVER ORE WAS ROASTED & THEN SPREAD OUT ON A COURTYARD WITH SOME MERCURY. MULES PULLING ROLLERS WERE THEN WALKED ROUND & ROUND THE YARD. THE PRODUCT WAS THEN WASHED, LEAVING A SPONGY METALLIC MIXTURE OF MERCURY & SILVER. WHEN HEATED, THE TWO METALS SEPARATED.

MERCURY TO MEXICO

THE SPANIARDS DISCOVERED RICH SILVER MINES IN MEXICO. TO EXTRACT THE SILVER FROM THE ORE, THE SO-CALLED 'PLATE FLEET' (WHICH BROUGHT THE SILVER BACK TO SPAIN) HAD TO SET OUT EVERY YEAR WITH AN EQUAL QUANTITY OF MERCURY MINED IN SPAIN. SILVER WAS LATER FOUND IN BOLIVIA BUT, FORTUNATELY, MERCURY WAS THEN DISCOVERED LOCALLY.

MERCURY AS METAL

MERCURY WAS FIRST FROZEN IN 1759. IT WAS THIS EXPERIMENT WHICH FINALLY CONVINCED SCIENTISTS THAT IT WAS AN ORDINARY METAL (EXCEPT FOR ITS LOW MELTING POINT).

MERCURY AS MEDICINE

MERCURY & ITS COMPOUNDS WERE POPULAR AS POTENT MEDICINES UP UNTIL THE 20TH CENTURY. MERCURIC COMPOUNDS TEND TO BE POISONOUS, WHICH MAY HAVE BEEN THE REASON FOR THEIR POPULARITY—AT LEAST THE PATIENT FELT SOME EFFECT AFTER TAKING THE MEDICINE. HOWEVER, NO ONE HAS CONCLUSIVELY PROVED THAT MERCURY IS INEFFECTIVE—THE NECESSARY TRIALS ARE CONSIDERED TO BE UNJUSTIFIABLY DANGEROUS.

USES OF MERCURY

WORLD PRODUCTION OF MERCURY IS NOW ABOUT ¼ MILLION TONS. ITS MAIN USES ARE IN THE CHEMICAL PROCESS FOR MAKING CAUSTIC SODA, AS A CATALYST IN THE PETROCHEMICAL INDUSTRY, IN DETONATORS & FUNGICIDES, IN MERCURY VAPOUR LAMPS & IN ELECTRICAL CONTACTS.

PRODUCTION

MERCURY POISONING

THE DEATH OF CHARLES II HAS BEEN ASCRIBED TO MERCURY POISONING. HE HAD BEEN SPENDING A LOT OF TIME AMUSING HIMSELF WITH AMATEURISH ALCHEMICAL EXPERIMENTS AT THE TIME OF HIS DEATH. IT MAY ALSO BE SIGNIFICANT THAT NEWTON RECORDED BOILING SEVERAL POUNDS OF MERCURY JUST BEFORE HIS PERIOD OF INSANITY (1692-3).

MERCURY FUNGICIDES

LARGE QUANTITIES OF MERCURY ARE USED TO MAKE FUNGICIDES. THESE ARE LIGHTLY DUSTED ON CEREAL SEEDS TO PREVENT FUNGUS DISEASES CALLED SMUT, BUNT & RUST. THESE FUNGI OFTEN USED TO RUIN CROPS &, AS THERE ARE NO SUITABLE ALTERNATIVES, THE ENVIRONMENTAL DANGERS OF MERCURY POISONING ARE CONSIDERED TO BE JUSTIFIABLE.

MERCURY IN MINAMATA

MERCURY POISONING WAS RESPONSIBLE FOR ONE OF THE WORST CASES OF INDUSTRIAL POLLUTION, THE MINAMATA DISASTER IN JAPAN. A COMPANY DUMPED LARGE QUANTITIES OF ORGANIC MERCURIC COMPOUNDS INTO THE SEA NEAR THE VILLAGE OF MINAMATA UNTIL THE 1960s. THE MERCURY ACCUMULATED IN THE BODIES OF THE LOCAL INHABITANTS. THERE ARE NOW 8/100 VICTIMS & NEW CASES ARE STILL BEING FOUND.

HOW TO COPY A PICTURE

ARRANGE PIECE OF GLASS ON TABLE. PLACE PICTURE TO BE COPIED ON ONE SIDE WITH A LIGHT ABOVE IT. PLACE BLANK SHEET OF PAPER ON OTHER SIDE. YOU CAN THEN OBTAIN A REVERSED REFLECTION OF THE PICTURE ON THE BLANK PAPER. WHEN VIEWED THROUGH GLASS, TRACE THIS WITH A PENCIL.

☆ METEORITES ☆
LARGE EXTRATERRESTRIAL LUMPS OF MATTER

METEORITE SCEPTICISM

IN THE 18TH CENTURY, SCIENTISTS DID NOT BELIEVE THAT STONES FELL FROM THE SKY. THEY THOUGHT THAT METEORITE SIGHTINGS WERE FIGMENTS OF THE PEASANTS' FERTILE IMAGINATION, & THAT THE METEORITES WERE MERELY STONES WHICH HAD BEEN STRUCK BY LIGHTNING. IT WAS NOT UNTIL A LARGE FALL OCCURRED IN A HEAVILY POPULATED PART OF FRANCE IN 1803, THAT THEIR EXTRATERRESTRIAL ORIGIN CAME TO BE ACCEPTED.

METEORITE POPULATION

ABOUT 75,000,000 METEORS, OR SHOOTING STARS, ENTER OUR ATMOSPHERE DAILY. ASTRONOMERS BELIEVE THAT MOST OF THESE ARE SMALL COMETS, WITH NO SOLID NUCLEI. ONLY ABOUT 500 METEORITES (WHICH HAVE SOLID NUCLEI) REACH THE EARTH BEFORE BURNING UP. OF THESE ABOUT 350 FALL IN THE SEA & MOST OF THE REST FALL UNNOTICED. ONLY ABOUT 6 PER YEAR ARE ANALYSED BY SCIENTIFIC LABORATORIES.

METEORITE NOISES

FALLING METEORITES PRODUCE A PUZZLING VARIETY OF SOUNDS (CAUSED BY COMPRESSION WAVES SIMILAR TO THOSE CREATED BY SUPERSONIC AIRCRAFT). METEORITES TEND TO BREAK UP IN THE ATMOSPHERE & EACH COMPONENT TRIGGERS OFF ITS OWN DETONATION, AUDIBLE UP TO 500KM. IN THE UPPER ATMOSPHERE THEY ALSO MAKE PECULIAR SINGING & BUZZING NOISES. CRACKLING, HISSING & RUSTLING NOISES HAVE ALSO BEEN HEARD.

METEORITE MYSTERY

METEORITES BECOME EXTREMELY HOT WHEN ENTERING THE ATMOSPHERE & THIS NOT ONLY MELTS THE EXTERIORS TO A SORT OF GLASS, BUT ALSO CAUSES MANY METEORITES OF LESS DURABLE COMPOSITION TO VAPORISE, LEAVING NO TRACE. SO WE STILL DO NOT KNOW THE COMPOSITION OF A LARGE PROPORTION OF THE METEORITES IN SPACE.

METEORITE VISIBILITY

METEORITES ARE ONLY VISIBLE IN FLIGHT BECAUSE OF THE LUMINOUS GAS & DUST CLOUD WHICH THEY PRODUCE. THE WEIGHT OF THE DUST EXPELLED IN THE UPPER ATMOSPHERE FAR EXCEEDS THAT OF THE FINAL METEORITE.

ONE CLASS OF METEORITE, THE CARBONIFEROUS CHONDITE, CONTAINS ORGANIC COMPOUNDS, INCLUDING AMINO ACIDS. THESE HAVE BEEN CLAIMED AS PROOF OF EXTRATERRESTRIAL LIFE, & ALSO AS THE 'SPARK' WHICH TRIGGERED OFF LIFE ON EARTH. THERE IS STRONG EVIDENCE THAT METEORITES HAVE AN EXTRATERRESTRIAL CHEMICAL EVOLUTION THAT PRECEDED THE ORIGIN OF LIFE ON EARTH.

METEORITE CASUALTIES

THE ONLY REPORTS OF ANY HUMAN DEATH FROM A METEORITE ARE 2 UNSUBSTANTIATED REPORTS FROM THE MIDDLE AGES OF ITALIAN MONKS BEING HIT. A CALF WAS STRUCK IN OHIO IN 1860, & A DOG WAS STRUCK IN EGYPT IN 1911. AN AMERICAN WOMAN WAS HIT ON THE ARM BY A METEORITE IN 1954. IT CRASHED THROUGH HER ROOF & RICOCHETED OFF THE RADIO.

HOW TO TAKE A PHOTO OF FRIENDS TALKING TO THEMSELVES

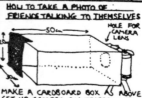

MAKE A CARDBOARD BOX AS ABOVE. SET UP CAMERA ON TRIPOD WITH FRIENDS TO ONE SIDE OF PICTURE & SET FOCUS & APERTURE. STICK BOX OVER LENS & DRAPE BLACK CLOTH OVER HALF OF BOX OPENING SO ONLY HALF OF PICTURE INCLUDING FRIENDS ARE EXPOSED. TAKE PHOTO, THEN MOVE CLOTH & FRIENDS TO OTHER HALF OF PICTURE & TAKE SECOND PHOTO WITHOUT WINDING ON FILM. BE CAREFUL NOT TO MOVE CAMERA BETWEEN PHOTOS.

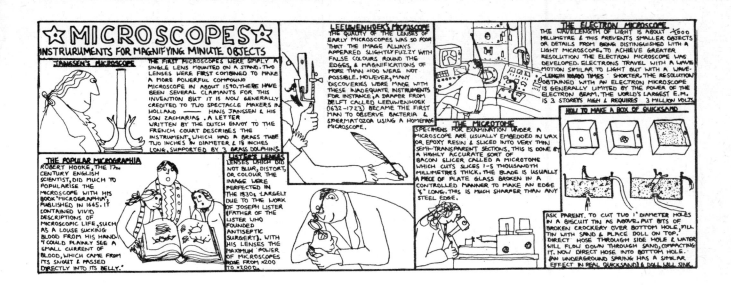

☆ MICROSCOPES ☆
INSTRUMENTS FOR MAGNIFYING MINUTE OBJECTS

JANSSEN'S MICROSCOPE
THE FIRST MICROSCOPES WERE SIMPLY A SINGLE LENS MOUNTED ON A STAND. TWO LENSES WERE FIRST COMBINED TO MAKE A MORE POWERFUL COMPOUND MICROSCOPE IN ABOUT 1590. THERE HAVE BEEN SEVERAL CLAIMANTS FOR THIS INVENTION BUT IT IS NOW GENERALLY CREDITED TO TWO SPECTACLE MAKERS IN HOLLAND — HANS JANSSEN & HIS SON ZACHARIAS. A LETTER WRITTEN BY THE DUTCH ENVOY TO THE FRENCH COURT DESCRIBES THE INSTRUMENT, WHICH HAD A BRASS TUBE TWO INCHES IN DIAMETER & 18 INCHES LONG, SUPPORTED BY 3 BRASS DOLPHINS.

THE POPULAR MICROGRAPHIA
ROBERT HOOKE, THE 17TH CENTURY ENGLISH SCIENTIST, DID MUCH TO POPULARISE THE MICROSCOPE WITH HIS BOOK 'MICROGRAPHIA' PUBLISHED IN 1665. IT CONTAINED VIVID DESCRIPTIONS OF MICROSCOPIC LIFE, SUCH AS A LOUSE SUCKING BLOOD FROM HIS HAND. "I COULD PLAINLY SEE A SMALL CURRENT OF BLOOD, WHICH CAME FROM ITS SNOUT & PASSED DIRECTLY INTO ITS BELLY."

LISTER'S LENSES
LENSES WHICH DID NOT BLUR, DISTORT, OR COLOUR THE IMAGE WERE PERFECTED IN THE 1830s, LARGELY DUE TO THE WORK OF JOSEPH LISTER (FATHER OF THE LISTER WHO FOUNDED ANTISEPTIC SURGERY). WITH HIS LENSES THE MAXIMUM POWER OF MICROSCOPES ROSE FROM x100 TO x1000.

LEEUWENHOEK'S MICROSCOPE
THE QUALITY OF THE LENSES OF EARLY MICROSCOPES WAS SO POOR THAT THE IMAGE ALWAYS APPEARED SLIGHTLY FUZZY WITH FALSE COLOURS ROUND THE EDGES, & MAGNIFICATIONS OF MORE THAN x100 WERE NOT POSSIBLE. HOWEVER, MANY DISCOVERIES WERE MADE WITH THESE INADEQUATE INSTRUMENTS. FOR INSTANCE, A DRAPER FROM DELFT CALLED LEEUWENHOEK (1632–1723) BECAME THE FIRST MAN TO OBSERVE BACTERIA & SPERMATOZOA USING A HOMEMADE MICROSCOPE.

THE MICROTOME
SPECIMENS FOR EXAMINATION UNDER A MICROSCOPE ARE USUALLY EMBEDDED IN WAX OR EPOXY RESIN & SLICED INTO VERY THIN SEMI-TRANSPARENT SECTIONS. THIS IS DONE BY A HIGHLY ACCURATE SORT OF BACON SLICER CALLED A MICROTOME WHICH CUTS SLICES 1-5 THOUSANDTH MILLIMETRES THICK. THE BLADE IS USUALLY A PIECE OF PLATE GLASS BROKEN IN A CONTROLLED MANNER TO MAKE AN EDGE ½" LONG. THIS IS MUCH SHARPER THAN ANY STEEL EDGE.

THE ELECTRON MICROSCOPE
THE WAVELENGTH OF LIGHT IS ABOUT 1/2000 MILLIMETRE & THIS PREVENTS SMALLER OBJECTS OR DETAILS FROM BEING DISTINGUISHED WITH A LIGHT MICROSCOPE. TO ACHIEVE GREATER RESOLUTION THE ELECTRON MICROSCOPE WAS DEVELOPED. ELECTRONS TRAVEL WITH A WAVE MOTION SIMILAR TO LIGHT BUT WITH A WAVELENGTH 100,000 TIMES SHORTER. THE RESOLUTION OBTAINED WITH AN ELECTRON MICROSCOPE IS GENERALLY LIMITED BY THE POWER OF THE ELECTRON BEAM. THE WORLD'S LARGEST E.M. IS 3 STOREYS HIGH & REQUIRES 3 MILLION VOLTS.

HOW TO MAKE A BOX OF QUICKSAND
ASK PARENT TO CUT TWO 1" DIAMETER HOLES IN A BISCUIT TIN AS ABOVE. PUT BITS OF BROKEN CROCKERY OVER BOTTOM HOLE, FILL TIN WITH SAND & PLACE DOLL ON TOP. DIRECT HOSE THROUGH SIDE HOLE & WATER WILL FLOW DOWN THROUGH SAND, COMPACTING IT. NOW DIRECT HOSE INTO BOTTOM HOLE. (AN UNDERGROUND SPRING HAS A SIMILAR EFFECT IN REAL QUICKSANDS) & DOLL WILL SINK.

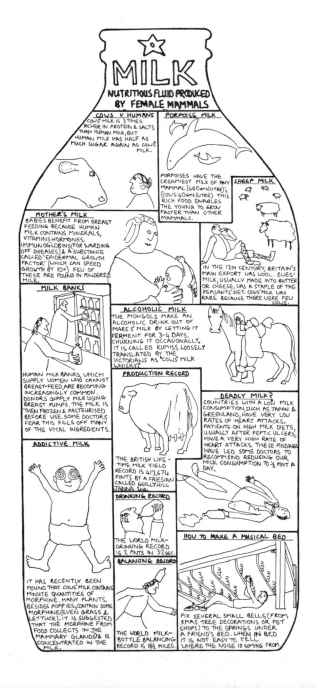

☆ MILK
NUTRITIOUS FLUID PRODUCED BY FEMALE MAMMALS

COWS V HUMANS
COWS' MILK IS 3 TIMES RICHER IN PROTEIN & SALTS THAN HUMAN MILK, BUT HUMAN MILK HAS HALF AS MUCH SUGAR AGAIN AS COWS' MILK.

PORPOISE MILK
PORPOISES HAVE THE CREAMIEST MILK OF ANY MAMMAL (460gm/LITRE) (COWS: 40gm/LITRE) THIS RICH FOOD ENABLES THE YOUNG TO GROW FASTER THAN OTHER MAMMALS.

SHEEP MILK
IN THE 13TH CENTURY, BRITAIN'S MAIN EXPORT WAS WOOL. EWES' MILK, USUALLY MADE INTO BUTTER OR CHEESE, WAS A STAPLE OF THE PEASANTS' DIET. COWS' MILK WAS RARE BECAUSE THERE WERE FEW COWS.

MOTHER'S MILK
BABIES BENEFIT FROM BREAST FEEDING BECAUSE HUMAN MILK CONTAINS MINERALS, VITAMINS, HORMONES, IMMUNOGLOBINS (FOR WARDING OFF DISEASES) & A SUBSTANCE CALLED 'EPIDERMAL GROWTH FACTOR' (WHICH CAN SPEED GROWTH BY 10x). FEW OF THESE ARE FOUND IN POWDERED MILK.

MILK BANKS
HUMAN MILK BANKS, WHICH SUPPLY WOMEN WHO CANNOT BREAST-FEED, ARE BECOMING INCREASINGLY COMMON. DONORS SUPPLY MILK USING BREAST PUMPS. THE MILK IS THEN FROZEN & PASTEURISED BEFORE USE. SOME DOCTORS FEAR THIS KILLS OFF MANY OF THE VITAL INGREDIENTS.

ALCOHOLIC MILK
THE MONGOLS MAKE AN ALCOHOLIC DRINK OUT OF MARES' MILK BY LETTING IT FERMENT FOR 3-4 DAYS, CHURNING IT OCCASIONALLY. IT IS CALLED KUMISS, LOOSELY TRANSLATED BY THE VICTORIANS AS "COWS' MILK WHISKY".

ADDICTIVE MILK
IT HAS RECENTLY BEEN FOUND THAT COWS' MILK CONTAINS MINUTE QUANTITIES OF MORPHINE. MANY PLANTS, BESIDES POPPIES, CONTAIN SOME MORPHINE (EVEN GRASS & LETTUCE). IT IS SUGGESTED THAT THE MORPHINE FROM FOOD COLLECTS IN THE MAMMARY GLANDS & IS CONCENTRATED IN THE MILK.

PRODUCTION RECORD
THE BRITISH LIFE-TIME MILK YIELD RECORD IS 413,674 PINTS BY A FRIESIAN CALLED GUILLYHILL JANNA 2ND.

DRINKING RECORD
THE WORLD MILK-DRINKING RECORD IS 2 PINTS IN 3.2 SEC.

BALANCING RECORD
THE WORLD MILK-BOTTLE BALANCING RECORD IS 18½ MILES.

DEADLY MILK?
COUNTRIES WITH A LOW MILK CONSUMPTION, SUCH AS JAPAN & GREENLAND, HAVE VERY LOW RATES OF HEART ATTACKS. PATIENTS ON HIGH MILK DIETS, USUALLY AFTER PEPTIC ULCERS, HAVE A VERY HIGH RATE OF HEART ATTACKS. THESE FINDINGS HAVE LED SOME DOCTORS TO RECOMMEND REDUCING OUR MILK CONSUMPTION TO ½ PINT A DAY.

HOW TO MAKE A MUSICAL BED
FIX SEVERAL SMALL BELLS (FROM XMAS TREE DECORATIONS OR PET SHOPS) TO THE SPRINGS UNDER A FRIEND'S BED. WHEN IN BED IT IS NOT EASY TO TELL WHERE THE NOISE IS COMING FROM.

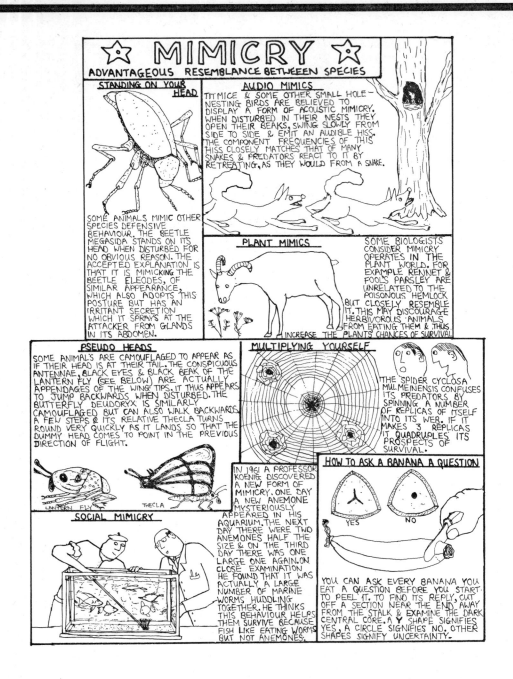

☆ MIMICRY ☆
ADVANTAGEOUS RESEMBLANCE BETWEEN SPECIES

STANDING ON YOUR HEAD

SOME ANIMALS MIMIC OTHER SPECIES DEFENSIVE BEHAVIOUR. THE BEETLE MEGASIDA STANDS ON ITS HEAD WHEN DISTURBED FOR NO OBVIOUS REASON. THE ACCEPTED EXPLANATION IS THAT IT IS MIMICKING THE BEETLE ELEODES, OF SIMILAR APPEARANCE, WHICH ALSO ADOPTS THIS POSTURE BUT HAS AN IRRITANT SECRETION WHICH IT SPRAYS AT THE ATTACKER FROM GLANDS IN ITS ABDOMEN.

AUDIO MIMICS

TITMICE & SOME OTHER SMALL HOLE-NESTING BIRDS ARE BELIEVED TO DISPLAY A FORM OF ACOUSTIC MIMICRY. WHEN DISTURBED IN THEIR NESTS THEY OPEN THEIR BEAKS, SWING SLOWLY FROM SIDE TO SIDE & EMIT AN AUDIBLE HISS. THE COMPONENT FREQUENCIES OF THIS HISS CLOSELY MATCHES THAT OF MANY SNAKES & PREDATORS REACT TO IT BY RETREATING, AS THEY WOULD FROM A SNAKE.

PLANT MIMICS

SOME BIOLOGISTS CONSIDER MIMICRY OPERATES IN THE PLANT WORLD. FOR EXAMPLE RENNET & FOOLS PARSLEY ARE UNRELATED TO THE POISONOUS HEMLOCK BUT CLOSELY RESEMBLE IT. THIS MAY DISCOURAGE HERBIVOROUS ANIMALS FROM EATING THEM & THUS INCREASE THE PLANTS CHANCES OF SURVIVAL.

PSEUDO HEADS

SOME ANIMALS ARE CAMOUFLAGED TO APPEAR AS IF THEIR HEAD IS AT THEIR TAIL. THE CONSPICUOUS ANTENNAE, BLACK EYES & BLACK BEAK OF THE LANTERN FLY (SEE BELOW) ARE ACTUALLY APPENDAGES OF THE WING TIPS. IT THUS APPEARS TO JUMP BACKWARDS WHEN DISTURBED. THE BUTTERFLY DEUDORYX IS SIMILARLY CAMOUFLAGED BUT CAN ALSO WALK BACKWARDS A FEW STEPS & ITS RELATIVE THECLA TURNS ROUND VERY QUICKLY AS IT LANDS SO THAT THE DUMMY HEAD COMES TO POINT IN THE PREVIOUS DIRECTION OF FLIGHT.

LANTERN FLY   THECLA

MULTIPLYING YOURSELF

THE SPIDER CYCLOSA MULMEINENSIS CONFUSES ITS PREDATORS BY SPINNING A NUMBER OF REPLICAS OF ITSELF INTO ITS WEB. IF IT MAKES 3 REPLICAS IT QUADRUPLES ITS PROSPECTS OF SURVIVAL.

IN 1961 A PROFESSOR KOENIG DISCOVERED A NEW FORM OF MIMICRY. ONE DAY A NEW ANEMONE MYSTERIOUSLY APPEARED IN HIS AQUARIUM. THE NEXT DAY THERE WERE TWO ANEMONES HALF THE SIZE & ON THE THIRD DAY THERE WAS ONE LARGE ONE AGAIN. ON CLOSE EXAMINATION HE FOUND THAT IT WAS ACTUALLY A LARGE NUMBER OF MARINE WORMS HUDDLING TOGETHER. HE THINKS THIS BEHAVIOUR HELPS THEM SURVIVE BECAUSE FISH LIKE EATING WORMS BUT NOT ANEMONES.

HOW TO ASK A BANANA A QUESTION

YES   NO

YOU CAN ASK EVERY BANANA YOU EAT A QUESTION BEFORE YOU START TO PEEL IT. TO FIND ITS REPLY, CUT OFF A SECTION NEAR THE END AWAY FROM THE STALK & EXAMINE THE DARK CENTRAL CORE. A Y SHAPE SIGNIFIES YES, A CIRCLE SIGNIFIES NO. OTHER SHAPES SIGNIFY UNCERTAINTY.

SOCIAL MIMICRY

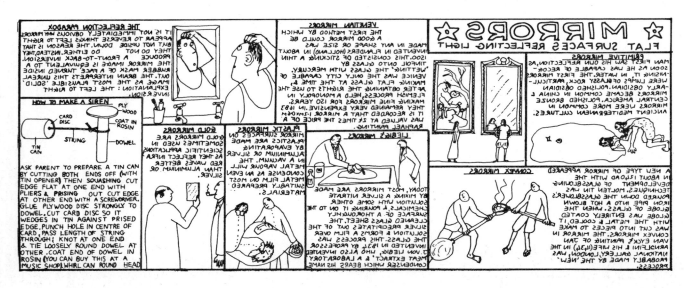

☆ MIRRORS ☆
FLAT SURFACES REFLECTING LIGHT

PRIMITIVE MIRRORS

MAN FIRST SAW HIS OWN REFLECTION, AS NARCISSUS DID, BY GAZING INTO STILL WATER. HE WAS CAPABLE OF RECOGNISING IT IN WATER. THE FIRST MIRRORS WERE LUMPS OF GLASSY ROCK, PARTICULARLY OBSIDIAN. POLISHED OBSIDIAN MIRRORS BECAME COMMON IN CHINA & CENTRAL AMERICA. POLISHED BRONZE MIRRORS WERE MORE COMMON IN ANCIENT MEDITERRANEAN CULTURES.

VENETIAN MIRRORS

THE FIRST METHOD BY WHICH MIRRORS COULD BE MADE IN ANY SHAPE OR SIZE WAS INVENTED IN FLANDERS (HOLLAND) IN ABOUT 1500. THIS CONSISTED OF STICKING A THIN TINFOIL ONTO GLASS BY "WETTING" THE GLASS WITH MERCURY. VENICE WAS THE ONLY CITY CAPABLE OF MAKING FLAT GLASS AT THE TIME & AFTER OBTAINING THE RIGHTS TO USE THE FLEMISH PROCESS, HELD A MONOPOLY IN MAKING FINE MIRRORS FOR 150 YEARS. THEY REMAINED VERY EXPENSIVE. IN 1837 IT IS RECORDED THAT A MIRROR 1.24×0.84 WAS VALUED AT 2× TIMES THE PRICE OF A RAPHAEL PAINTING.

COMPLEX MIRRORS

A NEW TYPE OF MIRROR APPEARED IN ABOUT 1840 WITH THE DEVELOPMENT OF GLASS-BLOWING TECHNIQUES. MOLTEN TIN WAS POURED DOWN THE GLASSBLOWER'S IRON PIPE INTO A HOT & BLOWN GLOBE OF GLASS. WHEN THE GLOBE WAS ENTIRELY COATED WITH THE METAL & COOLED, IT WAS CUT INTO PIECES TO MAKE CONVEX MIRRORS. THE MIRROR IN VAN EYCK'S PAINTING OF "JAN ARNOLFINI & HIS WIFE" (1434) IN THE NATIONAL GALLERY, LONDON, WAS PROBABLY MADE BY THE "NEW" PROCESS.

THE REFLECTION PARADOX

IT IS NOT IMMEDIATELY OBVIOUS WHY MIRRORS APPEAR TO REVERSE THINGS LEFT TO RIGHT BUT NOT UPSIDE DOWN. THE REASON IS THAT THEY DO NOT PRODUCE A FRONT-TO-BACK INVERSION. RUBBER MIRROR IMAGE IS EQUIVALENT TO A RUBBER MASK OF A FACE TURNED INSIDE OUT. THE BRAIN INTERPRETS THIS UNREAL IMAGE AS THE MOST PLAUSIBLE "SOLID" EXPLANATION: THE LEFT-TO-RIGHT INVERSION.

HOW TO MAKE A SIREN

FLY WOOD / CARD DISC / COAT IN ROSIN / STRING / DOWEL / TIN CAN

ASK PARENT TO PREPARE A TIN CAN BY CUTTING BOTH ENDS OFF (WITH TIN OPENER) THEN SQUASHING CUT EDGE FLAT AT ONE END WITH PLIERS & PRISING OUT CUT EDGE AT OTHER END WITH A SCREWDRIVER. GLUE PLYWOOD DISC STRONGLY TO DOWEL. CUT CARD DISC SO IT WEDGES IN TIN AGAINST PRISED EDGE. PUNCH HOLE IN CENTRE OF CARD, PASS LENGTH OF STRING THROUGH; KNOT AT ONE END & TIE LOOSELY ROUND DOWEL AT OTHER. COAT END OF DOWEL IN ROSIN (YOU CAN BUY THIS AT A MUSIC SHOP). WHIRL CAN ROUND HEAD

GOLD MIRRORS

GOLD MIRRORS ARE SOMETIMES USED IN SCIENTIFIC APPLICATIONS AS THEY REFLECT INFRA RED WAVES BETTER THAN ALUMINIUM OR SILVER.

PLASTIC MIRRORS

PLASTICS ARE MADE BY EVAPORATING ALUMINIUM OR SILVER ONTO THE VACUUM. THE FILM OF METAL IS ON MOST SUITABLY PREPARED MATERIALS.

LIEBIG'S MIRRORS

TODAY, MOST MIRRORS ARE MADE BY MIXING A SILVER NITRATE SOLUTION WITH SOME OTHER CHEMICALS & POURING IT ON TO THE SURFACE OF A THOROUGHLY CLEANED GLASS SHEET. THE SILVER PRECIPITATES OUT OF THE SOLUTION & FORMS A FILM OVER THE GLASS. THIS PROCESS WAS INVENTED IN 1835 BY PROFESSOR J. VON LIEBIG, WHO ALSO INVENTED MEAT EXTRACT, A LABORATORY CONDENSER WHICH BEARS HIS NAME

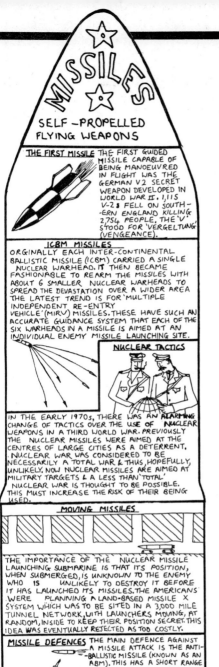

MISSILES
SELF-PROPELLED FLYING WEAPONS

THE FIRST MISSILE THE FIRST GUIDED MISSILE CAPABLE OF BEING MANOEUVRED IN FLIGHT WAS THE GERMAN V2 SECRET WEAPON DEVELOPED IN WORLD WAR II. 1,115 V-2s FELL ON SOUTHERN ENGLAND KILLING 2,754 PEOPLE. THE 'V' STOOD FOR 'VERGELTUNG' (VENGEANCE).

ICBM MISSILES
ORGINALLY EACH INTER-CONTINENTAL BALLISTIC MISSILE (ICBM) CARRIED A SINGLE NUCLEAR WARHEAD. IT THEN BECAME FASHIONABLE TO REARM THE MISSILES WITH ABOUT 6 SMALLER NUCLEAR WARHEADS TO SPREAD THE DEVASTATION OVER A WIDER AREA THE LATEST TREND IS FOR 'MULTIPLE INDEPENDENT RE-ENTRY VEHICLE' (MIRV) MISSILES. THESE HAVE SUCH AN ACCURATE GUIDANCE SYSTEM THAT EACH OF THE SIX WARHEADS IN A MISSILE IS AIMED AT AN INDIVIDUAL ENEMY MISSILE LAUNCHING SITE.

NUCLEAR TACTICS
IN THE EARLY 1970s, THERE WAS AN ALARMING CHANGE OF TACTICS OVER THE USE OF NUCLEAR WEAPONS IN A THIRD WORLD WAR. PREVIOUSLY THE NUCLEAR MISSILES WERE AIMED AT THE CENTRES OF LARGE CITIES AS A DETERRENT. NUCLEAR WAR WAS CONSIDERED TO BE NECESSARILY A TOTAL WAR & THUS, HOPEFULLY, UNLIKELY. NOW NUCLEAR MISSILES ARE AIMED AT MILITARY TARGETS & A LESS THAN 'TOTAL' NUCLEAR WAR IS THOUGHT TO BE POSSIBLE. THIS MUST INCREASE THE RISK OF THEIR BEING USED.

MOVING MISSILES
THE IMPORTANCE OF THE NUCLEAR MISSILE LAUNCHING SUBMARINE IS THAT ITS POSITION, WHEN SUBMERGED, IS UNKNOWN TO THE ENEMY WHO IS UNLIKELY TO DESTROY IT BEFORE IT HAS LAUNCHED ITS MISSILES. THE AMERICANS WERE PLANNING A LAND-BASED MISSILE X SYSTEM WHICH WAS TO BE SITED IN A 3,000 MILE TUNNEL NETWORK, WITH LAUNCHERS MOVING, AT RANDOM, INSIDE TO KEEP THEIR POSITION SECRET. THIS IDEA WAS EVENTUALLY REJECTED AS TOO COSTLY.

MISSILE DEFENCES THE MAIN DEFENCE AGAINST A MISSILE ATTACK IS THE ANTI-BALLISTIC MISSILE (KNOWN AS AN ABM). THIS HAS A SHORT RANGE & HOMES IN ON THE APPROACHING MISSILE'S RADAR OR ENGINE HEAT. THERE ARE ALSO DEVICES WHICH RELEASE FLARES & BITS OF SILVER PAPER TO CONFUSE THE MISSILE'S HEAT & RADAR SENSORS.

CRUISE MISSILES
U.S. AIR FORCE

THE CRUISE MISSILE IS ESSENTIALLY A PILOTLESS AIRCRAFT WHICH NAVIGATES TO ITS TARGET (ACCURATELY TO WITHIN 30 metres) USING MAPS FED INTO ITS COMPUTER. IT IS DIFFICULT TO DETECT IN ADVANCE AS IT FLIES VERY LOW (BELOW 100m) &, ON A RADAR SCREEN, APPEARS TO BE NO LARGER THAN MANY BIRDS. IT IS RELATIVELY CHEAP ———— ABOUT THE SAME AS THE COST OF A MODERN TANK & ONE-THIRTIETH OF THE COST OF A MODERN FIGHTER AIRCRAFT. THE FRIGHTENING POSSIBILITY IS THAT MANY SMALL COUNTRIES CAN NOW AFFORD TO HAVE A SMALL NUCLEAR FORCE.

HOW TO ATTACH A LOUD HORN TO A BICYCLE
BUY A PORTABLE AEROSOL FOG HORN FROM A YACHTING SHOP OR SHIP'S CHANDLER & A FRAME TO HOLD A WATER BOTTLE FROM A CYCLE SHOP. FIX WATER BOTTLE FRAME TO HANDLEBARS & SLIDE FOG HORN INTO IT.

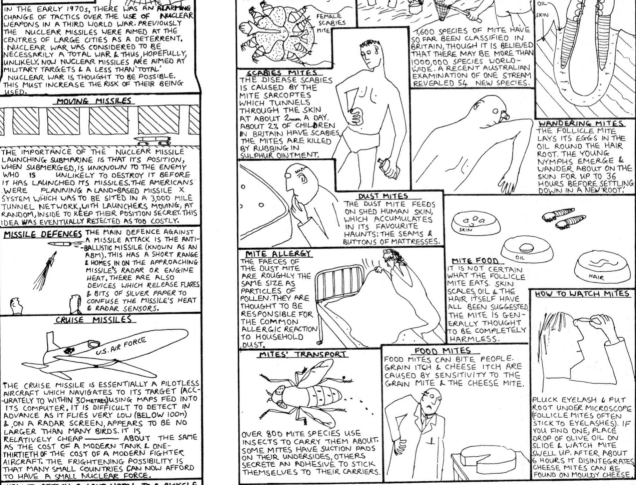

MITES
TINY ARACHNIDS WITH UNSEGMENTED BODIES

SPIDERY MITES
MITES ARE A PRIMITIVE FORM OF LIFE WHICH HAVE BEEN ON EARTH FOR 400 MILLION YEARS. THEY ARE CLASSED WITH SPIDERS AS THEY HAVE 8 LEGS (EXCEPT FOR THE YOUNG WHICH HAVE 6).

FEMALE SCABIES MITE

SCABIES MITES
THE DISEASE SCABIES IS CAUSED BY THE MITE SARCOPTES WHICH TUNNELS THROUGH THE SKIN AT ABOUT 2mm A DAY. ABOUT 2% OF CHILDREN IN BRITAIN HAVE SCABIES. THE MITES ARE KILLED BY RUBBING IN SULPHUR OINTMENT.

MITE ALLERGY
THE FAECES OF THE DUST MITE ARE ROUGHLY THE SAME SIZE AS PARTICLES OF POLLEN. THEY ARE THOUGHT TO BE RESPONSIBLE FOR THE COMMON ALLERGIC REACTION TO HOUSEHOLD DUST.

MITES' TRANSPORT
OVER 800 MITE SPECIES USE INSECTS TO CARRY THEM ABOUT. SOME MITES HAVE SUCTION PADS ON THEIR UNDERSIDES, OTHERS SECRETE AN ADHESIVE TO STICK THEMSELVES TO THEIR CARRIERS.

MASSES OF MITES
7,600 SPECIES OF MITE HAVE SO FAR BEEN CLASSIFIED IN BRITAIN, THOUGH IT IS BELIEVED THAT THERE MAY BE MORE THAN 1,000,000 SPECIES WORLDWIDE. A RECENT AUSTRALIAN EXAMINATION OF ONE STREAM REVEALED 54 NEW SPECIES.

DUST MITES
THE DUST MITE FEEDS ON SHED HUMAN SKIN, WHICH ACCUMULATES IN ITS FAVOURITE HAUNTS: THE SEAMS & BUTTONS OF MATTRESSES.

FOOD MITES
FOOD MITES CAN BITE PEOPLE. GRAIN ITCH & CHEESE ITCH ARE CAUSED BY SENSITIVITY TO THE GRAIN MITE & THE CHEESE MITE.

HUMAN MITES
MOST OF US CARRY FOLLICLE MITES (1/3mm LONG) IN THE WARM OILY SKIN ROUND THE ROOTS OF THE HAIR.

HAIR
OIL
SKIN

WANDERING MITES
THE FOLLICLE MITE LAYS ITS EGGS IN THE OIL ROUND THE HAIR ROOT. THE YOUNG NYMPHS EMERGE & WANDER ABOUT ON THE SKIN FOR UP TO 36 HOURS BEFORE SETTLING DOWN IN A NEW ROOT.

SKIN
OIL
HAIR

MITE FOOD
IT IS NOT CERTAIN WHAT THE FOLLICLE MITE EATS. SKIN SCALES, OIL & THE HAIR ITSELF HAVE ALL BEEN SUGGESTED. THE MITE IS GENERALLY THOUGHT TO BE COMPLETELY HARMLESS.

HOW TO WATCH MITES
PLUCK EYELASH & PUT ROOT UNDER MICROSCOPE (FOLLICLE MITES OFTEN STICK TO EYELASHES). IF YOU FIND ONE, PLACE DROP OF OLIVE OIL ON SLIDE & WATCH MITE SWELL UP. AFTER ABOUT 6 HOURS IT DISINTEGRATES CHEESE MITES CAN BE FOUND ON MOULDY CHEESE

☆ MODERN ARCHITECTURE ☆
RECENT BUILDING FASHIONS

HIGH LIVING
HIGH RISE FLATS ARE NO LONGER BEING BUILT IN BRITAIN BUT THEY ARE NOT UNPOPULAR EVERYWHERE. ALMOST THE ENTIRE POPULATION OF MADRID LIVE IN HIGH RISE FLATS & ARE SAID TO PREFER THEM. MORE THAN HALF THE POPULATION OF HONG KONG & SINGAPORE LIVE ABOVE THE 10TH FLOOR, BUT SHORTAGE OF SPACE DOES NOT LEAVE THEM MUCH OPTION.

SKYSCRAPERS
THE HIGHEST BUILDING BUILT ENTIRELY OF BRICKS IS 20 STOREYS HIGH (IN DENVER, COLORADO). HIGHER BUILDINGS REQUIRE A STRUCTURAL FRAME OF STEEL & CONCRETE TO HOLD THEM UP. THE WORLD'S HIGHEST BUILDING IS NOW THE SEARS TOWER (1,450ft, 109 STOREYS) IN CHICAGO. 16,700 PEOPLE WORK IN IT & IT IS 200ft HIGHER THAN THE EMPIRE STATE BUILDING.

ARCHITECTS' JOKES
SOME U.S. ARCHITECTS, REACTING AGAINST THE COLD, FORMAL NATURE OF MANY MODERN BUILDINGS, HAVE STARTED INCORPORATING JOKES IN THEIR DESIGNS. THE WALLS OF ONE BLOCK OF FLATS SPLAY OUT INTO A PILE OF RUBBLE, CAREFULLY ARRANGED & CEMENTED IN PLACE. THE ENTRANCE TO ONE SUPER-MARKET IS AN IRREGULAR LUMP OF THE BUILDING'S BRICKWORK WHICH SLIDES OUT ON RAILS.

POST MODERNISM
POST MODERNISM IS THE NAME GIVEN BY SOME ARCHITECTS TO A NUMBER OF CURRENTLY FASHIONABLE IDEAS. THEY CLAIM THAT THERE IS SOMETHING FUNDAMENTALLY INHUMAN ABOUT THE SCALE & FORMALITY OF MOST MODERN ARCHITECTURE. ONE IDEA IS TO INCREASE THE COMPLEXITY & IRREGULARITY OF THE SHAPE OF LARGE CITY BUILDINGS. ANOTHER IDEA IS TO START ADDING DECORATION (PEDIMENTS, FRIEZES, ARCHES ETC) TO BUILDINGS AGAIN. MANY ARCHITECTS DISMISS THEIR IDEAS AS BEING SOMEWHAT FRIVOLOUS. THIS IS PARTLY BECAUSE OF THEIR HABIT OF CALLING BUILDINGS 'DUCKS' OR 'DECORATED SHEDS' & PARTLY BECAUSE OF THEIR WORSHIP OF THE ODD BUILDINGS DESIGNED BY THE SURREALIST PAINTER GAUDI (NOTABLY BARCELONA CATHEDRAL).

HOW TO MAKE A PAPER SCREECHER
FOLD PAPER IN HALF. CUT TWO V-SHAPED NOTCHES FROM FOLDED EDGE FOLD EACH HALF BACK AS ABOVE. HOLD THE INSTRUMENT VERTICALLY BETWEEN THE FIRST & SECOND FINGERS & BRING IT TO YOUR LIPS. BLOW & IT WILL MAKE A PIERCING SCREECH.

EXPENSE
BRITAIN'S HIGHEST BUILDING IS THE WESTMINSTER BANK HQ IN THE CITY OF LONDON (600ft, 49 STOREYS). IT IS NOT QUITE FINISHED BUT IS EXPECTED TO TAKE THE WORLD RECORD FOR THE HIGHEST COST PER SQUARE FOOT OF OFFICE SPACE.

TECHNOLOGY

THE 1960s HAVE BEEN DESCRIBED AS THE HIGH TECHNOLOGY ERA OF BUILDING: THE ASSEMBLY ON-SITE OF FACTORY-MADE COMPONENTS - SUCH AS CONCRETE SLABS TO FORM THE BASIC BUILDING BLOCKS OF WALLS & FLOORS; HOWEVER THE NEW TECHNOLOGY DEMANDED PRECISION ASSEMBLY. THE CONCRETE PANELS WHICH SHOULD HAVE FITTED NEATLY TOGETHER OFTEN DID NOT; THE SEALS BETWEEN THE PANELS OFTEN LET IN WATER. THE GLC ESTIMATES THAT IT HAS SPENT £38 MILLION RECTIFYING FAULTS IN BUILDINGS LESS THAN TEN YEARS OLD. BRICKS & MORTAR ARE NOW BACK IN FASHION.

☆ MODERN ART ☆
CREATIONS INTENDED FOR VISUAL STIMULATION

MINIMALIST ART
MINIMAL ART IS A CLASSIFICATION GIVEN BY SOME CRITICS TO WORK THAT CONSISTS OF SIMPLE ARRANGEMENTS OF CUBES & OTHER SHAPES. THE CRITIC GREENBERG SEES THE MOVEMENT AS QUITE IMPORTANT IN 'SHRINKING THE AREA IN WHICH THINGS CAN SAFELY BE NON-ART'. THE ARTISTS HAVE VARIOUS THEORIES ABOUT THEIR WORK. ONE CALLED TONY SMITH USED TO BE AN ARCHITECT. HE TURNED TO MINIMALIST ART BECAUSE HE FELT THAT HIS BUILDINGS WERE TOO VULNERABLE TO ALTERATIONS WHICH WRECKED HIS INTENTIONS.

POP MUSIC & ART
BRITAIN'S SYSTEM OF ART EDUCATION IS LESS ACADEMIC & MORE LIBERAL THAN THAT OF MOST COUNTRIES. IT IS FREQUENTLY CRITICISED FOR THE LARGE NUMBER OF 'UNEMPLOYABLE' STUDENTS IT PRODUCES. HOWEVER, SOME SEE THIS FREEDOM AS A CAUSE FOR OUR DOMINANCE IN THE POP MUSIC WORLD. THE BEATLES HAD CLOSE CONNECTIONS WITH LIVERPOOL COLLEGE OF ART & PRACTICALLY EVERY MAJOR BRITISH POP-GROUP SINCE HAS HAD SOME KIND OF LINK WITH AN ART SCHOOL

PROLIFIC ART
THE MOST PROLIFIC LIVING ARTIST IS PROBABLY HERMAN H. SIMMS. HE WORKS AT DISNEYLAND PAINTING 'WHILE-YOU-WAIT' WATER COLOUR PORTRAITS. HE PRODUCED 9,803 IN 1973 ALONE.

HOW TO MAKE A REED INSTRUMENT FROM A STRAW
GRIP HERE WITH TEETH

CUT END OF PLASTIC DRINKING STRAW AS ABOVE. GRIP BETWEEN TEETH & BLOW. VARY POSITION IN MOUTH UNTIL YOU GET A BUZZING NOISE. YOU CAN LOWER THE PITCH OF THE BUZZ BY TAPING LENGTHS OF PLASTIC TUBE TO END OF STRAW & INCREASE THE VOLUME BY TAPING ON A FUNNEL.

SALEABLE ART
ONE TREND OF ART SINCE THE WAR HAS BEEN TO CONCERN ITSELF LESS & LESS WITH THE 'ART OBJECT' & MORE WITH THE PSYCHOLOGICAL EFFECT IT HAS ON THE SPECTATOR. THIS HAS ITS DISADVANTAGES AS COMMERCIAL ART GALLERIES & DEALERS DEPEND ON ARTISTS PRODUCING SALEABLE OBJECTS. CHRISTO, THE ARTIST FAMOUS FOR WRAPPING UP CLIFFS & BUILDINGS, HAS FOUND A WAY ROUND THE PROBLEM. HE PRODUCES VAST NUMBERS OF WORKING DRAWINGS & SKETCHES OF HIS PARCELS WHICH HE SELLS TO PAY FOR HIS PROJECTS

VALUABLE ART
THE HIGHEST PRICE EVER PAID FOR A PAINTING IN THE LIFETIME OF THE ARTIST IS £812,000 FOR A PICASSO IN 1969. POST-WAR MODERN ART HAS NOT USUALLY FETCHED SUCH HIGH PRICES. THE MOST EVER PAID FOR A BRITISH POST-WAR PAINTING IS £26,000 FOR A PAINTING OF A POPE IN 'CONVULSIVE HYSTERIA' BY FRANCIS BACON.

MODERN ART OR NOT
SOME CRITICS DO NOT THINK MODERN ART DESERVES THE NAME 'ART', OTHERS DO NOT CONSIDER IT TO BE MODERN. MANY CURRENT STYLES CAN BE SAID TO HAVE THEIR ROOTS IN THE WORK OF THE DADAISTS & DUCHAMP. DUCHAMP EXPERIMENTED WITH KINETIC ART & DISPLAYED 'READYMADES' (A PLATE RACK , A BICYCLE WHEEL & A LAVATORY SEAT THAT HE HAD BOUGHT) IN 1912. THE DADAISTS STAGED HAPPENINGS & PREACHED A PHILOSOPHY OF ANTI-ART (WHICH ADVOCATED THE INCLUSION OF EVERYTHING AS ART) IN THE 1930s.

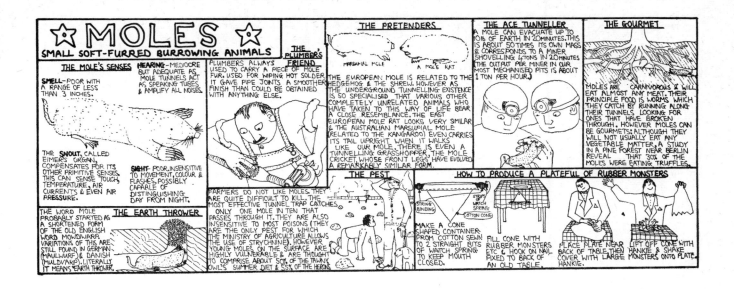

☆ MOLES ☆
SMALL SOFT-FURRED BURROWING ANIMALS

THE MOLE'S SENSES

SMELL - POOR WITH A RANGE OF LESS THAN 3 INCHES.

THE **SNOUT**, CALLED EIMER'S ORGAN, COMPENSATES FOR ITS OTHER PRIMITIVE SENSES. THIS CAN SENSE TOUCH, TEMPERATURE, AIR CURRENTS & EVEN AIR PRESSURE.

HEARING - MEDIOCRE BUT ADEQUATE AS MOLE TUNNELS ACT AS SPEAKING TUBES & AMPLIFY ALL NOISES.

SIGHT - POOR, INSENSITIVE TO MOVEMENT, COLOUR & FLASHES, POSSIBLY CAPABLE OF DISTINGUISHING DAY FROM NIGHT.

THE EARTH THROWER

THE WORD MOLE PROBABLY STARTED AS A SHORTENED FORM OF THE OLD ENGLISH WORD MOWDIWARP. VARIATIONS OF THIS ARE STILL FOUND IN GERMAN (MAULWARF) & DANISH (MULDVARP). LITERALLY IT MEANS 'EARTH THROWER'.

THE PLUMBER'S FRIEND

PLUMBERS ALWAYS USED TO CARRY A PIECE OF MOLE FUR. USED FOR WIPING HOT SOLDER IT GAVE PIPE JOINTS A SMOOTHER FINISH THAN COULD BE OBTAINED WITH ANYTHING ELSE.

THE PRETENDERS

MARSUPIAL MOLE   A MOLE RAT

THE EUROPEAN MOLE IS RELATED TO THE HEDGEHOG & THE SHREW. HOWEVER AS THE UNDERGROUND TUNNELLING EXISTENCE IS SO SPECIALISED THAT VARIOUS OTHER COMPLETELY UNRELATED ANIMALS WHO HAVE TAKEN TO THIS WAY OF LIFE BEAR A CLOSE RESEMBLANCE. THE EAST EUROPEAN MOLE RAT LOOKS VERY SIMILAR & THE AUSTRALIAN MARSUPIAL MOLE (RELATED TO THE KANGAROO) EVEN CARRIES ITS TAIL UPRIGHT WHEN IT WALKS LIKE OUR MOLE. THERE IS EVEN A TUNNELLING GRASSHOPPER, THE MOLE CRICKET, WHOSE FRONT LEGS HAVE EVOLVED A REMARKABLY SIMILAR FORM.

THE PEST

FARMERS DO NOT LIKE MOLES. THEY ARE QUITE DIFFICULT TO KILL. THE MOST EFFECTIVE TUNNEL TRAP CATCHES ONLY ONE MOLE IN TEN THAT PASSES THROUGH IT. THEY ARE ALSO INSENSITIVE TO MOST POISONS (THEY ARE THE ONLY PEST FOR WHICH THE MINISTRY OF AGRICULTURE ALLOWS THE USE OF STRYCHNINE). HOWEVER YOUNG MOLES ON THE SURFACE ARE HIGHLY VULNERABLE & ARE THOUGHT TO COMPRISE ABOUT 50% OF THE TAWNY OWL'S SUMMER DIET & 55% OF THE HERON'S.

THE ACE TUNNELLER

A MOLE CAN EVACUATE UP TO 10lb OF EARTH IN 20 MINUTES. THIS IS ABOUT 50 TIMES ITS OWN MASS & CORRESPONDS TO A MINER SHOVELLING 6 TONS IN 20 MINUTES. (THE OUTPUT PER MINER IN OUR MOST MECHANISED PITS IS ABOUT 1 TON PER HOUR.)

THE GOURMET

MOLES ARE CARNIVOROUS & WILL EAT ALMOST ANY MEAT. THEIR PRINCIPLE FOOD IS WORMS WHICH THEY CATCH BY RUNNING ALONG THEIR TUNNELS LOOKING FOR ONES THAT HAVE BROKEN THROUGH. HOWEVER MOLES CAN BE GOURMETS; ALTHOUGH THEY WILL NOT USUALLY EAT ANY VEGETABLE MATTER, A STUDY IN A PINE FOREST NEAR BERLIN REVEALED THAT 30% OF THE MOLES WERE EATING TRUFFLES.

HOW TO PRODUCE A PLATEFUL OF RUBBER MONSTERS

STRING BINDING / STRIP OF WATCH SPRING / COTTON CONE

MAKE A CONE SHAPED CONTAINER FROM COTTON SEWN TO 2 STRAIGHT BITS OF WATCH SPRING TO KEEP MOUTH CLOSED.

FILL CONE WITH RUBBER MONSTERS ETC & HOOK ON NAIL FIXED TO BACK OF AN OLD TABLE.

PLACE PLATE NEAR BACK OF TABLE THEN HANKIE & SHAKE COVER WITH LARGE MONSTERS ONTO PLATE. HANKIE.

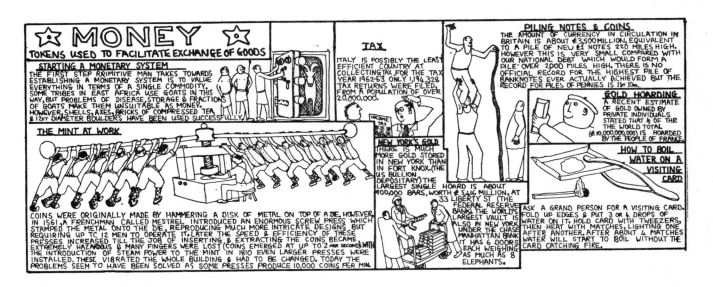

☆ MONEY ☆
TOKENS USED TO FACILITATE EXCHANGE OF GOODS

STARTING A MONETARY SYSTEM

THE FIRST STEP PRIMITIVE MAN TAKES TOWARDS ESTABLISHING A MONETARY SYSTEM IS TO VALUE EVERYTHING IN TERMS OF A SINGLE COMMODITY. SOME TRIBES IN EAST AFRICA USE GOATS IN THIS WAY, BUT PROBLEMS OF DISEASE, STORAGE & FRACTIONS OF GOATS MAKE THEM UNSUITABLE AS MONEY. HOWEVER SHELLS, AXES, BRICKS OF COMPRESSED TEA & 12FT DIAMETER BOULDERS HAVE BEEN USED SUCCESSFULLY.

THE MINT AT WORK

COINS WERE ORIGINALLY MADE BY HAMMERING A DISK OF METAL ON TOP OF A DIE. HOWEVER IN 1561, A FRENCHMAN CALLED MESTREL INTRODUCED AN ENORMOUS SCREW PRESS WHICH STAMPED THE METAL ONTO THE DIE, REPRODUCING MUCH MORE INTRICATE DESIGNS BUT REQUIRING UP TO 12 MEN TO OPERATE IT. LATER THE SPEED & EFFICIENCY OF THESE PRESSES INCREASED TILL THE JOB OF INSERTING & EXTRACTING THE COINS BECAME EXTREMELY HAZARDOUS & MANY FINGERS WERE LOST (COINS EMERGED AT UP TO 2 PER SECOND). WITH THE INTRODUCTION OF STEAM POWER TO THE MINT IN 1810 EVEN LARGER PRESSES WERE INSTALLED, THESE VIBRATED THE WHOLE BUILDING & HAD TO BE CHANGED. TODAY THE PROBLEMS SEEM TO HAVE BEEN SOLVED AS SOME PRESSES PRODUCE 10,000 COINS PER MIN.

TAX

ITALY IS POSSIBLY THE LEAST EFFICIENT COUNTRY AT COLLECTING TAX. FOR THE TAX YEAR 1962-63 ONLY 1,114,329 TAX RETURNS WERE FILED, FROM A POPULATION OF OVER 20,000,000.

INCOME TAX

NEW YORK'S GOLD

THERE IS MUCH MORE GOLD STORED IN NEW YORK THAN IN FORT KNOX. (THE US BULLION DEPOSITARY). THE LARGEST SINGLE HOARD IS ABOUT 700,000 BARS, WORTH £5,416 MILLION, AT 33 LIBERTY ST (THE FEDERAL RESERVE BANK). THE WORLD'S LARGEST VAULT IS ALSO IN NEW YORK UNDER THE CHASE MANHATTAN BANK. IT HAS 6 DOORS EACH WEIGHING AS MUCH AS 8 ELEPHANTS.

PILING NOTES & COINS

THE AMOUNT OF CURRENCY IN CIRCULATION IN BRITAIN IS ABOUT £3,500 MILLION, EQUIVALENT TO A PILE OF NEW £1 NOTES 220 MILES HIGH. HOWEVER THIS IS VERY SMALL COMPARED WITH OUR NATIONAL DEBT WHICH WOULD FORM A PILE OVER 2000 MILES HIGH. THERE IS NO OFFICIAL RECORD FOR THE HIGHEST PILE OF BANKNOTES EVER ACTUALLY ACHIEVED BUT THE RECORD FOR PILES OF PENNIES IS 11FT 10IN.

GOLD HOARDING

A RECENT ESTIMATE OF GOLD OWNED BY PRIVATE INDIVIDUALS STATED THAT ⅓ OF THE WORLD TOTAL (£10,000,000,000) IS HOARDED BY THE PEOPLE OF FRANCE.

HOW TO BOIL WATER ON A VISITING CARD

ASK A GRAND PERSON FOR A VISITING CARD. FOLD UP EDGES & PUT 3 OR 4 DROPS OF WATER ON IT. HOLD CARD WITH TWEEZERS, THEN HEAT WITH MATCHES, LIGHTING ONE AFTER ANOTHER. AFTER ABOUT 4 MATCHES WATER WILL START TO BOIL WITHOUT THE CARD CATCHING FIRE.

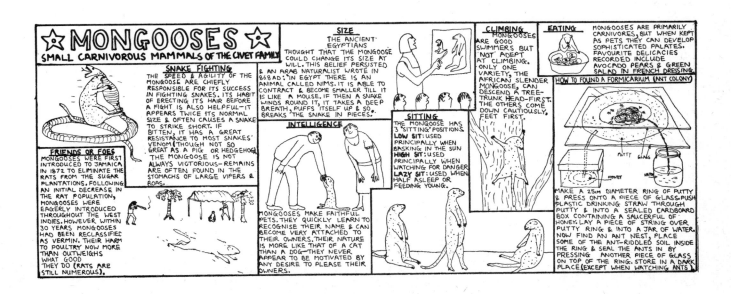

☆ MONGOOSES ☆
SMALL CARNIVOROUS MAMMALS OF THE CIVET FAMILY

SNAKE FIGHTING

THE SPEED & AGILITY OF THE MONGOOSE ARE CHIEFLY RESPONSIBLE FOR ITS SUCCESS IN FIGHTING SNAKES. ITS HABIT OF ERECTING ITS HAIR BEFORE A FIGHT IS ALSO HELPFUL - IT APPEARS TWICE ITS NORMAL SIZE & OFTEN CAUSES A SNAKE TO STRIKE SHORT. IF BITTEN, IT HAS A GREAT RESISTANCE TO MOST SNAKES' VENOM (THOUGH NOT SO GREAT AS A PIG OR HEDGEHOG). THE MONGOOSE IS NOT ALWAYS VICTORIOUS - REMAINS ARE OFTEN FOUND IN THE STOMACHS OF LARGE VIPERS & BOAS.

FRIENDS OR FOES

MONGOOSES WERE FIRST INTRODUCED TO JAMAICA IN 1872 TO ELIMINATE THE RATS FROM THE SUGAR PLANTATIONS. FOLLOWING AN INITIAL DECREASE IN THE RAT POPULATION, MONGOOSES WERE EAGERLY INTRODUCED THROUGHOUT THE WEST INDIES. HOWEVER WITHIN 30 YEARS MONGOOSES HAD BEEN RECLASSIFIED AS VERMIN. THEIR HARM TO POULTRY NOW OUTWEIGHS WHAT GOOD THEY DO (RATS ARE STILL NUMEROUS).

SIZE

THE ANCIENT EGYPTIANS THOUGHT THAT THE MONGOOSE COULD CHANGE ITS SIZE AT WILL. THIS BELIEF PERSISTED & AN ARAB NATURALIST WROTE IN 868 AD: 'IN EGYPT THERE IS AN ANIMAL CALLED NIMS. IT IS ABLE TO CONTRACT & BECOME SMALLER TILL IT IS LIKE A MOUSE, IF THEN A SNAKE WINDS ROUND IT, IT TAKES A DEEP BREATH, PUFFS ITSELF UP & SO BREAKS THE SNAKE IN PIECES.'

INTELLIGENCE

MONGOOSES MAKE FAITHFUL PETS. THEY QUICKLY LEARN TO RECOGNISE THEIR NAME & CAN BECOME VERY ATTACHED TO THEIR OWNERS. THEIR NATURE IS MORE LIKE THAT OF A CAT THAN A DOG AS THEY NEVER APPEAR TO BE MOTIVATED BY ANY DESIRE TO PLEASE THEIR OWNERS.

SITTING

THE MONGOOSE HAS 3 'SITTING' POSITIONS.
LOW SIT: USED PRINCIPALLY WHEN BASKING IN THE SUN
HIGH SIT: USED PRINCIPALLY WHEN WATCHING FOR DANGER
LAZY SIT: USED WHEN HALF ASLEEP OR FEEDING YOUNG.

CLIMBING

MONGOOSES ARE GOOD SWIMMERS BUT NOT ADEPT AT CLIMBING. ONLY ONE VARIETY, THE AFRICAN SLENDER MONGOOSE, CAN DESCEND A TREE-TRUNK HEAD-FIRST. THE OTHERS COME DOWN CAUTIOUSLY, FEET FIRST.

EATING

MONGOOSES ARE PRIMARILY CARNIVORES, BUT WHEN KEPT AS PETS THEY CAN DEVELOP SOPHISTICATED PALATES. FAVOURITE DELICACIES RECORDED INCLUDE AVOCADO PEARS & GREEN SALAD IN FRENCH DRESSING.

HOW TO FOUND A FORMICARIUM (ANT COLONY)

PUTTY / GLASS / HONEY

MAKE A 25CM DIAMETER RING OF PUTTY & PRESS ONTO A PIECE OF GLASS. PUSH PLASTIC DRINKING STRAW THROUGH PUTTY & INTO A SEALED CARDBOARD BOX CONTAINING A SAUCERFUL OF HONEY. LAY A PIECE OF STRING OVER PUTTY RING & INTO A JAR OF WATER. NOW FIND AN ANT NEST, PLACE SOME OF THE ANT-RIDDLED SOIL INSIDE THE RING & SEAL THE ANTS IN BY PRESSING ANOTHER PIECE OF GLASS ON TOP OF THE RING. STORE IN A DARK PLACE (EXCEPT WHEN WATCHING ANTS).

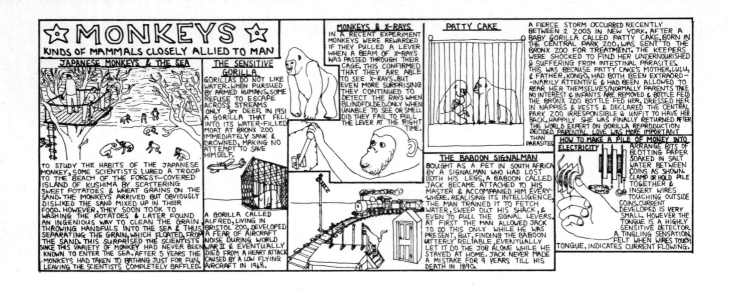

☆ MONKEYS ☆
KINDS OF MAMMALS CLOSELY ALLIED TO MAN

JAPANESE MONKEYS & THE SEA

TO STUDY THE HABITS OF THE JAPANESE MONKEY, SOME SCIENTISTS LURED A TROOP TO THE BEACH OF THE FOREST-COVERED ISLAND OF KUSHIMA BY SCATTERING SWEET POTATOES & WHEAT GRAINS ON THE SAND. THE MONKEYS ARRIVED BUT OBVIOUSLY DISLIKED THE SAND MIXED UP IN THEIR FOOD. HOWEVER, THEY SOON TOOK TO WASHING THE POTATOES & LATER FOUND AN INGENIOUS WAY TO CLEAN THE GRAIN, THROWING HANDFULS INTO THE SEA & THUS SEPARATING THE GRAIN, WHICH FLOATED, FROM THE SAND. THIS SURPRISED THE SCIENTISTS SINCE THIS VARIETY OF MONKEY HAD NEVER BEEN KNOWN TO ENTER THE SEA. AFTER 5 YEARS THE MONKEYS HAD TAKEN TO BATHING JUST FOR FUN, LEAVING THE SCIENTISTS COMPLETELY BAFFLED.

THE SENSITIVE GORILLA

GORILLAS DO NOT LIKE WATER. WHEN PURSUED BY ARMED HUMANS, SOME REFUSE TO ESCAPE ACROSS STREAMS ONLY 3FT DEEP. IN 1951 A GORILLA THAT FELL INTO ITS WATER-FILLED MOAT AT BRONX ZOO IMMEDIATELY SANK & DROWNED, MAKING NO ATTEMPT TO SAVE HIMSELF.

A GORILLA CALLED ALFRED, LIVING IN BRISTOL ZOO, DEVELOPED A FEAR OF AIRCRAFT NOISE DURING WORLD WAR II & EVENTUALLY DIED FROM A HEART ATTACK CAUSED BY A LOW FLYING AIRCRAFT IN 1948.

MONKEYS & X-RAYS

IN A RECENT EXPERIMENT MONKEYS WERE REWARDED IF THEY PULLED A LEVER WHEN A BEAM OF X-RAYS WAS PASSED THROUGH THEIR CAGE. THIS CONFIRMED THAT THEY ARE ABLE TO SEE X-RAYS. BUT EVEN MORE SURPRISING THEY CONTINUED TO DETECT THE RAYS WHEN BLINDFOLDED. ONLY WHEN UNABLE TO SEE OR SMELL DID THEY FAIL TO PULL THE LEVER AT THE RIGHT TIME.

PATTY CAKE

A FIERCE STORM OCCURRED RECENTLY BETWEEN 2 ZOOS IN NEW YORK. AFTER A BABY GORILLA CALLED PATTY CAKE, BORN IN THE CENTRAL PARK ZOO, WAS SENT TO THE BRONX ZOO FOR TREATMENT. THE KEEPERS WERE SHOCKED TO FIND HER UNDERNOURISHED & SUFFERING FROM INTESTINAL PARASITES. THIS WAS BECAUSE PATTY CAKE'S MOTHER, LULU, & FATHER, KONGO, HAD BOTH BEEN EXTRAORD-INARILY ATTENTIVE & HAD BEEN ALLOWED TO REAR HER THEMSELVES (NORMALLY PARENTS TAKE NO INTEREST & INFANTS ARE REMOVED & BOTTLE FED). THE BRONX ZOO BOTTLE FED HER, DRESSED HER IN NAPPIES & VESTS & DECLARED THE CENTRAL PARK ZOO IRRESPONSIBLE & UNFIT TO HAVE HER BACK. HAPPILY SHE WAS FINALLY RETURNED AFTER THE WORLD EXPERT ON GORILLA REPRODUCTION DECIDED PARENTAL LOVE WAS MORE IMPORTANT THAN PARASITES.

THE BABOON SIGNALMAN

BOUGHT AS A PET IN SOUTH AFRICA BY A SIGNALMAN WHO HAD LOST BOTH HIS LEGS, A BABOON CALLED JACK BECAME ATTACHED TO HIS MASTER & ACCOMPANIED HIM EVERY-WHERE, REALISING ITS INTELLIGENCE, THE MAN TRAINED IT TO FETCH WATER, SWEEP OUT HIS SHACK, & EVEN TO PULL THE SIGNAL LEVERS. AT FIRST THE MAN ALLOWED JACK TO DO THIS ONLY WHILE HE WAS PRESENT, BUT, FINDING THE BABOON UTTERLY RELIABLE, EVENTUALLY LET IT DO THE JOB ALONE WHILE HE STAYED AT HOME. JACK NEVER MADE A MISTAKE FOR 9 YEARS TILL HIS DEATH IN 1890.

HOW TO MAKE A PILE OF MONEY INTO ELECTRICITY

ARRANGE BITS OF BLOTTING PAPER SOAKED IN SALT WATER BETWEEN COINS AS SHOWN. CLAMP OR HOLD PILE TOGETHER & INSERT WIRES TOUCHING OUTSIDE COINS. CURRENT DEVELOPED IS VERY SMALL, HOWEVER THE TONGUE IS A HIGHLY SENSITIVE DETECTOR. A TINGLING SENSATION, FELT WHEN WIRES TOUCH TONGUE, INDICATES CURRENT FLOWING.

☆ MONKS ☆
MEN LIVING ASCETIC LIVES APART FROM THE WORLD

TRAPPISTS

'TRAPPIST MONKS ARE SAID TO GREET EACH OTHER DAILY WITH THE WORDS: FRÈRE, IL FAUT MOURIR' (BROTHER, WE ALL MUST DIE), OTHERWISE THEIR RULE OF SILENCE IS ABSOLUTE. THEY DIG THEIR OWN TOMBS A FEW SPADEFULS A DAY. IT IS SAID THEY DELIBERATELY CHOOSE UNHEALTHY, SWAMPY SITES IN THE HOPE OF DYING YOUNG, YET MANY TRAPPIST MONKS SEEM TO ENJOY EXTREMELY GOOD HEALTH.

MONACHISM & MASOCHISM

EXTREMES OF SELF TORTURE WERE NOT GENERALLY CONSIDERED TO BE DESIRABLE BY CHRISTIAN MONKS. HOWEVER THERE ARE RECORDS OF INDIVIDUALS WEARING IRON SHACKLES, HAVING THEMSELVES FLOGGED & SPENDING WEEKS IMMERSED IN ICY WATER. SOME MADE ARRANGEMENTS SO THAT THEY COULD NEVER SIT OR LIE DOWN. THE 'STYLITES' WERE CHRISTIAN MONKS WHO NEVER DESCENDED FROM THE TOP OF A COLUMN. THE 'DENDRITES' NEVER DESCENDED FROM A TREE.

DOUBLE HOUSES

GILBERT OF SEMPRINGHAM, A 12TH CENTURY LINCOLNSHIRE PRIEST, STARTED A CONVENT FOR 7 SPINSTERS OF HIS PARISH. THIS LED TO THE FOUNDATION OF 26 'DOUBLE-HOUSES', FOR BOTH NUNS & MONKS. THE SEXES HAD SEPARATE CLOISTERS, BUT WORSHIPPED TOGETHER IN A CHURCH WITH A PARTITION DOWN THE MIDDLE TO PREVENT THEM SEEING EACH OTHER.

RULES & REGULATIONS

MEDIEVAL MONASTERY LIFE WAS CLOSELY REGULATED. TRADITION HAS IT THAT THERE WERE EVEN RULES FOR GETTING INTO BED. MONKS HAD TO SLEEP IN THEIR SHIRTS, DRAWERS & GAITERS AND TAKE OFF THEIR SHOES UNDER THE BEDCLOTHES, & THEY WERE FORBIDDEN TO SING IN BED.

LUXURY

BY THE MIDDLE AGES MOST BENEDICTINE MONKS WERE LEADING QUITE A LUXURIOUS LIFE. SERVANTS GENERALLY OUTNUMBERED MONKS & GREAT CARE WAS TAKEN OVER THE CUISINE (MONKS WERE ALLOWED TO DRINK ALCOHOL & EAT ANYTHING EXCEPT THE FLESH OF FOUR FOOTED ANIMALS), EVEN THIS RESTRICTION WAS LIFTED FOR MONKS IN THE INFIRMARY.

HOW TO AVOID DOING A SUM

WRITE DOWN ANY THREE FIGURE NUMBER; FOR EXAMPLE: 423 REVERSE THE NUMBER: 324 SUBTRACT THE SMALLER FROM THE LARGER:

$$423 - 324 = 099$$

ADD THE RESULT TO ITS OWN REVERSE:

$$099 + 990 = 1089$$

THE AMAZING THING IS THAT ANY INITIAL 3 FIGURE NUMBER (PROVIDING THE LAST & FIRST DIGIT ARE NOT THE SAME) WILL GIVE THE SAME ANSWER.

THE CISTERCIANS

THE CISTERCIAN ORDER WAS FOUNDED IN 1098 AD BY SOME FRENCH BENEDICTINE MONKS WHO FELT THAT THEIR MONASTERY HAD BECOME SLACK. TO MAKE LIFE MORE UNCOMFORTABLE THEY FOUNDED THEIR MONASTERIES IN WILD, MOUNTAINOUS PLACES. THEY WOULD ACCEPT NO GIFTS EXCEPT LAND, WHICH THEY TILLED & ON WHICH THEY KEPT SHEEP. HOWEVER, BY THE MIDDLE AGES WOOL HAD BECOME SO VALUABLE THAT THE CISTERCIANS ACCIDENTALLY GREW RICH & THE ORDER BECAME LESS AUSTERE.

ST BENEDICT'S RULES

ST BENEDICT FOUNDED A SMALL MONASTERY AT MONTECASSINO BASED ON A SET OF RULES WHICH HE DEVISED IN ABOUT 535 AD. THESE INSISTED ON OBEDIENCE, STABILITY & 'CONVERSIO MORUM' (SELF IMPROVEMENT) & DIVIDED A MONK'S DAY INTO 3 PARTS: PRAYING (DURING THE 8 DAILY SERVICES), READING & LABOURING (MAKING FOOD, BOOKS & CLOTHES).

☆ MONUMENTS ☆
EDIFICES COMMEMORATING SOMETHING OR SOMEBODY

THE STATUE OF LIBERTY

BUILT & PAID FOR BY THE FRENCH TO COMMEMORATE THE UNION BETWEEN FRANCE & AMERICA IN THE WAR OF INDEPENDENCE. A SCULPTOR CALLED BARTHOLDI FIRST MADE A 9FT HIGH MODEL IN 1800 & THEN THE ENGINEER EIFFEL DESIGNED A FRAMEWORK TO SUPPORT THE FULL-SIZE VERSION (152 FT HIGH). THE OUTSIDE WAS MADE ENTIRELY OF COPPER SHEETS. THE THICKNESS OF A 2p PIECE, SHAPED BY HAMMERING OVER HUGE WOODEN PATTERNS. AFTER STANDING IN PARIS FOR A YEAR IT WAS SHIPPED TO NEW YORK & RE-ERECTED ON BEDLOWS ISLAND, PREVIOUSLY THE SITE OF NEW YORK'S PLAGUE HOSPITAL.

THE FATAL ATTRACTION OF THE EIFFEL TOWER
OVER 354 PEOPLE HAVE COMMITTED SUICIDE JUMPING FROM THE EIFFEL TOWER SINCE ITS OPENING IN 1889.

RUSSIA'S HUGE MOTHER
THE LARGEST STATUE IN THE WORLD IS AN ENORMOUS RUSSIAN PRE-STRESSED CONCRETE LADY 270FT HIGH. SHE IS A MEMORIAL TO THE BATTLE OF STALINGRAD & IS CALLED 'MOTHERLAND'.

POPE SIXTUS AND THE OBELISK
POPE SIXTUS WAS VERY KEEN TO HAVE AN OBELISK OUTSIDE ST PETER'S & WITHIN 4 MONTHS OF BECOMING POPE, IN 1586, HE HAD A FULL-SIZE WOODEN MODEL ERECTED TO SEE EXACTLY WHERE IT LOOKED BEST. HE THEN ORGANISED A COMPETITION FOR THE BEST METHOD OF MOVING THE WORLD'S LARGEST OBELISK (ORIGINALLY BUILT BY THE ANCIENT EGYPTIANS) TO HIS CHOSEN SITE. HE REJECTED ALL THE ENTRIES & GAVE THE JOB TO AN ENGINEER CALLED FONTANA. TERRIFIED OF HIS FATE LEST THE OBELISK SHOULD BREAK IN TRANSIT, FONTANA WISELY KEPT A RELAY OF POST HORSES PREPARED TO FACILITATE ESCAPE. HOWEVER THE OPERATION WAS SUCCESSFUL & HE RECEIVED A VAST PENSION.

PREHISTORIC MANPOWER
THE LARGEST BLOCKS AT STONEHENGE WEIGH 45 TONS & ARE ESTIMATED TO HAVE REQUIRED 550 MEN JUST TO PULL THEM UP A GENTLE 10% SLOPE. THE EARTHWORKS OF BRITAIN'S LARGEST SITE, AT AVEBURY, WILTSHIRE, WOULD HAVE REQUIRED ABOUT 15 MILLION MAN HOURS TO CREATE.

KING CHEOPS' PYRAMID
THE WORLD'S LARGEST PYRAMID IS COMPOSED OF 2.3 MILLION STONE BLOCKS, WEIGHING ½ TON EACH & WAS BUILT IN 2600 BC. IT HAS BEEN CALCULATED THAT ITS BASE AREA COULD HOLD WESTMINSTER ABBEY, ST PAUL'S CATHEDRAL, ST PETER'S (ROME), FLORENCE CATHEDRAL & MILAN CATHEDRAL.

HOW TO TRANSFER A NEWSPAPER PICTURE ONTO ANOTHER BIT OF PAPER
MIX 2 CUPS WATER, 1 CUP TURPS & 1 CUP LIQUID DETERGENT. SOAK PIECE OF PAPER IN MIXTURE, THEN LAY PAPER ON PICTURE & RUB CAREFULLY. REMOVE PAPER & MIXTURE WILL HAVE DISSOLVED THE NEWSPAPER INK & TRANSFERRED THE PICTURE.

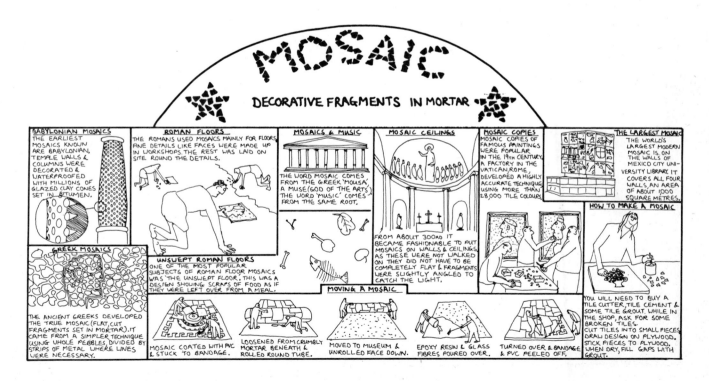

MOSAIC
DECORATIVE FRAGMENTS IN MORTAR

BABYLONIAN MOSAICS
THE EARLIEST MOSAICS KNOWN ARE BABYLONIAN, TEMPLE WALLS & COLUMNS WERE DECORATED & WATERPROOFED WITH MILLIONS OF GLAZED CLAY CONES SET IN BITUMEN.

GREEK MOSAICS
THE ANCIENT GREEKS DEVELOPED THE TRUE MOSAIC (FLAT, CUT FRAGMENTS SET IN MORTAR). IT CAME FROM A SIMPLER TECHNIQUE USING WHOLE PEBBLES, DIVIDED BY STRIPS OF METAL WHERE LINES WERE NECESSARY.

ROMAN FLOORS
THE ROMANS USED MOSAICS MAINLY FOR FLOORS. FINE DETAILS LIKE FACES WERE MADE UP IN WORKSHOPS, THE REST WAS LAID ON SITE ROUND THE DETAILS.

UNSWEPT ROMAN FLOORS
ONE OF THE MOST POPULAR SUBJECTS OF ROMAN FLOOR MOSAICS WAS 'THE UNSWEPT FLOOR', THIS WAS A DESIGN SHOWING SCRAPS OF FOOD AS IF THEY WERE LEFT OVER FROM A MEAL.

MOSAICS & MUSIC
THE WORD MOSAIC COMES FROM THE GREEK 'MOUSA', A MUSE (GOD OF THE ARTS). THE WORD 'MUSIC' COMES FROM THE SAME ROOT.

MOSAIC CEILINGS
FROM ABOUT 300AD IT BECAME FASHIONABLE TO PUT MOSAICS ON WALLS & CEILINGS, AS THESE WERE NOT WALKED ON THEY DID NOT HAVE TO BE COMPLETELY FLAT & FRAGMENTS WERE SLIGHTLY ANGLED TO CATCH THE LIGHT.

MOSAIC COPIES
MOSAIC COPIES OF FAMOUS PAINTINGS WERE POPULAR IN THE 19TH CENTURY. A FACTORY IN THE VATICAN, ROME, DEVELOPED A HIGHLY ACCURATE TECHNIQUE USING MORE THAN 28,000 TILE COLOURS.

THE LARGEST MOSAIC
THE WORLD'S LARGEST MODERN MOSAIC IS ON THE WALLS OF MEXICO CITY UNIVERSITY LIBRARY. IT COVERS ALL FOUR WALLS, AN AREA OF ABOUT 4000 SQUARE METRES.

MOVING A MOSAIC
MOSAIC COATED WITH PVC & STUCK TO BANDAGE.

LOOSENED FROM CRUMBLY MORTAR BENEATH & ROLLED ROUND TUBE.

MOVED TO MUSEUM & UNROLLED FACE DOWN.

EPOXY RESIN & GLASS FIBRES POURED OVER.

TURNED OVER & BANDAGE & PVC PEELED OFF.

HOW TO MAKE A MOSAIC
YOU WILL NEED TO BUY A TILE CUTTER, TILE CEMENT & SOME TILE GROUT. WHILE IN THE SHOP, ASK FOR SOME BROKEN TILES. CUT TILES INTO SMALL PIECES. DRAW DESIGN ON PLYWOOD. STICK PIECES TO PLYWOOD. WHEN DRY, FILL GAPS WITH GROUT.

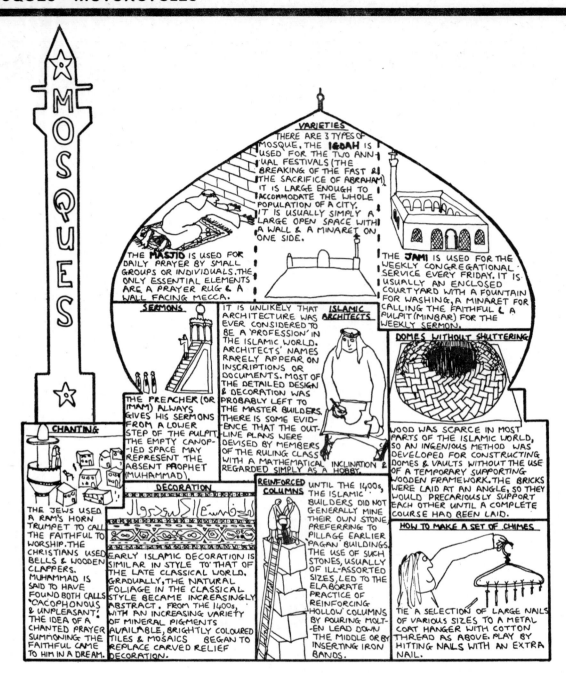

MOSQUES

VARIETIES

THERE ARE 3 TYPES OF MOSQUE. THE **IDGAH** IS USED FOR THE TWO ANNUAL FESTIVALS (THE BREAKING OF THE FAST & THE SACRIFICE OF ABRAHAM). IT IS LARGE ENOUGH TO ACCOMMODATE THE WHOLE POPULATION OF A CITY. IT IS USUALLY SIMPLY A LARGE OPEN SPACE WITH A WALL & A MINARET ON ONE SIDE.

THE **MASJID** IS USED FOR DAILY PRAYER BY SMALL GROUPS OR INDIVIDUALS. THE ONLY ESSENTIAL ELEMENTS ARE A PRAYER RUG & A WALL FACING MECCA.

THE **JAMI** IS USED FOR THE WEEKLY CONGREGATIONAL SERVICE EVERY FRIDAY. IT IS USUALLY AN ENCLOSED COURTYARD WITH A FOUNTAIN FOR WASHING, A MINARET FOR CALLING THE FAITHFUL & A PULPIT (MINBAR) FOR THE WEEKLY SERMON.

SERMONS

THE PREACHER (OR IMAM) ALWAYS GIVES HIS SERMONS FROM A LOWER STEP OF THE PULPIT. THE EMPTY CANOPIED SPACE MAY REPRESENT THE ABSENT PROPHET (MUHAMMAD).

ISLAMIC ARCHITECTS

IT IS UNLIKELY THAT ARCHITECTURE WAS EVER CONSIDERED TO BE A 'PROFESSION' IN THE ISLAMIC WORLD. ARCHITECTS' NAMES RARELY APPEAR ON INSCRIPTIONS OR DOCUMENTS. MOST OF THE DETAILED DESIGN & DECORATION WAS PROBABLY LEFT TO THE MASTER BUILDERS. THERE IS SOME EVIDENCE THAT THE OUTLINE PLANS WERE DEVISED BY MEMBERS OF THE RULING CLASS WITH A MATHEMATICAL INCLINATION & REGARDED SIMPLY AS A HOBBY.

DOMES WITHOUT SHUTTERING

WOOD WAS SCARCE IN MOST PARTS OF THE ISLAMIC WORLD, SO AN INGENIOUS METHOD WAS DEVELOPED FOR CONSTRUCTING DOMES & VAULTS WITHOUT THE USE OF A TEMPORARY SUPPORTING WOODEN FRAMEWORK. THE BRICKS WERE LAID AT AN ANGLE, SO THEY WOULD PRECARIOUSLY SUPPORT EACH OTHER UNTIL A COMPLETE COURSE HAD BEEN LAID.

CHANTING

THE JEWS USED A RAM'S HORN TRUMPET TO CALL THE FAITHFUL TO WORSHIP. THE CHRISTIANS USED BELLS & WOODEN CLAPPERS. MUHAMMAD IS SAID TO HAVE FOUND BOTH CALLS 'CACOPHONOUS & UNPLEASANT'. THE IDEA OF A CHANTED PRAYER SUMMONING THE FAITHFUL CAME TO HIM IN A DREAM.

DECORATION

EARLY ISLAMIC DECORATION IS SIMILAR IN STYLE TO THAT OF THE LATE CLASSICAL WORLD. GRADUALLY, THE NATURAL FOLIAGE IN THE CLASSICAL STYLE BECAME INCREASINGLY ABSTRACT. FROM THE 1400s, WITH AN INCREASING VARIETY OF MINERAL PIGMENTS AVAILABLE, BRIGHTLY COLOURED TILES & MOSAICS BEGAN TO REPLACE CARVED RELIEF DECORATION.

REINFORCED COLUMNS

UNTIL THE 1400s, THE ISLAMIC BUILDERS DID NOT GENERALLY MINE THEIR OWN STONE PREFERRING TO PILLAGE EARLIER PAGAN BUILDINGS. THE USE OF SUCH STONES, USUALLY OF ILL-ASSORTED SIZES, LED TO THE ELABORATE PRACTICE OF REINFORCING HOLLOW COLUMNS BY POURING MOLTEN LEAD DOWN THE MIDDLE OR BY INSERTING IRON BANDS.

HOW TO MAKE A SET OF CHIMES

TIE A SELECTION OF LARGE NAILS OF VARIOUS SIZES TO A METAL COAT HANGER WITH COTTON THREAD AS ABOVE. PLAY BY HITTING NAILS WITH AN EXTRA NAIL.

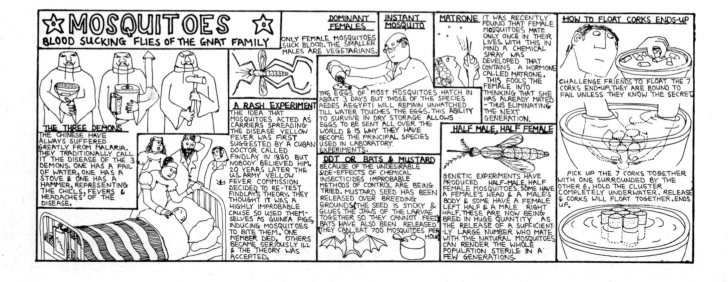

☆ MOSQUITOES ☆
BLOOD SUCKING FLIES OF THE GNAT FAMILY

THE THREE DEMONS

THE CHINESE HAVE ALWAYS SUFFERED GREATLY FROM MALARIA. THEY TRADITIONALLY CALL IT THE DISEASE OF THE 3 DEMONS. ONE HAS A PAIL OF WATER, ONE HAS A STOVE & ONE HAS A HAMMER, REPRESENTING THE CHILLS, FEVERS & HEADACHES OF THE DISEASE.

DOMINANT FEMALES

ONLY FEMALE MOSQUITOES SUCK BLOOD. THE SMALLER MALES ARE VEGETARIANS.

INSTANT MOSQUITO

THE EGGS OF MOST MOSQUITOES HATCH IN ABOUT 3 DAYS BUT THOSE OF THE SPECIES AEDES AEGYPTI WILL REMAIN UNHATCHED TILL WATER TOUCHES THE EGGS. THIS ABILITY TO SURVIVE IN DRY STORAGE ALLOWS EGGS TO BE SENT ALL OVER THE WORLD & IS WHY THEY HAVE BECOME THE PRINCIPAL SPECIES USED IN LABORATORY EXPERIMENTS.

A RASH EXPERIMENT

THE IDEA THAT MOSQUITOES ACTED AS CARRIERS SPREADING THE DISEASE YELLOW FEVER WAS FIRST SUGGESTED BY A CUBAN DOCTOR CALLED FINDLAY IN 1880 BUT NOBODY BELIEVED HIM. 20 YEARS LATER THE U.S. ARMY YELLOW FEVER COMMISSION DECIDED TO RE-TEST FINDLAY'S THEORY. THEY THOUGHT IT WAS A HIGHLY IMPROBABLE CAUSE SO USED THEMSELVES AS GUINEA PIGS, INDUCING MOSQUITOES TO BITE THEM. ONE MEMBER DIED, OTHERS BECAME SERIOUSLY ILL & THE THEORY WAS ACCEPTED.

DDT OR BATS & MUSTARD

BECAUSE OF THE UNDESIRABLE SIDE-EFFECTS OF CHEMICAL INSECTICIDES IMPROBABLE METHODS OF CONTROL ARE BEING TRIED. MUSTARD SEED HAS BEEN RELEASED OVER BREEDING GROUNDS. THE SEED IS STICKY & GLUES THE JAWS OF THE LARVAE TOGETHER SO THEY CANNOT FEED. BATS HAVE ALSO BEEN RELEASED. THEY CAN EAT 700 MOSQUITOES PER HOUR.

MATRONE

IT WAS RECENTLY FOUND THAT FEMALE MOSQUITOES MATE ONLY ONCE IN THEIR LIVES. WITH THIS IN MIND A CHEMICAL SPRAY WAS DEVELOPED THAT CONTAINS A HORMONE CALLED MATRONE. THIS FOOLS THE FEMALE INTO THINKING THAT SHE HAS ALREADY MATED – THUS ELIMINATING THE NEXT GENERATION.

HALF MALE, HALF FEMALE

GENETIC EXPERIMENTS HAVE PRODUCED HALF-MALE, HALF FEMALE MOSQUITOES. SOME HAVE A FEMALE'S HEAD & A MALE'S BODY & SOME HAVE A FEMALE LEFT HALF & A MALE RIGHT HALF. THESE ARE NOW BEING BRED IN HUGE QUANTITY AS THE RELEASE OF A SUFFICIENTLY LARGE NUMBER WHO MATE WITH THE NATURAL MOSQUITOES CAN RENDER THE WHOLE POPULATION STERILE IN A FEW GENERATIONS.

HOW TO FLOAT CORKS ENDS-UP

CHALLENGE FRIENDS TO FLOAT THE 7 CORKS END-UP. THEY ARE BOUND TO FAIL UNLESS THEY KNOW THE SECRET.

PICK UP THE 7 CORKS TOGETHER WITH ONE SURROUNDED BY THE OTHER 6. HOLD THE CLUSTER COMPLETELY UNDERWATER. RELEASE & CORKS WILL FLOAT TOGETHER, ENDS UP.

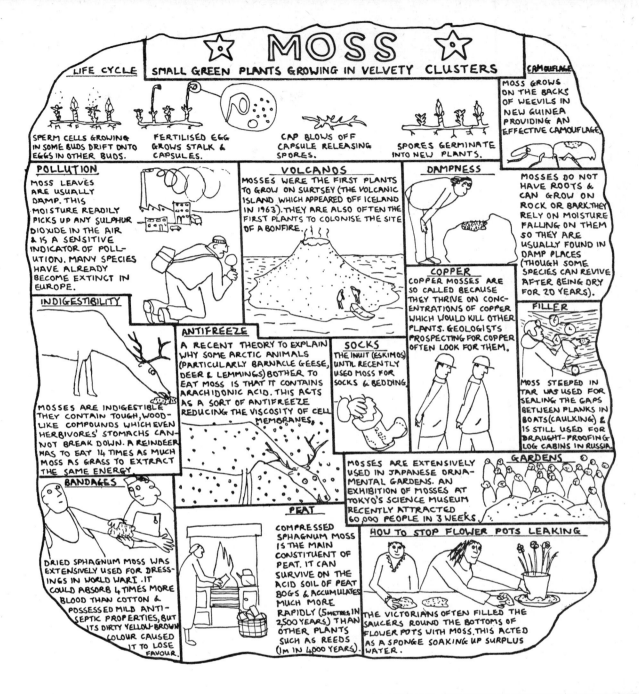

☆ MOSS ☆
SMALL GREEN PLANTS GROWING IN VELVETY CLUSTERS

LIFE CYCLE

SPERM CELLS GROWING IN SOME BUDS DRIFT ONTO EGGS IN OTHER BUDS.

FERTILISED EGG GROWS STALK & CAPSULES.

CAP BLOWS OFF CAPSULE RELEASING SPORES.

SPORES GERMINATE INTO NEW PLANTS.

CAMOUFLAGE

MOSS GROWS ON THE BACKS OF WEEVILS IN NEW GUINEA PROVIDING AN EFFECTIVE CAMOUFLAGE.

POLLUTION

MOSS LEAVES ARE USUALLY DAMP. THIS MOISTURE READILY PICKS UP ANY SULPHUR DIOXIDE IN THE AIR & IS A SENSITIVE INDICATOR OF POLLUTION. MANY SPECIES HAVE ALREADY BECOME EXTINCT IN EUROPE.

VOLCANOS

MOSSES WERE THE FIRST PLANTS TO GROW ON SURTSEY (THE VOLCANIC ISLAND WHICH APPEARED OFF ICELAND IN 1963). THEY ARE ALSO OFTEN THE FIRST PLANTS TO COLONISE THE SITE OF A BONFIRE.

DAMPNESS

MOSSES DO NOT HAVE ROOTS & CAN GROW ON ROCK OR BARK. THEY RELY ON MOISTURE FALLING ON THEM SO THEY ARE USUALLY FOUND IN DAMP PLACES (THOUGH SOME SPECIES CAN REVIVE AFTER BEING DRY FOR 20 YEARS).

COPPER

COPPER MOSSES ARE SO CALLED BECAUSE THEY THRIVE ON CONCENTRATIONS OF COPPER WHICH WOULD KILL OTHER PLANTS. GEOLOGISTS PROSPECTING FOR COPPER OFTEN LOOK FOR THEM.

INDIGESTIBILITY

MOSSES ARE INDIGESTIBLE THEY CONTAIN TOUGH, WOOD-LIKE COMPOUNDS WHICH EVEN HERBIVORES' STOMACHS CANNOT BREAK DOWN. A REINDEER HAS TO EAT 14 TIMES AS MUCH MOSS AS GRASS TO EXTRACT THE SAME ENERGY.

ANTIFREEZE

A RECENT THEORY TO EXPLAIN WHY SOME ARCTIC ANIMALS (PARTICULARLY BARNACLE GEESE, DEER & LEMMINGS) BOTHER TO EAT MOSS IS THAT IT CONTAINS ARACHIDONIC ACID. THIS ACTS AS A SORT OF ANTIFREEZE REDUCING THE VISCOSITY OF CELL MEMBRANES.

SOCKS

THE INUIT (ESKIMOS) UNTIL RECENTLY USED MOSS FOR SOCKS & BEDDING.

FILLER

MOSS STEEPED IN TAR WAS USED FOR SEALING THE GAPS BETWEEN PLANKS IN BOATS (CAULKING) & IS STILL USED FOR DRAUGHT-PROOFING LOG CABINS IN RUSSIA.

BANDAGES

DRIED SPHAGNUM MOSS WAS EXTENSIVELY USED FOR DRESSINGS IN WORLD WAR I. IT COULD ABSORB 4 TIMES MORE BLOOD THAN COTTON & POSSESSED MILD ANTISEPTIC PROPERTIES, BUT ITS DIRTY YELLOW-BROWN COLOUR CAUSED IT TO LOSE FAVOUR.

GARDENS

MOSSES ARE EXTENSIVELY USED IN JAPANESE ORNAMENTAL GARDENS. AN EXHIBITION OF MOSSES AT TOKYO'S SCIENCE MUSEUM RECENTLY ATTRACTED 60,000 PEOPLE IN 3 WEEKS.

PEAT

COMPRESSED SPHAGNUM MOSS IS THE MAIN CONSTITUENT OF PEAT. IT CAN SURVIVE ON THE ACID SOIL OF PEAT BOGS & ACCUMULATES MUCH MORE RAPIDLY (SMETRES IN 2500 YEARS) THAN OTHER PLANTS SUCH AS REEDS (1M IN 4000 YEARS).

HOW TO STOP FLOWER POTS LEAKING

THE VICTORIANS OFTEN FILLED THE SAUCERS ROUND THE BOTTOMS OF FLOWER POTS WITH MOSS. THIS ACTED AS A SPONGE SOAKING UP SURPLUS WATER.

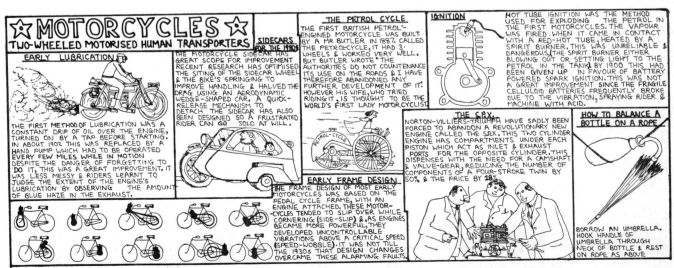

☆ MOTORCYCLES ☆
TWO-WHEELED MOTORISED HUMAN TRANSPORTERS

EARLY LUBRICATION

THE FIRST METHOD OF LUBRICATION WAS A CONSTANT DRIP OF OIL OVER THE ENGINE, TURNED ON BY A TAP BEFORE STARTING. IN ABOUT 1902 THIS WAS REPLACED BY A HAND PUMP WHICH HAD TO BE OPERATED EVERY FEW MILES WHILE IN MOTION DESPITE THE DANGER OF FORGETTING TO DO IT. THIS WAS A GREAT IMPROVEMENT. IT WAS LESS MESSY & RIDERS LEARNT TO JUDGE THE EXTENT OF THE ENGINE'S LUBRICATION BY OBSERVING THE AMOUNT OF BLUE HAZE IN THE EXHAUST.

SIDECARS FOR THE 1980s

THE MOTORCYCLE SIDECAR HAS GREAT SCOPE FOR IMPROVEMENT. RECENT RESEARCH HAS OPTIMISED THE SITING OF THE SIDECAR WHEEL & THE BIKE'S SPRINGING TO IMPROVE HANDLING & HALVED THE DRAG USING AN AERODYNAMIC WEDGE-SHAPED CAR. A QUICK-RELEASE MECHANISM TO DETACH THE SIDECAR HAS ALSO BEEN DESIGNED SO A FRUSTRATED RIDER CAN GO SOLO AT WILL.

THE PETROL CYCLE

THE FIRST BRITISH PETROL-ENGINED MOTORCYCLE WAS BUILT BY A MR BUTLER IN 1887. CALLED THE PETROL-CYCLE, IT HAD 3 WHEELS & WORKED VERY WELL. BUT BUTLER WROTE "THE AUTHORITIES DO NOT COUNTENANCE ITS USE ON THE ROADS & I HAVE THEREFORE ABANDONED ANY FURTHER DEVELOPMENT OF IT". HOWEVER HIS WIFE, WHO TRIED RIDING IT, IS THOUGHT TO BE THE WORLD'S FIRST LADY MOTORCYCLIST.

PETROL-CYCLE

EARLY FRAME DESIGN

THE FRAME DESIGN OF MOST EARLY MOTORCYCLES WAS BASED ON THE PEDAL CYCLE FRAME, WITH AN ENGINE ATTACHED. THESE MOTORCYCLES TENDED TO SLIP OVER WHILE CORNERING (SIDE-SLIP) & AS ENGINES BECAME MORE POWERFUL, THEY DEVELOPED UNCONTROLLABLE VIBRATIONS ABOVE A CRITICAL SPEED (SPEED-WOBBLE). IT WAS NOT TILL THE 1930s THAT DESIGN CHANGES OVERCAME THESE ALARMING FAULTS.

IGNITION

HOT TUBE IGNITION WAS THE METHOD USED FOR EXPLODING THE PETROL IN THE FIRST MOTORCYCLES. THE VAPOUR WAS FIRED WHEN IT CAME IN CONTACT WITH A RED-HOT TUBE, HEATED BY A SPIRIT BURNER. THIS WAS UNRELIABLE & DANGEROUS, (THE SPIRIT BURNER EITHER BLOWING OUT OR SETTING LIGHT TO THE PETROL IN THE TANK) BY 1900 THIS HAD BEEN GIVEN UP IN FAVOUR OF BATTERY POWERED SPARK IGNITION. THIS WAS NOT A GREAT IMPROVEMENT SINCE THE FRAGILE CELLULOID BATTERIES FREQUENTLY BROKE DUE TO THE VIBRATION, SPRAYING RIDER & MACHINE WITH ACID.

THE SRX

NORTON-VILLIERS-TRIUMPH HAVE SADLY BEEN FORCED TO ABANDON A REVOLUTIONARY NEW ENGINE CALLED THE SRX. THIS TWO CYLINDER ENGINE HAS COMPARTMENTS UNDER EACH PISTON WHICH ACT AS INLET & EXHAUST PORTS FOR THE OPPOSITE CYLINDER. THIS DISPENSES WITH THE NEED FOR A CAMSHAFT & VALVE-GEAR, REDUCING THE NUMBER OF COMPONENTS OF A FOUR-STROKE TWIN BY 50% & THE PRICE BY 28%.

HOW TO BALANCE A BOTTLE ON A ROPE

BORROW AN UMBRELLA. HOOK HANDLE OF UMBRELLA THROUGH NECK OF BOTTLE & REST ON ROPE AS ABOVE.

MOUNTAINEERING

CLIMBING NATURAL OBSTACLES

THE FIRST CLIMBS

ONE OF THE EARLIEST RECORDS OF ANYBODY CLIMBING A MOUNTAIN IS MOSES CLIMBING SINAI. ANOTHER EARLY CLIMBER WAS THE GREEK, PHILOSOPHER EMPEDOCLES, WHO CLIMBED MOUNT ETNA & COMMITTED SUICIDE JUMPING INTO THE VOLCANO.

LEONARDO'S CLIMB

LEONARDO DA VINCI TRIED TO CLIMB MONTE ROSA (5,000m) ON THE ITALIAN SWISS BORDER. HE GAVE UP AFTER 3,000m. HIS ACCOUNT OF A GLACIER CONJECTURED THAT IT HAD BEEN FORMED FROM LAYERS OF HAIL.

PETRARCH'S CLIMB

ONE OF THE FIRST DESCRIPTIONS OF A CLIMB UNDERTAKEN AS 'SPORT' WAS WRITTEN BY THE POET PETRARCH IN 1336. AFTER WRITING LYRICAL DESCRIPTIONS ABOUT HIS EXPERIENCE, HE FELT GUILTY ABOUT HIS EXHILARATION &, WHILE STILL ON THE SUMMIT, READ THE CONFESSIONS OF ST AUGUSTINE.

CLIMBING AS SPORT

UNTIL THE MID-19th CENTURY ALL KINDS OF QUASI SCIENTIFIC REASONS WERE GIVEN TO JUSTIFY ATTEMPTS TO CLIMB ANY MOUNTAIN. ONLY THEN DID MOUNTAINEERING COME TO BE REGARDED AS A RESPECTABLE SPORT. THIS WAS LARGELY THANKS TO A BARRISTER, SIR ALFRED WALLS, WHO WROTE VIVIDLY ABOUT THE CHALLENGE & THE BEAUTY OF HIS CLIMBING EXPERIENCES.

ROCK CLIMBING

CLIMBING IN BRITAIN DID NOT START UNTIL THE 1880s. PREVIOUSLY THE NATIVE BRITISH MOUNTAINS HAD SEEMED FAR TOO SMALL FOR THE EARLY CLIMBERS, WHO HAD BEEN INSPIRED BY THE ALPS.

CLIMBING & THE ROPE

AT ALL TIMES DURING A ROCK CLIMB, ONE CLIMBER MUST BE IN A SECURE POSITION (BELAY) WITH ONE END OF THE ROPE SECURED. ALL THE CLIMBERS ARE ATTACHED TO THIS ROPE, SO IF ANYONE FALLS THEY WILL NOT DROP FURTHER THAN THE LENGTH OF THE ROPE. FINDING A SUITABLE POSITION & PLACE TO FIX THE ROPE IS ONE OF THE GREATEST SKILLS OF ROCK CLIMBING. THE BELAY HAS TO BE VERY STRONG TO TAKE THE SHOCK OF HALTING THE FALL OF TWO OR MORE CLIMBERS. SPECIAL KNOTS ARE USED WHICH SLIP A CERTAIN DISTANCE BEFORE TIGHTENING & THUS HELP TO REDUCE THE JERK.

CLIMBING GADGETRY

DESPITE THE OBJECTIONS OF PURISTS, WHO FELT THAT EVEN ROPE WAS UNNECESSARY & 'CHEATING', MANY CLIMBING AIDS WERE INTRODUCED IN THE 1930s. THESE INCLUDED: CHROME MOLYBDENUM PITONS (SPIKES) WHICH GRIP THE ROCK BETTER & ARE STRONGER THAN THE TRADITIONAL MILD STEEL PITONS; EXPANSION BOLTS - WHICH CAN BE PLACED IN A CRACK & EXPANDED TO GRIP (PARTICULARLY USEFUL IN CLIMBING UNDER OVERHANGS); & CLIMBING HARNESSES WHICH CLIP ON TO THE ROPE & WILL SUPPORT THE BODY SAFELY.

HOW TO MAKE A BOOMERANG

CUT THE SHAPE BELOW OUT OF THICK CARD. REST IT ON THE EDGE OF A LARGE SQUARE OF CARD HELD IN ONE HAND. HIT OVERHANGING BRANCH OF BOOMERANG HARD WITH A STICK. WITH SOME PRACTICE IT WILL TAKE OFF, LOOP & RETURN.

TIED UNTIED TIED TIED UNTIED

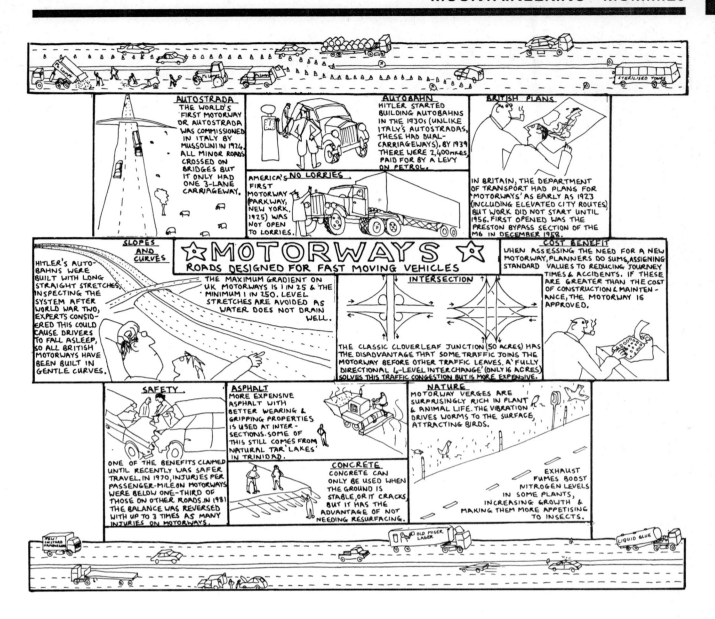

AUTOSTRADA
THE WORLD'S FIRST MOTORWAY OR AUTOSTRADA WAS COMMISSIONED IN ITALY BY MUSSOLINI IN 1924. ALL MINOR ROADS CROSSED ON BRIDGES BUT IT ONLY HAD ONE 3-LANE CARRIAGEWAY.

AMERICA'S FIRST MOTORWAY (PARKWAY, NEW YORK, 1925) WAS NOT OPEN TO LORRIES.

AUTOBAHN
HITLER STARTED BUILDING AUTOBAHNS IN THE 1930s (UNLIKE ITALY'S AUTOSTRADAS, THESE HAD DUAL-CARRIAGEWAYS). BY 1939 THERE WERE 2,400 MILES, PAID FOR BY A LEVY ON PETROL.

BRITISH PLANS
IN BRITAIN, THE DEPARTMENT OF TRANSPORT HAD PLANS FOR MOTORWAYS AS EARLY AS 1923 (INCLUDING ELEVATED CITY ROUTES) BUT WORK DID NOT START UNTIL 1956. FIRST OPENED WAS THE PRESTON BYPASS SECTION OF THE M6 IN DECEMBER 1958.

☆ MOTORWAYS ☆
ROADS DESIGNED FOR FAST MOVING VEHICLES

THE MAXIMUM GRADIENT ON UK MOTORWAYS IS 1 IN 25 & THE MINIMUM 1 IN 250. LEVEL STRETCHES ARE AVOIDED AS WATER DOES NOT DRAIN WELL.

SLOPES AND CURVES
HITLER'S AUTOBAHNS WERE BUILT WITH LONG STRAIGHT STRETCHES. INSPECTING THE SYSTEM AFTER WORLD WAR TWO, EXPERTS CONSIDERED THIS COULD CAUSE DRIVERS TO FALL ASLEEP, SO ALL BRITISH MOTORWAYS HAVE BEEN BUILT IN GENTLE CURVES.

INTERSECTION
THE CLASSIC CLOVERLEAF JUNCTION (50 ACRES) HAS THE DISADVANTAGE THAT SOME TRAFFIC JOINS THE MOTORWAY BEFORE OTHER TRAFFIC LEAVES. A 'FULLY DIRECTIONAL 4-LEVEL INTERCHANGE' (ONLY 16 ACRES) SOLVES THIS TRAFFIC CONGESTION BUT IS MORE EXPENSIVE.

COST BENEFIT
WHEN ASSESSING THE NEED FOR A NEW MOTORWAY, PLANNERS DO SUMS, ASSIGNING STANDARD VALUES TO REDUCING JOURNEY TIMES & ACCIDENTS. IF THESE ARE GREATER THAN THE COST OF CONSTRUCTION & MAINTENANCE, THE MOTORWAY IS APPROVED.

SAFETY
ONE OF THE BENEFITS CLAIMED UNTIL RECENTLY WAS SAFER TRAVEL. IN 1970, INJURIES PER PASSENGER-MILE ON MOTORWAYS WERE BELOW ONE-THIRD OF THOSE ON OTHER ROADS. IN 1981 THE BALANCE WAS REVERSED WITH UP TO 3 TIMES AS MANY INJURIES ON MOTORWAYS.

ASPHALT
MORE EXPENSIVE ASPHALT WITH BETTER WEARING & GRIPPING PROPERTIES IS USED AT INTERSECTIONS. SOME OF THIS STILL COMES FROM NATURAL 'TAR LAKES' IN TRINIDAD.

CONCRETE
CONCRETE CAN ONLY BE USED WHEN THE GROUND IS STABLE, OR IT CRACKS, BUT IT HAS THE ADVANTAGE OF NOT NEEDING RESURFACING.

NATURE
MOTORWAY VERGES ARE SURPRISINGLY RICH IN PLANT & ANIMAL LIFE. THE VIBRATION DRIVES WORMS TO THE SURFACE, ATTRACTING BIRDS.

EXHAUST FUMES BOOST NITROGEN LEVELS IN SOME PLANTS, INCREASING GROWTH & MAKING THEM MORE APPETISING TO INSECTS.

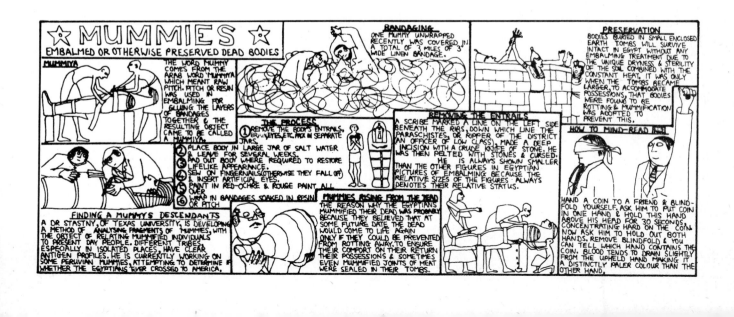

☆ MUMMIES ☆
EMBALMED OR OTHERWISE PRESERVED DEAD BODIES

MUMMIYA
THE WORD MUMMY COMES FROM THE ARAB WORD 'MUMMIYA' WHICH MEANT RAW PITCH. PITCH OR RESIN WAS USED IN EMBALMING FOR GLUING THE LAYERS OF BANDAGES TOGETHER & THE RESULTING OBJECT CAME TO BE CALLED A MUMMIYA.

THE PROCESS
1. REMOVE THE BODY'S ENTRAILS, BRAIN, EYES, ETC. PUT IN SEPARATE JARS.
2. PLACE BODY IN LARGE JAR OF SALT WATER & LEAVE FOR SEVERAL WEEKS.
3. PAD OUT BODY WHERE REQUIRED TO RESTORE LIFELIKE APPEARANCE.
4. SEW ON FINGERNAILS (OTHERWISE THEY FALL OFF) & INSERT ARTIFICIAL EYES.
5. PAINT IN RED-OCHRE & ROUGE PAINT ALL OVER.
6. WRAP IN BANDAGES SOAKED IN RESIN OR PITCH.

BANDAGING
ONE MUMMY UNWRAPPED RECENTLY WAS COVERED IN A TOTAL OF 3 MILES OF 3" WIDE LINEN BANDAGE.

PRESERVATION
BODIES BURIED IN SMALL ENCLOSED EARTH TOMBS WILL SURVIVE INTACT IN EGYPT WITHOUT ANY EMBALMING TREATMENT DUE TO THE UNIQUE DRYNESS & STERILITY OF THE SOIL COMBINED WITH THE CONSTANT HEAT. IT WAS ONLY WHEN THE TOMBS BECAME LARGER, TO ACCOMMODATE POSSESSIONS, THAT BODIES WERE FOUND TO BE ROTTING & MUMMIFICATION WAS ADOPTED TO PREVENT THIS.

REMOVING THE ENTRAILS
A SCRIBE MARKED A LINE ON THE LEFT SIDE BENEATH THE RIBS, DOWN WHICH LINE THE PARASCHISTES, OR RIPPER OF THE DISTRICT (AN OFFICER OF LOW CLASS), MADE A DEEP INCISION WITH A CRUDE KNIFE OF STONE. HE WAS THEN PELTED WITH STONES & CURSED. HE IS ALWAYS SHOWN SMALLER THAN THE OTHER FIGURES IN EGYPTIAN PICTURES OF EMBALMING BECAUSE THE RELATIVE SIZES OF THE FIGURES ALWAYS DENOTES THEIR RELATIVE STATUS.

FINDING A MUMMY'S DESCENDANTS
A DR STASTNY, OF TEXAS UNIVERSITY, IS DEVELOPING A METHOD OF ANALYSING FRAGMENTS OF MUMMIES, WITH THE OBJECT OF RELATING MUMMIFIED INDIVIDUALS TO PRESENT DAY PEOPLE. DIFFERENT TRIBES, ESPECIALLY IN ISOLATED PLACES, HAVE CLEAR ANTIGEN PROFILES. HE IS CURRENTLY WORKING ON SOME PERUVIAN MUMMIES, ATTEMPTING TO DETERMINE WHETHER THE EGYPTIANS EVER CROSSED TO AMERICA.

MUMMIES RISING FROM THE DEAD
THE REASON WHY THE EGYPTIANS MUMMIFIED THEIR DEAD WAS PROBABLY BECAUSE THEY BELIEVED THAT AT SOME FUTURE DATE THE DEAD WOULD COME TO LIFE AGAIN, ONLY IF THEY COULD BE PREVENTED FROM ROTTING AWAY. TO ENSURE THEIR COMFORT ON THEIR RETURN, THEIR POSSESSIONS & SOMETIMES EVEN MUMMIFIED JOINTS OF MEAT WERE SEALED IN THEIR TOMBS.

HOW TO MIND-READ
HAND A COIN TO A FRIEND & BLINDFOLD YOURSELF. ASK HIM TO PUT COIN IN ONE HAND & HOLD THIS HAND ABOVE HIS HEAD FOR 30 SECONDS, CONCENTRATING HARD ON THE COIN. NOW ASK HIM TO HOLD OUT BOTH HANDS. REMOVE BLINDFOLD & YOU CAN TELL WHICH HAND CONTAINS THE COIN. BLOOD TENDS TO DRAIN SLIGHTLY FROM THE UPHELD HAND MAKING IT A DISTINCTLY PALER COLOUR THAN THE OTHER HAND.

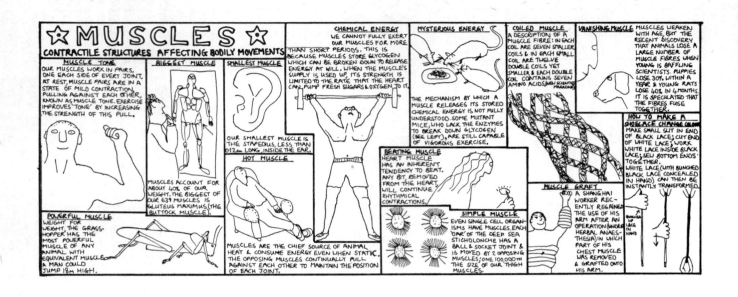

☆ MUSCLES ☆
CONTRACTILE STRUCTURES AFFECTING BODILY MOVEMENTS

MUSCLE TONE
OUR MUSCLES WORK IN PAIRS, ONE EACH SIDE OF EVERY JOINT. AT REST, MUSCLE PAIRS ARE IN A STATE OF MILD CONTRACTION, PULLING AGAINST EACH OTHER, KNOWN AS MUSCLE TONE. EXERCISE IMPROVES 'TONE' BY INCREASING THE STRENGTH OF THIS PULL.

BIGGEST MUSCLE

SMALLEST MUSCLE
OUR SMALLEST MUSCLE IS THE STAPEDIUS, LESS THAN 0.12cm LONG, INSIDE THE EAR.

HOT MUSCLE
MUSCLES ACCOUNT FOR ABOUT 40% OF OUR WEIGHT. THE BIGGEST OF OUR 639 MUSCLES IS GLUTEUS MAXIMUS (THE BUTTOCK MUSCLE).

POWERFUL MUSCLE
WEIGHT FOR WEIGHT, THE GRASSHOPPER HAS THE MOST POWERFUL MUSCLE OF ANY ANIMAL. WITH EQUIVALENT MUSCLE A MAN COULD JUMP 18m HIGH.

MUSCLES ARE THE CHIEF SOURCE OF ANIMAL HEAT & CONSUME ENERGY EVEN WHEN STATIC. THE OPPOSING MUSCLES CONTINUALLY PULL AGAINST EACH OTHER TO MAINTAIN THE POSITION OF EACH JOINT.

CHEMICAL ENERGY
WE CANNOT FULLY EXERT OUR MUSCLES FOR MORE THAN SHORT PERIODS. THIS IS BECAUSE MUSCLES STORE GLYCOGEN WHICH CAN BE BROKEN DOWN TO RELEASE ENERGY AT WILL. WHEN THE MUSCLE'S SUPPLY IS USED UP, ITS STRENGTH IS LIMITED TO THE RATE THAT THE HEART CAN PUMP FRESH SUGARS & OXYGEN TO IT.

THE MECHANISM BY WHICH A MUSCLE RELEASES ITS STORED CHEMICAL ENERGY IS NOT FULLY UNDERSTOOD. SOME MUTANT MICE, WHO LACK THE ENZYMES TO BREAK DOWN GLYCOGEN (SEE LEFT), ARE STILL CAPABLE OF VIGOROUS EXERCISE.

BEATING MUSCLE
HEART MUSCLE HAS AN INHERENT TENDENCY TO BEAT. ANY BIT REMOVED FROM THE HEART WILL CONTINUE RHYTHMICAL CONTRACTIONS.

SIMPLE MUSCLE
EVEN SINGLE CELL ORGANISMS HAVE MUSCLES. EACH 'ONE' OF THE DEEP SEA STICHOLONCHE HAS A BALL & SOCKET JOINT & IS MOVED BY 2 OPPOSING MUSCLES; ONE 100,000th THE SIZE OF OUR THIGH MUSCLES.

MYSTERIOUS ENERGY

COILED MUSCLE
A DESCRIPTION OF A MUSCLE FIBRE: IN EACH COIL ARE SEVEN SMALLER COILS & IN EACH SMALL COIL ARE TWELVE DOUBLE COILS YET SMALLER & EACH DOUBLE COIL CONTAINS SEVEN AMINO ACIDS (NEW SCIENTIST MAGAZINE).

VANISHING MUSCLE
MUSCLES WEAKEN WITH AGE, BUT THE RECENT DISCOVERY THAT ANIMALS LOSE A LARGE NUMBER OF MUSCLE FIBRES WHEN YOUNG IS BAFFLING SCIENTISTS. PUPPIES LOSE 30% WITHIN A YEAR & YOUNG RATS LOSE 40% IN 4 MONTHS. IT IS SPECULATED THAT THE FIBRES FUSE TOGETHER.

HOW TO MAKE A SHOELACE CHANGE COLOUR
MAKE SMALL SLIT IN END OF BLACK LACE; CUT END OF WHITE LACE; WORK WHITE LACE INSIDE BLACK LACE; SEW BOTTOM ENDS TOGETHER. WHITE LACE (WITH BUNCHED BLACK LACE CONCEALED IN HAND) CAN THEN BE INSTANTLY TRANSFORMED.

MUSCLE GRAFT
A SHANGHAI WORKER RECENTLY REGAINED THE USE OF HIS ARM AFTER AN OPERATION (UNDER HERBAL ANAESTHESIA) IN WHICH PART OF HIS CHEST MUSCLE WAS REMOVED & GRAFTED ONTO HIS ARM.

BUNCHED LACE IN HAND

☆ MUSIC ☆
THE ART OF EXPRESSION IN SOUND

SILENT MUSIC
THE INDIANS TRADITIONALLY BELIEVE THAT THERE ARE TWO TYPES OF SOUND. THE FIRST IS 'UNSTRUCK SOUND', THE MUSIC OF THE GODS, INAUDIBLE TO MEN, CREATED BY VIBRATION OF THE ETHER. THE SECOND IS STRUCK SOUND, MAN-MADE MUSIC, CREATED BY VIBRATION OF THE AIR. A TUNE IS SAID TO RESULT FROM A UNION BETWEEN PHYSICAL BREATH & THE FIRE OF INTELLECT.

THE INDIAN SCALE
THE INDIANS USE A 7 NOTE SCALE WITH SAME INTERVALS AS THE EUROPEAN MAJOR SCALE. THE NOTES ARE CALLED SA (THE KEY NOTE), RE, GA, MA, PA, DHA & NI. EACH NOTE REPRESENTS A PARTICULAR MOOD: SA & MA = TRANQUILLITY, RE = ANGER, GA & DHA = SOLEMNITY, PA = JOY & NI = SORROW. THE NOTES ARE ALSO LIKENED TO ANIMAL NOISES: E.G. RE = A COWS MOO, NI = AN ELEPHANTS TRUMPET ETC.

CHINESE INSTRUMENTS
THE CHINESE CLASSIFY THEIR INSTRUMENTS ACCORDING TO 8 CLASSES OF MATERIAL FROM WHICH THE NOISE STEMS.

THE CHINESE FOUNDATION
CHINESE MUSIC IS BASED ON A FOUNDATION NOTE WHICH WAS HELD TO BE ONE OF THE ETERNAL PRINCIPLES OF THE UNIVERSE. GREAT CARE HAD TO BE TAKEN TO DETERMINE THE EXACT PITCH OF THIS NOTE TO ENSURE THE WELL-BEING OF THE STATE. IN THE FIRST CENTURY BC AN IMPERIAL OFFICE OF MUSIC WAS SET UP TO STANDARDISE THE NOTE. IT WAS DECREED TO BE THE PITCH OBTAINED FROM BLOWING THROUGH A PIPE OF HEIGHT EQUAL TO 90 GRAINS OF MILLET OF AVERAGE SIZE LAID END TO END.

THE ORIGIN OF THE FLAT
IN THE 6TH CENTURY A.D. ST GREGORY SELECTED A SCALE OF 8 NOTES FOR USE IN CHURCH MUSIC. THESE WERE ADHERED TO FOR SOME 10 CENTURIES WITH ONE EXCEPTION. THE NOTE B WAS SOMETIMES FELT TO PRODUCE A 'FALSE RELATION OF SOUND' CALLED THE TRITONUS SO THEY SOMETIMES USED B FLAT. THIS IS THE ORIGIN OF OUR SYMBOL FOR A FLAT SINCE THIS CHANGE WAS INDICATED BY WRITING A SMALL ♭ INSTEAD OF A CAPITAL B.

METAL BELLS
STONE CHIMES
SILK STRINGS
BAMBOO FLUTES
WOOD PERCUSSIVE EFFECTS
SKIN DRUMS
GOURD WINDBOX FOR REED INSTRUMENT
CLAY PIPES

FOSSILISATION WRITING MUSIC
THE ISLAMIC WORLD NEVER DEVELOPED A SYSTEM OF MUSIC WRITING. PERFORMERS EXTEMPORISED, WITHIN DEFINED LIMITS, BUT TO PLAY THE SAME PIECE TWICE IN THE SAME WAY WAS UNTHINKABLE. ANY SYSTEM OF MUSIC WRITING WAS REGARDED AS DANGEROUS & LIABLE TO FOSSILISE THE INTERPRETATION

HOW TO FIND THE HEIGHT OF A CHURCH SPIRE
FIND A STICK TALLER THAN YOURSELF & MARK IT LEVEL WITH THE TOP OF YOUR HEAD. ASK SOMEONE TO MOVE SLOWLY FORWARD HOLDING STICK TILL, WITH YOUR EYE AT GROUND LEVEL THE MARK ON THE STICK IS IN LINE WITH THE TOP OF THE SPIRE. (SEE ABOVE). COUNT THE PACES FROM YOUR EYE TO THE STICK & TO THE BASE OF THE SPIRE. YOU CAN NOW FIND THE HEIGHT OF THE SPIRE FROM YOUR OWN HEIGHT, IN FEET, BY THIS SUM:

YOUR HEIGHT ✕ PACES TO SPIRE ÷ PACES TO STICK

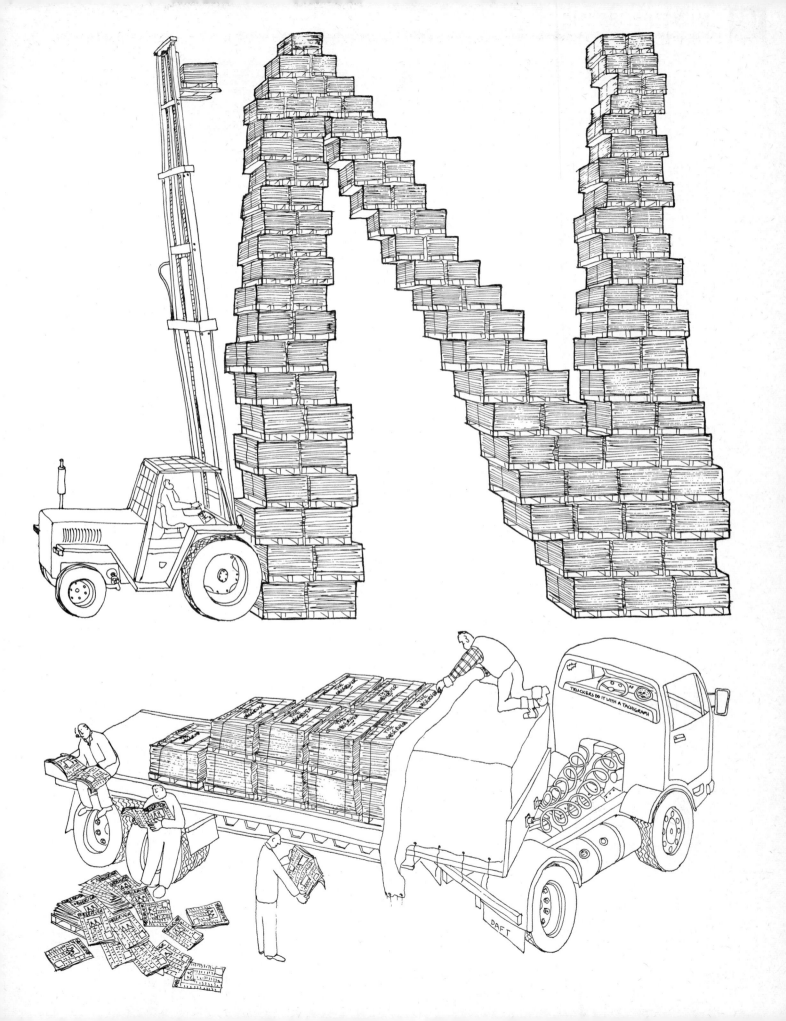

☆ NAMES ☆
THAT BY WHICH INDIVIDUALS ARE KNOWN

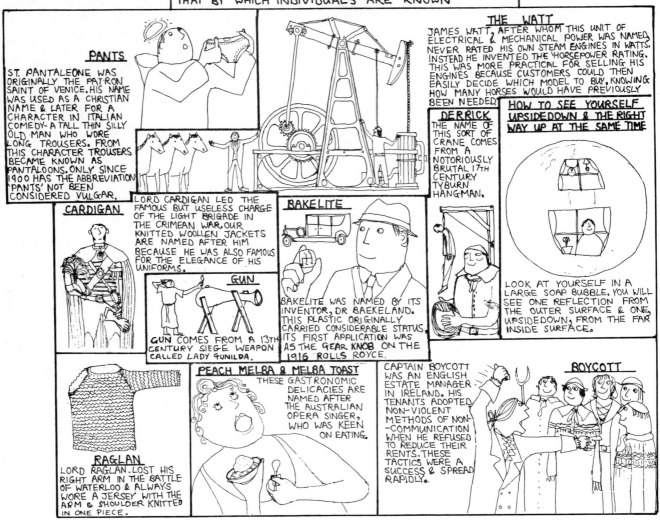

PANTS
ST. PANTALEONE WAS ORIGINALLY THE PATRON SAINT OF VENICE. HIS NAME WAS USED AS A CHRISTIAN NAME & LATER FOR A CHARACTER IN ITALIAN COMEDY- A TALL THIN SILLY OLD MAN WHO WORE LONG TROUSERS. FROM THIS CHARACTER TROUSERS BECAME KNOWN AS PANTALOONS. ONLY SINCE 1900 HAS THE ABBREVIATION 'PANTS' NOT BEEN CONSIDERED VULGAR.

CARDIGAN
LORD CARDIGAN LED THE FAMOUS BUT USELESS CHARGE OF THE LIGHT BRIGADE IN THE CRIMEAN WAR. OUR KNITTED WOOLLEN JACKETS ARE NAMED AFTER HIM BECAUSE HE WAS ALSO FAMOUS FOR THE ELEGANCE OF HIS UNIFORMS.

GUN
GUN COMES FROM A 13TH CENTURY SIEGE WEAPON CALLED LADY GUNILDA.

BAKELITE
BAKELITE WAS NAMED BY ITS INVENTOR, DR BAEKELAND. THIS PLASTIC ORIGINALLY CARRIED CONSIDERABLE STATUS. ITS FIRST APPLICATION WAS AS THE GEAR KNOB ON THE 1916 ROLLS ROYCE.

RAGLAN
LORD RAGLAN. LOST HIS RIGHT ARM IN THE BATTLE OF WATERLOO & ALWAYS WORE A JERSEY WITH THE ARM & SHOULDER KNITTED IN ONE PIECE.

PEACH MELBA & MELBA TOAST
THESE GASTRONOMIC DELICACIES ARE NAMED AFTER THE AUSTRALIAN OPERA SINGER, WHO WAS KEEN ON EATING.

THE WATT
JAMES WATT, AFTER WHOM THIS UNIT OF ELECTRICAL & MECHANICAL POWER WAS NAMED, NEVER RATED HIS OWN STEAM ENGINES IN WATTS. INSTEAD HE INVENTED THE 'HORSEPOWER' RATING. THIS WAS MORE PRACTICAL FOR SELLING HIS ENGINES BECAUSE CUSTOMERS COULD THEN EASILY DECIDE WHICH MODEL TO BUY, KNOWING HOW MANY HORSES WOULD HAVE PREVIOUSLY BEEN NEEDED.

DERRICK
THE NAME OF THIS SORT OF CRANE COMES FROM A NOTORIOUSLY BRUTAL 17TH CENTURY TYBURN HANGMAN.

HOW TO SEE YOURSELF UPSIDEDOWN & THE RIGHT WAY UP AT THE SAME TIME
LOOK AT YOURSELF IN A LARGE SOAP BUBBLE. YOU WILL SEE ONE REFLECTION FROM THE OUTER SURFACE & ONE, UPSIDEDOWN, FROM THE FAR INSIDE SURFACE.

BOYCOTT
CAPTAIN BOYCOTT WAS AN ENGLISH ESTATE MANAGER IN IRELAND. HIS TENANTS ADOPTED NON-VIOLENT METHODS OF NON-COMMUNICATION WHEN HE REFUSED TO REDUCE THEIR RENTS. THESE TACTICS WERE A SUCCESS & SPREAD RAPIDLY.

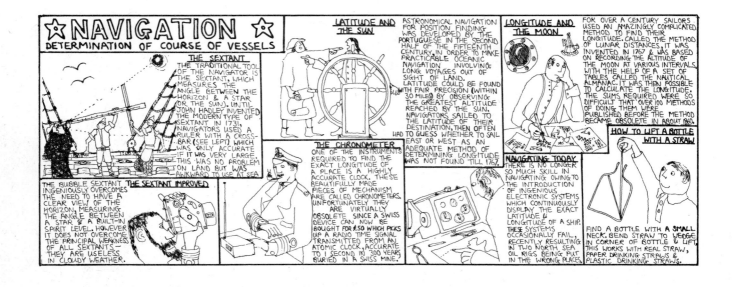

☆ NAVIGATION ☆
DETERMINATION OF COURSE OF VESSELS

THE SEXTANT
THE TRADITIONAL TOOL OF THE NAVIGATOR IS THE SEXTANT, WHICH MEASURES THE ANGLE BETWEEN THE HORIZON & A STAR (OR THE SUN). UNTIL JOHN HADLEY INVENTED THE MODERN TYPE OF SEXTANT IN 1731, NAVIGATORS USED A RULER WITH A CROSS-BAR (SEE LEFT) WHICH WAS ONLY ACCURATE IF IT WAS VERY LARGE. THIS WAS NO PROBLEM ON LAND BUT WAS AWKWARD TO USE AT SEA.

THE SEXTANT IMPROVED
THE BUBBLE SEXTANT INGENIOUSLY OVERCOMES THE NEED TO HAVE A CLEAR VIEW OF THE HORIZON, MEASURING THE ANGLE BETWEEN A STAR & A BUILT-IN SPIRIT LEVEL. HOWEVER IT DOES NOT OVERCOME THE PRINCIPAL WEAKNESS OF ALL SEXTANTS - THEY ARE USELESS IN CLOUDY WEATHER.

LATITUDE AND THE SUN
ASTRONOMICAL NAVIGATION FOR POSITION FINDING WAS DEVELOPED BY THE PORTUGUESE IN THE SECOND HALF OF THE FIFTEENTH CENTURY, IN ORDER TO MAKE PRACTICABLE OCEANIC NAVIGATION INVOLVING LONG VOYAGES OUT OF SIGHT OF LAND. LATITUDE COULD BE FOUND WITH FAIR PRECISION (WITHIN 30 MILES) BY OBSERVING THE GREATEST ALTITUDE REACHED BY THE SUN. NAVIGATORS SAILED TO THE LATITUDE OF THEIR DESTINATION, THEN OFTEN HAD TO GUESS WHETHER TO SAIL EAST OR WEST AS AN ADEQUATE METHOD OF DETERMINING LONGITUDE WAS NOT FOUND TILL 1767.

THE CHRONOMETER
ONE OF THE INSTRUMENTS REQUIRED TO FIND THE EXACT LONGITUDE OF A PLACE IS A HIGHLY ACCURATE CLOCK. THESE BEAUTIFULLY MADE PIECES OF MECHANISM ARE CALLED CHRONOMETERS. UNFORTUNATELY THEY ARE VIRTUALLY OBSOLETE SINCE A SWISS DEVICE CAN NOW BE BOUGHT FOR £50 WHICH PICKS UP A RADIO TIME SIGNAL TRANSMITTED FROM AN ATOMIC CLOCK, ACCURATE TO 1 SECOND IN 300 YEARS, BURIED IN A SWISS MINE.

LONGITUDE AND THE MOON
FOR OVER A CENTURY SAILORS USED AN AMAZINGLY COMPLICATED METHOD TO FIND THEIR LONGITUDE, CALLED THE METHOD OF LUNAR DISTANCES. IT WAS INVENTED IN 1767 & WAS BASED ON RECORDING THE ALTITUDE OF THE MOON AT VARIOUS INTERVALS WITH THE HELP OF A SET OF TABLES CALLED THE NAUTICAL ALMANAC. IT WAS THEN POSSIBLE TO CALCULATE THE LONGITUDE. THE SUMS REQUIRED WERE SO DIFFICULT THAT OVER 100 METHODS OF DOING THEM WERE PUBLISHED BEFORE THE METHOD BECAME OBSOLETE IN ABOUT 1860.

NAVIGATING TODAY
THERE IS NO LONGER SO MUCH SKILL IN NAVIGATING OWING TO THE INTRODUCTION OF INGENIOUS ELECTRONIC SYSTEMS WHICH CONTINUOUSLY DISPLAY THE EXACT LATITUDE & LONGITUDE OF A SHIP. THESE SYSTEMS OCCASIONALLY FAIL, RECENTLY RESULTING IN TWO NORTH SEA OIL RIGS BEING PUT IN THE WRONG PLACES.

HOW TO LIFT A BOTTLE WITH A STRAW
FIND A BOTTLE WITH A SMALL NECK, BEND STRAW TO WEDGE IN CORNER OF BOTTLE & LIFT. THIS WORKS WITH REAL STRAW, PAPER DRINKING STRAWS & PLASTIC DRINKING STRAWS.

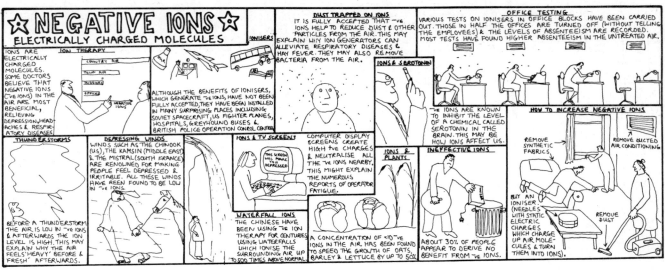

☆ NEGATIVE IONS ☆
ELECTRICALLY CHARGED MOLECULES

IONS ARE ELECTRICALLY CHARGED MOLECULES. SOME DOCTORS BELIEVE THAT NEGATIVE IONS (-ve IONS) IN THE AIR ARE MOST BENEFICIAL, RELIEVING DEPRESSION, HEADACHES & RESPIRATORY DISEASES.

ION THERAPY
COUNTRY AIR
TOWN AIR
INDOORS
OFFICE

IONISERS
ALTHOUGH THE BENEFITS OF IONISERS, WHICH GENERATE -ve IONS, HAVE NOT BEEN FULLY ACCEPTED, THEY HAVE BEEN INSTALLED IN MANY SURPRISING PLACES INCLUDING SOVIET SPACECRAFT, US FIGHTER PLANES, HOSPITALS, GREYHOUND BUSES & BRITISH POLICE OPERATION CONTROL CENTRES.

DUST TRAPPED ON IONS
IT IS FULLY ACCEPTED THAT -ve IONS HELP TO REDUCE DUST & OTHER PARTICLES FROM THE AIR. THIS MAY EXPLAIN WHY ION GENERATORS CAN ALLEVIATE RESPIRATORY DISEASES & HAY FEVER. THEY MAY ALSO REMOVE BACTERIA FROM THE AIR.

OFFICE TESTING
VARIOUS TESTS ON IONISERS IN OFFICE BLOCKS HAVE BEEN CARRIED OUT. THOSE IN HALF THE OFFICES ARE TURNED OFF (WITHOUT TELLING THE EMPLOYEES) & THE LEVELS OF ABSENTEEISM ARE RECORDED. MOST TESTS HAVE FOUND HIGHER ABSENTEEISM IN THE UNTREATED AIR.

IONS & SEROTONIN
-ve IONS ARE KNOWN TO INHIBIT THE LEVEL OF A CHEMICAL CALLED SEROTONIN IN THE BRAIN. THIS MAY BE HOW IONS AFFECT US.

THUNDERSTORMS
BEFORE A THUNDERSTORM THE AIR IS LOW IN -ve IONS & THE ION LEVEL IS HIGH. THIS MAY EXPLAIN WHY THE AIR FEELS 'HEAVY' BEFORE & 'FRESH' AFTERWARDS.

DEPRESSING WINDS
WINDS SUCH AS THE CHINOOK (US), THE KAMSIN (MIDDLE EAST) & THE MISTRAL (SOUTH FRANCE) ARE RENOWNED FOR MAKING PEOPLE FEEL DEPRESSED & IRRITABLE. ALL THESE WINDS HAVE BEEN FOUND TO BE LOW IN -ve IONS.

IONS & TV SCREENS
THIS SCREEN WILL MAKE YOU DEPRESSED
COMPUTER DISPLAY SCREENS CREATE HIGH +ve CHARGES & NEUTRALISE ALL THE -ve IONS NEARBY. THIS MIGHT EXPLAIN THE NUMEROUS REPORTS OF OPERATOR FATIGUE.

WATERFALL IONS
THE CHINESE HAVE BEEN USING -ve ION THERAPY FOR CENTURIES USING WATERFALLS WHICH IONISE THE SURROUNDING AIR UP TO 500 TIMES ABOVE NORMAL.

IONS & PLANTS
A CONCENTRATION OF x10 -ve IONS IN THE AIR HAS BEEN FOUND TO SPEED THE GROWTH OF OATS, BARLEY & LETTUCE BY UP TO 50%.

INEFFECTIVE IONS
ABOUT 30% OF PEOPLE APPEAR TO DERIVE NO BENEFIT FROM -ve IONS.

HOW TO INCREASE NEGATIVE IONS
REMOVE SYNTHETIC FABRICS.
REMOVE DUCTED AIR CONDITIONING.
BUY AN IONISER (NEEDLES WITH STATIC ELECTRIC CHARGES WHICH CHARGE UP AIR MOLECULES & TURN THEM INTO IONS).
REMOVE DUST.

☆ NEON ☆
GLOWING GAS IN SEALED GLASS TUBING

TESLA'S SIGN
IN THE 19TH CENTURY, POPULAR EXPERIMENTS INCLUDED GASES GLOWING IN TUBES AT LOW PRESSURES, WITH ELECTRICITY PASSING THROUGH THEM. THE YUGOSLAV PHYSICIST, TESLA, INVENTED ONE WHICH WAS USED FOR THE FIRST ELECTRIC SIGNS BUT UNFORTUNATELY, THE GAS QUICKLY BECAME CONTAMINATED & ITS LIFE WAS SHORT.

CLAUDE'S DISCOVERY
THE PRACTICAL NEON SIGN WAS PERFECTED BY THE FRENCHMAN GEORGE CLAUDE. AFTER DISCOVERING A CHEAP METHOD OF LIQUEFYING AIR & DISTILLING IT IN 1910, HE WAS LEFT WITH QUANTITIES OF NEON. EXPERIMENTING WITH USES FOR IT, HE STARTED MAKING SIGNS.

GLOWING GASES
ALL GASES WILL GLOW AT LOW PRESSURE WHEN ELECTRICITY IS PASSED THROUGH THEM. THE RARE GASES IN AIR (NEON, ARGON ETC) ARE MOST SUITABLE BECAUSE THEY NEED LESS VOLTAGE THAN MOST GASES.

CLAUDE'S PATENT
CLAUDE'S NEON LIGHT REMAINED A LABORATORY CURIOSITY UNTIL 1915, WHEN HE PERFECTED AN ELECTRODE THAT WOULD NOT CORRODE. HIS PATENTS GAVE HIM A MONOPOLY OF NEON SIGNS UNTIL ABOUT 1930. HE SOLD FRANCHISES TO MANY US FIRMS FOR £40,000 EACH PLUS ROYALTIES.

BENDING
THE BENDING IS HIGHLY SKILLED BECAUSE THE TUBE MUST NOT BE DISTORTED OR BECOME TOO THIN OR IT WILL BREAK WHEN THE AIR IS PUMPED OUT. GLASSBENDERS DON'T WEAR GLOVES SO THEY CAN FEEL THE HEAT OF THE GLASS.

PATTERN DRAWN ON ASBESTOS; GLASS HEATED, LAID OVER ASBESTOS; THEN BENT TO SHAPE.

FILLING
① ELECTRODES FUSED ONTO ENDS OF TUBE
② AIR PUMPED OUT & TUBE SEALED
③ HIGH VOLTAGE PASSED THROUGH TUBE TO CLEAN IT
④ NEON GAS SUCKED IN
⑤ TUBE RESEALED & CONNECTED TO TRANSFORMER

THE PROCESS IS ALMOST UNCHANGED SINCE CLAUDE'S PATENT
NEON 1920 1980

SIGN FASHIONS
IN THE LATE 1930s, THERE WERE HUNDREDS OF FIRMS PRODUCING NEON SIGNS. SINCE 1945, ILLUMINATED PERSPEX SIGNS HAVE BECOME POPULAR. TODAY, ALTHOUGH NEON IS RETURNING TO FASHION, THERE ARE FEW FIRMS STILL EQUIPPED TO USE IT.

BINGO
ORIENTAL HOTEL

FLASHERS
NEW YORK'S FIRST FLASHING ELECTRIC SIGN WAS SWITCHED ON & OFF MANUALLY (USUALLY BY A NEEDY MEDICAL STUDENT).

HOW TO MAKE A CANDLE LAST LONGER
CANDLES CAN BE MADE TO LAST LONGER BY DIPPING THEM IN VARNISH. WHEN IT HAS SET, THE VARNISH STRENGTHENS THE SIDES & STOPS WAX OVERFLOWING.
VARNISH

☆ NERVES ☆
FIBRES CONNECTING THE BRAIN TO ALL PARTS OF THE BODY

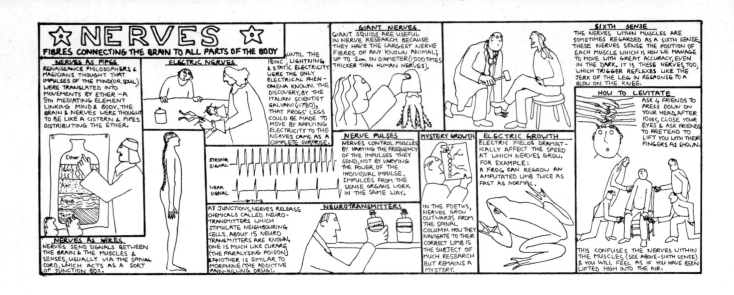

NERVES AS PIPES
RENAISSANCE PHILOSOPHERS & MAGICIANS THOUGHT THAT IMPULSES OF THE MIND (OR SOUL) WERE TRANSLATED INTO MOVEMENTS BY ETHER – A 5TH MEDIATING ELEMENT LINKING MIND & BODY. THE BRAIN & NERVES WERE THOUGHT TO BE LIKE A CISTERN & PIPES DISTRIBUTING THE ETHER.

NERVES AS WIRES
NERVES SEND SIGNALS BETWEEN THE BRAIN & THE MUSCLES & SENSES, USUALLY VIA THE SPINAL CORD, WHICH ACTS AS A SORT OF JUNCTION BOX.

ELECTRIC NERVES
UNTIL THE 18THC, LIGHTNING & STATIC ELECTRICITY WERE THE ONLY ELECTRICAL PHENOMENA KNOWN. THE DISCOVERY, BY THE ITALIAN SCIENTIST GALVANI (c1780), THAT FROGS' LEGS COULD BE MADE TO MOVE BY APPLYING ELECTRICITY TO THE NERVES CAME AS A COMPLETE SURPRISE.

GIANT NERVES
GIANT SQUIDS ARE USEFUL IN NERVE RESEARCH BECAUSE THEY HAVE THE LARGEST NERVE FIBRES OF ANY KNOWN ANIMAL; UP TO 2cm IN DIAMETER (1000 TIMES THICKER THAN HUMAN NERVES).

NERVE PULSES
NERVES CONTROL MUSCLES BY VARYING THE FREQUENCY OF THE IMPULSES THEY SEND, NOT BY VARYING THE POWER OF THE INDIVIDUAL IMPULSE. IMPULSES FROM THE SENSE ORGANS WORK IN THE SAME WAY.

STRONG SIGNAL

WEAK SIGNAL

TIME

AT JUNCTIONS, NERVES RELEASE CHEMICALS CALLED NEUROTRANSMITTERS WHICH STIMULATE NEIGHBOURING CELLS. ABOUT 15 NEUROTRANSMITTERS ARE KNOWN, ONE IS MUCH LIKE CURARE (THE PARALYSING POISON) & ANOTHER IS SIMILAR TO MORPHINE (THE ADDICTIVE PAIN-KILLING DRUG).

NEUROTRANSMITTERS

MYSTERY GROWTH
IN THE FOETUS, NERVES GROW OUTWARDS FROM THE SPINAL COLUMN. HOW THEY NAVIGATE TO THEIR CORRECT LIMB IS THE SUBJECT OF MUCH RESEARCH BUT REMAINS A MYSTERY.

ELECTRIC GROWTH
ELECTRIC FIELDS DRAMATICALLY AFFECT THE SPEED AT WHICH NERVES GROW. FOR EXAMPLE: A FROG CAN REGROW AN AMPUTATED LIMB TWICE AS FAST AS NORMAL.

SIXTH SENSE
THE NERVES WITHIN MUSCLES ARE SOMETIMES REGARDED AS A SIXTH SENSE, THESE NERVES SENSE THE POSITION OF EACH MUSCLE WHICH IS HOW WE MANAGE TO MOVE WITH GREAT ACCURACY, EVEN IN THE DARK. IT IS THESE NERVES TOO, WHICH TRIGGER REFLEXES LIKE THE JERK OF THE LEG IN RESPONSE TO A BLOW ON THE KNEE.

HOW TO LEVITATE
ASK 4 FRIENDS TO PRESS DOWN ON YOUR HEAD. AFTER 10 SEC, CLOSE YOUR EYES & ASK FRIENDS TO PRETEND TO LIFT YOU WITH THEIR FINGERS AS SHOWN.

THIS CONFUSES THE NERVES WITHIN THE MUSCLES (SEE ABOVE-SIXTH SENSE) & YOU WILL FEEL AS IF YOU HAVE BEEN LIFTED HIGH INTO THE AIR.

☆ NEWSPAPERS ☆
PERIODICAL PUBLICATIONS DISSEMINATING NEWS

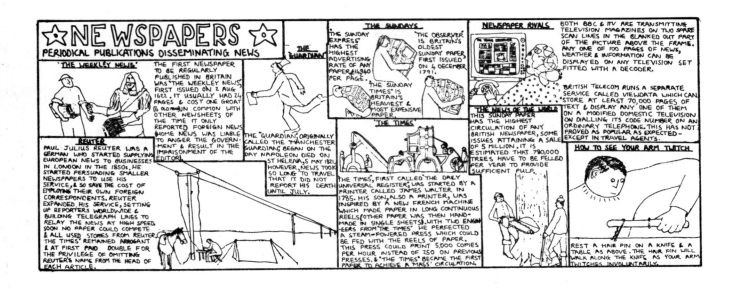

'THE WEEKLEY NEWS'
THE FIRST NEWSPAPER TO BE REGULARLY PUBLISHED IN BRITAIN WAS 'THE WEEKLEY NEWS', FIRST ISSUED ON 2 AUG 1622. IT USUALLY HAD 24 PAGES & COST ONE GROAT (4 OLD PENCE) IN COMMON WITH OTHER NEWSHEETS OF THE TIME IT ONLY REPORTED FOREIGN NEWS. HOME NEWS WAS LIABLE TO ANGER THE GOVERNMENT & RESULT IN THE IMPRISONMENT OF THE EDITOR.

REUTER
PAUL JULIUS REUTER WAS A GERMAN WHO STARTED SUPPLYING EUROPEAN NEWS TO BUSINESSES IN LONDON IN THE 1850s. HE STARTED PERSUADING SMALLER NEWSPAPERS TO USE HIS SERVICE, & SO SAVE THE COST OF EMPLOYING THEIR OWN FOREIGN CORRESPONDENTS. REUTER EXPANDED HIS SERVICE, SETTING UP REPORTERS WORLDWIDE & BUILDING TELEGRAPH LINES TO RELAY THE NEWS AT HIGH SPEED. SOON NO PAPER COULD COMPETE & ALL USED STORIES FROM REUTER. THE TIMES REMAINED ARROGANT & AT FIRST PAID DOUBLE FOR THE PRIVILEGE OF OMITTING REUTER'S NAME FROM THE HEAD OF EACH ARTICLE.

THE GUARDIAN
'THE GUARDIAN', ORIGINALLY CALLED THE 'MANCHESTER GUARDIAN', BEGAN ON THE DAY NAPOLEON DIED ON ST HELENA; 5 MAY 1821. HOWEVER, NEWS TOOK SO LONG TO TRAVEL THAT IT DID NOT REPORT HIS DEATH UNTIL JULY.

THE SUNDAYS
THE SUNDAY EXPRESS HAS THE HIGHEST ADVERTISING RATE OF ANY PAPER; £1,960 PER PAGE.
THE SUNDAY TIMES IS BRITAIN'S HEAVIEST & MOST EXPENSIVE PAPER.

THE OBSERVER IS BRITAIN'S OLDEST SUNDAY PAPER, FIRST ISSUED ON 4 DECEMBER 1791.

THE TIMES
THE TIMES, FIRST CALLED 'THE DAILY UNIVERSAL REGISTER', WAS STARTED BY A PRINTER CALLED JAMES WALTER IN 1785. HIS SON, ALSO A PRINTER, WAS INSPIRED BY A NEW FRENCH MACHINE WHICH MADE PAPER IN LONG CONTINUOUS REELS (OTHER PAPER WAS THEN HAND-MADE IN SINGLE SHEETS). WITH TWO ENGINEERS FROM 'THE TIMES' HE PERFECTED A STEAM-POWERED PRESS WHICH COULD BE FED WITH THE REELS OF PAPER. THIS PRESS COULD PRINT 5,000 COPIES PER HOUR INSTEAD OF 250 ON PREVIOUS PRESSES. & 'THE TIMES' BECAME THE FIRST PAPER TO ACHIEVE A MASS CIRCULATION.

NEWSPAPER RIVALS

THE NEWS OF THE WORLD
THIS SUNDAY PAPER HAS THE HIGHEST CIRCULATION OF ANY BRITISH NEWSPAPER, SOME ISSUES ATTAINING A SALE OF 5 MILLION. IT IS ESTIMATED THAT 780,000 TREES HAVE TO BE FELLED PER YEAR TO PROVIDE SUFFICIENT PULP.

BOTH BBC & ITV ARE TRANSMITTING TELEVISION MAGAZINES ON TWO SPARE SCAN LINES IN THE BLANKED OUT PART OF THE PICTURE ABOVE THE FRAME. ANY ONE OF 100 PAGES OF NEWS, WEATHER & INFORMATION CAN BE DISPLAYED ON ANY TELEVISION SET FITTED WITH A DECODER.

BRITISH TELECOM RUNS A SEPARATE SERVICE CALLED VIEWDATA WHICH CAN STORE AT LEAST 70,000 PAGES OF TEXT & DISPLAY ANY ONE OF THEM ON A MODIFIED DOMESTIC TELEVISION ON DIALLING ITS CODE NUMBER ON AN ORDINARY TELEPHONE. THIS HAS NOT PROVED AS POPULAR AS EXPECTED – EXCEPT IN TRAVEL AGENTS.

HOW TO SEE YOUR ARM TWITCH
REST A HAIR PIN ON A KNIFE & A TABLE AS ABOVE. THE HAIR PIN WILL WALK ALONG THE KNIFE AS YOUR ARM TWITCHES INVOLUNTARILY.

☆ NICKEL ☆
A WHITE MAGNETIC DUCTILE METAL

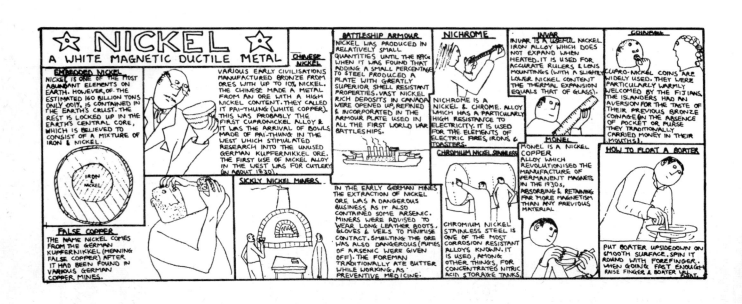

EMBEDDED NICKEL
NICKEL IS ONE OF THE MOST ABUNDANT ELEMENTS ON EARTH. HOWEVER, OF THE ESTIMATED 160 BILLION TONS, ONLY 0.01% IS CONTAINED IN THE EARTH'S CRUST. THE REST IS LOCKED UP IN THE EARTH'S CENTRAL CORE, WHICH IS BELIEVED TO CONSIST OF A MIXTURE OF IRON & NICKEL.

IRON & NICKEL

FALSE COPPER
THE NAME NICKEL COMES FROM THE GERMAN KUPFERNICKEL (MEANING FALSE COPPER) AFTER IT HAD BEEN FOUND IN VARIOUS GERMAN COPPER MINES.

CHINESE NICKEL
VARIOUS EARLY CIVILISATIONS MANUFACTURED BRONZE FROM ORES WITH UP TO 10% NICKEL. THE CHINESE MADE A METAL FROM AN ORE WITH A HIGH NICKEL CONTENT. THEY CALLED IT PAI-THUNG (WHITE COPPER). THIS WAS PROBABLY THE FIRST CUPRONICKEL ALLOY & IT WAS THE ARRIVAL OF BOWLS MADE OF PAI-THUNG IN THE WEST WHICH STIMULATED RESEARCH INTO THE UNUSED GERMAN KUPFERNICKEL ORE. THE FIRST USE OF NICKEL ALLOY IN THE WEST WAS FOR CUTLERY (IN ABOUT 1830).

SICKLY NICKEL MINERS
IN THE EARLY GERMAN MINES THE EXTRACTION OF NICKEL ORE WAS A DANGEROUS BUSINESS AS IT ALSO CONTAINED SOME ARSENIC. MINERS WERE ADVISED TO WEAR LONG LEATHER BOOTS, GLOVES & VEILS TO MINIMISE CONTACT. SMELTING THE ORE WAS ALSO DANGEROUS (FUMES OF ARSENIC WERE GIVEN OFF). THE FOREMAN TRADITIONALLY ATE BUTTER WHILE WORKING, AS PREVENTIVE MEDICINE.

BATTLESHIP ARMOUR
NICKEL WAS PRODUCED IN RELATIVELY SMALL QUANTITIES UNTIL THE 1890s WHEN IT WAS FOUND THAT ADDING A SMALL PERCENTAGE TO STEEL PRODUCED A PLATE WITH GREATLY SUPERIOR SHELL RESISTANT PROPERTIES. VAST NICKEL RICH DEPOSITS IN CANADA WERE OPENED UP, REFINED & INCORPORATED IN THE ARMOUR PLATE USED IN ALL THE FIRST WORLD WAR BATTLESHIPS.

CHROMIUM NICKEL STAINLESS
CHROMIUM NICKEL STAINLESS STEEL IS ONE OF THE MOST CORROSION RESISTANT ALLOYS KNOWN. IT IS USED, AMONG OTHER THINGS, FOR CONCENTRATED NITRIC ACID STORAGE TANKS.

NICHROME
NICHROME IS A NICKEL & CHROME ALLOY WHICH HAS A PARTICULARLY HIGH RESISTANCE TO ELECTRICITY. IT IS USED FOR THE ELEMENTS OF ELECTRIC FIRES, IRONS & TOASTERS.

MONEL
MONEL IS A NICKEL COPPER ALLOY WHICH REVOLUTIONISED THE MANUFACTURE OF PERMANENT MAGNETS IN THE 1930s, ABSORBING & RETAINING FAR MORE MAGNETISM THAN ANY PREVIOUS MATERIAL.

INVAR
INVAR IS A USEFUL NICKEL IRON ALLOY WHICH DOES NOT EXPAND WHEN HEATED. IT IS USED FOR ACCURATE RULERS & LENS MOUNTINGS (WITH A SLIGHTLY LOWER NICKEL CONTENT THE THERMAL EXPANSION EQUALS THAT OF GLASS).

COINAGE
CUPRO-NICKEL COINS ARE WIDELY USED. THEY WERE PARTICULARLY WARMLY WELCOMED BY THE FIJIANS. THE ISLANDERS HAD AN AVERSION FOR THE TASTE OF THEIR PREVIOUS BRONZE COINAGE (IN THE ABSENCE OF POCKET OR PURSE THEY TRADITIONALLY CARRIED MONEY IN THEIR MOUTHS).

HOW TO FLOAT A BOATER
PUT BOATER UPSIDEDOWN ON SMOOTH SURFACE. SPIN IT ROUND WITH FOREFINGER. WHEN GOING FAST ENOUGH RAISE FINGER & BOATER WILL FLOAT.

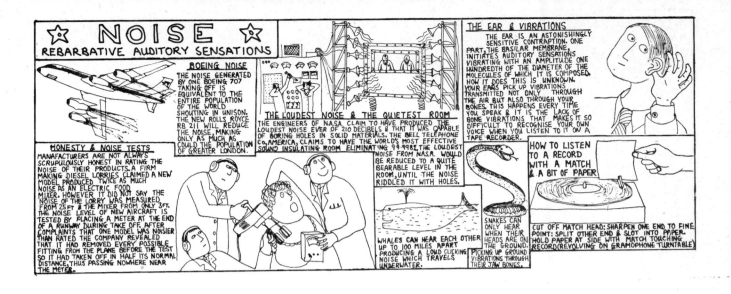

☆ NOISE ☆
REBARBATIVE AUDITORY SENSATIONS

BOEING NOISE
THE NOISE GENERATED BY ONE BOEING 707 TAKING OFF IS EQUIVALENT TO THE ENTIRE POPULATION OF THE WORLD SHOUTING IN UNISON. THE NEW ROLLS ROYCE RB 211 WILL REDUCE THE NOISE, MAKING ONLY AS MUCH AS COULD THE POPULATION OF GREATER LONDON.

HONESTY & NOISE TESTS
MANAFACTURERS ARE NOT ALWAYS SCRUPULOUSLY HONEST IN RATING THE NOISE OF THEIR PRODUCTS. A FIRM MAKING DIESEL LORRIES CLAIMED A NEW MODEL PRODUCED TWICE AS MUCH NOISE AS AN ELECTRIC FOOD MIXER. HOWEVER IT DID NOT SAY THE NOISE OF THE LORRY WAS MEASURED FROM 25FT & THE MIXER FROM ONLY 3FT. THE NOISE LEVEL OF NEW AIRCRAFT IS TESTED BY PLACING A METER AT THE END OF A RUNWAY DURING TAKE OFF. AFTER COMPLAINTS THAT ONE MODEL WAS NOISIER THAN RATED THE COMPANY REVEALED THAT IT HAD REMOVED EVERY POSSIBLE FITTING FROM THE PLANE BEFORE THE TEST SO IT HAD TAKEN OFF IN HALF ITS NORMAL DISTANCE, THUS PASSING NOWHERE NEAR THE METER.

THE LOUDEST NOISE & THE QUIETEST ROOM
THE ENGINEERS OF N.A.S.A. CLAIM TO HAVE PRODUCED THE LOUDEST NOISE EVER OF 210 DECIBELS & THAT IT WAS CAPABLE OF BORING HOLES IN SOLID MATERIALS. THE BELL TELEPHONE Co., AMERICA, CLAIMS TO HAVE THE WORLD'S MOST EFFECTIVE SOUND INSULATING ROOM ELIMINATING 99.99% THE LOUDEST NOISE FROM NASA. WOULD BE REDUCED TO A QUITE BEARABLE LEVEL IN THE ROOM, UNTIL THE NOISE RIDDLED IT WITH HOLES.

WHALES CAN HEAR EACH OTHER UP TO 100 MILES APART PRODUCING A LOUD CLICKING NOISE WHICH TRAVELS UNDERWATER.

SNAKES CAN ONLY HEAR WHEN THEIR HEADS ARE ON THE GROUND. PICKING UP GROUND VIBRATIONS THROUGH THEIR JAW BONES.

THE EAR & VIBRATIONS
THE EAR IS AN ASTONISHINGLY SENSITIVE CONTRAPTION. ONE PART, THE BASILAR MEMBRANE, INITIATES AUDITORY SENSATIONS VIBRATING WITH AN AMPLITUDE ONE HUNDREDTH OF THE DIAMETER OF THE MOLECULES OF WHICH IT IS COMPOSED. HOW IT DOES THIS IS UNKNOWN. YOUR EARS PICK UP VIBRATIONS TRANSMITTED NOT ONLY THROUGH THE AIR BUT ALSO THROUGH YOUR BONES. THIS HAPPENS EVERY TIME YOU SPEAK & IT IS THE LACK OF BONE VIBRATIONS THAT MAKES IT SO DIFFICULT TO RECOGNISE YOUR OWN VOICE WHEN YOU LISTEN TO IT ON A TAPE RECORDER.

HOW TO LISTEN TO A RECORD WITH A MATCH & A BIT OF PAPER
CUT OFF MATCH HEAD: SHARPEN ONE END TO FINE POINT: SPLIT OTHER END & SLOT INTO PAPER. HOLD PAPER AT SIDE WITH MATCH TOUCHING RECORD (REVOLVING ON GRAMOPHONE TURNTABLE).

☆ NURSERY RHYMES ☆
POETIC COMPOSITIONS FOR INFANTS

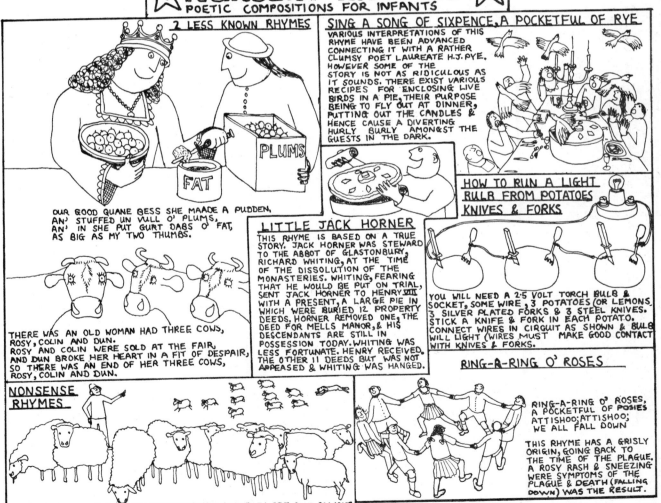

2 LESS KNOWN RHYMES

OUR GOOD QUANE BESS SHE MAADE A PUDDEN, AN' STUFFED UN VULL O' PLUMS, AN' IN SHE PUT GURT DABS O' FAT, AS BIG AS MY TWO THUMBS.

THERE WAS AN OLD WOMAN HAD THREE COWS, ROSY, COLIN AND DUN. ROSY AND COLIN WERE SOLD AT THE FAIR, AND DUN BROKE HER HEART IN A FIT OF DESPAIR, SO THERE WAS AN END OF HER THREE COWS, ROSY, COLIN AND DUN.

SING A SONG OF SIXPENCE, A POCKETFUL OF RYE
VARIOUS INTERPRETATIONS OF THIS RHYME HAVE BEEN ADVANCED CONNECTING IT WITH A RATHER CLUMSY POET LAUREATE H.J. PYE. HOWEVER SOME OF THE STORY IS NOT AS RIDICULOUS AS IT SOUNDS. THERE EXIST VARIOUS RECIPES FOR ENCLOSING LIVE BIRDS IN A PIE, THEIR PURPOSE BEING TO FLY OUT AT DINNER, PUTTING OUT THE CANDLES & HENCE CAUSE A DIVERTING HURLY BURLY AMONGST THE GUESTS IN THE DARK.

LITTLE JACK HORNER
THIS RHYME IS BASED ON A TRUE STORY. JACK HORNER WAS STEWARD TO THE ABBOT OF GLASTONBURY, RICHARD WHITING, AT THE TIME OF THE DISSOLUTION OF THE MONASTERIES. WHITING, FEARING THAT HE WOULD BE PUT ON TRIAL, SENT JACK HORNER TO HENRY VIII WITH A PRESENT, A LARGE PIE IN WHICH WERE BURIED 12 PROPERTY DEEDS. HORNER REMOVED ONE, THE DEED FOR MELLS MANOR, & HIS DESCENDANTS ARE STILL IN POSSESSION TODAY. WHITING WAS LESS FORTUNATE. HENRY RECEIVED THE OTHER 11 DEEDS BUT WAS NOT APPEASED & WHITING WAS HANGED.

HOW TO RUN A LIGHT BULB FROM POTATOES KNIVES & FORKS
YOU WILL NEED A 2.5 VOLT TORCH BULB & SOCKET, SOME WIRE, 3 POTATOES (OR LEMONS) 3 SILVER PLATED FORKS & 3 STEEL KNIVES. STICK A KNIFE & FORK IN EACH POTATO. CONNECT WIRES IN CIRCUIT AS SHOWN & BULB WILL LIGHT (WIRES MUST MAKE GOOD CONTACT WITH KNIVES & FORKS.

RING-A-RING O' ROSES
RING-A-RING O' ROSES, A POCKETFUL OF POSIES ATTISHOO; ATTISHOO; WE ALL FALL DOWN

THIS RHYME HAS A GRISLY ORIGIN, GOING BACK TO THE TIME OF THE PLAGUE. A ROSY RASH & SNEEZING WERE SYMPTOMS OF THE PLAGUE & DEATH (FALLING DOWN) WAS THE RESULT.

NONSENSE RHYMES
SOME RHYMES HAVE STRANGE VOCABULARIES BUT THEY ARE NOT ALWAYS COMPLETE NONSENSE. EENA MEENA MINA MO PROBABLY COMES FROM THE WORDS FOR 1,2,3&4 USED BY EAST ANGLIAN SHEPHERDS & HICKORY DICKORY DOCK FROM WORDS FOR 8,9&10 USED BY WESTMORLAND SHEPHERDS. WHEN RHYMES GET USED IN OTHER COUNTRIES THEY TEND TO KEEP THEIR SOUND RATHER THAN THEIR MEANING. IN DENMARK THERE IS A NONSENSE RHYME:

JECK OG JILL,
VENT OP DE HILL,
OG JILL KOM TOMBLING EFTER.

☆ NUTRITION ☆
THE SCIENCE OF EATING TO STAY HEALTHY

HEALTHY POISONS
HEALTH FOOD ADDICTS ARE KEEN TO EXPOSE ALL THE HARMFUL EFFECTS OF CHEMICAL FOOD ADDITIVES, BUT NATURAL FOODS ALSO CONTAIN MANY POISONOUS SUBSTANCES. APPLE PIPS, PLUM STONES, AND CHERRY STONES CAN YIELD PRUSSIC ACID, RHUBARB CONTAINS OXALIC ACID, POTATOES CONTAIN SOLANINE & NUTMEG CONTAINS A CHEMICAL SIMILAR TO LSD (MYRISTICIN). LARGE QUANTITIES OF SPINACH CAN CAUSE ANAEMIA; CABBAGE, ONIONS, RADISHES & TURNIPS CAN CAUSE GOITRE & BANANAS & SALT CAN INDUCE HIGH BLOOD PRESSURE.

KANGAROO MEAT
CHOLESTEROL, A CHEMICAL FOUND IN ANIMAL FATS, IS THOUGHT TO PROMOTE HEART ATTACKS. HOWEVER THERE IS ONE ANIMAL WHOSE MEAT HAS RECENTLY BEEN DISCOVERED TO BE CHOLESTEROL FREE. THE KANGAROO. AUSTRALIAN AGRICULTURISTS ARE SERIOUSLY CONSIDERING RANCHING DOMESTICATED KANGAROOS FOR HUMAN CONSUMPTION.

CARROTS
CARROTS REALLY DO HELP YOU SEE IN THE DARK. THE HUMAN METABOLISM CONVERTS CAROTENE TO VITAMIN A WHICH PROMOTES THE FORMATION OF A RETINAL PIGMENT ESSENTIAL FOR VISION AT LOW LIGHT LEVELS. HOWEVER, ANYTHING IN EXCESS CAN BE HARMFUL. IN 1973 A MAN DIED FROM CHRONIC VITAMIN A POISONING IN BRITAIN. HE HAD BEEN EATING HUNDREDS OF VITAMIN A TABLETS & A GALLON OF CARROT JUICE DAILY. THIS HAD TURNED HIS SKIN A BRIGHT ORANGE COLOUR AT HIS DEATH.

HEAVY BABIES
THE INCREASE IN THE NUMBER OF OVERWEIGHT BABIES IN BRITAIN IS WORRYING MANY DOCTORS. HEINZ ARE EXPERIMENTING REDUCING THE SUGAR CONTENT OF THEIR TINNED BABY FOODS BUT THEIR ATTEMPTS ARE HAMPERED BY THE FACT THAT CONSUMER APPRECIATION APPEARS TO BE DIRECTLY PROPORTIONAL TO SUGAR CONTENT.

THE NUMBER OF EGGS IN NOODLES
DETECTING THE EGG CONTENT OF NOODLES HAS BEEN THE SUBJECT OF INTENSIVE STUDY AT THE FRENCH INSTITUTE OF AGRONOMIC RESEARCH. PREVIOUS MACHINES COULD MEASURE ONLY THE YOLK CONTENT OR ONLY THE WHITE, BUT THIS WAS FELT TO BE INADEQUATE TO ENFORCE THE E.E.C. EDICT SPECIFYING MINIMUM TOTAL EGG CONTENT. THEY HAVE NOW SOLVED THE PROBLEM, INTRODUCING AN ELECTROPHORESIS NOODLE ANALYSER.

HOW TO MAKE MONEY OUT OF A SUGAR LUMP
CHALLENGE SOMEBODY TO BURN A SUGAR LUMP (HOLDING IT IN TWEEZERS OVER A CANDLE FLAME) WHEN HE FAILS, BET HIM YOU CAN DO IT. TO WIN BET SIMPLY COAT THE LUMP IN ASH (FROM A FIRE OR CIGARETTE) THE ASH ACTS AS A CATALYST & THE LUMP WILL NOW BURN.

VITAMIN C
THE BENEFICIAL EFFECTS OF TAKING LARGE DOSES OF VITAMIN C ARE STILL SCOFFED AT BY MANY DOCTORS. HOWEVER THE FIRST LARGE SCALE TEST BY TORONTO UNIVERSITY USING 1000 SUBJECTS SHOWED THAT THE 500 TAKING VITAMIN C HAD 30% FEWER DAYS OFF WORK DUE TO COLDS & FLU THAN THE 500 TAKING DUMMY PILLS (WITH A 1-IN-500 PROBABILITY THAT THIS OCCURRED BY CHANCE).

☆ NYLON ☆
COPOLYMER OF DICARBOXYLIC ACIDS & DIAMINES

DISCOVERY
NYLON WAS INVENTED IN AMERICA BY W. CAROTHERS, A CHEMIST, IN 1930. HE SUCCEEDED IN PRODUCING THE FIRST MAN-MADE CHEMICAL THAT CONTAINED LONG CHAIN MOLECULES (SIMILAR TO THOSE IN NATURAL FIBRES).

ONE MONTH LATER HIS ASSISTANT DISCOVERED THAT FROM THIS CHEMICAL (A GLUEY MASS) IT WAS POSSIBLE TO PULL OUT A FIBRE.

UNFORTUNATELY, THIS FIRST FIBRE WAS EASILY MELTED OR DISSOLVED & THE COMMERCIAL VARIETY (NYLON) WAS NOT PERFECTED FOR ANOTHER 7 YEARS.

CAROTHERS NEVER LIVED TO SEE THE SUCCESS OF HIS DISCOVERY. HE SUFFERED FROM DEPRESSION & COMMITTED SUICIDE IN 1937.

NYLON BRISTLE
THE FIRST NYLON PRODUCT WAS TOOTH-BRUSH BRISTLE (1938).

PRODUCTION
ABOUT 10% OF ALL FABRICS TODAY ARE MADE OF NYLON. WORLD PRODUCTION IS ABOUT 2.5 MILLION TONNES A YEAR.

'NATURAL LOOK' NYLON
FILAMENTS
CHOPPED FILAMENTS
SPUN CHOPPED FILAMENTS

MOST NYLON FABRICS ARE MADE OF NYLON FILAMENTS WHICH HAVE BEEN CHOPPED INTO SHORT UNEQUAL LENGTHS & THEN SPUN TO MAKE A YARN (LIKE NATURAL FIBRES).

NYLONS

NYLON STOCKINGS WERE LAUNCHED SIMULTANEOUSLY THROUGHOUT THE USA ON 15 MAY 1940. 12m GIANT STOCKINGED LEGS WERE BUILT FOR THE OCCASION. IN THE FIRST YEAR 64 MILLION PAIRS OF NYLONS WERE SOLD.

STRETCHING NYLON
THE LONG CHAIN MOLECULES IN NYLON ARE NORMALLY ARRANGED AT RANDOM. HOWEVER, IF A NYLON ROD IS STRETCHED TO A THIN FILAMENT THE LONG MOLECULES LINE UP & LOCK INTO EACH OTHER. THIS IS WHAT GIVES NYLON FILAMENTS THEIR STRENGTH.

RAW NYLON MOLECULES

STRETCHED NYLON MOLECULES

TOUGH NYLON
NYLON FIBRES ARE VERY TOUGH. EVEN BULLET-PROOF VESTS CAN BE MADE OF NYLON.

SOLID NYLON
NYLON IS NOT ONLY USED FOR FILAMENTS, IT CAN ALSO BE CAST INTO SOLID OBJECTS INCLUDING SHOE HEELS, FOOD BOXES & ELECTRIC DRILL CASINGS. IT IS ALSO USED FOR GEARS WHICH ARE INACCESSIBLE & CANNOT BE LUBRICATED.

SHINY NYLON
NYLON FILAMENTS (& HENCE NYLON CLOTHES) ARE NATURALLY SHINY. HOWEVER A WHITE POWDER (TITANIUM DIOXIDE) IS OFTEN ADDED TO THE CHEMICAL MIX TO MAKE MATT FILAMENTS.

COLD NYLON
NYLON GARMENTS TEND TO FEEL COLD WHEN FIRST PUT ON. THIS IS BECAUSE NYLON IS AN INSULATOR (& THUS WARMS UP SLOWLY) & BECAUSE ITS SMOOTH SURFACE INCREASES THE AREA OF SKIN CONTACT.

HOW TO DO A SIMPLE CARD TRICK
TURN BOTTOM CARD OF PACK BACK TO FRONT. ASK FRIEND TO PICK CARD. SECRETLY TURN PACK OVER. NOW ASK FRIEND TO MEMORISE HIS CARD & REPLACE IT. SHUFFLE PACK. THE BOTTOM CARD & CHOSEN CARD WILL BE THE ONLY ONES BACK TO FRONT.

NATURAL CRIMP
MOST NATURAL FIBRES ARE WAVY OR 'CRIMPED'. THIS CREATES FABRICS WHICH HAVE A LARGE AMOUNT OF AIR TRAPPED IN THEM GIVING GOOD INSULATION & MOISTURE ABSORPTION.

NYLON CRIMP
NYLON FILAMENTS CAN BE 'CRIMPED'. ONE METHOD (E.G. ACRILAN & ORLON) IS TO SPIN A MIXTURE OF HIGHLY STRETCHED & UNSTRETCHED FILAMENTS. WHEN THIS IS HEATED, THE HIGHLY STRETCHED FILAMENTS RELAX & SHRINK, CAUSING THE YARN TO 'CRIMP'.

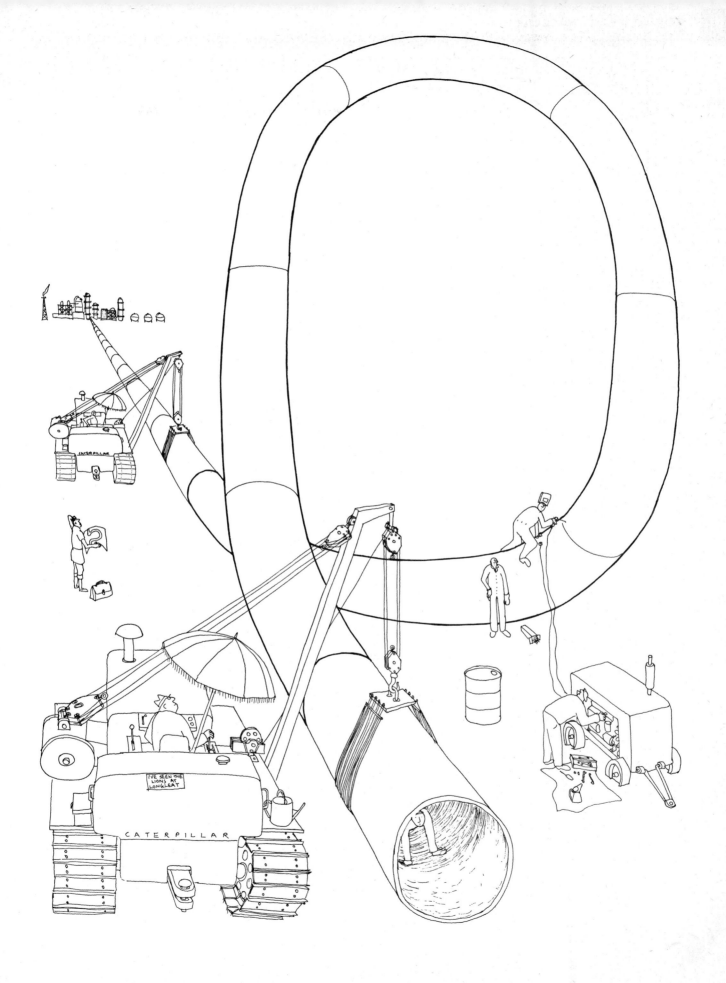

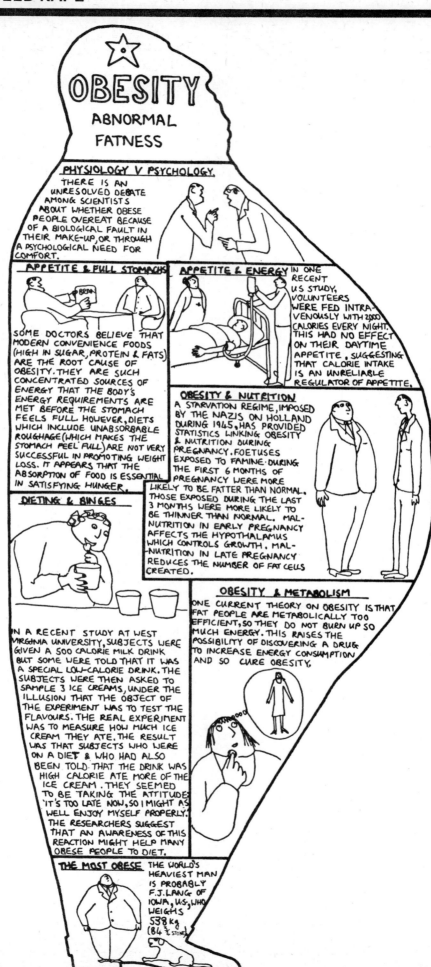

OBESITY

ABNORMAL FATNESS

PHYSIOLOGY V PSYCHOLOGY.

THERE IS AN UNRESOLVED DEBATE AMONG SCIENTISTS ABOUT WHETHER OBESE PEOPLE OVEREAT BECAUSE OF A BIOLOGICAL FAULT IN THEIR MAKE-UP, OR THROUGH A PSYCHOLOGICAL NEED FOR COMFORT.

APPETITE & FULL STOMACHS

SOME DOCTORS BELIEVE THAT MODERN CONVENIENCE FOODS (HIGH IN SUGAR, PROTEIN & FATS) ARE THE ROOT CAUSE OF OBESITY. THEY ARE SUCH CONCENTRATED SOURCES OF ENERGY THAT THE BODY'S ENERGY REQUIREMENTS ARE MET BEFORE THE STOMACH FEELS FULL. HOWEVER, DIETS WHICH INCLUDE UNABSORBABLE ROUGHAGE (WHICH MAKES THE STOMACH FEEL FULL) ARE NOT VERY SUCCESSFUL IN PROMOTING WEIGHT LOSS. IT APPEARS THAT THE ABSORPTION OF FOOD IS ESSENTIAL IN SATISFYING HUNGER.

APPETITE & ENERGY

IN ONE RECENT U.S. STUDY, VOLUNTEERS WERE FED INTRA-VENOUSLY WITH 2000 CALORIES EVERY NIGHT. THIS HAD NO EFFECT ON THEIR DAYTIME APPETITE, SUGGESTING THAT CALORIE INTAKE IS AN UNRELIABLE REGULATOR OF APPETITE.

OBESITY & NUTRITION

A STARVATION REGIME, IMPOSED BY THE NAZIS ON HOLLAND DURING 1945, HAS PROVIDED STATISTICS LINKING OBESITY & NUTRITION DURING PREGNANCY. FOETUSES EXPOSED TO FAMINE DURING THE FIRST 6 MONTHS OF PREGNANCY WERE MORE LIKELY TO BE FATTER THAN NORMAL. THOSE EXPOSED DURING THE LAST 3 MONTHS WERE MORE LIKELY TO BE THINNER THAN NORMAL. MAL-NUTRITION IN EARLY PREGNANCY AFFECTS THE HYPOTHALAMUS WHICH CONTROLS GROWTH. MAL-NUTRITION IN LATE PREGNANCY REDUCES THE NUMBER OF FAT CELLS CREATED.

DIETING & BINGES

IN A RECENT STUDY AT WEST VIRGINIA UNIVERSITY, SUBJECTS WERE GIVEN A 500 CALORIE MILK DRINK BUT SOME WERE TOLD THAT IT WAS A SPECIAL LOW-CALORIE DRINK. THE SUBJECTS WERE THEN ASKED TO SAMPLE 3 ICE CREAMS, UNDER THE ILLUSION THAT THE OBJECT OF THE EXPERIMENT WAS TO TEST THE FLAVOURS. THE REAL EXPERIMENT WAS TO MEASURE HOW MUCH ICE CREAM THEY ATE. THE RESULT WAS THAT SUBJECTS WHO WERE ON A DIET & WHO HAD ALSO BEEN TOLD THAT THE DRINK WAS HIGH CALORIE ATE MORE OF THE ICE CREAM. THEY SEEMED TO BE TAKING THE ATTITUDE 'IT'S TOO LATE NOW, SO I MIGHT AS WELL ENJOY MYSELF PROPERLY.' THE RESEARCHERS SUGGEST THAT AN AWARENESS OF THIS REACTION MIGHT HELP MANY OBESE PEOPLE TO DIET.

OBESITY & METABOLISM

ONE CURRENT THEORY ON OBESITY IS THAT FAT PEOPLE ARE METABOLICALLY TOO EFFICIENT, SO THEY DO NOT BURN UP SO MUCH ENERGY. THIS RAISES THE POSSIBILITY OF DISCOVERING A DRUG TO INCREASE ENERGY CONSUMPTION AND SO CURE OBESITY.

THE MOST OBESE

THE WORLD'S HEAVIEST MAN IS PROBABLY F.J. LANG OF IOWA, U.S. WHO WEIGHS 538 kg (84½ STONE)

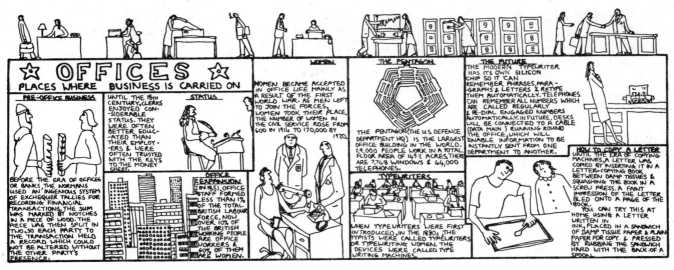

☆ OFFICES ☆
PLACES WHERE BUSINESS IS CARRIED ON

PRE-OFFICE BUSINESS
BEFORE THE ERA OF OFFICES OR BANKS, THE NORMANS USED AN INGENIOUS SYSTEM OF EXCHEQUER TALLIES FOR RECORDING FINANCIAL TRANSACTIONS. THE SUM WAS MARKED BY NOTCHES IN A PIECE OF WOOD. THE PIECE WAS THEN SPLIT IN TWO, SO EACH PARTY TO THE TRANSACTION HELD A RECORD WHICH COULD NOT BE ALTERED WITHOUT THE OTHER PARTY'S PRESENCE.

UNTIL THE 18TH CENTURY, CLERKS ENJOYED CONSIDERABLE STATUS. THEY WERE BETTER EDUCATED THAN THEIR EMPLOYERS & WERE OFTEN TRUSTED WITH THE KEYS TO THE MONEY CHEST.

STATUS

OFFICE EXPANSION
IN 1851, OFFICE STAFF FORMED LESS THAN 1% OF THE TOTAL BRITISH LABOUR FORCE. NOW OVER 10% OF THE BRITISH WORKING PEOPLE ARE OFFICE WORKERS & 60% OF THEM ARE WOMEN.

WOMEN
WOMEN BECAME ACCEPTED IN OFFICE LIFE MAINLY AS A RESULT OF THE FIRST WORLD WAR. AS MEN LEFT TO JOIN THE FORCES, WOMEN TOOK THEIR PLACE. THE NUMBER OF WOMEN IN THE CIVIL SERVICE ROSE FROM 600 IN 1914 TO 170,000 BY 1920.

THE PENTAGON
THE PENTAGON (THE U.S. DEFENCE DEPARTMENT HQ) IS THE LARGEST OFFICE BUILDING IN THE WORLD. 29,000 PEOPLE WORK IN A TOTAL FLOOR AREA OF 149.2 ACRES. THERE ARE 7,748 WINDOWS & 44,000 TELEPHONES.

TYPEWRITERS
WHEN TYPEWRITERS WERE FIRST INTRODUCED IN THE 1870s, THE TYPISTS WERE CALLED TYPEWRITERS OR TYPEWRITING WOMEN. THE DEVICES WERE CALLED TYPE WRITING MACHINES.

THE FUTURE
THE MODERN TYPEWRITER HAS ITS OWN SILICON CHIP SO IT CAN REMEMBER PHRASES, PARAGRAPHS & LETTERS & RETYPE THEM AUTOMATICALLY. TELEPHONES CAN REMEMBER ALL NUMBERS WHICH ARE CALLED REGULARLY & RE-DIAL ENGAGED NUMBERS AUTOMATICALLY. IN FUTURE, DESKS WILL BE CONNECTED TO A CABLE (DATA MAIN) RUNNING ROUND THE OFFICE, WHICH WILL ENABLE INFORMATION TO BE INSTANTLY SENT FROM ONE DEPARTMENT TO ANOTHER.

HOW TO COPY A LETTER
UNTIL THE ERA OF COPYING MACHINES, A LETTER WAS COPIED BY INSERTING IT IN A LETTER-COPYING BOOK BETWEEN DAMP TISSUES & SQUASHING THE BOOK IN A SCREW PRESS. A FAINT IMPRESSION OF THE LETTER BLED ONTO A PAGE OF THE BOOK. YOU CAN TRY THIS AT HOME USING A LETTER WRITTEN IN INK, PLACED IN A SANDWICH OF DAMP TISSUE PAPER & PLAIN PAPER FOR COPY. & PRESSED BY RUBBING THE SANDWICH HARD WITH THE BACK OF A SPOON.

☆ OIL SEED RAPE ☆
PROFITABLE SEED CROP WITH YELLOW FLOWERS

POPULAR RAPE
THE CROP WITH BRIGHT YELLOW FLOWERS, NOW SEEN IN MANY FIELDS IN SPRING & SUMMER, IS NOT MUSTARD, AS IS POPULARLY BELIEVED, BUT IS MOSTLY OIL SEED RAPE. IT HAS GROWN RAPIDLY IN POPULARITY FROM 5000 ACRES IN THE MID-1960s TO THE PRESENT 250,000 ACRES.

RAPE & TURNIPS
RAPE IS BOTANICALLY VERY SIMILAR TO TURNIPS - ALTHOUGH THE 'FRUIT' NEVER DEVELOPS, THE WORD 'RAPE' COMES FROM THE LATIN RAPA - TURNIP.

NASTY RAPE
RAPE SEEDS YIELD LARGE QUANTITIES OF OIL WHEN CRUSHED. UNFORTUNATELY, THE OIL FROM TRADITIONAL VARIETIES CONTAINS:

☆ ERUCIC ACID, WHICH CAN DAMAGE THE HEART.

☆ LINOLEIC ACID, WHICH MAKES COOKING OIL UNSTABLE & RESULTS IN A BAD TASTE.

☆ GLUCOSALINATES, WHICH ARE TOXIC TO ANIMALS & PREVENT THE ADDITION OF THE OIL TO ANIMAL FEEDS.

RAPE & MUSTARD
RAPE SEED LOOKS VERY SIMILAR TO MUSTARD SEED SO FARMERS ARE ADVISED NEVER TO PLANT RAPE WHERE MUSTARD HAS GROWN, TO AVOID CONTAMINATION.

SEASONAL RAPE
RAPE FLOWERS CAN BE SEEN THROUGHOUT THE SPRING & SUMMER. SOME RAPE IS PLANTED IN LATE SUMMER FOR HARVESTING EARLY THE NEXT SUMMER & SOME IS PLANTED IN THE SPRING FOR AN AUTUMN HARVEST.

DEAD RAPE
RAPE IS OFTEN SPRAYED WITH WEED-KILLER (DIQUAT) A FEW DAYS BEFORE HARVESTING. THIS COMPLETELY DESICCATES (DRIES OUT) THE LEAVES & STEMS, MAKING COMBINE HARVESTING EASIER & QUICKER.

RAPE CURRIES
DESPITE THE BITTER TASTE OF TRADITIONAL RAPE SEED OIL, IT IS USED FOR COOKING IN PARTS OF MALAYSIA. IT IS PARTICULARLY LIKED FOR FLAVOURING STRONG CURRIES.

RAPE V SOYA
RAPE HAS GREAT POTENTIAL AS A CROP FOR DEVELOPING COUNTRIES. IT CONTAINS AS MUCH PROTEIN AS SOYA BUT HAS TWICE AS MUCH OIL & THE EXTRACTION (BY CRUSHING) IS MUCH SIMPLER.

TASTY RAPE OIL
IN THE 1960s, STRAINS OF RAPE WERE DEVELOPED WITH 90% LESS ERUCIC ACID & GLUCOSALINATES. RAPE OIL IS NOW A MAJOR COMPONENT OF VEGETABLE COOKING OILS & MARGARINES & IS A VALUABLE ANIMAL FOOD (40% PROTEIN).

PROFITABLE RAPE
IN SOME PARTS OF BRITAIN, RAPE IS NOW A MORE PROFITABLE CROP THAN BARLEY OR WHEAT.

EUROPEAN RAPE
BRITAIN STILL GROWS MUCH LESS RAPE THAN MANY OTHER EUROPEAN COUNTRIES.

- POLAND
- FRANCE
- SWEDEN
- E. GERMANY
- W. GERMANY
- CZECH
- DENMARK
- UK

'000 TONS

HOW TO MAKE A GHOST COIN
HOLD TWO COINS BETWEEN THE TIPS OF YOUR FINGERS & RUB THEM RAPIDLY BACK & FORTH AGAINST EACH OTHER AS ABOVE. A THIRD 'GHOST' COIN WILL APPEAR BETWEEN THEM.

FLOWING RAPE
BECAUSE RAPE SEEDS ARE SMALL & ROUND THEY FLOW MORE EASILY THAN CEREAL GRAIN (WHEAT, BARLEY ETC), ALL HOLES IN TRAILERS, ELEVATORS & DRIERS HAVE TO BE BLOCKED WITH STICKY TAPE BEFORE USE.

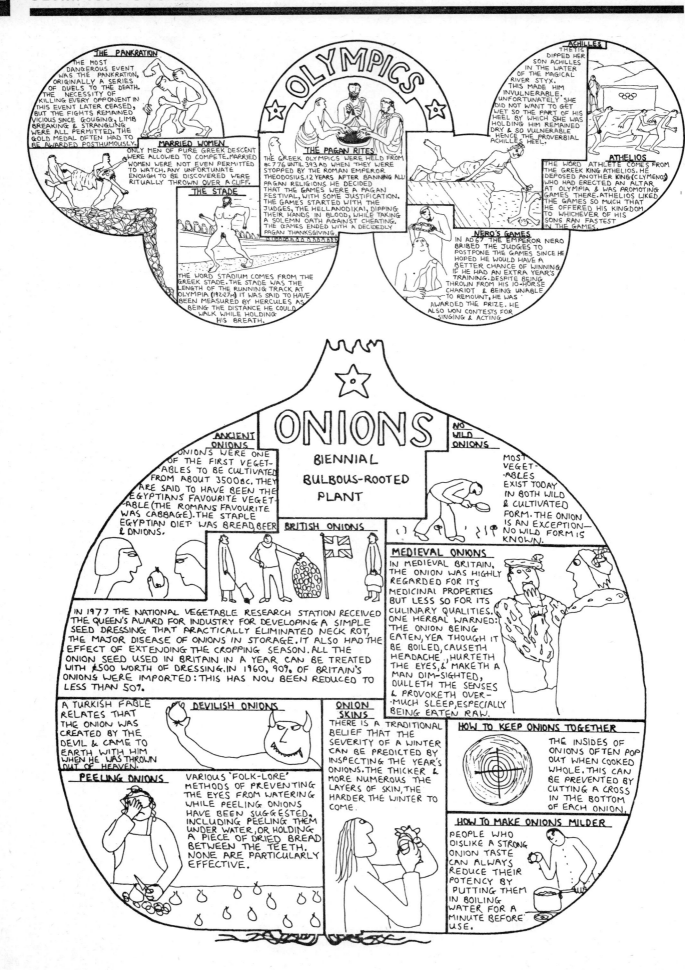

OLYMPICS

THE PANKRATION
THE MOST DANGEROUS EVENT WAS THE PANKRATION, ORIGINALLY A SERIES OF DUELS TO THE DEATH. THE NECESSITY OF KILLING EVERY OPPONENT IN THIS EVENT LATER CEASED, BUT THE FIGHTS REMAINED VICIOUS SINCE GOUGING, LIMB BREAKING & STRANGLING WERE ALL PERMITTED. THE GOLD MEDAL OFTEN HAD TO BE AWARDED POSTHUMOUSLY.

MARRIED WOMEN
ONLY MEN OF PURE GREEK DESCENT WERE ALLOWED TO COMPETE. MARRIED WOMEN WERE NOT EVEN PERMITTED TO WATCH. ANY UNFORTUNATE ENOUGH TO BE DISCOVERED WERE RITUALLY THROWN OVER A CLIFF.

THE STADE
THE WORD STADIUM COMES FROM THE GREEK STADE. THE STADE WAS THE LENGTH OF THE RUNNING TRACK AT OLYMPIA (192.27M). IT WAS SAID TO HAVE BEEN MEASURED BY HERCULES AS BEING THE DISTANCE HE COULD WALK WHILE HOLDING HIS BREATH.

THE PAGAN RITES
THE GREEK OLYMPICS WERE HELD FROM BC 776 UNTIL 393 AD WHEN THEY WERE STOPPED BY THE ROMAN EMPEROR THEODOSIUS. 12 YEARS AFTER BANNING ALL PAGAN RELIGIONS HE DECIDED THAT THE GAMES WERE A PAGAN FESTIVAL, WITH SOME JUSTIFICATION. THE GAMES STARTED WITH THE JUDGES, THE HELLANODIKAI, DIPPING THEIR HANDS IN BLOOD, WHILE TAKING A SOLEMN OATH AGAINST CHEATING. THE GAMES ENDED WITH A DECIDEDLY PAGAN THANKSGIVING.

NERO'S GAMES
IN AD 67 THE EMPEROR NERO BRIBED THE JUDGES TO POSTPONE THE GAMES SINCE HE HOPED HE WOULD HAVE A BETTER CHANCE OF WINNING IF HE HAD AN EXTRA YEAR'S TRAINING. DESPITE BEING THROWN FROM HIS 10-HORSE CHARIOT & BEING UNABLE TO REMOUNT, HE WAS AWARDED THE PRIZE. HE ALSO WON CONTESTS FOR SINGING & ACTING.

ACHILLES
THETIS DIPPED HER SON ACHILLES IN THE WATER OF THE MAGICAL RIVER STYX. THIS MADE HIM INVULNERABLE. UNFORTUNATELY SHE DID NOT WANT TO GET WET SO THE PART OF HIS HEEL BY WHICH SHE WAS HOLDING HIM REMAINED DRY & SO VULNERABLE. HENCE THE PROVERBIAL ACHILLES HEEL.

ATHELIOS
THE WORD ATHLETE COMES FROM THE GREEK KING ATHELIOS. HE DEPOSED ANOTHER KING (CLYMENOS) WHO HAD ERECTED AN ALTAR AT OLYMPIA & WAS PROMOTING GAMES THERE. ATHELIOS LIKED THE GAMES SO MUCH THAT HE OFFERED HIS KINGDOM TO WHICHEVER OF HIS SONS RAN FASTEST IN THE GAMES.

ONIONS
BIENNIAL BULBOUS-ROOTED PLANT

ANCIENT ONIONS
ONIONS WERE ONE OF THE FIRST VEGETABLES TO BE CULTIVATED FROM ABOUT 3500 BC. THEY ARE SAID TO HAVE BEEN THE EGYPTIANS FAVOURITE VEGETABLE (THE ROMANS FAVOURITE WAS CABBAGE). THE STAPLE EGYPTIAN DIET WAS BREAD, BEER & ONIONS.

NO WILD ONIONS
MOST VEGETABLES EXIST TODAY IN BOTH WILD & CULTIVATED FORM. THE ONION IS AN EXCEPTION—NO WILD FORM IS KNOWN.

BRITISH ONIONS
IN 1977 THE NATIONAL VEGETABLE RESEARCH STATION RECEIVED THE QUEEN'S AWARD FOR INDUSTRY FOR DEVELOPING A SIMPLE SEED DRESSING THAT PRACTICALLY ELIMINATED NECK ROT, THE MAJOR DISEASE OF ONIONS IN STORAGE. IT ALSO HAD THE EFFECT OF EXTENDING THE CROPPING SEASON. ALL THE ONION SEED USED IN BRITAIN IN A YEAR CAN BE TREATED WITH £500 WORTH OF DRESSING. IN 1960, 90% OF BRITAIN'S ONIONS WERE IMPORTED: THIS HAS NOW BEEN REDUCED TO LESS THAN 50%.

MEDIEVAL ONIONS
IN MEDIEVAL BRITAIN, THE ONION WAS HIGHLY REGARDED FOR ITS MEDICINAL PROPERTIES BUT LESS SO FOR ITS CULINARY QUALITIES. ONE HERBAL WARNED: THE ONION BEING EATEN, YEA THOUGH IT BE BOILED, CAUSETH HEADACHE, HURTETH THE EYES, & MAKETH A MAN DIM-SIGHTED, DULLETH THE SENSES & PROVOKETH OVER-MUCH SLEEP, ESPECIALLY BEING EATEN RAW.

DEVILISH ONIONS
A TURKISH FABLE RELATES THAT THE ONION WAS CREATED BY THE DEVIL & CAME TO EARTH WITH HIM WHEN HE WAS THROWN OUT OF HEAVEN.

ONION SKINS
THERE IS A TRADITIONAL BELIEF THAT THE SEVERITY OF A WINTER CAN BE PREDICTED BY INSPECTING THE YEAR'S ONIONS. THE THICKER & MORE NUMEROUS THE LAYERS OF SKIN, THE HARDER THE WINTER TO COME.

HOW TO KEEP ONIONS TOGETHER
THE INSIDES OF ONIONS OFTEN POP OUT WHEN COOKED WHOLE. THIS CAN BE PREVENTED BY CUTTING A CROSS IN THE BOTTOM OF EACH ONION.

PEELING ONIONS
VARIOUS 'FOLK-LORE' METHODS OF PREVENTING THE EYES FROM WATERING WHILE PEELING ONIONS HAVE BEEN SUGGESTED, INCLUDING PEELING THEM UNDER WATER, OR HOLDING A PIECE OF DRIED BREAD BETWEEN THE TEETH. NONE ARE PARTICULARLY EFFECTIVE.

HOW TO MAKE ONIONS MILDER
PEOPLE WHO DISLIKE A STRONG ONION TASTE CAN ALWAYS REDUCE THEIR POTENCY BY PUTTING THEM IN BOILING WATER FOR A MINUTE BEFORE USE.

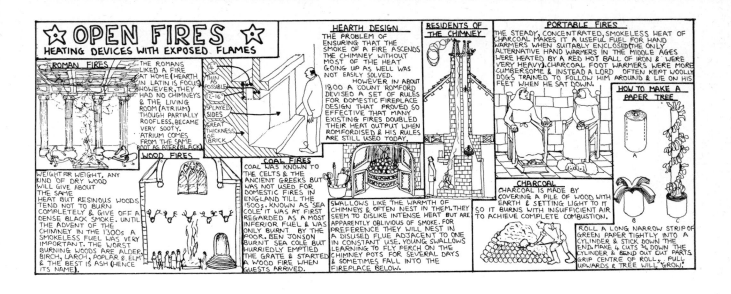

☆ OPEN FIRES ☆
HEATING DEVICES WITH EXPOSED FLAMES

ROMAN FIRES
THE ROMANS LIKED A FIRE AT HOME (HEARTH IN LATIN IS FOCUS) HOWEVER, THEY HAD NO CHIMNEYS & THE LIVING ROOM (ATRIUM) THOUGH PARTIALLY ROOFLESS, BECAME VERY SOOTY. ATRIUM COMES FROM THE SAME ROOT AS ATER (BLACK).

THIN AS POSSIBLE
12-16
SPLAYED SIDES
GREAT THICKNESS OF BRICK

WOOD FIRES
WEIGHT FOR WEIGHT, ANY KIND OF DRY WOOD WILL GIVE ABOUT THE SAME HEAT BUT RESINOUS WOODS TEND NOT TO BURN COMPLETELY & GIVE OFF A DENSE BLACK SMOKE. UNTIL THE ADVENT OF THE CHIMNEY IN THE 1300s A SMOKELESS FUEL WAS VERY IMPORTANT. THE WORST BURNING WOODS ARE ALDER, BIRCH, LARCH, POPLAR & ELM & THE BEST IS ASH (HENCE ITS NAME).

COAL FIRES
COAL WAS KNOWN TO THE CELTS & THE ANCIENT GREEKS BUT WAS NOT USED FOR DOMESTIC FIRES IN ENGLAND TILL THE 1500s. KNOWN AS 'SEA COLE' IT WAS AT FIRST REGARDED AS A MOST INFERIOR FUEL & WAS ONLY BURNT BY THE POOR. BEN JONSON BURNT SEA COLE BUT HURRIEDLY EMPTIED THE GRATE & STARTED A WOOD FIRE WHEN GUESTS ARRIVED.

HEARTH DESIGN
THE PROBLEM OF ENSURING THAT THE SMOKE OF A FIRE ASCENDS THE CHIMNEY WITHOUT MOST OF THE HEAT GOING UP AS WELL WAS NOT EASILY SOLVED. HOWEVER IN ABOUT 1800 A COUNT RUMFORD DEVISED A SET OF RULES FOR DOMESTIC FIREPLACE DESIGN THAT PROVED SO EFFECTIVE THAT MANY EXISTING FIRES DOUBLED THEIR HEAT OUTPUT WHEN ROMFORDISED & HIS RULES ARE STILL USED TODAY.

RESIDENTS OF THE CHIMNEY
SWALLOWS LIKE THE WARMTH OF CHIMNEYS & OFTEN NEST IN THEM. THEY SEEM TO DISLIKE INTENSE HEAT BUT ARE APPARENTLY OBLIVIOUS OF SMOKE. FOR PREFERENCE THEY WILL NEST IN A DISUSED FLUE ADJACENT TO ONE IN CONSTANT USE. YOUNG SWALLOWS LEARNING TO FLY PERCH ON THE CHIMNEY POTS FOR SEVERAL DAYS & SOMETIMES FALL INTO THE FIREPLACE BELOW.

PORTABLE FIRES
THE STEADY, CONCENTRATED, SMOKELESS HEAT OF CHARCOAL MAKES IT A USEFUL FUEL FOR HAND WARMERS WHEN SUITABLY ENCLOSED. THE ONLY ALTERNATIVE HAND WARMERS IN THE MIDDLE AGES WERE HEATED BY A RED HOT BALL OF IRON & WERE VERY HEAVY. CHARCOAL FOOT WARMERS WERE MORE CUMBERSOME & INSTEAD A LORD OFTEN KEPT WOOLLY DOGS TRAINED TO FOLLOW HIM AROUND & LIE ON HIS FEET WHEN HE SAT DOWN.

CHARCOAL
CHARCOAL IS MADE BY COVERING A PILE OF WOOD WITH EARTH & SETTING LIGHT TO IT SO IT BURNS WITH INSUFFICIENT AIR TO ACHIEVE COMPLETE COMBUSTION.

HOW TO MAKE A PAPER TREE
ROLL A LONG NARROW STRIP OF GREEN PAPER TIGHTLY INTO A CYLINDER & STICK DOWN THE END. MAKE 4 CUTS ¾ DOWN THE CYLINDER & BEND OUT CUT PARTS. GRIP CENTRE OF ROLL, PULL UPWARDS & TREE WILL 'GROW'.

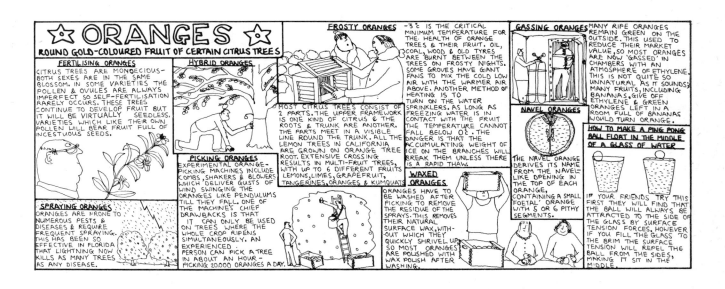

☆ ORANGES ☆
ROUND GOLD-COLOURED FRUIT OF CERTAIN CITRUS TREES

FERTILISING ORANGES
CITRUS TREES ARE MONOECIOUS – BOTH SEXES IN THE SAME BLOSSOM. IN SOME VARIETIES THE POLLEN & OVULES ARE ALWAYS IMPERFECT SO SELF-FERTILISATION RARELY OCCURS. THESE TREES CONTINUE TO DEVELOP FRUIT BUT IT WILL BE VIRTUALLY SEEDLESS. VARIETIES WHICH LIKE THEIR OWN POLLEN WILL BEAR FRUIT FULL OF INCESTUOUS SEEDS.

SPRAYING ORANGES
ORANGES ARE PRONE TO NUMEROUS PESTS & DISEASES & REQUIRE FREQUENT SPRAYING. THIS HAS BEEN SO EFFECTIVE IN FLORIDA THAT LIGHTNING NOW KILLS AS MANY TREES AS ANY DISEASE.

HYBRID ORANGES

PICKING ORANGES
EXPERIMENTAL ORANGE-PICKING MACHINES INCLUDE COMBS, SHAKERS & BLOWERS WHICH DELIVER GUSTS OF WIND SWINGING THE ORANGES LIKE PENDULUMS TILL THEY FALL. ONE OF THE MACHINE'S CHIEF DRAWBACKS IS THAT IT CAN ONLY BE USED ON TREES WHERE THE WHOLE CROP RIPENS SIMULTANEOUSLY. AN EXPERIENCED PERSON CAN PICK A TREE IN ABOUT AN HOUR – PICKING 20,000 ORANGES A DAY.

FROSTY ORANGES
-3°C IS THE CRITICAL MINIMUM TEMPERATURE FOR THE HEALTH OF ORANGE TREES & THEIR FRUIT. OIL, COAL, WOOD & OLD TYRES ARE BURNT BETWEEN THE TREES ON FROSTY NIGHTS. SOME GROVES HAVE GIANT FANS TO MIX THE COLD LOW AIR WITH THE WARMER AIR ABOVE. ANOTHER METHOD OF HEATING IS TO TURN ON THE WATER SPRINKLERS. AS LONG AS FREEZING WATER IS IN CONTACT WITH THE FRUIT THE TEMPERATURE CANNOT FALL BELOW 0°C. THE DANGER IS THAT THE ACCUMULATING WEIGHT OF ICE ON THE BRANCHES WILL BREAK THEM UNLESS THERE IS A RAPID THAW.

MOST CITRUS TREES CONSIST OF 2 PARTS. THE UPPER FRAMEWORK IS ONE KIND OF CITRUS & THE ROOTS & TRUNK ARE ANOTHER. THE PARTS MEET IN A VISIBLE LINE ROUND THE TRUNK. ALL THE LEMON TREES IN CALIFORNIA ARE GROWN ON ORANGE TREE ROOT. EXTENSIVE CROSSING RESULTS IN MULTI-FRUIT TREES, WITH UP TO 6 DIFFERENT FRUITS LEMONS, LIMES, GRAPEFRUIT, TANGERINES, ORANGES & KUMQUATS.

WAXED ORANGES
ORANGES HAVE TO BE WASHED AFTER PICKING TO REMOVE THE RESIDUE OF THE SPRAYS. THIS REMOVES THEIR NATURAL SURFACE WAX, WITHOUT WHICH THEY QUICKLY SHRIVEL UP, SO MOST ORANGES ARE POLISHED WITH WAX POLISH AFTER WASHING.

GASSING ORANGES
MANY RIPE ORANGES REMAIN GREEN ON THE OUTSIDE. THIS USED TO REDUCE THEIR MARKET VALUE, SO MOST ORANGES ARE NOW 'GASSED' IN CHAMBERS WITH AN ATMOSPHERE OF ETHYLENE. THIS IS NOT QUITE AS UNNATURAL AS IT SOUNDS; MANY FRUITS, INCLUDING BANANAS, GIVE OFF ETHYLENE & GREEN ORANGES LEFT IN A ROOM FULL OF BANANAS WOULD TURN ORANGE.

NAVEL ORANGES
THE NAVEL ORANGE DERIVES ITS NAME FROM THE NAVEL-LIKE OPENING IN THE TOP OF EACH ORANGE, CONTAINING A SMALL 'FOETAL' ORANGE WITH 5 OR 6 PITHY SEGMENTS.

HOW TO MAKE A PING PONG BALL FLOAT IN THE MIDDLE OF A GLASS OF WATER
IF YOUR FRIENDS TRY THIS FIRST THEY WILL FIND THAT THE BALL WILL ALWAYS BE ATTRACTED TO THE SIDE OF THE GLASS BY SURFACE TENSION FORCES. HOWEVER IF YOU FILL THE GLASS TO THE BRIM THE SURFACE TENSION WILL REPEL THE BALL FROM THE SIDES, MAKING IT SIT IN THE MIDDLE.

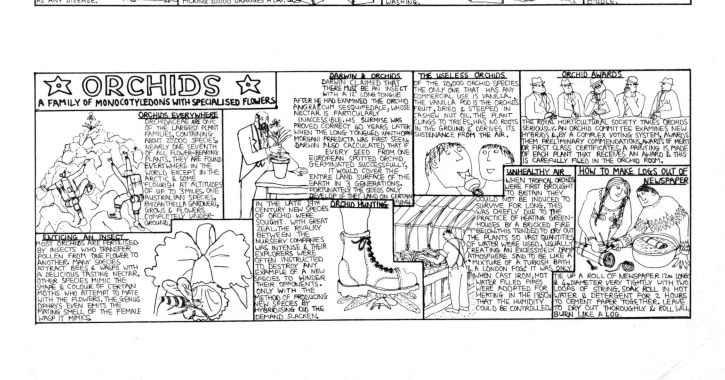

☆ ORCHIDS ☆
A FAMILY OF MONOCOTYLEDONS WITH SPECIALISED FLOWERS

ORCHIDS EVERYWHERE
ORCHIDACEAE ARE ONE OF THE LARGEST PLANT FAMILIES, CONTAINING ABOUT 20,000 SPECIES NEARLY ONE SEVENTH OF ALL FLOWER-BEARING PLANTS. THEY ARE FOUND EVERYWHERE IN THE WORLD EXCEPT IN THE ARCTIC & SOME FLOURISH AT ALTITUDES OF UP TO 3 MILES. ONE AUSTRALIAN SPECIES, RHIZANTHELLA GARDNERI, GROWS & FLOWERS COMPLETELY UNDERGROUND.

ENTICING AN INSECT
MOST ORCHIDS ARE FERTILISED BY INSECTS WHO TRANSFER POLLEN FROM ONE FLOWER TO ANOTHER. MANY SPECIES ATTRACT BEES & WASPS WITH A DELICIOUS TASTING NECTAR. OTHER SPECIES MIMIC THE SHAPE & COLOUR OF CERTAIN MOTHS WHO ATTEMPT TO MATE WITH THE FLOWERS. THE GENUS OPHRYS EVEN EMITS THE MATING SMELL OF THE FEMALE WASP IT MIMICS.

DARWIN & ORCHIDS
DARWIN CLAIMED THAT THERE MUST BE AN INSECT WITH A 12" LONG TONGUE AFTER HE HAD EXAMINED THE ORCHID ANGRAECUM SESQUIPEDALE, WHOSE NECTAR IS PARTICULARLY INACCESSIBLE. HIS SURMISE WAS PROVED CORRECT 40 YEARS LATER WHEN THE LONG TONGUED XANTHOPAN MORGANI PRAEDICTA WAS FIRST SEEN. DARWIN ALSO CALCULATED THAT IF EVERY SEED FROM ONE EUROPEAN SPOTTED ORCHID GERMINATED SUCCESSFULLY, IT WOULD COVER THE ENTIRE LAND SURFACE OF THE EARTH IN 3 GENERATIONS. FORTUNATELY THE SEEDS ONLY DEVELOP IF THEY LAND ON CERTAIN FUNGI.

ORCHID HUNTING
IN THE LATE 19TH CENTURY NEW SPECIES OF ORCHID WERE SOUGHT WITH GREAT ZEAL. THE RIVALRY BETWEEN THE NURSERY COMPANIES WAS INTENSE & THEIR EXPLORERS WERE OFTEN INSTRUCTED TO DESTROY ANY EXAMPLE OF A NEW SPECIES TO HINDER THEIR OPPONENTS. ONLY WITH THE METHOD OF PRODUCING NEW SPECIES BY HYBRIDISING DID THE DEMAND SLACKEN.

THE USEFUL ORCHIDS
OF THE 20,000 ORCHID SPECIES THE ONLY ONE THAT HAS ANY COMMERCIAL USE IS VANILLA. THE VANILLA POD IS THE ORCHID'S FRUIT, DRIED & STEEPED IN CASHEW NUT OIL. THE PLANT CLINGS TO TREES, HAS NO ROOTS IN THE GROUND & DERIVES ITS SUSTENANCE FROM THE AIR.

UNHEALTHY AIR
WHEN TROPICAL ORCHIDS WERE FIRST BROUGHT TO BRITAIN THEY COULD NOT BE INDUCED TO SURVIVE FOR LONG. THIS WAS CHIEFLY DUE TO THE PRACTICE OF HEATING GREENHOUSES BY A BRICKED FIRE. THIS TENDED TO DRY OUT THE PLANTS SO VAST QUANTITIES OF WATER WERE USED, USUALLY CREATING AN EXCESSIVELY DAMP ATMOSPHERE SAID TO BE LIKE A MIXTURE OF A TURKISH BATH & A LONDON FOG. IT WAS ONLY WHEN CAST IRON, HOT WATER FILLED PIPES WERE ADOPTED FOR HEATING IN THE 1850s THAT THE HUMIDITY COULD BE CONTROLLED.

ORCHID AWARDS
THE ROYAL HORTICULTURAL SOCIETY TAKES ORCHIDS SERIOUSLY. AN ORCHID COMMITTEE EXAMINES NEW HYBRIDS &, BY A COMPLEX VOTING SYSTEM, AWARDS THEM PRELIMINARY COMMENDATIONS, AWARDS OF MERIT OR FIRST CLASS CERTIFICATES. A PAINTING IS MADE OF EACH PLANT THAT RECEIVES AN AWARD & THIS IS CAREFULLY FILED IN THE ORCHID ROOM.

HOW TO MAKE LOGS OUT OF NEWSPAPER
TIE UP A ROLL OF NEWSPAPER 12" LONG & 4" DIAMETER VERY TIGHTLY WITH TWO LOOPS OF STRING. SOAK ROLL IN HOT WATER & DETERGENT FOR 2 HOURS TO CEMENT PAPER TOGETHER. LEAVE TO DRY OUT THOROUGHLY & ROLL WILL BURN LIKE A LOG.

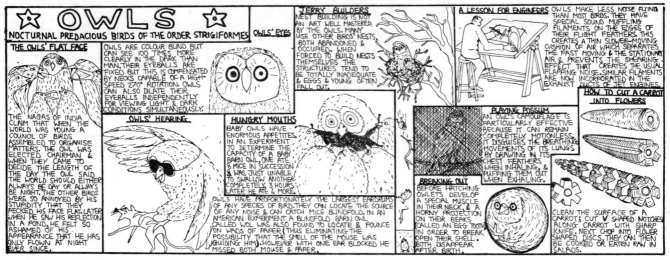

☆ OWLS ☆
NOCTURNAL PREDACIOUS BIRDS OF THE ORDER STRIGIFORMES

THE OWLS' FLAT FACE

THE NAGAS OF INDIA CLAIM THAT WHEN THE WORLD WAS YOUNG A COUNCIL OF BIRDS ASSEMBLED TO ORGANISE MATTERS. THE OWL WAS ELECTED CHAIRMAN & WHEN THEY CAME TO DECIDE THE LENGTH OF THE DAY THE OWL SAID THE WORLD SHOULD EITHER ALWAYS BE DAY OR ALWAYS BE NIGHT. THE OTHER BIRDS WERE SO ANNOYED BY HIS STUPIDITY THAT THEY PECKED HIS FACE FLAT. LATER WHEN HE SAW HIS REFLECTION IN A POND, HE FELT SO ASHAMED OF HIS APPEARANCE THAT THE HAS ONLY FLOWN AT NIGHT EVER SINCE.

OWLS' EYES

OWLS ARE COLOUR BLIND BUT CAN SEE 100 TIMES MORE CLEARLY IN THE DARK THAN MAN. THEIR EYEBALLS ARE FIXED BUT THIS IS COMPENSATED BY NECKS CAPABLE OF A HIGH SPEED 270° ROTATION. OWLS CAN ALSO DILATE THEIR EYEBALLS INDEPENDENTLY FOR VIEWING LIGHT & DARK CONDITIONS SIMULTANEOUSLY.

OWLS' HEARING

OWLS HAVE PROPORTIONALLY THE LARGEST EARDRUMS OF ANY SPECIES OF BIRD. THEY CAN LOCATE THE SOURCE OF ANY NOISE & CAN CATCH MICE BLINDFOLD. IN AN AMERICAN EXPERIMENT A BLINDFOLD BARN OWL CALLED WOL WAS ALSO FOUND TO LOCATE & POUNCE ON WADS OF PAPER (THUS ELIMINATING THE POSSIBILITY THAT THE SMELL OF THE MOUSE WAS GUIDING HIM). HOWEVER WITH ONE EAR BLOCKED HE MISSED BOTH MOUSE & PAPER.

HUNGRY MOUTHS

BABY OWLS HAVE ENORMOUS APPETITES. IN AN EXPERIMENT TO DETERMINE THE CAPACITY OF A BABY BARN OWL, ONE ATE 8 MICE IN SUCCESSION & WAS JUST UNABLE TO SWALLOW ANOTHER. COMPLETELY 3 HOURS LATER HE ATE 4 MORE.

JERRY BUILDERS

NEST BUILDING IS NOT AN ART WELL MASTERED BY THE OWLS. MANY USE OTHER BIRDS' NESTS, BOTH ABANDONED & OCCUPIED. WHEN FORCED TO BUILD NESTS THEMSELVES THE STRUCTURES TEND TO BE TOTALLY INADEQUATE & EGGS & YOUNG OFTEN FALL OUT.

PLAYING POSSUM

AN OWLS CAMOUFLAGE IS PARTICULARLY EFFECTIVE BECAUSE IT CAN REMAIN COMPLETELY MOTIONLESS. IT DISGUISES THE BREATHING MOVEMENTS OF ITS LUNGS BY DRAWING IN ITS CHEST FEATHERS WHEN INHALING, & PUFFING THEM OUT WHEN EXHALING.

BREAKING OUT

BEFORE HATCHING OWLETS DEVELOP A SPECIAL MUSCLE IN THEIR NECK, & A HORNY PROJECTION ON THEIR BEAKS CALLED AN EGG TOOTH IN ORDER TO BREAK OPEN THEIR SHELL. BOTH DISAPPEAR AFTER BIRTH.

A LESSON FOR ENGINEERS

OWLS MAKE LESS NOISE FLYING THAN MOST BIRDS. THEY HAVE SPECIAL SOUND MUFFLING FILAMENTS ON THE EDGES OF THEIR FLIGHT FEATHERS. THIS CREATES A THIN SLOWER-MOVING CUSHION OF AIR WHICH SEPARATES THE FAST MOVING & THE STATIONARY AIR & PREVENTS THE SHEARING EFFECT THAT CREATES THE USUAL FLAPPING NOISE. SIMILAR FILAMENTS ARE NOW INCORPORATED IN THE EXHAUST DUCTS OF JET ENGINES.

HOW TO CUT A CARROT INTO FLOWERS

CLEAN THE SURFACE OF A CARROT; CUT V SHAPED NOTCHES ALONG CARROT WITH SHARP KNIFE. NEXT CHOP INTO FLOWER SHAPED DISCS. THEY CAN THEN BE COOKED OR EATEN RAW IN SALADS.

OZONE
ALLOTROPIC FORM OF OXYGEN
☆ ☆

OZONE & ELECTRICITY

OZONE HAS A CHARACTERISTIC 'ELECTRICAL' SMELL; IT IS CREATED BY THE REACTION BETWEEN HIGH VOLTAGE ELECTRICITY & THE AIR. THE INDUSTRIAL MANUFACTURE OF OZONE IS BASED ON THIS REACTION. ITS MAIN INDUSTRIAL USE IS FOR PURIFYING WATER (IT IS A STRONG OXIDISING AGENT & KILLS ANY BACTERIA).

OZONE & AIR

THE UPPER ATMOSPHERE CONTAINS A GREAT DEAL OF OZONE, ESSENTIAL TO LIFE AS IT SHIELDS THE WORLD FROM MOST OF THE SUN'S RADIATION. THE EXTINCTION OF THE DINOSAURS HAS BEEN CREDITED TO A TEMPORARY DEPLETION OF THE OZONE LAYER.

OZONE & AEROSOLS

THE SCARE THAT THE CHEMICALS IN AEROSOL SPRAY CANS MIGHT BE DESTROYING THE WORLD'S OZONE LAYER IS NOW GENERALLY THOUGHT TO HAVE BEEN UNJUSTIFIED. THE NATURAL VARIATION CAUSED BY SUNSPOTS & SOLAR ACTIVITY IS ABOUT 20% & THIS DOES NOT APPEAR TO HAVE DISASTROUS CONSEQUENCES. CURRENT SCIENTIFIC OPINION IS THAT AEROSOLS MIGHT REDUCE THE OZONE LAYER BY A MAXIMUM OF 15%. METEOROLOGISTS BELIEVE THAT EVEN A 50% REDUCTION WOULD NOT AFFECT THE CLIMATE SIGNIFICANTLY, & DOCTORS CLAIM THAT SKIN CANCER COULD INCREASE BY, AT MOST, 0.3%.

OZONE & FRESH AIR

DESPITE THE LINK BETWEEN OZONE & 'FRESH' SEA AIR, THE GAS IS IN FACT MORE POISONOUS THAN CHLORINE, HYDROGEN CYANIDE & CARBON MONOXIDE, & CAUSES LUNG DAMAGE SIMILAR TO THE WORLD WAR I MUSTARD GASES. FRESH AIR 'IONISERS' USED TO BE MADE WHICH GENERATED OZONE & ADDED IT TO THE AIR TO REDUCE SMELLS. FORTUNATELY, MODERN IONISERS DO NOT DO THIS.

OZONE & POLLUTION

OZONE IN THE LOWER ATMOSPHERE IS CREATED FROM CAR EXHAUST GASES IN PARTS OF AMERICA. IT CAUSES IRRITATION TO THE LUNGS (ESPECIALLY TO ASTHMATICS), DAMAGE TO PLANT LEAVES & THE DECOMPOSITION OF CERTAIN PLASTICS. FORTUNATELY, THE CLIMATE IN BRITAIN IS TOO COLD & WINDY TO ENCOURAGE THE PHOTOCHEMICAL REACTIONS NECESSARY TO CREATE OZONE.

HOW TO PRINT YOUR OWN T-SHIRT

PIN PLAIN T-SHIRT TO A WOODEN BOARD & 'PRINT' DESIGN WITH WATERPROOF MARKER PENS. THESE DO NOT RUN & WILL SURVIVE SEVERAL WASHINGS.

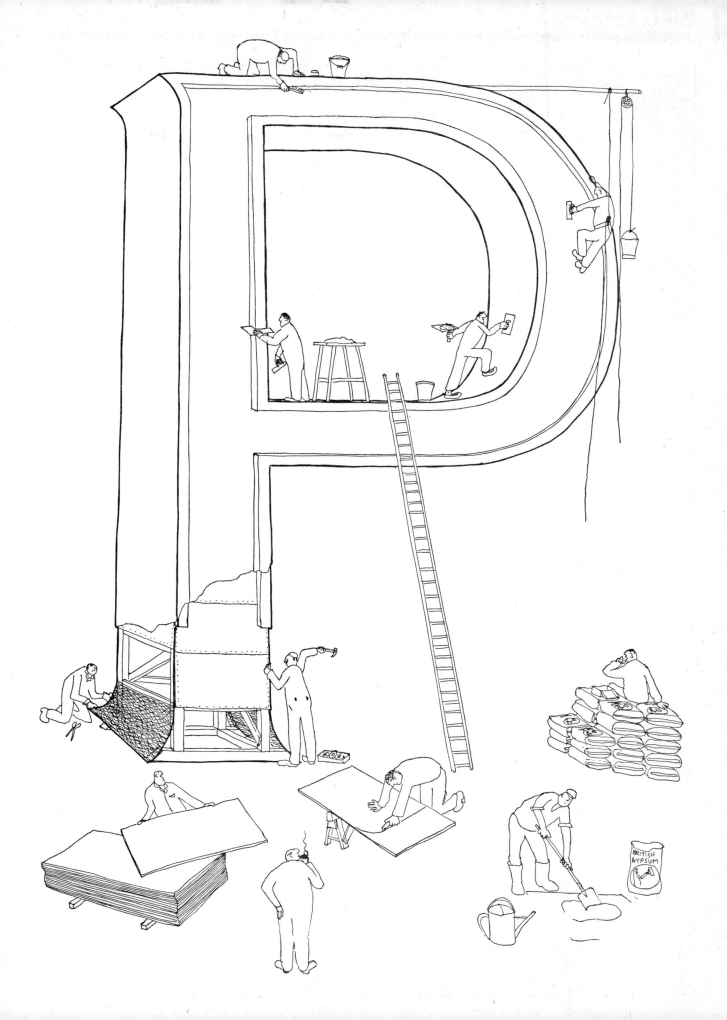

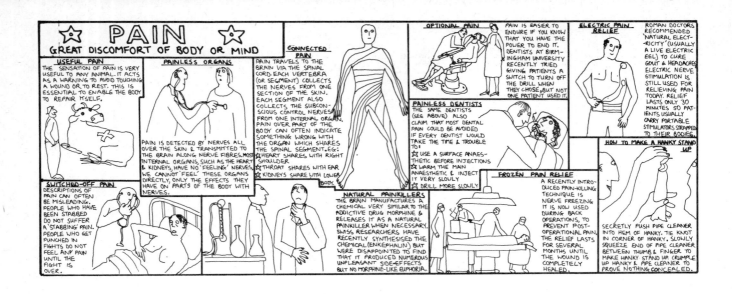

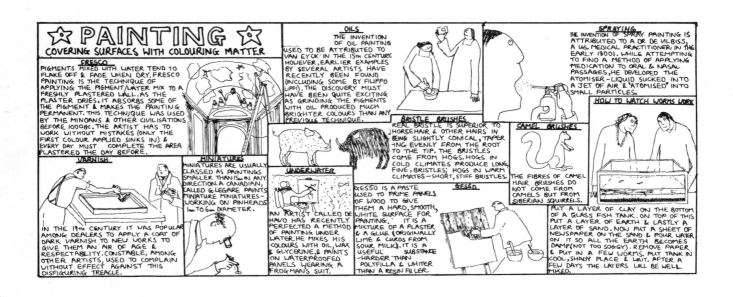

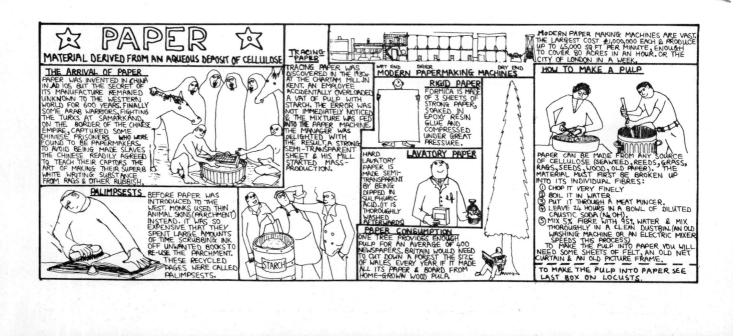

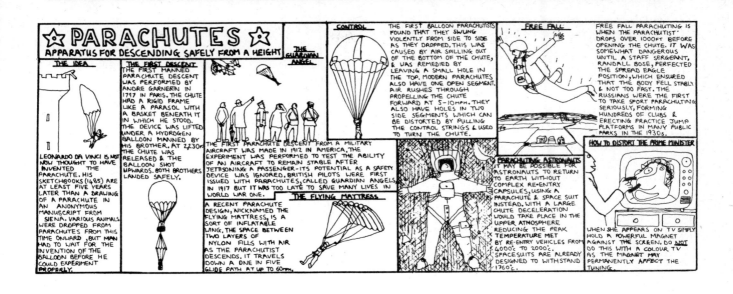

☆ PARACHUTES ☆
APPARATUS FOR DESCENDING SAFELY FROM A HEIGHT

THE IDEA
LEONARDO DA VINCI IS NOT NOW THOUGHT TO HAVE INVENTED THE PARACHUTE. HIS SKETCHBOOKS (1485) ARE AT LEAST FIVE YEARS LATER THAN A DRAWING OF A PARACHUTE IN AN ANONYMOUS MANUSCRIPT FROM SIENA. VARIOUS ANIMALS WERE DROPPED FROM PARACHUTES FROM THIS TIME ONWARD, BUT MAN HAD TO WAIT FOR THE INVENTION OF THE BALLOON BEFORE HE COULD EXPERIMENT PROPERLY.

THE FIRST DESCENT
THE FIRST MANNED PARACHUTE DESCENT WAS PERFORMED BY ANDRE GARNERIN IN 1797 IN PARIS. THE CHUTE HAD A RIGID FRAME LIKE A PARASOL WITH A BASKET BENEATH IT IN WHICH HE STOOD. THE DEVICE WAS LIFTED UNDER A HYDROGEN BALLOON MANNED BY HIS BROTHER. AT 2230m THE CHUTE WAS RELEASED & THE BALLOON SHOT UPWARDS. BOTH BROTHERS LANDED SAFELY.

THE GUARDIAN ANGEL

THE FIRST PARACHUTE DESCENT FROM A MILITARY AIRCRAFT WAS MADE IN 1912 IN AMERICA. THE EXPERIMENT WAS PERFORMED TO TEST THE ABILITY OF AN AIRCRAFT TO REMAIN STABLE AFTER JETTISONING A PASSENGER-ITS POTENTIAL AS A SAFETY DEVICE WAS IGNORED. BRITISH PILOTS WERE FIRST ISSUED WITH PARACHUTES, CALLED GUARDIAN ANGELS, IN 1917 BUT IT WAS TOO LATE TO SAVE MANY LIVES IN WORLD WAR ONE.

THE FLYING MATTRESS
A RECENT PARACHUTE DESIGN, NICKNAMED THE FLYING MATTRESS, IS A SORT OF INFLATABLE WING. THE SPACE BETWEEN TWO LAYERS OF NYLON FILLS WITH AIR AS THE PARACHUTIST DESCENDS. IT TRAVELS DOWN A ONE IN FIVE GLIDE PATH AT UP TO 60mph.

CONTROL
THE FIRST BALLOON PARACHUTISTS FOUND THAT THEY SWUNG VIOLENTLY FROM SIDE TO SIDE AS THEY DROPPED. THIS WAS CAUSED BY AIR SPILLING OUT OF THE BOTTOM OF THE CHUTE, & WAS REMEDIED BY LEAVING A SMALL HOLE IN THE TOP. MODERN PARACHUTES ALSO HAVE ONE OPEN SEGMENT. AIR RUSHES THROUGH PROPELLING THE CHUTE FORWARD AT 5-10mph. THEY ALSO HAVE HOLES IN TWO SIDE SEGMENTS WHICH CAN BE DISTORTED BY PULLING THE CONTROL STRINGS & USED TO TURN THE CHUTE.

PARACHUTING ASTRONAUTS
IT MAY BE POSSIBLE FOR ASTRONAUTS TO RETURN TO EARTH WITHOUT COMPLEX RE-ENTRY CAPSULES, USING A PARACHUTE & SPACE SUIT INSTEAD. WITH A LARGE CHUTE DECELERATION WOULD TAKE PLACE IN THE UPPER ATMOSPHERE REDUCING THE PEAK TEMPERATURE MET BY RE-ENTRY VEHICLES FROM 4000°C TO 2000°C. SPACESUITS ARE ALREADY DESIGNED TO WITHSTAND 1760°C.

FREE FALL
FREE FALL PARACHUTING IS WHEN THE PARACHUTIST DROPS OVER 1000FT BEFORE OPENING THE CHUTE. IT WAS SOMEWHAT DANGEROUS UNTIL A STAFF SERGEANT, RANDALL BOSE, PERFECTED THE SPREAD EAGLE POSITION, WHICH ENSURED THAT THE BODY FELL STABLY & NOT TOO FAST. THE RUSSIANS WERE THE FIRST TO TAKE SPORT PARACHUTING SERIOUSLY, FORMING HUNDREDS OF CLUBS & ERECTING PRACTICE JUMP PLATFORMS IN MANY PUBLIC PARKS IN THE 1930s.

HOW TO DISTORT THE PRIME MINISTER
WHEN SHE APPEARS ON TV SIMPLY HOLD A POWERFUL MAGNET AGAINST THE SCREEN. DO NOT DO THIS WITH A COLOUR TV AS THE MAGNET MAY PERMANENTLY AFFECT THE TUNING.

☆ PARASITES ☆
ANIMALS & PLANTS THAT LIVE & FEED ON ANOTHER

SIMPLICITY
THE STRUCTURE & DIGESTIVE SYSTEM OF PARASITES TEND TO BE VERY SIMPLE. THERE IS NO NEED FOR COMPLEXITY AS THE HOST PROVIDES SHELTER, WARMTH & ABUNDANT FOOD & WATER.

LIFE CYCLE OF FISH TAPE-WORM:

PLANKTON FISH MAN

PROFUSION
PRACTICALLY ALL ANIMALS HAVE BEEN FOUND TO HARBOUR AT LEAST ONE SPECIALLY ADAPTED PARASITE. THIS IMPLIES THAT THERE ARE MORE PARASITE SPECIES THAN ANIMALS.

DOMINANCE
RECENT EXPERIMENTS AT OHIO UNIVERSITY SUGGEST THAT DOMINANCE OF CERTAIN INDIVIDUALS AMONG SOCIAL ANIMALS MAY BE INFLUENCED BY PARASITES. DOMINANT LABORATORY MICE WERE FOUND TO HARBOUR FEWER PARASITES THAN THE REST.

MISTLETOE
MISTLETOE IS A PARASITE ON TREES AND IS PARTICULARLY DESTRUCTIVE IN THE SIVAJI REGION OF INDIA. SCIENTISTS HAVE NOW FOUND A SECOND MISTLETOE SPECIES WHICH IS PARASITIC ON THE HARMFUL VARIETY. THIS HAS NOW BEEN INTRODUCED IN INDIA & IS REDUCING THE DAMAGE.

ROTATING HEADED PARASITE
THE TERMITE PARASITE DEVESCOVINID CAN TWIST ITS HEAD ON ITS BODY FOR ANY NUMBER OF COMPLETE REVOLUTIONS. IT USES ITS HEAD ROTATION (UP TO 40 REVS A MINUTE) AS A FORM OF PROPULSION.

HOW TO MAKE CLEAR ICE CUBES
CLOUDINESS IN ICE CUBES IS CAUSED BY AIR DISSOLVED IN THE WATER. HEATING REMOVES THIS AIR SO CUBES MADE FROM VERY HOT WATER WILL BE CLEAR. PUT ICE TRAY IN POLYTHENE BAG TO AVOID CONDENSATION.

☆ PARLIAMENT ☆
A LEGISLATIVE BODY

ORIGINS
IN THE 13TH CENTURY, THE KINGS OF ENGLAND BEGAN TO SUMMON REPRESENTATIVES OF ALL THE BOROUGHS TO HELP RAISE TAXES. AT FIRST, THE REPRESENTATIVES HAD NO POWER & WERE RESENTED BY THEIR ELECTORS WHO HAD TO PAY THE SALARIES IN ADDITION TO THEIR OWN TAXES. HOWEVER, THE REPRESENTATIVES SLOWLY MANAGED TO WIN MORE & MORE CONCESSIONS IN EXCHANGE FOR RAISING THE TAXES. THEIR RISE TO POWER WAS COMPLETED IN THE 18TH CENTURY WHEN MINISTERS CAME TO BE ELECTED FROM THE REPRESENTATIVES (THE COMMONS) INSTEAD OF FROM THE LORDS.

AGES
THE YOUNGEST MP EVER WAS SIXTEEN (EDMUND WALLER, AMERSHAM, 1622). THE OLDEST WAS 98 (SAMUEL YOUNG, EAST CAVAN, 1918).

QUORUMS
A MINIMUM NUMBER OF 40 MPS IS REQUIRED FOR BUSINESS CARRIED ON IN THE HOUSE OF COMMONS TO BE VALID. THE HOUSE OF LORDS CAN FUNCTION LEGALLY WITH ONLY 3 MEMBERS PRESENT.

UNTIL THE REFORM ACT OF 1831, MEMBERS OF THE HOUSE OF COMMONS WERE ELECTED IN A VERY HAPHAZARD & CORRUPT WAY. SOME MPs REPRESENTED 'ROTTEN BOROUGHS' SUCH AS OLD SARUM (7 RESIDENTS) & DUNWICH (4 RESIDENTS & 2 MPs). TOWNS WHICH HAD COME INTO EXISTENCE SINCE 1600, SUCH AS BIRMINGHAM & MANCHESTER, HAD NO MPs. IN 1793 IT WAS ESTIMATED THAT (WITH A BRITISH POPULATION OF 8 MILLION) 257 MPS (THE MAJORITY) WERE BEING RETURNED BY ONLY 11,000 ELECTORS.

VOTING

ELIGIBILITY
THE AGE AT WHICH PEOPLE BECOME ELIGIBLE TO VOTE VARIES QUITE WIDELY FROM ONE COUNTRY TO ANOTHER. THE YOUNGEST IS NOW 15 IN THE PHILIPPINES & THE OLDEST IS 25 IN ANDORRA. BETWEEN 1918 & 1928, WOMEN IN BRITAIN WERE NOT ALLOWED TO VOTE UNTIL THEY REACHED 30.

REPRESENTATION
REPRESENTATION IS STILL NOT UNIFORM. THE LARGEST ELECTORATE FOR A SINGLE SEAT IS NOW ANTRIM SOUTH (126,444) & THE SMALLEST IS GLASGOW CENTRAL (19,826).

APATHY — VOTE FOR ANYBODY
THE RESIDENTS OF LONDON APPEAR TO BE THE MOST POLITICALLY APATHETIC IN BRITAIN. CHELSEA RECORDED THE LOWEST POLL IN THE LAST GENERAL ELECTION (57.3%). LONDON NORTH-EAST RECORDED THE LOWEST POLL IN THE EUROPEAN ELECTIONS (20.4%).

HOW TO MAKE A RUBBER STAMP
URGENT
ASK A GARAGE FOR AN OLD INNER TUBE FROM A CAR TYRE. CUT SHAPES FOR STAMP OUT OF RUBBER TUBE & STICK SHAPES TO BLOCK OF WOOD. USE STAMP WITH AN INK PAD FROM A STATIONER'S.

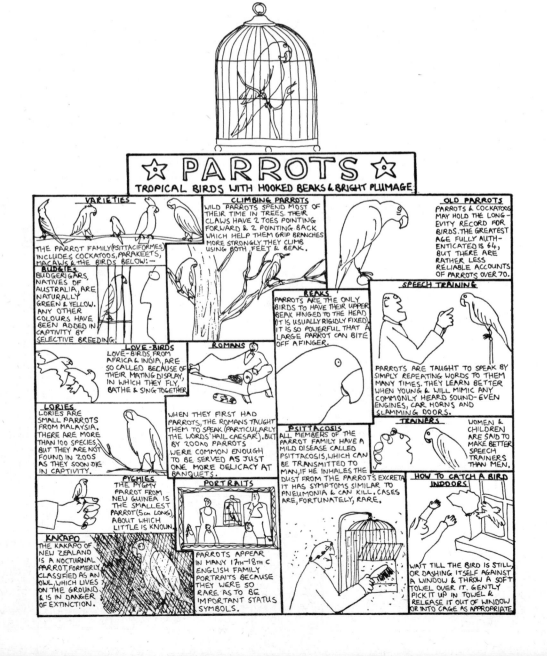

☆ PARROTS ☆
TROPICAL BIRDS WITH HOOKED BEAKS & BRIGHT PLUMAGE

VARIETIES
THE PARROT FAMILY (PSITTACIFORMES) INCLUDES COCKATOOS, PARAKEETS, MACAWS & THE BIRDS BELOW:—

BUDGIES
BUDGERIGARS, NATIVES OF AUSTRALIA, ARE NATURALLY GREEN & YELLOW. ANY OTHER COLOURS HAVE BEEN ADDED IN CAPTIVITY BY SELECTIVE BREEDING.

LOVE-BIRDS
LOVE-BIRDS, FROM AFRICA & INDIA, ARE SO CALLED BECAUSE OF THEIR MATING DISPLAY, IN WHICH THEY FLY, BATHE & SING TOGETHER.

LORIES
LORIES ARE SMALL PARROTS FROM MALAYSIA. THERE ARE MORE THAN 100 SPECIES, BUT THEY ARE NOT FOUND IN ZOOS AS THEY SOON DIE IN CAPTIVITY.

PYGMIES
THE PYGMY PARROT FROM NEW GUINEA IS THE SMALLEST PARROT (5cm LONG), ABOUT WHICH LITTLE IS KNOWN.

KAKAPO
THE KAKAPO OF NEW ZEALAND IS A NOCTURNAL PARROT, FORMERLY CLASSIFIED AS AN OWL, WHICH LIVES ON THE GROUND & IS IN DANGER OF EXTINCTION.

CLIMBING PARROTS
WILD PARROTS SPEND MOST OF THEIR TIME IN TREES. THEIR CLAWS HAVE 2 TOES POINTING FORWARD & 2 POINTING BACK WHICH HELP THEM GRIP BRANCHES MORE STRONGLY. THEY CLIMB USING BOTH FEET & BEAK.

ROMANS
WHEN THEY FIRST HAD PARROTS, THE ROMANS TAUGHT THEM TO SPEAK (PARTICULARLY THE WORDS 'HAIL CAESAR'). BUT BY 200 AD PARROTS WERE COMMON ENOUGH TO BE SERVED AS JUST ONE MORE DELICACY AT BANQUETS.

PORTRAITS
PARROTS APPEAR IN MANY 17TH–18TH C ENGLISH FAMILY PORTRAITS BECAUSE THEY WERE SO RARE AS TO BE IMPORTANT STATUS SYMBOLS.

BEAKS
PARROTS ARE THE ONLY BIRDS TO HAVE THEIR UPPER BEAK HINGED TO THE HEAD (IT IS USUALLY RIGIDLY FIXED) IT IS SO POWERFUL THAT A LARGE PARROT CAN BITE OFF A FINGER.

PSITTACOSIS
ALL MEMBERS OF THE PARROT FAMILY HAVE A MILD DISEASE CALLED PSITTACOSIS, WHICH CAN BE TRANSMITTED TO MAN, IF HE INHALES THE DUST FROM THE PARROT'S EXCRETA IT HAS SYMPTOMS SIMILAR TO PNEUMONIA & CAN KILL. CASES ARE, FORTUNATELY, RARE.

OLD PARROTS
PARROTS & COCKATOOS MAY HOLD THE LONGEVITY RECORD FOR BIRDS. THE GREATEST AGE FULLY AUTHENTICATED IS 64, BUT THERE ARE RATHER LESS RELIABLE ACCOUNTS OF PARROTS OVER 70.

SPEECH TRAINING
PARROTS ARE TAUGHT TO SPEAK BY SIMPLY REPEATING WORDS TO THEM MANY TIMES. THEY LEARN BETTER WHEN YOUNG & WILL MIMIC ANY COMMONLY HEARD SOUND — EVEN ENGINES, CAR HORNS AND SLAMMING DOORS.

TRAINERS
WOMEN & CHILDREN ARE SAID TO MAKE BETTER SPEECH TRAINERS THAN MEN.

HOW TO CATCH A BIRD INDOORS
WAIT TILL THE BIRD IS STILL OR DASHING ITSELF AGAINST A WINDOW & THROW A SOFT TOWEL OVER IT. GENTLY PICK IT UP IN TOWEL & RELEASE IT OUT OF WINDOW OR INTO CAGE AS APPROPRIATE

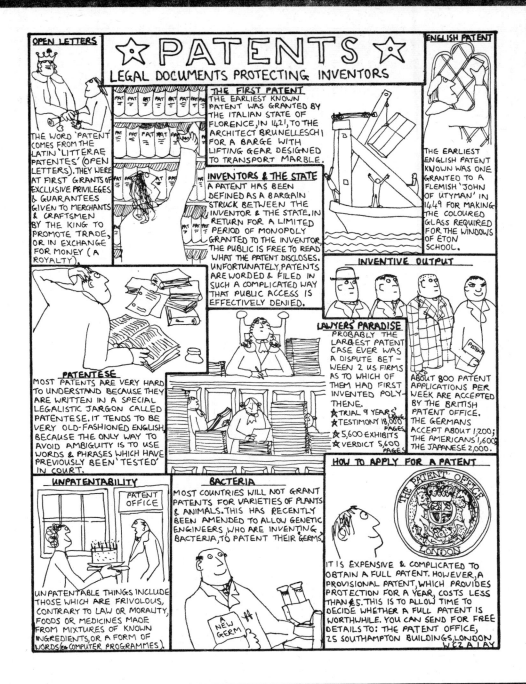

☆ PATENTS ☆
LEGAL DOCUMENTS PROTECTING INVENTORS

OPEN LETTERS

THE WORD 'PATENT' COMES FROM THE LATIN 'LITTERAE PATENTES' (OPEN LETTERS). THEY WERE AT FIRST GRANTS OF EXCLUSIVE PRIVILEGES & GUARANTEES GIVEN TO MERCHANTS & CRAFTSMEN BY THE KING TO PROMOTE TRADE, OR IN EXCHANGE FOR MONEY (A ROYALTY).

THE FIRST PATENT

THE EARLIEST KNOWN PATENT WAS GRANTED BY THE ITALIAN STATE OF FLORENCE, IN 1421, TO THE ARCHITECT BRUNELLESCHI FOR A BARGE WITH LIFTING GEAR DESIGNED TO TRANSPORT MARBLE.

INVENTORS & THE STATE

A PATENT HAS BEEN DEFINED AS A BARGAIN STRUCK BETWEEN THE INVENTOR & THE STATE, IN RETURN FOR A LIMITED PERIOD OF MONOPOLY GRANTED TO THE INVENTOR, THE PUBLIC IS FREE TO READ WHAT THE PATENT DISCLOSES. UNFORTUNATELY PATENTS ARE WORDED & FILED IN SUCH A COMPLICATED WAY THAT PUBLIC ACCESS IS EFFECTIVELY DENIED.

ENGLISH PATENT

THE EARLIEST ENGLISH PATENT KNOWN WAS ONE GRANTED TO A FLEMISH 'JOHN OF UTYMAN' IN 1449 FOR MAKING THE COLOURED GLASS REQUIRED FOR THE WINDOWS OF ETON SCHOOL.

INVENTIVE OUTPUT

ABOUT 800 PATENT APPLICATIONS PER WEEK ARE ACCEPTED BY THE BRITISH PATENT OFFICE. THE GERMANS ACCEPT ABOUT 1,200; THE AMERICANS 1,600; THE JAPANESE 2,000.

PATENTESE

MOST PATENTS ARE VERY HARD TO UNDERSTAND BECAUSE THEY ARE WRITTEN IN A SPECIAL LEGALISTIC JARGON CALLED PATENTESE. IT TENDS TO BE VERY OLD-FASHIONED ENGLISH, BECAUSE THE ONLY WAY TO AVOID AMBIGUITY IS TO USE WORDS & PHRASES WHICH HAVE PREVIOUSLY BEEN 'TESTED' IN COURT.

LAWYERS PARADISE

PROBABLY THE LARGEST PATENT CASE EVER WAS A DISPUTE BETWEEN 2 US FIRMS AS TO WHICH OF THEM HAD FIRST INVENTED POLYTHENE.
☆ TRIAL 9 YEARS
☆ TESTIMONY 18,000 PAGES
☆ 5,600 EXHIBITS
☆ VERDICT 5,600 PAGES

UNPATENTABILITY

UNPATENTABLE THINGS INCLUDE THOSE WHICH ARE FRIVOLOUS, CONTRARY TO LAW OR MORALITY, FOODS OR MEDICINES MADE FROM MIXTURES OF KNOWN INGREDIENTS, OR A FORM OF WORDS (eg COMPUTER PROGRAMMES).

BACTERIA

MOST COUNTRIES WILL NOT GRANT PATENTS FOR VARIETIES OF PLANTS & ANIMALS. THIS HAS RECENTLY BEEN AMENDED TO ALLOW GENETIC ENGINEERS WHO ARE INVENTING BACTERIA, TO PATENT THEIR GERMS.

A NEW GERM

HOW TO APPLY FOR A PATENT

IT IS EXPENSIVE & COMPLICATED TO OBTAIN A FULL PATENT. HOWEVER, A PROVISIONAL PATENT, WHICH PROVIDES PROTECTION FOR A YEAR, COSTS LESS THAN £5. THIS IS TO ALLOW TIME TO DECIDE WHETHER A FULL PATENT IS WORTHWHILE. YOU CAN SEND FOR FREE DETAILS TO: THE PATENT OFFICE, 25 SOUTHAMPTON BUILDINGS, LONDON WC2A 1AY

☆ PEARLS ☆
CONCRETIONS FORMED BY MOLLUSCS

PEARLS & THE GODS

MOST ANCIENT CIVILISATIONS BELIEVED THAT PEARLS WERE THE TEARS OF THE GODS. HOWEVER, IN PARTS OF INDIA IT WAS BELIEVED THAT IN THE BEGINNING WHEN THE GREAT GOD CREATED EARTH, FIRE, AIR & WATER, EACH OF THE ELEMENTS GAVE HIM A GIFT. THE AIR GAVE HIM A RAINBOW TO FORM A HALO ABOUT HIS HEAD; FIRE GAVE HIM A METEOR TO LIGHT HIS WAY; EARTH GAVE HIM A RUBY TO DECORATE HIS FOREHEAD & THE WATER GAVE HIM A PEARL TO WEAR OVER HIS HEART.

PEARL DIVERS

THE PEARL DIVERS OF THE PERSIAN GULF USED NO BREATHING APPARATUS. THEY JUMPED OVERBOARD HOLDING A ROCK (TO TAKE THEM TO THE BOTTOM QUICKLY), A BASKET (TO PUT THE OYSTERS IN) & A ROPE (TO HAUL THEM UP AGAIN). THEY DIVED FOR ABOUT A MINUTE 60-50 TIMES EVERY DAY FROM JUNE TO OCTOBER. THEY GREW VERY THIN DURING THE SEASON SINCE MUCH EATING CAUSES NAUSEA UNDERWATER.

WHY PEARLS ARE RARE

REAL PEARLS ARE VERY RARE. OYSTERS PRODUCE SEVERAL MILLION EGGS AT A TIME, WHICH HATCH INTO FREE-SWIMMING LARVAE, MOST ARE EATEN BY FISH. BUT THE FEW THAT SURVIVE 2 WEEKS HAVE BY THEN GROWN A SHELL & CAN ATTACH THEMSELVES TO A ROCK. FEW OF THE SURVIVORS CHOOSE GOOD LIVING PLACES & THE REST DIE OF STARVATION. ONE EGG IN 4,000,000 IS ESTIMATED TO REACH MATURITY. THEN VERY FEW OYSTERS HAPPEN TO SWALLOW A FOREIGN BODY & START COATING IT EVENLY WITH MOTHER-OF-PEARL. IN A SURVEY OF THE PERSIAN GULF BEDS 21 PEARLS WERE RECOVERED FROM 35,000 OYSTERS.

CULTURED PEARLS

CULTURED PEARLS ARE MADE BY INSERTING A BIT OF THE SHELL OF A GIANT PIG-TOE CLAM INTO THE FLESH OF AN OYSTER. IT IS THEN LEFT FOR SEVERAL YEARS WHILE THE OYSTER, IT IS HOPED, COATS THE NUCLEUS WITH MOTHER-OF-PEARL. CULTURED PEARLS ARE QUITE EXPENSIVE BECAUSE THE OYSTERS OFTEN DIE OR REJECT THE IMPLANT.

ARTIFICIAL PEARLS

THE BEST ARTIFICIAL PEARLS ARE MADE BY A FIRM IN MAJORCA. THEIR PROCESS IS SECRET BUT IS BASED ON COATING GLASS BEADS WITH MANY ALTERNATE LAYERS OF POWDERED FISH SCALES & BISMUTH OXYCHLORIDE (WHICH BRINGS OUT THE IRIDESCENCE).

DIGGING FOR PEARLS

PERHAPS THE EASIEST WAY TO FIND PEARLS IS TO DIG UNDERGROUND. SOME AMERICAN INDIANS HAD THE HABIT OF PLACING A PEARL IN THE MOUTH OF A DEAD PERSON, & 60,000 PEARLS HAVE BEEN DISCOVERED IN A SINGLE BURIAL MOUND.

HOW TO PERSUADE YOUR BRAIN THAT YOU HAVE TWO NOSES

CROSS FIRST & SECOND FINGERS OF ONE HAND. RUB NOSE WITH NOW INNER SURFACES OF THE CROSSED FINGERS (WHICH ARE NORMALLY THEIR OUTER EDGES) YOU WILL PROBABLY EXPERIENCE, BY TOUCH, 2 NOSES. THIS IS CALLED ARISTOTLES ILLUSION.

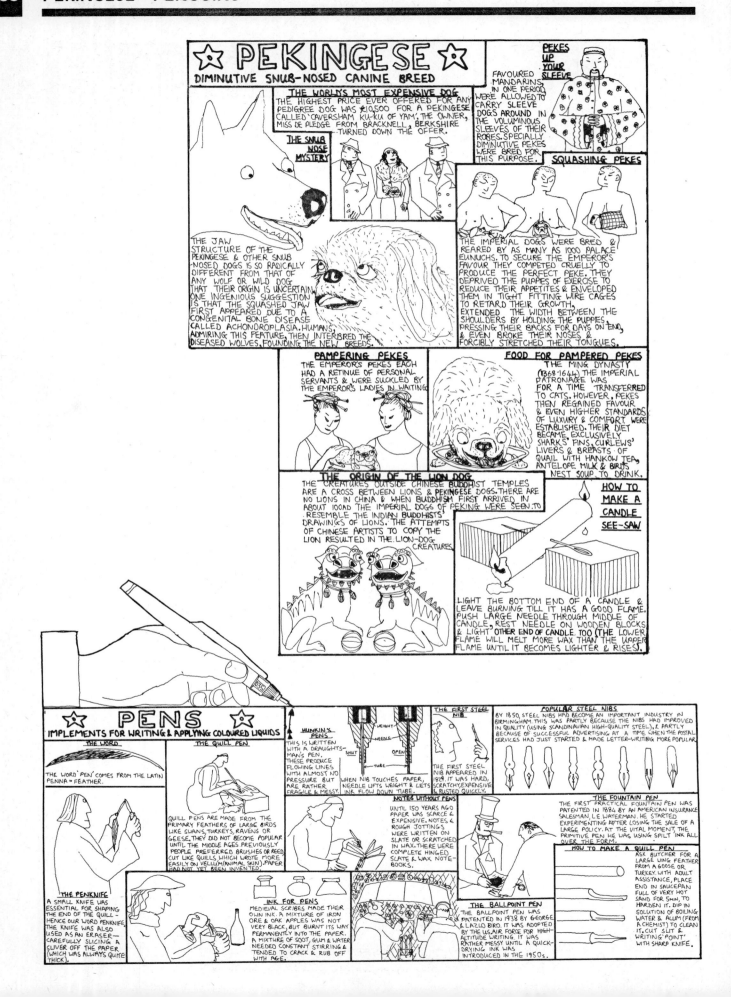

☆ PEKINGESE ☆
DIMINUTIVE SNUB-NOSED CANINE BREED

THE WORLD'S MOST EXPENSIVE DOG
THE HIGHEST PRICE EVER OFFERED FOR ANY PEDIGREE DOG WAS £10,500 FOR A PEKINGESE CALLED 'CAVERSHAM KU-KU OF YAM'. THE OWNER, MISS DE PLEDGE FROM BRACKNELL, BERKSHIRE TURNED DOWN THE OFFER.

PEKES UP YOUR SLEEVE
FAVOURED MANDARINS IN ONE PERIOD WERE ALLOWED TO CARRY SLEEVE DOGS AROUND IN THE VOLUMINOUS SLEEVES OF THEIR ROBES. SPECIALLY DIMINUTIVE PEKES WERE BRED FOR THIS PURPOSE.

THE SNUB NOSE MYSTERY
THE JAW STRUCTURE OF THE PEKINGESE & OTHER SNUB-NOSED DOGS IS SO RADICALLY DIFFERENT FROM THAT OF ANY WOLF OR WILD DOG THAT THEIR ORIGIN IS UNCERTAIN. ONE INGENIOUS SUGGESTION IS THAT THE SQUASHED JAW FIRST APPEARED DUE TO A CONGENITAL BONE DISEASE CALLED ACHONDROPLASIA. HUMANS, ADMIRING THIS FEATURE, THEN INTERBRED THE DISEASED WOLVES, FOUNDING THE NEW BREEDS.

SQUASHING PEKES
THE IMPERIAL DOGS WERE BRED & REARED BY AS MANY AS 1000 PALACE EUNUCHS. TO SECURE THE EMPEROR'S FAVOUR THEY COMPETED CRUELLY TO PRODUCE THE PERFECT PEKE. THEY DEPRIVED THE PUPPIES OF EXERCISE TO REDUCE THEIR APPETITES & ENVELOPED THEM IN TIGHT FITTING WIRE CAGES TO RETARD THEIR GROWTH, EXTENDED THE WIDTH BETWEEN THE SHOULDERS BY HOLDING THE PUPPIES PRESSING THEIR BACKS FOR DAYS ON END, & EVEN BROKE THEIR NOSES & FORCIBLY STRETCHED THEIR TONGUES.

PAMPERING PEKES
THE EMPEROR'S PEKES EACH HAD A RETINUE OF PERSONAL SERVANTS & WERE SUCKLED BY THE EMPEROR'S LADIES IN WAITING.

FOOD FOR PAMPERED PEKES
THE MING DYNASTY (1368-1644) THE IMPERIAL PATRONAGE WAS FOR A TIME TRANSFERRED TO CATS. HOWEVER, PEKES THEN REGAINED FAVOUR & EVEN HIGHER STANDARDS OF LUXURY & COMFORT WERE ESTABLISHED. THEIR DIET BECAME EXCLUSIVELY SHARKS' FINS, CURLEWS' LIVERS & BREASTS OF QUAIL WITH HANKOW TEA, ANTELOPE MILK & BIRDS NEST SOUP TO DRINK.

THE ORIGIN OF THE LION DOG
THE CREATURES OUTSIDE CHINESE BUDDHIST TEMPLES ARE A CROSS BETWEEN LIONS & PEKINGESE DOGS. THERE ARE NO LIONS IN CHINA & WHEN BUDDHISM FIRST ARRIVED IN ABOUT 100AD THE IMPERIAL DOGS OF PEKING WERE SEEN TO RESEMBLE THE INDIAN BUDDHISTS' DRAWINGS OF LIONS. THE ATTEMPTS OF CHINESE ARTISTS TO COPY THE LION RESULTED IN THE LION-DOG CREATURES.

HOW TO MAKE A CANDLE SEE-SAW
LIGHT THE BOTTOM END OF A CANDLE & LEAVE BURNING TILL IT HAS A GOOD FLAME. PUSH LARGE NEEDLE THROUGH MIDDLE OF CANDLE, REST NEEDLE ON WOODEN BLOCKS & LIGHT OTHER END OF CANDLE TOO (THE LOWER FLAME WILL MELT MORE WAX THAN THE UPPER FLAME UNTIL IT BECOMES LIGHTER & RISES).

☆ PENS ☆
IMPLEMENTS FOR WRITING & APPLYING COLOURED LIQUIDS

THE WORD
THE WORD 'PEN' COMES FROM THE LATIN PENNA = FEATHER.

THE QUILL PEN
QUILL PENS ARE MADE FROM THE PRIMARY FEATHERS OF LARGE BIRDS LIKE SWANS, TURKEYS, RAVENS OR GEESE. THEY DID NOT BECOME POPULAR UNTIL THE MIDDLE AGES. PREVIOUSLY PEOPLE PREFERRED BRUSHES OR REED CUT LIKE QUILLS WHICH WROTE MORE EASILY ON VELLUM (ANIMAL SKIN). PAPER HAD NOT YET BEEN INVENTED.

HUNKIN'S PENS
THIS IS WRITTEN WITH A DRAUGHTSMAN'S PEN. THESE PRODUCE FLOWING LINES WITH ALMOST NO PRESSURE BUT ARE RATHER FRAGILE & MESSY. WHEN NIB TOUCHES PAPER, NEEDLE LIFTS WEIGHT & LETS INK FLOW DOWN TUBE.

THE FIRST STEEL NIB
THE FIRST STEEL NIB APPEARED IN 1829. IT WAS HARD, SCRATCHY, EXPENSIVE & RUSTED QUICKLY.

POPULAR STEEL NIBS
BY 1850, STEEL NIBS HAD BECOME AN IMPORTANT INDUSTRY IN BIRMINGHAM. THIS WAS PARTLY BECAUSE THE NIBS HAD IMPROVED IN QUALITY (USING SCANDINAVIAN HIGH-QUALITY STEEL), & PARTLY BECAUSE OF SUCCESSFUL ADVERTISING AT A TIME WHEN THE POSTAL SERVICES HAD JUST STARTED & MADE LETTER-WRITING MORE POPULAR.

NOTES WITHOUT PENS
UNTIL 150 YEARS AGO PAPER WAS SCARCE & EXPENSIVE. NOTES & ROUGH JOTTINGS WERE WRITTEN ON SLATE OR SCRATCHED IN WAX. THERE WERE COMPLETE HINGED SLATE & WAX NOTE BOOKS.

THE FOUNTAIN PEN
THE FIRST PRACTICAL FOUNTAIN PEN WAS PATENTED IN 1884 BY AN AMERICAN INSURANCE SALESMAN, LE WATERMAN. HE STARTED EXPERIMENTING AFTER LOSING THE SALE OF A LARGE POLICY. AT THE VITAL MOMENT, THE PRIMITIVE PEN HE WAS USING SPILT INK ALL OVER THE FORM.

THE PENKNIFE
A SMALL KNIFE WAS ESSENTIAL FOR SHAPING THE END OF THE QUILL - HENCE OUR WORD PENKNIFE. THE KNIFE WAS ALSO USED AS AN ERASER - CAREFULLY SLICING A SLIVER OFF THE PAPER (WHICH WAS ALWAYS QUITE THICK).

INK FOR PENS
MEDIEVAL SCRIBES MADE THEIR OWN INK. A MIXTURE OF IRON ORE & OAK APPLES WAS NOT VERY BLACK, BUT BURNT ITS WAY PERMANENTLY INTO THE PAPER. A MIXTURE OF SOOT, GUM & WATER NEEDED CONSTANT STIRRING & TENDED TO CRACK & RUB OFF WITH AGE.

THE BALLPOINT PEN
THE BALLPOINT PEN WAS PATENTED IN 1938 BY GEORGE & LAZLO BIRO. IT WAS ADOPTED BY THE U.S. AIR FORCE FOR HIGH-ALTITUDE WRITING. IT WAS RATHER MESSY UNTIL A QUICK-DRYING INK WAS INTRODUCED IN THE 1950s.

HOW TO MAKE A QUILL PEN
ASK BUTCHER FOR A LARGE WING FEATHER FROM A GOOSE OR TURKEY. WITH ADULT ASSISTANCE, PLACE END IN SAUCEPAN FULL OF VERY HOT SAND FOR 5 MIN, TO HARDEN IT. DIP IN SOLUTION OF BOILING WATER & ALUM (FROM A CHEMIST) TO CLEAN IT. CUT SLIT & 'WRITING POINT' WITH SHARP KNIFE.

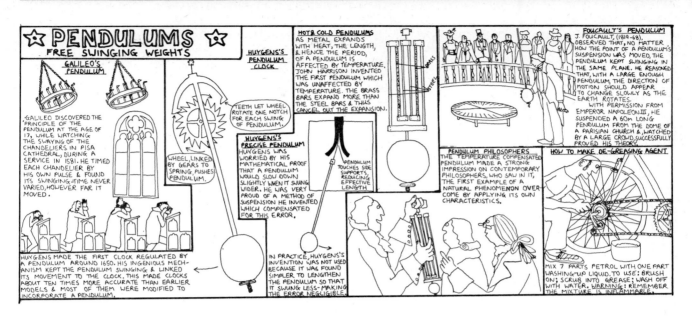

☆ PENDULUMS ☆
FREE SWINGING WEIGHTS

GALILEO'S PENDULUM

GALILEO DISCOVERED THE PRINCIPLE OF THE PENDULUM AT THE AGE OF 17, WHILE WATCHING THE SWAYING OF THE CHANDELIERS IN PISA CATHEDRAL, DURING A SERVICE IN 1581. HE TIMED EACH CHANDELIER BY HIS OWN PULSE & FOUND ITS SWINGING-TIME NEVER VARIED, HOWEVER FAR IT MOVED.

HUYGENS'S PENDULUM CLOCK

WHEEL, LINKED BY GEARS TO SPRING, PUSHES PENDULUM.

TEETH LET WHEEL ROTATE ONE NOTCH FOR EACH SWING OF PENDULUM.

HUYGENS'S PRECISE PENDULUM

HUYGENS WAS WORRIED BY HIS MATHEMATICAL PROOF THAT A PENDULUM WOULD SLOW DOWN SLIGHTLY WHEN IT SWUNG WIDER. HE WAS VERY PROUD OF A METHOD OF SUSPENSION HE INVENTED WHICH COMPENSATED FOR THIS ERROR.

PENDULUM TOUCHES SIDE SUPPORTS, REDUCING EFFECTIVE LENGTH

HUYGENS MADE THE FIRST CLOCK REGULATED BY A PENDULUM AROUND 1650. HIS INGENIOUS MECHANISM KEPT THE PENDULUM SWINGING & LINKED ITS MOVEMENT TO THE CLOCK. THIS MADE CLOCKS ABOUT TEN TIMES MORE ACCURATE THAN EARLIER MODELS & MOST OF THEM WERE MODIFIED TO INCORPORATE A PENDULUM.

IN PRACTICE, HUYGENS'S INVENTION WAS NOT USED BECAUSE IT WAS FOUND SIMPLER TO LENGTHEN THE PENDULUM SO THAT IT SWUNG LESS-MAKING THE ERROR NEGLIGIBLE.

HOT & COLD PENDULUMS

AS METAL EXPANDS WITH HEAT, THE LENGTH, & HENCE THE PERIOD, OF A PENDULUM IS AFFECTED BY TEMPERATURE. JOHN HARRISON INVENTED THE FIRST PENDULUM WHICH WAS UNAFFECTED BY TEMPERATURE. THE BRASS BARS EXPAND MORE THAN THE STEEL BARS & THUS CANCEL OUT THE EXPANSION.

PENDULUM PHILOSOPHERS

THE TEMPERATURE COMPENSATED PENDULUM MADE A STRONG IMPRESSION ON CONTEMPORARY PHILOSOPHERS, WHO SAW IN IT, THE FIRST EXAMPLE OF A NATURAL PHENOMENON OVERCOME BY APPLYING ITS OWN CHARACTERISTICS.

FOUCAULT'S PENDULUM

J. FOUCAULT, (1819-68), OBSERVED THAT, NO MATTER HOW THE POINT OF A PENDULUM'S SUSPENSION WAS MOVED, THE PENDULUM KEPT SWINGING IN THE SAME PLANE. HE REASONED THAT, WITH A LARGE ENOUGH PENDULUM, THE DIRECTION OF MOTION SHOULD APPEAR TO CHANGE SLOWLY AS THE EARTH ROTATES.
WITH PERMISSION FROM EMPEROR NAPOLEON III, HE SUSPENDED A 60M LONG PENDULUM FROM THE DOME OF A PARISIAN CHURCH & WATCHED BY A LARGE CROWD, SUCCESSFULLY PROVED HIS THEORY.

HOW TO MAKE DE-GREASING AGENT

MIX 7 PARTS PETROL WITH ONE PART WASHING-UP LIQUID. TO USE: BRUSH ON; SCRUB INTO GREASE; WASH OFF WITH WATER. WARNING: REMEMBER THE MIXTURE IS INFLAMMABLE.

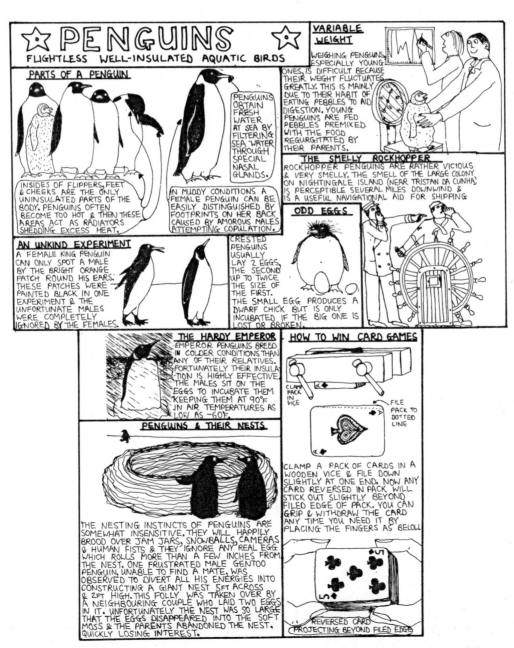

☆ PENGUINS ☆
FLIGHTLESS WELL-INSULATED AQUATIC BIRDS

PARTS OF A PENGUIN

PENGUINS OBTAIN FRESH WATER AT SEA BY FILTERING SEA WATER THROUGH SPECIAL NASAL GLANDS.

INSIDES OF FLIPPERS, FEET & CHEEKS ARE THE ONLY UNINSULATED PARTS OF THE BODY. PENGUINS OFTEN BECOME TOO HOT & THEN THESE AREAS ACT AS RADIATORS SHEDDING EXCESS HEAT.

IN MUDDY CONDITIONS A FEMALE PENGUIN CAN BE EASILY DISTINGUISHED BY FOOTPRINTS ON HER BACK CAUSED BY AMOROUS MALES ATTEMPTING COPULATION.

AN UNKIND EXPERIMENT

A FEMALE KING PENGUIN CAN ONLY SPOT A MALE BY THE BRIGHT ORANGE PATCH ROUND HIS EARS. THESE PATCHES WERE PAINTED BLACK IN ONE EXPERIMENT & THE UNFORTUNATE MALES WERE COMPLETELY IGNORED BY THE FEMALES.

CRESTED PENGUINS USUALLY LAY 2 EGGS, THE SECOND UP TO TWICE THE SIZE OF THE FIRST. THE SMALL EGG PRODUCES A DWARF CHICK BUT IS ONLY INCUBATED IF THE BIG ONE IS LOST OR BROKEN.

VARIABLE WEIGHT

WEIGHING PENGUINS, ESPECIALLY YOUNG ONES, IS DIFFICULT BECAUSE THEIR WEIGHT FLUCTUATES GREATLY. THIS IS MAINLY DUE TO THEIR HABIT OF EATING PEBBLES TO AID DIGESTION. YOUNG PENGUINS ARE FED PEBBLES PREMIXED WITH THE FOOD REGURGITATED BY THEIR PARENTS.

THE SMELLY ROCKHOPPER

ROCKHOPPER PENGUINS ARE RATHER VICIOUS & VERY SMELLY. THE SMELL OF THE LARGE COLONY ON NIGHTINGALE ISLAND (NEAR TRISTAN DA CUNHA) IS PERCEPTIBLE SEVERAL MILES DOWNWIND & IS A USEFUL NAVIGATIONAL AID FOR SHIPPING

ODD EGGS

THE HARDY EMPEROR

EMPEROR PENGUINS BREED IN COLDER CONDITIONS THAN ANY OF THEIR RELATIVES. FORTUNATELY THEIR INSULATION IS HIGHLY EFFECTIVE. THE MALES SIT ON THE EGGS TO INCUBATE THEM KEEPING THEM AT 90°F IN AIR TEMPERATURES AS LOW AS -60°F.

PENGUINS & THEIR NESTS

THE NESTING INSTINCTS OF PENGUINS ARE SOMEWHAT INSENSITIVE. THEY WILL HAPPILY BROOD OVER JAM JARS, SNOWBALLS, CAMERAS & HUMAN FISTS & THEY IGNORE ANY REAL EGG WHICH ROLLS MORE THAN A FEW INCHES FROM THE NEST. ONE FRUSTRATED MALE GENTOO PENGUIN, UNABLE TO FIND A MATE, WAS OBSERVED TO DIVERT ALL HIS ENERGIES INTO CONSTRUCTING A GIANT NEST 5FT ACROSS & 2FT HIGH. THIS FOLLY WAS TAKEN OVER BY A NEIGHBOURING COUPLE WHO LAID TWO EGGS IN IT. UNFORTUNATELY THE NEST WAS SO LARGE THAT THE EGGS DISAPPEARED INTO THE SOFT MOSS & THE PARENTS ABANDONED THE NEST, QUICKLY LOSING INTEREST.

HOW TO WIN CARD GAMES

CLAMP PACK IN VICE

FILE PACK TO DOTTED LINE

CLAMP A PACK OF CARDS IN A WOODEN VICE & FILE DOWN SLIGHTLY AT ONE END. NOW ANY CARD REVERSED IN PACK WILL STICK OUT SLIGHTLY BEYOND FILED EDGE OF PACK. YOU CAN GRIP & WITHDRAW THE CARD ANY TIME YOU NEED IT BY PLACING THE FINGERS AS BELOW.

REVERSED CARD PROJECTING BEYOND FILED EDGE

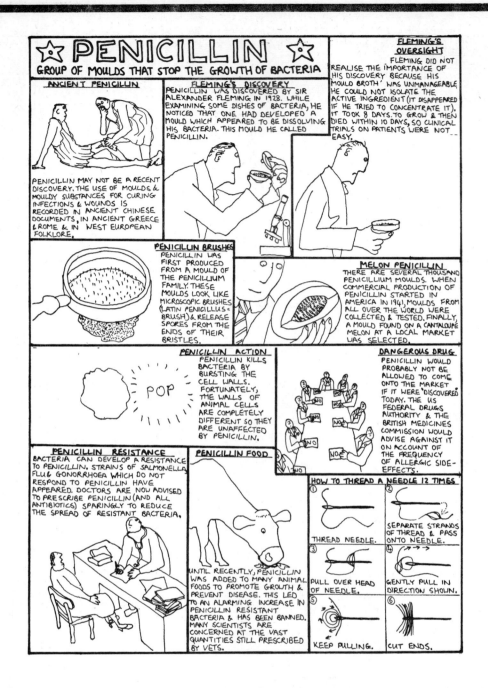

☆ PENICILLIN ☆
GROUP OF MOULDS THAT STOP THE GROWTH OF BACTERIA

ANCIENT PENICILLIN

PENICILLIN MAY NOT BE A RECENT DISCOVERY. THE USE OF MOULDS & MOULDY SUBSTANCES FOR CURING INFECTIONS & WOUNDS IS RECORDED IN ANCIENT CHINESE DOCUMENTS, IN ANCIENT GREECE & ROME & IN WEST EUROPEAN FOLKLORE.

FLEMING'S DISCOVERY

PENICILLIN WAS DISCOVERED BY SIR ALEXANDER FLEMING IN 1928. WHILE EXAMINING SOME DISHES OF BACTERIA, HE NOTICED THAT ONE HAD DEVELOPED A MOULD WHICH APPEARED TO BE DISSOLVING HIS BACTERIA. THIS MOULD HE CALLED PENICILLIN.

FLEMING'S OVERSIGHT

FLEMING DID NOT REALISE THE IMPORTANCE OF HIS DISCOVERY BECAUSE HIS 'MOULD BROTH' WAS UNMANAGEABLE. HE COULD NOT ISOLATE THE ACTIVE INGREDIENT (IT DISAPPEARED IF HE TRIED TO CONCENTRATE IT), IT TOOK 8 DAYS TO GROW & THEN DIED WITHIN 10 DAYS, SO CLINICAL TRIALS ON PATIENTS WERE NOT EASY.

PENICILLIN BRUSHES

PENICILLIN WAS FIRST PRODUCED FROM A MOULD OF THE PENICILLIUM FAMILY. THESE MOULDS LOOK LIKE MICROSCOPIC BRUSHES (LATIN PENICILLUS = BRUSH) & RELEASE SPORES FROM THE ENDS OF THEIR BRISTLES.

MELON PENICILLIN

THERE ARE SEVERAL THOUSAND PENICILLIUM MOULDS. WHEN COMMERCIAL PRODUCTION OF PENICILLIN STARTED IN AMERICA IN 1941, MOULDS FROM ALL OVER THE WORLD WERE COLLECTED & TESTED. FINALLY, A MOULD FOUND ON A CANTALOUPE MELON AT A LOCAL MARKET WAS SELECTED.

PENICILLIN ACTION

POP

PENICILLIN KILLS BACTERIA BY BURSTING THE CELL WALLS. FORTUNATELY, THE WALLS OF ANIMAL CELLS ARE COMPLETELY DIFFERENT SO THEY ARE UNAFFECTED BY PENICILLIN.

DANGEROUS DRUG

PENICILLIN WOULD PROBABLY NOT BE ALLOWED TO COME ONTO THE MARKET IF IT WERE "DISCOVERED" TODAY. THE US FEDERAL DRUGS AUTHORITY & THE BRITISH MEDICINES COMMISSION WOULD ADVISE AGAINST IT ON ACCOUNT OF THE FREQUENCY OF ALLERGIC SIDE-EFFECTS.

PENICILLIN RESISTANCE

BACTERIA CAN DEVELOP A RESISTANCE TO PENICILLIN. STRAINS OF SALMONELLA, FLU & GONORRHOEA WHICH DO NOT RESPOND TO PENICILLIN HAVE APPEARED. DOCTORS ARE NOW ADVISED TO PRESCRIBE PENICILLIN (AND ALL ANTIBIOTICS) SPARINGLY TO REDUCE THE SPREAD OF RESISTANT BACTERIA.

PENICILLIN FOOD

UNTIL RECENTLY, PENICILLIN WAS ADDED TO MANY ANIMAL FOODS TO PROMOTE GROWTH & PREVENT DISEASE. THIS LED TO AN ALARMING INCREASE IN PENICILLIN RESISTANT BACTERIA & HAS BEEN BANNED. MANY SCIENTISTS ARE CONCERNED AT THE VAST QUANTITIES STILL PRESCRIBED BY VETS.

HOW TO THREAD A NEEDLE 12 TIMES

① THREAD NEEDLE.

② SEPARATE STRANDS OF THREAD & PASS ONTO NEEDLE.

③ PULL OVER HEAD OF NEEDLE.

④ GENTLY PULL IN DIRECTION SHOWN.

⑤ KEEP PULLING.

⑥ CUT ENDS.

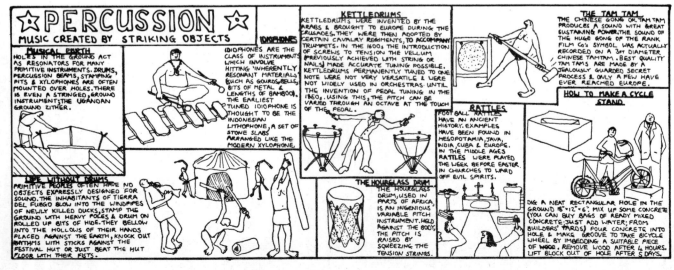

☆ PERCUSSION ☆
MUSIC CREATED BY STRIKING OBJECTS

MUSICAL EARTH

HOLES IN THE GROUND ACT AS RESONATORS FOR MANY PRIMITIVE INSTRUMENTS. DRUMS, PERCUSSION BEAMS, STAMPING PITS & XYLOPHONES ARE OFTEN MOUNTED OVER HOLES. THERE IS EVEN A STRINGED, GROUND INSTRUMENT; THE UGANDAN GROUND ZITHER.

IDIOPHONES

IDIOPHONES ARE THE CLASS OF INSTRUMENTS WHICH INVOLVE HITTING INHERENTLY RESONANT MATERIALS (SUCH AS GOURDS, BELLS, BITS OF METAL & LENGTHS OF BAMBOO). THE EARLIEST TUNED IDIOPHONE IS THOUGHT TO BE THE INDONESIAN LITHOPHONE, A SET OF STONE SLABS ARRANGED LIKE THE MODERN XYLOPHONE.

KETTLEDRUMS

KETTLEDRUMS WERE INVENTED BY THE ARABS & BROUGHT TO EUROPE DURING THE CRUSADES. THEY WERE THEN ADOPTED BY CERTAIN CAVALRY REGIMENTS, TO ACCOMPANY TRUMPETS. IN THE 1600s THE INTRODUCTION OF SCREWS TO TENSION THE VELLUM (PREVIOUSLY ACHIEVED WITH STRING OR NAILS) MADE ACCURATE TUNING POSSIBLE. KETTLEDRUMS PERMANENTLY TUNED TO ONE NOTE WERE NOT VERY VERSATILE & WERE NOT WIDELY USED IN ORCHESTRAS UNTIL THE INVENTION OF PEDAL TUNING IN THE 1860s. USING THIS, THE PITCH CAN BE VARIED THROUGH AN OCTAVE AT THE TOUCH OF THE PEDAL.

THE TAM TAM

THE CHINESE GONG OR TAM TAM PRODUCES A SOUND WITH GREAT SUSTAINING POWER. THE SOUND OF THE HUGE GONG OF THE RANK FILM Co's SYMBOL WAS ACTUALLY RECORDED ON A 3ft DIAMETER CHINESE TAMTAM. BEST QUALITY TAM TAMS ARE MADE BY A JEALOUSLY GUARDED SECRET PROCESS & ONLY A FEW HAVE EVER REACHED EUROPE.

RATTLES

FOOTBALL RATTLES HAVE AN ANCIENT HISTORY. EXAMPLES HAVE BEEN FOUND IN MESOPOTAMIA, JAVA, INDIA, CUBA & EUROPE. IN THE MIDDLE AGES RATTLES WERE PLAYED THE WEEK BEFORE EASTER IN CHURCHES TO WARD OFF EVIL SPIRITS.

LIFE WITHOUT DRUMS

PRIMITIVE PEOPLES OFTEN HAVE NO OBJECTS EXPRESSLY DESIGNED FOR SOUND. THE INHABITANTS OF TIERRA DEL FUEGO BLOW INTO THE WINDPIPES OF NEWLY KILLED DUCKS, STAMP THE GROUND WITH HEAVY POLES & DRUM ON ROLLED UP BITS OF HIDE. THEY BELLOW INTO THE HOLLOWS OF THEIR HANDS PLACED AGAINST THE EARTH, KNOCK OUT RHYTHMS WITH STICKS AGAINST THE FESTIVAL HUT OR JUST BEAT THE HUT FLOOR WITH THEIR FISTS.

THE HOURGLASS DRUM

THE HOURGLASS DRUM, USED IN PARTS OF AFRICA, IS AN INGENIOUS VARIABLE PITCH INSTRUMENT. HELD AGAINST THE BODY, THE PITCH IS RAISED BY SQUEEZING THE TENSION STRINGS.

HOW TO MAKE A CYCLE STAND

DIG A NEAT RECTANGULAR HOLE IN THE GROUND 18"×12"×6". MIX UP SOME CONCRETE (YOU CAN BUY BAGS OF READY MIXED CONCRETE; JUST ADD WATER; FROM BUILDERS' YARDS). POUR CONCRETE INTO HOLE & MAKE GROOVE TO TAKE BICYCLE WHEEL BY IMBEDDING A SUITABLE PIECE OF WOOD. REMOVE WOOD AFTER 4 HOURS. LIFT BLOCK OUT OF HOLE AFTER 5 DAYS.

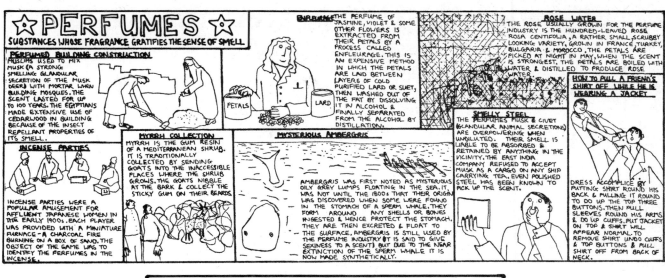

☆ PERFUMES ☆
SUBSTANCES WHOSE FRAGRANCE GRATIFIES THE SENSE OF SMELL

PERFUMED BUILDING CONSTRUCTION
MUSLIMS USED TO MIX MUSK (A STRONG SMELLING GLANDULAR SECRETION OF THE MUSK DEER) WITH MORTAR WHEN BUILDING MOSQUES. THE SCENT LASTED FOR UP TO 100 YEARS. THE EGYPTIANS MADE EXTENSIVE USE OF CEDARWOOD IN BUILDING BECAUSE OF THE INSECT REPELLANT PROPERTIES OF ITS SMELL.

INCENSE PARTIES
INCENSE PARTIES WERE A POPULAR AMUSEMENT FOR AFFLUENT JAPANESE WOMEN IN THE EARLY 1900s. EACH PLAYER WAS PROVIDED WITH A MINIATURE FURNACE – A CHARCOAL FIRE BURNING ON A BOX OF SAND. THE OBJECT OF THE GAME WAS TO IDENTIFY THE PERFUMES IN THE INCENSE.

MYRRH COLLECTION
MYRRH IS THE GUM RESIN OF A MEDITERRANEAN SHRUB. IT IS TRADITIONALLY COLLECTED BY SENDING GOATS INTO THE INACCESSIBLE PLACES WHERE THE SHRUB GROWS. THE GOATS NIBBLE AT THE BARK & COLLECT THE STICKY GUM ON THEIR BEARDS

ENFLEURAGE THE PERFUME OF JASMINE, VIOLET & SOME OTHER FLOWERS IS EXTRACTED FROM THEIR PETALS BY A PROCESS CALLED ENFLEURAGE. THIS IS AN EXPENSIVE METHOD IN WHICH THE PETALS ARE LAID BETWEEN LAYERS OF COLD PURIFIED LARD OR SUET, THEN WASHED OUT OF THE FAT BY DISSOLVING IT IN ALCOHOL & FINALLY SEPARATED FROM THE ALCOHOL BY DISTILLATION.

PETALS / LARD

MYSTERIOUS AMBERGRIS
AMBERGRIS WAS FIRST NOTED AS MYSTERIOUS OILY GREY LUMPS FLOATING IN THE SEA. IT WAS NOT UNTIL THE 1800s THAT THEIR ORIGIN WAS DISCOVERED WHEN SOME WERE FOUND IN THE STOMACH OF A SPERM WHALE. THEY FORM AROUND ANY SHELLS OR BONES INGESTED & HENCE PROTECT THE STOMACH. THEY ARE THEN EXCRETED & FLOAT TO THE SURFACE. AMBERGRIS IS STILL USED BY THE PERFUME INDUSTRY (IT IS SAID TO GIVE SEXINESS TO A SCENT) BUT DUE TO THE NEAR EXTINCTION OF THE SPERM WHALE IT IS NOW MADE SYNTHETICALLY.

ROSE WATER
THE ROSE USUALLY GROWN FOR THE PERFUME INDUSTRY IS THE HUNDRED-LEAVED ROSE ROSA CENTIFOLIA, A RATHER SMALL SCRUBBY LOOKING VARIETY, GROWN IN FRANCE, TURKEY, BULGARIA & MOROCCO. THE PETALS ARE PICKED AT NIGHT IN MAY, WHEN THE SCENT IS STRONGEST. THE PETALS ARE BOILED WITH WATER & DISTILLED TO PRODUCE ROSE WATER.

SMELLY STEEL
THE PERFUMES MUSK & CIVET (GLANDULAR ANIMAL SECRETIONS) ARE OVERPOWERING WHEN UNDILUTED. THEIR SMELL IS LIABLE TO BE ABSORBED & RETAINED BY ANYTHING IN THE VICINITY. THE EAST INDIA COMPANY REFUSED TO ACCEPT MUSK AS A CARGO ON ANY SHIP CARRYING TEA. EVEN POLISHED STEEL HAS BEEN KNOWN TO PICK UP THE SCENT.

HOW TO PULL A FRIEND'S SHIRT OFF WHILE HE IS WEARING A JACKET
DRESS ACCOMPLICE BY PUTTING SHIRT ROUND HIS BACK & PULLING IT ROUND TO DO UP THE TOP THREE BUTTONS. THEN PULL SLEEVES ROUND HIS ARMS & DO UP CUFFS. PUT JACKET ON TOP & SHIRT WILL APPEAR NORMAL. TO REMOVE SHIRT UNDO CUFFS & TOP BUTTONS & PULL SHIRT OFF FROM BACK OF NECK.

☆ PERPETUAL MOTION ☆
HYPOTHETICAL MECHANISMS

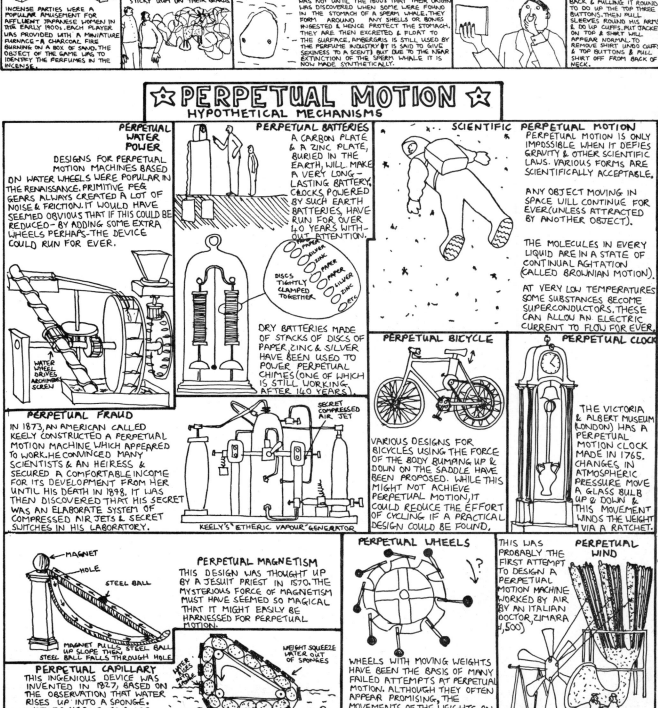

PERPETUAL WATER POWER
DESIGNS FOR PERPETUAL MOTION MACHINES BASED ON WATER WHEELS WERE POPULAR IN THE RENAISSANCE. PRIMITIVE PEG GEARS ALWAYS CREATED A LOT OF NOISE & FRICTION. IT WOULD HAVE SEEMED OBVIOUS THAT IF THIS COULD BE REDUCED – BY ADDING SOME EXTRA WHEELS PERHAPS – THE DEVICE COULD RUN FOR EVER.

WATER WHEEL DRIVES ARCHIMEDES SCREW

PERPETUAL FRAUD
IN 1873, AN AMERICAN CALLED KEELY CONSTRUCTED A PERPETUAL MOTION MACHINE WHICH APPEARED TO WORK. HE CONVINCED MANY SCIENTISTS & AN HEIRESS & SECURED A COMFORTABLE INCOME FOR ITS DEVELOPMENT FROM HER UNTIL HIS DEATH IN 1898. IT WAS THEN DISCOVERED THAT HIS SECRET WAS AN ELABORATE SYSTEM OF COMPRESSED AIR JETS & SECRET SWITCHES IN HIS LABORATORY.

SECRET COMPRESSED AIR JET

KEELY'S 'ETHERIC VAPOUR' GENERATOR

PERPETUAL BATTERIES
A CARBON PLATE & A ZINC PLATE, BURIED IN THE EARTH, WILL MAKE A VERY LONG-LASTING BATTERY. CLOCKS POWERED BY SUCH EARTH BATTERIES, HAVE RUN FOR OVER 40 YEARS WITHOUT ATTENTION.

DISCS TIGHTLY CLAMPED TOGETHER (PAPER SILVER ZINC PAPER SILVER ZINC ETC)

DRY BATTERIES MADE OF STACKS OF DISCS OF PAPER, ZINC & SILVER HAVE BEEN USED TO POWER PERPETUAL CHIMES (ONE OF WHICH IS STILL WORKING AFTER 140 YEARS).

PERPETUAL BICYCLE
VARIOUS DESIGNS FOR BICYCLES USING THE FORCE OF THE BODY BUMPING UP & DOWN ON THE SADDLE HAVE BEEN PROPOSED. WHILE THIS MIGHT NOT ACHIEVE PERPETUAL MOTION, IT COULD REDUCE THE EFFORT OF CYCLING IF A PRACTICAL DESIGN COULD BE FOUND.

SCIENTIFIC PERPETUAL MOTION
PERPETUAL MOTION IS ONLY IMPOSSIBLE WHEN IT DEFIES GRAVITY & OTHER SCIENTIFIC LAWS. VARIOUS FORMS ARE SCIENTIFICALLY ACCEPTABLE.

ANY OBJECT MOVING IN SPACE WILL CONTINUE FOR EVER (UNLESS ATTRACTED BY ANOTHER OBJECT).

THE MOLECULES IN EVERY LIQUID ARE IN A STATE OF CONTINUAL AGITATION (CALLED BROWNIAN MOTION).

AT VERY LOW TEMPERATURES SOME SUBSTANCES BECOME SUPERCONDUCTORS. THESE CAN ALLOW AN ELECTRIC CURRENT TO FLOW FOR EVER.

PERPETUAL CLOCK
THE VICTORIA & ALBERT MUSEUM (LONDON) HAS A PERPETUAL MOTION CLOCK MADE IN 1765. CHANGES IN ATMOSPHERIC PRESSURE MOVE A GLASS BULB UP & DOWN & THIS MOVEMENT WINDS THE WEIGHT VIA A RATCHET.

PERPETUAL MAGNETISM
THIS DESIGN WAS THOUGHT UP BY A JESUIT PRIEST IN 1570. THE MYSTERIOUS FORCE OF MAGNETISM MUST HAVE SEEMED SO MAGICAL THAT IT MIGHT EASILY BE HARNESSED FOR PERPETUAL MOTION.

MAGNET / HOLE / STEEL BALL
MAGNET PULLS STEEL BALL UP SLOPE THEN STEEL BALL FALLS THROUGH HOLE

PERPETUAL CAPILLARY
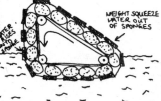
THIS INGENIOUS DEVICE WAS INVENTED IN 1827, BASED ON THE OBSERVATION THAT WATER RISES UP INTO A SPONGE. ANOTHER HEROIC FAILURE.

WATER RISES UP SPONGE / WEIGHT SQUEEZES WATER OUT OF SPONGES

PERPETUAL WHEELS
WHEELS WITH MOVING WEIGHTS HAVE BEEN THE BASIS OF MANY FAILED ATTEMPTS AT PERPETUAL MOTION. ALTHOUGH THEY OFTEN APPEAR PROMISING, THE MOVEMENTS OF THE WEIGHTS ON ONE SIDE ALWAYS CANCEL THE MOVEMENTS OF THE WEIGHTS ON THE OTHER.

PERPETUAL WIND
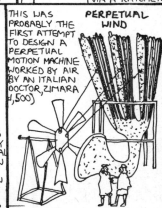
THIS WAS PROBABLY THE FIRST ATTEMPT TO DESIGN A PERPETUAL MOTION MACHINE WORKED BY AIR BY AN ITALIAN DOCTOR, ZIMARA (1500)

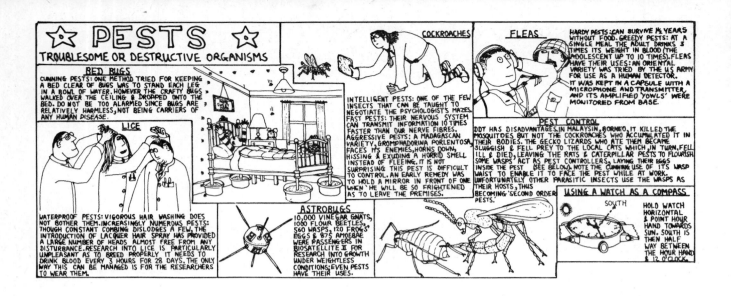

☆ PESTS ☆
TROUBLESOME OR DESTRUCTIVE ORGANISMS

BED BUGS
CUNNING PESTS: ONE METHOD TRIED FOR KEEPING A BED CLEAR OF BUGS WAS TO STAND EACH LEG IN A BOWL OF WATER. HOWEVER THE CRAFTY BUGS WALKED OVER THE CEILING & DROPPED ONTO THE BED. DO NOT BE TOO ALARMED SINCE BUGS ARE RELATIVELY HARMLESS, NOT BEING CARRIERS OF ANY HUMAN DISEASE.

LICE
WATERPROOF PESTS: VIGOROUS HAIR WASHING DOES NOT BOTHER THEM. INCREASINGLY NUMEROUS PESTS: THOUGH CONSTANT COMBING DISLODGES A FEW, THE INTRODUCTION OF LACQUER HAIR SPRAY HAS PROVIDED A LARGE NUMBER OF HEADS ALMOST FREE FROM ANY DISTURBANCE. RESEARCH INTO LICE IS PARTICULARLY UNPLEASANT AS TO BREED PROPERLY IT NEEDS TO DRINK BLOOD EVERY 3 HOURS FOR 28 DAYS. THE ONLY WAY THIS CAN BE MANAGED IS FOR THE RESEARCHERS TO WEAR THEM.

COCKROACHES
INTELLIGENT PESTS: ONE OF THE FEW INSECTS THAT CAN BE TAUGHT TO NEGOTIATE THE PSYCHOLOGISTS MAZES. FAST PESTS: THEIR NERVOUS SYSTEM CAN TRANSMIT INFORMATION 10 TIMES FASTER THAN OUR NERVE FIBRES. AGGRESSIVE PESTS: A MADAGASCAN VARIETY, GROMPHADORINA PORLENTOSA, FACES ITS ENEMIES, HORNS DOWN, HISSING & EXUDING A HORRID SMELL INSTEAD OF FLEEING. IT IS NOT SURPRISING THIS PEST IS DIFFICULT TO CONTROL. AN EARLY REMEDY WAS TO HOLD A MIRROR IN FRONT OF ONE WHEN 'HE WILL BE SO FRIGHTENED AS TO LEAVE THE PREMISES.

ASTROBUGS
10,000 VINEGAR GNATS, 1000 FLOUR BEETLES, 560 WASPS, 120 FROGS' EGGS & 875 AMOEBAE WERE PASSENGERS IN BIOSATELLITE II FOR RESEARCH INTO GROWTH UNDER WEIGHTLESS CONDITIONS: EVEN PESTS HAVE THEIR USES.

FLEAS
HARDY PESTS: CAN SURVIVE 1½ YEARS WITHOUT FOOD. GREEDY PESTS: AT A SINGLE MEAL THE ADULT DRINKS 3 TIMES ITS WEIGHT IN BLOOD (THE ADOLESCENT UP TO 10 TIMES). FLEAS HAVE THEIR USES: AN ORIENTAL VARIETY WAS TRIED BY THE US ARMY FOR USE AS A HUMAN DETECTOR. IT WAS KEPT IN A CAPSULE WITH A MICROPHONE AND TRANSMITTER, AND ITS AMPLIFIED 'YOWLS' WERE MONITORED FROM BASE.

PEST CONTROL
DDT HAS DISADVANTAGES. IN MALAYSIA, BORNEO, IT KILLED THE MOSQUITOES BUT NOT THE COCKROACHES WHO ACCUMULATED IT IN THEIR BODIES. THE GECKO LIZARDS WHO ATE THEM BECAME SLUGGISH & FELL PREY TO THE LOCAL CATS WHICH, IN TURN, FELL ILL & DIED, LEAVING THE RATS & CATERPILLAR PESTS TO FLOURISH. SOME WASPS' ACT AS PEST CONTROLLERS, LAYING THEIR EGGS INSIDE THE PEST   SEE BELOW. NOTE THE CUNNING USE OF ITS WASP WAIST TO ENABLE IT TO FACE THE PEST WHILE AT WORK. UNFORTUNATELY OTHER PARASITIC INSECTS USE THE WASPS AS THEIR HOSTS, THUS BECOMING 'SECOND ORDER PESTS.

USING A WATCH AS A COMPASS
SOUTH
HOLD WATCH HORIZONTAL & POINT HOUR HAND TOWARDS SUN. SOUTH IS THEN HALF WAY BETWEEN THE HOUR HAND & 12 O'CLOCK.

☆ PETROL ☆
A MIXTURE OF LIGHT VOLATILE HYDROCARBONS

AN UNWANTED DISCOVERY
PETROLEUM (ROCK OIL) WAS FIRST ENCOUNTERED BY THE AMERICANS DRILLING TO FIND SALT DEPOSITS. THEY HIT OIL AT LEAST 15 TIMES BETWEEN 1840 & 1860 & NO ATTEMPT WAS MADE TO COLLECT IT. IT WAS REGARDED AS A MENACE SQUIRTING OUT ALL OVER THE MEN & THEIR TOOLS. IN THE 1860s, WHEN PEOPLE BEGAN TO MAKE PARAFFIN FROM PART OF THE OIL, THE PETROL & MORE VOLATILE FRACTIONS WERE STILL REGARDED AS NOT ONLY USELESS BUT DANGEROUS.

THE FIRST PETROL PUMP
THE FIRST 'PETROL PUMP', USED FOR DISPENSING PARAFFIN, APPEARED IN 1885. IT WAS BUILT BY SYLVANUS BOWSER, INSPIRED BY A GROCER FRIEND WHO WAS RECEIVING COMPLAINTS THAT HIS BUTTER TASTED OF PARAFFIN (HIS PARAFFIN BARREL WAS LEAKING). INSTEAD OF MOVING OR MENDING THE OLD BARREL BOWSER MADE A LARGE TANK INCORPORATING A DEVICE FOR DISPENSING THE FUEL IN GIVEN QUANTITIES.

PARAFFIN
BEST BUTTER

THE CARGO IN A SUPERTANKER CONTAINS AS MUCH THERMAL ENERGY AS A POLARIS WARHEAD.

A GALLON OF PETROL CAN SPREAD TO A THIN FILM COVERING OVER 100 ACRES OF WATER

AN AMERICAN PHYSICIST, DR FONG, IS PROPOSING A WORLD WIDE SCHEME TO ADD 20% ALCOHOL TO PETROL. THIS WOULD INCREASE AN UNMODIFIED CAR'S PERFORMANCE & DECREASE ITS EXHAUST EMISSIONS. THE ALCOHOL WOULD BE PRODUCED BY THE FERMENTATION OF CORN. THIS PROCESS ONLY USES THE CORN STARCH & LEAVES THE PLANT CONTAINING 30% PROTEIN, IDEAL AS ANIMAL FEED. THE HUGE SCALE OF THIS NEW INDUSTRY WOULD LOWER THE PRICE OF ANIMAL FEED, LEADING TO CHEAPER MEAT. THE 60 MILLION ACRES NEEDED TO GROW ENOUGH EXTRA CORN COULD BE MARGINAL LAND RECLAIMED BY THE FUTURE UNEMPLOYED.

SPEAKING PETROL PUMPS
TALKING PETROL PUMPS WITH PRE-RECORDED INSTRUCTIONS HAVE RECENTLY BEEN TRIED AT SOME SELF-SERVICE GARAGES. B P, AFTER EXPERIMENTING WITH UNMANNED GARAGES, OVERCAME INITIAL SNAGS OF AUTOMATIC PUMPS CHEWING UP BANKNOTES & ACCEPTING FORGERIES (EVEN PHOTOCOPIES). HOWEVER THEY FOUND THAT A HIGH PERCENTAGE OF DRIVERS SEEMED TO BE INCAPABLE OF READING THE INSTRUCTIONS & MANY MOTORISTS DROVE AWAY FRUSTRATED OR SOAKED WITH PETROL.

ALCOHOLIC PANACEA
ALCOHOL

PUTTING OUT FIRES WITH PETROL
PETROL IS SOMETIMES USED FOR PUTTING OUT FIRES IN COTTON BALES. WATER IS USELESS BECAUSE THE BALES ARE SO TIGHTLY PACKED THAT IT CANNOT PENETRATE. PETROL WILL READILY SOAK TO THE BURNING CENTRE & DESTROY THE BLAZE WITHOUT IGNITING DUE TO THE LACK OF OXYGEN.

MILAGE
PENCE PER MILE, A FAMILY SALOON CAR IS NEARLY AS ECONOMIC TO RUN AS A BALLPOINT PEN.

HOW TO PUSH A KNITTING NEEDLE THROUGH A BALLOON
BLOW UP BALLOON, TIE IT UP & STICK 2 BITS OF SELLOTAPE ON IT - ON OPPOSITE SIDES. NOW YOU CAN PUSH KNITTING NEEDLE FIRMLY INTO TAPE, THROUGH BALLOON & OUT OTHER SIDE WITHOUT BALLOON BURSTING. THE TAPE PREVENTS THE PUNCTURE HOLES EXPANDING!

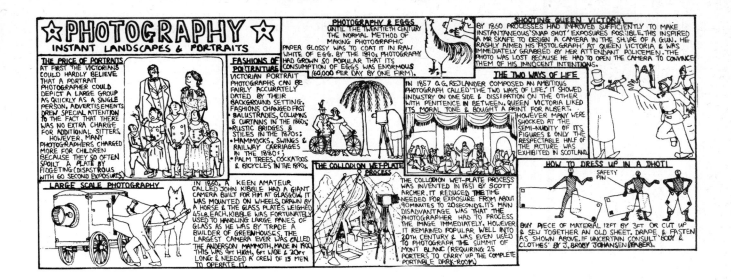

☆ PHOTOGRAPHY ☆
INSTANT LANDSCAPES & PORTRAITS

THE PRICE OF PORTRAITS
AT FIRST THE VICTORIANS COULD HARDLY BELIEVE THAT A PORTRAIT PHOTOGRAPHER COULD DEPICT A LARGE GROUP AS QUICKLY AS A SINGLE PERSON. ADVERTISEMENTS DREW SPECIAL ATTENTION TO THE FACT THAT THERE WAS NO EXTRA CHARGE FOR ADDITIONAL SITTERS. HOWEVER, MANY PHOTOGRAPHERS CHARGED MORE FOR CHILDREN BECAUSE THEY SO OFTEN SPOILT A PLATE BY FIDGETING (DISASTROUS WITH 60 SECOND EXPOSURES).

FASHIONS OF PORTRAITURE
VICTORIAN PORTRAIT PHOTOGRAPHS CAN BE FAIRLY ACCURATELY DATED BY THEIR BACKGROUND SETTING. FASHIONS CHANGED FAST.
- BALUSTRADES, COLUMNS & CURTAINS IN THE 1860s;
- RUSTIC BRIDGES & STILES IN THE 1870s;
- HAMMOCKS, SWINGS & RAILWAY CARRIAGES IN THE 1880s;
- PALM TREES, COCKATOOS & BICYCLES IN THE 1890s.

PHOTOGRAPHY & EGGS
UNTIL THE TWENTIETH CENTURY THE NORMAL METHOD OF MAKING PHOTOGRAPHIC PAPER GLOSSY WAS TO COAT IT IN RAW WHITE OF EGG. BY THE 1890s PHOTOGRAPHY HAD GROWN SO POPULAR THAT ITS CONSUMPTION OF EGGS WAS ENORMOUS (60,000 PER DAY BY ONE FIRM).

SHOOTING QUEEN VICTORIA
BY 1860 PROCESSES HAD IMPROVED SUFFICIENTLY TO MAKE INSTANTANEOUS 'SNAP SHOT' EXPOSURES POSSIBLE. THIS INSPIRED A MR SKAIFE TO DESIGN A CAMERA IN THE SHAPE OF A GUN. HE RASHLY AIMED HIS 'PISTOLGRAPH' AT QUEEN VICTORIA & WAS IMMEDIATELY GRABBED BY HER ATTENDANT POLICEMEN. THE PHOTO WAS LOST BECAUSE HE HAD TO OPEN THE CAMERA TO CONVINCE THEM OF HIS INNOCENT INTENTIONS.

THE TWO WAYS OF LIFE
IN 1857 O.G. REJLANDER COMPOSED AN AMBITIOUS PHOTOGRAPH CALLED 'THE TWO WAYS OF LIFE'. IT SHOWED INDUSTRY ON ONE SIDE & DISSIPATION ON THE OTHER WITH PENITENCE IN BETWEEN. QUEEN VICTORIA LIKED ITS MORAL TONE & BOUGHT A PRINT FOR ALBERT. HOWEVER MANY WERE SHOCKED AT THE SEMI-NUDITY OF ITS FIGURES & ONLY THE RESPECTABLE HALF OF THE PICTURE WAS EXHIBITED IN SCOTLAND.

LARGE SCALE PHOTOGRAPHY
IN 1860, A KEEN AMATEUR CALLED JOHN KIBBLE HAD A GIANT CAMERA BUILT FOR HIM AT GLASGOW. IT WAS MOUNTED ON WHEELS, DRAWN BY A HORSE & THE GLASS PLATES WEIGHED 45lb EACH. KIBBLE WAS FORTUNATELY USED TO HANDLING LARGE PANES OF GLASS AS HE WAS BY TRADE A BUILDER OF GREENHOUSES. THE LARGEST CAMERA EVER WAS CALLED THE ANDERSON MAMMOTH, MADE IN 1900. THIS WAS 9ft HIGH, 6ft WIDE & 20ft LONG & NEEDED A CREW OF 15 MEN TO OPERATE IT.

THE COLLODION WET-PLATE PROCESS
THE COLLODION WET-PLATE PROCESS WAS INVENTED IN 1851 BY SCOTT ARCHER. IT REDUCED THE TIME NEEDED FOR EXPOSURE FROM ABOUT 90 MINUTES TO 20 SECONDS. ITS MAIN DISADVANTAGE WAS THAT THE PHOTOGRAPHER HAD TO PROCESS THE IMAGE IMMEDIATELY. HOWEVER IT REMAINED POPULAR WELL INTO 20TH CENTURY & WAS EVEN USED TO PHOTOGRAPH THE SUMMIT OF MONT BLANC (REQUIRING 25 PORTERS TO CARRY UP THE COMPLETE PORTABLE DARK-ROOM).

HOW TO DRESS UP IN A DHOTI
BUY PIECE OF MATERIAL 12FT BY 3FT OR CUT UP & SEW TOGETHER AN OLD SHEET. DRAPE & FASTEN AS SHOWN ABOVE. IF UNCERTAIN CONSULT 'BODY & CLOTHES' BY J. BROBY JOHANSEN (FABER).

PHRASES
MANNER OF LINGUISTIC EXPRESSION

ABOVE BOARD
BOARD IS AN OLD ENGLISH WORD FOR TABLE. THE PHRASE COMES FROM THE PRACTICE OF CARD CHEATS HOLDING THEIR CARDS BELOW THE TABLE.

BLACK MARIA
THIS IS REPUTEDLY DERIVED FROM MARIA LEE, A LARGE, STRONG, BLACK LODGING HOUSE OWNER IN BOSTON, US, WHO OFTEN ASSISTED POLICE IN REMOVING THE DRUNK & DISORDERLY FROM HER HOUSE.

HIP HIP HURRAH
'HIP HIP' PROBABLY COMES FROM 'HEP, HEP', THE TRADITIONAL CRY OF THE JEW BAITERS OF MEDI-EVAL EUROPE. THE ORIGIN OF HURRAH IS UNCERTAIN. IT IS POSSIBLE THAT IT COMES FROM THE SLAVONIC 'HU RAJ' (TO PARADISE).

KICKING THE BUCKET
THE BUCKET IN THIS PHRASE ORIGINALLY RE-FERRED TO THE FRAME ON WHICH PIGS WERE HUNG AFTER SLAUGHTER.

LEFT IN THE LURCH
FROM THE GAME OF CRIBBAGE, DESCRIBING THE POSITION OF A PLAYER WHOSE SCORE IS UNDER 31 WHEN HIS OPPONENT REACHES 50.

LOCK, STOCK & BARREL
THIS ORIGINALLY REFERRED TO A GUN. THESE ARE THE THREE MAIN PARTS OF ANY GUN, SO THE PHRASE CAME TO MEAN 'COMPLETE'.

MAD AS A HATTER
ORIGINALLY 'MAD AS AN ATTER'. 'ATTER' IS THE SAXON WORD FOR ADDER OR VIPER. 'MAD' ORIGINALLY MEANT POISONOUS.

NUTS IN MAY
THIS COMES FROM 'KNOTS IN MAY' - BUNCHES OF BLOSSOM FROM THE HAWTHORN OR MAY TREE.

OUT OF SORTS
FIRST USED IN THE PRINTING INDUSTRY FOR A COMPOSITOR WHO COULD NOT GET ON WITH HIS WORK, BECAUSE HE WAS SHORT OF SOME LETTERS OF TYPE.

PIG IN A POKE
THIS COMES FROM AN OLD MARKET FRAUD. 'POKE' COMES FROM 'POCHE', WHICH MEANT BAG. THE TRADER PUT THE PIGLET INTO THE BAG FOR THE BUYER, BUT THEN SECRETLY SWAPPED IT FOR A SECOND BAG CONTAINING A KITTEN. 'LETTING THE CAT OUT OF THE BAG' COMES FROM THE SAME ORIGIN.

RAINING CATS & DOGS
THIS PROBABLY COMES FROM THE GREEK WORD 'CATADUPA' MEAN-ING WATERFALL.

UP TO SCRATCH
THIS COMES FROM EARLY BOXING MATCHES, WHEN CONTESTANTS HAD TO START EACH ROUND WITH THEIR LEFT FOOT ON A MARK SCRATCHED ON THE GROUND.

HOW TO GROW SALAD ON A SPONGE
PLACE SPONGE IN BOWL & POUR IN ONE cm OF WATER. SPRINKLE LETTUCE OR CRESS SEEDS ON SPONGE & LEAVE IN WARM LIGHT PLACE. WHEN SMALL PLANTS APPEAR, POUR SOME COLD TEA OR PLANT FOOD OVER TO ENCOURAGE GROWTH.

☆ PIANOS ☆
INSTRUMENTS WITH WIRES STRUCK BY HAMMERS MOVED BY KEYS

THE NEED FOR THE PIANO
BEFORE THE PIANO THE ONLY KEYBOARD INSTRUMENT WHOSE VOLUME VARIED WITH THE FORCE APPLIED TO THE KEYS WAS THE CLAVICHORD. UNFORTUNATELY THIS PRODUCED A VERY DELICATE SOUND MUCH QUIETER THAN THE HARPSICHORD & IT WAS DROWNED BY OTHER INSTRUMENTS. THE FIRST ATTEMPT TO BUILD A LOUDER, FINGER-RESPONSIVE INSTRUMENT CAME IN 1705. PANTALEON HEBENSTREIT CONSTRUCTED A GIANT DULCIMER WHICH HE PLAYED BY HITTING THE 200 STRINGS WITH STICKS. THE SOUND IMPRESSED MANY PEOPLE BUT THE INSTRUMENT WAS SO DIFFICULT TO PLAY THAT NOBODY ELSE MASTERED IT.

PIANO E FORTE
BARTOLOMMEO CHRISTOFORI MADE THE FIRST PRACTICAL PIANO IN ABOUT 1709, CALLING IT A 'GRAVICEMBALO COL PIANO E FORTE' (A KEYBOARD INSTRUMENT WITH SOFT & LOUD). HE PERFECTED THE FIRST MECHANISM WHICH PREVENTED A HAMMER FROM REMAINING IN CONTACT WITH ITS STRING (HENCE PREVENTING IT FROM VIBRATING). HOWEVER THE ITALIANS DID NOT APPRECIATE THE INNOVATION & CHRISTOFORI REVERTED TO MAKING KEYBOARD INSTRUMENTS LIKE THE HARPSICHORD IN WHICH THE STRINGS WERE PLUCKED.

THE WOODEN FRAME
THE CHIEF LIMITATION OF PIANOS IN THE EARLY 1800s WAS THEIR WOODEN FRAMES. THESE WERE FRAGILE & COULD ONLY BEAR STRINGS LIGHTER THAN ARE USED TODAY WHICH PRODUCED LESS VOLUME. LISZT PLAYED THEM WITH SUCH VIOLENCE THAT HE FREQUENTLY REQUIRED 3 INSTRUMENTS TO COMPLETE A CONCERT.

PIANO INFERNO
IN THE 1890s THE UPRIGHT IRON FRAME PIANO GAINED POPULARITY IN AMERICA SO QUICKLY THAT MANUFACTURERS WERE LEFT WITH AN EMBARRASSING QUANTITY OF HORIZONTAL 'SQUARE' PIANOS TAKEN IN PART EXCHANGE. THEY DISPOSED OF THEM IN FLAMBOYANT STYLE, CO-OPERATING TO BUILD A 50ft PYRAMID OF THE OBSOLETE PIANOS WHICH THEY SET FIRE TO IN 1903.

THE IRON FRAME
EUROPEAN INSTRUMENT MAKERS, USED TO WORKING WITH WOOD, WERE SUSPICIOUS OF THE USE OF METAL, & IT WAS LEFT TO AN AMERICAN CALLED BABCOCK TO CAST THE FIRST IRON PIANO FRAME IN 1825. THIS WAS DEVELOPED & PERFECTED BY AN IMMIGRANT CALLED STEINWEG, WHO ARRIVED IN AMERICA IN 1850 & CHANGED HIS NAME TO STEINWAY. THE IRON FRAME ENABLED MUCH LARGER HAMMERS TO BE USED WITH HEAVIER, LOUDER STRINGS, INCREASING THE MAXIMUM STRING TENSION FROM 3 TO 30 TONS. STEINWAY'S DESIGN HAS REMAINED VIRTUALLY UNCHANGED EVER SINCE.

PIANOS TODAY
ABOUT 2¼ MILLION HOMES IN BRITAIN HAVE PIANOS; FROM 6% IN LONDON TO 20% IN WALES & NORTH ENGLAND. MOST HAVE NOT BEEN TUNED IN THE LAST 2 YEARS (89% OF THOSE OWNED BY MANUAL WORKERS & OLD-AGE PENSIONERS)

HOW TO ETCH YOUR NAME ON AN EGG SHELL
PAINT NAME IN HOT MOLTEN WAX OR FAT. THEN IMMERSE EGG IN VINEGAR FOR 2 HOURS TO ETCH REMAINDER OF SHELL. REMOVE EGG & WASH OFF WAX WITH TURPS.

BRITAIN V AUSTRIA
IN THE EARLY 1800s THERE WERE 2 RIVAL PIANO MECHANISMS; THE ENGLISH, PERFECTED BY JOHN BROADWOOD, & THE VIENNESE PERFECTED BY JOHANN STEIN. BY 1850 THE VIENNESE HAD DISAPPEARED FROM THE MUSICAL SCENE. THIS WAS PARTLY DUE TO THE GREATER VOLUME OF THE ENGLISH PIANO, WHICH SUITED THE EMERGING ROMANTIC STYLE, & PARTLY TO BROADWOOD'S BUSINESS ACUMEN, ENERGETIC SALESMANSHIP & INTRODUCTION OF MASS PRODUCTION.

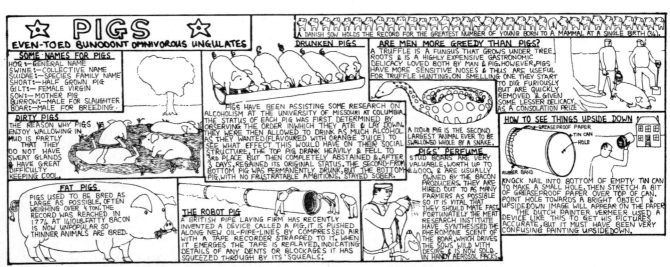

☆ PIGS ☆
EVEN-TOED BUNODONT OMNIVOROUS UNGULATES

A DANISH SOW HOLDS THE RECORD FOR THE GREATEST NUMBER OF YOUNG BORN TO A MAMMAL AT A SINGLE BIRTH (34).

SOME NAMES FOR PIGS
HOG:— GENERAL NAME
SWINE:— COLLECTIVE NAME
SUIDAE:— SPECIES FAMILY NAME
SHOAT:— HALF GROWN PIG
GILT:— FEMALE VIRGIN
SOW:— MOTHER PIG
BURROW:— MALE FOR SLAUGHTER
BOAR:— MALE FOR BREEDING

DIRTY PIGS
THE REASON WHY PIGS ENJOY WALLOWING IN MUD IS PARTLY THAT THEY DO NOT HAVE SWEAT GLANDS & HAVE GREAT DIFFICULTY KEEPING COOL.

DRUNKEN PIGS
PIGS HAVE BEEN ASSISTING SOME RESEARCH ON ALCOHOLISM AT THE UNIVERSITY OF MISSOURI AT COLUMBIA. THE STATUS OF EACH PIG WAS FIRST DETERMINED BY OBSERVING THE ORDER IN WHICH THEY ATE & LAY DOWN. THEY WERE THEN ALLOWED TO DRINK AS MUCH ALCOHOL AS THEY WANTED (FLAVOURED WITH ORANGE JUICE) TO SEE WHAT EFFECT THIS WOULD HAVE ON THEIR SOCIAL STRUCTURE. THE TOP PIG DRANK HEAVILY & FELL TO 3RD PLACE BUT THEN COMPLETELY ABSTAINED &, AFTER 3 DAYS, REGAINED ITS ORIGINAL STATUS. THE SECOND-FROM BOTTOM PIG WAS PERMANENTLY DRUNK, BUT THE BOTTOM PIG, WITH NO FRUSTRATABLE AMBITIONS, STAYED SOBER.

ARE MEN MORE GREEDY THAN PIGS?
A TRUFFLE IS A FUNGUS THAT GROWS UNDER TREE ROOTS & IS A HIGHLY EXPENSIVE GASTRONOMIC DELICACY LOVED BOTH BY MAN & PIG. HOWEVER, PIGS HAVE MORE SENSITIVE NOSES & THUS ARE USEFUL FOR TRUFFLE HUNTING. ON SMELLING ONE THEY START TO DIG FURIOUSLY BUT ARE QUICKLY REMOVED & GIVEN SOME LESSER DELICACY AS A CONSOLATION PRIZE

A 120LB PIG IS THE SECOND LARGEST ANIMAL EVER TO BE SWALLOWED WHOLE BY A SNAKE.

PIGS' PERFUME
STUD BOARS ARE VERY VALUABLE, WORTH UP TO £4000, & ARE USUALLY OWNED BY THE BACON PRODUCERS. THEY ARE HIRED OUT TO AS MANY FARMERS AS POSSIBLE SO IT IS VITAL THAT THEY SHOULD MATE FAST. FORTUNATELY THE MEAT RESEARCH INSTITUTE HAVE SYNTHESISED THE PHEROMONE SCENT OF THE BOAR WHICH DRIVES THE SOWS WILD WITH DESIRE & IS NOW SOLD IN HANDY AEROSOL PACKS.

HOW TO SEE THINGS UPSIDE DOWN
KNOCK NAIL INTO BOTTOM OF EMPTY TIN CAN TO MAKE A SMALL HOLE, THEN STRETCH A BIT OF GREASEPROOF PAPER OVER TOP OF CAN. POINT HOLE TOWARDS A BRIGHT OBJECT & UPSIDEDOWN IMAGE WILL APPEAR ON THE PAPER. THE DUTCH PAINTER VERMEER USED A DEVICE LIKE THIS TO GET HIS PICTURES ACCURATE, BUT IT MUST HAVE BEEN VERY CONFUSING PAINTING UPSIDEDOWN.

FAT PIGS
PIGS USED TO BE BRED AS LARGE AS POSSIBLE, OFTEN WEIGHING OVER ½ TON. THE RECORD WAS REACHED IN 1774 AT 1410LB. FATTY BACON IS NOW UNPOPULAR SO THINNER ANIMALS ARE BRED.

THE ROBOT PIG
A BRITISH PIPE LAYING FIRM HAS RECENTLY INVENTED A DEVICE CALLED A PIG. IT IS PUSHED ALONG NEW OIL-PIPE-LINES BY COMPRESSED AIR WITH A TAPE RECORDER STRAPPED TO IT. WHEN IT EMERGES THE TAPE IS REPLAYED, INDICATING DETAILS OF ANY DENTS OR BLOCKAGES IT HAS SQUEEZED THROUGH BY ITS 'SQUEALS'.

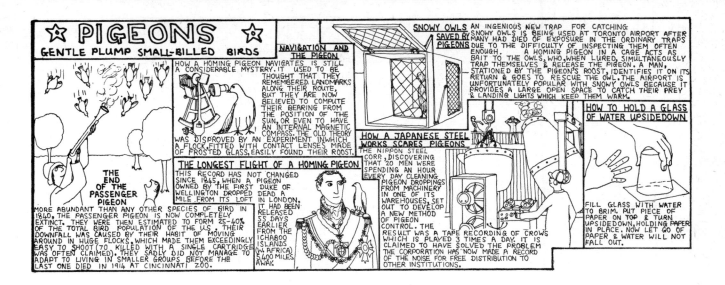

☆ PIGEONS ☆
GENTLE PLUMP SMALL-BILLED BIRDS

THE END OF THE PASSENGER PIGEON

MORE ABUNDANT THAN ANY OTHER SPECIES OF BIRD IN 1840, THE PASSENGER PIGEON IS NOW COMPLETELY EXTINCT. THEY WERE THEN ESTIMATED TO FORM 25-40% OF THE TOTAL BIRD POPULATION OF THE U.S. THEIR DOWNFALL WAS CAUSED BY THEIR HABIT OF MOVING AROUND IN HUGE FLOCKS, WHICH MADE THEM EXCEEDINGLY EASY TO SHOOT (70 KILLED WITH A SINGLE CARTRIDGE WAS OFTEN CLAIMED). THEY SADLY DID NOT MANAGE TO ADAPT TO LIVING IN SMALLER GROUPS BEFORE THE LAST ONE DIED IN 1914 AT CINCINNATI ZOO.

NAVIGATION AND THE PIGEON

HOW A HOMING PIGEON NAVIGATES IS STILL A CONSIDERABLE MYSTERY. IT USED TO BE THOUGHT THAT THEY REMEMBERED LANDMARKS ALONG THEIR ROUTE, BUT THEY ARE NOW BELIEVED TO COMPUTE THEIR BEARING FROM THE POSITION OF THE SUN, OR EVEN TO HAVE AN INTERNAL MAGNETIC COMPASS. THE OLD THEORY WAS DISPROVED BY AN EXPERIMENT IN WHICH A FLOCK, FITTED WITH CONTACT LENSES MADE OF FROSTED GLASS, EASILY FOUND THEIR ROOST.

THE LONGEST FLIGHT OF A HOMING PIGEON

THIS RECORD HAS NOT CHANGED SINCE 1845, WHEN A PIGEON OWNED BY THE FIRST DUKE OF WELLINGTON DROPPED DEAD IN LONDON. IT HAD BEEN RELEASED 55 DAYS EARLIER FROM THE ICHABOO ISLANDS (W. AFRICA) 5,400 MILES AWAY.

HOW A JAPANESE STEEL WORKS SCARES PIGEONS

THE NIPPON STEEL CORP., DISCOVERING THAT 20 MEN WERE SPENDING AN HOUR EVERY DAY CLEANING PIGEON DROPPINGS FROM MACHINERY IN ONE OF ITS WAREHOUSES, SET OUT TO DEVELOP A NEW METHOD OF PIGEON CONTROL. THE RESULT WAS A TAPE RECORDING OF CROWS WHICH IS PLAYED 3 TIMES A DAY. IT IS CLAIMED TO HAVE SOLVED THE PROBLEM & THE CORPORATION HAS NOW MADE A RECORD OF THE NOISE FOR FREE DISTRIBUTION TO OTHER INSTITUTIONS.

SNOWY OWLS SAVED BY PIGEONS

AN INGENIOUS NEW TRAP FOR CATCHING SNOWY OWLS IS BEING USED AT TORONTO AIRPORT AFTER MANY HAD DIED OF EXPOSURE IN THE ORDINARY TRAPS DUE TO THE DIFFICULTY OF INSPECTING THEM OFTEN ENOUGH. A HOMING PIGEON IN A CAGE ACTS AS BAIT TO THE OWLS, WHO, WHEN LURED, SIMULTANEOUSLY TRAP THEMSELVES & RELEASE THE PIGEON. A MAN, STATIONED BY THE PIGEON'S ROOST, IDENTIFIES IT ON ITS RETURN & GOES TO RESCUE THE OWL. THE AIRPORT IS UNFORTUNATELY POPULAR WITH SNOWY OWLS BECAUSE IT PROVIDES A LARGE OPEN SPACE TO CATCH THEIR PREY & LANDING LIGHTS WHICH KEEP THEM WARM.

HOW TO HOLD A GLASS OF WATER UPSIDE DOWN

FILL GLASS WITH WATER TO BRIM. PUT PIECE OF PAPER ON TOP & TURN UPSIDEDOWN, HOLDING PAPER IN PLACE. NOW LET GO OF PAPER & WATER WILL NOT FALL OUT.

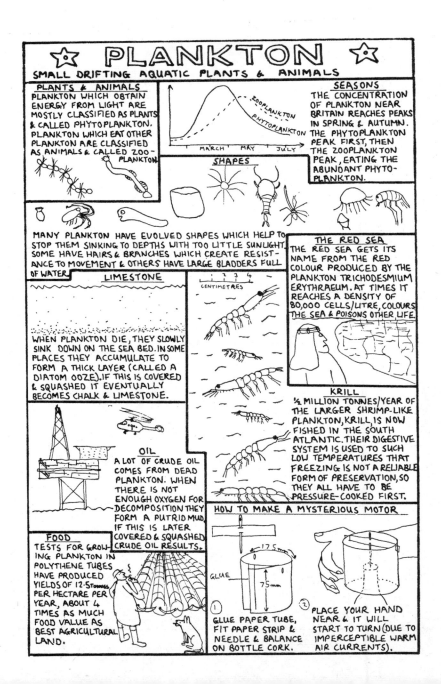

☆ PLANKTON ☆
SMALL DRIFTING AQUATIC PLANTS & ANIMALS

PLANTS & ANIMALS

PLANKTON WHICH OBTAIN ENERGY FROM LIGHT ARE MOSTLY CLASSIFIED AS PLANTS & CALLED PHYTOPLANKTON. PLANKTON WHICH EAT OTHER PLANKTON ARE CLASSIFIED AS ANIMALS & CALLED ZOO-PLANKTON.

SEASONS

THE CONCENTRATION OF PLANKTON NEAR BRITAIN REACHES PEAKS IN SPRING & AUTUMN. THE PHYTOPLANKTON PEAK FIRST, THEN THE ZOOPLANKTON PEAK, EATING THE ABUNDANT PHYTO-PLANKTON.

SHAPES

MANY PLANKTON HAVE EVOLVED SHAPES WHICH HELP TO STOP THEM SINKING TO DEPTHS WITH TOO LITTLE SUNLIGHT. SOME HAVE HAIRS & BRANCHES WHICH CREATE RESISTANCE TO MOVEMENT & OTHERS HAVE LARGE BLADDERS FULL OF WATER.

LIMESTONE

WHEN PLANKTON DIE, THEY SLOWLY SINK DOWN ON THE SEA BED. IN SOME PLACES THEY ACCUMULATE TO FORM A THICK LAYER (CALLED A DIATOM OOZE). IF THIS IS COVERED & SQUASHED IT EVENTUALLY BECOMES CHALK & LIMESTONE.

THE RED SEA

THE RED SEA GETS ITS NAME FROM THE RED COLOUR PRODUCED BY THE PLANKTON TRICHODESMIUM ERYTHRAEUM. AT TIMES IT REACHES A DENSITY OF 80,000 CELLS/LITRE, COLOURS THE SEA & POISONS OTHER LIFE.

KRILL

½ MILLION TONNES/YEAR OF THE LARGER SHRIMP-LIKE PLANKTON, KRILL, IS NOW FISHED IN THE SOUTH ATLANTIC. THEIR DIGESTIVE SYSTEM IS USED TO SUCH LOW TEMPERATURES THAT FREEZING IS NOT A RELIABLE FORM OF PRESERVATION, SO THEY ALL HAVE TO BE PRESSURE-COOKED FIRST.

OIL

A LOT OF CRUDE OIL COMES FROM DEAD PLANKTON. WHEN THERE IS NOT ENOUGH OXYGEN FOR DECOMPOSITION THEY FORM A PUTRID MUD. IF THIS IS LATER COVERED & SQUASHED CRUDE OIL RESULTS.

FOOD

TESTS FOR GROWING PLANKTON IN POLYTHENE TUBES HAVE PRODUCED YIELDS OF 12.5 TONNES PER HECTARE PER YEAR, ABOUT 4 TIMES AS MUCH FOOD VALUE AS BEST AGRICULTURAL LAND.

HOW TO MAKE A MYSTERIOUS MOTOR

(1) GLUE PAPER TUBE, FIT PAPER STRIP & NEEDLE & BALANCE ON BOTTLE CORK.

(2) PLACE YOUR HAND NEAR & IT WILL START TO TURN (DUE TO IMPERCEPTIBLE WARM AIR CURRENTS).

☆ PLATINUM ☆

RARE SILVER-COLOURED METAL WITH PROPERTIES SIMILAR TO GOLD

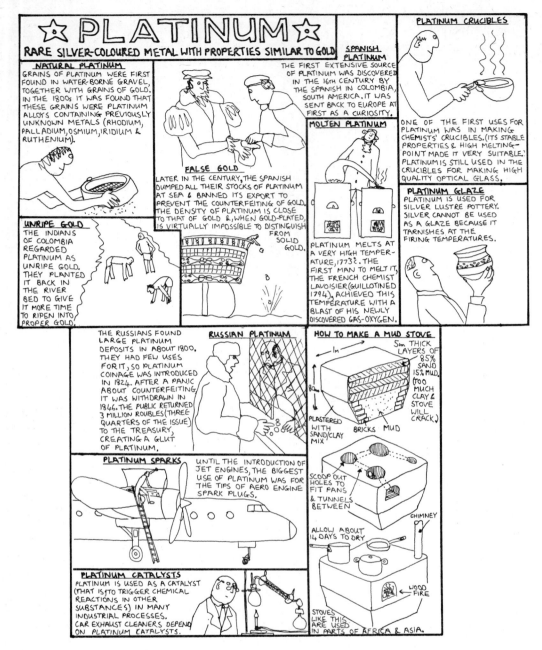

NATURAL PLATINUM

GRAINS OF PLATINUM WERE FIRST FOUND IN WATER-BORNE GRAVEL, TOGETHER WITH GRAINS OF GOLD. IN THE 1800s IT WAS FOUND THAT THESE GRAINS WERE PLATINUM ALLOYS CONTAINING PREVIOUSLY UNKNOWN METALS (RHODIUM, PALLADIUM, OSMIUM, IRIDIUM & RUTHENIUM).

UNRIPE GOLD

THE INDIANS OF COLOMBIA REGARDED PLATINUM AS UNRIPE GOLD. THEY PLANTED IT BACK IN THE RIVER BED TO GIVE IT MORE TIME TO RIPEN INTO PROPER GOLD.

SPANISH PLATINUM

THE FIRST EXTENSIVE SOURCE OF PLATINUM WAS DISCOVERED IN THE 16TH CENTURY BY THE SPANISH IN COLOMBIA, SOUTH AMERICA. IT WAS SENT BACK TO EUROPE AT FIRST AS A CURIOSITY.

FALSE GOLD

LATER IN THE CENTURY, THE SPANISH DUMPED ALL THEIR STOCKS OF PLATINUM AT SEA & BANNED ITS EXPORT TO PREVENT THE COUNTERFEITING OF GOLD. THE DENSITY OF PLATINUM IS CLOSE TO THAT OF GOLD &, WHEN GOLD-PLATED, IS VIRTUALLY IMPOSSIBLE TO DISTINGUISH FROM SOLID GOLD.

MOLTEN PLATINUM

PLATINUM MELTS AT A VERY HIGH TEMPERATURE, 1773°C. THE FIRST MAN TO MELT IT, THE FRENCH CHEMIST LAVOISIER (GUILLOTINED 1794), ACHIEVED THIS TEMPERATURE WITH A BLAST OF HIS NEWLY DISCOVERED GAS-OXYGEN.

PLATINUM CRUCIBLES

ONE OF THE FIRST USES FOR PLATINUM WAS IN MAKING CHEMISTS' CRUCIBLES. (ITS STABLE PROPERTIES & HIGH MELTING-POINT MADE IT VERY SUITABLE.) PLATINUM IS STILL USED IN THE CRUCIBLES FOR MAKING HIGH QUALITY OPTICAL GLASS.

PLATINUM GLAZE

PLATINUM IS USED FOR SILVER LUSTRE POTTERY. SILVER CANNOT BE USED AS A GLAZE BECAUSE IT TARNISHES AT THE FIRING TEMPERATURES.

RUSSIAN PLATINUM

THE RUSSIANS FOUND LARGE PLATINUM DEPOSITS IN ABOUT 1800. THEY HAD FEW USES FOR IT, SO PLATINUM COINAGE WAS INTRODUCED IN 1824. AFTER A PANIC ABOUT COUNTERFEITING IT WAS WITHDRAWN IN 1846. THE PUBLIC RETURNED 3 MILLION ROUBLES (THREE QUARTERS OF THE ISSUE) TO THE TREASURY, CREATING A GLUT OF PLATINUM.

PLATINUM SPARKS

UNTIL THE INTRODUCTION OF JET ENGINES, THE BIGGEST USE OF PLATINUM WAS FOR THE TIPS OF AERO ENGINE SPARK PLUGS.

PLATINUM CATALYSTS

PLATINUM IS USED AS A CATALYST (THAT IS, TO TRIGGER CHEMICAL REACTIONS IN OTHER SUBSTANCES) IN MANY INDUSTRIAL PROCESSES. CAR EXHAUST CLEANERS DEPEND ON PLATINUM CATALYSTS.

HOW TO MAKE A MUD STOVE

5cm THICK LAYERS OF 85% SAND 15% MUD. (TOO MUCH CLAY & STOVE WILL CRACK.)

PLASTERED WITH SAND/CLAY MIX

BRICKS   MUD

SCOOP OUT HOLES TO FIT PANS & TUNNELS BETWEEN

ALLOW ABOUT 14 DAYS TO DRY

CHIMNEY

WOOD FIRE

STOVES LIKE THIS ARE USED IN PARTS OF AFRICA & ASIA.

☆ PLAYING CARDS ☆

IMPLEMENTS OF GAMING, CONJURING & DIVINATION

THE OBSCURE ORIGINS

LONG BEFORE PLAYING CARDS APPEARED IN EUROPE, THE CHINESE HAD A SORT OF PACK WITH DESIGNS BASED ON THEIR PAPER MONEY. THE INDIANS HAD A PACK WITH RELIGIOUS DESIGNS BASED ON THE VARIOUS INCARNATIONS OF THE HINDU GOD VISHNU. IT IS NOT KNOWN EXACTLY HOW CARDS SPREAD TO EUROPE BUT THEIR FIRST MENTION OCCURS IN A SERMON OF 1377 CASTIGATING GAMBLING. THEIR POPULARITY SPREAD FAST & BY 1400 HAD ALREADY BEEN BANNED FOR ENCOURAGING GAMBLING IN FLORENCE, BASLE & OTHER CITIES.

TEACHING PACKS

IN THE 1600s EDUCATIONAL PACKS STARTED TO APPEAR. HERALDRY, AN ESSENTIAL PART OF THE EDUCATION OF GENTLEMEN, WAS THE USUAL SUBJECT. EACH CARD DEPICTED A SHIELD WITH A SHORT EXPLANATION IN ADDITION TO ITS VALUE & SUIT. OTHER SUBJECTS INCLUDED WARFARE, ASTRONOMY, GEOGRAPHY & EVEN CARVING, (ADVERTISED AS SHOWING THE BEST MANNER OF CUTTING UP ALL SORTS OF WILD & TAME FOWL, FISH & FLESH.)

GOD'S HEAD

TRANSFORMATION PACKS

IN 1809 A VOGUE STARTED FOR TRANSFORMATION PACKS. SO-CALLED BECAUSE THE PIPS ON EACH CARD WERE TRANSFORMED INTO PEOPLE & DESIGNS. GAMBLERS FOUND THEM DISTRACTING & PRODUCTION SOON CEASED.

A POPULAR IMPROVEMENT

MR DE LA RUE EARNED A PRECARIOUS LIVING MAKING STRAW HATS IN LONDON UNTIL HE PATENTED COLOUR PRINTED PLAYING CARDS IN 1832. HIS INVENTION WAS ENTHUSIASTICALLY WELCOMED BY GAMBLERS. THE DESIGN PRINTED ON THE BACK MASKED ANY FLAWS IN THE PAPER, THEREBY PREVENTING A CHEAT FROM RECOGNISING A CARD IN HIS OPPONENT'S HAND. IT ALSO REDUCED THE PRICE OF CARDS SINCE CHEAPER PAPER COULD BE USED.

AMERICAN INNOVATIONS

THE AMERICANS INVENTED DOUBLE ENDED CARDS, ALSO THE SATINED SURFACE & ROUNDED CORNERS NOW UNIVERSAL. THEY ATTEMPTED TO CHANGE THE COURT CARDS TO MORE APPROPRIATE FEDERAL SYMBOLS AFTER THE WAR OF INDEPENDENCE. QUEENS BECAME GODDESSES OF LIBERTY, KINGS BECAME INFANTRY OFFICERS & JACKS BECAME ARTILLERY OFFICERS. THESE NEVER GAINED MUCH POPULARITY.

NEW IDEAS

PLAYING CARD DESIGN HAS NOT CHANGED GREATLY SINCE 1900 DESPITE VARIOUS ATTEMPTS. WADDINGTONS TRIED MARKETING CIRCULAR CARDS IN THE 1920s, BARREL SHAPED CARDS IN THE 1950s, & ZULU SHIELD SHAPED CARDS IN 1954. DE LA RUE TRIED FIVE SUITED PACKS FOR BRIDGE IN 1935 & VARIOUS COMPANIES HAVE TRIED PRINTING EACH SUIT IN A DIFFERENT COLOUR TO AID RECOGNITION.

METAL CARDS

PACKS MADE OF SHEET IRON, WEIGHING 4KG WERE MADE IN VIENNA IN 1850. ALUMINIUM PACKS, TRIED IN 1901 IN AMERICA, WEIGHED ONLY 120 GMS BUT WERE NO MORE SUCCESSFUL.

HOW TO MAKE YOUR HANDS INTO A DOVE

ARRANGE HANDS AS ABOVE CLOSE TO WALL IN FRONT OF LIGHT. DOVE WILL APPEAR ON WALL.

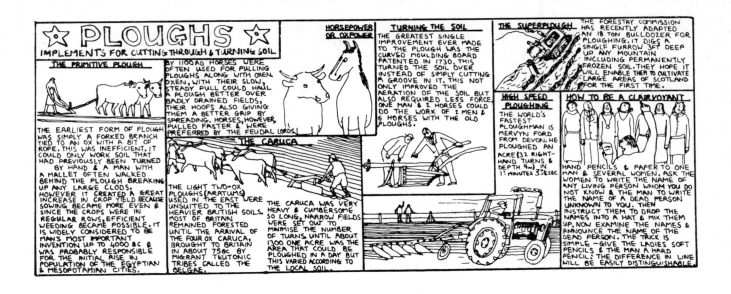

☆ PLOUGHS ☆
IMPLEMENTS FOR CUTTING THROUGH & TURNING SOIL

THE PRIMITIVE PLOUGH

THE EARLIEST FORM OF PLOUGH WAS SIMPLY A FORKED BRANCH TIED TO AN OX WITH A BIT OF ROPE. THIS WAS INEFFICIENT. IT COULD ONLY WORK SOIL THAT HAD PREVIOUSLY BEEN TURNED BY HAND & A MAN WITH A MALLET OFTEN WALKED BEHIND THE PLOUGH BREAKING UP ANY LARGE CLODS. HOWEVER IT CREATED A GREAT INCREASE IN CROP YIELD BECAUSE SOWING BECAME MORE EVEN & SINCE THE CROPS WERE IN REGULAR ROWS, EFFICIENT WEEDING BECAME POSSIBLE. IT IS WIDELY CONSIDERED TO BE MAN'S MOST IMPORTANT INVENTION UP TO 4000 BC & WAS PROBABLY RESPONSIBLE FOR THE INITIAL RISE IN POPULATION OF THE EGYPTIAN & MESOPOTAMIAN CITIES.

BY 1100AD HORSES WERE OFTEN USED FOR PULLING PLOUGHS ALONG WITH OXEN. OXEN, WITH THEIR SLOW, STEADY PULL COULD HAUL A PLOUGH BETTER OVER BADLY DRAINED FIELDS, THEIR HOOFS ALSO GIVING THEM A BETTER GRIP BY SPREADING. HORSES, HOWEVER PULLED FASTER & WERE PREFERRED BY THE FEUDAL LORDS.

THE CARUCA

THE LIGHT TWO-OX PLOUGHS (ARATRUMS) USED IN THE EAST WERE UNSUITED TO THE HEAVIER BRITISH SOILS. MOST OF BRITAIN REMAINED FORESTED UNTIL THE ARRIVAL OF THE FOUR OX CARUCA, BROUGHT TO BRITAIN IN ABOUT 75 BC BY MIGRANT TEUTONIC TRIBES CALLED THE BELGAE.

THE CARUCA WAS VERY HEAVY & CUMBERSOME SO LONG, NARROW FIELDS WERE SET OUT TO MINIMISE THE NUMBER OF TURNS UNTIL ABOUT 1300 ONE ACRE WAS THE AREA THAT COULD BE PLOUGHED IN A DAY BUT THIS VARIED ACCORDING TO THE LOCAL SOIL.

HORSEPOWER OR OXPOWER

TURNING THE SOIL

THE GREATEST SINGLE IMPROVEMENT EVER MADE TO THE PLOUGH WAS THE CURVED MOULDING BOARD PATENTED IN 1730. THIS TURNED THE SOIL OVER INSTEAD OF SIMPLY CUTTING A GROOVE IN IT. THIS NOT ONLY IMPROVED THE AERATION OF THE SOIL BUT ALSO REQUIRED LESS FORCE. ONE MAN & 2 HORSES COULD DO THE WORK OF 2 MEN & 6 HORSES WITH THE OLD PLOUGHS.

THE SUPERPLOUGH

THE FORESTRY COMMISSION HAS RECENTLY ADAPTED AN 18 TON BULLDOZER FOR PLOUGHING. IT DIGS A SINGLE FURROW 3FT DEEP UP ANY MOUNTAIN INCLUDING PERMANENTLY FROZEN SOIL. THEY HOPE IT WILL ENABLE THEM TO CULTIVATE LARGE AREAS OF SCOTLAND FOR THE FIRST TIME.

HIGH SPEED PLOUGHING

THE WORLD'S FASTEST PLOUGHMAN IS MERVYN FORD FROM DEVON. HE PLOUGHED AN ACRE (32 RIGHT-HAND TURNS & DEPTH 9IN) IN 11 MINUTES 33½SEC.

HOW TO BE A CLAIRVOYANT

HAND PENCILS & PAPER TO ONE MAN & SEVERAL WOMEN. ASK THE WOMEN TO WRITE THE NAME OF ANY LIVING PERSON WHOM YOU DO NOT KNOW & THE MAN TO WRITE THE NAME OF A DEAD PERSON UNKNOWN TO YOU. THEN INSTRUCT THEM TO DROP THE NAMES INTO A HAT & MIX THEM UP. NOW EXAMINE THE NAMES & ANNOUNCE THE NAME OF THE DEAD PERSON. THE TRICK IS SIMPLE — GIVE THE LADIES SOFT PENCILS & THE MAN A HARD PENCIL. THE DIFFERENCE IN LINE WILL BE EASILY DISTINGUISHABLE.

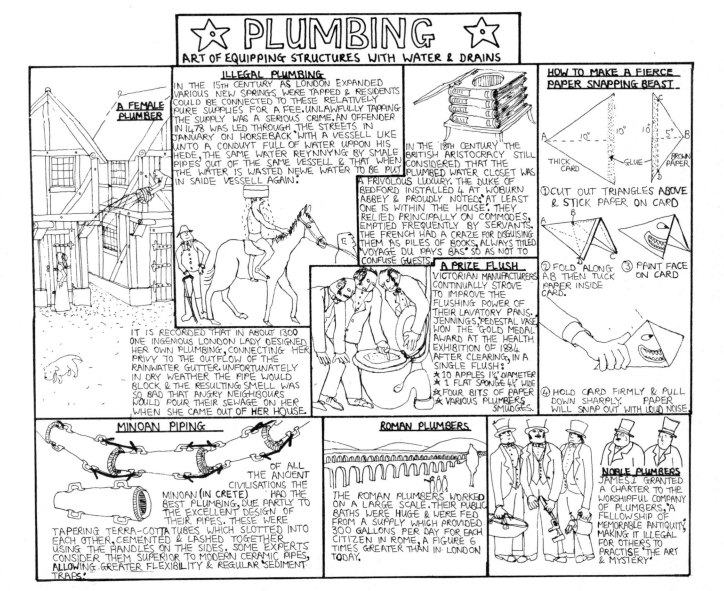

☆ PLUMBING ☆
ART OF EQUIPPING STRUCTURES WITH WATER & DRAINS

A FEMALE PLUMBER

IT IS RECORDED THAT IN ABOUT 1300 ONE INGENIOUS LONDON LADY DESIGNED HER OWN PLUMBING, CONNECTING HER PRIVY TO THE OUTFLOW OF THE RAINWATER GUTTER. UNFORTUNATELY IN DRY WEATHER THE PIPE WOULD BLOCK & THE RESULTING SMELL WAS SO BAD THAT ANGRY NEIGHBOURS WOULD POUR THEIR SEWAGE ON HER WHEN SHE CAME OUT OF HER HOUSE.

ILLEGAL PLUMBING

IN THE 15TH CENTURY AS LONDON EXPANDED VARIOUS NEW SPRINGS WERE TAPPED & RESIDENTS COULD BE CONNECTED TO THESE RELATIVELY PURE SUPPLIES FOR A FEE. UNLAWFULLY TAPPING THE SUPPLY WAS A SERIOUS CRIME. AN OFFENDER IN 1478 WAS LED THROUGH THE STREETS IN JANUARY ON HORSEBACK 'WITH A VESSELL LIKE UNTO A CONDUYT FULL OF WATER UPPON HIS HEDE, THE SAME WATER REYNNYNG BY SMALE PIPES OUT OF THE SAME VESSELL & THAT WHEN THE WATER IS WASTED NEWE WATER TO BE PUT IN SAIDE VESSELL AGAIN.'

IN THE 18TH CENTURY THE BRITISH ARISTOCRACY STILL CONSIDERED THAT THE PLUMBED WATER CLOSET WAS A FRIVOLOUS LUXURY. THE DUKE OF BEDFORD INSTALLED 4 AT WOBURN ABBEY & PROUDLY NOTED: 'AT LEAST ONE IS WITHIN THE HOUSE.' THEY RELIED PRINCIPALLY ON COMMODES, EMPTIED FREQUENTLY BY SERVANTS. THE FRENCH HAD A CRAZE FOR DISGUISING THEM AS PILES OF BOOKS, ALWAYS TITLED 'VOYAGE DU PAYS BAS' SO AS NOT TO CONFUSE GUESTS.

A PRIZE FLUSH

VICTORIAN MANUFACTURERS CONTINUALLY STROVE TO IMPROVE THE FLUSHING POWER OF THEIR LAVATORY PANS. JENNINGS' PEDESTAL VASE WON THE 'GOLD MEDAL' AWARD AT THE HEALTH EXHIBITION OF 1884 AFTER CLEARING, IN A SINGLE FLUSH:
★ 10 APPLES 1¾" DIAMETER
★ 1 FLAT SPONGE 4½" WIDE
★ FOUR BITS OF PAPER
★ VARIOUS PLUMBERS' SMUDGES.

HOW TO MAKE A FIERCE PAPER SNAPPING BEAST

① CUT OUT TRIANGLES ABOVE & STICK PAPER ON CARD
② FOLD ALONG A.B THEN TUCK PAPER INSIDE CARD.
③ PAINT FACE ON CARD
④ HOLD CARD FIRMLY & PULL DOWN SHARPLY. PAPER WILL SNAP OUT WITH LOUD NOISE.

MINOAN PIPING

OF ALL THE ANCIENT CIVILISATIONS THE MINOAN (IN CRETE) HAD THE BEST PLUMBING, DUE PARTLY TO THE EXCELLENT DESIGN OF THEIR PIPES. THESE WERE TAPERING TERRA-COTTA TUBES WHICH SLOTTED INTO EACH OTHER, CEMENTED & LASHED TOGETHER USING THE HANDLES ON THE SIDES. SOME EXPERTS CONSIDER THEM SUPERIOR TO MODERN CERAMIC PIPES, ALLOWING GREATER FLEXIBILITY & REGULAR 'SEDIMENT TRAPS.'

ROMAN PLUMBERS

THE ROMAN PLUMBERS WORKED ON A LARGE SCALE. THEIR PUBLIC BATHS WERE HUGE & WERE FED FROM A SUPPLY WHICH PROVIDED 300 GALLONS PER DAY FOR EACH CITIZEN IN ROME, A FIGURE 6 TIMES GREATER THAN IN LONDON TODAY.

NOBLE PLUMBERS

JAMES I GRANTED A CHARTER TO THE WORSHIPFUL COMPANY OF PLUMBERS, 'A FELLOWSHIP OF MEMORABLE ANTIQUITY', MAKING IT ILLEGAL FOR OTHERS TO PRACTISE 'THE ART & MYSTERY.'

☆ PLUTONIUM ☆
RADIOACTIVE MAN-MADE ELEMENT

APPEARANCE
PLUTONIUM RESEMBLES THE METAL NICKEL BUT TARNISHES QUICKLY & GROWS A POWDERY GREEN COATING OF PLUTONIUM OXIDE, AS THOUGH IT HAS GONE MOULDY. IF THE AIR IS DAMP IT MAY CATCH FIRE SPONTANEOUSLY & THE SMOKE IS EXTREMELY POISONOUS.

DISCOVERY
PLUTONIUM WAS FIRST CREATED IN 1940 AT BERKELEY, CALIFORNIA, USA, BY A PHYSICIST CALLED SEABORG, WHO WAS LATER AWARDED A NOBEL CHEMISTRY PRIZE FOR HIS WORK. THE ENTIRE WORLD'S SUPPLY WAS AT FIRST KEPT IN A MATCHBOX IN SEABORG'S DESK.

MANUFACTURE

ATOM BOMBS
PLUTONIUM WAS FIRST MANUFACTURED FOR USE AS NUCLEAR BOMBS. IF A LUMP OF PLUTONIUM LARGER THAN THE SIZE OF A GRAPEFRUIT IS ASSEMBLED, IT BECOMES UNSTABLE & STARTS AN UNCONTROLLABLE CHAIN REACTION (THE NUCLEAR EXPLOSION).
THE FIRST BOMBS CONTAINED TWO SMALL LUMPS OF PLUTONIUM HALF THE SIZE OF A GRAPEFRUIT. TO DETONATE THE BOMB, ONE LUMP IS SHOT AT THE OTHER (THE FASTER THE PARTS UNITE, THE BIGGER THE BANG).

PLUTONIUM IS MANUFACTURED AS A BY-PRODUCT FROM URANIUM FUELLED NUCLEAR REACTORS. ABOUT 1% OF THE URANIUM BECOMES PLUTONIUM IN THE REACTOR & THE USED REACTOR FUEL RODS ARE SENT TO A REPROCESSING PLANT TO EXTRACT THE PLUTONIUM. HERE THE RODS ARE CHOPPED INTO SMALL BITS & DISSOLVED IN NITRIC ACID. THE DISSOLVED RODS ARE THEN PASSED THROUGH A SERIES OF SOLVENTS WHICH EVENTUALLY ISOLATE PURE PLUTONIUM.

NUCLEAR REACTORS

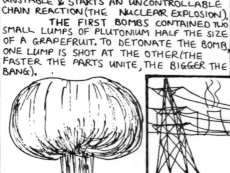

BREEDER REACTORS

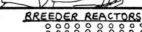
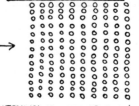

PLUTONIUM IS USED AS FUEL IN FAST BREEDER REACTORS WHICH PRODUCE MORE PLUTONIUM THAN THEY 'CONSUME' AS FUEL. THE PLUTONIUM IS SURROUNDED BY AN UNREACTIVE FORM OF URANIUM. AS THE PLUTONIUM REACTS, ITS RADIOACTIVE EMISSIONS CONVERT SOME OF THE SURROUNDING URANIUM INTO PLUTONIUM. THIS TECHNIQUE MULTIPLIES THE WORLD ENERGY SUPPLY 140 TIMES.

A LUMP OF PLUTONIUM SLIGHTLY SMALLER THAN THE GRAPEFRUIT NEEDED TO MAKE A BOMB WILL BECOME VERY HOT BUT WILL NOT EXPLODE. NUCLEAR POWER STATIONS COULD USE THIS HEAT TO GENERATE STEAM WHICH POWERS TURBINES & ELECTRIC GENERATORS.

REPROCESSING

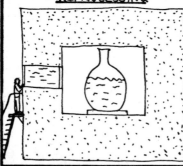

THE DESIGN OF REPROCESSING PLANTS IS COMPLICATED BY THE NEED TO SHIELD EVERY STAGE OF THE PROCESS IN 2m-THICK CONCRETE CELLS. THE EQUIPMENT HAS TO BE SIMPLE & HIGHLY RELIABLE AS THE CELLS ARE TOO RADIOACTIVE TO ENTER IF ANYTHING GOES WRONG.

HOW TO VANISH FROM A DOORWAY

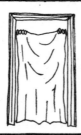

STAND IN DOORWAY HOLDING CLOTH RAISE CLOTH ABOVE HEAD SO AUDIENCE SEES ONLY YOUR HANDS. KEEPING HANDS STILL, MOVE SIDEWAYS OUT OF DOORWAY. DROP CLOTH & FLASH ARMS OUT OF SIGHT. THIS CAN LOOK VERY MYSTERIOUS WITH PRACTICE.

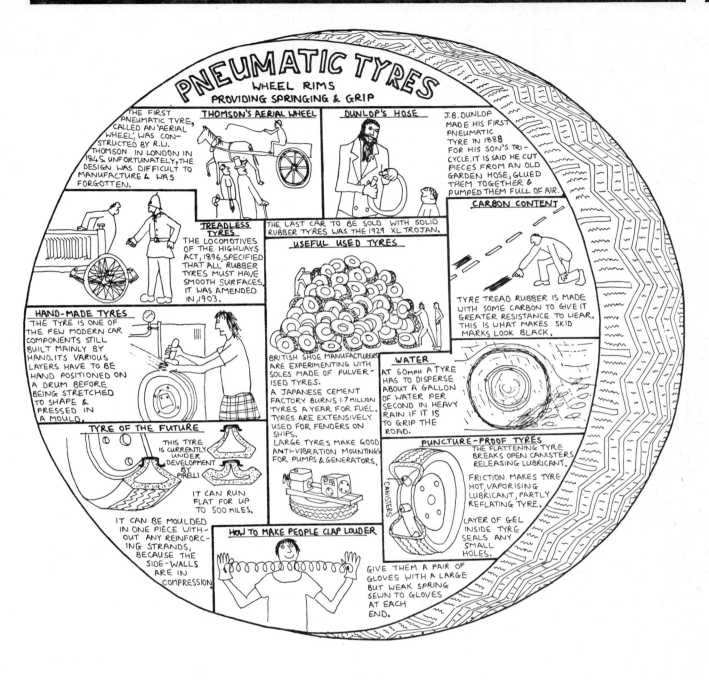

PNEUMATIC TYRES
WHEEL RIMS
PROVIDING SPRINGING & GRIP

THE FIRST PNEUMATIC TYRE, CALLED AN 'AERIAL WHEEL', WAS CONSTRUCTED BY R.W. THOMSON IN LONDON IN 1845. UNFORTUNATELY, THE DESIGN WAS DIFFICULT TO MANUFACTURE & WAS FORGOTTEN.

THOMSON'S AERIAL WHEEL

DUNLOP'S HOSE

J.B. DUNLOP MADE HIS FIRST PNEUMATIC TYRE IN 1888 FOR HIS SON'S TRICYCLE. IT IS SAID HE CUT PIECES FROM AN OLD GARDEN HOSE, GLUED THEM TOGETHER & PUMPED THEM FULL OF AIR.

TREADLESS TYRES
THE LOCOMOTIVES OF THE HIGHWAYS ACT, 1896, SPECIFIED THAT ALL RUBBER TYRES MUST HAVE SMOOTH SURFACES. IT WAS AMENDED IN 1903.

THE LAST CAR TO BE SOLD WITH SOLID RUBBER TYRES WAS THE 1929 XL TROJAN.

USEFUL USED TYRES

CARBON CONTENT

TYRE TREAD RUBBER IS MADE WITH SOME CARBON TO GIVE IT GREATER RESISTANCE TO WEAR. THIS IS WHAT MAKES SKID MARKS LOOK BLACK.

HAND-MADE TYRES
THE TYRE IS ONE OF THE FEW MODERN CAR COMPONENTS STILL BUILT MAINLY BY HAND. ITS VARIOUS LAYERS HAVE TO BE HAND POSITIONED ON A DRUM BEFORE BEING STRETCHED TO SHAPE & PRESSED IN A MOULD.

BRITISH SHOE MANUFACTURERS ARE EXPERIMENTING WITH SOLES MADE OF PULVERISED TYRES.
A JAPANESE CEMENT FACTORY BURNS 1.7 MILLION TYRES A YEAR FOR FUEL. TYRES ARE EXTENSIVELY USED FOR FENDERS ON SHIPS.
LARGE TYRES MAKE GOOD ANTI-VIBRATION MOUNTINGS FOR PUMPS & GENERATORS.

WATER
AT 60MPH A TYRE HAS TO DISPERSE ABOUT A GALLON OF WATER PER SECOND IN HEAVY RAIN IF IT IS TO GRIP THE ROAD.

TYRE OF THE FUTURE
THIS TYRE IS CURRENTLY UNDER DEVELOPMENT BY PIRELLI.
IT CAN RUN FLAT FOR UP TO 500 MILES.
IT CAN BE MOULDED IN ONE PIECE WITHOUT ANY REINFORCING STRANDS, BECAUSE THE SIDE-WALLS ARE IN COMPRESSION.

PUNCTURE-PROOF TYRES
THE FLATTENING TYRE BREAKS OPEN CANISTERS RELEASING LUBRICANT.
FRICTION MAKES TYRE HOT, VAPORISING LUBRICANT, PARTLY REFLATING TYRE.
LAYER OF GEL INSIDE TYRE SEALS ANY SMALL HOLES.

HOW TO MAKE PEOPLE CLAP LOUDER
GIVE THEM A PAIR OF GLOVES WITH A LARGE BUT WEAK SPRING SEWN TO GLOVES AT EACH END.

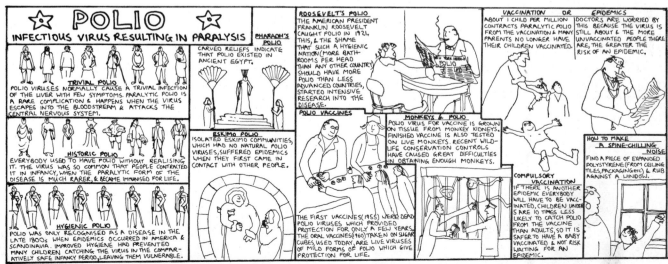

☆ POLIO ☆
INFECTIOUS VIRUS RESULTING IN PARALYSIS

TRIVIAL POLIO
POLIO VIRUSES NORMALLY CAUSE A TRIVIAL INFECTION OF THE LIVER WITH FEW SYMPTOMS. PARALYTIC POLIO IS A RARE COMPLICATION & HAPPENS WHEN THE VIRUS ESCAPES INTO THE BLOODSTREAM & ATTACKS THE CENTRAL NERVOUS SYSTEM.

HISTORIC POLIO
EVERYBODY USED TO HAVE POLIO WITHOUT REALISING IT. THE VIRUS WAS SO COMMON THAT PEOPLE CONTRACTED IT IN INFANCY, WHEN THE PARALYTIC FORM OF THE DISEASE IS MUCH RARER, & BECAME IMMUNISED FOR LIFE.

HYGIENIC POLIO
POLIO WAS ONLY RECOGNISED AS A DISEASE IN THE LATE 1800s WHEN EPIDEMICS OCCURRED IN AMERICA & SCANDINAVIA. IMPROVED HYGIENE HAD PREVENTED MANY CHILDREN CATCHING THE VIRUS IN THE COMPARATIVELY SAFE INFANCY PERIOD, LEAVING THEM VULNERABLE.

PHARAOH'S POLIO
CARVED RELIEFS INDICATE THAT POLIO EXISTED IN ANCIENT EGYPT.

ESKIMO POLIO
ISOLATED ESKIMO COMMUNITIES, WHICH HAD NO NATURAL POLIO VIRUSES, SUFFERED EPIDEMICS WHEN THEY FIRST CAME IN CONTACT WITH OTHER PEOPLE.

ROOSEVELT'S POLIO
THE AMERICAN PRESIDENT FRANKLIN ROOSEVELT CAUGHT POLIO IN 1921. THIS, & THE SHAME THAT SUCH A HYGIENIC NATION (MORE BATHROOMS PER HEAD THAN ANY OTHER COUNTRY) SHOULD HAVE MORE POLIO THAN LESS ADVANCED COUNTRIES, STARTED INTENSIVE RESEARCH INTO THE DISEASE.

POLIO VACCINES
THE FIRST VACCINES (1955) WERE DEAD POLIO VIRUSES WHICH PROVIDED PROTECTION FOR ONLY A FEW YEARS. THE ORAL VACCINES (1960) TAKEN ON SUGAR CUBES USED TODAY, ARE LIVE VIRUSES OF MILD FORMS OF POLIO WHICH GIVE PROTECTION FOR LIFE.

MONKEYS & POLIO
POLIO VIRUS FOR VACCINE IS GROWN ON TISSUE FROM MONKEY KIDNEYS. FINISHED VACCINE IS ALSO TESTED ON LIVE MONKEYS. RECENT WILDLIFE CONSERVATION CONTROLS HAVE CAUSED GREAT DIFFICULTIES IN OBTAINING ENOUGH MONKEYS.

COMPULSORY VACCINATION
IF THERE IS ANOTHER EPIDEMIC EVERYBODY WILL HAVE TO BE VACCINATED. CHILDREN UNDER 5 ARE 10 TIMES LESS LIKELY TO CATCH POLIO FROM THE VACCINE THAN ADULTS, SO IT IS SAFER TO HAVE A BABY VACCINATED & NOT RISK WAITING FOR AN EPIDEMIC.

VACCINATION OR EPIDEMICS
ABOUT 1 CHILD PER MILLION CONTRACTS PARALYTIC POLIO FROM THE VACCINATION & MANY PARENTS NO LONGER HAVE THEIR CHILDREN VACCINATED.

DOCTORS ARE WORRIED BY THIS BECAUSE THE VIRUS IS STILL ABOUT & THE MORE UNVACCINATED PEOPLE THERE ARE, THE GREATER THE RISK OF AN EPIDEMIC.

HOW TO MAKE A SPINE-CHILLING NOISE
FIND A PIECE OF EXPANDED POLYSTYRENE (FROM CEILING TILES, PACKAGING etc.) & RUB AGAINST A WINDOW.

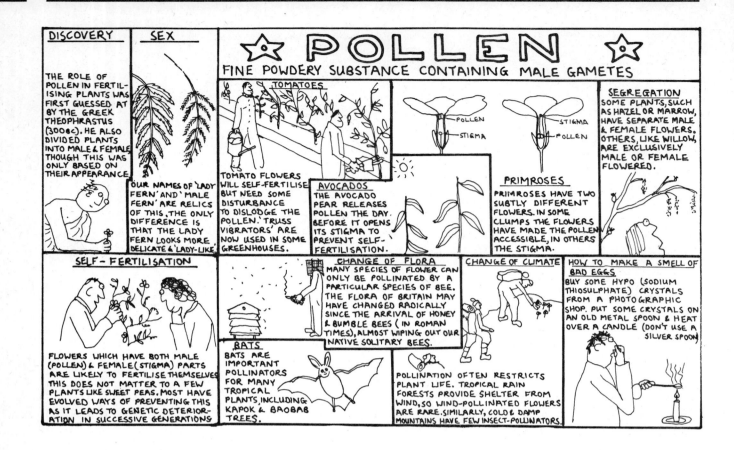

☆ POLLEN ☆
FINE POWDERY SUBSTANCE CONTAINING MALE GAMETES

DISCOVERY
THE ROLE OF POLLEN IN FERTILISING PLANTS WAS FIRST GUESSED AT BY THE GREEK THEOPHRASTUS (300BC). HE ALSO DIVIDED PLANTS INTO MALE & FEMALE THOUGH THIS WAS ONLY BASED ON THEIR APPEARANCE.

SEX
OUR NAMES OF 'LADY FERN' AND 'MALE FERN' ARE RELICS OF THIS, THE ONLY DIFFERENCE IS THAT THE LADY FERN LOOKS MORE DELICATE & 'LADY-LIKE'.

TOMATOES
TOMATO FLOWERS WILL SELF-FERTILISE BUT NEED SOME DISTURBANCE TO DISLODGE THE POLLEN. 'TRUSS VIBRATORS' ARE NOW USED IN SOME GREENHOUSES.

AVOCADOS
THE AVOCADO PEAR RELEASES POLLEN THE DAY BEFORE IT OPENS ITS STIGMA TO PREVENT SELF-FERTILISATION.

(diagram labels: POLLEN, STIGMA, STIGMA, POLLEN)

PRIMROSES
PRIMROSES HAVE TWO SUBTLY DIFFERENT FLOWERS. IN SOME CLUMPS THE FLOWERS HAVE MADE THE POLLEN ACCESSIBLE, IN OTHERS THE STIGMA.

SEGREGATION
SOME PLANTS, SUCH AS HAZEL OR MARROW, HAVE SEPARATE MALE & FEMALE FLOWERS. OTHERS, LIKE WILLOW, ARE EXCLUSIVELY MALE OR FEMALE FLOWERED.

SELF-FERTILISATION
FLOWERS WHICH HAVE BOTH MALE (POLLEN) & FEMALE (STIGMA) PARTS ARE LIKELY TO FERTILISE THEMSELVES THIS DOES NOT MATTER TO A FEW PLANTS LIKE SWEET PEAS. MOST HAVE EVOLVED WAYS OF PREVENTING THIS AS IT LEADS TO GENETIC DETERIORATION IN SUCCESSIVE GENERATIONS

BATS
BATS ARE IMPORTANT POLLINATORS FOR MANY TROPICAL PLANTS, INCLUDING KAPOK & BAOBAB TREES.

CHANGE OF FLORA
MANY SPECIES OF FLOWER CAN ONLY BE POLLINATED BY A PARTICULAR SPECIES OF BEE. THE FLORA OF BRITAIN MAY HAVE CHANGED RADICALLY SINCE THE ARRIVAL OF HONEY & BUMBLE BEES (IN ROMAN TIMES), ALMOST WIPING OUT OUR NATIVE SOLITARY BEES.

CHANGE OF CLIMATE
POLLINATION OFTEN RESTRICTS PLANT LIFE. TROPICAL RAIN FORESTS PROVIDE SHELTER FROM WIND, SO WIND-POLLINATED FLOWERS ARE RARE. SIMILARLY, COLD & DAMP MOUNTAINS HAVE FEW INSECT-POLLINATORS.

HOW TO MAKE A SMELL OF BAD EGGS
BUY SOME HYPO (SODIUM THIOSULPHATE) CRYSTALS FROM A PHOTOGRAPHIC SHOP. PUT SOME CRYSTALS ON AN OLD METAL SPOON & HEAT OVER A CANDLE (DON'T USE A SILVER SPOON)

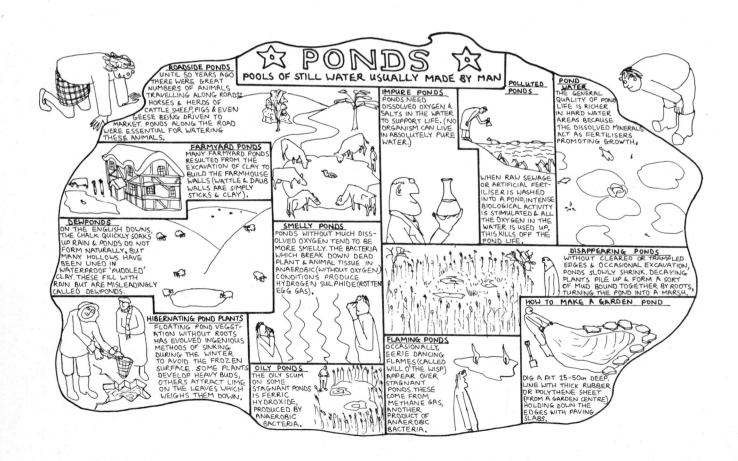

☆ PONDS ☆
POOLS OF STILL WATER USUALLY MADE BY MAN

ROADSIDE PONDS
UNTIL 50 YEARS AGO THERE WERE GREAT NUMBERS OF ANIMALS TRAVELLING ALONG ROADS: HORSES & HERDS OF CATTLE, SHEEP, PIGS & EVEN GEESE BEING DRIVEN TO MARKET. PONDS ALONG THE ROAD WERE ESSENTIAL FOR WATERING THESE ANIMALS.

FARMYARD PONDS
MANY FARMYARD PONDS RESULTED FROM THE EXCAVATION OF CLAY TO BUILD THE FARMHOUSE WALLS (WATTLE & DAUB WALLS ARE SIMPLY STICKS & CLAY).

DEWPONDS
ON THE ENGLISH DOWNS, THE CHALK QUICKLY SOAKS UP RAIN & PONDS DO NOT FORM NATURALLY, BUT MANY HOLLOWS HAVE BEEN LINED IN WATERPROOF 'PUDDLED' CLAY. THESE FILL WITH RAIN BUT ARE MISLEADINGLY CALLED DEWPONDS.

HIBERNATING POND PLANTS
FLOATING POND VEGETATION WITHOUT ROOTS HAS EVOLVED INGENIOUS METHODS OF SINKING DURING THE WINTER TO AVOID THE FROZEN SURFACE. SOME PLANTS DEVELOP HEAVY BUDS, OTHERS ATTRACT LIME ON THE LEAVES WHICH WEIGHS THEM DOWN.

SMELLY PONDS
PONDS WITHOUT MUCH DISSOLVED OXYGEN TEND TO BE MORE SMELLY. THE BACTERIA WHICH BREAK DOWN DEAD PLANT & ANIMAL TISSUE IN ANAEROBIC (WITHOUT OXYGEN) CONDITIONS PRODUCE HYDROGEN SULPHIDE (ROTTEN EGG GAS).

OILY PONDS
THE OILY SCUM ON SOME STAGNANT PONDS IS FERRIC HYDROXIDE, PRODUCED BY ANAEROBIC BACTERIA.

FLAMING PONDS
OCCASIONALLY, EERIE DANCING FLAMES (CALLED WILL O' THE WISP) APPEAR OVER STAGNANT PONDS. THESE COME FROM METHANE GAS, ANOTHER PRODUCT OF ANAEROBIC BACTERIA.

IMPURE PONDS
PONDS NEED DISSOLVED OXYGEN & SALTS IN THE WATER TO SUPPORT LIFE. (NO ORGANISM CAN LIVE IN ABSOLUTELY PURE WATER.)

POLLUTED PONDS
WHEN RAW SEWAGE OR ARTIFICIAL FERTILISER IS WASHED INTO A POND, INTENSE BIOLOGICAL ACTIVITY IS STIMULATED & ALL THE OXYGEN IN THE WATER IS USED UP, THIS KILLS OFF THE POND LIFE.

POND WATER
THE GENERAL QUALITY OF POND LIFE IS RICHER IN HARD WATER AREAS BECAUSE THE DISSOLVED MINERALS ACT AS FERTILISERS PROMOTING GROWTH.

DISAPPEARING PONDS
WITHOUT CLEARED OR TRAMPLED EDGES & OCCASIONAL EXCAVATION, PONDS SLOWLY SHRINK. DECAYING PLANTS PILE UP & FORM A SORT OF MUD BOUND TOGETHER BY ROOTS, TURNING THE POND INTO A MARSH.

HOW TO MAKE A GARDEN POND
DIG A PIT 25-50cm DEEP. LINE WITH THICK RUBBER OR POLYTHENE SHEET (FROM A GARDEN CENTRE) HOLDING DOWN THE EDGES WITH PAVING SLABS.

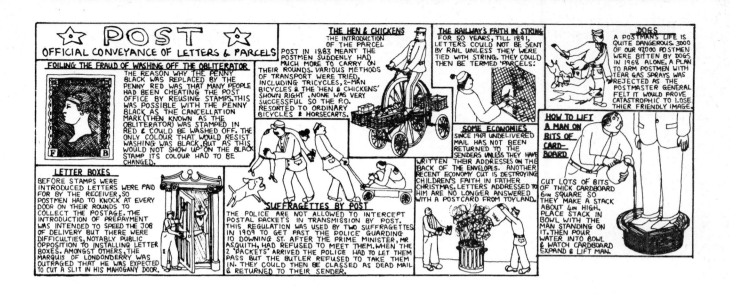

☆ POST ☆
OFFICIAL CONVEYANCE OF LETTERS & PARCELS

FOILING THE FRAUD OF WASHING OFF THE OBLITERATOR

THE REASON WHY THE PENNY BLACK WAS REPLACED BY THE PENNY RED WAS THAT MANY PEOPLE HAD BEEN CHEATING THE POST OFFICE BY REUSING STAMPS. THIS WAS POSSIBLE WITH THE PENNY BLACK AS THE CANCELLATION MARK (THEN KNOWN AS THE OBLITERATOR) WAS STAMPED IN RED & COULD BE WASHED OFF. THE ONLY COLOUR THAT WOULD RESIST WASHING WAS BLACK BUT AS THIS WOULD NOT SHOW UP ON THE BLACK STAMP ITS COLOUR HAD TO BE CHANGED.

LETTER BOXES

BEFORE STAMPS WERE INTRODUCED LETTERS WERE PAID FOR BY THE RECEIVER, SO POSTMEN HAD TO KNOCK AT EVERY DOOR ON THEIR ROUNDS TO COLLECT THE POSTAGE. THE INTRODUCTION OF PREPAYMENT WAS INTENDED TO SPEED THE JOB OF DELIVERY BUT THERE WERE DIFFICULTIES, NOTABLY PUBLIC OPPOSITION TO INSTALLING LETTER BOXES. AMONGST OTHERS, THE MARQUIS OF LONDONDERRY WAS OUTRAGED THAT HE WAS EXPECTED TO CUT A SLIT IN HIS MAHOGANY DOOR.

THE HEN & CHICKENS

THE INTRODUCTION OF THE PARCEL POST IN 1883 MEANT THE POSTMEN SUDDENLY HAD MUCH MORE TO CARRY ON THEIR ROUNDS. VARIOUS METHODS OF TRANSPORT WERE TRIED, INCLUDING TRICYCLES, 2-MAN BICYCLES & THE 'HEN & CHICKENS' SHOWN RIGHT. NONE WAS VERY SUCCESSFUL SO THE P.O. RESORTED TO ORDINARY BICYCLES & HORSECARTS.

SUFFRAGETTES BY POST

THE POLICE ARE NOT ALLOWED TO INTERCEPT POSTAL PACKETS IN TRANSMISSION BY POST. THIS REGULATION WAS USED BY TWO SUFFRAGETTES IN 1909 TO GET PAST THE POLICE GUARDING 10 DOWNING ST. AFTER THE PRIME MINISTER, MR ASQUITH, HAD REFUSED TO MEET THEM. WHEN THE 2 'PACKETS' ARRIVED THE POLICE HAD TO LET THEM PASS BUT THE BUTLER REFUSED TO TAKE THEM IN. THEY COULD THEN BE CLASSED AS DEAD MAIL & RETURNED TO THEIR SENDER.

THE RAILWAY'S FAITH IN STRING

FOR 50 YEARS, TILL 1891, LETTERS COULD NOT BE SENT BY RAIL UNLESS THEY WERE TIED WITH STRING. THEY COULD THEN BE TERMED 'PARCELS.'

SOME ECONOMIES

SINCE 1969 UNDELIVERED MAIL HAS NOT BEEN RETURNED TO THE SENDERS UNLESS THEY HAVE WRITTEN THEIR ADDRESSES ON THE BACK OF THE ENVELOPES. ANOTHER RECENT ECONOMY CUT IS DESTROYING CHILDREN'S FAITH IN FATHER CHRISTMAS. LETTERS ADDRESSED TO HIM ARE NO LONGER ANSWERED WITH A POSTCARD FROM TOYLAND.

DOGS

A POSTMAN'S LIFE IS QUITE DANGEROUS. 3000 OF OUR 97,000 POSTMEN WERE BITTEN BY DOGS IN 1968 ALONE. A PLAN TO ARM POSTMEN WITH TEAR GAS SPRAYS WAS REJECTED AS THE POSTMASTER GENERAL FELT IT WOULD PROVE CATASTROPHIC TO LOSE THEIR FRIENDLY IMAGE.

HOW TO LIFT A MAN ON BITS OF CARD-BOARD

CUT LOTS OF BITS OF THICK CARDBOARD 6in SQUARE SO THEY MAKE A STACK ABOUT 4in HIGH. PLACE STACK IN BOWL WITH THE MAN STANDING ON IT. THEN POUR WATER INTO BOWL & WATCH CARDBOARD EXPAND & LIFT MAN.

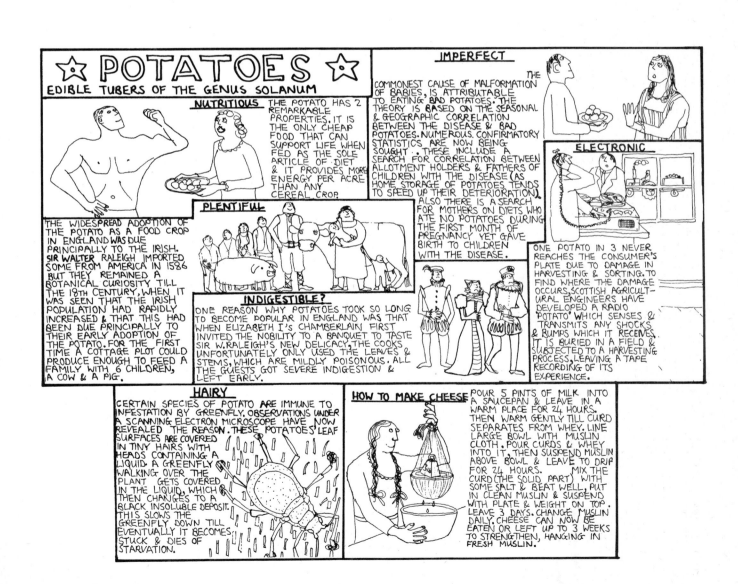

☆ POTATOES ☆
EDIBLE TUBERS OF THE GENUS SOLANUM

NUTRITIOUS

THE POTATO HAS 2 REMARKABLE PROPERTIES. IT IS THE ONLY CHEAP FOOD THAT CAN SUPPORT LIFE WHEN FED AS THE SOLE ARTICLE OF DIET & IT PROVIDES MORE ENERGY PER ACRE THAN ANY CEREAL CROP.

PLENTIFUL

THE WIDESPREAD ADOPTION OF THE POTATO AS A FOOD CROP IN ENGLAND WAS DUE PRINCIPALLY TO THE IRISH. SIR WALTER RALEIGH IMPORTED SOME FROM AMERICA IN 1586 BUT THEY REMAINED A BOTANICAL CURIOSITY TILL THE 18TH CENTURY, WHEN IT WAS SEEN THAT THE IRISH POPULATION HAD RAPIDLY INCREASED & THAT THIS HAD BEEN DUE PRINCIPALLY TO THEIR EARLY ADOPTION OF THE POTATO. FOR THE FIRST TIME A COTTAGE PLOT COULD PRODUCE ENOUGH TO FEED A FAMILY WITH 6 CHILDREN, A COW & A PIG.

INDIGESTIBLE?

ONE REASON WHY POTATOES TOOK SO LONG TO BECOME POPULAR IN ENGLAND WAS THAT WHEN ELIZABETH I's CHAMBERLAIN FIRST INVITED THE NOBILITY TO A BANQUET TO TASTE SIR W. RALEIGH'S NEW DELICACY, THE COOKS UNFORTUNATELY ONLY USED THE LEAVES & STEMS, WHICH ARE MILDLY POISONOUS. ALL THE GUESTS GOT SEVERE INDIGESTION & LEFT EARLY.

IMPERFECT

THE COMMONEST CAUSE OF MALFORMATION OF BABIES, IS ATTRIBUTABLE TO EATING BAD POTATOES. THE THEORY IS BASED ON THE SEASONAL & GEOGRAPHIC CORRELATION BETWEEN THE DISEASE & BAD POTATOES. NUMEROUS CONFIRMATORY STATISTICS ARE NOW BEING SOUGHT. THESE INCLUDE A SEARCH FOR CORRELATION BETWEEN ALLOTMENT HOLDERS & FATHERS OF CHILDREN WITH THE DISEASE (AS HOME STORAGE OF POTATOES TENDS TO SPEED UP THEIR DETERIORATION). ALSO THERE IS A SEARCH FOR MOTHERS ON DIETS WHO ATE NO POTATOES DURING THE FIRST MONTH OF PREGNANCY YET GAVE BIRTH TO CHILDREN WITH THE DISEASE.

ELECTRONIC

ONE POTATO IN 3 NEVER REACHES THE CONSUMER'S PLATE DUE TO DAMAGE IN HARVESTING & SORTING. TO FIND WHERE THE DAMAGE OCCURS, SCOTTISH AGRICULTURAL ENGINEERS HAVE DEVELOPED A RADIO 'POTATO' WHICH SENSES & TRANSMITS ANY SHOCKS & BUMPS WHICH IT RECEIVES. IT IS BURIED IN A FIELD & SUBJECTED TO A HARVESTING PROCESS, LEAVING A TAPE RECORDING OF ITS EXPERIENCE.

HAIRY

CERTAIN SPECIES OF POTATO ARE IMMUNE TO INFESTATION BY GREENFLY. OBSERVATIONS UNDER A SCANNING ELECTRON MICROSCOPE HAVE NOW REVEALED THE REASON. THESE POTATOES' LEAF SURFACES ARE COVERED IN TINY HAIRS WITH HEADS CONTAINING A LIQUID. A GREENFLY WALKING OVER THE PLANT GETS COVERED IN THE LIQUID, WHICH THEN CHANGES TO A BLACK INSOLUBLE DEPOSIT. THIS SLOWS THE GREENFLY DOWN TILL EVENTUALLY IT BECOMES STUCK & DIES OF STARVATION.

HOW TO MAKE CHEESE

POUR 5 PINTS OF MILK INTO A SAUCEPAN & LEAVE IN A WARM PLACE FOR 24 HOURS. THEN WARM GENTLY TILL CURD SEPARATES FROM WHEY. LINE LARGE BOWL WITH MUSLIN CLOTH. POUR CURDS & WHEY INTO IT, THEN SUSPEND MUSLIN ABOVE BOWL & LEAVE TO DRIP FOR 24 HOURS. MIX THE CURD (THE SOLID PART) WITH SOME SALT & BEAT WELL, PUT IN CLEAN MUSLIN & SUSPEND WITH PLATE & WEIGHT ON TOP. LEAVE 3 DAYS. CHANGE MUSLIN DAILY. CHEESE CAN NOW BE EATEN OR LEFT UP TO 3 WEEKS TO STRENGTHEN, HANGING IN FRESH MUSLIN.

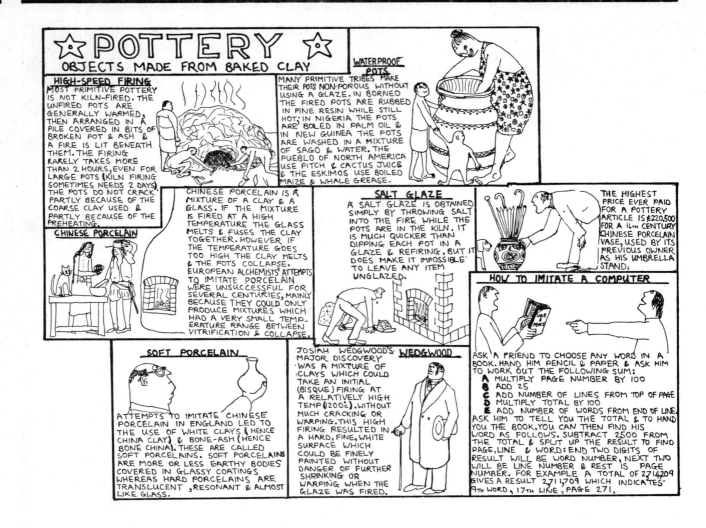

☆ POTTERY ☆
OBJECTS MADE FROM BAKED CLAY

HIGH-SPEED FIRING

MOST PRIMITIVE POTTERY IS NOT KILN-FIRED. THE UNFIRED POTS ARE GENERALLY WARMED, THEN ARRANGED IN A PILE COVERED IN BITS OF BROKEN POT & ASH & A FIRE IS LIT BENEATH THEM. THE FIRING RARELY TAKES MORE THAN 2 HOURS, EVEN FOR LARGE POTS (KILN FIRING SOMETIMES NEEDS 2 DAYS). THE POTS DO NOT CRACK, PARTLY BECAUSE OF THE COARSE CLAY USED & PARTLY BECAUSE OF THE PREHEATING.

WATERPROOF POTS

MANY PRIMITIVE TRIBES MAKE THEIR POTS NON-POROUS WITHOUT USING A GLAZE. IN BORNEO THE FIRED POTS ARE RUBBED IN PINE RESIN WHILE STILL HOT; IN NIGERIA THE POTS ARE BOILED IN PALM OIL & IN NEW GUINEA THE POTS ARE WASHED IN A MIXTURE OF SAGO & WATER. THE PUEBLO OF NORTH AMERICA USE PITCH & CACTUS JUICE & THE ESKIMOS USE BOILED MAIZE & WHALE GREASE.

CHINESE PORCELAIN

CHINESE PORCELAIN IS A MIXTURE OF A CLAY & A GLASS. IF THE MIXTURE IS FIRED AT A HIGH TEMPERATURE THE GLASS MELTS & FUSES THE CLAY TOGETHER. HOWEVER IF THE TEMPERATURE GOES TOO HIGH THE CLAY MELTS & THE POTS COLLAPSE. EUROPEAN ALCHEMISTS' ATTEMPTS TO IMITATE PORCELAIN WERE UNSUCCESSFUL FOR SEVERAL CENTURIES, MAINLY BECAUSE THEY COULD ONLY PRODUCE MIXTURES WHICH HAD A VERY SMALL TEMPERATURE RANGE BETWEEN VITRIFICATION & COLLAPSE.

SALT GLAZE

A SALT GLAZE IS OBTAINED SIMPLY BY THROWING SALT INTO THE FIRE WHILE THE POTS ARE IN THE KILN. IT IS MUCH QUICKER THAN DIPPING EACH POT IN A GLAZE & REFIRING, BUT IT DOES MAKE IT IMPOSSIBLE TO LEAVE ANY ITEM UNGLAZED.

THE HIGHEST PRICE EVER PAID FOR A POTTERY ARTICLE IS £220,500 FOR A 14TH CENTURY CHINESE PORCELAIN VASE, USED BY ITS PREVIOUS OWNER AS HIS UMBRELLA STAND.

HOW TO IMITATE A COMPUTER

ASK A FRIEND TO CHOOSE ANY WORD IN A BOOK. HAND HIM PENCIL & PAPER & ASK HIM TO WORK OUT THE FOLLOWING SUM:
A MULTIPLY PAGE NUMBER BY 100
B ADD 25
C ADD NUMBER OF LINES FROM TOP OF PAGE
D MULTIPLY TOTAL BY 100
E ADD NUMBER OF WORDS FROM END OF LINE.
ASK HIM TO TELL YOU THE TOTAL & TO HAND YOU THE BOOK. YOU CAN THEN FIND HIS WORD AS FOLLOWS. SUBTRACT 2500 FROM THE TOTAL & SPLIT UP THE RESULT TO FIND PAGE, LINE & WORD: END TWO DIGITS OF RESULT WILL BE WORD NUMBER, NEXT TWO WILL BE LINE NUMBER & REST IS PAGE NUMBER. FOR EXAMPLE A TOTAL OF 2714209 GIVES A RESULT 2711,709 WHICH INDICATES 9TH WORD, 17TH LINE, PAGE 271.

SOFT PORCELAIN

ATTEMPTS TO IMITATE CHINESE PORCELAIN IN ENGLAND LED TO THE USE OF WHITE CLAYS (HENCE CHINA CLAY) & BONE-ASH (HENCE BONE CHINA). THESE ARE CALLED SOFT PORCELAINS. SOFT PORCELAINS ARE MORE OR LESS EARTHY BODIES COVERED IN GLASSY COATINGS WHEREAS HARD PORCELAINS ARE TRANSLUCENT, RESONANT & ALMOST LIKE GLASS.

WEDGWOOD

JOSIAH WEDGWOOD'S MAJOR DISCOVERY WAS A MIXTURE OF CLAYS WHICH COULD TAKE AN INITIAL (BISQUE) FIRING AT A RELATIVELY HIGH TEMP (1200°C). WITHOUT MUCH CRACKING OR WARPING. THIS HIGH FIRING RESULTED IN A HARD, FINE, WHITE SURFACE WHICH COULD BE FINELY PAINTED WITHOUT DANGER OF FURTHER SHRINKING OR WARPING WHEN THE GLAZE WAS FIRED.

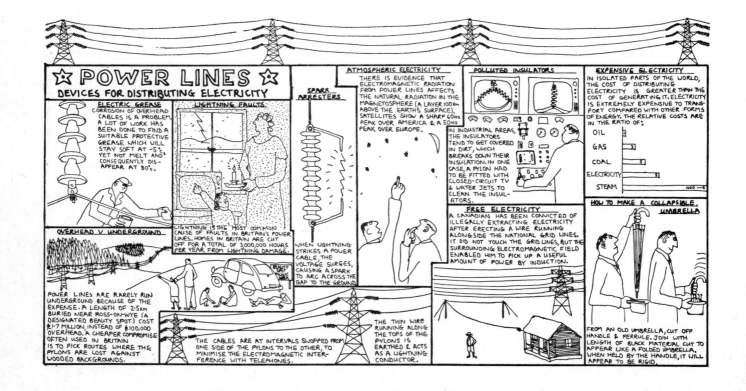

☆ POWER LINES ☆
DEVICES FOR DISTRIBUTING ELECTRICITY

ELECTRIC GREASE

CORROSION OF OVERHEAD CABLES IS A PROBLEM. A LOT OF WORK HAS BEEN DONE TO FIND A SUITABLE PROTECTIVE GREASE WHICH WILL STAY SOFT AT -5°C, YET NOT MELT AND CONSEQUENTLY DISAPPEAR AT 80°C.

LIGHTNING FAULTS

LIGHTNING IS THE MOST COMMON CAUSE OF FAULTS IN BRITAIN'S POWER LINES. HOMES IN BRITAIN ARE CUT OFF FOR A TOTAL OF 3,000,000 HOURS PER YEAR FROM LIGHTNING DAMAGE.

SPARK ARRESTERS

WHEN LIGHTNING STRIKES A POWER CABLE, THE VOLTAGE SURGES, CAUSING A SPARK TO ARC ACROSS THE GAP TO THE GROUND.

ATMOSPHERIC ELECTRICITY

THERE IS EVIDENCE THAT ELECTROMAGNETIC RADIATION FROM POWER LINES AFFECTS THE NATURAL RADIATION IN THE MAGNETOSPHERE (A LAYER 100 KM ABOVE THE EARTH'S SURFACE). SATELLITES SHOW A SHARP 60 Hz PEAK OVER AMERICA & A 50 Hz PEAK OVER EUROPE.

POLLUTED INSULATORS

IN INDUSTRIAL AREAS, THE INSULATORS TEND TO GET COVERED IN DIRT, WHICH BREAKS DOWN THEIR INSULATION. IN ONE CASE, A PYLON HAD TO BE FITTED WITH CLOSED-CIRCUIT TV & WATER JETS TO CLEAN THE INSULATORS.

EXPENSIVE ELECTRICITY

IN ISOLATED PARTS OF THE WORLD, THE COST OF DISTRIBUTING ELECTRICITY IS GREATER THAN THE COST OF GENERATING IT. ELECTRICITY IS EXTREMELY EXPENSIVE TO TRANSPORT COMPARED WITH OTHER FORMS OF ENERGY. THE RELATIVE COSTS ARE IN THE RATIO OF:

OIL
GAS
COAL
ELECTRICITY
STEAM

OVERHEAD V UNDERGROUND

POWER LINES ARE RARELY RUN UNDERGROUND BECAUSE OF THE EXPENSE. A LENGTH OF 2·5 KM BURIED NEAR ROSS-ON-WYE (A DESIGNATED BEAUTY SPOT) COST £1·7 MILLION, INSTEAD OF £100,000 OVERHEAD. A CHEAPER COMPROMISE OFTEN USED IN BRITAIN IS TO PICK ROUTES WHERE THE PYLONS ARE LOST AGAINST WOODED BACKGROUNDS.

THE CABLES ARE AT INTERVALS SWOPPED FROM ONE SIDE OF THE PYLONS TO THE OTHER, TO MINIMISE THE ELECTROMAGNETIC INTERFERENCE WITH TELEPHONES.

FREE ELECTRICITY

A CANADIAN HAS BEEN CONVICTED OF ILLEGALLY EXTRACTING ELECTRICITY AFTER ERECTING A WIRE RUNNING ALONGSIDE THE NATIONAL GRID LINES. IT DID NOT TOUCH THE GRID LINES, BUT THE SURROUNDING ELECTROMAGNETIC FIELD ENABLED HIM TO PICK UP A USEFUL AMOUNT OF POWER BY INDUCTION.

THE THIN WIRE RUNNING ALONG THE TOPS OF THE PYLONS IS EARTHED & ACTS AS A LIGHTNING CONDUCTOR.

HOW TO MAKE A COLLAPSIBLE UMBRELLA

FROM AN OLD UMBRELLA, CUT OFF HANDLE & FERRULE. JOIN WITH LENGTH OF BLACK MATERIAL CUT TO APPEAR LIKE A FOLDED UMBRELLA. WHEN HELD BY THE HANDLE, IT WILL APPEAR TO BE RIGID.

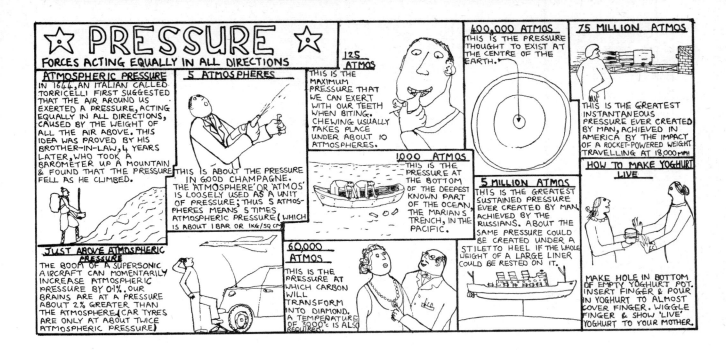

☆ PRESSURE ☆

FORCES ACTING EQUALLY IN ALL DIRECTIONS

ATMOSPHERIC PRESSURE
IN 1644, AN ITALIAN CALLED TORRICELLI FIRST SUGGESTED THAT THE AIR AROUND US EXERTED A PRESSURE, ACTING EQUALLY IN ALL DIRECTIONS, CAUSED BY THE WEIGHT OF ALL THE AIR ABOVE. THIS IDEA WAS PROVED BY HIS BROTHER-IN-LAW, 4 YEARS LATER, WHO TOOK A BAROMETER UP A MOUNTAIN & FOUND THAT THE PRESSURE FELL AS HE CLIMBED.

5 ATMOSPHERES
THIS IS ABOUT THE PRESSURE IN GOOD CHAMPAGNE. THE 'ATMOSPHERE' OR 'ATMOS' IS LOOSELY USED AS A UNIT OF PRESSURE; THUS 5 ATMOSPHERES MEANS 5 TIMES ATMOSPHERIC PRESSURE (WHICH IS ABOUT 1 BAR OR 1 KG/SQ CM)

125 ATMOS
THIS IS THE MAXIMUM PRESSURE THAT WE CAN EXERT WITH OUR TEETH WHEN BITING. CHEWING USUALLY TAKES PLACE UNDER ABOUT 10 ATMOSPHERES.

1000 ATMOS
THIS IS THE PRESSURE AT THE BOTTOM OF THE DEEPEST KNOWN PART OF THE OCEAN, THE MARIANS TRENCH, IN THE PACIFIC.

400,000 ATMOS
THIS IS THE PRESSURE THOUGHT TO EXIST AT THE CENTRE OF THE EARTH.

75 MILLION ATMOS
THIS IS THE GREATEST INSTANTANEOUS PRESSURE EVER CREATED BY MAN, ACHIEVED IN AMERICA BY THE IMPACT OF A ROCKET-POWERED WEIGHT TRAVELLING AT 18,000 MPH.

5 MILLION ATMOS
THIS IS THE GREATEST SUSTAINED PRESSURE EVER CREATED BY MAN, ACHIEVED BY THE RUSSIANS. ABOUT THE SAME PRESSURE COULD BE CREATED UNDER A STILETTO HEEL IF THE WHOLE WEIGHT OF A LARGE LINER COULD BE RESTED ON IT.

JUST ABOVE ATMOSPHERIC PRESSURE
THE BOOM OF A SUPERSONIC AIRCRAFT CAN MOMENTARILY INCREASE ATMOSPHERIC PRESSURE BY 0.1%. OUR BRAINS ARE AT A PRESSURE ABOUT 2% GREATER THAN THE ATMOSPHERE. (CAR TYRES ARE ONLY AT ABOUT TWICE ATMOSPHERIC PRESSURE)

60,000 ATMOS
THIS IS THE PRESSURE AT WHICH CARBON WILL TRANSFORM INTO DIAMOND. A TEMPERATURE OF 3000°C IS ALSO REQUIRED.

HOW TO MAKE YOGHURT LIVE
MAKE HOLE IN BOTTOM OF EMPTY YOGHURT POT. INSERT FINGER & POUR IN YOGHURT TO ALMOST COVER FINGER. WIGGLE FINGER & SHOW 'LIVE' YOGHURT TO YOUR MOTHER.

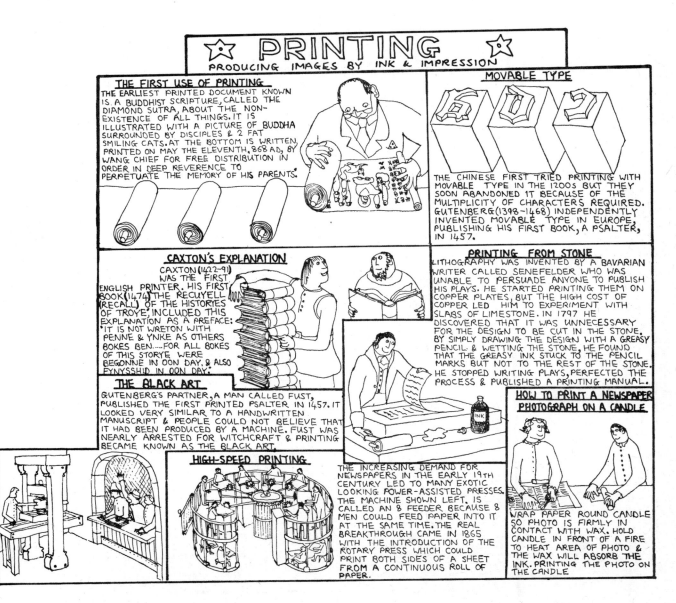

☆ PRINTING ☆

PRODUCING IMAGES BY INK & IMPRESSION

THE FIRST USE OF PRINTING
THE EARLIEST PRINTED DOCUMENT KNOWN IS A BUDDHIST SCRIPTURE, CALLED THE DIAMOND SUTRA, ABOUT THE NON-EXISTENCE OF ALL THINGS. IT IS ILLUSTRATED WITH A PICTURE OF BUDDHA SURROUNDED BY DISCIPLES & 2 FAT SMILING CATS. AT THE BOTTOM IS WRITTEN, PRINTED ON MAY THE ELEVENTH, 868 AD, BY WANG CHIEF FOR FREE DISTRIBUTION IN ORDER IN DEEP REVERENCE TO PERPETUATE THE MEMORY OF HIS PARENTS.

MOVABLE TYPE
THE CHINESE FIRST TRIED PRINTING WITH MOVABLE TYPE IN THE 1200S BUT THEY SOON ABANDONED IT BECAUSE OF THE MULTIPLICITY OF CHARACTERS REQUIRED. GUTENBERG (1398-1468) INDEPENDENTLY INVENTED MOVABLE TYPE IN EUROPE, PUBLISHING HIS FIRST BOOK, A PSALTER, IN 1457.

CAXTON'S EXPLANATION
CAXTON (1422-91) WAS THE FIRST ENGLISH PRINTER. HIS FIRST BOOK (1474), THE RECUYELL (RECALL) OF THE HISTORIES OF TROYE, INCLUDED THIS EXPLANATION AS A PREFACE: 'IT IS NOT WRETON WITH PENNE & YNKE AS OTHERS BOKES BEN.....FOR ALL BOKES OF THIS STORYE WERE BEGONNE IN OON DAY, & ALSO FYNYSSHID IN OON DAY.'

THE BLACK ART
GUTENBERG'S PARTNER, A MAN CALLED FUST, PUBLISHED THE FIRST PRINTED PSALTER IN 1457. IT LOOKED VERY SIMILAR TO A HANDWRITTEN MANUSCRIPT & PEOPLE COULD NOT BELIEVE THAT IT HAD BEEN PRODUCED BY A MACHINE. FUST WAS NEARLY ARRESTED FOR WITCHCRAFT & PRINTING BECAME KNOWN AS THE BLACK ART.

PRINTING FROM STONE
LITHOGRAPHY WAS INVENTED BY A BAVARIAN WRITER CALLED SENEFELDER WHO WAS UNABLE TO PERSUADE ANYONE TO PUBLISH HIS PLAYS. HE STARTED PRINTING THEM ON COPPER PLATES, BUT THE HIGH COST OF COPPER LED HIM TO EXPERIMENT WITH SLABS OF LIMESTONE. IN 1797 HE DISCOVERED THAT IT WAS UNNECESSARY FOR THE DESIGN TO BE CUT IN THE STONE. BY SIMPLY DRAWING THE DESIGN WITH A GREASY PENCIL & WETTING THE STONE, HE FOUND THAT THE GREASY INK STUCK TO THE PENCIL MARKS BUT NOT TO THE REST OF THE STONE. HE STOPPED WRITING PLAYS, PERFECTED THE PROCESS & PUBLISHED A PRINTING MANUAL.

HIGH-SPEED PRINTING
THE INCREASING DEMAND FOR NEWSPAPERS IN THE EARLY 19TH CENTURY LED TO MANY EXOTIC LOOKING POWER-ASSISTED PRESSES. THE MACHINE SHOWN LEFT, IS CALLED AN 8 FEEDER BECAUSE 8 MEN COULD FEED PAPER INTO IT AT THE SAME TIME. THE REAL BREAKTHROUGH CAME IN 1865 WITH THE INTRODUCTION OF THE ROTARY PRESS WHICH COULD PRINT BOTH SIDES OF A SHEET FROM A CONTINUOUS ROLL OF PAPER.

HOW TO PRINT A NEWSPAPER PHOTOGRAPH ON A CANDLE
WRAP PAPER ROUND CANDLE SO PHOTO IS FIRMLY IN CONTACT WITH WAX. HOLD CANDLE IN FRONT OF A FIRE TO HEAT AREA OF PHOTO & THE WAX WILL ABSORB THE INK, PRINTING THE PHOTO ON THE CANDLE

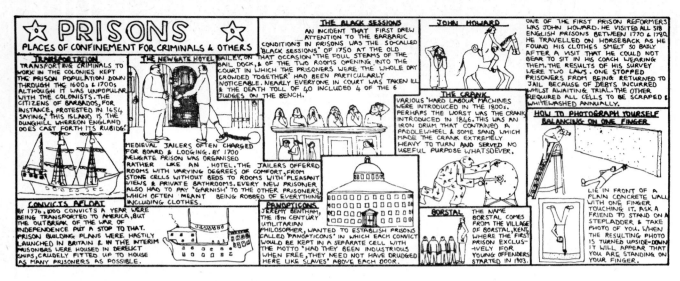

PRISONS
PLACES OF CONFINEMENT FOR CRIMINALS & OTHERS

TRANSPORTATION
TRANSPORTING CRIMINALS TO WORK IN THE COLONIES KEPT THE PRISON POPULATION DOWN THROUGH THE 1600s & 1700s ALTHOUGH IT WAS UNPOPULAR WITH THE COLONISTS. THE CITIZENS OF BARBADOS, FOR INSTANCE, PROTESTED IN 1654 SAYING, 'THIS ISLAND IS THE DUNGHILL WHEREON ENGLAND DOES CAST FORTH ITS RUBISH.'

CONVICTS AFLOAT
BY 1776, 1000 CONVICTS A YEAR WERE BEING TRANSPORTED TO AMERICA, BUT THE OUTBREAK OF THE WAR OF INDEPENDENCE PUT A STOP TO THAT. PRISON BUILDING PLANS WERE HASTILY LAUNCHED IN BRITAIN & IN THE INTERIM PRISONERS WERE HOUSED IN DERELICT SHIPS, CRUDELY FITTED UP TO HOUSE AS MANY PRISONERS AS POSSIBLE.

THE NEWGATE HOTEL
MEDIEVAL JAILERS OFTEN CHARGED FOR BOARD & LODGING. BY 1700 NEWGATE PRISON WAS ORGANISED RATHER LIKE AN HOTEL. THE JAILERS OFFERED ROOMS WITH VARYING DEGREES OF COMFORT, FROM STONE CELLS WITHOUT BEDS TO ROOMS WITH 'PLEASANT VIEWS' & PRIVATE BATHROOMS. EVERY NEW PRISONER ALSO HAD TO PAY 'GARNISH' TO THE OTHER PRISONERS WHICH OFTEN MEANT BEING ROBBED OF EVERYTHING INCLUDING CLOTHES.

THE BLACK SESSIONS
AN INCIDENT THAT FIRST DREW ATTENTION TO THE BARBARIC CONDITIONS IN PRISONS WAS THE SO-CALLED 'BLACK SESSIONS' OF 1750 AT THE OLD BAILEY. ON THAT OCCASION 'THE FOUL STEAMS OF THE BAIL DOCK, & OF THE TWO ROOMS OPENING INTO THE COURT IN WHICH THE PRISONERS WERE THE WHOLE DAY CROWDED TOGETHER' HAD BEEN PARTICULARLY NOTICEABLE. NEARLY EVERYONE IN COURT WAS TAKEN ILL & THE DEATH TOLL OF 40 INCLUDED 4 OF THE 6 JUDGES ON THE BENCH.

PANOPTICONS
JEREMY BENTHAM, THE 18TH CENTURY UTILITARIAN PHILOSOPHER, WANTED TO ESTABLISH PRISONS CALLED 'PANOPTICONS' IN WHICH EACH CONVICT WOULD BE KEPT IN A SEPARATE CELL WITH THE MOTTO 'HAD THEY BEEN INDUSTRIOUS WHEN FREE, THEY NEED NOT HAVE DRUDGED HERE LIKE SLAVES' ABOVE EACH DOOR.

JOHN HOWARD
ONE OF THE FIRST PRISON REFORMERS WAS JOHN HOWARD. HE VISITED ALL 518 ENGLISH PRISONS BETWEEN 1770 & 1780. HE TRAVELLED ON HORSEBACK AS HE FOUND THAT ON A VISIT THAT HE COULD NOT BEAR TO SIT IN HIS COACH WEARING THEM. THE RESULTS OF HIS SURVEY WERE TWO LAWS. ONE STOPPED PRISONERS FROM BEING RETURNED TO JAIL BECAUSE OF DEBTS INCURRED WHILST AWAITING TRIAL. THE OTHER REQUIRED ALL CELLS TO BE SCRAPED & WHITEWASHED ANNUALLY.

THE CRANK
VARIOUS 'HARD LABOUR' MACHINES WERE INTRODUCED IN THE 1800s. PERHAPS THE WORST WAS THE CRANK INTRODUCED IN 1846. THIS WAS AN IRON DRUM THAT CONTAINED A PADDLEWHEEL & SOME SAND WHICH MADE THE CRANK EXTREMELY HEAVY TO TURN AND SERVED NO USEFUL PURPOSE WHATSOEVER.

BORSTAL
THE NAME BORSTAL COMES FROM THE VILLAGE OF BORSTAL, KENT, WHERE THE FIRST PRISON EXCLUSIVELY FOR YOUNG OFFENDERS STARTED IN 1903.

HOW TO PHOTOGRAPH YOURSELF BALANCING ON ONE FINGER
LIE IN FRONT OF A PLAIN CONCRETE WALL WITH ONE FINGER TOUCHING IT. ASK A FRIEND TO STAND ON A STEPLADDER & TAKE PHOTO OF YOU. WHEN THE RESULTING PHOTO IS TURNED UPSIDE-DOWN IT WILL APPEAR THAT YOU ARE STANDING ON YOUR FINGER.

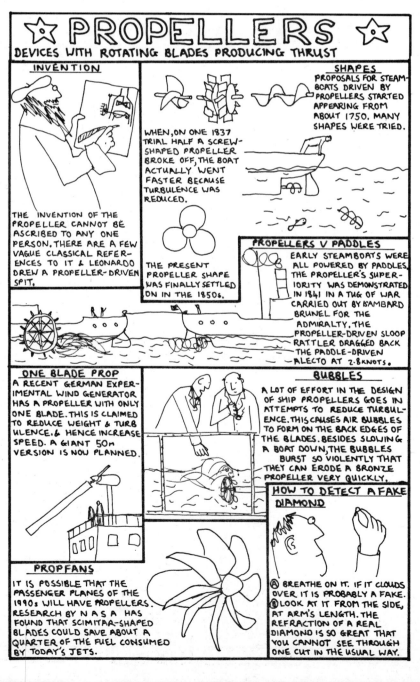

PROPELLERS
DEVICES WITH ROTATING BLADES PRODUCING THRUST

INVENTION
THE INVENTION OF THE PROPELLER CANNOT BE ASCRIBED TO ANY ONE PERSON. THERE ARE A FEW VAGUE CLASSICAL REFERENCES TO IT & LEONARDO DREW A PROPELLER-DRIVEN SPIT.

WHEN, ON ONE 1837 TRIAL HALF A SCREW-SHAPED PROPELLER BROKE OFF, THE BOAT ACTUALLY WENT FASTER BECAUSE TURBULENCE WAS REDUCED.

THE PRESENT PROPELLER SHAPE WAS FINALLY SETTLED ON IN THE 1850s.

SHAPES
PROPOSALS FOR STEAMBOATS DRIVEN BY PROPELLERS STARTED APPEARING FROM ABOUT 1750. MANY SHAPES WERE TRIED.

PROPELLERS V PADDLES
EARLY STEAMBOATS WERE ALL POWERED BY PADDLES. THE PROPELLER'S SUPERIORITY WAS DEMONSTRATED IN 1841 IN A TUG OF WAR CARRIED OUT BY ISAMBARD BRUNEL FOR THE ADMIRALTY. THE PROPELLER-DRIVEN SLOOP RATTLER DRAGGED BACK THE PADDLE-DRIVEN ALECTO AT 2.8 KNOTS.

ONE BLADE PROP
A RECENT GERMAN EXPERIMENTAL WIND GENERATOR HAS A PROPELLER WITH ONLY ONE BLADE. THIS IS CLAIMED TO REDUCE WEIGHT & TURBULENCE, & HENCE INCREASE SPEED. A GIANT 50m VERSION IS NOW PLANNED.

BUBBLES
A LOT OF EFFORT IN THE DESIGN OF SHIP PROPELLERS GOES IN ATTEMPTS TO REDUCE TURBULENCE. THIS CAUSES AIR BUBBLES TO FORM ON THE BACK EDGES OF THE BLADES. BESIDES SLOWING A BOAT DOWN, THE BUBBLES BURST SO VIOLENTLY THAT THEY CAN ERODE A BRONZE PROPELLER VERY QUICKLY.

HOW TO DETECT A FAKE DIAMOND
(A) BREATHE ON IT. IF IT CLOUDS OVER IT IS PROBABLY A FAKE.
(B) LOOK AT IT FROM THE SIDE, AT ARM'S LENGTH. THE REFRACTION OF A REAL DIAMOND IS SO GREAT THAT YOU CANNOT SEE THROUGH ONE CUT IN THE USUAL WAY.

PROPFANS
IT IS POSSIBLE THAT THE PASSENGER PLANES OF THE 1990s WILL HAVE PROPELLERS. RESEARCH BY N A S A HAS FOUND THAT SCIMITAR-SHAPED BLADES COULD SAVE ABOUT A QUARTER OF THE FUEL CONSUMED BY TODAY'S JETS.

☆ PROTECTIVE CLOTHING ☆

UTILITY GARMENTS DESIGNED FOR SAFETY

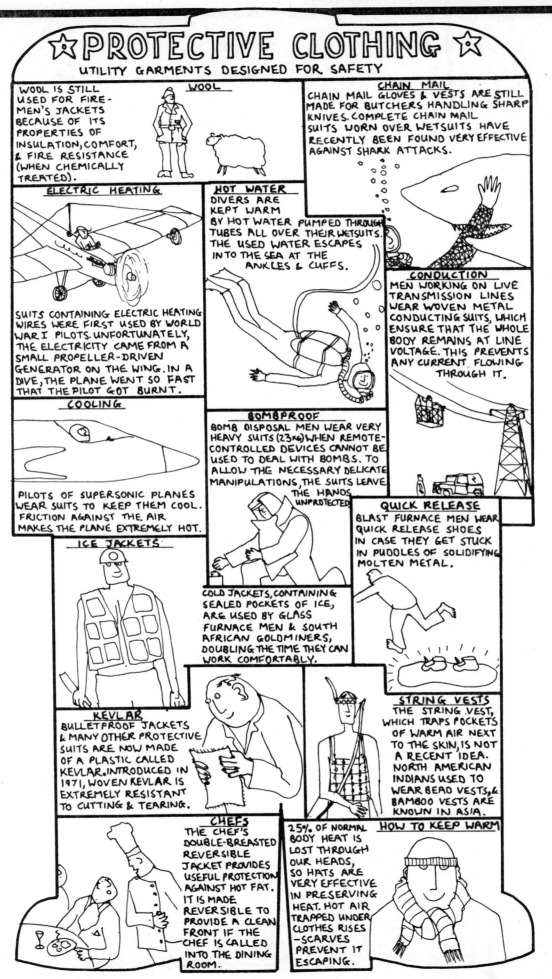

WOOL

WOOL IS STILL USED FOR FIREMEN'S JACKETS BECAUSE OF ITS PROPERTIES OF INSULATION, COMFORT, & FIRE RESISTANCE (WHEN CHEMICALLY TREATED).

CHAIN MAIL

CHAIN MAIL GLOVES & VESTS ARE STILL MADE FOR BUTCHERS HANDLING SHARP KNIVES. COMPLETE CHAIN MAIL SUITS WORN OVER WETSUITS HAVE RECENTLY BEEN FOUND VERY EFFECTIVE AGAINST SHARK ATTACKS.

ELECTRIC HEATING

SUITS CONTAINING ELECTRIC HEATING WIRES WERE FIRST USED BY WORLD WAR I PILOTS. UNFORTUNATELY, THE ELECTRICITY CAME FROM A SMALL PROPELLER-DRIVEN GENERATOR ON THE WING. IN A DIVE, THE PLANE WENT SO FAST THAT THE PILOT GOT BURNT.

HOT WATER

DIVERS ARE KEPT WARM BY HOT WATER PUMPED THROUGH TUBES ALL OVER THEIR WETSUITS. THE USED WATER ESCAPES INTO THE SEA AT THE ANKLES & CUFFS.

CONDUCTION

MEN WORKING ON LIVE TRANSMISSION LINES WEAR WOVEN METAL CONDUCTING SUITS, WHICH ENSURE THAT THE WHOLE BODY REMAINS AT LINE VOLTAGE. THIS PREVENTS ANY CURRENT FLOWING THROUGH IT.

COOLING

PILOTS OF SUPERSONIC PLANES WEAR SUITS TO KEEP THEM COOL. FRICTION AGAINST THE AIR MAKES THE PLANE EXTREMELY HOT.

BOMBPROOF

BOMB DISPOSAL MEN WEAR VERY HEAVY SUITS (23KG) WHEN REMOTE-CONTROLLED DEVICES CANNOT BE USED TO DEAL WITH BOMBS. TO ALLOW THE NECESSARY DELICATE MANIPULATIONS, THE SUITS LEAVE THE HANDS UNPROTECTED.

QUICK RELEASE

BLAST FURNACE MEN WEAR QUICK RELEASE SHOES IN CASE THEY GET STUCK IN PUDDLES OF SOLIDIFYING MOLTEN METAL.

ICE JACKETS

COLD JACKETS, CONTAINING SEALED POCKETS OF ICE, ARE USED BY GLASS FURNACE MEN & SOUTH AFRICAN GOLDMINERS, DOUBLING THE TIME THEY CAN WORK COMFORTABLY.

KEVLAR

BULLETPROOF JACKETS & MANY OTHER PROTECTIVE SUITS ARE NOW MADE OF A PLASTIC CALLED KEVLAR. INTRODUCED IN 1971, WOVEN KEVLAR IS EXTREMELY RESISTANT TO CUTTING & TEARING.

STRING VESTS

THE STRING VEST, WHICH TRAPS POCKETS OF WARM AIR NEXT TO THE SKIN, IS NOT A RECENT IDEA. NORTH AMERICAN INDIANS USED TO WEAR BEAD VESTS, & BAMBOO VESTS ARE KNOWN IN ASIA.

CHEFS

THE CHEF'S DOUBLE-BREASTED REVERSIBLE JACKET PROVIDES USEFUL PROTECTION AGAINST HOT FAT. IT IS MADE REVERSIBLE TO PROVIDE A CLEAN FRONT IF THE CHEF IS CALLED INTO THE DINING ROOM.

HOW TO KEEP WARM

25% OF NORMAL BODY HEAT IS LOST THROUGH OUR HEADS, SO HATS ARE VERY EFFECTIVE IN PRESERVING HEAT. HOT AIR TRAPPED UNDER CLOTHES RISES —SCARVES PREVENT IT ESCAPING.

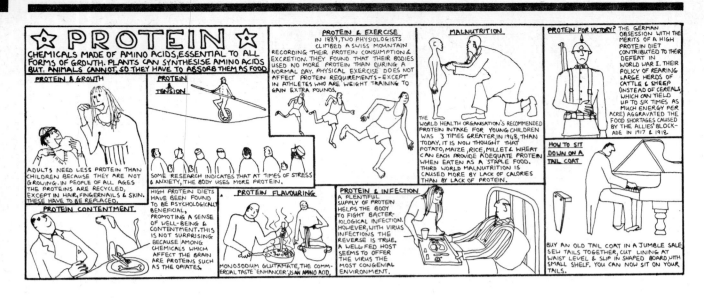

☆ PROTEIN ☆

CHEMICALS MADE OF AMINO ACIDS, ESSENTIAL TO ALL FORMS OF GROWTH. PLANTS CAN SYNTHESISE AMINO ACIDS BUT ANIMALS CANNOT, SO THEY HAVE TO ABSORB THEM AS FOOD.

PROTEIN & GROWTH
ADULTS NEED LESS PROTEIN THAN CHILDREN BECAUSE THEY ARE NOT GROWING. IN PEOPLE OF ALL AGES THE PROTEINS ARE RECYCLED, EXCEPT IN HAIR, FINGERNAILS & SKIN. THESE HAVE TO BE REPLACED.

PROTEIN & TENSION
SOME RESEARCH INDICATES THAT AT TIMES OF STRESS & ANXIETY, THE BODY USES MORE PROTEIN.

HIGH PROTEIN DIETS HAVE BEEN FOUND TO BE PSYCHOLOGICALLY BENEFICIAL, PROMOTING A SENSE OF WELL-BEING & CONTENTMENT. THIS IS NOT SURPRISING BECAUSE AMONG CHEMICALS WHICH AFFECT THE BRAIN ARE PROTEINS SUCH AS THE OPIATES.

PROTEIN CONTENTMENT.

PROTEIN FLAVOURING
MONOSODIUM GLUTAMATE, THE COMMERCIAL TASTE 'ENHANCER' IS AN AMINO ACID.

PROTEIN & EXERCISE
IN 1889, TWO PHYSIOLOGISTS CLIMBED A SWISS MOUNTAIN RECORDING THEIR PROTEIN CONSUMPTION & EXCRETION. THEY FOUND THAT THEIR BODIES USED NO MORE PROTEIN THAN DURING A NORMAL DAY. PHYSICAL EXERCISE DOES NOT AFFECT PROTEIN REQUIREMENTS – EXCEPT IN ATHLETES WHO ARE WEIGHT TRAINING TO GAIN EXTRA POUNDS.

PROTEIN & INFECTION
A PLENTIFUL SUPPLY OF PROTEIN HELPS THE BODY TO FIGHT BACTERIOLOGICAL INFECTION. HOWEVER, WITH VIRUS INFECTIONS THE REVERSE IS TRUE. A WELL-FED HOST SEEMS TO OFFER THE VIRUS THE MOST CONGENIAL ENVIRONMENT.

MALNUTRITION
THE WORLD HEALTH ORGANISATION'S RECOMMENDED PROTEIN INTAKE FOR YOUNG CHILDREN WAS 3 TIMES GREATER IN 1948, THAN TODAY. IT IS NOW THOUGHT THAT POTATO, MAIZE, RICE, MILLET & WHEAT CAN EACH PROVIDE ADEQUATE PROTEIN WHEN EATEN AS A STAPLE FOOD. THIRD WORLD MALNUTRITION IS CAUSED MORE BY LACK OF CALORIES THAN BY LACK OF PROTEIN.

PROTEIN FOR VICTORY?
THE GERMAN OBSESSION WITH THE MERITS OF A HIGH PROTEIN DIET CONTRIBUTED TO THEIR DEFEAT IN WORLD WAR I. THEIR POLICY OF REARING LARGE HERDS OF CATTLE & SHEEP (INSTEAD OF CEREALS, WHICH CAN YIELD UP TO SIX TIMES AS MUCH ENERGY PER ACRE) AGGRAVATED THE FOOD SHORTAGES CAUSED BY THE ALLIES' BLOCKADE IN 1917 & 1918.

HOW TO SIT DOWN ON A TAIL COAT
BUY AN OLD TAIL COAT IN A JUMBLE SALE. SEW TAILS TOGETHER, CUT LINING AT WAIST LEVEL & SLIP IN SHAPED BOARD WITH SMALL SHELF. YOU CAN NOW SIT ON YOUR TAILS.

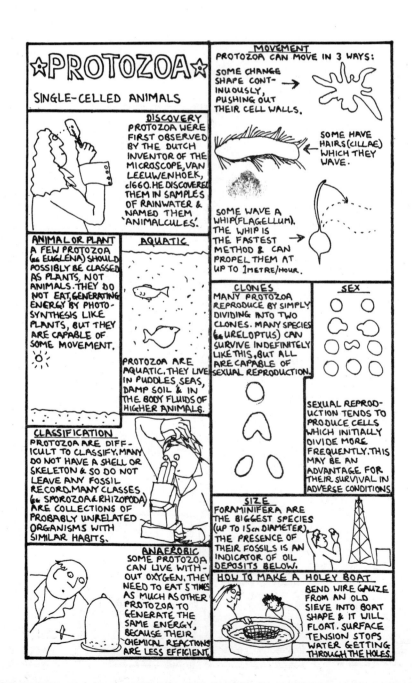

☆ PROTOZOA ☆

SINGLE-CELLED ANIMALS

DISCOVERY
PROTOZOA WERE FIRST OBSERVED BY THE DUTCH INVENTOR OF THE MICROSCOPE, VAN LEEUWENHOEK, c1660. HE DISCOVERED THEM IN SAMPLES OF RAINWATER & NAMED THEM 'ANIMALCULES'.

MOVEMENT
PROTOZOA CAN MOVE IN 3 WAYS:

SOME CHANGE SHAPE CONTINUOUSLY, PUSHING OUT THEIR CELL WALLS.

SOME HAVE HAIRS (CILLAE) WHICH THEY WAVE.

SOME WAVE A WHIP (FLAGELLUM). THE WHIP IS THE FASTEST METHOD & CAN PROPEL THEM AT UP TO 1 METRE/HOUR.

ANIMAL OR PLANT
A FEW PROTOZOA (e.g. EUGLENA) SHOULD POSSIBLY BE CLASSED AS PLANTS, NOT ANIMALS. THEY DO NOT EAT, GENERATING ENERGY BY PHOTOSYNTHESIS LIKE PLANTS, BUT THEY ARE CAPABLE OF SOME MOVEMENT.

AQUATIC
PROTOZOA ARE AQUATIC. THEY LIVE IN PUDDLES, SEAS, DAMP SOIL & IN THE BODY FLUIDS OF HIGHER ANIMALS.

CLONES
MANY PROTOZOA REPRODUCE BY SIMPLY DIVIDING INTO TWO CLONES. MANY SPECIES (e.g. UROLEPTUS) CAN SURVIVE INDEFINITELY LIKE THIS, BUT ALL ARE CAPABLE OF SEXUAL REPRODUCTION.

SEX
SEXUAL REPRODUCTION TENDS TO PRODUCE CELLS WHICH INITIALLY DIVIDE MORE FREQUENTLY. THIS MAY BE AN ADVANTAGE FOR THEIR SURVIVAL IN ADVERSE CONDITIONS.

CLASSIFICATION
PROTOZOA ARE DIFFICULT TO CLASSIFY. MANY DO NOT HAVE A SHELL OR SKELETON & SO DO NOT LEAVE ANY FOSSIL RECORD. MANY CLASSES (e.g. SPOROZOA & RHIZOPODA) ARE COLLECTIONS OF PROBABLY UNRELATED ORGANISMS WITH SIMILAR HABITS.

SIZE
FORAMINIFERA ARE THE BIGGEST SPECIES (UP TO 15cm DIAMETER). THE PRESENCE OF THEIR FOSSILS IS AN INDICATOR OF OIL DEPOSITS BELOW.

ANAEROBIC
SOME PROTOZOA CAN LIVE WITHOUT OXYGEN. THEY NEED TO EAT 5 TIMES AS MUCH AS OTHER PROTOZOA TO GENERATE THE SAME ENERGY, BECAUSE THEIR CHEMICAL REACTIONS ARE LESS EFFICIENT.

HOW TO MAKE A HOLEY BOAT
BEND WIRE GAUZE FROM AN OLD SIEVE INTO BOAT SHAPE & IT WILL FLOAT. SURFACE TENSION STOPS WATER GETTING THROUGH THE HOLES.

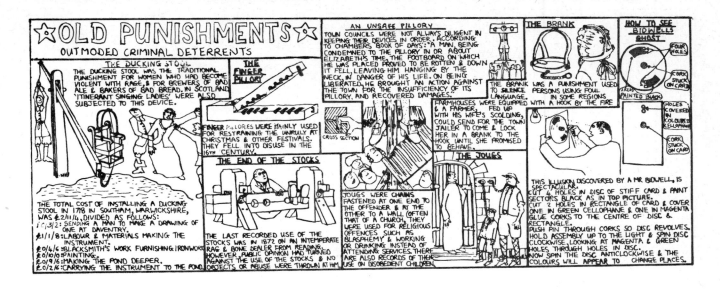

☆ OLD PUNISHMENTS ☆
OUTMODED CRIMINAL DETERRENTS

THE DUCKING STOOL
THE DUCKING STOOL WAS THE TRADITIONAL PUNISHMENT FOR WOMEN WHO HAD BECOME VIOLENT WITH RAGE, & FOR BREWERS OF BAD ALE & BAKERS OF BAD BREAD. IN SCOTLAND 'ITINERANT SINGING LADIES' WERE ALSO SUBJECTED TO THIS DEVICE.

THE TOTAL COST OF INSTALLING A DUCKING STOOL IN 1718 IN SOUTHAM, WARWICKSHIRE, WAS £2/11/4, DIVIDED AS FOLLOWS:
£0/3/2: SENDING A MAN TO MAKE A DRAWING OF ONE AT DAVENTRY.
£1/1/8: LABOUR & MATERIALS MAKING THE INSTRUMENT.
£0/4/6: BLACKSMITH'S WORK FURNISHING IRONWORK.
£0/10/0: PAINTING.
£0/9/6: MAKING THE POND DEEPER.
£0/2/6: CARRYING THE INSTRUMENT TO THE POND.

THE FINGER PILLORY
FINGER PILLORIES WERE MAINLY USED FOR RESTRAINING THE UNRULY AT CHRISTMAS & OTHER FESTIVALS. THEY FELL INTO DISUSE IN THE 16TH CENTURY.

THE END OF THE STOCKS
THE LAST RECORDED USE OF THE STOCKS WAS IN 1872 ON AN INTEMPERATE RAG & BONE DEALER FROM READING. HOWEVER, PUBLIC OPINION HAD TURNED AGAINST THE USE OF THE STOCKS & NO OBJECTS OR ABUSE WERE THROWN AT HIM.

AN UNSAFE PILLORY
TOWN COUNCILS WERE NOT ALWAYS DILIGENT IN KEEPING THEIR DEVICES IN ORDER. ACCORDING TO CHAMBERS BOOK OF DAYS: "A MAN, BEING CONDEMNED TO THE PILLORY IN OR ABOUT ELIZABETH'S TIME, THE FOOTBOARD ON WHICH HE WAS PLACED PROVED TO BE ROTTEN & DOWN IT FELL, LEAVING HIM HANGING BY THE NECK, IN DANGER OF HIS LIFE. ON BEING LIBERATED, HE BROUGHT AN ACTION AGAINST THE TOWN FOR THE INSUFFICIENCY OF ITS PILLORY, AND RECOVERED DAMAGES."

CROSS SECTION

THE JOUGS
JOUGS WERE CHAINS FASTENED AT ONE END TO THE OFFENDER & AT THE OTHER TO A WALL (OFTEN THAT OF A CHURCH). THEY WERE USED FOR RELIGIOUS OFFENCES SUCH AS BLASPHEMY & WORKING OR DRINKING INSTEAD OF ATTENDING SERVICES. THERE ARE ALSO RECORDS OF THEIR USE ON DISOBEDIENT CHILDREN.

THE BRANK
THE BRANK WAS A PUNISHMENT USED TO SILENCE PERSONS USING FOUL LANGUAGE. FARMHOUSES WERE EQUIPPED WITH A HOOK BY THE FIRE & A FARMER, FED UP WITH HIS WIFE'S SCOLDING, COULD SEND FOR THE TOWN JAILER TO COME & LOCK HER IN A BRANK TO THE HOOK UNTIL SHE PROMISED TO BEHAVE.

HOW TO SEE BIDWELL'S GHOST
THIS ILLUSION DISCOVERED BY A MR BIDWELL, IS SPECTACULAR. CUT 4 HOLES IN DISC OF STIFF CARD & PAINT SECTORS BLACK AS IN TOP PICTURE. CUT 2 HOLES IN RECTANGLE OF CARD & COVER ONE IN GREEN CELLOPHANE & ONE IN MAGENTA. GLUE CORKS TO THE CENTRE OF DISC & RECTANGLE. PUSH PIN THROUGH CORKS SO DISC REVOLVES. HOLD ASSEMBLY UP TO THE LIGHT & SPIN DISC CLOCKWISE, LOOKING AT MAGENTA & GREEN HOLES THROUGH HOLES IN DISC. NOW SPIN THE DISC ANTICLOCKWISE & THE COLOURS WILL APPEAR TO CHANGE PLACES.

FOUR HOLES / CORK STUCK ON CARD / AREAS PAINTED BLACK / HOLES COVERED IN COLOURED CELLOPHANE / CORK STUCK ON CARD

☆ PUPPETS ☆
DOLLS OR IMAGES MOVED BY WIRES OR HANDS

NEUROPASTES
THE GREEKS & ROMANS PRESENTED PUPPET SHOWS, PERFORMED BY NEUROPASTES (OR STRING PULLERS). MANY REGARDED THE PUPPET THEATRE AS SYMBOLIC OF HUMAN DESTINY. PLATO COMPARES MAN TO A MARIONETTE MANIPULATED BY THE HANDS OF THE GODS ACCORDING TO THEIR WHIMS.

PUNCH
THE ORIGIN OF PUNCH IS OBSCURE. SOME BELIEVE HE ARRIVED FROM FRANCE DURING THE REFORMATION (c1662), OTHERS BELIEVE HE EXISTED IN ELIZABETHAN ENGLAND. EITHER WAY HE IS A CLOSE RELATIVE OF PULCINELLA, A CHARACTER FROM THE EARLY ITALIAN THEATRE 'COMMEDIA DELL'ARTE'.

CHRISTIAN PUPPETS
THE EARLY CHRISTIAN CHURCH OFTEN USED MOVING FIGURINES TO REPRESENT THE SAINTS, THE VIRGIN MARY & CHRIST. EVEN CRUCIFIXES ON WHICH CHRIST'S EYES & MOUTH MOVED ARE KNOWN. THESE WERE MOSTLY DESTROYED IN THE 16TH CENTURY, ALTHOUGH SOME SURVIVE IN ITALY.

HIMMELREICH
PUPPETS HAVE BEEN POPULAR IN GERMANY SINCE THE MIDDLE AGES. ORIGINALLY THEY WERE CALLED 'HIMMELREICH' MEANING THE KINGDOM OF HEAVEN, AS THEY USED STRING PUPPETS & OFTEN LOWERED THEM ONTO THE STAGE AS IF ARRIVING FROM THE SKY.

BUNRAKU
THE JAPANESE HAVE A TRADITION OF LARGE PUPPETS, CALLED BUNRAKU, CONTROLLED FROM BEHIND BY PUPPETEERS DRESSED IN BLACK. THE PUPPETS MOVE THEIR FINGERS, MOUTHS, EYES & EYEBROWS. THREE PUPPETEERS ARE NEEDED TO MANIPULATE EACH PUPPET. APPRENTICES START BY CONTROLLING THE FEET, GRADUATING TO THE LEFT HAND & FINALLY TO THE HEAD & RIGHT HAND.

SPIRIT PUPPETS
SHADOW PUPPETS ARE FLAT CUT-OUT FIGURES WHICH APPEAR AS SILHOUETTES ON A LIGHTED SCREEN. THEY ARE TRADITIONALLY ASSOCIATED WITH THE SPIRITS OF THE DEAD. IT IS CALLED 'THE SCREEN OF DEATH' IN CHINA; 'CURTAIN OF THE DEPARTING' IN TURKEY; 'FOG & CLOUDS' IN JAVA; 'SCREEN OF DREAMS', 'VEIL OF THE DEPARTING', IN ARABIA.

REPLACEABLE MUPPETS
THE MUPPETS ARE MADE FROM EXPANDED POLYSTYRENE FOAM, WHICH IS VERY LIGHT & MAKES THEM LESS TIRING TO USE. UNFORTUNATELY, IT IS QUITE EASILY DAMAGED & MOST CHARACTERS HAVE TO HAVE NEW FACES EVERY YEAR.

PRUDISH PUPPETS
IN CHINA SHADOW PUPPET SHOWS WERE THE ONLY THEATRICAL ENTERTAINMENTS PERMITTED FOR RESPECTABLE WOMEN. THE STORIES WERE STRICTLY CENSORED & RATHER DULL.

HOW TO MAKE A LETTER BALANCE
CUT A 45cm LENGTH OF BROOMSTICK. NAIL A BIT OF CARD ACROSS TOP & TIE SMALL WEIGHT OR STONE TO BOTTOM. PLACE IN TALL GLASS JAR OF WATER. PUT KNOWN WEIGHTS ON CARD & MARK BROOMSTICK.

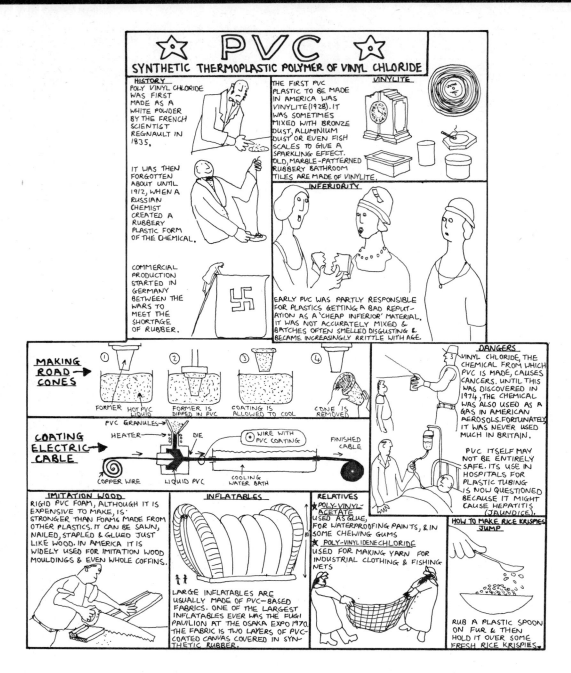

☆ PVC ☆

SYNTHETIC THERMOPLASTIC POLYMER OF VINYL CHLORIDE

HISTORY

POLY VINYL CHLORIDE WAS FIRST MADE AS A WHITE POWDER BY THE FRENCH SCIENTIST REGNAULT IN 1835.

IT WAS THEN FORGOTTEN ABOUT UNTIL 1912, WHEN A RUSSIAN CHEMIST CREATED A RUBBERY PLASTIC FORM OF THE CHEMICAL.

COMMERCIAL PRODUCTION STARTED IN GERMANY BETWEEN THE WARS TO MEET THE SHORTAGE OF RUBBER.

THE FIRST PVC PLASTIC TO BE MADE IN AMERICA WAS VINYLITE (1928). IT WAS SOMETIMES MIXED WITH BRONZE DUST, ALUMINIUM DUST OR EVEN FISH SCALES TO GIVE A SPARKLING EFFECT. OLD, MARBLE-PATTERNED RUBBERY BATHROOM TILES ARE MADE OF VINYLITE.

VINYLITE

INFERIORITY

EARLY PVC WAS PARTLY RESPONSIBLE FOR PLASTICS GETTING A BAD REPUTATION AS A 'CHEAP INFERIOR' MATERIAL. IT WAS NOT ACCURATELY MIXED & BATCHES OFTEN SMELLED DISGUSTING & BECAME INCREASINGLY BRITTLE WITH AGE.

MAKING ROAD CONES →

FORMER · HOT PVC LIQUID
FORMER IS DIPPED IN PVC
COATING IS ALLOWED TO COOL
CONE IS REMOVED

COATING ELECTRIC CABLE →

PVC GRANULES
HEATER
DIE
WIRE WITH PVC COATING
FINISHED CABLE
COPPER WIRE
LIQUID PVC
COOLING WATER BATH

DANGERS

VINYL CHLORIDE, THE CHEMICAL FROM WHICH PVC IS MADE, CAUSES CANCERS. UNTIL THIS WAS DISCOVERED IN 1974, THE CHEMICAL WAS ALSO USED AS A GAS IN AMERICAN AEROSOLS. FORTUNATELY IT WAS NEVER USED MUCH IN BRITAIN.

PVC ITSELF MAY NOT BE ENTIRELY SAFE. ITS USE IN HOSPITALS FOR PLASTIC TUBING IS NOW QUESTIONED BECAUSE IT MIGHT CAUSE HEPATITIS (JAUNDICE).

IMITATION WOOD

RIGID PVC FOAM, ALTHOUGH IT IS EXPENSIVE TO MAKE, IS STRONGER THAN FOAMS MADE FROM OTHER PLASTICS. IT CAN BE SAWN, NAILED, STAPLED & GLUED JUST LIKE WOOD. IN AMERICA IT IS WIDELY USED FOR IMITATION WOOD MOULDINGS & EVEN WHOLE COFFINS.

INFLATABLES

LARGE INFLATABLES ARE USUALLY MADE OF PVC-BASED FABRICS. ONE OF THE LARGEST INFLATABLES EVER WAS THE FUGI PAVILION AT THE OSAKA EXPO 1970. THE FABRIC IS TWO LAYERS OF PVC-COATED CANVAS COVERED IN SYNTHETIC RUBBER.

RELATIVES

★ POLY-VINYL-ACETATE USED AS GLUE, FOR WATERPROOFING PAINTS, & IN SOME CHEWING GUMS

★ POLY-VINYLIDENECHLORIDE USED FOR MAKING YARN FOR INDUSTRIAL CLOTHING & FISHING NETS

HOW TO MAKE RICE KRISPIES JUMP

RUB A PLASTIC SPOON ON FUR & THEN HOLD IT OVER SOME FRESH RICE KRISPIES.

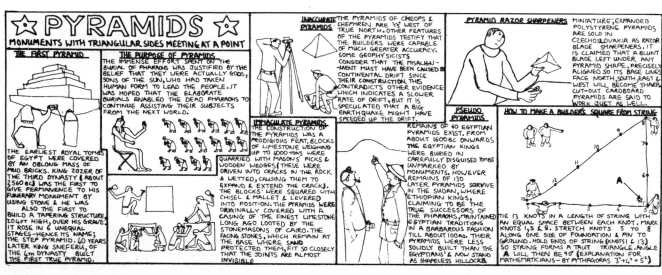

☆ PYRAMIDS ☆

MONUMENTS WITH TRIANGULAR SIDES MEETING AT A POINT

THE FIRST PYRAMID

THE EARLIEST ROYAL TOMBS OF EGYPT WERE COVERED BY AN OBLONG MASS OF MUD BRICKS. KING ZOZER OF THE THIRD DYNASTY (ABOUT 2560 BC) WAS THE FIRST TO GIVE PERMANENCE TO HIS FUNERARY MONUMENT BY USING STONE & HE WAS ALSO THE FIRST TO BUILD A TAPERING STRUCTURE. 204FT HIGH, OVER HIS GRAVE, IT ROSE IN 6 UNEQUAL STAGES—HENCE ITS NAME; THE STEP PYRAMID. 60 YEARS LATER KING SNEFERU, OF THE 4th DYNASTY BUILT THE FIRST TRUE PYRAMID.

THE PURPOSE OF PYRAMIDS

THE IMMENSE EFFORT SPENT ON THE BURIAL OF PHARAOHS WAS JUSTIFIED BY THE BELIEF THAT THEY WERE ACTUALLY GODS, SONS OF THE SUN, WHO HAD TAKEN HUMAN FORM TO LEAD THE PEOPLE. IT WAS HOPED THAT THE ELABORATE BURIALS ENABLED THE DEAD PHARAOHS TO CONTINUE ASSISTING THEIR SUBJECTS FROM THE NEXT WORLD.

INACCURATE PYRAMIDS

THE PYRAMIDS OF CHEOPS & CHEPHREN ARE 1/3° WEST OF TRUE NORTH. OTHER FEATURES OF THE PYRAMIDS TESTIFY THAT THE BUILDERS WERE CAPABLE OF MUCH GREATER ACCURACY. SOME GEOPHYSICISTS CONSIDER THAT THE MISALIGNMENT MUST HAVE BEEN CAUSED BY CONTINENTAL DRIFT SINCE THEIR CONSTRUCTION. THIS CONTRADICTS OTHER EVIDENCE WHICH INDICATES A SLOWER RATE OF DRIFT, BUT IT IS SPECULATED THAT A BIG EARTHQUAKE MIGHT HAVE SPEEDED UP THE DRIFT.

IMMACULATE PYRAMIDS

THE CONSTRUCTION OF THE PYRAMIDS WAS A PRODIGIOUS FEAT. BLOCKS OF LIMESTONE WEIGHING UP TO 1000 TONS WERE QUARRIED WITH MASONS' PICKS & WOODEN WEDGES (THESE WERE DRIVEN INTO CRACKS IN THE ROCK & WETTED, CAUSING THEM TO EXPAND & EXTEND THE CRACK). THE BLOCKS WERE SQUARED WITH CHISEL & MALLET & LEVERED INTO POSITION. THE PYRAMIDS WERE ORIGINALLY COVERED WITH A CASING OF THE FINEST LIMESTONE LONG AGO LOOTED BY THE STONEMASONS OF CAIRO. THE FACING STONES, WHICH REMAIN AT THE BASE WHERE SAND PROTECTED THEM, FIT SO CLOSELY THAT THE JOINTS ARE ALMOST INVISIBLE

PSEUDO PYRAMIDS

REMAINS OF 60 EGYPTIAN PYRAMIDS EXIST, FROM ABOUT 1600 BC ONWARDS THE EGYPTIAN KINGS WERE BURIED IN CAREFULLY DISGUISED TOMBS UNMARKED BY MONUMENTS. HOWEVER REMAINS OF 130 LATER PYRAMIDS SURVIVE IN THE SUDAN, WHERE ETHIOPIAN KINGS, CLAIMING TO BE THE TRUE SUCCESSORS OF THE PHARAOHS, MAINTAINED EGYPTIAN TRADITIONS IN A BARBAROUS FASHION TILL ABOUT 100 AD. THEIR PYRAMIDS WERE LESS SOLIDLY BUILT THAN THE EGYPTIANS' & NOW STAND AS SHAPELESS HILLOCKS.

PYRAMID RAZOR SHARPENERS

MINIATURE, EXPANDED POLYSTYRENE PYRAMIDS ARE SOLD IN CZECHOSLOVAKIA AS RAZOR BLADE SHARPENERS. IT IS CLAIMED THAT A BLUNT BLADE LEFT UNDER ANY PYRAMID SHAPE, PRECISELY ALIGNED SO ITS BASE LINES FACE NORTH, SOUTH, EAST & WEST WILL BECOME SHARP. CUT-OUT CARDBOARD PYRAMIDS ARE SAID TO WORK JUST AS WELL.

HOW TO MAKE A BUILDER'S SQUARE FROM STRING

TIE 13 KNOTS IN A LENGTH OF STRING WITH AN EQUAL SPACE BETWEEN EACH KNOT. MARK KNOTS 1, 5 & 8. STRETCH KNOTS 5 TO 8 ALONG ONE SIDE OF FOUNDATION & PIN TO GROUND. HOLD ENDS OF STRING (KNOTS 1 & 13) SO STRING FORMS A TAUT TRIANGLE. ANGLE A WILL THEN BE 90° (EXPLANATION FOR MATHEMATICIANS—BY PYTHAGORAS $3^2 + 4^2 = 5^2$)

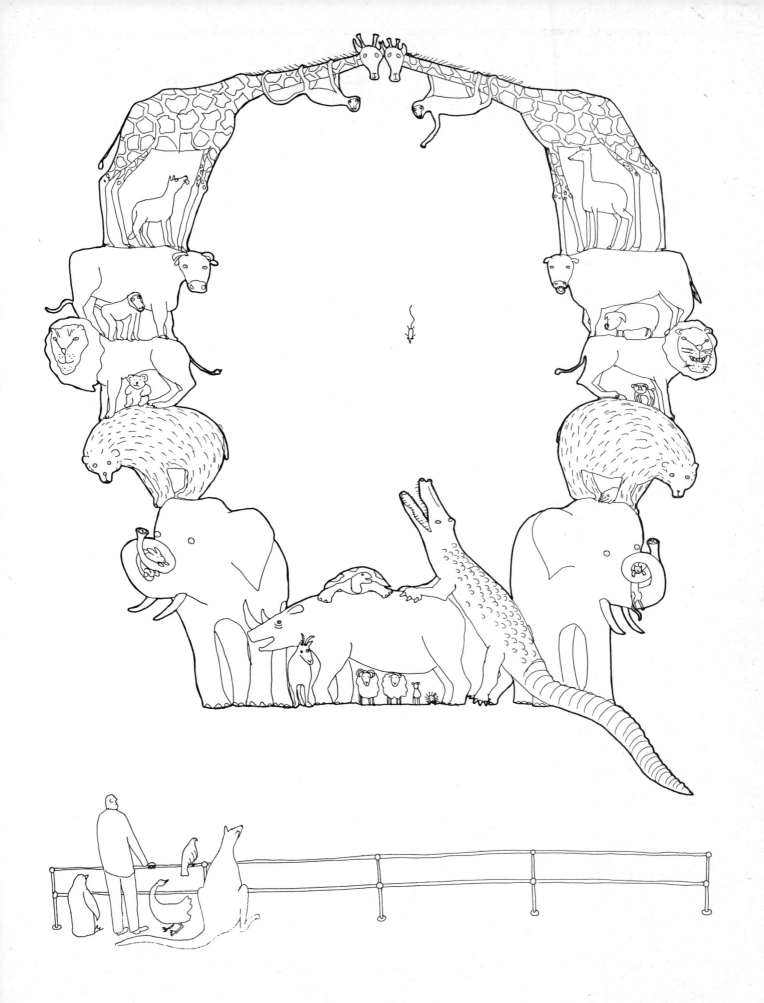

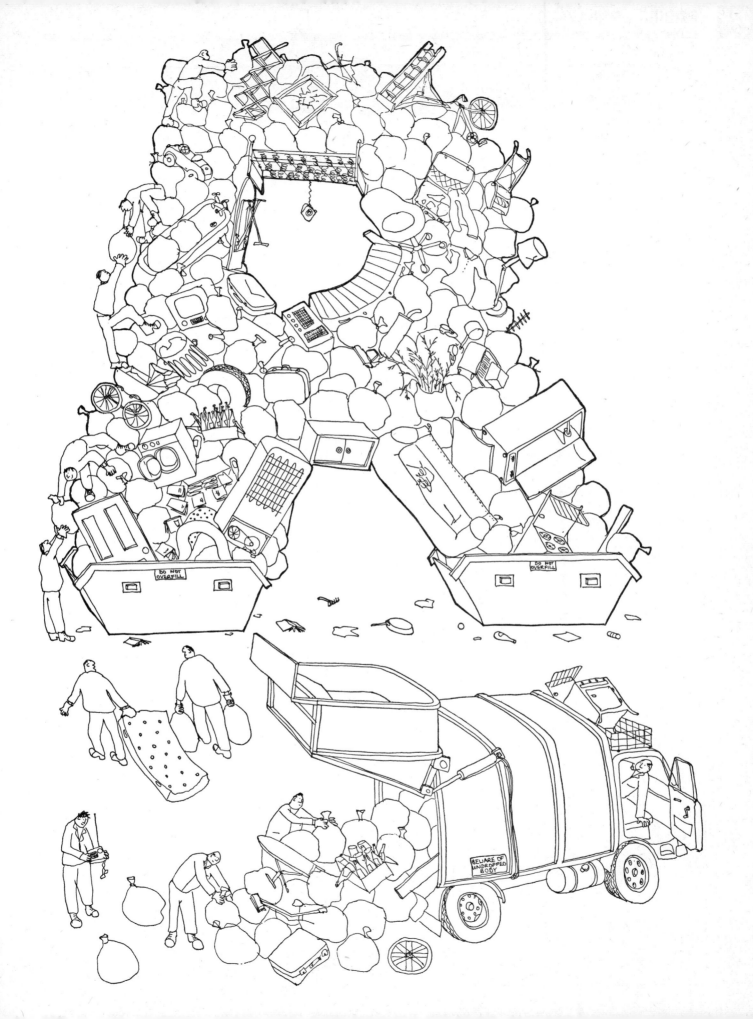

☆ RABIES ☆
INFECTIOUS VIRUS DISEASE TRANSMITTED BY SALIVA

SYMPTOMS
ABOUT 2 MONTHS AFTER BEING BITTEN THE VICTIM DEVELOPS A GREAT THIRST (BUT CANNOT SWALLOW) VISCOUS SALIVA & A TERRIFIED EXPRESSION. FITS OF MANIACAL EXCITEMENT & SPASMS MAY FOLLOW BEFORE HE DIES, ABOUT 5 DAYS LATER.

IN BRITAIN, THE MUZZLING OF ALL DOMESTIC DOGS WAS MADE COMPULSORY IN 1890 & UNMUZZLED DOGS WERE SHOT. IN 1892 THE PET LOVING LOBBY HAD THIS REPEALED & RABIES CASES INCREASED TO HIGHER LEVELS THAN EVER BEFORE.

QUARANTINE
USSR

1950
1969   1953
1970   1953
1977

IT HAS BEEN ARGUED THAT BRITAIN IS NOT AT RISK. EVEN THE RHINE STOPPED THE ADVANCE OF RABIES FOR 4 YEARS IN THE 1960s SO THE ENGLISH CHANNEL SHOULD BE AN EFFECTIVE BARRIER. SINCE 1970, ONLY ONE OF THE 75,000 ANIMALS IN QUARANTINE HAS DEVELOPED RABIES.

PASTEUR'S VACCINE
PASTEUR'S RABIES VACCINATIONS (1885) CONSISTED OF LIQUIDISED BRAIN CELLS OF INFECTED SHEEP, GIVEN AS SOON AS POSSIBLE AFTER THE BITE. THE COURSE CONSISTED OF 20 PAINFUL STOMACH WALL INJECTIONS, STARTING WITH INACTIVE CELLS FROM SHEEP DEAD 14 DAYS & BUILDING UP TO ACTIVE CELLS FROM FRESHLY KILLED SHEEP.

RESISTANCE
RABIES IS FATAL TO MOST MAMMALS EXCEPT VAMPIRE BATS & CERTAIN MONGOOSES.

ERADICATION
IN 1897 FRESH LEGISLATION, INCLUDING THE FIRST QUARANTINE RESTRICTIONS, WAS INTRODUCED & RABIES WAS ELIMINATED IN BRITAIN BY 1902.

MODERN VACCINE
PASTEUR'S VACCINE WAS USED UP TO THE 1950s. THE NEW SYNTHETIC VACCINE REQUIRES ONLY 4-6, LESS PAINFUL INJECTIONS.

FOX VACCINE
CURRENTLY A PROGRAMME OF FOX VACCINATION IS SUCCESSFULLY PREVENTING RABIES ENTERING SWISS VALLEYS. THE VACCINE IS MIXED WITH EGG & PUT IN CAPSULES HIDDEN INSIDE CHICKEN HEADS. THESE ARE DROPPED ROUND THE MOUTHS OF THE VALLEYS BY HELICOPTER.

FIERCE RABIES
STORIES OF VAMPIRES & WEREWOLVES PROBABLY STEM FROM RABID BATS & WOLVES, WHO CAN BITE WITH SUCH FEROCITY THAT THEY BREAK THEIR OWN JAWS.

FRIENDLY RABIES
MANY HIGHLY INFECTIOUS ANIMALS BECOME EXTREMELY FRIENDLY & APPROACHABLE FOR A BRIEF PERIOD BEFORE BECOMING FIERCE. THIS IS A SUBTLE ADAPTATION OF THE VIRUS WHICH INCREASES ITS CHANCES OF BEING PASSED ON.

POISONING
A FRENCH ATTEMPT TO CONTROL RABIES IN THE 1970s BY POISONING FOXES ROUND DIJON FAILED, CAUSING A RAPID SPREAD OF THE DISEASE. AS THE FOXES DIED, THEIR TERRITORIAL SYSTEM WAS DESTROYED, OTHER FOXES MOVED IN FROM SURROUNDING AREAS & CARRIED THE DISEASE WITH THEM.

HOW TO FILL AN EGG WITH CONFETTI
PIERCE TWO HOLES IN AN EGG WITH THE POINT OF A PAIR OF SCISSORS & BLOW OUT THE CONTENTS CAREFULLY ENLARGE ONE HOLE TO ABOUT 3mm & PUSH IN BITS OF CONFETTI. BREAK EGG OVER FRIEND'S HEAD.

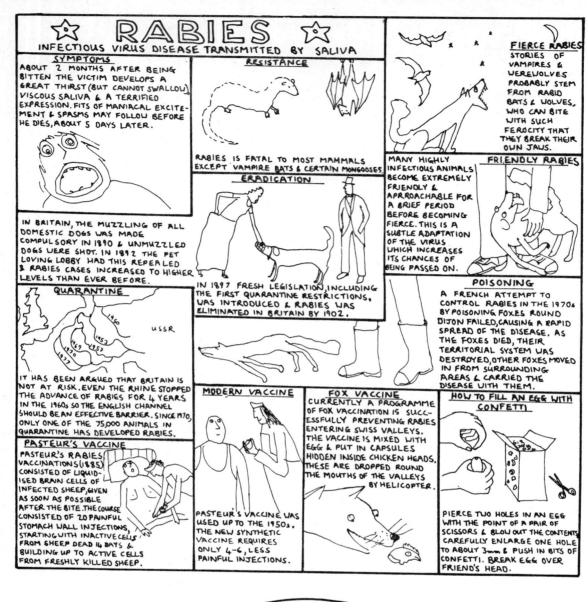

☆ RADAR ☆
THE DETECTION & LOCATION OF REMOTE OBJECTS BY RADIO WAVES

RADAR & ECHOES
THE PRINCIPLE OF RADAR IS SIMILAR TO THAT OF ACOUSTIC ECHOES. BOTH SOUND WAVES & RADIO WAVES CAN BE REFLECTED BY BUILDINGS & CLIFFS.

RADAR WORKS BY TRANSMITTING RADIO WAVE PULSES FROM DISTANT OBJECTS & PICKING UP THE REFLECTIONS. THE TIME LAPSE BETWEEN TRANSMISSION & REFLECTION IS PROPORTIONAL TO THE DISTANCE OF THE OBJECT.

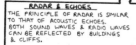

THE FIRST RADAR
IN 1934, THE AIR MINISTRY COMMISSIONED SIR ROBERT WATSON-WATT TO INVESTIGATE THE POSSIBILITY OF A DEATH RAY. HIS REPORT DISMISSED THE CONCEPT OF DEATH RAYS BUT CONSIDERED THE POSSIBILITY OF RADIO DETECTION. AFTER SEVERAL CONVINCING DEMONSTRATIONS, IN WHICH HE DETECTED AT RANGES OF UP TO 40 MILES (WITH EQUIPMENT MOUNTED IN THE BACK OF HIS MORRIS VAN), THE AIR MINISTRY'S FIRST PRACTICAL RADAR STATIONS WERE SET UP TO PROTECT THE THAMES ESTUARY.

SUPERIOR RADAR
IN WORLD WAR II, THE ALLIES' RADAR WAS SUPERIOR TO THE NAZIS' BECAUSE OF THE DISCOVERY OF THE CAVITY MAGNETRON: A DEVICE WHICH TRANSMITS MICROWAVE FREQUENCIES. THIS WAS MUCH SMALLER & MORE POWERFUL THAN PREVIOUS TRANSMITTERS, & IT REMAINED UNKNOWN TO THE NAZIS UNTIL THEY FOUND ONE IN A CRASHED PLANE IN 1943.

AWACS
THE MICROWAVES USED IN RADAR TRAVEL IN STRAIGHT LINES, SO RADAR CANNOT 'SEE' OVER THE HORIZON. TO 'INCREASE THE EFFECTIVE RANGE OF RADAR, AIRBORNE RADARS HAVE BEEN DEVELOPED CALLED 'AWACS' (ADVANCED WARNING & CONTROL SYSTEMS). THIS DETECTS ONLY MOVING OBJECTS & FILTERS OUT ANYTHING MOVING SLOWER THAN 90MPH SO THE RADAR IS NOT SWAMPED WITH ROAD TRAFFIC.

HIGH SPEED RADAR
THE LATEST RADARS ROTATE AT 750rpm (10 TIMES FASTER THAN THE TRADITIONAL TYPES). THIS GIVES A PICTURE WHICH DOESN'T FLICKER ON THE SCREEN & WHICH IS ACCURATE ENOUGH TO DISTINGUISH AIRCRAFT TYPES. IT CAN EVEN DETECT A DEAD HARE ON THE RUNWAY.

SECONDARY RADAR
ANY AIRCRAFT FLYING IN MILITARY CONTROLLED AIRSPACE HAS TO CARRY A SECONDARY RADAR. THIS PICKS UP SIGNALS FROM GROUND RADAR STATIONS & RE-TRANSMITS THEM, TOGETHER WITH A PULSED CODE INDICATING ITS IDENTITY & POSITION. ANY AIRCRAFT WHICH FAILS TO RESPOND IN THIS MANNER IS INTERCEPTED BY A FIGHTER PLANE & INSPECTED VISUALLY.

HOW TO MAKE A RACE TRACK FOR MARBLES
BUY A LUMP OF DAS MODELLING CLAY & ROLL IT OUT TO A 1cm THICK RECTANGLE SCOOP OUT TRACKS FOR MARBLES WITH LOOP OF WIRE. SMOOTH TRACKS WITH WETTED FINGER. WHEN DAS HAS SET, PLACE TRACK ON GENTLE SLOPE & ROCK FROM SIDE TO SIDE TO CONTROL MARBLES' DESCENT.

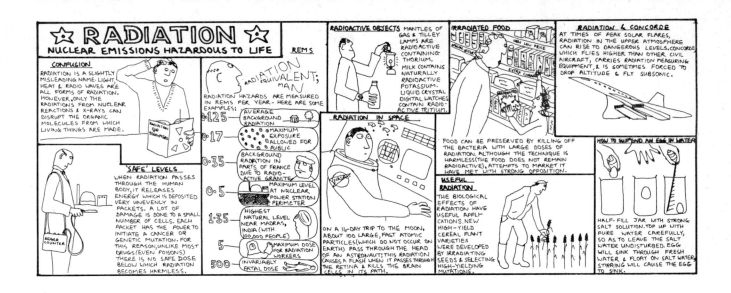

☆ RADIATION ☆
NUCLEAR EMISSIONS HAZARDOUS TO LIFE
REMS

CONFUSION
RADIATION IS A SLIGHTLY MISLEADING NAME. LIGHT, HEAT & RADIO WAVES ARE ALL FORMS OF RADIATION. HOWEVER, ONLY THE RADIATIONS FROM NUCLEAR REACTIONS & X-RAYS CAN DISRUPT THE ORGANIC MOLECULES FROM WHICH LIVING THINGS ARE MADE.

'SAFE' LEVELS
WHEN RADIATION PASSES THROUGH THE HUMAN BODY, IT RELEASES ENERGY WHICH IS DEPOSITED VERY UNEVENLY IN PACKETS. A LOT OF DAMAGE IS DONE TO A SMALL NUMBER OF CELLS. EACH PACKET HAS THE POWER TO INITIATE A CANCER OR GENETIC MUTATION. FOR THIS REASON, UNLIKE MOST DRUGS (EVEN POISONS) THERE IS NO SAFE DOSE BELOW WHICH RADIATION BECOMES HARMLESS.

RADIATION EQUIVALENT; MAN

RADIATION HAZARDS ARE MEASURED IN REMS PER YEAR – HERE ARE SOME EXAMPLES:
- 0·125 AVERAGE BACKGROUND RADIATION
- 0·17 MAXIMUM EXPOSURE ALLOWED FOR PUBLIC
- 0·35 BACKGROUND RADIATION IN PARTS OF FRANCE DUE TO RADIO-ACTIVE GRANITE
- 0·5 MAXIMUM LEVEL AT NUCLEAR POWER STATION PERIMETER
- 1·35 HIGHEST NATURAL LEVEL NEAR MADRAS, INDIA (WITH 100,000 PEOPLE)
- 5 MAXIMUM DOSE FOR RADIATION WORKERS
- 500 INVARIABLY FATAL DOSE

RADIOACTIVE OBJECTS
MANTLES OF GAS & TILLEY LAMPS ARE RADIOACTIVE CONTAINING THORIUM. MILK CONTAINS NATURALLY RADIOACTIVE POTASSIUM. LIQUID CRYSTAL DIGITAL WATCHES CONTAIN RADIO-ACTIVE TRITIUM.

RADIATION IN SPACE
ON A 14-DAY TRIP TO THE MOON, ABOUT 100 LARGE, FAST ATOMIC PARTICLES (WHICH DO NOT OCCUR ON EARTH) PASS THROUGH THE HEAD OF AN ASTRONAUT; THIS RADIATION CAUSES A FLASH WHEN IT PASSES THROUGH THE RETINA & KILLS THE BRAIN CELLS IN ITS PATH.

IRRADIATED FOOD
FOOD CAN BE PRESERVED BY KILLING OFF THE BACTERIA WITH LARGE DOSES OF RADIATION, ALTHOUGH THE TECHNIQUE IS HARMLESS (THE FOOD DOES NOT REMAIN RADIOACTIVE), ATTEMPTS TO MARKET IT HAVE MET WITH STRONG OPPOSITION.

USEFUL RADIATION
THE BIOLOGICAL EFFECTS OF RADIATION HAVE USEFUL APPLICATIONS. NEW HIGH-YIELD CEREAL PLANT VARIETIES WERE DEVELOPED BY IRRADIATING SEEDS & SELECTING HIGH-YIELDING MUTATIONS.

RADIATION & CONCORDE
AT TIMES OF PEAK SOLAR FLARES, RADIATION IN THE UPPER ATMOSPHERE CAN RISE TO DANGEROUS LEVELS. CONCORDE WHICH FLIES HIGHER THAN OTHER CIVIL AIRCRAFT, CARRIES RADIATION MEASURING EQUIPMENT, & IS SOMETIMES FORCED TO DROP ALTITUDE & FLY SUBSONIC.

HOW TO SUSPEND AN EGG IN WATER
HALF-FILL JAR WITH STRONG SALT SOLUTION. TOP UP WITH PURE WATER CAREFULLY, SO AS TO LEAVE THE SALT WATER UNDISTURBED. EGG WILL SINK THROUGH FRESH WATER & FLOAT ON SALT WATER. STIRRING WILL CAUSE THE EGG TO SINK.

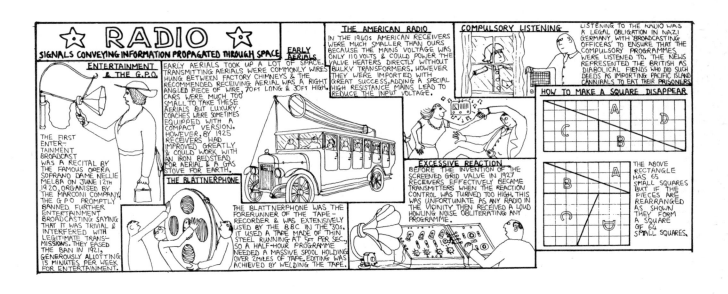

☆ RADIO ☆
SIGNALS CONVEYING INFORMATION PROPAGATED THROUGH SPACE

ENTERTAINMENT & THE G.P.O.
THE FIRST ENTERTAINMENT BROADCAST WAS A RECITAL BY THE FAMOUS OPERA SOPRANO DAME NELLIE MELBA ON JUNE 12TH 1920, ORGANISED BY THE MARCONI COMPANY. THE G.P.O PROMPTLY BANNED FURTHER ENTERTAINMENT BROADCASTING SAYING THAT IT WAS TRIVIAL & INTERFERED WITH LEGITIMATE TRANSMISSIONS. THEY EASED THE BAN IN 1921, GENEROUSLY ALLOTTING 15 MINUTES PER WEEK FOR ENTERTAINMENT.

EARLY AERIALS
EARLY AERIALS TOOK UP A LOT OF SPACE. TRANSMITTING AERIALS WERE COMMONLY WIRES HUNG BETWEEN FACTORY CHIMNEYS & THE RECOMMENDED RECEIVING AERIAL WAS A RIGHT ANGLED PIECE OF WIRE, 70FT LONG & 30FT HIGH. CARS WERE MUCH TOO SMALL TO TAKE THESE AERIALS BUT LUXURY COACHES WERE SOMETIMES EQUIPPED WITH A COMPACT VERSION. HOWEVER, BY 1925 RECEIVERS HAD IMPROVED GREATLY & COULD WORK WITH AN IRON BEDSTEAD FOR AERIAL & A GAS STOVE FOR EARTH.

THE BLATTNERPHONE
THE BLATTNERPHONE WAS THE FORERUNNER OF THE TAPE-RECORDER & WAS EXTENSIVELY USED BY THE B.B.C IN THE '30s. IT USED A TAPE MADE OF THIN STEEL RUNNING AT 5FT PER SEC., SO A HALF-HOUR PROGRAMME NEEDED A MASSIVE SPOOL HOLDING OVER 2MILES OF TAPE. EDITING WAS ACHIEVED BY WELDING THE TAPE.

THE AMERICAN RADIO
IN THE 1940s AMERICAN RECEIVERS WERE MUCH SMALLER THAN OURS BECAUSE THE MAINS VOLTAGE WAS ONLY 110 VOLTS & COULD POWER THE VALVE HEATERS DIRECTLY WITHOUT BULKY TRANSFORMERS. HOWEVER THEY WERE IMPORTED WITH GREAT SUCCESS, ADDING A SPECIAL HIGH RESISTANCE MAINS LEAD TO REDUCE THE INPUT VOLTAGE.

EXCESSIVE REACTION
BEFORE THE INVENTION OF THE SCREENED GRID VALVE IN 1927 RECEIVERS EFFECTIVELY BECAME TRANSMITTERS WHEN THE REACTION CONTROL WAS TURNED TOO HIGH. THIS WAS UNFORTUNATE AS ANY RADIO IN THE VICINITY THEN RECEIVED A LOUD HOWLING NOISE OBLITERATING ANY PROGRAMME.

COMPULSORY LISTENING
LISTENING TO THE RADIO WAS A LEGAL OBLIGATION IN NAZI GERMANY, WITH 'BROADCASTING OFFICERS' TO ENSURE THAT THE COMPULSORY PROGRAMMES WERE LISTENED TO. THE NEWS REPRESENTED THE BRITISH AS DIABOLICAL FIENDS WHO DID SUCH DEEDS AS IMPORTING PACIFIC ISLAND CANNIBALS TO EAT THEIR PRISONERS.

HOW TO MAKE A SQUARE DISAPPEAR
THE ABOVE RECTANGLE HAS 65 SMALL SQUARES BUT IF THE PIECES ARE REARRANGED AS SHOWN THEY FORM A SQUARE OF 64 SMALL SQUARES.

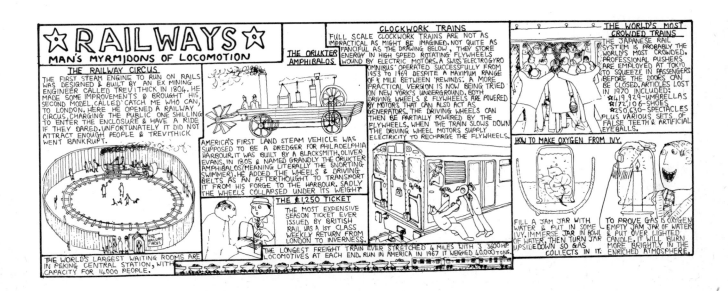

☆ RAILWAYS ☆
MAN'S MYRMIDONS OF LOCOMOTION

THE RAILWAY CIRCUS
THE FIRST STEAM ENGINE TO RUN ON RAILS WAS DESIGNED & BUILT BY AN EX MINING ENGINEER CALLED TREVITHICK IN 1804. HE MADE SOME IMPROVEMENTS & BROUGHT HIS SECOND MODEL, CALLED 'CATCH ME WHO CAN', TO LONDON. HERE HE OPENED A RAILWAY CIRCUS, CHARGING THE PUBLIC ONE SHILLING TO ENTER THE ENCLOSURE & HAVE A RIDE IF THEY DARED. UNFORTUNATELY IT DID NOT ATTRACT ENOUGH PEOPLE & TREVITHICK WENT BANKRUPT.

THE WORLD'S LARGEST WAITING ROOMS ARE IN PEKING CENTRAL STATION, WITH CAPACITY FOR 14,000 PEOPLE.

THE ORUKTER AMPHIBALOS
AMERICA'S FIRST LAND STEAM VEHICLE WAS SUPPOSED TO BE A DREDGER FOR PHILADELPHIA HARBOUR. IT WAS BUILT BY A BLACKSMITH, OLIVER EVANS, IN 1805 & NAMED GRANDLY THE ORUKTER AMPHIBALOS (MEANING LITERALLY THE SNORTING SWIMMER). HE ADDED THE WHEELS & DRIVING BELTS AS AN AFTERTHOUGHT TO TRANSPORT IT FROM HIS FORGE TO THE HARBOUR. SADLY THE WHEELS COLLAPSED UNDER ITS WEIGHT.

THE £1,250 TICKET
THE MOST EXPENSIVE SEASON TICKET EVER ISSUED BY BRITISH RAIL WAS A 1ST CLASS WEEKLY RETURN FROM LONDON TO INVERNESS.

THE LONGEST FREIGHT TRAIN EVER STRETCHED 4 MILES WITH 3 3600HP LOCOMOTIVES AT EACH END. RUN IN AMERICA IN 1967 IT WEIGHED 40,000 TONS.

CLOCKWORK TRAINS
FULL SCALE CLOCKWORK TRAINS ARE NOT AS IMPRACTICAL AS MIGHT BE IMAGINED, NOT QUITE AS FANCIFUL AS THE DRAWING BELOW. THEY STORE ENERGY IN HIGH SPEED ROTATING FLYWHEELS WOUND BY ELECTRIC MOTORS. A SWISS 'ELECTROGYRO' OMNIBUS' OPERATED SUCCESSFULLY FROM 1953 TO 1969 DESPITE A MAXIMUM RANGE OF ⅝ MILE BETWEEN 'REWINDS'. A MORE PRACTICAL VERSION IS NOW BEING TRIED ON NEW YORK'S UNDERGROUND. BOTH DRIVING WHEELS & FLYWHEELS ARE POWERED BY MOTORS THAT CAN ALSO ACT AS GENERATORS. THE DRIVING WHEELS CAN THEN BE PARTIALLY POWERED BY THE FLYWHEELS. WHEN THE TRAIN SLOWS DOWN THE DRIVING WHEEL MOTORS SUPPLY ELECTRICITY TO RECHARGE THE FLYWHEELS.

THE WORLD'S MOST CROWDED TRAINS
THE JAPANESE RAIL SYSTEM IS PROBABLY THE WORLD'S MOST CROWDED. PROFESSIONAL PUSHERS ARE EMPLOYED AT TOKYO TO SQUEEZE IN PASSENGERS BEFORE THE DOORS CAN BE CLOSED. ARTICLES LOST IN 1970 INCLUDED:
- ☆ 419,929 – UMBRELLAS
- ☆ 172,106 – SHOES
- ☆ 250,630 – SPECTACLES

PLUS VARIOUS SETS OF FALSE TEETH & ARTIFICIAL EYEBALLS.

HOW TO MAKE OXYGEN FROM IVY
FILL A JAM JAR WITH WATER & PUT IN SOME IVY. IMMERSE JAR IN BOWL OF WATER, THEN TURN JAR UPSIDE DOWN SO GAS COLLECTS IN IT.

TO PROVE GAS IS OXYGEN EMPTY JAM JAR OF WATER & PUT OVER LIGHTED CANDLE. IT WILL BURN MORE BRIGHTLY IN THE ENRICHED ATMOSPHERE.

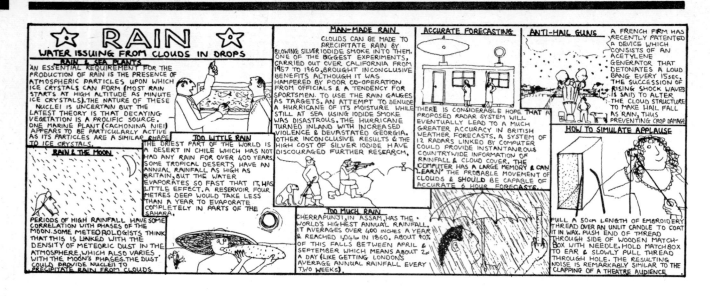

☆ RAIN ☆
WATER ISSUING FROM CLOUDS IN DROPS

RAIN & SEA PLANTS
AN ESSENTIAL REQUIREMENT FOR THE PRODUCTION OF RAIN IS THE PRESENCE OF ATMOSPHERIC PARTICLES UPON WHICH ICE CRYSTALS CAN FORM (MOST RAIN STARTS AT HIGH ALTITUDE AS MINUTE ICE CRYSTALS). THE NATURE OF THESE NUCLEI IS UNCERTAIN BUT THE LATEST THEORY IS THAT DECAYING VEGETATION IS A PROLIFIC SOURCE. ONE MARINE PLANT (CACHONINA NIEI) APPEARS TO BE PARTICULARLY ACTIVE AS ITS PARTICLES ARE A SIMILAR SHAPE TO ICE CRYSTALS.

RAIN & THE MOON
PERIODS OF HIGH RAINFALL HAVE SOME CORRELATION WITH PHASES OF THE MOON. SOME METEOROLOGISTS THINK THAT THIS IS LINKED WITH THE DENSITY OF METEORIC DUST IN THE ATMOSPHERE, WHICH ALSO VARIES WITH THE MOON'S PHASES. THE DUST COULD PROVIDE NUCLEI TO PRECIPITATE RAIN FROM CLOUDS.

TOO LITTLE RAIN
A DESERT IN CHILE WHICH HAS NOT HAD ANY RAIN FOR OVER 400 YEARS. SOME TROPICAL DESERTS HAVE AN ANNUAL RAINFALL AS HIGH AS BRITAIN, BUT THE WATER EVAPORATES SO FAST THAT IT HAS LITTLE EFFECT. A RESERVOIR FOUR METRES DEEP WOULD TAKE LESS THAN A YEAR TO EVAPORATE COMPLETELY IN PARTS OF THE SAHARA.

MAN-MADE RAIN
CLOUDS CAN BE MADE TO PRECIPITATE RAIN BY BLOWING SILVER IODIDE SMOKE INTO THEM. ONE OF THE BIGGEST EXPERIMENTS, CARRIED OUT OVER CALIFORNIA FROM 1957 TO 1960, BROUGHT INCONCLUSIVE BENEFITS ALTHOUGH IT WAS HAMPERED BY POOR CO-OPERATION FROM OFFICIALS & A TENDENCY FOR SPORTSMEN TO USE THE RAIN GAUGES AS TARGETS. AN ATTEMPT TO DENUDE A HURRICANE OF ITS MOISTURE WHILE STILL AT SEA USING IODIDE SMOKE WAS DISASTROUS. THE HURRICANE TURNED INLAND WITH INCREASED VIOLENCE & DEVASTATED GEORGIA. OTHER INCONCLUSIVE RESULTS & THE HIGH COST OF SILVER IODIDE HAVE DISCOURAGED FURTHER RESEARCH.

TOO MUCH RAIN
CHERRAPUNJI, IN ASSAM, HAS THE WORLD'S HIGHEST ANNUAL RAINFALL. IT AVERAGES OVER 400 INCHES A YEAR & REACHED 1,041 IN 1860. ABOUT 90% OF THIS FALLS BETWEEN APRIL & SEPTEMBER WHICH MEANS ABOUT 2" A DAY (LIKE GETTING LONDON'S AVERAGE ANNUAL RAINFALL EVERY TWO WEEKS).

ACCURATE FORECASTING
THERE IS CONSIDERABLE HOPE THAT A PROPOSED RADAR SYSTEM WILL EVENTUALLY LEAD TO A MUCH GREATER ACCURACY IN BRITISH WEATHER FORECASTS. A SYSTEM OF 12 RADARS LINKED BY COMPUTER COULD PROVIDE INSTANTANEOUS COUNTRYWIDE INFORMATION OF RAINFALL & CLOUD COVER. THE COMPUTER HAS A LARGE MEMORY & CAN 'LEARN' THE PROBABLE MOVEMENT OF CLOUDS & SHOULD BE CAPABLE OF ACCURATE 6 HOUR FORECASTS.

ANTI-HAIL GUNS
A FRENCH FIRM HAS RECENTLY PATENTED A DEVICE WHICH CONSISTS OF AN ACETYLENE GENERATOR THAT DETONATES A LOUD BANG EVERY 15 SEC. THE SUCCESSION OF RISING SHOCK WAVES IS SAID TO ALTER THE CLOUD STRUCTURE TO MAKE HAIL FALL AS RAIN, THUS PREVENTING CROP DAMAGE.

HOW TO SIMULATE APPLAUSE
PULL A 50cm LENGTH OF EMBROIDERY THREAD OVER AN UNLIT CANDLE TO COAT IT IN WAX. PUSH END OF THREAD THROUGH SIDE OF WOODEN MATCH-BOX WITH NEEDLE. HOLD MATCHBOX TO EAR & SLOWLY PULL THREAD THROUGH HOLE. THE RESULTING NOISE IS REMARKABLY SIMILAR TO THE CLAPPING OF A THEATRE AUDIENCE.

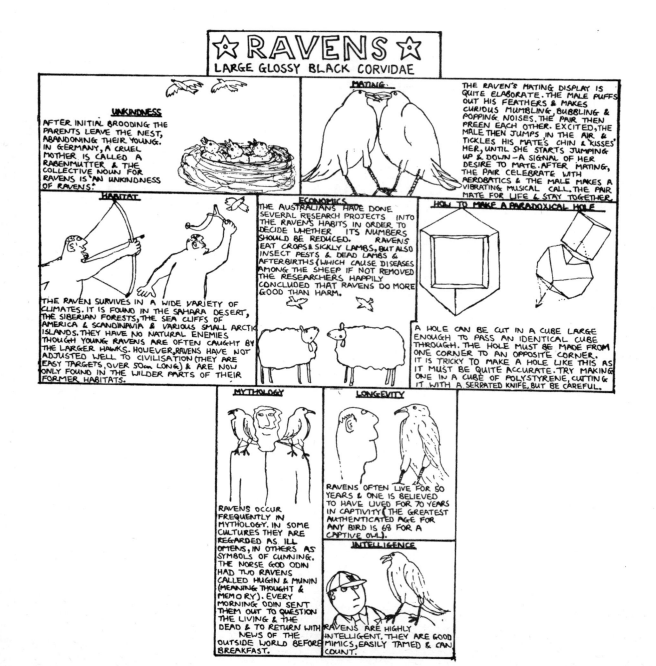

☆ RAVENS ☆
LARGE GLOSSY BLACK CORVIDAE

UNKINDNESS
AFTER INITIAL BROODING THE PARENTS LEAVE THE NEST, ABANDONING THEIR YOUNG. IN GERMANY, A CRUEL MOTHER IS CALLED A RABENMUTTER & THE COLLECTIVE NOUN FOR RAVENS IS 'AN UNKINDNESS OF RAVENS.'

MATING
THE RAVEN'S MATING DISPLAY IS QUITE ELABORATE. THE MALE PUFFS OUT HIS FEATHERS & MAKES CURIOUS MUMBLING, BUBBLING & POPPING NOISES. THE PAIR THEN PREEN EACH OTHER. EXCITED, THE MALE THEN JUMPS IN THE AIR & TICKLES HIS MATE'S CHIN & KISSES HER, UNTIL SHE STARTS JUMPING UP & DOWN — A SIGNAL OF HER DESIRE TO MATE. AFTER MATING, THE PAIR CELEBRATE WITH AEROBATICS & THE MALE MAKES A VIBRATING MUSICAL CALL. THE PAIR MATE FOR LIFE & STAY TOGETHER.

HABITAT
THE RAVEN SURVIVES IN A WIDE VARIETY OF CLIMATES. IT IS FOUND IN THE SAHARA DESERT, THE SIBERIAN FORESTS, THE SEA CLIFFS OF AMERICA & SCANDINAVIA & VARIOUS SMALL ARCTIC ISLANDS. THEY HAVE NO NATURAL ENEMIES THOUGH YOUNG RAVENS ARE OFTEN CAUGHT BY THE LARGER HAWKS. HOWEVER, RAVENS HAVE NOT ADJUSTED WELL TO CIVILISATION (THEY ARE EASY TARGETS, OVER 50cm LONG) & ARE NOW ONLY FOUND IN THE WILDER PARTS OF THEIR FORMER HABITATS.

ECONOMICS
THE AUSTRALIANS HAVE DONE SEVERAL RESEARCH PROJECTS INTO THE RAVEN'S HABITS IN ORDER TO DECIDE WHETHER ITS NUMBERS SHOULD BE REDUCED. RAVENS EAT CROPS & SICKLY LAMBS, BUT ALSO INSECT PESTS & DEAD LAMBS & AFTERBIRTHS (WHICH CAUSE DISEASES AMONG THE SHEEP IF NOT REMOVED). THE RESEARCHERS HAPPILY CONCLUDED THAT RAVENS DO MORE GOOD THAN HARM.

HOW TO MAKE A PARADOXICAL HOLE
A HOLE CAN BE CUT IN A CUBE LARGE ENOUGH TO PASS AN IDENTICAL CUBE THROUGH. THE HOLE MUST BE MADE FROM ONE CORNER TO AN OPPOSITE CORNER. IT IS TRICKY TO MAKE A HOLE LIKE THIS AS IT MUST BE QUITE ACCURATE. TRY MAKING ONE IN A CUBE OF POLYSTYRENE, CUTTING IT WITH A SERRATED KNIFE, BUT BE CAREFUL.

MYTHOLOGY
RAVENS OCCUR FREQUENTLY IN MYTHOLOGY. IN SOME CULTURES THEY ARE REGARDED AS ILL OMENS, IN OTHERS AS SYMBOLS OF CUNNING. THE NORSE GOD ODIN HAD TWO RAVENS CALLED HUGIN & MUNIN (MEANING THOUGHT & MEMORY). EVERY MORNING ODIN SENT THEM OUT TO QUESTION THE LIVING & THE DEAD & TO RETURN WITH NEWS OF THE OUTSIDE WORLD BEFORE BREAKFAST.

LONGEVITY
RAVENS OFTEN LIVE FOR 50 YEARS & ONE IS BELIEVED TO HAVE LIVED FOR 70 YEARS IN CAPTIVITY (THE GREATEST AUTHENTICATED AGE FOR ANY BIRD IS 68 FOR A CAPTIVE OWL).

INTELLIGENCE
RAVENS ARE HIGHLY INTELLIGENT. THEY ARE GOOD MIMICS, EASILY TAMED & CAN COUNT.

RATS
THE LARGER REPRESENTATIVES OF THE GENUS MUS

FOOD FOR RATS
ONE REASON THAT RATS ARE SO FREQUENTLY USED FOR RESEARCH IS THAT THEY WILL EAT ANY HUMAN FOOD. RESEARCHERS HAVE FOUND THAT FRESH FRUIT, MEAT, & PEANUT BUTTER ARE THEIR FAVOURITE FOODS & THAT CHEESE IS RELATIVELY UNATTRACTIVE. HOWEVER RATS WILL EAT ALMOST ANYTHING & ARE PARTICULARLY KEEN ON WARFARIN BASED POISONS TO WHICH SOME RATS HAVE BECOME IMMUNE. RATS HAVE EVEN GNAWED THROUGH A SHOPPING BASKET & A LAYER OF CARDBOARD TO GET AT SOME WARFARIN BEFORE THE PACKET WAS OPENED.

MORE FOOD FOR RATS
THE CONSERVATIONISTS CAMPAIGNING AGAINST THE USE OF FOOD PACKAGING ARE PERHAPS MISDIRECTING THEIR EFFORTS. RATS WERE RECENTLY FED UNDER LABORATORY CONDITIONS ON VARIOUS DIETS MADE UP OF BREAKFAST CEREALS & THEIR CONTAINERS. THE RESULTS SUGGEST THAT THE BOX CARDBOARD IS OFTEN MORE NUTRITIOUS THAN THE CEREALS INSIDE.

RATS AS FOOD ANALYSTS
RATS ARE BEING USED FOR A NEW METHOD OF ASSESSING THE NUTRITIONAL VALUES OF FOODS. RATS FED ON A BASE DIET OF 90% CARBOHYDRATE & 10% WHOLE COOKED EGG WILL STAY ALIVE BUT NOT GROW OR MATURE NORMALLY. THE NUTRITIONAL VALUE OF ANY PARTICULAR FOOD IS DETERMINED BY SUBSTITUTING THE FOOD FOR THE CARBOHYDRATE IN THE BASE DIET & RECORDING THE GROWTH RATE. UNLIKE THE TRADITIONAL METHOD OF ANALYSING FOODS THIS METHOD SHOWS THAT FREE RANGE EGGS ARE 9% MORE NUTRITIOUS THAN BATTERY EGGS, THAT FRESH MEAT IS TWICE AS GOOD AS TINNED MEAT & THAT FRESH MILK IS OVER 5 TIMES AS GOOD AS DRIED MILK.

WHERE RATS COME FROM
RATS ORIGINALLY CAME FROM EASTERN ASIA BUT THRIVED UNDER THE INFLUENCE OF MAN & SPREAD TO INFEST MOST ANCIENT CIVILISATIONS. HOWEVER BEFORE 1727 THE WORLD WAS PLAGUED ONLY BY BLACK RATS BUT THEN HORDES OF A NEW LARGER BROWN RAT SUDDENLY SPREAD FROM RUSSIA & WIPED OUT ALL THEIR COUSINS. THERE ARE NOW NO BLACK RATS LEFT EXCEPT IN THE TROPICS WHERE THE BROWN RAT IS UNSUITED.

SOME RESEARCHERS AT THE UNIVERSITY OF NEBRASKA HAVE BEEN INVESTIGATING THE INFLUENCE OF BROTHERS & SISTERS ON THE STABILITY OF YOUNG RATS. THEIR STABILITY WAS MEASURED BY RECORDING THEIR INCREASE IN HEART BEAT ON HEARING A LOUD BELL OR BEING GIVEN AN ELECTRIC SHOCK. THE RESULTS SHOWED THAT RATS WITHOUT BROTHERS & SISTERS WERE MORE STABLE. THIS IS SURPRISING SINCE OTHER RESEARCH HAS SHOWN THAT THE ONLY CHILDREN OF OTHER MAMMALS SUFFER FROM THE EFFECTS OF AN OVER-ATTENTIVE MOTHER.

HOW TO REAR A STABLE RAT

RAT RECOVERY
THE DIFFICULTY OF GETTING RID OF RATS IS PARTLY DUE TO THEIR HIGH REPRODUCTIVE RATE. FEMALES NORMALLY HAVE ABOUT 5 LITTERS OF UP TO 23 BABIES EACH YEAR. THIS MEANS THAT A POPULATION WILL QUICKLY RECOVER EVEN IF 95% HAVE BEEN EXTERMINATED. ONE PAIR OF RATS COULD HAVE 350,000,000 DESCENDANTS IN 3 YEARS IF THEY ALL SURVIVED.

HOW TO PUSH A 2p COIN THROUGH A ½" DIAMETER HOLE IN A PIECE OF CARD
THIS IS NOT AS DIFFICULT AS IT MIGHT SEEM. PLACE 2p ON TABLE & HOLD CARD BEHIND COIN. TO PUSH COIN THROUGH HOLE SIMPLY INSERT A PENCIL THROUGH HOLE & PUSH COIN ALONG WITH TIP OF PENCIL.

RECORDS

SOOTY CYLINDERS
THE FIRST MACHINE TO RECORD SOUND WAS THE PHONAUTOGRAPH, 1857. SOUNDS, FOCUSED BY A HORN, CAUSED A HOG'S HAIR TO VIBRATE & SCRATCH A LINE ON A ROTATING DRUM COVERED IN SOOT. THE SOUND COULD NOT BE REPLAYED.

TINFOIL CYLINDERS
THE FIRST MACHINE TO REPLAY SOUND WAS THOMAS EDISON'S 1877 PHONOGRAPH. IT WAS SIMILAR TO THE PHONAUTOGRAPH BUT SCRATCHED THE LINE IN TINFOIL INSTEAD OF SOOT. THE SOUND WAS REPLAYED BY RUNNING A BRISTLE OVER THE 'RECORDED' TINFOIL.

LOUD DISCS
THE FIRST RECORDS WERE CYLINDERS. FLAT DISCS WERE INTRODUCED AS CHILDREN'S TOYS IN THE 1890s. THE GROOVE WAS SCRATCHED ON A LAYER OF VARNISH ON A ZINC DISC WHICH WAS THEN ETCHED. THIS GAVE A MUCH LOUDER RECORDING & CYLINDERS SOON BECAME OBSOLETE.

HEAVYWEIGHT & LIGHTWEIGHT
THE MODERN STYLE LP, MADE OF VINYL, FIRST APPEARED IN 1948. IT REQUIRED A VERY SMALL NEEDLE WHICH RESTED LIGHTLY & AN ELECTRIC AMPLIFIER TO MAKE THE SOUND LOUD ENOUGH. (78RPM NEEDLES RESTED WITH A WEIGHT OF 100 GRAMS: MODERN LP NEEDLES NEED LESS THAN 5 GRAMS)

78RPM
33RPM

BACKWARD TESTING
THE STANDARD METHOD OF CHECKING NEWLY PRESSED DISCS IS TO PLAY THEM BACKWARDS. THE WAVEFORMS OF SCRATCHES ARE SYMMETRICAL & CAN THUS BE AUTOMATICALLY DISTINGUISHED FROM MUSICAL SOUNDS (WHICH ARE ASYMMETRICAL).

A GERMAN CHOCOLATE FIRM (STOLLWERCK) PRODUCED PLAYABLE RECORDS MADE OF CHOCOLATE COVERED IN TIN FOIL.

CHOCOLATE RECORDS
STOLLWERCK

INSECT RECORDS
UNTIL ABOUT 1950 RECORDS WERE MADE OF SHELLAC, A NATURAL RESIN PRODUCED BY INSECTS. WHICH CAME FROM SINGAPORE.

RECORDS
Produced by Tim Hunkin at Marsh Studios, Suffolk June/July 1981
Mixed at The Young Observer Editor Janet Crumbie

— ALL RIGHTS OF THE MANUFACTURER & OF THE OWNER OF THE RECORDED WORK RESERVED —

UNAUTHORISED PUBLIC READING BROADCASTING & COPYING OF THIS RECORD PROHIBITED

STEREO
SIDE ONE
TMT 271250

L
LONRHO RECORDS

LOUD GROOVES
LOUD SOUNDS NEED WIDER GROOVES THAN QUIET ONES. THIS IS WHY POP LPs ARE OFTEN SHORTER THAN CLASSICAL ONES. WHEN THE GROOVES ARE TOO CLOSE IT IS SOMETIMES POSSIBLE TO HEAR IN ADVANCE AN 'ECHO' OF A SOUND ON THE NEXT GROOVE.

DOUBLE TRACK RECORDS
SEVERAL DOUBLE GROOVE POP RECORDS HAVE BEEN RELEASED. TWO PARALLEL SPIRAL GROOVES ARE CUT & IT IS SIMPLY A MATTER OF CHANCE WHICH SPIRAL THE NEEDLE ENGAGES & THUS WHICH OF THE TWO TRACKS IS PLAYED (EG 'POP MUSIK' BY M).

REMIXED VINYL
NEW VINYL IS NORMALLY USED FOR CLASSICAL RECORDS. ALL THE REJECTS ARE REGROUND & THE RECYCLED VINYL IS USED FOR POP RECORDS. WITH THE INCREASE IN OIL PRICES, THE AVERAGE WEIGHT OF VINYL PER LP HAS BEEN REDUCED FROM 160G TO 120G SINCE 1974.

STRONG RECORDS
THE POINT OF A MODERN LP NEEDLE IS SO SMALL THAT OVER THE MICROSCOPIC AREA OF CONTACT IT EXERTS A HUGE PRESSURE. (UP TO 30,000 lb/sq in)

GROOVE IS SAME WIDTH AS A HUMAN HAIR
NO SOUND
MONO WAVES ON ONE SIDE OF GROOVE
STEREO ONE CHANNEL ON EACH SIDE OF GROOVE

SUCKING RECORD DECK
THERE IS NOW A CURE FOR WARPED RECORDS — A £1,500 TURNTABLE WITH A VACUUM PUMP WHICH SUCKS THE RECORD DOWN ONTO THE TURNTABLE, IRONING OUT THE WARP.

WATERY CLEANERS
MOST RECORD CLEANING FLUIDS CONTAIN OVER 99% DISTILLED WATER.

☆ RECYCLING ☆
RECLAIMING MATERIALS FOR FURTHER USE

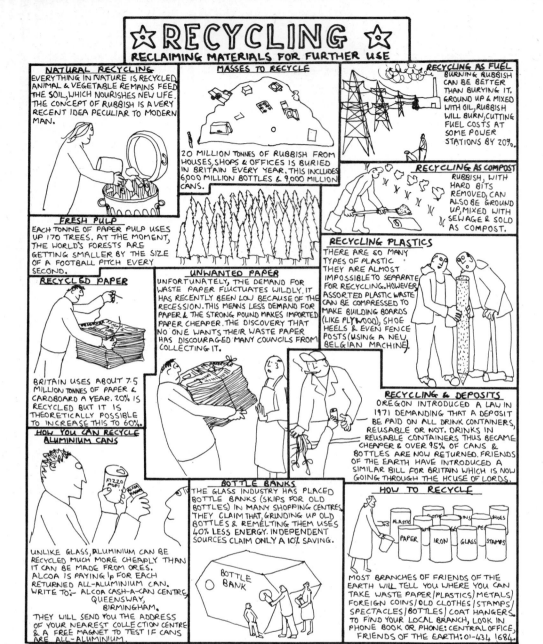

NATURAL RECYCLING
EVERYTHING IN NATURE IS RECYCLED. ANIMAL & VEGETABLE REMAINS FEED THE SOIL, WHICH NOURISHES NEW LIFE. THE CONCEPT OF RUBBISH IS A VERY RECENT IDEA PECULIAR TO MODERN MAN.

FRESH PULP
EACH TONNE OF PAPER PULP USES UP 170 TREES. AT THE MOMENT, THE WORLD'S FORESTS ARE GETTING SMALLER BY THE SIZE OF A FOOTBALL PITCH EVERY SECOND.

RECYCLED PAPER
BRITAIN USES ABOUT 7.5 MILLION TONNES OF PAPER & CARDBOARD A YEAR. 20% IS RECYCLED BUT IT IS THEORETICALLY POSSIBLE TO INCREASE THIS TO 60%.

HOW YOU CAN RECYCLE ALUMINIUM CANS
UNLIKE GLASS, ALUMINIUM CAN BE RECYCLED MUCH MORE CHEAPLY THAN IT CAN BE MADE FROM ORES. ALCOA IS PAYING 1p FOR EACH RETURNED ALL-ALUMINIUM CAN. WRITE TO:- ALCOA CASH-A-CAN CENTRE QUEENSWAY, BIRMINGHAM. THEY WILL SEND YOU THE ADDRESS OF YOUR NEAREST COLLECTION CENTRE & A FREE MAGNET TO TEST IF CANS ARE ALL-ALUMINIUM.

MASSES TO RECYCLE
20 MILLION TONNES OF RUBBISH FROM HOUSES, SHOPS & OFFICES IS BURIED IN BRITAIN EVERY YEAR. THIS INCLUDES 6,000 MILLION BOTTLES & 9,000 MILLION CANS.

UNWANTED PAPER
UNFORTUNATELY, THE DEMAND FOR WASTE PAPER FLUCTUATES WILDLY. IT HAS RECENTLY BEEN LOW BECAUSE OF THE RECESSION. THIS MEANS LESS DEMAND FOR PAPER & THE STRONG POUND MAKES IMPORTED PAPER CHEAPER. THE DISCOVERY THAT NO ONE WANTS THEIR WASTE PAPER HAS DISCOURAGED MANY COUNCILS FROM COLLECTING IT.

BOTTLE BANKS
THE GLASS INDUSTRY HAS PLACED BOTTLE BANKS (SKIPS FOR OLD BOTTLES) IN MANY SHOPPING CENTRES. THEY CLAIM THAT GRINDING UP OLD BOTTLES & REMELTING THEM USES 40% LESS ENERGY. INDEPENDENT SOURCES CLAIM ONLY A 10% SAVING.

BOTTLE BANK

RECYCLING AS FUEL
BURNING RUBBISH CAN BE BETTER THAN BURYING IT. GROUND UP & MIXED WITH OIL, RUBBISH WILL BURN, CUTTING FUEL COSTS AT SOME POWER STATIONS BY 20%.

RECYCLING AS COMPOST
RUBBISH, WITH HARD BITS REMOVED, CAN ALSO BE GROUND UP, MIXED WITH SEWAGE & SOLD AS COMPOST.

RECYCLING PLASTICS
THERE ARE SO MANY TYPES OF PLASTIC THEY ARE ALMOST IMPOSSIBLE TO SEPARATE FOR RECYCLING. HOWEVER ASSORTED PLASTIC WASTE CAN BE COMPRESSED TO MAKE BUILDING BOARDS (LIKE PLYWOOD), SHOE HEELS & EVEN FENCE POSTS (USING A NEW BELGIAN MACHINE).

RECYCLING & DEPOSITS
OREGON INTRODUCED A LAW IN 1971 DEMANDING THAT A DEPOSIT BE PAID ON ALL DRINK CONTAINERS, REUSABLE OR NOT. DRINKS IN REUSABLE CONTAINERS THUS BECAME CHEAPER & OVER 95% OF CANS & BOTTLES ARE NOW RETURNED. FRIENDS OF THE EARTH HAVE INTRODUCED A SIMILAR BILL FOR BRITAIN WHICH IS NOW GOING THROUGH THE HOUSE OF LORDS.

HOW TO RECYCLE
MOST BRANCHES OF FRIENDS OF THE EARTH WILL TELL YOU WHERE YOU CAN TAKE WASTE PAPER/PLASTICS/METALS/ FOREIGN COINS/OLD CLOTHES/STAMPS/ SPECTACLES/BOTTLES/COAT HANGERS. TO FIND YOUR LOCAL BRANCH, LOOK IN PHONE BOOK OR PHONE: CENTRAL OFFICE, FRIENDS OF THE EARTH: 01-434 1684.

☆ REFRIGERATION ☆
LOWERING THE TEMPERATURE OF OBJECTS

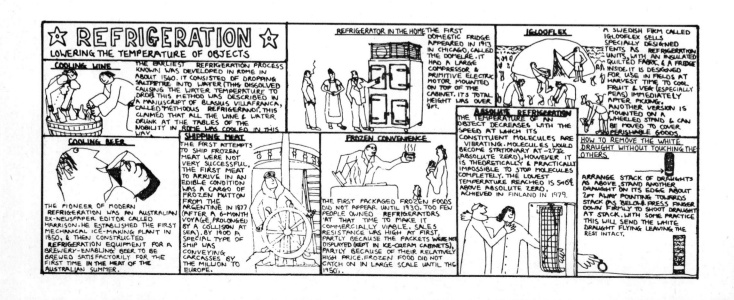

COOLING WINE
THE EARLIEST REFRIGERATION PROCESS KNOWN WAS DEVELOPED IN ROME IN ABOUT 1540. IT CONSISTED OF DROPPING SALTPETRE INTO WATER (THIS DISSOLVED CAUSING THE WATER TEMPERATURE TO DROP). THIS METHOD WAS DESCRIBED IN A MANUSCRIPT OF BLASIUS VILLAFRANCA, CALLED 'METHODUS REFRIGERANDI'. THIS CLAIMED THAT ALL THE WINE & WATER DRUNK AT THE TABLES OF THE NOBILITY IN ROME WAS COOLED IN THIS WAY.

COOLING BEER
THE PIONEER OF MODERN REFRIGERATION WAS AN AUSTRALIAN EX-NEWSPAPER EDITOR CALLED HARRISON. HE ESTABLISHED THE FIRST MECHANICAL ICE-MAKING PLANT IN 1850, & THEN CONSTRUCTED REFRIGERATION EQUIPMENT FOR A BREWERY - ENABLING BEER TO BE BREWED SATISFACTORILY FOR THE FIRST TIME IN THE HEAT OF THE AUSTRALIAN SUMMER.

SHIPPING MEAT
THE FIRST ATTEMPTS TO SHIP FROZEN MEAT WERE NOT VERY SUCCESSFUL. THE FIRST MEAT TO ARRIVE IN AN EDIBLE CONDITION WAS A CARGO OF FROZEN MUTTON FROM THE ARGENTINE IN 1877 (AFTER A 6-MONTH VOYAGE, PROLONGED BY A COLLISION AT SEA). BY 1900 A SPECIAL TYPE OF SHIP WAS CONVEYING CARCASSES BY THE MILLION TO EUROPE.

REFRIGERATOR IN THE HOME
THE FIRST DOMESTIC FRIDGE APPEARED IN 1913 IN CHICAGO, CALLED THE DOMELRE. IT HAD A LARGE COMPRESSOR & PRIMITIVE ELECTRIC MOTOR MOUNTED ON TOP OF THE CABINET. ITS TOTAL HEIGHT WAS OVER 9FT.

FROZEN CONVENIENCE
THE FIRST PACKAGED FROZEN FOODS DID NOT APPEAR UNTIL 1930. TOO FEW PEOPLE OWNED REFRIGERATORS 'AT THAT TIME TO MAKE IT COMMERCIALLY VIABLE. SALES RESISTANCE WAS HIGH AT FIRST, PARTLY BECAUSE THE PACKETS WERE NOT DISPLAYED (KEPT IN ICE-CREAM CABINETS), PARTLY BECAUSE OF THEIR RELATIVELY HIGH PRICE. FROZEN FOOD DID NOT CATCH ON IN LARGE SCALE UNTIL THE 1950s.

ABSOLUTE REFRIGERATION
THE TEMPERATURE OF AN OBJECT DECREASES WITH THE SPEED AT WHICH ITS CONSTITUENT MOLECULES ARE VIBRATING. MOLECULES WOULD BECOME STATIONARY AT -273°C (ABSOLUTE ZERO), HOWEVER IT IS THEORETICALLY & PRACTICALLY IMPOSSIBLE TO STOP MOLECULES COMPLETELY. THE LOWEST TEMPERATURE REACHED IS 5×10⁻⁸ ABOVE ABSOLUTE ZERO, ACHIEVED IN FINLAND IN 1979.

IGLOOFLEX
A SWEDISH FIRM CALLED IGLOOFLEX SELLS SPECIALLY DESIGNED TENTS AS REFRIGERATION UNITS, WITH AN INSULATED QUILTED FABRIC & A FRIDGE INSIDE. IT IS DESIGNED FOR USE IN FIELDS AT HARVEST TIME TO COOL FRUIT & VEG (ESPECIALLY PEAS) IMMEDIATELY AFTER PICKING. ANOTHER VERSION IS MOUNTED ON A WHEELED STAND & CAN BE MOVED TO COVER PERISHABLE GOODS.

HOW TO REMOVE THE WHITE DRAUGHT WITHOUT TOUCHING THE OTHERS
ARRANGE STACK OF DRAUGHTS AS ABOVE. STAND ANOTHER DRAUGHT ON ITS EDGE ABOUT 2FT AWAY POINTING TOWARDS STACK (AS BELOW). PRESS FINGER DOWN FIRMLY TO SHOOT DRAUGHT AT STACK. WITH SOME PRACTICE THIS WILL SEND THE WHITE DRAUGHT FLYING LEAVING THE REST INTACT.

☆ RELIABILITY ☆
MECHANICAL DEPENDABILITY & PREDICTABILITY

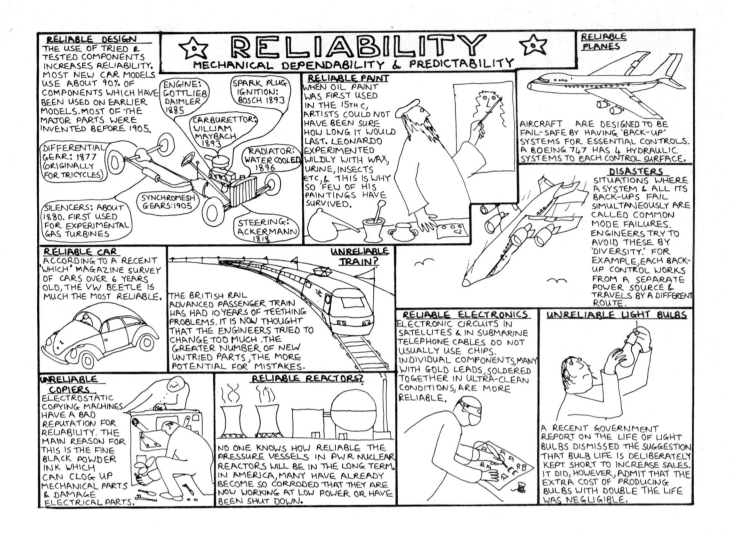

RELIABLE DESIGN

THE USE OF TRIED & TESTED COMPONENTS INCREASES RELIABILITY. MOST NEW CAR MODELS USE ABOUT 90% OF COMPONENTS WHICH HAVE BEEN USED ON EARLIER MODELS. MOST OF THE MAJOR PARTS WERE INVENTED BEFORE 1905.

ENGINE: GOTTLIEB DAIMLER 1885

SPARK PLUG IGNITION: BOSCH 1893

CARBURETTOR: WILLIAM MAYBACH 1893

RADIATOR: WATER COOLED 1896

DIFFERENTIAL GEAR: 1877 (ORIGINALLY FOR TRICYCLES)

SILENCERS: ABOUT 1880. FIRST USED FOR EXPERIMENTAL GAS TURBINES

SYNCHROMESH GEARS: 1905

STEERING: ACKERMANN 1818

RELIABLE PAINT

WHEN OIL PAINT WAS FIRST USED IN THE 15TH C, ARTISTS COULD NOT HAVE BEEN SURE HOW LONG IT WOULD LAST. LEONARDO EXPERIMENTED WILDLY WITH WAX, URINE, INSECTS ETC, & THIS IS WHY SO FEW OF HIS PAINTINGS HAVE SURVIVED.

RELIABLE PLANES

AIRCRAFT ARE DESIGNED TO BE FAIL-SAFE BY HAVING 'BACK-UP' SYSTEMS FOR ESSENTIAL CONTROLS. A BOEING 747 HAS 4 HYDRAULIC SYSTEMS TO EACH CONTROL SURFACE.

DISASTERS

SITUATIONS WHERE A SYSTEM & ALL ITS BACK-UPS FAIL SIMULTANEOUSLY ARE CALLED COMMON MODE FAILURES. ENGINEERS TRY TO AVOID THESE BY 'DIVERSITY.' FOR EXAMPLE, EACH BACK-UP CONTROL WORKS FROM A SEPARATE POWER SOURCE & TRAVELS BY A DIFFERENT ROUTE.

RELIABLE CAR

ACCORDING TO A RECENT 'WHICH' MAGAZINE SURVEY OF CARS OVER 6 YEARS OLD, THE VW BEETLE IS MUCH THE MOST RELIABLE.

UNRELIABLE TRAIN?

THE BRITISH RAIL ADVANCED PASSENGER TRAIN HAS HAD 10 YEARS OF TEETHING PROBLEMS. IT IS NOW THOUGHT THAT THE ENGINEERS TRIED TO CHANGE TOO MUCH. THE GREATER NUMBER OF NEW UNTRIED PARTS, THE MORE POTENTIAL FOR MISTAKES.

RELIABLE ELECTRONICS

ELECTRONIC CIRCUITS IN SATELLITES & IN SUBMARINE TELEPHONE CABLES DO NOT USUALLY USE CHIPS. INDIVIDUAL COMPONENTS, MANY WITH GOLD LEADS, SOLDERED TOGETHER IN ULTRA-CLEAN CONDITIONS, ARE MORE RELIABLE.

UNRELIABLE LIGHT BULBS

A RECENT GOVERNMENT REPORT ON THE LIFE OF LIGHT BULBS DISMISSED THE SUGGESTION THAT BULB LIFE IS DELIBERATELY KEPT SHORT TO INCREASE SALES. IT DID, HOWEVER, ADMIT THAT THE EXTRA COST OF PRODUCING BULBS WITH DOUBLE THE LIFE WAS NEGLIGIBLE.

UNRELIABLE COPIERS

ELECTROSTATIC COPYING MACHINES HAVE A BAD REPUTATION FOR RELIABILITY. THE MAIN REASON FOR THIS IS THE FINE BLACK POWDER INK WHICH CAN CLOG UP MECHANICAL PARTS & DAMAGE ELECTRICAL PARTS.

RELIABLE REACTORS?

NO ONE KNOWS HOW RELIABLE THE PRESSURE VESSELS IN PWR NUCLEAR REACTORS WILL BE IN THE LONG TERM. IN AMERICA, MANY HAVE ALREADY BECOME SO CORRODED THAT THEY ARE NOW WORKING AT LOW POWER OR HAVE BEEN SHUT DOWN.

☆ REMEDIES ☆
METHODS OF COMBATING HUMAN DISORDERS

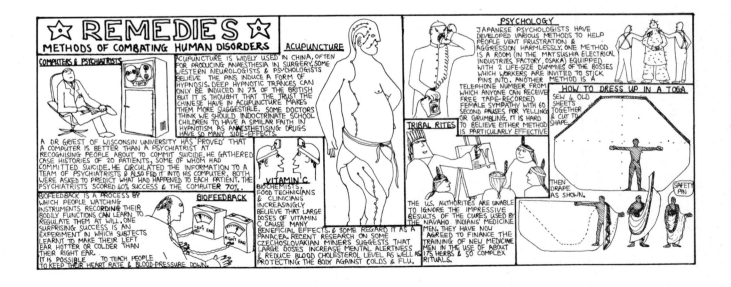

COMPUTERS & PSYCHIATRISTS

A DR GRIEST OF WISCONSIN UNIVERSITY HAS 'PROVED' THAT A COMPUTER IS BETTER THAN A PSYCHIATRIST AT RECOGNISING PEOPLE ABOUT TO COMMIT SUICIDE. HE GATHERED CASE HISTORIES OF 20 PATIENTS, SOME OF WHOM HAD COMMITTED SUICIDE. HE CIRCULATED THE INFORMATION TO A TEAM OF PSYCHIATRISTS & ALSO FED IT INTO HIS COMPUTER. BOTH WERE ASKED TO PREDICT WHAT HAD HAPPENED TO EACH PATIENT. THE PSYCHIATRISTS SCORED 40% SUCCESS & THE COMPUTER 70%.

BIOFEEDBACK

BIOFEEDBACK IS A PROCESS BY WHICH PEOPLE WATCHING INSTRUMENTS RECORDING THEIR BODILY FUNCTIONS CAN LEARN TO REGULATE THEM AT WILL. ONE SURPRISING SUCCESS IS AN EXPERIMENT IN WHICH SUBJECTS LEARNT TO MAKE THEIR LEFT EAR HOTTER OR COLDER THAN THEIR RIGHT EAR. IT IS POSSIBLE TO TEACH PEOPLE TO KEEP THEIR HEART RATE & BLOOD PRESSURE DOWN.

ACUPUNCTURE

ACUPUNCTURE IS WIDELY USED IN CHINA, OFTEN FOR PRODUCING ANAESTHESIA IN SURGERY. SOME WESTERN NEUROLOGISTS & PSYCHOLOGISTS BELIEVE THE PINS INDUCE A FORM OF HYPNOSIS. DEEP HYPNOTIC TRANCES CAN ONLY BE INDUCED IN 7% OF THE BRITISH BUT IT IS THOUGHT THAT THE TRUST THE CHINESE HAVE IN ACUPUNCTURE MAKES THEM MORE SUGGESTIBLE. SOME DOCTORS THINK WE SHOULD INDOCTRINATE SCHOOL CHILDREN TO HAVE A SIMILAR FAITH IN HYPNOTISM AS ANAESTHETISING DRUGS HAVE SO MANY SIDE-EFFECTS.

VITAMIN C

BIOCHEMISTS, FOOD TECHNICIANS & CLINICIANS INCREASINGLY BELIEVE THAT LARGE DOSES OF VITAMIN C CAUSE MANY BENEFICIAL EFFECTS. & SOME REGARD IT AS A PANACEA. RECENT RESEARCH ON SOME CZECHOSLOVAKIAN MINERS SUGGESTS THAT LARGE DOSES INCREASE MENTAL ALERTNESS & REDUCE BLOOD CHOLESTEROL LEVEL AS WELL AS PROTECTING THE BODY AGAINST COLDS & FLU.

PSYCHOLOGY

JAPANESE PSYCHOLOGISTS HAVE DEVELOPED VARIOUS METHODS TO HELP PEOPLE VENT FRUSTRATION & AGGRESSION HARMLESSLY. ONE METHOD IS A ROOM (IN THE MATSUSHIA ELECTRICAL INDUSTRIES FACTORY, OSAKA) EQUIPPED WITH 2 LIFE-SIZE DUMMIES OF THE BOSSES WHICH WORKERS ARE INVITED TO STICK PINS INTO. ANOTHER METHOD IS A TELEPHONE NUMBER FROM WHICH ANYONE CAN RECEIVE FREE TAPE-RECORDED FEMALE SYMPATHY WITH 60 SECOND PAUSES FOR YELLING OR GRUMBLING. IT IS HARD TO BELIEVE EITHER METHOD IS PARTICULARLY EFFECTIVE.

TRIBAL RITES

THE U.S. AUTHORITIES ARE UNABLE TO IGNORE THE IMPRESSIVE RESULTS OF THE CURES USED BY THE NAVAHO INDIANS' MEDICINE MEN. THEY HAVE NOW AGREED TO FINANCE THE TRAINING OF NEW MEDICINE MEN IN THE USE OF ABOUT 175 HERBS & 50 COMPLEX RITUALS.

HOW TO DRESS UP IN A TOGA

SEW 4 OLD SHEETS TOGETHER & CUT TO SHAPE.

THEN DRAPE AS SHOWN.

SAFETY PIN

☆ RICE ☆

AN ABUNDANT CULTIVATED GRASS WITH EDIBLE SEEDS

INTRODUCING RICE TO AMERICA

RICE FIRST ARRIVED IN AMERICA IN 1695. A SHIP BRINGING A CARGO OF RICE TO ENGLAND FROM MADAGASCAR WAS BLOWN OFF COURSE IN A STORM & TOOK SHELTER AT CHARLESTOWN, SOUTH CAROLINA. THE CAPTAIN GAVE THE COLONISTS SOME OF HIS CARGO IN RETURN FOR HELP IN REPAIRING HIS SHIP. THE GRAINS WERE PLANTED & GREW WITH SUCH SUCCESS THAT RICE QUICKLY BECAME SOUTH CAROLINA'S CHIEF EXPORT.

CULTIVATED RICE

THE PROCESS OF CULTIVATING RICE IS FIRST RECORDED IN HISTORY IN 2800BC WHEN A CHINESE EMPEROR PROCLAIMED THE ESTABLISHMENT OF AN ANNUAL CEREMONIAL RITUAL OF PLANTING RICE.

THE DANGER OF EATING FRIED RICE

ACCORDING TO THE MAGAZINE OF THE ASSOCIATION OF PUBLIC HEALTH INSPECTORS, FRIED RICE SERVED AT CHINESE RESTAURANTS MAY CAUSE FOOD POISONING. THIS IS CAUSED BY THE BACTERIUM BACILLUS CEREUS, WHICH WAS THOUGHT TO BE HARMLESS UNTIL RECENTLY, WHEN IT WAS PROVED TO HAVE CAUSED FOOD POISONING AMONG 600 NORWEGIANS WHO HAD EATEN A PARTICULAR VANILLA SAUCE. CEREUS GROWS BEST AT 30℃ & DEVELOPS ACTIVELY IN BOILED RICE STORED AT ROOM TEMPERATURE. UNFORTUNATELY SOME CHINESE RESTAURANTS PREPARE FRIED RICE BY BOILING RICE IN BULK, & THEN STORING IT AT ROOM TEMP TO BE FRIED UP WHEN REQUIRED. FORTUNATELY THE RESULTING POISONING IS USUALLY VERY MILD & NO ONE HAS EVER DIED FROM IT. (ALTHOUGH THE BACILLUS HAS CAUSED THE DEATH OF ONE TIGER IN CINCINNATI ZOO.)

RICE PAPER

RICE PAPER (THE EDIBLE PAPER USED ON THE BOTTOM OF MACAROON BISCUITS) IS A MISNOMER AS IT HAS NOTHING TO DO WITH RICE. IT CONSISTS OF THE PITH OF A SMALL TREE FROM TAIWAN (ARALIA PAPYIFERA) WHICH IS PEELED INTO THIN SHEETS WITH A SHARP KNIFE.

MECHANISATION

MECHANISATION OF RICE CULTIVATION IS HAMPERED BY THE TENDENCY OF LARGE MACHINES TO GET BOGGED DOWN IN THE WATERLOGGED CLAY SOIL WHERE RICE GROWS BEST. HOWEVER, THE AMERICANS HAVE SOLVED THE PROBLEMS AT GREAT EXPENSE, CLAIMING SPECTACULAR TIME SAVINGS. THEY CLAIM THAT TO CULTIVATE ONE TON OF RICE TAKES:

8 MAN HOURS	IN U.S.A.
80-150 "	BRAZIL
200 "	JAPAN
300 "	ASIA

ENEMIES OF RICE

RICE IS ATTACKED BY MANY DISEASES & PESTS WITH EVIL SOUNDING NAMES: ARMY WORMS, BLAST, RICE STINKBUGS, STALK BORERS, RICE WATER-WEEVILS. MIGRATING DUCKS ARE AN ADDITIONAL PEST IN CALIFORNIA. THEY ARRIVE JUST BEFORE HARVEST TIME & FIND THE RICE A PARTICULAR DELICACY.

HOW TO CRACK A HAZELNUT

SAW 2 CUTS HALFWAY THROUGH A PIECE OF A HAZELTREE BRANCH & GOUGE OUT NUT SIZED AREA BETWEEN CUTS WITH A PENKNIFE. GRIP ENDS OF NUTCRACKER & SQUEEZE NUT AS BELOW.

☆ RINGS ☆

ORNAMENTS FOR FINGERS

USEFUL RINGS

RINGS HAVE BEEN MADE WHICH INCLUDE SUNDIALS, WHISTLES, ASTROLABES, PIPE STOPPERS, WATCHES, KEYS & CAVITIES FOR PERFUMES & POISONS.

WEDDING RINGS

THE CUSTOM OF WEARING THE WEDDING RING ON THE FOURTH FINGER PROBABLY STEMS FROM THE ANCIENT EGYPTIAN BELIEF THAT A SPECIAL NERVE RAN DIRECTLY FROM IT TO THE HEART.

PAPAL RINGS

THE POPE HAS A SIGNET RING CALLED 'THE FISHERMAN'S RING' DEPICTING ST PETER IN A BOAT HOLDING A NET. THIS COMES FROM CHRIST'S WORDS (LUKE V 10) 'FROM HENCEFORTH THOU SHALT CATCH MEN'. THE RING IS BROKEN ON THE DEATH OF THE POPE & A NEW ONE MADE FOR HIS SUCCESSOR, TO PREVENT THE FRAUDULENT SEALING OF PAPAL DOCUMENTS

MEMORIAL RINGS

UNTIL THIS CENTURY, IT WAS QUITE COMMON FOR PEOPLE TO LEAVE INSTRUCTIONS IN THEIR WILLS FOR A NUMBER OF MEMORIAL RINGS TO BE MADE, WITH SUITABLE INSCRIPTIONS, FOR THEIR FRIENDS & RELATIVES.

HOLOLITHS

RINGS CUT OF SINGLE LARGE CRYSTALS OF PRECIOUS STONE ARE CALLED HOLOLITHS. THEY ARE EXTREMELY RARE AS SO MUCH OF THE ORIGINAL CRYSTAL IS WASTED.

TOE RINGS

THERE IS AN OLD HINDU TRADITION FOR WEARING RINGS WITH A SMALL MIRROR ATTACHED ON THE BIG TOE.

MONEY RINGS

THE ANCIENT GAULS AND BRITONS USED RINGS AS MONEY.

ALUMINIUM RINGS

IN WORLD WAR I, ALUMINIUM WAS STILL QUITE A RARE METAL. SOLDIERS USED TO SALVAGE THE ALUMINIUM FUSES FROM SHELLS, MELT THEM DOWN, & CAST & ENGRAVE INTRICATE RINGS.

HEALING RINGS

RINGS ARE OFTEN ASSOCIATED WITH HEALING. PLINY RECOMMENDED TRANSFERRING A RING FROM THE LEFT HAND TO THE MIDDLE FINGER OF THE RIGHT HAND AS A CURE FOR HICCUPS. CRAMP RINGS, WORN AS CURES FOR CRAMPS, CONVULSIONS & EPILEPSY, WERE POPULAR IN MEDIEVAL EUROPE. ONE TRIBE OF THE PHILIPPINES PUT RINGS ROUND THE WRISTS & ANKLES OF THE SERIOUSLY ILL TO STOP THE SOUL 'LEAVING' THE BODY.

ALARM RINGS

SOME INGENIOUS VICTORIAN ALARM RINGS WERE MADE WITH PINS. THE PIN PRICKED THE FINGER IF EVER THE STONE FELL OUT OF THE RING.

HOW TO REMOVE A RING

SOAK A LENGTH OF STRING IN SOAP-SUDS OR OIL & PASS ONE END THROUGH THE RING. WIND REST OF STRING TIGHTLY ROUND FINGER. LEAVE THE 'BANDAGE' ON FOR A FEW MINUTES, THEN SLOWLY UNWIND IT FROM THE RING END - THUS PULLING OFF RING.

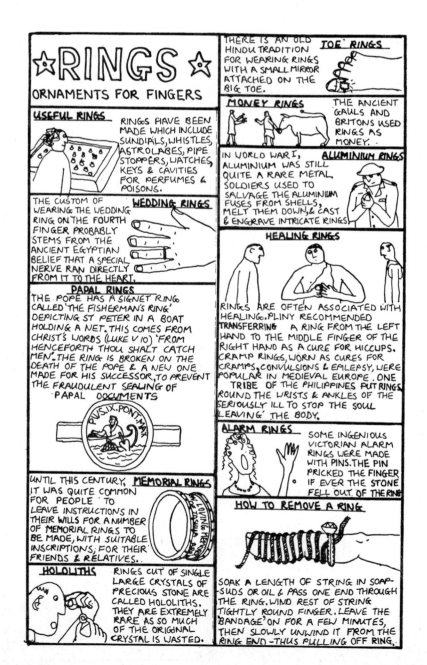

ROBOTS

MEDICAL ROBOTS

SOME MEDICAL SCHOOLS NOW USE COMPUTER-CONTROLLED HUMAN REPLICAS WHICH BREATHE, BLINK, HAVE AUDIBLE HEARTBEAT, & HAVE REACTIONS TO CERTAIN DRUGS. THEY ARE USED TO TEACH STUDENTS HOW TO DEAL WITH CARDIAC ARREST, CHANGE IN PULSE OR BLOOD PRESSURE & OTHER EMERGENCIES.

HUMAN ROBOTS

ACCORDING TO THE TALMUDIC TRADITION, GOD CREATED MAN IN A ROBOT-LIKE PROCESS. IN THE FIRST HOUR DUST WAS GATHERED FROM ALL PARTS OF THE WORLD; IN THE SECOND IT WAS KNEADED INTO A SHAPELESS MASS (GOLEM); IN THE THIRD HIS LIMBS WERE SHAPED; IN THE FOURTH A SOUL WAS INFUSED INTO HIM & IN THE FIFTH HE ROSE & STOOD ON HIS FEET.

TRAFFIC ROBOTS

THE GERMANS & THE FRENCH USE SIMPLE ROBOTS TO WARN MOTORISTS OF ROADWORKS. THE DUMMIES, WITH MECHANICAL WAVING FLAGS, ARE SAID TO BE MORE EFFECTIVE THAN SIGNS & LIGHTS. THE FRENCH MODEL SMILES; THE GERMAN ONE DOES NOT.

LIFELIKE ROBOTS

THE SIERRA ENGINEERING Co OF CALIFORNIA PRODUCES A WHOLE RANGE OF ACCURATE HUMAN REPLICAS FOR TESTING CAR SAFETY SYSTEMS, PLANE EJECTOR SEATS & SPACE EQUIPMENT. THEY EXUDE HUMAN TEMPERATURES & HAVE A PLASTIC SKIN BACKED BY FOAM WHICH APPROXIMATES TO THE RESILIENCE OF HUMAN FLESH. THEY ALSO HAVE SIMULATED BONES & INTERNAL ORGANS, ACCESSIBLE THROUGH A ZIP ON EACH SIDE.

GREEK ROBOT

THERE IS A ROBOT IN GREEK MYTHOLOGY, A GIANT MADE OF BRASS CALLED TALUS WHO GUARDED CRETE BY HEATING HIS BODY & HUGGING INTRUDERS TO DEATH.

DOMESTIC ROBOTS

THE IDEA OF A DOMESTIC ROBOT, TO CLEAN, WASH, COOK ETC, IS NOT NEW — THE ROBOT BELOW IS TAKEN FROM A VICTORIAN CARTOON. THE FIRST DOMESTIC ROBOT FOR RETAIL SALE IS EXPECTED TO REACH THE SHOPS IN AMERICA THIS YEAR SELLING AT ABOUT £2000. IT IS SAID TO MOP FLOORS, MOW LAWNS & DO SIMPLE COOKING.

MAN AMPLIFIERS

MAN AMPLIFIERS ARE MOTORISED FRAMEWORKS DESIGNED TO EXPAND A MAN'S STRENGTH. THE ONE ABOVE IS CALLED HARDIMAN, BUILT BY G.E.C. IT CAN BE DANGEROUS FOR THE OPERATOR. THE MACHINE CAN BE ACTIVATED BY AN INVOLUNTARY MOVEMENT & ATTEMPTS TO STOP IT CAN LEAD TO A RESONANT CHAIN REACTION, JERKING THE OPERATOR AROUND UNCONTROL-LABLY.

INTELLIGENT ROBOTS

AT THE MOMENT, THE MOST AMBITIOUS COMPUTERISED ROBOTS ARE CALIFORNIA UNIVERSITY'S SHAKEY — WHICH LOCATES AND MOVES DIFFERENT SHAPED WOODEN BLOCKS ON COMMAND & TOKYO UNIVERSITY'S WABOT ONE, WHICH RESPONDS TO VERBAL COMMANDS & PERFORMS SUCH TASKS AS LOCATING A GLASS, FILLING IT WITH WATER & CARRYING IT SOMEWHERE. THE MICROPROCESSOR WILL ENABLE MUCH LARGER MEMORIES TO BE BUILT IN. THIS WILL INCREASE THE POTENTIAL OF A ROBOT TO LEARN BY EXPERIENCE — AS DO OUR BRAINS.

HOW TO WALK WITH 3 LEGS

MAKE A FALSE LEG BY STUFFING A SOCK WITH NEWSPAPER & TYING TOP OF SOCK TO A STICK LONG ENOUGH TO REACH YOUR ELBOW. DRESS LEG IN SHOE & TROUSER LEG SIMILAR TO YOUR OWN. PRACTISE 3-LEGGED WALKING IN A MIRROR, HOLDING STICK BY YOUR SIDE. COMPLETE THE ILLUSION BY WEARING LONG COAT TO HIDE STICK — HOLDING IT THROUGH A COAT POCKET.

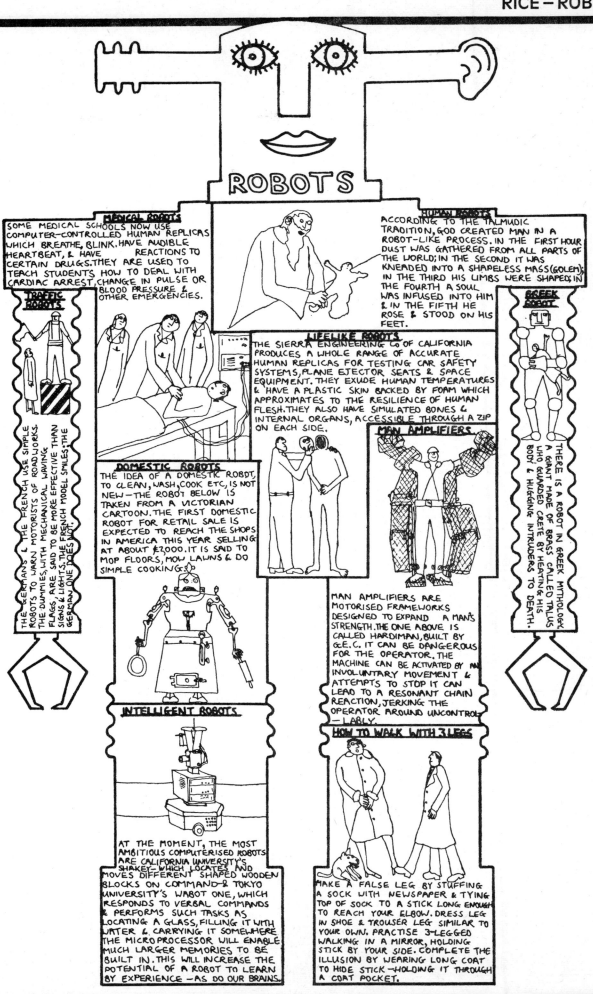

ROCKETS
AERODYNAMIC INFERNOS

MAJOR CONGREVES EXPERIMENT

IN 1789 THE BRITISH ARMY IN INDIA WAS ROUTED BY A LARGE BATTERY OF ROCKETS BELONGING TO HYDAR ALI, PRINCE OF MYSORE. THIS INSPIRED A MAJOR CONGREVE TO DEVELOP "THE SOULE OF ARTILLERY WITHOUT THE BODY" AS HE CALLED THE ROCKET. IN 1806 HIS DESIGN WAS TRIED AGAINST THE FRENCH FLEET IN BOULOGNE. UNFORTUNATELY THE WIND CARRIED THE ROCKETS AWAY FROM THE FLEET, BUT THE EXPERIMENT WAS CONSIDERED A SUCCESS AS THEY LANDED ON THE TOWN & CAUSED A LARGE FIRE.

THE TERRIBLE NEW WEAPON

EARLY REFERENCES TO ROCKETS WERE OFTEN MISLEADING. ONE MANUSCRIPT DESCRIBES A ROCKET AS "A SELF MOVING & COMBUSTING EGG" & ITS CONTENTS AS "THE LIFE, THE SOULE, & THE COALES OF THE BODY" (MEANING SULPHUR, SALTPETRE & CHARCOAL).

THE MAGEDEBURG EXPERIMENT

IN THE 1930s THE CITY COUNCIL OF MAGDEBURG BELIEVED THAT THE EARTH EXTENDED TO INFINITY IN ALL DIRECTIONS & THAT ITS SURFACE WAS THE INSIDE OF A HOLLOW SPHERE, WITH THE SUN AT THE CENTRE. THEY THOUGHT THEY WOULD PROVE THEIR THEORY IF THEY COULD SEND A ROCKET UP HIGH ENOUGH TO LAND IN AUSTRALIA. THEY OFFERED FUNDS TO THE GERMAN SOCIETY FOR SPACE RESEARCH, WHO WERE DELIGHTED TO HAVE SOME BACKING TO BUILD A SUITABLE LARGE ROCKET. IT WAS COMPLETED IN 1934 BUT CRASH-LANDED & EXPLODED, LEAVING THE THEORY UNPROVEN.

THE SPACE RACE

THE RUSSIANS HAD MUCH LARGER ROCKETS THAN THE AMERICANS IN THE 1950s. THEY HAD LAUNCHED A ½ TON SATELLITE CONTAINING THE DOG LAIKA BEFORE AMERICA GOT ITS FIRST 3LB SATELLITE (REFERRED TO BY KRUSCHEV AS "A MERE GRAPEFRUIT") ALOFT. THE REASON FOR THIS DISCREPANCY WAS IRONICALLY BECAUSE RUSSIA'S NUCLEAR TECHNOLOGY WAS MUCH MORE PRIMITIVE. THEIR ATOMIC BOMB WAS MUCH HEAVIER THAN THE AMERICANS' & THEY HAD DEVELOPED ENORMOUS ROCKETS TO CARRY IT.

ROCKET ASSAULT

THE U.S. DEVELOPED A ROCKET ASSAULT CRAFT IN WORLD WAR II WHICH HAD A FIREPOWER EQUAL TO 3 BATTLESHIPS. IT LACKED ACCURACY BUT CREATED A DEVASTATING PSYCHOLOGICAL IMPACT.

SATURN V

USED FOR THE APOLLO MISSIONS, SATURN IS THE WORLD'S LARGEST ROCKET. IT GULPS 13.4 TONS OF FUEL A SECOND ON TAKE OFF & GENERATES 175,600,000 H.P. IT IS SO VITAL FOR EVERYTHING TO FUNCTION CORRECTLY THAT MOST OF THE COMPUTERS INVOLVED ARE INSTALLED IN TRIPLICATE & THE MAJORITY DECISION IS ACTED UPON.

HOW TO MAKE A TEST TUBE GO POP WITHOUT BREAKING IT

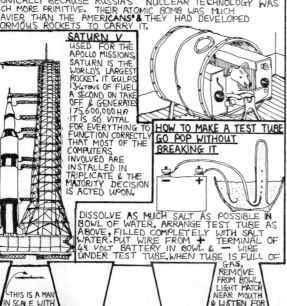

DISSOLVE AS MUCH SALT AS POSSIBLE IN BOWL OF WATER. ARRANGE TEST TUBE AS ABOVE, FILLED COMPLETELY WITH SALT WATER. PUT WIRE FROM + TERMINAL OF 4½ VOLT BATTERY IN BOWL & – WIRE UNDER TEST TUBE. WHEN TUBE IS FULL OF GAS, REMOVE FROM BOWL, LIGHT MATCH NEAR MOUTH & LISTEN FOR A STRANGE POP.

THIS IS A MAN IN SCALE WITH THE ROCKET ABOVE

ROPE
STRONG FLEXIBLE SUBSTANCE COMPOSED OF TWISTED FIBRES

PLASTIC ROPE

NYLON, POLYPROPYLENE & POLYESTER ROPES ARE ABOUT 3 TIMES AS STRONG AS A SISAL ROPE OF THE SAME DIAMETER. NATURAL ROPE IS STILL USEFUL IN SOME SITUATIONS AS "SYNTHETIC" ROPES DETERIORATE IN STRONG SUNLIGHT, HIGH TEMPERATURES & SOME CHEMICALS.

ROPE WALKS

ROPE CAN BE MADE FROM ANY LONG, THIN FIBRES. BUNDLES OF THE FIBRES ARE TWISTED TOGETHER TO FORM YARN. ROPE CONSISTS OF SEVERAL LENGTHS OF YARN TWISTED TOGETHER. THEY ARE TWISTED IN THE OPPOSITE DIRECTION TO THE COMPONENT YARNS, TO STOP THE ROPE UNTWISTING. ROPE IS TRADITIONALLY MADE IN LONG SHEDS CALLED ROPE WALKS. THE YARNS ARE LAID ON THE FLOOR & AN APPRENTICE ROTATES THEM AT ONE END WHILE THE ROPE MAKER WALKS DOWN THE SHED PICKING UP THE YARNS TO MAKE SURE THEY TWIST TOGETHER EVENLY.

EARLY ROPE

PALAEOLITHIC MAN USED ROPE. EVIDENCE REMAINS ON CAVE PAINTING & ON FRAGMENTS OF POTS DECORATED BY THE IMPRESSION OF ROPES. ROPE WAS ESSENTIAL TO ALL EARLY CIVILISATIONS FOR HAULING BUILDING MATERIALS AND MAKING BOATS. EVIDENCE OF ROPE-MAKING AS A SPECIALIST CRAFT EXISTS FROM 4000BC IN EGYPT; 2800BC IN CHINA; 400BC IN INDIA.

JUTE ROPE

JUTE IS THE COMMONEST SOFT VEGETABLE FIBRE USED FOR ROPE (ALSO FOR SACKING & WEBBING). IT COMES FROM THE STALKS OF A TROPICAL PLANT GROWN IN WATERLOGGED TROPICAL FIELDS. IT GROWS UP TO 18FT HIGH IN 4 MONTHS.

SISAL ROPE

SISAL ROPE IS STILL USED FOR COARSE STRING & ROPE AS THE FIBRES CAN BE GROWN RELATIVELY CHEAPLY. THE FIBRES COME FROM THE LEAVES OF A CACTUS-LIKE PLANT WHICH LOOKS LIKE A GIANT PINEAPPLE WITH 4FT LONG SPIKY LEAVES. ONCE THE CACTUS IS ESTABLISHED THE LEAVES CAN BE HARVESTED ANNUALLY.

HIGH CLIMBER ROPE

A SPECIAL HIGH-CLIMBER ROPE, WITH A STEEL CORE, HAS BEEN DEVELOPED FOR LUMBERJACKS WHEN CUTTING OFF THE TOPS OF TREES BEFORE FELLING. PREVIOUSLY ACCIDENTS OCCURRED WHEN ROPES WERE CHOPPED IN HALF BY LUMBERJACKS' AXES.

FATTEST & LONGEST ROPE

THE FATTEST ROPE EVER MADE WAS THE 15IN DIAMETER LAUNCHING ROPE FOR BRUNEL'S SHIP THE GREAT EASTERN (1858). THE LONGEST ROPE EVER (WITHOUT A SPLICE) WAS 10,000 FATHOMS (11.36 MILES) MADE IN 1874.

FORENSIC ROPE

THE POLICE FIND ROPE PARTICULARLY USEFUL FOR CRIME DETECTION. NO TWO ROPES ARE IDENTICAL & THIS ENABLES THE MANUFACTURER & LOCALITY OF PURCHASE TO BE TRACED FROM FRAGMENTS LEFT AT THE SCENE OF A CRIME.

WIRE ROPE

WIRE ROPE WAS INVENTED BY A GERMAN MINING OFFICIAL (W. ALBERT) IN 1834. IT HAD LIMITED USES UNTIL STEELMAKING & WIRE DRAWING PROCESSES WERE PERFECTED IN ABOUT 1900. IT IS ABOUT 10 TIMES AS STRONG AS NATURAL ROPE OF THE SAME SIZE.

HOW TO MAKE MATCHES FORM A STAR

BREAK 4 MATCHES IN HALF & ARRANGE (AS ABOVE) ON SMOOTH SURFACE. PUT DROP OF WATER INSIDE EACH V & MATCHES WILL MAGICALLY OPEN OUT TO FORM A STAR SHAPE.

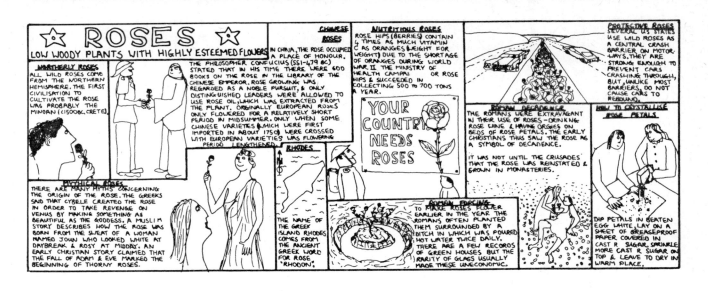

☆ ROSES ☆
LOW WOODY PLANTS WITH HIGHLY ESTEEMED FLOWERS

NORTHERLY ROSES
ALL WILD ROSES COME FROM THE NORTHERN HEMISPHERE. THE FIRST CIVILISATION TO CULTIVATE THE ROSE WAS PROBABLY THE MINOAN (c1500BC, CRETE).

MYTHICAL ROSES
THERE ARE MANY MYTHS CONCERNING THE ORIGIN OF THE ROSE. THE GREEKS SAID THAT CYBELE CREATED THE ROSE IN ORDER TO TAKE REVENGE ON VENUS BY MAKING SOMETHING AS BEAUTIFUL AS THE GODDESS. A MUSLIM STORY DESCRIBES HOW THE ROSE WAS BORN FROM THE SWEAT OF A WOMAN NAMED JOUN WHO LOOKED WHITE AT DAYBREAK & ROSY AT MIDDAY. AN EARLY CHRISTIAN STORY CLAIMED THAT THE FALL OF ADAM & EVE MARKED THE BEGINNING OF THORNY ROSES.

CHINESE ROSES
IN CHINA, THE ROSE OCCUPIED A PLACE OF HONOUR. THE PHILOSOPHER CONFUCIUS (551-479 BC) STATED THAT IN HIS TIME THERE WERE 600 BOOKS ON THE ROSE IN THE LIBRARY OF THE CHINESE EMPEROR. ROSE GROWING WAS REGARDED AS A NOBLE PURSUIT, & ONLY DISTINGUISHED LEADERS WERE ALLOWED TO USE ROSE OIL, WHICH WAS EXTRACTED FROM THE PLANT. ORIGINALLY EUROPEAN ROSES ONLY FLOWERED FOR A RELATIVELY SHORT PERIOD IN MIDSUMMER. ONLY WHEN SOME CHINESE VARIETIES (WHICH WERE FIRST IMPORTED IN ABOUT 1750) WERE CROSSED WITH EUROPEAN VARIETIES WAS FLOWERING PERIOD LENGTHENED.

RHODES
THE NAME OF THE GREEK ISLAND RHODES COMES FROM THE ANCIENT GREEK WORD FOR ROSE "RHODON".

NUTRITIOUS ROSES
ROSE HIPS (BERRIES) CONTAIN 4 TIMES AS MUCH VITAMIN C AS ORANGES, (WEIGHT FOR WEIGHT) DUE TO THE SHORTAGE OF ORANGES DURING WORLD WAR II THE MINISTRY OF HEALTH CAMPAIGN "YOUR COUNTRY NEEDS ROSE HIPS" & SUCCEEDED IN COLLECTING 500 TO 700 TONS A YEAR.

YOUR COUNTRY NEEDS ROSES

ROMAN FORCING
TO MAKE ROSES FLOWER EARLIER IN THE YEAR THE ROMANS OFTEN PLANTED THEM SURROUNDED BY A DITCH IN WHICH WAS POURED HOT WATER TWICE DAILY. THERE ARE A FEW RECORDS OF GREEN HOUSES BUT THE RARITY OF GLASS USUALLY MADE THESE UNECONOMIC.

ROMAN DECADENCE
THE ROMANS WERE EXTRAVAGANT IN THEIR USE OF ROSES – DRINKING ROSE WINE & HAVING ORGIES ON BEDS OF ROSE PETALS. THE EARLY CHRISTIANS THUS SAW THE ROSE AS A SYMBOL OF DECADENCE.

IT WAS NOT UNTIL THE CRUSADES THAT THE ROSE WAS REINSTATED & GROWN IN MONASTERIES.

PROTECTIVE ROSES
SEVERAL US STATES USE WILD ROSES AS A CENTRAL CRASH BARRIER ON MOTORWAYS. THEY ARE STRONG ENOUGH TO PREVENT CARS CRASHING THROUGH, BUT, UNLIKE MOST BARRIERS, DO NOT CAUSE CARS TO REBOUND.

HOW TO CRYSTALLISE ROSE PETALS
DIP PETALS IN BEATEN EGG WHITE, LAY ON A SHEET OF GREASEPROOF PAPER COVERED IN CAST R SUGAR, SPRINKLE MORE CAST R SUGAR ON TOP & LEAVE TO DRY IN A WARM PLACE.

☆ RUBBER ☆
VEGETABLE GUM COMMON IN TROPICAL TREES

RUBBER & THE AZTECS
THE AZTECS ATTACHED GREAT SIGNIFICANCE TO THIS STRANGE ELASTIC SOLID THAT BURNT WITH A DENSE BLACK SMOKE. THEY CALLED IT OLLI, A WORD WHICH ALSO MEANT BLOOD & IN THEIR PICTURE WRITING THE HEART WAS SYMBOLISED AS A BALL OF RUBBER. THE PRIESTS COVERED THEMSELVES WITH FRESH LIQUID LATEX & KEPT SOLIDIFIED LUMPS IN THE TEMPLES FOR HEALING & BURNING TO PRODUCE RAIN.

MR HANCOCK
THOMAS HANCOCK (1800-56) WAS THE FATHER OF THE MODERN RUBBER INDUSTRY. THE LIQUID LATEX FROM THE TREES WAS VERY DIFFICULT TO UTILISE AS IT SET TO A SOLID ELASTIC LUMP AFTER A FEW HOURS & IT WAS THEN IMPOSSIBLE TO REMOULD. HANCOCK STARTED MAKING ELASTIC BANDS THE SAME SIZE AS THE LUMPS HE RECEIVED BUT WHILE ATTEMPTING TO MAKE A MACHINE TO CUT THE LUMPS INTO BANDS HE MADE ONE WHICH WAS TOO VIOLENT & TRANSFORMED THE SHREDS INTO A GLUTINOUS BUT REMOULDABLE MASS. HE CALLED HIS MACHINE A MASTICATOR & WENT ON TO UNITE WITH CHARLES MACINTOSH TO MAKE WATERPROOF FABRICS.

RUBBER GLOVES
RUBBER GLOVES WERE THE BRAIN WAVE OF A SURGEON CALLED HALSTEAD. HE INTRODUCED THEM FOR ONE OF HIS NURSES WHO HAD AN ALLERGY TO CARBOLIC ACID & THEIR USE FOR KEEPING INCISIONS STERILE WAS ONLY REALISED LATER.

A RUBBER SKIN FOR DESERTS
THE UNISOL SOIL STABILISATION PROCESS IS A COATING OF RUBBER & OIL SPRAYED ON POOR SOIL. IT TRAPS MOISTURE & COMBATS EROSION, ALLOWING PLANTS TO ESTABLISH THEMSELVES

MR WICKHAM
SOUTH AMERICA HAD A MONOPOLY OF THE RUBBER TRADE UNTIL IT WAS DECIDED TO ATTEMPT TO ESTABLISH TREES IN CEYLON. AN EXPLORER CALLED WICKHAM WAS DISPATCHED TO COLLECT SEEDS IN 1878 &, DESPITE HAVING HIS BOAT & MONEY STOLEN, RETURNED IN RECORD TIME, CHARTERING ANOTHER VESSEL. KEW GARDENS THREW OUT MOST OF ITS TROPICAL PLANTS TO MAKE ROOM FOR HIS 70,000 SEEDS. 2,700 GREW INTO SAPLINGS & WERE RE-EXPORTED TO CEYLON

HOW TO SEPARATE A & B WITHOUT UNTYING ANY KNOTS
- PULL A's LOOP THROUGH B's RIGHT WRIST BAND FROM THE BACK.
- SLIP A's LOOP OVER BACK OF B's HAND.
- PULL A's LOOP BACK OUT OF B's WRIST.
- A & B WILL NOW BE DISENTANGLED.

☆ RUBBISH ☆
RAW MATERIALS FOR THE RECYCLING INDUSTRY

LUXURIOUS RUBBISH

TO PROVE THE POTENTIAL OF RUBBISH REYNOLDS ALUMINIUM Co. HAS BUILT A LUXURY HOUSE ENTIRELY FROM RECYCLED MATERIALS. IT IS MADE MAINLY FROM THEIR INDUSTRIAL METAL SCRAP BUT ALSO INCORPORATES

ASPHALT — OLD CAR TYRES, TAR & CRUSHED GLASS.
CEMENT — 50% FLY ASH FROM A POWER STATION.
ROOFING FELT — RECLAIMED PAPER FIBRES.
CARPETS — RECLAIMED NYLON FIBRES.
ROOFING TILES — WASTE PAPER & ASPHALT.
CENTRAL HEATING DUCTING — OLD ALUMINIUM CANS.
INSULATING FIBRE — CRUSHED GLASS & STEEL MILL SLAG.
MARBLE — QUARTZ CHIPS GLUED TOGETHER.
FLOOR TILES — WOOD CHIPS & WASTE VINYL.
GARDEN COMPOST — PROCESSED SEWAGE.

DEGRADABLE BOTTLES

THE SWEDES HAVE A CONTAINER MADE OF PVC LACED WITH POLYNYLIDENE CHLORIDE, ALUMINIUM FOIL & POLYSTYRENE GLUE WHICH IS SAID TO ROT IN SUNLIGHT. AN AMERICAN INVENTOR HAS BEEN GIVEN A £22,000 GRANT TO DEVELOP A BOTTLE THAT WILL DISSOLVE IN A POOL OF WATER WITH A WATERPROOF INNER COATING TO PREVENT ITS CONTENTS DISSOLVING IT. PERHAPS THE BEST INVENTION IS THE EDIBLE BOTTLE MADE FROM A SUBSTANCE SIMILAR TO ARTIFICIAL CREAM.

MILK BOTTLES

THE RETURNABLE MILK BOTTLE IS APPARENTLY BEING HANDLED INCREASINGLY WILDLY. IN 1963 BOTTLES LASTED AN AVERAGE OF 45 TRIPS BUT THIS HAS SINCE FALLEN TO 25. GLASGOW HAS THE WORST RECORD OF ANY CITY; BOTTLES AVERAGE ONLY 6 TRIPS.

CANNED ENERGY

WHILE ALUMINIUM CAN MANUFACTURERS SPONSOR VARIOUS RECYCLING SCHEMES THEY ARE NOT ENTIRELY ECOLOGICALLY VIRTUOUS. THE ENERGY NEEDED TO SMELT THE METAL FOR AN ALUMINIUM CAN IS 13 TIMES MORE THAN THAT NEEDED FOR THE ORDINARY STEEL ONES THEY ARE REPLACING.

CANS CONSUMED

SAVE PAPER SAVE TREES

THE AMOUNT OF WOOD PULP BRITAIN USES FOR PAPER REQUIRES A FOREST AREA THE SIZE OF WALES TO BE PULLED DOWN EVERY YEAR. WE AVOID THIS BY IMPORTING. OUR IMPORTS OF PAPER PRODUCTS & PULP COST MORE THAN WE RECEIVE FROM EXPORTING CARS.

WASTE IN A WASTEPLEX

BRITAIN'S FIRST WASTEPLEX IS BEING DEVELOPED AT STEVENAGE, HERTS. IT TAKES IN DOMESTIC REFUSE & PROCESSES IT WITH A VARIETY OF INGENIOUS MACHINES. THESE BURST ANY BAGS THAT THE RUBBISH ARRIVES IN, SEPARATE STEEL & OTHER METALS & THEN DISTIL THE REMAINDER TO PRODUCE VARIOUS OILS & A GLUEY SUBSTANCE SUITABLE FOR CAR TYRES.

RUBBISH

PAPER MANUFACTURERS ARE INCREASING THE PROPORTION OF WASTE PAPER THEY CAN INCORPORATE IN THEIR PRODUCTS BY INTRODUCING NEW MACHINES. IT IS IMPOSSIBLE TO MAKE HIGH QUALITY PAPER FROM WASTE BUT IT IS SUITABLE FOR MOST CARDBOARDS.

HOW TO CONFUSE YOUR FEET WITH BINOCULARS

TRY TO WALK ALONG A STRAIGHT LINE LOOKING AT YOUR FEET THROUGH BINOCULARS THE WRONG WAY ROUND. IT IS AMAZINGLY HARD TO STAY ON THE LINE. SEE IF ANY OF YOUR FRIENDS CAN DO IT.

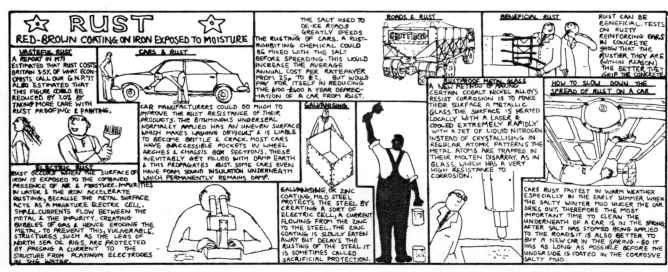

☆ RUST ☆
RED-BROWN COATING ON IRON EXPOSED TO MOISTURE

WASTEFUL RUST

A REPORT IN 1971 ESTIMATED THAT RUST COSTS BRITAIN 3.5% OF WHAT ECONOMISTS CALL OUR G.N.P. IT ALSO ESTIMATED THAT THIS FIGURE COULD BE REDUCED BY 20% BY TAKING MORE CARE WITH RUST PROOFING & PAINTING.

ELECTRIC RUST

RUST OCCURS WHEN THE SURFACE OF IRON IS EXPOSED TO THE COMBINED PRESENCE OF AIR & MOISTURE. IMPURITIES IN LATER & THE IRON ACCELERATE RUSTING, BECAUSE THE METAL SURFACE ACTS AS A MINIATURE ELECTRIC CELL. SMALL CURRENTS FLOW BETWEEN THE METAL & THE IMPURITY, CREATING BUBBLES OF GAS & HENCE ERODING THE METAL. TO PREVENT THIS, VULNERABLE STRUCTURES, SUCH AS THE LEGS OF NORTH SEA OIL RIGS, ARE PROTECTED BY PASSING A CURRENT TO THE STRUCTURE FROM PLATINUM ELECTRODES IN THE WATER.

CARS & RUST

CAR MANUFACTURERS COULD DO MUCH TO IMPROVE THE RUST RESISTANCE OF THEIR PRODUCTS. THE BITUMINOUS UNDERSEAL NORMALLY APPLIED HAS AN UNEVEN SURFACE WHICH MAKES WASHING DIFFICULT & IS LIABLE TO BECOME BRITTLE & CRACK. MOST CARS HAVE INACCESSIBLE POCKETS IN WHEEL ARCHES & CHASSIS BOX SECTIONS. THESE INEVITABLY GET FILLED WITH DAMP EARTH & THIS PROPAGATES RUST. SOME CARS EVEN HAVE FOAM SOUND INSULATION UNDERNEATH WHICH PERMANENTLY REMAINS DAMP.

THE SALT USED TO DE-ICE ROADS GREATLY SPEEDS THE RUSTING OF CARS. A RUST-INHIBITING CHEMICAL COULD BE MIXED WITH THE SALT BEFORE SPREADING. THIS WOULD INCREASE THE AVERAGE ANNUAL COST PER RATEPAYER FROM 25p TO £2, BUT WOULD PAY FOR ITSELF IN REDUCING THE £100 – £400 A YEAR DEPRECIATION OF A CAR FROM RUST.

GALVANISING

GALVANISING OR ZINC COATING MILD STEEL PROTECTS THE STEEL BY CREATING A SORT OF ELECTRIC CELL, A CURRENT FLOWING FROM THE ZINC TO THE STEEL. THE ZINC COATING IS SLOWLY EATEN AWAY BUT DELAYS THE RUSTING OF THE STEEL. IT IS SOMETIMES CALLED SACRIFICIAL PROTECTION.

ROADS & RUST

GRIT FLOW

BENEFICIAL RUST

RUST CAN BE BENEFICIAL. TESTS ON RUSTY REINFORCING BARS IN CONCRETE SHOW THAT THE RUSTIER THEY ARE (WITHIN REASON) THE BETTER THEY GRIP THE CONCRETE.

RUSTPROOF METAL GLASS

A NEW METHOD OF MAKING CERTAIN COBALT NICKEL ALLOYS RESIST CORROSION IS TO MAKE THEIR SURFACE A METALLIC GLASS. THE SURFACE IS HEATED LOCALLY WITH A LASER & COOLED EXTREMELY RAPIDLY WITH A JET OF LIQUID NITROGEN INSTEAD OF CRYSTALLISING IN REGULAR ATOMIC PATTERNS THE METAL ATOMS ARE TRAPPED IN THEIR MOLTEN DISARRAY, AS IN GLASS, WHICH HAS A VERY HIGH RESISTANCE TO CORROSION.

HOW TO SLOW DOWN THE SPREAD OF RUST ON A CAR

CARS RUST FASTEST IN WARM WEATHER ESPECIALLY IN THE EARLY SUMMER WHEN THE SALTY WINTER MUD UNDER THE CAR DRIES OUT. THEREFORE THE MOST IMPORTANT TIME TO CLEAN THE UNDERNEATH OF A CAR IS IN THE SPRING AFTER SALT HAS STOPPED BEING APPLIED TO THE ROADS. IT IS ALSO BETTER TO BUY A NEW CAR IN THE SPRING - SO IT HAS AS LONG AS POSSIBLE BEFORE THE UNDERSIDE IS COATED IN THE CORROSIVE SALTY MUD.

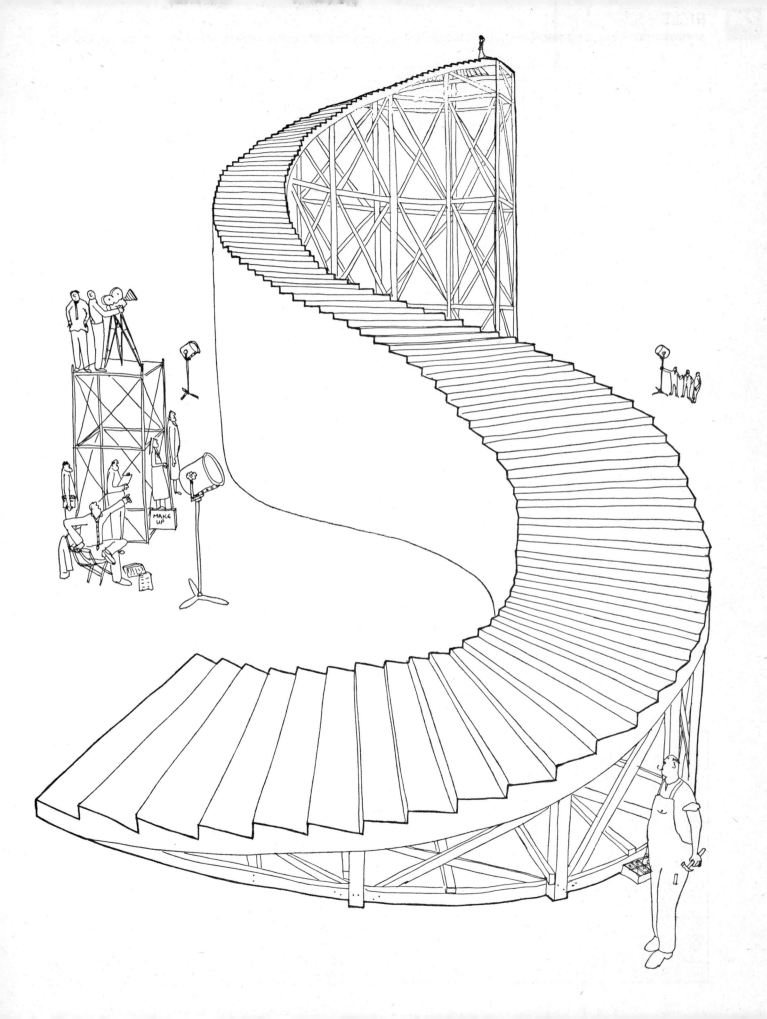

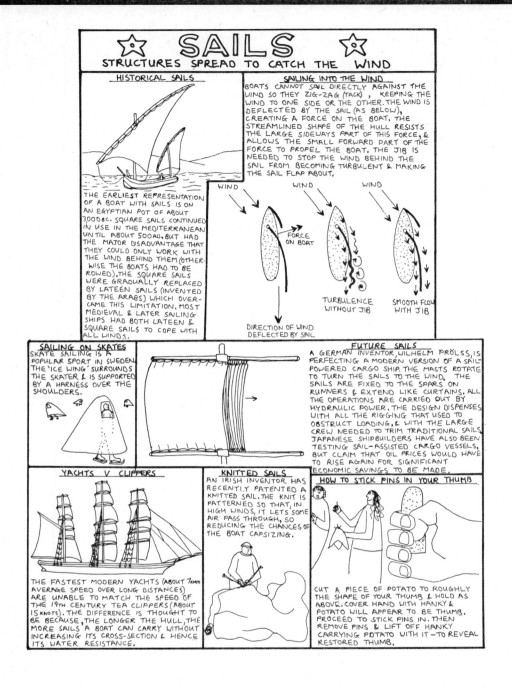

☆ SAILS ☆
STRUCTURES SPREAD TO CATCH THE WIND

HISTORICAL SAILS

THE EARLIEST REPRESENTATION OF A BOAT WITH SAILS IS ON AN EGYPTIAN POT OF ABOUT 3,000BC. SQUARE SAILS CONTINUED IN USE IN THE MEDITERRANEAN UNTIL ABOUT 500AD, BUT HAD THE MAJOR DISADVANTAGE THAT THEY COULD ONLY WORK WITH THE WIND BEHIND THEM (OTHERWISE THE BOATS HAD TO BE ROWED). THE SQUARE SAILS WERE GRADUALLY REPLACED BY LATEEN SAILS (INVENTED BY THE ARABS) WHICH OVERCAME THIS LIMITATION. MOST MEDIEVAL & LATER SAILING SHIPS HAD BOTH LATEEN & SQUARE SAILS TO COPE WITH ALL WINDS.

SAILING INTO THE WIND

BOATS CANNOT SAIL DIRECTLY AGAINST THE WIND SO THEY ZIG-ZAG (TACK), KEEPING THE WIND TO ONE SIDE OR THE OTHER. THE WIND IS DEFLECTED BY THE SAIL (AS BELOW), CREATING A FORCE ON THE BOAT. THE STREAMLINED SHAPE OF THE HULL RESISTS THE LARGE SIDEWAYS PART OF THIS LARGE FORCE, & ALLOWS THE SMALL FORWARD PART OF THE FORCE TO PROPEL THE BOAT. THE JIB IS NEEDED TO STOP THE WIND BEHIND THE SAIL FROM BECOMING TURBULENT & MAKING THE SAIL FLAP ABOUT.

WIND — FORCE ON BOAT

DIRECTION OF WIND DEFLECTED BY SAIL

WIND — TURBULENCE WITHOUT JIB

WIND — SMOOTH FLOW WITH JIB

SAILING ON SKATES

SKATE SAILING IS A POPULAR SPORT IN SWEDEN. THE 'ICE WING' SURROUNDS THE SKATER & IS SUPPORTED BY A HARNESS OVER THE SHOULDERS.

FUTURE SAILS

A GERMAN INVENTOR, WILHELM PRÖLSS, IS PERFECTING A MODERN VERSION OF A SAIL POWERED CARGO SHIP. THE MASTS ROTATE TO TURN THE SAILS TO THE WIND. THE SAILS ARE FIXED TO THE SPARS ON RUNNERS & EXTEND LIKE CURTAINS. ALL THE OPERATIONS ARE CARRIED OUT BY HYDRAULIC POWER. THE DESIGN DISPENSES WITH ALL THE RIGGING THAT USED TO OBSTRUCT LOADING, & WITH THE LARGE CREW NEEDED TO TRIM TRADITIONAL SAILS. JAPANESE SHIPBUILDERS HAVE ALSO BEEN TESTING SAIL-ASSISTED CARGO VESSELS, BUT CLAIM THAT OIL PRICES WOULD HAVE TO RISE AGAIN FOR SIGNIFICANT ECONOMIC SAVINGS TO BE MADE.

YACHTS V CLIPPERS

THE FASTEST MODERN YACHTS (ABOUT 7 KNOTS AVERAGE SPEED OVER LONG DISTANCES) ARE UNABLE TO MATCH THE SPEED OF THE 19TH CENTURY TEA CLIPPERS (ABOUT 15 KNOTS). THE DIFFERENCE IS THOUGHT TO BE BECAUSE, THE LONGER THE HULL, THE MORE SAILS A BOAT CAN CARRY WITHOUT INCREASING ITS CROSS-SECTION & HENCE ITS WATER RESISTANCE.

KNITTED SAILS

AN IRISH INVENTOR HAS RECENTLY PATENTED A KNITTED SAIL. THE KNIT IS PATTERNED SO THAT, IN HIGH WINDS, IT LETS SOME AIR PASS THROUGH, SO REDUCING THE CHANCES OF THE BOAT CAPSIZING.

HOW TO STICK PINS IN YOUR THUMB

CUT A PIECE OF POTATO TO ROUGHLY THE SHAPE OF YOUR THUMB & HOLD AS ABOVE. COVER HAND WITH HANKY & POTATO WILL APPEAR TO BE THUMB. PROCEED TO STICK PINS IN. THEN REMOVE PINS & LIFT OFF HANKY CARRYING POTATO WITH IT — TO REVEAL RESTORED THUMB.

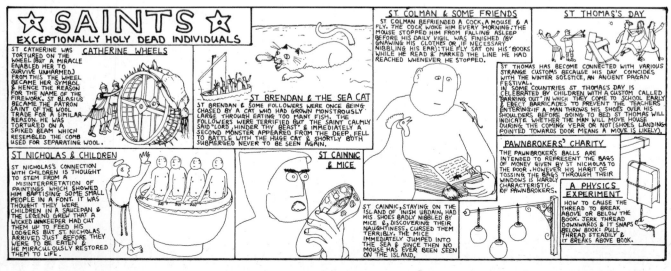

☆ SAINTS ☆
EXCEPTIONALLY HOLY DEAD INDIVIDUALS

CATHERINE WHEELS

ST CATHERINE WAS TORTURED ON THE WHEEL (BUT A MIRACLE ENABLED HER TO SURVIVE UNHARMED) FROM THIS THE WHEEL BECAME HER SYMBOL & HENCE THE REASON FOR THE NAME OF THE FIREWORK. ST BLASIUS BECAME THE PATRON SAINT OF THE WOOL TRADE FOR A SIMILAR REASON. HE WAS TORTURED ON A SPIKED BEAM WHICH RESEMBLED THE COMB USED FOR SEPARATING WOOL.

ST NICHOLAS & CHILDREN

ST NICHOLAS'S CONNECTION WITH CHILDREN IS THOUGHT TO STEM FROM A MISINTERPRETATION OF PAINTINGS WHICH SHOWED HIM BAPTISING SOME SMALL PEOPLE IN A FONT. IT WAS THOUGHT THEY WERE CHILDREN IN A SAUCEPAN & THE LEGEND GREW THAT A WICKED INNKEEPER HAD CUT THEM UP TO FEED HIS LODGERS BUT ST NICHOLAS ARRIVED JUST BEFORE THEY WERE TO BE EATEN & HE MIRACULOUSLY RESTORED THEM TO LIFE.

ST BRENDAN & THE SEA CAT

ST BRENDAN & SOME FOLLOWERS WERE ONCE BEING CHASED BY A CAT WHO HAD GROWN MONSTROUSLY LARGE THROUGH EATING TOO MANY FISH. THE FOLLOWERS WERE TERRIFIED BUT THE SAINT CALMLY SAID "LORD, HINDER THY BEAST" & IMMEDIATELY A SECOND MONSTER APPEARED FROM THE DEEP, FELL TO BATTLE WITH THE HUGE CAT & SHORTLY BOTH SUBMERGED NEVER TO BE SEEN AGAIN.

ST CAINNIC & MICE

ST CAINNIC, STAYING ON THE ISLAND OF INISH UBDAIN, HAD HIS SHOES BADLY NIBBLED BY MICE &, DISCOVERING THEIR NAUGHTINESS, CURSED THEM TERRIBLY. THE MICE IMMEDIATELY JUMPED INTO THE SEA & SINCE THEN NO MOUSE HAS EVER BEEN SEEN ON THE ISLAND.

ST COLMAN & SOME FRIENDS

ST COLMAN BEFRIENDED A COCK, A MOUSE & A FLY. THE COCK WOKE HIM EVERY MORNING; THE MOUSE STOPPED HIM FROM FALLING ASLEEP BEFORE HIS DAILY VIGIL WAS FINISHED (BY GNAWING HIS CLOTHES OR IF NECESSARY NIBBLING HIS EAR); THE FLY SAT ON HIS BOOKS WHILE HE READ & MARKED THE LINE HE HAD REACHED WHENEVER HE STOPPED.

ST THOMAS'S DAY

ST THOMAS HAS BECOME CONNECTED WITH VARIOUS STRANGE CUSTOMS BECAUSE HIS DAY COINCIDES WITH THE WINTER SOLSTICE, AN ANCIENT PAGAN FESTIVAL. IN SOME COUNTRIES ST THOMAS'S DAY IS CELEBRATED BY CHILDREN WITH A CUSTOM CALLED 'BARRING OUT' IN WHICH THEY COME TO SCHOOL EARLY & ERECT BARRICADES TO PREVENT THE TEACHERS ENTERING. IF A MAN THROWS HIS SHOES OVER HIS SHOULDERS, BEFORE GOING TO BED ST THOMAS WILL INDICATE WHETHER THE MAN WILL MOVE HOUSE DURING THE COMING YEAR OR NOT (SHOES LANDING POINTED TOWARDS DOOR MEANS A MOVE IS LIKELY).

PAWNBROKERS' CHARITY

THE PAWNBROKER'S BALLS ARE INTENDED TO REPRESENT THE BAGS OF MONEY GIVEN BY ST NICHOLAS TO THE POOR. HOWEVER HIS HABIT OF TOSSING THE BAGS THROUGH THEIR WINDOWS IS HARDLY CHARACTERISTIC OF PAWNBROKERS.

A PHYSICS EXPERIMENT

HOW TO CAUSE THE THREAD TO BREAK ABOVE OR BELOW THE BOOK. JERK THREAD DOWNWARDS & IT SNAPS BELOW BOOK. PULL THREAD STEADILY & IT BREAKS ABOVE BOOK.

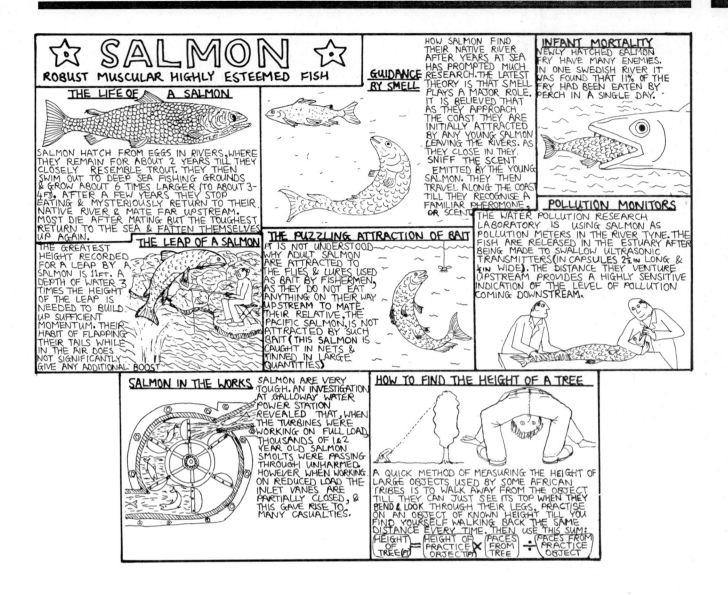

☆ SALMON ☆
ROBUST MUSCULAR HIGHLY ESTEEMED FISH

THE LIFE OF A SALMON

SALMON HATCH FROM EGGS IN RIVERS, WHERE THEY REMAIN FOR ABOUT 2 YEARS TILL THEY CLOSELY RESEMBLE TROUT. THEY THEN SWIM OUT TO DEEP SEA FISHING GROUNDS & GROW ABOUT 6 TIMES LARGER (TO ABOUT 3-4FT). AFTER A FEW YEARS THEY STOP EATING & MYSTERIOUSLY RETURN TO THEIR NATIVE RIVER & MATE FAR UPSTREAM. MOST DIE AFTER MATING BUT THE TOUGHEST RETURN TO THE SEA & FATTEN THEMSELVES UP AGAIN.

THE LEAP OF A SALMON

THE GREATEST HEIGHT RECORDED FOR A LEAP BY A SALMON IS 11FT. A DEPTH OF WATER 3 TIMES THE HEIGHT OF THE LEAP IS NEEDED TO BUILD UP SUFFICIENT MOMENTUM. THEIR HABIT OF FLAPPING THEIR TAILS WHILE IN THE AIR DOES NOT SIGNIFICANTLY GIVE ANY ADDITIONAL BOOST

GUIDANCE BY SMELL

HOW SALMON FIND THEIR NATIVE RIVER AFTER YEARS AT SEA HAS PROMPTED MUCH RESEARCH. THE LATEST THEORY IS THAT SMELL PLAYS A MAJOR ROLE. IT IS BELIEVED THAT AS THEY APPROACH THE COAST THEY ARE INITIALLY ATTRACTED BY ANY YOUNG SALMON LEAVING THE RIVERS. AS THEY CLOSE IN THEY SNIFF THE SCENT EMITTED BY THE YOUNG SALMON. THEY THEN TRAVEL ALONG THE COAST TILL THEY RECOGNISE A FAMILIAR PHEROMONE, OR SCENT.

THE PUZZLING ATTRACTION OF BAIT

IT IS NOT UNDERSTOOD WHY ADULT SALMON ARE ATTRACTED TO THE FLIES & LURES USED AS BAIT BY FISHERMEN, AS THEY DO NOT EAT ANYTHING ON THEIR WAY UPSTREAM TO MATE. THEIR RELATIVE, THE PACIFIC SALMON, IS NOT ATTRACTED BY SUCH BAIT (THIS SALMON IS CAUGHT IN NETS & TINNED IN LARGE QUANTITIES).

INFANT MORTALITY

NEWLY HATCHED SALMON FRY HAVE MANY ENEMIES. IN ONE SWEDISH RIVER IT WAS FOUND THAT 11% OF THE FRY HAD BEEN EATEN BY PERCH IN A SINGLE DAY.

POLLUTION MONITORS

THE WATER POLLUTION RESEARCH LABORATORY IS USING SALMON AS POLLUTION METERS IN THE RIVER TYNE. THE FISH ARE RELEASED IN THE ESTUARY AFTER BEING MADE TO SWALLOW ULTRASONIC TRANSMITTERS (IN CAPSULES 2½ IN LONG & ⅜ IN WIDE). THE DISTANCE THEY VENTURE UPSTREAM PROVIDES A HIGHLY SENSITIVE INDICATION OF THE LEVEL OF POLLUTION COMING DOWNSTREAM.

SALMON IN THE WORKS

SALMON ARE VERY TOUGH. AN INVESTIGATION AT GALLOWAY WATER POWER STATION REVEALED THAT, WHEN THE TURBINES WERE WORKING ON FULL LOAD, THOUSANDS OF 1 & 2 YEAR OLD SALMON SMOLTS WERE PASSING THROUGH UNHARMED. HOWEVER WHEN WORKING ON REDUCED LOAD THE INLET VANES ARE PARTIALLY CLOSED, & THIS GAVE RISE TO MANY CASUALTIES.

HOW TO FIND THE HEIGHT OF A TREE

A QUICK METHOD OF MEASURING THE HEIGHT OF LARGE OBJECTS USED BY SOME AFRICAN TRIBES IS TO WALK AWAY FROM THE OBJECT TILL THEY CAN JUST SEE ITS TOP WHEN THEY BEND & LOOK THROUGH THEIR LEGS. PRACTISE ON AN OBJECT OF KNOWN HEIGHT TILL YOU FIND YOURSELF WALKING BACK THE SAME DISTANCE EVERY TIME. THEN USE THIS SUM:

$$\text{HEIGHT OF TREE (FT)} = \text{HEIGHT OF PRACTICE OBJECT (FT)} \times \text{PACES FROM TREE} \div \text{PACES FROM PRACTICE OBJECT}$$

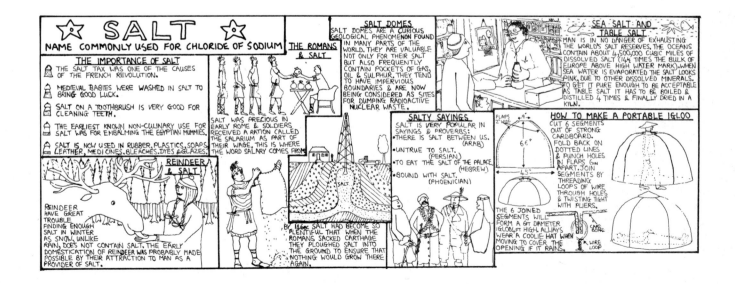

☆ SALT ☆
NAME COMMONLY USED FOR CHLORIDE OF SODIUM

THE IMPORTANCE OF SALT

- THE SALT TAX WAS ONE OF THE CAUSES OF THE FRENCH REVOLUTION.
- MEDIEVAL BABIES WERE WASHED IN SALT TO BRING GOOD LUCK.
- SALT ON A TOOTHBRUSH IS VERY GOOD FOR CLEANING TEETH.
- THE EARLIEST KNOWN NON-CULINARY USE FOR SALT WAS FOR EMBALMING THE EGYPTIAN MUMMIES.
- SALT IS NOW USED IN RUBBER, PLASTICS, SOAPS, LEATHER, MEDICINES, BLEACHES, DYES & GLAZES.

REINDEER & SALT

REINDEER HAVE GREAT TROUBLE FINDING ENOUGH SALT IN WINTER AS SNOW, UNLIKE RAIN, DOES NOT CONTAIN SALT. THE EARLY DOMESTICATION OF REINDEER WAS PROBABLY MADE POSSIBLE BY THEIR ATTRACTION TO MAN AS A PROVIDER OF SALT.

THE ROMANS & SALT

SALT WAS PRECIOUS IN EARLY ROME & SOLDIERS RECEIVED A RATION CALLED THE SALARIUM AS PART OF THEIR WAGE. THIS IS WHERE THE WORD SALARY COMES FROM.

BY 146BC SALT HAD BECOME SO PLENTIFUL THAT WHEN THE ROMANS SACKED CARTHAGE THEY PLOUGHED SALT INTO THE GROUND TO ENSURE THAT NOTHING WOULD GROW THERE AGAIN.

SALT DOMES

SALT DOMES ARE A CURIOUS GEOLOGICAL PHENOMENON FOUND IN MANY PARTS OF THE WORLD. THEY ARE VALUABLE NOT ONLY FOR THEIR SALT BUT ALSO FREQUENTLY CONTAIN POCKETS OF GAS, OIL & SULPHUR. THEY TEND TO HAVE IMPERVIOUS BOUNDARIES & ARE NOW BEING CONSIDERED AS SITES FOR DUMPING RADIOACTIVE NUCLEAR WASTE.

SALTY SAYINGS

SALT IS VERY POPULAR IN SAYINGS & PROVERBS:
- THERE IS SALT BETWEEN US. (ARAB)
- UNTRUE TO SALT. (PERSIAN)
- TO EAT THE SALT OF THE PALACE. (HEBREW)
- BOUND WITH SALT. (PHOENICIAN)

SEA SALT AND TABLE SALT

MAN IS IN NO DANGER OF EXHAUSTING THE WORLD'S SALT RESERVES. THE OCEANS CONTAIN ABOUT 4,500,000 CUBIC MILES OF DISSOLVED SALT (14½ TIMES THE BULK OF EUROPE ABOVE HIGH WATER MARK). WHEN SEA WATER IS EVAPORATED THE SALT LOOKS PINK, DUE TO OTHER DISSOLVED MINERALS. TO GET IT PURE ENOUGH TO BE ACCEPTABLE AS TABLE SALT IT HAS TO BE BOILED & DISTILLED 4 TIMES & FINALLY DRIED IN A KILN.

HOW TO MAKE A PORTABLE IGLOO

CUT 6 SEGMENTS OUT OF STRONG CARDBOARD. FOLD BACK ON DOTTED LINES & PUNCH HOLES IN FLAPS (⅜IN APART). JOIN SEGMENTS BY THREADING LOOPS OF WIRE THROUGH HOLES & TWISTING TIGHT WITH PLIERS.

THE 6 JOINED SEGMENTS WILL FORM A 6FT DIAMETER IGLOO, 5FT HIGH. ALWAYS WEAR A COOLIE HAT WHEN MOVING TO COVER THE OPENING IF IT RAINS.

FLAPS 2" WIDE
6'6"
4'3"
WIRE LOOP

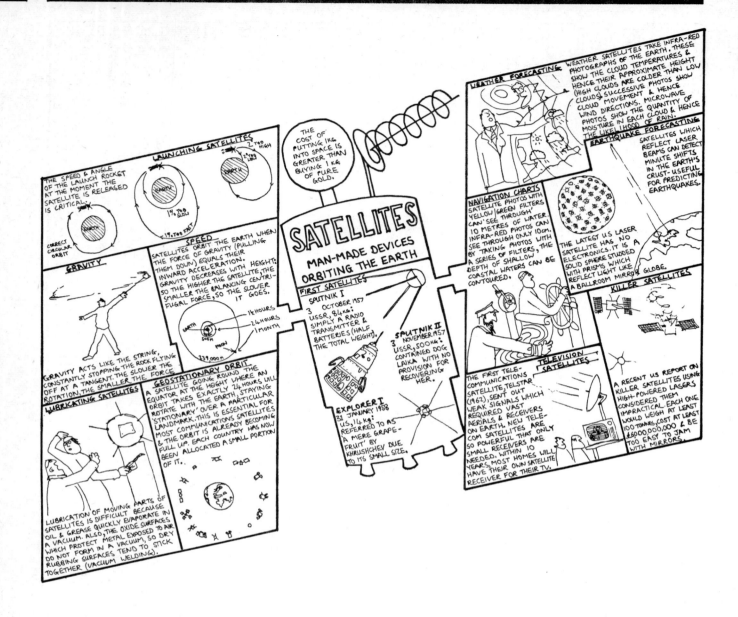

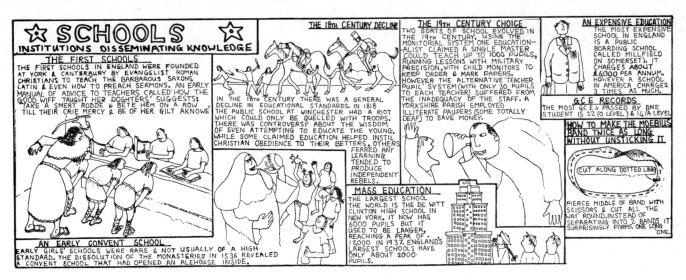

☆ SCHOOLS ☆
INSTITUTIONS DISSEMINATING KNOWLEDGE

THE FIRST SCHOOLS
THE FIRST SCHOOLS IN ENGLAND WERE FOUNDED AT YORK & CANTERBURY BY EVANGELIST ROMAN CHRISTIANS TO TEACH THE BARBAROUS SAXONS LATIN & EVEN HOW TO PREACH SERMONS. AN EARLY MANUAL OF ADVICE TO TEACHERS CALLED 'HOW THE GOOD WIFF TAUGHT HER DOGHTERS' SUGGESTS: TAKE A SMERT RODDE & BETE HEM ON A ROW TILL THEIR CRIE MERCY & BE OF HER GILT AKNOWE

AN EARLY CONVENT SCHOOL
EARLY GIRLS' SCHOOLS WERE RARE & NOT USUALLY OF A HIGH STANDARD. THE DISSOLUTION OF THE MONASTERIES IN 1536 REVEALED A CONVENT SCHOOL THAT HAD OPENED AN ALEHOUSE INSIDE.

THE 18TH CENTURY DECLINE
IN THE 18TH CENTURY THERE WAS A GENERAL DECLINE IN EDUCATIONAL STANDARDS. IN 1818 THE PUBLIC SCHOOL AT WINCHESTER HAD A RIOT WHICH COULD ONLY BE QUELLED WITH TROOPS. THERE WAS CONTROVERSY ABOUT THE WISDOM OF EVEN ATTEMPTING TO EDUCATE THE YOUNG. WHILE SOME CLAIMED EDUCATION HELPED INSTIL CHRISTIAN OBEDIENCE TO THEIR BETTERS, OTHERS FEARED ANY LEARNING TENDED TO PRODUCE INDEPENDENT REBELS.

MASS EDUCATION
THE LARGEST SCHOOL IN THE WORLD IS THE DE WITT CLINTON HIGH SCHOOL IN NEW YORK. IT NOW HAS 6000 PUPILS BUT IT USED TO BE LARGER, REACHING A PEAK OF 12,000 IN 1937. ENGLAND'S LARGEST SCHOOLS HAVE ONLY ABOUT 2000 PUPILS.

THE 19TH CENTURY CHOICE
TWO SORTS OF SCHOOL EVOLVED IN THE 19TH CENTURY. USING THE MONITORIAL SYSTEM, ONE EDUCATIONALIST CLAIMED A SINGLE MASTER COULD TEACH UP TO 1000 PUPILS, RUNNING LESSONS WITH MILITARY PRECISION, WITH CHILD MONITORS TO KEEP ORDER & MARK PAPERS. HOWEVER THE ALTERNATIVE 'TEACHER PUPIL' SYSTEM (WITH ONLY 30 PUPILS TO EACH TEACHER) SUFFERED FROM THE INADEQUACY OF THE STAFF. A YORKSHIRE PARISH EMPLOYED ILLITERATE PAUPERS (SOME TOTALLY DEAF) TO SAVE MONEY.

AN EXPENSIVE EDUCATION
THE MOST EXPENSIVE SCHOOL IN ENGLAND IS A PUBLIC BOARDING SCHOOL CALLED MILLFIELD (IN SOMERSET). IT CHARGES ABOUT £6000 PER ANNUM. HOWEVER A SCHOOL IN AMERICA CHARGES 3 TIMES AS MUCH.

GCE RECORDS
THE MOST GCE'S PASSED BY ONE STUDENT IS 22 (O LEVEL) & 14 (A LEVEL)

HOW TO MAKE THE MOEBIUS BAND TWICE AS LONG WITHOUT UNSTICKING IT
CUT ALONG DOTTED LINE

PIERCE MIDDLE OF BAND WITH SCISSORS & CUT ALL THE WAY ROUND. INSTEAD OF SEPARATING INTO 2 BANDS IT SURPRISINGLY FORMS ONE LONG ONE.

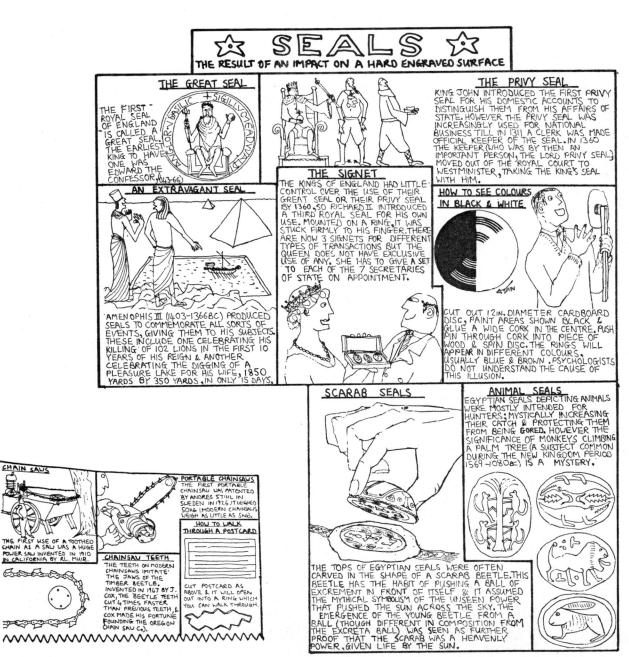

☆ SEALS ☆
THE RESULT OF AN IMPACT ON A HARD ENGRAVED SURFACE

THE GREAT SEAL
THE FIRST ROYAL SEAL OF ENGLAND IS CALLED A GREAT SEAL. THE EARLIEST KING TO HAVE ONE WAS EDWARD THE CONFESSOR (1043-66)

AN EXTRAVAGANT SEAL
AMENOPHIS III (1403-1366BC) PRODUCED SEALS TO COMMEMORATE ALL SORTS OF EVENTS, GIVING THEM TO HIS SUBJECTS. THESE INCLUDE ONE CELEBRATING HIS 'KILLING' OF 102 LIONS IN THE FIRST 10 YEARS OF HIS REIGN & ANOTHER CELEBRATING THE DIGGING OF A PLEASURE LAKE FOR HIS WIFE, 1850 YARDS BY 350 YARDS, IN ONLY 15 DAYS.

THE SIGNET
THE KINGS OF ENGLAND HAD LITTLE CONTROL OVER THE USE OF THEIR GREAT SEAL OR THEIR PRIVY SEAL BY 1360, SO RICHARD II INTRODUCED A THIRD ROYAL SEAL FOR HIS OWN USE. MOUNTED ON A RING, IT WAS STUCK FIRMLY TO HIS FINGER. THERE ARE NOW 3 SIGNETS FOR DIFFERENT TYPES OF TRANSACTIONS BUT THE QUEEN DOES NOT HAVE EXCLUSIVE USE OF ANY. SHE HAS TO GIVE A SET TO EACH OF THE 7 SECRETARIES OF STATE ON APPOINTMENT.

THE PRIVY SEAL
KING JOHN INTRODUCED THE FIRST PRIVY SEAL FOR HIS DOMESTIC ACCOUNTS TO DISTINGUISH THEM FROM HIS AFFAIRS OF STATE. HOWEVER THE PRIVY SEAL WAS INCREASINGLY USED FOR NATIONAL BUSINESS TILL IN 1311 A CLERK WAS MADE OFFICIAL KEEPER OF THE SEAL. IN 1360 THE KEEPER (WHO WAS BY THEN AN IMPORTANT PERSON, THE LORD PRIVY SEAL) MOVED OUT OF THE ROYAL COURT TO WESTMINSTER, TAKING THE KING'S SEAL WITH HIM.

HOW TO SEE COLOURS IN BLACK & WHITE
CUT OUT 12IN. DIAMETER CARDBOARD DISC, PAINT AREAS SHOWN BLACK & GLUE A WIDE CORK IN THE CENTRE. PUSH PIN THROUGH CORK INTO PIECE OF WOOD & SPIN DISC. THE RINGS WILL APPEAR IN DIFFERENT COLOURS, USUALLY BLUE & BROWN. PSYCHOLOGISTS DO NOT UNDERSTAND THE CAUSE OF THIS ILLUSION.

SPIN

CHAIN SAWS
THE FIRST USE OF A TOOTHED CHAIN AS A SAW WAS A HUGE POWER SAW INVENTED IN 1910 IN CALIFORNIA BY R.L. MUIR.

PORTABLE CHAINSAWS
THE FIRST PORTABLE CHAINSAW WAS PATENTED BY ANDRES STIHL IN SWEDEN IN 1926. IT WEIGHED 50KG (MODERN CHAINSAWS WEIGH AS LITTLE AS 5KG).

HOW TO WALK THROUGH A POSTCARD
CUT POSTCARD AS ABOVE & IT WILL OPEN OUT INTO A RING WHICH YOU CAN WALK THROUGH.

CHAINSAW TEETH
THE TEETH ON MODERN CHAINSAWS IMITATE THE JAWS OF THE TIMBER BEETLE, INVENTED IN 1947 BY J. COX, THE BEETLE TEETH CUT 4 TIMES FASTER THAN PREVIOUS TEETH, & COX MADE HIS FORTUNE FOUNDING THE OREGON CHAIN SAW CO.

SCARAB SEALS
THE TOPS OF EGYPTIAN SEALS WERE OFTEN CARVED IN THE SHAPE OF A SCARAB BEETLE. THIS BEETLE HAS THE HABIT OF PUSHING A BALL OF EXCREMENT IN FRONT OF ITSELF & IT ASSUMED THE MYTHICAL SYMBOLISM OF THE UNSEEN POWER THAT PUSHED THE SUN ACROSS THE SKY. THE EMERGENCE OF THE YOUNG BEETLE FROM A BALL (THOUGH DIFFERENT IN COMPOSITION FROM THE EXCRETA BALL) WAS SEEN AS FURTHER PROOF THAT THE SCARAB WAS A HEAVENLY POWER, GIVEN LIFE BY THE SUN.

ANIMAL SEALS
EGYPTIAN SEALS DEPICTING ANIMALS WERE MOSTLY INTENDED FOR HUNTERS; MYSTICALLY INCREASING THEIR CATCH & PROTECTING THEM FROM BEING GORED. HOWEVER THE SIGNIFICANCE OF MONKEYS CLIMBING A PALM TREE (A SUBJECT COMMON DURING THE NEW KINGDOM PERIOD 1569-1080BC) IS A MYSTERY.

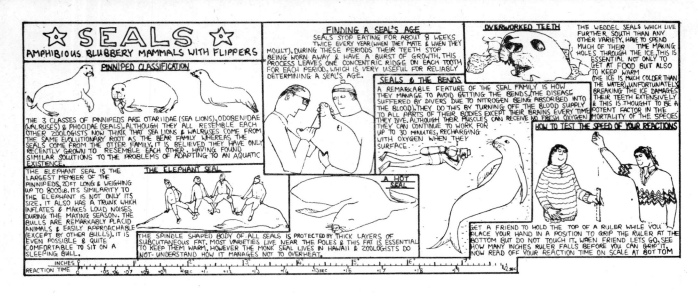

☆ SEALS ☆
AMPHIBIOUS BLUBBERY MAMMALS WITH FLIPPERS

PINNIPED CLASSIFICATION

THE 3 CLASSES OF PINNIPEDS ARE OTARIIDAE (SEA LIONS), ODOBENIDAE (WALRUSES) & PHOCIDAE (SEALS), ALTHOUGH THEY ALL RESEMBLE EACH OTHER ZOOLOGISTS NOW THINK THAT SEA LIONS & WALRUSES COME FROM THE SAME EVOLUTIONARY ROOT AS THE BEAR FAMILY WHEREAS THE SEALS COME FROM THE OTTER FAMILY. IT IS BELIEVED THEY HAVE ONLY RECENTLY GROWN TO RESEMBLE EACH OTHER, HAVING FOUND SIMILAR SOLUTIONS TO THE PROBLEMS OF ADAPTING TO AN AQUATIC EXISTENCE.

THE ELEPHANT SEAL

THE ELEPHANT SEAL IS THE LARGEST MEMBER OF THE PINNIPEDS. 20FT LONG & WEIGHING UP TO 8000LB. ITS SIMILARITY TO THE ELEPHANT IS NOT ONLY ITS SIZE, IT ALSO HAS A TRUNK WHICH INFLATES & MAKES LOUD NOISES DURING THE MATING SEASON. THE BULLS ARE REMARKABLY PLACID ANIMALS & EASILY APPROACHABLE (EXCEPT BY OTHER BULLS). IT IS EVEN POSSIBLE & QUITE COMFORTABLE TO SIT ON A SLEEPING BULL.

THE SPINDLE SHAPED BODY OF ALL SEALS IS PROTECTED BY THICK LAYERS OF SUBCUTANEOUS FAT. MOST VARIETIES LIVE NEAR THE POLES & THIS FAT IS ESSENTIAL TO KEEP THEM WARM. HOWEVER THE MONK SEAL LIVES IN HAWAII & ZOOLOGISTS DO NOT UNDERSTAND HOW IT MANAGES NOT TO OVERHEAT.

FINDING A SEAL'S AGE

SEALS STOP EATING FOR ABOUT 8 WEEKS TWICE EVERY YEAR (WHEN THEY MATE & WHEN THEY MOULT). DURING THESE PERIODS THEIR TEETH STOP BEING WORN AWAY & HAVE A BURST OF GROWTH. THIS PROCESS LEAVES ONE CONCENTRIC RIDGE ON EACH TOOTH FOR EACH PERIOD, WHICH IS VERY USEFUL FOR RELIABLY DETERMINING A SEAL'S AGE.

SEALS & THE BENDS

A REMARKABLE FEATURE OF THE SEAL FAMILY IS HOW THEY MANAGE TO AVOID GETTING THE BENDS, THE DISEASE SUFFERED BY DIVERS DUE TO NITROGEN BEING ABSORBED INTO THE BLOOD. THEY DO THIS BY TURNING OFF THE BLOOD SUPPLY TO ALL PARTS OF THEIR BODIES EXCEPT THEIR BRAINS EVERY TIME THEY DIVE. ALTHOUGH THEIR MUSCLES CAN RECEIVE NO FRESH OXYGEN THEY CAN CONTINUE TO WORK FOR UP TO 30 MINUTES, RECHARGING WITH OXYGEN WHEN THEY SURFACE.

A HOT SEAL

OVERWORKED TEETH

THE WEDDEL SEALS WHICH LIVE FURTHER SOUTH THAN ANY OTHER VARIETY, HAVE TO SPEND MUCH OF THEIR TIME MAKING HOLES THROUGH THE ICE, THIS IS ESSENTIAL NOT ONLY TO GET AT FOOD BUT ALSO TO KEEP WARM (THE ICE IS MUCH COLDER THAN THE WATER). UNFORTUNATELY BREAKING THE ICE DAMAGES THEIR TEETH EXTENSIVELY & THIS IS THOUGHT TO BE A POTENT FACTOR IN THE MORTALITY OF THE SPECIES.

HOW TO TEST THE SPEED OF YOUR REACTIONS

GET A FRIEND TO HOLD THE TOP OF A RULER WHILE YOU PLACE YOUR HAND IN A POSITION TO GRIP THE RULER AT THE BOTTOM BUT DO NOT TOUCH IT. WHEN FRIEND LETS GO, SEE HOW MANY INCHES RULER FALLS BEFORE YOU CAN GRIP IT. NOW READ OFF YOUR REACTION TIME ON SCALE AT BOTTOM

INCHES
REACTION TIME

☆ SEAWEED ☆
PRIMITIVE MARINE PLANTS LACKING ROOTS

SEAWEED & THE MOON

VARIOUS SEAWEEDS HAVE FORTNIGHTLY REPRODUCTIVE CYCLES WHICH ALWAYS START ON A SPRING TIDE BY SOME UNKNOWN MECHANISM. MORE MYSTERIOUS IS A SPECIES CALLED DICTYOTA, IT GROWS OFF THE COAST OF SOUTH CAROLINA & HAS A MONTHLY CYCLE WHICH ONLY STARTS ON A SPRING TIDE OF A NEW MOON & NEVER ON A SPRING TIDE OF A FULL MOON.

SEAWEED & SEWAGE

SEAWEED HAS RECENTLY BEEN TRIED FOR TREATING SEWAGE AS IT CAN PROVIDE OXYGEN NEEDED TO CAUSE THE DECOMPOSITION OF THE ORGANIC MATTER. THE EXPERIMENT FAILED BECAUSE BRITAIN DID NOT HAVE ENOUGH SUNSHINE TO KEEP THE PHOTOSYNTHETIC REACTIONS PRODUCING OXYGEN FAST ENOUGH.

SEAWEED & CABBAGES

SEAWEED MAKES GOOD MANURE ESPECIALLY FOR MANGOLDS, SWEDES, CABBAGES, ASPARAGUS & OTHER PLANTS THAT THRIVE ON LOTS OF SALT.

SEAWEED & WEATHERFORECASTING

LAMINARIA SACCHARINA IS THE SEAWEED TRADITIONALLY USED FOR WEATHERFORECASTING. WHEN DRIED THE FRONDS, OR EDGES, ARE BRITTLE IN DRY WEATHER BUT GO SOFT & SLIGHTLY STICKY ON THE APPROACH OF RAIN BECAUSE OF SUBSTANCES IN THE CELL WALLS WHICH ABSORB MOISTURE FROM THE AIR.

SEAWEED FOOD

THE MOST POPULAR JAPANESE SEAWEED FOOD IS PERHAPS KOMBU. THIS IS MADE FROM THE LARGE OARWEEDS, DRIED & CUT UP IN VARIOUS FORMS BLACK & WHITE PULPY KOMBU, SHREDDED KOMBU, FILMY KOMBU, HAIR KOMBU & SWEETCAKE KOMBU.

SEAWEED & ALGINIC ACID

THE SEAWEED GATHERING TRADE IS NOW FLOURISHING PROVIDING A WONDERFUL CHEMICAL CALLED ALGINIC ACID. THIS SUBSTANCE WAS DISCOVERED IN 1881 BUT REGARDED AS A SCIENTIFIC CURIOSITY TILL 1934 WHEN IT WAS FOUND TO BE USEFUL IN MAKING TRANSPARENT WRAPPING PAPER. IT IS NOW USED AS A THICKENER IN PRINTING INKS, IN ARTIFICIAL SILK (GIVING THE FIBRES STRENGTH WHILE BEING WOVEN), IN ICE CREAM (PREVENTING THE INGREDIENTS SEPARATING), IN WRAPPED CAKES (KEEPING THEM MOIST) & IN MEDICAL DRESSINGS (HELPING TO STOP BLEEDING).

SEAWEED BURNING

SOME SEAWEEDS, WHEN DRIED & BURNT IN A KILN, LEAVE VALUABLE CHEMICALS IN THEIR ASH. THE KELP BURNING INDUSTRY, AS IT WAS CALLED, ORIGINALLY PROVIDED SODA (Na_2CO_3) FOR MAKING GLASS. THEN THE SPANISH DISCOVERED A CHEAPER SOURCE OF SODA IN THE 1820s & THE KELP INDUSTRY COLLAPSED. FORTUNATELY THE ASH WAS THEN FOUND TO BE RICH IN IODINE & THE INDUSTRY REVIVED. THEN, IN 1877, A RICH DEPOSIT OF IODINE WAS DISCOVERED IN CHILE WHICH BANKRUPTED OUR INDUSTRY AGAIN.

HOW TO MAKE A LEAF SKELETON

PLACE A DEAD FAIRLY DRY LEAF ON A PIECE OF BLOTTING PAPER & BANG GENTLY WITH A CLOTHES BRUSH. THIS DISLODGES WEAKER MEMBRANE OF LEAF, LEAVING THE SKELETON. LEAVES FROM ANY DECIDUOUS TREE WILL WORK. (EVERGREENS ARE NOT SO SUCCESSFUL)

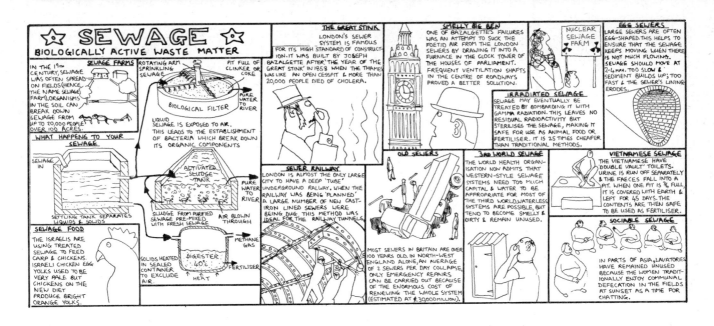

☆ SEWAGE ☆
BIOLOGICALLY ACTIVE WASTE MATTER

SEWAGE FARMS
IN THE 19th CENTURY, SEWAGE WAS OFTEN SPREAD ON FIELDS (HENCE THE NAME SEWAGE FARM). ORGANISMS IN THE SOIL CAN BREAK DOWN SEWAGE FROM UP TO 20,000 PEOPLE OVER 100 ACRES.

ROTATING ARM SPRINKLING SEWAGE

PIT FULL OF CLINKER OR COKE

BIOLOGICAL FILTER

PURE WATER TO RIVER

LIQUID SEWAGE IS EXPOSED TO AIR. THIS LEADS TO THE ESTABLISHMENT OF BACTERIA WHICH BREAK DOWN ITS ORGANIC COMPONENTS

WHAT HAPPENS TO YOUR SEWAGE
SEWAGE IN

ACTIVATED SLUDGE TANK

PURE WATER TO RIVER

SETTLING TANK SEPARATES LIQUIDS & SOLIDS

SLUDGE FROM PURIFIED SEWAGE PRE-MIXED WITH FRESH SEWAGE

AIR BLOWN THROUGH

SOLIDS HEATED IN SEALED CONTAINER TO EXCLUDE AIR.

DIGESTER 40°C

HEAT

METHANE GAS

FERTILISER

SEWAGE FOOD
THE ISRAELIS ARE USING TREATED SEWAGE TO FEED CARP & CHICKENS. ISRAELI CHICKEN EGG YOLKS USED TO BE VERY PALE BUT CHICKENS ON THE NEW DIET PRODUCE BRIGHT ORANGE YOLKS.

THE GREAT STINK
LONDON'S SEWER SYSTEM IS FAMOUS FOR ITS HIGH STANDARD OF CONSTRUCTION. IT WAS BUILT BY JOSEPH BAZALGETTE AFTER 'THE YEAR OF THE GREAT STINK' IN 1858 WHEN THE THAMES WAS LIKE AN OPEN CESSPIT & MORE THAN 20,000 PEOPLE DIED OF CHOLERA.

SEWER RAILWAY
LONDON IS ALMOST THE ONLY LARGE CITY TO HAVE A DEEP 'TUBE' UNDERGROUND RAILWAY. WHEN THE RAILWAY WAS BEING PLANNED A LARGE NUMBER OF NEW CAST-IRON LINED SEWERS WERE BEING DUG. THIS METHOD WAS IDEAL FOR THE RAILWAY TUNNELS.

SMELLY BIG BEN
ONE OF BAZALGETTE'S FAILURES WAS AN ATTEMPT TO SUCK THE FOETID AIR FROM THE LONDON SEWERS BY DRAWING IT INTO A FURNACE IN THE CLOCK TOWER OF THE HOUSES OF PARLIAMENT. FREQUENT VENTILATION SHAFTS IN THE CENTRE OF ROADWAYS PROVED A BETTER SOLUTION.

NUCLEAR SEWAGE FARM

EGG SEWERS
LARGE SEWERS ARE OFTEN EGG-SHAPED. THIS HELPS TO ENSURE THAT THE SEWAGE KEEPS MOVING WHEN THERE IS NOT MUCH FLOWING. SEWAGE SHOULD MOVE AT 2-4 M.P.H. TOO SLOW & SEDIMENT BUILDS UP; TOO FAST & THE SEWER'S LINING ERODES.

IRRADIATED SEWAGE
SEWAGE MAY EVENTUALLY BE TREATED BY BOMBARDING IT WITH GAMMA RADIATION. THIS LEAVES NO RESIDUAL RADIOACTIVITY BUT STERILISES THE SEWAGE, MAKING IT SAFE FOR USE AS ANIMAL FOOD OR FERTILISER. IT IS 25 TIMES CHEAPER THAN TRADITIONAL METHODS.

OLD SEWERS
MOST SEWERS IN BRITAIN ARE OVER 100 YEARS OLD. IN NORTH-WEST ENGLAND ALONE, AN AVERAGE OF 2 SEWERS PER DAY COLLAPSE. ONLY EMERGENCY REPAIRS CAN BE CARRIED OUT BECAUSE OF THE ENORMOUS COST OF RENEWING THE WHOLE SYSTEM (ESTIMATED AT £30,000 MILLION).

3rd WORLD SEWAGE
THE WORLD HEALTH ORGANISATION NOW ADMITS THAT WESTERN-STYLE SEWAGE SYSTEMS NEED TOO MUCH CAPITAL & WATER TO BE APPROPRIATE FOR MOST OF THE THIRD WORLD. WATERLESS SYSTEMS ARE POSSIBLE BUT TEND TO BECOME SMELLY & DIRTY & REMAIN UNUSED.

VIETNAMESE SEWAGE
THE VIETNAMESE HAVE DOUBLE VAULT' TOILETS. URINE IS RUN OFF SEPARATELY & THE FAECES FALL INTO A PIT. WHEN ONE PIT IS ¾ FULL, IT IS COVERED WITH EARTH & LEFT FOR 45 DAYS. THE CONTENTS ARE THEN SAFE TO BE USED AS FERTILISER.

SOCIABLE SEWAGE
IN PARTS OF ASIA, LAVATORIES HAVE REMAINED UNUSED BECAUSE THE WOMEN TRADITIONALLY ENJOY COMMUNAL DEFECATION IN THE FIELDS AT SUNSET AS A TIME FOR CHATTING.

☆ SEWING MACHINES ☆

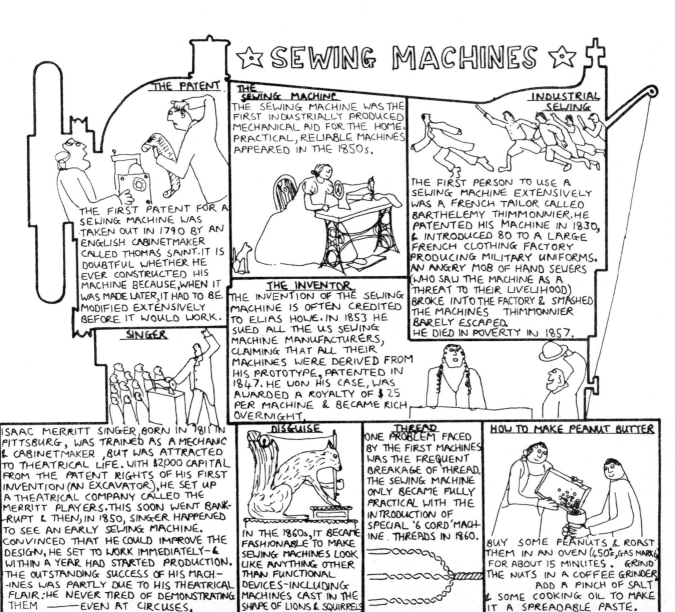

THE PATENT
THE FIRST PATENT FOR A SEWING MACHINE WAS TAKEN OUT IN 1790 BY AN ENGLISH CABINETMAKER CALLED THOMAS SAINT. IT IS DOUBTFUL WHETHER HE EVER CONSTRUCTED HIS MACHINE BECAUSE, WHEN IT WAS MADE LATER, IT HAD TO BE MODIFIED EXTENSIVELY BEFORE IT WOULD WORK.

THE SEWING MACHINE
THE SEWING MACHINE WAS THE FIRST INDUSTRIALLY PRODUCED MECHANICAL AID FOR THE HOME. PRACTICAL, RELIABLE MACHINES APPEARED IN THE 1850s.

THE INVENTOR
THE INVENTION OF THE SEWING MACHINE IS OFTEN CREDITED TO ELIAS HOWE. IN 1853 HE SUED ALL THE US SEWING MACHINE MANUFACTURERS, CLAIMING THAT ALL THEIR MACHINES WERE DERIVED FROM HIS PROTOTYPE, PATENTED IN 1847. HE WON HIS CASE, WAS AWARDED A ROYALTY OF $25 PER MACHINE & BECAME RICH OVERNIGHT.

INDUSTRIAL SEWING
THE FIRST PERSON TO USE A SEWING MACHINE EXTENSIVELY WAS A FRENCH TAILOR CALLED BARTHELEMY THIMMONNIER. HE PATENTED HIS MACHINE IN 1830, & INTRODUCED 80 TO A LARGE FRENCH CLOTHING FACTORY PRODUCING MILITARY UNIFORMS. AN ANGRY MOB OF HAND SEWERS (WHO SAW THE MACHINE AS A THREAT TO THEIR LIVELIHOOD) BROKE INTO THE FACTORY & SMASHED THE MACHINES. THIMMONNIER BARELY ESCAPED. HE DIED IN POVERTY IN 1857.

SINGER
ISAAC MERRITT SINGER, BORN IN 1811 IN PITTSBURG, WAS TRAINED AS A MECHANIC & CABINETMAKER, BUT WAS ATTRACTED TO THEATRICAL LIFE. WITH $2,000 CAPITAL FROM THE PATENT RIGHTS OF HIS FIRST INVENTION (AN EXCAVATOR), HE SET UP A THEATRICAL COMPANY CALLED THE MERRITT PLAYERS. THIS SOON WENT BANKRUPT & THEN, IN 1850, SINGER HAPPENED TO SEE AN EARLY SEWING MACHINE. CONVINCED THAT HE COULD IMPROVE THE DESIGN, HE SET TO WORK IMMEDIATELY & WITHIN A YEAR HAD STARTED PRODUCTION. THE OUTSTANDING SUCCESS OF HIS MACHINES WAS PARTLY DUE TO HIS THEATRICAL FLAIR: HE NEVER TIRED OF DEMONSTRATING THEM —— EVEN AT CIRCUSES.

DISGUISE
IN THE 1860s, IT BECAME FASHIONABLE TO MAKE SEWING MACHINES LOOK LIKE ANYTHING OTHER THAN FUNCTIONAL DEVICES - INCLUDING MACHINES CAST IN THE SHAPE OF LIONS & SQUIRRELS

THREAD
ONE PROBLEM FACED BY THE FIRST MACHINES WAS THE FREQUENT BREAKAGE OF THREAD. THE SEWING MACHINE ONLY BECAME FULLY PRACTICAL WITH THE INTRODUCTION OF SPECIAL '6 CORD' MACHINE THREADS IN 1860.

HOW TO MAKE PEANUT BUTTER
BUY SOME PEANUTS & ROAST THEM IN AN OVEN (450°F, GAS MARK 6) FOR ABOUT 15 MINUTES. GRIND THE NUTS IN A COFFEE GRINDER. ADD A PINCH OF SALT & SOME COOKING OIL TO MAKE IT A SPREADABLE PASTE.

☆ SHAVING ☆
PROCESS OF SCRAPING OFF FACIAL HAIR

THE PERILS OF A SHAVE
THE ROMANS HAD BARBERS' SHOPS BUT THEY WERE SOMETIMES HIGHLY DANGEROUS PLACES. A FAVOURITE HOBBY OF THE EMPEROR COMMODUS (AD 182-192) WAS TO COMMANDEER A BARBERS' SHOP & CUT OFF THE NOSES OF ALL THE CUSTOMERS.

MR GILLETTE'S INVENTION
'THE THING TO DO IS TO INVENT SOMETHING WHICH PEOPLE WILL HAVE TO HAVE, BUT WHICH THEY CAN USE, THROW AWAY, & BUY ANOTHER ONE'. THESE WORDS, FROM THE MAN WHO INVENTED THE DISPOSABLE BEER BOTTLE CAP, INSPIRED K.C. GILLETTE TO INVENT THE DISPOSABLE RAZOR BLADE. HE STARTED PRODUCTION IN 1903 & HAD RETIRED TO CALIFORNIA, A MILLIONAIRE, BY 1909.

UNSHAVEN JEWS
STRICT, ORTHODOX JEWS ARE NOT ALLOWED TO SHAVE. THE JEWISH ENCYCLOPEDIA SAYS THE REASON IS 'GOD GAVE MAN A BEARD TO DISTINGUISH HIM FROM WOMAN & IT IS THEREFORE WRONG TO ANTAGONISE NATURE'.

RAZOR BLADES & THE PYRAMIDS
THE MANY BRONZE EGYPTIAN RAZORS THAT HAVE BEEN FOUND PRESENT A CONSIDERABLE MYSTERY SINCE IT IS NOT KNOWN HOW BRONZE, A SOFT METAL, COULD HAVE BEEN KEPT SHARP. A CZECH RADIO ENGINEER CALLED DRBAL CLAIMS IT WAS THE INFLUENCE OF THE PYRAMIDS & THAT ANY BLADE PLACED UNDER A CORRECTLY ALIGNED PYRAMID SHAPE WILL BECOME SHARP. HE REASONS THAT THE METALLIC CRYSTAL STRUCTURE OF A BLADE IS PYRAMID SHAPED & THAT A RESONANT MAGNETIC FIELD IS SET UP THAT ENCOURAGES CRYSTAL GROWTH ON THE BLADE EDGE. BELIEF IN HIS THEORY IS QUITE WIDE SPREAD & MODEL EXPANDED POLYSTYRENE PYRAMIDS ARE NOW MANUFACTURED IN CZECHOSLOVAKIA CALLED CHEOPS PYRAMID RAZOR BLADE SHARPENERS.'

THE MODERN BLADE
MODERN RAZOR BLADES ARE COATED WITH CERAMIC CHROMIUM ALLOY, PTFE & ARE WONDERFULLY SHARP. IF A WHOLE BLADE LAID FLAT WAS THE SIZE OF A FOOTBALL PITCH (115 YARDS LONG) THE EDGE, ENLARGED PROPORTIONATELY, WOULD ONLY BE ABOUT THE THICKNESS OF THIS PIECE OF PAPER.

PRAYING FOR A BEARD
ST WILGEFORT'S STATUE STANDS IN WESTMINSTER ABBEY. SHE WAS A PORTUGUESE PRINCESS, ABOUT TO BE MARRIED AGAINST HER WILL, WHO PRAYED THAT SHE MIGHT BECOME SO UGLY THAT HER SUITOR WOULD CANCEL THE UNION. SHE MIRACULOUSLY GREW A BEARD (SUCCESSFULLY REPELLING THE SUITOR) & DEVOTED THE REST OF HER LIFE TO GOD.

HOW TO GROW A STALACTITE
BUY SOME EPSOM SALTS FROM A CHEMIST. DISSOLVE AS MUCH AS YOU CAN IN 2 GLASSES OF VERY HOT WATER. DRAPE A PIECE OF STRING BETWEEN THE GLASSES WITH BOTH ENDS IN THE SOLUTION. THE SOLUTION WILL THEN PASS ALONG THE STRING BY CAPILLARY ACTION & STALACTITE WILL CRYSTALLISE UNDER MIDDLE OF STRING.

☆ SHELLS ☆
HARD OUTER COVERINGS OF CERTAIN ORGANISMS

THE JAWS OF A GIANT CLAM
GIANT CLAMS WEIGH UP TO 600LB. & THE MUSCLE THAT CONNECTS THE TWO HALVES PROVIDES ENOUGH MEAT TO FILL FOUR PEOPLE. TO FIND THE FORCE EXERTED BY THIS MUSCLE A CLAM WAS FASTENED TO A POST WITH BUCKETS OF WATER HOOKED TO ITS LOWER LIP. 1960 LB. OF WATER WAS REQUIRED TO FORCE THE LIPS APART. THIS PRESSURE COULD EASILY TRAP A MAN IN THE SHELL BUT FORTUNATELY THEY CAN ONLY CLOSE THEIR MOUTHS RELATIVELY SLOWLY & THERE ARE NO RELIABLY AUTHENTICATED FATALITIES.

GOD AT HOME
THE SOUND OF THE SEA SUPPOSEDLY HEARD WHEN LARGE SHELLS ARE HELD CLOSE TO THE EAR HAS ALSO REPRESENTED THE VOICE OF A GOD TO MANY CIVILISATIONS. THE POLYNESIANS BELIEVED THAT A GOD LIVED IN EVERY TRUMPET SHELL.

TYRIAN PURPLE
THE ONLY BRIGHT PURPLE DYE AVAILABE TO THE ANCIENT MEDITERRANEAN CIVILISATIONS WAS A SECRETION OF THE SHELL 'MUREX BRANDARIS'. 8000 SPECIMENS WERE NEEDED TO PRODUCE ONE GRAM OF THE DYE (CALLED TYRIAN PURPLE AFTER TYRE, THE TOWN FROM WHICH IT WAS EXPORTED). PURPLE BECAME A SYMBOL OF THE ARISTOCRACY SINCE ONLY THE RICH COULD AFFORD IT.

DIGESTION
A UNIQUE FEATURE OF THE STOMACHS OF SHELLFISH IS A CRYSTALLINE, ROD-LIKE STRUCTURE WHICH ROTATES & ACTS AS A MIXER AIDING DIGESTION.

HOW TO MAKE FINGER PUPPETS
DRAW FACES ON FINGERS OF AN OLD GLOVE (PREFERABLY PLAIN PALE COLOUR) USING FELT-TIP PENS. CUT EARS OUT OF FELT & CLOTHES OUT OF SCRAPS OF FABRIC. STICK ON WITH COPYDEX. THREAD BITS OF WOOL INTO FINGERS FOR HAIR.

THE POLLUTED MUSSEL
A MUSSEL IS VERY EFFICIENT AT EXTRACTING CHEMICALS FROM SEA WATER, ACCUMULATING THEM IN ITS LIVER. THOSE LIVING IN EVEN SLIGHTLY POLLUTED WATER QUICKLY BECOME HIGHLY INDIGESTIBLE TO EAT SINCE THEY FILTER OVER 10 GALLONS OF WATER THROUGH THEIR SYSTEM EVERY DAY.

FRIED LIMPETS
LIMPETS ARE EDIBLE BUT A DOZEN SPECIMENS ARE REQUIRED FOR A SINGLE MOUTHFUL & MUCH PATIENCE IS REQUIRED TO REMOVE ANY FLESH FROM A SHELL. HOWEVER THEY ARE A TRADITIONAL FOOD ON THE ISLE OF MAN, FRIED & EATEN AT EASTER.

INTERRED FOR LIFE
A BIVALVE CALLED THE SHIPWORM SPENDS ITS LIFE EMBEDED IN WOOD, EQUIPPED WITH TEETH ON ITS SHELLS, IT STARTS BORING A TUNNEL AT AN EARLY AGE. IT CONTINUES TO GROW INSIDE & THE MOUTH OF THE TUNNEL SOON BECOMES TOO SMALL FOR IT EVER TO RETRACE ITS STEPS.

☆ SHIPBUILDING ☆
CONSTRUCTION OF WATERTIGHT DIRIGIBLE VESSELS

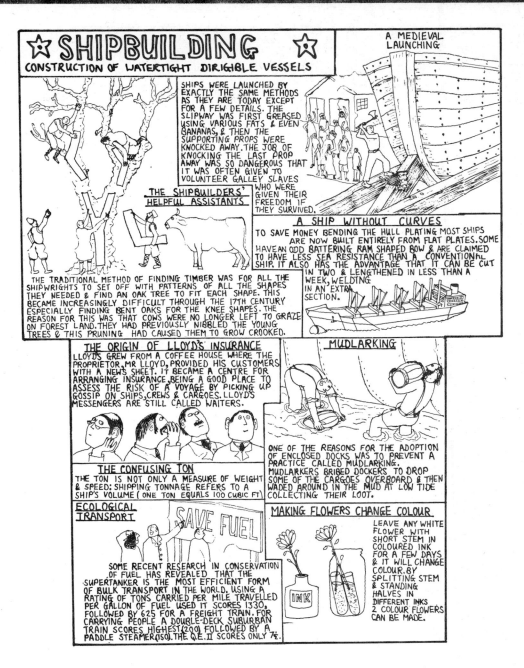

A MEDIEVAL LAUNCHING

SHIPS WERE LAUNCHED BY EXACTLY THE SAME METHODS AS THEY ARE TODAY EXCEPT FOR A FEW DETAILS. THE SLIPWAY WAS FIRST GREASED USING VARIOUS FATS & EVEN BANANAS, & THEN THE SUPPORTING PROPS WERE KNOCKED AWAY. THE JOB OF KNOCKING THE LAST PROP AWAY WAS SO DANGEROUS THAT IT WAS OFTEN GIVEN TO VOLUNTEER GALLEY SLAVES WHO WERE GIVEN THEIR FREEDOM IF THEY SURVIVED.

THE SHIPBUILDERS' HELPFUL ASSISTANTS

THE TRADITIONAL METHOD OF FINDING TIMBER WAS FOR ALL THE SHIPWRIGHTS TO SET OFF WITH PATTERNS OF ALL THE SHAPES THEY NEEDED & FIND AN OAK TREE TO FIT EACH SHAPE. THIS BECAME INCREASINGLY DIFFICULT THROUGH THE 17TH CENTURY ESPECIALLY FINDING BENT OAKS FOR THE KNEE SHAPES. THE REASON FOR THIS WAS THAT COWS WERE NO LONGER LEFT TO GRAZE ON FOREST LAND. THEY HAD PREVIOUSLY NIBBLED THE YOUNG TREES & THIS PRUNING HAD CAUSED THEM TO GROW CROOKED.

A SHIP WITHOUT CURVES

TO SAVE MONEY BENDING THE HULL PLATING MOST SHIPS ARE NOW BUILT ENTIRELY FROM FLAT PLATES. SOME HAVE AN ODD BATTERING RAM SHAPED BOW & ARE CLAIMED TO HAVE LESS SEA RESISTANCE THAN A CONVENTIONAL SHIP. IT ALSO HAS THE ADVANTAGE THAT IT CAN BE CUT IN TWO & LENGTHENED IN LESS THAN A WEEK, WELDING IN AN EXTRA SECTION.

THE ORIGIN OF LLOYD'S INSURANCE

LLOYDS GREW FROM A COFFEE HOUSE WHERE THE PROPRIETOR, MR LLOYD, PROVIDED HIS CUSTOMERS WITH A NEWS SHEET. IT BECAME A CENTRE FOR ARRANGING INSURANCE BEING A GOOD PLACE TO ASSESS THE RISK OF A VOYAGE BY PICKING UP GOSSIP ON SHIPS, CREWS & CARGOES. LLOYD'S MESSENGERS ARE STILL CALLED WAITERS.

MUDLARKING

ONE OF THE REASONS FOR THE ADOPTION OF ENCLOSED DOCKS WAS TO PREVENT A PRACTICE CALLED MUDLARKING. MUDLARKERS BRIBED DOCKERS TO DROP SOME OF THE CARGOES OVERBOARD & THEN WADED AROUND IN THE MUD AT LOW TIDE COLLECTING THEIR LOOT.

THE CONFUSING TON

THE TON IS NOT ONLY A MEASURE OF WEIGHT & SPEED: SHIPPING TONNAGE REFERS TO A SHIP'S VOLUME (ONE TON EQUALS 100 CUBIC FT)

ECOLOGICAL TRANSPORT

SAVE FUEL

SOME RECENT RESEARCH IN CONSERVATION OF FUEL HAS REVEALED THAT THE SUPERTANKER IS THE MOST EFFICIENT FORM OF BULK TRANSPORT IN THE WORLD. USING A RATING OF TONS CARRIED PER MILE TRAVELLED PER GALLON OF FUEL USED IT SCORES 1330, FOLLOWED BY 625 FOR A FREIGHT TRAIN. FOR CARRYING PEOPLE A DOUBLE-DECK SUBURBAN TRAIN SCORES HIGHEST (200) FOLLOWED BY A PADDLE STEAMER (150). THE Q.E.II SCORES ONLY 7½.

MAKING FLOWERS CHANGE COLOUR

LEAVE ANY WHITE FLOWER WITH SHORT STEM IN COLOURED INK FOR A FEW DAYS & IT WILL CHANGE COLOUR. BY SPLITTING STEM & STANDING HALVES IN DIFFERENT INKS 2 COLOUR FLOWERS CAN BE MADE.

INK

☆ SHIP FIGUREHEADS ☆
SYMBOLIC CARVINGS OF SHIPS BOWS

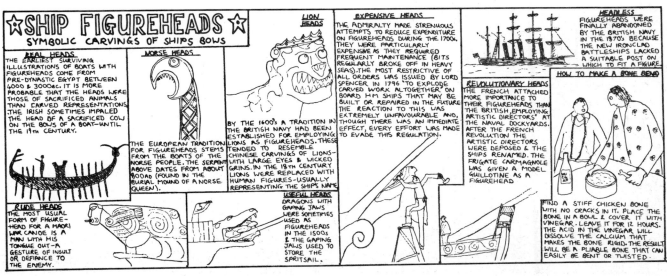

REAL HEADS
THE EARLIEST SURVIVING ILLUSTRATIONS OF BOATS WITH FIGUREHEADS COME FROM PRE-DYNASTIC EGYPT BETWEEN 4000 & 3000BC. IT IS MORE PROBABLE THAT THE HEADS WERE THOSE OF SACRIFICED ANIMALS THAN CARVED REPRESENTATIONS. THE IRISH SOMETIMES IMPALED THE HEAD OF A SACRIFICED COW ON THE BOWS OF A BOAT—UNTIL THE 19TH CENTURY.

NORSE HEADS
THE EUROPEAN TRADITION FOR FIGUREHEADS STEMS FROM THE BOATS OF THE NORSE PEOPLE. THE SERPENT ABOVE DATES FROM ABOUT 800AD (FOUND IN THE BURIAL MOUND OF A NORSE QUEEN).

LION HEADS
BY THE 1600's A TRADITION IN THE BRITISH NAVY HAD BEEN ESTABLISHED FOR EMPLOYING LIONS AS FIGUREHEADS. THESE TENDED TO RESEMBLE CHINESE CARVINGS OF LIONS WITH LARGE EYES & WICKED GRINS. IN THE 18TH CENTURY LIONS WERE REPLACED WITH HUMAN FIGURES—USUALLY REPRESENTING THE SHIPS NAME.

USEFUL HEADS
DRAGONS WITH GAPING JAWS WERE SOMETIMES USED AS FIGUREHEADS IN THE 1500s & THE GAPING JAWS USED TO STORE THE SPRITSAIL.

EXPENSIVE HEADS
THE ADMIRALTY MADE STRENUOUS ATTEMPTS TO REDUCE EXPENDITURE ON FIGUREHEADS DURING THE 1700s. THEY WERE PARTICULARLY EXPENSIVE AS THEY REQUIRED FREQUENT MAINTENANCE (BITS REGULARLY BROKE OFF IN HEAVY SEAS). THE MOST RESTRICTIVE OF ALL ORDERS WAS ISSUED BY LORD SPENCER IN 1796 "TO EXPLODE CARVED WORK ALTOGETHER" ON BOARD HM SHIPS THAT MAY BE BUILT OR REPAIRED IN THE FUTURE. THE REACTION TO THIS WAS EXTREMELY UNFAVOURABLE AND, THOUGH THERE WAS AN IMMEDIATE EFFECT, EVERY EFFORT WAS MADE TO EVADE THIS REGULATION.

REVOLUTIONARY HEADS
THE FRENCH ATTACHED MORE IMPORTANCE TO THEIR FIGUREHEADS THAN THE BRITISH, EMPLOYING ARTISTIC DIRECTORS AT THE NAVAL DOCKYARDS. AFTER THE FRENCH REVOLUTION THE ARTISTIC DIRECTORS WERE DEPOSED & THE SHIPS RENAMED. THE FRIGATE CARMAGNOLE WAS GIVEN A MODEL GUILLOTINE AS A FIGUREHEAD.

HEADLESS
FIGUREHEADS WERE FINALLY ABANDONED BY THE BRITISH NAVY IN THE 1870's BECAUSE THE NEW IRONCLAD BATTLESHIPS LACKED A SUITABLE POST ON WHICH TO FIT A FIGURE.

HOW TO MAKE A BONE BEND
FIND A STIFF CHICKEN BONE WITH NO CRACKS IN IT. PLACE THE BONE IN A BOWL & COVER IT WITH VINEGAR. LEAVE IT FOR 12 HOURS. THE ACID IN THE VINEGAR WILL DISSOLVE THE CALCIUM THAT MAKES THE BONE RIGID. THE RESULT WILL BE A PLIABLE BONE THAT CAN EASILY BE BENT OR TWISTED.

RUDE HEADS
THE MOST USUAL FORM OF FIGURE-HEAD FOR A MAORI WAR CANOE IS A MAN WITH HIS TONGUE OUT—A GESTURE OF INSULT OR DEFIANCE TO THE ENEMY.

☆ SHOES ☆
STIFF OUTER COVERINGS FOR HUMAN FEET

CORDWAINERS & COBBLERS
IN MEDIEVAL BRITAIN THE BEST SHOES WERE MADE OF A HARD-WEARING GOAT SKIN CALLED CORDWAIN, IMPORTED FROM SPAIN. SHOEMAKERS, CALLED CORDWAINERS, HAD A POWERFUL GUILD WHICH PREVENTED ORDINARY COBBLERS FROM BUYING CORDWAIN. (COBBLING WAS THEN A SPECIALISED TRADE, BUYING UP OLD SHOES & REMAKING THEM FOR RESALE.)

PIKED SHOES
IN THE 14th & 15th CENTURY SHOES WITH VERY LONG TOES (CALLED PIKED SHOES) WERE POPULAR DESPITE THEIR IMPRACTICAL SHAPE. THIS WAS POSSIBLY DUE TO THEIR SNOB APPEAL, AS A LAW OF 1420 FORBADE PERSONS WITH INCOMES UNDER £40 A YEAR FROM WEARING THEM. ATTEMPTS TO PREVENT THE NOBILITY TRIPPING THEMSELVES UP INCLUDED TYING THE PIKES TO THE KNEES. THIS APPARENTLY DID NOT SATISFY THE POPE AS IN 1468 HE ISSUED A 'PAPAL BULL' CURSING CORDWAINERS WHO PRODUCED PIKED SHOES LONGER THAN 11ins.

DUCK-BILLED TOES
IN THE 16th CENTURY THE BROAD TOE CAP BEGAN TO APPEAR. THIS BECAME INCREASINGLY DUCK-BILLED IN SHAPE TILL IT STOOD OUT FROM THE FOOT & WAS UP TO 9in WIDE. MARY TUDOR CURBED THIS SILLY FASHION BY ISSUING A DECLARATION FORBIDDING SHOES OVER 6in WIDE TO BE WORN IN COURT.

THE OLD-FASHIONED BUCKLE
THE CONSEQUENCES OF RAPIDLY CHANGING SHOE FASHIONS STARTED TO AFFECT MORE PEOPLE DURING THE INDUSTRIAL REVOLUTION. IN 1780 BIRMINGHAM WAS PRODUCING 2,500,000 SHOE BUCKLES PER YEAR. HOWEVER, BY 1790 BUCKLES WERE OUT OF FASHION, LEAVING 20,000 WORKERS UNEMPLOYED & STARVING. THE PRINCE OF WALES, ON RECEIVING A PETITION FROM THE BIRMINGHAM MAGNATES, WAS GREATLY SHOCKED & REVERTED TO WEARING BUCKLED SHOES. HIS GALLANT GESTURE UNFORTUNATELY DID NOT REVIVE THE FASHION.

BOW LEGGED BOOTS
IN THE 1680s IT WAS FASHIONABLE TO HAVE A BOWED GAIT SO ALL BOOTS WERE MADE WITH OUTWARD SLOPING HEELS.

PLATFORM SOLED SHOES
PLATFORM SOLES ARE NOT A NEW IDEA. CALLED CHOPINES, SHOES WITH HIGH CORK SOLES WERE HIGHLY FASHIONABLE AROUND 1600. ACCORDING TO CONTEMPORARY ACCOUNTS LADIES FREQUENTLY COULD NOT WALK IN THEM UNLESS SUPPORTED BY MAIDS ON BOTH SIDES. HOWEVER, THEY DID PREVENT LADIES GETTING THEIR DRESSES MUDDY & THE FASHION LASTED OVER 20 YEARS.

COMFORTABLE PLASTIC SHOES
THE MAIN PROBLEMS ENCOUNTERED IN DEVELOPING A PLASTIC SYNTHETIC LEATHER FOR SHOES ARE THAT IT MUST SLOWLY ALTER ITS SHAPE TO FIT THE FOOT & MUST TRANSMIT WATER & SWEAT LIKE REAL LEATHER. SO FAR, ATTEMPTS HAVE NOT BEEN VERY SUCCESSFUL BUT A PROCESS IS NOW BEING DEVELOPED IN WHICH A PLASTIC WILL BE SPRAY-MOULDED ON THE WEARER'S FOOT, OR ON A MODEL OF IT. THE SHOE WILL THEN BE MADE POROUS BY PUTTING IT UNDER AN ELECTRON GUN WHICH WILL RIDDLE THE PLASTIC WITH MINUTE HOLES.

HOW TO MAKE A RUBBER BAND
PICK SOME DANDELIONS. COAT A FINGER IN SAP FROM THE STEMS. ALLOW TO DRY, THEN ROLL OFF FINGER AS SHOWN ABOVE.

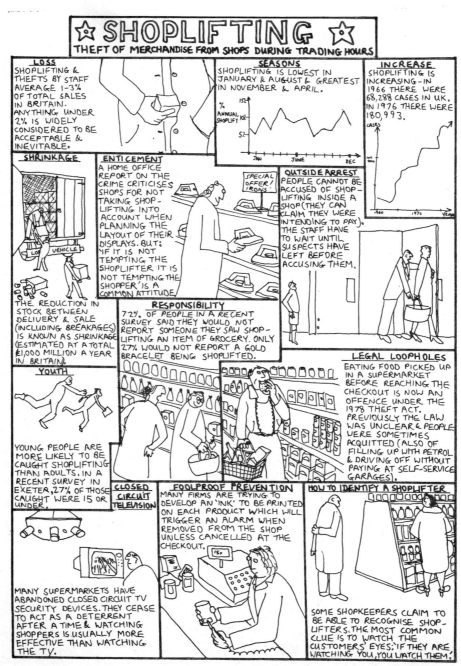

☆ SHOPLIFTING ☆
THEFT OF MERCHANDISE FROM SHOPS DURING TRADING HOURS

LOSS
SHOPLIFTING & THEFTS BY STAFF AVERAGE 1-3% OF TOTAL SALES IN BRITAIN. ANYTHING UNDER 2% IS WIDELY CONSIDERED TO BE ACCEPTABLE & INEVITABLE.

SEASONS
SHOPLIFTING IS LOWEST IN JANUARY & AUGUST & GREATEST IN NOVEMBER & APRIL.

INCREASE
SHOPLIFTING IS INCREASING - IN 1966 THERE WERE 68,288 CASES IN UK. IN 1976 THERE WERE 180,993.

SHRINKAGE
THE REDUCTION IN STOCK BETWEEN DELIVERY & SALE (INCLUDING BREAKAGES) IS KNOWN AS SHRINKAGE (ESTIMATED AT A TOTAL £1,000 MILLION A YEAR IN BRITAIN).

ENTICEMENT
A HOME OFFICE REPORT ON THE CRIME CRITICISES SHOPS FOR NOT TAKING SHOPLIFTING INTO ACCOUNT WHEN PLANNING THE LAYOUT OF THEIR DISPLAYS. BUT: 'IF IT IS NOT TEMPTING THE SHOPLIFTER IT IS NOT TEMPTING THE SHOPPER' IS A COMMON ATTITUDE.

OUTSIDE ARREST
PEOPLE CANNOT BE ACCUSED OF SHOPLIFTING INSIDE A SHOP (THEY CAN CLAIM THEY WERE INTENDING TO PAY). THE STAFF HAVE TO WAIT UNTIL SUSPECTS HAVE LEFT BEFORE ACCUSING THEM.

RESPONSIBILITY
72% OF PEOPLE IN A RECENT SURVEY SAID THEY WOULD NOT REPORT SOMEONE THEY SAW SHOPLIFTING AN ITEM OF GROCERY. ONLY 27% WOULD NOT REPORT A GOLD BRACELET BEING SHOPLIFTED.

YOUTH
YOUNG PEOPLE ARE MORE LIKELY TO BE CAUGHT SHOPLIFTING THAN ADULTS. IN A RECENT SURVEY IN EXETER, 27% OF THOSE CAUGHT WERE 15 OR UNDER.

LEGAL LOOPHOLES
EATING FOOD PICKED UP IN A SUPERMARKET BEFORE REACHING THE CHECKOUT IS NOW AN OFFENCE UNDER THE 1978 THEFT ACT. PREVIOUSLY THE LAW WAS UNCLEAR & PEOPLE WERE SOMETIMES ACQUITTED (ALSO OF FILLING UP WITH PETROL & DRIVING OFF WITHOUT PAYING AT SELF-SERVICE GARAGES).

CLOSED CIRCUIT TELEVISION
MANY SUPERMARKETS HAVE ABANDONED CLOSED CIRCUIT TV SECURITY DEVICES. THEY CEASE TO ACT AS A DETERRENT AFTER A TIME & WATCHING SHOPPERS IS USUALLY MORE EFFECTIVE THAN WATCHING THE TV.

FOOLPROOF PREVENTION
MANY FIRMS ARE TRYING TO DEVELOP AN 'INK' TO BE PRINTED ON EACH PRODUCT WHICH WILL TRIGGER AN ALARM WHEN REMOVED FROM THE SHOP UNLESS CANCELLED AT THE CHECKOUT.

HOW TO IDENTIFY A SHOPLIFTER
SOME SHOPKEEPERS CLAIM TO BE ABLE TO RECOGNISE SHOPLIFTERS. THE MOST COMMON CLUE IS TO WATCH THE CUSTOMERS' EYES: 'IF THEY ARE WATCHING YOU, YOU WATCH THEM.'

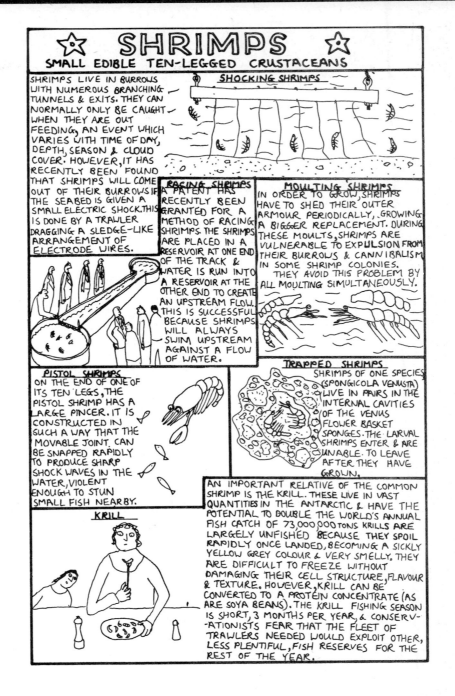

☆ SHRIMPS ☆
SMALL EDIBLE TEN-LEGGED CRUSTACEANS

SHRIMPS LIVE IN BURROWS WITH NUMEROUS BRANCHING TUNNELS & EXITS. THEY CAN NORMALLY ONLY BE CAUGHT WHEN THEY ARE OUT FEEDING, AN EVENT WHICH VARIES WITH TIME OF DAY, DEPTH, SEASON & CLOUD COVER. HOWEVER, IT HAS RECENTLY BEEN FOUND THAT SHRIMPS WILL COME OUT OF THEIR BURROWS IF THE SEABED IS GIVEN A SMALL ELECTRIC SHOCK. THIS IS DONE BY A TRAWLER DRAGGING A SLEDGE-LIKE ARRANGEMENT OF ELECTRODE WIRES.

SHOCKING SHRIMPS

RACING SHRIMPS
A PATENT HAS RECENTLY BEEN GRANTED FOR A METHOD OF RACING SHRIMPS. THE SHRIMPS ARE PLACED IN A RESERVOIR AT ONE END OF THE TRACK & WATER IS RUN INTO A RESERVOIR AT THE OTHER END TO CREATE AN UPSTREAM FLOW. THIS IS SUCCESSFUL BECAUSE SHRIMPS WILL ALWAYS SWIM UPSTREAM AGAINST A FLOW OF WATER.

MOULTING SHRIMPS
IN ORDER TO GROW, SHRIMPS HAVE TO SHED THEIR OUTER ARMOUR PERIODICALLY, GROWING A BIGGER REPLACEMENT. DURING THESE MOULTS, SHRIMPS ARE VULNERABLE TO EXPULSION FROM THEIR BURROWS & CANNIBALISM IN SOME SHRIMP COLONIES. THEY AVOID THIS PROBLEM BY ALL MOULTING SIMULTANEOUSLY.

PISTOL SHRIMPS
ON THE END OF ONE OF ITS TEN LEGS, THE PISTOL SHRIMP HAS A LARGE PINCER. IT IS CONSTRUCTED IN SUCH A WAY THAT THE MOVABLE JOINT CAN BE SNAPPED RAPIDLY TO PRODUCE SHARP SHOCK WAVES IN THE WATER, VIOLENT ENOUGH TO STUN SMALL FISH NEARBY.

TRAPPED SHRIMPS
SHRIMPS OF ONE SPECIES (SPONGICOLA VENUSTA) LIVE IN PAIRS IN THE INTERNAL CAVITIES OF THE VENUS FLOWER BASKET SPONGES. THE LARVAL SHRIMPS ENTER & ARE UNABLE TO LEAVE AFTER THEY HAVE GROWN.

KRILL
AN IMPORTANT RELATIVE OF THE COMMON SHRIMP IS THE KRILL. THESE LIVE IN VAST QUANTITIES IN THE ANTARCTIC & HAVE THE POTENTIAL TO DOUBLE THE WORLD'S ANNUAL FISH CATCH OF 73,000,000 TONS. KRILLS ARE LARGELY UNFISHED BECAUSE THEY SPOIL RAPIDLY ONCE LANDED, BECOMING A SICKLY YELLOW GREY COLOUR & VERY SMELLY. THEY ARE DIFFICULT TO FREEZE WITHOUT DAMAGING THEIR CELL STRUCTURE, FLAVOUR & TEXTURE. HOWEVER, KRILL CAN BE CONVERTED TO A PROTEIN CONCENTRATE (AS ARE SOYA BEANS). THE KRILL FISHING SEASON IS SHORT, 3 MONTHS PER YEAR, & CONSERVATIONISTS FEAR THAT THE FLEET OF TRAWLERS NEEDED WOULD EXPLOIT OTHER, LESS PLENTIFUL, FISH RESERVES FOR THE REST OF THE YEAR.

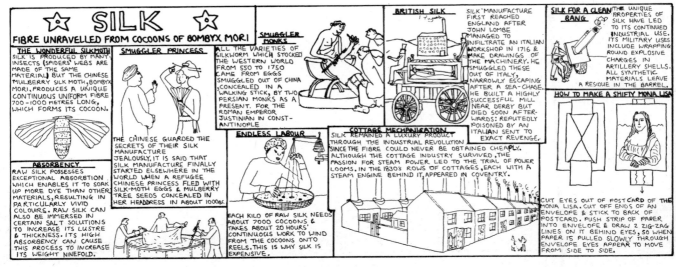

☆ SILK ☆
FIBRE UNRAVELLED FROM COCOONS OF BOMBYX MORI

THE WONDERFUL SILKMOTH
SILK IS PRODUCED BY MANY INSECTS (SPIDERS' WEBS ARE MADE OF THE SAME MATERIAL) BUT THE CHINESE MULBERRY SILK MOTH, BOMBYX MORI, PRODUCES A UNIQUE CONTINUOUS UNIFORM FIBRE 700-1000 METRES LONG, WHICH FORMS ITS COCOON.

ABSORBENCY
RAW SILK POSSESSES EXCEPTIONAL ABSORBTION WHICH ENABLES IT TO SOAK UP MORE DYE THAN OTHER MATERIALS, RESULTING IN PARTICULARLY VIVID COLOURS. RAW SILK CAN ALSO BE IMMERSED IN CERTAIN SALT SOLUTIONS TO INCREASE ITS LUSTRE & THICKNESS. ITS HIGH ABSORBENCY CAN CAUSE THIS PROCESS TO INCREASE ITS WEIGHT NINEFOLD.

SMUGGLER PRINCESS
THE CHINESE GUARDED THE SECRETS OF THEIR SILK MANUFACTURE JEALOUSLY. IT IS SAID THAT SILK MANUFACTURE FINALLY STARTED ELSEWHERE IN THE WORLD WHEN A REFUGEE CHINESE PRINCESS FLED WITH SILK-MOTH EGGS & MULBERRY TREE SEEDS CONCEALED IN HER HEADDRESS IN ABOUT 1000 BC.

SMUGGLER MONKS
ALL THE VARIETIES OF SILKWORM WHICH STOCKED THE WESTERN WORLD FROM 550 TO 1750 CAME FROM EGGS SMUGGLED OUT OF CHINA, CONCEALED IN A WALKING STICK, BY TWO PERSIAN MONKS AS A PRESENT FOR THE ROMAN EMPEROR JUSTINIAN IN CONSTANTINOPLE.

ENDLESS LABOUR
EACH KILO OF RAW SILK NEEDS ABOUT 7000 COCOONS & TAKES ABOUT 20 HOURS' CONTINUOUS WORK TO WIND FROM THE COCOONS ONTO REELS. THIS IS WHY SILK IS EXPENSIVE.

BRITISH SILK
SILK MANUFACTURE FIRST REACHED ENGLAND AFTER JOHN LOMBE MANAGED TO INFILTRATE AN ITALIAN WORKSHOP IN 1716 & MAKE DRAWINGS OF THE MACHINERY. HE SMUGGLED THESE OUT OF ITALY, NARROWLY ESCAPING AFTER A SEA-CHASE. HE BUILT A HIGHLY SUCCESSFUL MILL NEAR DERBY BUT DIED SOON AFTERWARDS: REPUTEDLY POISONED BY AN ITALIAN SENT TO EXACT REVENGE.

COTTAGE MECHANISATION
SILK REMAINED A LUXURY PRODUCT THROUGH THE INDUSTRIAL REVOLUTION SINCE THE FIBRE COULD NEVER BE OBTAINED CHEAPLY. ALTHOUGH THE COTTAGE INDUSTRY SURVIVED THE PASSION FOR STEAM POWER LED TO THE TRIAL OF POWER LOOMS. IN THE 1830s ROWS OF COTTAGES, EACH WITH A STEAM ENGINE BEHIND IT, APPEARED IN COVENTRY.

SILK FOR A CLEAN BANG
THE UNIQUE PROPERTIES OF SILK HAVE LED TO ITS CONTINUED INDUSTRIAL USE. ITS MILITARY USES INCLUDE WRAPPING ROUND EXPLOSIVE CHARGES IN ARTILLERY SHELLS. ALL SYNTHETIC MATERIALS LEAVE A RESIDUE IN THE BARREL.

HOW TO MAKE A SHIFTY MONA LISA
CUT EYES OUT OF POSTCARD OF THE MONA LISA. CUT OFF ENDS OF AN ENVELOPE & STICK TO BACK OF POSTCARD. PUSH STRIP OF PAPER INTO ENVELOPE & DRAW 2 ZIG-ZAG LINES ON IT BEHIND EYES, SO WHEN PAPER IS PULLED SLOWLY THROUGH ENVELOPE EYES APPEAR TO MOVE FROM SIDE TO SIDE.

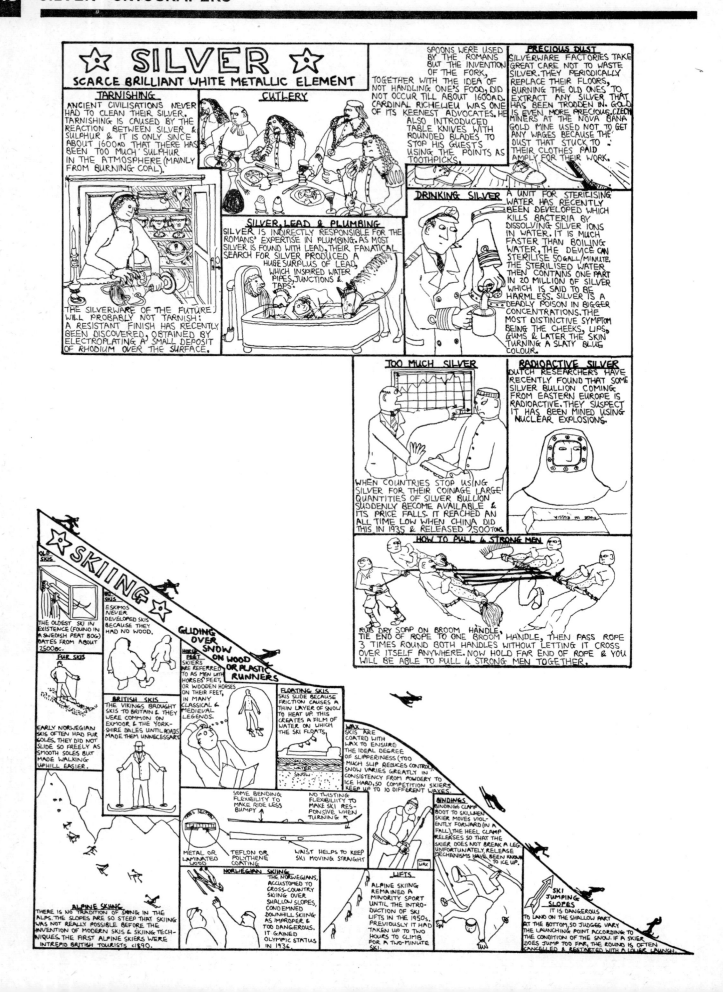

☆ SILVER ☆
SCARCE BRILLIANT WHITE METALLIC ELEMENT

TARNISHING
ANCIENT CIVILISATIONS NEVER HAD TO CLEAN THEIR SILVER. TARNISHING IS CAUSED BY THE REACTION BETWEEN SILVER & SULPHUR & IT IS ONLY SINCE ABOUT 1600AD THAT THERE HAS BEEN 'TOO MUCH' SULPHUR IN THE ATMOSPHERE (MAINLY FROM BURNING COAL).

THE SILVERWARE OF THE FUTURE WILL PROBABLY NOT TARNISH: A RESISTANT FINISH HAS RECENTLY BEEN DISCOVERED, OBTAINED BY ELECTROPLATING A SMALL DEPOSIT OF RHODIUM OVER THE SURFACE.

CUTLERY

SILVER, LEAD & PLUMBING
SILVER IS INDIRECTLY RESPONSIBLE FOR THE ROMANS' EXPERTISE IN PLUMBING. AS MOST SILVER IS FOUND WITH LEAD, THEIR FANATICAL SEARCH FOR SILVER PRODUCED A HUGE SURPLUS OF LEAD, WHICH INSPIRED WATER PIPES, JUNCTIONS & TAPS.

SPOONS WERE USED BY THE ROMANS BUT THE INVENTION OF THE FORK, TOGETHER WITH THE IDEA OF NOT HANDLING ONE'S FOOD, DID NOT OCCUR TILL ABOUT 1600AD. CARDINAL RICHELIEU WAS ONE OF ITS KEENEST ADVOCATES. HE ALSO INTRODUCED TABLE KNIVES WITH ROUNDED BLADES TO STOP HIS GUESTS USING THE POINTS AS TOOTHPICKS.

DRINKING SILVER
A UNIT FOR STERILISING WATER HAS RECENTLY BEEN DEVELOPED WHICH KILLS BACTERIA BY DISSOLVING SILVER IONS IN WATER. IT IS MUCH FASTER THAN BOILING WATER. THE DEVICE CAN STERILISE 50 GALL/MINUTE. THE STERILISED WATER THEN CONTAINS ONE PART IN 20 MILLION OF SILVER WHICH IS SAID TO BE HARMLESS. SILVER IS A DEADLY POISON IN BIGGER CONCENTRATIONS, THE MOST DISTINCTIVE SYMPTOM BEING THE CHEEKS, LIPS, GUMS & LATER THE SKIN TURNING A SLATY BLUE COLOUR.

PRECIOUS DUST
SILVERWARE FACTORIES TAKE GREAT CARE NOT TO WASTE SILVER. THEY PERIODICALLY REPLACE THEIR FLOORS, BURNING THE OLD ONES TO EXTRACT ANY SILVER THAT HAS BEEN TRODDEN IN. GOLD IS EVEN MORE PRECIOUS. CZECH MINERS AT THE NOVA BANA GOLD MINE USED NOT TO GET ANY WAGES BECAUSE THE DUST THAT STUCK TO THEIR CLOTHES PAID AMPLY FOR THEIR WORK.

TOO MUCH SILVER
WHEN COUNTRIES STOP USING SILVER FOR THEIR COINAGE LARGE QUANTITIES OF SILVER BULLION SUDDENLY BECOME AVAILABLE & ITS PRICE FALLS. IT REACHED AN ALL TIME LOW WHEN CHINA DID THIS IN 1935 & RELEASED 7,500 TONS.

RADIOACTIVE SILVER
DUTCH RESEARCHERS HAVE RECENTLY FOUND THAT SOME SILVER BULLION COMING FROM EASTERN EUROPE IS RADIOACTIVE. THEY SUSPECT IT HAS BEEN MINED USING NUCLEAR EXPLOSIONS.

HOW TO PULL 4 STRONG MEN
RUB DRY SOAP ON BROOM HANDLE. TIE END OF ROPE TO ONE BROOM HANDLE, THEN PASS ROPE 3 TIMES ROUND BOTH HANDLES WITHOUT LETTING IT CROSS OVER ITSELF ANYWHERE. NOW HOLD FAR END OF ROPE & YOU WILL BE ABLE TO PULL 4 STRONG MEN TOGETHER.

☆ SKIING ☆
GLIDING OVER SNOW ON WOOD OR PLASTIC RUNNERS

THE OLDEST SKI IN EXISTENCE (FOUND IN A SWEDISH PEAT BOG) DATES FROM ABOUT 2500BC.

FUR SKIS
EARLY NORWEGIAN SKIS OFTEN HAD FUR SOLES. THEY DID NOT SLIDE SO FREELY AS SMOOTH SOLES BUT MADE WALKING UPHILL EASIER.

ICE SKIS
ESKIMOS NEVER DEVELOPED SKIS BECAUSE THEY HAD NO WOOD.

BRITISH SKIS
THE VIKINGS BROUGHT SKIS TO BRITAIN & THEY WERE COMMON ON EXMOOR & THE YORKSHIRE DALES UNTIL ROADS MADE THEM UNNECESSARY.

HORSES' FEET
SKIERS ARE REFERRED TO AS MEN WITH HORSES' FEET, OR WOODEN HORSES ON THEIR FEET, IN MANY CLASSICAL & MEDIEVAL LEGENDS.

FLOATING SKIS
SKIS SLIDE BECAUSE FRICTION CAUSES A THIN LAYER OF SNOW TO HEAT UP. THIS CREATES A FILM OF WATER ON WHICH THE SKI FLOATS.

WATER
SNOW

WAX
SKIS ARE COATED WITH WAX TO ENSURE THE IDEAL DEGREE OF SLIPPERINESS (TOO MUCH SLIP REDUCES CONTROL). SNOW VARIES GREATLY IN CONSISTENCY FROM POWDERY TO ICE HARD, SO COMPETITION SKIERS KEEP UP TO 10 DIFFERENT WAXES.

SOME BENDING FLEXIBILITY TO MAKE RIDE LESS BUMPY

NO TWISTING FLEXIBILITY TO MAKE SKI RESPONSIVE WHEN TURNING

CROSS SECTION

METAL OR LAMINATED WOOD

TEFLON OR POLYTHENE COATING

WAIST HELPS TO KEEP SKI MOVING STRAIGHT

BINDINGS
BINDINGS CLAMP BOOT TO SKI. WHEN SKIER MOVES VIOLENTLY FORWARD (IN A FALL) THE HEEL CLAMP RELEASES SO THAT THE SKIER DOES NOT BREAK A LEG. UNFORTUNATELY, RELEASE MECHANISMS HAVE BEEN KNOWN TO ICE UP.

NORWEGIAN SKIING
THE NORWEGIANS, ACCUSTOMED TO CROSS-COUNTRY SKIING OVER SHALLOW SLOPES, CONDEMNED DOWNHILL SKIING AS IMPROPER & TOO DANGEROUS. IT GAINED OLYMPIC STATUS IN 1936.

ALPINE SKIING
THERE IS NO TRADITION OF SKIING IN THE ALPS. THE SLOPES ARE SO STEEP THAT SKIING WAS NOT REALLY POSSIBLE BEFORE THE INVENTION OF MODERN SKIS & SKIING TECHNIQUES. THE FIRST ALPINE SKIERS WERE INTREPID BRITISH TOURISTS c1890.

LIFTS
ALPINE SKIING REMAINED A MINORITY SPORT UNTIL THE INTRODUCTION OF SKI LIFTS IN THE 1950s. PREVIOUSLY IT HAD TAKEN UP TO TWO HOURS TO CLIMB FOR A TWO-MINUTE SKI.

SKI JUMPING SLOPES
IT IS DANGEROUS TO LAND ON THE SHALLOW PART AT THE BOTTOM, SO JUDGES VARY THE LAUNCHING POINT ACCORDING TO THE CONDITION OF THE SNOW. IF A SKIER DOES JUMP TOO FAR, THE ROUND IS OFTEN CANCELLED & RESTARTED WITH A LOWER LAUNCH.

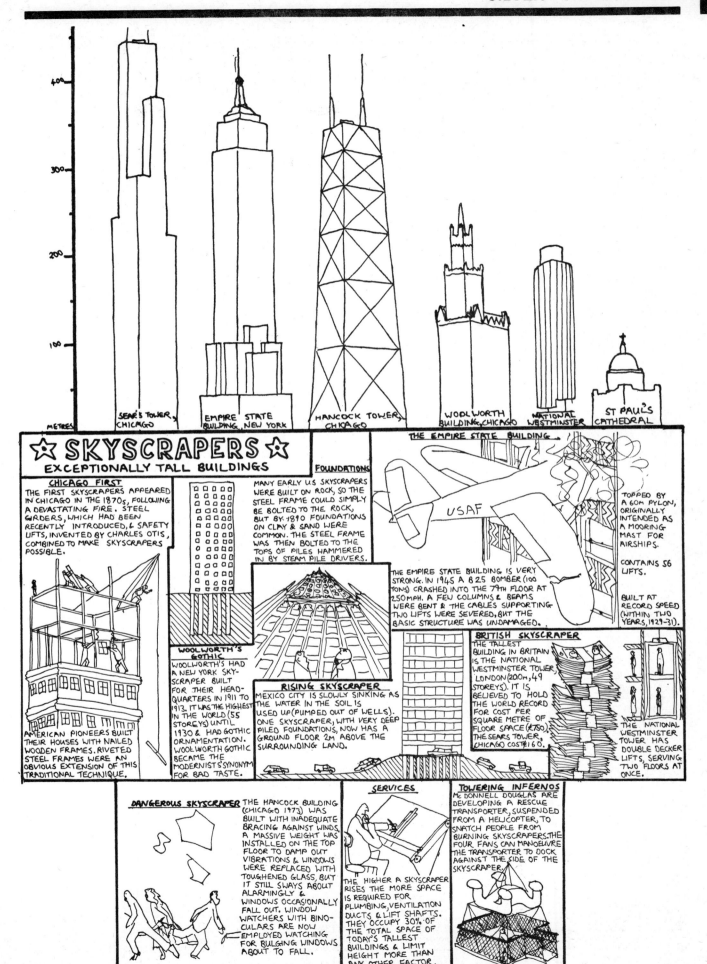

Height scale (metres): 400, 300, 200, 100

METRES

- SEARS TOWER, CHICAGO
- EMPIRE STATE BUILDING, NEW YORK
- HANCOCK TOWER, CHICAGO
- WOOLWORTH BUILDING, CHICAGO
- NATIONAL WESTMINSTER
- ST PAUL'S CATHEDRAL

☆ SKYSCRAPERS ☆
EXCEPTIONALLY TALL BUILDINGS

CHICAGO FIRST
THE FIRST SKYSCRAPERS APPEARED IN CHICAGO IN THE 1870s, FOLLOWING A DEVASTATING FIRE. STEEL GIRDERS, WHICH HAD BEEN RECENTLY INTRODUCED, & SAFETY LIFTS, INVENTED BY CHARLES OTIS, COMBINED TO MAKE SKYSCRAPERS POSSIBLE.

AMERICAN PIONEERS BUILT THEIR HOUSES WITH NAILED WOODEN FRAMES. RIVETED STEEL FRAMES WERE AN OBVIOUS EXTENSION OF THIS TRADITIONAL TECHNIQUE.

FOUNDATIONS
MANY EARLY U.S. SKYSCRAPERS WERE BUILT ON ROCK, SO THE STEEL FRAME COULD SIMPLY BE BOLTED TO THE ROCK, BUT BY 1890 FOUNDATIONS ON CLAY & SAND WERE COMMON. THE STEEL FRAME WAS THEN BOLTED TO THE TOPS OF PILES HAMMERED IN BY STEAM PILE DRIVERS.

WOOLWORTH'S GOTHIC
WOOLWORTH'S HAD A NEW YORK SKYSCRAPER BUILT FOR THEIR HEADQUARTERS IN 1911 TO 1913. IT WAS THE HIGHEST IN THE WORLD (55 STOREYS) UNTIL 1930 & HAD GOTHIC ORNAMENTATION. WOOLWORTH GOTHIC BECAME THE MODERNISTS' SYNONYM FOR BAD TASTE.

RISING SKYSCRAPER
MEXICO CITY IS SLOWLY SINKING AS THE WATER IN THE SOIL IS USED UP (PUMPED OUT OF WELLS). ONE SKYSCRAPER, WITH VERY DEEP PILED FOUNDATIONS, NOW HAS A GROUND FLOOR 2M ABOVE THE SURROUNDING LAND.

THE EMPIRE STATE BUILDING

USAF

THE EMPIRE STATE BUILDING IS VERY STRONG. IN 1945 A B25 BOMBER (100 TONS) CRASHED INTO THE 79TH FLOOR AT 250MPH. A FEW COLUMNS & BEAMS WERE BENT & THE CABLES SUPPORTING TWO LIFTS WERE SEVERED, BUT THE BASIC STRUCTURE WAS UNDAMAGED.

TOPPED BY A 60M PYLON, ORIGINALLY INTENDED AS A MOORING MAST FOR AIRSHIPS.

CONTAINS 56 LIFTS.

BUILT AT RECORD SPEED (WITHIN TWO YEARS, 1929-31).

BRITISH SKYSCRAPER
THE TALLEST BUILDING IN BRITAIN IS THE NATIONAL WESTMINSTER TOWER, LONDON (200M, 49 STOREYS). IT IS BELIEVED TO HOLD THE WORLD RECORD FOR COST PER SQUARE METRE OF FLOOR SPACE (£750), THE SEARS TOWER, CHICAGO COST £160.

THE NATIONAL WESTMINSTER TOWER HAS DOUBLE DECKER LIFTS, SERVING TWO FLOORS AT ONCE.

DANGEROUS SKYSCRAPER
THE HANCOCK BUILDING (CHICAGO 1973) WAS BUILT WITH INADEQUATE BRACING AGAINST WINDS. A MASSIVE WEIGHT WAS INSTALLED ON THE TOP FLOOR TO DAMP OUT VIBRATIONS & WINDOWS WERE REPLACED WITH TOUGHENED GLASS, BUT IT STILL SWAYS ABOUT ALARMINGLY & WINDOWS OCCASIONALLY FALL OUT. WINDOW WATCHERS WITH BINOCULARS ARE NOW EMPLOYED WATCHING FOR BULGING WINDOWS ABOUT TO FALL.

SERVICES
THE HIGHER A SKYSCRAPER RISES THE MORE SPACE IS REQUIRED FOR PLUMBING, VENTILATION DUCTS & LIFT SHAFTS. THEY OCCUPY 30% OF THE TOTAL SPACE OF TODAY'S TALLEST BUILDINGS & LIMIT HEIGHT MORE THAN ANY OTHER FACTOR.

TOWERING INFERNOS
McDONNELL DOUGLAS ARE DEVELOPING A RESCUE TRANSPORTER, SUSPENDED FROM A HELICOPTER, TO SNATCH PEOPLE FROM BURNING SKYSCRAPERS. THE FOUR FANS CAN MANOEUVRE THE TRANSPORTER TO DOCK AGAINST THE SIDE OF THE SKYSCRAPER.

☆ SKIN ☆
TISSUE FORMING OUTER COVERING OF VERTEBRATE BODY

TEEMING SKIN
WE HAVE 15-30 MILLION HARMLESS BACTERIA ON EACH SQUARE CENTIMETRE OF OUR SKIN. THEY CANNOT BE WASHED OFF, EVEN BY SURGEONS SCRUBBING UP BEFORE AN OPERATION.

PALE SKIN
VITAMIN D, NOT FOUND IN MANY FOODS, IS SYNTHESISED BY THE SKIN UNDER THE ACTION OF SUNLIGHT. PALE SKIN ABSORBS MORE SUNLIGHT THAN DARK SKIN & PEOPLE LIVING FAR FROM THE EQUATOR NEED TO ABSORB AS MUCH SUN AS POSSIBLE.

DARK SKIN
IN TROPICAL COUNTRIES, DARK SKIN IS AN ADVANTAGE AS IT PROTECTS AGAINST THE SUN'S ULTRA-VIOLET LIGHT WHICH CAN CAUSE SKIN CANCER.

ARTIFICIAL SKIN
AN INGENIOUS ARTIFICIAL SKIN HAS BEEN DEVELOPED FOR SEWING ON TO BURN PATIENTS. IT IS A THIN STRETCHY SILICONE FILM OVER A BIODEGRADABLE POLYMER LAYER ON WHICH NEW 'REAL' SKIN CAN GROW.

INHOSPITABLE SKIN
SKIN IS SALTY & ACID – AN INHOSPITABLE PLACE FOR ANY BACTERIA NOT SPECIFICALLY DESIGNED TO LIVE THERE. MANY HARMFUL BACTERIA SUCH AS TYPHOID, WHICH CAN NORMALLY SURVIVE FOR MANY WEEKS, DIE IN 20 MINUTES ON HEALTHY SKIN.

SWEATY EARS
SWEAT GLANDS INSIDE THE EAR HAVE BECOME MODIFIED TO PRODUCE EAR WAX. THIS CATCHES DIRT & PREVENTS IT REACHING THE EARDRUM.

HOW TO CLEAN VERY DIRTY SKIN
HAND CLEANERS & SOAPS OFTEN DON'T WORK SO WELL AS PUMICE STONE (FROM MOST CHEMISTS). THIS NATURAL VOLCANIC STONE HAS LOTS OF MINUTE HOLES WITH SHARP EDGES. IT SIMPLY RUBS OFF THE OUTER LAYER OF SKIN.

SWEATY PALMS
THE PALMS & SOLES HAVE SWEAT GLANDS WHICH ONLY REACT TO ADRENALIN IN THE BLOOD – NOT TO HEAT. THIS MAY HAVE EVOLVED AS AN AID TO GRIP WHILE FIGHTING – JUST AS MEN STILL SPIT ON THEIR HANDS BEFORE GRIPPING A SHOVEL.

SWEATY CHILDREN
CHILDREN CAN SWEAT MUCH MORE PROFUSELY THAN ADULTS. ALL SWEAT GLANDS ARE PRESENT AT BIRTH, SO THEY ARE MUCH CLOSER TOGETHER ON SMALL CHILDREN.

THICK SKIN
SKIN MAKES UP 16% OF OUR TOTAL BODY WEIGHT. IT IS MOSTLY ABOUT 1mm THICK BUT REACHES 3mm BETWEEN THE SHOULDER BLADES & ON OUR PALMS. HABITUALLY WALKING BAREFOOT DOUBLES THE THICKNESS OF SKIN ON THE SOLES TO ABOUT 10mm.

GROWING SKIN
NEW SKIN CELLS GROW UNDERNEATH THE SKIN, MOSTLY AT NIGHT. THEY TAKE ABOUT 48 DAYS TO REACH THE SURFACE. HERE THEY DIE & LIE FLAT, FORMING A MOISTURE BARRIER.

SELF-CLEANING SKIN
AFTER ABOUT TWO WEEKS, THE DEAD SURFACE CELLS FLAKE OFF & ARE REPLACED. THE GREAT ADVANTAGE OF THIS IS, HOWEVER DAMAGED OR DIRTY THE SKIN BECOMES IT IS SOON REPLACED.

DUSTY SKIN
SKIN IS SHED AS MINUTE SCALES, SMALL ENOUGH TO PASS THROUGH CLOTHING. IT IS OFTEN THE SOURCE OF MOST COMMON GREY HOUSE-HOLD DUST.

☆ SLANG ☆
UNDIGNIFIED COLLOQUIAL LANGUAGE

LATIN SLANG
THE ROMANS USED MANY SLANG TERMS – NOT RECOGNISED AS CLASSICAL LATIN. FOR EXAMPLE; TESTA, LITERALLY A BRICK OR POT, WAS USED AS SLANG FOR HEAD; UMBRA, LITERALLY A SHADOW, WAS USED TO REFER TO AN UNINVITED GUEST.

COCKNEY
THIS WORD PROBABLY COMES FROM 'COCKS' EGGS, A MEDIEVAL DELICACY. FROM THIS IT BECAME USED TO MEAN SPOILT CHILD, LATER A PAMPERED CITIZEN &, BY 1600, WAS IN USE AS SLANG FOR A LONDONER.

DEFINING SLANG
LINGUISTS HAVE DIFFICULTY DEFINING SLANG & DICTIONARY DEFINITIONS ARE VAGUE. A WORD MAY BE FELT DEFINITELY TO BE SLANG IN ONE SITUATION BUT TO BE PERFECTLY RESPECTABLE ENGLISH IN ANOTHER.

AMERICAN SLANG
SLANG IS COPIOUSLY DOCUMENTED & ANALYSED IN AMERICA. HIGH SCHOOLS ARE RICH SOURCES OF SLANG. A 1923 SURVEY OF WORDS USED FOR GIRL INCLUDED: A FLESH & BLOOD ANGEL, A WHIZZ, A PIPPIN, & A SWEET PATOOIE &, LESS FLATTERING, A PILL, A LEMON, A TOMATO, AN OILCAN, A CRUMB & A NUTCRACKER FACE.

HOW TO IMPROVISE SPECTACLES
PUSH A PIN THROUGH A SQUARE OF BLACK CARD. LOOK THROUGH THE HOLE & THE WORLD SHOULD APPEAR SHARP – AS IF YOU WERE WEARING SPECTACLES. THIS WORKS FOR MOST LONG & SHORT SIGHTED PEOPLE, ON THE SAME PRINCIPLE AS THE PIN HOLE CAMERA.

ROYAL SLANG
DURING THE 16TH CENTURY IT BECAME FASHIONABLE TO USE SLANG TERMS AT COURT. 3 GLOSSARIES OF THIEVES' SLANG WERE PUBLISHED – THE FIRST ATTEMPTS AT DICTIONARIES. TERMS FOR THIEVES INCLUDED PRIGGERS OF PRANCERS (HORSE THIEVES), FRESHWATER MARINERS (TRICKSTERS), BAWDY BASKETS (FEMALE THIEVES) & KITCHEN COVES (FEMALE, ORPHAN, TRAINEE THIEVES).

RHYMING SLANG
THE FIRST COLLECTION OF RHYMING SLANG WAS PUBLISHED IN 1857, CALLED 'THE VULGAR TONGUE'. AMONG THE ENTRIES ARE THE FOLLOWING: WHAT DO THEY REFER TO (ANSWERS BELOW) ① LEAN & LURCH ② UNCLE NED ③ TROUBLE & STRIFE

① CHURCH ② BED ③ WIFE

TASTY SLANG
THE CAFE SLANG BY WHICH ORDERS ARE CONVEYED FROM THE WAITERS TO THE KITCHEN IS RATHER UNAPPETISING. 'A SPLASH OF RED NOISE' (TOMATO SOUP), 'EVE WITH THE LID ON' (APPLE PIE), 'BOILED LEAVES' (TEA). 'TWO WITH THEIR EYES OPEN' (FRIED EGGS), 'ADAM & EVE ON A RAFT, WRECK 'EM' (SCRAMBLED EGGS)

INDIAN SLANG
THE COLONISATION OF INDIA ADDED MANY MODIFIED NATIVE WORDS TO THE ENGLISH LANGUAGE. CURRY, TODDY, VERANDAH, CHEROOT, PUKKA, LOOT & WALLAH ALL STARTED AS SLANG BUT SOME HAVE BECOME ACCEPTED AS STANDARD ENGLISH.

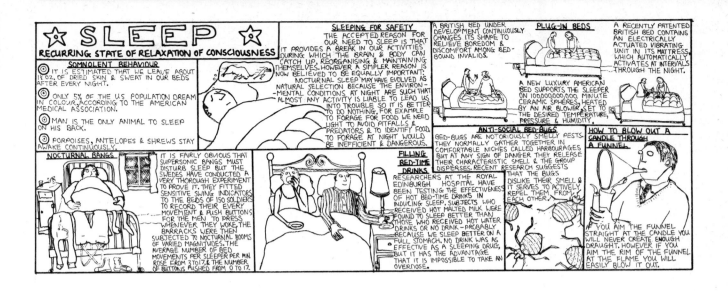

☆ SLEEP ☆
RECURRING STATE OF RELAXATION OF CONSCIOUSNESS

SOMNOLENT BEHAVIOUR
⊙ IT IS ESTIMATED THAT WE LEAVE ABOUT 1½ OZ. OF DRIED SKIN & SWEAT IN OUR BEDS AFTER EVERY NIGHT.

⊙ ONLY 5% OF THE U.S. POPULATION DREAM IN COLOUR, ACCORDING TO THE AMERICAN MEDICAL ASSOCIATION.

⊙ MAN IS THE ONLY ANIMAL TO SLEEP ON HIS BACK.

⊙ PORPOISES, ANTELOPES & SHREWS STAY AWAKE CONTINUOUSLY.

NOCTURNAL BANGS
IT IS FAIRLY OBVIOUS THAT SUPERSONIC BANGS MUST DISTURB SLEEP BUT THE SWEDES HAVE CONDUCTED A VERY THOROUGH EXPERIMENT TO PROVE IT. THEY FITTED SENSITIVE SWING INDICATORS TO THE BEDS OF 150 SOLDIERS TO RECORD THEIR EVERY MOVEMENT & PUSH BUTTONS FOR THE MEN TO PRESS WHENEVER THEY WOKE. THE BARRACKS WERE THEN SUBJECTED TO NOCTURNAL BOOMS OF VARIED MAGNITUDES. THE AVERAGE NUMBER OF BED MOVEMENTS PER SLEEPER PER MIN ROSE FROM 3 TO 17, & THE NUMBER OF BUTTONS PUSHED FROM 0 TO 17.

SLEEPING FOR SAFETY
THE ACCEPTED REASON FOR OUR NEED TO SLEEP IS THAT IT PROVIDES A BREAK IN OUR ACTIVITIES DURING WHICH THE BRAIN & BODY CAN CATCH UP, REORGANISING & MAINTAINING THEMSELVES. HOWEVER A SIMPLER REASON IS NOW BELIEVED TO BE EQUALLY IMPORTANT: NOCTURNAL SLEEP MAY HAVE EVOLVED AS NATURAL SELECTION BECAUSE THE ENVIRON-MENTAL CONDITIONS AT NIGHT ARE SUCH THAT ALMOST ANY ACTIVITY IS LIABLE TO LEAD US INTO TROUBLE SO IT IS BETTER TO DO NOTHING. FOR EXAMPLE TO FORAGE FOR FOOD WE NEED LIGHT TO AVOID PITFALLS & PREDATORS & TO IDENTIFY FOOD TO FORAGE AT NIGHT WOULD BE INEFFICIENT & DANGEROUS.

FILLING BED-TIME DRINKS
RESEARCHERS AT THE ROYAL EDINBURGH HOSPITAL HAVE BEEN TESTING THE EFFECTIVENESS OF HOT BED-TIME DRINKS IN INDUCING SLEEP. SUBJECTS WHO RECEIVED HOT MALTED MILK WERE FOUND TO SLEEP BETTER THAN THOSE WHO RECEIVED HOT WATER DRINKS OR NO DRINK – PROBABLY BECAUSE WE SLEEP BETTER ON A FULL STOMACH. NO DRINK WAS AS EFFECTIVE AS A SLEEPING DRUG, BUT IT HAS THE ADVANTAGE THAT IT IS IMPOSSIBLE TO TAKE AN OVERDOSE.

PLUG-IN BEDS
A BRITISH BED UNDER DEVELOPMENT CONTINUOUSLY CHANGES ITS SHAPE TO RELIEVE BOREDOM & DISCOMFORT AMONG BED-BOUND INVALIDS.

A RECENTLY PATENTED BRITISH BED CONTAINS AN ELECTRICALLY ACTUATED VIBRATING UNIT IN ITS MATTRESS WHICH AUTOMATICALLY ACTIVATES AT INTERVALS THROUGH THE NIGHT.

A NEW LUXURY AMERICAN BED SUPPORTS THE SLEEPER ON 100,000,000,000 MINUTE CERAMIC SPHERES, HEATED BY AN AIR BLOWER SET TO THE DESIRED TEMPERATURE, PRESSURE & HUMIDITY.

ANTI-SOCIAL BED-BUGS
BED-BUGS ARE NOTORIOUSLY SMELLY PESTS. THEY NORMALLY GATHER TOGETHER IN COMFORTABLE NICHES CALLED HARBOURAGES BUT AT ANY SIGN OF DANGER THEY RELEASE THEIR CHARACTERISTIC SMELL & THE GROUP DISPERSES. RECENT RESEARCH SUGGESTS THAT THE BUGS DISLIKE THEIR SMELL & IT SERVES TO ACTIVELY REPEL THEM FROM EACH OTHER.

HOW TO BLOW OUT A CANDLE THROUGH A FUNNEL
IF YOU AIM THE FUNNEL STRAIGHT AT THE CANDLE YOU WILL NEVER CREATE ENOUGH DRAUGHT. HOWEVER IF YOU AIM THE RIM OF THE FUNNEL AT THE FLAME YOU WILL EASILY BLOW IT OUT.

☆ SLUGS ☆
GASTROPOD MOLLUSCS

SLUGS & SNAILS
SLUGS ARE VERY SIMILAR TO SNAILS EXCEPT FOR THEIR LACK OF A PROTECTIVE SHELL. ALTHOUGH THIS MAKES SLUGS MORE VULNERABLE, THEY ARE MORE WIDESPREAD THAN SNAILS WHICH CAN ONLY LIVE IN AREAS RICH IN CALCIUM SALTS (TO HARDEN THE SHELL).

MINI SHELL
TESTACELLIDAE SLUGS HAVE A VESTIGIAL SHELL AT ONE END OF THE BODY TO PROTECT THE HEART.

MOVEMENT
TO SLUG, OR SLOG, IS TO BE SLOW (POSSIBLY FROM THE OLD SCANDINAVIAN SLOGG(E)). HENCE THE WORD SLUG. (THE FASTEST RECORDED SLUG'S SPEED IS 0.2 MPH.)

GIANTS
THE LARGEST SLUG (LIMAX CINEREONIGER) GROWS UP TO 30cm LONG. IT LIVES ON HILLSIDES & IN WOODLAND IN EUROPE.

SEX
SLUGS ARE HERMAPHRODITE. IN SOME SPECIES PARTNERS CAN SWOP SEXUAL ROLES BETWEEN MATINGS.

VITAMINS
A LACK OF B GROUP VITAMINS IN THE SLUG'S DIET STUNTS ITS GROWTH, SHORTENS ITS LIFE & INCLINES IT TO CANNIBALISM.

EYES & NOSE
EYE
SMELL RECEPTORS
NERVES TO BRAIN

SLUGS ARE BETTER AT SMELLING THAN SEEING. THEIR 'EYE' STALKS CAN DETECT THE SMELL OF MUSHROOMS FROM 1.2m.

AERODYNAMIC SLUGS
SLUGS ALWAYS CRAWL WITH THE WIND IF POSSIBLE. THIS MINIMISES THE LOSS OF WATER THROUGH EVAPORATION FROM THEIR MOIST SKIN.

SLUG PESTS
SLUGS ARE A MAJOR AGRICULTURAL PEST. IT IS ESTIMATED THAT THEY EAT 36,000 TONNES OF POTATOES A YEAR IN BRITAIN. THEY ALSO EAT WHEAT, SUGAR BEET & GREEN VEGETABLES.

SEA SLUG
THE SEA SLUG PROTECTS ITSELF WITH STING CELLS WHICH IT TAKES FROM THE JELLYFISH ON WHICH IT FEEDS. THE CELLS BECOME ATTACHED TO THE ENDS OF THE SLUG'S ARMS.

HOW TO TELL THE TEMPERATURE BY LISTENING TO A GRASSHOPPER
GRASSHOPPERS CLICK FASTER IN HOT WEATHER. THE NUMBER OF CLICKS IN 10 SECONDS IS APPROXIMATELY THE TEMPERATURE IN DEGREES CENTIGRADE.

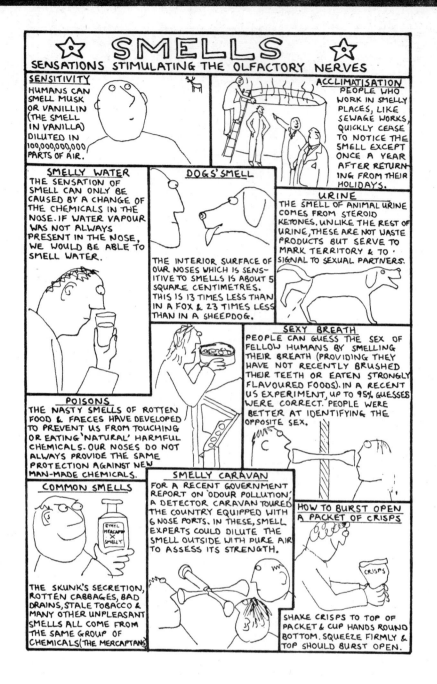

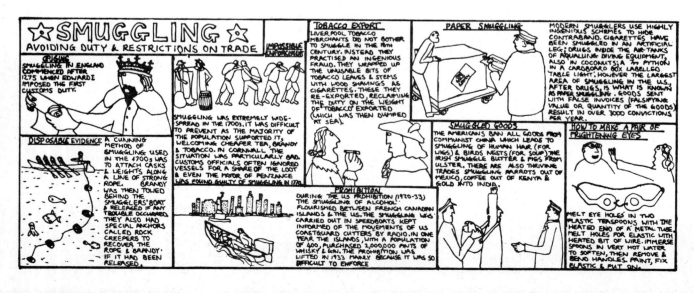

☆ SNAILS ☆
AIR-BREATHING GASTROPOD MOLLUSCS

SNAILS' TEETH

A SNAIL HAS ABOUT 25,600 TEETH & CAN CHEW THROUGH MOST MATERIALS. YOUNG SNAILS WILL EAT LIMESTONE ROCK TO PROVIDE THE CALCIUM FOR THEIR SHELLS, OR MAY RESORT TO CANNIBALISM, EATING EACH OTHERS' SHELLS. EDIBLE SNAILS USED TO BE TRANSPORTED IN WOODEN CRATES BUT MANY ESCAPED BY EATING THE WOOD.

SNAILS' SEX

SNAILS ARE HERMAPHRODITES. WHEN A COUPLE MATE, EACH ACTS BOTH AS A MALE & A FEMALE. THEY FERTILISE EACH OTHERS' EGGS & DIG PITS 15 DAYS LATER TO LAY THEM.

SNAILS & NOODLES

SNAILS REARED ON FARMS ARE QUITE EXPENSIVE TO FEED, CONSUMING VAST QUANTITIES OF ASSORTED VEGETABLES. HOWEVER, RECENT EXPERIMENTS SUGGEST THAT THEY ARE ALSO QUITE HAPPY EATING NOODLES – A DISCOVERY THAT COULD EVENTUALLY MAKE SNAILS A LESS EXPENSIVE DELICACY.

LIVING ON SNAIL MEAT

SNAILS COULD BECOME A STAPLE FOOD IN PARTS OF AFRICA. THE GROUND ON OIL PALM PLANTATIONS CAN BE SOWN WITH MANY SORTS OF VEGETATION SUITABLE FOR GRAZING LIVESTOCK. PAST ATTEMPTS IN NIGERIA FAILED BECAUSE CATTLE, SHEEP OR POULTRY NEEDED MORE MONEY TO BUY THAN THE NATIVES COULD USUALLY AFFORD. HOWEVER THE GIANT AFRICAN SNAIL HAS NOW BEEN FOUND TO FATTEN FAST ON SUCH LAND. 1000 SNAILS ON ¼ ACRE YIELD 170 lb OF SNAIL MEAT PER YEAR – WITH NO GREAT CAPITAL OUTLAY.

SNAILS, SAWDUST & ELECTRICITY

SNAIL FARMERS DO NOT NEED TO ERECT FENCES TO PREVENT THEIR LIVESTOCK ESCAPING. A LAYER OF DRY SAWDUST IS AN INSURMOUNTABLE OBSTACLE TO A SNAIL, PREVENTING IT FROM STICKING ITS STOMACH TO THE GROUND WITH ITS SALIVA. ANOTHER OBSTACLE NEVER CROSSED BY A SNAIL IS A LOW VOLTAGE A.C. ELECTRIC WIRE BURIED IN THE GROUND.

SNAILS & SOAP

2000 MILLION PEOPLE ARE AFFECTED BY BILHARZIA, A DISEASE TRANSMITTED BY THE WATER SNAIL. THE FREQUENT DISCOVERY OF DEAD SNAILS IN ETHIOPA HAS NOW LED TO A SIMPLE EFFECTIVE SNAIL POISON. THE DEAD SNAILS WERE ALWAYS FOUND DOWNSTREAM OF WASHING PLACES – POISONED BY THE ETHIOPIANS' SOAP MADE FROM BERRIES, COMMON IN MANY PARTS OF THE WORLD. PORTABLE MILLS ARE NOW BEING MADE TO EXTRACT THE SOAP-POISON.

SNAILS' SHELLS

ALL COMMON BRITISH SNAILS HAVE SHELLS COILED CLOCKWISE, EXCEPT FOR THE LIGHTNING WHELK WHOSE SHELL IS COILED ANTICLOCK-WISE & THE PERVERSE WHELK WHOSE SHELL MAY BE EITHER

HOW TO FIND WHETHER YOUR CUTLERY IS SOLID SILVER

PLACE A SUSPECT SPOON OR FORK IN A CUP WITH A SIMILAR SOLID SILVER PIECE. STICK A DRIED PEA TO THE HANDLE OF EACH WITH A DAB OF BUTTER. POUR BOILING WATER INTO CUP. IF THE PEA ON THE SUSPECT PIECE FALLS OFF SIMULTANEOUSLY WITH OTHER PEA THE PIECE IS SILVER; IF THE PEA FALLS OFF AFTER THE OTHER PEA THE PIECE IS NOT SOLID SILVER. SILVER CONDUCTS HEAT QUICKER THAN ANY OTHER METAL EXCEPT GOLD & MERCURY & PLATINUM.

MODEL T FORD CONVERTED FOR SNOW, 1913.

SPIRAL AUGER SNOW VEHICLE, U.S.1922.

DRUM SNOW VEHICLE, U.S.,1942 ENGINE INSIDE DRUM.

KAM SNO-BALL, 1957 TRACKS BOLT TO ANY CAR.

SKI-DOO, U.S., SINGLE POWERED TRACK UNDER SEAT.

SNOWMOBILE BUS, U.S., TRAVELS AT 50 mph.

☆ SNOW ☆
WATER FROZEN INTO SMALL 6 SIDED CRYSTALS

LABORATORY SNOW

MAKING SNOW IN A LABORATORY IS NOT SIMPLE. CHILLED WATER VAPOUR TENDS TO FREEZE ON THE SIDES OF ITS CONTAINER RATHER THAN FALL AS SNOW. IT WAS NOT UNTIL 1946 THAT SNOW WAS 'SYNTHESISED' BY COOLING THE WATER SUDDENLY TO -70°C.

DEEP SNOW

THE SNOWIEST RECORDED PLACE IN THE WORLD IS MOUNT RAINIER, WASHINGTON, US, WHERE AN AVERAGE OF 16.6m (575in) FALLS PER YEAR.

SNOW CRYSTALS STICK TOGETHER TO FORM LARGE FLAKES AT TEMPERATURES NEAR 0°. AT VERY LOW TEMPERATURES, SNOW FALLS AS A POWDER OF INDIVIDUAL CRYSTALS. VERY FINE, POWDERY SNOW, UNUSUAL IN BRITAIN, CAN PENETRATE CRACKS IN DOORS & WINDOWS & EVEN SUFFOCATE PEOPLE.

LIFE UNDER SNOW

ALTHOUGH THE AIR ABOVE MAY BE FAR BELOW FREEZING POINT, SMALL ANIMALS CAN LIVE IN RELATIVELY WARM (NEAR 0°C) SHELTERED DENS UNDER SNOW. MANY DO NOT HIBERNATE. VOLES, LEMMINGS & SHREWS LEAD ACTIVE LIVES, EATING STORED FOOD & REPRODUCING FREELY.

DUSTY SNOW

WHITE-OUT

WHEN A BLIZZARD IS STRONG ENOUGH, CLOUD MERGES INTO SNOW WITHOUT ANY VISIBLE HORIZON OR SHADOWS – A CONDITION KNOWN AS WHITE-OUT. ALL SENSE OF DIRECTION & EVEN BALANCE MAY BE LOST.

USEFUL SNOW

IN DEVON, CORN HAS GERMINATED & GROWN UP TO 75mm UNDER SNOW. IN MUCH OF THE US, SNOW COVER IS ESSENTIAL TO PROTECT CROPS PLANTED IN THE AUTUMN FROM COLD AIR TEMPERATURES. OCCASIONAL YEARS WITHOUT SNOW DO GREAT CROP DAMAGE.

ENCOURAGING SNOW

MANY REGIONS DEPEND ON THE SNOW MELTING IN THE SPRING FOR IRRIGATION. VARIOUS METHODS HAVE BEEN TRIED TO TRAP AS MUCH SNOW AS POSSIBLE. LEAVING STUBBLE & STRIPS OF UNCUT WHEAT, PLOUGHING RIDGES IN THE FIRST SNOWS, BUILDING HEDGES & TERRACING LAND ALL HELP TO INCREASE THE DEPTH OF SNOW & CROP YIELDS.

MELTERS

IN SOME PARTS OF AMERICA IT IS SO DIFFICULT TO FIND SUITABLE PLACES TO DUMP THE SNOW CLEARED FROM ROADS THAT IT IS TIPPED INTO VAST SNOW-MELTING MACHINES WITH OIL-FIRED BURNERS.

COWS ON SNOW

CATTLE CAN FEED THROUGH UP TO 150mm (6in) SNOW.

SHEEP ON SNOW

SHEEP CAN WALK THROUGH UP TO 300mm (12in) SNOW.

SHEEP IN SNOW

SHEEP CAN SURVIVE FOR SEVERAL WEEKS IN SNOW & EVEN GIVE BIRTH TO HEALTHY LAMBS.

HOW TO THREAD BEADS AT HIGH SPEED

STIFFEN END OF THREAD BY DIPPING IN NAIL POLISH. LINE BEADS UP ON CORRUGATED CARDBOARD WITH HOLES IN LINE & SIMPLY PUSH THREAD THROUGH.

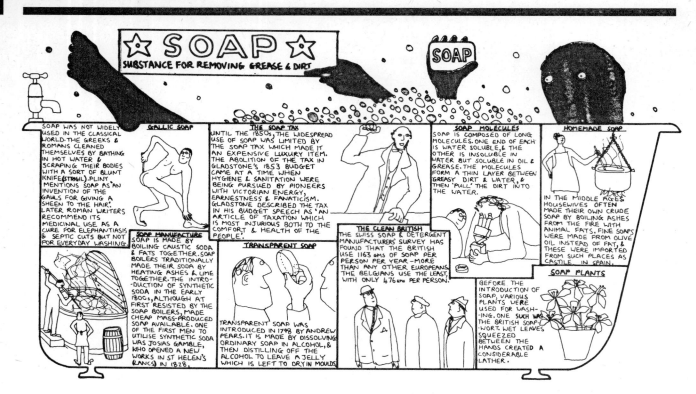

☆ SOAP ☆
SUBSTANCE FOR REMOVING GREASE & DIRT

SOAP WAS NOT WIDELY USED IN THE CLASSICAL WORLD. THE GREEKS & ROMANS CLEANED THEMSELVES BY BATHING IN HOT WATER & SCRAPING THEIR BODIES WITH A SORT OF BLUNT KNIFE (STRIGIL). PLINY MENTIONS SOAP AS AN INVENTION OF THE GAULS FOR GIVING A SHEEN TO THE HAIR. LATER ROMAN WRITERS RECOMMEND ITS MEDICINAL USE AS A CURE FOR ELEPHANTIASIS & SEPTIC CUTS BUT NOT FOR EVERYDAY WASHING.

GALLIC SOAP

SOAP MANUFACTURE
SOAP IS MADE BY BOILING CAUSTIC SODA & FATS TOGETHER. SOAP BOILERS TRADITIONALLY MADE THEIR SODA BY HEATING ASHES & LIME TOGETHER. THE INTRO-DUCTION OF SYNTHETIC SODA IN THE EARLY 1800s, ALTHOUGH AT FIRST RESISTED BY THE SOAP BOILERS, MADE CHEAP MASS-PRODUCED SOAP AVAILABLE. ONE OF THE FIRST MEN TO UTILISE SYNTHETIC SODA WAS JOSIAS GAMBLE, WHO OPENED A NEW WORKS IN ST HELEN'S (LANCS) IN 1828.

THE SOAP TAX
UNTIL THE 1850s, THE WIDESPREAD USE OF SOAP WAS LIMITED BY THE SOAP TAX WHICH MADE IT AN EXPENSIVE LUXURY ITEM. THE ABOLITION OF THE TAX IN GLADSTONE'S 1853 BUDGET CAME AT A TIME WHEN HYGIENE & SANITATION WERE BEING PURSUED BY PIONEERS WITH VICTORIAN ENERGY, EARNESTNESS & FANATICISM. GLADSTONE DESCRIBED THE TAX IN HIS BUDGET SPEECH AS 'AN ARTICLE OF TAXATION WHICH IS MOST INJURIOUS BOTH TO THE COMFORT & HEALTH OF THE PEOPLE'.

TRANSPARENT SOAP
TRANSPARENT SOAP WAS INTRODUCED IN 1748 BY ANDREW PEARS. IT IS MADE BY DISSOLVING ORDINARY SOAP IN ALCOHOL, & THEN DISTILLING OFF THE ALCOHOL TO LEAVE A JELLY WHICH IS LEFT TO DRY IN MOULDS.

SOAP MOLECULES
SOAP IS COMPOSED OF LONG MOLECULES. ONE END OF EACH IS WATER SOLUBLE, & THE OTHER IS INSOLUBLE IN WATER BUT SOLUBLE IN OIL & GREASE. THE MOLECULES FORM A THIN LAYER BETWEEN GREASY DIRT & WATER, & THEN 'PULL' THE DIRT INTO THE WATER.

THE CLEAN BRITISH
THE SWISS SOAP & DETERGENT MANUFACTURERS' SURVEY HAS FOUND THAT THE BRITISH USE 1163 GMS OF SOAP PER PERSON PER YEAR - MORE THAN ANY OTHER EUROPEANS. THE BELGIANS USE THE LEAST, WITH ONLY 476 GMS PER PERSON.

HOMEMADE SOAP
IN THE MIDDLE AGES, HOUSEWIVES OFTEN MADE THEIR OWN CRUDE SOAP BY BOILING ASHES FROM THE FIRE WITH ANIMAL FATS. FINE SOAPS WERE MADE FROM OLIVE OIL INSTEAD OF FAT, & THESE WERE IMPORTED FROM SUCH PLACES AS CASTILE IN SPAIN.

SOAP PLANTS
BEFORE THE INTRODUCTION OF SOAP, VARIOUS PLANTS WERE USED FOR WASH-ING. ONE SUCH WAS THE BRITISH SOAP-WORT. WET LEAVES SQUEEZED BETWEEN THE HANDS CREATED A CONSIDERABLE LATHER.

☆ SOIL ☆
TERRAIN CAPABLE OF SUSTAINING PLANT LIFE

COMPOST
A FERTILE SOIL MUST ABSORB RAINWATER & RETAIN IT FOR ENZYMES TO EXTRACT NUTRIENTS FROM IT INTO A FORM WHICH PLANT ROOTS CAN ABSORB. RAINWATER DOES NOT PENETRATE HEAVY CLAY SOILS & DRAINS STRAIGHT THROUGH SANDY SOIL. THE FUNCTION OF LIME & COMPOST IS MAINLY TO MAKE SOIL BETTER AT HOLDING RAINWATER. THEY GUM UP SAND & BREAK DOWN CLAY INTO LOOSE CRUMBS, CREATING WHAT GARDENERS CALL GOOD CRUMB STRUCTURE.

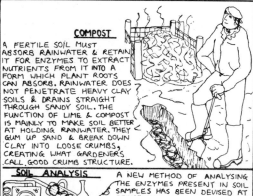

SOIL ANALYSIS
A NEW METHOD OF ANALYSING THE ENZYMES PRESENT IN SOIL SAMPLES HAS BEEN DEVISED AT BERKELEY UNIVERSITY, CALIFORNIA. EVERY SOIL HAS A UNIQUE ENZYME MAKE UP SO THE METHOD WILL BE USEFUL TO FORENSIC SCIENTISTS MATCHING SOIL FROM SUSPECTS' SHOES WITH SOIL FROM THE SCENE OF THE CRIME. ENZYME ACTIVITY ALSO VARIES WITH TIME SO IF SUSPECTS' SHOES ARE EXAMINED SOON ENOUGH (FROM TWO DAYS TO TWO MONTHS, DEPENDING ON THE SOIL TYPE), THE TIME THAT THE SHOES MET THE SOIL CAN BE ESTIMATED.

PRECIOUS METALS FROM THE SOIL
A RECENT GERMAN PATENT CLAIMS A REVOLUTIONARY METHOD FOR EXTRACTING TRACE ELEMENTS FROM SOIL. IT CLAIMS THAT FRUIT TREES DEPRIVED OF ESSENTIAL ELEMENTS SUCH AS CALCIUM POTASSIUM & IRON WILL ATTEMPT TO MAKE UP THE DEFICIENCY BY TAKING UP OTHER ELEMENTS PRESENT IN THE SOIL. THE SUBSTITUTE MINERALS ACCUMULATE IN THE FRUIT. USEFUL QUANTITIES OF URANIUM, THORIUM, & TITANIUM ARE REPORTED TO HAVE BEEN FOUND IN BANANAS GROWN IN THIS MANNER IN ECUADOR.

CULTIVATION WITHOUT SOIL
PLANT ROOTS NEED WATER & OXYGEN BUT IN MOST SOILS THESE ARE MUTUALLY EXCLUSIVE AS FLOODING PUSHES THE AIR OUT. THE 'NUTRIENT FILM TECHNIQUE' IS A METHOD OF PLANT CULTIVATION WHICH OVERCOMES THIS PROBLEM BY USING NO SOIL. THE PLANT IS FIXED UPRIGHT WITH THE ROOTS LYING ON A SLOPE. A CONSTANTLY CIRCULATING FILM OF NUTRIENT SOLUTION TRICKLES DOWN THE SLOPE, BATHING THE ROOTS IN AIR, WATER & A 'CAFETERIA SELECTION' OF NUTRIENTS.

HOW TO MAKE A CRYSTAL GARDEN
MIX 6 SPOONFULS WATER, 6 SP LAUNDRY BLUE, 6 SP SALT & ADD 6 SP AMMONIA. PLACE A FEW MATCHBOX-SIZED LUMPS OF BRICK OR CHARCOAL IN A 5 INCH SOUP BOWL & POUR IN MIXTURE. AS CRYSTALS START TO GROW PUT DROPS OF FOOD COLOURING ON LUMPS TO COLOUR CRYSTALS.

LIGHT & HEAVY SOIL
SANDY SOILS ARE DESCRIBED AS 'LIGHT' WHILE CLAYS ARE DESCRIBED AS 'HEAVY' ALTHOUGH A CUBIC FOOT OF SAND WEIGHS MORE THAN THE SAME VOLUME OF CLAY. SANDY SOILS ARE CALLED LIGHT BECAUSE THE LARGER PARTICLES MAKE IT EASIER TO DIG.

SOIL & STUBBLE

ORGANIC FARMERS OFTEN CLAIM THAT STRAW SHOULD BE PLOUGHED IN AFTER HARVEST RATHER THAN BURNT. LATEST RESEARCH BY THE BRITISH AGRICULTURAL RESEARCH INSTITUTE REFUTES THIS, CLAIMING THAT PLOUGHED-IN STRAW IS ONLY BENEFICIAL IF THERE IS A PARTICULARLY DRY AUTUMN. THE STRAW APPARENTLY CONTAINS SOME TOXINS WHICH SLOW THE GROWTH OF NEW SEEDLINGS & PROVIDES A HOME FOR MICRO ORGANISMS WHICH COMPETE WITH THE SEEDLINGS FOR NITROGEN.

SOLAR ENERGY
POWER FROM THE SUN

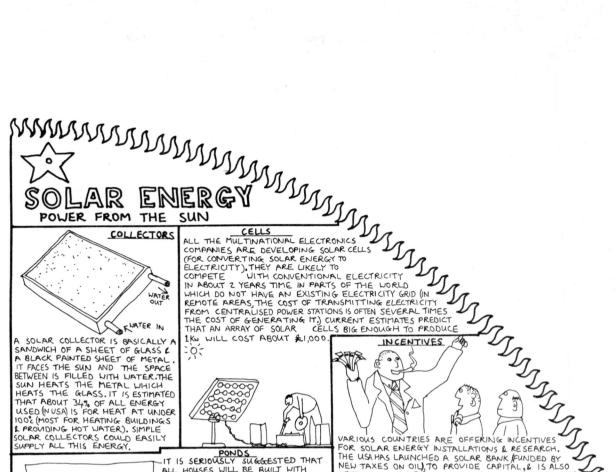

COLLECTORS

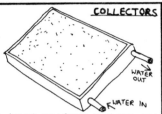

WATER OUT

WATER IN

A SOLAR COLLECTOR IS BASICALLY A SANDWICH OF A SHEET OF GLASS & A BLACK PAINTED SHEET OF METAL. IT FACES THE SUN AND THE SPACE BETWEEN IS FILLED WITH WATER. THE SUN HEATS THE METAL WHICH HEATS THE GLASS. IT IS ESTIMATED THAT ABOUT 34% OF ALL ENERGY USED (IN USA) IS FOR HEAT AT UNDER 100°C (MOST FOR HEATING BUILDINGS & PROVIDING HOT WATER). SIMPLE SOLAR COLLECTORS COULD EASILY SUPPLY ALL THIS ENERGY.

CELLS

ALL THE MULTINATIONAL ELECTRONICS COMPANIES ARE DEVELOPING SOLAR CELLS (FOR CONVERTING SOLAR ENERGY TO ELECTRICITY). THEY ARE LIKELY TO COMPETE WITH CONVENTIONAL ELECTRICITY IN ABOUT 2 YEARS TIME IN PARTS OF THE WORLD WHICH DO NOT HAVE AN EXISTING ELECTRICITY GRID (IN REMOTE AREAS, THE COST OF TRANSMITTING ELECTRICITY FROM CENTRALISED POWER STATIONS IS OFTEN SEVERAL TIMES THE COST OF GENERATING IT.) CURRENT ESTIMATES PREDICT THAT AN ARRAY OF SOLAR CELLS BIG ENOUGH TO PRODUCE 1KW WILL COST ABOUT £1,000.

INCENTIVES

VARIOUS COUNTRIES ARE OFFERING INCENTIVES FOR SOLAR ENERGY INSTALLATIONS & RESEARCH. THE USA HAS LAUNCHED A SOLAR BANK (FUNDED BY NEW TAXES ON OIL), TO PROVIDE CAPITAL, & IS ALSO OFFERING LARGE TAX REDUCTIONS FOR FACTORIES & HOUSES INCORPORATING SOLAR HEATING. SWEDEN HAS THE WORLD'S MOST AMBITIOUS PROGRAMME, AIMING TO TAKE FROM THE SUN ALL THE ENERGY IT NEEDS BY THE YEAR 2015. IT HAS PASSED STRINGENT NEW BUILDING REGULATIONS FOR INSULATION WHICH SHOULD REDUCE THE ENERGY REQUIRE-MENTS OF HOUSES BY ABOUT 40%, & IS SPENDING 4 TIMES AS MUCH ON SOLAR RESEARCH AS ON NUCLEAR RESEARCH.

PONDS

IT IS SERIOUSLY SUGGESTED THAT ALL HOUSES WILL BE BUILT WITH SOLAR PONDS IN THE NEAR FUTURE. SOLAR COLLECTORS WOULD HEAT UP THE POND IN THE SUMMER. THE WELL INSULATED POND WILL STAY WARM UNTIL WINTER WHEN THE WARM WATER CAN BE CIRCULATED THROUGH THE HOUSE. A SWEDISH SYSTEM HAS A POND WITH THE SOLAR COLLECTORS FLOATING ON TOP, SLOWLY ROTATING TO KEEP THEM FACING THE SUN. IT IS CLAIMED THAT THE WATER NEVER FALLS BELOW 30°C - EVEN AT THE END OF THE SWEDISH WINTER.

EXOTIC CELLS

RESEARCH ON EXOTIC TYPES OF SOLAR CELL INCLUDES:
★ WORK ON AMORPHOUS SILICON (POTENTIALLY 1/100th THE COST OF PRESENT CRYSTALLINE SILICON CELLS)
★ WORK ON OXIDES OF A RARE EARTH (RHODATE) AS AN ELECTRODE IN A BATTERY, IT APPEARS TO GENERATE HYDROGEN & ELECTRICITY FROM SOLAR ENERGY.
★ WORK ON ORGANIC CELLS. THESE COULD BE THE CHEAPEST OF ALL.

FACTS

★ THE SUN GENERATES ENERGY BY NUCLEAR FUSION REACTIONS IN ITS INTERIOR. THESE CAUSE IT TO LOSE FOUR MILLION TONS OF MATTER PER SECOND.

★ IF ONLY 1% OF THE SOLAR ENERY REACHING THE EARTH'S SURFACE COULD BE UTILISED WITH AN EFFICIENCY OF 5%, THE WHOLE OF THE EARTH'S POPULATION COULD ACHIEVE THE SAME ENERGY CONSUMPTION AS THE RICHEST PARTS OF THE WORLD.

HOW TO MAKE A SOLAR HOT WATER SYSTEM

VENT

TANK

HOT WATER

RADIATOR

COLD WATER

CIRCULATION TAP

THE SIMPLEST COLLECTORS ARE OLD DOMESTIC CENTRAL HEATING RADIATORS, PAINTED MATT BLACK. THESE ARE NOT QUITE AS EFFICIENT AS GLASS/METAL SANDWICHES, BUT THEY AVOID THE PROBLEMS OF WATER-TIGHT JOINTS. THE TANK MUST BE ABOVE THE PANEL TO MAKE THE WATER CIRCULATE BY NATURAL CONVECTION. ORDINARY GARDEN HOSE CAN BE USED TO JOIN COLLECTOR TO TANK. TANK SHOULD BE WELL INSULATED. FURTHER DETAILS CAN BE FOUND IN 'SURVIVAL SCRAPBOOK 5, ENERGY' (UNICORN BOOKS).

☆ SPEECH ☆
COMMUNICATIVE HUMAN NOISES ISSUING FROM MOUTHS

VOCAL CORDS
THE VOCAL CORDS VIBRATE AT DIFFERENT SPEEDS TO GIVE A SCALE OF MUSICAL NOTES. SPEECH WHICH DOES NOT USE VOCAL CORDS COMES OUT AS A WHISPER. MEN HAVE LOWER VOICES THAN WOMEN BECAUSE THEIR VOCAL CORDS ARE 50% LONGER & VIBRATE MORE SLOWLY.

VOCAL CORDS

VOWELS
THE SPACES IN FRONT OF & BEHIND THE TONGUE RESONATE AT TWO DIFFERENT FREQUENCIES ACCORDING TO THEIR SIZE (LIKE ORGAN PIPES). THESE DOUBLE RESONANCES MAKE THE COMPLICATED WAVE FORMS OF THE VOWELS.

CONSONANTS
CONSONANTS ARE MORE COMPLICATED TO SPEAK THAN VOWELS. THE NOSE IS USED FOR N, M, & NG. (EX) PLOSIVE BURSTS OF AIR ARE USED FOR P, B, T, D, K & G.

HOTTENTOTS SPEAK WHILE INHALING, MAKING EXPLOSIVE CLICKING NOISES WITH THEIR TONGUES.

IMITATION
SCIENTISTS HAVE BEEN SURPRISED TO DISCOVER THAT THE MOUTH MOVEMENTS OF PARENTS IN SPEAKING ARE IMITATED BY ONE-DAY-OLD BABIES, ALTHOUGH THEY DO NOT LEARN TO SPEAK FOR ALMOST 2 YEARS.

FAST TALKING
THE FASTEST SPEAKING RECORDED IN BRITAIN WAS A COMMENTARY ON A GREYHOUND RACE BY RAYMOND GLENDENNING (176 WORDS IN 30 SECONDS).

SYNTHESIS
COMPUTER VOICE SYNTHESISERS GENERATE 64 SOUNDS CALLED PHONEMES. THE MEMORY STORES WORDS AS SEQUENCES OF THESE PHONEMES. A SINGLE MODERN CHIP CAN STORE & SPEAK ABOUT 150 WORDS.

VISUALS v VERBALS
98% OF ADULTS LISTENING TO THE SOUND 'BA' WHILE WATCHING A VIDEO OF LIPS MOUTHING 'GA' ARE CONVINCED THEY HEAR THE SOUND 'DA'. THIS ILLUSION WORKS WITH OTHER SOUNDS & IS THOUGHT TO BE CAUSED BY THE BRAIN MAKING A GUESS, COMPROMISING THE INFORMATION RECEIVED.

COMPETENT MALEVOLENCE
A RECENT US STUDY ON PUBLIC SPEAKING HAS FOUND THAT THE FASTER THE SPEECH, THE MORE COMPETENT BUT THE LESS BENEVOLENT THE SPEAKER IS JUDGED TO BE.

SPEECH

ANALYSIS
COMPUTER VOICE RECOGNITION IS STILL PRIMITIVE. AT THE MOMENT THE MOST ADVANCED SYSTEM IS AN IBM MACHINE WHICH CAN CONVERT UP TO 1,000 WORDS INTO PRINT. UNFORTUNATELY IT TAKES OVER 100 MINUTES TO TRANSCRIBE A SENTENCE SPOKEN IN 30 SECONDS.

ANIMAL IGNORANCE
THE DIFFICULTY ANIMALS HAVE IN COMPREHENDING HUMAN SPEECH ARISES PARTLY BECAUSE THEY CAN HEAR MUCH HIGHER & LOWER NOTES THAN HUMANS. AS THEIR SOUND DETECTING NERVES ARE SPREAD OVER A WIDER RANGE THERE ARE FEWER AT SPEECH FREQUENCIES. THIS MAY PREVENT THEIR HEARING THE SUBTLE DIFFERENCES BETWEEN VOWELS ETC.

HOW TO STOP YOUR NOSE GOING RED
RUB YOUR EARS VIGOROUSLY & THE BLOOD SHOULD RUSH FROM YOUR NOSE TO THE EARS.

☆ SPICES ☆
PUNGENT & AROMATIC VEGETABLE SUBSTANCES

SAFFRON
SAFFRON IS MADE FROM THE STIGMAS OF THE FLOWERS OF A PARTICULAR TYPE OF CROCUS. IT USED TO BE GROWN IN ENGLAND (PRINCIPALLY ROUND SAFFRON WALDEN) BUT SINCE 11,000 STIGMAS HAVE TO BE PICKED FOR EACH OUNCE OF SAFFRON, IT BECAME UNECONOMIC AS LABOUR COSTS GREW & IS NOW THE MOST EXPENSIVE SPICE. HOWEVER THE ROMANS HAD SLAVES & USED IT LAVISHLY, EVEN PUTTING IT IN THEIR PUBLIC BATHS TO MAKE THE WATER YELLOW.

MUSTARD
MUSTARD COMES FROM THE SEEDS OF A RATHER WEEDY MEMBER OF THE CABBAGE FAMILY. IT IS SAID TO HAVE FIRST BEEN PLANTED IN AMERICA, BUT NOT AS A SPICE. SOME EXPLORING SPANISH MISSIONARIES CAST IT ALONG THEIR TRAIL, SO THEY COULD RETRACE THEIR STEPS THE NEXT SPRING BY FOLLOWING ITS BRIGHT YELLOW FLOWERS.

NUTMEG & MACE
BOTH NUTMEG & MACE COME FROM THE FRUIT OF THE TROPICAL NUTMEG TREE. THE FRUIT'S SKIN IS THROWN AWAY. THE FLESHY INSIDE IS MACE (WHEN DRIED) & THE KERNEL IS THE NUTMEG. WHEN NUTMEG WAS RARE & VALUABLE PEDLARS OFTEN CARVED IMITATION NUTMEGS OUT OF WOOD, DIPPED THEM IN NUTMEG OIL TO MAKE THEM SMELL & SOLD THEM AS REAL NUTMEGS.

VANILLA
VANILLA COMES FROM THE SEED PODS OF A MEXICAN ORCHID. IT WAS FIRST INTRODUCED TO THE WEST AS AN INGREDIENT OF AN AZTEC CHOCOLATE-BASED DRINK WHICH THE SPANISH EAGERLY EXPORTED. THE FIRST RECORD OF ANYONE ATTEMPTING TO TRY IT FOR FLAVOURING OTHER FOODS IS IN ENGLAND BY ELIZABETH I's SURGEON.

CINNAMON
CINNAMON COMES FROM THE BARK OF THE CINNAMON TREE. THE ARABS HAD A MONOPOLY IN THE CINNAMON TRADE & KEPT ITS SOURCE A CLOSE SECRET. THEY TOLD HERODOTUS, THE GREEK HISTORIAN, THAT CINNAMON TREES ONLY GREW ON THE SIDE OF ONE VERY STEEP CLIFF & CONTAINED THE NESTS OF SOME ENORMOUS FIERCE BIRDS. TO GET THE CINNAMON THEY SAID THAT THEY TOOK LARGE QUANTITIES OF MEAT TO THE BOTTOM OF THE CLIFF & THEN HASTILY RETIRED. THE GREEDY BIRDS WOULD THEN LOAD THEIR NESTS WITH SO MUCH MEAT THAT THE TREE WOULD BREAK & FALL TO THE GROUND WHERE THE ARABS COULD...

PEPPER – BLACK & WHITE
PEPPER COMES FROM THE DRIED BERRIES OF THE PEPPER VINE. WHITE PEPPER IS MADE BY PICKING THE BERRIES WHILE STILL SOFT & RUBBING OFF THE OUTER LAYERS BEFORE DRYING. BLACK PEPPER IS MADE USING THE WHOLE BERRY, PICKING IT LATER WHEN IT HAS GONE HARD. PEPPER INDIRECTLY CAUSED THE DISCOVERY OF AMERICA, SINCE COLUMBUS'S VOYAGE WAS THE SEARCH FOR A CHEAPER SOURCE OF PEPPER.

CLOVES
CLOVES ARE THE DRIED FLOWERS OF THE CLOVE TREE PICKED BEFORE THE BUDS HAVE OPENED.

HOW TO MAKE AN ALUMINIUM DAISY CHAIN
COLLECT ALUMINIUM RING-PULL CAN TOPS (ON ALL TINNED BEERS & SOFT DRINKS). JOIN TO EACH OTHER AS SHOWN (LEFT) TO MAKE NECKLACES, BRACELETS ETC.

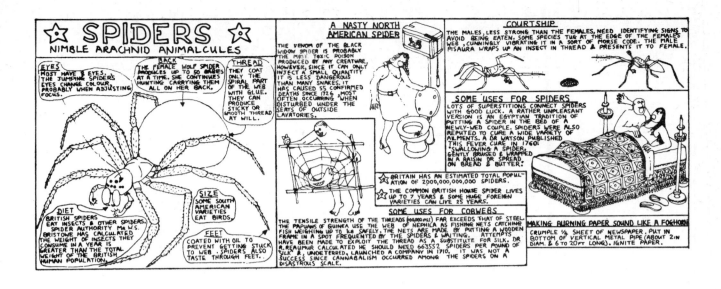

☆ SPIDERS ☆
NIMBLE ARACHNID ANIMALCULES

EYES
MOST HAVE 8 EYES. THE JUMPING SPIDER'S EYES CHANGE COLOUR, PROBABLY WHEN ADJUSTING FOCUS.

BACK
THE FEMALE WOLF SPIDER PRODUCES UP TO 50 BABIES AT A TIME. SHE CONTINUES HUNTING, CARRYING THEM ALL ON HER BACK.

THREAD
THEY COAT ONLY THE SPIRAL PART OF THE WEB WITH GLUE. THEY CAN PRODUCE STICKY OR SMOOTH THREAD AT WILL.

DIET
BRITISH SPIDERS EAT INSECTS & OTHER SPIDERS. SPIDER AUTHORITY Mr W.S. BRISTOWE HAS CALCULATED THE WEIGHT OF INSECTS THEY CONSUME IN A YEAR IS GREATER THAN THE TOTAL WEIGHT OF THE BRITISH HUMAN POPULATION.

SIZE
SOME SOUTH AMERICAN VARIETIES EAT BIRDS.

FEET
COATED WITH OIL TO PREVENT GETTING STUCK TO WEB. SPIDERS ALSO TASTE THROUGH FEET.

A NASTY NORTH AMERICAN SPIDER
THE VENOM OF THE BLACK WIDOW SPIDER IS PROBABLY THE MOST TOXIC POISON PRODUCED BY ANY CREATURE. HOWEVER, SINCE IT CAN ONLY INJECT A SMALL QUANTITY IT IS LESS DANGEROUS THAN MANY SNAKES. IT HAS CAUSED 55 CONFIRMED DEATHS SINCE 1726, MOST OFTEN OCCURRING WHEN DISTURBED UNDER THE SEATS OF OUTSIDE LAVATORIES.

COURTSHIP
THE MALES, LESS STRONG THAN THE FEMALES, NEED IDENTIFYING SIGNS TO AVOID BEING EATEN. SOME SPECIES TUG AT THE EDGE OF THE FEMALE'S WEB, CUNNINGLY VIBRATING IT IN A SORT OF MORSE CODE. THE MALE PISAURA WRAPS UP AN INSECT IN THREAD & PRESENTS IT TO FEMALE.

SOME USES FOR SPIDERS
LOTS OF SUPERSTITIONS CONNECT SPIDERS WITH GOOD LUCK. A RATHER UNPLEASANT VERSION IS AN EGYPTIAN TRADITION OF PUTTING A SPIDER IN THE BED OF A NEWLY-WED COUPLE. SPIDERS WERE ALSO REPUTED TO CURE A WIDE VARIETY OF AILMENTS. A DR WATSON PUBLISHED THIS FEVER CURE IN 1760: "SWALLOWING A SPIDER, GENTLY BRUISED & WRAPPED IN A RAISIN OR SPREAD ON BREAD & BUTTER."

☆ BRITAIN HAS AN ESTIMATED TOTAL POPULATION OF 2,000,000,000,000 SPIDERS.
☆ THE COMMON BRITISH HOUSE SPIDER LIVES UP TO 7 YEARS & SOME HUGE FOREIGN VARIETIES CAN LIVE 25 YEARS.

SOME USES FOR COBWEBS
THE TENSILE STRENGTH OF THE THREADS (60,000 psi) FAR EXCEEDS THAT OF STEEL. THE PAPUANS OF GUINEA USE THE WEB OF NEPHILA AS FISHING NETS CATCHING FISH WEIGHING UP TO 1lb SAFELY. THE NETS ARE MADE BY PUTTING A WOODEN FRAME IN A SPOT FREQUENTED BY THE SPIDERS & WAITING. ATTEMPTS HAVE BEEN MADE TO EXPLOIT THE THREAD AS A SUBSTITUTE FOR SILK. DR R. REAUMUR CALCULATED HE SHOULD NEED 663552 SPIDERS PER POUND OF SILK & UNDETERRED, LAUNCHED A COMPANY IN 1710. IT WAS NOT A SUCCESS SINCE CANNABALISM OCCURRED AMONG THE SPIDERS ON A DISASTROUS SCALE.

MAKING BURNING PAPER SOUND LIKE A FOGHORN
CRUMPLE ¼ SHEET OF NEWSPAPER. PUT IN BOTTOM OF VERTICAL METAL PIPE (ABOUT 2 in DIAM. & 6 to 20 ft LONG). IGNITE PAPER.

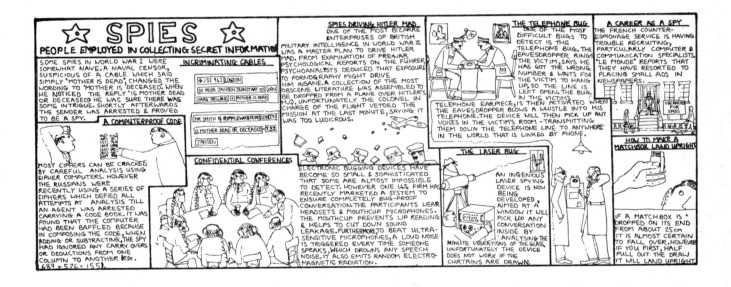

☆ SPIES ☆
PEOPLE EMPLOYED IN COLLECTING SECRET INFORMATION

SOME SPIES IN WORLD WAR I WERE SOMEWHAT NAIVE. A NAVAL CENSOR, SUSPICIOUS OF A CABLE WHICH SAID SIMPLY "MOTHER IS DEAD", CHANGED THE WORDING TO 'MOTHER IS DECEASED'. WHEN HE NOTICED THE REPLY 'IS MOTHER DEAD OR DECEASED' HE WAS SURE THERE WAS SOME INTRIGUE. SHORTLY AFTERWARDS THE SENDER WAS ARRESTED & PROVED TO BE A SPY.

INCRIMINATING CABLES

A COMPUTERPROOF CODE
MOST CIPHERS CAN BE CRACKED BY CAREFUL ANALYSIS USING CIPHER COMPUTERS. HOWEVER THE RUSSIANS WERE RECENTLY USING A SERIES OF CIPHERS WHICH DEFIED ALL ATTEMPTS AT ANALYSIS TILL AN AGENT WAS ARRESTED CARRYING A CODE BOOK. IT WAS FOUND THAT THE COMPUTER HAD BEEN BAFFLED BECAUSE IN COMPOSING THE CODE, WHEN ADDING OR SUBTRACTING, THE SPY HAD IGNORED ANY CARRY OVERS OR DEDUCTIONS FROM ONE COLUMN TO ANOTHER (eg. 689 + 576 = 155).

CONFIDENTIAL CONFERENCES

SPIES DRIVING HITLER MAD
ONE OF THE MOST BIZARRE ENTERPRISES OF BRITISH MILITARY INTELLIGENCE IN WORLD WAR II WAS A MASTER PLAN TO DRIVE HITLER MAD. FROM EXAMINATION OF PRE-WAR PSYCHOLOGICAL REPORTS ON THE FÜHRER PSYCHOANALYSTS DEDUCED THAT EXPOSURE TO PORNOGRAPHY MIGHT DRIVE HIM INSANE. A COLLECTION OF THE MOST OBSCENE LITERATURE WAS ASSEMBLED TO BE DROPPED FROM A PLANE OVER HITLER'S H.Q. UNFORTUNATELY THE COLONEL IN CHARGE OF THE FLIGHT VETOED THE MISSION AT THE LAST MINUTE, SAYING IT WAS TOO LUDICROUS.

ELECTRONIC BUGGING DEVICES HAVE BECOME SO SMALL & SOPHISTICATED THAT SOME ARE ALMOST IMPOSSIBLE TO DETECT. HOWEVER ONE U.S. FIRM HAS RECENTLY MARKETED A SYSTEM TO ENSURE COMPLETELY BUG-PROOF CONVERSATION. THE PARTICIPANTS WEAR HEADSETS & MOUTHCUP MICROPHONES. THE MOUTHCUP PREVENTS LIP READING & HELPS TO CUT DOWN SOUND LEAKAGE. FURTHERMORE TO BEAT ULTRA-SENSITIVE MICROPHONES, A LOUD NOISE IS TRIGGERED EVERY TIME SOMEONE SPEAKS, WHICH DROWNS ANY SPEECH NOISE. IT ALSO EMITS RANDOM ELECTRO-MAGNETIC RADIATION.

THE TELEPHONE BUG
ONE OF THE MOST DIFFICULT BUGS TO DETECT IS THE TELEPHONE BUG. THE EAVESDROPPER RINGS THE VICTIM, SAYS HE HAS GOT THE WRONG NUMBER & WAITS FOR THE VICTIM TO HANG UP, SO THE LINE IS LEFT OPEN. THE BUG, IN THE VICTIM'S TELEPHONE EARPIECE, IS THEN ACTIVATED WHEN THE EAVESDROPPER BLOWS A WHISTLE INTO HIS TELEPHONE. THE DEVICE WILL THEN PICK UP ANY VOICES IN THE VICTIM'S ROOM -TRANSMITTING THEM DOWN THE TELEPHONE LINE TO ANYWHERE IN THE WORLD THAT IS LINKED BY PHONE.

THE LASER BUG
AN INGENIOUS LASER SPYING DEVICE IS NOW BEING DEVELOPED. AIMED AT A WINDOW IT WILL PICK UP ANY CONVERSATION INSIDE BY ANALYSING THE MINUTE VIBRATIONS OF THE GLASS. UNFORTUNATELY THE DEVICE DOES NOT WORK IF THE CURTAINS ARE DRAWN.

A CAREER AS A SPY
THE FRENCH COUNTER-ESPIONAGE SERVICE IS HAVING TROUBLE RECRUITING, PARTICULARLY COMPUTER & COMMUNICATION SPECIALISTS. "LE MONDE" REPORTS THAT THEY HAVE RESORTED TO PLACING SMALL ADS IN NEWSPAPERS.

HOW TO MAKE A MATCHBOX LAND UPRIGHT
IF A MATCHBOX IS DROPPED ON ITS END FROM ABOUT 25 cm IT IS ALMOST CERTAIN TO FALL OVER. HOWEVER IF YOU FIRST, HALF PULL OUT THE DRAW, IT WILL LAND UPRIGHT.

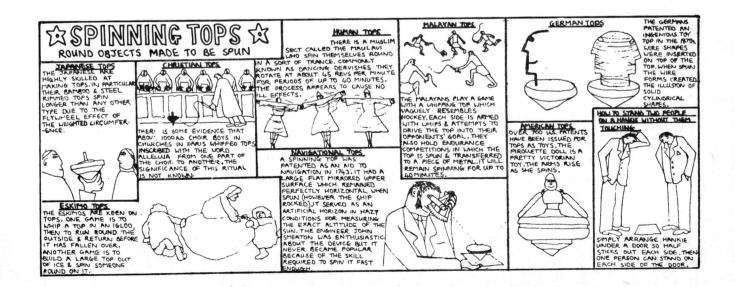

☆ SPINNING TOPS ☆
ROUND OBJECTS MADE TO BE SPUN

JAPANESE TOPS
THE JAPANESE ARE HIGHLY SKILLED AT MAKING TOPS. IN PARTICULAR THEIR BAMBOO & STEEL RIMMED TOPS SPIN LONGER THAN ANY OTHER TYPE DUE TO THE FLYWHEEL EFFECT OF THE WEIGHTED CIRCUMFER-ENCE.

ESKIMO TOPS
THE ESKIMOS ARE KEEN ON TOPS. ONE GAME IS TO WHIP A TOP IN AN IGLOO, THEN TO RUN ROUND THE OUTSIDE & RETURN BEFORE IT HAS FALLEN OVER. ANOTHER GAME IS TO BUILD A LARGE TOP OUT OF ICE & SPIN SOMEONE ROUND ON IT.

CHRISTIAN TOPS
THERE IS SOME EVIDENCE THAT ABOUT 1000 AD CHOIR BOYS IN CHURCHES IN PARIS WHIPPED TOPS INSCRIBED WITH THE WORD ALLELUIA FROM ONE PART OF THE CHOIR TO ANOTHER. THE SIGNIFICANCE OF THIS RITUAL IS NOT KNOWN.

HUMAN TOPS
THERE IS A MUSLIM SECT CALLED THE MAULAVI WHO SPIN THEMSELVES ROUND IN A SORT OF TRANCE. COMMONLY KNOWN AS DANCING DERVISHES THEY ROTATE AT ABOUT 45 REVS PER MINUTE FOR PERIODS OF UP TO 40 MINUTES. THE PROCESS APPEARS TO CAUSE NO ILL EFFECTS.

NAVIGATIONAL TOPS
A SPINNING TOP WAS PATENTED AS AN AID TO NAVIGATION IN 1743. IT HAD A LARGE FLAT MIRRORED UPPER SURFACE WHICH REMAINED PERFECTLY HORIZONTAL WHEN SPUN (HOWEVER THE SHIP ROCKED). IT SERVED AS AN ARTIFICIAL HORIZON IN HAZY CONDITIONS FOR MEASURING THE EXACT ALTITUDE OF THE SUN. THE ENGINEER JOHN SMEATON WAS ENTHUSIASTIC ABOUT THE DEVICE BUT IT NEVER BECAME POPULAR BECAUSE OF THE SKILL REQUIRED TO SPIN IT FAST ENOUGH.

MALAYAN TOPS
THE MALAYANS PLAY A GAME WITH A WHIPPING TOP WHICH VAGUELY RESEMBLES HOCKEY. EACH SIDE IS ARMED WITH WHIPS & ATTEMPTS TO DRIVE THE TOP INTO THEIR OPPONENTS' GOAL. THEY ALSO HOLD ENDURANCE COMPETITIONS IN WHICH THE TOP IS SPUN & TRANSFERRED TO A PIECE OF METAL. IT WILL REMAIN SPINNING FOR UP TO 40 MINUTES.

AMERICAN TOPS
OVER 700 U.S. PATENTS HAVE BEEN ISSUED FOR TOPS AS TOYS. THE PIROUETTE DOLL IS A PRETTY VICTORIAN TOY. THE ARMS RISE AS SHE SPINS.

GERMAN TOPS
THE GERMANS PATENTED AN INGENIOUS TOY TOP IN THE 1870s. WIRE SHAPES WERE INSERTED ON TOP OF THE TOP. WHEN SPUN THE WIRE FORMS CREATED THE ILLUSION OF SOLID CYLINDRICAL SHAPES.

HOW TO STAND TWO PEOPLE ON A HANKIE WITHOUT THEM TOUCHING
SIMPLY ARRANGE HANKIE UNDER A DOOR SO HALF STICKS OUT EACH SIDE. THEN ONE PERSON CAN STAND ON EACH SIDE OF THE DOOR.

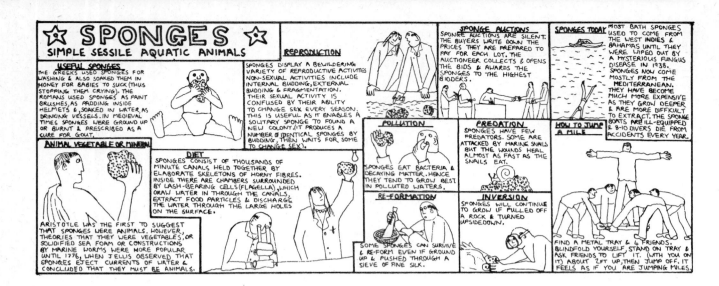

☆ SPONGES ☆
SIMPLE SESSILE AQUATIC ANIMALS

USEFUL SPONGES
THE GREEKS USED SPONGES FOR WASHING & ALSO SOAKED THEM IN HONEY FOR BABIES TO SUCK (THUS STOPPING THEM CRYING). THE ROMANS USED SPONGES AS PAINT BRUSHES, AS PADDING INSIDE HELMETS & SOAKED IN WATER AS DRINKING VESSELS. IN MEDIEVAL TIMES SPONGES WERE GROUND UP OR BURNT & PRESCRIBED AS A CURE FOR GOUT.

ANIMAL VEGETABLE OR MINERAL
ARISTOTLE WAS THE FIRST TO SUGGEST THAT SPONGES WERE ANIMALS. HOWEVER, THEORIES THAT THEY WERE VEGETABLES, OR SOLIDIFIED SEA FOAM OR CONSTRUCTIONS BY MARINE WORMS WERE MORE POPULAR UNTIL 1776, WHEN JELLIS OBSERVED THAT SPONGES EJECT CURRENTS OF WATER & CONCLUDED THAT THEY MUST BE ANIMALS.

DIET
SPONGES CONSIST OF THOUSANDS OF MINUTE CANALS HELD TOGETHER BY ELABORATE SKELETONS OF HORNY FIBRES. INSIDE THERE ARE CHAMBERS SURROUNDED BY LASH-BEARING CELLS (FLAGELLA), WHICH DRAW WATER IN THROUGH THE CANALS, EXTRACT FOOD PARTICLES & DISCHARGE THE WATER THROUGH THE LARGE HOLES ON THE SURFACE.

REPRODUCTION
SPONGES DISPLAY A BEWILDERING VARIETY OF REPRODUCTIVE ACTIVITIES. NON-SEXUAL ACTIVITIES INCLUDE INTERNAL BUDDING, EXTERNAL BUDDING & FRAGMENTATION. THEIR SEXUAL ACTIVITY IS CONFUSED BY THEIR ABILITY TO CHANGE SEX EVERY SEASON. THIS IS USEFUL AS IT ENABLES A SOLITARY SPONGE TO FOUND A NEW COLONY. (IT PRODUCES A NUMBER OF IDENTICAL SPONGES BY BUDDING, THEN WAITS FOR SOME TO CHANGE SEX).

SPONGE AUCTIONS
SPONGE AUCTIONS ARE SILENT. THE BUYERS WRITE DOWN THE PRICES THEY ARE PREPARED TO PAY FOR EACH LOT. THE AUCTIONEER COLLECTS & OPENS THE BIDS & AWARDS THE SPONGES TO THE HIGHEST BIDDERS.

POLLUTION
SPONGES EAT BACTERIA & DECAYING MATTER. HENCE THEY TEND TO GROW BEST IN POLLUTED WATERS.

RE-FORMATION
SOME SPONGES CAN SURVIVE & RE-FORM EVEN IF GROUND UP & PUSHED THROUGH A SIEVE OF FINE SILK.

PREDATION
SPONGES HAVE FEW PREDATORS. SOME ARE ATTACKED BY MARINE SNAILS BUT THE WOUNDS HEAL ALMOST AS FAST AS THE SNAILS EAT.

INVERSION
SPONGES WILL CONTINUE TO GROW IF PULLED OFF A ROCK & TURNED UPSIDEDOWN.

SPONGES TODAY
MOST BATH SPONGES USED TO COME FROM THE WEST INDIES & BAHAMAS UNTIL THEY WERE WIPED OUT BY A MYSTERIOUS FUNGUS DISEASE IN 1938. SPONGES NOW COME MOSTLY FROM THE MEDITERRANEAN. THEY HAVE BECOME MUCH MORE EXPENSIVE AS THEY GROW DEEPER & ARE MORE DIFFICULT TO EXTRACT. THE SPONGE BOATS ARE ILL-EQUIPPED & 8-10 DIVERS DIE FROM ACCIDENTS EVERY YEAR.

HOW TO JUMP A MILE
FIND A METAL TRAY & 4 FRIENDS. BLINDFOLD YOURSELF, STAND ON TRAY & ASK FRIENDS TO LIFT IT. (WITH YOU ON IT) ABOUT 2FT UP, THEN JUMP OFF. IT FEELS AS IF YOU ARE JUMPING MILES.

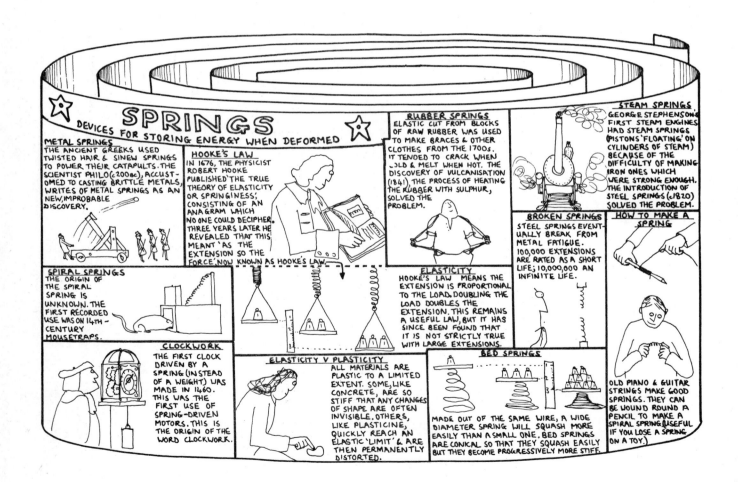

SPRINGS
DEVICES FOR STORING ENERGY WHEN DEFORMED

METAL SPRINGS
THE ANCIENT GREEKS USED TWISTED HAIR & SINEW SPRINGS TO POWER THEIR CATAPULTS. THE SCIENTIST PHILO (c200BC), ACCUSTOMED TO CASTING BRITTLE METALS, WRITES OF METAL SPRINGS AS AN NEW, IMPROBABLE DISCOVERY.

SPIRAL SPRINGS
THE ORIGIN OF THE SPIRAL SPRING IS UNKNOWN. THE FIRST RECORDED USE WAS ON 14TH-CENTURY MOUSETRAPS.

CLOCKWORK
THE FIRST CLOCK DRIVEN BY A SPRING (INSTEAD OF A WEIGHT) WAS MADE IN 1460. THIS WAS THE FIRST USE OF SPRING-DRIVEN MOTORS. THIS IS THE ORIGIN OF THE WORD CLOCKWORK.

HOOKE'S LAW
IN 1676, THE PHYSICIST ROBERT HOOKE PUBLISHED THE TRUE THEORY OF ELASTICITY OR SPRINGINESS, CONSISTING OF AN ANAGRAM WHICH NO ONE COULD DECIPHER. THREE YEARS LATER HE REVEALED THAT THIS MEANT 'AS THE EXTENSION SO THE FORCE' NOW KNOWN AS HOOKE'S LAW.

ELASTICITY V PLASTICITY
ALL MATERIALS ARE PLASTIC TO A LIMITED EXTENT. SOME, LIKE CONCRETE, ARE SO STIFF THAT ANY CHANGES OF SHAPE ARE OFTEN INVISIBLE. OTHERS, LIKE PLASTICINE, QUICKLY REACH AN ELASTIC 'LIMIT' & ARE THEN PERMANENTLY DISTORTED.

RUBBER SPRINGS
ELASTIC CUT FROM BLOCKS OF RAW RUBBER WAS USED TO MAKE BRACES & OTHER CLOTHES FROM THE 1700s. IT TENDED TO CRACK WHEN OLD & MELT WHEN HOT. THE DISCOVERY OF VULCANISATION (1841) THE PROCESS OF HEATING THE RUBBER WITH SULPHUR, SOLVED THE PROBLEM.

ELASTICITY
HOOKE'S LAW MEANS THE EXTENSION IS PROPORTIONAL TO THE LOAD. DOUBLING THE LOAD DOUBLES THE EXTENSION. THIS REMAINS A USEFUL LAW, BUT IT HAS SINCE BEEN FOUND THAT IT IS NOT STRICTLY TRUE WITH LARGE EXTENSIONS.

BED SPRINGS
MADE OUT OF THE SAME WIRE, A WIDE DIAMETER SPRING WILL SQUASH MORE EASILY THAN A SMALL ONE. BED SPRINGS ARE CONICAL SO THAT THEY SQUASH EASILY BUT THEY BECOME PROGRESSIVELY MORE STIFF.

STEAM SPRINGS
GEORGE STEPHENSON'S FIRST STEAM ENGINES HAD STEAM SPRINGS (PISTONS 'FLOATING' ON CYLINDERS OF STEAM) BECAUSE OF THE DIFFICULTY OF MAKING IRON ONES WHICH WERE STRONG ENOUGH. THE INTRODUCTION OF STEEL SPRINGS (c1820) SOLVED THE PROBLEM.

BROKEN SPRINGS
STEEL SPRINGS EVENTUALLY BREAK FROM METAL FATIGUE. 100,000 EXTENSIONS ARE RATED AS A SHORT LIFE; 10,000,000 AN INFINITE LIFE.

HOW TO MAKE A SPRING
OLD PIANO & GUITAR STRINGS MAKE GOOD SPRINGS. THEY CAN BE WOUND ROUND A PENCIL TO MAKE A SPIRAL SPRING (USEFUL IF YOU LOSE A SPRING ON A TOY.)

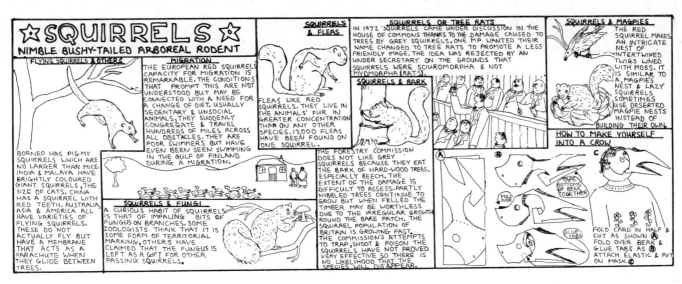

☆ SQUIRRELS ☆
NIMBLE BUSHY-TAILED ARBOREAL RODENT

FLYING SQUIRRELS & OTHERS

BORNEO HAS PIGMY SQUIRRELS WHICH ARE NO LARGER THAN MICE. INDIA & MALAYA HAVE BRIGHTLY COLOURED GIANT SQUIRRELS, THE SIZE OF CATS. CHINA HAS A SQUIRREL WITH RED TEETH. AUSTRALIA, ASIA & AMERICA ALL HAVE VARIETIES OF FLYING SQUIRRELS. THESE DO NOT ACTUALLY FLY BUT HAVE A MEMBRANE THAT ACTS AS A PARACHUTE WHEN THEY GLIDE BETWEEN TREES.

MIGRATION

THE EUROPEAN RED SQUIRRELS CAPACITY FOR MIGRATION IS REMARKABLE. THE CONDITIONS THAT PROMPT THIS ARE NOT UNDERSTOOD BUT MAY BE CONNECTED WITH A NEED FOR A CHANGE OF DIET. USUALLY SEDENTARY & UNSOCIAL ANIMALS, THEY SUDDENLY CONGREGATE & TRAVEL HUNDREDS OF MILES ACROSS ALL OBSTACLES. THEY ARE POOR SWIMMERS BUT HAVE EVEN BEEN SEEN SWIMMING IN THE GULF OF FINLAND DURING A MIGRATION.

SQUIRRELS & FUNGI

A CURIOUS HABIT OF SQUIRRELS IS THAT OF IMPALING BITS OF FUNGUS ON BRANCHES. SOME ZOOLOGISTS THINK THAT IT IS SOME FORM OF TERRITORIAL MARKING, OTHERS HAVE CLAIMED THAT THE FUNGUS IS LEFT AS A GIFT FOR OTHER PASSING SQUIRRELS.

SQUIRRELS & FLEAS

FLEAS LIKE RED SQUIRRELS. THEY LIVE IN THE ANIMALS' FUR IN GREATER CONCENTRATION THAN ON ANY OTHER SPECIES. 13,000 FLEAS HAVE BEEN FOUND ON ONE SQUIRREL.

SQUIRRELS & BARK

THE FORESTRY COMMISSION DOES NOT LIKE GREY SQUIRRELS BECAUSE THEY EAT THE BARK OF HARD-WOOD TREES, ESPECIALLY BEECH. THE EXTENT OF THE DAMAGE IS DIFFICULT TO ASSESS. PARTLY NIBBLED TREES CONTINUE TO GROW BUT WHEN FELLED THE TIMBER MAY BE WORTHLESS DUE TO THE IRREGULAR GROWTH ROUND THE BARE PATCH. THE SQUIRREL POPULATION OF BRITAIN IS GROWING FAST. THE COMMISSION'S ATTEMPTS TO TRAP, SHOOT & POISON THE SQUIRRELS HAVE NOT PROVED VERY EFFECTIVE SO THERE IS NO LIKELIHOOD THAT THE SPECIES WILL DISAPPEAR.

SQUIRRELS OR TREE RATS

IN 1972 'SQUIRRELS' CAME UNDER DISCUSSION IN THE HOUSE OF COMMONS THANKS TO THE DAMAGE CAUSED TO TREES BY GREY SQUIRRELS. ONE MP WANTED THEIR NAME CHANGED TO TREE RATS TO PROMOTE A LESS FRIENDLY IMAGE. THE IDEA WAS REJECTED BY AN UNDER SECRETARY ON THE GROUNDS THAT SQUIRRELS WERE SCIUROMORPHA & NOT MYOMORPHA (RATS).

SQUIRRELS & MAGPIES

THE RED SQUIRREL MAKES AN INTRICATE NEST OF INTERTWINED TWIGS LINED WITH MOSS. IT IS SIMILAR TO A MAGPIE'S NEST & LAZY SQUIRRELS SOMETIMES USE DESERTED MAGPIE NESTS INSTEAD OF BUILDING THEIR OWN.

HOW TO MAKE YOURSELF INTO A CROW

TAPE BOTTOMS OF BEAK TOGETHER

FOLD OVER

GLUE TABS

FOLD CARD IN HALF & CUT AS SHOWN (A) FOLD OVER BEAK & GLUE TABS AS (B) ATTACH ELASTIC & PUT ON MASK (C)

☆ STAMPS ☆
GUMMED LABELS INDICATING PAYMENT OF POSTAGE

FALSE START

THE FIRST ADHESIVE POSTAGE STAMPS WERE PRODUCED IN FRANCE IN 1653, ON A SUGGESTION MADE BY A MISTRESS OF MR FOUQUET, THE THEN GOVERNMENT INSPECTOR OF FINANCES. THEY WERE ABRUPTLY WITHDRAWN WHEN HE LOST HIS JOB A FEW MONTHS LATER.

FACES

QUEEN VICTORIA'S FACE WAS CHOSEN FOR THE FIRST STAMP, PARTLY BECAUSE A FACE IS DIFFICULT TO FORGE AS SMALL CHANGES ARE READILY NOTICEABLE.

POSTAGE ONE PENNY

POSTAGE ONE PENNY

GUM

AS EARLY AS 1852, A COMMONS SELECT COMMITTEE INVESTIGATED THE DANGER TO HEALTH FROM LICKING STAMPS. HOWEVER, THE GUM WAS PRONOUNCED HARMLESS.

TYPEWRITTEN

TYPEWRITTEN STAMPS HAVE BEEN USED IN UGANDA, THAILAND, ALBANIA & COLOMBIA. TYPEWRITERS WERE SUFFICIENTLY RARE UNTIL THE 1920s TO MAKE FORGERY UNLIKELY.

CANCELLATION

INKS WHICH RUN OR CHANGE COLOUR WHEN WETTED HAVE BEEN USED IN THE PAST TO STOP PEOPLE WASHING OFF CANCELLATION MARKS, BUT IMPROVEMENTS IN THE COMPOSITION OF THE CANCELLATION INK HAVE NOW MADE THIS UNNECESSARY.

REDONDA

REDONDA, AN UNINHABITED ISLAND IN THE CARIBBEAN, HAS HAD ITS OWN STAMPS SINCE 1979. IT IS OWNED BY ANTIGUA, WHICH ISSUED THE STAMPS INTENDING TO DEVELOP A TOURIST INDUSTRY.

ERRORS

NOT ONLY PRINTING ERRORS OCCUR ON STAMPS. ERRORS IN INSCRIPTIONS INCLUDE: ARAB GOLF (GULF) OMAN 1970; WALTER LILY (WATER LILY), COOK ISLANDS 1967.

BHUTAN

BHUTAN HAS PRODUCED: 3-D STAMPS (SIMILAR TO 3-D POSTCARDS); STAMPS WITH PLASTIC MOULDINGS OF SCULPTURAL RELIEFS; STEEL STAMPS (TO CELEBRATE ANNIVERSARY OF THE STEEL INDUSTRY) & MUSICAL STAMPS (MINIATURE RECORDS WHICH PLAYED THE NATIONAL ANTHEM).

DEVALUATION

GOVERNMENTS HAVE OCCASIONALLY MASS-PRODUCED ERRORS TO PREVENT RARITIES MAKING ANYBODY'S FORTUNE. HOWEVER, IN 1962 A US COLLECTOR SUCCESSFULLY OBTAINED AN INJUNCTION IN THE SUPREME COURT TO STOP THE POST OFFICE 'DEVALUING' A RARITY HE OWNED.

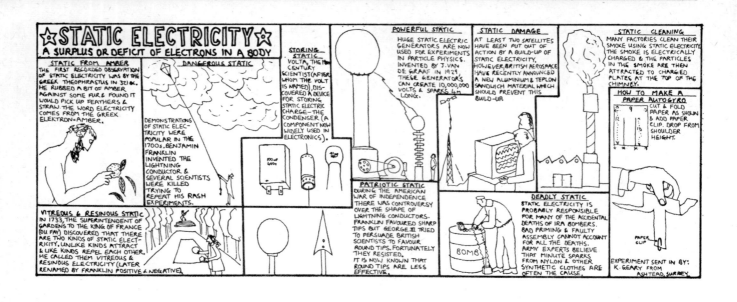

☆ STATIC ELECTRICITY ☆
A SURPLUS OR DEFICIT OF ELECTRONS IN A BODY

STATIC FROM AMBER
THE FIRST RECORDED OBSERVATION OF STATIC ELECTRICITY WAS BY THE GREEK THEOPHRASTUS IN 321 BC. HE RUBBED A BIT OF AMBER AGAINST SOME FUR & FOUND IT WOULD PICK UP FEATHERS & STRAW. THE WORD ELECTRICITY COMES FROM THE GREEK ELEKTRON=AMBER.

DANGEROUS STATIC
DEMONSTRATIONS OF STATIC ELECTRICITY WERE POPULAR IN THE 1700s. BENJAMIN FRANKLIN INVENTED THE LIGHTNING CONDUCTOR & SEVERAL SCIENTISTS WERE KILLED TRYING TO REPEAT HIS RASH EXPERIMENTS.

VITREOUS & RESINOUS STATIC
IN 1733, THE SUPERINTENDENT OF GARDENS TO THE KING OF FRANCE (DU FAY) DISCOVERED THAT THERE ARE TWO KINDS OF STATIC ELECTRICITY, UNLIKE KINDS ATTRACT & LIKE KINDS REPEL EACH OTHER. HE CALLED THEM VITREOUS & RESINOUS ELECTRICITY (LATER RENAMED BY FRANKLIN POSITIVE & NEGATIVE).

STORING STATIC
VOLTA, THE 18th CENTURY SCIENTIST (AFTER WHOM THE VOLT IS NAMED), DISCOVERED A DEVICE FOR STORING STATIC ELECTRIC CHARGE—THE CONDENSER (A COMPONENT NOW WIDELY USED IN ELECTRONICS).

PATRIOTIC STATIC
DURING THE AMERICAN WAR OF INDEPENDENCE THERE WAS CONTROVERSY OVER THE SHAPE OF LIGHTNING CONDUCTORS. FRANKLIN FAVOURED SHARP TIPS BUT GEORGE III TRIED TO PERSUADE BRITISH SCIENTISTS TO FAVOUR ROUND TIPS. FORTUNATELY THEY RESISTED. IT IS NOW KNOWN THAT ROUND TIPS ARE LESS EFFECTIVE.

POWERFUL STATIC
HUGE STATIC ELECTRIC GENERATORS ARE NOW USED FOR EXPERIMENTS IN PARTICLE PHYSICS. INVENTED BY J. VAN DE GRAAF IN 1929, THESE GENERATORS CAN CREATE 10,000,000 VOLTS & SPARKS 4m LONG.

STATIC DAMAGE
AT LEAST TWO SATELLITES HAVE BEEN PUT OUT OF ACTION BY A BUILD-UP OF STATIC ELECTRICITY. HOWEVER, BRITISH AEROSPACE HAVE RECENTLY ANNOUNCED A NEW ALUMINIUM & TEFLON SANDWICH MATERIAL WHICH SHOULD PREVENT THIS BUILD-UP.

DEADLY STATIC
STATIC ELECTRICITY IS PROBABLY RESPONSIBLE FOR MANY OF THE ACCIDENTAL DEATHS OF IRA BOMBERS. BAD PRIMING & FAULTY ASSEMBLY CANNOT ACCOUNT FOR ALL THE DEATHS. ARMY EXPERTS BELIEVE THAT MINUTE SPARKS FROM NYLON & OTHER SYNTHETIC CLOTHES ARE OFTEN THE CAUSE.

STATIC CLEANING
MANY FACTORIES CLEAN THEIR SMOKE USING STATIC ELECTRICITY. THE SMOKE IS ELECTRICALLY CHARGED & THE PARTICLES IN THE SMOKE ARE THEN ATTRACTED TO CHARGED PLATES AT THE TOP OF THE CHIMNEY.

HOW TO MAKE A PAPER AUTOGYRO
CUT & FOLD PAPER AS SHOWN & ADD PAPER CLIP. DROP FROM SHOULDER HEIGHT.

EXPERIMENT SENT IN BY: K. GEARY FROM ASHTEAD, SURREY.

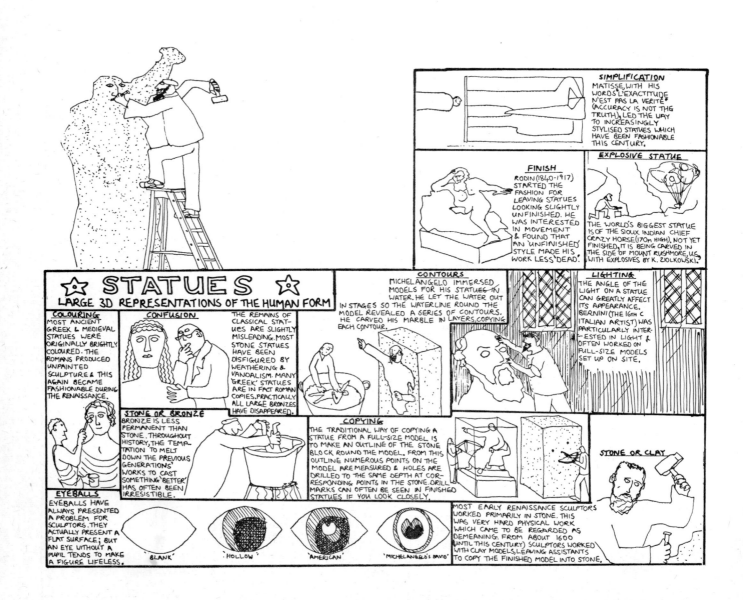

☆ STATUES ☆
LARGE 3D REPRESENTATIONS OF THE HUMAN FORM

COLOURING
MOST ANCIENT GREEK & MEDIEVAL STATUES WERE ORIGINALLY BRIGHTLY COLOURED. THE ROMANS PRODUCED UNPAINTED SCULPTURE & THIS AGAIN BECAME FASHIONABLE DURING THE RENAISSANCE.

CONFUSION
THE REMAINS OF CLASSICAL STATUES ARE SLIGHTLY MISLEADING. MOST STONE STATUES HAVE BEEN DISFIGURED BY WEATHERING & VANDALISM. MANY 'GREEK' STATUES ARE IN FACT ROMAN COPIES. PRACTICALLY ALL LARGE BRONZES HAVE DISAPPEARED.

STONE OR BRONZE
BRONZE IS LESS PERMANENT THAN STONE. THROUGHOUT HISTORY, THE TEMPTATION TO MELT DOWN THE PREVIOUS GENERATIONS' WORKS TO CAST SOMETHING 'BETTER' HAS OFTEN BEEN IRRESISTIBLE.

EYEBALLS
EYEBALLS HAVE ALWAYS PRESENTED A PROBLEM FOR SCULPTORS. THEY ACTUALLY PRESENT A FLAT SURFACE; BUT AN EYE WITHOUT A PUPIL TENDS TO MAKE A FIGURE LIFELESS.

'BLANK'   'HOLLOW'   'AMERICAN'   'MICHELANGELO'S DAVID'

CONTOURS
MICHELANGELO IMMERSED MODELS FOR HIS STATUES IN WATER. HE LET THE WATER OUT IN STAGES SO THE WATERLINE ROUND THE MODEL REVEALED A SERIES OF CONTOURS. HE CARVED HIS MARBLE IN LAYERS, COPYING EACH CONTOUR.

COPYING
THE TRADITIONAL WAY OF COPYING A STATUE FROM A FULL-SIZE MODEL IS TO MAKE AN OUTLINE OF THE STONE BLOCK ROUND THE MODEL. FROM THIS OUTLINE NUMEROUS POINTS ON THE MODEL ARE MEASURED & HOLES ARE DRILLED TO THE SAME DEPTH AT CORRESPONDING POINTS IN THE STONE. DRILL MARKS CAN OFTEN BE SEEN IN FINISHED STATUES IF YOU LOOK CLOSELY.

MOST EARLY RENAISSANCE SCULPTORS WORKED PRIMARILY IN STONE. THIS WAS VERY HARD PHYSICAL WORK WHICH CAME TO BE REGARDED AS DEMEANING. FROM ABOUT 1600 UNTIL THIS CENTURY SCULPTORS WORKED WITH CLAY MODELS, LEAVING ASSISTANTS TO COPY THE FINISHED MODEL INTO STONE.

SIMPLIFICATION
MATISSE, WITH HIS WORDS 'L'EXACTITUDE N'EST PAS LA VÉRITÉ' (ACCURACY IS NOT THE TRUTH), LED THE WAY TO INCREASINGLY STYLISED STATUES WHICH HAVE BEEN FASHIONABLE THIS CENTURY.

FINISH
RODIN (1840-1917) STARTED THE FASHION FOR LEAVING STATUES LOOKING SLIGHTLY UNFINISHED. HE WAS INTERESTED IN MOVEMENT & FOUND THAT AN 'UNFINISHED' STYLE MADE HIS WORK LESS 'DEAD'.

EXPLOSIVE STATUE
THE WORLD'S BIGGEST STATUE IS OF THE SIOUX INDIAN CHIEF CRAZY HORSE (170m HIGH). NOT YET FINISHED, IT IS BEING CARVED IN THE SIDE OF MOUNT RUSHMORE, US, WITH EXPLOSIVES BY K. ZIOLKOWSKI.

LIGHTING
THE ANGLE OF THE LIGHT ON A STATUE CAN GREATLY AFFECT ITS APPEARANCE. BERNINI (THE 16th C ITALIAN ARTIST) WAS PARTICULARLY INTERESTED IN LIGHT & OFTEN WORKED ON FULL-SIZE MODELS SET UP ON SITE.

STONE OR CLAY

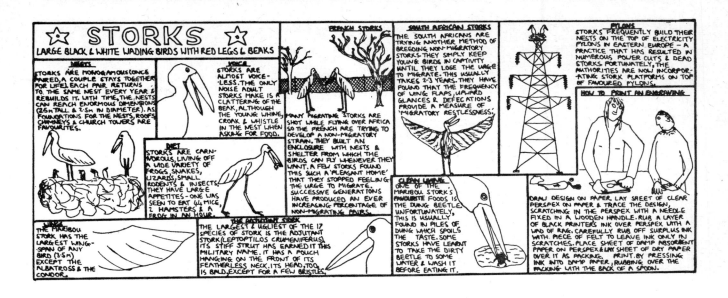

☆ STORKS ☆
LARGE BLACK & WHITE WADING BIRDS WITH RED LEGS & BEAKS

NESTS
STORKS ARE MONOGAMOUS (ONCE PAIRED, A COUPLE STAYS TOGETHER FOR LIFE) & EACH PAIR RETURNS TO THE SAME NEST EVERY YEAR & REBUILDS IT. WITH TIME, THE, THE, NESTS CAN REACH ENORMOUS DIMENSIONS (2.5m TALL & 2.5m IN DIAMETER). AS FOUNDATIONS FOR THE NESTS, ROOFS, CHIMNEYS & CHURCH TOWERS ARE FAVOURITES.

VOICE
STORKS ARE ALMOST VOICE-LESS. THE ONLY NOISE ADULT STORKS MAKE IS A CLATTERING OF THE BEAK, ALTHOUGH THE YOUNG WHINE, CROAK & WHISTLE IN THE NEST WHEN ASKING FOR FOOD.

DIET
STORKS ARE CARNIVOROUS, LIVING OFF A WIDE VARIETY OF FROGS, SNAKES, LIZARDS, SMALL RODENTS & INSECTS. THEY HAVE LARGE APPETITES - ONE WAS SEEN TO EAT 44 MICE, 2 HAMSTERS & A FROG IN AN HOUR.

WINGS
THE MARIBOU STORK HAS THE LARGEST WING-SPAN OF ANY BIRD (3.5m) EXCEPT THE ALBATROSS & THE CONDOR.

THE ADJUTANT STORK
THE LARGEST & UGLIEST OF THE 17 SPECIES OF STORK IS THE ADJUTANT STORK (LEPTOPTILOS CRUMENIFERUS). ITS STIFF STRUT HAS EARNED IT THIS MILITARY NAME. IT HAS A POUCH HANGING ON THE FRONT OF ITS FEATHERLESS NECK. ITS HEAD, TOO, IS BALD, EXCEPT FOR A FEW BRISTLES.

FRENCH STORKS
MANY MIGRATING STORKS ARE SHOT WHILE FLYING OVER AFRICA SO THE FRENCH ARE TRYING TO DEVELOP A NON-MIGRATORY STRAIN. THEY BUILT AN ENCLOSURE WITH NESTS & SHELTER FROM WHICH THE BIRDS CAN FLY WHENEVER THEY WANT. A FEW STORKS FOUND THIS SUCH A 'PLEASANT HOME' THAT THEY STOPPED FEELING THE URGE TO MIGRATE. SUCCESSIVE GENERATIONS HAVE PRODUCED AN EVER INCREASING PERCENTAGE OF NON-MIGRATING PAIRS.

SOUTH AFRICAN STORKS
THE SOUTH AFRICANS ARE TRYING ANOTHER METHOD OF BREEDING NON-MIGRATORY STORKS. THEY SIMPLY KEEP YOUNG BIRDS IN CAPTIVITY UNTIL THEY LOSE THE URGE TO MIGRATE. THIS USUALLY TAKES 2-3 YEARS. THEY HAVE FOUND THAT THE FREQUENCY OF WING FLAPS, UNAIMED GLANCES & DEFECATIONS PROVIDE A MEASURE OF 'MIGRATORY RESTLESSNESS'.

CLEAN LIVING
ONE OF THE MARIBOU STORK'S FAVOURITE FOODS IS THE DUNG BEETLE. UNFORTUNATELY, THIS IS USUALLY FOUND IN PILES OF DUNG WHICH SPOILS THE TASTE. SOME STORKS HAVE LEARNT TO TAKE THE DIRTY BEETLE TO SOME WATER & WASH IT BEFORE EATING IT.

PYLONS
STORKS FREQUENTLY BUILD THEIR NESTS ON THE TOP OF ELECTRICITY PYLONS IN EASTERN EUROPE - A PRACTICE THAT HAS RESULTED IN NUMEROUS POWER CUTS & DEAD STORKS. FORTUNATELY, THE AUTHORITIES ARE NOW INCORPORATING STORK PLATFORMS ON TOP OF FAVOURED PYLONS.

HOW TO PRINT AN ENGRAVING
DRAW DESIGN ON PAPER. LAY SHEET OF CLEAR PERSPEX ON PAPER & TRACE THE DESIGN, SCRATCHING IN THE PERSPEX WITH A NEEDLE FIXED IN A WOODEN HANDLE. RUB A LAYER OF BLACK PRINTER'S INK OVER PERSPEX WITH A WAD OF RAG. CAREFULLY RUB OFF SURPLUS INK WITH PIECE OF FELT TO LEAVE INK ONLY IN SCRATCHES. PLACE SHEET OF DAMP ABSORBENT PAPER ON PERSPEX & LAY SHEET OF DRY PAPER OVER IT AS PACKING. PRINT BY PRESSING INK INTO DAMP PAPER, RUBBING OVER THE PACKING WITH THE BACK OF A SPOON.

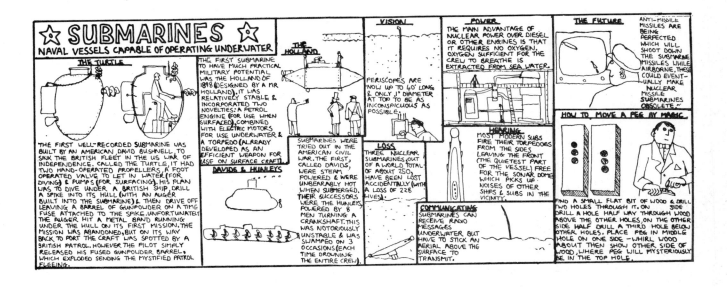

☆ SUBMARINES ☆
NAVAL VESSELS CAPABLE OF OPERATING UNDERWATER

THE TURTLE
THE FIRST WELL-RECORDED SUBMARINE WAS BUILT BY AN AMERICAN, DAVID BUSHNELL, TO SINK THE BRITISH FLEET IN THE US WAR OF INDEPENDENCE. CALLED THE TURTLE, IT HAD TWO HAND-OPERATED PROPELLERS, A FOOT OPERATED VALVE TO LET IN WATER (FOR DIVING) & PUMPS (FOR SURFACING). HIS PLAN WAS TO DIVE UNDER A BRITISH SHIP, DRILL A SPIKE INTO ITS HULL (WITH AN AUGER BUILT INTO THE SUBMARINE) & THEN DRIVE OFF LEAVING A BARREL OF GUNPOWDER ON A TIME FUSE ATTACHED TO THE SPIKE. UNFORTUNATELY THE AUGER HIT A METAL BAND RUNNING UNDER THE HULL ON ITS FIRST MISSION. THE MISSION WAS ABANDONED, BUT ON ITS WAY BACK TO PORT THE CRAFT WAS SPOTTED BY A BRITISH PATROL. HOWEVER, THE PILOT SIMPLY RELEASED HIS FUSED GUNPOWDER BARREL, WHICH EXPLODED SENDING THE MYSTIFIED PATROL FLEEING.

THE HOLLAND
THE FIRST SUBMARINE TO HAVE MUCH PRACTICAL MILITARY POTENTIAL WAS THE HOLLAND OF 1898 (DESIGNED BY A MR HOLLAND). IT WAS RELATIVELY STABLE & INCORPORATED TWO NOVELTIES: A PETROL ENGINE (FOR USE WHEN SURFACED) COMBINED WITH ELECTRIC MOTORS FOR USE UNDERWATER & A TORPEDO (ALREADY DEVELOPED AS AN EFFICIENT WEAPON FOR USE ON SURFACE CRAFT).

DAVIDS & HUNLEYS
SUBMARINES WERE TRIED OUT IN THE AMERICAN CIVIL WAR. THE FIRST, CALLED DAVIDS, WERE STEAM POWERED & WERE UNBEARABLY HOT WHEN SUBMERGED. THEIR SUCCESSORS WERE THE HUNLEYS POWERED BY 8 MEN TURNING A CRANKSHAFT. THIS WAS NOTORIOUSLY UNSTABLE & WAS SWAMPED ON 3 OCCASIONS (EACH TIME DROWNING THE ENTIRE CREW).

VISION
PERISCOPES ARE NOW UP TO 40' LONG & ONLY 1" DIAMETER AT TOP TO BE AS INCONSPICUOUS AS POSSIBLE.

LOSS
THREE NUCLEAR SUBMARINES, OUT OF A WORLD TOTAL OF ABOUT 250, HAVE BEEN LOST ACCIDENTALLY (WITH A LOSS OF 228 LIVES).

COMMUNICATIONS
SUBMARINES CAN RECEIVE RADIO MESSAGES UNDERWATER BUT HAVE TO STICK AN AERIAL ABOVE THE SURFACE TO TRANSMIT.

POWER
THE MAIN ADVANTAGE OF NUCLEAR POWER OVER DIESEL OR OTHER ENGINES IS THAT IT REQUIRES NO OXYGEN. OXYGEN SUFFICIENT FOR THE CREW TO BREATHE IS EXTRACTED FROM SEA WATER.

HEARING
MOST MODERN SUBS FIRE THEIR TORPEDOES FROM THE SIDES LEAVING THE FRONT (THE QUIETEST PART OF THE VESSEL) FREE FOR THE SONAR DOME WHICH PICKS UP NOISES OF OTHER SHIPS & SUBS IN THE VICINITY.

THE FUTURE
ANTI-MISSILE MISSILES ARE BEING PERFECTED WHICH WILL SHOOT DOWN THE SUBMARINE MISSILES WHILE AIRBORNE. THESE COULD EVENTUALLY MAKE NUCLEAR MISSILE SUBMARINES OBSOLETE.

HOW TO MOVE A PEG BY MAGIC
FIND A SMALL FLAT BIT OF WOOD & DRILL TWO HOLES THROUGH IT. ON ONE SIDE DRILL A HOLE HALF WAY THROUGH WOOD ABOVE THE OTHER HOLES, ON THE OTHER SIDE HALF DRILL A THIRD HOLE BELOW OTHER HOLES. PLACE PEG IN MIDDLE HOLE ON ONE SIDE - WHIRL WOOD ABOUT THEN SHOW OTHER SIDE OF WOOD, WHERE PEG WILL MYSTERIOUSLY BE IN THE TOP HOLE.

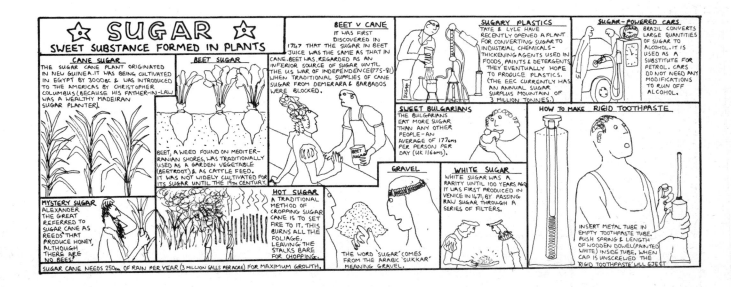

☆ SUGAR ☆
SWEET SUBSTANCE FORMED IN PLANTS

CANE SUGAR
THE SUGAR CANE PLANT ORIGINATED IN NEW GUINEA. IT WAS BEING CULTIVATED IN EGYPT BY 3000BC & WAS INTRODUCED TO THE AMERICAS BY CHRISTOPHER COLUMBUS (BECAUSE HIS FATHER-IN-LAW WAS A WEALTHY MADEIRAN SUGAR PLANTER).

MYSTERY SUGAR
ALEXANDER THE GREAT REFERRED TO SUGAR CANE AS REEDS THAT PRODUCE HONEY, ALTHOUGH THERE ARE NO BEES.

BEET SUGAR
BEET, A WEED FOUND ON MEDITERRANEAN SHORES, WAS TRADITIONALLY USED AS A GARDEN VEGETABLE (BEETROOT) & AS CATTLE FEED. IT WAS NOT WIDELY CULTIVATED FOR ITS SUGAR UNTIL THE 19TH CENTURY.

HOT SUGAR
A TRADITIONAL METHOD OF CROPPING SUGAR CANE IS TO SET FIRE TO IT. THIS BURNS ALL THE FOLIAGE, LEAVING THE STALKS BARE FOR CHOPPING.

BEET v CANE
IT WAS FIRST DISCOVERED IN 1747 THAT THE SUGAR IN BEET JUICE WAS THE SAME AS THAT IN CANE. BEET WAS REGARDED AS AN INFERIOR SOURCE OF SUGAR UNTIL THE US WAR OF INDEPENDENCE (1775-81) WHEN TRADITIONAL SUPPLIES OF CANE SUGAR FROM DEMERARA & BARBADOS WERE BLOCKED.

SWEET BULGARIANS
THE BULGARIANS EAT MORE SUGAR THAN ANY OTHER PEOPLE - AN AVERAGE OF 177gms PER PERSON PER DAY (UK 116gms).

GRAVEL
THE WORD 'SUGAR' COMES FROM THE ARABIC 'SUKKAR' MEANING GRAVEL.

SUGARY PLASTICS
TATE & LYLE HAVE RECENTLY OPENED A PLANT FOR CONVERTING SUGAR TO INDUSTRIAL CHEMICALS - THICKENING AGENTS USED IN FOODS, PAINTS & DETERGENTS. THEY EVENTUALLY HOPE TO PRODUCE PLASTICS. (THE EEC CURRENTLY HAS AN ANNUAL SUGAR SURPLUS MOUNTAIN OF 3 MILLION TONNES.)

WHITE SUGAR
WHITE SUGAR WAS A RARITY UNTIL 100 YEARS AGO. IT WAS FIRST PRODUCED IN VENICE IN 1471, BY PASSING RAW SUGAR THROUGH A SERIES OF FILTERS.

SUGAR-POWERED CARS
BRAZIL CONVERTS LARGE QUANTITIES OF SUGAR TO ALCOHOL. IT IS USED AS A SUBSTITUTE FOR PETROL. CARS DO NOT NEED ANY MODIFICATIONS TO RUN OFF ALCOHOL.

HOW TO MAKE RIGID TOOTHPASTE
INSERT METAL TUBE IN EMPTY TOOTHPASTE TUBE. PUSH SPRING & LENGTH OF WOODEN DOWEL (PAINTED WHITE) INSIDE TUBE. WHEN CAP IS UNSCREWED THE RIGID TOOTHPASTE WILL EJECT.

SUGAR CANE NEEDS 250cm OF RAIN PER YEAR (3 MILLION GALLS PER ACRE) FOR MAXIMUM GROWTH.

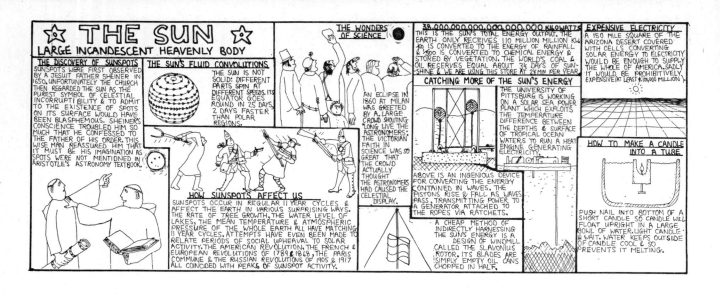

☆ THE SUN ☆
LARGE INCANDESCENT HEAVENLY BODY

THE DISCOVERY OF SUNSPOTS
SUNSPOTS WERE FIRST OBSERVED BY A JESUIT FATHER SHEINER IN 1650. UNFORTUNATELY THE CHURCH THEN REGARDED THE SUN AS THE PUREST SYMBOL OF CELESTIAL INCORRUPTIBILITY & TO ADMIT TO THE EXISTENCE OF SPOTS ON ITS SURFACE WOULD HAVE BEEN BLASPHEMOUS. SHEINER'S CONSCIENCE TROUBLED HIM SO MUCH THAT HE CONFESSED TO THE FATHER OF HIS ORDER. THIS WISE MAN REASSURED HIM THAT IT MUST BE HIS IMAGINATION AS SPOTS WERE NOT MENTIONED IN ARISTOTLE'S ASTRONOMY TEXTBOOK.

THE SUN'S FLUID CONVOLUTIONS
THE SUN IS NOT SOLID: DIFFERENT PARTS SPIN AT DIFFERENT SPEEDS. ITS EQUATOR GOES ROUND IN 25 DAYS, 2 DAYS FASTER THAN POLAR REGIONS.

HOW SUNSPOTS AFFECT US
SUNSPOTS OCCUR IN REGULAR 11 YEAR CYCLES & AFFECT THE EARTH IN VARIOUS SURPRISING WAYS. THE RATE OF TREE GROWTH, THE WATER LEVEL OF LAKES, THE MEAN TEMPERATURE & ATMOSPHERIC PRESSURE OF THE WHOLE EARTH ALL HAVE MATCHING 11 YEAR CYCLES. ATTEMPTS HAVE EVEN BEEN MADE TO RELATE PERIODS OF SOCIAL UPHEAVAL TO SOLAR ACTIVITY. THE AMERICAN REVOLUTION, THE FRENCH & EUROPEAN REVOLUTIONS OF 1789 & 1848, THE PARIS COMMUNE & THE RUSSIAN REVOLUTIONS OF 1905 & 1917 ALL COINCIDED WITH PEAKS OF SUNSPOT ACTIVITY.

THE WONDERS OF SCIENCE
AN ECLIPSE IN 1860 AT MILAN WAS GREETED BY A LARGE CROWD SHOUTING 'LONG LIVE THE ASTRONOMERS'. THE VICTORIAN FAITH IN SCIENCE WAS SO GREAT THAT THE CROWD ACTUALLY THOUGHT THE ASTRONOMERS HAD CAUSED THE CELESTIAL DISPLAY.

38,000,000,000,000,000,000 KILOWATTS
THIS IS THE SUN'S TOTAL ENERGY OUTPUT. THE EARTH ONLY RECEIVES 1/10 MILLION MILLION KW. 1/10 IS CONVERTED TO THE ENERGY OF RAINFALL & 1/500 IS CONVERTED TO CHEMICAL ENERGY & STORED BY VEGETATION. THE WORLD'S COAL & OIL RESERVES EQUAL ABOUT 3½ DAYS OF SUNSHINE & WE ARE USING THIS STORE AT 2½ MIN PER YEAR.

CATCHING MORE OF THE SUN'S ENERGY
THE UNIVERSITY OF PITTSBURG IS WORKING ON A SOLAR SEA POWER PLANT WHICH EXPLOITS THE TEMPERATURE DIFFERENCE BETWEEN THE DEPTHS & SURFACE OF TROPICAL OCEAN WATERS TO RUN A HEAT ENGINE GENERATING ELECTRICITY.

ABOVE IS AN INGENIOUS DEVICE FOR CONVERTING THE ENERGY CONTAINED IN WAVES. THE PISTONS RISE & FALL AS WAVES PASS, TRANSMITTING POWER TO A GENERATOR ATTACHED TO THE ROPES VIA RATCHETS.

A CHEAP METHOD OF INDIRECTLY HARNESSING THE SUN'S ENERGY IS A DESIGN OF WINDMILL CALLED THE SLAVONIUS ROTOR. ITS BLADES ARE SIMPLY EMPTY OIL CANS CHOPPED IN HALF.

EXPENSIVE ELECTRICITY
A 150 MILE SQUARE OF THE ARIZONA DESERT COVERED WITH CELLS CONVERTING SOLAR ENERGY TO ELECTRICITY WOULD BE ENOUGH TO SUPPLY THE WHOLE OF AMERICA. SADLY IT WOULD BE PROHIBITIVELY EXPENSIVE (AT LEAST £100,000 MILLION).

HOW TO MAKE A CANDLE INTO A TUBE
PUSH NAIL INTO BOTTOM OF A SHORT CANDLE SO CANDLE WILL FLOAT UPRIGHT IN A LARGE BOWL OF WATER. LIGHT CANDLE & WAIT. WATER KEEPS OUTSIDE OF CANDLE COOL & SO PREVENTS IT MELTING.

☆ SUNDIALS ☆
DEVICE FOR TELLING TIME BY SHADOWS CAST BY THE SUN

OBELISK TIME
THE ANCIENT EGYPTIANS USED OBELISKS, LIKE CLEOPATRA'S NEEDLE, AS SUNDIALS. THE SHADOW FELL ONTO MARKS CUT IN THE PAVEMENT BELOW.

LONG TIME

ARABIC TIME
THE EARLIEST KNOWN SUNDIALS (EGYPTIAN c2000BC) SIMPLY SHOW THE LENGTH OF SHADOWS HENCE THE PHRASE 'LENGTH OF TIME'.

UNEQUAL HOURS
THE ANCIENT EGYPTIANS WERE THE FIRST PEOPLE TO DIVIDE THE DAY INTO A FIXED NUMBER OF HOURS, THE HOUR VARYING IN LENGTH ACCORDING TO THE LENGTH OF THE DAYLIGHT PERIOD.

SUNDIAL ALARM
SOLAR ALARMS, IN WHICH SUNLIGHT PASSING THROUGH A LENS FIRED A SMALL CANNON, WERE POPULAR 18TH CENTURY SCIENTIFIC TOYS.

EQUAL HOURS (1/24 OF A DAY & A NIGHT) WERE AN ARABIC IDEA WHICH CAUGHT ON AFTER THE INVENTION OF MECHANICAL CLOCKS (c1400) THESE CLOCKS COULD NOT EASILY SHOW HOURS WHICH VARIED IN LENGTH.

EQUAL HOURS
SUNDIALS SHOWING 'EQUAL' HOURS FIRST APPEARED IN THE 14TH CENTURY-DESIGNED TO SET THE NEW, BUT RATHER INACCURATE, MECHANICAL CLOCKS.

UNEQUAL DAYS
AS CLOCKS IMPROVED IT WAS FOUND THAT SUNDIALS WERE NOT ALWAYS ACCURATE. BECAUSE THE MOTION OF THE EARTH ROUND THE SUN IS NOT PERFECTLY SYMMETRICAL THE LENGTH OF THE SOLAR DAY VARIES SLIGHTLY. THE CORRECTION FOR THIS, SEEN ON SOME SUNDIALS, IS CALLED THE 'EQUATION OF TIME'.

CLOUDS
SIR CHARLES WHEATSTONE, THE VICTORIAN SCIENTIST, INVENTED A SUNDIAL WHICH COULD WORK WHEN THE SKY WAS CLOUDY. IT CONTAINED A POLARISING FILTER & RELIED ON THE POLARISATION OF SUNLIGHT COMING THROUGH THE CLOUDS.

MEAN TIME
CLOCKS RECORD THE AVERAGE LENGTH OF A SOLAR DAY-HENCE 'MEAN' TIME.

WALES LATE
SUNDIALS ALSO HAVE TO BE CORRECTED FOR THEIR LONGITUDE. NOON IS WHEN THE SUN IS SOUTH OF GREENWICH. THE SUN IS SOUTH OF WALES UP TO 20 MINUTES LATER.

☆ HOW TO MAKE A SUNDIAL ☆

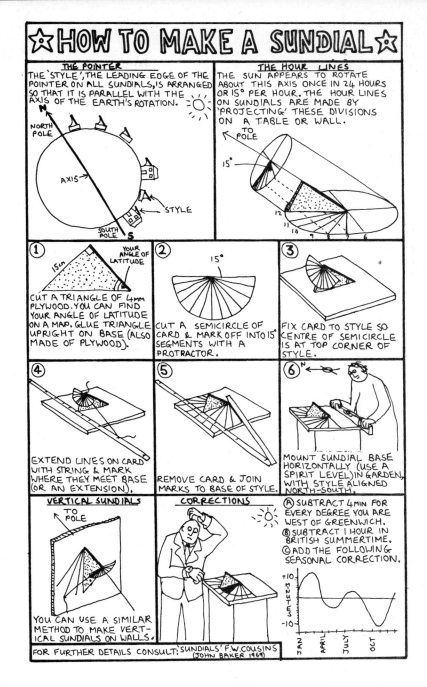

THE POINTER
THE 'STYLE', THE LEADING EDGE OF THE POINTER ON ALL SUNDIALS, IS ARRANGED SO THAT IT IS PARALLEL WITH THE AXIS OF THE EARTH'S ROTATION.

NORTH POLE
AXIS →
STYLE
SOUTH POLE

THE HOUR LINES
THE SUN APPEARS TO ROTATE ABOUT THIS AXIS ONCE IN 24 HOURS OR 15° PER HOUR. THE HOUR LINES ON SUNDIALS ARE MADE BY 'PROJECTING' THESE DIVISIONS ON A TABLE OR WALL.

TO POLE
15°

① CUT A TRIANGLE OF 4MM PLYWOOD. YOU CAN FIND YOUR ANGLE OF LATITUDE ON A MAP. GLUE TRIANGLE UPRIGHT ON BASE (ALSO MADE OF PLYWOOD).
YOUR ANGLE OF LATITUDE
15cm

② CUT A SEMICIRCLE OF CARD & MARK OFF INTO 15° SEGMENTS WITH A PROTRACTOR.
15°

③ FIX CARD TO STYLE SO CENTRE OF SEMICIRCLE IS AT TOP CORNER OF STYLE.

④ EXTEND LINES ON CARD WITH STRING & MARK WHERE THEY MEET BASE (OR AN EXTENSION).

⑤ REMOVE CARD & JOIN MARKS TO BASE OF STYLE.

⑥ MOUNT SUNDIAL BASE HORIZONTALLY (USE A SPIRIT LEVEL) IN GARDEN, WITH STYLE ALIGNED NORTH-SOUTH.

VERTICAL SUNDIALS
TO POLE
YOU CAN USE A SIMILAR METHOD TO MAKE VERTICAL SUNDIALS ON WALLS.

CORRECTIONS
Ⓐ SUBTRACT 4 MIN FOR EVERY DEGREE YOU ARE WEST OF GREENWICH.
Ⓑ SUBTRACT 1 HOUR IN BRITISH SUMMERTIME.
Ⓒ ADD THE FOLLOWING SEASONAL CORRECTION.

+10 / -10 MINUTES
JAN   APRIL   JULY   OCT

FOR FURTHER DETAILS CONSULT: 'SUNDIALS' F.W. COUSINS (JOHN BAKER 1969)

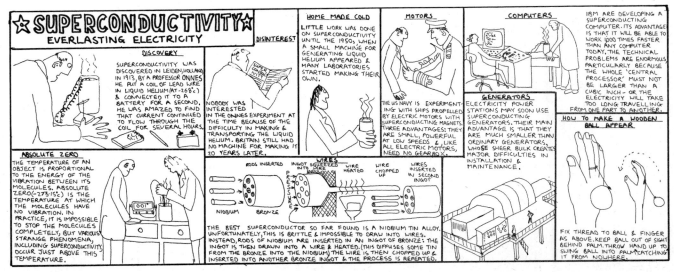

☆ SUPERCONDUCTIVITY ☆
EVERLASTING ELECTRICITY

DISCOVERY
SUPERCONDUCTIVITY WAS DISCOVERED IN LEIDEN, HOLLAND IN 1913, BY A PROFESSOR ONNES. HE PUT A COIL OF LEAD WIRE IN LIQUID HELIUM (AT -269°C) & CONNECTED IT TO A BATTERY FOR A SECOND. HE WAS AMAZED TO FIND THAT CURRENT CONTINUED TO FLOW THROUGH THE COIL FOR SEVERAL HOURS.

ABSOLUTE ZERO
THE TEMPERATURE OF AN OBJECT IS PROPORTIONAL TO THE ENERGY OF THE VIBRATION BETWEEN ITS MOLECULES. ABSOLUTE ZERO (-273.15°C) IS THE TEMPERATURE AT WHICH THE MOLECULES HAVE NO VIBRATION. IN PRACTICE, IT IS IMPOSSIBLE TO STOP THE MOLECULES COMPLETELY, BUT VARIOUS STRANGE PHENOMENA, INCLUDING SUPERCONDUCTIVITY, OCCUR JUST ABOVE THIS TEMPERATURE.

DISINTEREST
NOBODY WAS INTERESTED IN THE ONNES EXPERIMENT AT THE TIME BECAUSE OF THE DIFFICULTY IN MAKING & TRANSPORTING THE LIQUID HELIUM. BRITAIN STILL HAD NO MACHINE FOR MAKING IT 20 YEARS LATER.

HOME MADE COLD
LITTLE WORK WAS DONE ON SUPERCONDUCTIVITY UNTIL THE 1950s WHEN A SMALL MACHINE FOR GENERATING LIQUID HELIUM APPEARED & MANY LABORATORIES STARTED MAKING THEIR OWN.

MOTORS
THE US NAVY IS EXPERIMENTING WITH SHIPS PROPELLED BY ELECTRIC MOTORS WITH SUPERCONDUCTING MAGNETS. THESE HAVE THREE ADVANTAGES: THEY ARE SMALL, POWERFUL AT LOW SPEEDS & , LIKE ALL ELECTRIC MOTORS, NEED NO GEARBOX.

WIRES
RODS INSERTED | INGOT SQUEEZED INTO WIRE | WIRE HEATED | WIRE CHOPPED UP | WIRES INSERTED IN SECOND INGOT
NIOBIUM   BRONZE
PRESSURE

THE BEST SUPERCONDUCTOR SO FAR FOUND IS A NIOBIUM TIN ALLOY. UNFORTUNATELY, THIS IS BRITTLE & IMPOSSIBLE TO DRAW INTO WIRES. INSTEAD, RODS OF NIOBIUM ARE INSERTED IN AN INGOT OF BRONZE: THE INGOT IS THEN DRAWN INTO A WIRE & HEATED. (THIS DIFFUSES SOME TIN FROM THE BRONZE INTO THE NIOBIUM). THE WIRE IS THEN CHOPPED UP & INSERTED INTO ANOTHER BRONZE INGOT & THE PROCESS IS REPEATED.

COMPUTERS
IBM ARE DEVELOPING A SUPERCONDUCTING COMPUTER. ITS ADVANTAGE IS THAT IT WILL BE ABLE TO WORK 1000 TIMES FASTER THAN ANY COMPUTER TODAY. THE TECHNICAL PROBLEMS ARE ENORMOUS, PARTICULARLY BECAUSE THE WHOLE 'CENTRAL PROCESSOR' MUST NOT BE LARGER THAN A CUBIC INCH - OR THE ELECTRICITY WILL TAKE TOO LONG TRAVELLING FROM ONE PART TO ANOTHER.

GENERATORS
ELECTRICITY POWER STATIONS MAY SOON USE SUPERCONDUCTING GENERATORS. THEIR MAIN ADVANTAGE IS THAT THEY ARE MUCH SMALLER THAN ORDINARY GENERATORS, WHOSE SHEER BULK CREATES MAJOR DIFFICULTIES IN INSTALLATION & MAINTENANCE.

HOW TO MAKE A WOODEN BALL APPEAR
FIX THREAD TO BALL & FINGER AS ABOVE. KEEP BALL OUT OF SIGHT BEHIND PALM. THROW HAND UP TO SWING BALL INTO PALM, CATCHING IT FROM NOWHERE.

☆ SUPERSTITIONS ☆
IRRATIONAL BELIEFS IN OMENS & DIVINATIONS

THE FUTURE IN A MEAL

❶ A KNIFE RESTING ACROSS A SPOON AT A MEAL INDICATES A QUARREL IS IMMINENT.
❷ TWO TEASPOONS IN THE SAME CUP MEAN A MARRIAGE IS LIKELY.
❸ TWO WOMEN POURING TEA OUT OF THE SAME POT SIGNIFY A NEW BABY BEFORE THE END OF THE YEAR.
❹ HELPING SOMEONE TO SALT BRINGS BAD LUCK; HELP HIM TO SALT, HELP HIM TO SORROW.
❺ TAKING THE LAST PIECE OF BREAD & BUTTER ON A PLATE IS ALSO HIGHLY UNLUCKY. HOWEVER, IF THERE IS AN UNMARRIED LADY PRESENT, OFFER IT TO HER AS THIS DEED IS SAID TO BRING A HANDSOME HUSBAND & £10,000 A YEAR.

CUTTING YOUR NAILS

THE DAY ON WHICH YOU CUT YOUR NAILS IS HIGHLY SIGNIFICANT:

"A MAN HAD BETTER NE'ER BE BORN THAN HAVE HIS NAILS ON SUNDAY SHORN. CUT THEM ON MONDAY, CUT THEM FOR HEALTH; CUT THEM ON TUESDAY, CUT THEM FOR WEALTH; CUT THEM ON WEDNESDAY, CUT THEM FOR NEWS; CUT THEM ON THURSDAY FOR A NEW PAIR OF SHOES; CUT THEM ON FRIDAY, CUT THEM FOR SORROW; CUT THEM ON SATURDAY, SEE YOUR SWEETHEART TOMORROW."

THE SIGNIFICANCE OF SYMPTOMS

BURNING CHEEKS OR EARS MEAN SOMEONE IS TALKING ABOUT YOU. IT IS A FRIEND IF THE LEFT CHEEK BURNS, AN ENEMY IF THE RIGHT.

ITCHING PALMS MEAN MONEY. IF YOUR RIGHT HAND ITCHES YOU WILL RECEIVE SOME, IF THE LEFT, YOU WILL LOSE SOME.

WHITE SPECKS ON YOUR FINGERNAILS INDICATE A FORTHCOMING PRESENT. THE GIFT WILL ARRIVE WHEN THE SPECK REACHES THE EDGE OF THE NAIL.

THE FRAUDULENT MEDIUMS ACT

THIS ACT SUPERSEDED THE WITCHCRAFT ACT IN 1951. IT STATES THAT ANYBODY 'OFFERING TO CAST NATIVITIES & ANSWER ASTROLOGICAL QUESTIONS' MUST BE ABLE TO CONVINCE A COURT THAT HE OR SHE TRULY BELIEVES HIM OR HERSELF TO POSSESS 'CERTAIN POWERS' & TO BE GUILTY UNDER THE ACT, PREDICTING WITH INTENTION TO DECEIVE' MUST BE PROVEN.

STIRRING EGGS

ACCORDING TO SOME DRUIDS, STIRRING EGGS WIDDERSHINS (ANTICLOCK-WISE) IS AGAINST THE SUN & BRINGS MASSIVE DISASTERS, SO EGGS SHOULD ALWAYS BE STIRRED DEASIL (CLOCK-WISE).

SNEEZING

SNEEZE ON MONDAY, SNEEZE FOR DANGER, SNEEZE ON TUESDAY, KISS A STRANGER, SNEEZE ON WEDNESDAY, GET A LETTER, SNEEZE ON THURSDAY, SOMETHING BETTER, SNEEZE ON FRIDAY, SNEEZE FOR SORROW, SNEEZE ON SATURDAY, SEE YOUR TRUE LOVE TOMORROW, SNEEZE ON SUNDAY, BE HAPPY ALL THE WEEK THROUGH.

HOW TO CRACK A NUT

HANG A KNIFE BY A THREAD. PUSH A TUMBLER OF WATER UP TO IMMERSE THE HANDLE & THEN WITHDRAW. SOME DROPS OF WATER WILL FALL ON THE FLOOR. PLACE THE NUT WHERE THE DROPS FALL. BURN THE THREAD & KNIFE WILL FALL & CRACK NUT.

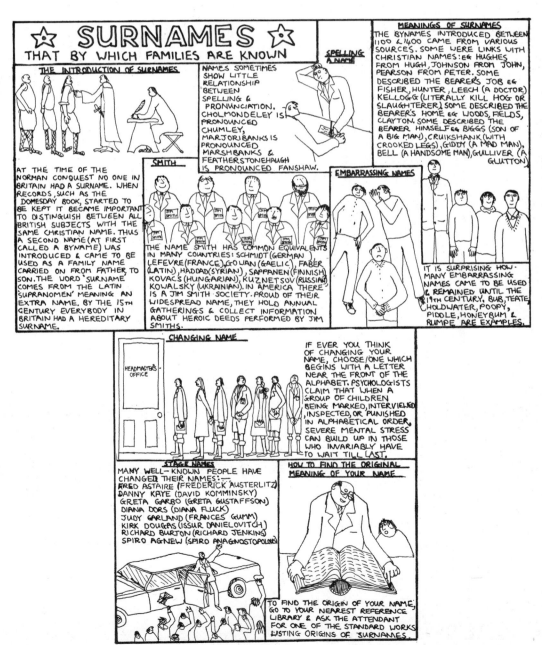

☆ SURNAMES ☆
THAT BY WHICH FAMILIES ARE KNOWN

THE INTRODUCTION OF SURNAMES

AT THE TIME OF THE NORMAN CONQUEST NO ONE IN BRITAIN HAD A SURNAME. WHEN RECORDS, SUCH AS THE DOMESDAY BOOK, STARTED TO BE KEPT IT BECAME IMPORTANT TO DISTINGUISH BETWEEN ALL BRITISH SUBJECTS WITH THE SAME CHRISTIAN NAME. THUS A SECOND NAME (AT FIRST CALLED A BYNAME) WAS INTRODUCED & CAME TO BE USED AS A FAMILY NAME CARRIED ON FROM FATHER TO SON. THE WORD 'SURNAME' COMES FROM THE LATIN 'SUPRANOMEN' MEANING AN EXTRA NAME. BY THE 15TH CENTURY EVERYBODY IN BRITAIN HAD A HEREDITARY SURNAME.

SPELLING A NAME

NAMES SOMETIMES SHOW LITTLE RELATIONSHIP BETWEEN SPELLING & PRONUNCIATION. CHOLMONDELEY IS PRONOUNCED CHUMLEY, MARJORIBANKS IS PRONOUNCED MARSHBANKS & FEATHERSTONEHAUGH IS PRONOUNCED FANSHAW.

SMITH

THE NAME SMITH HAS COMMON EQUIVALENTS IN MANY COUNTRIES: SCHMIDT (GERMAN) LEFEVRE (FRANCE), GOWAN (GAELIC), FABER (LATIN), HADDAD (SYRIAN), SAPPANEN (FINNISH), KOVACS (HUNGARIAN), KUZNETSOV (RUSSIAN), KOWALSKY (UKRAINIAN). IN AMERICA THERE IS A JIM SMITH SOCIETY. PROUD OF THEIR WIDESPREAD NAME, THEY HOLD ANNUAL GATHERINGS & COLLECT INFORMATION ABOUT HEROIC DEEDS PERFORMED BY JIM SMITHS.

MEANINGS OF SURNAMES

THE BYNAMES INTRODUCED BETWEEN 1100 & 1400 CAME FROM VARIOUS SOURCES. SOME WERE LINKS WITH CHRISTIAN NAMES: EG HUGHES FROM HUGH, JOHNSON FROM JOHN, PEARSON FROM PETER. SOME DESCRIBED THE BEARER'S JOB EG FISHER, HUNTER, LEECH (A DOCTOR) KELLOGG (LITERALLY KILL HOG OR SLAUGHTERER). SOME DESCRIBED THE BEARER'S HOME EG WOODS, FIELDS, CLAYTON. SOME DESCRIBED THE BEARER HIMSELF EG BIGGS (SON OF A BIG MAN), CRUIKSHANK (WITH CROOKED LEGS), GIDDY (A MAD MAN), BELL (A HANDSOME MAN), GULLIVER (A GLUTTON)

EMBARRASSING NAMES

IT IS SURPRISING HOW MANY EMBARRASSING NAMES CAME TO BE USED & REMAINED UNTIL THE 19TH CENTURY. BUB, TEATE, CHOLDWATER, POOPY, PIDDLE, HONEYBUM & RUMPE ARE EXAMPLES.

CHANGING NAME

HEADMASTER'S OFFICE

IF EVER YOU THINK OF CHANGING YOUR NAME, CHOOSE ONE WHICH BEGINS WITH A LETTER NEAR THE FRONT OF THE ALPHABET. PSYCHOLOGISTS CLAIM THAT WHEN A GROUP OF CHILDREN BEING MARKED, INTERVIEWED, INSPECTED, OR PUNISHED IN ALPHABETICAL ORDER, SEVERE MENTAL STRESS CAN BUILD UP IN THOSE WHO INVARIABLY HAVE TO WAIT TILL LAST.

STAGE NAMES

MANY WELL-KNOWN PEOPLE HAVE CHANGED THEIR NAMES:—
FRED ASTAIRE (FREDERICK AUSTERLITZ)
DANNY KAYE (DAVID KOMMINSKY)
GRETA GARBO (GRETA GUSTAFFSON)
DIANA DORS (DIANA FLUCK)
JUDY GARLAND (FRANCES GUMM)
KIRK DOUGLAS (ISSUR DANIELOVITCH)
RICHARD BURTON (RICHARD JENKINS)
SPIRO AGNEW (SPIRO ANAGNOSTOPOLIS)

HOW TO FIND THE ORIGINAL MEANING OF YOUR NAME

TO FIND THE ORIGIN OF YOUR NAME, GO TO YOUR NEAREST REFERENCE LIBRARY & ASK THE ATTENDANT FOR ONE OF THE STANDARD WORKS LISTING ORIGINS OF SURNAMES.

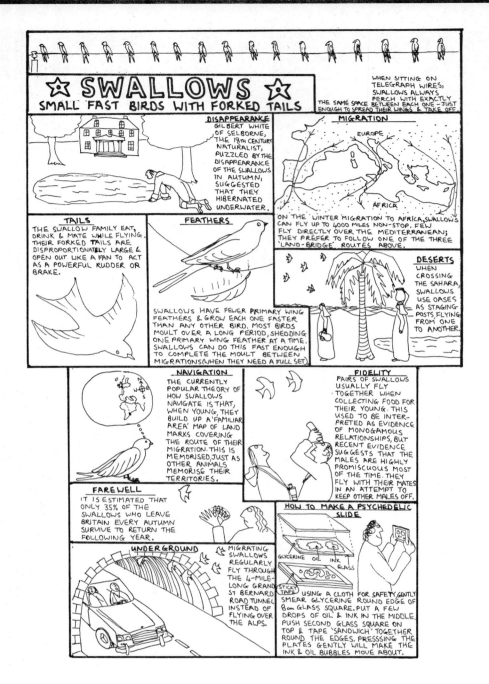

☆ SWALLOWS ☆
SMALL FAST BIRDS WITH FORKED TAILS

WHEN SITTING ON TELEGRAPH WIRES, SWALLOWS ALWAYS PERCH WITH EXACTLY THE SAME SPACE BETWEEN EACH ONE – JUST ENOUGH TO SPREAD THEIR WINGS & TAKE OFF.

DISAPPEARANCE
GILBERT WHITE OF SELBORNE, THE 18th CENTURY NATURALIST, PUZZLED BY THE DISAPPEARANCE OF THE SWALLOWS IN AUTUMN, SUGGESTED THAT THEY HIBERNATED UNDERWATER.

MIGRATION
EUROPE

AFRICA

ON THE WINTER MIGRATION TO AFRICA, SWALLOWS CAN FLY UP TO 4000 MILES NON-STOP. FEW FLY DIRECTLY OVER THE MEDITERRANEAN; THEY PREFER TO FOLLOW ONE OF THE THREE 'LAND-BRIDGE' ROUTES ABOVE.

TAILS
THE SWALLOW FAMILY EAT, DRINK & MATE WHILE FLYING. THEIR FORKED TAILS ARE DISPROPORTIONATELY LARGE & OPEN OUT LIKE A FAN TO ACT AS A POWERFUL RUDDER OR BRAKE.

FEATHERS
SWALLOWS HAVE FEWER PRIMARY WING FEATHERS & GROW EACH ONE FASTER THAN ANY OTHER BIRD. MOST BIRDS MOULT OVER A LONG PERIOD, SHEDDING ONE PRIMARY WING FEATHER AT A TIME. SWALLOWS CAN DO THIS FAST ENOUGH TO COMPLETE THE MOULT BETWEEN MIGRATIONS(WHEN THEY NEED A FULL SET).

DESERTS
WHEN CROSSING THE SAHARA, SWALLOWS USE OASES AS STAGING POSTS, FLYING FROM ONE TO ANOTHER.

NAVIGATION
THE CURRENTLY POPULAR THEORY OF HOW SWALLOWS NAVIGATE IS THAT, WHEN YOUNG, THEY BUILD UP A 'FAMILIAR AREA' MAP OF LAND MARKS COVERING THE ROUTE OF THEIR MIGRATION. THIS IS MEMORISED, JUST AS OTHER ANIMALS MEMORISE THEIR TERRITORIES.

FIDELITY
PAIRS OF SWALLOWS USUALLY FLY TOGETHER WHEN COLLECTING FOOD FOR THEIR YOUNG. THIS USED TO BE INTERPRETED AS EVIDENCE OF MONOGAMOUS RELATIONSHIPS, BUT RECENT EVIDENCE SUGGESTS THAT THE MALES ARE HIGHLY PROMISCUOUS MOST OF THE TIME. THEY FLY WITH THEIR MATES IN AN ATTEMPT TO KEEP OTHER MALES OFF.

FAREWELL
IT IS ESTIMATED THAT ONLY 35% OF THE SWALLOWS WHO LEAVE BRITAIN EVERY AUTUMN SURVIVE TO RETURN THE FOLLOWING YEAR.

HOW TO MAKE A PSYCHEDELIC SLIDE
GLYCERINE OIL INK
GLASS
STICKY TAPE
USING A CLOTH FOR SAFETY, GENTLY SMEAR GLYCERINE ROUND EDGE OF 8cm GLASS SQUARE. PUT A FEW DROPS OF OIL & INK IN THE MIDDLE. PUSH SECOND GLASS SQUARE ON TOP & TAPE 'SANDWICH' TOGETHER ROUND THE EDGES. PRESSSING THE PLATES GENTLY WILL MAKE THE INK & OIL BUBBLES MOVE ABOUT.

UNDERGROUND
MIGRATING SWALLOWS REGULARLY FLY THROUGH THE 4-MILE-LONG GRAND ST BERNARD ROAD TUNNEL INSTEAD OF FLYING OVER THE ALPS.

☆ SWANS ☆
LARGE STATELY LONG NECKED BIRDS OF THE DUCK FAMILY

AMAZING SWANS
SWANS HAVE 60 VERTEBRAE, MORE THAN GIRAFFES OR ANY OTHER BIRD OR MAMMAL.

THE MUTE SWAN WEIGHS UP TO 64lb, MORE THAN ANY OTHER FLYING BIRD IN BRITAIN & POSSIBLY THE WORLD.

FAITHFUL SWANS
85% OF THE SWANS IN A RECENT SURVEY WERE FOUND TO REMAIN WITH THE SAME PARTNER ALL THROUGH LIFE.

FAST SWANS
SWANS FLY AT ABOUT 30MPH IN STILL AIR. WHEN FLYING LONG DISTANCES THEY ADOPT A V FORMATION TO SAVE ENERGY. ALL, EXCEPT THE LEADER, ARE IN THE SLIPSTREAM OF THE ONE IN FRONT, WHICH CONSIDERABLY REDUCES THE AIR RESISTANCE. THEY ALSO ECONOMISE ON ENERGY BY FLYING HIGH WHEN WITH THE WIND & LOW WHEN AGAINST IT. (THE WIND IS ALWAYS LESS STRONG NEAR THE GROUND DUE TO DRAG.)

SWANS AT HOME
SWANS WILL MAKE THEIR HOME ON ANY QUIET PIECE OF WATER THAT IS OVER 30FT LONG & 8-18INCHES DEEP. THE DISTANCE IS NEEDED FOR TAKE OFF & THE DEPTH IS NEEDED FOR FEEDING FROM WEEDS ON THE BOTTOM.

VOCIFEROUS SWANS
THE MUTE SWAN IS CAPABLE OF A WIDE VARIETY OF NOISES. WHEN ANNOYED OR EXCITED IT EMITS A LOUD SNORT; WHEN VERY ANGRY THIS RISES TO A SHRILL TRUMPETING; WHEN FRIGHTENED IT HISSES LIKE A GOOSE; WHEN GREETING A FRIEND IT MAKES A GENTLER HISSING SOUND. WHEN THE MOTHER BIRD CALLS HER YOUNG SHE MAKES A YAPPING NOISE LIKE A DOG. THE MYTH OF THE SWAN SONG COMES FROM THE GREEKS. THEY THOUGHT SWANS WERE CAPABLE OF A LYRICAL SONG, BUT PERFORMED ONLY ONCE IN THEIR LIVES, JUST BEFORE DEATH.

HAZARDS FOR SWANS
SWANS HAVE EYES ON THE SIDES OF THEIR HEADS, GIVING THEM A COMPLETE CIRCULAR FIELD OF VISION. HOWEVER THIS LEAVES ONLY A VERY SMALL ANGLE IN FRONT WHICH IS VISIBLE THROUGH BOTH EYES (ESSENTIAL FOR JUDGING THE DISTANCE OF OBJECTS). THIS, COMBINED WITH THEIR LARGE WINGSPAN (UP TO 12FT) MAKES THEM HIGHLY VULNERABLE TO ELECTRICITY CABLES & ELECTROCUTION IS NOW THE GREATEST SINGLE CAUSE OF DEATH AMONG BRITISH SWANS.

POETIC SWANS
PYTHAGORAS BELIEVED THAT POETS TURNED INTO SWANS WHEN THEY DIED.

TASTY SWANS?
SWAN MEAT USED TO BE CONSIDERED A ROYAL DELICACY. ONE OCCASION WHEN IT IS SERVED NOW AT AN ANNUAL DINNER OF THE GUILD OF DYERS & VINTNERS. IT IS REPUTED TO CARVE WELL BUT TO TASTE RATHER OILY & LEATHERY.

HOW TO DRAW AN EGG
AN EGG
DRAW A HALF CIRCLE WITH COMPASSES FOR ROUND END OF EGG. TO DRAW POINTED END, STICK PAPER TO A ROLLING PIN OR CARDBOARD TUBE & THEN DRAW ROUND WITH COMPASSES TO JOIN 'FLAT' SEMICIRCLE

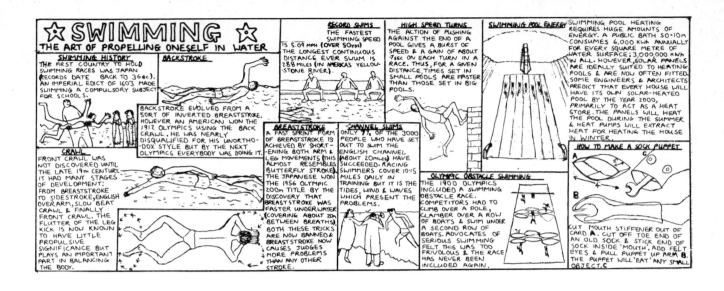

☆ SWIMMING ☆
THE ART OF PROPELLING ONESELF IN WATER

SWIMMING HISTORY
THE FIRST COUNTRY TO HOLD SWIMMING RACES WAS JAPAN (RECORDS DATE BACK TO 36BC). AN IMPERIAL EDICT OF 1603 MADE SWIMMING A COMPULSORY SUBJECT FOR SCHOOLS.

CRAWL
FRONT CRAWL WAS NOT DISCOVERED UNTIL THE LATE 19TH CENTURY. IT HAD MANY STAGES OF DEVELOPMENT: FROM BREASTSTROKE TO SIDESTROKE, ENGLISH OVERARM, SLOW BEAT CRAWL & FINALLY FRONT CRAWL. THE FLUTTER OF THE LEG KICK IS NOW KNOWN TO HAVE LITTLE PROPULSIVE SIGNIFICANCE BUT PLAYS AN IMPORTANT PART IN BALANCING THE BODY.

BACKSTROKE
BACKSTROKE EVOLVED FROM A SORT OF INVERTED BREASTSTROKE. HOWEVER AN AMERICAN WON THE 1912 OLYMPICS USING THE BACK CRAWL. HE WAS NEARLY DISQUALIFIED FOR HIS UNORTHODOX STYLE BUT BY THE NEXT OLYMPICS EVERYBODY WAS DOING IT.

BREASTSTROKE
A FAST SPRINT FORM OF BREASTSTROKE IS ACHIEVED BY SHORTENING BOTH ARM & LEG MOVEMENTS (THIS ALMOST RESEMBLES BUTTERFLY STROKE). THE JAPANESE WON THE 1956 OLYMPIC 200m TITLE BY THE DISCOVERY THAT BREASTSTROKE WAS FASTER UNDERWATER (COVERING ABOUT 20 BETWEEN BREATHS). BOTH THESE TRICKS ARE NOW BANNED & BREASTSTROKE NOW CAUSES JUDGES MORE PROBLEMS THAN ANY OTHER STROKE.

RECORD SWIMS
THE FASTEST SWIMMING SPEED IS 5.09 MPH (OVER 50yds). THE LONGEST CONTINUOUS DISTANCE EVER SWUM IS 288 MILES (IN AMERICA'S YELLOWSTONE RIVER).

HIGH SPEED TURNS
THE ACTION OF PUSHING AGAINST THE END OF A POOL GIVES A BURST OF SPEED & A GAIN OF ABOUT ⅓sec ON EACH TURN IN A RACE. THUS, FOR A GIVEN DISTANCE, TIMES SET IN SMALL POOLS ARE FASTER THAN THOSE SET IN BIG POOLS.

CHANNEL SWIMS
ONLY 7% OF THE 3000 PEOPLE WHO HAVE SET OUT TO SWIM THE ENGLISH CHANNEL (ABOUT 20miles) HAVE SUCCEEDED. RACING SWIMMERS COVER 10-15 MILES DAILY IN TRAINING BUT IT IS THE TIDES, WIND & WAVES WHICH PRESENT THE PROBLEMS.

OLYMPIC OBSTACLE SWIMMING
THE 1900 OLYMPICS INCLUDED A SWIMMING OBSTACLE RACE. COMPETITORS HAD TO CLIMB OVER A POLE, CLAMBER OVER A ROW OF BOATS & SWIM UNDER A SECOND ROW OF BOATS. ADVOCATES OF SERIOUS SWIMMING FELT THIS WAS TOO FRIVOLOUS & THE RACE HAS NEVER BEEN INCLUDED AGAIN.

SWIMMING POOL ENERGY
SWIMMING POOL HEATING REQUIRES HUGE AMOUNTS OF ENERGY. A PUBLIC BATH 50×10m CONSUMES 6,000 kWh ANNUALLY FOR EVERY SQUARE METRE OF WATER SURFACE; 3,000,000 kWh IN ALL. HOWEVER, SOLAR PANELS ARE IDEALLY SUITED TO HEATING POOLS & ARE NOW OFTEN FITTED. SOME ENGINEERS & ARCHITECTS PREDICT THAT EVERY HOUSE WILL HAVE ITS OWN SOLAR-HEATED POOL BY THE YEAR 2000, PRIMARILY TO ACT AS A HEAT STORE. THE PANELS WILL HEAT THE POOL DURING THE SUMMER & HEAT PUMPS WILL EXTRACT HEAT FOR HEATING THE HOUSE IN WINTER.

HOW TO MAKE A SOCK PUPPET
CUT MOUTH STIFFENER OUT OF CARD A. CUT OFF TOE END OF AN OLD SOCK & STICK END OF SOCK INSIDE 'MOUTH'. ADD FELT EYES & PULL PUPPET UP ARM B. THE PUPPET WILL 'EAT' ANY SMALL OBJECT. C

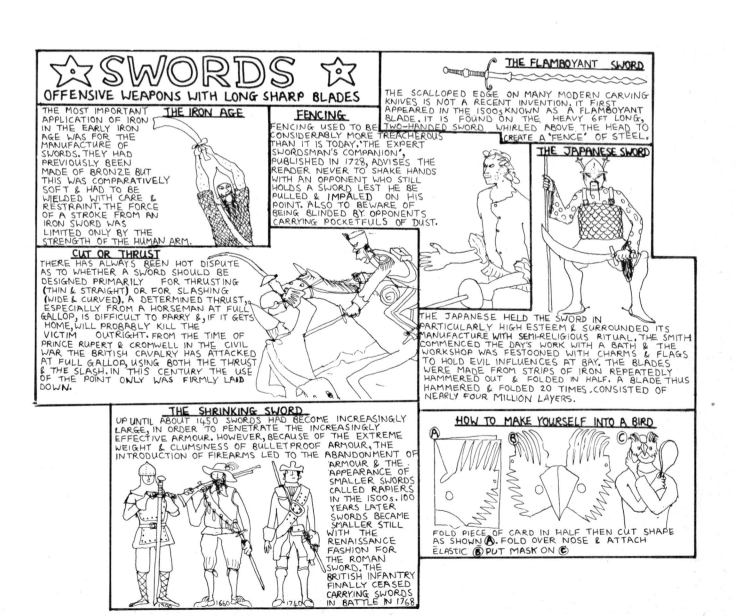

☆ SWORDS ☆
OFFENSIVE WEAPONS WITH LONG SHARP BLADES

THE IRON AGE
THE MOST IMPORTANT APPLICATION OF IRON IN THE EARLY IRON AGE WAS FOR THE MANUFACTURE OF SWORDS. THEY HAD PREVIOUSLY BEEN MADE OF BRONZE BUT THIS WAS COMPARATIVELY SOFT & HAD TO BE WIELDED WITH CARE & RESTRAINT. THE FORCE OF A STROKE FROM AN IRON SWORD WAS LIMITED ONLY BY THE STRENGTH OF THE HUMAN ARM.

CUT OR THRUST
THERE HAS ALWAYS BEEN HOT DISPUTE AS TO WHETHER A SWORD SHOULD BE DESIGNED PRIMARILY FOR THRUSTING (THIN & STRAIGHT) OR FOR SLASHING (WIDE & CURVED). A DETERMINED THRUST, ESPECIALLY FROM A HORSEMAN AT FULL GALLOP, IS DIFFICULT TO PARRY &, IF IT GETS HOME, WILL PROBABLY KILL THE VICTIM OUTRIGHT. FROM THE TIME OF PRINCE RUPERT & CROMWELL IN THE CIVIL WAR THE BRITISH CAVALRY HAS ATTACKED AT FULL GALLOP, USING BOTH THE THRUST & THE SLASH. IN THIS CENTURY THE USE OF THE POINT ONLY WAS FIRMLY LAID DOWN.

FENCING
FENCING USED TO BE CONSIDERABLY MORE TREACHEROUS THAN IT IS TODAY. 'THE EXPERT SWORDSMAN'S COMPANION', PUBLISHED IN 1728, ADVISES THE READER NEVER TO SHAKE HANDS WITH AN OPPONENT WHO STILL HOLDS A SWORD LEST HE BE PULLED & IMPALED ON HIS POINT. ALSO TO BEWARE OF BEING BLINDED BY OPPONENTS CARRYING POCKETFULS OF DUST.

THE FLAMBOYANT SWORD
THE SCALLOPED EDGE ON MANY MODERN CARVING KNIVES IS NOT A RECENT INVENTION. IT FIRST APPEARED IN THE 1500s KNOWN AS A FLAMBOYANT BLADE. IT IS FOUND ON THE HEAVY 6FT LONG, TWO-HANDED SWORD WHIRLED ABOVE THE HEAD TO CREATE A 'FENCE' OF STEEL.

THE JAPANESE SWORD
THE JAPANESE HELD THE SWORD IN PARTICULARLY HIGH ESTEEM & SURROUNDED ITS MANUFACTURE WITH SEMI-RELIGIOUS RITUAL. THE SMITH COMMENCED THE DAY'S WORK WITH A BATH & THE WORKSHOP WAS FESTOONED WITH CHARMS & FLAGS TO HOLD EVIL INFLUENCES AT BAY. THE BLADES WERE MADE FROM STRIPS OF IRON REPEATEDLY HAMMERED OUT & FOLDED IN HALF. A BLADE THUS HAMMERED & FOLDED 20 TIMES, CONSISTED OF NEARLY FOUR MILLION LAYERS.

THE SHRINKING SWORD
UP UNTIL ABOUT 1450 SWORDS HAD BECOME INCREASINGLY LARGE, IN ORDER TO PENETRATE THE INCREASINGLY EFFECTIVE ARMOUR. HOWEVER, BECAUSE OF THE EXTREME WEIGHT & CLUMSINESS OF BULLETPROOF ARMOUR, THE INTRODUCTION OF FIREARMS LED TO THE ABANDONMENT OF ARMOUR & THE APPEARANCE OF SMALLER SWORDS CALLED RAPIERS IN THE 1500s. 100 YEARS LATER SWORDS BECAME SMALLER STILL WITH THE RENAISSANCE FASHION FOR THE ROMAN SWORD. THE BRITISH INFANTRY FINALLY CEASED CARRYING SWORDS IN BATTLE IN 1768.

HOW TO MAKE YOURSELF INTO A BIRD
FOLD PIECE OF CARD IN HALF THEN CUT SHAPE AS SHOWN A. FOLD OVER NOSE & ATTACH ELASTIC B PUT MASK ON C

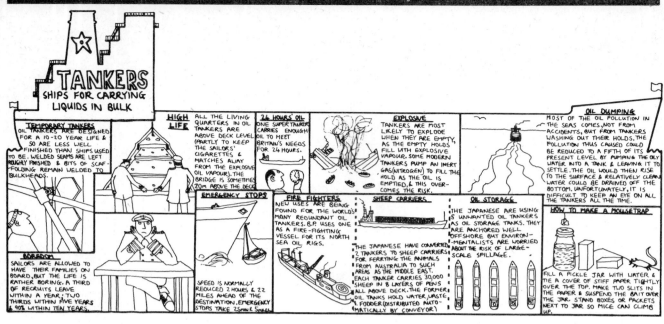

☆ TANKERS ☆
SHIPS FOR CARRYING LIQUIDS IN BULK

TEMPORARY TANKERS
OIL TANKERS ARE DESIGNED FOR A 10-20 YEAR LIFE & SO ARE LESS WELL FINISHED THAN SHIPS USED TO BE. WELDED SEAMS ARE LEFT ROUGHLY FINISHED & BITS OF SCAFFOLDING REMAIN WELDED TO BULKHEADS.

HIGH LIFE
ALL THE LIVING QUARTERS IN OIL TANKERS ARE ABOVE DECK LEVEL (PARTLY TO KEEP THE SAILORS' CIGARETTES & MATCHES AWAY FROM THE EXPLOSIVE OIL VAPOUR). THE BRIDGE IS SOMETIMES 20m ABOVE THE DECK.

24 HOURS' OIL
ONE SUPERTANKER CARRIES ENOUGH OIL TO MEET BRITAIN'S NEEDS FOR 24 HOURS.

EXPLOSIVE
TANKERS ARE MOST LIKELY TO EXPLODE WHEN THEY ARE EMPTY, AS THE EMPTY HOLDS FILL WITH EXPLOSIVE VAPOUR. SOME MODERN TANKERS PUMP AN INERT GAS (NITROGEN) TO FILL THE HOLD AS THE OIL IS EMPTIED, & THIS OVERCOMES THE RISK.

OIL DUMPING
MOST OF THE OIL POLLUTION IN THE SEAS COMES, NOT FROM ACCIDENTS, BUT FROM TANKERS WASHING OUT THEIR HOLDS. THE POLLUTION THUS CAUSED COULD BE REDUCED TO A FIFTH OF ITS PRESENT LEVEL BY PUMPING THE OILY WATER INTO A TANK & LEAVING IT TO SETTLE. THE OIL WOULD THEN RISE TO THE SURFACE & RELATIVELY CLEAN WATER COULD BE DRAINED OFF THE BOTTOM. UNFORTUNATELY, IT IS DIFFICULT TO KEEP AN EYE ON ALL THE TANKERS ALL THE TIME.

BOREDOM
SAILORS ARE ALLOWED TO HAVE THEIR FAMILIES ON BOARD, BUT THE LIFE IS RATHER BORING. A THIRD OF RECRUITS LEAVE WITHIN A YEAR; TWO THIRDS WITHIN FIVE YEARS & 90% WITHIN TEN YEARS.

EMERGENCY STOPS
SPEED IS NORMALLY REDUCED 2 HOURS & 22 MILES AHEAD OF THE DESTINATION. EMERGENCY STOPS TAKE 2.5mn & 5mls.

FIRE FIGHTERS
NEW USES ARE BEING FOUND FOR THE WORLD'S MANY REDUNDANT OIL TANKERS. B.P. USES ONE AS A FIRE-FIGHTING VESSEL FOR ITS NORTH SEA OIL RIGS.

SHEEP CARRIERS
THE JAPANESE HAVE CONVERTED 2 TANKERS TO SHEEP CARRIERS FOR FERRYING THE ANIMALS FROM AUSTRALIA TO SUCH AREAS AS THE MIDDLE EAST. EACH TANKER CARRIES 30,000 SHEEP IN 8 LAYERS OF PENS ALL ABOVE DECK. THE FORMER OIL TANKS HOLD WATER, WASTE & FODDER (DISTRIBUTED AUTOMATICALLY BY CONVEYOR).

OIL STORAGE
THE JAPANESE ARE USING 5 UNWANTED OIL TANKERS AS OIL STORAGE TANKS. THEY ARE ANCHORED WELL OFFSHORE BUT ENVIRONMENTALISTS ARE WORRIED ABOUT THE RISK OF LARGE-SCALE SPILLAGE.

HOW TO MAKE A MOUSETRAP
FILL A PICKLE JAR WITH WATER & TIE A COVER OF STIFF PAPER TIGHTLY OVER THE TOP. MAKE TWO SLITS IN THE PAPER & SUSPEND THE BAIT OVER THE JAR. STAND BOXES OR PACKETS NEXT TO JAR SO MICE CAN CLIMB UP.

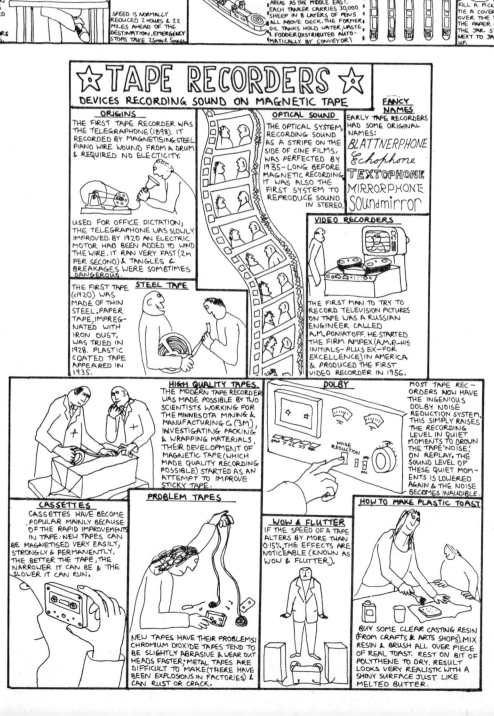

☆ TAPE RECORDERS ☆
DEVICES RECORDING SOUND ON MAGNETIC TAPE

ORIGINS
THE FIRST TAPE RECORDER WAS THE TELEGRAPHONE (1898). IT RECORDED BY MAGNETISING STEEL PIANO WIRE WOUND FROM A DRUM & REQUIRED NO ELECTICITY.

USED FOR OFFICE DICTATION, THE TELEGRAPHONE WAS SLOWLY IMPROVED. BY 1920 AN ELECTRIC MOTOR HAD BEEN ADDED TO WIND THE WIRE. IT RAN VERY FAST (2m PER SECOND) & TANGLES & BREAKAGES WERE SOMETIMES DANGEROUS.

STEEL TAPE
THE FIRST TAPE (c1920) WAS MADE OF THIN STEEL. PAPER TAPE, IMPREGNATED WITH IRON DUST, WAS TRIED IN 1928. PLASTIC COATED TAPE APPEARED IN 1935.

OPTICAL SOUND
THE OPTICAL SYSTEM, RECORDING SOUND AS A STRIPE ON THE SIDE OF CINE FILMS, WAS PERFECTED BY 1935 – LONG BEFORE MAGNETIC RECORDING. IT WAS ALSO THE FIRST SYSTEM TO REPRODUCE SOUND IN STEREO.

FANCY NAMES
EARLY TAPE RECORDERS HAD SOME ORIGINAL NAMES:
BLATTNERPHONE
Echophone
TEXTOPHONE
MIRRORPHONE
SOUNDmirror

VIDEO RECORDERS
THE FIRST MAN TO TRY TO RECORD TELEVISION PICTURES ON TAPE WAS A RUSSIAN ENGINEER CALLED A.M. PONIATOFF. HE STARTED THE FIRM AMPEX (A.M.P.–HIS INITIALS – PLUS EX–FOR EXCELLENCE) IN AMERICA & PRODUCED THE FIRST VIDEO RECORDER IN 1956.

HIGH QUALITY TAPES
THE MODERN TAPE RECORDER WAS MADE POSSIBLE BY TWO SCIENTISTS WORKING FOR THE MINNESOTA MINING & MANUFACTURING Co. (3M), INVESTIGATING PACKING & WRAPPING MATERIALS. THEIR DEVELOPMENT OF MAGNETIC TAPE (WHICH MADE QUALITY RECORDING POSSIBLE) STARTED AS AN ATTEMPT TO IMPROVE STICKY TAPE.

DOLBY
MOST TAPE RECORDERS NOW HAVE THE INGENIOUS DOLBY NOISE REDUCTION SYSTEM. THIS SIMPLY RAISES THE RECORDING LEVEL IN QUIET MOMENTS TO DROWN THE TAPE 'NOISE'. ON REPLAY, THE SOUND LEVEL OF THESE QUIET MOMENTS IS LOWERED AGAIN & THE NOISE BECOMES INAUDIBLE.

CASSETTES
CASSETTES HAVE BECOME POPULAR MAINLY BECAUSE OF THE RAPID IMPROVEMENTS IN TAPE. NEW TAPES CAN BE MAGNETISED VERY EASILY, STRONGLY & PERMANENTLY. THE BETTER THE TAPE, THE NARROWER IT CAN BE & THE SLOWER IT CAN RUN.

PROBLEM TAPES
NEW TAPES HAVE THEIR PROBLEMS: CHROMIUM DIOXIDE TAPES TEND TO BE SLIGHTLY ABRASIVE & WEAR OUT HEADS FASTER; METAL TAPES ARE DIFFICULT TO MAKE (THERE HAVE BEEN EXPLOSIONS IN FACTORIES) & CAN RUST OR CRACK.

WOW & FLUTTER
IF THE SPEED OF A TAPE ALTERS BY MORE THAN 0.15%, THE EFFECTS ARE NOTICEABLE (KNOWN AS WOW & FLUTTER).

HOW TO MAKE PLASTIC TOAST
BUY SOME CLEAR CASTING RESIN (FROM CRAFTS & ARTS SHOPS). MIX RESIN & BRUSH ALL OVER PIECE OF REAL TOAST. REST ON BIT OF POLYTHENE TO DRY. RESULT LOOKS VERY REALISTIC WITH A SHINY SURFACE JUST LIKE MELTED BUTTER.

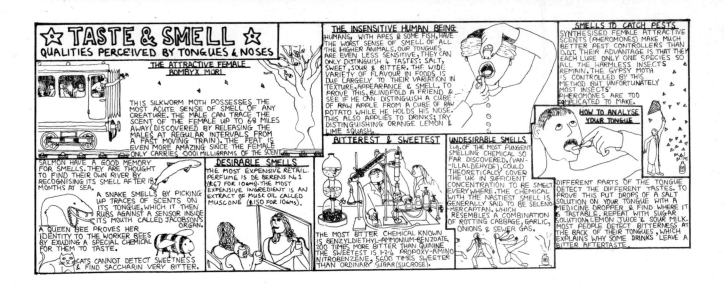

☆ TASTE & SMELL ☆
QUALITIES PERCEIVED BY TONGUES & NOSES

THE ATTRACTIVE FEMALE BOMBYX MORI

THIS SILKWORM MOTH POSSESSES THE MOST ACUTE SENSE OF SMELL OF ANY CREATURE. THE MALE CAN TRACE THE SCENT OF THE FEMALE UP TO 6·8 MILES AWAY (DISCOVERED BY RELEASING THE MALES AT REGULAR INTERVALS FROM A FAST MOVING TRAIN). THE FEAT IS EVEN MORE AMAZING SINCE THE FEMALE ONLY CARRIES ·0001 MILLIGRAMS OF THE SCENT.

SALMON HAVE A GOOD MEMORY FOR SMELLS. THEY ARE THOUGHT TO FIND THEIR OWN RIVER BY RECOGNISING ITS SMELL AFTER 18 MONTHS AT SEA.

A SNAKE SMELLS BY PICKING UP TRACES OF SCENTS ON ITS TONGUE, WHICH IT THEN RUBS AGAINST A SENSOR INSIDE ITS MOUTH CALLED JACOBSON'S ORGAN.

A QUEEN BEE PROVES HER IDENTITY TO THE WORKER BEES BY EXUDING A SPECIAL CHEMICAL FOR THEM TO TASTE.

CATS CANNOT DETECT SWEETNESS & FIND SACCHARIN VERY BITTER.

DESIRABLE SMELLS

THE MOST EXPENSIVE RETAIL PERFUME IS DE BERENS No 1 (£67 FOR 10 GMS). THE MOST EXPENSIVE INGREDIENT IS AN EXTRACT OF MUSK OIL CALLED MUSCONE (£150 FOR 10 GMS).

THE INSENSITIVE HUMAN BEING

HUMANS, WITH APES & SOME FISH, HAVE THE WORST SENSE OF SMELL OF ALL THE HIGHER ANIMALS. OUR TONGUES ARE EVEN LESS SENSITIVE. THEY CAN ONLY DISTINGUISH 4 TASTES: SALT, SWEET, SOUR & BITTER. THE WIDE VARIETY OF FLAVOUR IN FOODS IS DUE LARGELY TO THEIR VARIATION IN TEXTURE, APPEARANCE & SMELL. TO PROVE THIS, BLINDFOLD A FRIEND & SEE IF HE CAN DISTINGUISH A CUBE OF RAW APPLE FROM A CUBE OF RAW POTATO WHILE HE HOLDS HIS NOSE. THIS ALSO APPLIES TO DRINKS; TRY DISTINGUISHING ORANGE LEMON & LIME SQUASH.

BITTEREST & SWEETEST

THE MOST BITTER CHEMICAL KNOWN IS BENZYLDIETHYL-AMMONIUM-BENZOATE 200 TIMES MORE BITTER THAN QUININE. THE SWEETEST IS 1-2-4 PROPOXY-AMINO NITROBENZENE, 5600 TIMES SWEETER THAN ORDINARY SUGAR (SUCROSE).

UNDESIRABLE SMELLS

2LB. OF THE MOST PUNGENT SMELLING CHEMICAL SO FAR DISCOVERED, (VANILLALDEHYDE), COULD THEORETICALLY COVER THE UK IN SUFFICIENT CONCENTRATION TO BE SMELT EVERYWHERE. THE CHEMICAL WITH THE NASTIEST SMELL IS GENERALLY SAID TO BE SELENO-MERCAPTAN. WHICH RESEMBLES A COMBINATION OF ROTTING CABBAGE, GARLIC, ONIONS & SEWER GAS.

SMELLS TO CATCH PESTS

SYNTHESISED FEMALE ATTRACTIVE SCENTS (PHEROMONES) MAKE MUCH BETTER PEST CONTROLLERS THAN D.D.T. THEIR ADVANTAGE IS THAT THEY EACH LURE ONLY ONE SPECIES SO ALL THE HARMLESS INSECTS REMAIN. THE GYPSY MOTH IS CONTROLLED BY THIS METHOD BUT UNFORTUNATELY MOST INSECTS' PHEROMONES ARE TOO COMPLICATED TO MAKE.

HOW TO ANALYSE YOUR TONGUE

DIFFERENT PARTS OF THE TONGUE DETECT THE DIFFERENT TASTES. TO PROVE THIS PUT DROPS OF A SALT SOLUTION ON YOUR TONGUE WITH A MEDICINE DROPPER & FIND WHERE IT TASTABLE. REPEAT WITH SUGAR SOLUTION, LEMON JUICE & SOUR MILK. MOST PEOPLE DETECT BITTERNESS AT THE BACK OF THEIR TONGUES, WHICH EXPLAINS WHY SOME DRINKS LEAVE A BITTER AFTERTASTE.

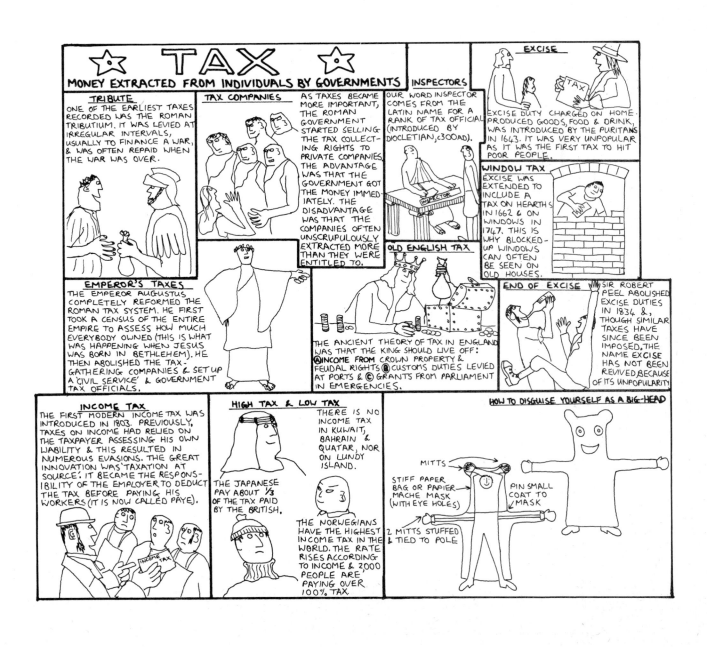

☆ TAX ☆
MONEY EXTRACTED FROM INDIVIDUALS BY GOVERNMENTS

TRIBUTE

ONE OF THE EARLIEST TAXES RECORDED WAS THE ROMAN TRIBUTIUM. IT WAS LEVIED AT IRREGULAR INTERVALS, USUALLY TO FINANCE A WAR, & WAS OFTEN REPAID WHEN THE WAR WAS OVER.

TAX COMPANIES

AS TAXES BECAME MORE IMPORTANT, THE ROMAN GOVERNMENT STARTED SELLING THE TAX COLLECTING RIGHTS TO PRIVATE COMPANIES. THE ADVANTAGE WAS THAT THE GOVERNMENT GOT THE MONEY IMMEDIATELY. THE DISADVANTAGE WAS THAT THE COMPANIES OFTEN UNSCRUPULOUSLY EXTRACTED MORE THAN THEY WERE ENTITLED TO.

INSPECTORS

OUR WORD INSPECTOR COMES FROM THE LATIN NAME FOR A RANK OF TAX OFFICIAL (INTRODUCED BY DIOCLETIAN, c300AD).

EXCISE

EXCISE DUTY CHARGED ON HOME PRODUCED GOODS, FOOD & DRINK, WAS INTRODUCED BY THE PURITANS IN 1643. IT WAS VERY UNPOPULAR AS IT WAS THE FIRST TAX TO HIT POOR PEOPLE.

WINDOW TAX

EXCISE WAS EXTENDED TO INCLUDE A TAX ON HEARTHS IN 1662 & ON WINDOWS IN 1747. THIS IS WHY BLOCKED-UP WINDOWS CAN OFTEN BE SEEN ON OLD HOUSES.

EMPEROR'S TAXES

THE EMPEROR AUGUSTUS COMPLETELY REFORMED THE ROMAN TAX SYSTEM. HE FIRST TOOK A CENSUS OF THE ENTIRE EMPIRE TO ASSESS HOW MUCH EVERYBODY OWNED (THIS IS WHAT WAS HAPPENING WHEN JESUS WAS BORN IN BETHLEHEM). HE THEN ABOLISHED THE TAX-GATHERING COMPANIES & SET UP A 'CIVIL SERVICE' & GOVERNMENT TAX OFFICIALS.

OLD ENGLISH TAX

THE ANCIENT THEORY OF TAX IN ENGLAND WAS THAT THE KING SHOULD LIVE OFF: (A) INCOME FROM CROWN PROPERTY & FEUDAL RIGHTS (B) CUSTOMS DUTIES LEVIED AT PORTS & (C) GRANTS FROM PARLIAMENT IN EMERGENCIES.

END OF EXCISE

SIR ROBERT PEEL ABOLISHED EXCISE DUTIES IN 1834 &, THOUGH SIMILAR TAXES HAVE SINCE BEEN IMPOSED, THE NAME EXCISE HAS NOT BEEN REVIVED BECAUSE OF ITS UNPOPULARITY.

INCOME TAX

THE FIRST MODERN INCOME TAX WAS INTRODUCED IN 1803. PREVIOUSLY, TAXES ON INCOME HAD RELIED ON THE TAXPAYER ASSESSING HIS OWN LIABILITY & THIS RESULTED IN NUMEROUS EVASIONS. THE GREAT INNOVATION WAS 'TAXATION AT SOURCE'. IT BECAME THE RESPONSIBILITY OF THE EMPLOYER TO DEDUCT THE TAX BEFORE PAYING HIS WORKERS (IT IS NOW CALLED PAYE).

HIGH TAX & LOW TAX

THE JAPANESE PAY ABOUT 1/3 OF THE TAX PAID BY THE BRITISH.

THERE IS NO INCOME TAX IN KUWAIT, BAHRAIN & QUATAR, NOR ON LUNDY ISLAND.

THE NORWEGIANS HAVE THE HIGHEST INCOME TAX IN THE WORLD. THE RATE RISES ACCORDING TO INCOME & 2,000 PEOPLE ARE PAYING OVER 100% TAX.

HOW TO DISGUISE YOURSELF AS A BIG-HEAD

MITTS

STIFF PAPER BAG OR PAPIER MACHE MASK (WITH EYE HOLES)

PIN SMALL COAT TO MASK

2 MITTS STUFFED & TIED TO POLE

☆ TEA ☆
REFRESHING BEVERAGE INFUSED FROM LEAVES

THE ORIGIN OF TEA
THERE ARE MANY LEGENDS SURROUNDING THE ORIGIN OF TEA. ONE IS THAT A BUDDHIST MONK CALLED DHARUMA WHO KEPT FALLING ASLEEP WHILE HE WAS MEDITATING CUT OFF HIS EYELIDS AS A SOLUTION. WHERE HIS EYELIDS FELL THE FIRST TEA PLANTS GREW, TO HELP OTHERS STAY AWAKE WITHOUT RESORTING TO SUCH EXTREMES.

ODD TASTES
GREAT CARE HAS TO BE TAKEN IN STORING TEA TO ENSURE THAT IT DOES NOT PICK UP ANY UNWANTED FLAVOURS. TEA IN CHESTS PACKED NEXT TO ORANGES OR EVEN BANANAS CAN BE DETECTED BY A TEA TASTER. ONE JAPANESE EMPEROR WAS SO FUSSY ABOUT THE QUALITY OF HIS TEA THAT SCOUTS ALWAYS PRECEDED THE DELIVERY OF HIS SUPPLY TO MAKE PEASANTS PUT OUT FIRES & STOP OTHER SMELLY ACTIVITIES.

OLD STEWED TEA
TEA WAS FIRST SERVED TO THE PUBLIC IN ENGLAND IN 1657 AT A COFFEE HOUSE IN LONDON CALLED GARRAWAYS. IT COULD NOT HAVE TASTED VERY PLEASANT AS IT WAS BREWED IN BULK & KEPT IN A CASK FROM WHICH IT WAS DRAWN & HEATED UP WHEN REQUIRED.

QUICK BREW TEA
QUICK-BREW TEAS WERE MADE POSSIBLE BY THE INVENTION IN 1950 OF A NEW METHOD OF PROCESSING FRESH LEAVES AFTER PICKING. INSTEAD OF ROLLING THE LEAVES UNDERFOOT (THE ORTHODOX METHOD) THE C.T.C. (CRUSHING, TEARING, CURLING) MACHINE IS USED. THIS BREAKS UP THE LEAF MORE THOROUGHLY & ENABLES THE FLAVOUR TO BE MORE EASILY EXTRACTED.

TEA IN TIBET
THE TIBETANS ADD YAK BUTTER OR RANCID GOAT BUTTER TO THEIR TEA INSTEAD OF MILK.

TEA IN BRITAIN
THE BRITISH DRINK TEA IN LARGE QUANTITIES. WE IMPORT ABOUT 500 MILLION POUNDS A YEAR, NEARLY 5 TIMES MORE THAN THE WHOLE OF THE REST OF EUROPE.

TEA IN RUSSIA
THE RUSSIANS DRINK TEA ADDING LOTS OF SUGAR & LEMON OR SOMETIMES JAM.

TEA IN CHINA
THE CHINESE ONLY ADOPTED OUR METHOD OF INFUSING TEA ABOUT 500 YEARS AGO. PREVIOUSLY THEY BOILED THE POWDERED LEAVES WITH RICE CAKES TO A THICK SYRUP.

ADULTERATED TEA
TEA HAS BEEN SUBJECT TO ALL SORTS OF ADULTERATIONS. PROCESSED WILLOW, SLOE, ELDER & ASH LEAVES HAVE ALL BEEN ADDED, ALSO FLOOD DAMAGED TEA COATED WITH THE POISONOUS COLOURING PRUSSIAN BLUE. THE COMMONEST ADULTERATION, MUCH PRACTISED IN CHINA IN THE 19TH CENTURY, WAS 'MALOO', SIMPLY REDRIED USED TEA LEAVES, FROM THEIR TEAPOTS, TIPPED INTO THE CHESTS FOR EXPORT.

HOW TO MAKE YOGURT
PUT 1 PINT OF MILK (OR POWDERED MILK & WATER RECONSTITUTED) IN CLEAN SAUCEPAN. HEAT TILL A TEASPOON DIPPED IN FEELS AS HOT AS YOU CAN BEAR ON YOUR WRIST. ADD 1 TABLESPOON OF BOUGHT YOGURT, COVER WITH LID, WRAP CLOTH ROUND TO INSULATE & LEAVE IN A WARM PLACE FOR AT LEAST 7 HOURS.

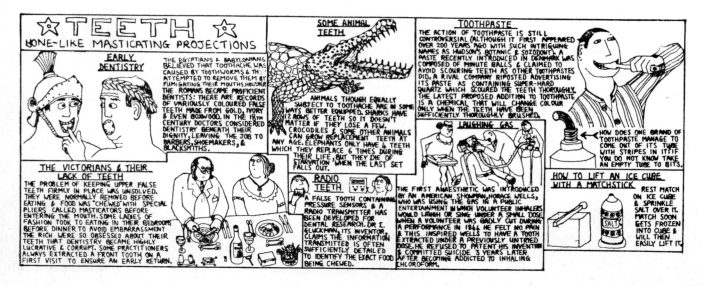

☆ TEETH ☆
BONE-LIKE MASTICATING PROJECTIONS

EARLY DENTISTRY
THE EGYPTIANS & BABYLONIANS BELIEVED THAT TOOTHACHE WAS CAUSED BY TOOTHWORMS & THEY ATTEMPTED TO REMOVE THEM BY FUMIGATING THEIR MOUTHS. HOWEVER THE ROMANS BECAME PROFICIENT DENTISTS: THERE ARE RECORDS OF VARIOUSLY COLOURED FALSE TEETH MADE FROM GOLD, IVORY & EVEN BOXWOOD. IN THE 19TH CENTURY DOCTORS CONSIDERED DENTISTRY BENEATH THEIR DIGNITY, LEAVING THE JOB TO BARBERS, SHOEMAKERS, & BLACKSMITHS.

SOME ANIMAL TEETH
ANIMALS THOUGH EQUALLY SUBJECT TO TOOTHACHE ARE IN SOME WAYS BETTER EQUIPPED. SHARKS HAVE 2 ROWS OF TEETH SO IT DOESN'T MATTER IF THEY LOSE A FEW. CROCODILES & SOME OTHER ANIMALS CAN GROW REPLACEMENT TEETH AT ANY AGE. ELEPHANTS ONLY HAVE 4 TEETH WHICH THEY REPLACE 6 TIMES DURING THEIR LIFE, BUT THEY DIE OF STARVATION WHEN THE LAST SET FALLS OUT.

TOOTHPASTE
THE ACTION OF TOOTHPASTE IS STILL CONTROVERSIAL (ALTHOUGH IT FIRST APPEARED OVER 200 YEARS AGO WITH SUCH INTRIGUING NAMES AS HUDSON'S BOTANIC & SOZODONT). A PASTE RECENTLY INTRODUCED IN DENMARK WAS COMPOSED OF MINUTE BALLS & CLAIMED TO AVOID SCOURING TEETH AS OTHER TOOTHPASTES DID. A RIVAL COMPANY RIPOSTED ADVERTISING ITS PASTE AS CONTAINING SUPER-HARD QUARTZ WHICH SCOURED THE TEETH THOROUGHLY. THE LATEST PROPOSED ADDITION TO TOOTHPASTE IS A CHEMICAL THAT WILL CHANGE COLOUR ONLY WHEN THE TEETH HAVE BEEN SUFFICIENTLY THOROUGHLY BRUSHED.

THE VICTORIANS & THEIR LACK OF TEETH
THE PROBLEM OF KEEPING UPPER FALSE TEETH FIRMLY IN PLACE WAS UNSOLVED. THEY WERE NORMALLY REMOVED BEFORE EATING & FOOD WAS 'CHEWED' WITH SPECIAL PLIERS CALLED MASTICATORS BEFORE ENTERING THE MOUTH. SOME LADIES OF FASHION TOOK TO EATING IN THEIR BEDROOMS BEFORE DINNER TO AVOID EMBARRASSMENT. THE RICH WERE SO OBSESSED ABOUT THEIR TEETH THAT DENTISTRY BECAME HIGHLY LUCRATIVE & CORRUPT. SOME PRACTITIONERS ALWAYS EXTRACTED A FRONT TOOTH ON A FIRST VISIT TO ENSURE AN EARLY RETURN.

RADIO TEETH
A FALSE TOOTH CONTAINING PRESSURE SENSORS & A RADIO TRANSMITTER HAS BEEN DEVELOPED FOR DENTAL RESEARCH. DR I. GLUCKMAN, ITS INVENTOR, CLAIMS THE INFORMATION TRANSMITTED IS OFTEN SUFFICIENTLY DETAILED TO IDENTIFY THE EXACT FOOD BEING CHEWED.

LAUGHING GAS
THE FIRST ANAESTHETIC WAS INTRODUCED BY AN AMERICAN SHOWMAN, HORACE WELLS, WHO WAS USING THE GAS IN A PUBLIC ENTERTAINMENT IN WHICH VOLUNTEER INHALERS WOULD LAUGH OR SING UNDER A SMALL DOSE. WHEN A VOLUNTEER WAS BADLY CUT DURING A PERFORMANCE IN 1844 HE FELT NO PAIN & THIS INSPIRED WELLS TO HAVE A TOOTH EXTRACTED UNDER A PREVIOUSLY UNTRIED DOSE. HE REFUSED TO PATENT HIS INVENTION & COMMITTED SUICIDE 3 YEARS LATER AFTER BECOMING ADDICTED TO INHALING CHLOROFORM.

HOW DOES ONE BRAND OF TOOTHPASTE MANAGE TO COME OUT OF ITS TUBE WITH STRIPES IN IT? IF YOU DO NOT KNOW TAKE AN EMPTY TUBE TO BITS.

HOW TO LIFT AN ICE CUBE WITH A MATCHSTICK
REST MATCH ON ICE CUBE & SPRINKLE SALT OVER IT. MATCH SOON GETS FROZEN INTO CUBE & WILL THEN EASILY LIFT IT.

SALT

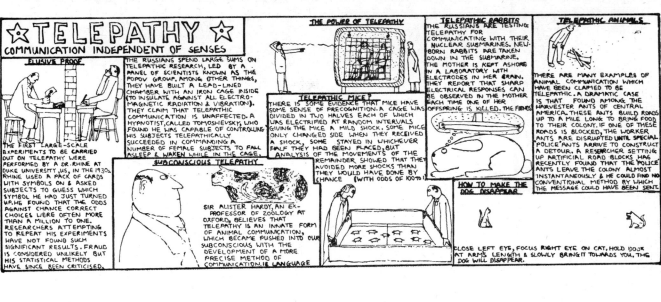

☆ TELEPATHY ☆
COMMUNICATION INDEPENDENT OF SENSES

ELUSIVE PROOF

THE FIRST LARGE-SCALE EXPERIMENTS TO BE CARRIED OUT ON TELEPATHY WERE PERFORMED BY A DR. RHINE AT DUKE UNIVERSITY, US, IN THE 1930s. RHINE USED A PACK OF CARDS WITH SYMBOLS ON & ASKED SUBJECTS TO GUESS WHICH SYMBOL HE HAD JUST TURNED UP. HE FOUND THAT THE ODDS AGAINST CHANCE CORRECT CHOICES WERE OFTEN MORE THAN A MILLION TO ONE. RESEARCHERS ATTEMPTING TO REPEAT HIS EXPERIMENTS HAVE NOT FOUND SUCH SIGNIFICANT RESULTS. FRAUD IS CONSIDERED UNLIKELY BUT HIS STATISTICAL METHODS HAVE SINCE BEEN CRITICISED.

THE RUSSIANS SPEND LARGE SUMS ON TELEPATHIC RESEARCH, LED BY A PANEL OF SCIENTISTS KNOWN AS THE POPOV GROUP. AMONG OTHER THINGS, THEY HAVE BUILT A LEAD-LINED CHAMBER WITH AN IRON CAGE INSIDE (TO INSULATE AGAINST ALL ELECTRO-MAGNETIC RADIATION & VIBRATION). THEY CLAIM THAT TELEPATHIC COMMUNICATION IS UNAFFECTED. A HYPNOTIST, CALLED TOMOSHEVSKY, WHO FOUND HE WAS CAPABLE OF CONTROLLING HIS SUBJECTS TELEPATHICALLY SUCCEEDED IN COMMANDING A NUMBER OF FEMALE SUBJECTS TO FALL ASLEEP & WAKEN WHILE IN THE CAGE.

SUBCONSCIOUS TELEPATHY

SIR ALISTER HARDY, AN EX-PROFESSOR OF ZOOLOGY AT OXFORD, BELIEVES THAT TELEPATHY IS AN INNATE FORM OF ANIMAL COMMUNICATION, WHICH BECAME PUSHED INTO OUR SUBCONSCIOUS WITH THE DEVELOPMENT OF A MORE PRECISE METHOD OF COMMUNICATION, I.E. LANGUAGE.

THE POWER OF TELEPATHY

TELEPATHIC MICE?

THERE IS SOME EVIDENCE THAT MICE HAVE SOME SENSE OF PRECOGNITION. A CAGE WAS DIVIDED IN TWO HALVES EACH OF WHICH WAS ELECTRIFIED AT RANDOM INTERVALS GIVING THE MICE A MILD SHOCK. SOME MICE ONLY CHANGED SIDE WHEN THEY RECEIVED A SHOCK, SOME STAYED IN WHICHEVER HALF THEY HAD BEEN PLACED, BUT ANALYSIS OF THE MOVEMENTS OF THE REMAINDER SHOWED THAT THEY AVOIDED MORE SHOCKS THAN THEY WOULD HAVE DONE BY CHANCE (WITH ODDS OF 100 TO 1).

TELEPATHIC RABBITS

THE RUSSIANS ARE TESTING TELEPATHY FOR COMMUNICATING WITH THEIR NUCLEAR SUBMARINES. NEW-BORN RABBITS ARE TAKEN DOWN IN THE SUBMARINE. THE MOTHER IS KEPT ASHORE IN A LABORATORY WITH ELECTRODES IN HER BRAIN. THEY REPORT THAT SHARP ELECTRICAL RESPONSES CAN BE OBSERVED IN THE MOTHER EACH TIME ONE OF HER OFFSPRING IS KILLED. THE FIENDS.

HOW TO MAKE THE DOG DISAPPEAR

CLOSE LEFT EYE, FOCUS RIGHT EYE ON CAT, HOLD BOOK AT ARMS LENGTH & SLOWLY BRING IT TOWARDS YOU. THE DOG WILL DISAPPEAR.

TELEPATHIC ANIMALS

THERE ARE MANY EXAMPLES OF ANIMAL COMMUNICATION WHICH HAVE BEEN CLAIMED TO BE TELEPATHIC. A DRAMATIC CASE IS THAT FOUND AMONG THE HARVESTER ANTS OF CENTRAL AMERICA. THESE ANTS BUILD ROADS UP TO A MILE LONG TO BRING FOOD TO THEIR COLONY. IF ONE OF THESE ROADS IS DISRUPTED, THE WORKER ANTS ARE DISRUPTED UNTIL SPECIAL 'POLICE' ANTS ARRIVE TO CONSTRUCT A DETOUR. A RESEARCHER SETTING UP ARTIFICIAL ROAD BLOCKS HAS RECENTLY FOUND THAT THE POLICE ANTS LEAVE THE COLONY ALMOST INSTANTANEOUSLY & HE COULD FIND NO CONVENTIONAL METHOD BY WHICH THE MESSAGE COULD HAVE BEEN SENT.

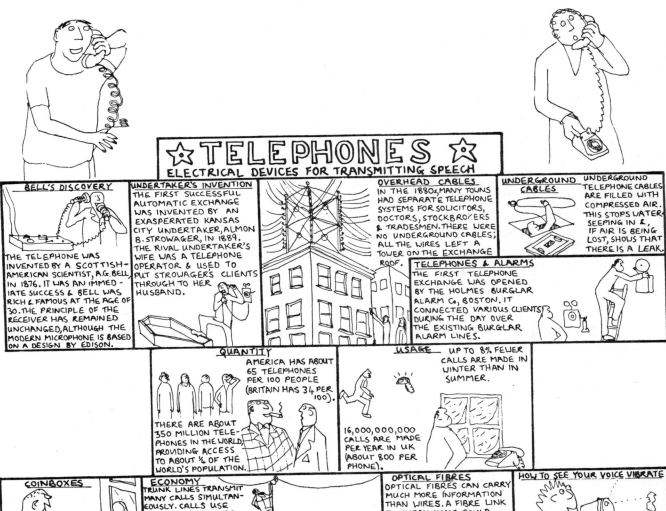

☆ TELEPHONES ☆
ELECTRICAL DEVICES FOR TRANSMITTING SPEECH

BELL'S DISCOVERY

THE TELEPHONE WAS INVENTED BY A SCOTTISH-AMERICAN SCIENTIST, A.G. BELL IN 1876. IT WAS AN IMMED-IATE SUCCESS & BELL WAS RICH & FAMOUS AT THE AGE OF 30. THE PRINCIPLE OF THE RECEIVER HAS REMAINED UNCHANGED, ALTHOUGH THE MODERN MICROPHONE IS BASED ON A DESIGN BY EDISON.

UNDERTAKER'S INVENTION

THE FIRST SUCCESSFUL AUTOMATIC EXCHANGE WAS INVENTED BY AN EXASPERATED KANSAS CITY UNDERTAKER, ALMON B. STROWAGER, IN 1889. THE RIVAL UNDERTAKER'S WIFE WAS A TELEPHONE OPERATOR & USED TO PUT STROWAGER'S CLIENTS THROUGH TO HER HUSBAND.

OVERHEAD CABLES

IN THE 1880s, MANY TOWNS HAD SEPARATE TELEPHONE SYSTEMS FOR SOLICITORS, DOCTORS, STOCKBROKERS & TRADESMEN. THERE WERE NO UNDERGROUND CABLES; ALL THE WIRES LEFT A TOWER ON THE EXCHANGE ROOF.

UNDERGROUND CABLES

UNDERGROUND TELEPHONE CABLES ARE FILLED WITH COMPRESSED AIR. THIS STOPS WATER SEEPING IN &, IF AIR IS BEING LOST, SHOWS THAT THERE IS A LEAK.

TELEPHONES & ALARMS

THE FIRST TELEPHONE EXCHANGE WAS OPENED BY THE HOLMES BURGLAR ALARM Co, BOSTON. IT CONNECTED VARIOUS CLIENTS DURING THE DAY OVER THE EXISTING BURGLAR ALARM LINES.

QUANTITY

AMERICA HAS ABOUT 65 TELEPHONES PER 100 PEOPLE (BRITAIN HAS 34 PER 100).

THERE ARE ABOUT 350 MILLION TELE-PHONES IN THE WORLD, PROVIDING ACCESS TO ABOUT ¼ OF THE WORLD'S POPULATION.

USAGE

UP TO 8% FEWER CALLS ARE MADE IN WINTER THAN IN SUMMER.

16,000,000,000 CALLS ARE MADE PER YEAR IN UK (ABOUT 800 PER PHONE).

COINBOXES

UNTIL 1921 COINBOXES WERE MADE OF WOOD, EXCEPT FOR DOCKLAND AREAS WHERE TOUGHER STEEL BOXES WERE ERECTED.

ECONOMY

TRUNK LINES TRANSMIT MANY CALLS SIMULTAN-EOUSLY. CALLS USE DIFFERENT CARRIER FREQUENCIES (LIKE RADIO STATIONS) TO SEPARATE THEM.

USEFUL PAUSES

ONLY 50% OF THE TIME DURING A TELEPHONE CALL IS SPENT SPEAKING. ON INTERCONTINENTAL LINES, EQUIPMENT AUTOMATICALLY BREAKS THE LINE DURING PAUSES IN SPEECH. THE PAUSES FROM SEVERAL DIFFERENT LINES ARE COMB-INED TO CREATE AN EXTRA LINE.

OPTICAL FIBRES

OPTICAL FIBRES CAN CARRY MUCH MORE INFORMATION THAN WIRES. A FIBRE LINK TO EVERY HOME COULD PROVIDE CABLE TELEVISION AS WELL AS TELEPHONE CALLS. ALTHOUGH THIS IS AT PRESENT UNECONOMIC, FIBRE IS FAST BECOMING CHEAPER.

HOW TO SEE YOUR VOICE VIBRATE

☆ CUT BOTTOM OFF EMPTY TIN WITH TIN OPENER.
☆ TIE STRETCHED BIT OF RUBBER (BALLOON) OVER ONE END.
☆ GLUE PIECE OF MIRROR ON RUBBER, OFF CENTRE.
☆ HOLD TIN SO SUN IS REFLECTED FROM MIRROR ONTO WALL.
☆ VIBRATING REFLECTION WILL MAKE PATTERNS AS YOU SPEAK.

☆ TENTS ☆

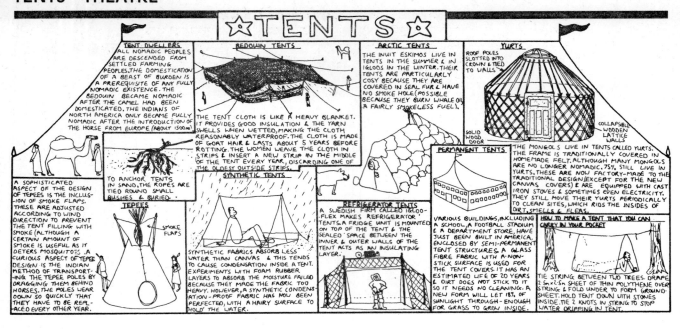

TENT DWELLERS
ALL NOMADIC PEOPLES ARE DESCENDED FROM SETTLED FARMING PEOPLES. THE DOMESTICATION OF A BEAST OF BURDEN IS A PREREQUISITE OF ANY FULLY NOMADIC EXISTENCE. THE BEDOUIN BECAME NOMADIC AFTER THE CAMEL HAD BEEN DOMESTICATED. THE INDIANS OF NORTH AMERICA ONLY BECAME FULLY NOMADIC AFTER THE INTRODUCTION OF THE HORSE FROM EUROPE (ABOUT 1500AD).

A SOPHISTICATED ASPECT OF THE DESIGN OF TEPEES IS THE INCLUSION OF SMOKE FLAPS. THESE ARE ADJUSTED ACCORDING TO WIND DIRECTION TO PREVENT THE TENT FILLING WITH SMOKE (ALTHOUGH A CERTAIN AMOUNT OF SMOKE IS USEFUL AS IT DETERS MOSQUITOES). A CURIOUS ASPECT OF TEPEE DESIGN IS THE INDIAN METHOD OF TRANSPORTING THE TEPEE POLES BY DRAGGING THEM BEHIND HORSES. THE POLES WEAR DOWN SO QUICKLY THAT THEY HAVE TO BE REPLACED EVERY OTHER YEAR.

TO ANCHOR TENTS IN SAND, THE ROPES ARE TIED ROUND SMALL BUSHES & BURIED.

TEPEES — SMOKE FLAPS

BEDOUIN TENTS
THE TENT CLOTH IS LIKE A HEAVY BLANKET. IT PROVIDES GOOD INSULATION & THE YARN SWELLS WHEN WETTED, MAKING THE CLOTH REASONABLY WATERPROOF. THE CLOTH IS MADE OF GOAT HAIR & LASTS ABOUT 5 YEARS BEFORE ROTTING. THE WOMEN WEAVE THE CLOTH IN STRIPS & INSERT A NEW STRIP IN THE MIDDLE OF THE TENT EVERY YEAR, DISCARDING ONE OF THE OLDEST OUTSIDE STRIPS.

SYNTHETIC TENTS
SYNTHETIC FABRICS ABSORB LESS WATER THAN CANVAS & THIS TENDS TO CAUSE CONDENSATION INSIDE A TENT. EXPERIMENTS WITH FOAM RUBBER LAYERS TO ABSORB THE MOISTURE FAILED BECAUSE THEY MADE THE FABRIC TOO HEAVY. HOWEVER, A SYNTHETIC CONDENSATION-PROOF FABRIC HAS NOW BEEN PERFECTED, WITH A HAIRY SURFACE TO 'HOLD' THE WATER.

ARCTIC TENTS
THE INUIT ESKIMOS LIVE IN TENTS IN THE SUMMER & IN IGLOOS IN THE WINTER. THEIR TENTS ARE PARTICULARLY COSY BECAUSE THEY ARE COVERED IN SEAL FUR & HAVE NO SMOKE HOLE (POSSIBLE BECAUSE THEY BURN WHALE OIL, A FAIRLY SMOKELESS FUEL).

REFRIGERATOR TENTS
A SWEDISH FIRM CALLED IGLOO-FLEX MAKES REFRIGERATOR TENTS. A FRIDGE UNIT IS MOUNTED ON TOP OF THE TENT & THE SEALED SPACE BETWEEN THE INNER & OUTER WALLS OF THE TENT ACTS AS AN INSULATING LAYER.

PERMANENT TENTS
VARIOUS BUILDINGS, INCLUDING A SCHOOL, A FOOTBALL STADIUM & A DEPARTMENT STORE, HAVE JUST BEEN BUILT IN AMERICA, ENCLOSED BY SEMI-PERMANENT TENT STRUCTURES. A GLASS FIBRE FABRIC WITH A NON-STICK SURFACE IS USED FOR THE TENT COVERS. IT HAS AN ESTIMATED LIFE OF 20 YEARS & DIRT DOES NOT STICK TO IT SO IT NEEDS NO CLEANING. A NEW FORM WILL LET 18% OF SUNLIGHT THROUGH - ENOUGH FOR GRASS TO GROW INSIDE.

YURTS
ROOF POLES SLOTTED INTO CROWN & TIED TO WALLS. SOLID WOOD DOOR. COLLAPSIBLE WOODEN LATTICE WALLS.

THE MONGOLS LIVE IN TENTS CALLED YURTS. THE FRAME IS TRADITIONALLY COVERED IN HOMEMADE FELT. ALTHOUGH MANY MONGOLS ARE NO LONGER NOMADIC, 75% STILL LIVE IN YURTS. THESE ARE NOW FACTORY-MADE TO THE TRADITIONAL DESIGN (EXCEPT FOR THE NEW CANVAS COVERS) & ARE EQUIPPED WITH CAST IRON STOVES & SOMETIMES EVEN ELECTRICITY. THEY STILL MOVE THEIR YURTS PERIODICALLY TO CLEAN SITES, WHICH RIDS THE INSIDES OF DIRT, SMELLS & FLEAS.

HOW TO MAKE A TENT THAT YOU CAN CARRY IN YOUR POCKET
TIE THE STRING BETWEEN TWO TREES. DRAPE 2.5m x 1.5m SHEET OF THIN POLYTHENE OVER STRING & FOLD UNDER TO FORM GROUNDSHEET. HOLD TENT DOWN WITH STONES INSIDE. TIE 2 KNOTS IN STRING TO STOP WATER DRIPPING IN TENT.

☆ TENNIS ☆
GAME HITTING BALL OVER NET WITH RACKETS

PRIMITIVE TENNIS
FRENCH MONASTERIES ARE RECORDED AS HAVING REAL TENNIS COURTS AS EARLY AS 1050. THE FRENCH ALSO PLAYED A GAME CALLED 'LA LONGUE PAUME' WHICH ENTAILED HITTING A CORK BALL OVER AN EARTH MOUND.

MODERN TENNIS
THE RISE IN POPULARITY OF LAWN TENNIS OCCURRED IN THE 1880s, LARGELY FROM A GAME PATENTED BY A MAJOR WINGFIELD IN 1874. THIS REQUIRED A COURT SHAPED LIKE AN HOUR GLASS WITH A NET IN THE MIDDLE & WAS CALLED SPHAIRISTIKÉ. HE PUBLICISED ITS VIRTUES WIDELY & THOUGH THE SHAPE OF THE COURT & SOME RULES WERE CHANGED IT DEVELOPED INTO LAWN TENNIS.

DEUCE
DEUCE (THE TENNIS TERM FOR A SCORE OF 40 ALL) COMES FROM THE FRENCH DEUX (TWO) IMPLYING TWO CONSECUTIVE POINTS TO WIN.

LOVE
LOVE (THE TENNIS TERM FOR ZERO) IS PROBABLY A CORRUPTION OF THE FRENCH L'OEUF (THE EGG) THE SAME IDEA AS THE DUCK IN CRICKET.

SCORING
THE ODD SCORING SYSTEM (15, 30, 40, GAME) IS DERIVED FROM THE DAYS OF REAL TENNIS WHEN IT WAS THE CUSTOM TO USE A CLOCK FACE TO RECORD THE SCORES.

RACKETS
DESPITE TRIALS WITH NUMEROUS SYNTHETIC MATERIALS MOST FIRST-CLASS PLAYERS STILL PREFER RACKETS STRUNG WITH SHEEP GUT. ABOUT 7 SHEEP ARE NEEDED TO FURNISH SUFFICIENT GUT FOR A SINGLE RACKET.

TENNIS BALLS
COLOURED BALLS WERE FIRST PERMITTED IN 1970 BECAUSE OF THE DIFFICULTY OF SEEING WHITE BALLS AGAINST THE LIGHTS IN INDOOR MATCHES. THEY ARE NOW USED OUTSIDE AS WELL, AS THEY SHOW UP BETTER ON COLOUR TV. OPINIONS VARY WHETHER THE AIR INSIDE THE BALL SHOULD BE UNDER PRESSURE OR NOT. IT USUALLY IS, BUT THE SWEDES TEND TO PREFER UNPRESSURISED BALLS.

LONGEST MATCH
THE LONGEST MATCH EVER RECORDED LASTED 100 HOURS & 10MIN, PLAYED BY 2 ARMY OFFICERS IN SOUTH AFRICA.

FASTEST SERVE
THE FASTEST SERVICE EVER RECORDED IS 136mph BY W. TILDEN IN 1936.

RICHEST PLAYER
BJORN BORG WON $100 000 IN 1979 THE MOST EVER WON BY A TENNIS PLAYER IN A YEAR. THIS IS ABOUT TWICE AS MUCH AS THAT WON BY ANY GOLFER IN A YEAR.

HOW TO MAKE A CRYSTAL GARDEN
MIX 6 TABLESPOONS WATER, 6TSP LAUNDRY BLUE, 6TSP SALT & ADD 6TSP AMMONIA. PUT A FEW MATCHBOX SIZED LUMPS OF BRICK OR CHARCOAL IN A SOUP BOWL & POUR IN MIXTURE. AS CRYSTALS START TO GROW PUT DROPS OF FOOD COLOURING ON LUMPS TO COLOUR CRYSTALS.

☆ THERMOMETERS ☆
INSTRUMENTS FOR MEASURING TEMPERATURE

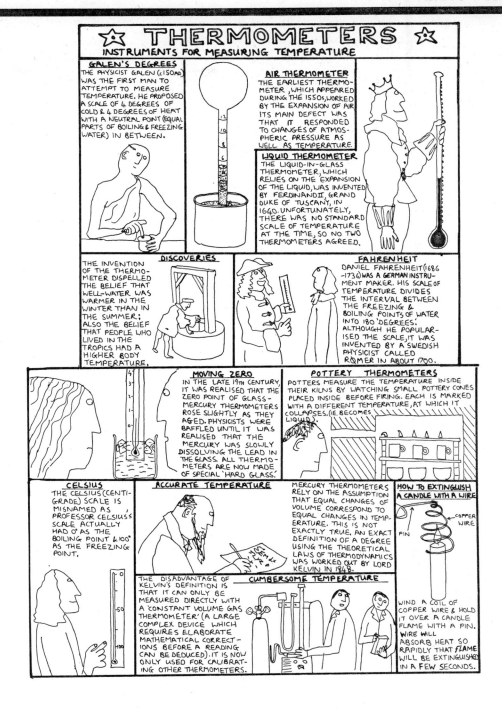

GALEN'S DEGREES
THE PHYSICIST GALEN (c150AD) WAS THE FIRST MAN TO ATTEMPT TO MEASURE TEMPERATURE. HE PROPOSED A SCALE OF 4 DEGREES OF COLD & 4 DEGREES OF HEAT WITH A NEUTRAL POINT (EQUAL PARTS OF BOILING & FREEZING WATER) IN BETWEEN.

AIR THERMOMETER
THE EARLIEST THERMOMETER, WHICH APPEARED DURING THE 1550s, WORKED BY THE EXPANSION OF AIR. ITS MAIN DEFECT WAS THAT IT RESPONDED TO CHANGES OF ATMOSPHERIC PRESSURE AS WELL AS TEMPERATURE.

LIQUID THERMOMETER
THE LIQUID-IN-GLASS THERMOMETER, WHICH RELIES ON THE EXPANSION OF THE LIQUID, WAS INVENTED BY FERDINAND II, GRAND DUKE OF TUSCANY, IN 1640. UNFORTUNATELY, THERE WAS NO STANDARD SCALE OF TEMPERATURE AT THE TIME, SO NO TWO THERMOMETERS AGREED.

DISCOVERIES
THE INVENTION OF THE THERMOMETER DISPELLED THE BELIEF THAT WELL-WATER WAS WARMER IN THE WINTER THAN IN THE SUMMER; ALSO THE BELIEF THAT PEOPLE WHO LIVED IN THE TROPICS HAD A HIGHER BODY TEMPERATURE.

FAHRENHEIT
DANIEL FAHRENHEIT (1686-1736) WAS A GERMAN INSTRUMENT MAKER. HIS SCALE OF TEMPERATURE DIVIDES THE INTERVAL BETWEEN THE FREEZING & BOILING POINTS OF WATER INTO 180 DEGREES. ALTHOUGH HE POPULARISED THE SCALE, IT WAS INVENTED BY A SWEDISH PHYSICIST CALLED RØMER IN ABOUT 1700.

MOVING ZERO
IN THE LATE 19th CENTURY, IT WAS REALISED THAT THE ZERO POINT OF GLASS-MERCURY THERMOMETERS ROSE SLIGHTLY AS THEY AGED. PHYSICISTS WERE BAFFLED UNTIL IT WAS REALISED THAT THE MERCURY WAS SLOWLY DISSOLVING THE LEAD IN THE GLASS. ALL THERMOMETERS ARE NOW MADE OF SPECIAL 'HARD GLASS'.

POTTERY THERMOMETERS
POTTERS MEASURE THE TEMPERATURE INSIDE THEIR KILNS BY WATCHING SMALL POTTERY CONES PLACED INSIDE BEFORE FIRING. EACH IS MARKED WITH A DIFFERENT TEMPERATURE, AT WHICH IT COLLAPSES. (IE. BECOMES LIQUID).

CELSIUS
THE CELSIUS (CENTIGRADE) SCALE IS MISNAMED AS PROFESSOR CELSIUS'S SCALE ACTUALLY HAD 0° AS THE BOILING POINT & 100° AS THE FREEZING POINT.

ACCURATE TEMPERATURE
MERCURY THERMOMETERS RELY ON THE ASSUMPTION THAT EQUAL CHANGES OF VOLUME CORRESPOND TO EQUAL CHANGES IN TEMPERATURE. THIS IS NOT EXACTLY TRUE. AN EXACT DEFINITION OF A DEGREE USING THE THEORETICAL LAWS OF THERMODYNAMICS WAS WORKED OUT BY LORD KELVIN IN 1848.

CUMBERSOME TEMPERATURE
THE DISADVANTAGE OF KELVIN'S DEFINITION IS THAT IT CAN ONLY BE MEASURED DIRECTLY WITH A 'CONSTANT VOLUME GAS THERMOMETER' (A LARGE COMPLEX DEVICE WHICH REQUIRES ELABORATE MATHEMATICAL CORRECTIONS BEFORE A READING CAN BE DEDUCED). IT IS NOW ONLY USED FOR CALIBRATING OTHER THERMOMETERS.

HOW TO EXTINGUISH A CANDLE WITH A WIRE
WIND A COIL OF COPPER WIRE & HOLD IT OVER A CANDLE FLAME WITH A PIN. WIRE WILL ABSORB HEAT SO RAPIDLY THAT *FLAME WILL BE EXTINGUISHED* IN A FEW SECONDS.

☆ THEATRE ☆
THE PERFORMANCE OF STORIES & SPECTACLE BY ACTORS

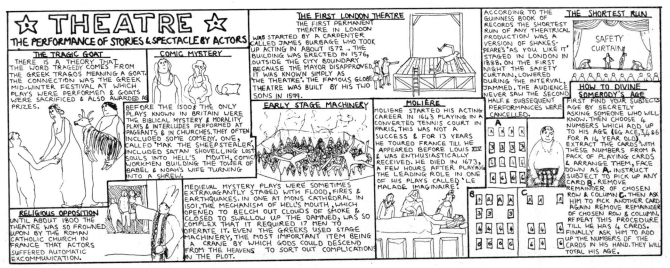

THE TRAGIC GOAT
THERE IS A THEORY THAT THE WORD TRAGEDY COMES FROM THE GREEK TRAGOS MEANING A GOAT. THE CONNECTION WAS THE GREEK MID-WINTER FESTIVAL AT WHICH PLAYS WERE PERFORMED & GOATS WERE SACRIFICED & ALSO AWARDED AS PRIZES.

COMIC MYSTERY
BEFORE THE 1500s THE ONLY PLAYS KNOWN IN BRITAIN WERE THE BIBLICAL MYSTERY & MORALITY PLAYS & INTERLUDES PERFORMED AT PAGEANTS & IN CHURCHES. THEY OFTEN INCLUDED SOME COMEDY. ONE, CALLED 'MAK THE SHEEPSTEALER', INCLUDED SATAN SHOVELLING LOST SOULS INTO HELL'S MOUTH, COMIC WORKMEN BUILDING THE TOWER OF BABEL & NOAH'S WIFE TURNING INTO A SHREW.

RELIGIOUS OPPOSITION
UNTIL ABOUT 1800 THE THEATRE WAS SO FROWNED UPON BY THE ROMAN CATHOLIC CHURCH IN FRANCE THAT ACTORS SUFFERED AUTOMATIC EXCOMMUNICATION.

THE FIRST LONDON THEATRE
THE FIRST PERMANENT THEATRE IN LONDON WAS STARTED BY A CARPENTER CALLED JAMES BURBAGE WHO TOOK UP ACTING IN ABOUT 1572. THE BUILDING WAS ERECTED IN 1576, OUTSIDE THE CITY BOUNDARY BECAUSE THE MAYOR DISAPPROVED. IT WAS KNOWN SIMPLY AS 'THE THEATRE'. THE FAMOUS GLOBE THEATRE WAS BUILT BY HIS TWO SONS IN 1599.

EARLY STAGE MACHINERY
MEDIEVAL MYSTERY PLAYS WERE SOMETIMES EXTRAVAGANTLY STAGED WITH FLOOD, FIRES & EARTHQUAKES. IN ONE AT MONS CATHEDRAL IN 1501, THE MECHANISM OF HELL'S MOUTH, WHICH OPENED TO BELCH OUT CLOUDS OF SMOKE & CLOSED TO SWALLOW UP THE DAMNED, WAS SO COMPLEX THAT IT REQUIRED 17 MEN TO OPERATE IT. EVEN THE GREEKS USED STAGE MACHINERY, THE MOST IMPORTANT ITEM BEING A CRANE BY WHICH GODS COULD DESCEND FROM THE HEAVENS TO SORT OUT COMPLICATIONS IN THE PLOT.

MOLIÈRE
MOLIÈRE STARTED HIS ACTING CAREER IN 1643 PLAYING IN A CONVERTED TENNIS COURT IN PARIS. THIS WAS NOT A SUCCESS & FOR 13 YEARS HE TOURED FRANCE TILL HE APPEARED BEFORE LOUIS XIV & WAS ENTHUSIASTICALLY RECEIVED. HE DIED IN 1673, A FEW HOURS AFTER PLAYING THE LEADING ROLE IN ONE OF HIS PLAYS CALLED 'LE MALADE IMAGINAIRE'.

THE SHORTEST RUN
ACCORDING TO THE GUINNESS BOOK OF RECORDS THE SHORTEST RUN OF ANY THEATRICAL PRODUCTION WAS A VERSION OF SHAKESPEARE'S 'AS YOU LIKE IT' STAGED IN LONDON IN 1888. ON THE FIRST NIGHT THE SAFETY CURTAIN, LOWERED DURING THE INTERVAL, JAMMED. THE AUDIENCE NEVER SAW THE SECOND HALF & SUBSEQUENT PERFORMANCES WERE CANCELLED.

HOW TO DIVINE SOMEBODY'S AGE
FIRST FIND YOUR SUBJECTS AGE BY SECRETLY ASKING SOMEONE WHO WILL KNOW. THEN CHOOSE 4 NUMBERS WHICH ADD UP TO HIS AGE (EG ACE, 3, 4 & 6 FOR A 14 YEAR OLD). EXTRACT THE CARDS WITH THESE NUMBERS FROM A PACK OF PLAYING CARDS & ARRANGE THEM, FACE DOWN AS **A**. INSTRUCT SUBJECT TO PICK UP ANY CARD **B**. REMOVE REMAINDER OF CHOSEN ROW & COLUMN **C**. THEN ASK HIM TO PICK ANOTHER CARD AGAIN REMOVE REMAINDER OF CHOSEN ROW & COLUMN. REPEAT THIS PROCEDURE TILL HE HAS 4 CARDS. FINALLY ASK HIM TO ADD UP THE NUMBERS OF THE CARDS IN HIS HAND. THEY WILL TOTAL HIS AGE.

☆ THRUSHES
SONGBIRDS OF THE FAMILY TURDINAE

ROMAN DELICACY
THE ROMANS REGARDED THRUSHES AS A DELICACY, REARING THEM IN AVIARIES WHERE THEY WERE FATTENED ON A PASTE OF BRUISED FIGS & FLOUR.

WORMS
IT IS NOT KNOWN EXACTLY HOW THRUSHES DETECT WORMS. THEY APPEAR TO STRIKE WHEN NONE OF THE WORM IS VISIBLE ABOVE GROUND.

RELATIVES
THRUSHES ARE CLOSELY RELATED TO BLACKBIRDS, REDWINGS AND FIELDFARES. VARIOUS EXOTIC THRUSHES ALSO VISIT BRITAIN.

ANTING
ANOTHER METHOD OF REMOVING PARASITES IS ANTING. THE THRUSHES SQUASH ANTS ALONG THEIR WINGS & TAILS, KILLING THE PARASITES WITH THE FORMIC ACID FROM THE ANTS. THEY ALSO LET LIVE ANTS, WHICH EAT THE PARASITES, CRAWL OVER THEIR PLUMAGE.

ODD MATES
SONG THRUSHES SOMETIMES MATE, OR SHARE NESTS WITH, THEIR CLOSE RELATIVE THE BLACKBIRD. ROBINS HAVE ALSO BEEN OBSERVED TENDING NESTING SONG THRUSHES.

SLUGS & SNAILS
THE SONG THRUSH'S DIET INCLUDES SLUGS & SNAILS. IT BREAKS OPEN SNAIL SHELLS BY SMASHING THEM AGAINST ROCKS & PREPARES SLUGS BY WIPING OFF THE SLIME ON GRASS.

ELECTRONIC TRILL
RESEARCHERS AT SUSSEX UNIVERSITY BELIEVE THAT SONG THRUSHES HAVE RECENTLY STARTED TO IMITATE THE ELECTRONIC WARBLE OF TRIMPHONES. IT IS KNOWN THAT THE YOUNG NEED TO LISTEN TO THEIR PARENTS TO DEVELOP THEIR OWN SONGS & IT IS THOUGHT THAT THEY WILL ALSO LEARN TO IMITATE OTHER SIMILAR SOUNDS.

SUNBATHING
THRUSHES HAVE BEEN KNOWN TO SUNBATHE, BY LYING, WINGS EXTENDED, ON THE GROUND, FOR UP TO 30 MIN. THIS PROBABLY INDUCES PARASITES IN THE FEATHERS TO MOVE, & SO MAKES THEM EASIER TO DISLODGE BY PREENING.

HOW TO MAKE A BIRDCAKE
MAKE A SMALL HOLE IN THE BOTTOM OF A HALF COCONUT & PUSH STRING THROUGH. FILL COCONUT WITH BREAD CRUSTS, CRUMBS, & WARM, MELTED FAT. WHEN FAT SETS, SUSPEND COCONUT UPSIDE-DOWN IN GARDEN.

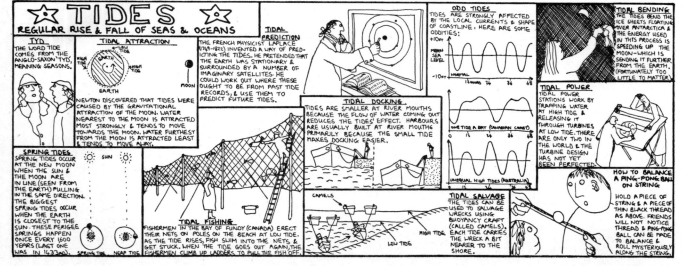

☆ TIDES ☆
REGULAR RISE & FALL OF SEAS & OCEANS

TYD
THE WORD TIDE COMES FROM THE ANGLO-SAXON 'TYD', MEANING SEASONS.

TIDAL ATTRACTION
NEWTON DISCOVERED THAT TIDES WERE CAUSED BY THE GRAVITATIONAL ATTRACTION OF THE MOON. WATER NEAREST TO THE MOON IS ATTRACTED MOST STRONGLY & TENDS TO MOVE TOWARDS THE MOON. WATER FURTHEST FROM THE MOON IS ATTRACTED LEAST & TENDS TO MOVE AWAY.

SPRING TIDES
SPRING TIDES OCCUR AT THE NEW MOON WHEN THE SUN & THE MOON ARE IN LINE (SEEN FROM THE EARTH) PULLING IN THE SAME DIRECTION. THE BIGGEST SPRING TIDES OCCUR WHEN THE EARTH IS CLOSEST TO THE SUN. THESE PERIGEE SPRINGS HAPPEN ONCE EVERY 1600 YEARS (LAST ONE WAS IN 1433 AD).

TIDAL PREDICTION
THE FRENCH PHYSICIST LAPLACE (1749-1827) INVENTED A WAY OF PREDICTING THE TIDES. HE PRETENDED THAT THE EARTH WAS STATIONARY & SURROUNDED BY A NUMBER OF IMAGINARY SATELLITES. HE COULD WORK OUT WHERE THESE OUGHT TO BE FROM PAST TIDE RECORDS, & USE THEM TO PREDICT FUTURE TIDES.

TIDAL DOCKING
TIDES ARE SMALLER AT RIVER MOUTHS BECAUSE THE FLOW OF WATER COMING OUT REDUCES THE TIDES' EFFECT. HARBOURS ARE USUALLY BUILT AT RIVER MOUTHS PRIMARILY BECAUSE THE SMALL TIDE MAKES DOCKING EASIER.

TIDAL FISHING
FISHERMEN IN THE BAY OF FUNDY (CANADA) ERECT THEIR NETS ON POLES ON THE BEACH AT LOW TIDE. AS THE TIDE RISES, FISH SWIM INTO THE NETS & GET STUCK. WHEN THE TIDE GOES OUT AGAIN, THE FISHERMEN CLIMB UP LADDERS TO PULL THE FISH OFF.

ODD TIDES
TIDES ARE STRONGLY AFFECTED BY THE LOCAL CURRENTS & SHAPE OF COASTLINE. HERE ARE SOME ODDITIES:

TWO TIDES A DAY

ONE TIDE A DAY (CANADIAN COAST)

UNEQUAL HIGH TIDES (AUSTRALIA)

TIDAL SALVAGE
THE TIDES CAN BE USED TO SALVAGE WRECKS USING BUOYANCY CRAFT (CALLED CAMELS). EACH TIDE CARRIES THE WRECK A BIT NEARER TO THE SHORE.

TIDAL BENDING
THE TIDES BEND THE ICE SHEETS FLOATING OVER ANTARCTICA & THE ENERGY USED IN THIS PROCESS IS SPEEDING UP THE MOON—WHICH IS SENDING IT FURTHER FROM THE EARTH. (FORTUNATELY TOO LITTLE TO MATTER)

TIDAL POWER
TIDAL POWER STATIONS WORK BY TRAPPING WATER AT HIGH TIDE & RELEASING IT THROUGH TURBINES AT LOW TIDE. THERE ARE ONLY TWO IN THE WORLD & THE TURBINE DESIGN HAS NOT YET BEEN PERFECTED.

HOW TO BALANCE A PING-PONG BALL ON STRING
HOLD A PIECE OF STRING & A PIECE OF THIN BLACK THREAD AS ABOVE. FRIENDS WILL NOT NOTICE THREAD & PING-PONG BALL CAN BE MADE TO BALANCE & ROLL MYSTERIOUSLY ALONG THE STRING.

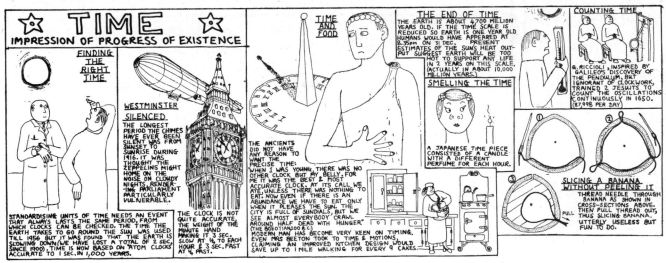

☆ TIME ☆
IMPRESSION OF PROGRESS OF EXISTENCE

FINDING THE RIGHT TIME

WESTMINSTER SILENCED
THE LONGEST PERIOD THE CHIMES HAVE EVER BEEN SILENT WAS FROM SUNSET TO SUNRISE DURING 1916. IT WAS THOUGHT THE ZEPPELINS MIGHT HOME IN ON THE NOISE ON CLOUDY NIGHTS, RENDERING PARLIAMENT PARTICULARLY VULNERABLE.

STANDARDISING UNITS OF TIME NEEDS AN EVENT THAT ALWAYS LASTS THE SAME PERIOD, FROM WHICH CLOCKS CAN BE CHECKED. THE TIME THE EARTH TAKES TO GO ROUND THE SUN WAS USED TILL 1956 BUT IT WAS FOUND THAT THE EARTH IS SLOWING DOWN (WE HAVE LOST A TOTAL OF 2 SEC. SINCE 1900). TIME IS NOW BASED ON ATOM CLOCKS ACCURATE TO 1 SEC. IN 1,000 YEARS.

THE CLOCK IS NOT QUITE ACCURATE. THE WEIGHT OF THE MINUTE HAND MAKING IT 3 SEC. SLOW AT ¼ TO EACH HOUR & 3 SEC. FAST AT ¼ PAST.

TIME AND FOOD
THE ANCIENTS DID NOT HAVE ANY REASON TO WANT THE PRECISE TIME: 'WHEN I WAS YOUNG, THERE WAS NO OTHER CLOCK BUT MY BELLY, FOR ME IT WAS THE BEST & MOST ACCURATE CLOCK. AT ITS CALL WE ATE, UNLESS THERE WAS NOTHING TO EAT. NOW EVEN IF THERE IS AN ABUNDANCE WE HAVE TO EAT ONLY WHEN IT PLEASES THE SUN. THE CITY IS FULL OF SUNDIALS, BUT WE SEE ALMOST EVERYBODY CRAWL AROUND HALF DEAD WITH HUNGER' (THE BOEOTIAN,100 B.C.)
MODERN MAN HAS BECOME VERY KEEN ON TIMING. EVEN MRS BEETON TOOK TO TIME & MOTIONS, CLAIMING AN IMPROVED KITCHEN DESIGN WOULD SAVE UP TO 1 MILE WALKING FOR EVERY 9 CAKES.

THE END OF TIME
THE EARTH IS ABOUT 4,700 MILLION YEARS OLD. IF THE TIME SCALE IS REDUCED SO EARTH IS ONE YEAR OLD HUMANS WOULD HAVE APPEARED AT 8.35PM ON 31 DEC. PRESENT ESTIMATES OF THE SUN'S HEAT OUTPUT SUGGEST EARTH WILL BE TOO HOT TO SUPPORT ANY LIFE IN 2 YEARS ON THIS SCALE (ACTUALLY IN ABOUT 10,000 MILLION YEARS.)

SMELLING THE TIME
A JAPANESE TIME PIECE CONSISTED OF A CANDLE WITH A DIFFERENT PERFUME FOR EACH HOUR.

COUNTING TIME
G. RICCIOLI, INSPIRED BY GALILEO'S DISCOVERY OF THE PENDULUM, BUT IGNORANT OF CLOCKWORK, TRAINED 2 JESUITS TO COUNT THE OSCILLATIONS CONTINUOUSLY IN 1650. (87,998 PER DAY)

SLICING A BANANA WITHOUT PEELING IT
THREAD NEEDLE THROUGH CROSS-SECTIONS ABOVE. THEN PULL THREAD OUT, THUS SLICING BANANA. UTTERLY USELESS BUT FUN TO DO.

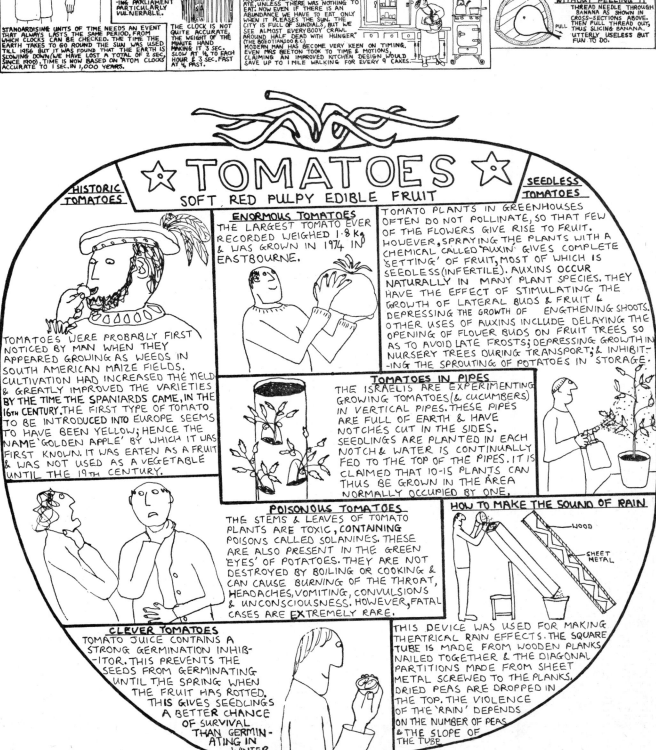

☆ TOMATOES ☆
SOFT RED PULPY EDIBLE FRUIT

HISTORIC TOMATOES
TOMATOES WERE PROBABLY FIRST NOTICED BY MAN WHEN THEY APPEARED GROWING AS WEEDS IN SOUTH AMERICAN MAIZE FIELDS. CULTIVATION HAD INCREASED THE YIELD & GREATLY IMPROVED THE VARIETIES BY THE TIME THE SPANIARDS CAME, IN THE 16TH CENTURY. THE FIRST TYPE OF TOMATO TO BE INTRODUCED INTO EUROPE SEEMS TO HAVE BEEN YELLOW; HENCE THE NAME 'GOLDEN APPLE' BY WHICH IT WAS FIRST KNOWN. IT WAS EATEN AS A FRUIT & WAS NOT USED AS A VEGETABLE UNTIL THE 19TH CENTURY.

ENORMOUS TOMATOES
THE LARGEST TOMATO EVER RECORDED WEIGHED 1.8 Kg & WAS GROWN IN 1974 IN EASTBOURNE.

SEEDLESS TOMATOES
TOMATO PLANTS IN GREENHOUSES OFTEN DO NOT POLLINATE, SO THAT FEW OF THE FLOWERS GIVE RISE TO FRUIT. HOWEVER, SPRAYING THE PLANTS WITH A CHEMICAL CALLED 'AUXIN' GIVES COMPLETE 'SETTING' OF FRUIT, MOST OF WHICH IS SEEDLESS (INFERTILE). AUXINS OCCUR NATURALLY IN MANY PLANT SPECIES. THEY HAVE THE EFFECT OF STIMULATING THE GROWTH OF LATERAL BUDS & FRUIT & DEPRESSING THE GROWTH OF LENGTHENING SHOOTS. OTHER USES OF AUXINS INCLUDE DELAYING THE OPENING OF FLOWER BUDS ON FRUIT TREES SO AS TO AVOID LATE FROSTS; DEPRESSING GROWTH IN NURSERY TREES DURING TRANSPORT; & INHIBITING THE SPROUTING OF POTATOES IN STORAGE.

TOMATOES IN PIPES
THE ISRAELIS ARE EXPERIMENTING GROWING TOMATOES (& CUCUMBERS) IN VERTICAL PIPES. THESE PIPES ARE FULL OF EARTH & HAVE NOTCHES CUT IN THE SIDES. SEEDLINGS ARE PLANTED IN EACH NOTCH & WATER IS CONTINUALLY FED TO THE TOP OF THE PIPES. IT IS CLAIMED THAT 10-15 PLANTS CAN THUS BE GROWN IN THE AREA NORMALLY OCCUPIED BY ONE.

POISONOUS TOMATOES
THE STEMS & LEAVES OF TOMATO PLANTS ARE TOXIC, CONTAINING POISONS CALLED SOLANINES. THESE ARE ALSO PRESENT IN THE GREEN 'EYES' OF POTATOES. THEY ARE NOT DESTROYED BY BOILING OR COOKING & CAN CAUSE BURNING OF THE THROAT, HEADACHES, VOMITING, CONVULSIONS & UNCONSCIOUSNESS. HOWEVER, FATAL CASES ARE EXTREMELY RARE.

HOW TO MAKE THE SOUND OF RAIN
WOOD
SHEET METAL

THIS DEVICE WAS USED FOR MAKING THEATRICAL RAIN EFFECTS. THE SQUARE TUBE IS MADE FROM WOODEN PLANKS NAILED TOGETHER & THE DIAGONAL PARTITIONS MADE FROM SHEET METAL SCREWED TO THE PLANKS. DRIED PEAS ARE DROPPED IN THE TOP. THE VIOLENCE OF THE 'RAIN' DEPENDS ON THE NUMBER OF PEAS & THE SLOPE OF THE TUBE

CLEVER TOMATOES
TOMATO JUICE CONTAINS A STRONG GERMINATION INHIBITOR. THIS PREVENTS THE SEEDS FROM GERMINATING UNTIL THE SPRING WHEN THE FRUIT HAS ROTTED. THIS GIVES SEEDLINGS A BETTER CHANCE OF SURVIVAL THAN GERMINATING IN WINTER

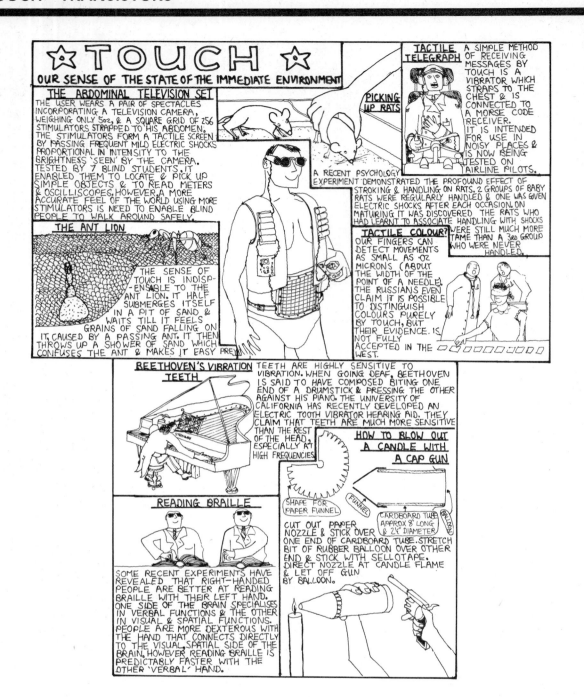

☆ TOUCH ☆
OUR SENSE OF THE STATE OF THE IMMEDIATE ENVIRONMENT

THE ABDOMINAL TELEVISION SET
THE USER WEARS A PAIR OF SPECTACLES INCORPORATING A TELEVISION CAMERA, WEIGHING ONLY 5oz, & A SQUARE GRID OF 256 STIMULATORS STRAPPED TO HIS ABDOMEN. THE STIMULATORS FORM A TACTILE SCREEN BY PASSING FREQUENT MILD ELECTRIC SHOCKS PROPORTIONAL IN INTENSITY TO THE BRIGHTNESS 'SEEN' BY THE CAMERA. TESTED BY 7 BLIND STUDENTS, IT ENABLED THEM TO LOCATE & PICK UP SIMPLE OBJECTS & TO READ METERS & OSCILLOSCOPES. HOWEVER A MORE ACCURATE FEEL OF THE WORLD USING MORE STIMULATORS IS NEED TO ENABLE BLIND PEOPLE TO WALK AROUND SAFELY.

THE ANT LION
THE SENSE OF TOUCH IS INDISP-ENSABLE TO THE ANT LION. IT HALF SUBMERGES ITSELF IN A PIT OF SAND & WAITS TILL IT FEELS GRAINS OF SAND FALLING ON IT, CAUSED BY A PASSING ANT. IT THEN THROWS UP A SHOWER OF SAND WHICH CONFUSES THE ANT & MAKES IT EASY PREY.

PICKING UP RATS
A RECENT PSYCHOLOGY EXPERIMENT DEMONSTRATED THE PROFOUND EFFECT OF STROKING & HANDLING ON RATS. 2 GROUPS OF BABY RATS WERE REGULARLY HANDLED & ONE WAS GIVEN ELECTRIC SHOCKS AFTER EACH OCCASION. ON MATURING IT WAS DISCOVERED THE RATS WHO HAD LEARNT TO ASSOCIATE HANDLING WITH SHOCKS WERE STILL MUCH MORE TAME THAN A 3RD GROUP WHO WERE NEVER HANDLED.

TACTILE TELEGRAPH
A SIMPLE METHOD OF RECEIVING MESSAGES BY TOUCH IS A VIBRATOR WHICH STRAPS TO THE CHEST & IS CONNECTED TO A MORSE CODE RECEIVER. IT IS INTENDED FOR USE IN NOISY PLACES & IS NOW BEING TESTED ON AIRLINE PILOTS.

TACTILE COLOUR?
OUR FINGERS CAN DETECT MOVEMENTS AS SMALL AS ·02 MICRONS (ABOUT THE WIDTH OF THE POINT OF A NEEDLE). THE RUSSIANS EVEN CLAIM IT IS POSSIBLE TO DISTINGUISH COLOURS PURELY BY TOUCH, BUT THEIR EVIDENCE IS NOT FULLY ACCEPTED IN THE WEST.

BEETHOVEN'S VIBRATION TEETH
TEETH ARE HIGHLY SENSITIVE TO VIBRATION. WHEN GOING DEAF, BEETHOVEN IS SAID TO HAVE COMPOSED BITING ONE END OF A DRUMSTICK & PRESSING THE OTHER AGAINST HIS PIANO. THE UNIVERSITY OF CALIFORNIA HAS RECENTLY DEVELOPED AN ELECTRIC TOOTH VIBRATOR HEARING AID. THEY CLAIM THAT TEETH ARE MUCH MORE SENSITIVE THAN THE REST OF THE HEAD, ESPECIALLY AT HIGH FREQUENCIES.

HOW TO BLOW OUT A CANDLE WITH A CAP GUN
SHAPE FOR PAPER FUNNEL
FUNNEL
BALLOON
CARDBOARD TUBE APPROX 8' LONG & 2¼' DIAMETER
CUT OUT PAPER NOZZLE & STICK OVER ONE END OF CARDBOARD TUBE. STRETCH BIT OF RUBBER BALLOON OVER OTHER END & STICK WITH SELLOTAPE. DIRECT NOZZLE AT CANDLE FLAME & LET OFF GUN BY BALLOON.

READING BRAILLE
SOME RECENT EXPERIMENTS HAVE REVEALED THAT RIGHT-HANDED PEOPLE ARE BETTER AT READING BRAILLE WITH THEIR LEFT HAND. ONE SIDE OF THE BRAIN SPECIALISES IN VERBAL FUNCTIONS & THE OTHER IN VISUAL & SPATIAL FUNCTIONS. PEOPLE ARE MORE DEXTEROUS WITH THE HAND THAT CONNECTS DIRECTLY TO THE VISUAL SPATIAL SIDE OF THE BRAIN. HOWEVER READING BRAILLE IS PREDICTABLY FASTER WITH THE OTHER 'VERBAL' HAND.

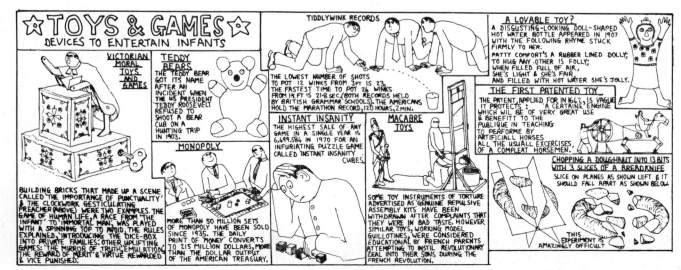

☆ TOYS & GAMES ☆
DEVICES TO ENTERTAIN INFANTS

VICTORIAN MORAL TOYS AND GAMES
BUILDING BRICKS THAT MADE UP A SCENE CALLED 'THE IMPORTANCE OF PUNCTUALITY' & THE CLOCKWORK GESTICULATING PREACHER (ABOVE) WERE TWO EXAMPLES. THE GAME OF HUMAN LIFE, A RACE FROM THE INFANT TO IMMORTAL MAN, WAS PLAYED WITH A SPINNING TOP TO AVOID THE RULES EXPLAINED, INTRODUCING THE DICE-BOX INTO PRIVATE FAMILIES. OTHER UPLIFTING GAMES: THE MIRROR OF TRUTH, EMULATION, THE REWARD OF MERIT & VIRTUE REWARDED & VICE PUNISHED.

TEDDY BEARS
THE TEDDY BEAR GOT ITS NAME AFTER AN INCIDENT WHEN THE US PRESIDENT TEDDY ROOSEVELT REFUSED TO SHOOT A BEAR CUB ON A HUNTING TRIP IN 1903.

MONOPOLY
MORE THAN 50 MILLION SETS OF MONOPOLY HAVE BEEN SOLD SINCE 1935. THE DAILY PRINT OF 'MONEY' CONVERTS TO 215 MILLION DOLLARS, MORE THAN THE DOLLAR OUTPUT OF THE AMERICAN TREASURY.

TIDDLYWINK RECORDS
THE LOWEST NUMBER OF SHOTS TO POT 12 WINKS FROM 3FT IS 23. THE FASTEST TIME TO POT 24 WINKS FROM 1¼FT IS 21·8 SEC. (BOTH RECORDS HELD BY BRITISH GRAMMAR SCHOOLS). THE AMERICANS HOLD THE MARATHON RECORD, 120 HOURS, 2 MIN.

INSTANT INSANITY
THE HIGHEST SALE OF ANY GAME IN A SINGLE YEAR IS 6,499,584 IN 1970 FOR AN INFURIATING PUZZLE GAME CALLED INSTANT INSANITY CUBES.

MACABRE TOYS
SOME TOY INSTRUMENTS OF TORTURE ADVERTISED AS GENUINE REPULSIVE ASSEMBLY KITS HAVE BEEN WITHDRAWN AFTER COMPLAINTS THAT THEY WERE IN BAD TASTE. HOWEVER SIMILAR TOYS, WORKING MODEL GUILLOTINES, WERE CONSIDERED EDUCATIONAL BY FRENCH PARENTS ATTEMPTING TO INSTIL REVOLUTIONARY ZEAL INTO THEIR SONS DURING THE FRENCH REVOLUTION.

A LOVABLE TOY?
A DISGUSTING-LOOKING DOLL-SHAPED HOT WATER BOTTLE APPEARED IN 1907 WITH THE FOLLOWING RHYME STUCK FIRMLY TO HER.
PATTY COMFORT'S A RUBBER LINED DOLLY;
TO HUG ANY OTHER IS FOLLY;
WHEN FILLED FULL OF AIR,
SHE'S LIGHT & SHE'S FAIR,
AND FILLED WITH HOT WATER SHE'S JOLLY.

THE FIRST PATENTED TOY
THE PATENT, APPLIED FOR IN 1642, IS VAGUE IT PROTECTS: 'A CERTAINE ENGINE WHICH WIL BE OF VERY GREAT USE & BENEFITT TO THE PUBLIQUE IN TEACHING TO PERFORME BY ARTIFICIALL HORSES ALL THE USUALL EXCERCISES OF A COMPLEAT HORSEMEN.'

CHOPPING A DOUGHNUT INTO 13 BITS WITH 3 SLICES OF A BREADKNIFE
SLICE ON PLANES AS SHOWN LEFT & IT SHOULD FALL APART AS SHOWN BELOW.
THIS EXPERIMENT IS AMAZINGLY DIFFICULT.

☆ TRADE NAMES ☆
NAMES DESIGNATING PRODUCTS & MANUFACTURERS

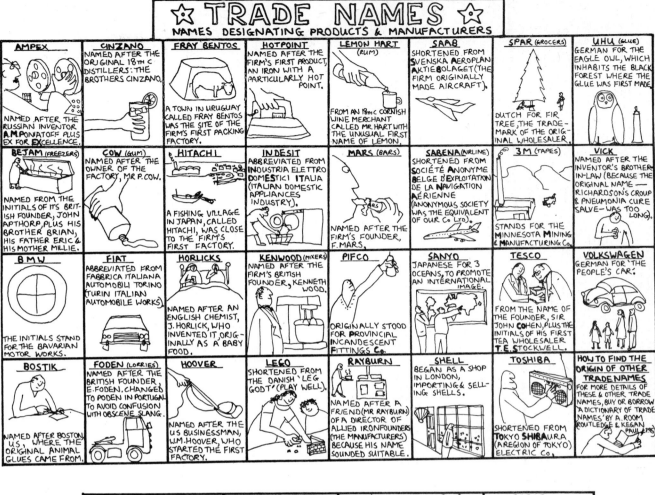

AMPEX
NAMED AFTER THE RUSSIAN INVENTOR A.M. PONIATOFF PLUS EX FOR EXCELLENCE.

CINZANO
NAMED AFTER THE ORIGINAL 18th C DISTILLERS: THE BROTHERS CINZANO.

FRAY BENTOS
A TOWN IN URUGUAY CALLED FRAY BENTOS WAS THE SITE OF THE FIRM'S FIRST PACKING FACTORY.

HOTPOINT
NAMED AFTER THE FIRM'S FIRST PRODUCT, AN IRON WITH A PARTICULARLY HOT POINT.

LEMON HART (RUM)
FROM AN 18th C CORNISH WINE MERCHANT CALLED MR HART WITH THE UNUSUAL FIRST NAME OF LEMON.

SAAB
SHORTENED FROM SVENSKA AEROPLAN AKTIEBOLAGET (THE FIRM ORIGINALLY MADE AIRCRAFT).

SPAR (GROCERS)
DUTCH FOR FIR TREE, THE TRADE-MARK OF THE ORIGINAL WHOLESALER.

UHU (GLUE)
GERMAN FOR THE EAGLE OWL, WHICH INHABITS THE BLACK FOREST WHERE THE GLUE WAS FIRST MADE.

BEJAM (FREEZERS)
NAMED FROM THE INITIALS OF ITS BRITISH FOUNDER, JOHN APTHORP, PLUS HIS BROTHER BRIAN, HIS FATHER ERIC & HIS MOTHER MILLIE.

COW (GUM)
NAMED AFTER THE OWNER OF THE FACTORY, MR P. COW.

HITACHI
A FISHING VILLAGE IN JAPAN, CALLED HITACHI, WAS CLOSE TO THE FIRM'S FIRST FACTORY.

INDESIT
ABBREVIATED FROM INDUSTRIA ELETTRO DOMESTICI ITALIA (ITALIAN DOMESTIC APPLIANCES INDUSTRY).

MARS (BARS)
NAMED AFTER THE FIRM'S FOUNDER, F. MARS.

SABENA (AIRLINE)
SHORTENED FROM SOCIÉTÉ ANONYME BELGE D'EXPLOITATION DE LA NAVIGATION AÉRIENNE (ANONYMOUS SOCIETY WAS THE EQUIVALENT OF OUR CO. LTD).

3M (TAPES)
STANDS FOR THE MINNESOTA MINING & MANUFACTURING Co.

VICK
NAMED AFTER THE INVENTOR'S BROTHER IN-LAW (BECAUSE THE ORIGINAL NAME – RICHARDSON'S CROUP & PNEUMONIA CURE SALVE – WAS TOO LONG).

BMW
THE INITIALS STAND FOR THE BAVARIAN MOTOR WORKS.

FIAT
ABBREVIATED FROM FABBRICA ITALIANA AUTOMOBILI TORINO (TURIN ITALIAN AUTOMOBILE WORKS).

HORLICKS
NAMED AFTER AN ENGLISH CHEMIST, J. HORLICK, WHO INVENTED IT, ORIGINALLY AS A BABY FOOD.

KENWOOD (MIXERS)
NAMED AFTER THE FIRM'S BRITISH FOUNDER, KENNETH WOOD.

PIFCO
ORIGINALLY STOOD FOR PROVINCIAL INCANDESCENT FITTINGS Co.

SANYO
JAPANESE FOR 3 OCEANS, TO PROMOTE AN INTERNATIONAL IMAGE.

TESCO
FROM THE NAME OF THE FOUNDER, SIR JOHN COHEN, PLUS THE INITIALS OF HIS FIRST TEA WHOLESALER T.E. STOCKWELL.

VOLKSWAGEN
GERMAN FOR 'THE PEOPLE'S CAR'.

BOSTIK
NAMED AFTER BOSTON, US, WHERE THE ORIGINAL ANIMAL GLUES CAME FROM.

FODEN (LORRIES)
NAMED AFTER THE BRITISH FOUNDER E. FODEN, CHANGED TO FODEN IN PORTUGAL TO AVOID CONFUSION WITH OBSCENE SLANG.

HOOVER
NAMED AFTER THE US BUSINESSMAN, W.M. HOOVER, WHO STARTED THE FIRST FACTORY.

LEGO
SHORTENED FROM THE DANISH 'LEG GODT' (PLAY WELL).

RAYBURN
NAMED AFTER A FRIEND (MR RAYBURN) OF A DIRECTOR OF ALLIED IRONFOUNDERS (THE MANUFACTURERS) BECAUSE HIS NAME SOUNDED SUITABLE.

SHELL
BEGAN AS A SHOP IN LONDON, IMPORTING & SELLING SHELLS.

TOSHIBA
SHORTENED FROM TOKYO SHIBAURA (A REGION OF TOKYO) ELECTRIC Co.

HOW TO FIND THE ORIGIN OF OTHER TRADE NAMES
FOR MORE DETAILS OF THESE & OTHER TRADE NAMES, BUY OR BORROW 'A DICTIONARY OF TRADE NAMES' BY A. ROOM (ROUTLEDGE & KEGAN PAUL £7.95)

DISCOVERY
THE PRINCIPLE OF THE TRANSISTOR IS BASED ON WORK DONE IN THE 1870s. A GERMAN ENGINEER CALLED BRAUN DISCOVERED THAT WHEN A WIRE TOUCHED CERTAIN CRYSTALS, ELECTRICITY WOULD FLOW FREELY IN ONE DIRECTION ONLY.

THE CAT'S WHISKER
THE FIRST USE OF BRAUN'S INVENTION WAS IN EARLY RADIO RECEIVERS. THE BEST POINT FOR THE WIRE TO TOUCH THE CRYSTAL WAS CRITICAL, SO IT WAS MADE ADJUSTABLE & CALLED A CAT'S WHISKER.

RADIO
A TRANSMITTER SUPERIMPOSES SPEECH ONTO A HIGH FREQUENCY RADIO WAVE WHICH TRAVELS THROUGH THE AIR. THE CAT'S WHISKER IN THE RECEIVER BLOCKS OFF THE RADIO WAVE, SO THE SPEECH CAN BE PICKED UP THROUGH THE EARPHONES.

RADAR
THE CAT'S WHISKER WAS REPLACED BY VALVES IN THE 1920s. HOWEVER, INTEREST REVIVED IN WORLD WAR II WHEN IT WAS FOUND THAT A CRYSTAL WORKED BETTER FOR THE HIGH FREQUENCIES USED IN RADAR RECEIVERS.

AMPLIFICATION
IN 1947, EXPERIMENTS WERE MADE PUTTING TWO WHISKERS ON A CRYSTAL OF GERMANIUM AT THE BELL TELEPHONE LABORATORIES (NEW JERSEY). IT WAS FOUND THAT A SMALL AMOUNT OF CURRENT PASSING FROM ONE WHISKER TO THE CRYSTAL COULD CONTROL A BIGGER CURRENT FROM THE OTHER WHISKER – THE FIRST TRANSISTOR AMPLIFIER.

☆ TRANSISTORS ☆
ELECTRIC DEVICES FOR SWITCHING & AMPLIFICATION

A GERMANIUM SANDWICH
THE FIRST PRACTICAL TRANSISTOR WAS MADE IN 1950 BY ADDING IMPURITIES TO PARTS OF A GERMANIUM CRYSTAL, ALTERING ITS ELECTRICAL CHARACTERISTICS. THE AREAS BETWEEN THE IMPURITIES ACTED LIKE THE 2 WHISKER CONTACTS.

USEFUL TRANSISTORS
THE FIRST TRANSISTOR RADIOS APPEARED IN 1955. THEY WERE AN IMMEDIATE SUCCESS, MAKING THE FIRST TRULY PORTABLE RADIO.

MODERN TRANSISTORS
THE MOST COMMON SORT OF TRANSISTOR INSIDE SILICON CHIPS IS THE FIELD EFFECT TRANSISTOR. THE CURRENT FLOWING THROUGH THE SILICON CHANNEL IS CONTROLLED BY THE VOLTAGE ACROSS IT.

NO VOLTAGE — BIG CURRENT
SMALL VOLTAGE — SMALL CURRENT
LARGE VOLTAGE — NO CURRENT

MAKING TRANSISTORS
CHIPS OFTEN CONTAIN MILLIONS OF TRANSISTORS. THEY ARE MADE BY LAYING A SERIES OF MINUTE STENCIL MASKS OVER A WAFER OF SILICON & EXPOSING IT TO VAPOURS WHICH DIFFUSE IMPURITIES INTO THE SILICON. CONTACTS & CONDUCTING PATHS ARE THEN ETCHED ON TOP WITH SIMILAR MASKS.

SMALLER TRANSISTORS
MUCH CURRENT RESEARCH IS AIMED AT REDUCING THE SIZE OF CHIPS' TRANSISTORS TO MAKE COMPUTERS SMALLER & FASTER. IT IS DIFFICULT TO MAKE THE MASKS FINE ENOUGH & DIFFICULT TO REDUCE THE HEAT GENERATED BY EACH TRANSISTOR.

TOOTH TRANSISTOR
MR HENRY KOCH (US) COMPLAINED OF HEARING MUSIC IN HIS HEAD. IT WAS EVENTUALLY FOUND THAT A BIT OF CARBORUNDUM FROM A DENTIST'S DRILL INSIDE ONE OF HIS TEETH WAS ACTING AS A TRANSISTOR. THIS WAS PICKING UP MUSIC FROM A POWERFUL RADIO TRANSMITTER NEARBY.

TRUMPETS

LOUD RAUCOUS WIND INSTRUMENTS

SHELLFISH TRUMPETS

IT HAS BEEN SUGGESTED THAT THE METHOD OF RAISING SOUND WAVES BY THE VIBRATION OF THE LIPS WAS DISCOVERED WHILE EATING SHELLFISH. ONE OF THE EARLIEST FORMS OF LIP-VOICED INSTRUMENT IS THE SPIRAL SHELL. IN ORDER TO REMOVE THE SHELLFISH CONCEALED INSIDE, IT WAS NECESSARY TO BREAK OFF THE TIP OF THE SHELL & TO PUSH OR BLOW OUT THE FISH. WITH THE FINAL BLAST THAT HERALDED THE MEAL, THE VIBRATION OF THE LIPS WAS DISCOVERED.

DIDGERIDOOS

IT IS DIFFICULT TO DETERMINE WHETHER SOME PRIMITIVE INSTRUMENTS WERE USED FOR SHOUTING THROUGH, AS MEGAPHONES, OR FOR BLOWING (VIBRATING THE LIPS) AS TRUMPETS. THE ABORIGINES HAVE AN INSTRUMENT CALLED A DIDGERIDOO WHICH IS USED FOR BOTH. A BASE NOTE IS SOUNDED WITH THE LIPS WHILE THE PLAYER ELICITS OTHER HARMONIES BY HUMMING OR ROARING AT THE SAME TIME.

HOLES & SLIDES

NOT UNTIL THE LATE 1800s WERE MANY TRUMPETS CAPABLE OF A FULL CHROMATIC SCALE. SOME TRUMPETS WERE MADE IN THE EARLY 1800s WITH SIDE HOLES (AS IN FLUTES etc), BUT NOTES PLAYED WITH OPEN HOLES ALWAYS SOUNDED THINNER THAN THOSE WITH ALL HOLES CLOSED. A SLIDE TRUMPET, LIKE A SMALL TROMBONE, WAS ALSO POPULAR IN ENGLAND IN THIS PERIOD. THE VALVE TRUMPET WAS INVENTED IN GERMANY IN 1815, BUT WAS NOT GENERALLY ACCEPTED UNTIL ABOUT 1900.

VALVE TRUMPETS

THE RISE IN POPULARITY OF VALVED BRASS INSTRUMENTS IS PRIMARILY DUE TO ADOLF SAX —A GERMAN WHO SETTLED IN PARIS IN 1841. HE BECAME INFLUENTIAL & MANAGED TO CARRY OUT EXTENSIVE REFORMS IN FRENCH ARMY BANDS— EQUIPPING THEM WITH A RANGE OF VALVED BRASS INSTRUMENTS OF HIS OWN DESIGN —AMONG THEM THE SAXOPHONE.

STRAIGHT TRUMPETS

THE ROMANS WERE THE FIRST TO ATTEMPT TO BEND THE TUBING OF THEIR TRUMPETS. STRAIGHT 3-5m LONG TRUMPETS WERE COMMON IN CHINA & TIBET, THE BELL BEING HELD BY A SMALL BOY.

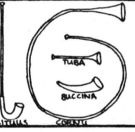

TUBA
BUCCINA
LITUUS
CORNU

'RAUCOUS' TRUMPETS

THE ROMANS WERE KEEN ON TRUMPETS & USED 4 VARIETIES IN THEIR ARMIES: THE LITUUS, THE TUBA, THE CORNU & THE BUCCINA. YOU NEEDED GREAT ENERGY TO PLAY THEM, SHOWN BY THE DISCOVERY OF FACE BANDAGES WITH SOME INSTRUMENTS. THEY ALL PRODUCED LOUD IMPURE NOTES & WERE NICKNAMED 'STRIDOR', 'RUDIS', 'RAUCUS' & 'HORRIBILIS'.

HOW TO MAKE A DUOPRINT

COLOUR A SHEET OF PAPER WITH WAX CRAYONS —LEAVING NO AREA UNCOVERED. COVER THIS WITH BLACK CRAYON SO NO COLOUR SHOWS THROUGH. COVER PAPER WITH A SECOND SHEET & DRAW ON IT IN BALLPOINT PEN. SEPARATE THE SHEETS & THE BLACK CRAYON WILL HAVE STUCK TO THE UNDERSIDE OF THE SECOND SHEET WHERE PRESSED, CREATING TWO INTERESTING PRINTS.

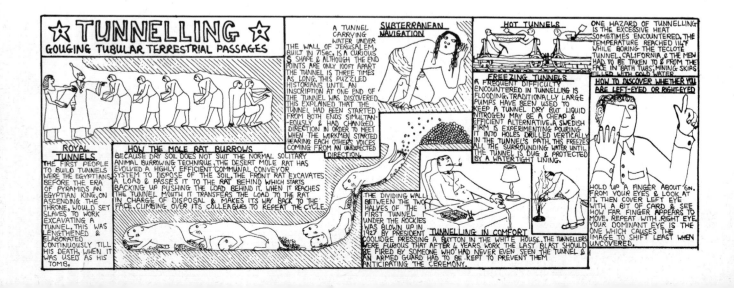

☆ TUNNELLING ☆
GOUGING TUBULAR TERRESTRIAL PASSAGES

ROYAL TUNNELS

THE FIRST PEOPLE TO BUILD TUNNELS WERE THE EGYPTIANS. BEFORE THE ERA OF PYRAMIDS AN EGYPTIAN KING, ON ASCENDING THE THRONE, WOULD SET SLAVES TO WORK EXCAVATING A TUNNEL. THIS WAS LENGTHENED & ELABORATED CONTINUOUSLY TILL HIS DEATH, WHEN IT WAS USED AS HIS TOMB.

HOW THE MOLE RAT BURROWS

BECAUSE DRY SOIL DOES NOT SUIT THE NORMAL SOLITARY ANIMAL BURROWING TECHNIQUE, THE DESERT MOLE RAT HAS EVOLVED A HIGHLY EFFICIENT COMMUNAL CONVEYOR SYSTEM TO DISPOSE OF THE SOIL. THE FRONT RAT EXCAVATES A LOAD & PASSES IT TO THE RAT BEHIND WHICH STARTS BACKING UP PUSHING THE LOAD BEHIND IT. WHEN IT REACHES THE TUNNEL MOUTH IT TRANSFERS THE LOAD TO THE RAT IN CHARGE OF DISPOSAL & MAKES ITS WAY BACK TO THE FACE, CLIMBING OVER ITS COLLEAGUES TO REPEAT THE CYCLE.

A TUNNEL CARRYING WATER UNDER THE WALL OF JERUSALEM, BUILT IN 715BC, IS A CURIOUS S SHAPE & ALTHOUGH THE END POINTS ARE ONLY 100FT APART THE TUNNEL IS THREE TIMES AS LONG. THIS PUZZLED HISTORIANS UNTIL AN INSCRIPTION AT ONE END OF THE TUNNEL WAS DISCOVERED. THIS EXPLAINED THAT THE TUNNEL HAD BEEN STARTED FROM BOTH ENDS SIMULTANEOUSLY & HAD CHANGED DIRECTION IN ORDER TO MEET WHEN THE WORKMEN STARTED HEARING EACH OTHER'S VOICES COMING FROM AN UNEXPECTED DIRECTION.

SUBTERRANEAN NAVIGATION

THE DIVIDING WALL BETWEEN THE TWO HALVES OF THE FIRST TUNNEL UNDER THE ROCKIES WAS BLOWN UP IN 1927 BY PRESIDENT COOLIDGE PRESSING A BUTTON IN THE WHITE HOUSE. THE TUNNELLERS WERE FURIOUS THAT AFTER 4 YEARS WORK THE LAST BLAST SHOULD BE FIRED BY SOMEONE WHO HAD NEVER EVEN SEEN THE TUNNEL & AN ARMED GUARD HAD TO BE KEPT TO PREVENT THEM ANTICIPATING THE CEREMONY.

TUNNELLING IN COMFORT

HOT TUNNELS

ONE HAZARD OF TUNNELLING IS THE EXCESSIVE HEAT SOMETIMES ENCOUNTERED. THE TEMPERATURE REACHED 114°F WHILE BORING THE TECLOTE TUNNEL, CALIFORNIA & THE MEN HAD TO BE TAKEN TO & FROM THE FACE IN BATH TUBS, MINING SKIPS FILLED WITH COLD WATER.

FREEZING TUNNELS

A FREQUENT DIFFICULTY ENCOUNTERED IN TUNNELLING IS FLOODING. TRADITIONALLY LARGE PUMPS HAVE BEEN USED TO KEEP A TUNNEL DRY BUT LIQUID NITROGEN MAY BE A CHEAP & EFFICIENT ALTERNATIVE. A SWEDISH FIRM IS EXPERIMENTING POURING IT INTO HOLES DRILLED VERTICALLY IN THE TUNNEL'S PATH. THIS FREEZES ALL THE SURROUNDING WATER UNTIL THE TUNNEL IS DUG & PROTECTED BY A WATERTIGHT LINING.

HOW TO DISCOVER WHETHER YOU ARE LEFT-EYED OR RIGHT-EYED

HOLD UP A FINGER ABOUT 6IN. FROM YOUR EYES & LOOK AT IT, THEN COVER LEFT EYE WITH A BIT OF CARD & SEE HOW FAR FINGER APPEARS TO MOVE. REPEAT WITH RIGHT EYE. YOUR DOMINANT EYE IS THE ONE WHICH CAUSES THE IMAGE TO SHIFT LEAST WHEN UNCOVERED.

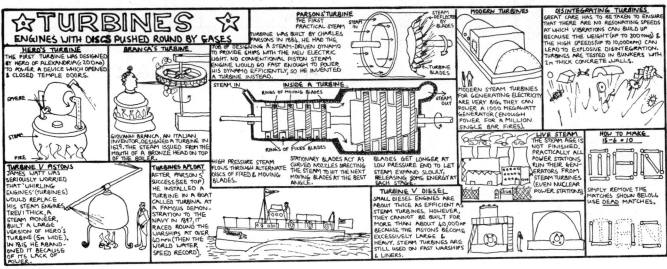

☆ TURBINES ☆
ENGINES WITH DISCS PUSHED ROUND BY GASES

HERO'S TURBINE
THE FIRST TURBINE WAS DESIGNED BY HERO OF ALEXANDRIA (c.200AD) TO POWER A DEVICE WHICH OPENED & CLOSED TEMPLE DOORS.

SPHERE
STEAM
FIRE

BRANCA'S TURBINE
GIOVANNI BRANCA, AN ITALIAN INVENTOR, DESIGNED A TURBINE IN 1629. THE STEAM ISSUED FROM THE MOUTH OF A BRONZE HEAD ON TOP OF THE BOILER.

PARSONS' TURBINE
THE FIRST PRACTICAL STEAM TURBINE WAS BUILT BY CHARLES PARSONS IN 1884. HE HAD THE JOB OF DESIGNING A STEAM-DRIVEN DYNAMO TO PROVIDE SHIPS WITH THE NEW ELECTRIC LIGHT. NO CONVENTIONAL PISTON STEAM ENGINE WOULD GO FAST ENOUGH TO POWER HIS DYNAMO EFFICIENTLY, SO HE INVENTED A TURBINE INSTEAD.

STEAM IN
STEAM DEFLECTED BY BLADES
TURBINE BLADES

INSIDE A TURBINE
STEAM IN
RINGS OF MOVING BLADES
STEAM OUT
RINGS OF FIXED BLADES

HIGH PRESSURE STEAM FLOWS THROUGH ALTERNATE DISCS OF FIXED & MOVING BLADES.

STATIONARY BLADES ACT AS CURVED NOZZLES DIRECTING THE STEAM TO HIT THE NEXT MOVING BLADES AT THE BEST ANGLE.

BLADES GET LONGER AT LOW PRESSURE END TO LET STEAM EXPAND SLOWLY, RELEASING SOME ENERGY AT EACH STAGE.

MODERN TURBINES
MODERN STEAM TURBINES FOR GENERATING ELECTRICITY ARE VERY BIG. THEY CAN POWER A 1000 MEGAWATT GENERATOR (ENOUGH POWER FOR A MILLION SINGLE BAR FIRES).

DISINTEGRATING TURBINES
GREAT CARE HAS TO BE TAKEN TO ENSURE THAT THERE ARE NO RESONATING SPEEDS AT WHICH VIBRATIONS CAN BUILD UP BECAUSE THE WEIGHT (UP TO 300 TONS) & THE HIGH SPEEDS (UP TO 10,000 RPM) CAN LEAD TO EXPLOSIVE DISINTEGRATION. TURBINES ARE TESTED IN BUNKERS WITH 2M THICK CONCRETE WALLS.

TURBINE V PISTONS
JAMES WATT WAS SERIOUSLY WORRIED THAT 'WHIRLING ENGINES' (TURBINES) WOULD REPLACE HIS STEAM ENGINES. TREVITHICK, A STEAM PIONEER, BUILT A LARGE VERSION OF HERO'S TURBINE (5m WIDE). IN 1815 HE ABANDONED IT BECAUSE OF ITS LACK OF POWER.

TURBINES AFLOAT
AFTER PARSONS' SUCCESS (SEE TOP) HE INSTALLED A TURBINE IN A BOAT CALLED TURBINIA AT A FAMOUS DEMONSTRATION TO THE NAVY IN 1897. IT RACED ROUND THE WARSHIPS AT OVER 40 MPH (THEN THE WORLD WATER SPEED RECORD).

TURBINE V DIESEL
SMALL DIESEL ENGINES ARE ABOUT TWICE AS EFFICIENT AS STEAM TURBINES. HOWEVER, THEY CANNOT BE BUILT FOR MORE THAN ABOUT 40,000HP BECAUSE THE PISTONS BECOME EXCESSIVELY LARGE & HEAVY. STEAM TURBINES ARE STILL USED ON FAST WARSHIPS & LINERS.

LIVE STEAM
THE STEAM AGE IS NOT FINISHED. PRACTICALLY ALL POWER STATIONS RUN THEIR GENERATORS FROM STEAM TURBINES (EVEN NUCLEAR POWER STATIONS).

HOW TO MAKE
15 − 6 = 10
SIMPLY REMOVE THE MATCHES SHOWN BELOW. USE DEAD MATCHES.

☆ TWINS ☆
INDIVIDUALS CONCEIVED SIMULTANEOUSLY

OMINOUS TWINS
THE IBO OF NIGERIA TRADITIONALLY SAW THE BIRTH OF TWINS AS A BAD OMEN. THEY THREW AWAY ANY FOOD, WATER & FIREWOOD LEFT FROM THE NIGHT OF THE BIRTH.

INCESTUOUS TWINS
THE YUROK INDIANS OF NORTH AMERICA KILLED THE FEMALE OF A MALE-FEMALE PAIR FOR FEAR THEY HAD COMMITTED INCEST IN THE WOMB.

HEAVENLY TWINS
THE COCOPAS INDIANS OF NORTH AMERICA TREATED TWINS PARTICULARLY WELL. THEY BELIEVED TWINS WERE VISITORS FROM HEAVEN & WOULD RETURN THERE IF THEY DID NOT ENJOY LIFE ON EARTH.

WILD TWINS
IN PARTS OF UGANDA TWINS WERE SEEN ALMOST AS WILD ANIMALS & HAD A REPUTATION FOR BEING SO FEARLESS THAT THEY WERE USED TO LEAD CHARGES IN WARS.

TWIN FATHERS
THE SALIVA TRIBE OF SOUTH AMERICA BELIEVED THAT TWINS MUST HAVE DIFFERENT FATHERS. THE MOTHER WAS OFTEN WHIPPED BY HER HUSBAND FOR ADULTERY.

FRATERNAL TWINS
FRATERNAL TWINS OCCUR ABOUT 1 IN 125 BIRTHS, WHEN TWO SEPARATE EGGS ARE FERTILISED SIMULTANEOUSLY. THEY DO NOT SHARE THE SAME GENES & CAN BE OPPOSITE SEXES.

IDENTICAL TWINS
THESE OCCUR ABOUT 1 IN 500 BIRTHS WHEN A SINGLE EGG SPLITS IN HALF SHORTLY AFTER FERTILISATION. THEY ARE ALWAYS THE SAME SEX & PHYSICALLY IDENTICAL BECAUSE THEY HAVE THE SAME GENES.

TWIN ARMADILLOS
MOST ANIMALS WHICH HAVE MULTIPLE BIRTHS CONCEIVE BY FERTILISING MANY EGGS SIMULTANEOUSLY. THE NINE-BANDED ARMADILLO IS AN EXCEPTION. THE MALE FERTILISES ONE EGG WHICH LATER SPLITS- SO THE YOUNG ARE IDENTICAL TWINS.

NUTRITION
SHEEP ARE OFTEN OVERFED BEFORE MATING TO INCREASE LITTER SIZE. THE INCIDENCE OF HUMAN TWINS FELL SLIGHTLY DURING WORLD WAR II BECAUSE OF MALNUTRITION IN COUNTRIES WHERE FOOD WAS SCARCE.

AGE
(graph: % BIRTHS TWINS vs AGE, 20 30 40 50)
WOMEN ARE MOST LIKELY TO HAVE TWINS BETWEEN 30 & 40 BECAUSE THEY RELEASE TWO EGGS AT A TIME MORE FREQUENTLY DURING THIS PERIOD.

TESTING FOR TWINS
A TRADITIONAL METHOD OF DETECTING TWINS WAS TO HAVE 2 DOCTORS LISTENING TO & CALLING OUT THE FOETUS'S HEARTBEAT. IF THEIR CALLS DID NOT COINCIDE IT WAS ASSUMED THAT THERE WERE TWO FOETUSES.

HEREDITY
SISTERS OF MOTHERS OF TWINS ARE 2.5 TIMES MORE LIKELY TO HAVE TWINS THAN NORMAL. SISTERS OF FRATERNAL TWINS ARE 4 TIMES MORE LIKELY TO HAVE TWINS THAN NORMAL.

RACE
(graph: % BIRTHS TWINS — AFRICANS, EUROPEANS, JAPANESE)
IT IS NOT KNOWN WHY LIKELIHOOD OF TWINS VARIES WITH RACE.

ONLY 50% OF TWINS ARE NOW DETECTED BEFORE BIRTH. HOWEVER A HORMONE HAS RECENTLY BEEN IDENTIFIED WHICH IS PRESENT AT MUCH HIGHER LEVELS IN WOMEN BEARING TWINS. IT IS HOPED THIS WILL PROVIDE A RELIABLE TEST FOR TWINS AFTER ONLY 6 WEEKS OF PREGNANCY.

FREQUENCY
MORE FREQUENT INTERCOURSE INCREASES THE LIKELIHOOD OF A SECOND EGG BEING FERTILISED.

DRUGS
FERTILITY DRUGS CAN INCREASE THE CHANCE OF TWINS FROM 1 IN 100 TO 1 IN 4.

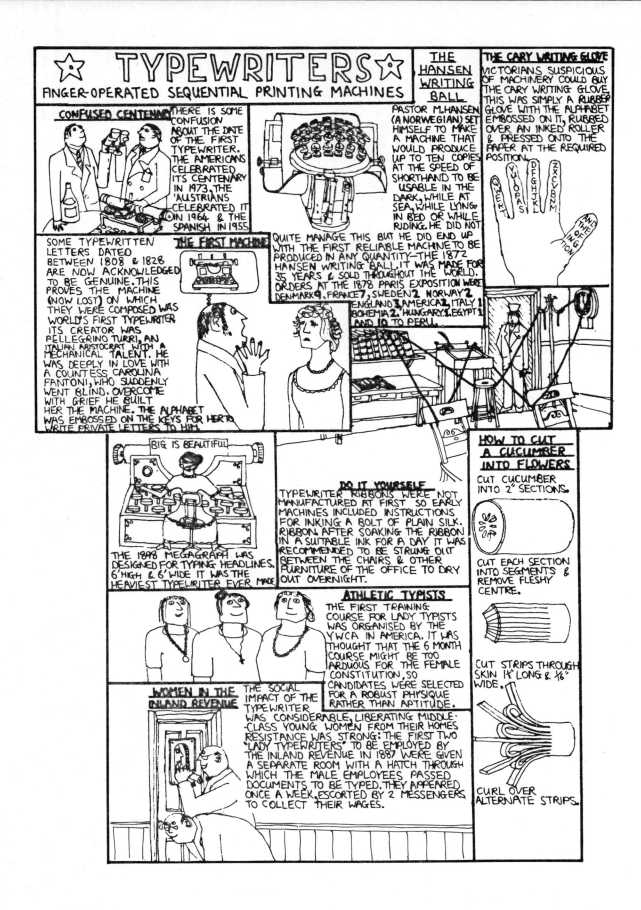

☆ TYPEWRITERS ☆
FINGER-OPERATED SEQUENTIAL PRINTING MACHINES

CONFUSED CENTENARY

THERE IS SOME CONFUSION ABOUT THE DATE OF THE FIRST TYPEWRITER. THE AMERICANS CELEBRATED ITS CENTENARY IN 1973, THE 'AUSTRIANS' CELEBRATED IT IN 1964 & THE SPANISH IN 1955.

SOME TYPEWRITTEN LETTERS DATED BETWEEN 1808 & 1828 ARE NOW ACKNOWLEDGED TO BE GENUINE. THIS PROVES THE MACHINE (NOW LOST) ON WHICH THEY WERE COMPOSED WAS WORLD'S FIRST TYPEWRITER. ITS CREATOR WAS PELLEGRINO TURRI, AN ITALIAN ARISTOCRAT WITH A MECHANICAL TALENT. HE WAS DEEPLY IN LOVE WITH A COUNTESS CAROLINA FANTONI, WHO SUDDENLY WENT BLIND. OVERCOME WITH GRIEF HE BUILT HER THE MACHINE. THE ALPHABET WAS EMBOSSED ON THE KEYS FOR HER TO WRITE PRIVATE LETTERS TO HIM.

THE FIRST MACHINE

THE HANSEN WRITING BALL

PASTOR M. HANSEN (A NORWEGIAN) SET HIMSELF TO MAKE A MACHINE THAT WOULD PRODUCE UP TO TEN COPIES AT THE SPEED OF SHORTHAND TO BE USABLE IN THE DARK, WHILE AT SEA, WHILE LYING IN BED OR WHILE RIDING. HE DID NOT QUITE MANAGE THIS BUT HE DID END UP WITH THE FIRST RELIABLE MACHINE TO BE PRODUCED IN ANY QUANTITY—THE 1872 HANSEN WRITING BALL. IT WAS MADE FOR 35 YEARS & SOLD THROUGHOUT THE WORLD. ORDERS AT THE 1878 PARIS EXPOSITION WERE DENMARK 9, FRANCE 7, SWEDEN 2, NORWAY 2, ENGLAND 3, AMERICA 2, ITALY 1, BOHEMIA 2, HUNGARY 1, EGYPT 1 AND 10 TO PERU.

THE CARY WRITING GLOVE

VICTORIANS SUSPICIOUS OF MACHINERY COULD BUY THE CARY WRITING GLOVE. THIS WAS SIMPLY A RUBBER GLOVE WITH THE ALPHABET EMBOSSED ON IT, RUBBED OVER AN INKED ROLLER & PRESSED ONTO THE PAPER AT THE REQUIRED POSITION.

BIG IS BEAUTIFUL

THE 1898 MEGAGRAPH WAS DESIGNED FOR TYPING HEADLINES. 6' HIGH & 6' WIDE IT WAS THE HEAVIEST TYPEWRITER EVER MADE.

DO IT YOURSELF

TYPEWRITER RIBBONS WERE NOT MANUFACTURED AT FIRST SO EARLY MACHINES INCLUDED INSTRUCTIONS FOR INKING A BOLT OF PLAIN SILK RIBBON. AFTER SOAKING THE RIBBON IN A SUITABLE INK FOR A DAY IT WAS RECOMMENDED TO BE STRUNG OUT BETWEEN THE CHAIRS & OTHER FURNITURE OF THE OFFICE TO DRY OUT OVERNIGHT.

ATHLETIC TYPISTS

THE FIRST TRAINING COURSE FOR LADY TYPISTS WAS ORGANISED BY THE YWCA IN AMERICA. IT WAS THOUGHT THAT THE 6 MONTH COURSE MIGHT BE TOO ARDUOUS FOR THE FEMALE CONSTITUTION, SO CANDIDATES WERE SELECTED FOR A ROBUST PHYSIQUE RATHER THAN APTITUDE.

WOMEN IN THE INLAND REVENUE

THE SOCIAL IMPACT OF THE TYPEWRITER WAS CONSIDERABLE, LIBERATING MIDDLE-CLASS YOUNG WOMEN FROM THEIR HOMES. RESISTANCE WAS STRONG: THE FIRST TWO 'LADY TYPEWRITERS' TO BE EMPLOYED BY THE INLAND REVENUE IN 1887 WERE GIVEN A SEPARATE ROOM WITH A HATCH THROUGH WHICH THE MALE EMPLOYEES PASSED DOCUMENTS TO BE TYPED. THEY APPEARED ONCE A WEEK, ESCORTED BY 2 MESSENGERS TO COLLECT THEIR WAGES.

HOW TO CUT A CUCUMBER INTO FLOWERS

CUT CUCUMBER INTO 2" SECTIONS.

CUT EACH SECTION INTO SEGMENTS & REMOVE FLESHY CENTRE.

CUT STRIPS THROUGH SKIN 1¼" LONG & 1/16" WIDE.

CURL OVER ALTERNATE STRIPS.

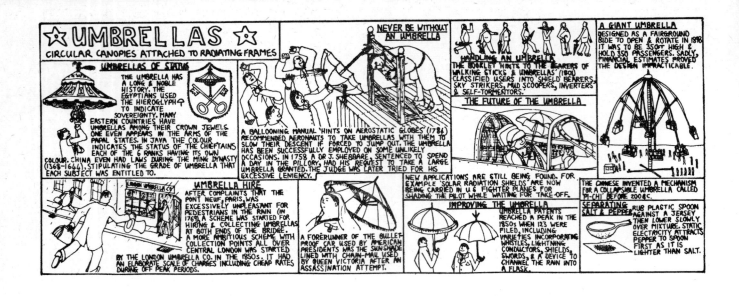

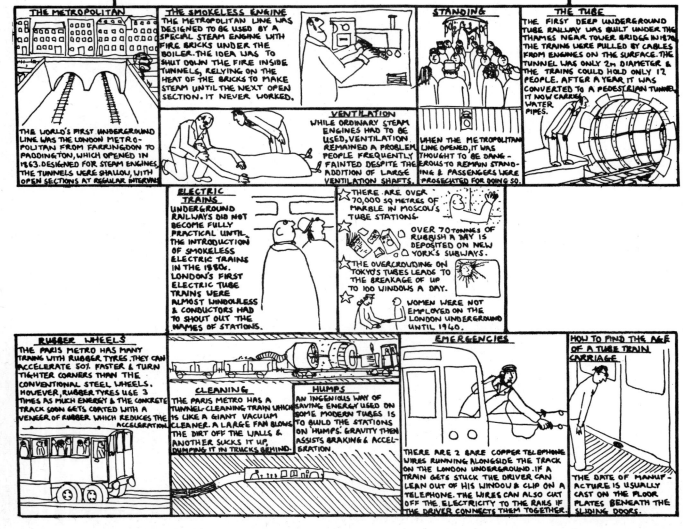

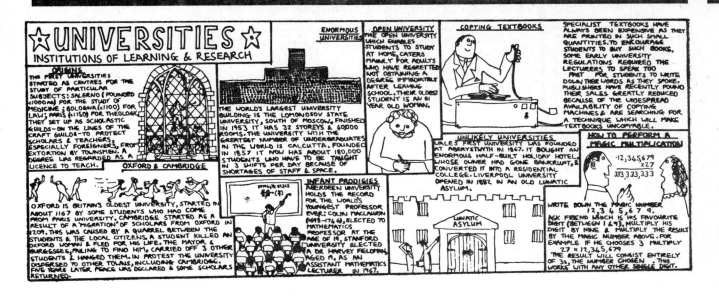

☆ UNIVERSITIES ☆
INSTITUTIONS OF LEARNING & RESEARCH

ORIGINS
THE FIRST UNIVERSITIES STARTED AS CENTRES FOR THE STUDY OF PARTICULAR SUBJECTS: SALERNO (FOUNDED c1000AD) FOR THE STUDY OF MEDICINE ; BOLOGNA (c1100) FOR LAW; PARIS (c1150) FOR THEOLOGY. THEY SET UP AS SCHOLASTIC GUILDS - ON THE LINES OF THE CRAFT GUILDS - TO PROTECT SCHOLARS & TEACHERS, ESPECIALLY FOREIGNERS, FROM EXTORTION BY TOWNSMEN. A DEGREE WAS REGARDED AS A LICENCE TO TEACH.

OXFORD & CAMBRIDGE
OXFORD IS BRITAIN'S OLDEST UNIVERSITY, STARTED IN ABOUT 1167 BY SOME STUDENTS WHO HAD COME FROM PARIS UNIVERSITY. CAMBRIDGE STARTED AS A RESULT OF A "MIGRATION" OF SCHOLARS FROM OXFORD IN 1209. THIS WAS CAUSED BY A QUARREL BETWEEN THE STUDENTS & THE LOCAL CITIZENS. A STUDENT KILLED AN OXFORD WOMAN & FLED FOR HIS LIFE. THE MAYOR & BURGESSES, FAILING TO FIND HIM, CARRIED OFF 3 OTHER STUDENTS & HANGED THEM. IN PROTEST THE UNIVERSITY DISPERSED TO OTHER TOWNS, INCLUDING CAMBRIDGE. FIVE YEARS LATER PEACE WAS DECLARED & SOME SCHOLARS RETURNED.

ENORMOUS UNIVERSITIES
THE WORLD'S LARGEST UNIVERSITY BUILDING IS THE LOMONOSOV STATE UNIVERSITY, SOUTH OF MOSCOW. FINISHED IN 1953 IT HAS 32 STOREYS & 40000 ROOMS. THE UNIVERSITY WITH THE GREATEST NUMBER OF UNDERGRADUATES IN THE WORLD IS CALCUTTA. FOUNDED IN 1857 IT NOW HAS ABOUT 180,000 STUDENTS WHO HAVE TO BE TAUGHT IN 3 SHIFTS PER DAY BECAUSE OF SHORTAGES OF STAFF & SPACE.

INFANT PRODIGIES
ABERDEEN UNIVERSITY HOLDS THE RECORD FOR THE WORLD'S YOUNGEST PROFESSOR EVER: COLIN MACLAURIN (1698-1746), ELECTED TO MATHEMATICS PROFESSOR AT THE AGE OF 19. STANFORD UNIVERSITY ELECTED A DR HARVEY FRIEDMAN, AGED 19, AS AN ASSISTANT MATHEMATICS LECTURER IN 1967.

OPEN UNIVERSITY
THE OPEN UNIVERSITY WHICH ENABLES STUDENTS TO STUDY AT HOME, CATERS MAINLY FOR ADULTS WHO HAVE REGRETTED NOT OBTAINING A DEGREE IMMEDIATELY AFTER LEAVING SCHOOL. THEIR OLDEST STUDENT IS AN 81 YEAR OLD WOMAN.

UNLIKELY UNIVERSITIES
WALES' FIRST UNIVERSITY WAS FOUNDED AT ABERYSTWYTH IN 1867. IT BOUGHT AN ENORMOUS HALF-BUILT HOLIDAY HOTEL, WHOSE OWNER HAD GONE BANKRUPT, & CONVERTED IT INTO A RESIDENTIAL COLLEGE. LIVERPOOL UNIVERSITY OPENED IN 1882 IN AN OLD LUNATIC ASYLUM.

LUNATIC ASYLUM

COPYING TEXTBOOKS
SPECIALIST TEXTBOOKS HAVE ALWAYS BEEN EXPENSIVE AS THEY ARE PRINTED IN SUCH SMALL QUANTITIES. TO ENCOURAGE STUDENTS TO BUY SUCH BOOKS, SOME EARLY UNIVERSITY REGULATIONS REQUIRED THE LECTURERS TO SPEAK TOO FAST FOR STUDENTS TO WRITE DOWN THEIR WORDS AS THEY SPOKE. PUBLISHERS HAVE RECENTLY FOUND THEIR SALES GREATLY REDUCED BECAUSE OF THE WIDESPREAD AVAILABILITY OF COPYING MACHINES & ARE SEARCHING FOR A TECHNIQUE WHICH WILL MAKE TEXTBOOKS UNCOPYABLE.

HOW TO PERFORM A MAGIC MULTIPLICATION

$$12,345,679 \times 27 = 333,333,333$$

WRITE DOWN THE MAGIC NUMBER 12,345,679. ASK FRIEND WHICH IS HIS FAVOURITE DIGIT (BETWEEN 1 & 9), MULTIPLY HIS DIGIT BY NINE & MULTIPLY THE RESULT BY THE MAGIC NUMBER ABOVE. FOR EXAMPLE IF HE CHOOSES 3 MULTIPLY $27 \times 12,345,679$. THE RESULT WILL CONSIST ENTIRELY OF 3's, THE NUMBER CHOSEN. THIS WORKS WITH ANY OTHER SINGLE DIGIT.

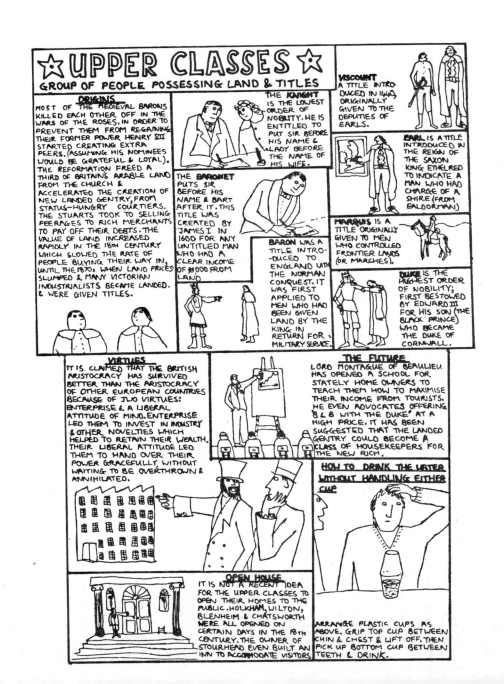

☆ UPPER CLASSES ☆
GROUP OF PEOPLE POSSESSING LAND & TITLES

ORIGINS
MOST OF THE MEDIEVAL BARONS KILLED EACH OTHER OFF IN THE WARS OF THE ROSES. IN ORDER TO PREVENT THEM FROM REGAINING THEIR FORMER POWER HENRY VII STARTED CREATING EXTRA PEERS. (ASSUMING HIS NOMINEES WOULD BE GRATEFUL & LOYAL). THE REFORMATION FREED A THIRD OF BRITAIN'S ARABLE LAND FROM THE CHURCH & ACCELERATED THE CREATION OF NEW LANDED GENTRY, FROM STATUS-HUNGRY COURTIERS. THE STUARTS TOOK TO SELLING PEERAGES TO RICH MERCHANTS TO PAY OFF THEIR DEBTS. THE VALUE OF LAND INCREASED RAPIDLY IN THE 18TH CENTURY WHICH SLOWED THE RATE OF PEOPLE BUYING THEIR WAY IN, UNTIL THE 1870s WHEN LAND PRICES SLUMPED & MANY VICTORIAN INDUSTRIALISTS BECAME LANDED, & WERE GIVEN TITLES.

THE KNIGHT
IS THE LOWEST ORDER OF NOBILITY. HE IS ENTITLED TO PUT SIR BEFORE HIS NAME & LADY BEFORE THE NAME OF HIS WIFE.

THE BARONET
PUTS SIR BEFORE HIS NAME & BART AFTER IT. THIS TITLE WAS CREATED BY JAMES I IN 1600 FOR ANY UNTITLED MAN WHO HAD A CLEAR INCOME OF £1000 FROM LAND.

BARON
WAS A TITLE INTRODUCED TO ENGLAND WITH THE NORMAN CONQUEST. IT WAS FIRST APPLIED TO MEN WHO HAD BEEN GIVEN LAND BY THE KING IN RETURN FOR MILITARY SERVICE.

VISCOUNT
A TITLE INTRODUCED IN 1440, ORIGINALLY GIVEN TO THE DEPUTIES OF EARLS.

EARL
IS A TITLE INTRODUCED IN THE REIGN OF THE SAXON KING ETHELRED TO INDICATE A MAN WHO HAD CHARGE OF A SHIRE (FROM EALDORMAN)

MARQUIS
IS A TITLE ORIGINALLY GIVEN TO MEN WHO CONTROLLED FRONTIER LANDS (OR MARCHES).

DUKE
IS THE HIGHEST ORDER OF NOBILITY; FIRST BESTOWED BY EDWARD III FOR HIS SON (THE BLACK PRINCE) WHO BECAME THE DUKE OF CORNWALL.

VIRTUES
IT IS CLAIMED THAT THE BRITISH ARISTOCRACY HAS SURVIVED BETTER THAN THE ARISTOCRACY OF OTHER EUROPEAN COUNTRIES BECAUSE OF TWO VIRTUES: ENTERPRISE & A LIBERAL ATTITUDE OF MIND. ENTERPRISE LED THEM TO INVEST IN INDUSTRY & OTHER NOVELTIES WHICH HELPED TO RETAIN THEIR WEALTH. THEIR LIBERAL ATTITUDE LED THEM TO HAND OVER THEIR POWER GRACEFULLY, WITHOUT WAITING TO BE OVERTHROWN & ANNIHILATED.

THE FUTURE
LORD MONTAGUE OF BEAULIEU HAS OPENED A SCHOOL FOR STATELY HOME OWNERS TO TEACH THEM HOW TO MAXIMISE THEIR INCOME FROM TOURISTS. HE EVEN ADVOCATES OFFERING "B & B WITH THE DUKE" AT A HIGH PRICE. IT HAS BEEN SUGGESTED THAT THE LANDED GENTRY COULD BECOME A CLASS OF HOUSEKEEPERS FOR THE NEW RICH.

HOW TO DRINK THE WATER WITHOUT HANDLING EITHER CUP
ARRANGE PLASTIC CUPS AS ABOVE. GRIP TOP CUP BETWEEN CHIN & CHEST & LIFT OFF. THEN PICK UP BOTTOM CUP BETWEEN TEETH & DRINK.

OPEN HOUSE
IT IS NOT A RECENT IDEA FOR THE UPPER CLASSES TO OPEN THEIR HOMES TO THE PUBLIC. HOLKHAM, WILTON, BLENHEIM & CHATSWORTH WERE ALL OPENED ON CERTAIN DAYS IN THE 18TH CENTURY. THE OWNER OF STOURHEAD EVEN BUILT AN INN TO ACCOMMODATE VISITORS.

☆ UTOPIAS ☆
REAL OR IMAGINARY SOCIETIES CONSIDERED TO BE PERFECT

SPARTA

ACCOUNTS OF THE ANCIENT GREEK MILITARY STATE OF SPARTA ARE PART MYTH & PART HISTORY. LATER WRITERS LOOKED BACK ON IT AS A FORM OF UTOPIA.

SPARTA WAS VERY AUSTERE. PERSONAL WEALTH, TRAVEL, DOMESTICITY & EVEN CRAFTSMANSHIP WERE SUPPRESSED. ADULTERY WAS ENCOURAGED BUT EACH BABY WAS INSPECTED AT BIRTH BY THE ELDERS & DROPPED DOWN A DEEP CAVE IF NOT 'HEALTHY' ENOUGH.

THE MILLENARISTS

REFERENCES IN THE BOOK OF REVELATIONS LED SOME EARLY CHRISTIANS (MILLENARISTS) TO BELIEVE THAT THERE WOULD EVENTUALLY BE A HEAVEN ON EARTH.

IN 1420 THE HUSSITES, A BOHEMIAN MILLENARIST SECT, CONVINCED THAT THE TIME FOR HEAVEN ON EARTH HAD COME, SEIZED THE TOWN OF TABOR (CZECHOSLOVAKIA). THEY LIVED BY WARFARE, KEEPING THEIR BOOTY IN A COMMUNAL PIT IN THE TOWN. THEY WERE DEFEATED IN 1434 & 13,000 OF THE ARMY OF 18,000 WERE MASSACRED.

NO PLACE

THE WORD UTOPIA WAS INVENTED BY THE ENGLISH WRITER SIR THOMAS MORE (c1515). HE TOOK IT FROM THE GREEK OU=NOT+TOPOS= PLACE OR EUTOPIA=GOOD PLACE.

MORE'S 'UTOPIA' IS A COMMUNAL ISLAND. LAWS AGAINST SEDUCTION & CORRUPTION ARE STRICT, GAMES & TRAVEL ARE RESTRICTED. ALL RELIGIONS ARE TOLERATED BUT ANYONE WHO BECOMES TOO HEATED ABOUT RELIGIOUS MATTERS IS BANISHED. TO PLACATE ANGRY CHURCHMEN, MORE CALLED THE STORYTELLER OF HIS BOOK HYTHLODAY (DISPENSER OF NONSENSE).

THE DIGGERS

THE ENCLOSURES, RESTRICTING ACCESS TO LAND BY THE POOR, CAUSED A FAMOUS ATTEMPT AT A UTOPIAN REFORM. WINSTANLEY, THE ENGLISH REFORMER, & 30 'DIGGERS' OR 'LEVELLERS' OCCUPIED SOME WASTE GROUND IN SURREY IN 1649 & STARTED CULTIVATING IT.

THEIR CROPS & PROPERTY WERE ATTACKED & BURNT SEVERAL TIMES BY ANGRY LOCALS BUT EACH TIME THE DIGGERS RETURNED—UNTIL A PARSON WOODFORD LED A PARTICULARLY VIOLENT ATTACK IN 1650.

THE SHAKERS

BY THE MID-1700s THERE WAS ALREADY A STRONG FEELING THAT INDUSTRIAL CAPITALISM WAS UNNATURAL & CREATING INHUMAN CONDITIONS. MANY SECTS, MOSTLY RELIGIOUS, SET OFF FOR AMERICA TO FOUND THEIR UTOPIAS.

ONE SECT, THE SHAKERS, BELIEVED THEIR VILLAGES WERE EACH A SMALL PART OF THE GARDEN OF EDEN. THEIR LIFE CENTRED ON RELIGIOUS MEETINGS & ECSTATIC WHIRLING & SHAKING. THEY WERE NOT ALLOWED TO HAVE CHILDREN BUT RECRUITED MORE THAN 6,000 MEMBERS.

TOLSTOY'S COMMUNES

SEVERAL UTOPIAN 'COMMUNIST' COLONIES WERE FOUNDED BY TOLSTOY'S SUPPORTERS IN BRITAIN IN THE 1890s.

NONE LASTED LONG. THE MORE COMMITTED & ENERGETIC MEMBERS DID THE WORK OF EVERYBODY ELSE. THOSE WHO LEFT DID SO WITH THE BEST CLOTHES & ANY AVAILABLE MONEY.

MEGASTRUCTURES

MANY TECHNOLOGICAL UTOPIAS HAVE BEEN PROPOSED - CULMINATING IN 1960s 'MEGASTRUCTURES' WHICH WOULD CONTAIN WHOLE CITIES WITH MOVABLE 'PLUG-IN' HOMES. FLOATING & WALKING CITIES WERE ALSO SUGGESTED.

ARCOSANTI (ARIZONA) IS AN EXPERIMENTAL 'HIGH-TECH' UTOPIA, DESIGNED TO HOUSE 3,000 PEOPLE IN CLOSE PROXIMITY. ITS FOUNDER, SOLERI, BELIEVES THAT THE AWESOMENESS OF THE STRUCTURE & THE COMPLEXITY OF ITS CONSTRUCTION ARE POSITIVE ALTERNATIVES TO WAR, SQUALOR & SOCIAL STRIFE.

CHRISTIANIA

DURING THE 1960s, MANY HIPPIES STARTED UTOPIAN COMMUNITES TO ESCAPE FROM THE MODERN INDUSTRIAL WORLD.

ONE OF THE MOST FAMOUS IS THE TOWN OF CHRISTIANIA, DENMARK. ABANDONED ARMY BARRACKS, OCCUPIED BY SQUATTERS IN 1971, HAVE DEVELOPED INTO A TOWN OF ABOUT 1,000 PEOPLE. DESPITE CONTINUAL THREATS OF EVICTION, THEY PAY NO TAX & ORGANISE THEIR OWN POLICING & SOCIAL SERVICES.

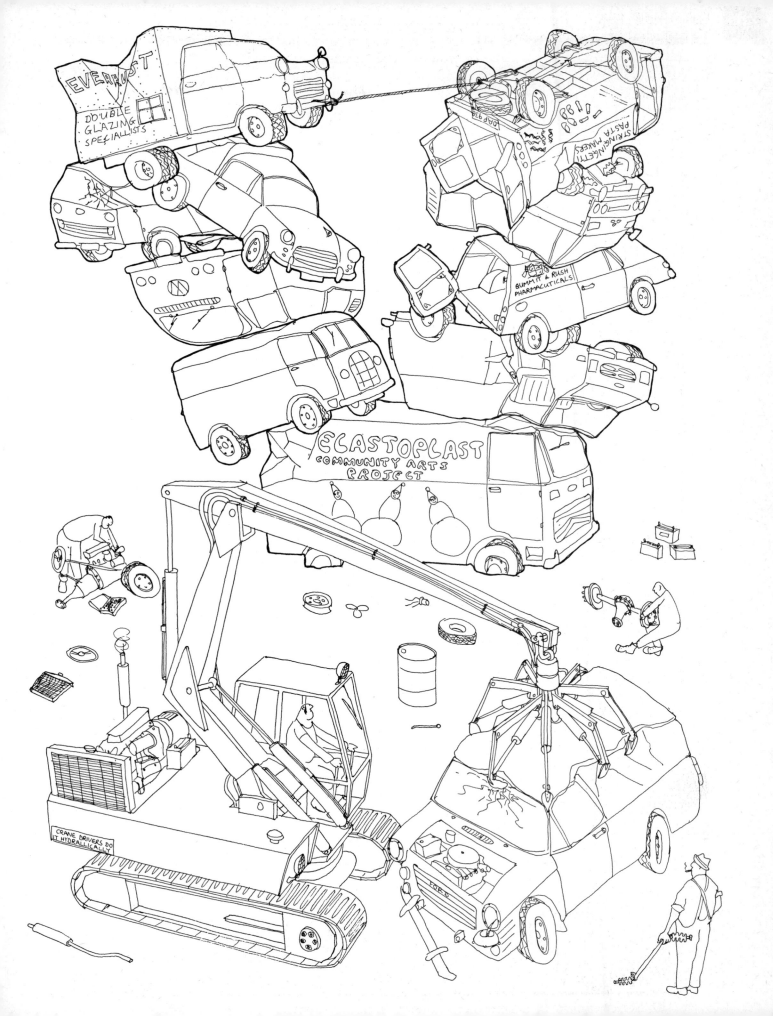

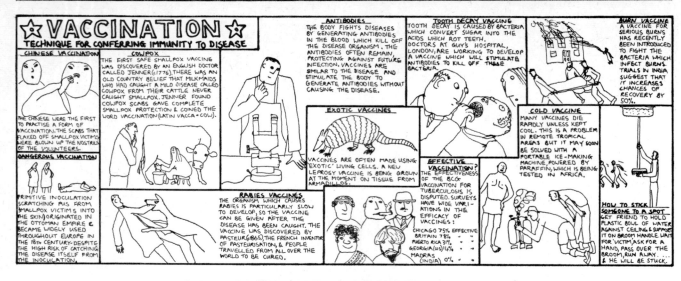

☆ VACCINATION ☆
TECHNIQUE FOR CONFERRING IMMUNITY TO DISEASE

CHINESE VACCINATION
THE CHINESE WERE THE FIRST TO PRACTISE A FORM OF VACCINATION. THE SCABS THAT FLAKED OFF SMALLPOX VICTIMS WERE BLOWN UP THE NOSTRILS OF THE VOLUNTEERS.

DANGEROUS VACCINATION
PRIMITIVE INOCULATION SCRATCHING PUS FROM SMALLPOX VICTIMS INTO THE SKIN) ORIGINATED IN THE OTTOMAN EMPIRE & BECAME WIDELY USED THROUGHOUT EUROPE IN THE 18TH CENTURY. DESPITE THE HIGH RISK OF CATCHING THE DISEASE ITSELF FROM THE INOCULATION.

COWPOX
THE FIRST SAFE SMALLPOX VACCINE WAS DISCOVERED BY AN ENGLISH DOCTOR CALLED JENNER (1796). THERE WAS AN OLD COUNTRY BELIEF THAT MILKMAIDS WHO HAD CAUGHT A MILD DISEASE CALLED COWPOX FROM THEIR CATTLE NEVER CAUGHT SMALLPOX. JENNER FOUND COWPOX SCABS GAVE COMPLETE SMALLPOX PROTECTION & COINED THE WORD VACCINATION (LATIN VACCA = COW).

RABIES VACCINES
THE ORGANISM WHICH CAUSES RABIES IS PARTICULARLY SLOW TO DEVELOP, SO THE VACCINE CAN BE GIVEN AFTER THE DISEASE HAS BEEN CAUGHT. THE VACCINE WAS DISCOVERED BY PASTEUR (1885), THE FRENCH INVENTOR OF PASTEURISATION, & PEOPLE TRAVELLED FROM ALL OVER THE WORLD TO BE CURED.

ANTIBODIES
THE BODY FIGHTS DISEASES BY GENERATING ANTIBODIES IN THE BLOOD WHICH KILL OFF THE DISEASE ORGANISM. THE ANTIBODIES OFTEN REMAIN, PROTECTING AGAINST FUTURE INFECTION. VACCINES ARE SIMILAR TO THE DISEASE AND STIMULATE THE BODY TO GENERATE ANTIBODIES WITHOUT CAUSING THE DISEASE.

EXOTIC VACCINES
VACCINES ARE OFTEN MADE USING 'EXOTIC' LIVING CELLS. A NEW LEPROSY VACCINE IS BEING GROUND AT THE MOMENT ON TISSUE FROM ARMADILLOS.

EFFECTIVE VACCINATION?
THE EFFECTIVENESS OF THE BCG VACCINATION FOR TUBERCULOSIS IS DISPUTED. SURVEYS HAVE WIDE VARIATIONS IN THE EFFICACY OF VACCINES:

CHICAGO 75% EFFECTIVE
BRITAIN 78%
PUERTO RICA 31%
GEORGIA (US) 14%
MADRAS (INDIA) 0%

TOOTH DECAY VACCINE
TOOTH DECAY IS CAUSED BY BACTERIA WHICH CONVERT SUGAR INTO THE ACIDS WHICH ROT TEETH. DOCTORS AT GUY'S HOSPITAL, LONDON, ARE WORKING TO DEVELOP A VACCINE WHICH WILL STIMULATE ANTIBODIES TO KILL OFF THOSE BACTERIA.

COLD VACCINE
MANY VACCINES DIE RAPIDLY UNLESS KEPT COOL. THIS IS A PROBLEM IN REMOTE TROPICAL AREAS BUT IT MAY SOON BE SOLVED WITH A PORTABLE ICE-MAKING MACHINE POWERED BY PARAFFIN, WHICH IS BEING TESTED IN AFRICA.

BURN VACCINE
A VACCINE FOR SERIOUS BURNS HAS RECENTLY BEEN INTRODUCED TO FIGHT THE BACTERIA WHICH INFECT BURNS. TRIALS IN INDIA SUGGEST THAT IT INCREASES CHANCES OF RECOVERY BY 50%.

HOW TO STICK SOMEONE TO A SPOT
GET FRIEND TO HOLD PLASTIC BOWL OF WATER AGAINST CEILING & SUPPORT IT ON BROOM HANDLE. WAIT FOR 'VICTIM', ASK FOR A HAND, PASS OVER THE BROOM, RUN AWAY... & HE WILL BE STUCK.

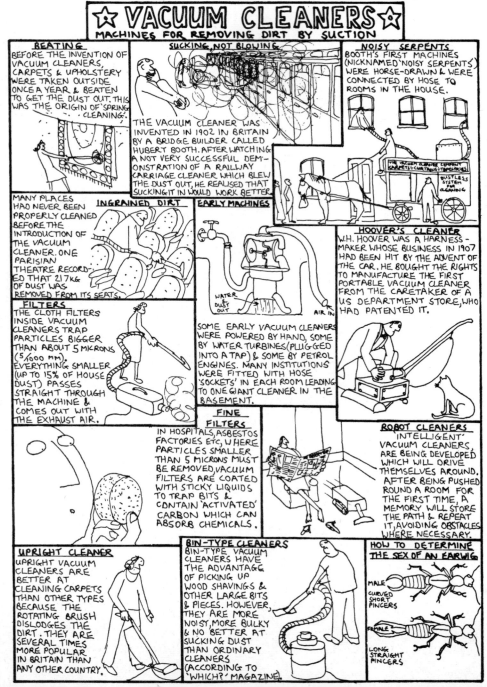

☆ VACUUM CLEANERS ☆
MACHINES FOR REMOVING DIRT BY SUCTION

BEATING
BEFORE THE INVENTION OF VACUUM CLEANERS, CARPETS & UPHOLSTERY WERE TAKEN OUTSIDE ONCE A YEAR & BEATEN TO GET THE DUST OUT. THIS WAS THE ORIGIN OF 'SPRING CLEANING'.

SUCKING, NOT BLOWING
THE VACUUM CLEANER WAS INVENTED IN 1902 IN BRITAIN BY A BRIDGE BUILDER CALLED HUBERT BOOTH. AFTER WATCHING A NOT VERY SUCCESSFUL DEMONSTRATION OF A RAILWAY CARRIAGE CLEANER WHICH BLEW THE DUST OUT, HE REALISED THAT SUCKING IT IN WOULD WORK BETTER.

NOISY SERPENTS
BOOTH'S FIRST MACHINES (NICKNAMED 'NOISY SERPENTS') WERE HORSE-DRAWN & WERE CONNECTED BY HOSE TO ROOMS IN THE HOUSE.

INGRAINED DIRT
MANY PLACES HAD NEVER BEEN PROPERLY CLEANED BEFORE THE INTRODUCTION OF THE VACUUM CLEANER. ONE PARISIAN THEATRE RECORDED THAT 217 KG OF DUST WAS REMOVED FROM ITS SEATS.

EARLY MACHINES
SOME EARLY VACUUM CLEANERS WERE POWERED BY HAND, SOME BY WATER TURBINES (PLUGGED INTO A TAP) & SOME BY PETROL ENGINES. MANY INSTITUTIONS WERE FITTED WITH HOSE 'SOCKETS' IN EACH ROOM LEADING TO ONE GIANT CLEANER IN THE BASEMENT.

WATER & DUST OUT

AIR IN

HOOVER'S CLEANER
W.H. HOOVER WAS A HARNESS-MAKER WHOSE BUSINESS IN 1907 HAD BEEN HIT BY THE ADVENT OF THE CAR. HE BOUGHT THE RIGHTS TO MANUFACTURE THE FIRST PORTABLE VACUUM CLEANER FROM THE CARETAKER OF A US DEPARTMENT STORE, WHO HAD PATENTED IT.

FILTERS
THE CLOTH FILTERS INSIDE VACUUM CLEANERS TRAP PARTICLES BIGGER THAN ABOUT 5 MICRONS (5/1000 MM). EVERYTHING SMALLER (UP TO 15% OF HOUSE DUST) PASSES STRAIGHT THROUGH THE MACHINE & COMES OUT WITH THE EXHAUST AIR.

FINE FILTERS
IN HOSPITALS, ASBESTOS FACTORIES ETC, WHERE PARTICLES SMALLER THAN 5 MICRONS MUST BE REMOVED, VACUUM FILTERS ARE COATED WITH STICKY LIQUIDS TO TRAP BITS & CONTAIN 'ACTIVATED' CARBON WHICH CAN ABSORB CHEMICALS.

ROBOT CLEANERS
'INTELLIGENT' VACUUM CLEANERS ARE BEING DEVELOPED WHICH WILL DRIVE THEMSELVES AROUND. AFTER BEING PUSHED ROUND A ROOM FOR THE FIRST TIME, A MEMORY WILL STORE THE PATH & REPEAT IT, AVOIDING OBSTACLES WHERE NECESSARY.

UPRIGHT CLEANER
UPRIGHT VACUUM CLEANERS ARE BETTER AT CLEANING CARPETS THAN OTHER TYPES BECAUSE THE ROTATING BRUSH DISLODGES THE DIRT. THEY ARE SEVERAL TIMES MORE POPULAR IN BRITAIN THAN ANY OTHER COUNTRY.

BIN-TYPE CLEANERS
BIN-TYPE VACUUM CLEANERS HAVE THE ADVANTAGE OF PICKING UP WOOD SHAVINGS & OTHER LARGE BITS & PIECES. HOWEVER, THEY ARE MORE NOISY, MORE BULKY & NO BETTER AT SUCKING DUST THAN ORDINARY CLEANERS (ACCORDING TO 'WHICH?' MAGAZINE).

HOW TO DETERMINE THE SEX OF AN EARWIG
MALE — CURVED SHORT PINCERS
FEMALE — LONG STRAIGHT PINCERS

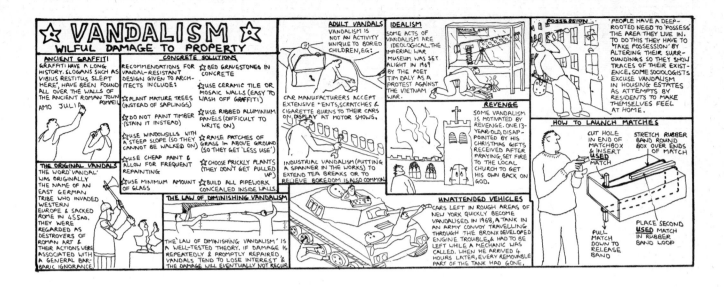

☆ VANDALISM ☆
WILFUL DAMAGE TO PROPERTY

ANCIENT GRAFFITI
Graffiti have a long history. Slogans such as 'Vibius Restitus slept here' have been found all over the walls of the ancient Roman town Pompeii.

AMO JULIA

THE ORIGINAL VANDALS
The word 'Vandal' was originally the name of an East German tribe who invaded Western Europe & sacked Rome in 455AD. They were regarded as destroyers of Roman art & their actions were associated with a general barbaric ignorance.

CONCRETE SOLUTIONS
Recommendations for vandal-resistant design given to architects include:
☆ Plant mature trees (instead of saplings)
☆ Do not paint timber (stain it instead)
☆ Use windowsills with a steep slope (so they cannot be walked on)
☆ Use cheap paint & allow for frequent repainting
☆ Use minimum amount of glass
☆ Bed gravestones in concrete
☆ Use ceramic tile or mosaic walls (easy to wash off graffiti)
☆ Use ribbed aluminium panels (difficult to write on)
☆ Raise patches of grass 1m above ground (so they get 'less use')
☆ Choose prickly plants (they don't get pulled up)
☆ Build all pipework concealed inside walls.

THE LAW OF DIMINISHING VANDALISM
The 'law of diminishing vandalism' is a well-tested theory. If damage is repeatedly & promptly repaired, vandals tend to lose interest & the damage will eventually not recur.

ADULT VANDALS
Vandalism is not an activity unique to bored children, e.g.:

Car manufacturers accept extensive 'dents, scratches & cigarette burns to their cars on display at motor shows.

Industrial vandalism (putting a spanner in the works) to extend tea breaks or to relieve boredom is also common.

IDEALISM
Some acts of vandalism are ideological. The Imperial War Museum was set alight in 1969 by the poet Tim Daly as a protest against the Vietnam war.

REVENGE
Some vandalism is motivated by revenge. One 13-year-old, disappointed by his Christmas gifts received after praying, set fire to the local church to get his own back on God.

UNATTENDED VEHICLES
Cars left in rough areas of New York quickly become vandalised. In 1968, a tank in an army convoy travelling through the Bronx developed engine trouble, & had to be left while a mechanic was called. When he arrived 4 hours later, every removable part of the tank had gone.

POSSESSION
'People have a deep-rooted need to possess' the area they live in. To do this they have to 'take possession' by altering their surroundings so they show traces of their existence. Some sociologists excuse vandalism in housing estates as attempts by residents to make themselves feel at home.

HOW TO LAUNCH MATCHES
Cut hole in end of matchbox & insert USED match
Stretch rubber band round box over ends of match
Pull match down to release band
Place second USED match in rubber band loop

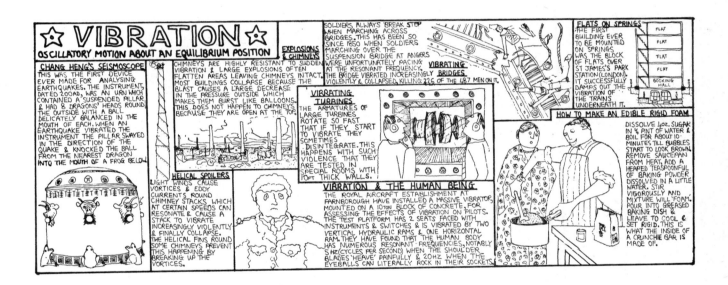

☆ VIBRATION ☆
OSCILLATORY MOTION ABOUT AN EQUILIBRIUM POSITION

CHANG HENG'S SEISMOSCOPE
This was the first device ever made for analysing earthquakes. The instrument, dated 200AD, was an urn which contained a suspended pillar & had 8 dragons' heads round the outside with a ball delicately balanced in the mouth of each. When an earthquake vibrated the instrument the pillar swayed in the direction of the quake & knocked the ball from the nearest dragon into the mouth of a frog below.

EXPLOSIONS & CHIMNEYS
Chimneys are highly resistant to sudden vibration & large explosions often flatten areas leaving chimneys intact. Most buildings collapse because the blast causes a large decrease in the pressure outside which makes them burst like balloons. This does not happen to chimneys because they are open at the top.

HELICAL SPOILERS
Light winds cause vortices & eddy currents round chimney stacks which at certain speeds can resonate & cause a stack to vibrate increasingly violently & finally collapse. The helical fins round some chimneys prevent this happening by breaking up the vortices.

Soldiers always break step when marching across bridges. This has been so since 1850 when soldiers marching over the suspension bridge at Angers were unfortunately pacing at the resonant frequency. The bridge vibrated increasingly violently & collapsed, killing 226 of the 487 men on it.

VIBRATING BRIDGES

VIBRATING TURBINES
The armatures of large turbines rotate so fast that if they start to vibrate they sometimes disintegrate. This happens with such violence that they are tested in special rooms with 10ft thick walls.

VIBRATION & THE HUMAN BEING
The Royal Aircraft Establishment at Farnborough have installed a massive vibrator mounted on a 10ton block of concrete, for assessing the effects of vibration on pilots. The test platform has 2 seats faced with instruments & switches & is vibrated by two vertical hydraulic rams & one horizontal ram. They have found that the human body has numerous resonant frequencies, notably 5Hz (cycles per second) when the shoulder blades 'heave' painfully & 20Hz when the eyeballs can literally rock in their sockets.

FLATS ON SPRINGS
The first building ever to be mounted on springs was the block of flats over St James's Park station (London). It successfully damps out the vibration of the trains underneath it.

FLAT
FLAT
FLAT
FLAT
BOOKING HALL

HOW TO MAKE AN EDIBLE RIGID FOAM
Dissolve 4oz. sugar in ¼ pint of water & boil for about 10 minutes till bubbles start to look brown. Remove saucepan from heat, add a heaped teaspoonful of baking powder dissolved in a little water. Stir vigorously and mixture will 'foam'. Pour into greased baking dish & leave to cool & set rigid. This is what the inside of a crunchie bar is made of.

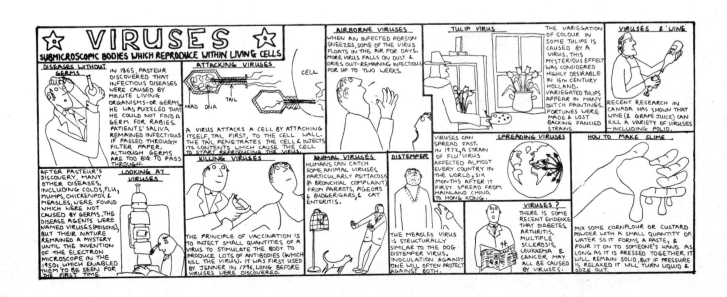

☆ VIRUSES ☆
SUBMICROSCOPIC BODIES WHICH REPRODUCE WITHIN LIVING CELLS

DISEASES WITHOUT GERMS
In 1865, Pasteur discovered that infectious diseases were caused by minute living organisms - or germs. He was puzzled that he could not find a germ for rabies. Patients' saliva remained infectious if passed through filter paper, although germs are too big to pass through.

After Pasteur's discovery, many other diseases, including colds, flu, mumps, chickenpox & measles, were found which were not caused by germs. The disease agents were named viruses (poisons), but their nature remained a mystery until the invention of the electron microscope in the 1950s, which enabled them to be seen for the first time.

LOOKING AT VIRUSES

ATTACKING VIRUSES
HEAD DNA
TAIL
A virus attacks a cell by attaching itself, tail first, to the cell wall. The tail penetrates the cell & injects its contents which cause the cell to start reproducing the virus.

KILLING VIRUSES
The principle of vaccination is to inject small quantities of a virus to stimulate the body to produce lots of antibodies (which kill the virus). It was first used by Jenner in 1796, long before viruses were discovered.

AIRBORNE VIRUSES
When an infected person sneezes, some of the virus floats in the air for days. More virus falls on dust & dries out - remaining infectious for up to two weeks.

CELL

ANIMAL VIRUSES
Humans can catch some animal viruses, particularly psittacosis (a bronchial complaint) from parrots, pigeons & budgerigars, & cat enteritis.

DISTEMPER
The measles virus is structurally similar to the dog distemper virus. Inoculation against one will often protect against both.

TULIP VIRUS
The variegation of colour in some tulips is caused by a virus. This mysterious effect was considered highly desirable in 16th century Holland. Variegated tulips appear in many Dutch paintings. Fortunes were made & lost backing fancied strains.

SPREADING VIRUSES
Viruses can spread fast. In 1972, a strain of flu virus affected almost every country in the world, six months after it first spread from mainland China to Hong Kong.

VIRUSES?
There is some recent evidence that diabetes, arthritis, multiple sclerosis, leukaemia & cancer may all be caused by viruses.

VIRUSES & 'WINE
Recent research in Canada has shown that wine (& grape juice) can kill a variety of viruses - including polio.

HOW TO MAKE SLIME
Mix some cornflour or custard powder with a small quantity of water so it forms a paste, & pour it on to someone's hand. As long as it is pressed together it will remain solid, but if pressure is relaxed it will turn liquid & ooze out.

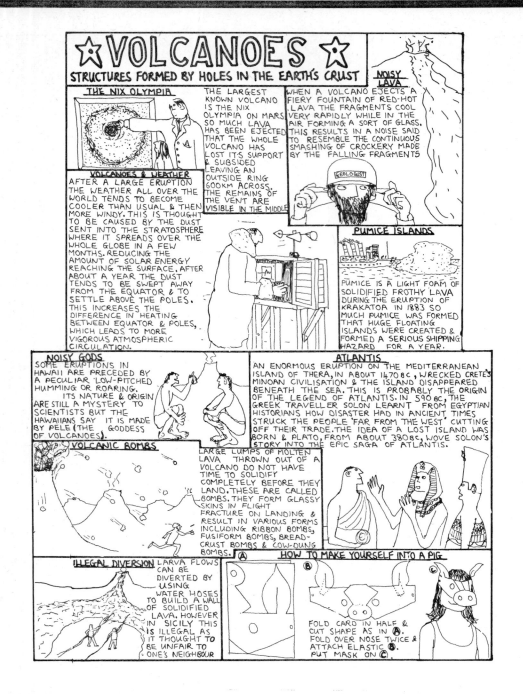

☆ VOLCANOES ☆
STRUCTURES FORMED BY HOLES IN THE EARTH'S CRUST

THE NIX OLYMPIA

THE LARGEST KNOWN VOLCANO IS THE NIX OLYMPIA ON MARS. SO MUCH LAVA HAS BEEN EJECTED THAT THE WHOLE VOLCANO HAS LOST ITS SUPPORT & SUBSIDED LEAVING AN OUTSIDE RING 600KM ACROSS. THE REMAINS OF THE VENT ARE VISIBLE IN THE MIDDLE.

NOISY LAVA

WHEN A VOLCANO EJECTS A FIERY FOUNTAIN OF RED-HOT LAVA THE FRAGMENTS COOL VERY RAPIDLY WHILE IN THE AIR FORMING A SORT OF GLASS. THIS RESULTS IN A NOISE SAID TO RESEMBLE THE CONTINUOUS SMASHING OF CROCKERY MADE BY THE FALLING FRAGMENTS

VOLCANOES & WEATHER

AFTER A LARGE ERUPTION THE WEATHER ALL OVER THE WORLD TENDS TO BECOME COOLER THAN USUAL & THEN MORE WINDY. THIS IS THOUGHT TO BE CAUSED BY THE DUST SENT INTO THE STRATOSPHERE WHERE IT SPREADS OVER THE WHOLE GLOBE IN A FEW MONTHS, REDUCING THE AMOUNT OF SOLAR ENERGY REACHING THE SURFACE. AFTER ABOUT A YEAR THE DUST TENDS TO BE SWEPT AWAY FROM THE EQUATOR & TO SETTLE ABOVE THE POLES. THIS INCREASES THE DIFFERENCE IN HEATING BETWEEN EQUATOR & POLES, WHICH LEADS TO MORE VIGOROUS ATMOSPHERIC CIRCULATION.

PUMICE ISLANDS

PUMICE IS A LIGHT FOAM OF SOLIDIFIED FROTHY LAVA DURING THE ERUPTION OF KRAKATOA IN 1883 SO MUCH PUMICE WAS FORMED THAT HUGE FLOATING ISLANDS WERE CREATED & FORMED A SERIOUS SHIPPING HAZARD FOR A YEAR.

NOISY GODS

SOME ERUPTIONS IN HAWAII ARE PRECEDED BY A PECULIAR 'LOW-PITCHED' HUMMING OR ROARING. ITS NATURE & ORIGIN ARE STILL A MYSTERY TO SCIENTISTS BUT THE HAWAIIANS SAY IT IS MADE BY PELE (THE GODDESS OF VOLCANOES).

ATLANTIS

AN ENORMOUS ERUPTION ON THE MEDITERRANEAN ISLAND OF THERA, IN ABOUT 1470 BC, WRECKED CRETE'S MINOAN CIVILISATION & THE ISLAND DISAPPEARED BENEATH THE SEA. THIS IS PROBABLY THE ORIGIN OF THE LEGEND OF ATLANTIS. IN 590 BC, THE GREEK TRAVELLER SOLON LEARNT FROM EGYPTIAN HISTORIANS HOW DISASTER HAD IN ANCIENT TIMES STRUCK THE PEOPLE 'FAR FROM THE WEST' CUTTING OFF THEIR TRADE. THE IDEA OF A LOST ISLAND WAS BORN & PLATO, FROM ABOUT 380 BC, WOVE SOLON'S STORY INTO THE EPIC SAGA OF ATLANTIS.

VOLCANIC BOMBS

LARGE LUMPS OF MOLTEN LAVA THROWN OUT OF A VOLCANO DO NOT HAVE TIME TO SOLIDIFY COMPLETELY BEFORE THEY LAND. THESE ARE CALLED BOMBS. THEY FORM GLASSY SKINS IN FLIGHT FRACTURE ON LANDING & RESULT IN VARIOUS FORMS INCLUDING RIBBON BOMBS, FUSIFORM BOMBS, BREAD-CRUST BOMBS & COW-DUNG BOMBS.

ILLEGAL DIVERSION

LAVA FLOWS CAN BE DIVERTED BY USING WATER HOSES TO BUILD A WALL OF SOLIDIFIED LAVA. HOWEVER IN SICILY THIS IS ILLEGAL AS IT THOUGHT TO BE UNFAIR TO ONE'S NEIGHBOUR

HOW TO MAKE YOURSELF INTO A PIG

FOLD CARD IN HALF & CUT SHAPE AS IN Ⓐ. FOLD OVER NOSE TWICE & ATTACH ELASTIC Ⓑ. PUT MASK ON Ⓒ.

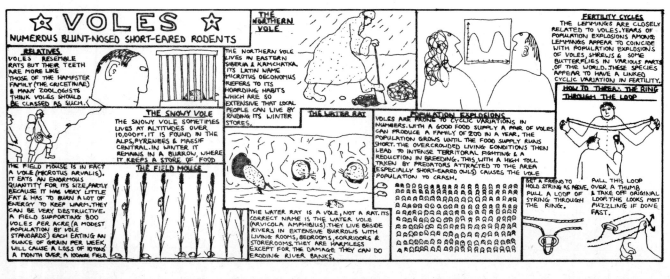

☆ VOLES ☆
NUMEROUS BLUNT-NOSED SHORT-EARED RODENTS

RELATIVES
VOLES RESEMBLE RATS BUT THEIR TEETH ARE MORE LIKE THOSE OF THE HAMSTER FAMILY (THE CRICETINAE) & MANY ZOOLOGISTS THINK VOLES SHOULD BE CLASSED AS SUCH.

THE NORTHERN VOLE
THE NORTHERN VOLE LIVES IN EASTERN SIBERIA & KAMCHATKA. ITS LATIN NAME MICROTUS OECONOMUS REFERS TO ITS HOARDING HABITS WHICH ARE SO EXTENSIVE THAT LOCAL PEOPLE CAN LIVE BY RAIDING ITS WINTER STORES.

FERTILITY CYCLES
THE LEMMINGS ARE CLOSELY RELATED TO VOLES. YEARS OF POPULATION EXPLOSIONS AMONG LEMMINGS APPEAR TO COINCIDE WITH POPULATION EXPLOSIONS OF VOLES, SHREWS & SOME BUTTERFLIES IN VARIOUS PARTS OF THE WORLD. THESE SPECIES APPEAR TO HAVE A LINKED CYCLIC VARIATION IN FERTILITY.

THE SNOWY VOLE
THE SNOWY VOLE SOMETIMES LIVES AT ALTITUDES OVER 10,000 FT. IT IS FOUND IN THE ALPS, PYRENEES & MASSIF CENTRAL. IN WINTER IT REMAINS IN A BURROW, WHERE IT KEEPS A STORE OF FOOD

THE FIELD MOUSE
THE FIELD MOUSE IS IN FACT A VOLE (MICROTUS ARVALIS). IT EATS AN ENORMOUS QUANTITY FOR ITS SIZE, PARTLY BECAUSE IT HAS VERY LITTLE FAT & HAS TO BURN A LOT OF ENERGY TO KEEP WARM. THEY CAN BE VERY DESTRUCTIVE. A FIELD SUPPORTING 800 VOLES PER ACRE (A MODEST POPULATION BY VOLE STANDARDS) EACH EATING AN OUNCE OF GRAIN PER WEEK, WILL CAUSE A LOSS OF 10 TONS A MONTH OVER A 100 ACRE FIELD.

THE WATER RAT
THE WATER RAT IS A VOLE, NOT A RAT. ITS CORRECT NAME IS THE WATER VOLE (ARVICOLA AMPHIBIUS). THEY LIVE BESIDE RIVERS IN EXTENSIVE BURROWS WITH LIVING ROOMS, BEDROOMS, CORRIDORS & STOREROOMS. THEY ARE HARMLESS EXCEPT FOR THE DAMAGE THEY CAN DO ERODING RIVER BANKS.

POPULATION EXPLOSIONS
VOLES ARE PRONE TO CYCLIC VARIATIONS IN NUMBERS. WITH A GOOD FOOD SUPPLY A PAIR OF VOLES CAN PRODUCE A FAMILY OF 200 IN A YEAR. THE POPULATION GROWS UNTIL THE FOOD SUPPLY RUNS SHORT. THE OVERCROWDED LIVING CONDITIONS THEN LEAD TO INTENSE TERRITORIAL FIGHTING & A REDUCTION IN BREEDING. THIS, WITH A HIGH TOLL TAKEN BY PREDATORS ATTRACTED TO THE AREA (ESPECIALLY SHORT-EARED OWLS) CAUSES THE VOLE POPULATION TO CRASH.

HOW TO THREAD THE RING THROUGH THE LOOP
GET A FRIEND TO HOLD STRING AS ABOVE. PULL A LOOP OF STRING THROUGH THE RING.

PULL THIS LOOP OVER A THUMB & TAKE OFF ORIGINAL LOOP. THIS LOOKS MOST PUZZLING IF DONE FAST.

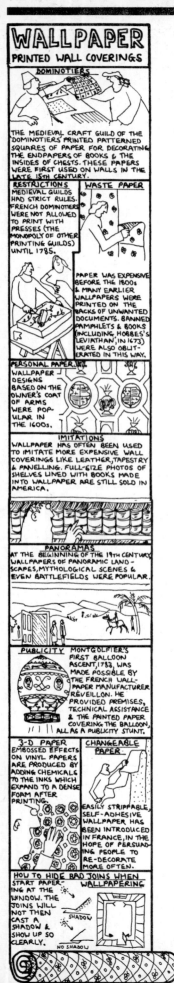

WALLPAPER
PRINTED WALL COVERINGS

DOMINOTIERS

THE MEDIEVAL CRAFT GUILD OF THE 'DOMINOTIERS' PRINTED PATTERNED SQUARES OF PAPER FOR DECORATING THE ENDPAPERS OF BOOKS & THE INSIDES OF CHESTS. THESE PAPERS WERE FIRST USED ON WALLS IN THE LATE 15TH CENTURY.

RESTRICTIONS
MEDIEVAL GUILDS HAD STRICT RULES. FRENCH DOMINOTIERS WERE NOT ALLOWED TO PRINT WITH PRESSES (THE MONOPOLY OF OTHER PRINTING GUILDS) UNTIL 1785.

WASTE PAPER
PAPER WAS EXPENSIVE BEFORE THE 1800s & MANY EARLIER WALLPAPERS WERE PRINTED ON THE BACKS OF UNWANTED DOCUMENTS. BANNED PAMPHLETS & BOOKS (INCLUDING HOBBES'S LEVIATHAN, IN 1673) WERE ALSO OBLITERATED IN THIS WAY.

PERSONAL PAPER
WALLPAPER DESIGNS BASED ON THE OWNER'S COAT OF ARMS WERE POPULAR IN THE 1600s.

IMITATIONS
WALLPAPER HAS OFTEN BEEN USED TO IMITATE MORE EXPENSIVE WALL COVERINGS LIKE LEATHER, TAPESTRY & PANELLING. FULL-SIZE PHOTOS OF SHELVES LINED WITH BOOKS MADE INTO WALLPAPER ARE STILL SOLD IN AMERICA.

PANORAMAS
AT THE BEGINNING OF THE 19TH CENTURY WALLPAPERS OF PANORAMIC LANDSCAPES, MYTHOLOGICAL SCENES & EVEN BATTLEFIELDS WERE POPULAR.

PUBLICITY
MONTGOLFIER'S FIRST BALLOON ASCENT, 1783, WAS MADE POSSIBLE BY THE FRENCH WALLPAPER MANUFACTURER RÉVEILLON. HE PROVIDED PREMISES, TECHNICAL ASSISTANCE & THE PAINTED PAPER COVERING THE BALLOON, ALL AS A PUBLICITY STUNT.

3-D PAPER
EMBOSSED EFFECTS ON VINYL PAPERS ARE PRODUCED BY ADDING CHEMICALS TO THE INKS WHICH EXPAND TO A DENSE FOAM AFTER PRINTING.

CHANGEABLE PAPER
EASILY STRIPPABLE, SELF-ADHESIVE WALLPAPER HAS BEEN INTRODUCED IN FRANCE, IN THE HOPE OF PERSUADING PEOPLE TO RE-DECORATE MORE OFTEN.

HOW TO HIDE BAD JOINS WHEN WALLPAPERING
START PAPERING AT THE WINDOW. THE JOINS WILL NOT THEN CAST A SHADOW & SHOW UP SO CLEARLY.

SHADOW

NO SHADOW

☆ WATCHES ☆
SMALL TIMEPIECES WORN BY PEOPLE

EGGS
THE EARLIEST PORTABLE CLOCKS (c1550) ARE KNOWN AS NUREMBURG EGGS. THEY WERE DESIGNED TO BE HUNG FROM THE NECK, LIKE THE SCENT BOTTLES OF THE PERIOD.

HAIRSPRINGS

MINUTES
THE HAIRSPRING IMPROVED THE ACCURACY OF WATCHES SO MUCH THAT A MINUTE HAND BECAME USEABLE. AT FIRST TWIN HANDS WERE FOUND CONFUSING & MINUTES WERE SHOWN ON A SEPARATE DIAL.

ROTATION
SOME PRECISION 19TH CENTURY WATCHES HAD MOVEMENTS WHICH SLOWLY ROTATED IN THE CASE. THIS EVENED OUT ANY IMBALANCE & FRICTION. AS WATCHES IMPROVED THIS WAS NO LONGER FOUND NECESSARY.

JEWELS
JEWELS WERE FIRST USED IN 1671 TO REDUCE THE FRICTION IN BEARINGS. THE METHOD OF DRILLING HOLES THROUGH THE JEWELS (DRILLBITS COATED IN POWDERED DIAMOND) REMAINED THE SECRET OF A FEW ENGLISH WATCHMAKERS FOR 100 YEARS.

THE HAIRSPRING WAS INTRODUCED BY THE DUTCH SCIENTIST HUYGENS IN 1675. THIS PERFORMS THE SAME FUNCTION AS GRAVITY ON A PENDULUM, GIVING THE WHEEL A 'NATURAL' CONSTANT FREQUENCY.

OIL
OIL IS THE BANE OF ALL MECHANICAL WATCHES. AFTER A TIME IT FORMS EITHER A 'GRINDING PASTE' WITH QUARTZ DUST FROM THE AIR OR A HARD COAT LIKE VARNISH.

WRIST WATCHES
WRIST WATCHES ARE SURPRISINGLY RECENT, FIRST GAINING POPULARITY WITH ARTILLERY OFFICERS IN W.W.I.

GEARS
ENLARGED TO THE SAME SCALE, THE GEARS ON WATCHES ARE NO MORE ACCURATE THAN THE BIG WOODEN GEARS ON OLD WINDMILLS.

QUARTZ
QUARTZ WATCHES HAVE A TINY PIECE OF QUARTZ WHICH VIBRATES (LIKE A TUNING FORK). IT IS MOUNTED IN A MINUTE VACUUM CHAMBER. THE ELECTRONICS KEEP THE QUARTZ VIBRATING & COUNT THE VIBRATIONS.

SPEAKING WATCHES
HITACHI HAVE PATENTED A FLAT TRANSPARENT LOUDSPEAKER WHICH CAN BE MOUNTED IN A LIQUID CRYSTAL WATCH DISPLAY. THE LOUDSPEAKER ALSO ACTS AS A MICROPHONE, SO WRISTWATCH WALKIE-TALKIES WILL SOON APPEAR.

HOW TO USE A WATCH AS A COMPASS
SOUTH

HOLD WATCH LEVEL & TURN IT SO HOUR HAND FACES SUN. HALF WAY BETWEEN 12 o'CLOCK & HOUR HAND WILL THEN POINT ROUGHLY SOUTH.

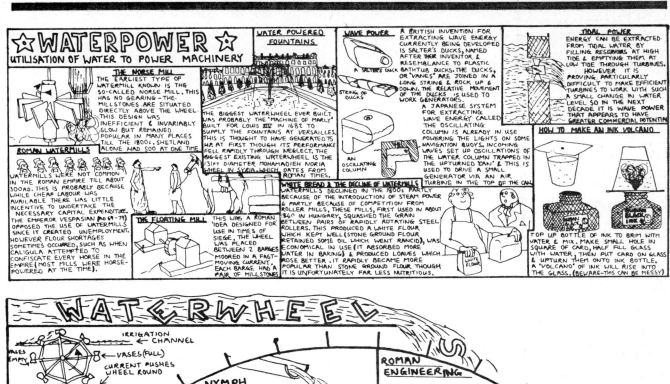

☆ WATERPOWER ☆
UTILISATION OF WATER TO POWER MACHINERY

THE NORSE MILL
THE EARLIEST TYPE OF WATERMILL KNOWN IS THE SO-CALLED NORSE MILL. THIS HAS NO GEARING – THE MILLSTONES ARE SITUATED DIRECTLY ABOVE THE WHEEL. THIS DESIGN WAS INEFFICIENT & INVARIABLY SLOW BUT REMAINED POPULAR IN MANY PLACES TILL THE 1800s. SHETLAND ALONE HAD 500 AT ONE TIME.

ROMAN WATERMILLS
WATERMILLS WERE NOT COMMON IN THE ROMAN EMPIRE TILL ABOUT 300AD. THIS IS PROBABLY BECAUSE WHILE CHEAP LABOUR WAS AVAILABLE THERE WAS LITTLE INCENTIVE TO UNDERTAKE THE NECESSARY CAPITAL EXPENDITURE. THE EMPEROR VESPASIAN (AD 69–79) OPPOSED THE USE OF WATERMILLS SINCE IT CREATED UNEMPLOYMENT. HOWEVER FLOUR SHORTAGES SOMETIMES OCCURRED, SUCH AS WHEN CALIGULA ATTEMPTED TO CONFISCATE EVERY HORSE IN THE EMPIRE (MOST MILLS WERE HORSE-POWERED AT THE TIME).

THE FLOATING MILL
THIS WAS A ROMAN 'IDEA' DESIGNED FOR USE IN TIMES OF SIEGE. THE WHEEL WAS PLACED BETWEEN 2 BARGES MOORED IN A FAST-MOVING CURRENT. EACH BARGE HAD A PAIR OF MILLSTONES.

WATER POWERED FOUNTAINS
THE BIGGEST WATERWHEEL EVER BUILT WAS PROBABLY THE 'MACHINE OF MARLY' BUILT FOR LOUIS XIV IN 1682 TO SUPPLY THE FOUNTAINS AT VERSAILLES. THIS IS THOUGHT TO HAVE GENERATED 75 H.P. AT FIRST THOUGH ITS PERFORMANCE FELL RAPIDLY THROUGH NEGLECT. THE BIGGEST EXISTING WATERWHEEL IS THE 131FT DIAMETER MOHAMADIEH NORIA WHEEL IN SYRIA, WHICH DATES FROM ROMAN TIMES.

WHITE BREAD & THE DECLINE OF WATERMILLS
WATERMILLS DECLINED IN THE 1800s PARTLY BECAUSE OF THE INTRODUCTION OF STEAM POWER & PARTLY BECAUSE OF COMPETITION FROM ROLLER MILLS. THESE MILLS, FIRST USED IN ABOUT 1840 IN HUNGARY, SQUASHED THE GRAIN BETWEEN PAIRS OF RAPIDLY ROTATING STEEL ROLLERS. THIS PRODUCED A WHITE FLOUR WHICH KEPT WELL (STONE GROUND FLOUR RETAINED SOME OIL WHICH WENT RANCID), WAS ECONOMICAL IN USE (IT ABSORBED MORE WATER IN BAKING) & PRODUCED LOAVES WHICH ROSE BETTER. IT RAPIDLY BECAME MORE POPULAR THAN STONE GROUND FLOUR THOUGH IT IS UNFORTUNATELY FAR LESS NUTRITIOUS.

WAVE POWER
A BRITISH INVENTION FOR EXTRACTING WAVE ENERGY CURRENTLY BEING DEVELOPED IS SALTER'S DUCKS, NAMED AFTER THEIR INVENTOR & RESEMBLANCE TO PLASTIC.
A SALTERS DUCK BATHTUB DUCKS. THE DUCKS, OR 'VANES' ARE JOINED IN A LONG STRING & ROCK UP & DOWN. THE RELATIVE MOVEMENT OF THE DUCKS IS USED TO WORK GENERATORS.
A JAPANESE SYSTEM FOR EXTRACTING WAVE ENERGY CALLED THE OSCILLATING COLUMN IS ALREADY IN USE POWERING THE LIGHTS ON SOME NAVIGATION BUOYS. INCOMING WAVES SET UP OSCILLATIONS OF THE WATER COLUMN TRAPPED IN THE UPTURNED CAN' & THIS IS USED TO DRIVE A SMALL GENERATOR VIA AN AIR TURBINE IN THE TOP OF THE CAN.

TIDAL POWER
ENERGY CAN BE EXTRACTED FROM TIDAL WATER BY FILLING RESERVOIRS AT HIGH TIDE & EMPTYING THEM AT LOW TIDE THROUGH TURBINES. HOWEVER IT IS PROVING PARTICULARLY DIFFICULT TO MAKE EFFICIENT TURBINES TO WORK WITH SUCH A SMALL CHANGE IN WATER LEVEL SO IN THE NEXT DECADE IT IS WAVE POWER THAT APPEARS TO HAVE GREATER COMMERCIAL POTENTIAL.

HOW TO MAKE AN INK VOLCANO
TOP UP BOTTLE OF INK TO BRIM WITH WATER & MIX. MAKE SMALL HOLE IN SQUARE OF CARD, HALF FILL GLASS WITH WATER, THEN PUT CARD ON GLASS & UPTURN THEM ONTO INK BOTTLE. A 'VOLCANO' OF INK WILL RISE INTO THE GLASS. (BEWARE–THIS CAN BE MESSY)

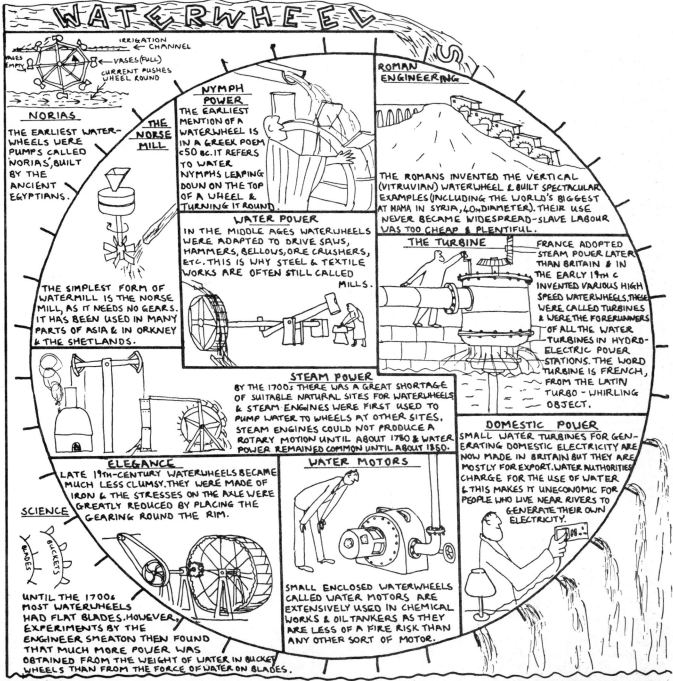

WATERWHEEL

IRRIGATION ← CHANNEL
VASES EMPTY
VASES (FULL)
CURRENT PUSHES WHEEL ROUND

NORIAS
THE EARLIEST WATER-WHEELS WERE PUMPS CALLED 'NORIAS', BUILT BY THE ANCIENT EGYPTIANS.

THE NORSE MILL
THE SIMPLEST FORM OF WATERMILL IS THE NORSE MILL, AS IT NEEDS NO GEARS. IT HAS BEEN USED IN MANY PARTS OF ASIA & IN ORKNEY & THE SHETLANDS.

NYMPH POWER
THE EARLIEST MENTION OF A WATERWHEEL IS IN A GREEK POEM c50 BC. IT REFERS TO WATER NYMPHS LEAPING DOWN ON THE TOP OF A WHEEL & TURNING IT ROUND.

WATER POWER
IN THE MIDDLE AGES WATERWHEELS WERE ADAPTED TO DRIVE SAWS, HAMMERS, BELLOWS, ORE CRUSHERS, ETC. THIS IS WHY STEEL & TEXTILE WORKS ARE OFTEN STILL CALLED MILLS.

ROMAN ENGINEERING
THE ROMANS INVENTED THE VERTICAL (VITRUVIAN) WATERWHEEL & BUILT SPECTACULAR EXAMPLES (INCLUDING THE WORLD'S BIGGEST AT HAMA IN SYRIA, 40m DIAMETER). THEIR USE NEVER BECAME WIDESPREAD – SLAVE LABOUR WAS TOO CHEAP & PLENTIFUL.

THE TURBINE
FRANCE ADOPTED STEAM POWER LATER THAN BRITAIN & IN THE EARLY 19TH C INVENTED VARIOUS HIGH SPEED WATERWHEELS. THESE WERE CALLED TURBINES & WERE THE FORERUNNERS OF ALL THE WATER TURBINES IN HYDRO-ELECTRIC POWER STATIONS. THE WORD TURBINE IS FRENCH, FROM THE LATIN TURBO – WHIRLING OBJECT.

STEAM POWER
BY THE 1700s THERE WAS A GREAT SHORTAGE OF SUITABLE NATURAL SITES FOR WATERWHEELS & STEAM ENGINES WERE FIRST USED TO PUMP WATER TO WHEELS AT OTHER SITES. STEAM ENGINES COULD NOT PRODUCE A ROTARY MOTION UNTIL ABOUT 1780 & WATER POWER REMAINED COMMON UNTIL ABOUT 1850.

DOMESTIC POWER
SMALL WATER TURBINES FOR GENERATING DOMESTIC ELECTRICITY ARE NOW MADE IN BRITAIN BUT THEY ARE MOSTLY FOR EXPORT. WATER AUTHORITIES CHARGE FOR THE USE OF WATER & THIS MAKES IT UNECONOMIC FOR PEOPLE WHO LIVE NEAR RIVERS TO GENERATE THEIR OWN ELECTRICITY.

ELEGANCE
LATE 19TH-CENTURY WATERWHEELS BECAME MUCH LESS CLUMSY. THEY WERE MADE OF IRON & THE STRESSES ON THE AXLE WERE GREATLY REDUCED BY PLACING THE GEARING ROUND THE RIM.

SCIENCE
BLADES / BUCKETS
UNTIL THE 1700s MOST WATERWHEELS HAD FLAT BLADES. HOWEVER, EXPERIMENTS BY THE ENGINEER SMEATON THEN FOUND THAT MUCH MORE POWER WAS OBTAINED FROM THE WEIGHT OF WATER IN BUCKET WHEELS THAN FROM THE FORCE OF WATER ON BLADES.

WATER MOTORS
SMALL ENCLOSED WATERWHEELS CALLED WATER MOTORS ARE EXTENSIVELY USED IN CHEMICAL WORKS & OIL TANKERS AS THEY ARE LESS OF A FIRE RISK THAN ANY OTHER SORT OF MOTOR.

☆ WEATHER ☆
ATMOSPHERIC PHENOMENA OF THE TROPOSPHERE

BAD WEATHER

BRITAIN HAS AN AVERAGE OF SIX LIGHTNING STRIKES PER YEAR IN EVERY SQUARE MILE. FOR THUNDER LOVERS THE BEST PLACE IN THE WORLD IS BOGO, INDONESIA, AVERAGING 322 DAYS WITH THUNDER EACH YEAR.

DANGEROUS WEATHER

WORSE THAN THE BIBLICAL SHOWERS OF TOADS WAS A CYCLONE IN 1856 AT HARRODSBURG, IN KENTUCKY, WHICH STRUCK A FACTORY MAKING KNITTING NEEDLES. THE RESULTING SHOWER KILLED SEVERAL PEOPLE.

FOG: VERY EXPANSIVE STUFF. PAIL OF WATER PRODUCES ENOUGH FOG TO COVER THE WHOLE OF LONDON 50FT DEEP. FOR ALL FOG LOVERS THE BEST PLACE IN THE WORLD IS OFF THE LABRADOR COAST, WITH AN ANNUAL AVERAGE OF 120 TOTALLY FOGGY DAYS.

WEATHERFORECASTING AND COWS

COWS ARE SUCH CLEVER ANIMALS THEY OFTEN LIE DOWN BEFORE IT STARTS TO RAIN, KEEPING A PATCH OF GRASS DRY. THEY ALSO RARELY LIE UNDER TREES, THUS AVOIDING BEING STRUCK BY LIGHTNING.

INDOOR WEATHER

BEFORE CENTRAL HEATING THERE WAS NOT MUCH POINT IN HAVING A VERY LARGE BUILDING AS TEMPERATURE CHANGES CAUSED CLOUDS & RAIN INSIDE. THIS WAS A CONSIDERABLE PROBLEM IN THE GOODYEAR ZEPPELIN HANGAR, IN INDIANA.

HOW TO DRAW WEATHERFORECASTERS

WEATHER FORECASTERS ARE SOLID IMPERVIOUS MEN. THEY ARE NOT VERY DECORATIVE BUT COME AS A RELIEF AFTER SERIOUS TELEVISION, DRAWING A COMPLETE WEATHERMAN IS PRACTICALLY IMPOSSIBLE SINCE THEIR FEET NEVER APPEAR.

THE ACCURACY OF WEATHERFORECASTS

THERE ARE ABOUT 2000 WEATHER STATIONS REPORTING EVERY TWO HOURS IN THE NORTHERN HEMISPHERE AND THE FORECASTERS CLAIM TO BE ABLE TO PREDICT THE CONDITIONS 10 HOURS IN ADVANCE WITH 85% ACCURACY. IS IT WORTH IT? THERE IS A SIMPLER METHOD THAT WORKS NEARLY AS WELL. THERE IS A BETTER THAN 50% CHANCE THAT THE CONDITIONS ON ANY DAY WILL BE THE SAME AS ON THE PREVIOUS DAY.

A GRASSHOPPER THERMOMETER

COUNT THE NUMBER OF CLICKS PER MINUTE, DIVIDE BY 4 & ADD 40 FOR ROUGH GUIDE TO TEMPERATURE IN FARENHEIT.

← THE PATH OF THE NORTH POLE FROM 1908 to 1910

A PATH AS RANDOM AS THIS IS OBVIOUSLY HIGHLY UNPREDICT-ABLE. IT HAS BEEN CALCULATED THAT IF THE ICE CAPS WERE TO MELT, MEAN SEA LEVEL WOULD RISE 50FT, IMMERSING MOST OF ENGLAND. EVERY WELL EQUIPPED HOME NEEDS A BOAT.

HOW TO WALK THROUGH A POSTCARD

CUT POSTCARD AS SHOWN, THEN EXPAND INTO SORT OF PAPER CHAIN & WALK THROUGH VERY GENTLY.

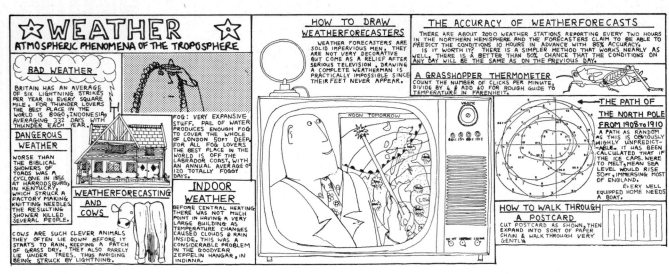

☆ WEDDINGS ☆
CEREMONIES MARKING UNION OF MAN & WOMAN

MARRIAGE BY CAPTURE & PURCHASE

ANCIENT BRITONS OFTEN SECURED WIVES SIMPLY BY CAPTURING GIRLS FROM OTHER FAMILIES. AN EARLY ATTEMPT TO LEGISLATE AGAINST THIS PRACTICE WAS MADE BY ETHELBERT, KING OF KENT, IN ABOUT 600AD. HE DECREED THAT ANY MAN FOUND GUILTY OF CARRYING AWAY A MAID SHOULD PAY 50s. TO HER OWNER. IF A MAN CARRIED AWAY A MARRIED WOMAN HE COULD KEEP HER ONLY IF HE PROVIDED A REPLACEMENT, AT HIS OWN COST, TO THE INJURED HUSBAND.

SAXON MALE CHAUVINISTS

THE WORD 'WED' COMES FROM THE SAXON WORD FOR THE SUM OF MONEY, OR PLEDGE, GIVEN TO THE BRIDE'S FATHER BY THE GROOM. IN RETURN THE FATHER WOULD HAND A SLIPPER TO THE GROOM WHO PROMPTLY USED IT TO HIT HIS BRIDE ON HER HEAD (TO SIGNIFY THAT HE WAS NOW HER MASTER). THE SLIPPER WAS LATER CARRIED INTO THE BRIDAL CHAMBER & HUNG ABOVE THE HUSBAND'S SIDE OF THE BED.

PORCH MARRIAGE

UNTIL ABOUT 1550 CHRISTIAN MARRIAGES WERE ALWAYS PERFORMED IN THE PORCH OUTSIDE THE CHURCH. AFTER THE CEREMONY EVERYONE WENT INSIDE FOR A NUPTIAL MASS.

MEDIEVAL DIVORCE

DIVORCE COULD BE OBTAINED WITH SURPRISING EASE BY MEDIEVAL LORDS. A LORD SIMPLY INVENTED SOME EVIDENCE THAT HE WAS RELATED TO HIS WIFE. THIS AUTOMATICALLY NULLIFIED THE MARRIAGE. AS A MAN COULD NOT MARRY A RELATIVE AS DISTANT AS A THIRD COUSIN, EVEN BY MARRIAGE, ANY EVIDENCE WAS DIFFICULT TO DISPROVE.

SYMBOLIC CONFETTI

AN ELIZABETHAN ALTERNATIVE TO CONFETTI WAS TO THROW A SYMBOL OF THE GROOM'S TRADE: NAILS FOR A BLACKSMITH, BITS OF CLOTH FOR A TAILOR, WOOD-SHAVINGS FOR A CARPENTER, WOOL FOR A WEAVER, CAKE FOR A BAKER, GRAIN FOR A FARMER PAPER FOR A CLERK, ETC.

A DISAPPOINTING CAKE

WHEN PRESIDENT NIXON'S DAUGHTER PAT WAS MARRIED IN 1971 THE TRADITIONAL WEDDING CAKE WAS REPLACED BY A LIGHT LEMON SPONGE. THE WHITE HOUSE CHEF PUBLISHED A SMALL-SCALE VERSION OF THE RECIPE IN ADVANCE TO ENABLE ALL ZEALOUS AMERICANS TO EAT THE SAME CAKE ON THE WEDDING DAY. HOWEVER THERE WAS A MISTAKE IN THE PUBLISHED RECIPE WHICH CAUSED THE CAKE TO HAVE A CONSISTENCY OF GLUE ON THE OUTSIDE AND SOUP INSIDE.

INSTANT MARRIAGE

A FASHION DEVELOPED IN THE 1700s FOR SECRET MARRIAGES BY SPECIAL LICENCE. THIS RESULTED IN A TRADE OF INSTANT WEDDINGS PERFORMED BY MINISTERS OF DUBIOUS AUTHENTICITY IN PUBS & BARBERS SHOPS. THE MARRIAGE ACT OF 1753 PUT AN END TO THIS PRACTICE IN ENGLAND & SENT THE TRADE TO GRETNA GREEN, JUST OVER THE SCOTTISH BORDER.

HOW TO PHOTOGRAPH YOUR FRIENDS SITTING ON YOUR HANDS

ARRANGE FRIENDS AS BELOW ON A LARGE FIELD OR PLAYGROUND. WHEN LOOKING THROUGH CAMERA B & C MUST BE POSITIONED EXACTLY ABOVE A'S HAND. THE RESULTING PHOTOGRAPH IS A MOST CONVINCING PUZZLE.

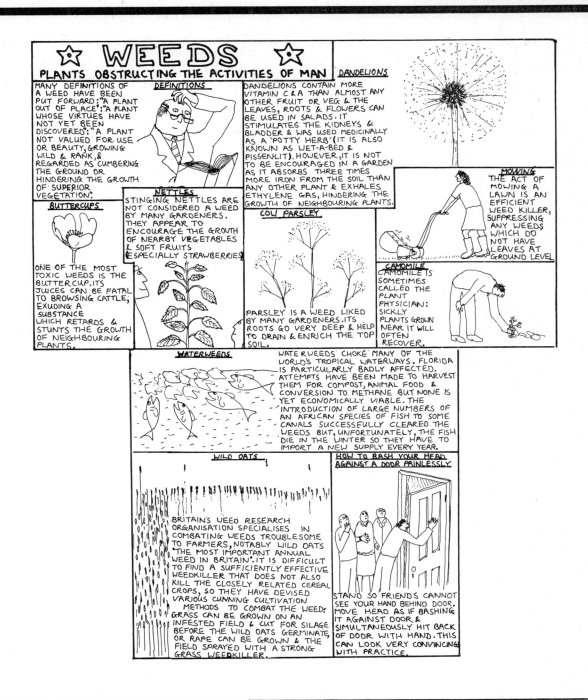

☆ WEEDS ☆
PLANTS OBSTRUCTING THE ACTIVITIES OF MAN

DEFINITIONS

MANY DEFINITIONS OF A WEED HAVE BEEN PUT FORWARD: "A PLANT OUT OF PLACE"; "A PLANT WHOSE VIRTUES HAVE NOT YET BEEN DISCOVERED"; "A PLANT NOT VALUED FOR USE OR BEAUTY, GROWING WILD & RANK, & REGARDED AS CUMBERING THE GROUND OR HINDERING THE GROWTH OF SUPERIOR VEGETATION".

BUTTERCUPS

ONE OF THE MOST TOXIC WEEDS IS THE BUTTERCUP. ITS JUICES CAN BE FATAL TO BROWSING CATTLE, EXUDING A SUBSTANCE WHICH RETARDS & STUNTS THE GROWTH OF NEIGHBOURING PLANTS.

NETTLES

STINGING NETTLES ARE NOT CONSIDERED A WEED BY MANY GARDENERS. THEY APPEAR TO ENCOURAGE THE GROWTH OF NEARBY VEGETABLES & SOFT FRUITS (ESPECIALLY STRAWBERRIES).

COW PARSLEY

PARSLEY IS A WEED LIKED BY MANY GARDENERS. ITS ROOTS GO VERY DEEP & HELP TO DRAIN & ENRICH THE TOP SOIL.

DANDELIONS

DANDELIONS CONTAIN MORE VITAMIN C & A THAN ALMOST ANY OTHER FRUIT OR VEG & THE LEAVES, ROOTS & FLOWERS CAN BE USED IN SALADS. IT STIMULATES THE KIDNEYS & BLADDER & WAS USED MEDICINALLY AS A 'POTTY HERB' (IT IS ALSO KNOWN AS WET-A-BED & PISSENLIT). HOWEVER, IT IS NOT TO BE ENCOURAGED IN A GARDEN AS IT ABSORBS THREE TIMES MORE IRON FROM THE SOIL THAN ANY OTHER PLANT & EXHALES ETHYLENE GAS, HINDERING THE GROWTH OF NEIGHBOURING PLANTS.

MOWING

THE ACT OF MOWING A LAWN IS AN EFFICIENT WEED KILLER, SUPPRESSING ANY WEEDS WHICH DO NOT HAVE LEAVES AT GROUND LEVEL

CAMOMILE

CAMOMILE IS SOMETIMES CALLED THE PLANT PHYSICIAN: SICKLY PLANTS GROWN NEAR IT WILL OFTEN RECOVER.

WATERWEEDS

WATERWEEDS CHOKE MANY OF THE WORLD'S TROPICAL WATERWAYS. FLORIDA IS PARTICULARLY BADLY AFFECTED. ATTEMPTS HAVE BEEN MADE TO HARVEST THEM FOR COMPOST, ANIMAL FOOD & CONVERSION TO METHANE BUT NONE IS YET ECONOMICALLY VIABLE. THE INTRODUCTION OF LARGE NUMBERS OF AN AFRICAN SPECIES OF FISH TO SOME CANALS SUCCESSFULLY CLEARED THE WEEDS BUT, UNFORTUNATELY, THE FISH DIE IN THE WINTER SO THEY HAVE TO IMPORT A NEW SUPPLY EVERY YEAR.

WILD OATS

BRITAIN'S WEED RESEARCH ORGANISATION SPECIALISES IN COMBATING WEEDS TROUBLESOME TO FARMERS, NOTABLY WILD OATS 'THE MOST IMPORTANT ANNUAL WEED IN BRITAIN'. IT IS DIFFICULT TO FIND A SUFFICIENTLY EFFECTIVE WEEDKILLER THAT DOES NOT ALSO KILL THE CLOSELY RELATED CEREAL CROPS, SO THEY HAVE DEVISED VARIOUS CUNNING CULTIVATION METHODS TO COMBAT THE WEED: GRASS CAN BE GROWN ON AN INFESTED FIELD & CUT FOR SILAGE BEFORE THE WILD OATS GERMINATE, OR RAPE CAN BE GROWN & THE FIELD SPRAYED WITH A STRONG GRASS WEEDKILLER.

HOW TO BASH YOUR HEAD AGAINST A DOOR PAINLESSLY

STAND SO FRIENDS CANNOT SEE YOUR HAND BEHIND DOOR. MOVE HEAD AS IF BASHING IT AGAINST DOOR & SIMULTANEOUSLY HIT BACK OF DOOR WITH HAND. THIS CAN LOOK VERY CONVINCING WITH PRACTICE.

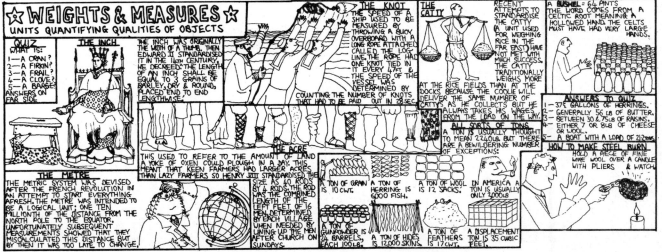

☆ WEIGHTS & MEASURES ☆
UNITS QUANTIFYING QUALITIES OF OBJECTS

QUIZ

WHAT IS:
1 – A CRAN?
2 – A FIRKIN?
3 – A FRAIL?
4 – A CLOVE?
5 – A BARGE?

ANSWERS ON FAR SIDE

THE INCH

THE INCH WAS ORIGINALLY THE WIDTH OF A THUMB, THEN EDWARD II STANDARDISED IT IN THE 14TH CENTURY, HE DECREED 'THE LENGTH OF AN INCH SHALL BE EQUAL TO 3 GRAINS OF BARLEY, DRY & ROUND, PLACED END TO END LENGTHWISE'.

THE METRE

THE METRIC SYSTEM WAS DEVISED AFTER THE FRENCH REVOLUTION IN AN ATTEMPT TO START EVERYTHING AFRESH. THE METRE WAS INTENDED TO BE A LOGICAL UNIT: ONE TEN MILLIONTH OF THE DISTANCE FROM THE NORTH POLE TO THE EQUATOR. UNFORTUNATELY SUBSEQUENT MEASUREMENTS SHOWED THAT THEY MISCALCULATED THIS DISTANCE BUT BY THEN IT WAS TOO LATE TO CHANGE.

THE KNOT

THE SPEED OF A SHIP USED TO BE MEASURED BY THROWING A BUOY OVERBOARD WITH A LONG ROPE ATTACHED CALLED THE LOG LINE. THE ROPE HAD ONE KNOT TIED IN IT EVERY 47FT & THE SPEED OF THE VESSEL WAS DETERMINED BY COUNTING THE NUMBER OF KNOTS THAT HAD TO BE PAID OUT IN 28 SEC.

THE ACRE

THIS USED TO REFER TO THE AMOUNT OF LAND A YOKE OF OXEN COULD PLOUGH IN A DAY. THIS MEANT THAT KEEN FARMERS HAD LARGER ACRES THAN LAZY FARMERS SO HENRY VIII STANDARDISED THE SIZE AS 40 RODS BY 4 RODS. THE ROD WAS THE COMBINED LENGTH OF THE LEFT FEET OF 16 MEN DETERMINED BY EACH VILLAGE WHEN NEEDED BY LINING UP THE MEN AFTER CHURCH ON SUNDAYS.

THE CATTY

RECENT ATTEMPTS TO STANDARDISE THE CATTY (A UNIT USED FOR WEIGHING RICE IN THE FAR EAST) HAVE NOT MET WITH MUCH SUCCESS. THE CATTY TRADITIONALLY WEIGHS MORE AT THE RICE FIELDS THAN AT THE DOCKS BECAUSE THE COOLIE WILL DELIVER THE SAME NUMBER OF CATTYS AS HE COLLECTS BUT HE ALWAYS TAKES HIS WAGES FROM THE LOAD ON THE WAY.

ALL SORTS OF TONS

A TON IS USUALLY THOUGHT TO MEAN 2240LB. BUT THERE ARE A BEWILDERING NUMBER OF EXCEPTIONS:

A TON OF GRAIN IS 10 CWT.

A TON OF HERRING IS 6000 FISH.

A TON OF GUNPOWDER IS 24 BARRELS, EACH 100LB.

A TON OF WOOL IS 12 SACKS.

IN AMERICA A TON IS USUALLY ONLY 2000LB.

A TON OF HIDES IS 12,000 SKINS.

A TON OF FEATHERS IS 17 CWT.

A DISPLACEMENT TON IS 35 CUBIC FEET.

A BUSHEL = 64 PINTS THE WORD COMES FROM A CELTIC ROOT MEANING A HOLLOWED HAND. THE CELTS MUST HAVE HAD VERY LARGE HANDS.

ANSWERS TO QUIZ

1 – 37½ GALLONS OF HERRINGS.
2 – GENERALLY 56 LB OF BUTTER.
3 – BETWEEN 30 & 75LB OF RAISINS.
4 – EITHER 7 OR 8LB OF CHEESE OR WOOL.
5 – A BOAT WITH A LOAD OF 21½ TONS.

HOW TO MAKE STEEL BURN

HOLD A PIECE OF FINE WIRE WOOL OVER A CANDLE WITH PLIERS & WATCH

☆ WEIGHT LIFTING ☆
COMPETITIVE LIFTING OF HEAVY OBJECTS

GREEK WEIGHTLIFTING
VARIOUS HUGE BOULDERS IN GREECE ARE INSCRIBED WITH THE NAMES OF ANCIENT GREEK ATHLETES ALLEGED TO HAVE LIFTED THEM.

MANHOOD STONES

MANHOOD STONES CAN BE FOUND IN SOME SCOTTISH CASTLES. LAIRDS HAD TO LIFT THEM TO PROVE THEIR MANHOOD.

DUMB-BELLS
THE ORIGINAL DUMB-BELL WAS A SHORT CANE, WITH A SOLID BELL-SHAPED LUMP OF LEAD ON THE END. IT WAS USED BY THE ENGLISH NOBILITY FOR STRENGTHENING EXERCISES IN THE 16TH CENTURY.

STONE-LIFTING

STONE-LIFTING CONTESTS ARE POPULAR IN THE BASQUE REGIONS OF FRANCE & SPAIN. CONTESTANTS HAVE TO LIFT A HEAVY STONE TO THE SHOULDER AS MANY TIMES AS POSSIBLE IN ONE MINUTE.

OLYMPIC WEIGHTLIFTING
IN THE OLYMPICS, CONTESTANTS DO A TWO-HAND SNATCH (LIFTING THE BAR-BELLS FROM THE FLOOR TO ARMS' LENGTH OVERHEAD IN ONE MOVEMENT. RECORD: 200.5kg) — FOLLOWED BY A TWO-HAND CLEAN & JERK (LIFTING THE BAR-BELLS TO THE SHOULDER. RECORD:256kg). THE TWO SCORES ARE ADDED TOGETHER FOR THE FINAL TOTAL

THE ONLY BRITISH CHAMP

THE ONLY BRITISH LIFTER TO WIN AN OLYMPIC TITLE WAS LAUNCETON ELLIOT IN 1896.

THE WORLD RECORD
THE GREATEST WEIGHT EVER LIFTED IS 2·84 TONNES. IT WAS A BACK LIFT OFF TRESTLES BY PAUL ANDERSON (US) IN 1957.

THE FEMALE RECORD

THE FEMALE RECORD FOR A TWO-HAND CLEAN & JERK (SEE 'OLYMPIC WEIGHTLIFTING') IS 121kg BY KATIE SANDWINA (GERMANY).

IMPRESSIVE LIFTING FEATS
HERMANN GORNER (GERMANY) LIFTED 24 MEN SITTING ON A PLANK IN 1921 ON THE SOLES OF HIS FEET. HE ALSO CARRIED A ¾ TONNE PIANO ON HIS BACK FOR 16 METRES

HOLLOW WEIGHTS

BEFORE DETACHABLE DISC WEIGHTS WERE INTRODUCED, BAR-BELLS HAD HOLLOW BALLS OF IRON AT EACH END WHICH WERE PROGRESSIVELY FILLED WITH SAND.

WEIGHTLIFTING DRUGS
WEIGHTLIFTING RECORDS HAVE IMPROVED GREATLY WITH THE USE OF ANABOLIC STEROID DRUGS, WHICH STIMULATE MUSCLE GROWTH. THE DRUG REMAINS EFFECTIVE FOR MORE THAN 6 MONTHS, SO DRUG TESTS, WHICH WORK ONLY IF GIVEN WITHIN 14 DAYS OF THE DRUG BEING TAKEN, CANNOT HOPE TO PREVENT THEIR USE.

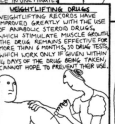

HOW TO MAKE A BALLOON CHANGE COLOUR
PUSH A YELLOW BALLOON INSIDE A BLUE BALLOON. BLOW UP INNER BALLOON & TIE IT; THEN BLOW UP OUTER BALLOON FURTHER & TIE IT.
• SHOW BALLOON TO AUDIENCE & COVER IT WITH A CLOTH.
• DISTRACT ATTENTION FROM NOISE & INSERT PIN TO PUNCTURE OUTER BALLOON ONLY.
• REMOVE CLOTH TO REVEAL YELLOW BALLOON.

☆ WELDING ☆
TECHNIQUE OF JOINING METALS BY MELTING

OXYACETYLENE WELDING

FOR OVER 6000 YEARS MAN HAS KNOWN HOW TO WELD METALS TOGETHER BY HEATING THEM IN A CHARCOAL FIRE. HOWEVER THIS TECHNIQUE IS LIMITED TO SMALL ITEMS. THE INVENTION OF THE BLOWTORCH IN 1887 FOR BURNING AIR OR OXYGEN WITH COAL GAS OR HYDROGEN BY T. FLETCHER OF WARRINGTON WAS A GREAT STEP FORWARD, BUT IT WAS NOT UNTIL THE OXYGEN & ACETYLENE TORCH WAS PERFECTED (ABOUT 1900) THAT A HOT ENOUGH FLAME WAS MADE TO MELT & WELD IRON & STEEL.

ELECTRIC WELDING
VOLTA PERFORMED THE FIRST ELECTRIC WELDING IN 1800. WHILE DEMONSTRATING TO NAPOLEON THE BATTERY HE HAD INVENTED, HE MELTED SOME IRON WIRE CONNECTED BETWEEN A HUGE BANK OF HIS BATTERIES. A RUSSIAN, N.G. SLAVIANOFF, FIRST PATENTED ARC WELDING IN 1880. THE METALS TO BE WELDED WERE CONNECTED TO ONE TERMINAL OF A LARGE BATTERY AND A CARBON ROD CONNECTED TO THE OTHER TERMINAL. IF THE ROD WAS HELD CLOSE TO THE METAL A CONTINUOUS SPARK (THE ARC) LEAPT FROM ROD TO METAL. INTO THIS ARC HE DROPPED SMALL METAL SHAVINGS WHICH FUSED THE WELD TOGETHER.

FRICTION WELDING

AN INGENIOUS RECENT PROCESS USED FOR WELDING TWO TUBES TOGETHER IS FRICTION WELDING. ONE TUBE IS ROTATED IN A LATHE WHILE THE OTHER TUBE IS CLAMPED & PUSHED AGAINST THE FIRST TO GENERATE HEAT BY FRICTION. AT THE RIGHT TEMPERATURE THE FIXED TUBE IS RELEASED & THE JOIN FUSES TOGETHER.

ACETYLENE
ACETYLENE WAS DISCOVERED IN 1892 BY THEOBALD WILSON IN THE US DURING AN ATTEMPT TO MAKE THE METAL CALCIUM BY HEATING LIME & IRON TOGETHER. DISGUSTED BY HIS FAILURE HE HURLED THE BLACK RESIDUE INTO A NEARBY CREEK. A GREAT SEETHING & BUBBLING IMMEDIATELY STARTED & THE GAS (ACETYLENE) WAS FOUND TO BE INFLAMMABLE. THE FIRST USE FOUND FOR IT WAS LIGHTING. MANY HOUSES IN SCOTLAND WERE LIT BY ACETYLENE PIPED FROM A PLANT IN FOYERS, INVERNESS-SHIRE. EARLY ATTEMPTS TO COMPRESS IT IN CYLINDERS LED TO FATAL ACCIDENTS & IT WAS NOT UNTIL IT WAS DISCOVERED THAT IT COULD BE SAFELY DISSOLVED IN CYLINDERS OF ACETONE (1901) THAT IT BECAME AVAILABLE FOR WELDING.

LASER WELDING
LASER WELDING HAS GREAT POTENTIAL FOR THE FUTURE BUT IS FRAUGHT WITH PROBLEMS. THE RUBY LASER IS HIGHLY EFFICIENT AT WELDING SMALL ITEMS BUT LARGE SCALE WELDING CAN ONLY BE DONE WITH A GAS LASER. THIS REQUIRES MASSIVE PUMPS, HEAT EXCHANGERS & POWER SUPPLIES (IT IS ONLY 10% EFFICIENT). THE BEAM IS INVISIBLE, IN THE INFRA-RED BAND, WHICH MAKES IT DIFFICULT TO GUIDE & INCREASES THE DANGER OF REFLECTING THE BEAM WHERE IT IS UNWANTED. IN PRACTICE A SECONDARY VISIBLE LASER IS USUALLY SUPERIMPOSED ON THE MAIN BEAM.

RUSSIAN WELDING

METALS CAN BE WELDED BY PUSHING THEM TOGETHER AT HIGH PRESSURE WITHOUT ANY HEAT. THE RUSSIANS ARE PARTICULARLY GOOD AT THIS. THEY HAVE ONE SIMPLE DEVICE IN WHICH THE COMPONENTS TO BE WELDED ARE PLACED UNDER A RAM FULL OF WATER. IN THE NORTH THE WATER IS FROZEN SIMPLY BY OPENING THE DOOR; IT EXPANDS AS IT FREEZES & FORCES THE COMPONENTS TOGETHER AT 20,000 ATMOSPHERES.

HOW TO MAKE A MAGICIAN'S TABLE

COVER LARGE CARDBOARD BOX WITH PAPER TABLE CLOTH. CUT ROUND HOLE IN BOX TOP & PAPER. PAINT BLACK SPOTS ON REST OF PAPER TO DISGUISE HOLE. TO PERFORM: PLACE HAT ON TABLE OVER HOLE, THEN FRIEND INSIDE BOX CAN FILL HAT WITH THINGS

☆ WHALES ☆
ORDER OF MAMMALS ADAPTED FOR AN AQUATIC LIFE

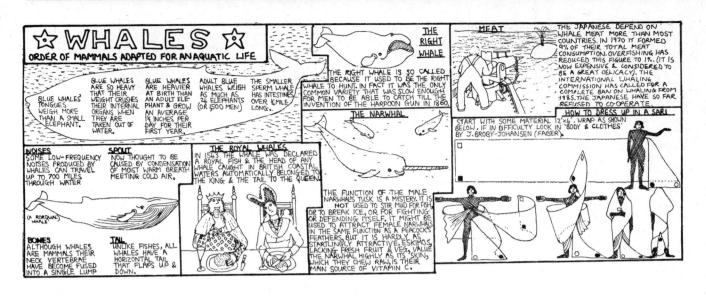

BLUE WHALES TONGUES WEIGH MORE THAN A SMALL ELEPHANT.

BLUE WHALES ARE SO HEAVY THAT THEIR WEIGHT CRUSHES THEIR INTERNAL ORGANS WHEN THEY ARE TAKEN OUT OF WATER.

BLUE WHALES ARE HEAVIER AT BIRTH THAN AN ADULT ELEPHANT & GROW AN AVERAGE 1½ INCHES PER DAY FOR THEIR FIRST YEAR.

ADULT BLUE WHALES WEIGH AS MUCH AS 24 ELEPHANTS (OR 1500 MEN)

THE SMALLER SPERM WHALE HAS INTESTINES OVER ½ MILE LONG.

THE RIGHT WHALE

THE RIGHT WHALE IS SO CALLED BECAUSE IT USED TO BE THE RIGHT WHALE TO HUNT. IN FACT IT WAS THE ONLY COMMON VARIETY THAT WAS SLOW ENOUGH FOR MEN TO BE ABLE TO CATCH TILL THE INVENTION OF THE HARPOON GUN IN 1860.

THE NARWHAL

MEAT

THE JAPANESE DEPEND ON WHALE MEAT MORE THAN MOST COUNTRIES. IN 1970 IT FORMED 9% OF THEIR TOTAL MEAT CONSUMPTION. OVERFISHING HAS REDUCED THIS FIGURE TO 1%. (IT IS NOW EXPENSIVE & CONSIDERED TO BE A GREAT DELICACY). THE INTERNATIONAL WHALING COMMISSION HAS CALLED FOR A COMPLETE BAN ON WHALING FROM 1985. THE JAPANESE HAVE SO FAR REFUSED TO CO-OPERATE.

HOW TO DRESS UP IN A SARI

START WITH SOME MATERIAL 12'×4'. WRAP AS SHOWN BELOW. IF IN DIFFICULTY LOOK IN 'BODY & CLOTHES' BY J. BROBY-JOHANSEN (FABER)

NOISES
SOME LOW-FREQUENCY NOISES PRODUCED BY WHALES CAN TRAVEL UP TO 700 MILES THROUGH WATER

SPOUT
NOW THOUGHT TO BE CAUSED BY CONDENSATION OF MOIST WARM BREATH MEETING COLD AIR.

THE ROYAL WHALES
IN 1515 THE WHALE WAS DECLARED A ROYAL FISH & THE HEAD OF ANY WHALE CAUGHT IN BRITISH COASTAL WATERS AUTOMATICALLY BELONGED TO THE KING & THE TAIL TO THE QUEEN.

(A RORQUAL WHALE)

BONES
ALTHOUGH WHALES ARE MAMMALS THEIR NECK VERTEBRAE HAVE BECOME FUSED INTO A SINGLE LUMP

TAIL
UNLIKE FISHES, ALL WHALES HAVE A HORIZONTAL TAIL THAT FLAPS UP & DOWN.

THE FUNCTION OF THE MALE NARWHALS TUSK IS A MYSTERY. IT IS NOT USED TO STIR MUD FOR FISH OR TO BREAK ICE, OR FOR FIGHTING OR DEFENDING ITSELF. IT MIGHT BE USED TO ATTRACT FEMALE NARWHALS IN THE SAME FUNCTION AS A PEACOCK'S FEATHERS, BUT IT IS HARDLY AS STARTLINGLY ATTRACTIVE. ESKIMOS, LACKING FRESH FRUIT & VEG, VALUE THE NARWHAL HIGHLY AS ITS 'SKIN', WHICH THEY CHEW RAW, IS THEIR MAIN SOURCE OF VITAMIN C.

☆ WHISKY ☆
SPIRIT MADE BY DISTILLATION OF FERMENTED CEREALS

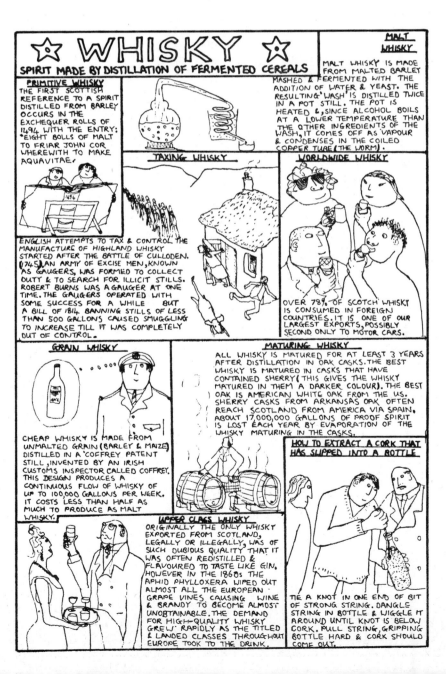

PRIMITIVE WHISKY
THE FIRST SCOTTISH REFERENCE TO A SPIRIT DISTILLED FROM BARLEY OCCURS IN THE EXCHEQUER ROLLS OF 1494 WITH THE ENTRY: 'EIGHT BOLLS OF MALT TO FRIAR JOHN COR WHEREWITH TO MAKE AQUAVITAE.'

MALT WHISKY
MALT WHISKY IS MADE FROM MALTED BARLEY MASHED & FERMENTED WITH THE ADDITION OF WATER & YEAST. THE RESULTING 'WASH' IS DISTILLED TWICE IN A POT STILL. THE POT IS HEATED &, SINCE ALCOHOL BOILS AT A LOWER TEMPERATURE THAN THE OTHER INGREDIENTS OF THE WASH, IT COMES OFF AS VAPOUR & CONDENSES IN THE COILED COPPER TUBE (THE WORM).

TAXING WHISKY
ENGLISH ATTEMPTS TO TAX & CONTROL THE MANUFACTURE OF HIGHLAND WHISKY STARTED AFTER THE BATTLE OF CULLODEN (1745). AN ARMY OF EXCISE MEN, KNOWN AS GAUGERS, WAS FORMED TO COLLECT DUTY & TO SEARCH FOR ILLICIT STILLS. ROBERT BURNS WAS A GAUGER AT ONE TIME. THE GAUGERS OPERATED WITH SOME SUCCESS FOR A WHILE BUT A BILL OF 1814 BANNING STILLS OF LESS THAN 500 GALLONS CAUSED SMUGGLING TO INCREASE TILL IT WAS COMPLETELY OUT OF CONTROL.

WORLDWIDE WHISKY
OVER 78% OF SCOTCH WHISKY IS CONSUMED IN FOREIGN COUNTRIES. IT IS ONE OF OUR LARGEST EXPORTS, POSSIBLY SECOND ONLY TO MOTOR CARS.

GRAIN WHISKY
CHEAP WHISKY IS MADE FROM UNMALTED GRAIN (BARLEY & MAIZE) DISTILLED IN A 'COFFREY PATENT STILL, INVENTED BY AN IRISH CUSTOMS INSPECTOR CALLED COFFREY. THIS DESIGN PRODUCES A CONTINUOUS FLOW OF WHISKY OF UP TO 100,000 GALLONS PER WEEK. IT COSTS LESS THAN HALF AS MUCH TO PRODUCE AS MALT WHISKY.

MATURING WHISKY
ALL WHISKY IS MATURED FOR AT LEAST 3 YEARS AFTER DISTILLATION IN OAK CASKS. THE BEST WHISKY IS MATURED IN CASKS THAT HAVE CONTAINED SHERRY (THIS GIVES THE WHISKY MATURED IN THEM A DARKER COLOUR). THE BEST OAK IS AMERICAN WHITE OAK FROM THE US. SHERRY CASKS FROM ARKANSAS OAK OFTEN REACH SCOTLAND FROM AMERICA VIA SPAIN. ABOUT 17,000,000 GALLONS OF PROOF SPIRIT IS LOST EACH YEAR BY EVAPORATION OF THE WHISKY MATURING IN THE CASKS.

HOW TO EXTRACT A CORK THAT HAS SLIPPED INTO A BOTTLE
TIE A KNOT IN ONE END OF STRONG STRING. DANGLE STRING IN BOTTLE & WIGGLE IT AROUND UNTIL KNOT IS BELOW CORK. PULL STRING, GRIPPING BOTTLE HARD & CORK SHOULD COME OUT.

UPPER CLASS WHISKY
ORIGINALLY THE ONLY WHISKY EXPORTED FROM SCOTLAND, LEGALLY OR ILLEGALLY, WAS OF SUCH DUBIOUS QUALITY THAT IT WAS OFTEN REDISTILLED & FLAVOURED TO TASTE LIKE GIN. HOWEVER IN THE 1860s THE APHID PHYLLOXERA WIPED OUT ALMOST ALL THE EUROPEAN GRAPE VINES CAUSING WINE & BRANDY TO BECOME ALMOST UNOBTAINABLE. THE DEMAND FOR HIGH-QUALITY WHISKY GREW RAPIDLY AS THE TITLED & LANDED CLASSES THROUGHOUT EUROPE TOOK TO THE DRINK.

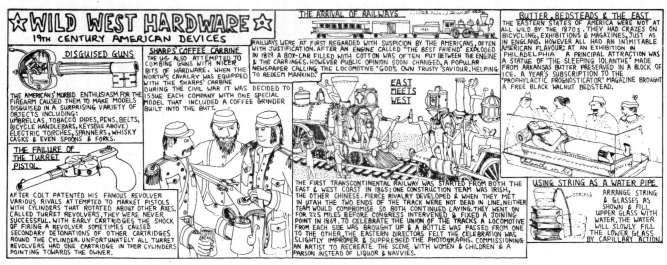

☆ WILD WEST HARDWARE ☆
19TH CENTURY AMERICAN DEVICES

DISGUISED GUNS

THE AMERICANS' MORBID ENTHUSIASM FOR THE FIREARM CAUSED THEM TO MAKE MODELS DISGUISED IN A SURPRISING VARIETY OF OBJECTS INCLUDING: UMBRELLAS, TOBACCO PIPES, PENS, BELTS, BICYCLE HANDLEBARS, KEYS (SEE ABOVE) ELECTRIC TORCHES, SPANNERS, WHISKY CASKS & EVEN SPOONS & FORKS.

THE FAILURE OF THE TURRET PISTOL

AFTER COLT PATENTED HIS FAMOUS REVOLVER VARIOUS RIVALS ATTEMPTED TO MARKET PISTOLS WITH CYLINDERS THAT ROTATED ABOUT OTHER AXES, CALLED TURRET REVOLVERS, THEY WERE NEVER SUCCESSFUL. WITH EARLY CARTRIDGES THE SHOCK OF FIRING A REVOLVER SOMETIMES CAUSED SECONDARY DETONATIONS OF OTHER CARTRIDGES ROUND THE CYLINDER. UNFORTUNATELY ALL TURRET REVOLVERS HAD ONE CARTRIDGE IN THEIR CYLINDERS POINTING TOWARDS THE OWNER.

SHARPS' COFFEE CARBINE

THE U.S. ALSO ATTEMPTED TO COMBINE GUNS WITH NICER BITS OF HARDWARE. WHEN THE NORTH'S CAVALRY WAS EQUIPPED WITH THE SHARPS' CARBINE DURING THE CIVIL WAR IT WAS DECIDED TO ISSUE EACH COMPANY WITH ONE SPECIAL MODEL THAT INCLUDED A COFFEE GRINDER BUILT INTO THE BUTT.

THE ARRIVAL OF RAILWAYS

RAILWAYS WERE AT FIRST REGARDED WITH SUSPICION BY THE AMERICANS, OFTEN WITH JUSTIFICATION. AFTER AN ENGINE CALLED "THE BEST FRIEND" EXPLODED IN 1829 A BOX-CAR FILLED WITH COTTON WAS OFTEN PUT BETWEEN THE ENGINE & THE CARRIAGES. HOWEVER PUBLIC OPINION SOON CHANGED, A POPULAR NEWSPAPER CALLING THE LOCOMOTIVE "GOD'S OWN TRUSTY SAVIOUR, HELPING TO REDEEM MANKIND."

EAST MEETS WEST

THE FIRST TRANSCONTINENTAL RAILWAY WAS STARTED FROM BOTH THE EAST & WEST COAST IN 1865; ONE CONSTRUCTION TEAM WAS IRISH, THE OTHER CHINESE. FIERCE RIVALRY DEVELOPED & WHEN THEY MET IN UTAH THE TWO ENDS OF THE TRACK WERE NOT DEAD IN LINE. NEITHER TEAM WOULD COMPROMISE SO BOTH CONTINUED LAYING. THEY WENT ON FOR 225 MILES BEFORE CONGRESS INTERVENED & FIXED A JOINING POINT IN 1869. TO CELEBRATE THE UNION OF THE TRACKS A LOCOMOTIVE FROM EACH SIDE WAS BROUGHT UP & A BOTTLE WAS PASSED FROM ONE TO THE OTHER. THE EASTERN DIRECTORS FELT THE CELEBRATION WAS SLIGHTLY IMPROPER & SUPPRESSED THE PHOTOGRAPHS, COMMISSIONING AN ARTIST TO RECREATE THE SCENE WITH WOMEN & CHILDREN & A PARSON INSTEAD OF LIQUOR & NAVVIES.

BUTTER, BEDSTEADS & THE EAST

THE EASTERN STATES OF AMERICA WERE NOT AT ALL WILD BY THE 1870s. THEY HAD CRAZES ON BICYCLING, EXHIBITIONS & MAGAZINES, JUST AS IN ENGLAND. HOWEVER ALL HAD AN INIMITABLE AMERICAN FLAVOUR: AT AN EXHIBITION IN PHILADELPHIA A PRINCIPAL ATTRACTION WAS A STATUE OF "THE SLEEPING IOLANTHE" MADE FROM ARKANSAS BUTTER PRESERVED IN A BLOCK OF ICE. A YEAR'S SUBSCRIPTION TO THE "PROPHYLACTIC PROGNOSTICATOR" MAGAZINE BROUGHT A FREE BLACK WALNUT BEDSTEAD.

USING STRING AS A WATER PIPE

ARRANGE STRING & GLASSES AS SHOWN & FILL UPPER GLASS WITH WATER. THE WATER WILL SLOWLY FILL THE LOWER GLASS BY CAPILLARY ACTION.

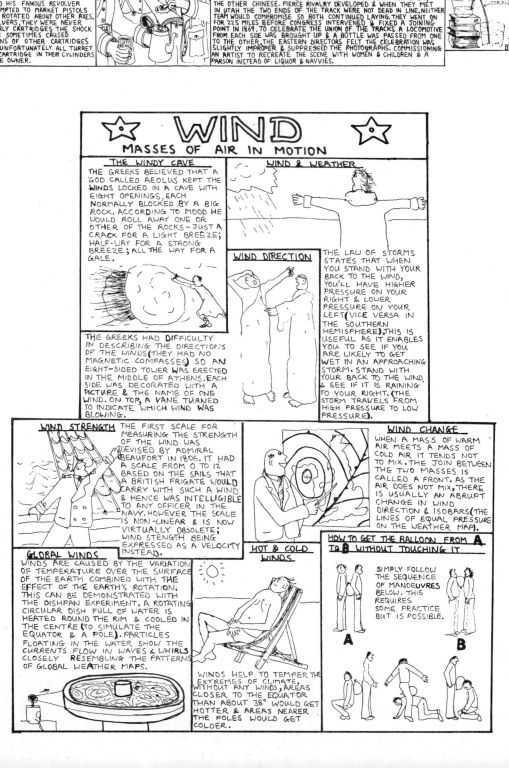

☆ WIND ☆
MASSES OF AIR IN MOTION

THE WINDY CAVE

THE GREEKS BELIEVED THAT A GOD CALLED AEOLUS KEPT THE WINDS LOCKED IN A CAVE WITH EIGHT OPENINGS, EACH NORMALLY BLOCKED BY A BIG ROCK. ACCORDING TO MOOD HE WOULD ROLL AWAY ONE OR OTHER OF THE ROCKS – JUST A CRACK FOR A LIGHT BREEZE; HALF-WAY FOR A STRONG BREEZE; ALL THE WAY FOR A GALE.

THE GREEKS HAD DIFFICULTY IN DESCRIBING THE DIRECTIONS OF THE WINDS (THEY HAD NO MAGNETIC COMPASSES) SO AN EIGHT-SIDED TOWER WAS ERECTED IN THE MIDDLE OF ATHENS. EACH SIDE WAS DECORATED WITH A PICTURE & THE NAME OF ONE WIND. ON TOP, A VANE TURNED TO INDICATE WHICH WIND WAS BLOWING.

WIND & WEATHER

WIND DIRECTION

THE LAW OF STORMS STATES THAT WHEN YOU STAND WITH YOUR BACK TO THE WIND, YOU'LL HAVE HIGHER PRESSURE ON YOUR RIGHT & LOWER PRESSURE ON YOUR LEFT (VICE VERSA IN THE SOUTHERN HEMISPHERE). THIS IS USEFUL AS IT ENABLES YOU TO SEE IF YOU ARE LIKELY TO GET WET IN AN APPROACHING STORM. STAND WITH YOUR BACK TO THE WIND & SEE IF IT IS RAINING TO YOUR RIGHT. (THE STORM TRAVELS FROM HIGH PRESSURE TO LOW PRESSURE).

WIND STRENGTH

THE FIRST SCALE FOR MEASURING THE STRENGTH OF THE WIND WAS DEVISED BY ADMIRAL BEAUFORT IN 1806. IT HAD A SCALE FROM 0 TO 12 BASED ON THE SAILS THAT A BRITISH FRIGATE WOULD CARRY WITH SUCH A WIND & HENCE WAS INTELLIGIBLE TO ANY OFFICER IN THE NAVY. HOWEVER THE SCALE IS NON-LINEAR & IS NOW VIRTUALLY OBSOLETE; WIND STRENGTH BEING EXPRESSED AS A VELOCITY INSTEAD.

GLOBAL WINDS

WINDS ARE CAUSED BY THE VARIATION OF TEMPERATURE OVER THE SURFACE OF THE EARTH COMBINED WITH THE EFFECT OF THE EARTH'S ROTATION. THIS CAN BE DEMONSTRATED WITH THE DISHPAN EXPERIMENT. A ROTATING CIRCULAR DISH FULL OF WATER IS HEATED ROUND THE RIM & COOLED IN THE CENTRE (TO SIMULATE THE EQUATOR & A POLE). PARTICLES FLOATING IN THE WATER SHOW THE CURRENTS FLOW IN WAVES & WHIRLS CLOSELY RESEMBLING THE PATTERNS OF GLOBAL WEATHER MAPS.

HOT & COLD WINDS

WINDS HELP TO TEMPER THE EXTREMES OF CLIMATE. WITHOUT ANY WINDS, AREAS CLOSER TO THE EQUATOR THAN ABOUT 38° WOULD GET HOTTER & AREAS NEARER THE POLES WOULD GET COLDER.

WIND CHANGE

WHEN A MASS OF WARM AIR MEETS A MASS OF COLD AIR IT TENDS NOT TO MIX. THE JOIN BETWEEN THE TWO MASSES IS CALLED A FRONT. AS THE AIR DOES NOT MIX, THERE IS USUALLY AN ABRUPT CHANGE IN WIND DIRECTION & ISOBARS (THE LINES OF EQUAL PRESSURE ON THE WEATHER MAP).

HOW TO GET THE BALLOON FROM A TO B WITHOUT TOUCHING IT

SIMPLY FOLLOW THE SEQUENCE OF MANOEUVRES BELOW. THIS REQUIRES SOME PRACTICE BUT IS POSSIBLE.

A

B

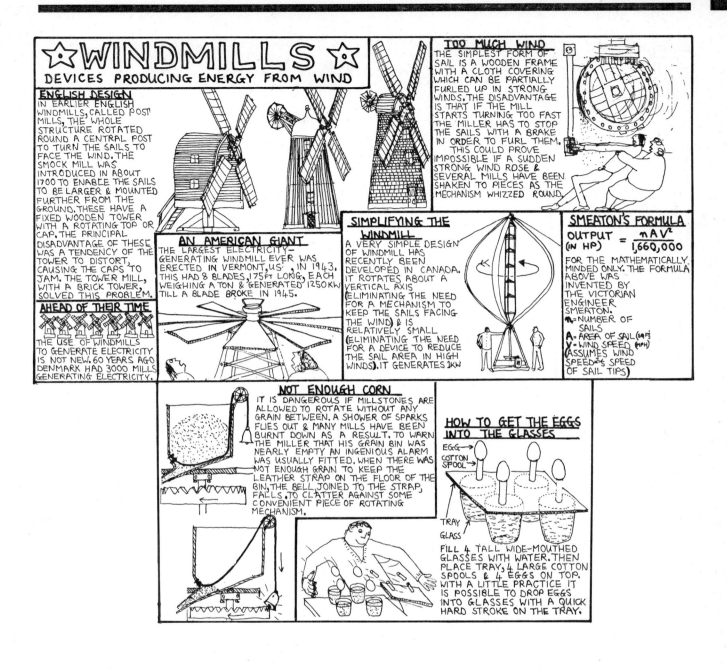

☆ WINDMILLS ☆
DEVICES PRODUCING ENERGY FROM WIND

ENGLISH DESIGN

IN EARLIER ENGLISH WINDMILLS, CALLED POST MILLS, THE WHOLE STRUCTURE ROTATED ROUND A CENTRAL POST TO TURN THE SAILS TO FACE THE WIND. THE SMOCK MILL WAS INTRODUCED IN ABOUT 1700 TO ENABLE THE SAILS TO BE LARGER & MOUNTED FURTHER FROM THE GROUND. THESE HAVE A FIXED WOODEN TOWER WITH A ROTATING TOP OR CAP. THE PRINCIPAL DISADVANTAGE OF THESE WAS A TENDENCY OF THE TOWER TO DISTORT, CAUSING THE CAPS TO JAM. THE TOWER MILL, WITH A BRICK TOWER, SOLVED THIS PROBLEM.

AHEAD OF THEIR TIME

THE USE OF WINDMILLS TO GENERATE ELECTRICITY IS NOT NEW. 60 YEARS AGO DENMARK HAD 3000 MILLS GENERATING ELECTRICITY.

AN AMERICAN GIANT

THE LARGEST ELECTRICITY-GENERATING WINDMILL EVER WAS ERECTED IN VERMONT, US, IN 1943. THIS HAD 8 BLADES, 175FT LONG, EACH WEIGHING A TON & GENERATED 1250KW TILL A BLADE BROKE IN 1945.

TOO MUCH WIND

THE SIMPLEST FORM OF SAIL IS A WOODEN FRAME WITH A CLOTH COVERING WHICH CAN BE PARTIALLY FURLED UP IN STRONG WINDS. THE DISADVANTAGE IS THAT IF THE MILL STARTS TURNING TOO FAST THE MILLER HAS TO STOP THE SAILS WITH A BRAKE IN ORDER TO FURL THEM. THIS COULD PROVE IMPOSSIBLE IF A SUDDEN STRONG WIND ROSE & SEVERAL MILLS HAVE BEEN SHAKEN TO PIECES AS THE MECHANISM WHIZZED ROUND.

SIMPLIFYING THE WINDMILL

A VERY SIMPLE DESIGN OF WINDMILL HAS RECENTLY BEEN DEVELOPED IN CANADA. IT ROTATES ABOUT A VERTICAL AXIS (ELIMINATING THE NEED FOR A MECHANISM TO KEEP THE SAILS FACING THE WIND) & IS RELATIVELY SMALL (ELIMINATING THE NEED FOR A DEVICE TO REDUCE THE SAIL AREA IN HIGH WINDS). IT GENERATES 1KW

SMEATON'S FORMULA

$$\text{OUTPUT (IN HP)} = \frac{nAV^2}{1,660,000}$$

FOR THE MATHEMATICALLY MINDED ONLY. THE FORMULA ABOVE WAS INVENTED BY THE VICTORIAN ENGINEER SMEATON.
n = NUMBER OF SAILS
A = AREA OF SAIL (SQ FT)
V = WIND SPEED (MPH)
(ASSUMES WIND SPEED = SPEED OF SAIL TIPS)

NOT ENOUGH CORN

IT IS DANGEROUS IF MILLSTONES ARE ALLOWED TO ROTATE WITHOUT ANY GRAIN BETWEEN. A SHOWER OF SPARKS FLIES OUT & MANY MILLS HAVE BEEN BURNT DOWN AS A RESULT. TO WARN THE MILLER THAT HIS GRAIN BIN WAS NEARLY EMPTY AN INGENIOUS ALARM WAS USUALLY FITTED. WHEN THERE WAS NOT ENOUGH GRAIN TO KEEP THE LEATHER STRAP ON THE FLOOR OF THE BIN, THE BELL JOINED TO THE STRAP FALLS TO CLATTER AGAINST SOME CONVENIENT PIECE OF ROTATING MECHANISM.

HOW TO GET THE EGGS INTO THE GLASSES

EGG →
COTTON SPOOL →
TRAY
GLASS

FILL 4 TALL WIDE-MOUTHED GLASSES WITH WATER. THEN PLACE TRAY, 4 LARGE COTTON SPOOLS & 4 EGGS ON TOP. WITH A LITTLE PRACTICE IT IS POSSIBLE TO DROP EGGS INTO GLASSES WITH A QUICK HARD STROKE ON THE TRAY.

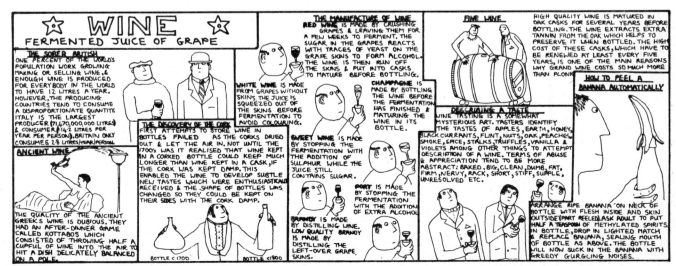

☆ WINE ☆
FERMENTED JUICE OF GRAPE

THE SOBER BRITISH

ONE PERCENT OF THE WORLD'S POPULATION WORK GROWING, MAKING OR SELLING WINE, & ENOUGH WINE IS PRODUCED FOR EVERYBODY IN THE WORLD TO HAVE 12 LITRES A YEAR. HOWEVER, THE PRODUCING COUNTRIES TEND TO CONSUME A DISPROPORTIONATE QUANTITY. ITALY IS THE LARGEST PRODUCER (7,470,000,000 LITRES & CONSUMES 114.2 LITRES PER YEAR PER PERSON). BRITAIN ONLY CONSUMES 2.8 LITRES/YEAR/PERSON.

ANCIENT WINE

THE QUALITY OF THE ANCIENT GREEKS WINE IS DUBIOUS. THEY HAD AN AFTER-DINNER GAME CALLED KOTTABOS WHICH CONSISTED OF THROWING HALF A CUPFUL OF WINE INTO THE AIR TO HIT A DISH DELICATELY BALANCED ON A POLE.

THE DISCOVERY OF THE CORK

FIRST ATTEMPTS TO STORE WINE IN BOTTLES FAILED AS THE CORKS DRIED OUT & LET THE AIR IN. NOT UNTIL THE 1700's WAS IT REALISED THAT WINE KEPT IN A CORKED BOTTLE COULD KEEP MUCH LONGER THAN WINE KEPT IN A CASK, IF THE CORK WAS KEPT DAMP. THIS ENABLED THE WINE TO DEVELOP SUBTLE NEW TASTES WHICH WERE ENTHUSIASTICALLY RECEIVED & THE SHAPE OF BOTTLES WAS CHANGED SO THEY COULD BE KEPT ON THEIR SIDES WITH THE CORK DAMP.

BOTTLE c 1700   BOTTLE c 1800

THE MANUFACTURE OF WINE

RED WINE IS MADE BY CRUSHING GRAPES & LEAVING THEM FOR A FEW WEEKS TO FERMENT. THE SUGAR IN THE GRAPES REACTS WITH TRACES OF YEAST ON THE GRAPE SKINS TO FORM ALCOHOL. THE WINE IS THEN RUN OFF THE SKINS & PUT INTO CASKS TO MATURE BEFORE BOTTLING.

WHITE WINE IS MADE FROM GRAPES WITHOUT SKINS. THE JUICE IS SQUEEZED OUT OF THE SKINS BEFORE FERMENTATION TO AVOID COLOURING.

CHAMPAGNE IS MADE BY BOTTLING THE WINE BEFORE THE FERMENTATION HAS FINISHED & MATURING THE WINE IN ITS BOTTLE.

SWEET WINE IS MADE BY STOPPING THE FERMENTATION WITH THE ADDITION OF SULPHUR WHILE THE JUICE STILL CONTAINS SUGAR.

PORT IS MADE BY STOPPING THE FERMENTATION WITH THE ADDITION OF EXTRA ALCOHOL.

BRANDY IS MADE BY DISTILLING WINE. LOW QUALITY BRANDY IS MADE BY DISTILLING THE LEFT-OVER GRAPE SKINS.

FINE WINE

HIGH QUALITY WINE IS MATURED IN OAK CASKS FOR SEVERAL YEARS BEFORE BOTTLING. THE WINE EXTRACTS EXTRA TANNIN FROM THE OAK WHICH HELPS TO PRESERVE IT WHEN BOTTLED. THE HIGH COST OF THESE CASKS, WHICH HAVE TO BE RENEWED AT LEAST EVERY FIVE YEARS, IS ONE OF THE MAIN REASONS WHY GRAND WINE COSTS SO MUCH MORE THAN PLONK.

DESCRIBING A TASTE

WINE TASTING IS A SOMEWHAT MYSTERIOUS ART. TASTERS IDENTIFY THE TASTES OF APPLES, EARTH, HONEY, BLACK CURRANTS, FLINT, NUTS, OAK, PEACHES, SMOKE, SPICE, STALKS, TRUFFLES, VANILLA & VIOLETS AMONG OTHER THINGS TO ATTEMPT DESCRIPTION OF A WINE. TERMS OF ABUSE & APPRECIATION TEND TO BE MORE ABSTRACT: BAKED, BIG, CLEAN, DUMB, FAT, FIRM, NERVY, RACK, SHORT, STIFF, SUPPLE, UNRESOLVED ETC.

HOW TO PEEL A BANANA AUTOMATICALLY

ARRANGE RIPE BANANA ON NECK OF BOTTLE WITH FLESH INSIDE AND SKIN OUTSIDE (PART PEELED). ASK ADULT TO PUT HALF A TEASPOON OF METHYLATED SPIRITS IN BOTTLE, DROP IN LIGHTED MATCH & REPLACE BANANA, SEALING MOUTH OF BOTTLE AS ABOVE. THE BOTTLE WILL NOW SUCK IN THE BANANA WITH GREEDY GURGLING NOISES.

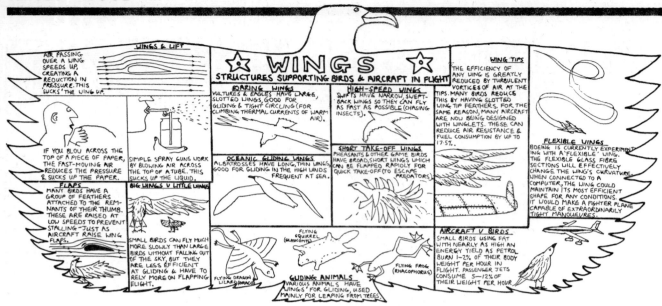

☆ WINGS ☆
STRUCTURES SUPPORTING BIRDS & AIRCRAFT IN FLIGHT

WINGS & LIFT

AIR PASSING OVER A WING SPEEDS UP, CREATING A REDUCTION IN PRESSURE. THIS 'SUCKS' THE WING UP.

IF YOU BLOW ACROSS THE TOP OF A PIECE OF PAPER, THE FAST-MOVING AIR REDUCES THE PRESSURE & SUCKS UP THE PAPER.

SIMPLE SPRAY GUNS WORK BY BLOWING AIR ACROSS THE TOP OF A TUBE. THIS SUCKS UP THE LIQUID.

FLAPS

MANY BIRDS HAVE A GROUP OF FEATHERS ATTACHED TO THE REMNANTS OF THEIR THUMB. THESE ARE RAISED AT LOW SPEEDS TO PREVENT STALLING – JUST AS AIRCRAFT RAISE WING FLAPS.

BIG WINGS V LITTLE WINGS

SMALL BIRDS CAN FLY MUCH MORE SLOWLY THAN LARGE BIRDS WITHOUT FALLING OUT OF THE SKY, BUT THEY ARE LESS EFFICIENT AT GLIDING & HAVE TO RELY MORE ON FLAPPING FLIGHT.

SOARING WINGS

VULTURES & EAGLES HAVE LARGE, SLOTTED WINGS, GOOD FOR GLIDING & TIGHT CIRCLING (FOR CLIMBING THERMAL CURRENTS OF WARM AIR).

OCEANIC GLIDING WINGS

ALBATROSSES HAVE LONG, THIN WINGS GOOD FOR GLIDING IN THE HIGH WINDS FREQUENT AT SEA.

HIGH-SPEED WINGS

SWIFTS HAVE NARROW SWEPT-BACK WINGS SO THEY CAN FLY AS FAST AS POSSIBLE (CHASING INSECTS).

SHORT TAKE-OFF WINGS

PHEASANTS & OTHER GAME BIRDS HAVE BROAD, SHORT WINGS WHICH CAN BE FLAPPED RAPIDLY FOR QUICK TAKE-OFF (TO ESCAPE PREDATORS).

GLIDING ANIMALS

VARIOUS ANIMALS HAVE 'WINGS' FOR GLIDING, USED MAINLY FOR LEAPING FROM TREES.

FLYING DRAGON LIZARD (DRACO)

FLYING SQUIRREL (GLAUCOMYS)

FLYING FROG (RHACOPHORUS)

WING TIPS

THE EFFICIENCY OF ANY WING IS GREATLY REDUCED BY TURBULENT VORTICES OF AIR AT THE TIPS. MANY BIRDS REDUCE THIS BY HAVING SLOTTED WING TIP FEATHERS. FOR THE SAME REASON, MANY AIRCRAFT ARE NOW BEING DESIGNED WITH WINGLETS. THESE CAN REDUCE AIR RESISTANCE & FUEL CONSUMPTION BY UP TO 17.5%.

AIRCRAFT V BIRDS

SMALL BIRDS USING FAT WITH NEARLY AS HIGH AN ENERGY YIELD AS PETROL BURN 1–2% OF THEIR BODY WEIGHT PER HOUR IN FLIGHT. PASSENGER JETS CONSUME 5–12% OF THEIR WEIGHT PER HOUR

FLEXIBLE WINGS

BOEING IS CURRENTLY EXPERIMENTING WITH A 'FLEXIBLE' WING. THE FLEXIBLE GLASS FIBRE SECTIONS WILL EFFECTIVELY CHANGE THE WING'S CURVATURE. WHEN CONNECTED TO A COMPUTER, THE WING COULD MAINTAIN ITS MOST EFFICIENT SHAPE FOR ANY CONDITIONS. IT WOULD MAKE A FIGHTER PLANE CAPABLE OF EXTRAORDINARILY TIGHT MANOEUVRES.

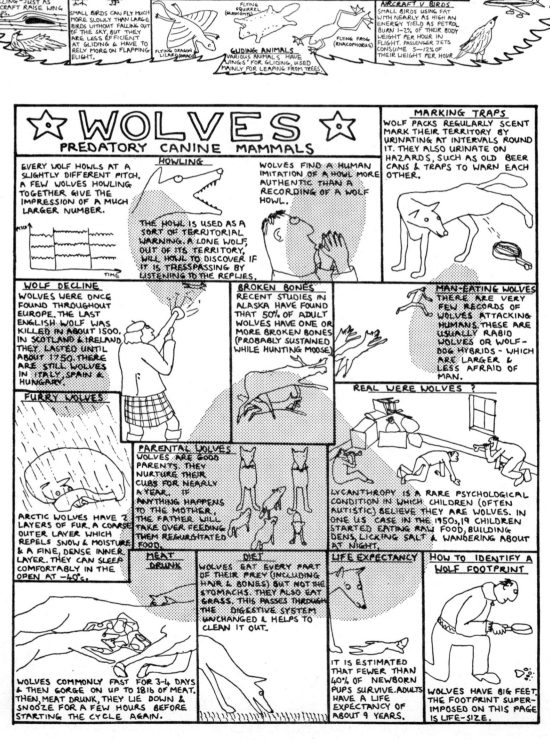

☆ WOLVES ☆
PREDATORY CANINE MAMMALS

HOWLING

EVERY WOLF HOWLS AT A SLIGHTLY DIFFERENT PITCH. A FEW WOLVES HOWLING TOGETHER GIVE THE IMPRESSION OF A MUCH LARGER NUMBER.

THE HOWL IS USED AS A SORT OF TERRITORIAL WARNING. A LONE WOLF, OUT OF ITS TERRITORY, WILL HOWL TO DISCOVER IF IT IS TRESPASSING BY LISTENING TO THE REPLIES.

WOLVES FIND A HUMAN IMITATION OF A HOWL MORE AUTHENTIC THAN A RECORDING OF A WOLF HOWL.

MARKING TRAPS

WOLF PACKS REGULARLY SCENT MARK THEIR TERRITORY BY URINATING AT INTERVALS ROUND IT. THEY ALSO URINATE ON HAZARDS, SUCH AS OLD BEER CANS & TRAPS TO WARN EACH OTHER.

WOLF DECLINE

WOLVES WERE ONCE FOUND THROUGHOUT EUROPE. THE LAST ENGLISH WOLF WAS KILLED IN ABOUT 1500. IN SCOTLAND & IRELAND THEY LASTED UNTIL ABOUT 1750. THERE ARE STILL WOLVES IN ITALY, SPAIN & HUNGARY.

BROKEN BONES

RECENT STUDIES IN ALASKA HAVE FOUND THAT 50% OF ADULT WOLVES HAVE ONE OR MORE BROKEN BONES (PROBABLY SUSTAINED WHILE HUNTING MOOSE).

MAN-EATING WOLVES

THERE ARE VERY FEW RECORDS OF WOLVES ATTACKING HUMANS. THESE ARE USUALLY RABID WOLVES OR WOLF-DOG HYBRIDS – WHICH ARE LARGER & LESS AFRAID OF MAN.

FURRY WOLVES

ARCTIC WOLVES HAVE 2 LAYERS OF FUR. A COARSE OUTER LAYER WHICH REPELS SNOW & MOISTURE & A FINE, DENSE INNER LAYER. THEY CAN SLEEP COMFORTABLY IN THE OPEN AT –40°C.

PARENTAL WOLVES

WOLVES ARE GOOD PARENTS. THEY NURTURE THEIR CUBS FOR NEARLY A YEAR. IF ANYTHING HAPPENS TO THE MOTHER, THE FATHER WILL TAKE OVER FEEDING THEM REGURGITATED FOOD.

REAL WEREWOLVES?

LYCANTHROPY IS A RARE PSYCHOLOGICAL CONDITION IN WHICH CHILDREN (OFTEN AUTISTIC) BELIEVE THEY ARE WOLVES. IN ONE US CASE IN THE 1950s, 19 CHILDREN STARTED EATING RAW FOOD, BUILDING DENS, LICKING SALT & WANDERING ABOUT AT NIGHT.

MEAT DRUNK

WOLVES COMMONLY FAST FOR 3–4 DAYS & THEN GORGE ON UP TO 18lb OF MEAT. THEN, MEAT DRUNK, THEY LIE DOWN & SNOOZE FOR A FEW HOURS BEFORE STARTING THE CYCLE AGAIN.

DIET

WOLVES EAT EVERY PART OF THEIR PREY (INCLUDING HAIR & BONES) BUT NOT THE STOMACHS. THEY ALSO EAT GRASS. THIS PASSES THROUGH THE DIGESTIVE SYSTEM UNCHANGED & HELPS TO CLEAN IT OUT.

LIFE EXPECTANCY

IT IS ESTIMATED THAT FEWER THAN 40% OF NEWBORN PUPS SURVIVE. ADULTS HAVE A LIFE EXPECTANCY OF ABOUT 9 YEARS.

HOW TO IDENTIFY A WOLF FOOTPRINT

WOLVES HAVE BIG FEET. THE FOOTPRINT SUPERIMPOSED ON THIS PAGE IS LIFE-SIZE.

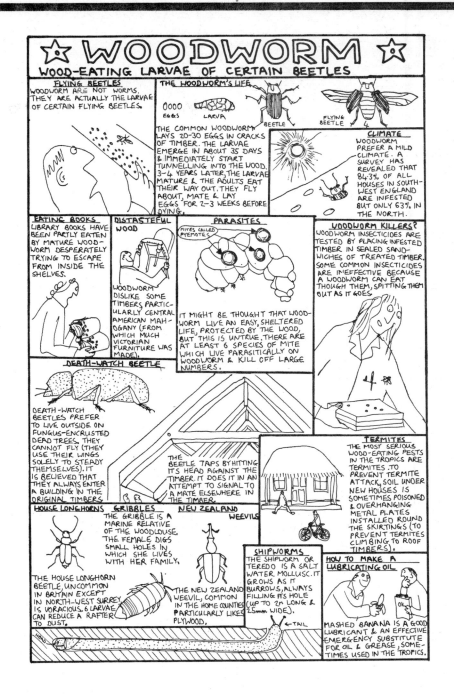

☆ WOODWORM ☆
WOOD-EATING LARVAE OF CERTAIN BEETLES

FLYING BEETLES
WOODWORM ARE NOT WORMS. THEY ARE ACTUALLY THE LARVAE OF CERTAIN FLYING BEETLES.

THE WOODWORM'S LIFE
oooo EGGS   LARVA   BEETLE   FLYING BEETLE

THE COMMON WOODWORM LAYS 20-30 EGGS IN CRACKS OF TIMBER. THE LARVAE EMERGE IN ABOUT 35 DAYS & IMMEDIATELY START TUNNELLING INTO THE WOOD. 3-4 YEARS LATER, THE LARVAE MATURE & THE ADULTS EAT THEIR WAY OUT. THEY FLY ABOUT, MATE & LAY EGGS FOR 2-3 WEEKS BEFORE DYING.

CLIMATE
WOODWORM PREFER A MILD CLIMATE. A SURVEY HAS REVEALED THAT 84.3% OF ALL HOUSES IN SOUTH-WEST ENGLAND ARE INFESTED BUT ONLY 63% IN THE NORTH.

EATING BOOKS
LIBRARY BOOKS HAVE BEEN PARTLY EATEN BY MATURE WOODWORM DESPERATELY TRYING TO ESCAPE FROM INSIDE THE SHELVES.

DISTASTEFUL WOOD
WOODWORM DISLIKE SOME TIMBERS PARTICULARLY CENTRAL AMERICAN MAHOGANY (FROM WHICH MUCH VICTORIAN FURNITURE WAS MADE).

PARASITES
MITES CALLED PYEMOTES

IT MIGHT BE THOUGHT THAT WOODWORM LIVE AN EASY, SHELTERED LIFE, PROTECTED BY THE WOOD, BUT THIS IS UNTRUE. THERE ARE AT LEAST 6 SPECIES OF MITE WHICH LIVE PARASITICALLY ON WOODWORM & KILL OFF LARGE NUMBERS.

WOODWORM KILLERS?
WOODWORM INSECTICIDES ARE TESTED BY PLACING INFESTED TIMBER IN SEALED SANDWICHES OF TREATED TIMBER. SOME COMMON INSECTICIDES ARE INEFFECTIVE BECAUSE A WOODWORM CAN EAT THOUGH THEM, SPITTING THEM OUT AS IT GOES

DEATH-WATCH BEETLE
DEATH-WATCH BEETLES PREFER TO LIVE OUTSIDE ON FUNGUS-ENCRUSTED DEAD TREES. THEY CANNOT FLY (THEY USE THEIR WINGS SOLELY TO STEADY THEMSELVES). IT IS BELIEVED THAT THEY ALWAYS ENTER A BUILDING IN THE ORIGINAL TIMBERS

THE BEETLE TAPS BY HITTING ITS HEAD AGAINST THE TIMBER. IT DOES IT IN AN ATTEMPT TO SIGNAL TO A MATE ELSEWHERE IN THE TIMBER.

TERMITES
THE MOST SERIOUS WOOD-EATING PESTS IN THE TROPICS ARE TERMITES. TO PREVENT TERMITE ATTACK, SOIL UNDER NEW HOUSES IS SOMETIMES POISONED & OVERHANGING METAL PLATES INSTALLED ROUND THE SKIRTINGS (TO PREVENT TERMITES CLIMBING TO ROOF TIMBERS).

HOUSE LONGHORNS
THE HOUSE LONGHORN BEETLE, UNCOMMON IN BRITAIN EXCEPT IN NORTH-WEST SURREY IS VORACIOUS. 6 LARVAE CAN REDUCE A RAFTER TO DUST.

GRIBBLES
THE GRIBBLE IS A MARINE RELATIVE OF THE WOODLOUSE. THE FEMALE DIGS SMALL HOLES IN WHICH SHE LIVES WITH HER FAMILY.

NEW ZEALAND WEEVILS
THE NEW ZEALAND WEEVIL, COMMON IN THE HOME COUNTIES PARTICULARLY LIKES PLYWOOD.

SHIPWORMS
THE SHIPWORM OR TEREDO IS A SALT WATER MOLLUSC. IT GROWS AS IT BURROWS, ALWAYS FILLING ITS HOLE (UP TO 2n LONG & 25mm WIDE).

← TAIL
HEAD

HOW TO MAKE A LUBRICATING OIL
MASHED BANANA IS A GOOD LUBRICANT & AN EFFECTIVE EMERGENCY SUBSTITUTE FOR OIL & GREASE, SOMETIMES USED IN THE TROPICS.

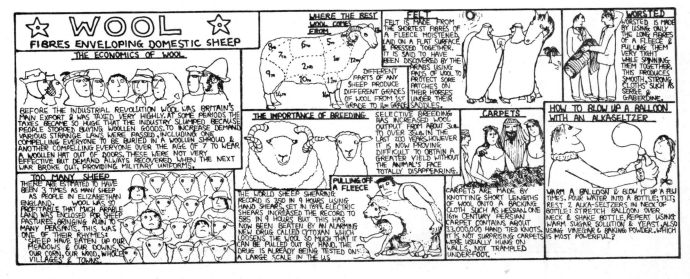

☆ WOOL ☆
FIBRES ENVELOPING DOMESTIC SHEEP

THE ECONOMICS OF WOOL
BEFORE THE INDUSTRIAL REVOLUTION WOOL WAS BRITAIN'S MAIN EXPORT & WAS TAXED VERY HIGHLY. AT SOME PERIODS THE TAXES BECAME SO HUGE THAT THE INDUSTRY SLUMPED BECAUSE PEOPLE STOPPED BUYING WOOLLEN GOODS. TO INCREASE DEMAND VARIOUS STRANGE LAWS WERE PASSED, INCLUDING ONE COMPELLING EVERYONE TO BE BURIED IN A WOOLLEN SHROUD & ANOTHER COMPELLING EVERYONE OVER THE AGE OF 7 TO WEAR A WOOLLEN HAT OUT OF DOORS. THESE WERE NOT VERY EFFECTIVE BUT DEMAND ALWAYS RECOVERED WHEN THE NEXT WAR BROKE OUT, PROVIDING MILITARY UNIFORMS.

TOO MANY SHEEP
THERE ARE ESTIMATED TO HAVE BEEN 3 TIMES AS MANY SHEEP AS PEOPLE IN ELIZABETHAN ENGLAND. WOOL WAS SO PROFITABLE THAT MUCH ARABLE LAND WAS ENCLOSED FOR SHEEP PASTURES, BRINGING RUIN TO MANY PEASANTS. THIS WAS ONE OF THEIR RHYMES:
"SHEEP HAVE EATEN UP OUR MEADOWS & OUR DOWNS, OUR CORN, OUR WOOD, WHOLE VILLAGES & TOWNS."

WHERE THE BEST WOOL COMES FROM
DIFFERENT PARTS OF ANY SHEEP PRODUCE DIFFERENT GRADES OF WOOL FROM 1ST GRADE TO 14th GRADE

THE IMPORTANCE OF BREEDING
SELECTIVE BREEDING HAS INCREASED WOOL OUTPUT FROM ABOUT 3LB. TO OVER 35LB. IN THE LAST 200 YEARS. HOWEVER IT IS NOW PROVING DIFFICULT TO OBTAIN A GREATER YIELD WITHOUT THE ANIMAL'S FACE TOTALLY DISAPPEARING.

PULLING OFF A FLEECE
THE WORLD SHEEP SHEARING RECORD IS 350 IN 9 HOURS USING HAND SHEARS, SET IN 1899. ELECTRIC SHEARS INCREASED THE RECORD TO 585 IN 9 HOURS BUT THIS HAS NOW BEEN BEATEN BY AN ALARMING NEW DRUG CALLED CYTOXAN WHICH LOOSENS THE WOOL SO MUCH THAT IT CAN BE PULLED OUT BY HAND. THE DRUG IS ALREADY BEING TESTED ON A LARGE SCALE IN THE US

FELT
FELT IS MADE FROM THE SHORTEST FIBRES OF A FLEECE MOISTENED LAID ON A FLAT SURFACE & PRESSED TOGETHER. IT IS SAID TO HAVE BEEN DISCOVERED BY THE ARABS USING PADS OF WOOL TO PROTECT SORE PATCHES ON THEIR HORSES UNDER THEIR SADDLES.

CARPETS
CARPETS ARE MADE BY KNOTTING SHORT LENGTHS OF WOOL ONTO A BACKING CLOTH SUCH AS HESSIAN. ONE 16TH CENTURY PERSIAN CARPET CONTAINS ABOUT 33,000,000 HAND TIED KNOTS. IT IS NOT SURPRISING CARPETS WERE USUALLY HUNG ON WALLS, NOT TRAMPLED UNDER-FOOT.

WORSTED
WORSTED IS MADE BY USING ONLY THE LONG FIBRES OF A FLEECE & PULLING THEM VERY TIGHT WHILE SPINNING THEM TOGETHER. THIS PRODUCES SMOOTH, STRONG CLOTHS SUCH AS SERGE & GABERDINE.

HOW TO BLOW UP A BALLOON WITH AN ALKASELTZER
WARM A BALLOON & BLOW IT UP A FEW TIMES. POUR WATER INTO A BOTTLE; TILT; REST 2 ALKA-SELTZERS IN NECK OF BOTTLE; STRETCH BALLOON OVER NECK & HOLD. TRY REPEAT USING WARM SUGAR SOLUTION & YEAST, ALSO USING VINEGAR & BAKING POWDER. WHICH IS MOST POWERFUL?

☆ WORMS ☆
INVERTEBRATE ANIMALS LIVING IN DAMP EARTH

WORMS & THE GARDENER

WORMS ARE WONDERFULLY GOOD FOR THE FERTILITY OF THE SOIL. THEY AERATE THE SOIL & IMPROVE THE DRAINAGE. THEY SORT THE SOIL PARTICLES BY REJECTING LARGE BITS & CONSUMING & EXCRETING THE SMALL BITS. THEIR EXCRETA CONTAIN VALUABLE CHEMICALS FOR ENRICHING THE SOIL. THEY ALSO REDUCE ACIDITY OR ALKALINITY OF A SOIL SINCE THEIR EXCRETA ARE MORE NEUTRAL THAN THE PARENT SOIL. TO AUGMENT THEIR ACTIVITY ATTEMPTS HAVE BEEN MADE TO INTRODUCE EXTRA WORMS INTO CULTIVATED SOILS. UNFORTUNATELY THESE HAVE PROVED INEFFECTIVE EXCEPT FOR AN INITIAL INCREASE IN YIELD CAUSED BY THE FERTILISING EFFECT OF DEAD WORMS.

MEDICINAL WORMS

THE WORMS USED IN MANY PRIMITIVE MEDICINAL POTIONS MAY WELL HAVE BEEN EFFECTIVE. CERTAIN TROPICAL SPECIES HAVE BEEN FOUND TO CONTAIN FEVER-REDUCING & ANTI-ASTHMATIC PROPERTIES. THE BRITISH WORM IS EXCEPTIONALLY RICH IN VITAMIN D.

WORMS' REPRODUCTION

WORMS ARE HERMAPHRODITES, HAVING BOTH MALE & FEMALE SEX ORGANS. WHEN TWO WORMS MATE, EACH FERTILISES THE OTHER. THE MALE & FEMALE ORGANS ARE AT OPPOSITE ENDS OF THE BODY WHICH IS SAID TO HELP PREVENT SELF-FERTILISATION.

WORMS' SKELETONS

WORMS & THE ARCHAEOLOGIST

WORMS ARE AS HELPFUL TO ARCHAEOLOGISTS AS THEY ARE TO FARMERS. THE ACTION OF WORMS CAUSES ANY OBJECT LEFT ON THE GROUND TO SINK PROGRESSIVELY IN. THEY SEEM TO PREFER BURROWING BENEATH SOLID OBJECTS, PROBABLY FOR PROTECTION. EVERY TIME A BURROW COLLAPSES THE OBJECT SINKS A BIT. THIS HAS HELPED TO PRESERVE MANY ANTIQUITIES.

THE BODY OF A WORM

THE BODY OF A WORM HAS 4 CONCENTRIC LAYERS, THE GUT IN THE MIDDLE, 2 LAYERS OF MUSCLE ON THE OUTSIDE WITH A LIQUID-FILLED SPACE BETWEEN. THIS LAYER IS KNOWN AS THE FLUID SKELETON, BECAUSE WHEN THE WORM TENSES ITS MUSCLES THE FLUID IS PUT UNDER PRESSURE MAKING THE BODY RIGID & ENABLING IT TO GRIP THE SIDES OF ITS BURROW.

WORMS & REGENERATION

IF AN EARTHWORM IS CHOPPED IN TWO ONLY THE FRONT END HAS ANY CHANCE OF SURVIVING, REGENERATING THE MISSING SEGMENTS. MANY OTHER TYPES OF WORM HAVE A BETTER REGENERATIVE ABILITY. SOME SYLLID POLYCHAETES DEVELOP NEW HEADS AT REGULAR INTERVALS ALONG THE BODY, EACH PART EVENTUALLY BREAKING OFF AS A SEPARATE INDIVIDUAL.

WORMS & VIBRATION

VIBRATION TENDS TO BRING WORMS TO THE SURFACE. A DRAMATIC RESULT OF THIS PHENOMENON IS THE LARGE NUMBER OF CROWS THAT HAVE APPEARED ON MOTORWAY VERGES EATING UP THE SURFACE WORMS.

HOW TO MAKE A MAGNETIC THEATRE

OPEN PAPER CLIPS OUT TO RIGHT ANGLES, GLUE CARDBOARD CUT-OUT FIGURES TO CLIPS. USE CARDBOARD BOX AS STAGE & MOVE FIGURES AROUND WITH MAGNET BELOW STAGE.

☆ WRITING ☆
SYSTEMS OF PERPETUATING VOCAL COMMUNICATION

HOW ALPHABETS STARTED

THE FIRST 'WRITING' WAS BASED ON PICTURES OF OBJECTS (PICTOGRAMS)

(EGYPTIAN) (MESOPOTAMIAN) (CHINESE)

IDEAS & ACTIONS WERE SOMETIMES REPRESENTED BY COMBINATIONS OF OBJECTS (IDEOGRAMS)

(EGYPTIAN) EYE+TEARS = WEEP
(CHINESE) RECTANGLE(MOUTH) +VAPOUR=SPEECH
(EGYPTIAN) SPLIT REED+ VIAL=WRITING

THE SUMERIANS DEVELOPED A SYSTEM OF USING THE SAME OBJECT FOR ALL THE WORDS THAT SOUNDED ROUGHLY THE SAME (HIEROGLYPHICS). THIS WAS LATER SIMPLIFIED BY THE PHOENICIANS WHO USED ONE OBJECT TO REPRESENT EACH HARD SOUND (AN ALPHABET LACKING VOWELS)

ALPHA & BETA

THE LETTER A COMES FROM THE PHOENICIAN PICTOGRAM FOR ALEPH, AN OX. THE GREEKS ADOPTED THE SYMBOL, TURNED ON ITS SIDE, TO SIGNIFY THE SOUND OF 'A' & FORGOT IT WAS A PICTURE OF AN OX'S HEAD. B HAS ALSO BEEN TURNED ON ITS SIDE, IT CAME FROM BETH, THE PHOENICIAN PICTOGRAM FOR A HOUSE.

THE 65 VARIETIES

THERE ARE NOW 65 ALPHABETS IN USE. ROTOKAS IS THE SHORTEST (11 LETTERS) & CAMBODIAN IS THE LONGEST (74 LETTERS).

THE PEN & THE SWORD

THE ROMANS WROTE ON WAXED PLATES USING METAL STYLUS PENS. THESE HAD THE ADVANTAGE OF ALSO SERVING AS WEAPONS. THE CONSPIRATORS KILLED JULIUS CAESAR WITH THEIR PENS.

THE FIRST PAPER

THE DISCOVERY OF PAPER IS SAID TO HAVE BEEN MADE IN 100 A.D. BY A TSAI LUN, WHILE ATTEMPTING TO IMITATE A MATERIAL CERTAIN WASPS CONSTRUCT THEIR HIVES FROM. HE BOILED, BEAT & WASHED PIECES OF BARK, LINEN RAGS & OLD FISHING NETS & PRODUCED A SOFT TOUGH WHITE SHEET, GREATLY SUPERIOR TO THE SQUASHED REEDS (PAPYRUS) THEN IN USE.

READIMIX

THE LARGEST LETTERS IN THE WORLD ARE 180m HIGH ON A HILLSIDE SIGN IN NULLARBOR, WESTERN AUSTRALIA.

THE SMALLEST WRITING EVER WAS ACHIEVED AT CORNELL UNIVERSITY WHERE 16 LETTERS WERE ETCHED ON A .03mm SALT CRYSTAL WITH AN ELECTRON MICROSCOPE

CHINESE PRINTING

THE INVENTION OF PRINTING WITH MOVABLE TYPE WAS FIRST MADE BY PI CHENG IN 1040 A.D. USING PICTOGRAMS CARVED INTO A BLOCK OF CLAY. UNFORTUNATELY THE CHINESE WRITTEN LANGUAGE HAD 40,000 CHARACTERS & THE METHOD DID NOT PROVE POPULAR. THIS CAUSED A LACK OF CHEAPLY ACCESSIBLE KNOWLEDGE WHICH IS THOUGHT TO BE PARTLY RESPONSIBLE FOR CHINA NOT DEVELOPING A TECHNOLOGICAL SOCIETY.

HOW TO MAKE A TEDDY BEAR VANISH

EYE HOLE · GLASS · BLACK CARD · LIGHTS

FIND A BOX WITH A LID & PAINT INSIDE BLACK. BUY GLASS TO FIT ACROSS DIAGONAL & POLISH IT. ALSO BUY 6 BULBS (6v), SOCKETS & BATTERIES. STICK EVERYTHING INSIDE BOX. PUNCH SMALL EYE HOLE; CONNECT BULBS & PUT ON LID. (OMITTED IN DRAWING).

BEAR VISIBLE   BEAR INVISIBLE

(GLASS WILL ONLY REFLECT BEAR WHEN LIGHTS ON LEFT OF GLASS ARE LIT.)

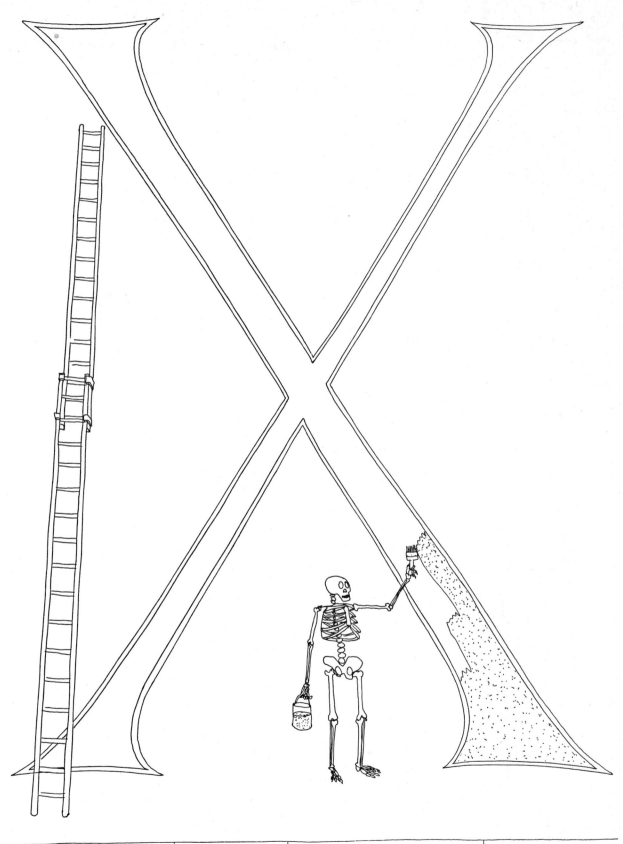

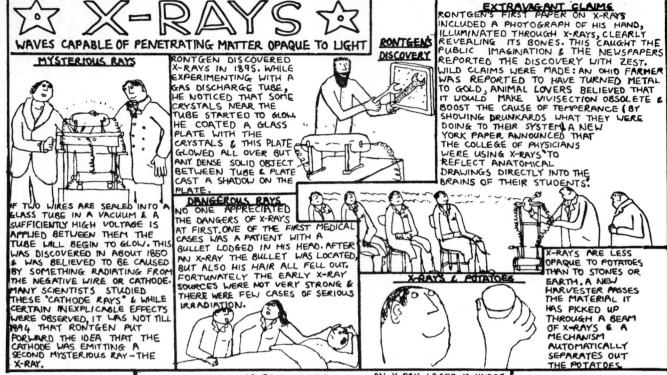

☆ X-RAYS ☆

WAVES CAPABLE OF PENETRATING MATTER OPAQUE TO LIGHT

MYSTERIOUS RAYS

IF TWO WIRES ARE SEALED INTO A GLASS TUBE IN A VACUUM & A SUFFICIENTLY HIGH VOLTAGE IS APPLIED BETWEEN THEM THE TUBE WILL BEGIN TO GLOW. THIS WAS DISCOVERED IN ABOUT 1850 & WAS BELIEVED TO BE CAUSED BY SOMETHING RADIATING FROM THE NEGATIVE WIRE OR CATHODE. MANY SCIENTISTS STUDIED THESE "CATHODE RAYS" & WHILE CERTAIN INEXPLICABLE EFFECTS WERE OBSERVED, IT WAS NOT TILL 1894 THAT RONTGEN PUT FORWARD THE IDEA THAT THE CATHODE WAS EMITTING A SECOND MYSTERIOUS RAY — THE X-RAY.

RONTGEN DISCOVERED X-RAYS IN 1895. WHILE EXPERIMENTING WITH A GAS DISCHARGE TUBE, HE NOTICED THAT SOME CRYSTALS NEAR THE TUBE STARTED TO GLOW. HE COATED A GLASS PLATE WITH THE CRYSTALS & THIS PLATE GLOWED ALL OVER BUT ANY DENSE SOLID OBJECT BETWEEN TUBE & PLATE CAST A SHADOW ON THE PLATE.

DANGEROUS RAYS

NO ONE APPRECIATED THE DANGERS OF X-RAYS AT FIRST. ONE OF THE FIRST MEDICAL CASES WAS A PATIENT WITH A BULLET LODGED IN HIS HEAD. AFTER AN X-RAY THE BULLET WAS LOCATED, BUT ALSO HIS HAIR ALL FELL OUT. FORTUNATELY THE EARLY X-RAY SOURCES WERE NOT VERY STRONG & THERE WERE FEW CASES OF SERIOUS IRRADIATION.

RONTGEN'S DISCOVERY

EXTRAVAGANT CLAIMS

RONTGEN'S FIRST PAPER ON X-RAYS INCLUDED A PHOTOGRAPH OF HIS HAND, ILLUMINATED THROUGH X-RAYS, CLEARLY REVEALING ITS BONES. THIS CAUGHT THE PUBLIC IMAGINATION & THE NEWSPAPERS REPORTED THE DISCOVERY WITH ZEST. WILD CLAIMS WERE MADE: AN OHIO FARMER WAS REPORTED TO HAVE TURNED METAL TO GOLD, ANIMAL LOVERS BELIEVED THAT IT WOULD MAKE VIVISECTION OBSOLETE & BOOST THE CAUSE OF TEMPERANCE (BY SHOWING DRUNKARDS WHAT THEY WERE DOING TO THEIR SYSTEM). A NEW YORK PAPER ANNOUNCED THAT THE COLLEGE OF PHYSICIANS WERE USING X-RAYS "TO REFLECT ANATOMICAL DRAWINGS DIRECTLY INTO THE BRAINS OF THEIR STUDENTS."

X-RAYS & POTATOES

X-RAYS ARE LESS OPAQUE TO POTATOES THAN TO STONES OR EARTH. A NEW HARVESTER PASSES THE MATERIAL IT HAS PICKED UP THROUGH A BEAM OF X-RAYS & A MECHANISM AUTOMATICALLY SEPARATES OUT THE POTATOES.

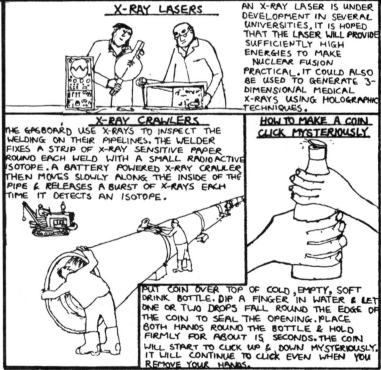

X-RAY LASERS

AN X-RAY LASER IS UNDER DEVELOPMENT IN SEVERAL UNIVERSITIES. IT IS HOPED THAT THE LASER WILL PROVIDE SUFFICIENTLY HIGH ENERGIES TO MAKE NUCLEAR FUSION PRACTICAL. IT COULD ALSO BE USED TO GENERATE 3-DIMENSIONAL MEDICAL X-RAYS USING HOLOGRAPHIC TECHNIQUES.

X-RAY CRAWLERS

THE GASBOARD USE X-RAYS TO INSPECT THE WELDING ON THEIR PIPELINES. THE WELDER FIXES A STRIP OF X-RAY SENSITIVE PAPER ROUND EACH WELD WITH A SMALL RADIOACTIVE ISOTOPE. A BATTERY POWERED X-RAY CRAWLER THEN MOVES SLOWLY ALONG THE INSIDE OF THE PIPE & RELEASES A BURST OF X-RAYS EACH TIME IT DETECTS AN ISOTOPE.

HOW TO MAKE A COIN CLICK MYSTERIOUSLY

PUT COIN OVER TOP OF COLD, EMPTY, SOFT DRINK BOTTLE. DIP A FINGER IN WATER & LET ONE OR TWO DROPS FALL ROUND THE EDGE OF THE COIN TO SEAL THE OPENING. PLACE BOTH HANDS ROUND THE BOTTLE & HOLD FIRMLY FOR ABOUT 15 SECONDS. THE COIN WILL START TO CLICK UP & DOWN MYSTERIOUSLY. IT WILL CONTINUE TO CLICK EVEN WHEN YOU REMOVE YOUR HANDS.

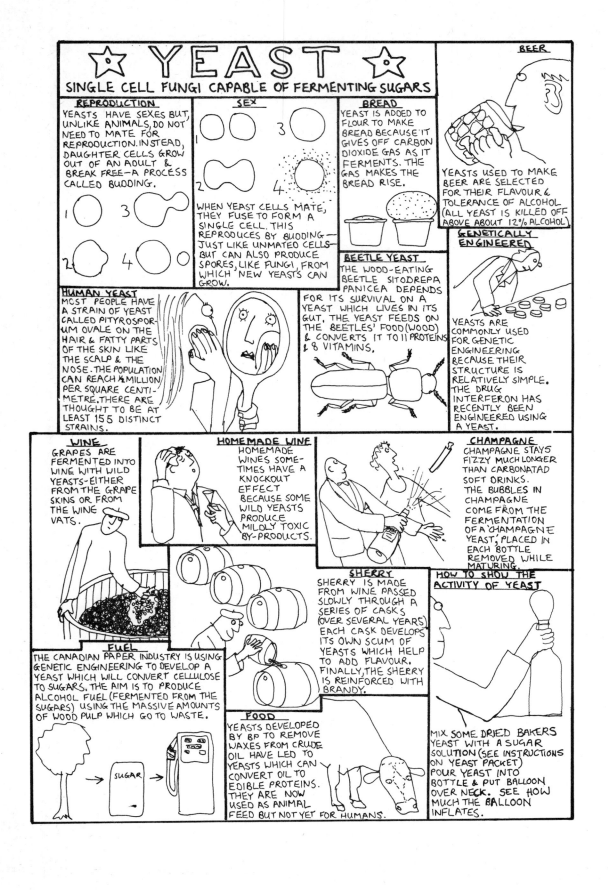

☆ YEAST ☆
SINGLE CELL FUNGI CAPABLE OF FERMENTING SUGARS

REPRODUCTION
YEASTS HAVE SEXES BUT, UNLIKE ANIMALS, DO NOT NEED TO MATE FOR REPRODUCTION. INSTEAD, DAUGHTER CELLS GROW OUT OF AN ADULT & BREAK FREE - A PROCESS CALLED BUDDING.

SEX
WHEN YEAST CELLS MATE, THEY FUSE TO FORM A SINGLE CELL. THIS REPRODUCES BY BUDDING - JUST LIKE UNMATED CELLS - BUT CAN ALSO PRODUCE SPORES, LIKE FUNGI, FROM WHICH NEW YEASTS CAN GROW.

BREAD
YEAST IS ADDED TO FLOUR TO MAKE BREAD BECAUSE IT GIVES OFF CARBON DIOXIDE GAS AS IT FERMENTS. THE GAS MAKES THE BREAD RISE.

BEER
YEASTS USED TO MAKE BEER ARE SELECTED FOR THEIR FLAVOUR & TOLERANCE OF ALCOHOL (ALL YEAST IS KILLED OFF ABOVE ABOUT 12% ALCOHOL)

BEETLE YEAST
THE WOOD-EATING BEETLE SITODREPA PANICEA DEPENDS FOR ITS SURVIVAL ON A YEAST WHICH LIVES IN ITS GUT. THE YEAST FEEDS ON THE BEETLES' FOOD (WOOD) & CONVERTS IT TO 11 PROTEINS & 8 VITAMINS.

GENETICALLY ENGINEERED
YEASTS ARE COMMONLY USED FOR GENETIC ENGINEERING BECAUSE THEIR STRUCTURE IS RELATIVELY SIMPLE. THE DRUG INTERFERON HAS RECENTLY BEEN ENGINEERED USING A YEAST.

HUMAN YEAST
MOST PEOPLE HAVE A STRAIN OF YEAST CALLED PITYROSPORUM OVALE ON THE HAIR & FATTY PARTS OF THE SKIN LIKE THE SCALP & THE NOSE. THE POPULATION CAN REACH ½ MILLION PER SQUARE CENTIMETRE. THERE ARE THOUGHT TO BE AT LEAST 155 DISTINCT STRAINS.

WINE
GRAPES ARE FERMENTED INTO WINE WITH WILD YEASTS - EITHER FROM THE GRAPE SKINS OR FROM THE WINE VATS.

HOMEMADE WINE
HOMEMADE WINES SOMETIMES HAVE A KNOCKOUT EFFECT BECAUSE SOME WILD YEASTS PRODUCE MILDLY TOXIC BY-PRODUCTS.

CHAMPAGNE
CHAMPAGNE STAYS FIZZY MUCH LONGER THAN CARBONATAD SOFT DRINKS. THE BUBBLES IN CHAMPAGNE COME FROM THE FERMENTATION OF A 'CHAMPAGNE YEAST' PLACED IN EACH BOTTLE REMOVED WHILE MATURING.

SHERRY
SHERRY IS MADE FROM WINE PASSED SLOWLY THROUGH A SERIES OF CASKS (OVER SEVERAL YEARS) EACH CASK DEVELOPS ITS OWN SCUM OF YEASTS WHICH HELP TO ADD FLAVOUR. FINALLY, THE SHERRY IS REINFORCED WITH BRANDY.

FUEL
THE CANADIAN PAPER INDUSTRY IS USING GENETIC ENGINEERING TO DEVELOP A YEAST WHICH WILL CONVERT CELLULOSE TO SUGARS. THE AIM IS TO PRODUCE ALCOHOL FUEL (FERMENTED FROM THE SUGARS) USING THE MASSIVE AMOUNTS OF WOOD PULP WHICH GO TO WASTE.

SUGAR

FOOD
YEASTS DEVELOPED BY BP TO REMOVE WAXES FROM CRUDE OIL HAVE LED TO YEASTS WHICH CAN CONVERT OIL TO EDIBLE PROTEINS. THEY ARE NOW USED AS ANIMAL FEED BUT NOT YET FOR HUMANS.

HOW TO SHOW THE ACTIVITY OF YEAST
MIX SOME DRIED BAKERS YEAST WITH A SUGAR SOLUTION (SEE INSTRUCTIONS ON YEAST PACKET) POUR YEAST INTO BOTTLE & PUT BALLOON OVER NECK. SEE HOW MUCH THE BALLOON INFLATES.

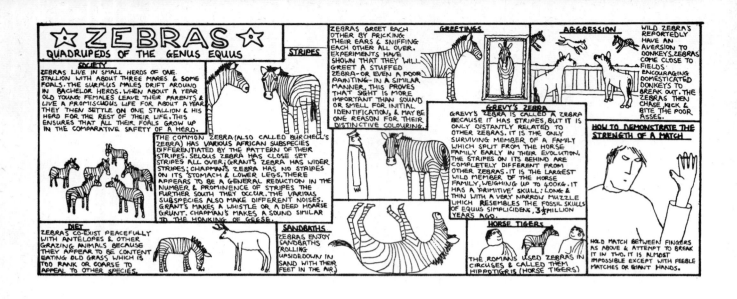

☆ ZEBRAS ☆
QUADRUPEDS OF THE GENUS EQUUS

SOCIETY
ZEBRAS LIVE IN SMALL HERDS OF ONE STALLION WITH ABOUT THREE MARES & SOME FOALS. THE SURPLUS MALES DRIFT AROUND IN BACHELOR HERDS. WHEN ABOUT A YEAR OLD YOUNG FEMALES LEAVE THEIR PARENTS & LIVE A PROMISCUOUS LIFE FOR ABOUT A YEAR. THEY THEN SETTLE ON ONE STALLION & HIS HERD FOR THE REST OF THEIR LIFE. THIS ENSURES THAT ALL THEIR FOALS GROW UP IN THE COMPARATIVE SAFETY OF A HERD.

THE COMMON ZEBRA (ALSO CALLED BURCHELL'S ZEBRA) HAS VARIOUS AFRICAN SUBSPECIES DIFFERENTIATED BY THE PATTERN OF THEIR STRIPES. SELOUS ZEBRA HAS CLOSE SET STRIPES ALL OVER; GRANTS ZEBRA HAS WIDER STRIPES; CHAPMANS ZEBRA HAS NO STRIPES ON ITS STOMACH & LOWER LEGS. THERE APPEARS TO BE A GENERAL REDUCTION IN THE NUMBER & PROMINENCE OF STRIPES THE FURTHER SOUTH THEY OCCUR. THE VARIOUS SUBSPECIES ALSO MAKE DIFFERENT NOISES. GRANT'S MAKES A WHISTLE OR A DEEP HOARSE GRUNT. CHAPMAN'S MAKES A SOUND SIMILAR TO THE HONKING OF GEESE.

DIET
ZEBRAS CO-EXIST PEACEFULLY WITH ANTELOPES & OTHER GRAZING ANIMALS BECAUSE THEY APPEAR TO BE CONTENT EATING OLD GRASS WHICH IS TOO RANK OR COARSE TO APPEAL TO OTHER SPECIES.

STRIPES
ZEBRAS GREET EACH OTHER BY PRICKING THEIR EARS & SNIFFING EACH OTHER ALL OVER. EXPERIMENTS HAVE SHOWN THAT THEY WILL GREET A STUFFED ZEBRA-OR EVEN A POOR PAINTING- IN A SIMILAR MANNER. THIS PROVES THAT SIGHT IS MORE IMPORTANT THAN SOUND OR SMELL FOR INITIAL IDENTIFICATION, & MAY BE ONE REASON FOR THEIR DISTINCTIVE COLOURING.

SANDBATHS
ZEBRAS ENJOY SANDBATHS (ROLLING UPSIDEDOWN IN SAND WITH THEIR FEET IN THE AIR.)

GREETINGS

AGGRESSION

WILD ZEBRA'S REPORTEDLY HAVE AN AVERSION TO DONKEYS. ZEBRAS COME CLOSE TO FIELDS ENCOURAGING DOMESTICATED DONKEYS TO BREAK OUT. THE ZEBRAS THEN CHASE KICK & BITE THE POOR ASSES.

GREVY'S ZEBRA
GREVY'S ZEBRA IS CALLED A ZEBRA BECAUSE IT HAS STRIPES, BUT IT IS ONLY DISTANTLY RELATED TO OTHER ZEBRAS. IT IS THE ONLY SURVIVING MEMBER OF A FAMILY WHICH SPLIT FROM THE HORSE FAMILY EARLY IN THEIR EVOLUTION. THE STRIPES ON ITS BEHIND ARE COMPLETELY DIFFERENT FROM OTHER ZEBRAS. IT IS THE LARGEST WILD MEMBER OF THE HORSE FAMILY, WEIGHING UP TO 400KG. IT HAS A 'PRIMITIVE' SKULL: LONG & THIN WITH A VERY NARROW MUZZLE WHICH RESEMBLES THE FOSSIL SKULLS OF EQUUS SIMPLICIDENS, $3\frac{1}{2}$ MILLION YEARS AGO.

HORSE TIGERS
THE ROMANS USED ZEBRAS IN CIRCUSES & CALLED THEM HIPPOTIGRIS (HORSE TIGERS)

HOW TO DEMONSTRATE THE STRENGTH OF A MATCH
HOLD MATCH BETWEEN FINGERS AS ABOVE & ATTEMPT TO BREAK IT IN TWO. IT IS ALMOST IMPOSSIBLE EXCEPT WITH FEEBLE MATCHES OR GIANT HANDS.

☆ ZOOS ☆

ROYAL ZOOS
MOST MODERN EUROPEAN ZOOS STEM FROM PRIVATE ROYAL COLLECTIONS. THE BRITISH ROYAL COLLECTION WAS STARTED BY HENRY I IN THE 12th C AT WOODSTOCK (OXFORDSHIRE). THE COLLECTION WAS TRANSFERRED TO REGENT'S PARK WHEN LONDON ZOO OPENED IN 1828.

SELF-SUSTAINING ZOOS
INSTEAD OF THE COMPREHENSIVE COLLECTIONS OF THE PAST, LONDON ZOO NOW CONCENTRATES ON SPECIES WHICH CAN FORM SELF-SUSTAINING GROUPS. THE NUMBER OF MONKEY SPECIES HAS BEEN REDUCED TO 16 FROM 50 IN 1966. 87% OF THE ANIMALS NOW IN THE ZOO WERE BORN THERE.

ARTIFICIAL BREEDING
LONDON ZOO HAS THE WORLD RECORD FOR SUCCESSFUL BREEDING OF CAPTIVE ANIMALS. IT HAS PERFECTED METHODS OF ARTIFICIAL INSEMINATION & INDUCTION OF OVULATION FOR MANY SPECIES. IT IS HOPED TO USE THESE METHODS FOR BREEDING THREATENED SPECIES.

ZOO BOOM
SINCE 1950 THERE HAS BEEN A ZOO BOOM IN BRITAIN (FROM 14 TO OVER 150). MOST NEW ZOOS UNDERTAKE NO RESEARCH & ARE RUN AS COMMERCIAL ENTERTAINMENT BUSINESSES.

NEW ZOO

ZOOS AT HOME
BEFORE THE 1976 DANGEROUS WILD ANIMALS ACT, THERE WAS NO LAW TO STOP PEOPLE KEEPING TIGERS, POLAR BEARS, OR ANY WILD ANIMAL AT HOME.

ZOOS V HUNGER
JUST BEFORE THE FRENCH REVOLUTION, A HUNGRY MOB WENT TO LOUIS XVI 's ZOO AT VERSAILLES COMPLAINING THAT IT WAS SHAMEFUL TO FEED 'ORNAMENTAL' ANIMALS WHEN PEOPLE WERE STARVING & THAT, IN ANY CASE, THE ANIMALS HAD A RIGHT TO BE FREE. THEY RELEASED ALL THE ANIMALS EXCEPT THE DANGEROUS ONES. THEN HUNGER OVERCAME THE MOB & THEY GAVE CHASE, KILLING & EATING THE LOT.

PETTING ZOOS
PETTING ZOOS', WHERE CHILDREN ARE ENCOURAGED TO TOUCH THE ANIMALS, HAVE RECENTLY BECOME POPULAR IN THE US. ANIMAL LOVERS ACCUSE THESE ZOOS OF CRUELTY, AS THE ANIMALS' TEETH & CLAWS ARE USUALLY REMOVED FOR SAFETY.

HOW TO REMOVE A DENT FROM A PING PONG BALL
PLACE BALL IN PAN OF WATER & HEAT SLOWLY. AIR INSIDE BALL WILL EXPAND, PLASTIC WILL SOFTEN & DENT WILL POP OUT. REMOVE BALL QUICKLY TO PREVENT IT BURSTING.

ROMAN ZOOS
THE ROMANS KEPT LARGE NUMBERS OF WILD ANIMALS, BUT USED THEM ALL FOR GLADIATORIAL BATTLES. NERO ONCE PITTED A COMPANY OF HORSEMEN AGAINST 300 LIONS & 400 BEARS.

EGYPTIAN ZOOS
THE EARLIEST KNOWN COLLECTION OF ANIMALS WAS FORMED IN THE 3rd DYNASTY ANCIENT EGYPT c2000BC AT PUZURISH (NOW IN IRAQ). SPECIMENS OF SACRED ANIMALS, SUCH AS LIONS, BABOONS & IBIS, WERE OFTEN KEPT IN EGYPTIAN TEMPLES.

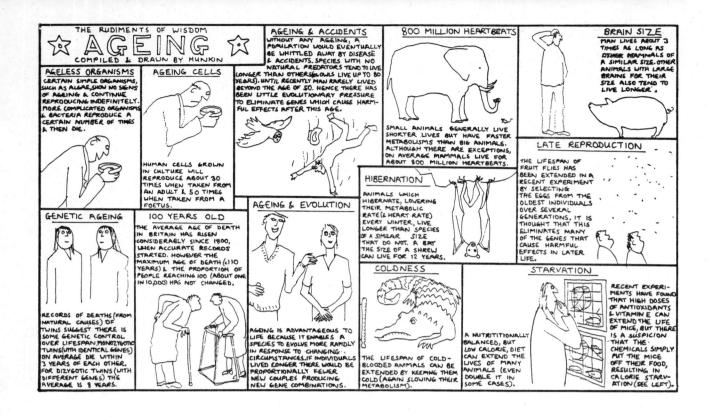

THE RUDIMENTS OF WISDOM ☆ AGEING ☆
COMPILED & DRAWN BY HUNKIN

AGELESS ORGANISMS
CERTAIN SIMPLE ORGANISMS, SUCH AS ALGAE, SHOW NO SIGNS OF AGEING & CONTINUE REPRODUCING INDEFINITELY. MORE COMPLICATED ORGANISMS & BACTERIA REPRODUCE A CERTAIN NUMBER OF TIMES & THEN DIE.

AGEING CELLS
HUMAN CELLS GROWN IN CULTURE WILL REPRODUCE ABOUT 30 TIMES WHEN TAKEN FROM AN ADULT & 50 TIMES WHEN TAKEN FROM A FOETUS.

GENETIC AGEING
RECORDS OF DEATHS (FROM NATURAL CAUSES) OF TWINS SUGGEST THERE IS SOME GENETIC CONTROL OVER LIFESPAN. MONOZYGOTIC TWINS (WITH IDENTICAL GENES) ON AVERAGE DIE WITHIN 3 YEARS OF EACH OTHER. FOR DIZYGOTIC TWINS (WITH DIFFERENT GENES) THE AVERAGE IS 8 YEARS.

100 YEARS OLD
THE AVERAGE AGE OF DEATH IN BRITAIN HAS RISEN CONSIDERABLY SINCE 1800, WHEN ACCURATE RECORDS STARTED. HOWEVER THE MAXIMUM AGE OF DEATH (<110 YEARS) & THE PROPORTION OF PEOPLE REACHING 100 (ABOUT ONE IN 10,000) HAS NOT CHANGED.

AGEING & ACCIDENTS
WITHOUT ANY AGEING, A POPULATION WOULD EVENTUALLY BE WHITTLED AWAY BY DISEASE & ACCIDENTS. SPECIES WITH NO NATURAL PREDATORS TEND TO LIVE LONGER THAN OTHERS (OWLS LIVE UP TO 80 YEARS). UNTIL RECENTLY MAN RARELY LIVED BEYOND THE AGE OF 50. HENCE THERE HAS BEEN LITTLE EVOLUTIONARY PRESSURE TO ELIMINATE GENES WHICH CAUSE HARMFUL EFFECTS AFTER THIS AGE.

AGEING & EVOLUTION
AGEING IS ADVANTAGEOUS TO LIFE BECAUSE IT ENABLES A SPECIES TO EVOLVE MORE RAPIDLY IN RESPONSE TO CHANGING CIRCUMSTANCES. IF INDIVIDUALS LIVED LONGER THERE WOULD BE PROPORTIONALLY FEWER NEW COUPLES PRODUCING NEW GENE COMBINATIONS.

800 MILLION HEARTBEATS
SMALL ANIMALS GENERALLY LIVE SHORTER LIVES BUT HAVE FASTER METABOLISMS THAN BIG ANIMALS. ALTHOUGH THERE ARE EXCEPTIONS, ON AVERAGE MAMMALS LIVE FOR ABOUT 800 MILLION HEARTBEATS.

HIBERNATION
ANIMALS WHICH HIBERNATE, LOWERING THEIR METABOLIC RATE (& HEART RATE) EVERY WINTER, LIVE LONGER THAN SPECIES OF A SIMILAR SIZE THAT DO NOT. A BAT THE SIZE OF A SHREW CAN LIVE FOR 12 YEARS.

COLDNESS
THE LIFESPAN OF COLD-BLOODED ANIMALS CAN BE EXTENDED BY KEEPING THEM COLD (AGAIN SLOWING THEIR METABOLISM).

BRAIN SIZE
MAN LIVES ABOUT 3 TIMES AS LONG AS OTHER MAMMALS OF A SIMILAR SIZE. OTHER ANIMALS WITH LARGE BRAINS FOR THEIR SIZE ALSO TEND TO LIVE LONGER.

LATE REPRODUCTION
THE LIFESPAN OF FRUIT FLIES HAS BEEN EXTENDED IN A RECENT EXPERIMENT BY SELECTING THE EGGS FROM THE OLDEST INDIVIDUALS OVER SEVERAL GENERATIONS. IT IS THOUGHT THAT THIS ELIMINATES MANY OF THE GENES THAT CAUSE HARMFUL EFFECTS IN LATER LIFE.

STARVATION
A NUTRITIONALLY BALANCED, BUT LOW CALORIE, DIET CAN EXTEND THE LIVES OF MANY ANIMALS (EVEN DOUBLE IT IN SOME CASES).

RECENT EXPERIMENTS HAVE FOUND THAT HIGH DOSES OF ANTIOXIDANTS & VITAMIN E CAN EXTEND THE LIFE OF MICE, BUT THERE IS A SUSPICION THAT THE CHEMICALS SIMPLY PUT THE MICE OFF THEIR FOOD, RESULTING IN CALORIE STARVATION (SEE LEFT).

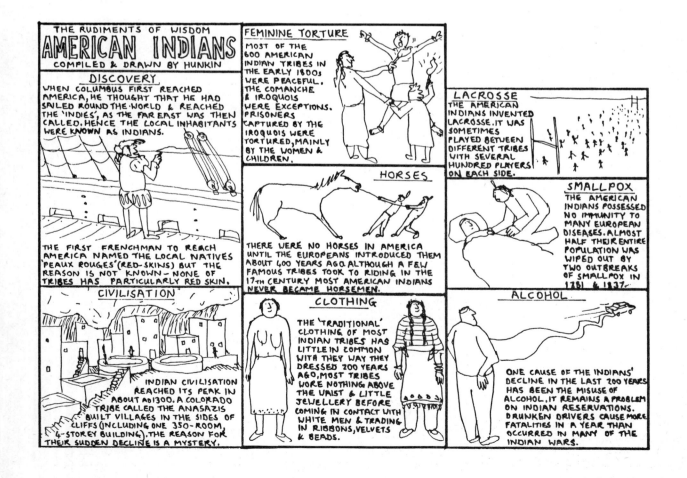

THE RUDIMENTS OF WISDOM AMERICAN INDIANS
COMPILED & DRAWN BY HUNKIN

DISCOVERY
WHEN COLUMBUS FIRST REACHED AMERICA, HE THOUGHT THAT HE HAD SAILED ROUND THE WORLD & REACHED THE 'INDIES', AS THE FAR EAST WAS THEN CALLED. HENCE THE LOCAL INHABITANTS WERE KNOWN AS INDIANS.

THE FIRST FRENCHMAN TO REACH AMERICA NAMED THE LOCAL NATIVES 'PEAUX ROUGES' (RED-SKINS) BUT THE REASON IS NOT KNOWN – NONE OF TRIBES HAS PARTICULARLY RED SKIN.

CIVILISATION
INDIAN CIVILISATION REACHED ITS PEAK IN ABOUT AD 1300. A COLORADO TRIBE CALLED THE ANASAZIS BUILT VILLAGES IN THE SIDES OF CLIFFS (INCLUDING ONE 350-ROOM 4-STOREY BUILDING). THE REASON FOR THEIR SUDDEN DECLINE IS A MYSTERY.

FEMININE TORTURE
MOST OF THE 600 AMERICAN INDIAN TRIBES IN THE EARLY 1800s WERE PEACEFUL. THE COMANCHE & IROQUOIS WERE EXCEPTIONS. PRISONERS CAPTURED BY THE IROQUOIS WERE TORTURED, MAINLY BY THE WOMEN & CHILDREN.

HORSES
THERE WERE NO HORSES IN AMERICA UNTIL THE EUROPEANS INTRODUCED THEM ABOUT 400 YEARS AGO. ALTHOUGH A FEW FAMOUS TRIBES TOOK TO RIDING IN THE 17TH CENTURY MOST AMERICAN INDIANS NEVER BECAME HORSEMEN.

CLOTHING
THE 'TRADITIONAL' CLOTHING OF MOST INDIAN TRIBES HAS LITTLE IN COMMON WITH THEY WAY THEY DRESSED 200 YEARS AGO. MOST TRIBES WORE NOTHING ABOVE THE WAIST & LITTLE JEWELLERY BEFORE COMING IN CONTACT WITH WHITE MEN & TRADING IN RIBBONS, VELVETS & BEADS.

LACROSSE
THE AMERICAN INDIANS INVENTED LACROSSE. IT WAS SOMETIMES PLAYED BETWEEN DIFFERENT TRIBES WITH SEVERAL HUNDRED PLAYERS ON EACH SIDE.

SMALLPOX
THE AMERICAN INDIANS POSSESSED NO IMMUNITY TO MANY EUROPEAN DISEASES. ALMOST HALF THEIR ENTIRE POPULATION WAS WIPED OUT BY TWO OUTBREAKS OF SMALLPOX IN 1781 & 1837.

ALCOHOL
ONE CAUSE OF THE INDIANS' DECLINE IN THE LAST 200 YEARS HAS BEEN THE MISUSE OF ALCOHOL. IT REMAINS A PROBLEM ON INDIAN RESERVATIONS. DRUNKEN DRIVERS CAUSE MORE FATALITIES IN A YEAR THAN OCCURRED IN MANY OF THE INDIAN WARS.

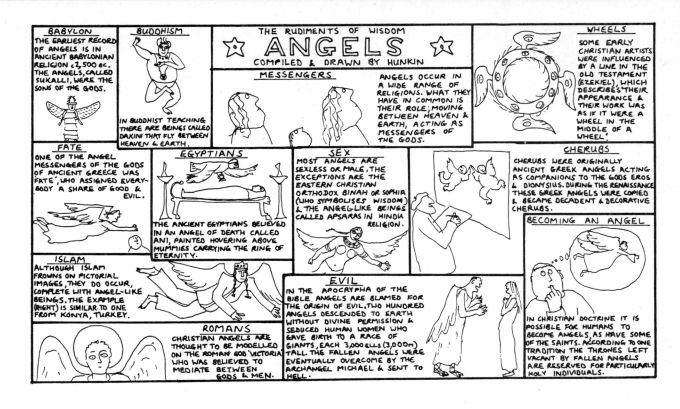

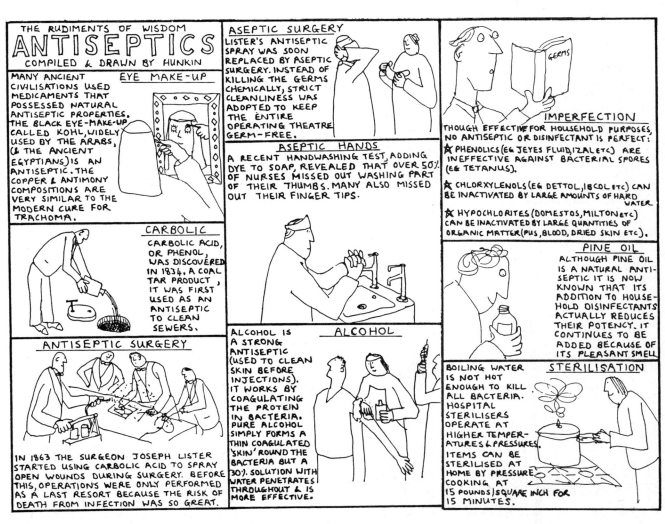

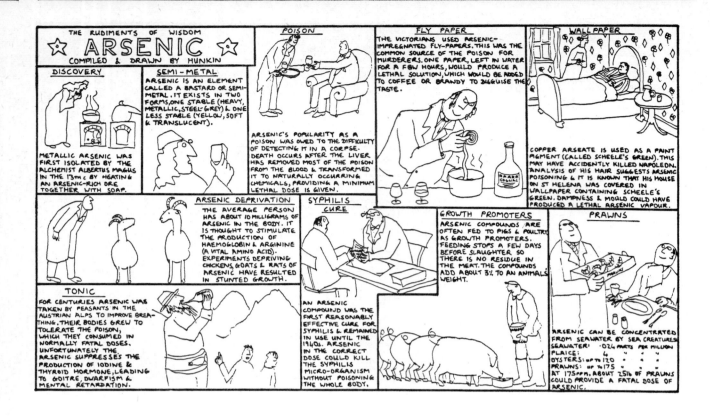

THE RUDIMENTS OF WISDOM
☆ **ARSENIC** ☆
COMPILED & DRAWN BY HUNKIN

DISCOVERY
METALLIC ARSENIC WAS FIRST ISOLATED BY THE ALCHEMIST ALBERTUS MAGUS IN THE 13TH C BY HEATING AN ARSENIC-RICH ORE TOGETHER WITH SOAP.

SEMI – METAL
ARSENIC IS AN ELEMENT CALLED A BASTARD OR SEMI-METAL. IT EXISTS IN TWO FORMS, ONE STABLE (HEAVY, METALLIC, STEEL-GREY) & ONE LESS STABLE (YELLOW, SOFT & TRANSLUCENT).

POISON
ARSENIC'S POPULARITY AS A POISON WAS OWED TO THE DIFFICULTY OF DETECTING IT IN A CORPSE. DEATH OCCURS AFTER THE LIVER HAS REMOVED MOST OF THE POISON FROM THE BLOOD & TRANSFORMED IT TO NATURALLY OCCURRING CHEMICALS, PROVIDING A MINIMUM LETHAL DOSE IS GIVEN.

FLY PAPER
THE VICTORIANS USED ARSENIC-IMPREGNATED FLY-PAPERS. THIS WAS THE COMMON SOURCE OF THE POISON FOR MURDERERS. ONE PAPER, LEFT IN WATER FOR A FEW HOURS, WOULD PRODUCE A LETHAL SOLUTION, WHICH WOULD BE ADDED TO COFFEE OR BRANDY TO DISGUISE THE TASTE.

WALLPAPER
COPPER ARSEATE IS USED AS A PAINT PIGMENT (CALLED SCHEELE'S GREEN). THIS MAY HAVE ACCIDENTLY KILLED NAPOLEON. ANALYSIS OF HIS HAIR SUGGESTS ARSENIC POISONING & IT IS KNOWN THAT HIS HOUSE ON ST HELENA WAS COVERED IN WALLPAPER CONTAINING SCHEELE'S GREEN. DAMPNESS & MOULD COULD HAVE PRODUCED A LETHAL ARSENIC VAPOUR.

ARSENIC DEPRIVATION
THE AVERAGE PERSON HAS ABOUT 10 MILLIGRAMS OF ARSENIC IN THE BODY. IT IS THOUGHT TO STIMULATE THE PRODUCTION OF HAEMOGLOBIN & ARGININE (A VITAL AMINO ACID). EXPERIMENTS DEPRIVING CHICKENS, GOATS & RATS OF ARSENIC HAVE RESULTED IN STUNTED GROWTH.

SYPHILIS CURE
AN ARSENIC COMPOUND WAS THE FIRST REASONABLY EFFECTIVE CURE FOR SYPHILIS & REMAINED IN USE UNTIL THE 1940s. ARSENIC IN THE CORRECT DOSE COULD KILL THE SYPHILIS MICRO-ORGANISM WITHOUT POISONING THE WHOLE BODY.

GROWTH PROMOTERS
ARSENIC COMPOUNDS ARE OFTEN FED TO PIGS & POULTRY AS GROWTH PROMOTERS. FEEDING STOPS A FEW DAYS BEFORE SLAUGHTER SO THERE IS NO RESIDUE IN THE MEAT. THE COMPOUNDS ADD ABOUT 3% TO AN ANIMAL'S WEIGHT.

PRAWNS
ARSENIC CAN BE CONCENTRATED FROM SEAWATER BY SEA CREATURES.
SEAWATER: ·024 PARTS PER MILLION
PLAICE: 4
OYSTERS: UP TO 120
PRAWNS: UP TO 175
AT 175PPM, ABOUT 25% OF PRAWNS COULD PROVIDE A FATAL DOSE OF ARSENIC.

TONIC
FOR CENTURIES ARSENIC WAS TAKEN BY PEASANTS IN THE AUSTRIAN ALPS TO IMPROVE BREATHING. THEIR BODIES GREW TO TOLERATE THE POISON, WHICH THEY CONSUMED IN NORMALLY FATAL DOSES. UNFORTUNATELY THE ARSENIC SUPPRESSES THE PRODUCTION OF IODINE & THYROID HORMONE, LEADING TO GOITRE, DWARFISM & MENTAL RETARDATION.

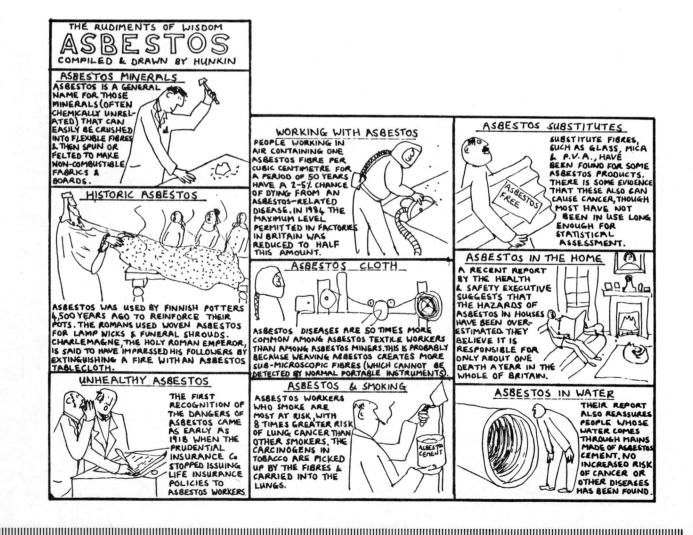

THE RUDIMENTS OF WISDOM
ASBESTOS
COMPILED & DRAWN BY HUNKIN

ASBESTOS MINERALS
ASBESTOS IS A GENERAL NAME FOR THOSE MINERALS (OFTEN CHEMICALLY UNRELATED) THAT CAN EASILY BE CRUSHED INTO FLEXIBLE FIBRES & THEN SPUN OR FELTED TO MAKE NON-COMBUSTIBLE FABRICS & BOARDS.

HISTORIC ASBESTOS
ASBESTOS WAS USED BY FINNISH POTTERS 4,500 YEARS AGO TO REINFORCE THEIR POTS. THE ROMANS USED WOVEN ASBESTOS FOR LAMP WICKS & FUNERAL SHROUDS. CHARLEMAGNE, THE HOLY ROMAN EMPEROR, IS SAID TO HAVE IMPRESSED HIS FOLLOWERS BY EXTINGUISHING A FIRE WITH AN ASBESTOS TABLECLOTH.

UNHEALTHY ASBESTOS
THE FIRST RECOGNITION OF THE DANGERS OF ASBESTOS CAME AS EARLY AS 1918 WHEN THE PRUDENTIAL INSURANCE Co STOPPED ISSUING LIFE INSURANCE POLICIES TO ASBESTOS WORKERS.

WORKING WITH ASBESTOS
PEOPLE WORKING IN AIR CONTAINING ONE ASBESTOS FIBRE PER CUBIC CENTIMETRE FOR A PERIOD OF 50 YEARS HAVE A 2-5% CHANCE OF DYING FROM AN ASBESTOS-RELATED DISEASE. IN 1984 THE MAXIMUM LEVEL PERMITTED IN FACTORIES IN BRITAIN WAS REDUCED TO HALF THIS AMOUNT.

ASBESTOS CLOTH
ASBESTOS DISEASES ARE 50 TIMES MORE COMMON AMONG ASBESTOS TEXTILE WORKERS THAN AMONG ASBESTOS MINERS. THIS IS PROBABLY BECAUSE WEAVING ASBESTOS CREATES MORE SUB-MICROSCOPIC FIBRES (WHICH CANNOT BE DETECTED BY NORMAL PORTABLE INSTRUMENTS).

ASBESTOS & SMOKING
ASBESTOS WORKERS WHO SMOKE ARE MOST AT RISK, WITH 8 TIMES GREATER RISK OF LUNG CANCER THAN OTHER SMOKERS. THE CARCINOGENS IN TOBACCO ARE PICKED UP BY THE FIBRES & CARRIED INTO THE LUNGS.

ASBESTOS SUBSTITUTES
SUBSTITUTE FIBRES, SUCH AS GLASS, MICA & P.V.A., HAVE BEEN FOUND FOR SOME ASBESTOS PRODUCTS. THERE IS SOME EVIDENCE THAT THESE ALSO CAN CAUSE CANCER, THOUGH MOST HAVE NOT BEEN IN USE LONG ENOUGH FOR STATISTICAL ASSESSMENT.

ASBESTOS IN THE HOME
A RECENT REPORT BY THE HEALTH & SAFETY EXECUTIVE SUGGESTS THAT THE HAZARDS OF ASBESTOS IN HOUSES HAVE BEEN OVER-ESTIMATED. THEY BELIEVE IT IS RESPONSIBLE FOR ONLY ABOUT ONE DEATH A YEAR IN THE WHOLE OF BRITAIN.

ASBESTOS IN WATER
THEIR REPORT ALSO REASSURES PEOPLE WHOSE WATER COMES THROUGH MAINS MADE OF ASBESTOS CEMENT. NO INCREASED RISK OF CANCER OR OTHER DISEASES HAS BEEN FOUND.

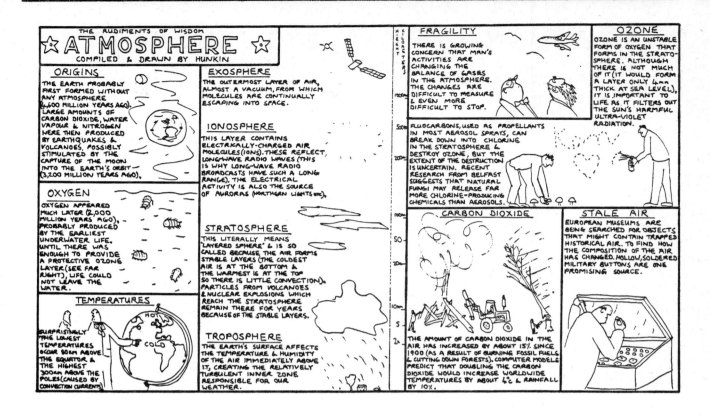

☆ ATMOSPHERE ☆
THE RUDIMENTS OF WISDOM
COMPILED & DRAWN BY HUNKIN

ORIGINS
THE EARTH PROBABLY FIRST FORMED WITHOUT ANY ATMOSPHERE (4,600 MILLION YEARS AGO). LARGE AMOUNTS OF CARBON DIOXIDE, WATER VAPOUR & NITROGEN WERE THEN PRODUCED BY EARTHQUAKES & VOLCANOS, POSSIBLY STIMULATED BY THE CAPTURE OF THE MOON INTO THE EARTH'S ORBIT (3,200 MILLION YEARS AGO).

OXYGEN
OXYGEN APPEARED MUCH LATER (2,000 MILLION YEARS AGO), PROBABLY PRODUCED BY THE EARLIEST UNDERWATER LIFE. UNTIL THERE WAS ENOUGH TO PROVIDE A PROTECTIVE OZONE LAYER (SEE FAR RIGHT), LIFE COULD NOT LEAVE THE WATER.

TEMPERATURES
SURPRISINGLY THE LOWEST TEMPERATURES OCCUR 80km ABOVE THE EQUATOR & THE HIGHEST 300km ABOVE THE POLES (CAUSED BY CONVECTION CURRENTS).

EXOSPHERE
THE OUTERMOST LAYER OF AIR, ALMOST A VACUUM, FROM WHICH MOLECULES ARE CONTINUALLY ESCAPING INTO SPACE.

IONOSPHERE
THIS LAYER CONTAINS ELECTRICALLY-CHARGED AIR MOLECULES (IONS). THESE REFLECT LONG-WAVE RADIO WAVES (THIS IS WHY LONG-WAVE RADIO BROADCASTS HAVE SUCH A LONG RANGE). THE ELECTRICAL ACTIVITY IS ALSO THE SOURCE OF AURORAS (NORTHERN LIGHTS etc).

STRATOSPHERE
THIS LITERALLY MEANS 'LAYERED SPHERE' & IS SO CALLED BECAUSE THE AIR FORMS STABLE LAYERS (THE COLDEST AIR IS AT THE BOTTOM & THE WARMEST IS AT THE TOP SO THERE IS LITTLE CONVECTION). PARTICLES FROM VOLCANOES & NUCLEAR EXPLOSIONS WHICH REACH THE STRATOSPHERE REMAIN THERE FOR YEARS BECAUSE OF THE STABLE LAYERS.

TROPOSPHERE
THE EARTH'S SURFACE AFFECTS THE TEMPERATURE & HUMIDITY OF THE AIR IMMEDIATELY ABOVE IT, CREATING THE RELATIVELY TURBULENT INNER ZONE RESPONSIBLE FOR OUR WEATHER.

FRAGILITY
THERE IS GROWING CONCERN THAT MAN'S ACTIVITIES ARE CHANGING THE BALANCE OF GASES IN THE ATMOSPHERE. THE CHANGES ARE DIFFICULT TO MEASURE & EVEN MORE DIFFICULT TO STOP.

FLUOCARBONS, USED AS PROPELLANTS IN MOST AEROSOL SPRAYS, CAN BREAK DOWN INTO CHLORINE IN THE STRATOSPHERE & DESTROY OZONE, BUT THE EXTENT OF THE DESTRUCTION IS UNCERTAIN. RECENT RESEARCH FROM BELFAST SUGGESTS THAT NATURAL FUNGI MAY RELEASE FAR MORE CHLORINE-PRODUCING CHEMICALS THAN AEROSOLS.

CARBON DIOXIDE
THE AMOUNT OF CARBON DIOXIDE IN THE AIR HAS INCREASED BY ABOUT 15% SINCE 1900 (AS A RESULT OF BURNING FOSSIL FUELS & CUTTING DOWN FORESTS). COMPUTER MODELS PREDICT THAT DOUBLING THE CARBON DIOXIDE WOULD INCREASE WORLDWIDE TEMPERATURES BY ABOUT 4°C & RAINFALL BY 10%.

OZONE
OZONE IS AN UNSTABLE FORM OF OXYGEN THAT FORMS IN THE STRATOSPHERE. ALTHOUGH THERE IS NOT MUCH OF IT (IT WOULD FORM A LAYER ONLY 4mm THICK AT SEA LEVEL), IT IS IMPORTANT TO LIFE AS IT FILTERS OUT THE SUN'S HARMFUL ULTRA-VIOLET RADIATION.

STALE AIR
EUROPEAN MUSEUMS ARE BEING SEARCHED FOR OBJECTS THAT MIGHT CONTAIN TRAPPED HISTORICAL AIR, TO FIND HOW THE COMPOSITION OF THE AIR HAS CHANGED. HOLLOW, SOLDERED MILITARY BUTTONS ARE ONE PROMISING SOURCE.

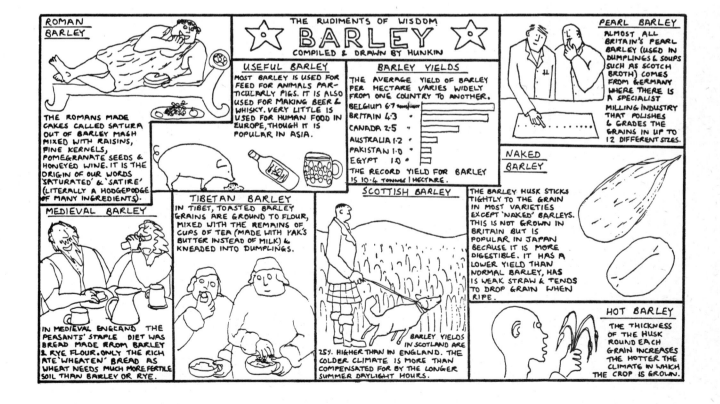

☆ BARLEY ☆
THE RUDIMENTS OF WISDOM
COMPILED & DRAWN BY HUNKIN

ROMAN BARLEY
THE ROMANS MADE CAKES CALLED SATURA OUT OF BARLEY MASH MIXED WITH RAISINS, PINE KERNELS, POMEGRANATE SEEDS & HONEYED WINE. IT IS THE ORIGIN OF OUR WORDS 'SATURATED' & 'SATIRE' (LITERALLY A HODGEPODGE OF MANY INGREDIENTS).

MEDIEVAL BARLEY
IN MEDIEVAL ENGLAND THE PEASANTS' STAPLE DIET WAS BREAD MADE FROM BARLEY & RYE FLOUR. ONLY THE RICH ATE 'WHEATEN' BREAD AS WHEAT NEEDS MUCH MORE FERTILE SOIL THAN BARLEY OR RYE.

USEFUL BARLEY
MOST BARLEY IS USED FOR FEED FOR ANIMALS PARTICULARLY PIGS. IT IS ALSO USED FOR MAKING BEER & WHISKY. VERY LITTLE IS USED FOR HUMAN FOOD IN EUROPE, THOUGH IT IS POPULAR IN ASIA.

TIBETAN BARLEY
IN TIBET, TOASTED BARLEY GRAINS ARE GROUND TO FLOUR, MIXED WITH THE REMAINS OF CUPS OF TEA (MADE WITH YAK'S BUTTER INSTEAD OF MILK) & KNEADED INTO DUMPLINGS.

BARLEY YIELDS
THE AVERAGE YIELD OF BARLEY PER HECTARE VARIES WIDELY FROM ONE COUNTRY TO ANOTHER.

Country	Yield (tonnes/hectare)
BELGIUM	6·7
BRITAIN	4·3
CANADA	2·5
AUSTRALIA	1·2
PAKISTAN	1·0
EGYPT	1·0

THE RECORD YIELD FOR BARLEY IS 10·4 TONNES/HECTARE.

SCOTTISH BARLEY
BARLEY YIELDS IN SCOTLAND ARE 25% HIGHER THAN IN ENGLAND. THE COLDER CLIMATE IS MORE THAN COMPENSATED FOR BY THE LONGER SUMMER DAYLIGHT HOURS.

PEARL BARLEY
ALMOST ALL BRITAIN'S PEARL BARLEY (USED IN DUMPLINGS & SOUPS SUCH AS SCOTCH BROTH) COMES FROM GERMANY WHERE THERE IS A SPECIALIST MILLING INDUSTRY THAT POLISHES & GRADES THE GRAINS IN UP TO 12 DIFFERENT SIZES.

NAKED BARLEY
THE BARLEY HUSK STICKS TIGHTLY TO THE GRAIN IN MOST VARIETIES EXCEPT 'NAKED' BARLEYS. THIS IS NOT GROWN IN BRITAIN BUT IS POPULAR IN JAPAN BECAUSE IT IS MORE DIGESTIBLE. IT HAS A LOWER YIELD THAN NORMAL BARLEY, HAS A WEAK STRAW & TENDS TO DROP GRAIN WHEN RIPE.

HOT BARLEY
THE THICKNESS OF THE HUSK ROUND EACH GRAIN INCREASES THE HOTTER THE CLIMATE IN WHICH THE CROP IS GROWN.

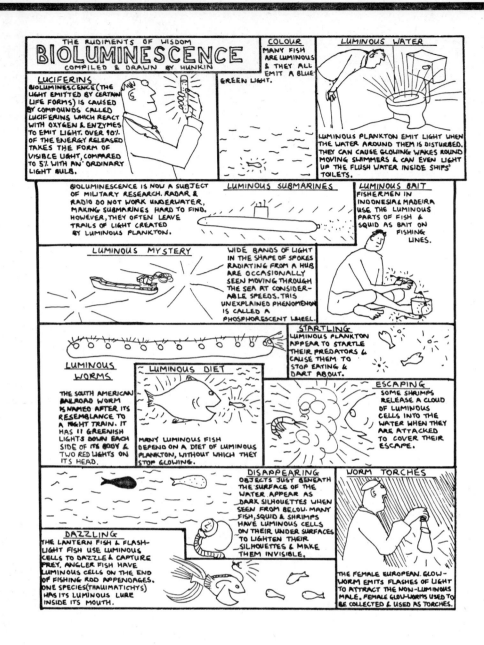

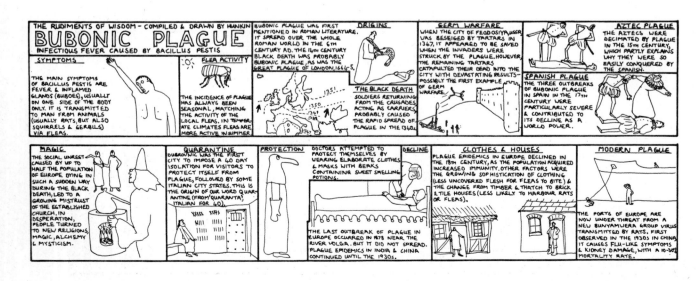

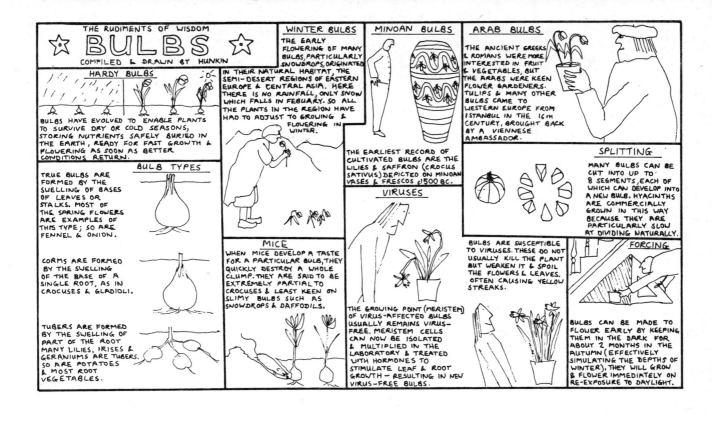

THE RUDIMENTS OF WISDOM ☆ BULBS ☆
COMPILED & DRAWN BY HUNKIN

HARDY BULBS
BULBS HAVE EVOLVED TO ENABLE PLANTS TO SURVIVE DRY OR COLD SEASONS, STORING NUTRIENTS SAFELY BURIED IN THE EARTH, READY FOR FAST GROWTH & FLOWERING AS SOON AS BETTER CONDITIONS RETURN.

BULB TYPES
TRUE BULBS ARE FORMED BY THE SWELLING OF BASES OF LEAVES OR STALKS. MOST OF THE SPRING FLOWERS ARE EXAMPLES OF THIS TYPE; SO ARE FENNEL & ONION.

CORMS ARE FORMED BY THE SWELLING OF THE BASE OF A SINGLE ROOT, AS IN CROCUSES & GLADIOLI.

TUBERS ARE FORMED BY THE SWELLING OF PART OF THE ROOT. MANY LILIES, IRISES & GERANIUMS ARE TUBERS. SO ARE POTATOES & MOST ROOT VEGETABLES.

WINTER BULBS
THE EARLY FLOWERING OF MANY BULBS, PARTICULARLY SNOWDROPS, ORIGINATED IN THEIR NATURAL HABITAT, THE SEMI-DESERT REGIONS OF EASTERN EUROPE & CENTRAL ASIA. HERE THERE IS NO RAINFALL, ONLY SNOW WHICH FALLS IN FEBUARY. SO ALL THE PLANTS IN THE REGION HAVE HAD TO ADJUST TO GROWING & FLOWERING IN WINTER.

MICE
WHEN MICE DEVELOP A TASTE FOR A PARTICULAR BULB, THEY QUICKLY DESTROY A WHOLE CLUMP. THEY ARE SAID TO BE EXTREMELY PARTIAL TO CROCUSES & LEAST KEEN ON SLIMY BULBS SUCH AS SNOWDROPS & DAFFODILS.

MINOAN BULBS
THE EARLIEST RECORD OF CULTIVATED BULBS ARE THE LILIES & SAFFRON (CROCUS SATIVUS) DEPICTED ON MINOAN VASES & FRESCOS c1500 BC.

VIRUSES
THE GROWING POINT (MERISTEM) OF VIRUS-AFFECTED BULBS USUALLY REMAINS VIRUS-FREE. MERISTEM CELLS CAN NOW BE ISOLATED & MULTIPLIED IN THE LABORATORY & TREATED WITH HORMONES TO STIMULATE LEAF & ROOT GROWTH – RESULTING IN NEW VIRUS-FREE BULBS.

ARAB BULBS
THE ANCIENT GREEKS & ROMANS WERE MORE INTERESTED IN FRUIT & VEGETABLES, BUT THE ARABS WERE KEEN FLOWER GARDENERS. TULIPS & MANY OTHER BULBS CAME TO WESTERN EUROPE FROM ISTANBUL IN THE 16TH CENTURY, BROUGHT BACK BY A VIENNESE AMBASSADOR.

BULBS ARE SUSCEPTIBLE TO VIRUSES. THESE DO NOT USUALLY KILL THE PLANT BUT WEAKEN IT & SPOIL THE FLOWERS & LEAVES, OFTEN CAUSING YELLOW STREAKS.

SPLITTING
MANY BULBS CAN BE CUT INTO UP TO 8 SEGMENTS, EACH OF WHICH CAN DEVELOP INTO A NEW BULB. HYACINTHS ARE COMMERCIALLY GROWN IN THIS WAY BECAUSE THEY ARE PARTICULARLY SLOW AT DIVIDING NATURALLY.

FORCING
BULBS CAN BE MADE TO FLOWER EARLY BY KEEPING THEM IN THE DARK FOR ABOUT 2 MONTHS IN THE AUTUMN (EFFECTIVELY SIMULATING THE DEPTHS OF WINTER). THEY WILL GROW & FLOWER IMMEDIATELY ON RE-EXPOSURE TO DAYLIGHT.

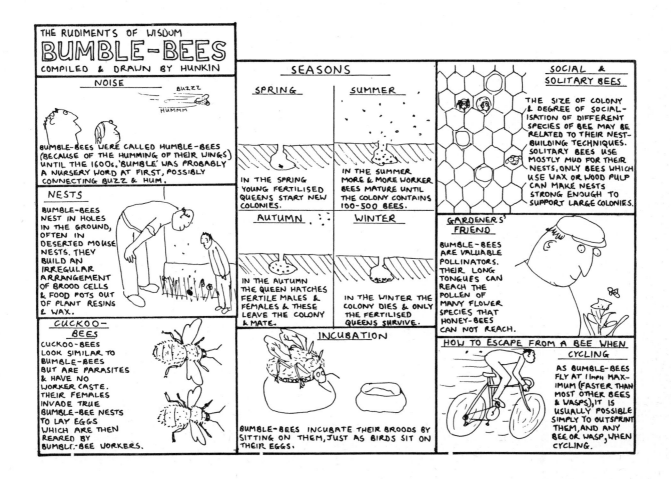

THE RUDIMENTS OF WISDOM BUMBLE-BEES
COMPILED & DRAWN BY HUNKIN

NOISE
BUZZ
HUMMM
BUMBLE-BEES WERE CALLED HUMBLE-BEES (BECAUSE OF THE HUMMING OF THEIR WINGS) UNTIL THE 1600s. 'BUMBLE' WAS PROBABLY A NURSERY WORD AT FIRST, POSSIBLY CONNECTING BUZZ & HUM.

NESTS
BUMBLE-BEES NEST IN HOLES IN THE GROUND, OFTEN IN DESERTED MOUSE NESTS. THEY BUILD AN IRREGULAR ARRANGEMENT OF BROOD CELLS & FOOD POTS OUT OF PLANT RESINS & WAX.

CUCKOO-BEES
CUCKOO-BEES LOOK SIMILAR TO BUMBLE-BEES BUT ARE PARASITES & HAVE NO WORKER CASTE. THEIR FEMALES INVADE TRUE BUMBLE-BEE NESTS TO LAY EGGS WHICH ARE THEN REARED BY BUMBLE-BEE WORKERS.

SEASONS

SPRING
IN THE SPRING YOUNG FERTILISED QUEENS START NEW COLONIES.

SUMMER
IN THE SUMMER MORE & MORE WORKER BEES MATURE UNTIL THE COLONY CONTAINS 100-500 BEES.

AUTUMN
IN THE AUTUMN THE QUEEN HATCHES FERTILE MALES & FEMALES & THESE LEAVE THE COLONY & MATE.

WINTER
IN THE WINTER THE COLONY DIES & ONLY THE FERTILISED QUEENS SURVIVE.

INCUBATION
BUMBLE-BEES INCUBATE THEIR BROODS BY SITTING ON THEM, JUST AS BIRDS SIT ON THEIR EGGS.

SOCIAL & SOLITARY BEES
THE SIZE OF COLONY & DEGREE OF SOCIAL-ISATION OF DIFFERENT SPECIES OF BEE MAY BE RELATED TO THEIR NEST-BUILDING TECHNIQUES. SOLITARY BEES USE MOSTLY MUD FOR THEIR NESTS, ONLY BEES WHICH USE WAX OR WOOD PULP CAN MAKE NESTS STRONG ENOUGH TO SUPPORT LARGE COLONIES.

GARDENERS' FRIEND
BUMBLE-BEES ARE VALUABLE POLLINATORS. THEIR LONG TONGUES CAN REACH THE POLLEN OF MANY FLOWER SPECIES THAT HONEY-BEES CAN NOT REACH.

HOW TO ESCAPE FROM A BEE WHEN CYCLING
AS BUMBLE-BEES FLY AT 11mph MAXIMUM (FASTER THAN MOST OTHER BEES & WASPS), IT IS USUALLY POSSIBLE SIMPLY TO OUTSPRINT THEM, AND ANY BEE OR WASP, WHEN CYCLING.

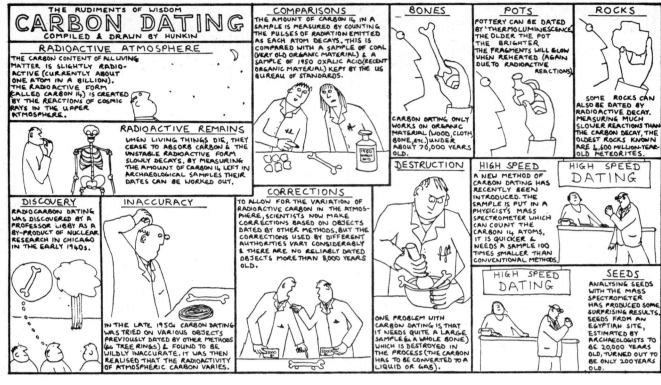

THE RUDIMENTS OF WISDOM
CARBON DATING
COMPILED & DRAWN BY HUNKIN

RADIOACTIVE ATMOSPHERE
THE CARBON CONTENT OF ALL LIVING MATTER IS SLIGHTLY RADIO-ACTIVE (CURRENTLY ABOUT ONE ATOM IN A BILLION). THE RADIOACTIVE FORM (CALLED CARBON 14) IS CREATED BY THE REACTIONS OF COSMIC RAYS IN THE UPPER ATMOSPHERE.

RADIOACTIVE REMAINS
WHEN LIVING THINGS DIE, THEY CEASE TO ABSORB CARBON & THE UNSTABLE RADIOACTIVE FORM SLOWLY DECAYS. BY MEASURING THE AMOUNT OF CARBON 14 LEFT IN ARCHAEOLOGICAL SAMPLES THEIR DATES CAN BE WORKED OUT.

DISCOVERY
RADIOCARBON DATING WAS DISCOVERED BY A PROFESSOR LIBBY AS A BY-PRODUCT OF NUCLEAR RESEARCH IN CHICAGO IN THE EARLY 1940s.

INACCURACY
IN THE LATE 1950s CARBON DATING WAS TRIED ON VARIOUS OBJECTS PREVIOUSLY DATED BY OTHER METHODS (eg TREE RINGS) & FOUND TO BE WILDLY INACCURATE. IT WAS THEN REALISED THAT THE RADIOACTIVITY OF ATMOSPHERIC CARBON VARIES.

COMPARISONS
THE AMOUNT OF CARBON 14 IN A SAMPLE IS MEASURED BY COUNTING THE PULSES OF RADIATION EMITTED AS EACH ATOM DECAYS. THIS IS COMPARED WITH A SAMPLE OF COAL (VERY OLD ORGANIC MATERIAL) & A SAMPLE OF 1950 OXALIC ACID (RECENT ORGANIC MATERIAL) KEPT BY THE US BUREAU OF STANDARDS.

CORRECTIONS
TO ALLOW FOR THE VARIATION OF RADIOACTIVE CARBON IN THE ATMOS-PHERE, SCIENTISTS NOW MAKE CORRECTIONS BASED ON OBJECTS DATED BY OTHER METHODS. BUT THE CORRECTIONS USED BY DIFFERENT AUTHORITIES VARY CONSIDERABLY & THERE ARE NO RELIABLY DATED OBJECTS MORE THAN 8,000 YEARS OLD.

BONES
CARBON DATING ONLY WORKS ON ORGANIC MATERIAL (WOOD, CLOTH, BONE, ETC.) UNDER ABOUT 70,000 YEARS OLD.

DESTRUCTION
ONE PROBLEM WITH CARBON DATING IS THAT IT NEEDS QUITE A LARGE SAMPLE (eg A WHOLE BONE) WHICH IS DESTROYED IN THE PROCESS (THE CARBON HAS TO BE CONVERTED TO A LIQUID OR GAS).

POTS
POTTERY CAN BE DATED BY 'THERMOLUMINESCENCE' THE OLDER THE POT THE BRIGHTER THE FRAGMENTS WILL GLOW WHEN REHEATED (AGAIN DUE TO RADIOACTIVE REACTIONS)

HIGH SPEED
A NEW METHOD OF CARBON DATING HAS RECENTLY BEEN INTRODUCED. THE SAMPLE IS PUT IN A PHYSICIST'S MASS SPECTROMETER WHICH CAN COUNT THE CARBON 14 ATOMS. IT IS QUICKER & NEEDS A SAMPLE 100 TIMES SMALLER THAN CONVENTIONAL METHODS.

HIGH SPEED DATING

ROCKS
SOME ROCKS CAN ALSO BE DATED BY RADIOACTIVE DECAY. MEASURING MUCH SLOWER REACTIONS THAN THE CARBON DECAY, THE OLDEST ROCKS KNOWN ARE 4,600 MILLION-YEAR-OLD METEORITES.

HIGH SPEED DATING

SEEDS
ANALYSING SEEDS WITH THE MASS SPECTROMETER HAS PRODUCED SOME SURPRISING RESULTS. SEEDS FROM AN EGYPTIAN SITE, ESTIMATED BY ARCHAEOLOGISTS TO BE 20,000 YEARS OLD, TURNED OUT TO BE ONLY 200 YEARS OLD.

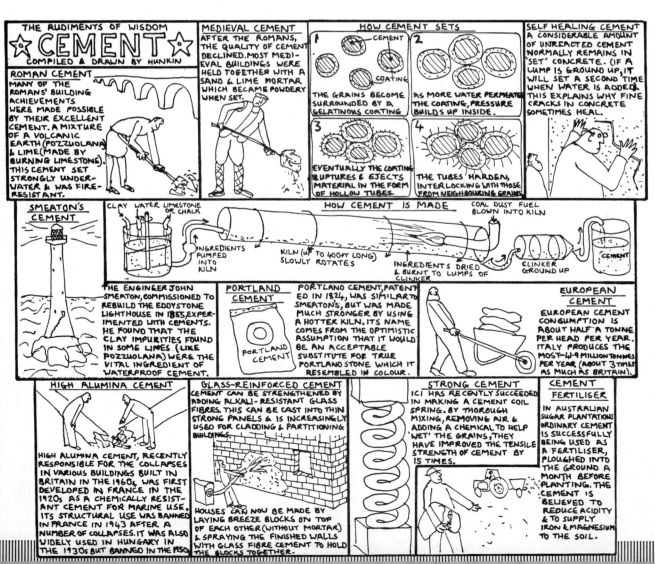

THE RUDIMENTS OF WISDOM
☆ CEMENT ☆
COMPILED & DRAWN BY HUNKIN

ROMAN CEMENT
MANY OF THE ROMANS' BUILDING ACHIEVEMENTS WERE MADE POSSIBLE BY THEIR EXCELLENT CEMENT. A MIXTURE OF A VOLCANIC EARTH (POZZUOLANA) & LIME (MADE BY BURNING LIMESTONE). THIS CEMENT SET STRONGLY UNDER-WATER & WAS FIRE-RESISTANT.

MEDIEVAL CEMENT
AFTER THE ROMANS, THE QUALITY OF CEMENT DECLINED. MOST MEDI-EVAL BUILDINGS WERE HELD TOGETHER WITH A SAND & LIME MORTAR WHICH BECAME POWDERY WHEN SET.

HOW CEMENT SETS
1. THE GRAINS BECOME SURROUNDED BY A GELATINOUS COATING
2. AS MORE WATER PERMEATES THE COATING, PRESSURE BUILDS UP INSIDE.
3. EVENTUALLY THE COATING RUPTURES & EJECTS MATERIAL IN THE FORM OF HOLLOW TUBES.
4. THE TUBES HARDEN, INTERLOCKING WITH THOSE FROM NEIGHBOURING GRAINS.

SELF HEALING CEMENT
A CONSIDERABLE AMOUNT OF UNREACTED CEMENT NORMALLY REMAINS IN 'SET' CONCRETE. (IF A LUMP IS GROUND UP, IT WILL SET A SECOND TIME WHEN WATER IS ADDED.) THIS EXPLAINS WHY FINE CRACKS IN CONCRETE SOMETIMES HEAL.

SMEATON'S CEMENT
THE ENGINEER JOHN SMEATON, COMMISSIONED TO REBUILD THE EDDYSTONE LIGHTHOUSE IN 1855, EXPER-IMENTED WITH CEMENTS. HE FOUND THAT THE CLAY IMPURITIES FOUND IN SOME LIMES (LIKE POZZUOLANA) WERE THE VITAL INGREDIENT OF WATERPROOF CEMENT.

HOW CEMENT IS MADE
CLAY WATER LIMESTONE OR CHALK
INGREDIENTS PUMPED INTO KILN
KILN (UP TO 400FT LONG) SLOWLY ROTATES
COAL DUST FUEL BLOWN INTO KILN
INGREDIENTS DRIED & BURNT TO LUMPS OF CLINKER
CLINKER GROUND UP
CEMENT

PORTLAND CEMENT
PORTLAND CEMENT, PATENT-ED IN 1824, WAS SIMILAR TO SMEATON'S, BUT WAS MADE MUCH STRONGER BY USING A HOTTER KILN. ITS NAME COMES FROM THE OPTIMISTIC ASSUMPTION THAT IT WOULD BE AN ACCEPTABLE SUBSTITUTE FOR TRUE PORTLAND STONE WHICH IT RESEMBLED IN COLOUR.

EUROPEAN CEMENT
EUROPEAN CEMENT CONSUMPTION IS ABOUT HALF A TONNE PER HEAD PER YEAR. ITALY PRODUCES THE MOST—41.9 MILLION TONNES PER YEAR (ABOUT 3 TIMES AS MUCH AS BRITAIN).

HIGH ALUMINA CEMENT
HIGH ALUMINA CEMENT, RECENTLY RESPONSIBLE FOR THE COLLAPSES IN VARIOUS BUILDINGS BUILT IN BRITAIN IN THE 1960s, WAS FIRST DEVELOPED IN FRANCE IN THE 1920s AS A CHEMICALLY RESIST-ANT CEMENT FOR MARINE USE. ITS STRUCTURAL USE WAS BANNED IN FRANCE IN 1943 AFTER A NUMBER OF COLLAPSES. IT WAS ALSO WIDELY USED IN HUNGARY IN THE 1930s BUT BANNED IN THE 1950s

GLASS-REINFORCED CEMENT
CEMENT CAN BE STRENGTHENED BY ADDING ALKALI-RESISTANT GLASS FIBRES. THIS CAN BE CAST INTO THIN STRONG PANELS & IS INCREASINGLY USED FOR CLADDING & PARTITIONING BUILDINGS.
HOUSES CAN NOW BE MADE BY LAYING BREEZE BLOCKS ON TOP OF EACH OTHER (WITHOUT MORTAR) & SPRAYING THE FINISHED WALLS WITH GLASS FIBRE CEMENT TO HOLD THE BLOCKS TOGETHER.

STRONG CEMENT
ICI HAS RECENTLY SUCCEEDED IN MAKING A CEMENT COIL SPRING. BY THOROUGH MIXING, REMOVING AIR & ADDING A CHEMICAL TO HELP 'WET' THE GRAINS, THEY HAVE IMPROVED THE TENSILE STRENGTH OF CEMENT BY 15 TIMES.

CEMENT FERTILISER
IN AUSTRALIAN SUGAR PLANTATIONS ORDINARY CEMENT IS SUCCESSFULLY BEING USED AS A FERTILISER, PLOUGHED INTO THE GROUND A MONTH BEFORE PLANTING. THE CEMENT IS BELIEVED TO REDUCE ACIDITY & TO SUPPLY IRON & MAGNESIUM TO THE SOIL.

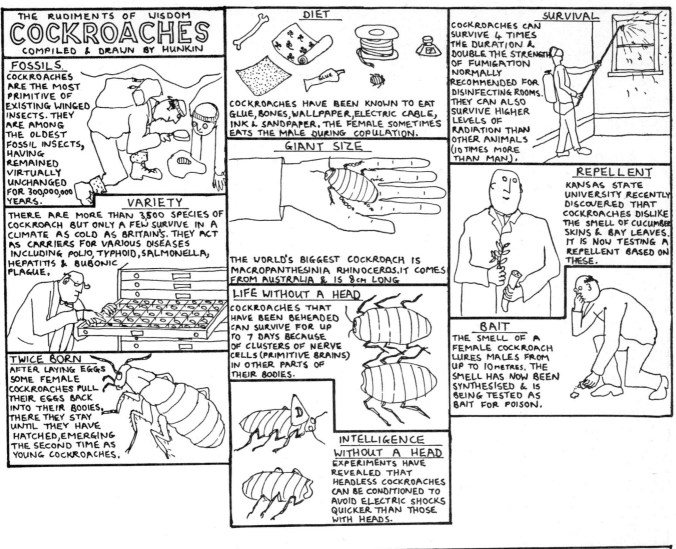

THE RUDIMENTS OF WISDOM
COCKROACHES
COMPILED & DRAWN BY HUNKIN

FOSSILS
COCKROACHES ARE THE MOST PRIMITIVE OF EXISTING WINGED INSECTS. THEY ARE AMONG THE OLDEST FOSSIL INSECTS, HAVING REMAINED VIRTUALLY UNCHANGED FOR 300,000,000 YEARS.

VARIETY
THERE ARE MORE THAN 3,500 SPECIES OF COCKROACH BUT ONLY A FEW SURVIVE IN A CLIMATE AS COLD AS BRITAIN'S. THEY ACT AS CARRIERS FOR VARIOUS DISEASES INCLUDING POLIO, TYPHOID, SALMONELLA, HEPATITIS & BUBONIC PLAGUE.

TWICE BORN
AFTER LAYING EGGS SOME FEMALE COCKROACHES PULL THEIR EGGS BACK INTO THEIR BODIES. THERE THEY STAY UNTIL THEY HAVE HATCHED, EMERGING THE SECOND TIME AS YOUNG COCKROACHES.

DIET
COCKROACHES HAVE BEEN KNOWN TO EAT GLUE, BONES, WALLPAPER, ELECTRIC CABLE, INK & SANDPAPER. THE FEMALE SOMETIMES EATS THE MALE DURING COPULATION.

GIANT SIZE
THE WORLD'S BIGGEST COCKROACH IS MACROPANTHESINIA RHINOCEROS. IT COMES FROM AUSTRALIA & IS 8CM LONG

LIFE WITHOUT A HEAD
COCKROACHES THAT HAVE BEEN BEHEADED CAN SURVIVE FOR UP TO 7 DAYS BECAUSE OF CLUSTERS OF NERVE CELLS (PRIMITIVE BRAINS) IN OTHER PARTS OF THEIR BODIES.

INTELLIGENCE WITHOUT A HEAD
EXPERIMENTS HAVE REVEALED THAT HEADLESS COCKROACHES CAN BE CONDITIONED TO AVOID ELECTRIC SHOCKS QUICKER THAN THOSE WITH HEADS.

SURVIVAL
COCKROACHES CAN SURVIVE 4 TIMES THE DURATION & DOUBLE THE STRENGTH OF FUMIGATION NORMALLY RECOMMENDED FOR DISINFECTING ROOMS. THEY CAN ALSO SURVIVE HIGHER LEVELS OF RADIATION THAN OTHER ANIMALS (10 TIMES MORE THAN MAN).

REPELLENT
KANSAS STATE UNIVERSITY RECENTLY DISCOVERED THAT COCKROACHES DISLIKE THE SMELL OF CUCUMBER SKINS & BAY LEAVES. IT IS NOW TESTING A REPELLENT BASED ON THESE.

BAIT
THE SMELL OF A FEMALE COCKROACH LURES MALES FROM UP TO 10 METRES. THE SMELL HAS NOW BEEN SYNTHESISED & IS BEING TESTED AS BAIT FOR POISON.

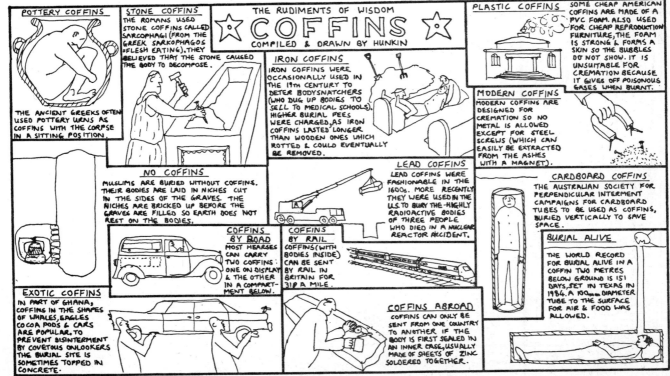

THE RUDIMENTS OF WISDOM
☆ COFFINS ☆
COMPILED & DRAWN BY HUNKIN

POTTERY COFFINS
THE ANCIENT GREEKS OFTEN USED POTTERY URNS AS COFFINS WITH THE CORPSE IN A SITTING POSITION.

STONE COFFINS
THE ROMANS USED STONE COFFINS CALLED SARCOPHAGI (FROM THE GREEK SARKOPHAGOS =FLESH EATING). THEY BELIEVED THAT THE STONE CAUSED THE BODY TO DECOMPOSE.

IRON COFFINS
IRON COFFINS WERE OCCASIONALLY USED IN THE 19TH CENTURY TO DETER BODYSNATCHERS (WHO DUG UP BODIES TO SELL TO MEDICAL SCHOOLS). HIGHER BURIAL FEES WERE CHARGED, AS IRON COFFINS LASTED LONGER THAN WOODEN ONES WHICH ROTTED & COULD EVENTUALLY BE REMOVED.

NO COFFINS
MUSLIMS ARE BURIED WITHOUT COFFINS. THEIR BODIES ARE LAID IN NICHES CUT IN THE SIDES OF THE GRAVES. THE NICHES ARE BRICKED UP BEFORE THE GRAVES ARE FILLED SO EARTH DOES NOT REST ON THE BODIES.

COFFINS BY ROAD
MOST HEARSES CAN CARRY TWO COFFINS, ONE ON DISPLAY & THE OTHER IN A COMPARTMENT BELOW.

COFFINS BY RAIL
COFFINS (WITH BODIES INSIDE) CAN BE SENT BY RAIL IN BRITAIN FOR 31P A MILE.

LEAD COFFINS
LEAD COFFINS WERE FASHIONABLE IN THE 1600s. MORE RECENTLY THEY WERE USED IN THE U.S. TO BURY THE HIGHLY RADIOACTIVE BODIES OF THREE PEOPLE WHO DIED IN A NUCLEAR REACTOR ACCIDENT.

EXOTIC COFFINS
IN PART OF GHANA, COFFINS IN THE SHAPES OF WHALES, EAGLES, COCOA PODS & CARS ARE POPULAR. TO PREVENT DISINTERMENT BY COVETOUS ONLOOKERS THE BURIAL SITE IS SOMETIMES TOPPED IN CONCRETE.

COFFINS ABROAD
COFFINS CAN ONLY BE SENT FROM ONE COUNTRY TO ANOTHER IF THE BODY IS FIRST SEALED IN AN INNER CASE, USUALLY MADE OF SHEETS OF ZINC SOLDERED TOGETHER.

PLASTIC COFFINS
SOME CHEAP AMERICAN COFFINS ARE MADE OF A PVC FOAM. ALSO USED FOR CHEAP REPRODUCTION FURNITURE, THE FOAM IS STRONG & FORMS A SKIN SO THE BUBBLES DO NOT SHOW. IT IS UNSUITABLE FOR CREMATION BECAUSE IT GIVES OFF POISONOUS GASES WHEN BURNT.

MODERN COFFINS
MODERN COFFINS ARE DESIGNED FOR CREMATION SO NO METAL IS ALLOWED EXCEPT FOR STEEL SCREWS (WHICH CAN EASILY BE EXTRACTED FROM THE ASHES WITH A MAGNET).

CARDBOARD COFFINS
THE AUSTRALIAN SOCIETY FOR PERPENDICULAR INTERMENT CAMPAIGNS FOR CARDBOARD TUBES TO BE USED AS COFFINS, BURIED VERTICALLY TO SAVE SPACE.

BURIAL ALIVE
THE WORLD RECORD FOR BURIAL ALIVE IN A COFFIN TWO METRES BELOW GROUND IS 151 DAYS, SET IN TEXAS IN 1984. A 100mm DIAMETER TUBE TO THE SURFACE FOR AIR & FOOD WAS ALLOWED.

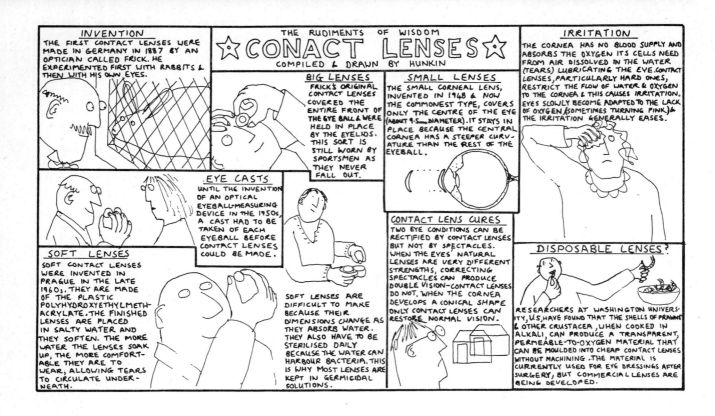

THE RUDIMENTS OF WISDOM
☆ CONACT LENSES ☆
COMPILED & DRAWN BY HUNKIN

INVENTION
THE FIRST CONTACT LENSES WERE MADE IN GERMANY IN 1887 BY AN OPTICIAN CALLED FRICK. HE EXPERIMENTED FIRST WITH RABBITS & THEN WITH HIS OWN EYES.

BIG LENSES
FRICK'S ORIGINAL CONTACT LENSES COVERED THE ENTIRE FRONT OF THE EYE BALL & WERE HELD IN PLACE BY THE EYELIDS. THIS SORT IS STILL WORN BY SPORTSMEN AS THEY NEVER FALL OUT.

SMALL LENSES
THE SMALL CORNEAL LENS, INVENTED IN 1948 & NOW THE COMMONEST TYPE, COVERS ONLY THE CENTRE OF THE EYE (ABOUT 9.5mm DIAMETER). IT STAYS IN PLACE BECAUSE THE CENTRAL CORNEA HAS A STEEPER CURVATURE THAN THE REST OF THE EYEBALL.

IRRITATION
THE CORNEA HAS NO BLOOD SUPPLY AND ABSORBS THE OXYGEN ITS CELLS NEED FROM AIR DISSOLVED IN THE WATER (TEARS) LUBRICATING THE EYE. CONTACT LENSES, PARTICULARLY HARD ONES, RESTRICT THE FLOW OF WATER & OXYGEN TO THE CORNEA & THIS CAUSES IRRITATION. EYES SLOWLY BECOME ADAPTED TO THE LACK OF OXYGEN (SOMETIMES TURNING PINK) & THE IRRITATION GENERALLY EASES.

EYE CASTS
UNTIL THE INVENTION OF AN OPTICAL EYEBALL-MEASURING DEVICE IN THE 1950s, A CAST HAD TO BE TAKEN OF EACH EYEBALL BEFORE CONTACT LENSES COULD BE MADE.

SOFT LENSES
SOFT CONTACT LENSES WERE INVENTED IN PRAGUE IN THE LATE 1960s. THEY ARE MADE OF THE PLASTIC POLYHYDROXYETHYLMETHACRYLATE. THE FINISHED LENSES ARE PLACED IN SALTY WATER AND THEY SOFTEN. THE MORE WATER THE LENSES SOAK UP, THE MORE COMFORTABLE THEY ARE TO WEAR, ALLOWING TEARS TO CIRCULATE UNDERNEATH.

SOFT LENSES ARE DIFFICULT TO MAKE BECAUSE THEIR DIMENSIONS CHANGE AS THEY ABSORB WATER. THEY ALSO HAVE TO BE STERILISED DAILY BECAUSE THE WATER CAN HARBOUR BACTERIA. THIS IS WHY MOST LENSES ARE KEPT IN GERMICIDAL SOLUTIONS.

CONTACT LENS CURES
TWO EYE CONDITIONS CAN BE RECTIFIED BY CONTACT LENSES BUT NOT BY SPECTACLES. WHEN THE EYES' NATURAL LENSES ARE VERY DIFFERENT STRENGTHS, CORRECTING SPECTACLES CAN PRODUCE DOUBLE VISION—CONTACT LENSES DO NOT. WHEN THE CORNEA DEVELOPS A CONICAL SHAPE ONLY CONTACT LENSES CAN RESTORE NORMAL VISION.

DISPOSABLE LENSES?
RESEARCHERS AT WASHINGTON UNIVERSITY, U.S. HAVE FOUND THAT THE SHELLS OF PRAWNS & OTHER CRUSTACEA, WHEN COOKED IN ALKALI, CAN PRODUCE A TRANSPARENT, PERMEABLE-TO-OXYGEN MATERIAL THAT CAN BE MOULDED INTO CHEAP CONTACT LENSES WITHOUT MACHINING. THE MATERIAL IS CURRENTLY USED FOR EYE DRESSINGS AFTER SURGERY, BUT COMMERCIAL LENSES ARE BEING DEVELOPED.

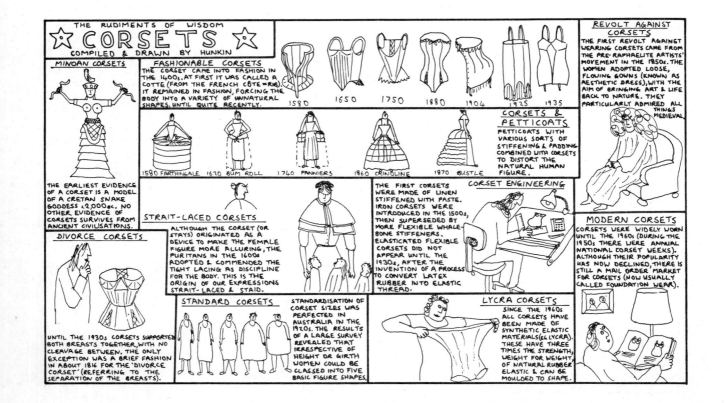

THE RUDIMENTS OF WISDOM
☆ CORSETS ☆
COMPILED & DRAWN BY HUNKIN

MINOAN CORSETS

FASHIONABLE CORSETS
THE CORSET CAME INTO FASHION IN THE 1400s. AT FIRST IT WAS CALLED A COTTE (FROM THE FRENCH CÔTE = RIB). IT REMAINED IN FASHION, FORCING THE BODY INTO A VARIETY OF UNNATURAL SHAPES, UNTIL QUITE RECENTLY.

1580   1650   1750   1880   1904   1925   1935

REVOLT AGAINST CORSETS
THE FIRST REVOLT AGAINST WEARING CORSETS CAME FROM THE PRE-RAPHAELITE ARTISTS' MOVEMENT IN THE 1850s. THE WOMEN ADOPTED LOOSE, FLOWING GOWNS (KNOWN AS AESTHETIC DRESS), WITH THE AIM OF BRINGING ART & LIFE BACK TO NATURE. THEY PARTICULARLY ADMIRED ALL THINGS MEDIEVAL.

THE EARLIEST EVIDENCE OF A CORSET IS A MODEL OF A CRETAN SNAKE GODDESS c.2,000BC. NO OTHER EVIDENCE OF CORSETS SURVIVES FROM ANCIENT CIVILISATIONS.

1580 FARTHINGALE   1620 BUM ROLL   1740 PANNIERS   1860 CRINOLINE   1870 BUSTLE

CORSETS & PETTICOATS
PETTICOATS WITH VARIOUS SORTS OF STIFFENING & PADDING COMBINED WITH CORSETS TO DISTORT THE NATURAL HUMAN FIGURE.

DIVORCE CORSETS

STRAIT-LACED CORSETS
ALTHOUGH THE CORSET (OR STAYS) ORIGINATED AS A DEVICE TO MAKE THE FEMALE FIGURE MORE ALLURING, THE PURITANS IN THE 1600s ADOPTED & COMMENDED THE TIGHT LACING AS DISCIPLINE FOR THE BODY. THIS IS THE ORIGIN OF OUR EXPRESSIONS STRAIT-LACED AND STAID.

CORSET ENGINEERING
THE FIRST CORSETS WERE MADE OF LINEN STIFFENED WITH PASTE. IRON CORSETS WERE INTRODUCED IN THE 1500s, THEN SUPERSEDED BY MORE FLEXIBLE WHALEBONE STIFFENERS. ELASTICATED FLEXIBLE CORSETS DID NOT APPEAR UNTIL THE 1930s, AFTER THE INVENTION OF A PROCESS TO CONVERT LATEX RUBBER INTO ELASTIC THREAD.

MODERN CORSETS
CORSETS WERE WIDELY WORN UNTIL THE 1960s (DURING THE 1950s THERE WERE ANNUAL NATIONAL CORSET WEEKS). ALTHOUGH THEIR POPULARITY HAS NOW DECLINED, THERE IS STILL A MAIL ORDER MARKET FOR CORSETS (NOW USUALLY CALLED FOUNDATION WEAR).

UNTIL THE 1930s CORSETS SUPPORTED BOTH BREASTS TOGETHER, WITH NO CLEAVAGE BETWEEN. THE ONLY EXCEPTION WAS A BRIEF FASHION IN ABOUT 1816 FOR THE 'DIVORCE CORSET' (REFERRING TO THE SEPARATION OF THE BREASTS).

STANDARD CORSETS
STANDARDISATION OF CORSET SIZES WAS PERFECTED IN AUSTRALIA IN THE 1920s. THE RESULTS OF A LARGE SURVEY REVEALED THAT IRRESPECTIVE OF HEIGHT OR GIRTH WOMEN COULD BE CLASSED INTO FIVE BASIC FIGURE SHAPES.

LYCRA CORSETS
SINCE THE 1960s ALL CORSETS HAVE BEEN MADE OF SYNTHETIC ELASTIC MATERIALS (e.g. LYCRA). THESE HAVE THREE TIMES THE STRENGTH, WEIGHT FOR WEIGHT, OF NATURAL RUBBER ELASTIC & CAN BE MOULDED TO SHAPE.

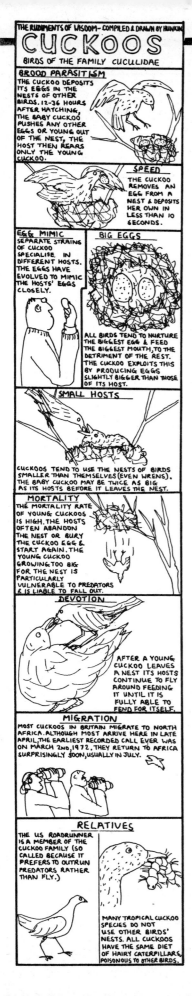

THE RUDIMENTS OF WISDOM – COMPILED & DRAWN BY HUNKIN
CUCKOOS
BIRDS OF THE FAMILY CUCULIDAE

BROOD PARASITISM
THE CUCKOO DEPOSITS ITS EGGS IN THE NESTS OF OTHER BIRDS. 12-36 HOURS AFTER HATCHING, THE BABY CUCKOO PUSHES ANY OTHER EGGS OR YOUNG OUT OF THE NEST, THE HOST THEN REARS ONLY THE YOUNG CUCKOO.

SPEED
THE CUCKOO REMOVES AN EGG FROM A NEST & DEPOSITS HER OWN IN LESS THAN 10 SECONDS.

EGG MIMIC
SEPARATE STRAINS OF CUCKOO SPECIALISE IN DIFFERENT HOSTS. THE EGGS HAVE EVOLVED TO MIMIC THE HOSTS' EGGS CLOSELY.

BIG EGGS
ALL BIRDS TEND TO NURTURE THE BIGGEST EGG & FEED THE BIGGEST MOUTH, TO THE DETRIMENT OF THE REST. THE CUCKOO EXPLOITS THIS BY PRODUCING EGGS SLIGHTLY BIGGER THAN THOSE OF ITS HOST.

SMALL HOSTS
CUCKOOS TEND TO USE THE NESTS OF BIRDS SMALLER THAN THEMSELVES (EVEN WRENS). THE BABY CUCKOO MAY BE TWICE AS BIG AS ITS HOSTS BEFORE IT LEAVES THE NEST.

MORTALITY
THE MORTALITY RATE OF YOUNG CUCKOOS IS HIGH. AS THE HOSTS OFTEN ABANDON THE NEST OR BURY THE CUCKOO EGG & START AGAIN. THE YOUNG CUCKOO GROWING TOO BIG FOR THE NEST IS PARTICULARLY VULNERABLE TO PREDATORS & IS LIABLE TO FALL OUT.

DEVOTION
AFTER A YOUNG CUCKOO LEAVES A NEST ITS HOSTS CONTINUE TO FLY AROUND FEEDING IT UNTIL IT IS FULLY ABLE TO FEND FOR ITSELF.

MIGRATION
MOST CUCKOOS IN BRITAIN MIGRATE TO NORTH AFRICA. ALTHOUGH MOST ARRIVE HERE IN LATE APRIL, THE EARLIEST RECORDED CALL EVER WAS ON MARCH 2ND, 1972, THEY RETURN TO AFRICA SURPRISINGLY SOON, USUALLY IN JULY.

RELATIVES
THE US ROADRUNNER IS A MEMBER OF THE CUCKOO FAMILY (SO CALLED BECAUSE IT PREFERS TO OUTRUN PREDATORS RATHER THAN FLY.)

MANY TROPICAL CUCKOO SPECIES DO NOT USE OTHER BIRDS' NESTS. ALL CUCKOOS HAVE THE SAME DIET OF HAIRY CATERPILLARS, POISONOUS TO OTHER BIRDS.

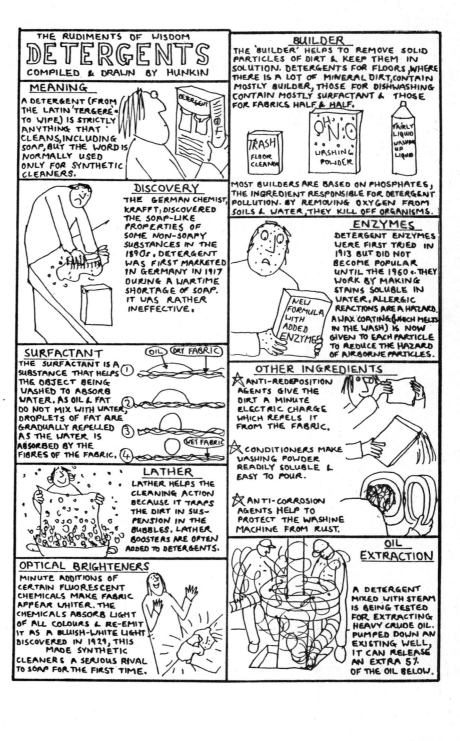

THE RUDIMENTS OF WISDOM
DETERGENTS
COMPILED & DRAWN BY HUNKIN

MEANING
A DETERGENT (FROM THE LATIN 'TERGERE = TO WIPE') IS STRICTLY ANYTHING THAT CLEANS, INCLUDING SOAP, BUT THE WORD IS NORMALLY USED ONLY FOR SYNTHETIC CLEANERS.

DISCOVERY
THE GERMAN CHEMIST, KRAFFT, DISCOVERED THE SOAP-LIKE PROPERTIES OF SOME NON-SOAPY SUBSTANCES IN THE 1890s. DETERGENT WAS FIRST MARKETED IN GERMANY IN 1917 DURING A WARTIME SHORTAGE OF SOAP. IT WAS RATHER INEFFECTIVE.

SURFACTANT
THE SURFACTANT IS A SUBSTANCE THAT HELPS THE OBJECT BEING WASHED TO ABSORB WATER. AS OIL & FAT DO NOT MIX WITH WATER, DROPLETS OF FAT ARE GRADUALLY REPELLED AS THE WATER IS ABSORBED BY THE FIBRES OF THE FABRIC.

OIL — DRY FABRIC
WET FABRIC

LATHER
LATHER HELPS THE CLEANING ACTION BECAUSE IT TRAPS THE DIRT IN SUSPENSION IN THE BUBBLES. LATHER BOOSTERS ARE OFTEN ADDED TO DETERGENTS.

OPTICAL BRIGHTENERS
MINUTE ADDITIONS OF CERTAIN FLUORESCENT CHEMICALS MAKE FABRIC APPEAR WHITER. THE CHEMICALS ABSORB LIGHT OF ALL COLOURS & RE-EMIT IT AS A BLUISH-WHITE LIGHT DISCOVERED IN 1929, THIS MADE SYNTHETIC CLEANERS A SERIOUS RIVAL TO SOAP FOR THE FIRST TIME.

BUILDER
THE 'BUILDER' HELPS TO REMOVE SOLID PARTICLES OF DIRT & KEEP THEM IN SOLUTION. DETERGENTS FOR FLOORS, WHERE THERE IS A LOT OF MINERAL DIRT, CONTAIN MOSTLY BUILDER, THOSE FOR DISHWASHING CONTAIN MOSTLY SURFACTANT & THOSE FOR FABRICS HALF & HALF.

TRASH FLOOR CLEANER
WASHING POWDER
FAIRLY LIQUID WASHING UP LIQUID

MOST BUILDERS ARE BASED ON PHOSPHATES, THE INGREDIENT RESPONSIBLE FOR DETERGENT POLLUTION. BY REMOVING OXYGEN FROM SOILS & WATER, THEY KILL OFF ORGANISMS.

ENZYMES
DETERGENT ENZYMES WERE FIRST TRIED IN 1913 BUT DID NOT BECOME POPULAR UNTIL THE 1960s. THEY WORK BY MAKING STAINS SOLUBLE IN WATER. ALLERGIC REACTIONS ARE A HAZARD. A WAX COATING (WHICH MELTS IN THE WASH) IS NOW GIVEN TO EACH PARTICLE TO REDUCE THE HAZARD OF AIRBORNE PARTICLES.

NEW FORMULA WITH ADDED ENZYMES

OTHER INGREDIENTS
☆ ANTI-REDEPOSITION AGENTS GIVE THE DIRT A MINUTE ELECTRIC CHARGE WHICH REPELS IT FROM THE FABRIC.

☆ CONDITIONERS MAKE WASHING POWDER READILY SOLUBLE & EASY TO POUR.

☆ ANTI-CORROSION AGENTS HELP TO PROTECT THE WASHING MACHINE FROM RUST.

OIL EXTRACTION
A DETERGENT MIXED WITH STEAM IS BEING TESTED FOR EXTRACTING HEAVY CRUDE OIL. PUMPED DOWN AN EXISTING WELL, IT CAN RELEASE AN EXTRA 5% OF THE OIL BELOW.

THE RUDIMENTS OF WISDOM
DOMESTICATED ANIMALS
COMPILED & DRAWN BY HUNKIN

DOMESTICATED EVOLUTION

DOMESTICATION REMOVES THE PRESSURE OF NATURAL SELECTION FROM THE EVOLUTION OF ANY ANIMAL. BESIDES CHARACTERISTICS DELIBERATELY INBRED, ALL DOMESTICATED ANIMALS TEND TO CHANGE IN CERTAIN SIMILAR WAYS:

REDUCTION IN TAUTNESS OF SKIN: FLABBY NECKS, DROOPING EARS ETC.

DOMESTICATED   WILD

MOTTLED & PIEBALD PATTERNING NOT KNOWN IN WILD ANIMALS.

SHORTENING OF SKELETAL STRUCTURES, PARTICULARLY NECK & LEGS.

RETENTION OF JUVENILE CHARACTERISTICS, LIKE THE SHAPE OF THE SKULL.

DOGS
DOGS WERE DOMESTICATED SEVERAL THOUSAND YEARS BEFORE ANY OTHER ANIMAL & BEFORE MAN SETTLED DOWN INTO AGRICULTURAL COMMUNITIES.

MAN'S RELATIONSHIP WITH DOGS IS THOUGHT TO HAVE STARTED WITH WILD DOGS SCAVENGING SCRAPS LEFT BY HUMANS & HUMANS ACCEPTING THE DOGS SIMPLY AS PETS.

PRIMITIVE PET-KEEPING
SOME ABORIGINES TIE UP YOUNG DINGOS, WALLABIES, RATS & EVEN FROGS IN THEIR CAMPS. THE ANIMALS ARE NOT REGULARLY FED & OFTEN DIE, BUT SOME LEARN TO FEND FOR THEMSELVES IN THE CAMP & STAY WHEN THEY ARE RELEASED AS ADULTS.

REINDEER
IT IS THOUGHT THAT REINDEER WERE ATTRACTED TO HUMAN CAMPS BY THE SALT IN HUMAN URINE. MEN CAPTURED & TAMED YOUNG DEER AS DECOYS TO ATTRACT THE WILD DEER THEY HUNTED.

HYENAS
SOME ANIMALS ARE NO LONGER DOMESTICATED. THE ANCIENT EGYPTIANS KEPT HYENAS & EARLY SWISS LAKE-DWELLERS KEPT FOXES.

HERD DOMESTICATION
HERD ANIMALS, USED TO BEING SOCIABLE TO EACH OTHER, ARE MORE READILY SOCIABLE TO OTHER ANIMAL SPECIES. ALL BUT ONE OF OUR FAMILIAR DOMESTIC ANIMALS WERE ORIGINALLY HERD ANIMALS, THE EXCEPTION BEING THE CAT.

CATS
THE CATS WHICH FIRST CAME INTO CONTACT WITH HUMANS WERE SMALL WILD CATS WHICH HUNTED AROUND GRANARIES IN THE MIDDLE EAST (10,000BC). THEY BECAME A SACRED ANIMAL TO THE ANCIENT EGYPTIANS & WERE FED AT THEIR TEMPLES. THE EXPORT OF DOMESTICATED CATS WAS BANNED & NONE REACHED THE OUTSIDE WORLD UNTIL ABOUT 300BC.

LIONS
LION TAMERS PREFER TO USE WILD LIONS, CAUGHT & TRAINED WHEN ADULTS. THEY RETAIN A FEAR OF MAN WHICH MAKES THEM SAFER TO HANDLE THAN LIONS BORN & BRED IN CAPTIVITY.

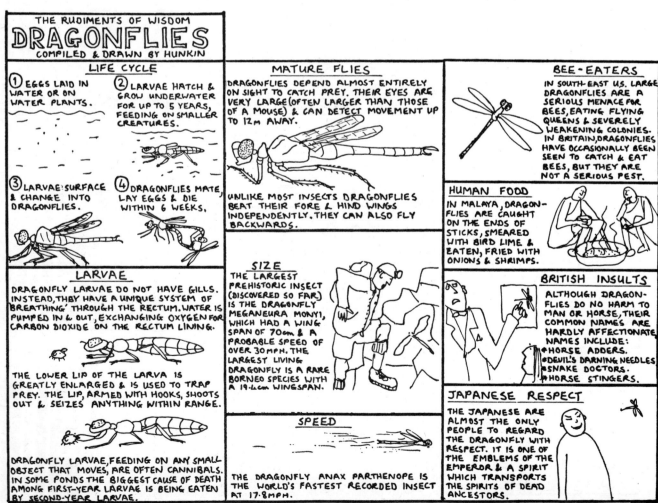

THE RUDIMENTS OF WISDOM
DRAGONFLIES
COMPILED & DRAWN BY HUNKIN

LIFE CYCLE
① EGGS LAID IN WATER OR ON WATER PLANTS.

② LARVAE HATCH & GROW UNDERWATER FOR UP TO 5 YEARS, FEEDING ON SMALLER CREATURES.

③ LARVAE SURFACE & CHANGE INTO DRAGONFLIES.

④ DRAGONFLIES MATE, LAY EGGS & DIE WITHIN 6 WEEKS.

LARVAE
DRAGONFLY LARVAE DO NOT HAVE GILLS. INSTEAD, THEY HAVE A UNIQUE SYSTEM OF 'BREATHING' THROUGH THE RECTUM. WATER IS PUMPED IN & OUT, EXCHANGING OXYGEN FOR CARBON DIOXIDE ON THE RECTUM LINING.

THE LOWER LIP OF THE LARVA IS GREATLY ENLARGED & IS USED TO TRAP PREY. THE LIP, ARMED WITH HOOKS, SHOOTS OUT & SEIZES ANYTHING WITHIN RANGE.

DRAGONFLY LARVAE, FEEDING ON ANY SMALL OBJECT THAT MOVES, ARE OFTEN CANNIBALS. IN SOME PONDS THE BIGGEST CAUSE OF DEATH AMONG FIRST-YEAR LARVAE IS BEING EATEN BY SECOND-YEAR LARVAE.

MATURE FLIES
DRAGONFLIES DEPEND ALMOST ENTIRELY ON SIGHT TO CATCH PREY. THEIR EYES ARE VERY LARGE (OFTEN LARGER THAN THOSE OF A MOUSE) & CAN DETECT MOVEMENT UP TO 12m AWAY.

UNLIKE MOST INSECTS DRAGONFLIES BEAT THEIR FORE & HIND WINGS INDEPENDENTLY. THEY CAN ALSO FLY BACKWARDS.

SIZE
THE LARGEST PREHISTORIC INSECT (DISCOVERED SO FAR) IS THE DRAGONFLY MEGANEURA MONYI, WHICH HAD A WING SPAN OF 70cm & A PROBABLE SPEED OF OVER 30 MPH. THE LARGEST LIVING DRAGONFLY IS A RARE BORNEO SPECIES WITH A 19.4cm WINGSPAN.

SPEED
THE DRAGONFLY ANAX PARTHENOPE IS THE WORLD'S FASTEST RECORDED INSECT AT 17.8 MPH.

BEE-EATERS
IN SOUTH-EAST U.S. LARGE DRAGONFLIES ARE A SERIOUS MENACE FOR BEES, EATING FLYING QUEENS & SEVERELY WEAKENING COLONIES. IN BRITAIN, DRAGONFLIES HAVE OCCASIONALLY BEEN SEEN TO CATCH & EAT BEES, BUT THEY ARE NOT A SERIOUS PEST.

HUMAN FOOD
IN MALAYA, DRAGONFLIES ARE CAUGHT ON THE ENDS OF STICKS, SMEARED WITH BIRD LIME & EATEN, FRIED WITH ONIONS & SHRIMPS.

BRITISH INSULTS
ALTHOUGH DRAGONFLIES DO NO HARM TO MAN OR HORSE, THEIR COMMON NAMES ARE HARDLY AFFECTIONATE. NAMES INCLUDE:
+ HORSE ADDERS.
+ DEVIL'S DARNING NEEDLES.
+ SNAKE DOCTORS.
+ HORSE STINGERS.

JAPANESE RESPECT
THE JAPANESE ARE ALMOST THE ONLY PEOPLE TO REGARD THE DRAGONFLY WITH RESPECT. IT IS ONE OF THE EMBLEMS OF THE EMPEROR & A SPIRIT WHICH TRANSPORTS THE SPIRITS OF DEAD ANCESTORS.

THE RUDIMENTS OF WISDOM
DRINKING WATER
COMPILED & DRAWN BY HUNKIN

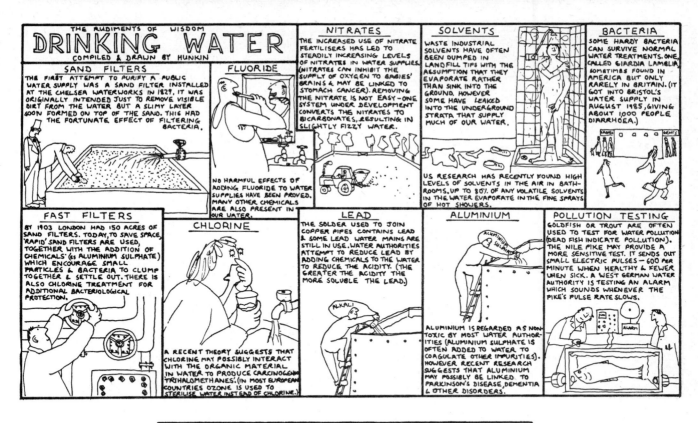

SAND FILTERS
THE FIRST ATTEMPT TO PURIFY A PUBLIC WATER SUPPLY WAS A SAND FILTER INSTALLED AT THE CHELSEA WATERWORKS IN 1827. IT WAS ORIGINALLY INTENDED JUST TO REMOVE VISIBLE DIRT FROM THE WATER BUT A SLIMY LAYER SOON FORMED ON TOP OF THE SAND. THIS HAD THE FORTUNATE EFFECT OF FILTERING BACTERIA.

FLUORIDE
NO HARMFUL EFFECTS OF ADDING FLUORIDE TO WATER SUPPLIES HAVE BEEN PROVED. MANY OTHER CHEMICALS ARE ALSO PRESENT IN OUR WATER.

NITRATES
THE INCREASED USE OF NITRATE FERTILISERS HAS LED TO STEADILY INCREASING LEVELS OF NITRATES IN WATER SUPPLIES. (NITRATES CAN INHIBIT THE SUPPLY OF OXYGEN TO BABIES' BRAINS & MAY BE LINKED TO STOMACH CANCER). REMOVING THE NITRATE IS NOT EASY – ONE SYSTEM UNDER DEVELOPMENT CONVERTS THE NITRATES TO BICARBONATES, RESULTING IN SLIGHTLY FIZZY WATER.

SOLVENTS
WASTE INDUSTRIAL SOLVENTS HAVE OFTEN BEEN DUMPED IN LANDFILL TIPS WITH THE ASSUMPTION THAT THEY EVAPORATE RATHER THAN SINK INTO THE GROUND. HOWEVER SOME HAVE LEAKED INTO THE UNDERGROUND STRATA THAT SUPPLY MUCH OF OUR WATER.

US RESEARCH HAS RECENTLY FOUND HIGH LEVELS OF SOLVENTS IN THE AIR IN BATHROOMS. UP TO 80% OF ANY VOLATILE SOLVENTS IN THE WATER EVAPORATE IN THE FINE SPRAYS OF HOT SHOWERS.

BACTERIA
SOME HARDY BACTERIA CAN SURVIVE NORMAL WATER TREATMENTS. ONE, CALLED GIARDIA LAMBLIA, SOMETIMES FOUND IN AMERICA BUT ONLY RARELY IN BRITAIN. (IT GOT INTO BRISTOL'S WATER SUPPLY IN AUGUST 1985, GIVING ABOUT 1,000 PEOPLE DIARRHOEA.)

FAST FILTERS
BY 1903 LONDON HAD 150 ACRES OF SAND FILTERS. TODAY, TO SAVE SPACE, 'RAPID' SAND FILTERS ARE USED, TOGETHER WITH THE ADDITION OF CHEMICALS (AS ALUMINIUM SULPHATE) WHICH ENCOURAGE SMALL PARTICLES & BACTERIA TO CLUMP TOGETHER & SETTLE OUT. THERE IS ALSO CHLORINE TREATMENT FOR ADDITIONAL BACTERIOLOGICAL PROTECTION.

CHLORINE
A RECENT THEORY SUGGESTS THAT CHLORINE MAY POSSIBLY INTERACT WITH THE ORGANIC MATERIAL IN WATER TO PRODUCE CARCINOGENIC TRIHALOMETHANES. (IN MOST EUROPEAN COUNTRIES OZONE IS USED TO STERILISE WATER INSTEAD OF CHLORINE.)

LEAD
THE SOLDER USED TO JOIN COPPER PIPES CONTAINS LEAD & SOME LEAD WATER MAINS ARE STILL IN USE. WATER AUTHORITIES ATTEMPT TO REDUCE LEAD BY ADDING CHEMICALS TO THE WATER TO REDUCE THE ACIDITY. (THE GREATER THE ACIDITY THE MORE SOLUBLE THE LEAD.)

ALUMINIUM
ALUMINIUM IS REGARDED AS NON-TOXIC BY MOST WATER AUTHORITIES (ALUMINIUM SULPHATE IS OFTEN ADDED TO WATER TO COAGULATE OTHER IMPURITIES). HOWEVER RECENT RESEARCH SUGGESTS THAT ALUMINIUM MAY POSSIBLY BE LINKED TO PARKINSON'S DISEASE, DEMENTIA & OTHER DISORDERS.

POLLUTION TESTING
GOLDFISH OR TROUT ARE OFTEN USED TO TEST FOR WATER POLLUTION (DEAD FISH INDICATE POLLUTION). THE NILE PIKE MAY PROVIDE A MORE SENSITIVE TEST. IT SENDS OUT SMALL ELECTRIC PULSES – 600 PER MINUTE WHEN HEALTHY & FEWER WHEN SICK. A WEST GERMAN WATER AUTHORITY IS TESTING AN ALARM WHICH SOUNDS WHENEVER THE PIKE'S PULSE RATE SLOWS.

THE RUDIMENTS OF WISDOM
ELECTRICAL POLLUTION
COMPILED & DRAWN BY HUNKIN

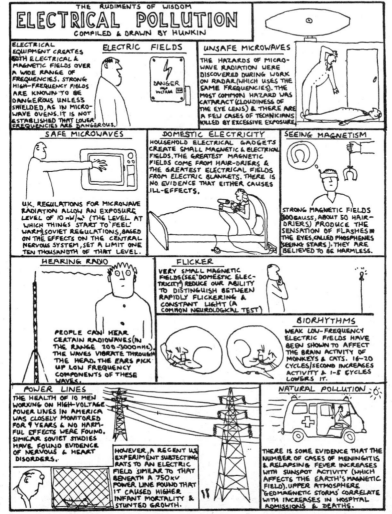

ELECTRICAL EQUIPMENT CREATES BOTH ELECTRICAL & MAGNETIC FIELDS OVER A WIDE RANGE OF FREQUENCIES. STRONG HIGH-FREQUENCY FIELDS ARE KNOWN TO BE DANGEROUS UNLESS SHIELDED, AS IN MICRO-WAVE OVENS. IT IS NOT ESTABLISHED THAT LOWER FREQUENCIES ARE DANGEROUS.

ELECTRIC FIELDS
DANGER HIGH VOLTAGE

UNSAFE MICROWAVES
THE HAZARDS OF MICRO-WAVE RADIATION WERE DISCOVERED DURING WORK ON RADAR (WHICH USES THE SAME FREQUENCIES). THE MOST COMMON HAZARD WAS CATARACT (CLOUDINESS OF THE EYE LENS) & THERE ARE A FEW CASES OF TECHNICIANS KILLED BY EXCESSIVE EXPOSURE.

SAFE MICROWAVES
U.K. REGULATIONS FOR MICROWAVE RADIATION ALLOW AN EXPOSURE LEVEL OF 10 mW/m² (THE LEVEL AT WHICH THINGS START TO 'FEEL' WARM). SOVIET REGULATIONS, BASED ON THE EFFECTS ON THE CENTRAL NERVOUS SYSTEM, SET A LIMIT ONE TEN THOUSANDTH OF THAT LEVEL.

DOMESTIC ELECTRICITY
HOUSEHOLD ELECTRICAL GADGETS CREATE SMALL MAGNETIC & ELECTRICAL FIELDS. THE GREATEST MAGNETIC FIELDS COME FROM HAIR-DRIERS & THE GREATEST ELECTRICAL FIELDS FROM ELECTRIC BLANKETS. THERE IS NO EVIDENCE THAT EITHER CAUSES ILL-EFFECTS.

SEEING MAGNETISM
STRONG MAGNETIC FIELDS (500 GAUSS, ABOUT 50 HAIR-DRIERS) PRODUCE THE SENSATION OF FLASHES IN THE EYES, CALLED PHOSPHENES (SEEING STARS). THEY ARE BELIEVED TO BE HARMLESS.

HEARING RADIO
PEOPLE CAN HEAR CERTAIN RADIOWAVES (IN THE RANGE 200-3000 mHz). THE WAVES VIBRATE THROUGH THE HEAD. THE EARS PICK UP LOW FREQUENCY COMPONENTS OF THESE WAVES.

FLICKER
VERY SMALL MAGNETIC FIELDS (SEE 'DOMESTIC ELEC-TRICITY') REDUCE OUR ABILITY TO DISTINGUISH BETWEEN RAPIDLY FLICKERING & CONSTANT LIGHT (A COMMON NEUROLOGICAL TEST)

BIORHYTHMS
WEAK LOW-FREQUENCY ELECTRIC FIELDS HAVE BEEN SHOWN TO AFFECT THE BRAIN ACTIVITY OF MONKEYS & CATS. 16-20 CYCLES/SECOND INCREASES ACTIVITY & 1-5 CYCLES LOWERS IT.

POWER LINES
THE HEALTH OF 10 MEN WORKING ON HIGH-VOLTAGE POWER LINES IN AMERICA WAS CLOSELY MONITORED FOR 9 YEARS & NO HARM-FUL EFFECTS WERE FOUND. SIMILAR SOVIET STUDIES HAVE FOUND EVIDENCE OF NERVOUS & HEART DISORDERS.

HOWEVER, A RECENT US EXPERIMENT SUBJECTING RATS TO AN ELECTRIC FIELD SIMILAR TO THAT BENEATH A 750kV POWER LINE FOUND THAT IT CAUSED HIGHER INFANT MORTALITY & STUNTED GROWTH.

NATURAL POLLUTION
THERE IS SOME EVIDENCE THAT THE NUMBER OF CASES OF MENINGITIS & RELAPSING FEVER INCREASES WITH SUNSPOT ACTIVITY (WHICH AFFECTS THE EARTH'S MAGNETIC FIELD). UPPER ATMOSPHERE GEOMAGNETIC STORMS CORRELATE WITH INCREASES IN HOSPITAL ADMISSIONS & DEATHS.

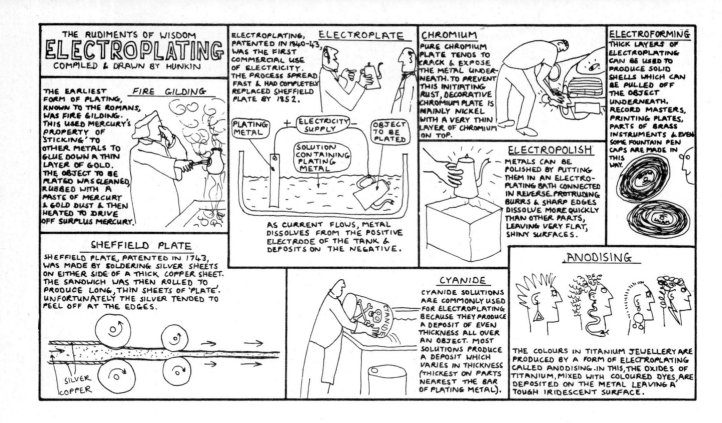

THE RUDIMENTS OF WISDOM
ELECTROPLATING
COMPILED & DRAWN BY HUNKIN

FIRE GILDING
THE EARLIEST FORM OF PLATING, KNOWN TO THE ROMANS, WAS FIRE GILDING. THIS USED MERCURY'S PROPERTY OF 'STICKING' TO OTHER METALS TO GLUE DOWN A THIN LAYER OF GOLD. THE OBJECT TO BE PLATED WAS CLEANED, RUBBED WITH A PASTE OF MERCURY & GOLD DUST & THEN HEATED TO DRIVE OFF SURPLUS MERCURY.

SHEFFIELD PLATE
SHEFFIELD PLATE, PATENTED IN 1743, WAS MADE BY SOLDERING SILVER SHEETS ON EITHER SIDE OF A THICK COPPER SHEET. THE SANDWICH WAS THEN ROLLED TO PRODUCE LONG, THIN SHEETS OF 'PLATE'. UNFORTUNATELY THE SILVER TENDED TO PEEL OFF AT THE EDGES.

SILVER
COPPER

ELECTROPLATING, PATENTED IN 1840-43, WAS THE FIRST COMMERCIAL USE OF ELECTRICITY. THE PROCESS SPREAD FAST & HAD COMPLETELY REPLACED SHEFFIELD PLATE BY 1852.

ELECTROPLATE
PLATING METAL
+ ELECTRICITY SUPPLY
OBJECT TO BE PLATED
SOLUTION CONTAINING PLATING METAL

AS CURRENT FLOWS, METAL DISSOLVES FROM THE POSITIVE ELECTRODE OF THE TANK & DEPOSITS ON THE NEGATIVE.

CYANIDE
CYANIDE SOLUTIONS ARE COMMONLY USED FOR ELECTROPLATING BECAUSE THEY PRODUCE A DEPOSIT OF EVEN THICKNESS ALL OVER AN OBJECT. MOST SOLUTIONS PRODUCE A DEPOSIT WHICH VARIES IN THICKNESS (THICKEST ON PARTS NEAREST THE BAR OF PLATING METAL).

CHROMIUM
PURE CHROMIUM PLATE TENDS TO CRACK & EXPOSE THE METAL UNDERNEATH. TO PREVENT THIS INITIATING RUST, DECORATIVE CHROMIUM PLATE IS MAINLY NICKEL WITH A VERY THIN LAYER OF CHROMIUM ON TOP.

ELECTROPOLISH
METALS CAN BE POLISHED BY PUTTING THEM IN AN ELECTROPLATING BATH CONNECTED IN REVERSE. PROTRUDING BURRS & SHARP EDGES DISSOLVE MORE QUICKLY THAN OTHER PARTS, LEAVING VERY FLAT, SHINY SURFACES.

ELECTROFORMING
THICK LAYERS OF ELECTROPLATING CAN BE USED TO PRODUCE SOLID SHELLS WHICH CAN BE PULLED OFF THE OBJECT UNDERNEATH. RECORD MASTERS, PRINTING PLATES, PARTS OF BRASS INSTRUMENTS & EVEN SOME FOUNTAIN PEN CAPS ARE MADE IN THIS WAY.

ANODISING
THE COLOURS IN TITANIUM JEWELLERY ARE PRODUCED BY A FORM OF ELECTROPLATING CALLED ANODISING. IN THIS, THE OXIDES OF TITANIUM, MIXED WITH COLOURED DYES, ARE DEPOSITED ON THE METAL LEAVING A TOUGH IRIDESCENT SURFACE.

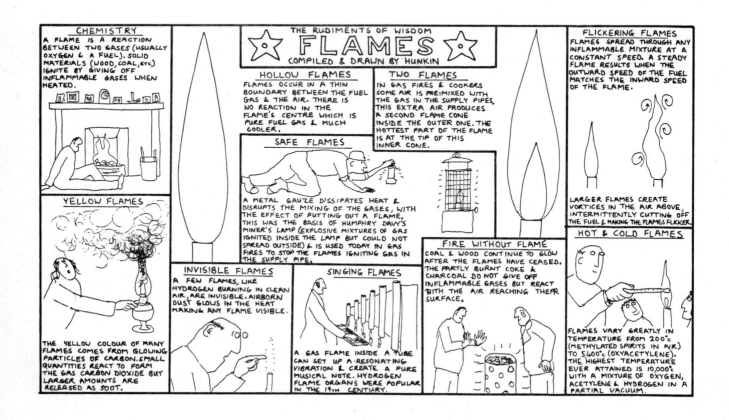

CHEMISTRY
A FLAME IS A REACTION BETWEEN TWO GASES (USUALLY OXYGEN & A FUEL). SOLID MATERIALS (WOOD, COAL, etc) IGNITE BY GIVING OFF INFLAMMABLE GASES WHEN HEATED.

YELLOW FLAMES
THE YELLOW COLOUR OF MANY FLAMES COMES FROM GLOWING PARTICLES OF CARBON. SMALL QUANTITIES REACT TO FORM THE GAS CARBON DIOXIDE BUT LARGER AMOUNTS ARE RELEASED AS SOOT.

THE RUDIMENTS OF WISDOM
☆ FLAMES ☆
COMPILED & DRAWN BY HUNKIN

HOLLOW FLAMES
FLAMES OCCUR IN A THIN BOUNDARY BETWEEN THE FUEL GAS & THE AIR. THERE IS NO REACTION IN THE FLAME'S CENTRE WHICH IS PURE FUEL GAS & MUCH COOLER.

SAFE FLAMES
A METAL GAUZE DISSIPATES HEAT & DISRUPTS THE MIXING OF THE GASES, WITH THE EFFECT OF PUTTING OUT A FLAME. THIS WAS THE BASIS OF HUMPHRY DAVY'S MINER'S LAMP (EXPLOSIVE MIXTURES OF GAS IGNITED INSIDE THE LAMP BUT COULD NOT SPREAD OUTSIDE) & IS USED TODAY IN GAS FIRES TO STOP THE FLAMES IGNITING GAS IN THE SUPPLY PIPE.

INVISIBLE FLAMES
A FEW FLAMES, LIKE HYDROGEN BURNING IN CLEAN AIR, ARE INVISIBLE. AIRBORN DUST GLOWS IN THE HEAT MAKING ANY FLAME VISIBLE.

SINGING FLAMES
A GAS FLAME INSIDE A TUBE CAN SET UP A RESONATING VIBRATION & CREATE A PURE MUSICAL NOTE. HYDROGEN FLAME ORGANS WERE POPULAR IN THE 19TH CENTURY.

TWO FLAMES
IN GAS FIRES & COOKERS SOME AIR IS PRE-MIXED WITH THE GAS IN THE SUPPLY PIPES. THIS EXTRA AIR PRODUCES A SECOND FLAME CONE INSIDE THE OUTER ONE. THE HOTTEST PART OF THE FLAME IS AT THE TIP OF THIS INNER CONE.

FIRE WITHOUT FLAME
COAL & WOOD CONTINUE TO GLOW AFTER THE FLAMES HAVE CEASED. THE PARTLY BURNT COKE & CHARCOAL DO NOT GIVE OFF INFLAMMABLE GASES BUT REACT WITH THE AIR REACHING THEIR SURFACE.

FLICKERING FLAMES
FLAMES SPREAD THROUGH ANY INFLAMMABLE MIXTURE AT A CONSTANT SPEED. A STEADY FLAME RESULTS WHEN THE OUTWARD SPEED OF THE FUEL MATCHES THE INWARD SPEED OF THE FLAME.

LARGER FLAMES CREATE VORTICES IN THE AIR ABOVE, INTERMITTENTLY CUTTING OFF THE FUEL & MAKING THE FLAMES FLICKER.

HOT & COLD FLAMES
FLAMES VARY GREATLY IN TEMPERATURE FROM 200°C (METHYLATED SPIRITS IN AIR) TO 5,400°C (OXYACETYLENE). THE HIGHEST TEMPERATURE EVER ATTAINED IS 10,000°C WITH A MIXTURE OF OXYGEN, ACETYLENE & HYDROGEN IN A PARTIAL VACUUM.

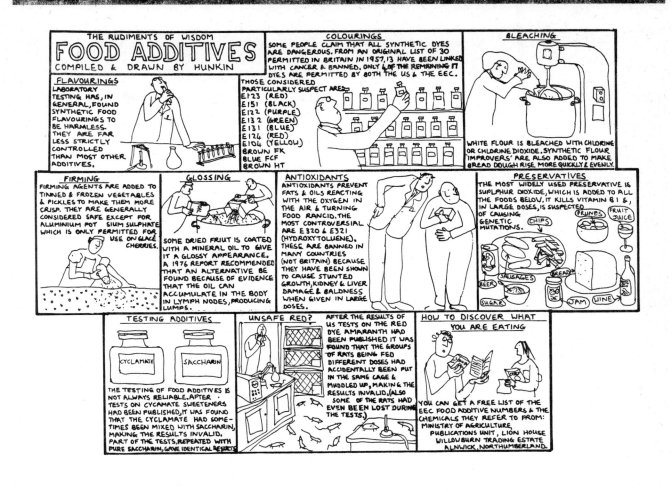

THE RUDIMENTS OF WISDOM
FOOD ADDITIVES
COMPILED & DRAWN BY HUNKIN

FLAVOURINGS
LABORATORY TESTING HAS, IN GENERAL, FOUND SYNTHETIC FOOD FLAVOURINGS TO BE HARMLESS. THEY ARE FAR LESS STRICTLY CONTROLLED THAN MOST OTHER ADDITIVES.

COLOURINGS
SOME PEOPLE CLAIM THAT ALL SYNTHETIC DYES ARE DANGEROUS. FROM AN ORIGINAL LIST OF 30 PERMITTED IN BRITAIN IN 1957, 13 HAVE BEEN LINKED WITH CANCER & BANNED. ONLY 4 OF THE REMAINING 17 DYES ARE PERMITTED BY BOTH THE US & THE EEC.

THOSE CONSIDERED PARTICULARLY SUSPECT ARE:
E123 (RED)
E151 (BLACK)
E122 (PURPLE)
E132 (GREEN)
E131 (BLUE)
E124 (RED)
E104 (YELLOW)
BROWN FK
BLUE FCF
BROWN HT

BLEACHING
WHITE FLOUR IS BLEACHED WITH CHLORINE OR CHLORINE DIOXIDE. SYNTHETIC FLOUR 'IMPROVERS' ARE ALSO ADDED TO MAKE BREAD DOUGH RISE MORE QUICKLY & EVENLY.

FIRMING
FIRMING AGENTS ARE ADDED TO TINNED & FROZEN VEGETABLES & PICKLES TO MAKE THEM MORE CRISP. THEY ARE GENERALLY CONSIDERED SAFE EXCEPT FOR ALUMINIUM POTASSIUM SULPHATE WHICH IS ONLY PERMITTED FOR USE ON GLACÉ CHERRIES.

GLOSSING
SOME DRIED FRUIT IS COATED WITH A MINERAL OIL TO GIVE IT A GLOSSY APPEARANCE. A 1976 REPORT RECOMMENDED THAT AN ALTERNATIVE BE FOUND BECAUSE OF EVIDENCE THAT THE OIL CAN ACCUMULATE IN THE BODY IN LYMPH NODES, PRODUCING LUMPS.

ANTIOXIDANTS
ANTIOXIDANTS PREVENT FATS & OILS REACTING WITH THE OXYGEN IN THE AIR & TURNING FOOD RANCID. THE MOST CONTROVERSIAL ARE E320 & E321 (HYDROXYTOLUENE). THESE ARE BANNED IN MANY COUNTRIES (NOT BRITAIN) BECAUSE THEY HAVE BEEN SHOWN TO CAUSE STUNTED GROWTH, KIDNEY & LIVER DAMAGE & BALDNESS WHEN GIVEN IN LARGE DOSES.

PRESERVATIVES
THE MOST WIDELY USED PRESERVATIVE IS SULPHUR DIOXIDE, WHICH IS ADDED TO ALL THE FOODS BELOW. IT KILLS VITAMIN B1 &, IN LARGE DOSES, IS SUSPECTED OF CAUSING GENETIC MUTATIONS.

CHIPS
PRUNES
FRUIT JUICE
BEER
SAUSAGES
BREAD
SUGAR
JAM
WINE

TESTING ADDITIVES
CYCLAMATE   SACCHARIN

THE TESTING OF FOOD ADDITIVES IS NOT ALWAYS RELIABLE. AFTER TESTS ON CYCLAMATE SWEETENERS HAD BEEN PUBLISHED, IT WAS FOUND THAT THE CYCLAMATE HAD SOMETIMES BEEN MIXED WITH SACCHARIN, MAKING THE RESULTS INVALID. PART OF THE TESTS, REPEATED WITH PURE SACCHARIN, GAVE IDENTICAL RESULTS.

UNSAFE RED?
AFTER THE RESULTS OF US TESTS ON THE RED DYE AMARANTH HAD BEEN PUBLISHED IT WAS FOUND THAT THE GROUPS OF RATS BEING FED DIFFERENT DOSES HAD ACCIDENTALLY BEEN PUT IN THE SAME CAGE & MUDDLED UP, MAKING THE RESULTS INVALID. (ALSO SOME OF THE RATS HAD EVEN BEEN LOST DURING THE TESTS.)

HOW TO DISCOVER WHAT YOU ARE EATING
YOU CAN GET A FREE LIST OF THE EEC FOOD ADDITIVE NUMBERS & THE CHEMICALS THEY REFER TO FROM:
MINISTRY OF AGRICULTURE
PUBLICATIONS UNIT, LION HOUSE
WILLOWBURN TRADING ESTATE
ALNWICK, NORTHUMBERLAND.

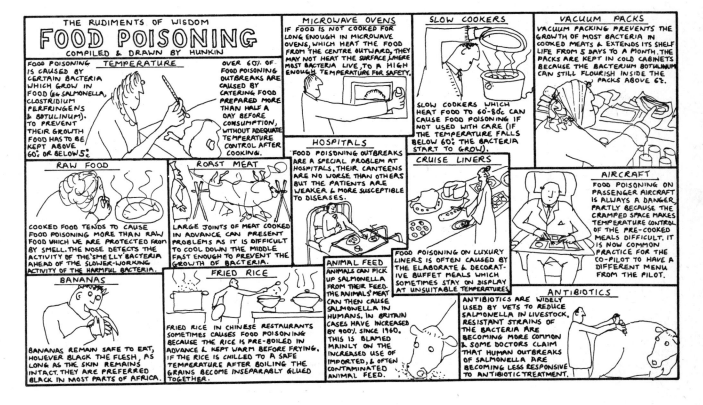

THE RUDIMENTS OF WISDOM
FOOD POISONING
COMPILED & DRAWN BY HUNKIN

TEMPERATURE
FOOD POISONING IS CAUSED BY CERTAIN BACTERIA WHICH GROW IN FOOD (EG SALMONELLA, CLOSTRIDIUM PERFRINGENS & BOTULINUM). TO PREVENT THEIR GROWTH FOOD HAS TO BE KEPT ABOVE 60°C OR BELOW 5°C.

OVER 60% OF FOOD POISONING OUTBREAKS ARE CAUSED BY CATERING FOOD PREPARED MORE THAN HALF A DAY BEFORE CONSUMPTION, WITHOUT ADEQUATE TEMPERATURE CONTROL AFTER COOKING.

MICROWAVE OVENS
IF FOOD IS NOT COOKED FOR LONG ENOUGH IN MICROWAVE OVENS, WHICH HEAT THE FOOD FROM THE CENTRE OUTWARD, THEY MAY NOT HEAT THE SURFACE (WHERE MOST BACTERIA LIVE) TO A HIGH ENOUGH TEMPERATURE FOR SAFETY.

SLOW COOKERS
SLOW COOKERS WHICH HEAT FOOD TO 60°-80°C CAN CAUSE FOOD POISONING IF NOT USED WITH CARE (IF THE TEMPERATURE FALLS BELOW 60°C THE BACTERIA START TO GROW).

VACUUM PACKS
VACUUM PACKING PREVENTS THE GROWTH OF MOST BACTERIA IN COOKED MEATS & EXTENDS ITS SHELF LIFE FROM 5 DAYS TO A MONTH. THE PACKS ARE KEPT IN COLD CABINETS BECAUSE THE BACTERIUM BOTULINUM CAN STILL FLOURISH INSIDE THE PACKS ABOVE 6°C.

RAW FOOD
COOKED FOOD TENDS TO CAUSE FOOD POISONING MORE THAN RAW FOOD WHICH WE ARE PROTECTED FROM BY SMELL. THE NOSE DETECTS THE ACTIVITY OF THE 'SMELLY' BACTERIA AHEAD OF THE SLOWER-WORKING ACTIVITY OF THE HARMFUL BACTERIA.

ROAST MEAT
LARGE JOINTS OF MEAT COOKED IN ADVANCE CAN PRESENT PROBLEMS AS IT IS DIFFICULT TO COOL DOWN THE MIDDLE FAST ENOUGH TO PREVENT THE GROWTH OF BACTERIA.

HOSPITALS
FOOD POISONING OUTBREAKS ARE A SPECIAL PROBLEM AT HOSPITALS. THEIR CANTEENS ARE NO WORSE THAN OTHERS BUT THE PATIENTS ARE WEAKER & MORE SUSCEPTIBLE TO DISEASES.

CRUISE LINERS
FOOD POISONING ON LUXURY LINERS IS OFTEN CAUSED BY THE ELABORATE & DECORATIVE BUFFET MEALS WHICH SOMETIMES STAY ON DISPLAY AT UNSUITABLE TEMPERATURES.

AIRCRAFT
FOOD POISONING ON PASSENGER AIRCRAFT IS ALWAYS A DANGER PARTLY BECAUSE THE CRAMPED SPACE MAKES TEMPERATURE CONTROL OF THE PRE-COOKED MEALS DIFFICULT. IT IS NOW COMMON PRACTICE FOR THE CO-PILOT TO HAVE A DIFFERENT MENU FROM THE PILOT.

BANANAS
BANANAS REMAIN SAFE TO EAT, HOWEVER BLACK THE FLESH, AS LONG AS THE SKIN REMAINS INTACT. THEY ARE PREFERRED BLACK IN MOST PARTS OF AFRICA.

FRIED RICE
FRIED RICE IN CHINESE RESTAURANTS SOMETIMES CAUSES FOOD POISONING BECAUSE THE RICE IS PRE-BOILED IN ADVANCE & KEPT WARM BEFORE FRYING. IF THE RICE IS CHILLED TO A SAFE TEMPERATURE AFTER BOILING THE GRAINS BECOME INSEPARABLY GLUED TOGETHER.

ANIMAL FEED
ANIMALS CAN PICK UP SALMONELLA FROM THEIR FEED. THE ANIMALS' MEAT CAN THEN CAUSE SALMONELLA IN HUMANS. IN BRITAIN CASES HAVE INCREASED BY 900% SINCE 1960. THIS IS BLAMED MAINLY ON THE INCREASED USE OF IMPORTED, & OFTEN CONTAMINATED ANIMAL FEED.

ANTIBIOTICS
ANTIBIOTICS ARE WIDELY USED BY VETS TO REDUCE SALMONELLA IN LIVESTOCK. RESISTANT STRAINS OF THE BACTERIA ARE BECOMING MORE COMMON & SOME DOCTORS CLAIM THAT HUMAN OUTBREAKS OF SALMONELLA ARE BECOMING LESS RESPONSIVE TO ANTIBIOTIC TREATMENT.

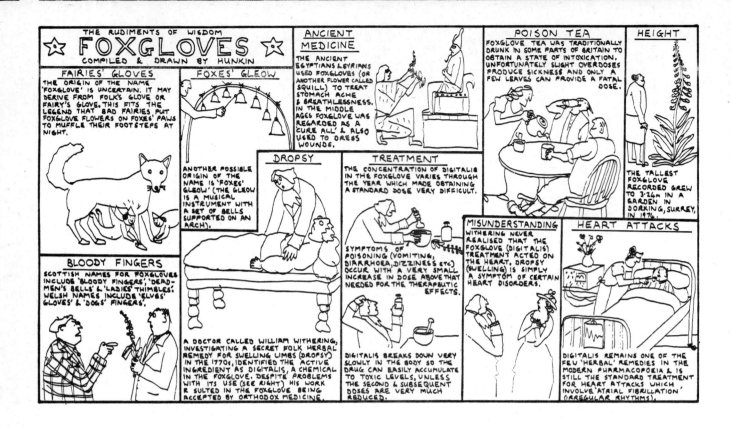

THE RUDIMENTS OF WISDOM ☆ FOXGLOVES ☆
COMPILED & DRAWN BY HUNKIN

FAIRIES' GLOVES
THE ORIGIN OF THE NAME 'FOXGLOVE' IS UNCERTAIN. IT MAY DERIVE FROM FOLK'S GLOVE OR FAIRY'S GLOVE. THIS FITS THE LEGEND THAT BAD FAIRIES PUT FOXGLOVE FLOWERS ON FOXES' PAWS TO MUFFLE THEIR FOOTSTEPS AT NIGHT.

FOXES' GLEOW
ANOTHER POSSIBLE ORIGIN OF THE NAME IS 'FOXES' GLEOW' (THE GLEOW IS A MUSICAL INSTRUMENT WITH A SET OF BELLS SUPPORTED ON AN ARCH).

BLOODY FINGERS
SCOTTISH NAMES FOR FOXGLOVES INCLUDE 'BLOODY FINGERS', 'DEAD-MEN'S BELLS' & 'LADIES THIMBLES'. WELSH NAMES INCLUDE 'ELVES' GLOVES' & 'DOGS' FINGERS'.

DROPSY
A DOCTOR CALLED WILLIAM WITHERING, INVESTIGATING A SECRET FOLK HERBAL REMEDY FOR SWELLING LIMBS (DROPSY) IN THE 1770s, IDENTIFIED THE ACTIVE INGREDIENT AS DIGITALIS, A CHEMICAL IN THE FOXGLOVE. DESPITE PROBLEMS WITH ITS USE (SEE RIGHT) HIS WORK RESULTED IN THE FOXGLOVE BEING ACCEPTED BY ORTHODOX MEDICINE.

ANCIENT MEDICINE
THE ANCIENT EGYPTIANS & SYRIANS USED FOXGLOVES (OR ANOTHER FLOWER CALLED SQUILL) TO TREAT STOMACH ACHE & BREATHLESSNESS. IN THE MIDDLE AGES FOXGLOVE WAS REGARDED AS A 'CURE ALL' & ALSO USED TO DRESS WOUNDS.

TREATMENT
THE CONCENTRATION OF DIGITALIS IN THE FOXGLOVE VARIES THROUGH THE YEAR WHICH MADE OBTAINING A STANDARD DOSE VERY DIFFICULT.

SYMPTOMS OF POISONING (VOMITING, DIARRHOEA, DIZZINESS etc) OCCUR WITH A VERY SMALL INCREASE IN DOSE ABOVE THAT NEEDED FOR THE THERAPEUTIC EFFECTS.

DIGITALIS BREAKS DOWN VERY SLOWLY IN THE BODY SO THE DRUG CAN EASILY ACCUMULATE TO TOXIC LEVELS, UNLESS THE SECOND & SUBSEQUENT DOSES ARE VERY MUCH REDUCED.

POISON TEA
FOXGLOVE TEA WAS TRADITIONALLY DRUNK IN SOME PARTS OF BRITAIN TO OBTAIN A STATE OF INTOXICATION. UNFORTUNATELY SLIGHT OVERDOSES PRODUCE SICKNESS AND ONLY A FEW LEAVES CAN PROVIDE A FATAL DOSE.

MISUNDERSTANDING
WITHERING NEVER REALISED THAT THE FOXGLOVE (DIGITALIS) TREATMENT ACTED ON THE HEART. DROPSY (SWELLING) IS SIMPLY A SYMPTOM OF CERTAIN HEART DISORDERS.

HEIGHT
THE TALLEST FOXGLOVE RECORDED GREW TO 3·24m IN A GARDEN IN DORKING, SURREY, IN 1976.

HEART ATTACKS
DIGITALIS REMAINS ONE OF THE FEW 'HERBAL' REMEDIES IN THE MODERN PHARMACOPOEIA & IS STILL THE STANDARD TREATMENT FOR HEART ATTACKS WHICH INVOLVE 'ATRIAL FIBRILLATION' (IRREGULAR RHYTHMS).

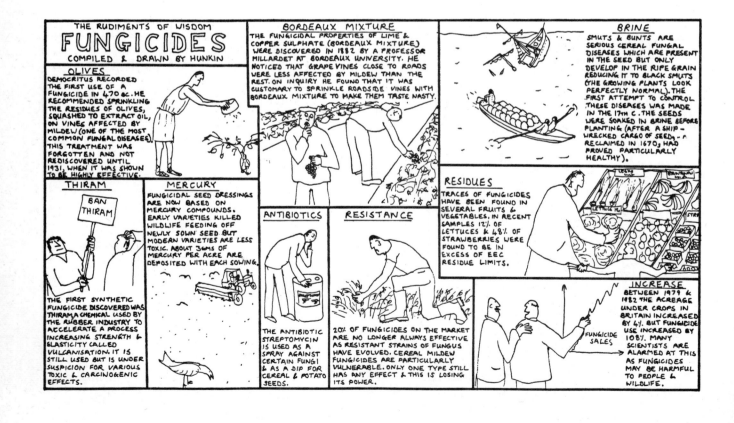

THE RUDIMENTS OF WISDOM FUNGICIDES
COMPILED & DRAWN BY HUNKIN

OLIVES
DEMOCRITUS RECORDED THE FIRST USE OF A FUNGICIDE IN 470 BC. HE RECOMMENDED SPRINKLING THE RESIDUES OF OLIVES, SQUASHED TO EXTRACT OIL, ON VINES AFFECTED BY MILDEW (ONE OF THE MOST COMMON FUNGAL DISEASES). THIS TREATMENT WAS FORGOTTEN AND NOT REDISCOVERED UNTIL 1931, WHEN IT WAS SHOWN TO BE HIGHLY EFFECTIVE.

THIRAM
THE FIRST SYNTHETIC FUNGICIDE DISCOVERED WAS THIRAM A CHEMICAL USED BY THE RUBBER INDUSTRY TO ACCELERATE A PROCESS INCREASING STRENGTH & ELASTICITY CALLED VULCANISATION. IT IS STILL USED BUT IS UNDER SUSPICION FOR VARIOUS TOXIC & CARCINOGENIC EFFECTS.

MERCURY
FUNGICIDAL SEED DRESSINGS ARE NOW BASED ON MERCURY COMPOUNDS. EARLY VARIETIES KILLED WILDLIFE FEEDING OFF NEWLY SOWN SEED BUT MODERN VARIETIES ARE LESS TOXIC. ABOUT 3gms OF MERCURY PER ACRE ARE DEPOSITED WITH EACH SOWING.

BORDEAUX MIXTURE
THE FUNGICIDAL PROPERTIES OF LIME & COPPER SULPHATE (BORDEAUX MIXTURE) WERE DISCOVERED IN 1882 BY A PROFESSOR MILLARDET AT BORDEAUX UNIVERSITY. HE NOTICED THAT GRAPE VINES CLOSE TO ROADS WERE LESS AFFECTED BY MILDEW THAN THE REST. ON INQUIRY HE FOUND THAT IT WAS CUSTOMARY TO SPRINKLE ROADSIDE VINES WITH BORDEAUX MIXTURE TO MAKE THEM TASTE NASTY.

ANTIBIOTICS
THE ANTIBIOTIC STREPTOMYCIN IS USED AS A SPRAY AGAINST CERTAIN FUNGI & AS A DIP FOR CEREAL & POTATO SEEDS.

RESISTANCE
20% OF FUNGICIDES ON THE MARKET ARE NO LONGER ALWAYS EFFECTIVE AS RESISTANT STRAINS OF FUNGUS HAVE EVOLVED. CEREAL MILDEW FUNGICIDES ARE PARTICULARLY VULNERABLE. ONLY ONE TYPE STILL HAS ANY EFFECT & THIS IS LOSING ITS POWER.

BRINE
SMUTS & BUNTS ARE SERIOUS CEREAL FUNGAL DISEASES WHICH ARE PRESENT IN THE SEED BUT ONLY DEVELOP IN THE RIPE GRAIN REDUCING IT TO BLACK SMUTS (THE GROWING PLANTS LOOK PERFECTLY NORMAL). THE FIRST ATTEMPT TO CONTROL THESE DISEASES WAS MADE IN THE 17TH C. THE SEEDS WERE SOAKED IN BRINE BEFORE PLANTING (AFTER A SHIP-WRECKED CARGO OF SEED - RECLAIMED IN 1670, HAD PROVED PARTICULARLY HEALTHY).

RESIDUES
TRACES OF FUNGICIDES HAVE BEEN FOUND IN SEVERAL FRUITS & VEGETABLES. IN RECENT SAMPLES 12% OF LETTUCES & 48% OF STRAWBERRIES WERE FOUND TO BE IN EXCESS OF EEC RESIDUE LIMITS.

INCREASE
BETWEEN 1979 & 1982 THE ACREAGE UNDER CROPS IN BRITAIN INCREASED BY 4% BUT FUNGICIDE USE INCREASED BY 108%. MANY SCIENTISTS ARE ALARMED AT THIS AS FUNGICIDES MAY BE HARMFUL TO PEOPLE & WILDLIFE.

SOME VITAL STATISTICS FROM FRANCE
COMPILED & DRAWN BY HUNKIN

FRANCE IS THE LARGEST COUNTRY IN EUROPE (544,000 KM²), MORE THAN TWICE THE SIZE OF BRITAIN (244,100 KM²).

EUROPE'S LONGEST EVER RECORDED TRAFFIC JAM (109 MILES) OCCURRED OUTSIDE LYON IN 1980. ONE PERSON IN 2,500 DIES ON THE ROADS EVERY YEAR IN FRANCE, MORE THAN ANY OTHER EUROPEAN COUNTRY (BRITAIN: ONE IN 5,500).

BEDS ARE MORE EXPENSIVE IN FRANCE THAN IN ANY OTHER E.E.C. COUNTRY. AVERAGE PRICES ARE 15% HIGHER THAN IN BRITAIN.

PARIS HAS THE LARGEST SEWAGE WORKS IN EUROPE, TREATING 440,000,000 GALLONS PER DAY.

IN FRANCE THERE ARE MORE DEATHS FROM DISEASES OF THE DIGESTIVE SYSTEM (6·2% BRITAIN 2·5%) & FEWER DEATHS FROM HEART DISEASE (38% BRITAIN 51%) THAN IN ANY OTHER EUROPEAN COUNTRY.

A MONSIEUR 'MANGETOUT' LOTITO HOLDS THE WORLD RECORD FOR EATING A COMPLETE BICYCLE IN 10 DAYS AT EVREY. THE METAL WAS GROUND INTO FILINGS & THE TYRES WERE STEWED.

THE WORLD'S GREATEST WELFARE BENEFIT FRAUD OCCURRED IN MARSEILLES. ANTHONY MORENO OBTAINED 23,000,000 FRANCS (£2·3 MILLION) IN 8 YEARS BY CLAIMING FOR 197 FAMILIES & 3,000 CHILDREN.

FRANCE IS THE MOST HEAVILY POLICED COUNTRY IN EUROPE, WITH ONE POLICEMAN FOR EVERY 221 PEOPLE (BRITAIN HAS ONE FOR EVERY 512).

SOME VITAL STATISTICS FROM GERMANY
COMPILED & DRAWN BY HUNKIN

GERMANY'S POPULATION IS DECLINING AT A RATE OF 1·5% PER YEAR. IT HAS THE LOWEST BIRTHRATE IN THE WORLD–10·1 BIRTHS PER 1000 PEOPLE PER YEAR (13·5 PER 1,000 IN BRITAIN).

THERE ARE 12 TRACTORS & 2·9 COMBINE HARVESTERS PER 100 HECTARES IN GERMANY, THE MOST ANYWHERE IN EUROPE (BRITAIN HAS 2·7 TRACTORS & 1·5 COMBINES PER 100 HECTARES).

THE GERMANS ARE THE WORLD'S BIGGEST BEER DRINKERS, CONSUMING AN AVERAGE OF 324 PINTS PER PERSON PER YEAR (BRITONS DRINK 258 PINTS).

GERMANY PRODUCES MORE APPLES (1,839,000 TONS A YEAR) THAN ANY OTHER EUROPEAN COUNTRY (BRITAIN: 370,000 TONS).

THE WORLD'S LARGEST COOLING TOWER (170m HIGH) IS IN GERMANY AT A NUCLEAR POWER STATION NEAR UENTROP.

24% OF GERMAN WOMEN POSSESS SOME DIAMOND JEWELLERY, THE HIGHEST FIGURE IN EUROPE.

THE WORLD'S LARGEST EXCAVATOR IS IN USE AT A LIGNITE (LOW GRADE COAL) MINE NEAR HAMBURG. THE 13,000 TON MACHINE CAN EXCAVATE 200,000 CUBIC METRES A DAY.

CARS IN GERMANY ARE THE CHEAPEST IN EUROPE, COSTING 35% LESS THAN IN BRITAIN. ORDINARY NAILS, HOWEVER, ARE THE MOST EXPENSIVE IN EUROPE—20% MORE THAN IN BRITAIN.

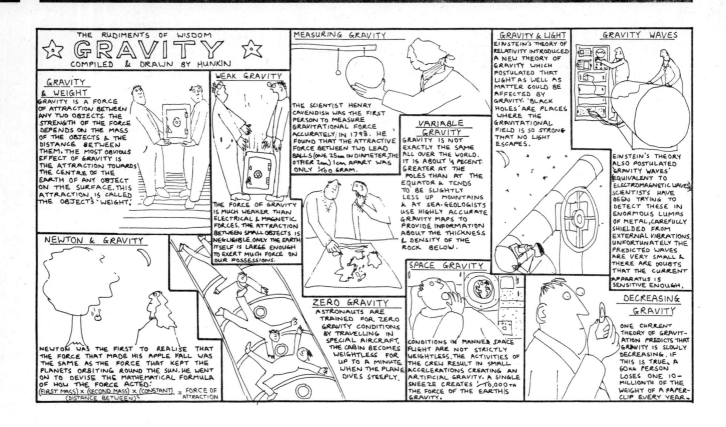

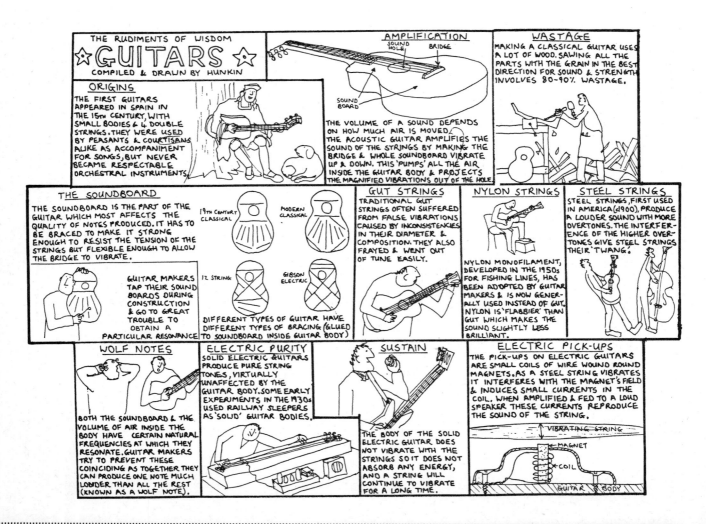

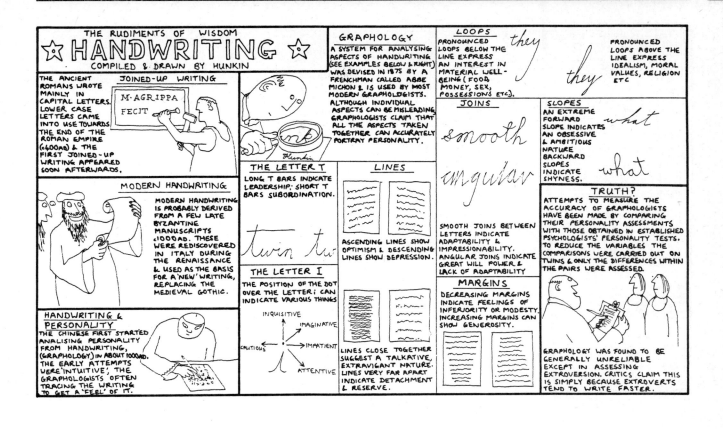

THE RUDIMENTS OF WISDOM
☆ HANDWRITING ☆
COMPILED & DRAWN BY HUNKIN

JOINED-UP WRITING

THE ANCIENT ROMANS WROTE MAINLY IN CAPITAL LETTERS. LOWER CASE LETTERS CAME INTO USE TOWARDS THE END OF THE ROMAN EMPIRE (400AD) & THE FIRST JOINED-UP WRITING APPEARED SOON AFTERWARDS.

M.AGRIPPA FECIT

MODERN HANDWRITING

MODERN HANDWRITING IS PROBABLY DERIVED FROM A FEW LATE BYZANTINE MANUSCRIPTS c1000AD. THESE WERE REDISCOVERED IN ITALY DURING THE RENAISSANCE & USED AS THE BASIS FOR A 'NEW' WRITING, REPLACING THE MEDIEVAL GOTHIC.

HANDWRITING & PERSONALITY

THE CHINESE FIRST STARTED ANALISING PERSONALITY FROM HANDWRITING, (GRAPHOLOGY) IN ABOUT 1000AD. THE EARLY ATTEMPTS WERE 'INTUITIVE', THE GRAPHOLOGISTS OFTEN TRACING THE WRITING TO GET A 'FEEL' OF IT.

GRAPHOLOGY

A SYSTEM FOR ANALYSING ASPECTS OF HANDWRITING (SEE EXAMPLES BELOW & RIGHT) WAS DEVISED IN 1875 BY A FRENCHMAN CALLED ABBE MICHON & IS USED BY MOST MODERN GRAPHOLOGISTS. ALTHOUGH INDIVIDUAL ASPECTS CAN BE MISLEADING, GRAPHOLOGISTS CLAIM THAT ALL THE ASPECTS TAKEN TOGETHER CAN ACCURATELY PORTRAY PERSONALITY.

THE LETTER T

LONG T BARS INDICATE LEADERSHIP; SHORT T BARS SUBORDINATION.

twin tw

THE LETTER I

THE POSITION OF THE DOT OVER THE LETTER i CAN INDICATE VARIOUS THINGS

INQUISITIVE

IMAGINATIVE

CAUTIOUS → IMPATIENT

ATTENTIVE

LINES

ASCENDING LINES SHOW OPTIMISM & DESCENDING LINES SHOW DEPRESSION.

LINES CLOSE TOGETHER SUGGEST A TALKATIVE, EXTRAVIGANT NATURE. LINES VERY FAR APART INDICATE DETACHMENT & RESERVE.

LOOPS

PRONOUNCED LOOPS BELOW THE LINE EXPRESS AN INTEREST IN MATERIAL WELL-BEING (FOOD, MONEY, SEX, POSSESSIONS ETC).

they

they

PRONOUNCED LOOPS ABOVE THE LINE EXPRESS IDEALISM, MORAL VALUES, RELIGION ETC

JOINS

smooth

angular

SMOOTH JOINS BETWEEN LETTERS INDICATE ADAPTABILITY & IMPRESSIONABILITY. ANGULAR JOINS INDICATE GREAT WILL POWER & LACK OF ADAPTABILITY

MARGINS

DECREASING MARGINS INDICATE FEELINGS OF INFERIORITY OR MODESTY. INCREASING MARGINS CAN SHOW GENEROSITY.

SLOPES

AN EXTREME FORWARD SLOPE INDICATES AN OBSESSIVE & AMBITIOUS NATURE. BACKWARD SLOPES INDICATE SHYNESS.

what

what

TRUTH?

ATTEMPTS TO MEASURE THE ACCURACY OF GRAPHOLOGISTS HAVE BEEN MADE BY COMPARING THEIR PERSONALITY ASSESSMENTS WITH THOSE OBTAINED IN ESTABLISHED PSYCHOLOGISTS' PERSONALITY TESTS. TO REDUCE THE VARIABLES THE COMPARISONS WERE CARRIED OUT ON TWINS & ONLY THE DIFFERENCES WITHIN THE PAIRS WERE ASSESSED.

GRAPHOLOGY WAS FOUND TO BE GENERALLY UNRELIABLE EXCEPT IN ASSESSING EXTROVERSION. CRITICS CLAIM THIS IS SIMPLY BECAUSE EXTROVERTS TEND TO WRITE FASTER.

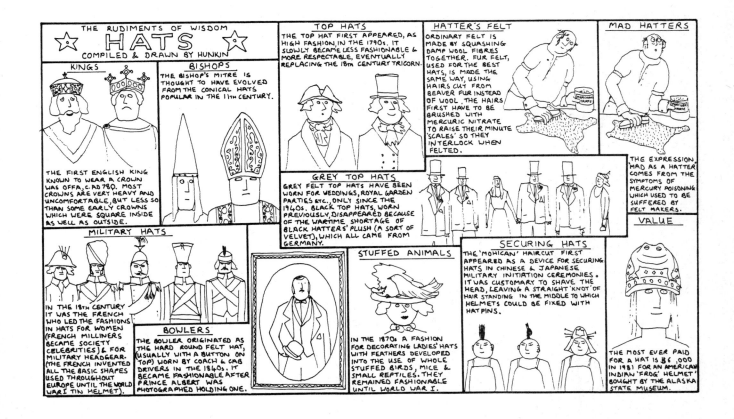

THE RUDIMENTS OF WISDOM
☆ HATS ☆
COMPILED & DRAWN BY HUNKIN

KINGS

THE FIRST ENGLISH KING KNOWN TO WEAR A CROWN WAS OFFA, c.AD 780. MOST CROWNS ARE VERY HEAVY AND UNCOMFORTABLE, BUT LESS SO THAN SOME EARLY CROWNS WHICH WERE SQUARE INSIDE AS WELL AS OUTSIDE.

BISHOPS

THE BISHOP'S MITRE IS THOUGHT TO HAVE EVOLVED FROM THE CONICAL HATS POPULAR IN THE 11TH CENTURY.

MILITARY HATS

IN THE 18TH CENTURY IT WAS THE FRENCH WHO LED THE FASHIONS IN HATS FOR WOMEN (FRENCH MILLINERS BECAME SOCIETY CELEBRITIES) & FOR MILITARY HEADGEAR. (THE FRENCH INVENTED ALL THE BASIC SHAPES USED THROUGHOUT EUROPE UNTIL THE WORLD WAR I TIN HELMET).

BOWLERS

THE BOWLER ORIGINATED AS THE HARD ROUND FELT HAT, (USUALLY WITH A BUTTON ON TOP) WORN BY COACH & CAB DRIVERS IN THE 1840s. IT BECAME FASHIONABLE AFTER PRINCE ALBERT WAS PHOTOGRAPHED HOLDING ONE.

TOP HATS

THE TOP HAT FIRST APPEARED, AS HIGH FASHION, IN THE 1790s. IT SLOWLY BECAME LESS FASHIONABLE & MORE RESPECTABLE, EVENTUALLY REPLACING THE 18TH CENTURY TRICORN.

GREY TOP HATS

GREY FELT TOP HATS HAVE BEEN WORN FOR WEDDINGS, ROYAL GARDEN PARTIES ETC., ONLY SINCE THE 1940s. BLACK TOP HATS, WORN PREVIOUSLY, DISAPPEARED BECAUSE OF THE WARTIME SHORTAGE OF BLACK HATTERS' PLUSH (A SORT OF VELVET), WHICH ALL CAME FROM GERMANY.

STUFFED ANIMALS

IN THE 1870s A FASHION FOR DECORATING LADIES' HATS WITH FEATHERS DEVELOPED INTO THE USE OF WHOLE STUFFED BIRDS, MICE & SMALL REPTILES. THEY REMAINED FASHIONABLE UNTIL WORLD WAR I.

HATTER'S FELT

ORDINARY FELT IS MADE BY SQUASHING DAMP WOOL FIBRES TOGETHER. FUR FELT, USED FOR THE BEST HATS, IS MADE THE SAME WAY, USING HAIRS CUT FROM BEAVER FUR INSTEAD OF WOOL. THE HAIRS FIRST HAVE TO BE BRUSHED WITH MERCURIC NITRATE TO RAISE THEIR MINUTE 'SCALES' SO THEY INTERLOCK WHEN FELTED.

SECURING HATS

THE 'MOHICAN' HAIRCUT FIRST APPEARED AS A DEVICE FOR SECURING HATS IN CHINESE & JAPANESE MILITARY INITIATION CEREMONIES. IT WAS CUSTOMARY TO SHAVE THE HEAD, LEAVING A STRAIGHT 'KNOT' OF HAIR STANDING IN THE MIDDLE TO WHICH HELMETS COULD BE FIXED WITH HAT PINS.

MAD HATTERS

THE EXPRESSION 'MAD AS A HATTER' COMES FROM THE SYMPTOMS OF MERCURY POISONING WHICH USED TO BE SUFFERED BY FELT MAKERS.

VALUE

THE MOST EVER PAID FOR A HAT IS $6,000 IN 1981 FOR AN AMERICAN INDIAN 'FROG' HELMET BOUGHT BY THE ALASKA STATE MUSEUM.

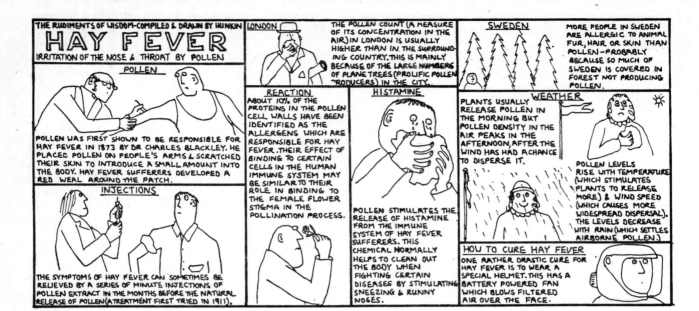

HAY FEVER

THE RUDIMENTS OF WISDOM-COMPILED & DRAWN BY HUNKIN

IRRITATION OF THE NOSE & THROAT BY POLLEN

POLLEN

POLLEN WAS FIRST SHOWN TO BE RESPONSIBLE FOR HAY FEVER IN 1873 BY DR CHARLES BLACKLEY. HE PLACED POLLEN ON PEOPLE'S ARMS & SCRATCHED THEIR SKIN TO INTRODUCE A SMALL AMOUNT INTO THE BODY. HAY FEVER SUFFERERS DEVELOPED A RED WEAL AROUND THE PATCH.

INJECTIONS

THE SYMPTOMS OF HAY FEVER CAN SOMETIMES BE RELIEVED BY A SERIES OF MINUTE INJECTIONS OF POLLEN EXTRACT IN THE MONTHS BEFORE THE NATURAL RELEASE OF POLLEN (A TREATMENT FIRST TRIED IN 1911).

LONDON

THE POLLEN COUNT (A MEASURE OF ITS CONCENTRATION IN THE AIR) IN LONDON IS USUALLY HIGHER THAN IN THE SURROUNDING COUNTRY. THIS IS MAINLY BECAUSE OF THE LARGE NUMBERS OF PLANE TREES (PROLIFIC POLLEN PRODUCERS) IN THE CITY.

REACTION

ABOUT 10% OF THE PROTEINS IN THE POLLEN CELL WALLS HAVE BEEN IDENTIFIED AS THE ALLERGENS WHICH ARE RESPONSIBLE FOR HAY FEVER. THEIR EFFECT OF BINDING TO CERTAIN CELLS IN THE HUMAN IMMUNE SYSTEM MAY BE SIMILAR TO THEIR ROLE IN BINDING TO THE FEMALE FLOWER STIGMA IN THE POLLINATION PROCESS.

HISTAMINE

POLLEN STIMULATES THE RELEASE OF HISTAMINE FROM THE IMMUNE SYSTEM OF HAY FEVER SUFFERERS. THIS CHEMICAL NORMALLY HELPS TO CLEAN OUT THE BODY WHEN FIGHTING CERTAIN DISEASES BY STIMULATING SNEEZING & RUNNY NOSES.

SWEDEN

MORE PEOPLE IN SWEDEN ARE ALLERGIC TO ANIMAL FUR, HAIR OR SKIN THAN POLLEN – PROBABLY BECAUSE SO MUCH OF SWEDEN IS COVERED IN FOREST NOT PRODUCING POLLEN.

WEATHER

PLANTS USUALLY RELEASE POLLEN IN THE MORNING BUT POLLEN DENSITY IN THE AIR PEAKS IN THE AFTERNOON, AFTER THE WIND HAS HAD A CHANCE TO DISPERSE IT.

POLLEN LEVELS RISE WITH TEMPERATURE (WHICH STIMULATES PLANTS TO RELEASE MORE) & WIND SPEED (WHICH CAUSES MORE WIDESPREAD DISPERSAL). THE LEVELS DECREASE WITH RAIN (WHICH SETTLES AIRBORNE POLLEN.)

HOW TO CURE HAY FEVER

ONE RATHER DRASTIC CURE FOR HAY FEVER IS TO WEAR A SPECIAL HELMET. THIS HAS A BATTERY POWERED FAN WHICH BLOWS FILTERED AIR OVER THE FACE.

☆ HYDROFOILS ☆

THE RUDIMENTS OF WISDOM

COMPILED & DRAWN BY HUNKIN

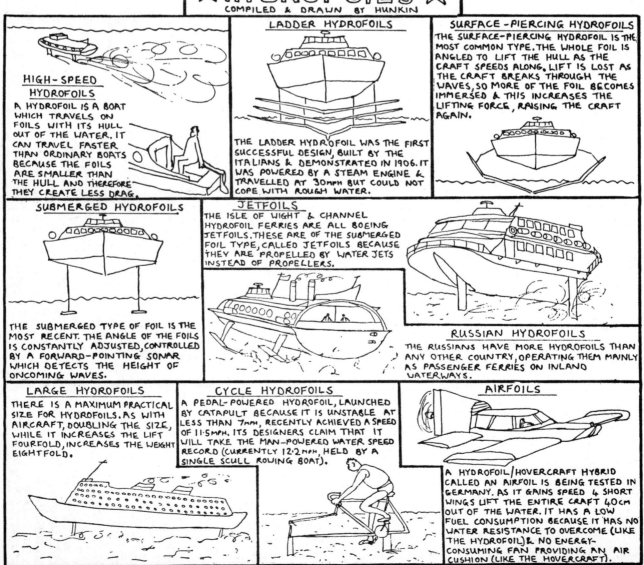

HIGH-SPEED HYDROFOILS

A HYDROFOIL IS A BOAT WHICH TRAVELS ON FOILS WITH ITS HULL OUT OF THE WATER. IT CAN TRAVEL FASTER THAN ORDINARY BOATS BECAUSE THE FOILS ARE SMALLER THAN THE HULL AND THEREFORE THEY CREATE LESS DRAG.

LADDER HYDROFOILS

THE LADDER HYDROFOIL WAS THE FIRST SUCCESSFUL DESIGN, BUILT BY THE ITALIANS & DEMONSTRATED IN 1906. IT WAS POWERED BY A STEAM ENGINE & TRAVELLED AT 30MPH BUT COULD NOT COPE WITH ROUGH WATER.

SURFACE-PIERCING HYDROFOILS

THE SURFACE-PIERCING HYDROFOIL IS THE MOST COMMON TYPE. THE WHOLE FOIL IS ANGLED TO LIFT THE HULL AS THE CRAFT SPEEDS ALONG. LIFT IS LOST AS THE CRAFT BREAKS THROUGH THE WAVES, SO MORE OF THE FOIL BECOMES IMMERSED & THIS INCREASES THE LIFTING FORCE, RAISING THE CRAFT AGAIN.

SUBMERGED HYDROFOILS

THE SUBMERGED TYPE OF FOIL IS THE MOST RECENT. THE ANGLE OF THE FOILS IS CONSTANTLY ADJUSTED, CONTROLLED BY A FORWARD-POINTING SONAR WHICH DETECTS THE HEIGHT OF ONCOMING WAVES.

JETFOILS

THE ISLE OF WIGHT & CHANNEL HYDROFOIL FERRIES ARE ALL BOEING JETFOILS. THESE ARE OF THE SUBMERGED FOIL TYPE, CALLED JETFOILS BECAUSE THEY ARE PROPELLED BY WATER JETS INSTEAD OF PROPELLERS.

RUSSIAN HYDROFOILS

THE RUSSIANS HAVE MORE HYDROFOILS THAN ANY OTHER COUNTRY, OPERATING THEM MAINLY AS PASSENGER FERRIES ON INLAND WATERWAYS.

LARGE HYDROFOILS

THERE IS A MAXIMUM PRACTICAL SIZE FOR HYDROFOILS. AS WITH AIRCRAFT, DOUBLING THE SIZE, WHILE IT INCREASES THE LIFT FOURFOLD, INCREASES THE WEIGHT EIGHTFOLD.

CYCLE HYDROFOILS

A PEDAL-POWERED HYDROFOIL, LAUNCHED BY CATAPULT BECAUSE IT IS UNSTABLE AT LESS THAN 7MPH, RECENTLY ACHIEVED A SPEED OF 11.5MPH. ITS DESIGNERS CLAIM THAT IT WILL TAKE THE MAN-POWERED WATER SPEED RECORD (CURRENTLY 12.2MPH, HELD BY A SINGLE SCULL ROWING BOAT).

AIRFOILS

A HYDROFOIL/HOVERCRAFT HYBRID CALLED AN AIRFOIL IS BEING TESTED IN GERMANY. AS IT GAINS SPEED 4 SHORT WINGS LIFT THE ENTIRE CRAFT 40CM OUT OF THE WATER. IT HAS A LOW FUEL CONSUMPTION BECAUSE IT HAS NO WATER RESISTANCE TO OVERCOME (LIKE THE HYDROFOIL) & NO ENERGY-CONSUMING FAN PROVIDING AN AIR CUSHION (LIKE THE HOVERCRAFT).

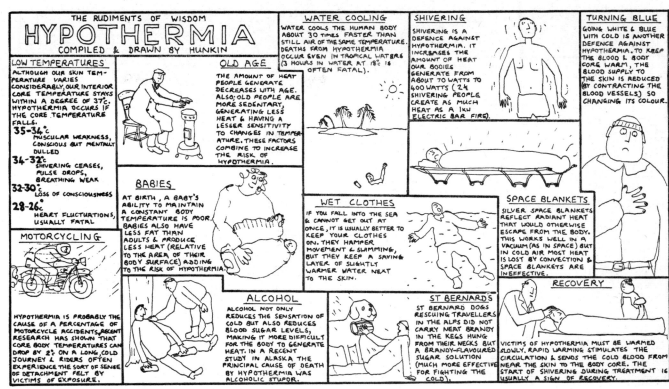

THE RUDIMENTS OF WISDOM
HYPOTHERMIA
COMPILED & DRAWN BY HUNKIN

LOW TEMPERATURES
ALTHOUGH OUR SKIN TEMPERATURE VARIES CONSIDERABLY, OUR INTERIOR CORE TEMPERATURE STAYS WITHIN A DEGREE OF 37°C. HYPOTHERMIA OCCURS IF THE CORE TEMPERATURE FALLS.

35-34°C MUSCULAR WEAKNESS, CONSCIOUS BUT MENTALLY DULLED

34-32°C SHIVERING CEASES, PULSE DROPS, BREATHING WEAK

32-30°C LOSS OF CONSCIOUSNESS

28-26°C HEART FLUCTUATIONS, USUALLY FATAL

MOTORCYCLING
HYPOTHERMIA IS PROBABLY THE CAUSE OF A PERCENTAGE OF MOTORCYCLE ACCIDENTS. RECENT RESEARCH HAS SHOWN THAT CORE BODY TEMPERATURES CAN DROP BY 2° ON A LONG COLD JOURNEY & RIDERS OFTEN EXPERIENCE THE SORT OF SENSE OF DETACHMENT FELT BY VICTIMS OF EXPOSURE.

OLD AGE
THE AMOUNT OF HEAT PEOPLE GENERATE DECREASES WITH AGE. ALSO, OLD PEOPLE ARE MORE SEDENTARY, GENERATING LESS HEAT & HAVING A LESSER SENSITIVITY TO CHANGES IN TEMPERATURE. THESE FACTORS COMBINE TO INCREASE THE RISK OF HYPOTHERMIA.

BABIES
AT BIRTH, A BABY'S ABILITY TO MAINTAIN A CONSTANT BODY TEMPERATURE IS POOR. BABIES ALSO HAVE LESS FAT THAN ADULTS & PRODUCE LESS HEAT (RELATIVE TO THE AREA OF THEIR BODY SURFACE) ADDING TO THE RISK OF HYPOTHERMIA.

ALCOHOL
ALCOHOL NOT ONLY REDUCES THE SENSATION OF COLD BUT ALSO REDUCES BLOOD SUGAR LEVELS, MAKING IT MORE DIFFICULT FOR THE BODY TO GENERATE HEAT. IN A RECENT STUDY IN ALASKA THE PRINCIPAL CAUSE OF DEATH BY HYPOTHERMIA WAS ALCOHOLIC STUPOR.

WATER COOLING
WATER COOLS THE HUMAN BODY ABOUT 30 TIMES FASTER THAN STILL AIR OF THE SAME TEMPERATURE. DEATHS FROM HYPOTHERMIA OCCUR EVEN IN TROPICAL WATERS (3 HOURS IN WATER AT 18°C IS OFTEN FATAL).

WET CLOTHES
IF YOU FALL INTO THE SEA & CANNOT GET OUT AT ONCE, IT IS USUALLY BETTER TO KEEP YOUR CLOTHES ON. THEY HAMPER MOVEMENT & SWIMMING, BUT THEY KEEP A SAVING LAYER OF SLIGHTLY WARMER WATER NEXT TO THE SKIN.

ST BERNARDS
ST BERNARD DOGS RESCUING TRAVELLERS IN THE ALPS DID NOT CARRY NEAT BRANDY IN THE KEGS HUNG FROM THEIR NECKS BUT A BRANDY-FLAVOURED SUGAR SOLUTION (MUCH MORE EFFECTIVE FOR FIGHTING THE COLD).

SHIVERING
SHIVERING IS A DEFENCE AGAINST HYPOTHERMIA. IT INCREASES THE AMOUNT OF HEAT OUR BODIES GENERATE FROM ABOUT 70 WATTS TO 400 WATTS (24 SHIVERING PEOPLE CREATE AS MUCH HEAT AS A 1KW ELECTRIC BAR FIRE).

SPACE BLANKETS
SILVER SPACE BLANKETS REFLECT RADIANT HEAT THAT WOULD OTHERWISE ESCAPE FROM THE BODY. THIS WORKS WELL IN A VACUUM (AS IN SPACE) BUT IN COLD AIR MOST HEAT IS LOST BY CONVECTION & SPACE BLANKETS ARE INEFFECTIVE.

TURNING BLUE
GOING WHITE & BLUE WITH COLD IS ANOTHER DEFENCE AGAINST HYPOTHERMIA. TO KEEP THE BLOOD & BODY CORE WARM, THE BLOOD SUPPLY TO THE SKIN IS REDUCED (BY CONTRACTING THE BLOOD VESSELS) SO CHANGING ITS COLOUR.

RECOVERY
VICTIMS OF HYPOTHERMIA MUST BE WARMED SLOWLY. RAPID WARMING STIMULATES THE CIRCULATION & SENDS THE COLD BLOOD FROM NEAR THE SKIN TO THE BODY CORE. THE START OF SHIVERING DURING TREATMENT IS USUALLY A SIGN OF RECOVERY.

GOAT BOATS
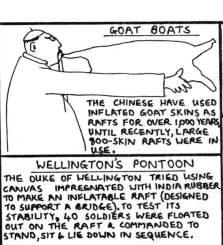
THE CHINESE HAVE USED INFLATED GOAT SKINS AS RAFTS FOR OVER 1,000 YEARS. UNTIL RECENTLY, LARGE 800-SKIN RAFTS WERE IN USE.

WELLINGTON'S PONTOON
THE DUKE OF WELLINGTON TRIED USING CANVAS IMPREGNATED WITH INDIA RUBBER TO MAKE AN INFLATABLE RAFT (DESIGNED TO SUPPORT A BRIDGE). TO TEST ITS STABILITY, 40 SOLDIERS WERE FLOATED OUT ON THE RAFT & COMMANDED TO STAND, SIT & LIE DOWN IN SEQUENCE.

THE BOAT CLOAK
THE FIRST INFLATABLE BOAT WAS MADE BY A LT HALKETT IN 1844. IT WAS INCORPORATED INTO A CLOAK IN THE FORM OF AN INSET OVAL PANEL WHICH COULD BE INFLATED. THE BOAT CLOAK WAS USED ON SEVERAL ARCTIC EXPEDITIONS.

THE RUDIMENTS OF WISDOM
INFLATABLE BOATS
COMPILED & DRAWN BY HUNKIN

PLEASURE BOATS
TODAY'S INFLATABLE BOATS ARE BASED ON THE DESIGNS OF THE BRITISH INVENTOR R.F. DAGNELL. HIS COMPANY SOLD A RANGE OF INFLATABLES IN THE 1930s. THEY CAME WITH TUBES TO CONNECT THEM TO CAR EXHAUST PIPES (THE EXHAUST GASES WERE USED TO INFLATE THE BOATS).

SURVIVAL BOATS
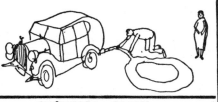
INFLATABLE BOATS WERE FIRST MASS-PRODUCED IN WORLD WAR TWO. BY 1941 ALL FIGHTER PILOTS HAD ONE FITTED TO THEIR PARACHUTE PACKS. THESE WERE ALSO THE FIRST CRAFT TO INFLATE AUTOMATICALLY FROM A GAS CYLINDER. THEY SAVED OVER 7,000 AIRMEN DURING THE WAR.

ROTTEN BOATS
SUNLIGHT ROTS NATURAL RUBBER SO THE EARLY INFLATABLES WERE NEVER VERY DURABLE OR POPULAR. IN THE 1950s A CHEMICAL COATING CALLED HYPALON WAS DEVELOPED WHICH PREVENTED THE ROT.

LIFE BOATS

THE FIRST INFLATABLE INSHORE LIFE BOATS CAME INTO SERVICE IN 1963. THEIR FIRST RESCUE WAS AT ABERYSTWYTH WHEN 3 PEOPLE & A DOG WERE SAVED.

UNSINKABLE BOATS
INFLATABLE BOATS ARE TOO FLEXIBLE TO TRAVEL FAST IN ROUGH SEAS. HOWEVER BY ADDING A RIGID BOTTOM THEY CAN BE MADE EXCEPTIONALLY STABLE. THE RECENT 'ATLANTIC' CLASS LIFEBOATS ARE RIGID INFLATABLES, WITH THE BUOYANCY TUBES FIXED TO A SHALLOW FIBREGLASS HULL.

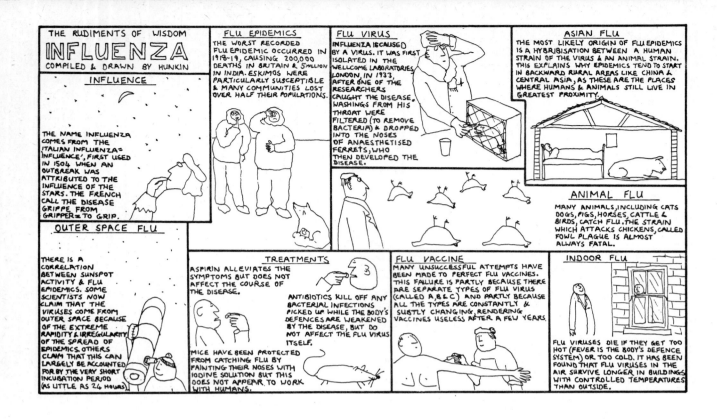

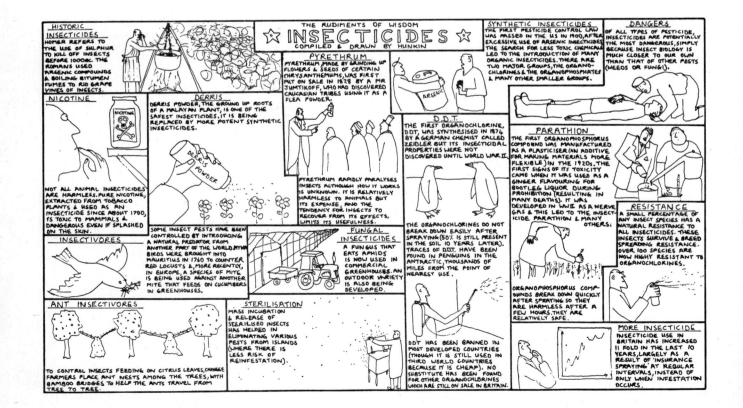

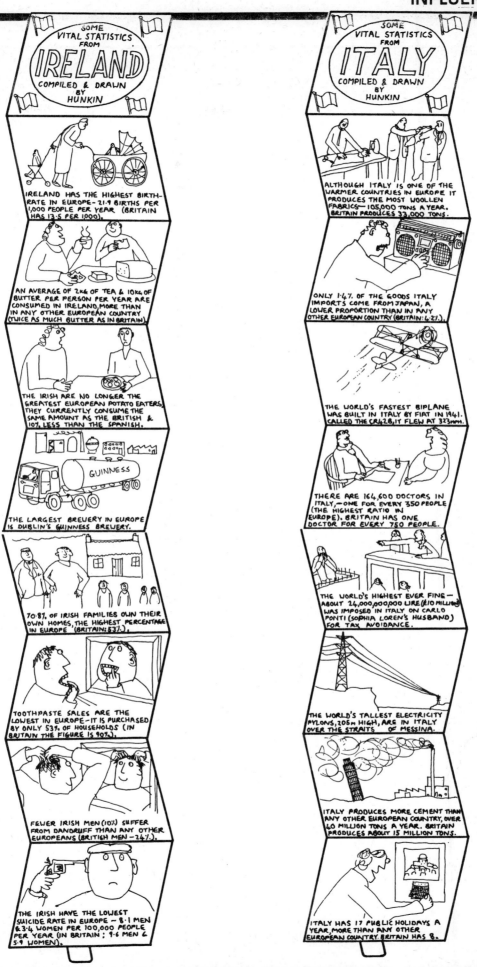

SOME VITAL STATISTICS FROM IRELAND
COMPILED & DRAWN BY HUNKIN

IRELAND HAS THE HIGHEST BIRTH-RATE IN EUROPE – 21.9 BIRTHS PER 1,000 PEOPLE PER YEAR (BRITAIN HAS 13.5 PER 1000).

AN AVERAGE OF 2kg OF TEA & 10kg OF BUTTER PER PERSON PER YEAR ARE CONSUMED IN IRELAND, MORE THAN IN ANY OTHER EUROPEAN COUNTRY (TWICE AS MUCH BUTTER AS IN BRITAIN).

THE IRISH ARE NO LONGER THE GREATEST EUROPEAN POTATO EATERS, THEY CURRENTLY CONSUME THE SAME AMOUNT AS THE BRITISH & 10% LESS THAN THE SPANISH.

THE LARGEST BREWERY IN EUROPE IS DUBLIN'S GUINNESS BREWERY.

70.8% OF IRISH FAMILIES OWN THEIR OWN HOMES, THE HIGHEST PERCENTAGE IN EUROPE (BRITAIN: 53%).

TOOTHPASTE SALES ARE THE LOWEST IN EUROPE – IT IS PURCHASED BY ONLY 53% OF HOUSEHOLDS (IN BRITAIN THE FIGURE IS 90%).

FEWER IRISH MEN (10%) SUFFER FROM DANDRUFF THAN ANY OTHER EUROPEANS (BRITISH MEN – 24%).

THE IRISH HAVE THE LOWEST SUICIDE RATE IN EUROPE – 8.1 MEN & 3.4 WOMEN PER 100,000 PEOPLE PER YEAR (IN BRITAIN: 9.6 MEN & 5.9 WOMEN).

SOME VITAL STATISTICS FROM ITALY
COMPILED & DRAWN BY HUNKIN

ALTHOUGH ITALY IS ONE OF THE WARMER COUNTRIES IN EUROPE IT PRODUCES THE MOST WOOLLEN FABRICS – 105,000 TONS A YEAR. BRITAIN PRODUCES 33,000 TONS.

ONLY 1.4% OF THE GOODS ITALY IMPORTS COME FROM JAPAN, A LOWER PROPORTION THAN IN ANY OTHER EUROPEAN COUNTRY (BRITAIN: 6.2%).

THE WORLD'S FASTEST BIPLANE WAS BUILT IN ITALY BY FIAT IN 1941. CALLED THE CR428, IT FLEW AT 323mph.

THERE ARE 164,600 DOCTORS IN ITALY, – ONE FOR EVERY 350 PEOPLE (THE HIGHEST RATIO IN EUROPE). BRITAIN HAS ONE DOCTOR FOR EVERY 750 PEOPLE.

THE WORLD'S HIGHEST EVER FINE – ABOUT 24,000,000,000 LIRE (£10 MILLION) WAS IMPOSED IN ITALY ON CARLO PONTI (SOPHIA LOREN'S HUSBAND) FOR TAX AVOIDANCE.

THE WORLD'S TALLEST ELECTRICITY PYLONS, 205m HIGH, ARE IN ITALY OVER THE STRAITS OF MESSINA.

ITALY PRODUCES MORE CEMENT THAN ANY OTHER EUROPEAN COUNTRY, OVER 40 MILLION TONS A YEAR. BRITAIN PRODUCES ABOUT 15 MILLION TONS.

ITALY HAS 17 PUBLIC HOLIDAYS A YEAR, MORE THAN ANY OTHER EUROPEAN COUNTRY. BRITAIN HAS 8.

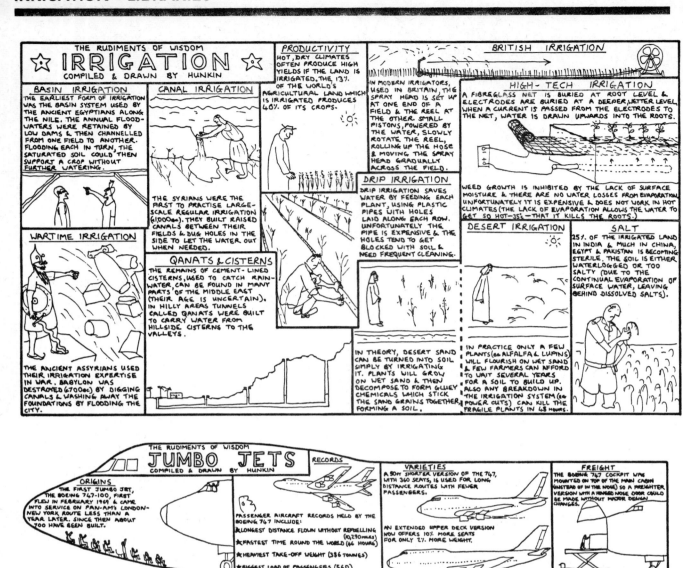

THE RUDIMENTS OF WISDOM
☆ IRRIGATION ☆
COMPILED & DRAWN BY HUNKIN

BASIN IRRIGATION
THE EARLIEST FORM OF IRRIGATION WAS THE BASIN SYSTEM USED BY THE ANCIENT EGYPTIANS ALONG THE NILE. THE ANNUAL FLOOD-WATERS WERE RETAINED BY LOW DAMS & THEN CHANNELLED FROM ONE FIELD TO ANOTHER. FLOODING EACH IN TURN, THE SATURATED SOIL COULD THEN SUPPORT A CROP WITHOUT FURTHER WATERING.

CANAL IRRIGATION
THE SYRIANS WERE THE FIRST TO PRACTISE LARGE-SCALE REGULAR IRRIGATION (1000BC). THEY BUILT RAISED CANALS BETWEEN THEIR FIELDS & DUG HOLES IN THE SIDE TO LET THE WATER OUT WHEN NEEDED.

WARTIME IRRIGATION
THE ANCIENT ASSYRIANS USED THEIR IRRIGATION EXPERTISE IN WAR. BABYLON WAS DESTROYED (670OBC) BY DIGGING CANALS & WASHING AWAY THE FOUNDATIONS BY FLOODING THE CITY.

QANATS & CISTERNS
THE REMAINS OF CEMENT-LINED CISTERNS, USED TO CATCH RAIN-WATER, CAN BE FOUND IN MANY PARTS OF THE MIDDLE EAST (THEIR AGE IS UNCERTAIN). IN HILLY AREAS TUNNELS CALLED QANATS WERE BUILT TO CARRY WATER FROM HILLSIDE CISTERNS TO THE VALLEYS.

PRODUCTIVITY
HOT, DRY CLIMATES OFTEN PRODUCE HIGH YIELDS IF THE LAND IS IRRIGATED. THE 13% OF THE WORLD'S AGRICULTURAL LAND WHICH IS IRRIGATED PRODUCES 40% OF ITS CROPS.

IN MODERN IRRIGATORS, USED IN BRITAIN, THE SPRAY HEAD IS SET UP AT ONE END OF A FIELD & THE REEL AT THE OTHER SMALL PISTONS, POWERED BY THE WATER, SLOWLY ROTATE THE REEL, ROLLING UP THE HOSE & MOVING THE SPRAY HEAD GRADUALLY ACROSS THE FIELD.

DRIP IRRIGATION
DRIP IRRIGATION SAVES WATER BY FEEDING EACH PLANT, USING PLASTIC PIPES WITH HOLES LAID ALONG EACH ROW. UNFORTUNATELY THE PIPE IS EXPENSIVE & THE HOLES TEND TO GET BLOCKED WITH SOIL & NEED FREQUENT CLEANING.

IN THEORY, DESERT SAND CAN BE TURNED INTO SOIL SIMPLY BY IRRIGATING IT. PLANTS WILL GROW ON WET SAND & THEN DECOMPOSE TO FORM GLUEY CHEMICALS WHICH STICK THE SAND GRAINS TOGETHER, FORMING A SOIL.

BRITISH IRRIGATION

HIGH-TECH IRRIGATION
A FIBREGLASS NET IS BURIED AT ROOT LEVEL & ELECTRODES ARE BURIED AT A DEEPER, WETTER LEVEL. WHEN A CURRENT IS PASSED FROM THE ELECTRODES TO THE NET, WATER IS DRAWN UPWARDS INTO THE ROOTS.

WEED GROWTH IS INHIBITED BY THE LACK OF SURFACE MOISTURE & THERE ARE NO WATER LOSSES FROM EVAPORATION. UNFORTUNATELY IT IS EXPENSIVE & DOES NOT WORK IN HOT CLIMATES (THE LACK OF EVAPORATION ALLOWS THE WATER TO GET SO HOT – 35% – THAT IT KILLS THE ROOTS.)

DESERT IRRIGATION

SALT
25% OF THE IRRIGATED LAND IN INDIA & MUCH IN CHINA, EGYPT & PAKISTAN IS BECOMING STERILE. THE SOIL IS EITHER WATERLOGGED OR TOO SALTY (DUE TO THE CONTINUAL EVAPORATION OF SURFACE WATER, LEAVING BEHIND DISSOLVED SALTS).

IN PRACTICE ONLY A FEW PLANTS (eg ALFALFA & LUPINS) WILL FLOURISH ON WET SAND & FEW FARMERS CAN AFFORD TO WAIT SEVERAL YEARS FOR A SOIL TO BUILD UP. ALSO ANY BREAKDOWN IN THE IRRIGATION SYSTEM (eg POWER CUTS) CAN KILL THE FRAGILE PLANTS IN 48 HOURS.

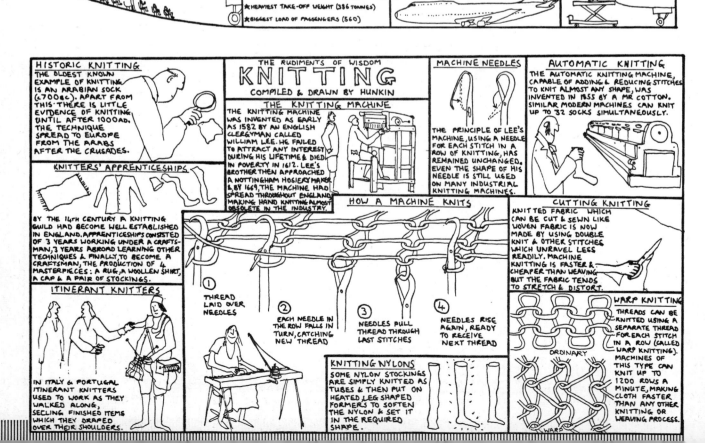

THE RUDIMENTS OF WISDOM
JUMBO JETS
COMPILED & DRAWN BY HUNKIN

ORIGINS
THE FIRST JUMBO JET, THE BOEING 747-100, FIRST FLEW IN FEBRUARY 1969 & CAME INTO SERVICE ON PAN-AM'S LONDON-NEW YORK ROUTE LESS THAN A YEAR LATER. SINCE THEN ABOUT 700 HAVE BEEN BUILT.

RECORDS
PASSENGER AIRCRAFT RECORDS HELD BY THE BOEING 747 INCLUDE:
★ LONGEST DISTANCE FLOWN WITHOUT REFUELLING (10,290 miles)
★ FASTEST TIME ROUND THE WORLD (46 HOURS)
★ HEAVIEST TAKE-OFF WEIGHT (386 TONNES)
★ BIGGEST LOAD OF PASSENGERS (560)

VARIETIES
A 50FT SHORTER VERSION OF THE 747, WITH 360 SEATS, IS USED FOR LONG DISTANCE ROUTES WITH FEWER PASSENGERS.

AN EXTENDED UPPER DECK VERSION NOW OFFERS 10% MORE SEATS FOR ONLY 2% MORE WEIGHT.

FREIGHT
THE BOEING 747 COCKPIT WAS MOUNTED ON TOP OF THE MAIN CABIN (INSTEAD OF IN THE NOSE) SO A FREIGHTER VERSION WITH A HINGED NOSE DOOR COULD BE MADE WITHOUT MAJOR DESIGN CHANGES.

HISTORIC KNITTING
THE OLDEST KNOWN EXAMPLE OF KNITTING IS AN ARABIAN SOCK (c700BC). APART FROM THIS THERE IS LITTLE EVIDENCE OF KNITTING UNTIL AFTER 1000AD. THE TECHNIQUE SPREAD TO EUROPE FROM THE ARABS AFTER THE CRUSADES.

KNITTERS' APPRENTICESHIPS
BY THE 14th CENTURY A KNITTING GUILD HAD BECOME WELL ESTABLISHED IN ENGLAND. APPRENTICESHIPS CONSISTED OF 3 YEARS WORKING UNDER A CRAFTS-MAN, 3 YEARS ABROAD LEARNING OTHER TECHNIQUES & FINALLY, TO BECOME A CRAFTSMAN, THE PRODUCTION OF 4 MASTERPIECES: A RUG, A WOOLLEN SHIRT, A CAP & A PAIR OF STOCKINGS.

ITINERANT KNITTERS
IN ITALY & PORTUGAL ITINERANT KNITTERS USED TO WORK AS THEY WALKED ALONG, SELLING FINISHED ITEMS WHICH THEY DRAPED OVER THEIR SHOULDERS.

THE RUDIMENTS OF WISDOM
KNITTING
COMPILED & DRAWN BY HUNKIN

THE KNITTING MACHINE
THE KNITTING MACHINE WAS INVENTED AS EARLY AS 1582 BY AN ENGLISH CLERGYMAN CALLED WILLIAM LEE. HE FAILED TO ATTRACT ANY INTEREST DURING HIS LIFETIME & DIED IN POVERTY IN 1612. LEE'S BROTHER THEN APPROACHED A NOTTINGHAM HOSIERY MAKER & BY 1669, THE MACHINE HAD SPREAD THROUGHOUT ENGLAND MAKING HAND KNITTING ALMOST OBSOLETE IN THE INDUSTRY.

HOW A MACHINE KNITS
① THREAD LAID OVER NEEDLES
② EACH NEEDLE IN THE ROW FALLS IN TURN, CATCHING NEW THREAD
③ NEEDLES PULL THREAD THROUGH LAST STITCHES
④ NEEDLES RISE AGAIN, READY TO RECEIVE NEXT THREAD

KNITTING NYLONS
SOME NYLON STOCKINGS ARE SIMPLY KNITTED AS TUBES & THEN PUT ON HEATED LEG SHAPED FORMERS TO SOFTEN THE NYLON & SET IT IN THE REQUIRED SHAPE.

MACHINE NEEDLES
THE PRINCIPLE OF LEE'S MACHINE, USING A NEEDLE FOR EACH STITCH IN A ROW OF KNITTING, HAS REMAINED UNCHANGED. EVEN THE SHAPE OF HIS NEEDLE IS STILL USED ON MANY INDUSTRIAL KNITTING MACHINES.

AUTOMATIC KNITTING
THE AUTOMATIC KNITTING MACHINE, CAPABLE OF ADDING & REDUCING STITCHES TO KNIT ALMOST ANY SHAPE, WAS INVENTED IN 1855 BY A MR COTTON. SIMILAR MODERN MACHINES CAN KNIT UP TO 32 SOCKS SIMULTANEOUSLY.

CUTTING KNITTING
KNITTED FABRIC WHICH CAN BE CUT & SEWN LIKE WOVEN FABRIC IS NOW MADE BY USING DOUBLE KNIT & OTHER STITCHES WHICH UNRAVEL LESS READILY. MACHINE KNITTING IS FASTER & CHEAPER THAN WEAVING BUT THE FABRIC TENDS TO STRETCH & DISTORT.

WARP KNITTING
THREADS CAN BE KNITTED USING A SEPARATE THREAD FOR EACH STITCH IN A ROW (CALLED WARP KNITTING). MACHINES OF THIS TYPE CAN KNIT UP TO 1200 ROWS A MINUTE, MAKING CLOTH FASTER THAN ANY OTHER KNITTING OR WEAVING PROCESS.

ORDINARY

WARP

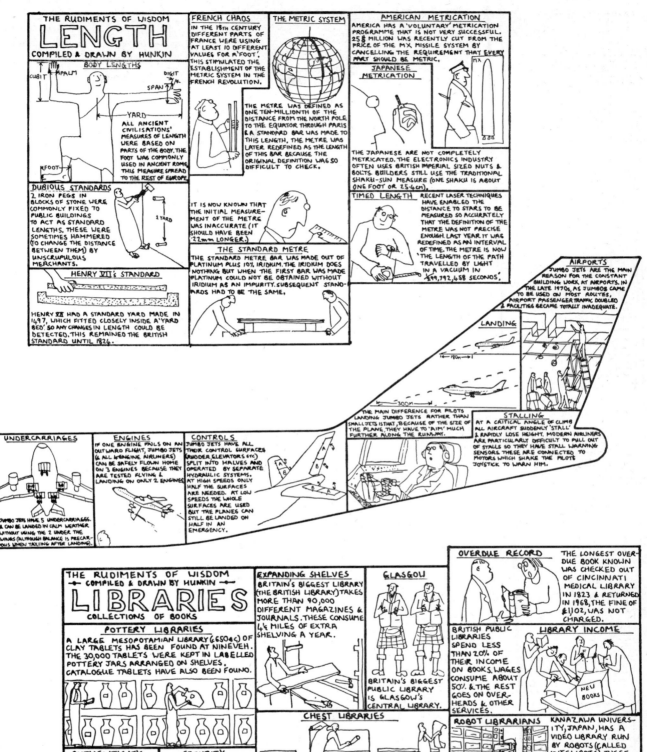

THE RUDIMENTS OF WISDOM
LENGTH
COMPILED & DRAWN BY HUNKIN

BODY LENGTHS
CUBIT · PALM · DIGIT · SPAN · YARD · FOOT

ALL ANCIENT CIVILISATIONS' MEASURES OF LENGTH WERE BASED ON PARTS OF THE BODY. THE FOOT WAS COMMONLY USED IN ANCIENT ROME. THIS MEASURE SPREAD TO THE REST OF EUROPE.

DUBIOUS STANDARDS
2 IRON PEGS IN BLOCKS OF STONE WERE COMMONLY FIXED TO PUBLIC BUILDINGS TO ACT AS STANDARD LENGTHS. THESE WERE SOMETIMES HAMMERED (TO CHANGE THE DISTANCE BETWEEN THEM) BY UNSCRUPULOUS MERCHANTS.

1 YARD

HENRY VII's STANDARD
HENRY VII HAD A STANDARD YARD MADE IN 1497, WHICH FITTED CLOSELY INSIDE A 'YARD BED' SO ANY CHANGES IN LENGTH COULD BE DETECTED. THIS REMAINED THE BRITISH STANDARD UNTIL 1824.

FRENCH CHAOS
IN THE 18TH CENTURY DIFFERENT PARTS OF FRANCE WERE USING AT LEAST 10 DIFFERENT VALUES FOR A 'FOOT'. THIS STIMULATED THE ESTABLISHMENT OF THE METRIC SYSTEM IN THE FRENCH REVOLUTION.

IT IS NOW KNOWN THAT THE INITIAL MEASUREMENT OF THE METRE WAS INACCURATE (IT SHOULD HAVE BEEN .22mm LONGER.)

THE STANDARD METRE
THE STANDARD METRE BAR WAS MADE OUT OF PLATINUM PLUS 10% IRIDIUM. THE IRIDIUM DOES NOTHING BUT WHEN THE FIRST BAR WAS MADE PLATINUM COULD NOT BE OBTAINED WITHOUT IRIDIUM AS AN IMPURITY. SUBSEQUENT STANDARDS HAD TO BE THE SAME.

THE METRIC SYSTEM
THE METRE WAS DEFINED AS ONE TEN-MILLIONTH OF THE DISTANCE FROM THE NORTH POLE TO THE EQUATOR THROUGH PARIS & A STANDARD BAR WAS MADE TO THIS LENGTH. THE METRE WAS LATER REDEFINED AS THE LENGTH OF THIS BAR BECAUSE THE ORIGINAL DEFINITION WAS SO DIFFICULT TO CHECK.

AMERICAN METRICATION
AMERICA HAS A 'VOLUNTARY' METRICATION PROGRAMME THAT IS NOT VERY SUCCESSFUL. 25½ MILLION WAS RECENTLY CUT FROM THE PRICE OF THE MX MISSILE SYSTEM BY CANCELLING THE REQUIREMENT THAT EVERY PART SHOULD BE METRIC.

JAPANESE METRICATION
THE JAPANESE ARE NOT COMPLETELY METRICATED. THE ELECTRONICS INDUSTRY OFTEN USES BRITISH IMPERIAL SIZED NUTS & BOLTS. BUILDERS STILL USE THE TRADITIONAL SHAKU-SUN MEASURE (ONE SHAKU IS ABOUT ONE FOOT OR 25.4cm).

TIMED LENGTH
RECENT LASER TECHNIQUES HAVE ENABLED THE DISTANCE TO STARS TO BE MEASURED SO ACCURATELY THAT THE DEFINITION OF THE METRE WAS NOT PRECISE ENOUGH. LAST YEAR IT WAS REDEFINED AS AN INTERVAL OF TIME. THE METRE IS NOW 'THE LENGTH OF THE PATH TRAVELLED BY LIGHT IN A VACUUM IN 1/299,792,458 SECONDS'.

AIRPORTS
JUMBO JETS ARE THE MAIN REASON FOR THE CONSTANT BUILDING WORK AT AIRPORTS. IN THE LATE 1970s, AS JUMBOS CAME TO BE USED ON MOST ROUTES, AIRPORT PASSENGER TRAFFIC DOUBLED & FACILITIES BECAME TOTALLY INADEQUATE.

LANDING
190m · 300m

THE MAIN DIFFERENCE FOR PILOTS LANDING JUMBO JETS RATHER THAN SMALL JETS IS THAT, BECAUSE OF THE SIZE OF THE PLANE, THEY HAVE TO 'AIM' MUCH FURTHER ALONG THE RUNWAY.

STALLING
AT A CRITICAL ANGLE OF CLIMB ALL AIRCRAFT SUDDENLY 'STALL' & RAPIDLY LOSE HEIGHT. MODERN AIRLINERS ARE PARTICULARLY DIFFICULT TO PULL OUT OF STALLS SO THEY HAVE STALL WARNING SENSORS. THESE ARE CONNECTED TO MOTORS WHICH SHAKE THE PILOTS JOYSTICK TO WARN HIM.

UNDERCARRIAGES
JUMBO JETS HAVE 5 UNDERCARRIAGES & CAN BE LANDED IN CALM WEATHER WITHOUT USING THE 2 UNDER THE WINGS (ALTHOUGH BALANCE IS PRECARIOUS WHEN TAXIING AFTER LANDING).

ENGINES
IF ONE ENGINE FAILS ON AN OUTWARD FLIGHT, JUMBO JETS (& ALL 4-ENGINE AIRLINERS) CAN BE SAFELY FLOWN HOME ON 3 ENGINES BECAUSE THEY ARE TESTED FLYING & LANDING ON ONLY 2 ENGINES.

CONTROLS
JUMBO JETS HAVE ALL THEIR CONTROL SURFACES (RUDDER, ELEVATORS ETC) SPLIT INTO HALVES AND OPERATED BY SEPARATE HYDRAULIC SYSTEMS. AT HIGH SPEEDS ONLY HALF THE SURFACES ARE NEEDED. AT LOW SPEEDS THE WHOLE SURFACES ARE USED BUT THE PLANES CAN STILL BE LANDED ON HALF IN AN EMERGENCY.

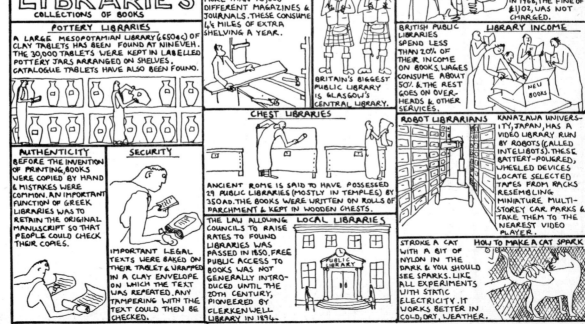

THE RUDIMENTS OF WISDOM
COMPILED & DRAWN BY HUNKIN
LIBRARIES
COLLECTIONS OF BOOKS

POTTERY LIBRARIES
A LARGE MESOPOTAMIAN LIBRARY (650 BC) OF CLAY TABLETS HAS BEEN FOUND AT NINEVEH. THE 30,000 TABLETS WERE KEPT IN LABELLED POTTERY JARS ARRANGED ON SHELVES. CATALOGUE TABLETS HAVE ALSO BEEN FOUND.

AUTHENTICITY
BEFORE THE INVENTION OF PRINTING, BOOKS WERE COPIED BY HAND & MISTAKES WERE COMMON. AN IMPORTANT FUNCTION OF GREEK LIBRARIES WAS TO RETAIN THE ORIGINAL MANUSCRIPT SO THAT PEOPLE COULD CHECK THEIR COPIES.

SECURITY
IMPORTANT LEGAL TEXTS WERE BAKED ON THEIR TABLET & WRAPPED IN A CLAY ENVELOPE ON WHICH THE TEXT WAS REPEATED. ANY TAMPERING WITH THE TEXT COULD THEN BE CHECKED.

EXPANDING SHELVES
BRITAIN'S BIGGEST LIBRARY (THE BRITISH LIBRARY) TAKES MORE THAN 90,000 DIFFERENT MAGAZINES & JOURNALS. THESE CONSUME 4½ MILES OF EXTRA SHELVING A YEAR.

CHEST LIBRARIES
ANCIENT ROME IS SAID TO HAVE POSSESSED 29 PUBLIC LIBRARIES (MOSTLY IN TEMPLES) BY 350 AD. THE BOOKS WERE WRITTEN ON ROLLS OF PARCHMENT & KEPT IN WOODEN CHESTS.

LOCAL LIBRARIES
THE LAW ALLOWING COUNCILS TO RAISE RATES TO FOUND LIBRARIES WAS PASSED IN 1850. FREE PUBLIC ACCESS TO BOOKS WAS NOT GENERALLY INTRODUCED UNTIL THE 20TH CENTURY, PIONEERED BY CLERKENWELL LIBRARY IN 1894.

PUBLIC LIBRARY

GLASGOW
BRITAIN'S BIGGEST PUBLIC LIBRARY IS GLASGOW'S CENTRAL LIBRARY.

OVERDUE RECORD
THE LONGEST OVERDUE BOOK KNOWN WAS CHECKED OUT OF CINCINNATI MEDICAL LIBRARY IN 1823 & RETURNED IN 1968. THE FINE OF £2102 WAS NOT CHARGED.

BRITISH PUBLIC LIBRARIES SPEND LESS THAN 20% OF THEIR INCOME ON BOOKS. WAGES CONSUME ABOUT 50% & THE REST GOES ON OVERHEADS & OTHER SERVICES.

LIBRARY INCOME
NEW BOOKS

ROBOT LIBRARIANS
KANAZAWA UNIVERSITY, JAPAN, HAS A VIDEO LIBRARY RUN BY ROBOTS (CALLED INTELIBOTS). THESE BATTERY-POWERED, WHEELED DEVICES LOCATE SELECTED TAPES FROM RACKS RESEMBLING MINIATURE MULTI-STOREY CAR PARKS & TAKE THEM TO THE NEAREST VIDEO PLAYER.

HOW TO MAKE A CAT SPARK
STROKE A CAT WITH A BIT OF NYLON IN THE DARK & YOU SHOULD SEE SPARKS. LIKE ALL EXPERIMENTS WITH STATIC ELECTRICITY, IT WORKS BETTER IN COLD, DRY WEATHER.

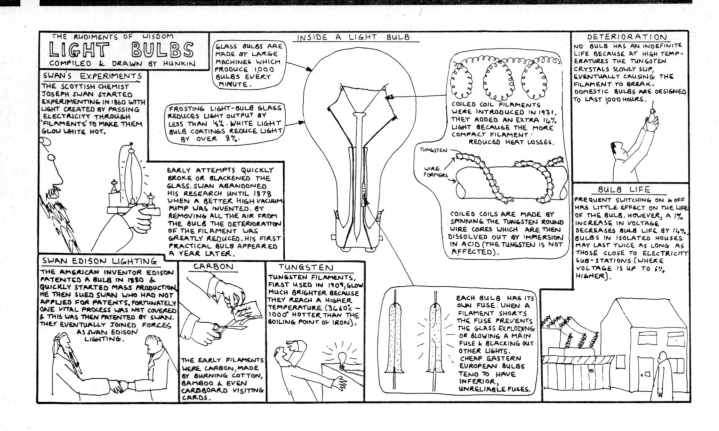

THE RUDIMENTS OF WISDOM
LIGHT BULBS
COMPILED & DRAWN BY HUNKIN

SWAN'S EXPERIMENTS
THE SCOTTISH CHEMIST JOSEPH SWAN STARTED EXPERIMENTING IN 1860 WITH LIGHT CREATED BY PASSING ELECTRICITY THROUGH 'FILAMENTS' TO MAKE THEM GLOW WHITE HOT.

EARLY ATTEMPTS QUICKLY BROKE OR BLACKENED THE GLASS. SWAN ABANDONED HIS RESEARCH UNTIL 1878 WHEN A BETTER HIGH VACUUM PUMP WAS INVENTED. BY REMOVING ALL THE AIR FROM THE BULB THE DETERIORATION OF THE FILAMENT WAS GREATLY REDUCED. HIS FIRST PRACTICAL BULB APPEARED A YEAR LATER.

SWAN EDISON LIGHTING
THE AMERICAN INVENTOR EDISON PATENTED A BULB IN 1880 & QUICKLY STARTED MASS PRODUCTION. HE THEN SUED SWAN WHO HAD NOT APPLIED FOR PATENTS. FORTUNATELY ONE VITAL PROCESS WAS NOT COVERED & THIS WAS THEN PATENTED BY SWAN. THEY EVENTUALLY JOINED FORCES AS SWAN EDISON LIGHTING.

GLASS BULBS ARE MADE BY LARGE MACHINES WHICH PRODUCE 1000 BULBS EVERY MINUTE.

FROSTING LIGHT-BULB GLASS REDUCES LIGHT OUTPUT BY LESS THAN 4%. WHITE LIGHT BULB COATINGS REDUCE LIGHT BY OVER 8%.

INSIDE A LIGHT BULB

CARBON
THE EARLY FILAMENTS WERE CARBON, MADE BY BURNING COTTON, BAMBOO & EVEN CARDBOARD VISITING CARDS.

TUNGSTEN
TUNGSTEN FILAMENTS, FIRST USED IN 1909, GLOW MUCH BRIGHTER BECAUSE THEY REACH A HIGHER TEMPERATURE (3660°C – 1000° HOTTER THAN THE BOILING POINT OF IRON).

COILED COIL FILAMENTS WERE INTRODUCED IN 1931. THEY ADDED AN EXTRA 14% LIGHT BECAUSE THE MORE COMPACT FILAMENT REDUCED HEAT LOSSES.

TUNGSTEN
WIRE FORMERS

COILED COILS ARE MADE BY SPINNING THE TUNGSTEN ROUND WIRE CORES WHICH ARE THEN DISSOLVED OUT BY IMMERSION IN ACID (THE TUNGSTEN IS NOT AFFECTED).

EACH BULB HAS ITS OWN FUSE. WHEN A FILAMENT SHORTS THE FUSE PREVENTS THE GLASS EXPLODING OR BLOWING A MAIN FUSE & BLACKING OUT OTHER LIGHTS. CHEAP EASTERN EUROPEAN BULBS TEND TO HAVE INFERIOR, UNRELIABLE FUSES.

DETERIORATION
NO BULB HAS AN INDEFINITE LIFE BECAUSE AT HIGH TEMPERATURES THE TUNGSTEN CRYSTALS SLOWLY SLIP, EVENTUALLY CAUSING THE FILAMENT TO BREAK. DOMESTIC BULBS ARE DESIGNED TO LAST 1000 HOURS.

BULB LIFE
FREQUENT SWITCHING ON & OFF HAS LITTLE EFFECT ON THE LIFE OF THE BULB. HOWEVER, A 1% INCREASE IN VOLTAGE DECREASES BULB LIFE BY 14%. BULBS IN ISOLATED HOUSES MAY LAST TWICE AS LONG AS THOSE CLOSE TO ELECTRICITY SUB-STATIONS (WHERE VOLTAGE IS UP TO 6% HIGHER).

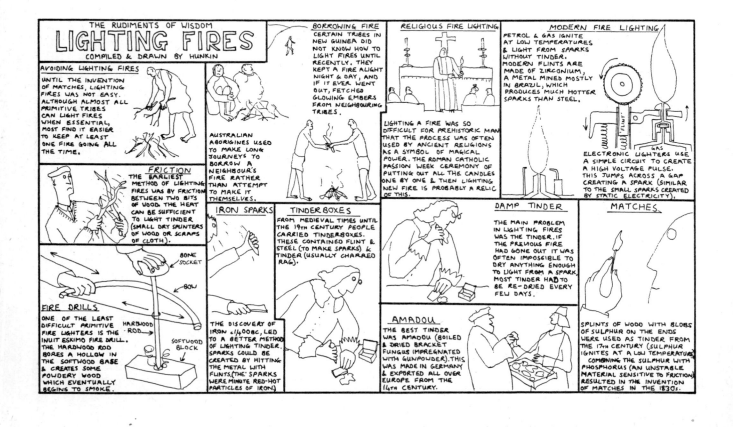

THE RUDIMENTS OF WISDOM
LIGHTING FIRES
COMPILED & DRAWN BY HUNKIN

AVOIDING LIGHTING FIRES
UNTIL THE INVENTION OF MATCHES, LIGHTING FIRES WAS NOT EASY. ALTHOUGH ALMOST ALL PRIMITIVE TRIBES CAN LIGHT FIRES WHEN ESSENTIAL, MOST FIND IT EASIER TO KEEP AT LEAST ONE FIRE GOING ALL THE TIME.

FRICTION
THE EARLIEST METHOD OF LIGHTING FIRES WAS BY FRICTION BETWEEN TWO BITS OF WOOD. THE HEAT CAN BE SUFFICIENT TO LIGHT TINDER (SMALL DRY SPLINTERS OF WOOD OR SCRAPS OF CLOTH).

BONE SOCKET
BOW

FIRE DRILLS
ONE OF THE LEAST DIFFICULT PRIMITIVE FIRE LIGHTERS IS THE INUIT ESKIMO FIRE DRILL. THE HARDWOOD ROD BORES A HOLLOW IN THE SOFTWOOD BASE & CREATES SOME POWDERY WOOD WHICH EVENTUALLY BEGINS TO SMOKE.

HARDWOOD ROD
SOFTWOOD BLOCK

BORROWING FIRE
CERTAIN TRIBES IN NEW GUINEA DID NOT KNOW HOW TO LIGHT FIRES UNTIL RECENTLY. THEY KEPT A FIRE ALIGHT NIGHT & DAY, AND IF IT EVER WENT OUT, FETCHED GLOWING EMBERS FROM NEIGHBOURING TRIBES.

AUSTRALIAN ABORIGINES USED TO MAKE LONG JOURNEYS TO BORROW A NEIGHBOUR'S FIRE RATHER THAN ATTEMPT TO MAKE IT THEMSELVES.

IRON SPARKS
THE DISCOVERY OF IRON c/4000BC, LED TO A BETTER METHOD OF LIGHTING TINDER. SPARKS COULD BE CREATED BY HITTING THE METAL WITH FLINTS. (THE 'SPARKS' WERE MINUTE RED-HOT PARTICLES OF IRON).

RELIGIOUS FIRE LIGHTING
LIGHTING A FIRE WAS SO DIFFICULT FOR PREHISTORIC MAN THAT THE PROCESS WAS OFTEN USED BY ANCIENT RELIGIONS AS A SYMBOL OF MAGICAL POWER. THE ROMAN CATHOLIC PASSION WEEK CEREMONY OF PUTTING OUT ALL THE CANDLES ONE BY ONE & THEN LIGHTING NEW FIRE IS PROBABLY A RELIC OF THIS.

TINDERBOXES
FROM MEDIEVAL TIMES UNTIL THE 19TH CENTURY PEOPLE CARRIED TINDERBOXES. THESE CONTAINED FLINT & STEEL (TO MAKE SPARKS) & TINDER (USUALLY CHARRED RAG).

AMADOU
THE BEST TINDER WAS AMADOU (BOILED & DRIED BRACKET FUNGUS IMPREGNATED WITH GUNPOWDER). THIS WAS MADE IN GERMANY & EXPORTED ALL OVER EUROPE FROM THE 14TH CENTURY.

MODERN FIRE LIGHTING
PETROL & GAS IGNITE AT LOW TEMPERATURES & LIGHT FROM SPARKS WITHOUT TINDER. MODERN FLINTS ARE MADE OF ZIRCONIUM, A METAL MINED MOSTLY IN BRAZIL, WHICH PRODUCES MUCH HOTTER SPARKS THAN STEEL.

FLINT
GAS

ELECTRONIC LIGHTERS USE A SIMPLE CIRCUIT TO CREATE A HIGH VOLTAGE PULSE. THIS JUMPS ACROSS A GAP CREATING A SPARK (SIMILAR TO THE SMALL SPARKS CREATED BY STATIC ELECTRICITY).

DAMP TINDER
THE MAIN PROBLEM IN LIGHTING FIRES WAS THE TINDER. IF THE PREVIOUS FIRE HAD GONE OUT IT WAS OFTEN IMPOSSIBLE TO DRY ANYTHING ENOUGH TO LIGHT FROM A SPARK. MOST TINDER HAD TO BE RE-DRIED EVERY FEW DAYS.

MATCHES
SPLINTS OF WOOD WITH BLOBS OF SULPHUR ON THE ENDS WERE USED AS TINDER FROM THE 17TH CENTURY (SULPHUR IGNITES AT A LOW TEMPERATURE). COMBINING THE SULPHUR WITH PHOSPHORUS (AN UNSTABLE MATERIAL SENSITIVE TO FRICTION) RESULTED IN THE INVENTION OF MATCHES IN THE 1830s.

THE RUDIMENTS OF WISDOM – COMPILED & DRAWN BY HUNKIN

MODERN POISONS
MAN-MADE SUBSTANCES HARMFUL TO LIFE

LETHAL DISCOVERIES

HUMPHRY DAVY, THE 18TH-CENTURY CHEMIST, BELIEVED IN TESTING ALL THE CHEMICALS HE USED. HE DIED OF POISONING AGED 33.

THE 19TH-CENTURY SWEDISH CHEMIST BERZELIUS WAS POISONED BY THE ELEMENT SELENIUM WHICH HE DISCOVERED.

MARIE CURIE'S EXPERIMENTS WITH RADIUM CAUSED HER DEATH FROM LEUKEMIA.

LEAD

THE DANGERS OF LEAD WERE DISCOVERED IN ABOUT 1800 DURING INVESTIGATIONS INTO A DISEASE KNOWN AS 'DEVONSHIRE CHOLIC'. IT WAS FOUND TO BE CAUSED BY THE LEAD CONTAINERS USED FOR MAKING CIDER.

FATAL DOSES

FAMILIAR CHEMICAL POISONS ARE MILD IN COMPARISON WITH SOME RADIOACTIVE SUBSTANCES.

LETHAL DOSE 50%

THE DOSE OF A POISON NEEDED TO KILL AN ADULT VARIES ENORMOUSLY FROM ONE INDIVIDUAL TO ANOTHER. EXPERIMENTAL RESULTS ARE EXPRESSED IN TERMS OF THE, LETHAL DOSE TO KILL 50% OF ANY SAMPLE GROUP OF SUBJECTS, KNOWN AS 'LD 50'.

A ROUGH FORM OF JUSTICE IN MEDIEVAL SOCIETIES CONSISTED OF GIVING THE ACCUSED A ROUGHLY 'LD 50' DOSE OF A POISON. THOSE WHO SURVIVED WERE DEEMED TO BE INNOCENT.

NERVE GAS

MODERN NERVE GASES WERE DEVELOPED DURING INSECTICIDE RESEARCH IN BRITAIN (THEY ARE CLOSELY RELATED TO MALATHION, USED TO KILL GREENFLY ON ROSES). THEY DISRUPT THE NERVOUS SYSTEM, CAUSING EXCESSIVE SWEATING, VOMITING, PARALYSIS & DEATH.

TROOPS IN DANGER OF BEING ATTACKED WITH NERVE GASES TAKE PILLS TO NEUTRALISE ITS EFFECTS. THE PILLS NOW INCLUDE VALIUM TO COUNTER THE EFFECTS OF THE OTHER INGREDIENTS, WHICH HAVE CAUSED MENTAL DISTURBANCES IN A FEW SOLDIERS.

MURDER

MURDER BY POISON HAS DECLINED THIS CENTURY AS FORENSIC METHODS HAVE IMPROVED, REDUCING THE CHANCES OF A POISON GOING UNDETECTED.

DEATH WATCH

MANY HAZARDOUS CHEMICALS DO NOT PRODUCE ANY SYMPTOMS FOR 15-25 YEARS. THE ROYAL SOCIETY OF CHEMISTRY NOW KEEPS RECORDS OF HOW ITS MEMBERS DIE, WHICH MAY EVENTUALLY HELP TO IDENTIFY NEW & UNSUSPECTED DANGERS.

POISON CENTRES

MOST COUNTRIES HAVE 'POISON CENTRES' WHERE DOCTORS CAN PHONE FOR SPECIALIST ADVICE. IN FRANCE, THE CENTRES ALSO ACCEPT CALLS DIRECTLY FROM THE PUBLIC.

ANTIFREEZE

THE ANTIDOTE FOR POISONING BY ANTIFREEZE (GLYCOL) & METHS IS PURE ALCOHOL (INJECTED INTO THE BLOOD).

TREATMENT

FEW POISONS HAVE EFFECTIVE ANTIDOTES. TREATMENT USUALLY CONSISTS OF MEASURES TO KEEP THE PATIENT BREATHING & THE ADMINISTERING OF LARGE QUANTITIES OF A HARMLESS SOLVENT.

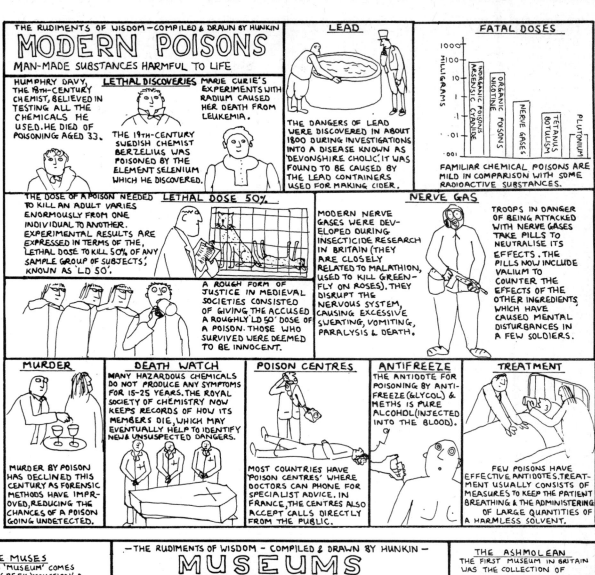

.– THE RUDIMENTS OF WISDOM – COMPILED & DRAWN BY HUNKIN –

MUSEUMS
BUILDINGS FOR EXHIBITING, STUDYING & PRESERVING HISTORICAL OBJECTS

THE MUSES

THE WORD 'MUSEUM' COMES FROM THE GREEK 'MOUSEION', A TEMPLE DEDICATED TO THE MUSES (THE GODDESSES OF SONG & THE ARTS WHO PROVIDED INSPIRATION FOR ARTISTS).

THE WORD 'MUSEUM' WAS NOT USED IN ITS MODERN SENSE UNTIL THE 1600s. EARLY COLLECTIONS OF OBJECTS WERE OFTEN CALLED 'CABINETS OF CURIOSITIES'.

THE GREEKS

THE ANCIENT GREEKS WERE THE FIRST TO COLLECT WORKS OF ART & DISPLAY THEM PUBLICLY. THE IDEA WAS THEN LOST UNTIL THE RENAISSANCE WHEN THE ITALIAN NOBILITY EXHIBITED THEIR COLLECTIONS AS SYMBOLS OF SOCIAL STATUS.

THE GALLERY

IT WAS A RENAISSANCE FASHION TO HOUSE PAINTINGS IN LONG ROOMS WHICH USUALLY HAD WINDOWS ON ONE SIDE (THE EARLIEST STILL SURVIVING IS THE UFFIZI IN FLORENCE). THIS IS THE ORIGIN OF THE TERM ART 'GALLERY'.

THE ASHMOLEAN

THE FIRST MUSEUM IN BRITAIN WAS THE COLLECTION OF ELIAS ASHMOLE, BEQUEATHED TO THE UNIVERSITY OF OXFORD IN 1683 (THE ASHMOLEAN MUSEUM). THE EXHIBITS WERE DIVIDED INTO 'NATURAL' & 'ARTIFICIAL'. VISITORS WERE CHARGED ON LEAVING ACCORDING TO THE TIME SPENT INSIDE.

THE V & A

THE VICTORIA & ALBERT MUSEUM WAS FOUNDED AFTER AN OUTCRY ABOUT THE POOR DESIGN OF BRITISH GOODS, REVEALED BY THE GREAT EXHIBITION OF 1851. THIS ALSO LED TO THE FOUNDATION OF SOME OF THE FIRST ART SCHOOLS.

THE BRITISH MUSEUM

THE BRITISH MUSEUM OPENED IN 1753. VISITORS HAD TO APPLY FOR A TICKET 2 WEEKS IN ADVANCE &, IF APPROVED, WERE THEN RUSHED ROUND THE ENTIRE COLLECTION IN 2-HOUR CONDUCTED TOURS.

FREE ENTRY

WHEN THE IMPERIAL GALLERY, VIENNA, ABOLISHED ADMISSION CHARGES IN THE 1770s, MANY ARTISTS OBJECTED, CLAIMING THAT THE PRESENCE OF THE GENERAL PUBLIC WOULD DISTURB THE SILENT CONTEMPLATION OF THEIR WORKS OF ART BY THE UPPER CLASSES.

SNOB APPEAL

A SURVEY OF LONDON MUSEUMS REVEALED THAT THE GREAT MAJORITY OF VISITORS WERE MIDDLE CLASS. THE NATURAL HISTORY MUSEUM ATTRACTED THE GREATEST NUMBER OF LOWER INCOME GROUP VISITORS & THE TATE GALLERY THE FEWEST.

ACREAGE

THE WORLD'S BIGGEST MUSEUM IS NEW YORK'S NATURAL HISTORY MUSEUM, COVERING 23 ACRES, THE BRITISH MUSEUM COVERS 17.5 ACRES.

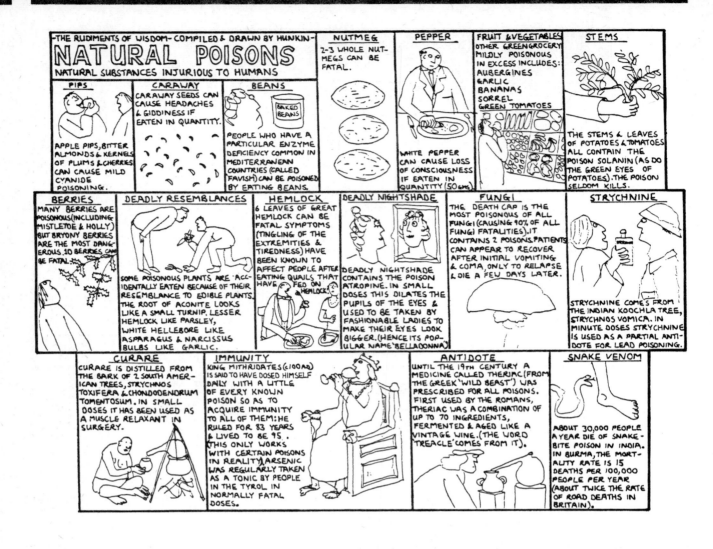

NATURAL POISONS
-THE RUDIMENTS OF WISDOM- COMPILED & DRAWN BY HUNKIN-

NATURAL SUBSTANCES INJURIOUS TO HUMANS

PIPS: APPLE PIPS, BITTER ALMONDS & KERNELS OF PLUMS & CHERRIES CAN CAUSE MILD CYANIDE POISONING.

CARAWAY: CARAWAY SEEDS CAN CAUSE HEADACHES & GIDDINESS IF EATEN IN QUANTITY.

BEANS: PEOPLE WHO HAVE A PARTICULAR ENZYME DEFICIENCY COMMON IN MEDITERRANEAN COUNTRIES (CALLED FAVISH) CAN BE POISONED BY EATING BEANS.

NUTMEG: 2-3 WHOLE NUTMEGS CAN BE FATAL.

PEPPER: WHITE PEPPER CAN CAUSE LOSS OF CONSCIOUSNESS IF EATEN IN QUANTITY (50 gms).

FRUIT & VEGETABLES: OTHER GREENGROCERY MILDLY POISONOUS IN EXCESS INCLUDES: AUBERGINES, GARLIC, BANANAS, SORREL, GREEN TOMATOES.

STEMS: THE STEMS & LEAVES OF POTATOES & TOMATOES ALL CONTAIN THE POISON SOLANIN (AS DO THE GREEN EYES OF POTATOES). THE POISON SELDOM KILLS.

BERRIES: MANY BERRIES ARE POISONOUS (INCLUDING MISTLETOE & HOLLY) BUT BRYONY BERRIES ARE THE MOST DANGEROUS. 10 BERRIES CAN BE FATAL.

DEADLY RESEMBLANCES: SOME POISONOUS PLANTS ARE ACCIDENTALLY EATEN BECAUSE OF THEIR RESEMBLANCE TO EDIBLE PLANTS. THE ROOT OF ACONITE LOOKS LIKE A SMALL TURNIP, LESSER HEMLOCK LIKE PARSLEY, WHITE HELLEBORE LIKE ASPARAGUS & NARCISSUS BULBS LIKE GARLIC.

HEMLOCK: 6 LEAVES OF GREAT HEMLOCK CAN BE FATAL. SYMPTOMS (TINGLING OF THE EXTREMITIES & TIREDNESS) HAVE BEEN KNOWN TO AFFECT PEOPLE AFTER EATING QUAILS THAT HAVE FED ON HEMLOCK.

DEADLY NIGHTSHADE: DEADLY NIGHTSHADE CONTAINS THE POISON ATROPINE. IN SMALL DOSES THIS DILATES THE PUPILS OF THE EYES & USED TO BE TAKEN BY FASHIONABLE LADIES TO MAKE THEIR EYES LOOK BIGGER. (HENCE ITS POPULAR NAME 'BELLADONNA')

FUNGI: THE DEATH CAP IS THE MOST POISONOUS OF ALL FUNGI (CAUSING 90% OF ALL FUNGI FATALITIES). IT CONTAINS 2 POISONS. PATIENTS CAN APPEAR TO RECOVER AFTER INITIAL VOMITING & COMA, ONLY TO RELAPSE & DIE A FEW DAYS LATER.

STRYCHNINE: STRYCHNINE COMES FROM THE INDIAN KOOCHLA TREE, STRYCHNOS VOMICA. IN MINUTE DOSES STRYCHNINE IS USED AS A PARTIAL ANTIDOTE FOR LEAD POISONING.

CURARE: CURARE IS DISTILLED FROM THE BARK OF 2 SOUTH AMERICAN TREES, STRYCHNOS TOXIFERA & CHONDODENDRUM TOMENTOSUM. IN SMALL DOSES IT HAS BEEN USED AS A MUSCLE RELAXANT IN SURGERY.

IMMUNITY: KING MITHRIDATES (c.100 AD) IS SAID TO HAVE DOSED HIMSELF DAILY WITH A LITTLE OF EVERY KNOWN POISON SO AS TO ACQUIRE IMMUNITY TO ALL OF THEM: HE RULED FOR 83 YEARS & LIVED TO BE 95. THIS ONLY WORKS WITH CERTAIN POISONS. IN REALITY, ARSENIC WAS REGULARLY TAKEN AS A TONIC BY PEOPLE IN THE TYROL IN NORMALLY FATAL DOSES.

ANTIDOTE: UNTIL THE 19TH CENTURY A MEDICINE CALLED THERIAC (FROM THE GREEK 'WILD BEAST') WAS PRESCRIBED FOR ALL POISONS. FIRST USED BY THE ROMANS, THERIAC WAS A COMBINATION OF UP TO 70 INGREDIENTS, FERMENTED & AGED LIKE A VINTAGE WINE. (THE WORD 'TREACLE' COMES FROM IT).

SNAKE VENOM: ABOUT 30,000 PEOPLE A YEAR DIE OF SNAKE-BITE POISON IN INDIA. IN BURMA, THE MORTALITY RATE IS 15 DEATHS PER 100,000 PEOPLE PER YEAR (ABOUT TWICE THE RATE OF ROAD DEATHS IN BRITAIN).

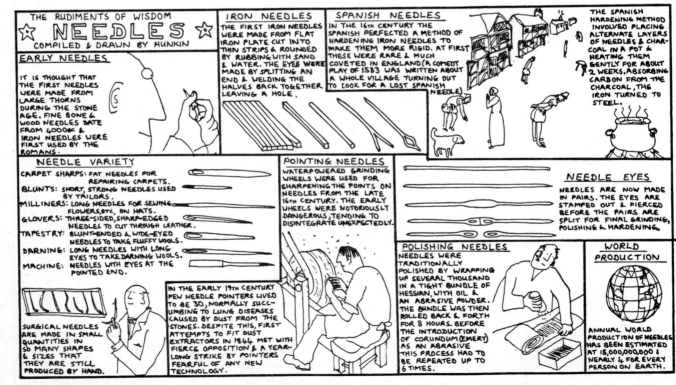

NEEDLES
THE RUDIMENTS OF WISDOM ☆ NEEDLES ☆ COMPILED & DRAWN BY HUNKIN

EARLY NEEDLES: IT IS THOUGHT THAT THE FIRST NEEDLES WERE MADE FROM LARGE THORNS DURING THE STONE AGE. FINE BONE & WOOD NEEDLES DATE FROM 6,000BC & IRON NEEDLES WERE FIRST USED BY THE ROMANS.

IRON NEEDLES: THE FIRST IRON NEEDLES WERE MADE FROM FLAT IRON PLATE CUT INTO THIN STRIPS & ROUNDED BY RUBBING WITH SAND & WATER. THE EYES WERE MADE BY SPLITTING AN END & WELDING THE HALVES BACK TOGETHER LEAVING A HOLE.

SPANISH NEEDLES: IN THE 16TH CENTURY THE SPANISH PERFECTED A METHOD OF HARDENING IRON NEEDLES TO MAKE THEM MORE RIGID. AT FIRST THESE WERE RARE & MUCH COVETED IN ENGLAND (A COMEDY PLAY OF 1583 WAS WRITTEN ABOUT A WHOLE VILLAGE TURNING OUT TO LOOK FOR A LOST SPANISH NEEDLE).

THE SPANISH HARDENING METHOD INVOLVED PLACING ALTERNATE LAYERS OF NEEDLES & CHARCOAL IN A POT & HEATING THEM GENTLY FOR ABOUT 2 WEEKS. ABSORBING CARBON FROM THE CHARCOAL, THE IRON TURNED TO STEEL.

NEEDLE VARIETY:
- CARPET SHARPS: FAT NEEDLES FOR REPAIRING CARPETS.
- BLUNTS: SHORT, STRONG NEEDLES USED BY TAILORS.
- MILLINERS: LONG NEEDLES FOR SEWING FLOWERS, ETC, ON HATS.
- GLOVERS: THREE-SIDED, SHARP-EDGED NEEDLES TO CUT THROUGH LEATHER.
- TAPESTRY: BLUNT-ENDED & WIDE-EYED NEEDLES TO TAKE FLUFFY WOOLS.
- DARNING: LONG NEEDLES WITH LONG EYES TO TAKE DARNING WOOLS.
- MACHINE: NEEDLES WITH EYES AT THE POINTED END.

POINTING NEEDLES: WATER-POWERED GRINDING WHEELS WERE USED FOR SHARPENING THE POINTS ON NEEDLES FROM THE LATE 16TH CENTURY. THE EARLY WHEELS WERE NOTORIOUSLY DANGEROUS, TENDING TO DISINTEGRATE UNEXPECTEDLY.

NEEDLE EYES: NEEDLES ARE NOW MADE IN PAIRS. THE EYES ARE STAMPED OUT & PIERCED BEFORE THE PAIRS ARE SPLIT FOR FINAL GRINDING, POLISHING & HARDENING.

SURGICAL NEEDLES ARE MADE IN SMALL QUANTITIES IN SO MANY SHAPES & SIZES THAT THEY ARE STILL PRODUCED BY HAND.

IN THE EARLY 19TH CENTURY FEW NEEDLE POINTERS LIVED TO BE 30, NORMALLY SUCCUMBING TO LUNG DISEASES CAUSED BY DUST FROM THE STONES. DESPITE THIS, FIRST ATTEMPTS TO FIT DUST EXTRACTORS IN 1844 MET WITH FIERCE OPPOSITION & A YEAR-LONG STRIKE BY POINTERS FEARFUL OF ANY NEW TECHNOLOGY.

POLISHING NEEDLES: NEEDLES WERE TRADITIONALLY POLISHED BY WRAPPING UP SEVERAL THOUSAND IN A TIGHT BUNDLE OF HESSIAN WITH OIL & AN ABRASIVE POWDER. THE BUNDLE WAS THEN ROLLED BACK & FORTH FOR 8 HOURS. BEFORE THE INTRODUCTION OF CORUNDUM (EMERY) AS AN ABRASIVE THIS PROCESS HAD TO BE REPEATED UP TO 6 TIMES.

WORLD PRODUCTION: ANNUAL WORLD PRODUCTION OF NEEDLES HAS BEEN ESTIMATED AT 15,000,000,000 & NEARLY 4 FOR EVERY PERSON ON EARTH.

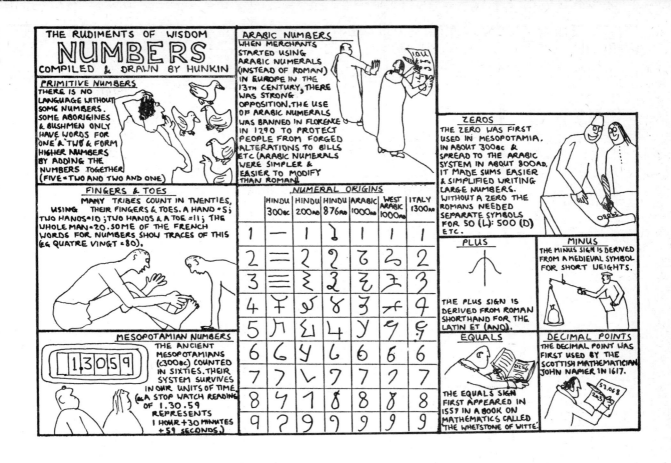

THE RUDIMENTS OF WISDOM
NUMBERS
COMPILED & DRAWN BY HUNKIN

PRIMITIVE NUMBERS
THERE IS NO LANGUAGE WITHOUT SOME NUMBERS. SOME ABORIGINES & BUSHMEN ONLY HAVE WORDS FOR ONE & TWO & FORM HIGHER NUMBERS BY ADDING THE NUMBERS TOGETHER (FIVE = TWO AND TWO AND ONE)

FINGERS & TOES
MANY TRIBES COUNT IN TWENTIES, USING THEIR FINGERS & TOES. A HAND = 5; TWO HANDS = 10; TWO HANDS & A TOE = 11; THE WHOLE MAN = 20. SOME OF THE FRENCH WORDS FOR NUMBERS SHOW TRACES OF THIS (E.G. QUATRE VINGT = 80).

MESOPOTAMIAN NUMBERS
THE ANCIENT MESOPOTAMIANS (C300BC) COUNTED IN SIXTIES. THEIR SYSTEM SURVIVES IN OUR UNITS OF TIME (E.G. A STOP WATCH READING OF 1.30.59 REPRESENTS 1 HOUR + 30 MINUTES + 59 SECONDS.)

ARABIC NUMBERS
WHEN MERCHANTS STARTED USING ARABIC NUMERALS (INSTEAD OF ROMAN) IN EUROPE IN THE 13th CENTURY, THERE WAS STRONG OPPOSITION. THE USE OF ARABIC NUMERALS WAS BANNED IN FLORENCE IN 1290 TO PROTECT PEOPLE FROM FORGED ALTERATIONS TO BILLS ETC (ARABIC NUMERALS WERE SIMPLER & EASIER TO MODIFY THAN ROMAN).

NUMERAL ORIGINS

	HINDU 300BC	HINDU 200AD	HINDU 876AD	ARABIC 1000AD	WEST ARABIC 1000AD	ITALY 1300AD
1	—	ı	I	ı	ı	1
2	=	2	2	2	2	2
3	≡	ξ	3	3	3	3
4	Ψ	ප	8	3	Ӿ	4
5	Ո	ЯԼ	4	Ƴ	9	5
6	6	५	6	6	6	6
7	7	レ	7	7	7	7
8	8	५	1	8	8	8
9	9	3	9	9	9	9

ZEROS
THE ZERO WAS FIRST USED IN MESOPOTAMIA IN ABOUT 300BC & SPREAD TO THE ARABIC SYSTEM IN ABOUT 800AD. IT MADE SUMS EASIER & SIMPLIFIED WRITING LARGE NUMBERS. WITHOUT A ZERO THE ROMANS NEEDED SEPARATE SYMBOLS FOR 50 (L); 500 (D) ETC.

PLUS
THE PLUS SIGN IS DERIVED FROM ROMAN SHORTHAND FOR THE LATIN ET (AND).

MINUS
THE MINUS SIGN IS DERIVED FROM A MEDIEVAL SYMBOL FOR SHORT WEIGHTS.

EQUALS
THE EQUALS SIGN FIRST APPEARED IN 1557 IN A BOOK ON MATHEMATICS CALLED 'THE WHETSTONE OF WITTE.'

DECIMAL POINTS
THE DECIMAL POINT WAS FIRST USED BY THE SCOTTISH MATHEMATICIAN JOHN NAPIER IN 1617.

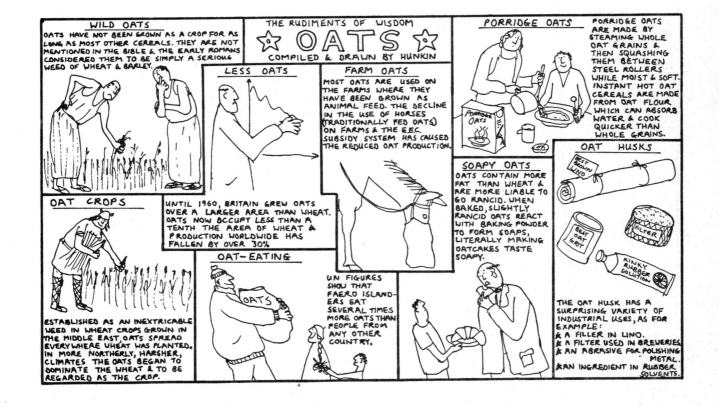

THE RUDIMENTS OF WISDOM
☆ OATS ☆
COMPILED & DRAWN BY HUNKIN

WILD OATS
OATS HAVE NOT BEEN GROWN AS A CROP FOR AS LONG AS MOST OTHER CEREALS. THEY ARE NOT MENTIONED IN THE BIBLE & THE EARLY ROMANS CONSIDERED THEM TO BE SIMPLY A SERIOUS WEED OF WHEAT & BARLEY.

OAT CROPS
ESTABLISHED AS AN INEXTRICABLE WEED IN WHEAT CROPS GROWN IN THE MIDDLE EAST, OATS SPREAD EVERYWHERE WHEAT WAS PLANTED. IN MORE NORTHERLY, HARSHER, CLIMATES THE OATS BEGAN TO DOMINATE THE WHEAT & TO BE REGARDED AS THE CROP.

LESS OATS
UNTIL 1960, BRITAIN GREW OATS OVER A LARGER AREA THAN WHEAT. OATS NOW OCCUPY LESS THAN A TENTH THE AREA OF WHEAT & PRODUCTION WORLDWIDE HAS FALLEN BY OVER 30%

FARM OATS
MOST OATS ARE USED ON THE FARMS WHERE THEY HAVE BEEN GROWN AS ANIMAL FEED. THE DECLINE IN THE USE OF HORSES (TRADITIONALLY FED OATS) ON FARMS & THE E.E.C. SUBSIDY SYSTEM HAS CAUSED THE REDUCED OAT PRODUCTION.

OAT-EATING
UN FIGURES SHOW THAT FAERO ISLANDERS EAT SEVERAL TIMES MORE OATS THAN PEOPLE FROM ANY OTHER COUNTRY.

PORRIDGE OATS
PORRIDGE OATS ARE MADE BY STEAMING WHOLE OAT GRAINS & THEN SQUASHING THEM BETWEEN STEEL ROLLERS WHILE MOIST & SOFT. INSTANT HOT OAT CEREALS ARE MADE FROM OAT FLOUR WHICH CAN ABSORB WATER & COOK QUICKER THAN WHOLE GRAINS.

SOAPY OATS
OATS CONTAIN MORE FAT THAN WHEAT & ARE MORE LIABLE TO GO RANCID. WHEN BAKED, SLIGHTLY RANCID OATS REACT WITH BAKING POWDER TO FORM SOAPS, LITERALLY MAKING OATCAKES TASTE SOAPY.

OAT HUSKS
THE OAT HUSK HAS A SURPRISING VARIETY OF INDUSTRIAL USES, AS FOR EXAMPLE:
★ A FILLER IN LINO.
★ A FILTER USED IN BREWERIES
★ AN ABRASIVE FOR POLISHING METAL.
★ AN INGREDIENT IN RUBBER SOLVENTS.

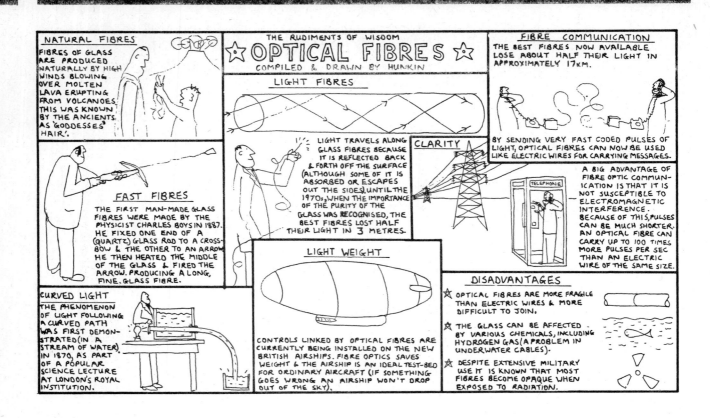

NATURAL FIBRES

FIBRES OF GLASS ARE PRODUCED NATURALLY BY HIGH WINDS BLOWING OVER MOLTEN LAVA ERUPTING FROM VOLCANOES. THIS WAS KNOWN BY THE ANCIENTS AS 'GODDESSES' HAIR'.

FAST FIBRES

THE FIRST MAN-MADE GLASS FIBRES WERE MADE BY THE PHYSICIST CHARLES BOYS IN 1887. HE FIXED ONE END OF A (QUARTZ) GLASS ROD TO A CROSS-BOW & THE OTHER TO AN ARROW. HE THEN HEATED THE MIDDLE OF THE GLASS & FIRED THE ARROW, PRODUCING A LONG, FINE, GLASS FIBRE.

CURVED LIGHT

THE PHENOMENON OF LIGHT FOLLOWING A CURVED PATH WAS FIRST DEMONSTRATED (IN A STREAM OF WATER) IN 1870, AS PART OF A POPULAR SCIENCE LECTURE AT LONDON'S ROYAL INSTITUTION.

THE RUDIMENTS OF WISDOM
☆ OPTICAL FIBRES ☆
COMPILED & DRAWN BY HUNKIN

LIGHT FIBRES

LIGHT TRAVELS ALONG GLASS FIBRES BECAUSE IT IS REFLECTED BACK & FORTH OFF THE SURFACE (ALTHOUGH SOME OF IT IS ABSORBED OR ESCAPES OUT THE SIDES) UNTIL THE 1970s, WHEN THE IMPORTANCE OF THE PURITY OF THE GLASS WAS RECOGNISED, THE BEST FIBRES LOST HALF THEIR LIGHT IN 3 METRES.

LIGHT WEIGHT

CONTROLS LINKED BY OPTICAL FIBRES ARE CURRENTLY BEING INSTALLED ON THE NEW BRITISH AIRSHIPS. FIBRE OPTICS SAVES WEIGHT & THE AIRSHIP IS AN IDEAL TEST-BED FOR ORDINARY AIRCRAFT (IF SOMETHING GOES WRONG AN AIRSHIP WON'T DROP OUT OF THE SKY).

CLARITY

FIBRE COMMUNICATION

THE BEST FIBRES NOW AVAILABLE LOSE ABOUT HALF THEIR LIGHT IN APPROXIMATELY 17KM.

BY SENDING VERY FAST CODED PULSES OF LIGHT, OPTICAL FIBRES CAN NOW BE USED LIKE ELECTRIC WIRES FOR CARRYING MESSAGES.

A BIG ADVANTAGE OF FIBRE OPTIC COMMUNICATION IS THAT IT IS NOT SUSCEPTIBLE TO ELECTROMAGNETIC INTERFERENCE. BECAUSE OF THIS, PULSES CAN BE MUCH SHORTER. AN OPTICAL FIBRE CAN CARRY UP TO 100 TIMES MORE PULSES PER SEC THAN AN ELECTRIC WIRE OF THE SAME SIZE.

DISADVANTAGES

☆ OPTICAL FIBRES ARE MORE FRAGILE THAN ELECTRIC WIRES & MORE DIFFICULT TO JOIN.

☆ THE GLASS CAN BE AFFECTED BY VARIOUS CHEMICALS, INCLUDING HYDROGEN GAS (A PROBLEM IN UNDERWATER CABLES).

☆ DESPITE EXTENSIVE MILITARY USE IT IS KNOWN THAT MOST FIBRES BECOME OPAQUE WHEN EXPOSED TO RADIATION.

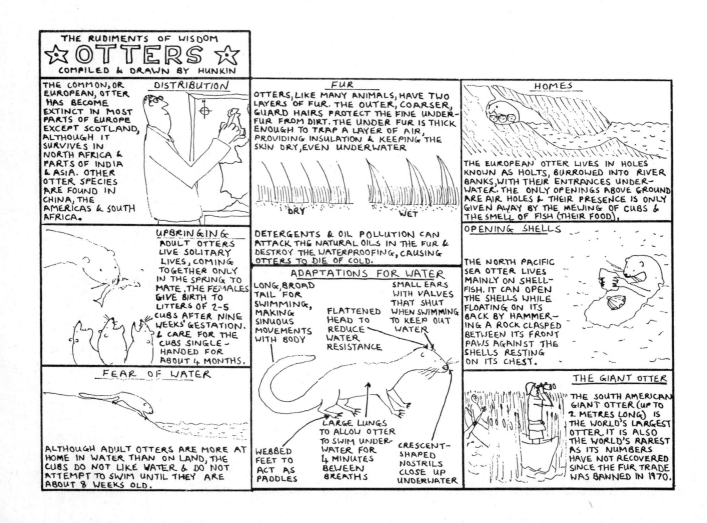

THE RUDIMENTS OF WISDOM
☆ OTTERS ☆
COMPILED & DRAWN BY HUNKIN

DISTRIBUTION

THE COMMON, OR EUROPEAN, OTTER HAS BECOME EXTINCT IN MOST PARTS OF EUROPE EXCEPT SCOTLAND, ALTHOUGH IT SURVIVES IN NORTH AFRICA & PARTS OF INDIA & ASIA. OTHER OTTER SPECIES ARE FOUND IN CHINA, THE AMERICAS & SOUTH AFRICA.

UPBRINGING

ADULT OTTERS LIVE SOLITARY LIVES, COMING TOGETHER ONLY IN THE SPRING TO MATE. THE FEMALES GIVE BIRTH TO LITTERS OF 2-5 CUBS AFTER NINE WEEKS' GESTATION & CARE FOR THE CUBS SINGLE-HANDED FOR ABOUT 4 MONTHS.

FEAR OF WATER

ALTHOUGH ADULT OTTERS ARE MORE AT HOME IN WATER THAN ON LAND, THE CUBS DO NOT LIKE WATER & DO NOT ATTEMPT TO SWIM UNTIL THEY ARE ABOUT 8 WEEKS OLD.

FUR

OTTERS, LIKE MANY ANIMALS, HAVE TWO LAYERS OF FUR. THE OUTER, COARSER, GUARD HAIRS PROTECT THE FINE UNDER-FUR FROM DIRT. THE UNDER FUR IS THICK ENOUGH TO TRAP A LAYER OF AIR, PROVIDING INSULATION & KEEPING THE SKIN DRY, EVEN UNDERWATER.

DRY   WET

DETERGENTS & OIL POLLUTION CAN ATTACK THE NATURAL OILS IN THE FUR & DESTROY THE WATERPROOFING, CAUSING OTTERS TO DIE OF COLD.

ADAPTATIONS FOR WATER

LONG, BROAD TAIL FOR SWIMMING, MAKING SINUOUS MOVEMENTS WITH BODY

SMALL EARS WITH VALVES THAT SHUT WHEN SWIMMING TO KEEP OUT WATER

FLATTENED HEAD TO REDUCE WATER RESISTANCE

WEBBED FEET TO ACT AS PADDLES

LARGE LUNGS TO ALLOW OTTER TO SWIM UNDER-WATER FOR 4 MINUTES BETWEEN BREATHS

CRESCENT-SHAPED NOSTRILS CLOSE UP UNDERWATER

HOMES

THE EUROPEAN OTTER LIVES IN HOLES KNOWN AS HOLTS, BURROWED INTO RIVER BANKS, WITH THEIR ENTRANCES UNDER-WATER. THE ONLY OPENINGS ABOVE GROUND ARE AIR HOLES & THEIR PRESENCE IS ONLY GIVEN AWAY BY THE MEWING OF CUBS & THE SMELL OF FISH (THEIR FOOD).

OPENING SHELLS

THE NORTH PACIFIC SEA OTTER LIVES MAINLY ON SHELL-FISH. IT CAN OPEN THE SHELLS WHILE FLOATING ON ITS BACK BY HAMMER-ING A ROCK CLASPED BETWEEN ITS FRONT PAWS AGAINST THE SHELLS RESTING ON ITS CHEST.

THE GIANT OTTER

THE SOUTH AMERICAN GIANT OTTER (UP TO 2 METRES LONG) IS THE WORLD'S LARGEST OTTER. IT IS ALSO THE WORLD'S RAREST AS ITS NUMBERS HAVE NOT RECOVERED SINCE THE FUR TRADE WAS BANNED IN 1970.

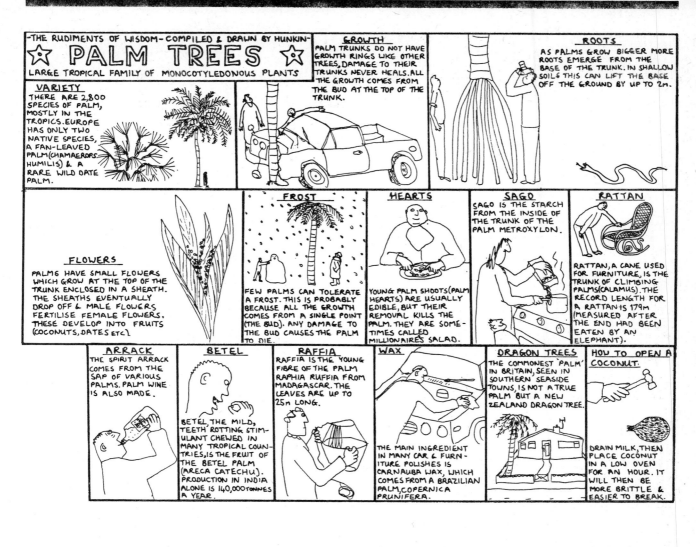

-THE RUDIMENTS OF WISDOM-COMPILED & DRAWN BY HUNKIN-

☆ PALM TREES ☆

LARGE TROPICAL FAMILY OF MONOCOTYLEDONOUS PLANTS

VARIETY
THERE ARE 2,800 SPECIES OF PALM, MOSTLY IN THE TROPICS. EUROPE HAS ONLY TWO NATIVE SPECIES, A FAN-LEAVED PALM (CHAMAEROPS HUMILIS) & A RARE WILD DATE PALM.

GROWTH
PALM TRUNKS DO NOT HAVE GROWTH RINGS LIKE OTHER TREES, DAMAGE TO THEIR TRUNKS NEVER HEALS. ALL THE GROWTH COMES FROM THE BUD AT THE TOP OF THE TRUNK.

ROOTS
AS PALMS GROW BIGGER MORE ROOTS EMERGE FROM THE BASE OF THE TRUNK. IN SHALLOW SOILS THIS CAN LIFT THE BASE OFF THE GROUND BY UP TO 2m.

FLOWERS
PALMS HAVE SMALL FLOWERS WHICH GROW AT THE TOP OF THE TRUNK ENCLOSED IN A SHEATH. THE SHEATHS EVENTUALLY DROP OFF & MALE FLOWERS FERTILISE FEMALE FLOWERS. THESE DEVELOP INTO FRUITS (COCONUTS, DATES ETC.)

FROST
FEW PALMS CAN TOLERATE A FROST. THIS IS PROBABLY BECAUSE ALL THE GROWTH COMES FROM A SINGLE POINT (THE BUD). ANY DAMAGE TO THE BUD CAUSES THE PALM TO DIE.

HEARTS
YOUNG PALM SHOOTS (PALM HEARTS) ARE USUALLY EDIBLE, BUT THEIR REMOVAL KILLS THE PALM. THEY ARE SOME-TIMES CALLED MILLIONAIRES SALAD.

SAGO
SAGO IS THE STARCH FROM THE INSIDE OF THE TRUNK OF THE PALM METROXYLON.

RATTAN
RATTAN, A CANE USED FOR FURNITURE, IS THE TRUNK OF CLIMBING PALMS (CALAMUS). THE RECORD LENGTH FOR A RATTAN IS 179m (MEASURED AFTER THE END HAD BEEN EATEN BY AN ELEPHANT).

ARRACK
THE SPIRIT ARRACK COMES FROM THE SAP OF VARIOUS PALMS. PALM WINE IS ALSO MADE.

BETEL
BETEL, THE MILD, TEETH ROTTING STIM-ULANT CHEWED IN MANY TROPICAL COUN-TRIES, IS THE FRUIT OF THE BETEL PALM (ARECA CATECHU). PRODUCTION IN INDIA ALONE IS 140,000 TONNES A YEAR.

RAFFIA
RAFFIA IS THE YOUNG FIBRE OF THE PALM RAPHIA RUFFIA FROM MADAGASCAR. THE LEAVES ARE UP TO 25m LONG.

WAX
THE MAIN INGREDIENT IN MANY CAR & FURN-ITURE POLISHES IS CARNAUBA WAX, WHICH COMES FROM A BRAZILIAN PALM, COPERNICA PRUNIFERA.

DRAGON TREES
THE COMMONEST 'PALM' IN BRITAIN, SEEN IN SOUTHERN SEASIDE TOWNS, IS NOT A TRUE PALM BUT A NEW ZEALAND DRAGON TREE.

HOW TO OPEN A COCONUT
DRAIN MILK, THEN PLACE COCONUT IN A LOW OVEN FOR AN HOUR. IT WILL THEN BE MORE BRITTLE & EASIER TO BREAK.

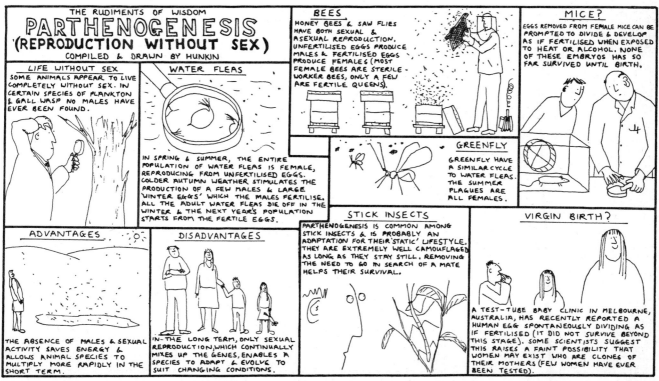

THE RUDIMENTS OF WISDOM

PARTHENOGENESIS
(REPRODUCTION WITHOUT SEX)
COMPILED & DRAWN BY HUNKIN

LIFE WITHOUT SEX
SOME ANIMALS APPEAR TO LIVE COMPLETELY WITHOUT SEX. IN CERTAIN SPECIES OF PLANKTON & GALL WASP NO MALES HAVE EVER BEEN FOUND.

WATER FLEAS
IN SPRING & SUMMER, THE ENTIRE POPULATION OF WATER FLEAS IS FEMALE, REPRODUCING FROM UNFERTILISED EGGS. COLDER AUTUMN WEATHER STIMULATES THE PRODUCTION OF A FEW MALES & LARGE 'WINTER EGGS' WHICH THE MALES FERTILISE. ALL THE ADULT WATER FLEAS DIE OFF IN THE WINTER & THE NEXT YEAR'S POPULATION STARTS FROM THE FERTILE EGGS.

BEES
HONEY BEES & SAW FLIES HAVE BOTH SEXUAL & ASEXUAL REPRODUCTION. UNFERTILISED EGGS PRODUCE MALES & FERTILISED EGGS PRODUCE FEMALES (MOST FEMALE BEES ARE STERILE WORKER BEES, ONLY A FEW ARE FERTILE QUEENS).

GREENFLY
GREENFLY HAVE A SIMILAR CYCLE TO WATER FLEAS. THE SUMMER PLAGUES ARE ALL FEMALES.

MICE?
EGGS REMOVED FROM FEMALE MICE CAN BE PROMPTED TO DIVIDE & DEVELOP AS IF FERTILISED WHEN EXPOSED TO HEAT OR ALCOHOL. NONE OF THESE EMBRYOS HAS SO FAR SURVIVED UNTIL BIRTH.

STICK INSECTS
PARTHENOGENESIS IS COMMON AMONG STICK INSECTS & IS PROBABLY AN ADAPTATION FOR THEIR 'STATIC' LIFESTYLE. THEY ARE EXTREMELY WELL CAMOUFLAGED AS LONG AS THEY STAY STILL. REMOVING THE NEED TO GO IN SEARCH OF A MATE HELPS THEIR SURVIVAL.

ADVANTAGES
THE ABSENCE OF MALES & SEXUAL ACTIVITY SAVES ENERGY & ALLOWS ANIMAL SPECIES TO MULTIPLY MORE RAPIDLY IN THE SHORT TERM.

DISADVANTAGES
IN THE LONG TERM, ONLY SEXUAL REPRODUCTION, WHICH CONTINUALLY MIXES UP THE GENES, ENABLES A SPECIES TO ADAPT & EVOLVE TO SUIT CHANGING CONDITIONS.

VIRGIN BIRTH?
A TEST-TUBE BABY CLINIC IN MELBOURNE, AUSTRALIA, HAS RECENTLY REPORTED A HUMAN EGG SPONTANEOUSLY DIVIDING AS IF FERTILISED (IT DID NOT SURVIVE BEYOND THIS STAGE). SOME SCIENTISTS SUGGEST THIS RAISES A FAINT POSSIBILITY THAT WOMEN MAY EXIST WHO ARE CLONES OF THEIR MOTHERS (FEW WOMEN HAVE EVER BEEN TESTED).

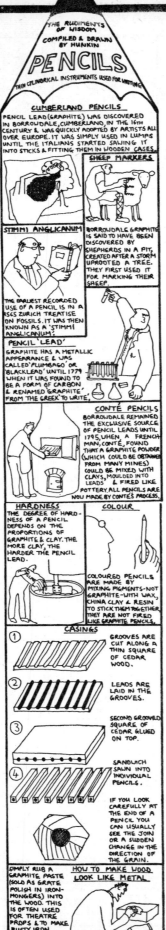

THE RUDIMENTS OF WISDOM
COMPILED & DRAWN BY HUNKIN

PENCILS
THIN CYLINDRICAL INSTRUMENTS USED FOR WRITING

CUMBERLAND PENCILS
PENCIL LEAD (GRAPHITE) WAS DISCOVERED IN BORROWDALE, CUMBERLAND, IN THE 16TH CENTURY & WAS QUICKLY ADOPTED BY ARTISTS ALL OVER EUROPE. IT WAS SIMPLY USED IN LUMPS UNTIL THE ITALIANS STARTED SAWING IT INTO STICKS & FITTING THEM IN WOODEN CASES.

SHEEP MARKERS
BORROWDALE GRAPHITE IS SAID TO HAVE BEEN DISCOVERED BY SHEPHERDS IN A PIT, CREATED AFTER A STORM UPROOTED A TREE. THEY FIRST USED IT FOR MARKING THEIR SHEEP.

STIMMI ANGLICANUM
THE EARLIEST RECORDED USE OF A PENCIL IS IN A 1565 ZURICH TREATISE ON FOSSILS. IT WAS THEN KNOWN AS A 'STIMMI ANGLICANUM'.

PENCIL 'LEAD'
GRAPHITE HAS A METALLIC APPEARANCE & WAS CALLED 'PLUMBAGO' OR 'BLACKLEAD' UNTIL 1779 WHEN IT WAS FOUND TO BE A FORM OF CARBON & RENAMED 'GRAPHITE' FROM THE GREEK 'TO WRITE'.

CONTÉ PENCILS
BORROWDALE REMAINED THE EXCLUSIVE SOURCE OF PENCIL LEADS UNTIL 1795, WHEN A FRENCHMAN, CONTÉ, FOUND THAT A GRAPHITE POWDER (WHICH COULD BE OBTAINED FROM MANY MINES) COULD BE MIXED WITH CLAYS, MOULDED INTO LEADS & FIRED LIKE POTTERY. ALL PENCILS ARE NOW MADE BY CONTÉ'S PROCESS.

HARDNESS
THE DEGREE OF HARDNESS OF A PENCIL DEPENDS ON THE PROPORTIONS OF GRAPHITE & CLAY. THE MORE CLAY, THE HARDER THE PENCIL LEAD.

COLOUR
COLOURED PENCILS ARE MADE BY MIXING PIGMENTS - NOT GRAPHITE - WITH WAX, CHINA CLAY & RESIN TO STICK THEM TOGETHER. THEY ARE NOT FIRED LIKE GRAPHITE PENCILS.

CASINGS
① GROOVES ARE CUT ALONG A THIN SQUARE OF CEDAR WOOD.

② LEADS ARE LAID IN THE GROOVES.

③ SECOND GROOVED SQUARE OF CEDAR GLUED ON TOP.

④ SANDWICH SAWN INTO INDIVIDUAL PENCILS.

IF YOU LOOK CAREFULLY AT THE END OF A PENCIL YOU CAN USUALLY SEE THE JOIN OR A SUDDEN CHANGE IN THE DIRECTION OF THE GRAIN.

HOW TO MAKE WOOD LOOK LIKE METAL
SIMPLY RUB A GRAPHITE PASTE (SOLD AS GRATE POLISH IN IRONMONGERS) INTO THE WOOD. THIS IS OFTEN USED FOR THEATRE PROPS & TO MAKE RUSTY IRON LOOK NEW.

THE RUDIMENTS OF WISDOM
PHOSPHORESCENCE
COMPILED & DRAWN BY HUNKIN

GLOWING STONE
THE FIRST SUBSTANCE EVER PRODUCED THAT GLOWED IN THE DARK WAS BOLOGNA STONE. AN AMATEUR ALCHEMIST SYNTHESISED IT IN 1602 BY HEATING A LOCAL MINERAL WITH CHARCOAL. AT FIRST, ALCHEMISTS WERE CONVINCED THAT THEY HAD FOUND THE MAGICAL PHILOSOPHER'S STONE FOR TURNING ALL METALS TO GOLD.

PHOSPHORUS
THE ELEMENT PHOSPHORUS DERIVES ITS NAME FROM ITS PROPERTY OF GLOWING IN THE DARK (FROM THE GREEK 'PHOROS' = LIGHT BEARING). LIKE MOST LUMINOUS PAINTS, PHOSPHORUS GLOWS BY RE-EMITTING ENERGY PREVIOUSLY ABSORBED FROM BRIGHT LIGHT.

GLOWING MEDICINE
PHOSPHORUS WAS DISCOVERED BY ALCHEMISTS IN THE LATE 1600s, DISTILLED FROM URINE AT RED HEAT. ITS 'MAGICAL' PROPERTY LED TO THE PRESCRIPTION OF GLOWING PILLS FOR ALL SORTS OF ILLNESSES (ALTHOUGH IT IS A POTENT POISON, PILLS CONTAINING PHOSPHORUS REMAINED IN BRITISH CHEMISTS' STOCKS UNTIL THE 1950s)

GLOWING POISON
PHOSPHORUS WAS OFTEN USED AS A POISON BY MURDERERS - IT IS DIFFICULT TO DETECT BECAUSE ITS COMPOUNDS OCCUR NATURALLY IN THE BODY. ONE INTENDED VICTIM WAS SAVED BY THE POISON'S PHOSPHORESCENCE. HE NOTICED THAT HIS SOUP WAS GLOWING WHILE CARRYING IT TO THE TABLE THROUGH A DARK CORRIDOR.

HOT GLOW
SOME CHEMICALS, LIKE FLUORSPAR, ABSORB BRIGHT LIGHT BUT DO NOT GLOW IN THE DARK UNTIL THEY ARE WARMED. AT ROOM TEMPERATURE THE ENERGY IS 'FROZEN' IN.

ORGANIC GLOW
CERTAIN ORGANIC CHEMICALS, CALLED LUCIFERINS CAN REACT WITH ENZYMES & OXYGEN & RELEASE ENERGY IN THE FORM OF LIGHT. THIS IS HOW GLOW-WORMS, FIREFLIES & MANY FISH & PLANKTON GLOW.

CHEMICAL GLOW
SOME CHEMICALS WHICH REACT WITH EACH OTHER TO PRODUCE LIGHT ARE USED FOR EMERGENCY LIGHTING (BY MOUNTAINEERS & YACHTSMEN). LIGHT STICKS CONTAIN TWO CHEMICALS, ONE INSIDE A GLASS VIAL. WHEN THIS IS BROKEN, THE CHEMICALS MIX & GLOW FOR SEVERAL HOURS.

RADIOACTIVE GLOW
SOME LUMINOUS WATCHES ARE PAINTED WITH RADIOACTIVE PAINT. THE ENERGY RELEASED BY THE RADIOACTIVE SUBSTANCE (TRITIUM IN MODERN WATCHES & RADIUM IN OLDER ONES) STIMULATES A SECOND CHEMICAL TO GLOW.

HOW TO SEE RADIOACTIVITY
TAKE AN OLD RADIUM PAINTED LUMINOUS WATCH INTO A DARK PLACE. WAIT FOR ABOUT 15 MINUTES UNTIL YOUR EYES BECOME ADJUSTED TO THE DARK. YOU WILL THEN BE ABLE TO SEE SMALL FLASHES AS INDIVIDUAL RADIOACTIVE ATOMS DECAY.

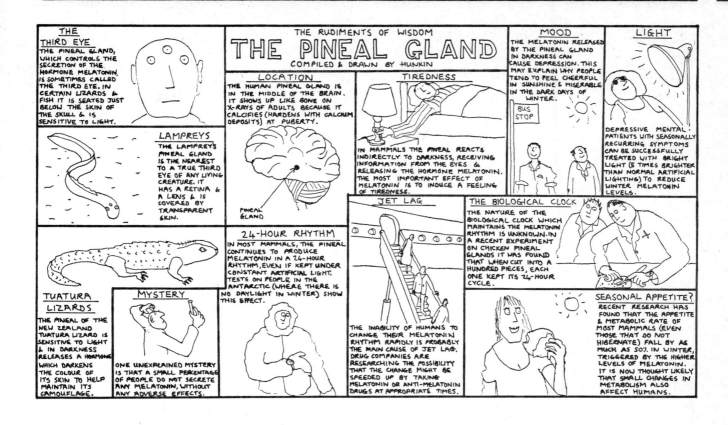

THE THIRD EYE

THE PINEAL GLAND, WHICH CONTROLS THE SECRETION OF THE HORMONE MELATONIN, IS SOMETIMES CALLED THE THIRD EYE. IN CERTAIN LIZARDS & FISH IT IS SEATED JUST BELOW THE SKIN OF THE SKULL & IS SENSITIVE TO LIGHT.

LAMPREYS

THE LAMPREY'S PINEAL GLAND IS THE NEAREST TO A TRUE THIRD EYE OF ANY LIVING CREATURE. IT HAS A RETINA & A LENS & IS COVERED BY TRANSPARENT SKIN.

TUATURA LIZARDS

THE PINEAL OF THE NEW ZEALAND TUATURA LIZARD IS SENSITIVE TO LIGHT & IN DARKNESS RELEASES A HORMONE WHICH DARKENS THE COLOUR OF ITS SKIN TO HELP MAINTAIN ITS CAMOUFLAGE.

MYSTERY

ONE UNEXPLAINED MYSTERY IS THAT A SMALL PERCENTAGE OF PEOPLE DO NOT SECRETE ANY MELATONIN, WITHOUT ANY ADVERSE EFFECTS.

THE RUDIMENTS OF WISDOM
THE PINEAL GLAND
COMPILED & DRAWN BY HUNKIN

LOCATION

THE HUMAN PINEAL GLAND IS IN THE MIDDLE OF THE BRAIN. IT SHOWS UP LIKE BONE ON X-RAYS OF ADULTS BECAUSE IT CALCIFIES (HARDENS WITH CALCIUM DEPOSITS) AT PUBERTY.

PINEAL GLAND

24-HOUR RHYTHM

IN MOST MAMMALS, THE PINEAL CONTINUES TO PRODUCE MELATONIN IN A 24-HOUR RHYTHM, EVEN IF KEPT UNDER CONSTANT ARTIFICIAL LIGHT. TESTS ON PEOPLE IN THE ANTARCTIC (WHERE THERE IS NO DAYLIGHT IN WINTER) SHOW THIS EFFECT.

TIREDNESS

IN MAMMALS THE PINEAL REACTS INDIRECTLY TO DARKNESS, RECEIVING INFORMATION FROM THE EYES & RELEASING THE HORMONE MELATONIN. THE MOST IMPORTANT EFFECT OF MELATONIN IS TO INDUCE A FEELING OF TIREDNESS.

JET LAG

THE INABILITY OF HUMANS TO CHANGE THEIR MELATONIN RHYTHM RAPIDLY IS PROBABLY THE MAIN CAUSE OF JET LAG. DRUG COMPANIES ARE RESEARCHING THE POSSIBILITY THAT THE CHANGE MIGHT BE SPEEDED UP BY TAKING MELATONIN OR ANTI-MELATONIN DRUGS AT APPROPRIATE TIMES.

MOOD

THE MELATONIN RELEASED BY THE PINEAL GLAND IN DARKNESS CAN CAUSE DEPRESSION. THIS MAY EXPLAIN WHY PEOPLE TEND TO FEEL CHEERFUL IN SUNSHINE & MISERABLE IN THE DARK DAYS OF WINTER.

BUS STOP

LIGHT

DEPRESSIVE MENTAL PATIENTS WITH SEASONALLY RECURRING SYMPTOMS CAN BE SUCCESSFULLY TREATED WITH BRIGHT LIGHT (5 TIMES BRIGHTER THAN NORMAL ARTIFICIAL LIGHTING) TO REDUCE WINTER MELATONIN LEVELS.

THE BIOLOGICAL CLOCK

THE NATURE OF THE BIOLOGICAL CLOCK WHICH MAINTAINS THE MELATONIN RHYTHM IS UNKNOWN. IN A RECENT EXPERIMENT ON CHICKEN PINEAL GLANDS IT WAS FOUND THAT WHEN CUT INTO A HUNDRED PIECES, EACH ONE KEPT ITS 24-HOUR CYCLE.

SEASONAL APPETITE?

RECENT RESEARCH HAS FOUND THAT THE APPETITE & METABOLIC RATE OF MOST MAMMALS (EVEN THOSE THAT DO NOT HIBERNATE) FALL BY AS MUCH AS 50% IN WINTER, TRIGGERED BY THE HIGHER LEVELS OF MELATONIN. IT IS NOW THOUGHT LIKELY THAT SMALL CHANGES IN METABOLISM ALSO AFFECT HUMANS.

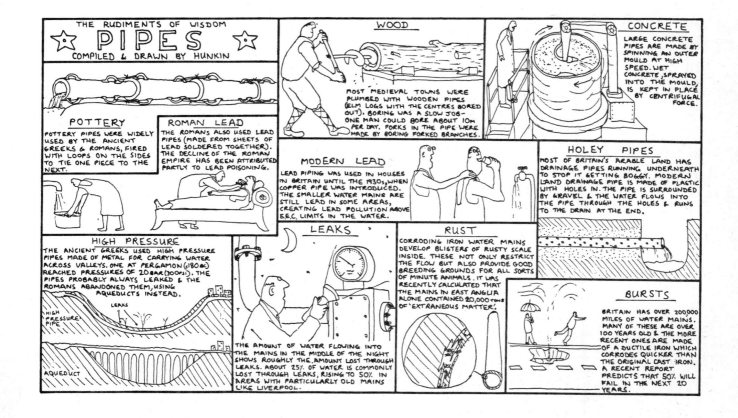

THE RUDIMENTS OF WISDOM
☆ PIPES ☆
COMPILED & DRAWN BY HUNKIN

POTTERY

POTTERY PIPES WERE WIDELY USED BY THE ANCIENT GREEKS & ROMANS, FIRED WITH LOOPS ON THE SIDES TO TIE ONE PIECE TO THE NEXT.

ROMAN LEAD

THE ROMANS ALSO USED LEAD PIPES (MADE FROM SHEETS OF LEAD SOLDERED TOGETHER). THE DECLINE OF THE ROMAN EMPIRE HAS BEEN ATTRIBUTED PARTLY TO LEAD POISONING.

HIGH PRESSURE

THE ANCIENT GREEKS USED HIGH PRESSURE PIPES MADE OF METAL FOR CARRYING WATER ACROSS VALLEYS. ONE AT PERGAMON (180 BC) REACHED PRESSURES OF 20 BAR (300 PSI). THE PIPES PROBABLY ALWAYS LEAKED & THE ROMANS ABANDONED THEM, USING AQUEDUCTS INSTEAD.

HIGH PRESSURE PIPE

LEAKS

AQUEDUCT

WOOD

MOST MEDIEVAL TOWNS WERE PLUMBED WITH WOODEN PIPES (ELM LOGS WITH THE CENTRES BORED OUT). BORING WAS A SLOW JOB - ONE MAN COULD BORE ABOUT 10M PER DAY. FORKS IN THE PIPE WERE MADE BY BORING FORKED BRANCHES.

MODERN LEAD

LEAD PIPING WAS USED IN HOUSES IN BRITAIN UNTIL THE 1930s, WHEN COPPER PIPE WAS INTRODUCED. THE SMALLER WATER MAINS ARE STILL LEAD IN SOME AREAS, CREATING LEAD POLLUTION ABOVE E.E.C. LIMITS IN THE WATER.

LEAKS

THE AMOUNT OF WATER FLOWING INTO THE MAINS IN THE MIDDLE OF THE NIGHT SHOWS ROUGHLY THE AMOUNT LOST THROUGH LEAKS. ABOUT 25% OF WATER IS COMMONLY LOST THROUGH LEAKS, RISING TO 50% IN AREAS WITH PARTICULARLY OLD MAINS LIKE LIVERPOOL.

RUST

CORRODING IRON WATER MAINS DEVELOP BLISTERS OF RUSTY SCALE INSIDE. THESE NOT ONLY RESTRICT THE FLOW BUT ALSO PROVIDE GOOD BREEDING GROUNDS FOR ALL SORTS OF MINUTE ANIMALS. IT WAS RECENTLY CALCULATED THAT THE MAINS IN EAST ANGLIA ALONE CONTAINED 20,000 TONS OF 'EXTRANEOUS MATTER'.

CONCRETE

LARGE CONCRETE PIPES ARE MADE BY SPINNING AN OUTER MOULD AT HIGH SPEED. WET CONCRETE, SPRAYED INTO THE MOULD, IS KEPT IN PLACE BY CENTRIFUGAL FORCE.

HOLEY PIPES

MOST OF BRITAIN'S ARABLE LAND HAS DRAINAGE PIPES RUNNING UNDERNEATH TO STOP IT GETTING BOGGY. MODERN LAND DRAINAGE PIPE IS MADE OF PLASTIC WITH HOLES IN. THE PIPE IS SURROUNDED BY GRAVEL & THE WATER FLOWS INTO THE PIPE THROUGH THE HOLES & RUNS TO THE DRAIN AT THE END.

BURSTS

BRITAIN HAS OVER 200,000 MILES OF WATER MAINS. MANY OF THESE ARE OVER 100 YEARS OLD & THE MORE RECENT ONES ARE MADE OF A DUCTILE IRON WHICH CORRODES QUICKER THAN THE ORIGINAL CAST IRON. A RECENT REPORT PREDICTS THAT 50% WILL FAIL IN THE NEXT 20 YEARS.

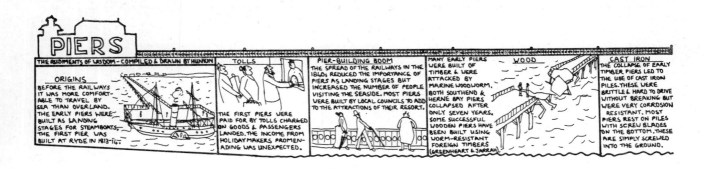

PIERS

THE RUDIMENTS OF WISDOM – COMPILED & DRAWN BY HUNKIN

ORIGINS
BEFORE THE RAILWAYS IT WAS MORE COMFORTABLE TO TRAVEL BY SEA THAN OVERLAND. THE EARLY PIERS WERE BUILT AS LANDING STAGES FOR STEAMBOATS. THE FIRST PIER WAS BUILT AT RYDE IN 1813-14.

TOLLS
THE FIRST PIERS WERE PAID FOR BY TOLLS CHARGED ON GOODS & PASSENGERS LANDED. THE INCOME FROM HOLIDAYMAKERS PROMENADING WAS UNEXPECTED.

PIER-BUILDING BOOM
THE SPREAD OF THE RAILWAYS IN THE 1860s REDUCED THE IMPORTANCE OF PIERS AS LANDING STAGES BUT INCREASED THE NUMBER OF PEOPLE VISITING THE SEASIDE. MOST PIERS WERE BUILT BY LOCAL COUNCILS TO ADD TO THE ATTRACTIONS OF THEIR RESORT.

MANY EARLY PIERS WERE BUILT OF TIMBER & WERE ATTACKED BY MARINE WOODWORM. BOTH SOUTHEND & HERNE BAY PIERS COLLAPSED AFTER ONLY SEVEN YEARS. SOME SUCCESSFUL WOODEN PIERS HAVE BEEN BUILT USING WORM-RESISTANT FOREIGN TIMBERS (GREENHEART & JARRAH).

WOOD

CAST IRON
THE COLLAPSE OF EARLY TIMBER PIERS LED TO THE USE OF CAST IRON PILES. THESE WERE BRITTLE & HARD TO DRIVE WITHOUT BREAKING BUT WERE VERY CORROSION RESISTANT. MOST PIERS REST ON PILES WITH SCREW BLADES ON THE BOTTOM. THESE ARE SIMPLY SCREWED INTO THE GROUND.

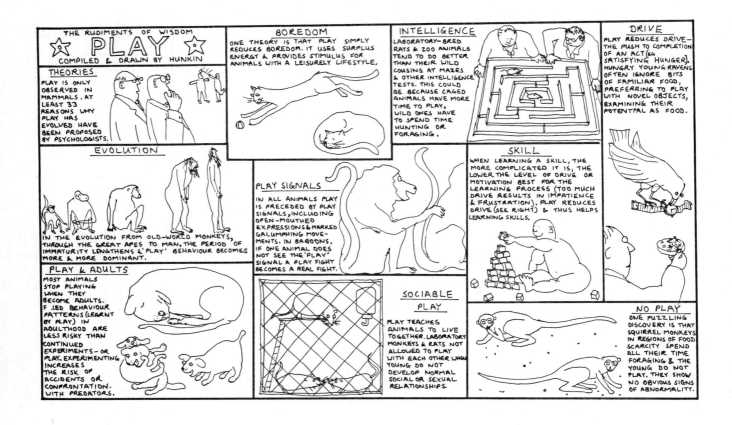

☆ PLAY ☆

THE RUDIMENTS OF WISDOM
COMPILED & DRAWN BY HUNKIN

THEORIES
PLAY IS ONLY OBSERVED IN MAMMALS. AT LEAST 33 REASONS WHY PLAY HAS EVOLVED HAVE BEEN PROPOSED BY PSYCHOLOGISTS.

EVOLUTION
IN THE EVOLUTION FROM OLD-WORLD MONKEYS, THROUGH THE GREAT APES TO MAN, THE PERIOD OF IMMATURITY LENGTHENS & 'PLAY' BEHAVIOUR BECOMES MORE & MORE DOMINANT.

PLAY & ADULTS
MOST ANIMALS STOP PLAYING WHEN THEY BECOME ADULTS. FIXED BEHAVIOUR PATTERNS (LEARNT BY PLAY) IN ADULTHOOD ARE LESS RISKY THAN CONTINUED EXPERIMENTS – OR PLAY. EXPERIMENTING INCREASES THE RISK OF ACCIDENTS OR CONFRONTATION WITH PREDATORS.

BOREDOM
ONE THEORY IS THAT PLAY SIMPLY REDUCES BOREDOM. IT USES SURPLUS ENERGY & PROVIDES STIMULUS FOR ANIMALS WITH A LEISURELY LIFESTYLE.

PLAY SIGNALS
IN ALL ANIMALS PLAY IS PRECEDED BY PLAY SIGNALS, INCLUDING OPEN-MOUTHED EXPRESSIONS & MARKED GALUMPHING MOVEMENTS. IN BABOONS, IF ONE ANIMAL DOES NOT SEE THE 'PLAY' SIGNAL A PLAY FIGHT BECOMES A REAL FIGHT.

SOCIABLE PLAY
PLAY TEACHES ANIMALS TO LIVE TOGETHER. LABORATORY MONKEYS & RATS NOT ALLOWED TO PLAY WITH EACH OTHER WHEN YOUNG DO NOT DEVELOP NORMAL SOCIAL OR SEXUAL RELATIONSHIPS.

INTELLIGENCE
LABORATORY-BRED RATS & ZOO ANIMALS TEND TO DO BETTER THAN THEIR WILD COUSINS AT MAZES & OTHER INTELLIGENCE TESTS. THIS COULD BE BECAUSE CAGED ANIMALS HAVE MORE TIME TO PLAY. WILD ONES HAVE TO SPEND TIME HUNTING OR FORAGING.

SKILL
WHEN LEARNING A SKILL, THE MORE COMPLICATED IT IS, THE LOWER THE LEVEL OF DRIVE OR MOTIVATION BEST FOR THE LEARNING PROCESS (TOO MUCH DRIVE RESULTS IN IMPATIENCE & FRUSTRATION). PLAY REDUCES DRIVE (SEE RIGHT) & THUS HELPS LEARNING SKILLS.

DRIVE
PLAY REDUCES DRIVE – THE PUSH TO COMPLETION OF AN ACT (EG SATISFYING HUNGER). HUNGRY YOUNG RAVENS OFTEN IGNORE BITS OF FAMILIAR FOOD, PREFERRING TO PLAY WITH NOVEL OBJECTS, EXAMINING THEIR POTENTIAL AS FOOD.

NO PLAY
ONE PUZZLING DISCOVERY IS THAT SQUIRREL MONKEYS IN REGIONS OF FOOD SCARCITY SPEND ALL THEIR TIME FORAGING & THE YOUNG DO NOT PLAY. THEY SHOW NO OBVIOUS SIGNS OF ABNORMALITY.

PLYWOOD

THE RUDIMENTS OF WISDOM
COMPILED & DRAWN BY HUNKIN

BEDS
THE EARLIEST KNOWN EXAMPLE OF PLYWOOD IS THE LABURNUM HEADPIECE OF A BEDSTEAD FOUND IN THE TOMB OF TUTANKHAMUN'S GRANDPARENTS. SOME ANCIENT EGYPTIAN SARCOPHAGUSES WERE MADE OF 6 LAYERS OF WOOD GLUED TOGETHER.

SMALL SHEETS
18TH-CENTURY CABINET MAKERS MADE SMALL BITS OF PLYWOOD BY SAWING THE LAYERS (PLIES) & GLUING THEM TOGETHER WITH THE GRAIN IN ALTERNATE DIRECTIONS. THESE WERE USED IN PLACES WHERE STRENGTH WAS IMPORTANT.

LARGE SHEETS
LARGE PLYWOOD SHEETS WERE NOT MADE UNTIL THE INVENTION OF THE ROTARY VENEER CUTTER IN THE 1890s. THIS PEELED A THIN CONTINUOUS STRIP OFF A ROTATING LOG, PREVIOUSLY SOFTENED BY STEAM.

BOATS
THE FIRST PLYWOOD BOATS WERE THAMES LAUNCHES BUILT IN THE 1890s. ALTERNATE LAYERS OF THIN WOOD & WATERPROOF CANVAS WERE SEWN TOGETHER ON LARGE SEWING MACHINES. THERE WAS NO RELIABLE WATERPROOF GLUE AT THE TIME.

AEROPLANES
PLYWOOD WAS FIRST WIDELY USED FOR BUILDING AEROPLANES IN WORLD WAR ONE. THIS STIMULATED RESEARCH AS HIGH-QUALITY PLY WAS NEEDED, PARTICULARLY FOR THE WINGS.

TESTING
MANY PIERS ARE NOW IN POOR STRUCTURAL CONDITION & HAVE TO BE TESTED AT INTERVALS, COMMONLY BY ERECTING TEMPORARY WATER TANKS ON THE DECK & FILLING THEM TO SIMULATE A CROWDED PIER.

ORIENTAL INFLUENCE
MOST OF THE FINEST PIERS WERE DESIGNED BY AN ENGINEER PREVIOUSLY EMPLOYED ON THE EAST INDIA RAILWAY, CALLED EUGINUS BIRCH. HE INTRODUCED THE SCREW PILE & IS RESPONSIBLE FOR MUCH OF THE ORIENTAL ARCHITECTURE.

SCREW PILES

SAILPOWER
SOME EARLY PIER RAILWAYS HAD WAGONS POWERED BY SAIL.

END OF THE PIER
THE LAST PIER TO BE BUILT WAS AT FLEETWOOD, LANCS, IN 1909. DEAL PIER WAS REBUILT IN CONCRETE IN 1945.

MANY PIERS WERE BREACHED IN WORLD WAR II TO PREVENT THEIR BEING USED AS LANDING STAGES. SOUTHEND PIER, HOWEVER, WAS USED AS A CONVOY ASSEMBLY POINT, FORTIFIED WITH PILL BOXES & ANTI-AIRCRAFT GUNS, & RENAMED H.M.S. LEIGH.

FORTIFIED PIER

– THE RUDIMENTS OF WISDOM – COMPILED & DRAWN BY HUNKIN –

☆ POLYTHENE ☆
THERMOPLASTIC POLYMER OF ETHYLENE

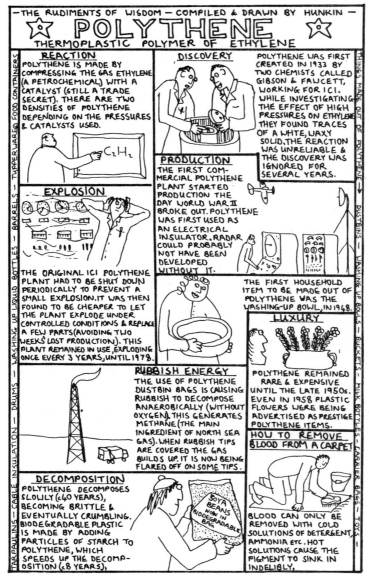

REACTION
POLYTHENE IS MADE BY COMPRESSING THE GAS ETHYLENE (A PETROCHEMICAL) WITH A CATALYST (STILL A TRADE SECRET). THERE ARE TWO DENSITIES OF POLYTHENE DEPENDING ON THE PRESSURES & CATALYSTS USED.

C_2H_2

DISCOVERY
POLYTHENE WAS FIRST CREATED IN 1933 BY TWO CHEMISTS CALLED GIBSON & FAWCETT, WORKING FOR ICI. WHILE INVESTIGATING THE EFFECT OF HIGH PRESSURES ON ETHYLENE THEY FOUND TRACES OF A WHITE, WAXY SOLID. THE REACTION WAS UNRELIABLE & THE DISCOVERY WAS IGNORED FOR SEVERAL YEARS.

PRODUCTION
THE FIRST COMMERCIAL POLYTHENE PLANT STARTED PRODUCTION THE DAY WORLD WAR II BROKE OUT. POLYTHENE WAS FIRST USED AS AN ELECTRICAL INSULATOR. RADAR COULD PROBABLY NOT HAVE BEEN DEVELOPED WITHOUT IT.

EXPLOSION
THE ORIGINAL ICI POLYTHENE PLANT HAD TO BE SHUT DOWN PERIODICALLY TO PREVENT A SMALL EXPLOSION. IT WAS THEN FOUND TO BE CHEAPER TO LET THE PLANT EXPLODE UNDER CONTROLLED CONDITIONS & REPLACE A FEW PARTS (AVOIDING TWO WEEKS LOST PRODUCTION). THIS PLANT REMAINED IN USE, EXPLODING ONCE EVERY 3 YEARS, UNTIL 1978.

THE FIRST HOUSEHOLD ITEM TO BE MADE OUT OF POLYTHENE WAS THE WASHING-UP BOWL, IN 1948.

LUXURY
POLYTHENE REMAINED RARE & EXPENSIVE UNTIL THE LATE 1950s. EVEN IN 1958 PLASTIC FLOWERS WERE BEING ADVERTISED AS PRESTIGE POLYTHENE ITEMS.

RUBBISH ENERGY
THE USE OF POLYTHENE DUSTBIN BAGS IS CAUSING RUBBISH TO DECOMPOSE ANAEROBICALLY (WITHOUT OXYGEN). THIS GENERATES METHANE (THE MAIN INGREDIENT OF NORTH SEA GAS). WHEN RUBBISH TIPS ARE COVERED THE GAS BUILDS UP. IT IS NOW BEING FLARED OFF ON SOME TIPS.

HOW TO REMOVE BLOOD FROM A CARPET
BLOOD CAN ONLY BE REMOVED WITH COLD SOLUTIONS OF DETERGENT, AMMONIA ETC. HOT SOLUTIONS CAUSE THE PIGMENT TO SINK IN INDELIBLY.

DECOMPOSITION
POLYTHENE DECOMPOSES SLOWLY (<40 YEARS), BECOMING BRITTLE & EVENTUALLY CRUMBLING. BIODEGRADABLE PLASTIC IS MADE BY ADDING PARTICLES OF STARCH TO POLYTHENE, WHICH SPEEDS UP THE DECOMPOSITION (<8 YEARS).

SOYA BEANS NOW IN BIODEGRADABLE BAG

(Vertical side text:) TUPPERWARE – FOOD CONTAINERS – BARRELS – LIQUID BOTTLES – DRUMS – INSULATION – CABLE – TARPAULINS – WASHING-UP BOWLS – BUCKETS – MILK BOTTLES – CARRIER BAGS – TOYS – THINGS MADE OUT OF POLYTHENE – DUSTBINS – WASHING-UP BOWLS –

BREAKING
MANY LIVES WERE LOST IN WORLD WAR ONE WHEN PLYWOOD PLANES MYSTERIOUSLY BROKE UP IN FLIGHT. IT WAS FINALLY DISCOVERED THAT CUTTING THE PLIES LEFT THE SURFACE BRUISED & WEAK & THAT THE PRESSING SEALED THE FIBRES SO THE GLUE COULD NOT PENETRATE. UNDER STRESS THE WEAK SURFACE LAYER SIMPLY PEELED OFF. SINCE THEN OUTER FACES OF QUALITY PLY HAVE ALWAYS BEEN SANDED TO REOPEN THE GRAIN.

ROTTING
THE LARGEST EVER PLYWOOD SHEETS WERE MADE IN THE US IN 1946 & MEASURED 2.7m x 15.2m.
THOUSANDS OF GLIDERS WERE MADE OUT OF PLYWOOD DURING WORLD WAR TWO. THESE WERE STORED OUTSIDE & PREVENTING THE PLYWOOD FROM ROTTING BECAME A CONSIDERABLE PROBLEM. ENGINEERS INSPECTED IT BY SMELLING THE PLYWOOD TO CHECK FOR MOULDY STENCHES.

HARDBOARD
TO MAKE HARDBOARD, WOOD CHIPS ARE HEATED WITH HIGH-PRESSURE STEAM & SHOT THROUGH A GUN. THIS SUDDEN PRESSURE REDUCTION REDUCES THE CHIPS TO PULP & DRIVES OUT LIGNIN, THE NATURAL SUBSTANCE WHICH GLUES THE WOOD TOGETHER. THE GLUEY PULP IS THEN PRESSED TO MAKE HARDBOARD.

WATERTIGHT?
WATERPROOF PLYWOOD, GLUED WITH PHENOL FORMALDEHYDE, DID NOT APPEAR UNTIL THE 1940s. NO PLYWOOD IS TRULY WATERPROOF AS WATER EVENTUALLY SEEPS IN AT THE EDGES THROUGH THE END-GRAIN TIMBERS.

HOUSES
MANY MODERN HOUSES WHICH APPEAR TO BE BRICK ARE ACTUALLY SUPPORTED BY PLYWOOD & TIMBER FRAMES INSIDE (THE BRICK SKIN IS SIMPLY DECORATION). SOME EXPERTS DISTRUST THIS FORM OF BUILDING BECAUSE IF ANY WATER REACHES THE FRAMEWORK IT WILL QUICKLY DETERIORATE.

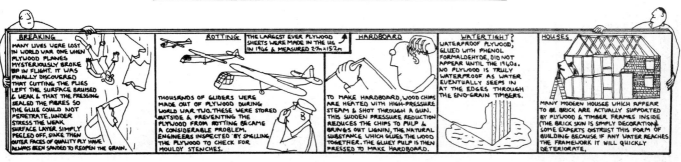

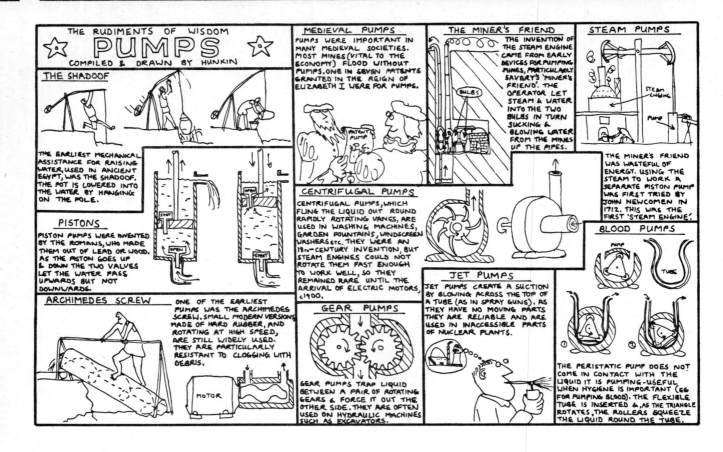

THE RUDIMENTS OF WISDOM ☆ PUMPS ☆
COMPILED & DRAWN BY HUNKIN

THE SHADOOF
THE EARLIEST MECHANICAL ASSISTANCE FOR RAISING WATER, USED IN ANCIENT EGYPT, WAS THE SHADOOF. THE POT IS LOWERED INTO THE WATER BY HANGING ON THE POLE.

PISTONS
PISTON PUMPS WERE INVENTED BY THE ROMANS, WHO MADE THEM OUT OF LEAD OR WOOD. AS THE PISTON GOES UP & DOWN THE TWO VALVES LET THE WATER PASS UPWARDS BUT NOT DOWNWARDS.

ARCHIMEDES SCREW
ONE OF THE EARLIEST PUMPS WAS THE ARCHIMEDES SCREW. SMALL MODERN VERSIONS MADE OF HARD RUBBER, AND ROTATING AT HIGH SPEED, ARE STILL WIDELY USED. THEY ARE PARTICULARLY RESISTANT TO CLOGGING WITH DEBRIS.

MEDIEVAL PUMPS
PUMPS WERE IMPORTANT IN MANY MEDIEVAL SOCIETIES. MOST MINES (VITAL TO THE ECONOMY) FLOOD WITHOUT PUMPS. ONE IN SEVEN PATENTS GRANTED IN THE REIGN OF ELIZABETH I WERE FOR PUMPS.

CENTRIFUGAL PUMPS
CENTRIFUGAL PUMPS, WHICH FLING THE LIQUID OUT ROUND RAPIDLY ROTATING VANES, ARE USED IN WASHING MACHINES, GARDEN FOUNTAINS, WINDSCREEN WASHERS ETC. THEY WERE AN 18TH-CENTURY INVENTION, BUT STEAM ENGINES COULD NOT ROTATE THEM FAST ENOUGH TO WORK WELL, SO THEY REMAINED RARE UNTIL THE ARRIVAL OF ELECTRIC MOTORS, c1900.

GEAR PUMPS
GEAR PUMPS TRAP LIQUID BETWEEN A PAIR OF ROTATING GEARS & FORCE IT OUT THE OTHER SIDE. THEY ARE OFTEN USED ON HYDRAULIC MACHINES SUCH AS EXCAVATORS.

THE MINER'S FRIEND
THE INVENTION OF THE STEAM ENGINE CAME FROM EARLY DEVICES FOR PUMPING MINES, PARTICULARLY SAVERY'S 'MINER'S FRIEND'. THE OPERATOR LET STEAM & WATER INTO THE TWO BULBS IN TURN SUCKING & BLOWING WATER FROM THE MINES UP THE PIPES.

JET PUMPS
JET PUMPS CREATE A SUCTION BY BLOWING ACROSS THE TOP OF A TUBE (AS IN SPRAY GUNS). AS THEY HAVE NO MOVING PARTS THEY ARE RELIABLE AND ARE USED IN INACCESSIBLE PARTS OF NUCLEAR PLANTS.

STEAM PUMPS
THE MINER'S FRIEND WAS WASTEFUL OF ENERGY. USING THE STEAM TO WORK A SEPARATE PISTON PUMP WAS FIRST TRIED BY JOHN NEWCOMEN IN 1712. THIS WAS THE FIRST 'STEAM ENGINE'.

BLOOD PUMPS
THE PERISTALTIC PUMP DOES NOT COME IN CONTACT WITH THE LIQUID IT IS PUMPING - USEFUL WHEN HYGIENE IS IMPORTANT (EG FOR PUMPING BLOOD). THE FLEXIBLE TUBE IS INSERTED &, AS THE TRIANGLE ROTATES, THE ROLLERS SQUEEZE THE LIQUID ROUND THE TUBE.

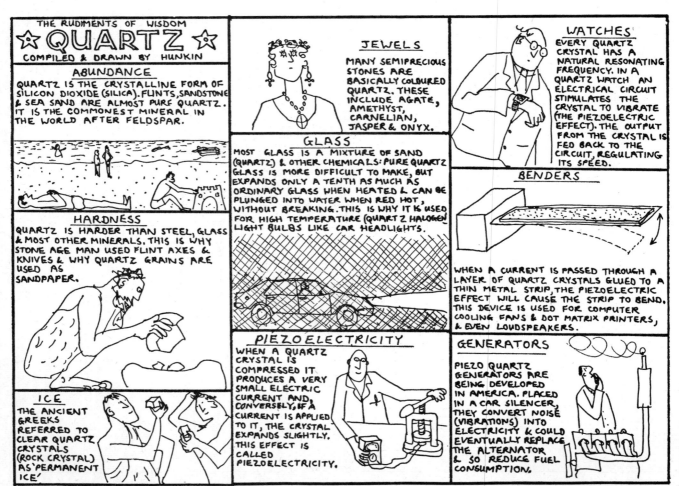

THE RUDIMENTS OF WISDOM ☆ QUARTZ ☆
COMPILED & DRAWN BY HUNKIN

ABUNDANCE
QUARTZ IS THE CRYSTALLINE FORM OF SILICON DIOXIDE (SILICA). FLINTS, SANDSTONE & SEA SAND ARE ALMOST PURE QUARTZ. IT IS THE COMMONEST MINERAL IN THE WORLD AFTER FELDSPAR.

HARDNESS
QUARTZ IS HARDER THAN STEEL, GLASS & MOST OTHER MINERALS. THIS IS WHY STONE AGE MAN USED FLINT AXES & KNIVES & WHY QUARTZ GRAINS ARE USED AS SANDPAPER.

ICE
THE ANCIENT GREEKS REFERRED TO CLEAR QUARTZ CRYSTALS (ROCK CRYSTAL) AS 'PERMANENT ICE'

JEWELS
MANY SEMIPRECIOUS STONES ARE BASICALLY COLOURED QUARTZ. THESE INCLUDE AGATE, AMETHYST, CARNELIAN, JASPER & ONYX.

GLASS
MOST GLASS IS A MIXTURE OF SAND (QUARTZ) & OTHER CHEMICALS. PURE QUARTZ GLASS IS MORE DIFFICULT TO MAKE, BUT EXPANDS ONLY A TENTH AS MUCH AS ORDINARY GLASS WHEN HEATED & CAN BE PLUNGED INTO WATER WHEN RED HOT, WITHOUT BREAKING. THIS IS WHY IT IS USED FOR HIGH TEMPERATURE (QUARTZ HALOGEN) LIGHT BULBS LIKE CAR HEADLIGHTS.

PIEZOELECTRICITY
WHEN A QUARTZ CRYSTAL IS COMPRESSED IT PRODUCES A VERY SMALL ELECTRIC CURRENT AND, CONVERSELY, IF A CURRENT IS APPLIED TO IT, THE CRYSTAL EXPANDS SLIGHTLY. THIS EFFECT IS CALLED PIEZOELECTRICITY.

WATCHES
EVERY QUARTZ CRYSTAL HAS A NATURAL RESONATING FREQUENCY. IN A QUARTZ WATCH AN ELECTRICAL CIRCUIT STIMULATES THE CRYSTAL TO VIBRATE (THE PIEZOELECTRIC EFFECT). THE OUTPUT FROM THE CRYSTAL IS FED BACK TO THE CIRCUIT, REGULATING ITS SPEED.

BENDERS
WHEN A CURRENT IS PASSED THROUGH A LAYER OF QUARTZ CRYSTALS GLUED TO A THIN METAL STRIP, THE PIEZOELECTRIC EFFECT WILL CAUSE THE STRIP TO BEND. THIS DEVICE IS USED FOR COMPUTER COOLING FANS & DOT MATRIX PRINTERS, & EVEN LOUDSPEAKERS.

GENERATORS
PIEZO QUARTZ GENERATORS ARE BEING DEVELOPED IN AMERICA. PLACED IN A CAR SILENCER, THEY CONVERT NOISE (VIBRATIONS) INTO ELECTRICITY & COULD EVENTUALLY REPLACE THE ALTERNATOR & SO REDUCE FUEL CONSUMPTION.

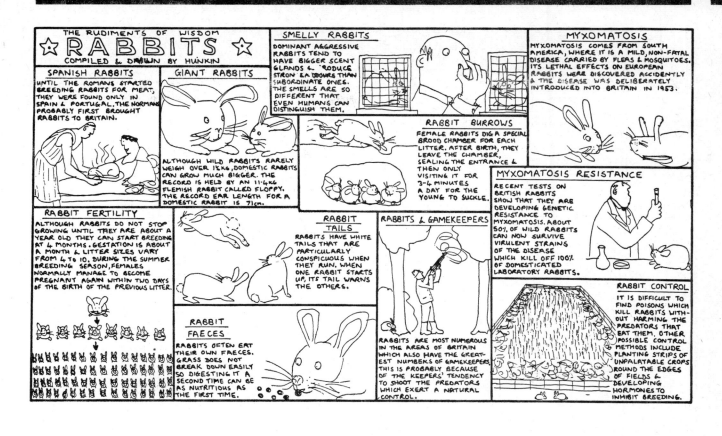

THE RUDIMENTS OF WISDOM ☆ RABBITS ☆
COMPILED & DRAWN BY HUNKIN

SPANISH RABBITS
UNTIL THE ROMANS STARTED BREEDING RABBITS FOR MEAT, THEY WERE FOUND ONLY IN SPAIN & PORTUGAL. THE NORMANS PROBABLY FIRST BROUGHT RABBITS TO BRITAIN.

GIANT RABBITS
ALTHOUGH WILD RABBITS RARELY WEIGH OVER 1½kg, DOMESTIC RABBITS CAN GROW MUCH BIGGER. THE RECORD IS HELD BY AN 11·4kg FLEMISH RABBIT CALLED FLOPPY. THE RECORD EAR LENGTH FOR A DOMESTIC RABBIT IS 71cm.

SMELLY RABBITS
DOMINANT AGGRESSIVE RABBITS TEND TO HAVE BIGGER SCENT GLANDS & PRODUCE STRONGER ODOURS THAN SUBORDINATE ONES. THE SMELLS ARE SO DIFFERENT THAT EVEN HUMANS CAN DISTINGUISH THEM.

MYXOMATOSIS
MYXOMATOSIS COMES FROM SOUTH AMERICA, WHERE IT IS A MILD, NON-FATAL DISEASE CARRIED BY FLEAS & MOSQUITOES. ITS LETHAL EFFECTS ON EUROPEAN RABBITS WERE DISCOVERED ACCIDENTLY & THE DISEASE WAS DELIBERATELY INTRODUCED INTO BRITAIN IN 1953.

RABBIT BURROWS
FEMALE RABBITS DIG A SPECIAL BROOD CHAMBER FOR EACH LITTER. AFTER BIRTH, THEY LEAVE THE CHAMBER, SEALING THE ENTRANCE & THEN ONLY VISITING IT FOR 3-4 MINUTES A DAY FOR THE YOUNG TO SUCKLE.

MYXOMATOSIS RESISTANCE
RECENT TESTS ON BRITISH RABBITS SHOW THAT THEY ARE DEVELOPING GENETIC RESISTANCE TO MYXOMATOSIS. ABOUT 50% OF WILD RABBITS CAN NOW SURVIVE VIRULENT STRAINS OF THE DISEASE WHICH KILL OFF 100% OF DOMESTICATED LABORATORY RABBITS.

RABBIT FERTILITY
ALTHOUGH RABBITS DO NOT STOP GROWING UNTIL THEY ARE ABOUT A YEAR OLD THEY CAN START BREEDING AT 4 MONTHS. IN JUDAISM GESTATION IS ABOUT A MONTH & LITTER SIZES VARY FROM 4 TO 10. DURING THE SUMMER BREEDING SEASON, FEMALES NORMALLY MANAGE TO BECOME PREGNANT AGAIN WITHIN TWO DAYS OF THE BIRTH OF THE PREVIOUS LITTER.

RABBIT TAILS
RABBITS HAVE WHITE TAILS THAT ARE PARTICULARLY CONSPICUOUS WHEN THEY RUN. WHEN ONE RABBIT STARTS UP, ITS TAIL WARNS THE OTHERS.

RABBITS & GAMEKEEPERS
RABBITS ARE MOST NUMEROUS IN THE AREAS OF BRITAIN WHICH HAVE THE GREATEST NUMBERS OF GAMEKEEPERS. THIS IS PROBABLY BECAUSE OF THE KEEPERS' TENDENCY TO SHOOT THE PREDATORS WHICH EXERT A NATURAL CONTROL.

RABBIT FAECES
RABBITS OFTEN EAT THEIR OWN FAECES. GRASS DOES NOT BREAK DOWN EASILY SO DIGESTING IT A SECOND TIME CAN BE AS NUTRITIOUS AS THE FIRST TIME.

RABBIT CONTROL
IT IS DIFFICULT TO FIND POISONS WHICH KILL RABBITS WITHOUT HARMING THE PREDATORS THAT EAT THEM. OTHER POSSIBLE CONTROL METHODS INCLUDE PLANTING STRIPS OF UNPALATABLE CROPS ROUND THE EDGES OF FIELDS & DEVELOPING HORMONES TO INHIBIT BREEDING.

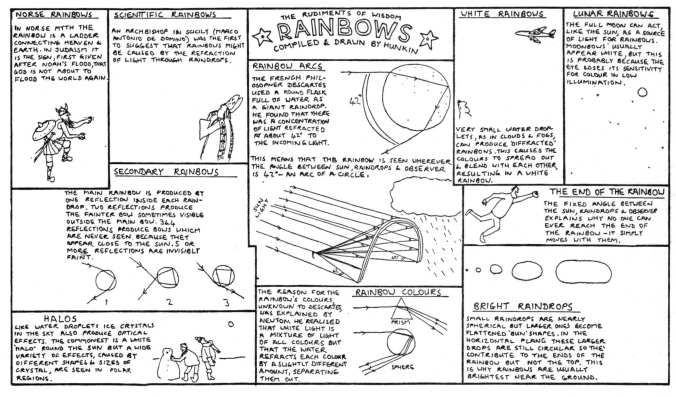

NORSE RAINBOWS
IN NORSE MYTH THE RAINBOW IS A LADDER CONNECTING HEAVEN & EARTH. IN JUDAISM IT IS THE SIGN, FIRST GIVEN AFTER NOAH'S FLOOD, THAT GOD IS NOT ABOUT TO FLOOD THE WORLD AGAIN.

SCIENTIFIC RAINBOWS
AN ARCHBISHOP IN SICILY (MARCO ANTONIO DE DOMINIS) WAS THE FIRST TO SUGGEST THAT RAINBOWS MIGHT BE CAUSED BY THE REFRACTION OF LIGHT THROUGH RAINDROPS.

THE RUDIMENTS OF WISDOM ☆ RAINBOWS ☆
COMPILED & DRAWN BY HUNKIN

RAINBOW ARCS
THE FRENCH PHILOSOPHER DESCARTES USED A ROUND FLASK FULL OF WATER AS A GIANT RAINDROP. HE FOUND THAT THERE WAS A CONCENTRATION OF LIGHT REFRACTED AT ABOUT 42° TO THE INCOMING LIGHT.

THIS MEANS THAT THE RAINBOW IS SEEN WHEREVER THE ANGLE BETWEEN SUN, RAINDROPS & OBSERVER IS 42° – AN ARC OF A CIRCLE.

WHITE RAINBOWS
VERY SMALL WATER DROPLETS, AS IN CLOUDS & FOGS, CAN PRODUCE 'DIFFRACTED' RAINBOWS. THIS CAUSES THE COLOURS TO SPREAD OUT & BLEND WITH EACH OTHER RESULTING IN A WHITE RAINBOW.

LUNAR RAINBOWS
THE FULL MOON CAN ACT, LIKE THE SUN, AS A SOURCE OF LIGHT FOR RAINBOWS. 'MOONBOWS' USUALLY APPEAR WHITE, BUT THIS IS PROBABLY BECAUSE THE EYE LOSES ITS SENSITIVITY FOR COLOUR IN LOW ILLUMINATION.

SECONDARY RAINBOWS
THE MAIN RAINBOW IS PRODUCED BY ONE REFLECTION INSIDE EACH RAINDROP. TWO REFLECTIONS PRODUCE THE FAINTER BOW SOMETIMES VISIBLE OUTSIDE THE MAIN BOW. 3 & 4 REFLECTIONS PRODUCE BOWS WHICH ARE NEVER SEEN BECAUSE THEY APPEAR CLOSE TO THE SUN. 5 OR MORE REFLECTIONS ARE INVISIBLY FAINT.

HALOS
LIKE WATER DROPLETS ICE CRYSTALS IN THE SKY ALSO PRODUCE OPTICAL EFFECTS. THE COMMONEST IS A WHITE 'HALO' ROUND THE SUN BUT A WIDE VARIETY OF EFFECTS, CAUSED BY DIFFERENT SHAPES & SIZES OF CRYSTAL, ARE SEEN IN POLAR REGIONS.

RAINBOW COLOURS
THE REASON FOR THE RAINBOW'S COLOURS, UNKNOWN TO DESCARTES, WAS EXPLAINED BY NEWTON. HE REALISED THAT WHITE LIGHT IS A MIXTURE OF LIGHT OF ALL COLOURS BUT THAT THE WATER REFRACTS EACH COLOUR BY A SLIGHTLY DIFFERENT AMOUNT, SEPARATING THEM OUT.

PRISM

SPHERE

THE END OF THE RAINBOW
THE FIXED ANGLE BETWEEN THE SUN, RAINDROPS & OBSERVER EXPLAINS WHY NO ONE CAN EVER REACH THE END OF THE RAINBOW – IT SIMPLY MOVES WITH THEM.

BRIGHT RAINDROPS
SMALL RAINDROPS ARE NEARLY SPHERICAL BUT LARGER ONES BECOME FLATTENED 'BUN' SHAPES. IN THE HORIZONTAL PLANE THESE LARGER DROPS ARE STILL CIRCULAR SO THEY CONTRIBUTE TO THE ENDS OF THE RAINBOW BUT NOT THE TOP. THIS IS WHY RAINBOWS ARE USUALLY BRIGHTEST NEAR THE GROUND.

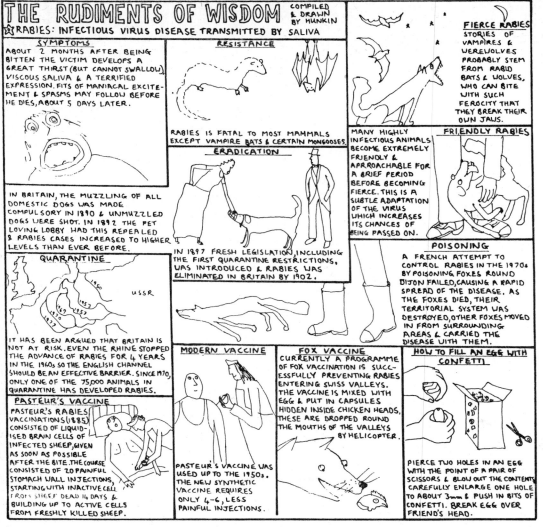

THE RUDIMENTS OF WISDOM

COMPILED & DRAWN BY HUNKIN

☆ RABIES: INFECTIOUS VIRUS DISEASE TRANSMITTED BY SALIVA

SYMPTOMS

ABOUT 2 MONTHS AFTER BEING BITTEN THE VICTIM DEVELOPS A GREAT THIRST (BUT CANNOT SWALLOW) VISCOUS SALIVA & A TERRIFIED EXPRESSION. FITS OF MANIACAL EXCITEMENT & SPASMS MAY FOLLOW BEFORE HE DIES, ABOUT 5 DAYS LATER.

IN BRITAIN, THE MUZZLING OF ALL DOMESTIC DOGS WAS MADE COMPULSORY IN 1890 & UNMUZZLED DOGS WERE SHOT. IN 1892 THE PET LOVING LOBBY HAD THIS REPEALED & RABIES CASES INCREASED TO HIGHER LEVELS THAN EVER BEFORE.

QUARANTINE

USSR

IT HAS BEEN ARGUED THAT BRITAIN IS NOT AT RISK. EVEN THE RHINE STOPPED THE ADVANCE OF RABIES FOR 4 YEARS IN THE 1960s SO THE ENGLISH CHANNEL SHOULD BE AN EFFECTIVE BARRIER. SINCE 1970, ONLY ONE OF THE 75,000 ANIMALS IN QUARANTINE HAS DEVELOPED RABIES.

PASTEUR'S VACCINE

PASTEUR'S RABIES VACCINATIONS (1885) CONSISTED OF LIQUIDISED BRAIN CELLS OF INFECTED SHEEP, GIVEN AS SOON AS POSSIBLE AFTER THE BITE. THE COURSE CONSISTED OF 20 PAINFUL STOMACH WALL INJECTIONS, STARTING WITH INACTIVE CELLS FROM SHEEP DEAD 14 DAYS & BUILDING UP TO ACTIVE CELLS FROM FRESHLY KILLED SHEEP.

RESISTANCE

RABIES IS FATAL TO MOST MAMMALS EXCEPT VAMPIRE BATS & CERTAIN MONGOOSES.

ERADICATION

IN 1897 FRESH LEGISLATION, INCLUDING THE FIRST QUARANTINE RESTRICTIONS, WAS INTRODUCED & RABIES WAS ELIMINATED IN BRITAIN BY 1902.

MODERN VACCINE

PASTEUR'S VACCINE WAS USED UP TO THE 1950s. THE NEW SYNTHETIC VACCINE REQUIRES ONLY 4-6, LESS PAINFUL INJECTIONS.

FOX VACCINE

CURRENTLY A PROGRAMME OF FOX VACCINATION IS SUCCESSFULLY PREVENTING RABIES ENTERING SWISS VALLEYS. THE VACCINE IS MIXED WITH EGG & PUT IN CAPSULES HIDDEN INSIDE CHICKEN HEADS, THESE ARE DROPPED ROUND THE MOUTHS OF THE VALLEYS BY HELICOPTER.

FIERCE RABIES

STORIES OF VAMPIRES & WEREWOLVES PROBABLY STEM FROM RABID BATS & WOLVES, WHO CAN BITE WITH SUCH FEROCITY THAT THEY BREAK THEIR OWN JAWS.

FRIENDLY RABIES

MANY HIGHLY INFECTIOUS ANIMALS BECOME EXTREMELY FRIENDLY & APPROACHABLE FOR A BRIEF PERIOD BEFORE BECOMING FIERCE. THIS IS A SUBTLE ADAPTATION OF THE VIRUS WHICH INCREASES ITS CHANCES OF BEING PASSED ON.

POISONING

A FRENCH ATTEMPT TO CONTROL RABIES IN THE 1970s BY POISONING FOXES ROUND DIJON FAILED, CAUSING A RAPID SPREAD OF THE DISEASE. AS THE FOXES DIED, THEIR TERRITORIAL SYSTEM WAS DESTROYED, OTHER FOXES MOVED IN FROM SURROUNDING AREAS & CARRIED THE DISEASE WITH THEM.

HOW TO FILL AN EGG WITH CONFETTI

PIERCE TWO HOLES IN AN EGG WITH THE POINT OF A PAIR OF SCISSORS & BLOW OUT THE CONTENTS CAREFULLY ENLARGE ONE HOLE TO ABOUT 3mm & PUSH IN BITS OF CONFETTI. BREAK EGG OVER FRIEND'S HEAD.

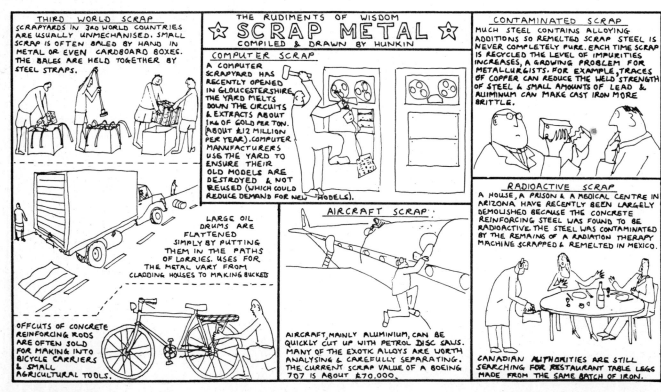

THE RUDIMENTS OF WISDOM
☆ SCRAP METAL ☆
COMPILED & DRAWN BY HUNKIN

THIRD WORLD SCRAP

SCRAPYARDS IN 3RD WORLD COUNTRIES ARE USUALLY UNMECHANISED. SMALL SCRAP IS OFTEN BALED BY HAND IN METAL OR EVEN CARDBOARD BOXES. THE BALES ARE HELD TOGETHER BY STEEL STRAPS.

LARGE OIL DRUMS ARE FLATTENED SIMPLY BY PUTTING THEM IN THE PATHS OF LORRIES. USES FOR THE METAL VARY FROM CLADDING HOUSES TO MAKING BUCKETS.

OFFCUTS OF CONCRETE REINFORCING RODS ARE OFTEN SOLD FOR MAKING INTO BICYCLE CARRIERS & SMALL AGRICULTURAL TOOLS.

COMPUTER SCRAP

A COMPUTER SCRAPYARD HAS RECENTLY OPENED IN GLOUCESTERSHIRE. THE YARD MELTS DOWN THE CIRCUITS & EXTRACTS ABOUT 1KG OF GOLD PER TON (ABOUT £12 MILLION PER YEAR). COMPUTER MANUFACTURERS USE THE YARD TO ENSURE THEIR OLD MODELS ARE DESTROYED & NOT REUSED (WHICH COULD REDUCE DEMAND FOR NEW MODELS).

AIRCRAFT SCRAP

AIRCRAFT, MAINLY ALUMINIUM, CAN BE QUICKLY CUT UP WITH PETROL DISC SAWS. MANY OF THE EXOTIC ALLOYS ARE WORTH ANALYSING & CAREFULLY SEPARATING. THE CURRENT SCRAP VALUE OF A BOEING 707 IS ABOUT £70,000.

CONTAMINATED SCRAP

MUCH STEEL CONTAINS ALLOYING ADDITIONS SO REMELTED SCRAP STEEL IS NEVER COMPLETELY PURE. EACH TIME SCRAP IS RECYCLED THE LEVEL OF IMPURITIES INCREASES, A GROWING PROBLEM FOR METALLURGISTS. FOR EXAMPLE, TRACES OF COPPER CAN REDUCE THE WELD STRENGTH OF STEEL & SMALL AMOUNTS OF LEAD & ALUMINIUM CAN MAKE CAST IRON MORE BRITTLE.

RADIOACTIVE SCRAP

A HOUSE, A PRISON & A MEDICAL CENTRE IN ARIZONA HAVE RECENTLY BEEN LARGELY DEMOLISHED BECAUSE THE CONCRETE REINFORCING STEEL WAS FOUND TO BE RADIOACTIVE. THE STEEL WAS CONTAMINATED BY THE REMAINS OF A RADIATION THERAPY MACHINE SCRAPPED & REMELTED IN MEXICO.

CANADIAN AUTHORITIES ARE STILL SEARCHING FOR RESTAURANT TABLE LEGS MADE FROM THE SAME BATCH OF IRON.

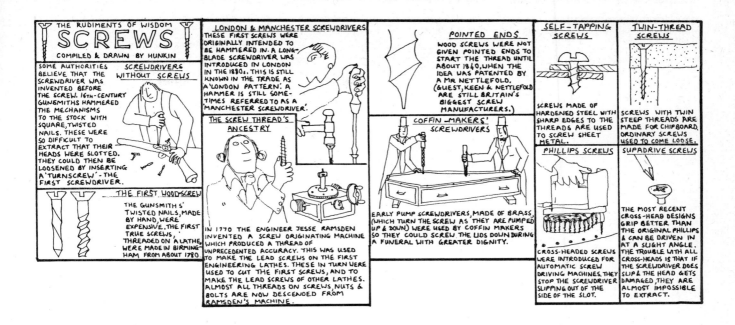

THE RUDIMENTS OF WISDOM
SCREWS
COMPILED & DRAWN BY HUNKIN

SCREWDRIVERS WITHOUT SCREWS

SOME AUTHORITIES BELIEVE THAT THE SCREWDRIVER WAS INVENTED BEFORE THE SCREW. 16TH-CENTURY GUNSMITHS HAMMERED THE MECHANISMS TO THE STOCK WITH SQUARE, TWISTED NAILS. THESE WERE SO DIFFICULT TO EXTRACT THAT THEIR HEADS WERE SLOTTED. THEY COULD THEN BE LOOSENED BY INSERTING A 'TURNSCREW' – THE FIRST SCREWDRIVER.

THE FIRST WOODSCREW

THE GUNSMITH'S TWISTED NAILS, MADE BY HAND, WERE EXPENSIVE. THE FIRST TRUE SCREWS, THREADED ON A LATHE, WERE MADE IN BIRMINGHAM FROM ABOUT 1780.

LONDON & MANCHESTER SCREWDRIVERS

THESE FIRST SCREWS WERE ORIGINALLY INTENDED TO BE HAMMERED IN. A LONG-BLADE SCREWDRIVER WAS INTRODUCED IN LONDON IN THE 1880s. THIS IS STILL KNOWN IN THE TRADE AS A 'LONDON PATTERN'. A HAMMER IS STILL SOMETIMES REFERRED TO AS A 'MANCHESTER SCREWDRIVER'.

THE SCREW THREAD'S ANCESTRY

IN 1770 THE ENGINEER JESSE RAMSDEN INVENTED A SCREW ORIGINATING MACHINE WHICH PRODUCED A THREAD OF UNPRECEDENTED ACCURACY. THIS WAS USED TO MAKE THE LEAD SCREWS ON THE FIRST ENGINEERING LATHES. THESE IN TURN WERE USED TO CUT THE FIRST SCREWS, AND TO MAKE THE LEAD SCREWS OF OTHER LATHES. ALMOST ALL THREADS ON SCREWS, NUTS & BOLTS ARE NOW DESCENDED FROM RAMSDEN'S MACHINE.

POINTED ENDS

WOOD SCREWS WERE NOT GIVEN POINTED ENDS TO START THE THREAD UNTIL ABOUT 1840, WHEN THE IDEA WAS PATENTED BY A MR NETTLEFOLD. (GUEST, KEEN & NETTLEFOLD ARE STILL BRITAIN'S BIGGEST SCREW MANUFACTURERS.)

COFFIN-MAKERS' SCREWDRIVERS

EARLY PUMP SCREWDRIVERS, MADE OF BRASS, (WHICH TURN THE SCREW AS THEY ARE PUMPED UP & DOWN) WERE USED BY COFFIN MAKERS SO THEY COULD SCREW THE LIDS DOWN DURING A FUNERAL WITH GREATER DIGNITY.

SELF-TAPPING SCREWS

SCREWS MADE OF HARDENED STEEL WITH SHARP EDGES TO THE THREADS ARE USED TO SCREW SHEET METAL.

TWIN-THREAD SCREWS

SCREWS WITH TWIN STEEP THREADS ARE MADE FOR CHIPBOARD. ORDINARY SCREWS USED TO COME LOOSE.

PHILLIPS SCREWS

CROSS-HEADED SCREWS WERE INTRODUCED FOR AUTOMATIC SCREW DRIVING MACHINES. THEY STOP THE SCREWDRIVER SLIPPING OUT OF THE SIDE OF THE SLOT.

SUPADRIVE SCREWS

THE MOST RECENT CROSS-HEAD DESIGNS GRIP BETTER THAN THE ORIGINAL PHILLIPS & CAN BE DRIVEN IN AT A SLIGHT ANGLE. THE TROUBLE WITH ALL CROSS-HEADS IS THAT IF THE SCREWDRIVER DOES SLIP & THE HEAD GETS DAMAGED, THEY ARE ALMOST IMPOSSIBLE TO EXTRACT.

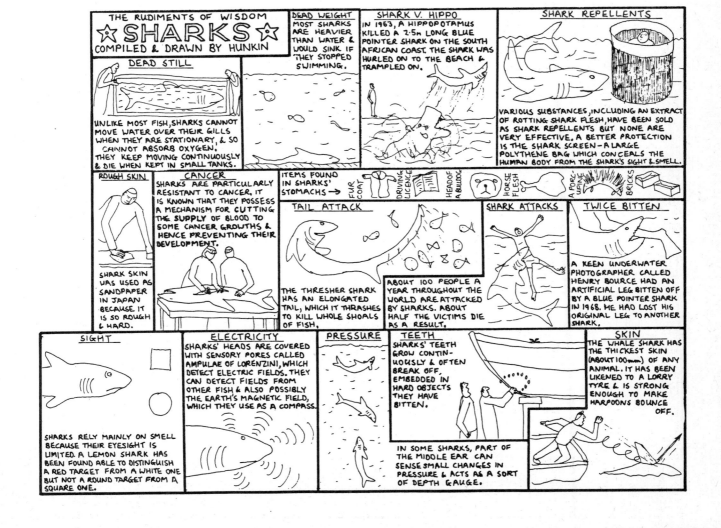

THE RUDIMENTS OF WISDOM
☆ SHARKS ☆
COMPILED & DRAWN BY HUNKIN

DEAD STILL

UNLIKE MOST FISH, SHARKS CANNOT MOVE WATER OVER THEIR GILLS WHEN THEY ARE STATIONARY, & SO CANNOT ABSORB OXYGEN. THEY KEEP MOVING CONTINUOUSLY & DIE WHEN KEPT IN SMALL TANKS.

DEAD WEIGHT

MOST SHARKS ARE HEAVIER THAN WATER & WOULD SINK IF THEY STOPPED SWIMMING.

SHARK V. HIPPO

IN 1963, A HIPPOPOTAMUS KILLED A 2.5m LONG BLUE POINTER SHARK ON THE SOUTH AFRICAN COAST. THE SHARK WAS HURLED ON TO THE BEACH & TRAMPLED ON.

SHARK REPELLENTS

VARIOUS SUBSTANCES, INCLUDING AN EXTRACT OF ROTTING SHARK FLESH, HAVE BEEN SOLD AS SHARK REPELLENTS BUT NONE ARE VERY EFFECTIVE. A BETTER PROTECTION IS THE SHARK SCREEN – A LARGE POLYTHENE BAG WHICH CONCEALS THE HUMAN BODY FROM THE SHARK'S SIGHT & SMELL.

ROUGH SKIN

SHARK SKIN WAS USED AS SANDPAPER IN JAPAN BECAUSE IT IS SO ROUGH & HARD.

CANCER

SHARKS ARE PARTICULARLY RESISTANT TO CANCER. IT IS KNOWN THAT THEY POSSESS A MECHANISM FOR CUTTING THE SUPPLY OF BLOOD TO SOME CANCER GROWTHS & HENCE PREVENTING THEIR DEVELOPMENT.

ITEMS FOUND IN SHARKS' STOMACHS → FUR COAT, DRIVING LICENCE, HEAD OF A BULLDOG, HORSE FLESH, A PORCUPINE, BRICKS.

TAIL ATTACK

THE THRESHER SHARK HAS AN ELONGATED TAIL, WHICH IT THRASHES TO KILL WHOLE SHOALS OF FISH.

SHARK ATTACKS

ABOUT 100 PEOPLE A YEAR THROUGHOUT THE WORLD ARE ATTACKED BY SHARKS. ABOUT HALF THE VICTIMS DIE AS A RESULT.

TWICE BITTEN

A KEEN UNDERWATER PHOTOGRAPHER CALLED HENRY BOURCE HAD AN ARTIFICIAL LEG BITTEN OFF BY A BLUE POINTER SHARK IN 1968. HE HAD LOST HIS ORIGINAL LEG TO ANOTHER SHARK.

SIGHT

SHARKS RELY MAINLY ON SMELL BECAUSE THEIR EYESIGHT IS LIMITED. A LEMON SHARK HAS BEEN FOUND ABLE TO DISTINGUISH A RED TARGET FROM A WHITE ONE BUT NOT A ROUND TARGET FROM A SQUARE ONE.

ELECTRICITY

SHARKS' HEADS ARE COVERED WITH SENSORY PORES CALLED AMPULAE OF LORENZINI, WHICH DETECT ELECTRIC FIELDS. THEY CAN DETECT FIELDS FROM OTHER FISH & ALSO POSSIBLY THE EARTH'S MAGNETIC FIELD, WHICH THEY USE AS A COMPASS.

PRESSURE

IN SOME SHARKS, PART OF THE MIDDLE EAR CAN SENSE SMALL CHANGES IN PRESSURE & ACTS AS A SORT OF DEPTH GAUGE.

TEETH

SHARKS' TEETH GROW CONTINUOUSLY & OFTEN BREAK OFF, EMBEDDED IN HARD OBJECTS THEY HAVE BITTEN.

SKIN

THE WHALE SHARK HAS THE THICKEST SKIN (ABOUT 100mm) OF ANY ANIMAL. IT HAS BEEN LIKENED TO A LORRY TYRE & IS STRONG ENOUGH TO MAKE HARPOONS BOUNCE OFF.

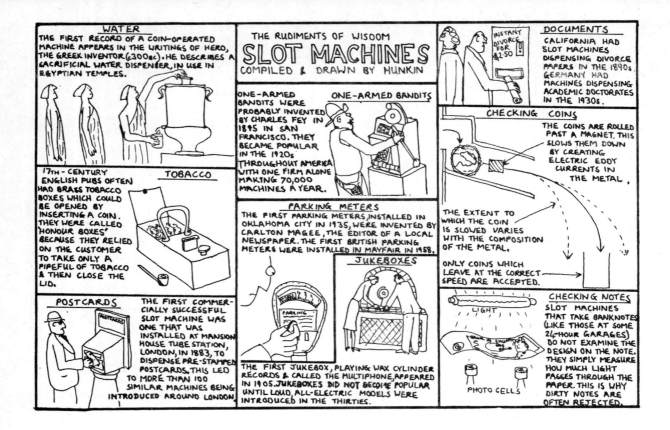

WATER

THE FIRST RECORD OF A COIN-OPERATED MACHINE APPEARS IN THE WRITINGS OF HERO, THE GREEK INVENTOR (c.300 BC). HE DESCRIBES A SACRIFICIAL WATER DISPENSER, IN USE IN EGYPTIAN TEMPLES.

TOBACCO

17TH-CENTURY ENGLISH PUBS OFTEN HAD BRASS TOBACCO BOXES WHICH COULD BE OPENED BY INSERTING A COIN. THEY WERE CALLED 'HONOUR BOXES' BECAUSE THEY RELIED ON THE CUSTOMER TO TAKE ONLY A PIPEFUL OF TOBACCO & THEN CLOSE THE LID.

POSTCARDS

THE FIRST COMMERCIALLY SUCCESSFUL SLOT MACHINE WAS ONE THAT WAS INSTALLED AT MANSION HOUSE TUBE STATION, LONDON, IN 1883, TO DISPENSE PRE-STAMPED POSTCARDS. THIS LED TO MORE THAN 100 SIMILAR MACHINES BEING INTRODUCED AROUND LONDON.

THE RUDIMENTS OF WISDOM
SLOT MACHINES
COMPILED & DRAWN BY HUNKIN

ONE-ARMED BANDITS

ONE-ARMED BANDITS WERE PROBABLY INVENTED BY CHARLES FEY IN 1895 IN SAN FRANCISCO. THEY BECAME POPULAR IN THE 1920s THROUGHOUT AMERICA WITH ONE FIRM ALONE MAKING 70,000 MACHINES A YEAR.

PARKING METERS

THE FIRST PARKING METERS, INSTALLED IN OKLAHOMA CITY IN 1935, WERE INVENTED BY CARLTON MAGEE, THE EDITOR OF A LOCAL NEWSPAPER. THE FIRST BRITISH PARKING METERS WERE INSTALLED IN MAYFAIR IN 1958.

JUKEBOXES

THE FIRST JUKEBOX, PLAYING WAX CYLINDER RECORDS & CALLED THE MULTIPHONE, APPEARED IN 1905. JUKEBOXES DID NOT BECOME POPULAR UNTIL LOUD, ALL-ELECTRIC MODELS WERE INTRODUCED IN THE THIRTIES.

DOCUMENTS

CALIFORNIA HAD SLOT MACHINES DISPENSING DIVORCE PAPERS IN THE 1890s. GERMANY HAD MACHINES DISPENSING ACADEMIC DOCTORATES IN THE 1930s.

INSTANT DIVORCE FOR $2.50

CHECKING COINS

THE COINS ARE ROLLED PAST A MAGNET. THIS SLOWS THEM DOWN BY CREATING ELECTRIC EDDY CURRENTS IN THE METAL.

THE EXTENT TO WHICH THE COIN IS SLOWED VARIES WITH THE COMPOSITION OF THE METAL.

ONLY COINS WHICH LEAVE AT THE CORRECT SPEED ARE ACCEPTED.

CHECKING NOTES

LIGHT

SLOT MACHINES THAT TAKE BANKNOTES (LIKE THOSE AT SOME 24-HOUR GARAGES) DO NOT EXAMINE THE DESIGN ON THE NOTE. THEY SIMPLY MEASURE HOW MUCH LIGHT PASSES THROUGH THE PAPER. THIS IS WHY DIRTY NOTES ARE OFTEN REJECTED.

PHOTO CELLS

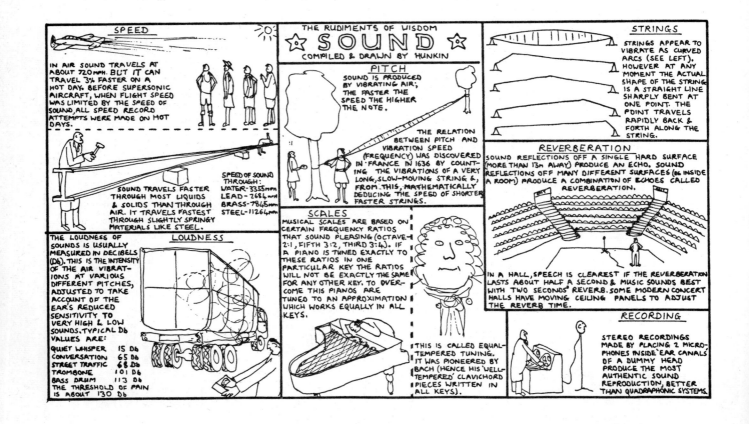

SPEED

IN AIR SOUND TRAVELS AT ABOUT 720 mph. BUT IT CAN TRAVEL 3% FASTER ON A HOT DAY. BEFORE SUPERSONIC AIRCRAFT, WHEN FLIGHT SPEED WAS LIMITED BY THE SPEED OF SOUND, ALL SPEED RECORD ATTEMPTS WERE MADE ON HOT DAYS.

SOUND TRAVELS FASTER THROUGH MOST LIQUIDS & SOLIDS THAN THROUGH AIR. IT TRAVELS FASTEST THROUGH SLIGHTLY SPRINGY MATERIALS LIKE STEEL.

SPEED OF SOUND THROUGH:
WATER – 3355 mph
LEAD – 2684 mph
BRASS – 7845 mph
STEEL – 11264 mph

LOUDNESS

THE LOUDNESS OF SOUNDS IS USUALLY MEASURED IN DECIBELS (Db). THIS IS THE INTENSITY OF THE AIR VIBRATIONS AT VARIOUS DIFFERENT PITCHES, ADJUSTED TO TAKE ACCOUNT OF THE EAR'S REDUCED SENSITIVITY TO VERY HIGH & LOW SOUNDS. TYPICAL Db VALUES ARE:

QUIET WHISPER   15 Db
CONVERSATION   65 Db
STREET TRAFFIC   68 Db
TROMBONE   101 Db
BASS DRUM   113 Db
THE THRESHOLD OF PAIN IS ABOUT 130 Db

THE RUDIMENTS OF WISDOM
☆ SOUND ☆
COMPILED & DRAWN BY HUNKIN

PITCH

SOUND IS PRODUCED BY VIBRATING AIR; THE FASTER THE SPEED THE HIGHER THE NOTE.

THE RELATION BETWEEN PITCH AND VIBRATION SPEED (FREQUENCY) WAS DISCOVERED IN FRANCE IN 1636 BY COUNTING THE VIBRATIONS OF A VERY LONG, SLOW-MOVING STRING &, FROM THIS, MATHEMATICALLY DEDUCING THE SPEED OF SHORTER FASTER STRINGS.

SCALES

MUSICAL SCALES ARE BASED ON CERTAIN FREQUENCY RATIOS THAT SOUND PLEASING (OCTAVE-2:1, FIFTH 3:2, THIRD 3:4). IF A PIANO IS TUNED EXACTLY TO THESE RATIOS IN ONE PARTICULAR KEY THE RATIOS WILL NOT BE EXACTLY THE SAME FOR ANY OTHER KEY. TO OVERCOME THIS PIANOS ARE TUNED TO AN APPROXIMATION WHICH WORKS EQUALLY IN ALL KEYS.

THIS IS CALLED EQUAL-TEMPERED TUNING. IT WAS PIONEERED BY BACH (HENCE HIS 'WELL-TEMPERED' CLAVICHORD PIECES WRITTEN IN ALL KEYS).

STRINGS

STRINGS APPEAR TO VIBRATE AS CURVED ARCS (SEE LEFT). HOWEVER AT ANY MOMENT THE ACTUAL SHAPE OF THE STRING IS A STRAIGHT LINE SHARPLY BENT AT ONE POINT. THE POINT TRAVELS RAPIDLY BACK & FORTH ALONG THE STRING.

REVERBERATION

SOUND REFLECTIONS OFF A SINGLE HARD SURFACE (MORE THAN 13m AWAY) PRODUCE AN ECHO. SOUND REFLECTIONS OFF MANY DIFFERENT SURFACES (e.g. INSIDE A ROOM) PRODUCE A COMBINATION OF ECHOES CALLED REVERBERATION.

IN A HALL, SPEECH IS CLEAREST IF THE REVERBERATION LASTS ABOUT HALF A SECOND & MUSIC SOUNDS BEST WITH TWO SECONDS' REVERB. SOME MODERN CONCERT HALLS HAVE MOVING CEILING PANELS TO ADJUST THE REVERB TIME.

RECORDING

STEREO RECORDINGS MADE BY PLACING 2 MICROPHONES INSIDE 'EAR CANALS' OF A DUMMY HEAD PRODUCE THE MOST AUTHENTIC SOUND REPRODUCTION, BETTER THAN QUADRAPHONIC SYSTEMS.

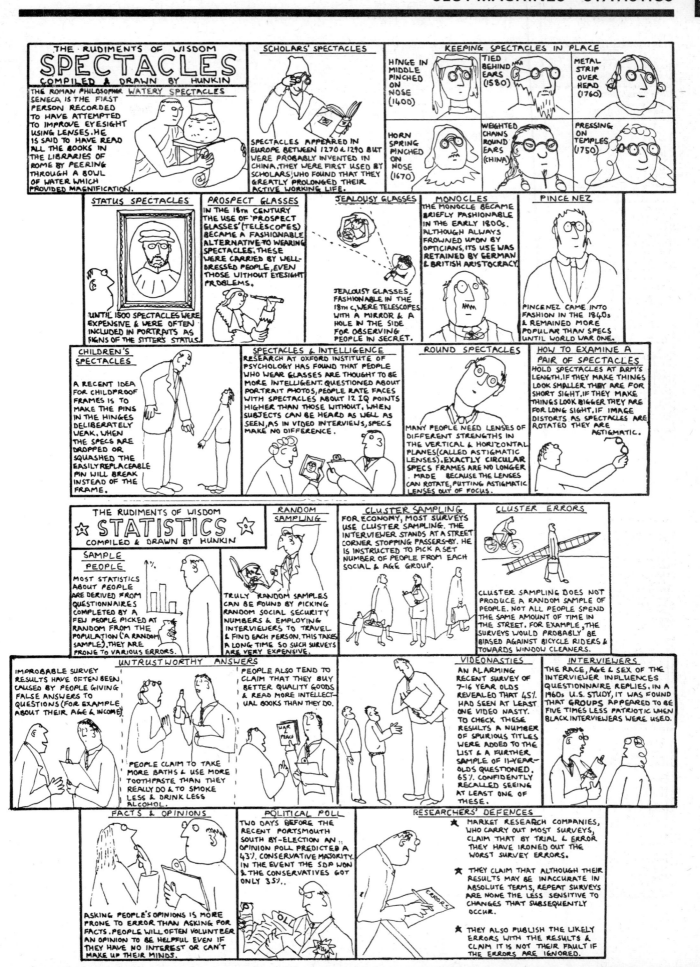

THE RUDIMENTS OF WISDOM
SPECTACLES
COMPILED & DRAWN BY HUNKIN

WATERY SPECTACLES
THE ROMAN PHILOSOPHER SENECA IS THE FIRST PERSON RECORDED TO HAVE ATTEMPTED TO IMPROVE EYESIGHT USING LENSES. HE IS SAID TO HAVE READ ALL THE BOOKS IN THE LIBRARIES OF ROME BY PEERING THROUGH A BOWL OF WATER WHICH PROVIDED MAGNIFICATION.

SCHOLARS' SPECTACLES
SPECTACLES APPEARED IN EUROPE BETWEEN 1270 & 1290 BUT WERE PROBABLY INVENTED IN CHINA. THEY WERE FIRST USED BY SCHOLARS, WHO FOUND THAT THEY GREATLY PROLONGED THEIR ACTIVE WORKING LIFE.

KEEPING SPECTACLES IN PLACE
HINGE IN MIDDLE PINCHED ON NOSE (1400)
TIED BEHIND EARS (1580)
METAL STRIP OVER HEAD (1760)
HORN SPRING PINCHED ON NOSE (1670)
WEIGHTED CHAINS ROUND EARS (CHINA)
PRESSING ON TEMPLES (1750)

STATUS SPECTACLES
UNTIL 1500 SPECTACLES WERE EXPENSIVE & WERE OFTEN INCLUDED IN PORTRAITS AS SIGNS OF THE SITTERS STATUS.

PROSPECT GLASSES
IN THE 18TH CENTURY THE USE OF 'PROSPECT GLASSES' (TELESCOPES) BECAME A FASHIONABLE ALTERNATIVE TO WEARING SPECTACLES. THESE WERE CARRIED BY WELL-DRESSED PEOPLE, EVEN THOSE WITHOUT EYESIGHT PROBLEMS.

JEALOUSY GLASSES
JEALOUSY GLASSES, FASHIONABLE IN THE 18TH C, WERE TELESCOPES WITH A MIRROR & A HOLE IN THE SIDE FOR OBSERVING PEOPLE IN SECRET.

MONOCLES
THE MONOCLE BECAME BRIEFLY FASHIONABLE IN THE EARLY 1800s. ALTHOUGH ALWAYS FROWNED UPON BY OPTICIANS, ITS USE WAS RETAINED BY GERMAN & BRITISH ARISTOCRACY.

PINCE NEZ
PINCE NEZ CAME INTO FASHION IN THE 1840s & REMAINED MORE POPULAR THAN SPECS UNTIL WORLD WAR ONE.

CHILDREN'S SPECTACLES
A RECENT IDEA FOR CHILDPROOF FRAMES IS TO MAKE THE PINS IN THE HINGES DELIBERATELY WEAK. WHEN THE SPECS ARE DROPPED OR SQUASHED THE EASILY REPLACEABLE PIN WILL BREAK INSTEAD OF THE FRAME.

SPECTACLES & INTELLIGENCE
RESEARCH AT OXFORD INSTITUTE OF PSYCHOLOGY HAS FOUND THAT PEOPLE WHO WEAR GLASSES ARE THOUGHT TO BE MORE INTELLIGENT. QUESTIONED ABOUT PORTRAIT PHOTOS, PEOPLE RATE FACES WITH SPECTACLES ABOUT 12 IQ POINTS HIGHER THAN THOSE WITHOUT. WHEN SUBJECTS CAN BE HEARD AS WELL AS SEEN, AS IN VIDEO INTERVIEWS, SPECS MAKE NO DIFFERENCE.

ROUND SPECTACLES
MANY PEOPLE NEED LENSES OF DIFFERENT STRENGTHS IN THE VERTICAL & HORIZONTAL PLANES (CALLED ASTIGMATIC LENSES). EXACTLY CIRCULAR SPECS FRAMES ARE NO LONGER MADE BECAUSE THE LENSES CAN ROTATE, PUTTING ASTIGMATIC LENSES OUT OF FOCUS.

HOW TO EXAMINE A PAIR OF SPECTACLES
HOLD SPECTACLES AT ARM'S LENGTH. IF THEY MAKE THINGS LOOK SMALLER THEY ARE FOR SHORT SIGHT. IF THEY MAKE THINGS LOOK BIGGER THEY ARE FOR LONG SIGHT. IF IMAGE DISTORTS AS SPECTACLES ARE ROTATED THEY ARE ASTIGMATIC.

THE RUDIMENTS OF WISDOM
☆ STATISTICS ☆
COMPILED & DRAWN BY HUNKIN

SAMPLE PEOPLE
MOST STATISTICS ABOUT PEOPLE ARE DERIVED FROM QUESTIONNAIRES COMPLETED BY A FEW PEOPLE PICKED AT RANDOM FROM THE POPULATION ('A RANDOM SAMPLE'), THEY ARE PRONE TO VARIOUS ERRORS.

RANDOM SAMPLING
TRULY RANDOM SAMPLES CAN BE FOUND BY PICKING RANDOM SOCIAL SECURITY NUMBERS & EMPLOYING INTERVIEWERS TO TRAVEL & FIND EACH PERSON. THIS TAKES A LONG TIME SO SUCH SURVEYS ARE VERY EXPENSIVE.

CLUSTER SAMPLING
FOR ECONOMY, MOST SURVEYS USE CLUSTER SAMPLING. THE INTERVIEWER STANDS AT A STREET CORNER STOPPING PASSERS-BY. HE IS INSTRUCTED TO PICK A SET NUMBER OF PEOPLE FROM EACH SOCIAL & AGE GROUP.

CLUSTER ERRORS
CLUSTER SAMPLING DOES NOT PRODUCE A RANDOM SAMPLE OF PEOPLE. NOT ALL PEOPLE SPEND THE SAME AMOUNT OF TIME IN THE STREET. FOR EXAMPLE, THE SURVEYS WOULD PROBABLY BE BIASED AGAINST BICYCLE RIDERS & TOWARDS WINDOW CLEANERS.

UNTRUSTWORTHY ANSWERS
IMPROBABLE SURVEY RESULTS HAVE OFTEN BEEN CAUSED BY PEOPLE GIVING FALSE ANSWERS TO QUESTIONS (FOR EXAMPLE ABOUT THEIR AGE & INCOME).

PEOPLE CLAIM TO TAKE MORE BATHS & USE MORE TOOTHPASTE THAN THEY REALLY DO & TO SMOKE LESS & DRINK LESS ALCOHOL.

PEOPLE ALSO TEND TO CLAIM THAT THEY BUY BETTER QUALITY GOODS & READ MORE INTELLECTUAL BOOKS THAN THEY DO.

VIDEONASTIES
AN ALARMING RECENT SURVEY OF 7-16 YEAR OLDS REVEALED THAT 45% HAD SEEN AT LEAST ONE VIDEO NASTY. TO CHECK THESE RESULTS A NUMBER OF SPURIOUS TITLES WERE ADDED TO THE LIST & A FURTHER SAMPLE OF 11-YEAR-OLDS QUESTIONED. 68% CONFIDENTLY RECALLED SEEING AT LEAST ONE OF THESE.

INTERVIEWERS
THE RACE, AGE & SEX OF THE INTERVIEWER INFLUENCES QUESTIONNAIRE REPLIES. IN A 1960s U.S. STUDY, IT WAS FOUND THAT GROUPS APPEARED TO BE FIVE TIMES LESS PATRIOTIC WHEN BLACK INTERVIEWERS WERE USED.

FACTS & OPINIONS
ASKING PEOPLE'S OPINIONS IS MORE PRONE TO ERROR THAN ASKING FOR FACTS. PEOPLE WILL OFTEN VOLUNTEER AN OPINION TO BE HELPFUL EVEN IF THEY HAVE NO INTEREST OR CAN'T MAKE UP THEIR MINDS.

POLITICAL POLL
TWO DAYS BEFORE THE RECENT PORTSMOUTH SOUTH BY-ELECTION AN OPINION POLL PREDICTED A 43% CONSERVATIVE MAJORITY. IN THE EVENT THE SDP WON & THE CONSERVATIVES GOT ONLY 35%.

RESEARCHERS' DEFENCES
★ MARKET RESEARCH COMPANIES, WHO CARRY OUT MOST SURVEYS, CLAIM THAT BY TRIAL & ERROR THEY HAVE IRONED OUT THE WORST SURVEY ERRORS.

★ THEY CLAIM THAT ALTHOUGH THEIR RESULTS MAY BE INACCURATE IN ABSOLUTE TERMS, REPEAT SURVEYS ARE NONE THE LESS SENSITIVE TO CHANGES THAT SUBSEQUENTLY OCCUR.

★ THEY ALSO PUBLISH THE LIKELY ERRORS WITH THE RESULTS & CLAIM IT IS NOT THEIR FAULT IF THE ERRORS ARE IGNORED.

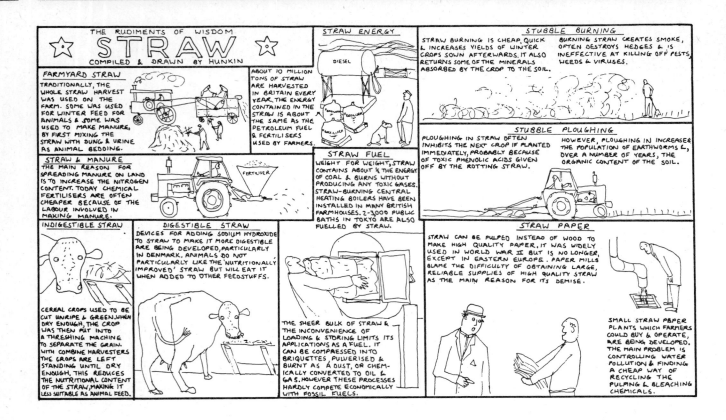

THE RUDIMENTS OF WISDOM ☆ STRAW ☆
COMPILED & DRAWN BY HUNKIN

FARMYARD STRAW
TRADITIONALLY, THE WHOLE STRAW HARVEST WAS USED ON THE FARM. SOME WAS USED FOR WINTER FEED FOR ANIMALS & SOME WAS USED TO MAKE MANURE, BY FIRST MIXING THE STRAW WITH DUNG & URINE AS ANIMAL BEDDING.

STRAW & MANURE
THE MAIN REASON FOR SPREADING MANURE ON LAND IS TO INCREASE THE NITROGEN CONTENT. TODAY CHEMICAL FERTILISERS ARE OFTEN CHEAPER BECAUSE OF THE LABOUR INVOLVED IN MAKING MANURE.

INDIGESTIBLE STRAW
CEREAL CROPS USED TO BE CUT UNRIPE & GREEN, WHEN DRY ENOUGH, THE CROP WAS THEN PUT INTO A THRESHING MACHINE TO SEPARATE THE GRAIN. WITH COMBINE HARVESTERS THE CROPS ARE LEFT STANDING UNTIL DRY ENOUGH, THIS REDUCES THE NUTRITIONAL CONTENT OF THE STRAW, MAKING IT LESS SUITABLE AS ANIMAL FEED.

DIGESTIBLE STRAW
DEVICES FOR ADDING SODIUM HYDROXIDE TO STRAW TO MAKE IT MORE DIGESTIBLE ARE BEING DEVELOPED, PARTICULARLY IN DENMARK. ANIMALS DO NOT PARTICULARLY LIKE THE 'NUTRITIONALLY IMPROVED' STRAW BUT WILL EAT IT WHEN ADDED TO OTHER FEEDSTUFFS.

STRAW ENERGY
ABOUT 10 MILLION TONS OF STRAW ARE HARVESTED IN BRITAIN EVERY YEAR. THE ENERGY CONTAINED IN THE STRAW IS ABOUT THE SAME AS THE PETROLEUM FUEL & FERTILISERS USED BY FARMERS.

STRAW FUEL
WEIGHT FOR WEIGHT, STRAW CONTAINS ABOUT ½ THE ENERGY OF COAL & BURNS WITHOUT PRODUCING ANY TOXIC GASES. STRAW-BURNING CENTRAL HEATING BOILERS HAVE BEEN INSTALLED IN MANY BRITISH FARMHOUSES. 2-3000 PUBLIC BATHS IN TOKYO ARE ALSO FUELLED BY STRAW.

THE SHEER BULK OF STRAW & THE INCONVENIENCE OF LOADING & STORING LIMITS ITS APPLICATIONS AS A FUEL. IT CAN BE COMPRESSED INTO BRIQUETTES, PULVERISED & BURNT AS A DUST, OR CHEMICALLY CONVERTED TO OIL & GAS. HOWEVER THESE PROCESSES HARDLY COMPETE ECONOMICALLY WITH FOSSIL FUELS.

STUBBLE BURNING
STRAW BURNING IS CHEAP, QUICK & INCREASES YIELDS OF WINTER CROPS SOWN AFTERWARDS. IT ALSO RETURNS SOME OF THE MINERALS ABSORBED BY THE CROP TO THE SOIL.

BURNING STRAW CREATES SMOKE, OFTEN DESTROYS HEDGES & IS INEFFECTIVE AT KILLING OFF PESTS, WEEDS & VIRUSES.

STUBBLE PLOUGHING
PLOUGHING IN STRAW OFTEN INHIBITS THE NEXT CROP IF PLANTED IMMEDIATELY, PROBABLY BECAUSE OF TOXIC PHENOLIC ACIDS GIVEN OFF BY THE ROTTING STRAW.

HOWEVER, PLOUGHING IN INCREASES THE POPULATION OF EARTHWORMS &, OVER A NUMBER OF YEARS, THE ORGANIC CONTENT OF THE SOIL.

STRAW PAPER
STRAW CAN BE PULPED INSTEAD OF WOOD TO MAKE HIGH QUALITY PAPER. IT WAS WIDELY USED IN WORLD WAR II BUT IS NO LONGER, EXCEPT IN EASTERN EUROPE. PAPER MILLS BLAME THE DIFFICULTY OF OBTAINING LARGE, RELIABLE SUPPLIES OF HIGH QUALITY STRAW AS THE MAIN REASON FOR ITS DEMISE.

SMALL STRAW PAPER PLANTS WHICH FARMERS COULD BUY & OPERATE, ARE BEING DEVELOPED. THE MAIN PROBLEM IS CONTROLLING WATER POLLUTION & FINDING A CHEAP WAY OF RECYCLING THE PULPING & BLEACHING CHEMICALS.

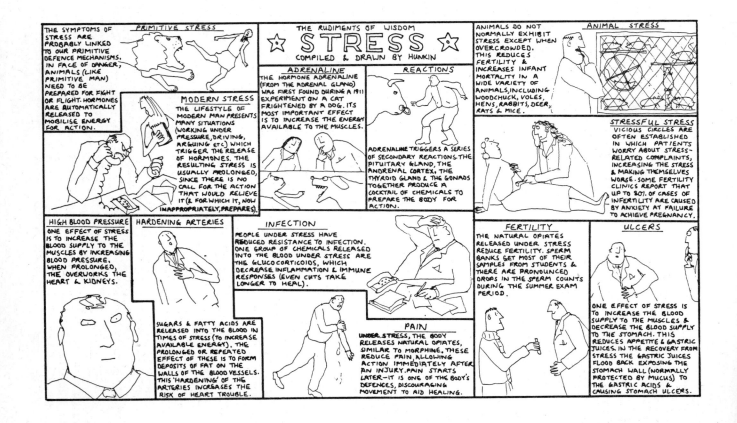

THE RUDIMENTS OF WISDOM ☆ STRESS ☆
COMPILED & DRAWN BY HUNKIN

PRIMITIVE STRESS
THE SYMPTOMS OF STRESS ARE PROBABLY LINKED TO OUR PRIMITIVE DEFENCE MECHANISMS. IN FACE OF DANGER, ANIMALS (LIKE PRIMITIVE MAN) NEED TO BE PREPARED FOR FIGHT OR FLIGHT. HORMONES ARE AUTOMATICALLY RELEASED TO MOBILISE ENERGY FOR ACTION.

MODERN STRESS
THE LIFESTYLE OF MODERN MAN PRESENTS MANY SITUATIONS (WORKING UNDER PRESSURE, DRIVING, ARGUING ETC) WHICH TRIGGER THE RELEASE OF HORMONES. THE RESULTING STRESS IS USUALLY PROLONGED, SINCE THERE IS NO CALL FOR THE ACTION THAT WOULD RELIEVE IT (& FOR WHICH IT, NOW INAPPROPRIATELY, PREPARES).

ADRENALINE
THE HORMONE ADRENALINE (FROM THE ADRENAL GLAND) WAS FIRST FOUND DURING A 1911 EXPERIMENT ON A CAT FRIGHTENED BY A DOG. ITS MOST IMPORTANT EFFECT IS TO INCREASE THE ENERGY AVAILABLE TO THE MUSCLES.

REACTIONS
ADRENALINE TRIGGERS A SERIES OF SECONDARY REACTIONS. THE PITUITARY GLAND, THE ADRENAL CORTEX, THE THYROID GLAND & THE GONADS TOGETHER PRODUCE A COCKTAIL OF CHEMICALS TO PREPARE THE BODY FOR ACTION.

ANIMAL STRESS
ANIMALS DO NOT NORMALLY EXHIBIT STRESS EXCEPT WHEN OVERCROWDED. THIS REDUCES FERTILITY & INCREASES INFANT MORTALITY IN A WIDE VARIETY OF ANIMALS, INCLUDING WOODCHUCK, VOLES, HENS, RABBITS, DEER, RATS & MICE.

STRESSFUL STRESS
VICIOUS CIRCLES ARE OFTEN ESTABLISHED IN WHICH PATIENTS WORRY ABOUT STRESS-RELATED COMPLAINTS, INCREASING THE STRESS & MAKING THEMSELVES WORSE. SOME FERTILITY CLINICS REPORT THAT UP TO 80% OF CASES OF INFERTILITY ARE CAUSED BY ANXIETY AT FAILURE TO ACHIEVE PREGNANCY.

HIGH BLOOD PRESSURE
ONE EFFECT OF STRESS IS TO INCREASE THE BLOOD SUPPLY TO THE MUSCLES BY INCREASING BLOOD PRESSURE. WHEN PROLONGED, THIS OVERWORKS THE HEART & KIDNEYS.

HARDENING ARTERIES
SUGARS & FATTY ACIDS ARE RELEASED INTO THE BLOOD IN TIMES OF STRESS (TO INCREASE AVAILABLE ENERGY). THE PROLONGED OR REPEATED EFFECT OF THESE IS TO FORM DEPOSITS OF FAT ON THE WALLS OF THE BLOOD VESSELS. THIS 'HARDENING' OF THE ARTERIES INCREASES THE RISK OF HEART TROUBLE.

INFECTION
PEOPLE UNDER STRESS HAVE REDUCED RESISTANCE TO INFECTION. ONE GROUP OF CHEMICALS RELEASED INTO THE BLOOD UNDER STRESS ARE THE GLUCOCORTICOIDS, WHICH DECREASE INFLAMMATION & IMMUNE RESPONSES (EVEN CUTS TAKE LONGER TO HEAL).

PAIN
UNDER STRESS, THE BODY RELEASES NATURAL OPIATES, SIMILAR TO MORPHINE. THESE REDUCE PAIN ALLOWING ACTION IMMEDIATELY AFTER AN INJURY. PAIN STARTS LATER – IT IS ONE OF THE BODY'S DEFENCES, DISCOURAGING MOVEMENT TO AID HEALING.

FERTILITY
THE NATURAL OPIATES RELEASED UNDER STRESS REDUCE FERTILITY. SPERM BANKS GET MOST OF THEIR SAMPLES FROM STUDENTS & THERE ARE PRONOUNCED DROPS IN THE SPERM COUNTS DURING THE SUMMER EXAM PERIOD.

ULCERS
ONE EFFECT OF STRESS IS TO INCREASE THE BLOOD SUPPLY TO THE MUSCLES & DECREASE THE BLOOD SUPPLY TO THE STOMACH. THIS REDUCES APPETITE & GASTRIC JUICES. IN THE RECOVERY FROM STRESS THE GASTRIC JUICES FLOOD BACK EXPOSING THE STOMACH WALL (NORMALLY PROTECTED BY MUCUS) TO THE GASTRIC ACIDS & CAUSING STOMACH ULCERS.

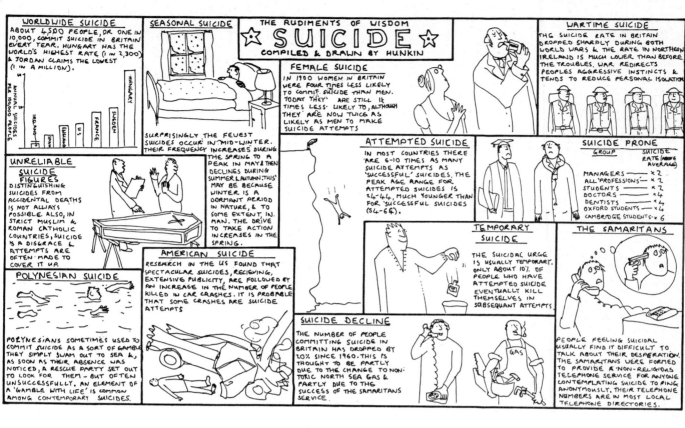

THE RUDIMENTS OF WISDOM
☆ SUICIDE ☆
COMPILED & DRAWN BY HUNKIN

WORLDWIDE SUICIDE
ABOUT 4,500 PEOPLE, OR ONE IN 10,000, COMMIT SUICIDE IN BRITAIN EVERY YEAR. HUNGARY HAS THE WORLD'S HIGHEST RATE (1 IN 2,300) & JORDAN CLAIMS THE LOWEST (1 IN A MILLION).

SEASONAL SUICIDE
SURPRISINGLY THE FEWEST SUICIDES OCCUR IN MID-WINTER. THEIR FREQUENCY INCREASES DURING THE SPRING TO A PEAK IN MAY & THEN DECLINES DURING SUMMER & AUTUMN. THIS MAY BE BECAUSE WINTER IS A DORMANT PERIOD IN NATURE, & TO SOME EXTENT IN MAN. THE DRIVE TO TAKE ACTION INCREASES IN THE SPRING.

FEMALE SUICIDE
IN 1900 WOMEN IN BRITAIN WERE FOUR TIMES LESS LIKELY TO COMMIT SUICIDE THAN MEN. TODAY THEY ARE STILL 1½ TIMES LESS LIKELY TO, ALTHOUGH THEY ARE NOW TWICE AS LIKELY AS MEN TO MAKE SUICIDE ATTEMPTS

WARTIME SUICIDE
THE SUICIDE RATE IN BRITAIN DROPPED SHARPLY DURING BOTH WORLD WARS & THE RATE IN NORTHERN IRELAND IS MUCH LOWER THAN BEFORE THE TROUBLES. WAR REDIRECTS PEOPLES AGGRESSIVE INSTINCTS & TENDS TO REDUCE PERSONAL ISOLATION.

UNRELIABLE SUICIDE FIGURES
DISTINGUISHING SUICIDES FROM ACCIDENTAL DEATHS IS NOT ALWAYS POSSIBLE. ALSO, IN STRICT MUSLIM & ROMAN CATHOLIC COUNTRIES, SUICIDE IS A DISGRACE & ATTEMPTS ARE OFTEN MADE TO COVER IT UP.

ATTEMPTED SUICIDE
IN MOST COUNTRIES THERE ARE 6-10 TIMES AS MANY SUICIDE ATTEMPTS AS 'SUCCESSFUL' SUICIDES. THE PEAK AGE RANGE FOR ATTEMPTED SUICIDES IS 24-44, MUCH YOUNGER THAN FOR 'SUCCESSFUL' SUICIDES (54-64).

SUICIDE PRONE

GROUP	SUICIDE RATE (ABOVE AVERAGE)
MANAGERS	× 2
ALL 'PROFESSIONS'	× 2
STUDENTS	× 2
DOCTORS	× 4
DENTISTS	× 4
OXFORD STUDENTS	× 4
CAMBRIDGE STUDENTS	× 6

POLYNESIAN SUICIDE
POLYNESIANS SOMETIMES USED TO COMMIT SUICIDE AS A SORT OF GAMBLE. THEY SIMPLY SWAM OUT TO SEA &, AS SOON AS THEIR ABSENCE WAS NOTICED, A RESCUE PARTY SET OUT TO LOOK FOR THEM - BUT OFTEN UNSUCCESSFULLY. AN ELEMENT OF A 'GAMBLE WITH LIFE' IS COMMON AMONG CONTEMPORARY SUICIDES.

AMERICAN SUICIDE
RESEARCH IN THE US FOUND THAT SPECTACULAR SUICIDES, RECIEVING EXTENSIVE PUBLICITY, ARE FOLLOWED BY AN INCREASE IN THE NUMBER OF PEOPLE KILLED IN CAR CRASHES. IT IS PROBABLE THAT SOME CRASHES ARE SUICIDE ATTEMPTS

TEMPORARY SUICIDE
THE SUICIDAL URGE IS USUALLY TEMPORARY. ONLY ABOUT 10% OF PEOPLE WHO HAVE ATTEMPTED SUICIDE EVENTUALLY KILL THEMSELVES IN SUBSEQUENT ATTEMPTS

SUICIDE DECLINE
THE NUMBER OF PEOPLE COMMITTING SUICIDE IN BRITAIN HAS DROPPED BY 20% SINCE 1960. THIS IS THOUGHT TO BE PARTLY DUE TO THE CHANGE TO NON-TOXIC NORTH SEA GAS & PARTLY DUE TO THE SUCCESS OF THE SAMARITANS SERVICE.

THE SAMARITANS
PEOPLE FEELING SUICIDAL USUALLY FIND IT DIFFICULT TO TALK ABOUT THEIR DESPERATION. THE SAMARITANS WERE FORMED TO PROVIDE A 'NON-RELIGIOUS' TELEPHONE SERVICE FOR ANYONE CONTEMPLATING SUICIDE TO RING ANONYMOUSLY. THEIR TELEPHONE NUMBERS ARE IN MOST LOCAL TELEPHONE DIRECTORIES.

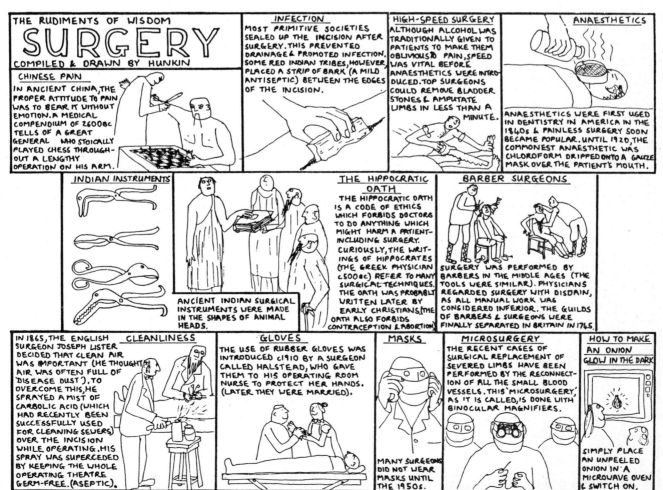

THE RUDIMENTS OF WISDOM
SURGERY
COMPILED & DRAWN BY HUNKIN

CHINESE PAIN
IN ANCIENT CHINA, THE PROPER ATTITUDE TO PAIN WAS TO BEAR IT WITHOUT EMOTION. A MEDICAL COMPENDIUM OF 2600BC TELLS OF A GREAT GENERAL WHO STOICALLY PLAYED CHESS THROUGH-OUT A LENGTHY OPERATION ON HIS ARM.

INFECTION
MOST PRIMITIVE SOCIETIES SEALED UP THE INCISION AFTER SURGERY. THIS PREVENTED DRAINAGE & PROMOTED INFECTION. SOME RED INDIAN TRIBES, HOWEVER, PLACED A STRIP OF BARK (A MILD ANTISEPTIC) BETWEEN THE EDGES OF THE INCISION.

HIGH-SPEED SURGERY
ALTHOUGH ALCOHOL WAS TRADITIONALLY GIVEN TO PATIENTS TO MAKE THEM OBLIVIOUS TO PAIN, SPEED WAS VITAL BEFORE ANAESTHETICS WERE INTRODUCED. TOP SURGEONS COULD REMOVE BLADDER STONES & AMPUTATE LIMBS IN LESS THAN A MINUTE.

ANAESTHETICS
ANAESTHETICS WERE FIRST USED IN DENTISTRY IN AMERICA IN THE 1840s & PAINLESS SURGERY SOON BECAME POPULAR. UNTIL 1920, THE COMMONEST ANAESTHETIC WAS CHLOROFORM DRIPPED ONTO A GAUZE MASK OVER THE PATIENT'S MOUTH.

INDIAN INSTRUMENTS
ANCIENT INDIAN SURGICAL INSTRUMENTS WERE MADE IN THE SHAPES OF ANIMAL HEADS.

THE HIPPOCRATIC OATH
THE HIPPOCRATIC OATH IS A CODE OF ETHICS WHICH FORBIDS DOCTORS TO DO ANYTHING WHICH MIGHT HARM A PATIENT-INCLUDING SURGERY. CURIOUSLY, THE WRITINGS OF HIPPOCRATES (THE GREEK PHYSICIAN c500BC) REFER TO MANY SURGICAL TECHNIQUES. THE OATH WAS PROBABLY WRITTEN LATER BY EARLY CHRISTIANS (THE OATH ALSO FORBIDS CONTRACEPTION & ABORTION)

BARBER SURGEONS
SURGERY WAS PERFORMED BY BARBERS IN THE MIDDLE AGES (THE TOOLS WERE SIMILAR). PHYSICIANS REGARDED SURGERY WITH DISDAIN, AS ALL MANUAL WORK WAS CONSIDERED INFERIOR. THE GUILDS OF BARBERS & SURGEONS WERE FINALLY SEPARATED IN BRITAIN IN 1745.

CLEANLINESS
IN 1865, THE ENGLISH SURGEON JOSEPH LISTER DECIDED THAT CLEAN AIR WAS IMPORTANT (HE THOUGHT AIR WAS OFTEN FULL OF 'DISEASE DUST'), TO OVERCOME THIS, HE SPRAYED A MIST OF CARBOLIC ACID (WHICH HAD RECENTLY BEEN SUCCESSFULLY USED FOR CLEANING SEWERS) OVER THE INCISION WHILE OPERATING. HIS SPRAY WAS SUPERCEDED BY KEEPING THE WHOLE OPERATING THEATRE GERM-FREE. (ASEPTIC).

GLOVES
THE USE OF RUBBER GLOVES WAS INTRODUCED c1910 BY A SURGEON CALLED HALSTEAD, WHO GAVE THEM TO HIS OPERATING ROOM NURSE TO PROTECT HER HANDS. (LATER THEY WERE MARRIED).

MASKS
MANY SURGEONS DID NOT WEAR MASKS UNTIL THE 1950s.

MICROSURGERY
THE RECENT CASES OF SURGICAL REPLACEMENT OF SEVERED LIMBS HAVE BEEN PERFORMED BY THE RECONNECT-ION OF ALL THE SMALL BLOOD VESSELS. THIS 'MICROSURGERY', AS IT IS CALLED, IS DONE WITH BINOCULAR MAGNIFIERS.

HOW TO MAKE AN ONION GLOW IN THE DARK
SIMPLY PLACE AN UNPEELED ONION IN A MICROWAVE OVEN & SWITCH ON.

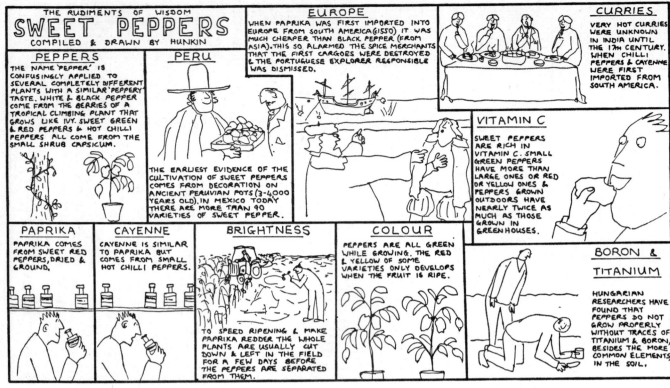

THE RUDIMENTS OF WISDOM — SWEET PEPPERS
COMPILED & DRAWN BY HUNKIN

PEPPERS
THE NAME 'PEPPER' IS CONFUSINGLY APPLIED TO SEVERAL COMPLETELY DIFFERENT PLANTS WITH A SIMILAR 'PEPPERY' TASTE. WHITE & BLACK PEPPER COME FROM THE BERRIES OF A TROPICAL CLIMBING PLANT THAT GROWS LIKE IVY. SWEET GREEN & RED PEPPERS & HOT CHILLI PEPPERS ALL COME FROM THE SMALL SHRUB CAPSICUM.

PERU
THE EARLIEST EVIDENCE OF THE CULTIVATION OF SWEET PEPPERS COMES FROM DECORATION ON ANCIENT PERUVIAN POTS (3-4000 YEARS OLD). IN MEXICO TODAY THERE ARE MORE THAN 90 VARIETIES OF SWEET PEPPER.

EUROPE
WHEN PAPRIKA WAS FIRST IMPORTED INTO EUROPE FROM SOUTH AMERICA (1550) IT WAS MUCH CHEAPER THAN BLACK PEPPER (FROM ASIA). THIS SO ALARMED THE SPICE MERCHANTS THAT THE FIRST CARGOES WERE DESTROYED & THE PORTUGUESE EXPLORER RESPONSIBLE WAS DISMISSED.

CURRIES
VERY HOT CURRIES WERE UNKNOWN IN INDIA UNTIL THE 17th CENTURY. WHEN CHILLI PEPPERS & CAYENNE WERE FIRST IMPORTED FROM SOUTH AMERICA.

VITAMIN C
SWEET PEPPERS ARE RICH IN VITAMIN C. SMALL GREEN PEPPERS HAVE MORE THAN LARGE ONES OR RED OR YELLOW ONES & PEPPERS GROWN OUTDOORS HAVE NEARLY TWICE AS MUCH AS THOSE GROWN IN GREENHOUSES.

PAPRIKA
PAPRIKA COMES FROM SWEET RED PEPPERS, DRIED & GROUND.

CAYENNE
CAYENNE IS SIMILAR TO PAPRIKA BUT COMES FROM SMALL HOT CHILLI PEPPERS.

BRIGHTNESS
TO SPEED RIPENING & MAKE PAPRIKA REDDER THE WHOLE PLANTS ARE USUALLY CUT DOWN & LEFT IN THE FIELD FOR A FEW DAYS BEFORE THE PEPPERS ARE SEPARATED FROM THEM.

COLOUR
PEPPERS ARE ALL GREEN WHILE GROWING. THE RED & YELLOW OF SOME VARIETIES ONLY DEVELOPS WHEN THE FRUIT IS RIPE.

BORON & TITANIUM
HUNGARIAN RESEARCHERS HAVE FOUND THAT PEPPERS DO NOT GROW PROPERLY WITHOUT TRACES OF TITANIUM & BORON, BESIDES THE MORE COMMON ELEMENTS IN THE SOIL.

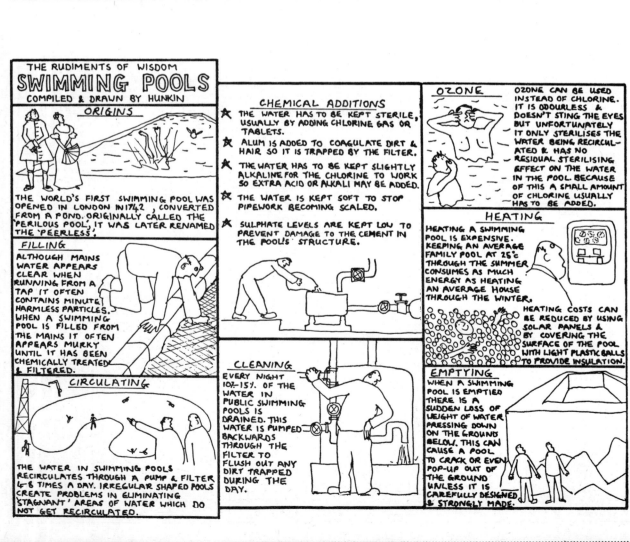

THE RUDIMENTS OF WISDOM — SWIMMING POOLS
COMPILED & DRAWN BY HUNKIN

ORIGINS
THE WORLD'S FIRST SWIMMING POOL WAS OPENED IN LONDON IN 1742, CONVERTED FROM A POND. ORIGINALLY CALLED THE 'PERILOUS POOL', IT WAS LATER RENAMED THE 'PEERLESS'.

FILLING
ALTHOUGH MAINS WATER APPEARS CLEAR WHEN RUNNING FROM A TAP IT OFTEN CONTAINS MINUTE HARMLESS PARTICLES. WHEN A SWIMMING POOL IS FILLED FROM THE MAINS IT OFTEN APPEARS MURKY UNTIL IT HAS BEEN CHEMICALLY TREATED & FILTERED.

CIRCULATING
THE WATER IN SWIMMING POOLS RECIRCULATES THROUGH A PUMP & FILTER 4-8 TIMES A DAY. IRREGULAR SHAPED POOLS CREATE PROBLEMS IN ELIMINATING 'STAGNANT' AREAS OF WATER WHICH DO NOT GET RECIRCULATED.

CHEMICAL ADDITIONS
★ THE WATER HAS TO BE KEPT STERILE, USUALLY BY ADDING CHLORINE GAS OR TABLETS.

★ ALUM IS ADDED TO COAGULATE DIRT & HAIR SO IT IS TRAPPED BY THE FILTER.

★ THE WATER HAS TO BE KEPT SLIGHTLY ALKALINE FOR THE CHLORINE TO WORK SO EXTRA ACID OR ALKALI MAY BE ADDED.

★ THE WATER IS KEPT SOFT TO STOP PIPEWORK BECOMING SCALED.

★ SULPHATE LEVELS ARE KEPT LOW TO PREVENT DAMAGE TO THE CEMENT IN THE POOL'S STRUCTURE.

CLEANING
EVERY NIGHT 10%-15% OF THE WATER IN PUBLIC SWIMMING POOLS IS DRAINED. THIS WATER IS PUMPED BACKWARDS THROUGH THE FILTER TO FLUSH OUT ANY DIRT TRAPPED DURING THE DAY.

OZONE
OZONE CAN BE USED INSTEAD OF CHLORINE. IT IS ODOURLESS & DOESN'T STING THE EYES BUT UNFORTUNATELY IT ONLY STERILISES THE WATER BEING RECIRCULATED & HAS NO RESIDUAL STERILISING EFFECT ON THE WATER IN THE POOL. BECAUSE OF THIS A SMALL AMOUNT OF CHLORINE USUALLY HAS TO BE ADDED.

HEATING
HEATING A SWIMMING POOL IS EXPENSIVE. KEEPING AN AVERAGE FAMILY POOL AT 25°C THROUGH THE SUMMER CONSUMES AS MUCH ENERGY AS HEATING AN AVERAGE HOUSE THROUGH THE WINTER.

HEATING COSTS CAN BE REDUCED BY USING SOLAR PANELS & BY COVERING THE SURFACE OF THE POOL WITH LIGHT PLASTIC BALLS TO PROVIDE INSULATION.

EMPTYING
WHEN A SWIMMING POOL IS EMPTIED THERE IS A SUDDEN LOSS OF WEIGHT OF WATER PRESSING DOWN ON THE GROUND BELOW. THIS CAN CAUSE A POOL TO CRACK OR EVEN POP-UP OUT OF THE GROUND UNLESS IT IS CAREFULLY DESIGNED & STRONGLY MADE.

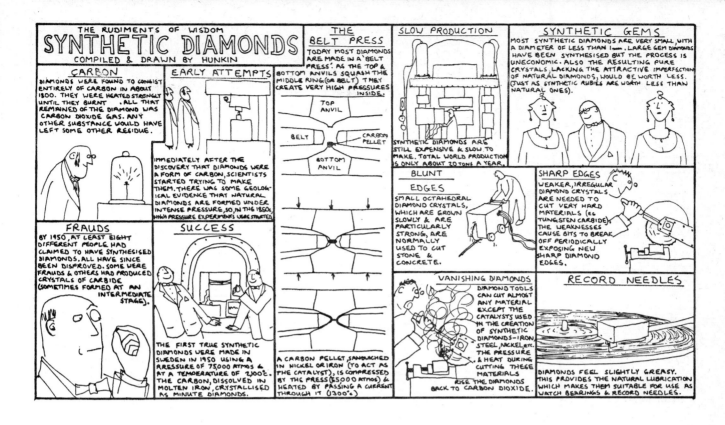

THE RUDIMENTS OF WISDOM
SYNTHETIC DIAMONDS
COMPILED & DRAWN BY HUNKIN

CARBON
DIAMONDS WERE FOUND TO CONSIST ENTIRELY OF CARBON IN ABOUT 1800. THEY WERE HEATED STRONGLY UNTIL THEY BURNT. ALL THAT REMAINED OF THE DIAMOND WAS CARBON DIOXIDE GAS. ANY OTHER SUBSTANCE WOULD HAVE LEFT SOME OTHER RESIDUE.

EARLY ATTEMPTS
IMMEDIATELY AFTER THE DISCOVERY THAT DIAMONDS WERE A FORM OF CARBON, SCIENTISTS STARTED TRYING TO MAKE THEM. THERE WAS SOME GEOLOGICAL EVIDENCE THAT NATURAL DIAMONDS ARE FORMED UNDER INTENSE PRESSURE, SO, IN THE 1850s, HIGH PRESSURE EXPERIMENTS WERE STARTED.

THE BELT PRESS
TODAY MOST DIAMONDS ARE MADE IN A 'BELT PRESS'. AS THE TOP & MIDDLE RING (OR BELT) THEY CREATE VERY HIGH PRESSURES INSIDE.

TOP ANVIL / BELT / CARBON PELLET / BOTTOM ANVIL

BOTTOM ANVILS SQUASH THE MIDDLE RING (OR BELT) THEY CREATE VERY HIGH PRESSURES INSIDE.

A CARBON PELLET, SANDWICHED IN NICKEL OR IRON (TO ACT AS THE CATALYST), IS COMPRESSED BY THE PRESS (55000 ATMOS) & HEATED BY PASSING A CURRENT THROUGH IT (1300°c)

SLOW PRODUCTION
SYNTHETIC DIAMONDS ARE STILL EXPENSIVE & SLOW TO MAKE. TOTAL WORLD PRODUCTION IS ONLY ABOUT 20 TONS A YEAR.

SYNTHETIC GEMS
MOST SYNTHETIC DIAMONDS ARE VERY SMALL, WITH A DIAMETER OF LESS THAN 1mm. LARGE GEM DIAMONDS HAVE BEEN SYNTHESISED BUT THE PROCESS IS UNECONOMIC. ALSO THE RESULTING PURE CRYSTALS, LACKING THE ATTRACTIVE IMPERFECTION OF NATURAL DIAMONDS, WOULD BE WORTH LESS (JUST AS SYNTHETIC RUBIES ARE WORTH LESS THAN NATURAL ONES).

FRAUDS
BY 1950, AT LEAST EIGHT DIFFERENT PEOPLE HAD CLAIMED TO HAVE SYNTHESISED DIAMONDS. ALL HAVE SINCE BEEN DISPROVED. SOME WERE FRAUDS & OTHERS HAD PRODUCED CRYSTALS OF CARBIDE (SOMETIMES FORMED AT AN INTERMEDIATE STAGE).

SUCCESS
THE FIRST TRUE SYNTHETIC DIAMONDS WERE MADE IN SWEDEN IN 1950 USING A PRESSURE OF 75000 ATMOS & AT A TEMPERATURE OF 2000°c. THE CARBON, DISSOLVED IN MOLTEN IRON, CRYSTALLISED AS MINUTE DIAMONDS.

BLUNT EDGES
SMALL OCTAHEDRAL DIAMOND CRYSTALS, WHICH ARE GROWN SLOWLY & ARE PARTICULARLY STRONG, ARE NORMALLY USED TO CUT STONE & CONCRETE.

SHARP EDGES
WEAKER, IRREGULAR DIAMOND CRYSTALS ARE NEEDED TO CUT VERY HARD MATERIALS (EG TUNGSTEN CARBIDE). THE WEAKNESSES CAUSE BITS TO BREAK OFF PERIODICALLY EXPOSING NEW SHARP DIAMOND EDGES.

VANISHING DIAMONDS
DIAMOND TOOLS CAN CUT ALMOST ANY MATERIAL EXCEPT THE CATALYSTS USED IN THE CREATION OF SYNTHETIC DIAMONDS—IRON, STEEL, NICKEL etc. THE PRESSURE & HEAT DURING CUTTING THESE MATERIALS RISE THE DIAMONDS BACK TO CARBON DIOXIDE.

RECORD NEEDLES
DIAMONDS FEEL SLIGHTLY GREASY. THIS PROVIDES THE NATURAL LUBRICATION WHICH MAKES THEM SUITABLE FOR USE AS WATCH BEARINGS & RECORD NEEDLES.

THE RUDIMENTS OF WISDOM
☆ TANKS ☆
COMPILED & DRAWN BY HUNKIN

THE STEAM TANK
A SUGGESTION FOR AN ARMOURED STEAM TRACTION ENGINE FITTED WITH A GUN & SCYTHES WAS SUBMITTED TO THE BRITISH GOVERNMENT IN 1855. IT WAS REJECTED ON THE GROUNDS THAT IT WAS UNCIVILISED.

FAILURES
IMPRACTICAL VEHICLES TESTED IN WORLD WAR I INCLUDED A PAIR OF STEAM ENGINES LINKED SIDE BY SIDE RUNNING ASTRIDE A TRENCH TO BURY THE TROOPS SHELTERING IN IT. THE RUSSIANS TRIED A TANK WITH 9 METRE DIAMETER WHEELS.

PRACTICALITY
IN 1915 THE WAR OFFICE PRODUCED A SPECIFICATION FOR A BULLETPROOF VEHICLE THAT WOULD CLIMB A 1·7m BANK & CROSS A 1·7m DITCH. TWO PROTOTYPES, CALLED 'LITTLE WILLIE' & 'MOTHER' WERE BUILT IN LINCOLN & MASS PRODUCTION STARTED IN FEBRUARY 1916.

THE FIRST DESIGN
THE FIRST MODELS HAD TAIL WHEELS FOR STEERING. LATER VERSIONS SIMPLY USED THE TRACKS: THE TANKS TURNED WHEN ONE TRACK WENT FASTER THAN THE OTHER.

THE TRACKS WENT OVER THE TOP OF THE TANK SO OAK POLES COULD BE BOLTED ACROSS BOTH TRACKS TO PROVIDE MORE GRIP WHEN THE TANK GOT STUCK.

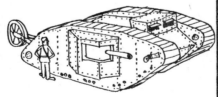

THE TANK CARRIED A CREW OF ABOUT 10. FOUR MEN WERE NEEDED TO DRIVE IT (COMMANDER, DRIVER & TWO GEARBOX OPERATORS).

THE PETROL TANK CARRIED 45 GALLONS, ENOUGH FOR 12 MILES AT 4 MPH. EVERY 70 MILES THE TANK NEEDED A WORKSHOP OVERHAUL.

SECRECY
IN ORDER TO KEEP THE NATURE OF THESE NEW WEAPONS SECRET THEY WERE REFERRED TO AS 'TANKS', FROM THEIR RESEMBLANCE TO LARGE WATER TANKS.

TRIUMPH
TANKS REMAINED A BATTLEFIELD ODDITY UNTIL NOVEMBER 1917, WHEN A MASSED TANK ATTACK AT CAMBRAI BREACHED A 12-MILE SECTION OF THE GERMAN FRONT. THIS CONVINCED GENERALS OF THEIR VALUE & STARTED A RUSH TO PRODUCE TANKS BY ALL COUNTRIES INVOLVED.

RELIABILITY
TANKS DO NOT HAVE A GOOD RELIABILITY RECORD. IN WORLD WAR II 75% OF TANK LOSSES WERE DUE TO MECHANICAL FAILURES. TANKS COULD RARELY ADVANCE MORE THAN 300 MILES WITHOUT PAUSING FOR REPAIRS.

VULNERABILITY
MODERN TANKS STILL HAVE A POOR RECORD OF RELIABILITY (PARTLY DUE TO THE HIGH LEVELS OF VIBRATION). THEY ARE ALSO VULNERABLE TO THE NEW 'ARMOUR PIERCING FIN STABILISED DISCARDING SABOT' SHELL WHICH IS CLAIMED TO PENETRATE ANY KNOWN ARMOUR.

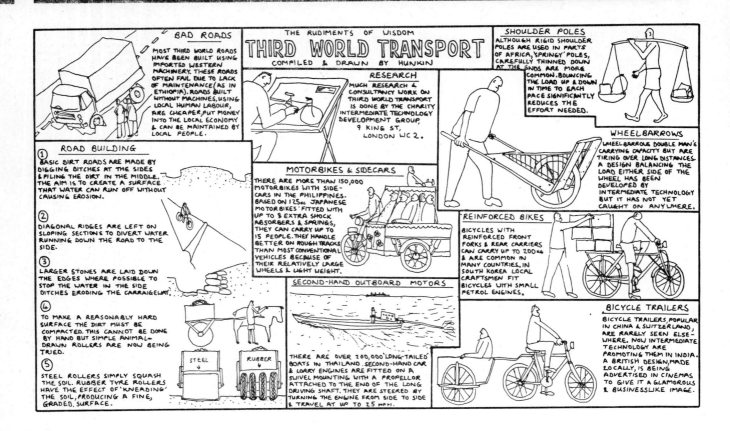

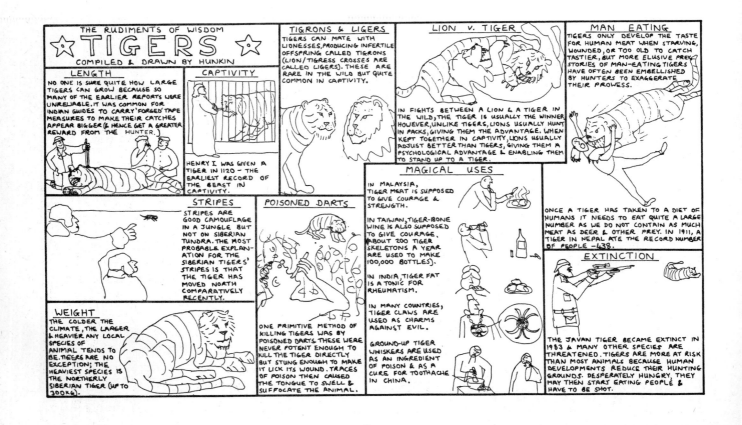

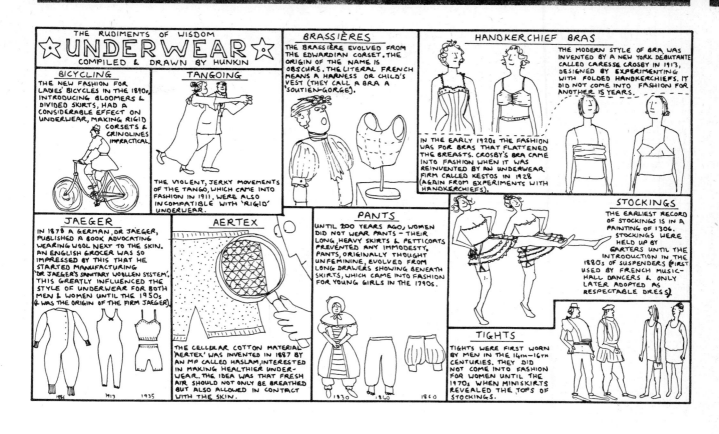

THE RUDIMENTS OF WISDOM
☆ UNDERWEAR ☆
COMPILED & DRAWN BY HUNKIN

BICYCLING
THE NEW FASHION FOR LADIES' BICYCLES IN THE 1890s, INTRODUCING BLOOMERS & DIVIDED SKIRTS, HAD A CONSIDERABLE EFFECT ON UNDERWEAR, MAKING RIGID CORSETS & CRINOLINES IMPRACTICAL.

TANGOING
THE VIOLENT, JERKY MOVEMENTS OF THE TANGO, WHICH CAME INTO FASHION IN 1911, WERE ALSO INCOMPATIBLE WITH 'RIGID' UNDERWEAR.

BRASSIÈRES
THE BRASSIÈRE EVOLVED FROM THE EDWARDIAN CORSET. THE ORIGIN OF THE NAME IS OBSCURE. THE LITERAL FRENCH MEANS A HARNESS OR CHILD'S VEST (THEY CALL A BRA A 'SOUTIEN-GORGE').

HANDKERCHIEF BRAS
THE MODERN STYLE OF BRA WAS INVENTED BY A NEW YORK DEBUTANTE CALLED CARESSE CROSBY IN 1913, DESIGNED BY EXPERIMENTING WITH FOLDED HANDKERCHIEFS. IT DID NOT COME INTO FASHION FOR ANOTHER 15 YEARS.

IN THE EARLY 1920s THE FASHION WAS FOR BRAS THAT FLATTENED THE BREASTS. CROSBY'S BRA CAME INTO FASHION WHEN IT WAS REINVENTED BY AN UNDERWEAR FIRM CALLED KESTOS IN 1928 (AGAIN FROM EXPERIMENTS WITH HANDKERCHIEFS).

JAEGER
IN 1878 A GERMAN, DR JAEGER, PUBLISHED A BOOK ADVOCATING WEARING WOOL NEXT TO THE SKIN. AN ENGLISH GROCER WAS SO IMPRESSED BY THIS THAT HE STARTED MANUFACTURING 'DR JAEGER'S SANITARY WOOLLEN SYSTEM'. THIS GREATLY INFLUENCED THE STYLE OF UNDERWEAR FOR BOTH MEN & WOMEN UNTIL THE 1950s (& WAS THE ORIGIN OF THE FIRM JAEGER).

AERTEX
THE CELLULAR COTTON MATERIAL 'AERTEX' WAS INVENTED IN 1887 BY AN MP CALLED HASLAM, INTERESTED IN MAKING HEALTHIER UNDERWEAR. THE IDEA WAS THAT FRESH AIR SHOULD NOT ONLY BE BREATHED BUT ALSO ALLOWED IN CONTACT WITH THE SKIN.

PANTS
UNTIL 200 YEARS AGO, WOMEN DID NOT WEAR PANTS – THEIR LONG, HEAVY SKIRTS & PETTICOATS PREVENTED ANY IMMODESTY. PANTS, ORIGINALLY THOUGHT UNFEMININE, EVOLVED FROM LONG DRAWERS SHOWING BENEATH SKIRTS, WHICH CAME INTO FASHION FOR YOUNG GIRLS IN THE 1790s.

STOCKINGS
THE EARLIEST RECORD OF STOCKINGS IS IN A PAINTING OF 1306. STOCKINGS WERE HELD UP BY GARTERS UNTIL THE INTRODUCTION IN THE 1880s OF SUSPENDERS (FIRST USED BY FRENCH MUSIC-HALL DANCERS & ONLY LATER ADOPTED AS RESPECTABLE DRESS).

TIGHTS
TIGHTS WERE FIRST WORN BY MEN IN THE 14th–16th CENTURIES. THEY DID NOT COME INTO FASHION FOR WOMEN UNTIL THE 1970s WHEN MINISKIRTS REVEALED THE TOPS OF STOCKINGS.

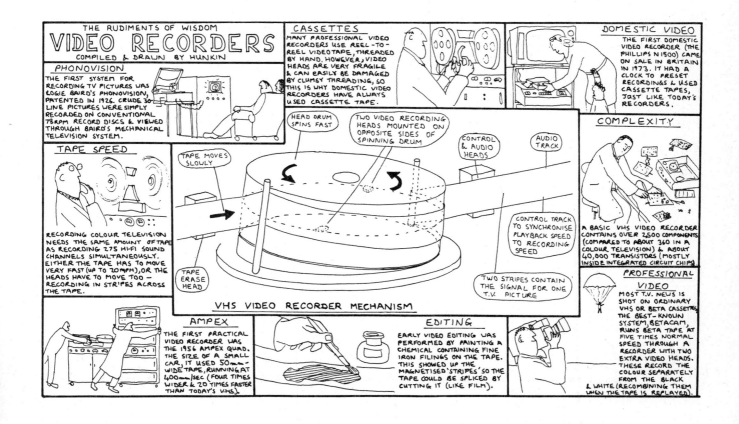

THE RUDIMENTS OF WISDOM
VIDEO RECORDERS
COMPILED & DRAWN BY HUNKIN

PHONOVISION
THE FIRST SYSTEM FOR RECORDING TV PICTURES WAS LOGIE BAIRD'S PHONOVISION, PATENTED IN 1926. CRUDE 30-LINE PICTURES WERE SIMPLY RECORDED ON CONVENTIONAL 78 RPM RECORD DISCS & VIEWED THROUGH BAIRD'S MECHANICAL TELEVISION SYSTEM.

CASSETTES
MANY PROFESSIONAL VIDEO RECORDERS USE REEL-TO-REEL VIDEOTAPE, THREADED BY HAND. HOWEVER, VIDEO HEADS ARE VERY FRAGILE & CAN EASILY BE DAMAGED BY CLUMSY THREADING, SO THIS IS WHY DOMESTIC VIDEO RECORDERS HAVE ALWAYS USED CASSETTE TAPE.

DOMESTIC VIDEO
THE FIRST DOMESTIC VIDEO RECORDER (THE PHILLIPS N1500) CAME ON SALE IN BRITAIN IN 1973. IT HAD A CLOCK TO PRESET RECORDINGS & USED CASSETTE TAPES, JUST LIKE TODAY'S RECORDERS.

TAPE SPEED
RECORDING COLOUR TELEVISION NEEDS THE SAME AMOUNT OF TAPE AS RECORDING 275 HI-FI SOUND CHANNELS SIMULTANEOUSLY. EITHER THE TAPE HAS TO MOVE VERY FAST (UP TO 20 MPH), OR THE HEADS HAVE TO MOVE TOO – RECORDING IN STRIPES ACROSS THE TAPE.

HEAD DRUM SPINS FAST

TAPE MOVES SLOWLY

TWO VIDEO RECORDING HEADS MOUNTED ON OPPOSITE SIDES OF SPINNING DRUM

CONTROL & AUDIO HEADS

AUDIO TRACK

TAPE ERASE HEAD

CONTROL TRACK TO SYNCHRONISE PLAYBACK SPEED TO RECORDING SPEED

TWO STRIPES CONTAIN THE SIGNAL FOR ONE T.V. PICTURE

VHS VIDEO RECORDER MECHANISM

COMPLEXITY
A BASIC VHS VIDEO RECORDER CONTAINS OVER 2500 COMPONENTS (COMPARED TO ABOUT 360 IN A COLOUR TELEVISION) & ABOUT 40,000 TRANSISTORS (MOSTLY INSIDE INTEGRATED CIRCUIT CHIPS).

AMPEX
THE FIRST PRACTICAL VIDEO RECORDER WAS THE 1956 AMPEX QUAD, THE SIZE OF A SMALL CAR. IT USED 50 mm WIDE TAPE, RUNNING AT 400 mm/SEC (FOUR TIMES WIDER & 20 TIMES FASTER THAN TODAY'S VHS).

EDITING
EARLY VIDEO EDITING WAS PERFORMED BY PAINTING A CHEMICAL CONTAINING FINE IRON FILINGS ON THE TAPE. THIS SHOWED UP THE MAGNETISED 'STRIPES' SO THE TAPE COULD BE SPLICED BY CUTTING IT (LIKE FILM).

PROFESSIONAL VIDEO
MOST T.V. NEWS IS SHOT ON ORDINARY VHS OR BETA CASSETTES. THE BEST-KNOWN SYSTEM, BETACAM, RUNS BETA TAPE AT FIVE TIMES NORMAL SPEED THROUGH A RECORDER WITH TWO EXTRA VIDEO HEADS. THESE RECORD THE COLOUR SEPARATELY FROM THE BLACK & WHITE (RECOMBINING THEM WHEN THE TAPE IS REPLAYED).

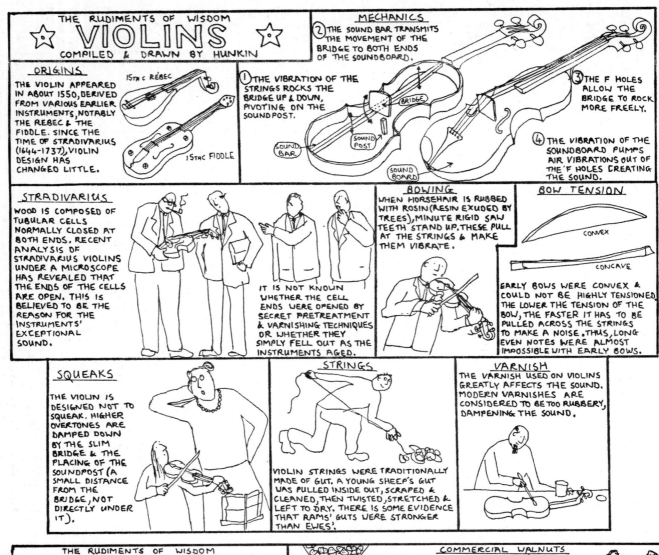

THE RUDIMENTS OF WISDOM
☆ VIOLINS ☆
COMPILED & DRAWN BY HUNKIN

ORIGINS
THE VIOLIN APPEARED IN ABOUT 1550, DERIVED FROM VARIOUS EARLIER INSTRUMENTS, NOTABLY THE REBEC & THE FIDDLE. SINCE THE TIME OF STRADIVARIUS (1644-1737), VIOLIN DESIGN HAS CHANGED LITTLE.

15th c REBEC
15th c FIDDLE

MECHANICS
② THE SOUND BAR TRANSMITS THE MOVEMENT OF THE BRIDGE TO BOTH ENDS OF THE SOUNDBOARD.

① THE VIBRATION OF THE STRINGS ROCKS THE BRIDGE UP & DOWN, PIVOTING ON THE SOUNDPOST.

③ THE F HOLES ALLOW THE BRIDGE TO ROCK MORE FREELY.

④ THE VIBRATION OF THE SOUNDBOARD PUMPS AIR VIBRATIONS OUT OF THE F HOLES CREATING THE SOUND.

BRIDGE
SOUND BAR
SOUND POST
SOUND BOARD

STRADIVARIUS
WOOD IS COMPOSED OF TUBULAR CELLS NORMALLY CLOSED AT BOTH ENDS. RECENT ANALYSIS OF STRADIVARIUS VIOLINS UNDER A MICROSCOPE HAS REVEALED THAT THE ENDS OF THE CELLS ARE OPEN. THIS IS BELIEVED TO BE THE REASON FOR THE INSTRUMENTS' EXCEPTIONAL SOUND.

IT IS NOT KNOWN WHETHER THE CELL ENDS WERE OPENED BY SECRET PRETREATMENT & VARNISHING TECHNIQUES OR WHETHER THEY SIMPLY FELL OUT AS THE INSTRUMENTS AGED.

BOWING
WHEN HORSEHAIR IS RUBBED WITH ROSIN (RESIN EXUDED BY TREES), MINUTE RIGID SAW TEETH STAND UP. THESE PULL AT THE STRINGS & MAKE THEM VIBRATE.

BOW TENSION
CONVEX
CONCAVE

EARLY BOWS WERE CONVEX & COULD NOT BE HIGHLY TENSIONED. THE LOWER THE TENSION OF THE BOW, THE FASTER IT HAS TO BE PULLED ACROSS THE STRINGS TO MAKE A NOISE. THUS, LONG EVEN NOTES WERE ALMOST IMPOSSIBLE WITH EARLY BOWS.

SQUEAKS
THE VIOLIN IS DESIGNED NOT TO SQUEAK. HIGHER OVERTONES ARE DAMPED DOWN BY THE SLIM BRIDGE & THE PLACING OF THE SOUNDPOST (A SMALL DISTANCE FROM THE BRIDGE, NOT DIRECTLY UNDER IT).

STRINGS
VIOLIN STRINGS WERE TRADITIONALLY MADE OF GUT. A YOUNG SHEEP'S GUT WAS PULLED INSIDE OUT, SCRAPED & CLEANED, THEN TWISTED, STRETCHED & LEFT TO DRY. THERE IS SOME EVIDENCE THAT RAMS' GUTS WERE STRONGER THAN EWES'.

VARNISH
THE VARNISH USED ON VIOLINS GREATLY AFFECTS THE SOUND. MODERN VARNISHES ARE CONSIDERED TO BE TOO RUBBERY, DAMPENING THE SOUND.

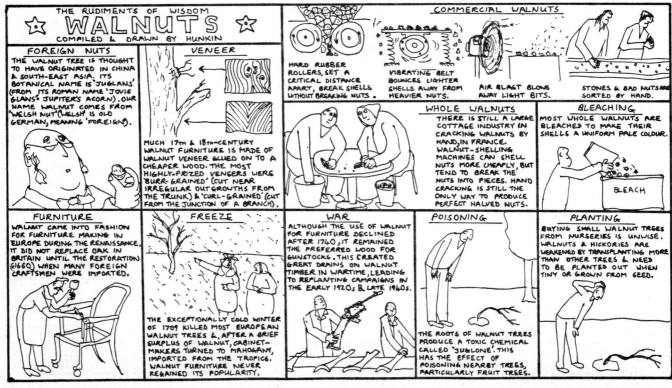

THE RUDIMENTS OF WISDOM
☆ WALNUTS ☆
COMPILED & DRAWN BY HUNKIN

FOREIGN NUTS
THE WALNUT TREE IS THOUGHT TO HAVE ORIGINATED IN CHINA & SOUTH-EAST ASIA. ITS BOTANICAL NAME IS 'JUGLANS' (FROM ITS ROMAN NAME 'JOVIS GLANS' JUPITER'S ACORN). OUR NAME WALNUT COMES FROM 'WELSH NUT' (WELSH IS OLD GERMAN, MEANING 'FOREIGN').

VENEER
MUCH 17TH & 18TH-CENTURY WALNUT FURNITURE IS MADE OF WALNUT VENEER GLUED ON TO A CHEAPER WOOD. THE MOST HIGHLY-PRIZED VENEERS WERE 'BURR-GRAINED' (CUT NEAR IRREGULAR OUTGROWTHS FROM THE TRUNK) & 'CURL-GRAINED' (CUT FROM THE JUNCTION OF A BRANCH).

COMMERCIAL WALNUTS
HARD RUBBER ROLLERS, SET A CRITICAL DISTANCE APART, BREAK SHELLS WITHOUT BREAKING NUTS.

VIBRATING BELT BOUNCES LIGHTER SHELLS AWAY FROM HEAVIER NUTS.

AIR BLAST BLOWS AWAY LIGHT BITS.

STONES & BAD NUTS ARE SORTED BY HAND.

WHOLE WALNUTS
THERE IS STILL A LARGE COTTAGE INDUSTRY IN CRACKING WALNUTS BY HAND, IN FRANCE. WALNUT-SHELLING MACHINES CAN SHELL NUTS MORE CHEAPLY, BUT TEND TO BREAK THE NUTS INTO PIECES. HAND CRACKING IS STILL THE ONLY WAY TO PRODUCE PERFECT HALVED NUTS.

BLEACHING
MOST WHOLE WALNUTS ARE BLEACHED TO MAKE THEIR SHELLS A UNIFORM PALE COLOUR.

BLEACH

FURNITURE
WALNUT CAME INTO FASHION FOR FURNITURE MAKING IN EUROPE DURING THE RENAISSANCE. IT DID NOT REPLACE OAK IN BRITAIN UNTIL THE RESTORATION (1660) WHEN MANY FOREIGN CRAFTSMEN WERE IMPORTED.

FREEZE
THE EXCEPTIONALLY COLD WINTER OF 1709 KILLED MOST EUROPEAN WALNUT TREES &, AFTER A BRIEF SURPLUS OF WALNUT, CABINET-MAKERS TURNED TO MAHOGANY, IMPORTED FROM THE TROPICS. WALNUT FURNITURE NEVER REGAINED ITS POPULARITY.

WAR
ALTHOUGH THE USE OF WALNUT FOR FURNITURE DECLINED AFTER 1740, IT REMAINED THE PREFERRED WOOD FOR GUNSTOCKS. THIS CREATED GREAT DRAINS ON WALNUT TIMBER IN WARTIME, LEADING TO REPLANTING CAMPAIGNS IN THE EARLY 1920s & LATE 1940s.

POISONING
THE ROOTS OF WALNUT TREES PRODUCE A TOXIC CHEMICAL CALLED 'JUGLONE'. THIS HAS THE EFFECT OF POISONING NEARBY TREES, PARTICULARLY FRUIT TREES.

PLANTING
BUYING SMALL WALNUT TREES FROM NURSERIES IS UNWISE. WALNUTS & HICKORIES ARE WEAKENED BY TRANSPLANTING MORE THAN OTHER TREES & NEED TO BE PLANTED OUT WHEN TINY OR GROWN FROM SEED.

THE RUDIMENTS OF WISDOM
WASHING MACHINES
COMPILED & DRAWN BY HUNKIN

EARLY AUTOMATION?

THE EARLIEST FORM OF AUTO-MATIC WASHING WAS THE NAUTICAL PRACTICE OF TOWING CLOTHES BEHIND THE SHIP. THE COMBINATION OF AGITATION & A CONSTANT FLOW OF CLEAN WATER WASHED REASONABLY EFFECTIVELY.

MANUAL MACHINES

THE FIRST WASHING MACHINES APPEARED IN THE 1860s. THEY WERE SIMPLY WOODEN BOXES WHICH COULD BE TURNED BY A HANDLE, TUMBLING THE CLOTHES OVER EACH OTHER.

SHOCKING MACHINES

MOTORISED MACHINES, POWERED BY ELECTRICITY, STEAM & PETROL, WERE GRADUALLY INTRODUCED. MANY ELECTRIC MACHINES OF THE 1920s HAD THE MOTOR POSITIONED UNDER THE TUB, WHERE IT TENDED TO GET WET & DELIVER POWERFUL ELECTRIC SHOCKS.

COAL-FIRED MACHINES

SOME ELECTRIC WASHING MACHINES MADE IN GERMANY IN THE 1920s HAD COAL-FIRED HEATING—A GRATE UNDERNEATH THE WASHING DRUM.

AUTOMATIC MACHINES

THE FIRST FULLY AUTOMATIC ELECTRIC WASHING MACHINE WAS THE 'THOR', PATENTED IN AMERICA IN 1907. IT WAS NOT A SUCCESS, PARTLY BECAUSE SERVANT LABOUR WAS STILL CHEAP & PLENTIFUL. AUTOMATICS DID NOT BECOME POPULAR UNTIL THE 1950s.

DRYING

MOST EARLY MACHINES WERE FITTED WITH WRINGERS. SOME AMERICAN MACHINES OF THE 1950s HAD RUBBER TUBS WHICH COLLAPSED & SQUEEZED THE CLOTHES DRY. THE SPIN-DRIER WAS INVENTED IN THE 1890s BUT DID NOT BECOME POPULAR UNTIL THE 1960s.

LATHER

FRONT LOADERS WORK BY BASHING THE CLOTHES AGAINST THE SIDES OF THE DRUM (LIKE BEATING CLOTHES ON ROCKS). HIGH-LATHER POWDERS DO NOT WORK WELL BECAUSE THEY 'CUSHION' THE IMPACT.

VIBRATION

THE INERTIA OF A LOAD OF WASHING SPINNING AT FULL SPEED IS CONSIDERABLE. BOTH DRUM & MACHINE BASE NEED CONCRETE WEIGHTS TO STABILISE THEM. TO ENSURE THE CLOTHES ARE DISTRIBUTED EVENLY ROUND THE DRUM (SO THE LOAD IS BALANCED), THE SPIN SPEED IS USUALLY INCREASED GRADUALLY IN STEPS.

ECONOMY

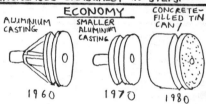

ALUMINIUM CASTING | SMALLER ALUMINIUM CASTING | CONCRETE-FILLED TIN CAN!
1960 | 1970 | 1980

IN THE LAST 20 YEARS, GREAT INGENUITY HAS GONE INTO REDUCING THE COST OF MANUFACTURING WASHING MACHINES. FOR EXAMPLE, THE DESIGN OF THE PULLEY & BEARING ON THE BACK OF A WASHING DRUM SHOWN ABOVE.

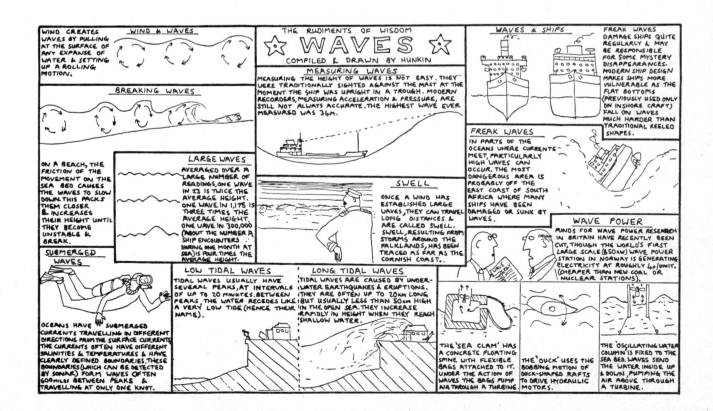

WIND & WAVES

WIND CREATES WAVES BY PULLING AT THE SURFACE OF ANY EXPANSE OF WATER & SETTING UP A ROLLING MOTION.

BREAKING WAVES

ON A BEACH, THE FRICTION OF THE MOVEMENT ON THE SEA BED CAUSES THE WAVES TO SLOW DOWN. THIS PACKS THEM CLOSER & INCREASES THEIR HEIGHT UNTIL THEY BECOME UNSTABLE & BREAK.

SUBMERGED WAVES

OCEANS HAVE SUBMERGED CURRENTS TRAVELLING IN DIFFERENT DIRECTIONS FROM THE SURFACE CURRENTS. THE CURRENTS OFTEN HAVE DIFFERENT SALINITIES & TEMPERATURES & HAVE CLEARLY DEFINED BOUNDARIES. THESE BOUNDARIES (WHICH CAN BE DETECTED BY SONAR) FORM WAVES OFTEN 600 MILES BETWEEN PEAKS & TRAVELLING AT ONLY ONE KNOT.

THE RUDIMENTS OF WISDOM
☆ WAVES ☆
COMPILED & DRAWN BY HUNKIN

MEASURING WAVES

MEASURING THE HEIGHT OF WAVES IS NOT EASY. THEY WERE TRADITIONALLY SIGHTED AGAINST THE MAST AT THE MOMENT THE SHIP WAS UPRIGHT IN A TROUGH. MODERN RECORDERS, MEASURING ACCELERATION & PRESSURE, ARE STILL NOT ALWAYS ACCURATE. THE HIGHEST WAVE EVER MEASURED WAS 34m.

LARGE WAVES

AVERAGED OVER A LARGE NUMBER OF READINGS, ONE WAVE IN 23 IS TWICE THE AVERAGE HEIGHT. ONE WAVE IN 1,175 IS THREE TIMES THE AVERAGE HEIGHT. ONE WAVE IN 300,000 (ABOUT THE NUMBER A SHIP ENCOUNTERS DURING ONE MONTH AT SEA) IS FOUR TIMES THE AVERAGE HEIGHT.

SWELL

ONCE A WIND HAS ESTABLISHED LARGE WAVES, THEY CAN TRAVEL LONG DISTANCES & ARE CALLED SWELL. SWELL, RESULTING FROM STORMS AROUND THE FALKLANDS, HAS BEEN TRACED AS FAR AS THE CORNISH COAST.

LOW TIDAL WAVES

TIDAL WAVES USUALLY HAVE SEVERAL PEAKS, AT INTERVALS OF UP TO 20 MINUTES. BETWEEN PEAKS THE WATER RECEDES LIKE A VERY LOW TIDE (HENCE THEIR NAME).

LONG TIDAL WAVES

TIDAL WAVES ARE CAUSED BY UNDER-WATER EARTHQUAKES & ERUPTIONS. THEY ARE OFTEN UP TO 20km LONG BUT USUALLY LESS THAN 50cm HIGH IN THE OPEN SEA. THEY INCREASE RAPIDLY IN HEIGHT WHEN THEY REACH SHALLOW WATER.

WAVES & SHIPS

FREAK WAVES DAMAGE SHIPS QUITE REGULARLY & MAY BE RESPONSIBLE FOR SOME MYSTERY DISAPPEARANCES. MODERN SHIP DESIGN MAKES SHIPS MORE VULNERABLE AS THE FLAT BOTTOMS (PREVIOUSLY USED ONLY ON INSHORE CRAFT) FALL ON WAVES MUCH HARDER THAN TRADITIONAL KEELED SHAPES.

FREAK WAVES

IN PARTS OF THE OCEANS WHERE CURRENTS MEET, PARTICULARLY HIGH WAVES CAN OCCUR. THE MOST DANGEROUS AREA IS PROBABLY OFF THE EAST COAST OF SOUTH AFRICA WHERE MANY SHIPS HAVE BEEN DAMAGED OR SUNK BY WAVES.

WAVE POWER

FUNDS FOR WAVE POWER RESEARCH IN BRITAIN HAVE RECENTLY BEEN CUT, THOUGH THE WORLD'S FIRST LARGE SCALE (850kw) WAVE POWER STATION IN NORWAY IS GENERATING ELECTRICITY AT ROUGHLY 4p/UNIT. (CHEAPER THAN NEW COAL OR NUCLEAR STATIONS).

THE 'SEA CLAM' HAS A CONCRETE FLOATING SPINE WITH FLEXIBLE BAGS ATTACHED TO IT. UNDER THE ACTION OF WAVES THE BAGS PUMP AIR THROUGH A TURBINE.

THE 'DUCK' USES THE BOBBING MOTION OF DUCK-SHAPED RAFTS TO DRIVE HYDRAULIC MOTORS.

THE 'OSCILLATING WATER COLUMN' IS FIXED TO THE SEA BED. WAVES SEND THE WATER INSIDE UP & DOWN, PUMPING THE AIR ABOVE THROUGH A TURBINE.

THE RUDIMENTS OF WISDOM
☆ WAX ☆
COMPILED & DRAWN BY HUNKIN

VARIETY
THE WORD 'WAX' ORIGINALLY REFERRED ONLY TO BEESWAX. IT IS NOW USED FOR ANYTHING WHICH RESEMBLES BEESWAX, INCLUDING A LARGE NUMBER OF UNRELATED CHEMICALS.

OZOCERITE
A SOLID MINERAL WAX CALLED OZOCERITE IS MINED IN RUSSIA. IT OCCURS IN DEPOSITS SIMILAR TO CRUDE OIL & IS USED FOR CANDLES & SHOE POLISH.

STATUES
THE ANCIENT EGYPTIANS MADE STATUETTES & IMITATION FRUITS OUT OF BEESWAX. THE GREEKS ALSO MADE WAX DOLLS & ROMAN PATRICIANS KEPT WAX MASKS OF THEIR ANCESTORS.

WAXWORKS
WAXWORK FIGURES DO NOT LAST FOR EVER. AS THE WAX DARKENS & DETERIORATES, THE PLASTER MOULDS FOR EACH HEAD ARE KEPT & REPLACEMENT HEADS CAST PERIODICALLY.

OLD CANDLES
CANDLES USED TO BE MADE BY DIPPING LENGTHS OF COTTON IN MOLTEN BEESWAX (FOR RICH PEOPLE) OR SMELLY TALLOW (FOR POOR PEOPLE). THE WICK DID NOT DROP OFF AS THE CANDLE BURNT & HAD TO BE TRIMMED EVERY FEW MINUTES.

NEW CANDLES
MODERN CANDLES HAVE PLAITED WICKS WHICH AUTOMATICALLY BURN DOWN WITH THE CANDLE (PATENTED IN 1825). CANDLES ARE MADE IN METAL MOULDS FROM PARAFFIN WAX, A PETROCHEMICAL FIRST USED IN ABOUT 1850. (BEESWAX WAS TOO STICKY FOR MOULDING.)

WICK THREADED — WAX POURED — MOULD PARTED

UNWANTED WAX
CRUDE OIL CONTAINS A CERTAIN AMOUNT OF WAX, MOSTLY PARAFFIN WAX. ENGINE OIL HAS TO BE DE-WAXED TO STOP ANY WAX SOLIDIFYING AT LOW TEMPERATURES & BLOCKING THE OILWAYS.

WATERPROOFING
WAXES ARE SPRAYED ON CITRUS FRUIT, MUCH FOOD PACKAGING & SOMETIMES ON FRESH CONCRETE TO RETAIN MOISTURE. THEY ARE INCORPORATED IN MANY SUBSTANCES, EVEN CHIPBOARD, TO INCREASE WATER RESISTANCE & ARE ADDED TO CAR TYRE RUBBER TO SLOW DOWN THE DETERIORATION FROM THE SUN & OZONE.

WAX SWITCHING
SWITCH

PARAFFIN WAXES EXPAND CONSIDERABLY ON MELTING. MANY THERMOSTATS (TEMPERATURE SWITCHES) CONTAIN WAXES MIXED TO MELT AT THE REQUIRED TEMPERATURE. THE EXPANSION OPERATES THE SWITCH.

WAX — METAL CASE

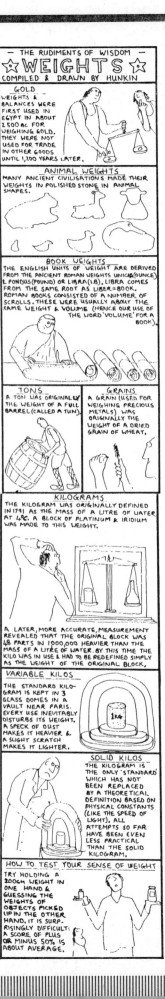

— THE RUDIMENTS OF WISDOM —
☆ WEIGHTS ☆
COMPILED & DRAWN BY HUNKIN

GOLD
WEIGHTS & BALANCES WERE FIRST USED IN EGYPT IN ABOUT 2,500 BC FOR WEIGHING GOLD. THEY WERE NOT USED FOR TRADE IN OTHER GOODS UNTIL 1,200 YEARS LATER.

ANIMAL WEIGHTS
MANY ANCIENT CIVILISATIONS MADE THEIR WEIGHTS IN POLISHED STONE IN ANIMAL SHAPES.

BOOK WEIGHTS
THE ENGLISH UNITS OF WEIGHT ARE DERIVED FROM THE ANCIENT ROMAN WEIGHTS UNCIA (OUNCE) & PONDUS (POUND) OR LIBRA (LB). LIBRA COMES FROM THE SAME ROOT AS LIBER = BOOK. ROMAN BOOKS CONSISTED OF A NUMBER OF SCROLLS. THESE WERE USUALLY ABOUT THE SAME WEIGHT & VOLUME (HENCE OUR USE OF THE WORD 'VOLUME' FOR A BOOK).

TONS
A TON WAS ORIGINALLY THE WEIGHT OF A FULL BARREL (CALLED A TUN).

GRAINS
A GRAIN (USED FOR WEIGHING PRECIOUS METALS) WAS ORIGINALLY THE WEIGHT OF A DRIED GRAIN OF WHEAT.

KILOGRAMS
THE KILOGRAM WAS ORIGINALLY DEFINED IN 1791 AS THE MASS OF A LITRE OF WATER AT 4°C. A BLOCK OF PLATINUM & IRIDIUM WAS MADE TO THIS WEIGHT.

A LATER, MORE ACCURATE, MEASUREMENT REVEALED THAT THE ORIGINAL BLOCK WAS 48 PARTS IN 1,000,000 HEAVIER THAN THE MASS OF A LITRE OF WATER. BY THIS TIME THE KILO WAS IN USE & HAD TO BE REDEFINED SIMPLY AS THE WEIGHT OF THE ORIGINAL BLOCK.

VARIABLE KILOS
THE STANDARD KILOGRAM IS KEPT IN 3 GLASS DOMES IN A VAULT NEAR PARIS. EVERY USE INEVITABLY DISTURBS ITS WEIGHT. A SPECK OF DUST MAKES IT HEAVIER & A SLIGHT SCRATCH MAKES IT LIGHTER.

1KG

SOLID KILOS
THE KILOGRAM IS THE ONLY 'STANDARD' WHICH HAS NOT BEEN REPLACED BY A THEORETICAL DEFINITION BASED ON PHYSICAL CONSTANTS (LIKE THE SPEED OF LIGHT). ALL ATTEMPTS SO FAR HAVE BEEN EVEN LESS PRACTICAL THAN THE SOLID KILOGRAM.

HOW TO TEST YOUR SENSE OF WEIGHT
TRY HOLDING A 200GM WEIGHT IN ONE HAND & GUESSING THE WEIGHTS OF OBJECTS PICKED UP IN THE OTHER HAND. IT IS SURPRISINGLY DIFFICULT: A SCORE OF PLUS OR MINUS 50% IS ABOUT AVERAGE.

THE RUDIMENTS OF WISDOM
WEEDKILLERS
COMPILED & DRAWN BY HUNKIN

PROLIFIC WEEDS
MOST CEREAL PLANTS PRODUCE ONLY 25-30 SEEDS. MANY WEEDS ARE MORE PROLIFIC: POPPIES—17,000 SEEDS, RAGWORT—63,000 SEEDS, RUSHES—50,000. AN ACRE OF MIXED WEEDS HAS BEEN ESTIMATED TO PRODUCE 5,000,000,000 SEEDS.

SIMPLE WEED-KILLERS

THE FIRST WEEDKILLERS KILLED ALL PLANT LIFE OF THIS TYPE, ONLY SODIUM CHLORATE IS STILL WIDELY USED, BECAUSE IT BREAKS DOWN IN THE SOIL.

HORMONE KILLERS
IN THE 1940s SCIENTISTS DEVELOPED THE HORMONE WEEDKILLERS, 24D & MCPA, WHICH DISRUPT PLANT GROWTH. A FEW DROPS CAUSE TWISTING, CONTORTION & TUMOUR-LIKE GROWTHS BEFORE DEATH.

HORMONE SAFETY
24D & MCPA ARE RELATIVELY NON-POISONOUS, WITH LITTLE EVIDENCE OF CARCINOGENIC ACTIVITY. THEY BREAK DOWN IN THE SOIL AFTER SPRAYING.

2 4 5 T
2 4 5 T IS CLOSELY RELATED TO 24D BUT IS MORE EFFECTIVE AGAINST WOODY PLANTS (HENCE ITS USE IN VIETNAM). 2 4 5 T IS OFTEN CONTAMINATED WITH THE POISON DIOXIN DURING MANUFACTURE. ITS USE IS RESTRICTED IN THE U.S. BUT NOT IN BRITAIN.

PARAQUAT
PARAQUAT KILLS ALL PLANT LIFE (& IS HIGHLY TOXIC TO MAMMALS) BUT IMMEDIATELY BECOMES HARMLESS ON REACHING THE SOIL. IT IS USED AS AN ALTERNATIVE TO PLOUGHING (SEEDS CAN BE DRILLED DIRECTLY INTO THE SOIL AFTER APPLYING PARAQUAT), REDUCING SOIL EROSION.

SELECTIVE WEEDKILLERS
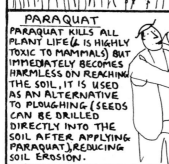
ONE OF THE FIRST 'SELECTIVE' WEEDKILLERS (THAT DO NOT HARM CROP PLANTS) WAS SULPHURIC ACID. EXTENSIVELY USED IN THE 1930s, IT HARMLESSLY RAN OFF THE LEAVES OF THE CEREAL BUT CLUNG TO & BURNT THE RELATIVELY ROUGH LEAVES OF THE WEEDS.

NEW WEEDKILLERS

MCPA & 24D KILL BROAD-LEAVED WEEDS ONLY. THEIR EXTENSIVE USE HAS LED TO OTHER WEEDS SUCH AS POPPIES & CHARLOCK TAKING OVER, WHICH HAS REQUIRED THE DEVELOPMENT OF MANY OTHER ORGANIC WEEDKILLERS.

WEEDKILLERS & SOIL
WEEDKILLERS GENERALLY DO LITTLE HARM TO THE MICRO-ORGANISMS IN THE SOIL, & SOME ACTUALLY STIMULATE THEM BY ACTING AS 'FOOD.' RECENT EVIDENCE FROM THE U.S. SUGGESTS THAT CERTAIN WEEDKILLERS ARE BECOMING INEFFECTIVE AS SOIL MICRO-ORGANISMS HAVE EVOLVED TO EAT THEM BEFORE THEY GET TO THE WEEDS.

LESS WEEDKILLER
BRITAIN'S WEED RESEARCH ORGANISATION HAS FOUND THAT ONLY A QUARTER OF THE RECOMMENDED DOSE OF WEEDKILLER IS OFTEN NECESSARY. 72% OF WEEDS SURVIVE A SINGLE QUARTER-DOSE SPRAY BUT WHEN THIS IS REPEATED AT INTERVALS, AS IS RECOMMENDED, THIS FIGURE FALLS TO 14%.

WEEDKILLERS & WILDLIFE
ALTHOUGH MOST WEEDKILLERS ARE NOT TOXIC TO ANIMALS THEY HAVE ENDANGERED MANY SPECIES WHICH FEED OFF WEEDS, PARTICULARLY BUTTERFLIES, SIMPLY BY REMOVING THEIR FOOD SUPPLY.

ANIMAL WEEDKILLERS
ANIMALS CAN BE USEFUL IN CONTROLLING WEEDS:
★ RAGWORT, POISONOUS TO CATTLE, CAN BE CHECKED BY GRAZING SHEEP.
★ GEESE WEED U.S. MINT FIELDS (THEY LIKE THE WEEDS BUT NOT THE MINT).
★ PIGS WILL DIG UP BRACKEN ROOTS.
★ GOATS WILL EAT ALMOST ANYTHING.

WEEDKILLERS & THE N.F.U.
THE NATIONAL FARMERS' UNION IS CAMPAIGNING FOR A BAN ON THE 'ESTER HORMONE' GROUP OF WEEDKILLERS. THIS IS NOT BECAUSE OF THEIR TOXICITY BUT BECAUSE OF THEIR TENDENCY TO VAPORISE AND DRIFT FROM LEAF SURFACES, KILLING WILDLIFE AND NEIGHBOURING CROPS.

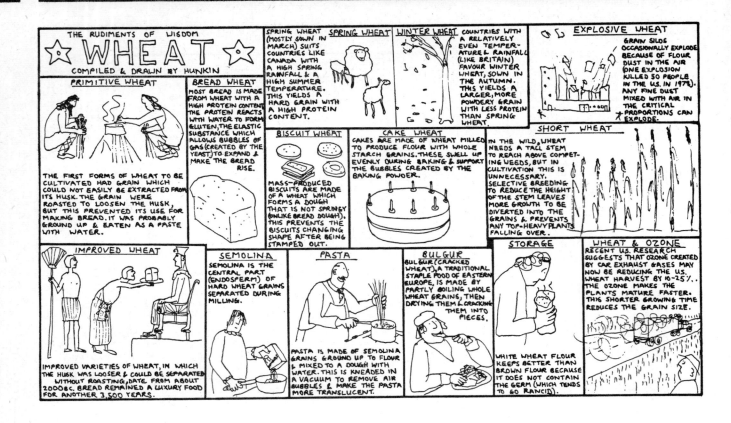

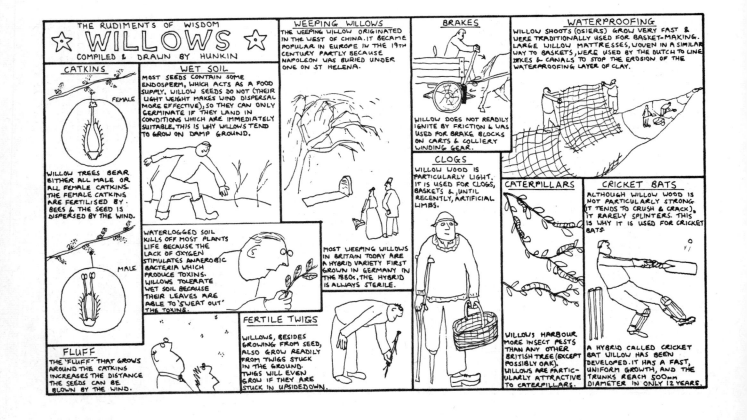

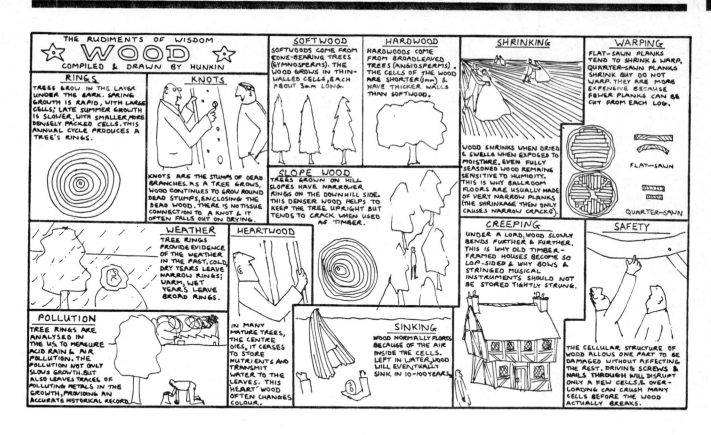

THE RUDIMENTS OF WISDOM
☆ WOOD ☆
COMPILED & DRAWN BY HUNKIN

RINGS
TREES GROW IN THE LAYER UNDER THE BARK. SPRING GROWTH IS RAPID, WITH LARGE CELLS; LATE SUMMER GROWTH IS SLOWER, WITH SMALLER, MORE DENSELY PACKED CELLS. THIS ANNUAL CYCLE PRODUCES A TREE'S RINGS.

KNOTS
KNOTS ARE THE STUMPS OF DEAD BRANCHES. AS A TREE GROWS, WOOD CONTINUES TO GROW ROUND DEAD STUMPS, ENCLOSING THE DEAD WOOD. THERE IS NO TISSUE CONNECTION TO A KNOT & IT OFTEN FALLS OUT ON DRYING.

SOFTWOOD
SOFTWOODS COME FROM CONE-BEARING TREES (GYMNOSPERMS). THE WOOD GROWS IN THIN-WALLED CELLS, EACH ABOUT 3mm LONG.

HARDWOOD
HARDWOODS COME FROM BROADLEAVED TREES (ANGIOSPERMS). THE CELLS OF THE WOOD ARE SHORTER (1mm) & HAVE THICKER WALLS THAN SOFTWOOD.

SLOPE WOOD
TREES GROWN ON HILL SLOPES HAVE NARROWER RINGS ON THE DOWNHILL SIDE. THIS DENSER WOOD HELPS TO KEEP THE TREE UPRIGHT BUT TENDS TO CRACK WHEN USED AS TIMBER.

WEATHER
TREE RINGS PROVIDE EVIDENCE OF THE WEATHER IN THE PAST. COLD DRY YEARS LEAVE NARROW RINGS; WARM, WET YEARS LEAVE BROAD RINGS.

HEARTWOOD
IN MANY MATURE TREES, THE CENTRE DIES, IT CEASES TO STORE NUTRIENTS AND TRANSMIT WATER TO THE LEAVES. THIS 'HEART' WOOD OFTEN CHANGES COLOUR.

POLLUTION
TREE RINGS ARE ANALYSED IN THE US TO MEASURE ACID RAIN & AIR POLLUTION. THE POLLUTION NOT ONLY SLOWS GROWTH BUT ALSO LEAVES TRACES OF POLLUTING METALS IN THE GROWTH, PROVIDING AN ACCURATE HISTORICAL RECORD.

SINKING
WOOD NORMALLY FLOATS BECAUSE OF THE AIR INSIDE THE CELLS. LEFT IN WATER, WOOD WILL EVENTUALLY SINK IN 10-100 YEARS.

SHRINKING
WOOD SHRINKS WHEN DRIED & SWELLS WHEN EXPOSED TO MOISTURE, EVEN FULLY SEASONED WOOD REMAINS SENSITIVE TO HUMIDITY. THIS IS WHY BALLROOM FLOORS ARE USUALLY MADE OF VERY NARROW PLANKS (THE SHRINKAGE THEN ONLY CAUSES NARROW CRACKS).

WARPING
FLAT-SAWN PLANKS TEND TO SHRINK & WARP. QUARTER-SAWN PLANKS SHRINK BUT DO NOT WARP. THEY ARE MORE EXPENSIVE BECAUSE FEWER PLANKS CAN BE CUT FROM EACH LOG.

FLAT-SAWN

QUARTER-SAWN

CREEPING
UNDER A LOAD, WOOD SLOWLY BENDS FURTHER & FURTHER. THIS IS WHY OLD TIMBER-FRAMED HOUSES BECOME SO LOP-SIDED & WHY BOWS & STRINGED MUSICAL INSTRUMENTS SHOULD NOT BE STORED TIGHTLY STRUNG.

SAFETY
THE CELLULAR STRUCTURE OF WOOD ALLOWS ONE PART TO BE DAMAGED WITHOUT AFFECTING THE REST, DRIVING SCREWS & NAILS THROUGH WILL DISRUPT ONLY A FEW CELLS, & OVER-LOADING CAN CRUSH MANY CELLS BEFORE THE WOOD ACTUALLY BREAKS.

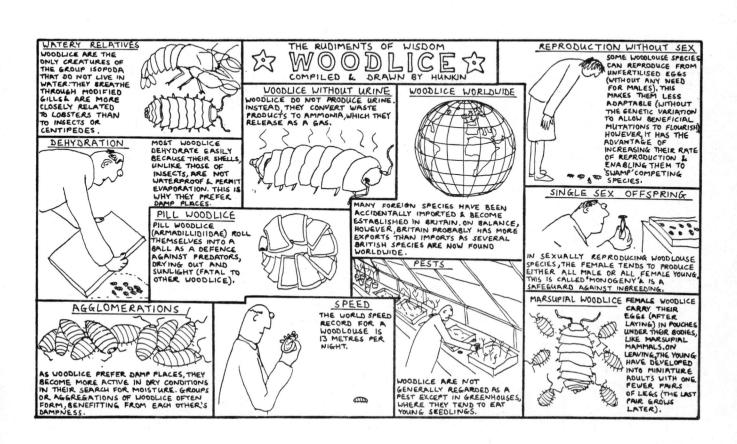

WATERY RELATIVES
WOODLICE ARE THE ONLY CREATURES OF THE GROUP ISOPODA THAT DO NOT LIVE IN WATER. THEY BREATHE THROUGH MODIFIED GILLS & ARE MORE CLOSELY RELATED TO LOBSTERS THAN TO INSECTS OR CENTIPEDES.

DEHYDRATION
MOST WOODLICE DEHYDRATE EASILY BECAUSE THEIR SHELLS, UNLIKE THOSE OF INSECTS, ARE NOT WATERPROOF & PERMIT EVAPORATION. THIS IS WHY THEY PREFER DAMP PLACES.

PILL WOODLICE
PILL WOODLICE (ARMADILLIDIIDAE) ROLL THEMSELVES INTO A BALL AS A DEFENCE AGAINST PREDATORS, DRYING OUT AND SUNLIGHT (FATAL TO OTHER WOODLICE).

AGGLOMERATIONS
AS WOODLICE PREFER DAMP PLACES, THEY BECOME MORE ACTIVE IN DRY CONDITIONS IN THEIR SEARCH FOR MOISTURE. GROUPS OR AGGREGATIONS OF WOODLICE OFTEN FORM, BENEFITTING FROM EACH OTHER'S DAMPNESS.

THE RUDIMENTS OF WISDOM
☆ WOODLICE ☆
COMPILED & DRAWN BY HUNKIN

WOODLICE WITHOUT URINE
WOODLICE DO NOT PRODUCE URINE. INSTEAD, THEY CONVERT WASTE PRODUCTS TO AMMONIA, WHICH THEY RELEASE AS A GAS.

WOODLICE WORLDWIDE
MANY FOREIGN SPECIES HAVE BEEN ACCIDENTALLY IMPORTED & BECOME ESTABLISHED IN BRITAIN. ON BALANCE, HOWEVER, BRITAIN PROBABLY HAS MORE EXPORTS THAN IMPORTS AS SEVERAL BRITISH SPECIES ARE NOW FOUND WORLDWIDE.

PESTS
WOODLICE ARE NOT GENERALLY REGARDED AS A PEST EXCEPT IN GREENHOUSES, WHERE THEY TEND TO EAT YOUNG SEEDLINGS.

SPEED
THE WORLD SPEED RECORD FOR A WOODLOUSE IS 13 METRES PER NIGHT.

REPRODUCTION WITHOUT SEX
SOME WOODLOUSE SPECIES CAN REPRODUCE FROM UNFERTILISED EGGS (WITHOUT ANY NEED FOR MALES). THIS MAKES THEM LESS ADAPTABLE (WITHOUT THE GENETIC VARIATION TO ALLOW BENEFICIAL MUTATIONS TO FLOURISH) HOWEVER IT HAS THE ADVANTAGE OF INCREASING THEIR RATE OF REPRODUCTION & ENABLING THEM TO 'SWAMP' COMPETING SPECIES.

SINGLE SEX OFFSPRING
IN SEXUALLY REPRODUCING WOODLOUSE SPECIES, THE FEMALE TENDS TO PRODUCE EITHER ALL MALE OR ALL FEMALE YOUNG. THIS IS CALLED 'MONOGENY' & IS A SAFEGUARD AGAINST INBREEDING.

MARSUPIAL WOODLICE
FEMALE WOODLICE CARRY THEIR EGGS (AFTER LAYING) IN POUCHES UNDER THEIR BODIES, LIKE MARSUPIAL MAMMALS. ON LEAVING, THE YOUNG HAVE DEVELOPED INTO MINIATURE ADULTS WITH ONE FEWER PAIRS OF LEGS (THE LAST PAIR GROWS LATER).

THE RUDIMENTS OF WISDOM
☆ WOUNDS ☆
COMPILED & DRAWN BY HUNKIN

ELASTOPLAST
ANCIENT EGYPTIAN SURGICAL RECORDS DESCRIBE ADHESIVE PLASTERS FOR PULLING WOUND EDGES TOGETHER.

STITCHES
SOME TRIBES IN SOUTH AFRICA USED CURVED ACACIA THORNS AS STITCHES WITH VEGETABLE FIBRE 'STRING' HOLDING THE ENDS TOGETHER.

HIPPOCRATES
HIPPOCRATES (c400BC) TAUGHT THAT WOUNDS SHOULD BE KEPT DRY & THE EDGES BROUGHT TOGETHER AS CLOSELY AS POSSIBLE TO ALLOW FAST HEALING WITHOUT INFECTION. THIS IS BASICALLY THE PRACTICE TODAY.

GALEN
GALEN (c150AD) BELIEVED THAT INFECTION & PUS WERE ESSENTIAL TO THE HEALING PROCESS. WOUNDS WERE SEARED WITH RED-HOT IRONS OR BOILING OIL OR COVERED IN OINTMENTS TO MAKE THEM SEPTIC, EVEN IF THEY HAD BEEN CLEAN AT THE START. UNFORTUNATELY HIS WRITINGS, NOT THOSE OF HIPPOCRATES, WERE FOLLOWED BY DOCTORS RIGHT UP TO THE 19th C.

OINTMENT
ONE MEDIEVAL WOUND OINTMENT USED BY A SUCCESSFUL TURIN SURGEON CONSISTED OF NEW-BORN PUPPIES BOILED IN OIL & FIXED WITH EARTHWORMS IN TURPENTINE.

ADRENALIN
SERIOUS WOUNDS ARE OFTEN NOT PAINFUL AT FIRST BECAUSE THEY STIMULATE THE RELEASE OF THE HORMONE ADRENALIN (ALLOWING INJURED PEOPLE TO WALK MILES IF NECESSARY TO REACH ASSISTANCE). HOWEVER, ADRENALIN REDUCES THE NUMBER OF ANTIBODIES & WHITE CELLS IN THE BLOOD & SLOWS HEALING, SO SOOTHING INJURED PEOPLE HAS SPECIFIC THERAPEUTIC VALUE.

INSULATION
WOUNDS ARE MORE LIKELY TO BECOME INFECTED AT LOW TEMPERATURES & HEAL QUICKEST AT BODY TEMPERATURE (40°C). AN IMPORTANT FUNCTION OF A DRESSING IS TO INSULATE THE WOUND TO KEEP IT WARM.

HISTAMINE
FOR THE FIRST FEW DAYS THE AREA ROUND A WOUND BECOMES RED, SWOLLEN & INFLAMED. THIS IS DUE TO THE HORMONE HISTAMINE, WHICH ENLARGES THE BLOOD VESSELS TO LET A GREATER SUPPLY THROUGH TO FIGHT INFECTION & FACILITATE HEALING.

SOLUBLE STITCHES
STITCHES TO INTERNAL ORGANS ARE MADE OF CAT GUT (ACTUALLY STERILISED SHEEP OR CATTLE GUT) OR CERTAIN PLASTICS. THESE DO NOT HAVE TO BE REMOVED BECAUSE THEY ARE DISSOLVED & EVENTUALLY ABSORBED BY THE BODY.

SHAVING
RECENT EVIDENCE SUGGESTS THAT SHAVING THE SITE OF AN INCISION BEFORE AN OPERATION (TO MAKE STITCHING EASIER) IS NOT A GOOD IDEA. BY NOT SHAVING, THE INFECTION RATE WAS REDUCED TO ONE NINTH, PROBABLY BECAUSE OF THE LACK OF SUPERFICIAL SKIN ABRASIONS.

SUPERGLUE
SUPERGLUE HAS BEEN TRIED INSTEAD OF STITCHES BY ARMY SURGEONS IN RECENT WARS. IT IS QUITE EFFECTIVE FOR SOME INTERNAL STITCHING BUT UNSUITABLE FOR SKIN AS THE GLUE ACTS AS A BARRIER WHICH SLOWS HEALING & INCREASES THE RISK OF INFECTION.

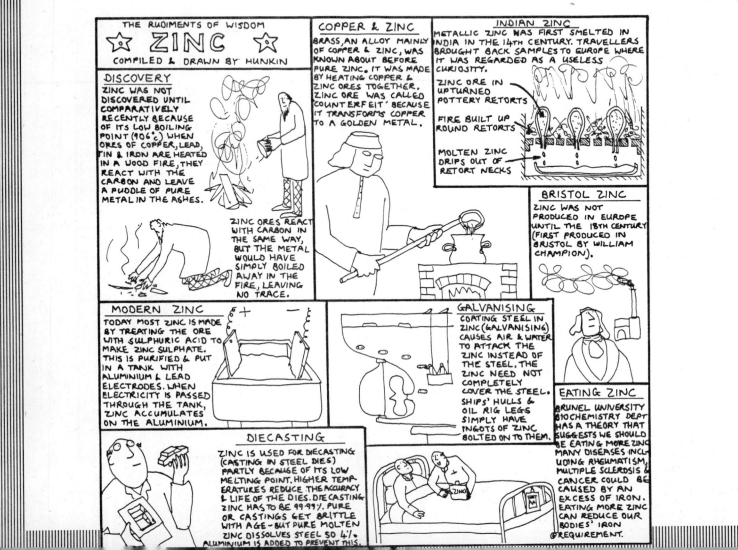

THE RUDIMENTS OF WISDOM
☆ ZINC ☆
COMPILED & DRAWN BY HUNKIN

DISCOVERY
ZINC WAS NOT DISCOVERED UNTIL COMPARATIVELY RECENTLY BECAUSE OF ITS LOW BOILING POINT (906°C) WHEN ORES OF COPPER, LEAD, TIN & IRON ARE HEATED IN A WOOD FIRE, THEY REACT WITH THE CARBON AND LEAVE A PUDDLE OF PURE METAL IN THE ASHES.

ZINC ORES REACT WITH CARBON IN THE SAME WAY, BUT THE METAL WOULD HAVE SIMPLY BOILED AWAY IN THE FIRE, LEAVING NO TRACE.

COPPER & ZINC
BRASS, AN ALLOY MAINLY OF COPPER & ZINC, WAS KNOWN ABOUT BEFORE PURE ZINC. IT WAS MADE BY HEATING COPPER & ZINC ORES TOGETHER. ZINC ORE WAS CALLED 'COUNTERFEIT' BECAUSE IT TRANSFORMS COPPER TO A GOLDEN METAL.

INDIAN ZINC
METALLIC ZINC WAS FIRST SMELTED IN INDIA IN THE 14TH CENTURY. TRAVELLERS BROUGHT BACK SAMPLES TO EUROPE WHERE IT WAS REGARDED AS A USELESS CURIOSITY.

ZINC ORE IN UPTURNED POTTERY RETORTS
FIRE BUILT UP ROUND RETORTS
MOLTEN ZINC DRIPS OUT OF RETORT NECKS

BRISTOL ZINC
ZINC WAS NOT PRODUCED IN EUROPE UNTIL THE 18TH CENTURY (FIRST PRODUCED IN BRISTOL BY WILLIAM CHAMPION).

MODERN ZINC
TODAY MOST ZINC IS MADE BY TREATING THE ORE WITH SULPHURIC ACID TO MAKE ZINC SULPHATE. THIS IS PURIFIED & PUT IN A TANK WITH ALUMINIUM & LEAD ELECTRODES. WHEN ELECTRICITY IS PASSED THROUGH THE TANK, ZINC ACCUMULATES ON THE ALUMINIUM.

GALVANISING
COATING STEEL IN ZINC (GALVANISING) CAUSES AIR & WATER TO ATTACK THE ZINC INSTEAD OF THE STEEL. THE ZINC NEED NOT COMPLETELY COVER THE STEEL. SHIPS' HULLS & OIL RIG LEGS SIMPLY HAVE INGOTS OF ZINC BOLTED ON TO THEM.

EATING ZINC
BRUNEL UNIVERSITY BIOCHEMISTRY DEPT HAS A THEORY THAT SUGGESTS WE SHOULD BE EATING MORE ZINC. MANY DISEASES INCLUDING RHEUMATISM, MULTIPLE SCLEROSIS & CANCER COULD BE CAUSED BY AN EXCESS OF IRON. EATING MORE ZINC CAN REDUCE OUR BODIES' IRON REQUIREMENT.

DIECASTING
ZINC IS USED FOR DIECASTING (CASTING IN STEEL DIES) PARTLY BECAUSE OF ITS LOW MELTING POINT. HIGHER TEMPERATURES REDUCE THE ACCURACY & LIFE OF THE DIES. DIECASTING ZINC HAS TO BE 99·99% PURE OR CASTINGS GET BRITTLE WITH AGE - BUT PURE MOLTEN ZINC DISSOLVES STEEL SO 4% ALUMINIUM IS ADDED TO PREVENT THIS.

Index of Experiments

Subject Index

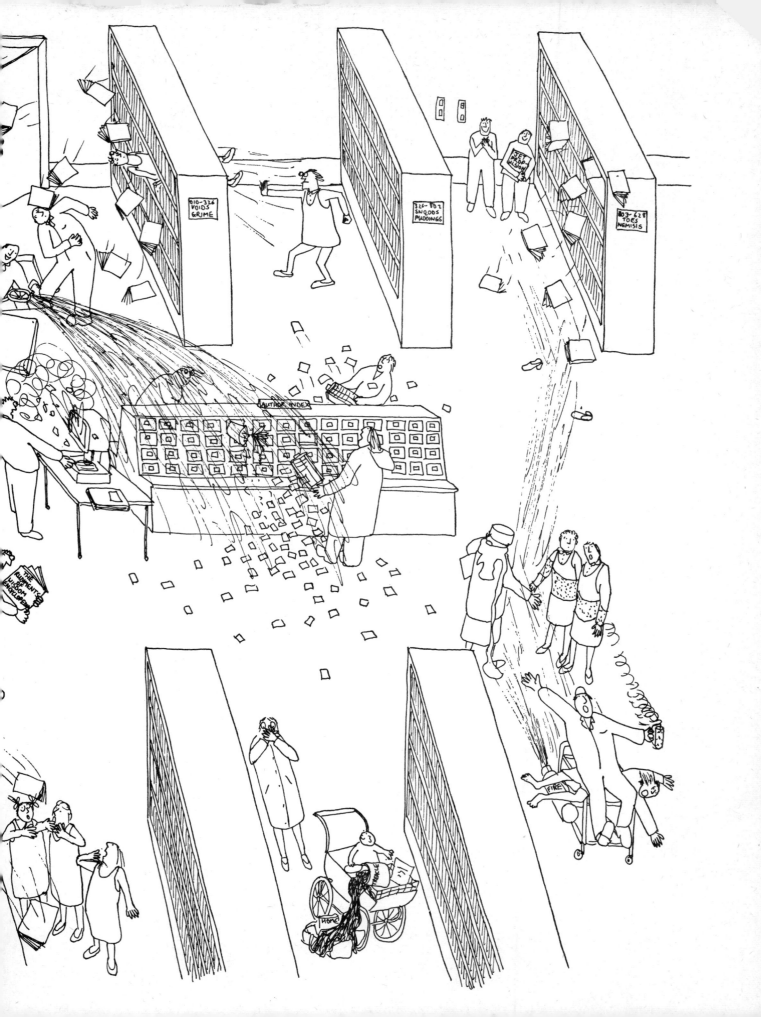